LUTHER'S WORKS

LUTHER'S WORKS

COMPANION VOLUME

SIXTEENTH-CENTURY BIOGRAPHIES OF MARTIN LUTHER

Justus Jonas and Michael Coelius
Johann Bugenhagen
Philip Melanchthon
Johann Walter
Johann Mathesius

Edited by
CHRISTOPHER BOYD BROWN

CONCORDIA PUBLISHING HOUSE • SAINT LOUIS

Unless otherwise indicated, Scripture quotations in this volume are translated from Luther's writings or from Luther's German Bible.

Quotations marked LW are from *Luther's Works*, American Edition: volumes 1–30 © 1955–76 and volumes 57–60, 67–69, 75–79 © 2009–16 Concordia Publishing House; volumes 31–54 © 1957–86 Augsburg Fortress.

The image of Martin Luther (below, p. 7) from the 1546 Wittenberg printing of Justus Jonas and Michael Coelius, *Report on the Christian Departure of the Reverend Dr. Martin Luther*, is courtesy of Concordia Seminary Library Special Collections, St. Louis, MO.

Manufactured in the United States of America

Library of Congress Cataloging-in-Publication Data

Luther, Martin, 1483–1546.
    [Selections, English. 2014]
    Luther's works : Sixteenth-century biographies of Martin Luther / edited by Christopher Boyd Brown.
        p. cm. — (Luther's works)
    Includes indexes.
    ISBN 9780758614049
    I. Christopher Boyd Brown. II. Title. III. Series.
    BS2615.54.L8813   2009
    226.5'07—dc22   2009011458

1 2 3 4 5 6 7 8 9 10   27 26 25 24 23 22 21 20 19 18

CONTENTS

GENERAL INTRODUCTION

SINCE the publication of the American edition of *Luther's Works* in English began in 1955 under the general editorship of Jaroslav Pelikan and Helmut Lehmann, there has been an explosion in the translation of Luther into the languages of the globe. Scholarship on Luther continues to flourish not only in its traditional northern European seats and its newer homes in North America but also throughout the world, as theologians, pastors, and scholars direct their attention to the reformer's theology and historical influence.

Although the first fifty-four volumes of the American edition are the most extensive collection of Luther's works in translation, they do not contain everything that has attracted the attention of historians and theologians in subsequent decades nor everything that Luther's contemporaries and successors esteemed and republished. The new volumes of *Luther's Works*, though not attempting to translate all of Luther into English, are intended to reflect both modern and sixteenth-century interests and to expand the coverage of genres underrepresented in the existing volumes, such as Luther's sermons and disputations.

The goal of the translation is to allow Luther to speak in modern English yet as a man of the sixteenth century. The translators have been asked to resist bowdlerizing Luther's language to conform to modern sensibilities about society and gender—or scatology. Editorial introductions and notes are offered to familiarize the reader with the particular circumstances of each text and its theological and social context.

The primary basis for the English translation is the comprehensive Weimar edition (*D. Martin Luthers Werke: Kritische Gesamtausgabe*, Weimar: H. Böhlau, 1883–), supplemented where possible by edited texts from more recent editions of Luther's selected works. Scholars able to work in Luther's own German and Latin will want to consult the Weimar edition and its notes, especially for textual issues. The equivalent page numbers from the Weimar edition (or other original source) are printed at the top of the page in each new volume of the American edition and approximate page breaks are marked with a stroke (|).

References to Luther in the notes are given from the American edition of *Luther's Works* wherever possible, and otherwise from the Weimar edition. In the case of texts scheduled for translation in future volumes, both the

Weimar reference and the prospective volume in the American edition are given. With each substantive Luther citation, the short title of the work has been given along with its date, for the convenience of the reader. Where the dates of original composition and of publication differ by more than a year, both are indicated, separated by a slash.

Biblical passages within Luther's works have been rendered in fidelity to Luther's own text, even when this differs from modern critical texts or conventional English translations. Necessary expansions of partial references have been rendered in brackets from the appropriate edition of Luther's German Bible, from the Vulgate (including Luther's 1529 revision thereof), or in consultation with Luther's translation of the passage in his lectures, as appropriate. This approach has made it impossible to use any single English translation throughout, though the English Standard Version (ESV) has been used as a starting point where possible or, occasionally, the Authorized or Douay versions where these correspond more closely to Luther's own text. Biblical language has been modernized after the model of the ESV, including the use of "you" as the second person form throughout.

A comparison of the present volumes with the Weimar edition will immediately reveal the profound debt that the editors of the American edition, past and present, owe to the long succession of Weimar editors. But the publication of these texts in a new English edition affords the opportunity to draw on the accumulation of decades of scholarship since the appearance of many of the Weimar volumes, as well as on new electronic resources, and thus, on occasion, to make some new contribution in token repayment of that vast scholarly debt. Although the present edition is addressed chiefly to scholars, pastors, and theologians working in English, whether as a first language or a language of scholarship, it is hoped that the annotations and the translations of difficult texts may be of service even to those working with Luther in the original tongues.

Even now, amid the fifth century after his death, Luther remains an epochal figure in the history of the Christian Church, a prominent shaper of the religious and cultural history of the West and a provocative voice still heard and engaged by theologians, pastors, and laity around the world as a witness to the Gospel of Jesus Christ. The editor and publisher trust that these new volumes of *Luther's Works* in English will, in harmony with the original goals of the American edition, serve their readers with much that has proved and will prove its "importance for the faith, life, and history of the Christian Church."

C. B. B.

ABBREVIATIONS

AC	Augsburg Confession
ACCS	*Ancient Christian Commentary on Scripture*. Edited by Thomas C. Oden. 29 volumes. Downers Grove, IL: InterVarsity Press, 1998–2007.
ADB	*Allgemeine Deutsche Biographie*. Edited by Historische Kommission bei der Bayerischen Königlichen Akademie der Wissenschaften. Leipzig: Duncker & Humblot, 1875–1912. Reprinted, 1967–71.
ADRRG	*Akten der deutschen Reichsreligionsgespräche im 16. Jahrhundert*. Göttingen: Vandenhoeck & Ruprecht, 2000–.
Aland	Kurt Aland. *Hilfsbuch zum Lutherstudium*. 4th edition. Bielefeld: Luther-Verlag, 1996. Cited by main catalog number, postil number (Po), sermon number (Pr), or letter number (Br).
ANF	*The Ante-Nicene Fathers: Translations of the Writings of the Fathers down to A.D. 325*. Edited by Alexander Roberts and James Donaldson. Revised by A. Cleveland Coxe. 10 volumes. Buffalo: Christian Literature Publishing Co., 1885–96. Reprint, Peabody, MA: Hendrickson, 1994.
Ap	Apology of the Augsburg Confession
ARG	*Archiv für Reformationsgeschichte*
ASD	*Opera omnia Desiderii Erasmi Roterodami*. Amsterdam: North-Holland, 1969–.
Baseley	Joel R. Baseley, trans. *Festival Sermons of Martin Luther: The Church Postils*. Dearborn, MI: Mark V Publications, 2005.
BBKL	*Biographisch-bibliographisches Kirchenlexicon*. Edited by Friedrich Wilhelm Bautz. Hamm: Bautz, 1970–.
Brecht	Martin Brecht. *Martin Luther*. Translated by James L. Schaaf. 3 volumes. Minneapolis: Fortress, 1985–93.
BSELK	*Die Bekenntnisschriften der evangelisch-lutherischen Kirche*. Edited by Irene Dingel. Göttingen: Vandenhoeck & Ruprecht, 2014.
BSLK	*Die Bekenntnisschriften der evangelisch-lutherischen Kirche*. 12th edition. Göttingen: Vandenhoeck & Ruprecht, 1998.
CCath	*Corpus Catholicorum*. Münster: Aschendorff, 1919–.

CCCM	*Corpus Christianorum: Continuatio Mediaeualis*. Turnhout: Brepols, 1971–.
CCSL	*Corpus Christianorum: Series Latina*. Turnhout: Brepols, 1953–.
CF	*Cistercian Fathers Series*. Kalamazoo, MI: Cistercian Publications, 1970–.
Concordia	*Concordia: The Lutheran Confessions*. 2nd edition. Edited by Paul T. McCain et al. St. Louis: Concordia, 2006.
CR	*Corpus Reformatorum*. Volumes 1–28: *Philippi Melanthonis Opera quae supersunt omnia*. Edited by C. G. Bretschneider and H. E. Bindseil. Halle: C. A. Schwetschke, 1834–60. Volumes 29–87: *Ioannis Calvini Opera quae supersunt omnia*. Edited by W. Baum, E. Cunitz, E. Reuss. Braunschweig: C. A. Schwetschke et filius, 1863–1900. Volumes 88–: *Huldreich Zwinglis Sämtliche Werke*. Edited by Emil Egli et al. Leipzig: Heinsius, 1905–.
CSEL	*Corpus scriptorum ecclesiasticorum Latinorum*. Vienna: Verlag der Österreichischen Akademie der Wissenschaften, 1866–.
CWE	*Collected Works of Erasmus*. Toronto: University of Toronto Press, 1974–. Corresponding page references to the Latin editions of Erasmus (ASD, LB) are provided throughout CWE.
DB	*Deutsche Bibel*. Luther's published German translation of the Bible (1522–46), edited in WA DB 6–12.
Denzinger	Heinrich Denzinger, ed. *Enchiridion symbolorum definitionum et declarationum de rebus fidei et morum*. 34th edition. Edited by Adolf Schönmetzer. Freiburg: Herder, 1967. Roy J. Deferrari, trans. *The Sources of Catholic Dogma*. St. Louis: Herder, 1957. Cited according to the older paragraph numbers on the inner margin of the Latin edition, corresponding to the enumeration of the English edition.
DRA	*Deutsche Reichstagsakten unter Kaiser Karl V. Deutsche Reichstagsakten, jüngere Reihe*. Edited by Adolf Wrede. 20 volumes. Göttingen: Vandenhoeck & Ruprecht, 1962–2001.
DuCange	Charles du Fresne du Cange et al., eds. *Glossarium mediæ et infimæ latinitatis*. 10 volumes. Niort: L. Favre, 1883–87. http://ducange.enc.sorbonne.fr/
DWB	Jacob Grimm and Wilhelm Grimm. *Deutsches Wörterbuch*. 16 volumes in 32. Leipzig: S. Hirzel, 1854–1960.
E	*D. Martin Luthers sämmtliche Werke*. 67 volumes. Frankfurt and Erlangen: Carl Heyder, 1826–57.
E var. arg.	*D. Martini Lutheri opera latina varii argumenti ad reformationis historiam imprimis pertinentia*. 7 volumes. Frankfurt and Erlangen: Heyder & Zimmer, 1865–73.

FC   *Fathers of the Church*. Edited by Ludwig Schopp. New York: Fathers of the Church, 1947–.

FC SD   Solid Declaration of the Formula of Concord

Friedberg   Emil Friedberg, ed. *Corpus Iuris Canonici*. 2 volumes. Leipzig: Tauchnitz, 1879. Reprint, Graz: Akademische Druck- u. Verlagsanstalt, 1959.

GCS   *Die griechischen christlichen Schriftsteller der ersten drei Jahrhunderte*. Berlin: Akad.-Verlag, 1897–.

HRED   *The Holy Roman Empire: A Dictionary Handbook*. Edited by Jonathan W. Zophy. Westport, CT: Greenwood Press, 1980.

Jena Ger / Lat   Jena edition of Luther's works. *Die erste [–achte] Teil aller Bücher und Schrifften des thewren/ selingen Mans Doc[tor] Mart[ini] Lutheri*. 8 volumes. Jena: Christian Rödinger and heirs, 1555–58. *Tomus primus [–quartus] omnium operum Reverendi Patris D. M. L.* 4 volumes. Jena: Christian Rödinger and heirs, 1556–58.

Klug   Eugene Klug, ed. *Sermons of Martin Luther: The House Postils*. Grand Rapids: Baker Books, 1996 (3 volumes = volumes 5–7 of *The Complete Sermons of Martin Luther*. Grand Rapids: Baker Books, 2000).

Kolb-Wengert   Robert Kolb and Timothy J. Wengert, eds. *The Book of Concord: The Confessions of the Evangelical Lutheran Church*. Minneapolis: Fortress, 2000.

LA   *Legenda Aurea*. Edited by Theodor Graesse. Leipzig: Libraria Arnoldiana, 1850. Reprint, Osnabrück: Zeller, 1965. William Granger Ryan, trans. *The Golden Legend: Readings on the Saints*. 2 volumes. Princeton: Princeton University Press, 1993. Cited by volume and page from the English edition, as well as by number.

LCC   *Library of Christian Classics*. Edited by John T. McNeill and Henry P. van Dusen. Philadelphia: Westminster Press, 1953–.

Lenker   John Nicholas Lenker, ed. *Sermons of Martin Luther: The Church Postils*. Grand Rapids: Baker Books, 1996 (8 volumes in 4; reprinted as volumes 1–4 of *The Complete Sermons of Martin Luther*. Grand Rapids: Baker Books, 2000. Originally published as volumes 7–14 of *The Precious and Sacred Writings of Martin Luther*. Minneapolis: Lutherans in All Lands/Luther Press, 1904–9).

LH   *Luthers Leben in Predigten*. Edited by Georg Loesche. Bibliothek deutscher Schriftsteller aus Böhmen 9. Prague: J. G. Calve/Josef Koch, 1898.

LH²   *Luthers Leben in Predigten*. 2nd edition. Edited by Georg Loesche. Bibliothek deutscher Schriftsteller aus Böhmen 9. Prague: J. G. Calve/Josef Koch, 1906.

LJB   *Lutherjahrbuch.* Göttingen: Vandenhoeck & Ruprecht, 1919–.

Loeb   *Loeb Classical Library.* Cambridge, MA: Harvard University Press, 1912–.

Loy   Martin Luther. *Sermons on the Gospels for the Sundays and Principal Festivals of the Church Year.* Edited by Matthias Loy. 2 volumes. Rock Island, IL: Augustana Book Concern, 1871. A partial English translation of Veit Dietrich's 1544 edition of the *House Postil.*

LQ   *Lutheran Quarterly.* Milwaukee: Lutheran Quarterly, 1987–.

LSB   The Commission on Worship of The Lutheran Church—Missouri Synod. *Lutheran Service Book.* St. Louis: Concordia, 2006.

LSC   *Luther: Letters of Spiritual Counsel.* Edited by Theodore Tappert. LCC 18. Philadelphia, Westminster: 1960.

LW   *Luther's Works: American Edition.* Volumes 1–30: Edited by Jaroslav Pelikan. St. Louis: Concordia, 1955–76. Volumes 31–55: Edited by Helmut Lehmann. Philadelphia/Minneapolis: Muhlenberg/ Fortress, 1957–86. Volumes 56–82: Edited by Christopher Boyd Brown and Benjamin T. G. Mayes. St. Louis: Concordia: 2009–.

LXX   Septuagint

MBW   *Melanchthons Briefwechsel.* Edited by Heinz Scheible. Stuttgart-Bad Canstatt: Frommann-Holzboog, 1977–.

MSA   *Melanchthons Werke in Auswahl.* [*Studienausgabe.*] Edited by Robert Stupperich. 7 volumes. Gütersloh: Gerd Mohn, 1951–75.

NDB   *Neue Deutsche Biographie.* Edited by Die Historische Kommission bei der Bayerischen Königlichen Akademie der Wissenschaften. Berlin: Duncker & Humblot, 1953–.

NPNF[1]   *A Select Library of the Christian Church: Nicene and Post-Nicene Fathers: First Series.* Edited by Philip Schaff. 14 volumes. New York, 1886–89. Reprint, Peabody, MA: Hendrickson, 1994.

NPNF[2]   *A Select Library of the Christian Church: Nicene and Post-Nicene Fathers: Second Series.* Edited by Philip Schaff and Henry Wace. 14 volumes. New York, 1890–1900. Reprint, Peabody, MA: Hendrickson, 1994.

OCD   *Oxford Classical Dictionary.* 4th edition. Edited by Simon Hornblower, Antony Spawforth, and Esther Eidinow. Oxford: Oxford University Press, 2012.

ODCC   *The Oxford Dictionary of the Christian Church.* 3rd edition revised. Edited by F. L. Cross. Oxford: Oxford University Press, 2005.

OER   *The Oxford Encyclopedia of the Reformation.* Edited by Hans J. Hillerbrand. 4 volumes. New York: Oxford University Press, 1996.

PG   *Patrologiae cursus completus: Series Graeca.* Edited by J.-P. Migne. 161 volumes in 167. Petit-Montrouge: Apud J. P. Migne, 1857–66.

PL   *Patrologiae cursus completus: Series Latina.* Edited by J.-P. Migne. 221 volumes in 223. Paris: Garnier Fratres, 1844–64.

SCJ   *The Sixteenth Century Journal*

Sehling   Emil Sehling et al., eds. *Die evangelischen Kirchenordnungen des XVI. Jahrhunderts.* Volumes 1–5: Leipzig: O. R. Reisland, 1902–13. Volumes 6–: Tübingen: Mohr (Paul Siebeck), 1957–.

StL   Dr. *Martin Luthers sämmtliche Schriften: Neue revidirte Stereotypausgabe.* Edited by Johann Georg Walch. 23 volumes in 25. St. Louis: Concordia, 1880–1910.

Tanner   Norman P. Tanner, ed. *Decrees of the Ecumenical Councils.* 2 volumes. London: Sheed & Ward; Washington, DC: Georgetown University Press, 1990.

Thiele   Ernst Thiele. *Luthers Sprichwörtersammlung.* Weimar: Hermann Böhlaus Nachfolger, 1900. Reprint, Leipzig: Reprint-Verlag. Cited by number and page, e.g., Thiele no. 42, pp. 121–23.

TLH   *The Lutheran Hymnal.* St. Louis: Concordia, 1941.

Tr   Treatise on the Power and Primacy of the Pope

VD16   *Verzeichnis der im deutschen Sprachbereich erschienenen Drucke des XVI. Jahrhunderts.* Edited by Irmgard Bezzel. 25 volumes. Stuttgart: Hiersemann, 1983–2000. http://vd16.de

Vg   Vulgate translation of the Bible

WA   *D. Martin Luthers Werke: Kritische Gesamtausgabe.* 73 volumes in 85. Weimar: H. Böhlau, 1883–.

WA Ar   *Archiv zur Weimarer Ausgabe der Werke Martin Luthers: Texte und Untersuchungen.* Cologne: Böhlau Verlag, 1981–.

WA Br   *D. Martin Luthers Werke: Briefwechsel.* 18 volumes. Weimar: H. Böhlau, 1930–.

WA DB   *D. Martin Luthers Werke: Deutsche Bibel.* 12 volumes in 15. Weimar: H. Böhlau, 1906–.

WA N   *Revisionsnachtrag* ["revision-addenda"] for select volumes of the Weimar edition. *D. Martin Luthers Werke: Kritische Gesamtausgabe, Revisionsnachtrag.* 6 volumes. Weimar: H. Böhlaus Nachfolger, 1963–74. Cited by the volume to which it refers and page number of the *Revisionsnachtrag* volume, e.g., WA 30/2N:154.

WA TR   *D. Martin Luthers Werke: Tischreden.* 6 volumes. Weimar: H. Böhlau, 1912–21.

Wackernagel	Philipp Wackernagel, ed. *Das deutsche Kirchenlied von der ältesten Zeit bis zu Anfang des 17. Jahrhunderts.* 5 volumes. Leipzig: Teubner, 1864–77.
Wander	Karl Friedrich Wilhelm Wander. *Deutsches Sprichwörter Lexikon.* 5 volumes. Leipzig: Brockhaus, 1867–80. Reprint, Darmstadt: Wissenschaftliche Buchgesellschaft, 2007. Cited by volume and page, then word and number, e.g., Wander 2:212, "Gott" no. 22.
Witt Ger / Lat	Wittenberg edition of Luther's works. *Der Erste [–zwölfte] Teil der Bücher D. Mart[ini] Luth[eri].* 12 volumes. Wittenberg: Hans Lufft, 1539–59. *Tomus primus [–septimus] omnium operum reverendi Domini Martini Lutheri, Doctoris Theologiae.* 7 volumes. Wittenberg: Hans Lufft, Peter Seitz's heirs, and Thomas Klug, 1545–57.
WSA	*The Works of St. Augustine: A Translation for the Twenty-first Century.* Edited by Edmund Hill and John E. Rotelle. In three series. Hyde Park, NY: New City Press, 1990–.

VOLUME INTRODUCTION

MARTIN Luther has been the subject of hundreds of biographies in the last five hundred years, and the Reformation anniversary has called forth the latest wave. The long succession of Luther biographies stretches back to Luther's own autobiographical efforts, which were quickly supplemented by his colleagues, friends, and students as they sought to collect his works, narrate his history, and reflect on the significance of his life and teaching. The present volume seeks to present some of these earliest sources for the reformer's biography, making most of them accessible in English for the first time.

Luther's Autobiography and Works

Luther never produced a full-scale autobiography, though he did begin to conceive of such a project in the last years of his life. He took a hand in publishing accounts of certain key events in his early career: the *Proceedings at Augsburg*, for example, offered Luther's own perspective on his 1518 encounter with the papal legate Cardinal Cajetan;[1] and a Wittenberg account of Luther's 1521 trial at Worms was likely compiled with his help.[2] Many of Luther's autobiographical statements were called forth in response to controversy: when, for example, he was accused in 1520 of being of Bohemian descent (and therefore a dangerous Hussite heretic), Luther responded with an account of his birth in Eisleben, childhood in Mansfeld, and education and family connections in Eisenach.[3] Luther's 1521 treatise *Judgment on Monastic Vows* included a public dedication to his father in which he recounted his entrance into the monastery.[4] In the early 1540s, when Duke Henry of Braunschweig (1489–1568)[5] accused Luther and the late Elector Frederick the Wise (1463–1525) of having deliberately provoked

---

[1] LW 31:253–92.

[2] *Acta et res gestae D. M. Lutheri in comitiis principum Wormatiae* (1521), WA 7:818–41, translated in *Luther at the Diet of Worms* (1521), LW 32:105–23.

[3] Luther to Spalatin, January 14, 1520, LW 48:144–46.

[4] Luther to Hans Luther, November 21, 1521, LW 48:329–36.

[5] See below, p. 27 n. 6.

the "Lutheran rumpus,"[6] Luther responded with his own detailed narrative of the Indulgence Controversy in his 1541 polemic *Against Hanswurst*.[7]

Luther's conversations with his colleagues and students also provided an important occasion for autobiographical reflection. His *Table Talk*, written down by students beginning in 1529, contain a great deal of reminiscence about the events of his early career—in many cases much more information than stems from the time when the events happened.[8] These autobiographical reminiscences in the *Table Talk* become more frequent in the last years of Luther's life, from about 1539 onward, produced by a combination of Luther's own intensifying self-reflection and the biographical interests of the students gathered at his table in those years, particularly Johann Mathesius.

Luther's remarks at table have provided later biographers with many of the details that have become iconic in discussions of his life. It is the *Table Talk*, for example, that contains the story of the vow Luther made to St. Anne near Stotternheim amid a thunderstorm (first appearing in 1539)[9] or the accounts of his Reformation "breakthrough" which place it "in this tower" or "*in cloaca*."[10] The reliability of the *Table Talk* can, of course, be questioned, though it is implausible that Luther's students would have deliberately falsified notes they had taken for their own private memorial.[11] On some points, the varying biographical information in the *Table Talk* evidently reflects Luther's own uncertainty—even about his own birthdate.[12] Luther's *Table Talk* did not appear in print until a selection was edited for publication in 1566 by Luther's student and last assistant, Johann Aurifaber.[13] Nevertheless,

---

[6] On the accusation of instigating the Indulgence Controversy, see below, Melanchthon, *Preface*, pp. 67–68. On Elector Frederick, see below, p. 68 n. 82.

[7] LW 41:231–36.

[8] See Volker Leppin, *Martin Luther*, 2nd ed. (Darmstadt: Wissenschaftliche Buchgesellschaft, 2010).

[9] *Table Talk* no. 4707 (1539), WA TR 4:440; cf. below, Mathesius, *History*, p. 122.

[10] *Table Talk* no. 1681 (1532), WA TR 2:177; no. 3232a–b (1532), WA TR 3:228; no. 3232c (1532), LW 54:193–94.

[11] See Katharina Bärenfänger, Volker Leppin, and Stefan Michel, eds., *Martin Luthers Tischreden: Neuansätze der Forschung* (Tübingen: Mohr Siebeck, 2013); Michael Beyer, "Tischreden," in *Luther Handbuch*, ed. Albrecht Beutel (Tübingen: Mohr Siebeck, 2005).

[12] See below, pp. liv–lv and n. 182 there. Cf. below, Mathesius, *History*, p. 114.

[13] Johann Aurifaber, ed., *Tischreden oder Colloquia Doct[or] Mart[in] Luthers* (Eisleben: U. Gaubisch, 1566) [VD16 L6748], edited in WA TR 6. A selected English translation was made in the nineteenth century by William Hazlitt, *The Table Talk or Familiar Discourse of Martin Luther* (London: Bogue, 1848), with many subsequent printings. On Aurifaber's *Table Talk*, see Robert Kolb, *Martin Luther as Prophet, Teacher, and Hero: Images of the Reformer, 1520–1620* (Grand Rapids: Baker, 1999), pp. 152–54; Ernst Kroker, "Tischreden aus Johannes Aurifabers Sammlung FB," WA TR 6:xi–xxxix. Aurifaber (1519–75) had studied in Wittenberg from 1537 to 1540 and then served as Luther's professional assistant from 1545 until Luther's death. From

manuscript collections had circulated among Luther's students and admirers throughout the previous decades and formed a key source for their biographies of the reformer. Sometimes Luther's oral reminiscences also found their way into the published work of his students.[14]

Luther's correspondence with his friends also contained occasional pieces of autobiography, such as his 1520 report to Georg Spalatin on his ancestry.[15] The letters themselves are an essential source for modern biographers for Luther's day-to-day life and activities, as well as his connections beyond Wittenberg. Luther, however (unlike his contemporary Erasmus [ca. 1467–1536]),[16] was reluctant to see his correspondence published.[17] Apart from the numerous open letters he wrote, which were public by their

---

1540 to 1544, Aurifaber had been a tutor for the sons of Count Albert of Mansfeld (see below, p. xxviii n. 54)—Vollrad (1520–78), John [Hans] (ca. 1532–67), and Carl (1534–94)—with whom he would maintain relationships for the rest of his life. After his service to Luther, Count Albert asked Aurifaber to serve as a chaplain during the Smalcaldic War. In 1561, Aurifaber published two volumes of Luther's letters in Eisleben with Count Vollrad's support, dedicating the first volume of this work to Count Carl. In 1565, Aurifaber began publishing the first two volumes of the Eisleben edition of Luther's works, containing material not edited in the Wittenberg or Jena editions, but publication ceased before a planned third volume could be completed. Aurifaber did continue, however, with his collection of Luther's *Table Talk* in 1566. See the introduction by Christopher Boyd Brown, LW 69:xvi; Kolb, *Luther as Prophet, Teacher, and Hero*, pp. 150–53; William R. Russell, "Aurifaber, Johannes," *OER* 1:101–2; Robert J. Christman, *Doctrinal Controversy and Lay Religiosity in Late Reformation Germany: The Case of Mansfeld* (Boston: Brill, 2012), p. 40.

[14] See, e.g., Martin Lohrmann, "A Newly Discovered Report of Luther's Reformation Breakthrough from Johannes Bugenhagen's 1550 Jonah Commentary," *LQ* 22, no. 3 (2008): 324–30.

[15] See above, p. xvii n. 3. On Spalatin, see below, p. 136 n. 121.

[16] Desiderius Erasmus was the leading northern humanist scholar of his day, advocating the study of pagan as well as Christian classics instead of scholastic "sophistry" as the foundation of authentic Christianity, the *philosophia Christi*. His correspondence was first collected and published in 1515 and in regularly expanded editions thereafter. Erasmus edited the works of many church fathers as well as published the first printed Greek New Testament in 1516, work which Luther quickly drew upon in his own study and teaching. Although many contemporaries perceived Luther and Erasmus as allies, Erasmus' own public posture toward Luther was one of studied reserve and careful neutrality until he finally published a theological critique of Luther in his *Discussion of Free Will* (1525) (CWE 76), to which Luther responded with *Bondage of the Will* (1525) (LW 33:3–295). On Erasmus, see Erika Rummel, *Erasmus* (New York: Continuum, 2004); Lewis Spitz, *The Religious Renaissance of the German Humanists* (Cambridge, MA: Harvard University Press, 1963), pp. 197–266.

[17] See *Table Talk* no. 5170 (1540), WA TR 4:691–92. On the history of editions of Luther's correspondence, see Hans Volz and Eike Wolgast, "Geschichte der Lutherbriefeditionen des 16. bis 20. Jahrhunderts," WA Br 14:353–631; Kolb, *Luther as Prophet, Teacher, and Hero*, pp. 151–52.

nature, and a few other exceptions,[18] it was not until the end of his life that his students began to consider publishing his letters. The earliest of these collections presented selections of Luther's letters of pastoral comfort [*Trostschriften*] addressed to Christians in the midst of spiritual temptation [*Anfechtungen*] or persecution. The first, edited by Luther's frequent editorial collaborator Caspar Cruciger Sr., appeared the year before Luther's death.[19] Cruciger's collection saw numerous reprintings before being revised and expanded by Georg Rörer in 1554.[20] A separate collection of similar purpose was published by Aurifaber in 1547 and was followed by an expanded edition in 1550.[21]

---

[18] See *Martini Lutheri Epistolarum Farrago* (Hagenau: Johann Setzer, 1525) [VD16 L4656]; Volz and Wolgast, "Geschichte der Lutherbriefeditionen," WA Br 14:571–72.

[19] *Etliche Trostschrifften und predigten, fur die so in tods und ander not und anfechtung sind* (Wittenberg: Hans Lufft, 1545) [VD16 L3463]—though the colophon, fol. Q6v, gives the date as 1544. See Volz and Wolgast, "Geschichte der Lutherbriefeditionen," WA Br 14:360–63, 572–75; Kolb, *Luther as Prophet, Teacher, and Hero*, p. 166. Cruciger (1504–48), who had heard Luther and Johann Eck (see below, p. 154 n. 89) debate when he was a student in Leipzig, came to Wittenberg to complete his studies in 1521. After a period as rector of the Latin school in Magdeburg, Cruciger was called back in April 1528 to the Wittenberg faculty and as preacher at the Castle Church. He became one of Luther's most trusted editors, working on the *Summer Postil* as well as collaborating on the first volumes of the Wittenberg edition of Luther's works. On Cruciger, see the introduction by Benjamin T. G. Mayes, LW 77:xiii–xiv; Timothy J. Wengert, "Caspar Cruciger, 1504–1548: The Case of the Disappearing Reformer," *SCJ* 20, no. 3 (Autumn 1989): 417–41. See also Luther to Nicolaus Gerbel, November 27, 1535, where he called Cruciger his "Elisha": WA Br 7:329. Cruciger had a son of the same name, Caspar Cruciger Jr. (1525–97), but, in this volume, references to "Caspar Cruciger" without further specification are to the elder Cruciger.

[20] *Etliche Trostschrifften und Predigten des Ehrwird[igen] Herrn Doct. Mart. Luth. für die so in Todes/ und ander not und anfechtung sind* (Jena: Christian Rödinger, 1554) [VD16 L3480–3481]. See Volz and Wolgast, "Geschichte der Lutherbriefeditionen," WA Br 14:409–11, 592–602; Kolb, *Luther as Prophet, Teacher, and Hero*, p. 166. Georg Rörer (1492–1557) came to Wittenberg in 1522 after study in Leipzig; he was ordained deacon in Wittenberg in 1525. Soon after his arrival, he began taking stenographic notes on Luther's preaching and some of his lecturing, an activity that he continued throughout Luther's life, eventually receiving official support for his activities in the form of a stipend from the Wittenberg town council. Rörer would record the deliberations over the Bible translation as well. His notes were the source of many of the sermons, lectures, and other material printed during Luther's lifetime; in 1537, he was appointed editor of the Wittenberg edition of Luther's works (Witt Lat and Witt Ger). On Rörer, see Marilyn J. Harran, "Rörer, Georg," *OER* 3:450; the introductions by Christopher Boyd Brown, LW 69:3–4; 58:xxv–xxviii; Reinhold Jauernig, "Magister Georg Rörer: Im Dienst der 'Werke Luthers,'" in Karl Brinkel and Herbert von Hintzenstern, eds., *Luthers Freunde und Schüler in Thüringen*, vol. 1 (Berlin: Evangelische Verlagsanstalt, 1961), pp. 155–61. Rörer's extant manuscripts are described in WA Br 14:175–282.

[21] *Etliche schoene Trostschriffte, des Ehrwirdigen Herrn Doctoris Martini Lutheri* (Erfurt: Wolfgang Stürmer, 1547) [VD16 L4705]; WA 60:574–75. On the 1550 edition [VD16 L4995], see Volz and Wolgast, "Geschichte der Lutherbriefeditionen," WA Br 14:365–69, 576–77.

Amid the theological and political challenges faced by Lutherans after the defeat of the Smalcaldic League and the emperor's efforts to impose the Augsburg Interim to regulate religious practice,[22] the different parties appealed to Luther's views. In 1549, Matthias Flacius (1520–75), a leader of the Gnesio-Lutheran critics of Philip Melanchthon, published an edition of Luther's correspondence from the Coburg during the 1530 Diet of Augsburg to support the Gnesio-Lutheran refusal to accept compromise with Roman Catholic theology or practice.[23]

As in the case of the *Table Talk*, the first systematic effort to collect, edit, and publish Luther's correspondence as a whole was made by Aurifaber.[24] Having long worked at collecting copies of Luther's letters from correspondents and library collections, the first volume of his edition of Luther's correspondence, from the years 1507 to 1521, appeared in 1556, containing 249 letters by Luther. A second volume, with Luther's letters from 1522 to 1528, was published in 1565, containing 393 letters by the reformer.[25] Aurifaber's prefaces to these volumes offered his own brief narrative of Luther's life during the years covered. Although he had already assembled the manuscript for a third volume containing 475 of Luther's letters from 1530 to 1546, it was never published because of the disappointing sales of the first two volumes.[26] Thus only a portion of Luther's full correspondence was available for his early modern readers and biographers.

---

[22] After the military defeat of the Smalcaldic League in 1547, the Augsburg Interim of 1548, drafted by a committee of Roman Catholic theologians and the Lutheran Johann Agricola (see below, p. 345 n. 134) and issued under imperial authority, sought to impose on Protestant cities and territories conformity with traditional Roman Catholic practices. Lutherans were divided between those who, like Melanchthon, regarded it as an unfortunate but endurable imposition by the ruling authorities, and those who rejected it as an intolerable compromise of Evangelical confession: see below, p. lxxxv; p. 199 n. 88. For the text of the Augsburg Interim, see Robert Kolb and James A. Nestingen, eds., *Sources and Contexts of the Book of Concord* (Minneapolis: Fortress, 2001), pp. 144–96.

[23] *Aliquot Epistolae Reverendi Patris Piae Memoriae D. Martini Lutheri quibusdam Theologis ad Augustana comitia. Anno 1530. Scriptae* (Magdeburg: Michael Lotter, 1549) [VD16 L3274–3275]. See Volz and Wolgast, "Geschichte der Lutherbriefeditionen," WA Br 14:400–408, 587–92; Kolb, *Luther as Prophet, Teacher, and Hero*, pp. 40–42.

[24] See Volz and Wolgast, "Geschichte der Lutherbriefeditionen," WA Br 14:363–400; Kolb, *Luther as Prophet, Teacher, and Hero*, pp. 151–52.

[25] See Volz and Wolgast, "Geschichte der Lutherbriefeditionen," WA Br 14:375–91, 577–83.

[26] See Volz and Wolgast, "Geschichte der Lutherbriefeditionen," WA Br 14:391–92. Aurifaber's manuscript is preserved in the collection of the Herzog August Bibliothek in Wolfenbüttel. The one-year gap between the two published volumes and Aurifaber's third manuscript volume is apparently because Aurifaber had originally intended to include the 1529 correspondence in the second volume, but the material had to be omitted because of length.

Luther's lectures and sermons also contained occasional reflections on his life—especially his time as a monk.[27] As in the *Table Talk*, these autobiographical discussions in public speaking seem to become more frequent in the last years of Luther's life. In a 1545 sermon, for example, we find Luther's only direct account of climbing the *Scala Sancta* in Rome.[28] In his Genesis lectures, Luther recollects his apprehension at celebrating his first Mass; his scandalized shock as a monk when he read St. Bonaventure praising marriage; and the influence of his monastic superior Johann von Staupitz.[29]

Of course, Luther's published writings, in addition to whatever bits of information about Luther's biography they contained, were themselves a major part of the history of his life, thought, and influence. The earliest efforts to collect Luther's published works and present them together, in chronological order or topically, date back to the first years of the Reformation. Already in 1518 the eminent Basel humanist printer Johann Froben (1470–1527) gathered Luther's available Latin publications to that time in a single volume; the book proved to be Froben's most successful publication, to the chagrin of Erasmus.[30] Froben's Latin volume was reprinted in Strassburg and in Basel, where the competing printer Andreas Cratander (d. 1540) expanded the collection to two Latin volumes in 1520.[31] Cratander accompanied this edition with a one-volume collection of Luther's German works, which was also reprinted in Strassburg.[32] These early collections, however, were undertaken by enterprising printers; Luther himself played no role in planning, assembling, or editing them.

---

[27] See, e.g., *Lectures on Galatians* (1531/1535), LW 27:13; sermons of February 23, 1539, LW 58:10; January 6, 1544, LW 58:60–61; January 20, 1544, LW 58:86; May 10, 1545, LW 58:135; May 31, 1545, LW 58:157; December 25, 1544, LW 58:197; June 7, 1545, LW 58:236–37; August 12, 1545, LW 58:272–73; September 6, 1545, LW 58:286; November 1, 1545, LW 58:318; and January 6, 1546, LW 58:364. Cf. the introduction by Christopher Boyd Brown, LW 58:xvii.

[28] Sermon for Trinity 24, November 15, 1545, LW 58:337.

[29] *Lectures on Genesis* (1535–45/1544–54), LW 4:341; 5:36 (cf. LW 1:135; 4:303–4); 5:47; 7:192. On Bonaventure, see below, p. 456 n. 204. On Staupitz, see below, p. lvi n. 194.

[30] *Ad Leonem X. Pontificem Maximum . . .* (Basel: Johann Froben, 1518) [VD16 L3407]. See Hans Volz and Eike Wolgast, "Geschichte der Luther-Ausgaben vom 16. bis zum 19. Jahrhundert," WA 60:431–50, 455–58, 607–11; Kolb, *Luther as Prophet, Teacher, and Hero*, pp. 139–41; Andrew Pettegree, *Brand Luther* (New York: Penguin, 2015), p. 107.

[31] *Prima [Secunda] Pars Operum Reverendi Patris, Ac Sacrae Theologiae Doctoris Martini Lutherii, Augustiniani Wittenbergensis* (Basel: Andreas Cratander, 1520) [VD16 L3410]. The Basel printer Adam Petri (1454–1525/1527) sought to produce a similar two-volume set [VD16 L3411] but never printed the second volume.

[32] *Martini Luthers der waren göttlichen schrifft Doctors/ Augustiner zů Wittenbergk/ mancherley buechlin und tractetlin* (Basel: Cratander, 1520) [VD16 L3307]. See Volz and Wolgast, "Geschichte der Luther-Ausgaben," WA 60:450–54, 459–60, 611–12.

CATALOG OR INDEX OF ALL THE BOOKS AND WRITINGS PUBLISHED BY DR. MARTIN LUTHER, 1518–33 (1533)[33]

A new proposal for publishing Luther's collected works was advanced in 1528 by the Zwickau city clerk Stephan Roth, who had studied in Wittenberg from 1523 to 1527.[34] Roth had sought to establish himself as an editor of Luther's sermons, albeit not always with Luther's own consent or prior knowledge. His volumes of postil sermons—a summer collection, festival collection, and winter collection—both supplemented and competed with the postil volumes prepared in Wittenberg under Luther's auspices. In Roth's 1528 edition of Luther's *Winter Postil*, he announced his intention "to have all Luther's books printed in order, one after the other, divided into sections, just as he himself has given his consent and permission to do."[35] Roth's work on this plan resulted in the appearance of a *Directory or Index of All the Books and Writings Published by Dr. Martin Luther* from the Wittenberg press of his brother-in-law Georg Rhau (1488–1548) later that same year.[36]

Although Roth claimed to have Luther's consent for his proposal, the *Directory* appeared without any preface or other endorsement from Luther, and in fact the relationship between Luther and Roth was deteriorating: first, because of Luther's growing dissatisfaction with Roth's editorial work and apparent profiteering, and then because of Roth's involvement, as city clerk, with what Luther judged to be the unwarranted and illegitimate dismissal of one of the Zwickau preachers. As a result, Luther regarded the members of the Zwickau government as excommunicated, a breach which was not reconciled, in Roth's case, until 1536.[37]

Roth's plan for an edition of Luther's works never came to fruition—though Roth did later assist with the preparation of materials for the Wittenberg edition—but his organized list of Luther's works did serve those who wished to evaluate and fill in their own collections of Luther's treatises. The *Directory* was thus republished in Wittenberg in 1533 as the *Catalog,*

---

[33] *Catalogus oder Register aller Bücher und schrifften, D. Mart. Luth. durch jn ausgelassen, vom jar. M. D. XVIII. bis jns .XXXIII. Mit einer Vorrhede* (Wittenberg: Hans Lufft, 1533) [VD16 L3449], 16 leaves in octavo. Aland 121 (WA 38:132–34; 60:3–15). See below, *Catalog*, pp. 1–4.

[34] On Stephan Roth (1492–1546) and his publishing efforts, see the introduction by Benjamin T. G. Mayes, LW 75:xvii–xxii; Volz and Wolgast, "Geschichte der Luther-Ausgaben," WA 60:461–62.

[35] WA 21:189.

[36] *Verzeychung und Register/ aller Buecher und schrifften/ D. Mart. Luth. durch yhn ausgelassen Vom Jar M. D. xviij. bis yns acht vnd zwenzigst* (Wittenberg: Georg Rhau, 1528) [VD16 L3447].

[37] See Brecht 2:440–45.

this time from the press of Hans Lufft (1495–1584) and now bearing Luther's own short preface.

Lufft's 1533 printing added works that had appeared since Roth's list had been prepared in 1528. The *Catalog* was divided into works in Latin and works in German, each section further subdivided by genre, in roughly chronological order within each subdivision, though with only scattered indications of exact date. The Latin section included six "sermons," ten "treatises" [*libelli*], eight "commentaries," the Wittenberg revisions of parts of the Vulgate Bible, seven treatises translated from German, eighteen prefaces to books by others, and twenty-five "apologetic" works. The German section listed twenty-four "expository" works [*Auslegung*], sixteen "sermons," forty-seven "books of doctrine and exhortation," fifty-six "exhortations," the German translation of the Bible, thirty-three prefaces to books by others, forty-nine "controversial" books, eleven "open letters," and forty-two sermons and German expositions that originally had been delivered orally.[38]

Luther's preface deprecated the publication of his own works in favor of Holy Scripture. Nevertheless, he estimated that his writings could be valuable as a witness to the history of the progress of God's Word. He warned that his early works would be found to yield too much to the papacy; contrary to the charges brought against him by his Roman Catholic opponents, the fact that his later works, by contrast, dealt "solely and purely" with Christ was evidence not of contradiction but of his own deepening understanding of the Scriptures. This preface is translated by Matthew Carver below (pp. 1–4) on the basis of the 1533 Wittenberg printing as edited in the Weimar edition (WA 38:133–34).

Despite the failure of Roth's original plans, Luther's 1533 preface developed a framework for the presentation of his writing that he took up again when the Wittenberg edition of his works began publication at the end of the decade. For most of the rest of the 1530s, Luther continued to resist efforts to arrange the publication of his collected works, temporizing over a 1536 proposal from the Strassburg printer Wendel Rihel (d. 1555) and the humanist theologian Wolfgang Capito (1478–1541) by saying he would rather devour his own books, like Saturn, to prevent their publication, and suggesting his Wittenberg colleague Caspar Cruciger as editor instead.[39] But by 1539, Luther had given his consent to an edition of his works to be undertaken in

---

[38] For the list, see WA 60:4–15.

[39] See Luther to Wolfgang Capito, July 9, 1537, WA Br 8:99–100; Volz and Wolgast, "Geschichte der Luther-Ausgaben," WA 60:563–64; Pettegree, *Brand Luther*, pp. 273–74.

Wittenberg, appearing from the press of Hans Lufft, with his longtime scribe Georg Rörer and editoral assistant Cruciger as editors.[40]

As in Roth's design, the Wittenberg edition of Luther's works was to be divided into separate Latin and German series. The German series was arranged by genre—a first volume of exposition of New Testament Epistles followed by a second volume of controversial works—though the extent of Luther's exegetical works meant that most of the following volumes contained biblical exposition of some description. The Latin series was intended to be arranged chronologically, with the first volume presenting material from the years 1517 to 1520 and the second volume offering material from 1521 to 1527—though, again, the extent of exegetical material meant that a strict chronological scheme was largely abandoned for the subsequent volumes. The Wittenberg editors included much contextual material from official sources and from Luther's opponents, as well as related works by Melanchthon and some others, making the first two Latin volumes in particular a kind of historical and biographical narrative in their own right.[41] The Jena edition of Luther's works, which began to appear in 1555 under the auspices of the deposed elector John Frederick[42] as a theological and literary competitor to the Wittenberg edition, amplified this biographical character by adopting a more consistent chronological scheme throughout its series of German and Latin volumes.[43] The two volumes of Johann Aurifaber's Eisleben edition, appearing in 1564–65 (a third volume was planned but never published), continued a chronological

---

[40] After 1551, Georg Major (1502–74; see below, p. 300 n. 88) took over the editorship of the Wittenberg edition as Rörer first left Saxony for Denmark and then in 1552 accepted the call to oversee the competing Jena edition of Luther's works.

[41] See Kolb, *Luther as Prophet, Teacher, and Hero*, pp. 141–46; Volz and Wolgast, "Geschichte der Luther-Ausgaben," WA 60:464–95; lists of the contents of each volume in the Wittenberg edition are found in Kurt Aland, *Hilfsbuch zum Lutherstudium*, 4th ed. (Bielefeld: Luther-Verlag, 1996), pp. 549–60 (Witt Ger), pp. 561–67 (Witt Lat).

[42] John Frederick "The Magnanimous" (1503–54), who in 1532 succeeded his father, John the Steadfast (1468–1532), as elector of Saxony, was a committed defender of Lutheranism. After the defeat of the Smalcaldic League by Emperor Charles V in 1547, John Frederick was imprisoned and stripped of the electoral dignity, which was transferred to his cousin Duke Maurice of Albertine Saxony (see below, p. lxxiii), who thus also gained control of Wittenberg and its university. When John Frederick was freed in 1552 and assumed rule over a reduced Saxon duchy centered at Weimar, he patronized efforts to support authentic Lutheranism, including the Jena edition of Luther's works and the establishment of the University of Jena in 1558 (cf. below, p. lxxiv, p. 199 n. 88). Cf. Günther Wartenburg, "Saxony," *OER* 3:490.

[43] See Kolb, *Luther as Prophet, Teacher, and Hero*, pp. 146–50; Volz and Wolgast, "Geschichte der Luther-Ausgaben," WA 60:495–543; lists of the contents of each volume in the Jena edition are found in Aland, *Hilfsbuch*, pp. 569–81 (Jena Ger), pp. 583–87 (Jena Lat).

arrangement, though because of their supplementary character they could not so easily be read as a narrative.[44]

It was only with the Wittenberg edition of his works that Luther himself was directly involved, composing prefaces for the two volumes that appeared before his death.[45] Luther's 1539 preface to the first volume of the Wittenberg edition of his German writings (LW 34:279–88) took up some of the themes of his 1533 preface to the *Catalog*, emphasizing the superiority of the Bible—now translated into German—to his own books. Luther went on to articulate his famous method of theological study: *oratio, meditatio, tentatio*. The historical perspective of the 1533 preface, with its awareness of his theological development, was taken up in Luther's March 1545 preface to the first volume of the Latin series of the Wittenberg edition of his works, recounting the years 1517 to 1521 (LW 34:323–38). With its description of Luther's "breakthrough" in interpreting Paul amid his preparations to lecture on the Psalms, the 1545 preface was the culmination of Luther's own autobiographical efforts—and has become the source of interminable debates among modern scholars about the dating and character of Luther's theological development. It was intended as the first installment in an autobiographical series, but Luther died before writing the intended preface for the second Latin volume.[46] Instead, the continuation of his biography fell to Melanchthon, who took a different tack, focusing on Luther's youth instead of continuing with the controversies of the 1520s.[47] Thus the task of writing Luther's complete biography was left to others.

[44] See Kolb, *Luther as Prophet, Teacher, and Hero*, p. 150; Volz and Wolgast, "Geschichte der Luther-Ausgaben," WA 60:544–48; lists of the contents of the Eisleben edition are found in Aland, *Hilfsbuch*, pp. 589–93.

[45] The 1548 second German volume (Witt Ger 2) appeared with "Dr. Martin Luther's Preface, Composed before His Passing," but this was in fact a pastiche assembled by Rörer from the last pages of Luther's 1539 *Against the Antinomians* (LW 47:115–19) and the last portion of Luther's 1535 preface to Rhegius, *Refutation* (LW 60:88–90), linked by a middle section of unknown authorship and origin. See WA 54:468–77 and the introduction there by Otto Albrecht, pp. 459–67; and the introduction by Robert Kolb, LW 60:86.

[46] *Preface to the Latin Writings* (1545), LW 34:338.

[47] See below, Melanchthon, *Preface*, pp. 56–69.

JUSTUS JONAS AND MICHAEL COELIUS, *REPORT ON THE CHRISTIAN DEPARTURE OF THE REVEREND DR. MARTIN LUTHER FROM THIS MORTAL LIFE* (1546)[48]

Luther's death in Eisleben in the early morning hours of February 18, 1546, inevitably ushered in a new phase in Luther's biography, as the task of interpreting Luther's life now fell to his colleagues and students—and to his opponents. False reports of Luther's demise, produced by Roman Catholic critics, had already circulated, to one of which Luther had responded in his 1545 pamphlet *An Italian Lie concerning Dr. Martin Luther's Death.*[49] Yet if enemies elsewhere expected Luther's death, it seems to have come as a surprise to his immediate circle of colleagues and friends, not least because it had been expected for so long. From the time of his serious illness in the winter of 1536–37, Luther had regarded his death as imminent.[50] Yet his health had shown signs of improvement in 1544 and 1545, and Luther had traveled more in those years than he had for many years previously. Although he briefly suffered from vertigo on the final stage of his trip to Eisleben, Luther was as concerned with the health of Melanchthon (who had been too sick to travel) and Justus Jonas (who had injured his leg) as he was with his own.[51] Because of the conflicting expectations that friends and foes brought to Luther's last days, the narration and interpretation of the reformer's death became a key to defining his legacy.[52]

The fact that it was in Eisleben—the town of his birth in the county of Mansfeld—that Luther also departed mortal life was a fortuitous (or providential) coincidence.[53] Luther had maintained ties of relation and friendship to his boyhood home throughout his life, but his visits in person had been rare. The counts of Mansfeld were an old Thuringian noble family who enjoyed

---

[48] *Vom Christlichen abschied aus diesem toedlichen leben des Ehrwirdigen Herrn D. Martini Lutheri bericht durch D. Justum Jonam M. Michaelem Celium vnd ander die dabey gewesen kurtz zusamen gezogen* (Wittenberg: Georg Rhau, 1546) [VD16 ZV20628, J905], 16 leaves in quarto. WA 54:478–86 (introduction), 487–96 (text). See below, pp. 5–22.

[49] LW 34:361–66.

[50] See Brecht 3:185–88; and the introduction by Christopher Boyd Brown, LW 58:xvi.

[51] See Luther to Katharina Luther, February 1, 10, and 14, 1546, LW 50:290–92, 306, 312; and to Melanchthon, February 1, 1546, LW 50:292–95.

[52] Ninety sixteenth-century texts reporting on Luther's death are compiled in Christoph Schubart, *Die Berichte über Luthers Tod und Begräbnis: Texte und Untersuchungen* (Weimar: Böhlau, 1917). The *Report* by Jonas and Coelius is included as no. 69, pp. 59–68. On Luther's final stay in Eisleben, see Brecht 3:369–77.

[53] On the county of Mansfeld and its religious and political alignments in the sixteenth century, see Christman, *Doctrinal Controversy and Lay Religiosity in Late Reformation Germany*, pp. 15–47.

independence under direct fealty to the emperor [*Reichsunmittelbarkeit*] and had the advantage of presiding over a lucrative copper mining industry in their territories. Since 1501, however, the family had been divided into three lines, identified by the relative positions of their residences in the castle overlooking the town of Mansfeld (Tal Mansfeld). The brothers Count Albert of the Hinterort line and Count Gebhard of the Mittelort line became early supporters of the Reformation.[54] In 1525, at Luther's recommendation, they had appointed Johann Agricola (1494–1566), who was still Luther's friend and supporter at the time, as a pastor and teacher in Eisleben, where he remained until he was expelled in 1540 after falling out with Luther in the Antinomian Controversy.[55] More enduring was their appointment of Michael Coelius as court preacher at Mansfeld. Coelius had been rector of the Latin school in Döbeln, in Meissen, where both Johann Mathesius and Johann Walter were his students.[56] Having been ordained a priest, Coelius attended the Leipzig disputation in 1519 and became an adherent and friend of Luther. In Mansfeld, he became a winsome voice for the Reformation, defending it among its opponents and maintaining peace among its supporters.[57] Meanwhile, Counts Albert and Gebhard took active roles in the military and political defense of the Reformation movement, supporting the Augsburg Confession and joining the Smalcaldic League.

Albert and Gerhard's cousin Count Hoyer, on the other hand, remained a staunch adherent of the traditional religion, leading to conflict in those towns where the different branches of the family exercised joint jurisdiction. In Eisleben itself, the main town church of St. Andreas remained divided until 1540 when Hoyer died. Roman Catholic services were held in the morning, and Evangelical preaching by Luther's friend, the former Augustinian friar Caspar Güttel (1471–1542), was offered in

---

[54] Count Albert IV (1480–1560) founded Eisleben Neustadt in 1514. He was a strong supporter of Luther, and he and his brother, Count Gebhard VII (1478–1558), opened an Evangelical school in Eisleben in 1525, following consultations with Luther. Despite resistance from their cousin, Count Hoyer (1484–1540) of the Vorderort line, Albert was able to establish afternoon Evangelical services at St. Andreas Church in Eisleben, the last Roman Catholic church in town. See Christman, *Doctrinal Controversy and Lay Religiosity in Late Reformation Germany*, pp. 26–28.

[55] On Agricola, see below, p. 345 n. 134, pp. 372–73 n. 32, p. 412 n. 105, p. 414 nn. 116–17.

[56] On Mathesius, see below, pp. lxxx–lxxxvi; on Walter, see below, pp. lxxi–lxxv.

[57] Michael Coelius [Caelius] (1492–1559), pastor of the castle church of Mansfeld since 1525, maintained peace with colleagues Cyriakus Spangenberg (1528–1604) and Johann Agricola while opposing the lapsed Lutheran Georg Witzel. After Luther's death, Coelius joined the rest of the Mansfeld clergy in opposing the Augsburg Interim and Majorism. See Adolf Brecher, "Caelius, Michael," *ADB* 3:680–81; Christman, *Doctrinal Controversy and Lay Religiosity in Late Reformation Germany*, p. 27.

the afternoon.[58] Between 1533 and 1538, the Roman Catholic preacher under Count Hoyer's patronage was Georg Witzel (1501–73), a lapsed Lutheran who sought to persuade the people of Eisleben to return to the old religion as well.[59]

Upon Hoyer's death without issue in 1540, his nephews Count Philip (1502–46) and Count John [Hans] George (1515–79) accepted the Reformation as well, a step made easier by the fact that their political allies in Albertine Saxony had also done so after the death of Duke George the Bearded in 1539. The new common religious position among the three lines of Mansfeld counts did not, however, mean the end of conflict. Their jurisdiction still overlapped, and agreement on shared responsibility for the churches and schools of the county was elusive, to say nothing of the administration and taxation of the mines. Moreover, Count Albert had proven a shrewder financial administrator than his relatives and had, despite Luther's criticism, taken advantage of the distress of his brother, Gebhard, to expand his own power relative to the other counts.[60]

These conflicts finally drew Luther back to his homeland in the county Mansfeld for several trips in 1545 and 1546. In early October 1545, Luther and Melanchthon traveled together to Eisleben, apparently at Count Albert's invitation, to lay the groundwork for discussions. By early December, the different branches of the family had agreed to accept Luther as facilitator,[61] and Luther and Melanchthon traveled back to Mansfeld at Christmas to begin negotiations. Melanchthon became ill, however, and the Wittenbergers had to return home at the beginning of January 1546, setting a date of January 25 for their return and the resumption of talks.[62]

Melanchthon failed to recover in time to travel, so Luther set off for Eisleben without him on January 23, 1546, accompanied instead by his three sons, Johannes (Hans) (1526–75), Martin (1531–65), and Paul (1533–93); his secretary Johann Aurifaber; and his servant [famulus] Ambrosius Rutfeldt from Delitzsch.[63] Luther was delayed in Halle because of ice and flooding on the Saale River, and he preached there on January 26 before he

---

[58] On Güttel, see the introduction by Robert J. Christman, LW 60:245–46.

[59] On Witzel, see the introduction by Robert Kolb, LW 60:24–27.

[60] See Brecht 3:369; Luther to Count Albert of Mansfeld, February 23, 1542, WA Br 9:626–29.

[61] Luther to Count Albert of Mansfeld, December 6, 1545, LW 50:281–84.

[62] On the way back to Wittenberg, Luther preached at Halle on Epiphany, January 6, 1546: see LW 58:357–69.

[63] On Ambrosius Rutfeldt, see Schubart, Die Berichte über Luthers Tod und Begräbnis, p. 8; and WA 54:481.

was able to continue toward Mansfeld.[64] The superintendent in Halle was Justus Jonas [Jodocus Koch] (1493–1555), who had come to Halle from Wittenberg to begin Evangelical preaching in 1541, when Luther's old opponent Cardinal Albert of Brandenburg withdrew from the city. In 1542, Jonas became the first Evangelical superintendent in Halle as the city adopted a Lutheran church order. Jonas was Luther's friend and longtime colleague: he had been trained as a jurist and theologian and was a professor of canon law in Erfurt when he first heard Luther at Leipzig in 1519. In 1521, Jonas accompanied the Wittenbergers from Erfurt to Worms; while there he was offered a new appointment to the faculty in Wittenberg. Over their years of association, Jonas translated many of Luther's Latin works into German (and vice versa) for publication. Before his work in Halle, Jonas had helped draft church ordinances for Anhalt, Zerbst, and ducal Saxony.[65] He joined Luther's party as they left Halle for Eisleben. Thus it happened that Jonas also became Luther's companion on his last earthly journey.

Luther's party was received at the borders of county Mansfeld by a mounted escort and arrived in Eisleben on January 28. To maintain impartiality, Luther did not stay in one of the town palaces of the counts, but in a house belonging to the town government of Eisleben, occupied by the town clerk Johann Albrecht and his family, who served as Luther's host.[66] Luther's sons spent at least part of the time with family in Mansfeld rather than remaining continuously with their father in Eisleben.[67]

The negotiations among the counts began the day after Luther's arrival and continued for nearly three weeks, until February 16 and 17. In addition to the Mansfeld counts from the three branches of the family, Prince

---

[64] *Sermon on the Conversion of St. Paul*, LW 58:370–84. This sermon was published posthumously in April 1546, edited by the Halle preacher Matthias Wanckel (1511–71), along with Luther's Halle sermon of January 6: see the introduction by Christopher Boyd Brown, LW 58:351–54.

[65] On Jonas, see Robert Rosin, "Jonas, Justus," *OER* 2:352–53; Peter G. Bietenholz and Thomas B. Deutscher, eds., *Contemporaries of Erasmus: A Biographical Register of the Renaissance and Reformation* (Toronto: University of Toronto Press, 1985–87), 2:244–47.

[66] According to Jonas and Coelius, *Report* (see below, p. 17), Luther stayed in "Dr. Drachstedt's house": i.e., a house that had been owned by the jurist Dr. Philipp Drachstedt (ca. 1468–1539); had passed after his death to his son, Barthel Drachstedt (d. 1560); and was then sold to the town (see Schubart, *Die Berichte über Luthers Tod und Begräbnis*, p. 125). Although the house has been identified since the eighteenth century as the house at Andreaskirchplatz 7 in Eisleben, this may rest on a confusion of properties belonging to Barthel Drachstedt and his father, making the actual location of the house in which Luther died am Markt 56.

[67] See below, Jonas and Coelius, *Report*, p. 11 (and n. 24 there) and p. 20.

Wolfgang of Anhalt[68] and Count John Henry of Schwarzburg,[69] longtime supporters of Luther, also participated. Meanwhile, Luther preached four times in St. Andreas: on January 31, February 2, February 7, and February 15; he also took part in an ordination on February 14.[70] The negotiations on February 16 resulted in an enduring agreement as to the organization of the church and schools in the county of Mansfeld, though the settlement of economic and political matters achieved the following day was not so definitive.[71] By the time of the final session on February 17, Luther's health had declined so much that he was unable to participate.

Luther died in Eisleben early on the morning of February 18. He was attended in his last hours by Jonas, Coelius, and Aurifaber, along with his servant Ambrose. Luther's sons Martin and Paul were present in the house (Johannes was apparently still with relatives in Tal Mansfeld). Count Albert and his wife, Anna, called upon Luther in his illness and supplied medicine, leaving behind one of the count's counselors, Conrad von Wolframsdorf.[72] When Luther's condition grew worse, the two Eisleben town physicians— a Dr. Ludwig and the recent Wittenberg graduate Master Simon Wild— were summoned,[73] and Albert and his wife returned. Count John Henry of Schwarzburg arrived just before Luther's final breath. When Luther's heart had stopped, the Roman Catholic town apothecary, Johann Landau (though not mentioned in the account of Jonas and Coelius), was summoned to

---

[68] Wolfgang (1492–1566), prince of Anhalt-Köthen, had signed the Augsburg Confession in 1530 (see Kolb-Wengert, pp. 104–5; *Concordia*, p. 63); Luther to Nicholas Hausmann, July 6, 1530, LW 49:349–50; Franz Kindscher, "Wolfgang," *ADB* 44:68–72.

[69] Count John Henry of Schwarzburg (1496–1555) had corresponded with Luther already in 1522 about introducing the Reformation in his territories: see Luther to John Henry of Schwarzburg, December 12, 1522, WA Br 2:626–28; Brecht 2:72. On his participation together with Prince Wolfgang in the Mansfeld negotiations, see Brecht 3:374.

[70] For these sermons, see *Four Sermons Preached in Eisleben* (1546), LW 58:397–460; 51:381–92. On the question of the dating of the last sermon to February 15 or February 14, see the introduction by John W. Doberstein, LW 51:383; the introduction by Christopher Boyd Brown, LW 58:402; Brecht 3:372.

[71] See Christman, *Doctrinal Controversy and Lay Religiosity in Late Reformation Germany*, pp. 35–36; Brecht 3:374.

[72] On Anna, countess of Mansfeld, see below, p. 13 n. 40. On Conrad von Wolframsdorf, see below, p. 12 n. 29.

[73] Simon Wild [Bildaeus] (ca. 1520–60) was a protégé of the Zwickau town clerk and some-time-friend of Stephan Roth (see above, p. xxiii n. 34). Wild had studied at Wittenberg from 1539 to 1545, earning a master's degree, and then became a town physician in Eisleben after a brief return to Zwickau. See Georg Buchwald, "Simon Wilde aus Zwickau: Ein Wittenberger Studentenleben zur Zeit der Reformation," *Mitteilungen der Deutschen Gesellschaft zur Erforschung Vaterländischer Sprache* 9, no. 1 (1894): 61–111. Dr. Ludwig cannot be further identified; he would have been, with a doctorate in medicine, the senior town physician.

administer an enema in an attempt to revive him. In death, Luther was seen by many of the rest of the nobility and townspeople of Eisleben—first while lying on a bed of cushions, and then in a pewter coffin in the Drachstedt house before a public funeral service was held in St. Andreas on February 19. Although the counts of Mansfeld wished to have Luther buried there, they acceded to the request of the Saxon elector to have his body returned to Wittenberg. The cortege departed Eisleben on February 20 and arrived in Wittenberg on February 22, having stopped the intervening nights in Halle and in Bitterfeld.

Luther's final hours and death were thus well-witnessed, and several of those present made reports. Jonas wrote a detailed account immediately on February 18, at four o'clock in the morning, in a letter to Elector John Frederick. There he asked the elector to convey the news to Luther's wife, Katharina;[74] to Melanchthon; and to the Wittenberg city pastor Johann Bugenhagen, as well as to the university.[75] Jonas then wrote to Bugenhagen as well, though the letter has been lost.[76] Aurifaber wrote briefly to the Halle clerk Michael Gutt and to the Leipzig superintendent Johann Pfeffinger (1493–1573).[77] Count Albert and Prince Wolfgang both wrote briefly to the Saxon elector—to speak only of eyewitnesses.[78] Two painters—an anonymous artist from Eisleben and Lucas Furtenagel from Halle—made images of Luther in death.[79]

---

[74] Katharina Luther, née von Bora (1499–1552), from a minor Saxon noble family, had entered the cloister at an early age, taking vows as a Cistercian nun in 1515. In 1523, she and eleven other nuns escaped the convent at Nimbschen and came to Wittenberg for refuge, where Katharina was the last of the former nuns to accept a husband (see the introduction by Christopher Boyd Brown, LW 69:333–34). Her marriage to Luther in 1525 (see below, Mathesius, *History*, p. 227) produced scandal throughout Catholic Europe. Nevertheless, their marriage, which produced six children (Johannes [Hans], Elisabeth, Magdalena, Martin, Paul, and Margaretha), and the Luther household (including in addition to the children several orphan relatives and student boarders), which Katharina capably managed, became a model of Lutheran domesticity. See Martin Brecht, "Luther, Katharina," *OER* 2:460–61; Ernst Kroker, *The Mother of the Reformation: The Amazing Life and Story of Katharine Luther*, trans. Mark DeGarmeaux (St. Louis: Concordia, 2013); Kirsi Stjerna, *Women and the Reformation* (Malden, MA: Blackwell, 2009), pp. 51–70.

[75] Jonas to Elector John Frederick, February 18, 1546 (Schubart, *Die Berichte über Luthers Tod und Begräbnis*, no. 1, pp. 1–6).

[76] See Schubart, *Die Berichte über Luthers Tod und Begräbnis*, no. 3, p. 10.

[77] Schubart, *Die Berichte über Luthers Tod und Begräbnis*, nos. 5–6, pp. 11–12.

[78] Schubart, *Die Berichte über Luthers Tod und Begräbnis*, nos. 7 and 9, pp. 12–14.

[79] See below, Jonas and Coelius, *Report*, p. 18. Lucas Furtenagel [Fortenagel] (1505–46) was a Hallensian painter, trained in Augsburg under Hans Burgkmair (1473–1531). A portrait of Burgkmair and his wife, now in the Vienna Kunsthistorisches Museum, is ascribed to Furtenagel. Of his efforts to memorialize Luther (which may have been repeated the following day, when the coffin was in the church: see Schubart, *Die Berichte über Luthers Tod*

Both Jonas, who preached at Luther's Eisleben memorial service on February 19, and Coelius, who preached the following morning before the funeral procession departed the town, delivered sermons which reflected on Luther's life and the events surrounding his death and their significance; these sermons were later repeated in Halle and then published.[80] The apothecary, Johann Landau, a Roman Catholic, later composed his own report, sent to Georg Witzel, which the controversialist Johann Cochlaeus had translated into Latin and printed as part of his own anti-Lutheran polemic.[81] Its historical value is qualified not only by its point of view but also because it was not composed until some three months after Luther's death. Some of its details about dates, for example, are demonstrably incorrect.[82]

It was Jonas, who had written the first report of Luther's death to Elector John Frederick, who was responsible for the official published report that related and interpreted Luther's death for a wider audience, assisted by Coelius and Aurifaber—though since Aurifaber was the junior partner in the undertaking, his participation as author was mentioned only at the end of the document.[83] Already the day after Luther's death such a report was expected; Coelius promised its publication in his sermon on February 20 (or at least by the time the sermon was repeated in Halle). Elector John Frederick supported these plans with his own mandate, and the report appeared from

---

und Begräbnis, p. 79), there survives a pen drawing in the Staatliche Museum in Berlin. The anonymous Eisleben painter may have been associated with the Cranach workshop, and his work may have served as the basis for Lucas Cranach's (1472–1553) images of Luther in death, such as the painting now in the Hanover Niedersächsische Landesgalerie—but it may also be the case that the Eisleben artist's work is simply lost and Furtenagel's image or images provided the model for Cranach. See Georg Stuhlfauth, *Die Bildnisse D. Martin Luthers im Tode* (Weimar: Böhlau, 1927); Johannes Ficker, "Die Bildnisse Luthers aus der Zeit seines Lebens," *LJB* 16 (1934): 140–42; Alfred Dieck, "Cranachs Gemälde des toten Luther in Hannover und das Problem der Luther-Totenbilder," *Niederdeutsche Beiträge zur Kunstgeschichte* 2 (1962): 191–218.

[80] See Schubart, *Die Berichte über Luthers Tod und Begräbnis*, no. 15, pp. 17–18, and no. 28, pp. 29–32. The sermons delivered by Jonas and Coelius in Eisleben were revised for publication as *Zwo Tröstliche Predigt vber der Leich D. Doc. Martini Luther zu Eisleben den XIX. und XX. Februarii gethan durch D. Doct: Justum Joham, M. Michaelem Celium, Anno 1546* (Wittenberg: G. Rhau, 1546) [VD16 J899]. According to fol. A2r, the sermons were later repeated in Halle (though not while Luther's remains were there: see below, p. 19), and the notes behind the printed version were taken during their delivery there, rather than from the preachers' manuscripts or from notes taken in Eisleben.

[81] On Cochlaeus, see below, pp. lxvii–lxx.

[82] See Landau to Georg Witzel, before June 9, 1546, in Schubart, *Die Berichte über Luthers Tod und Begräbnis*, no. 78, pp. 74–80. Cf. the introduction by Christopher Boyd Brown, LW 58:403; and Schubart's analysis, *Die Berichte über Luthers Tod und Begräbnis*, pp. 110–13.

[83] See below, Jonas and Coelius, *Report*, p. 22.

Georg Rhau's Wittenberg presses just after the middle of March.[84] It was reprinted across Germany and in French and English translations.[85]

Jonas and his fellow authors were concerned to show that Luther had died peacefully, steadfast in faith in Jesus Christ—not attended by any of the terrors or ill omens that his enemies had anticipated—and relying upon God's Word rather than the traditional last rites of the medieval church. Luther's prayers, therefore, were central to their narrative: his repetition of Ps. 31:5 and Luke 23:46 (also an echo of the Compline liturgy) and other biblical texts; and especially Luther's prayer commending his soul to God, in confidence in Christ and His salvation—and in defiance of the pope. This prayer had been mentioned in the early epistolary reports as well as in the funeral sermons and was copied separately as a memorial, reflecting its importance as a witness to Luther's faith.[86]

Yet the report of the days before Luther's death made by Jonas and Coelius conveyed not only his piety but his conviviality and humor as well, as he discussed theology, food, and wine in turn. It was this aspect of Luther's last days which hostile reports found especially offensive, seeking to mock his eating and drinking and laughing with his companions—as well as his family connections to a wife and children—as unworthy of a supposed man of God.[87] For Jonas, Coelius, Aurifaber, and their Lutheran readers, however, Luther's faith, confidence, and human affection were exemplary, evidence of God's work to preserve the Gospel in the world as well as in Luther's heart.

---

[84] See the summary in Karl Drescher's preface, WA 54:43–44.

[85] In addition to the two Wittenberg printings [VD16 J905, ZV20628], there were editions in Augsburg [VD16 ZV8745–8746], Erfurt [VD16 ZV8749], Frankfurt am Main [VD16 J900], Hanover [VD16 J882], Constance [VD16 ZV27824], Magdeburg [VD16 J901–903], Nürnberg [VD16 J883, J904], Regensburg [J884], Strassburg [VD16 J885], Ulm [VD16 J886], and Zwickau [VD16 ZV8748], as well as an edition without indicated location [VD16 ZV8744]. A French edition appeared in Basel [VD16 ZV27825] and an English edition in Wesel [VD16 ZV25460]. On the incorporation of the *Report* by Jonas and Coelius in Johann Pollicarius' compilation, see below, p. lxiii.

[86] See below, p. xxxviii; Jonas and Coelius, *Report*, pp. 13–14. Cf. Melanchthon, "Oral Report on Luther's Death," in Schubart, *Die Berichte über Luthers Tod und Begräbnis*, no. 21, pp. 22–24, published in Pollicarius' collection; Schubart, *Die Berichte über Luthers Tod und Begräbnis*, pp. 95–96; Carolyn R. S. Lenz, "A Recently Discovered Manuscript Account of Luther's Last Prayer," *ARG* 66 (1975): 79–92.

[87] See, e.g., Landau, in Schubart, *Die Berichte über Luthers Tod und Begräbnis*, no. 78, pp. 76–77 (cf. his criticism of the Eisleben citizens charged with keeping watch over Luther's coffin for "drinking good beer" in place of a requiem Mass, p. 79); Johann Cochlaeus, *The Deeds and Writings of Dr. Martin Luther*, in Elizabeth Vandiver, Ralph Keen, and Thomas D. Frazel, trans. and eds., *Luther's Lives: Two Contemporary Accounts of Martin Luther* (Manchester, UK: Manchester University Press, 2002), pp. 350–54.

The present translation, by Matthew Carver, is made from the German text of the 1546 Wittenberg printing as edited in WA 54:487–96.[88]

JOHANN BUGENHAGEN, *A CHRISTIAN SERMON FOR THE FUNERAL AND BURIAL OF THE REVEREND DR. MARTIN LUTHER* (1546)[89]

The news of Luther's death arrived in Wittenberg on the morning of February 19, with the letters from Jonas to the elector and to Bugenhagen.[90] Melanchthon took responsibility for making a public announcement to the students when they had gathered for his series of lectures on Romans.[91] He briefly described Luther's last hours, as Jonas had narrated them, and read Luther's prayer of commendation to God in full.[92] Finally, Melanchthon lamented: "Alas! The horseman and chariot of Israel has perished [2 Kings 2:12], who guided the Church in these last days of the world's old age. For the doctrine concerning remission of sins and faith in the Son of God was not grasped by human wisdom, but it has been manifested by God through this man, who, we see, was stirred up by God. Let us therefore love the memory of this man and the kind of doctrine which he passed on, and with what equanimity we can muster, let us contemplate the tremendous calamities and great upheavals which will follow upon this event. O Son of God, Immanuel, You who were crucified and raised for us, I pray that You would rule, preserve, and defend Your Church! Amen."[93]

When Luther's funeral procession returned his remains to Wittenberg on February 22, 1546, the solemnity was a public occasion such as the town had seldom witnessed. The closest parallels were the funerals of the electors Frederick the Wise and John the Steadfast, in 1525 and 1532 respectively, at

---

[88] The Weimar text is superior to the edition in Schubart, *Die Berichte über Luthers Tod und Begräbnis*, no. 69, pp. 59–68. For the translation here, see below, pp. 5–22. An older English translation appeared in Martin Ebon, trans. and ed., *The Last Days of Luther: By Justus Jonas, Michael Coelius, and Others*, intro. Theodore G. Tappert (Garden City, NY: Doubleday, 1970).

[89] *Eine Christliche Predigt/ über der Leich und begrebnis/ des Ehrwirdigen D. Martini Luthers/ durch Ern Johan Bugenhagen Pomern/ Doctor/ und Pfarherr der Kirchen zu Wittemberg/ gethan* (Wittenberg: Georg Rhau, 1546) [VD16 B9274], 13 leaves in quarto.

[90] See Melanchthon to Jonas, February 19, 1546, CR 6:56–57.

[91] See CR 6:57–59.

[92] See below, Jonas and Coelius, *Report*, p. 14.

[93] Melanchthon's announcement was published as part of the collection of materials on Luther made by Johann Pollicarius (see below, p. lxiii). See the full translation of Melanchthon's announcement to the students in Vandiver et al., *Luther's Lives*, pp. 38–40.

which Luther himself had preached.[94] For Luther's funeral, the electoral government, visiting nobility, university, and town government all took part, along with Luther's family, led by Katharina and their children. Jonas and Coelius reported that the press of students, townspeople, and others who filled the streets and market square in Wittenberg were a throng such as had never before been seen.[95]

At the elector's arrangement, Luther's funeral service and burial took place not in the city church of St. Mary's but in the Castle Church. The liturgy seems to have followed Luther's 1542 recommendations in his *Preface to the Burial Hymns*.[96] In keeping with the composite character of the event, there were two oral addresses given: a funeral sermon delivered in German by Bugenhagen, as pastor and superintendent of the church in Wittenberg; and an oration in Latin given by Melanchthon, speaking for the university community. After both Bugenhagen and Melanchthon had spoken, Luther's burial took place in a grave just in front of the pulpit, not far from the graves of the electors Frederick and John before the altar of the Castle Church.

Johann Bugenhagen (1485–1558), from Pomerania (hence his frequent epithet "Pomeranus" or "Pommer"), who had come to Wittenberg in 1521, had enjoyed a long and close association with Luther.[97] While serving as a priest, Bugenhagen had come to identify himself as a Christian humanist under the influence of Erasmus, and he overcame his initial offense at Luther's provocative writing to embrace his proclamation of the Gospel. In Wittenberg, Bugenhagen lectured on biblical books privately until he received his doctorate in 1533 and became a regular professor in the university. In addition to his own published exegetical and theological works, whose insight Luther highly valued,[98] Bugenhagen also translated works by Luther into the Low German dialect.

The most important sphere of Bugenhagen's activity, however, was pastoral. In 1523, he was chosen as pastor of the Wittenberg parish, responsible for preaching and pastoral care. Bugenhagen also applied his talents to the administration of the church, helping to draft ordinances for the Wittenberg

---

[94] See *Two Sermons for the Burial of Elector Frederick the Wise* (1525), WA 17/1:196–227 (LW 56); *Two Funeral Sermons* (1532), LW 51:229–55.

[95] See below, Jonas and Coelius, *Report*, pp. 20–21.

[96] LW 53:325–31; cf. below, Jonas and Coelius, *Report*, p. 20.

[97] On Bugenhagen, see Kurt K. Hendel, "Johannes Bugenhagen: Reformer beyond the Limelight," in *Johannes Bugenhagen: Selected Writings*, ed. Kurt K. Hendel (Minneapolis: Fortress, 2015), 1:1–75.

[98] See Luther's prefaces to Bugenhagen, *Interpretation of the Psalms* (1524), LW 59:82–87; and to Bugenhagen's edition of Athanasius, *Against the Idolatry of the Gentiles* (1532), LW 59:342–47.

church and school and traveling to organize Evangelical churches in the cities of Braunschweig, Hamburg, and Lübeck and in the territories of Pomerania, Denmark, and Braunschweig-Wolfenbüttel. His absences created many opportunities for Luther to step into the Wittenberg pulpit. Yet Bugenhagen's pastoral presence in Wittenberg was crucial, for it was Bugenhagen who presided at Luther's wedding and served as the reformer's own pastor and confessor.

To Bugenhagen, therefore, also fell the task of preaching at Luther's funeral, with a sermon that brought together elements that became an enduring part of Lutheran memory of the reformer (a word which Bugenhagen helped to associate indelibly with Luther). Bugenhagen's sermon reflected his own deep grief even as it expressed thanksgiving for God's work accomplished through Luther, "this lofty teacher and prophet, the reformer of the Church whom God sent" not only to the Church in Germany but also "in many foreign nations." Although to his opponents he may have seemed "too severe and presumptuous," Luther was animated with divine boldness by God's Spirit to stand firm against the devil, "the wretched pope and numerous sects and tyrants," and "so many shameful idolatries and commandments of men."[99]

Bugenhagen reinforced his depiction of Luther's role by turning to the Apocalypse to identify Luther with the "angel flying through the midst of the heavens, having an eternal Gospel to proclaim" (Rev. 14:6-7).[100] The connection was not new, having already been proposed in 1522 by Luther's friend, the former Augustinian Michael Stifel, in a piece of popular verse.[101] Nor was it necessarily so audacious as it may appear: in late medieval tradition, the Dominican St. Vincent Ferrer (1350–1419) had self-consciously applied the Revelation 14 text and its imagery to himself, an appropriation that was incorporated into his iconography and liturgical memorial.[102]

Bugenhagen also appealed to a more recent tradition of prophecy, identifying Luther as the "swan" who had been foretold a century before by the

---

[99] See below, Bugenhagen, *Christian Sermon*, pp. 25–26.

[100] See below, Bugenhagen, *Christian Sermon*, p. 27.

[101] Michael Stifel [Stiefel], *Von der Christfermigen/ rechtegegrundten leer Doctoris Martini Luthers/ ain überauß schön kunstlich Lied* (Augsburg: Philipp Ulhart Sr., 1522) [VD16 S9019–9020]. For the verse "Johannis thut uns schreiben," see Wackernagel 3:74–79, no. 107; Rebecca Wagner Oettinger, *Music as Propaganda in the German Reformation* (Aldershot: Ashgate, 2001), p. 305. On Stifel (ca. 1487–1567), see Richard Ernest Walker, "Stifel, Michael," *OER* 4:112–13; Luther, *Sermon for the Wedding of Michael Stifel* (1528), WA 27:384–90 (LW 56).

[102] See *ODCC*, 3rd ed., s.v. "Vincent Ferrer"; Friedrich Wilhelm Bautz, "Ferrer, Vincenz," *BBKL* 11:20–21; on Ferrer's identification with the angel of Revelation 14, see Andrew Pradel, *St. Vincent Ferrer: The Angel of the Judgment*, trans. T. A. Dixon (Rockford, IL: Tan Books, 2000), from the French edition of 1875.

"goose" John [Jan] Hus (1369–1415), the Czech theologian and reformer who, having denounced abuses and immorality among the clergy, had been condemned and burned at the Council of Constance.[103] Luther himself had first appealed to this "prophecy" (in fact a conflation of statements made by Hus and his associate Jerome of Prague [ca. 1379–1416]) in the wake of the Diet of Augsburg.[104] The connection between Luther and Hus served to anchor Luther's ministry in the history of God's work in the Church, assuring Bugenhagen's listeners that God remained their protector even after Luther's death.[105]

Yet even as Bugenhagen sought to portray Luther as a biblical and world-historical figure, one who had "carried out his mandate in the supreme office of apostle and prophet,"[106] he also presented Luther as a well-known local presence, a friend and colleague in ministry. An extended digression about the ministry of Luther and Bugenhagen during the illness and death of Luther's brother-in-law Ambrose Berndt[107] offers not only a parallel to Luther's peaceful departure from the world but also a picture of Luther as pastor.

Bugenhagen concludes with an account of Luther's own death, focusing on his prayers and faithful commendation into God's hands.[108] Bugenhagen beseeches God to preserve Luther's teaching among his successors, exhorting his listeners against ingratitude, and calling upon them to pray for the Church in the words of Luther's own hymn "Lord, Keep Us Steadfast in Your Word."[109] Finally, the opponents of the Gospel are warned of impending judgment in the words of Luther's "prophecy" against the pope.[110] With its juxtaposition of the biblical and universal with the intensely local and personal, Bugenhagen's sermon for Luther's funeral shaped the sixteenth-century memorial of Luther among his colleagues and students.

---

[103] Hus was also associated with the distribution of Communion to the laity in both kinds (including the cup), though this seems to have first become a major issue among his followers after his death. On the reception of Hus by Luther and in the sixteenth-century Reformation in general, see Phillip N. Haberkern, *Patron Saint and Prophet: Jan Hus in the Bohemian and German Reformations* (New York: Oxford University Press, 2016), especially pp. 149–62. Cf. Luther, preface to the second volume of the works of Hus (1524), LW 59:97–101; preface and afterword to Hus, *Three Letters* (1536), LW 60:122–33; preface to Hus, *Some Very Godly and Erudite Letters* (1537), LW 60:152–57.

[104] On Hus' "prophecy," see Haberkern, *Patron Saint and Prophet*, pp. 188–89.

[105] Cf. Haberkern, *Patron Saint and Prophet*, pp. 248–59, on Bugenhagen's sermon.

[106] See below, Bugenhagen, *Christian Sermon*, p. 29.

[107] See below, Bugenhagen, *Christian Sermon*, pp. 31–33.

[108] See above, p. xxxiv; and below, Bugenhagen, *Christian Sermon*, p. 33.

[109] See below, Bugenhagen, *Christian Sermon*, p. 34.

[110] See below, Bugenhagen, *Christian Sermon*, p. 35.

Bugenhagen's sermon was quickly printed in Wittenberg by Georg Rhau,[111] followed by separate editions elsewhere, before being incorporated into collections on Luther's death and biography.[112] The translation of Bugenhagen's *Christian Sermon* in this volume has been made by Matthew Carver from the 1546 Wittenberg printing, consulted in the digitized exemplar of the Bavarian State Library in Munich.[113]

PHILIP MELANCHTHON, *ORATION AT THE FUNERAL OF DR. MARTIN LUTHER* (1546)[114]

Philip Melanchthon's reminiscence of Luther was, like Bugenhagen's, based on a long and fruitful collaboration. Melanchthon (1497–1560), holding a master's degree in the liberal arts from Tübingen, had come to Wittenberg in 1518 to assume a professorship in Greek. Although a young man of only twenty-one years, he was already a promising humanist who had developed under the patronage of his uncle, the Hebraist Johann Reuchlin.[115] Having taken the first theological degree in Wittenberg, Melanchthon lectured on the New Testament as well as on classical texts, in both the arts and the theological faculties. Alongside Luther, Melanchthon became the most prominent public exponent of the Wittenberg theology.[116] His published commentaries on New Testament books and, above all, his *Loci communes*

---

[111] The 1546 Wittenberg editions by Georg Rhau [VD16 B9274, ZV2697] are distinguished by the variation of Bugenhagen's title as "*Pfarrherr*" or "*Pfarrher*" on the title page. Some copies give evidence of the haste of printing: the copy of VD16 ZV2697 from the Wartburg library digitized at the University of Jena, for example, leaves a page of type out of place on the verso of the title page.

[112] In 1546, separate editions of Bugenhagen's *Christian Sermon* also appeared at Augsburg [VD16 B9270], Frankfurt am Main [VD16 B9271], Magdeburg [VD16 B9269], Zwickau [VD16 B9275], and an edition without indicated location [VD16 ZV2696].

[113] See below, pp. 23–35. The translation here may be compared with Kurt K. Hendel, trans., "A Christian sermon over the body and at the funeral of the venerable Dr. Martin Luther, preached by Mr. Johann Bugenhagen Pomeranus, doctor and pastor of the church in Wittenberg," in *Johannes Bugenhagen: Selected Writings* (Minneapolis: Fortress, 2015), 1:111–23.

[114] *Oratio in Funere Reverendi Viri D. Martini Lutheri, Recitata Vitebergae a Philippo Melanchthone* (Leipzig: Valentin Babst, 1546) [VD16 M3849], 8 leaves in octavo, edited in CR 11:726–34. On the complex history of early printings of Melanchthon's *Oration* and their variations in text, see below, pp. xliv–liii.

[115] On Reuchlin, see below, p. 132 n. 100.

[116] On Melanchthon, see Heinz Scheible, "Melanchthon, Philipp," *OER* 3:41–45; and the essays collected in Timothy J. Wengert, *Philip Melanchthon, Speaker of the Reformation: Wittenberg's Other Reformer* (Burlington, VT: Ashgate, 2010).

projected his influence beyond the Wittenberg classroom across Europe.[117] He took a leading role in the organization of schools and churches, particularly through his participation in the Saxon visitations of 1528–30.[118] Because Luther, under the imperial ban since the Diet of Worms in 1521, was confined to electoral Saxony and other friendly territories, Melanchthon was the leading representative of the Evangelical theologians at imperial diets and colloquies, above all at the 1530 Diet of Augsburg, where Melanchthon was chief drafter of the Augsburg Confession.[119]

Differences in approach and emphasis between Luther and Melanchthon were usually appreciated on both sides of the collaboration as advantageous to their shared cause.[120] Frequently, Luther defended Melanchthon against critics who claimed to be speaking on Luther's behalf, such as Johann Agricola and Conrad Cordatus—though Luther's response was more qualified in the latter case.[121] Even in the 1540s, as differences between Luther and Melanchthon in articulating the doctrine of the Lord's Supper became apparent, Luther refrained from openly criticizing his colleague.[122] After Luther's death, Melanchthon's legacy would become controversial, as many Lutherans (themselves students of both Melanchthon and Luther) found Melanchthon's accommodation to imperial religious policy in the wake of the 1547 defeat of the Smalcaldic League to be intolerable and, partly in light of the suspicions thus engendered, questioned some

---

[117] For the various English editions of Melanchthon's *Loci communes*, see below, p. 189 n. 30. On Melanchthon's commentaries, see Luther's prefaces to Melanchthon, *Annotations on Romans and Corinthians* (1522), LW 59:18–22, and to Melanchthon, *Exposition of Colossians* (1529), LW 59:248–50, and the introductions by Timothy J. Wengert there, as well as Wengert, *Philip Melanchthon's "Annotations in Johannem" of 1523 in Relation to Its Predecessors and Contemporaries*, Travaux d'humanisme et Renaissance 220 (Geneva: Droz, 1987).

[118] See *Instructions for the Visitors* (1528), LW 40:263–320.

[119] For the Augsburg Confession, see Kolb-Wengert, pp. 27–105; *Concordia*, pp. 21–63. On Melanchthon's participation in the colloquies, see below, Mathesius, *History*, pp. 310–11, 324–26, 395–96, 489–93.

[120] See Timothy J. Wengert, "Luther and Melanchthon—Melanchthon and Luther," *LJB* 66 (1999): 55–88, reprinted in Wengert, *Philip Melanchthon, Speaker of the Reformation*.

[121] On the controversies with Agricola and Cordatus, see below, pp. 345 n. 134, 372–73 n. 32, 416 n. 134. Cordatus (1480–1546) was an Austrian humanist and theologian who had first come to Wittenberg in 1524. After circulating through several positions, Cordatus was recommended by Luther for the pastorate in Neimeck, near Wittenberg, from which post in 1537 he accused Melanchthon of teaching that good works were necessary for salvation. See Robert Rosin, "Cordatus, Conrad," *OER* 1:430.

[122] See, e.g., *Brief Confession* (1544), LW 38:279–319; Charles P. Arand, James A. Nestingen, and Robert Kolb, *The Lutheran Confessions: History and Theology of the Book of Concord* (Minneapolis: Fortress, 2012), pp. 161–70.

of Melanchthon's other theological positions as well.[123] Yet Melanchthon's funeral oration predates those later controversies, and it would be anachronistic to project them back onto it.

Melanchthon's Latin oration for Luther, delivered in the Castle Church on February 22, 1546, after Bugenhagen's German sermon, was part of an established custom for prominent public funerals in Wittenberg. Melanchthon previously had delivered such orations at the funerals of the Saxon electors Frederick the Wise and John the Steadfast in 1525 and 1532 respectively.[124] The corpus of Melanchthon's orations also contains a 1539 funeral oration for the Wittenberg professor of civil law Sebald Münster, read by Veit Oertel from Winsheim (1501–70),[125] as well as one for Dorothea of Denmark, duchess of Prussia (1504–47), delivered by Georg Sabinus (1508–60).[126] Melanchthon's funeral orations are examples of epideictic oratory: the *genus demonstrativum*, concerned with praise and blame, as Melanchthon had described it in his rhetorical handbooks.[127]

In the funeral oration for Luther, Melanchthon plays on the expectations of this genre.[128] After a proemium strongly resembling those of his other funeral orations, making reference to public lamentation and the orator's hesitation to speak because of his own grief, Melanchthon announces that he

---

[123] See Arand et al., *Lutheran Confessions*, pp. 171–216.

[124] CR 11:90–98, 223–27.

[125] CR 11:457–66.

[126] CR 11:763–75. Other biographical orations (not explicitly characterized as "funeral" orations) followed: of Caspar Cruciger, in 1549 on the anniversary of his 1548 death (CR 11:833–41); of Sibylle of Cleves, wife of Elector John Frederick of Saxony, in 1553 (CR 12:61–68); of George of Anhalt in 1554 (CR 12:68–79); of the jurist Hieronymus Schurff in 1554 (CR 12:86–94); and of Johann Bugenhagen in 1558 (CR 12:295–307).

[127] See Melanchthon, *Elementa Rhetorices*, ed. and trans. Volkhard Wels, 2nd ed. (Berlin: Weidler, 2001), pp. 130–37.

[128] On the *Oration*, see James Michael Weiss, "Erasmus at Luther's Funeral," *SCJ* 16 (1985): 91–114; Timothy J. Wengert, "The First Biography of Martin Luther, Compiled by Johannes Pollicarius," in *Memoria—theologische Synthese—Autoritätenkonflikt: Die Rezeption Luthers und Melanchthons in der Schülergeneration*, ed. Irene Dingel (Tübingen: Mohr Siebeck, 2016), pp. 15–44, especially pp. 31–35; Naomichi Masaki, "Luther-Memoria on the Occasion of His Death," in *Memoria—theologische Synthese—Autoritätenkonflikt: Die Rezeption Luthers und Melanchthons in der Schülergeneration*, ed. Irene Dingel (Tübingen: Mohr Siebeck, 2016), pp. 69–87, especially pp. 81–84; Robert Kolb, *For All the Saints: Changing Perceptions of Martyrdom and Sainthood in the Lutheran Reformation* (Macon, GA: Mercer University Press, 1987), pp. 105–7; Kolb, *Luther as Prophet, Teacher, and Hero*, pp. 34–37; and Siegfried Bräuer, "Die Überlieferung von Melanchthons Leichenrede auf Luther," in *Humanismus und Wittenberger Reformation: Festgabe anlässlich des 500. Geburtstages des Praeceptor Germaniae Philipp Melanchthon am 16. Februar 1997*, ed. Michael Beyer and Günther Wartenberg (Leipzig: Evangelische Verlagsanstalt, 1996), pp. 185–252.

will not be following the usual patterns of personal encomium or biography but will focus instead on the central topic of Luther's office in the Church.

Although this was a departure from the straightforward model of biographical narrative which Melanchthon recommended for epideictic orations dealing with *persons* (and which he followed in many of the other biographical orations),[129] it reflected Melanchthon's advice for speaking about a person's notable *deeds* which were deserving of commemoration and thanksgiving, in which case he allowed great flexibility in introducing topics drawn from other genres of speech.[130] For older members of the Wittenberg audience, this pattern would have recalled the approach Melanchthon had used in his orations for the Saxon electors, in which he had focused on their office and rule as princes rather than on their personal biographies. Melanchthon's attention to Luther's teaching—and the rhetorical effort to anticipate and respond to criticisms of it—also recalls his orations on the great teachers of the Church, especially the 1539 *Oration on the Life of Augustine*.[131]

In the *Oration*, Melanchthon thus makes Luther's status as a hero called and stirred up by God to be a teacher in the Church the central theme, supported by description of God's providential government of His Church and exhortation to render the thanks due to God. Rather than interpreting Luther in the terms Bugenhagen had used—as a prophet or apostle, or as the angel of Revelation 14—Melanchthon places Luther in a succession of teachers extending from Adam through the patriarchs and prophets, to Christ and the apostles, through the fathers of the Church and certain medieval theologians—or, as Melanchthon summarizes, "Isaiah, the Baptist, Paul, Augustine, Luther."[132]

Melanchthon then addresses a series of objections to Luther's ministry, in the course of which Melanchthon has opportunity to describe Luther's doctrine and character.[133] First, Melanchthon anticipates the charge that Luther has disturbed the Church. Melanchthon instead ascribes blame for any disturbances to the "godless . . . who refuse to hear the Son of God,"[134] and goes on to give an elegant summary of Luther's teaching on repentance,

---

[129] Melanchthon, *Elementa Rhetorices*, pp. 130–31. Melanchthon's preface to Witt Lat 2 is much closer to the narrative model: see below, *Preface*, pp. 53–80.

[130] Melanchthon, *Elementa Rhetorices*, pp. 132–37.

[131] CR 11:446–56. The *Oratio de vita Augustini* is, however, biographical in organization.

[132] See below, Melanchthon, *Oration*, p. 43. Cf. Peter Fraenkel, *Testimonia Patrum: The Function of the Patristic Argument in the Theology of Philip Melanchthon* (Geneva: Droz, 1961), pp. 160–61.

[133] According to Melanchthon, *Elementa Rhetorices*, pp. 132–33, such confutations and confirmations are a necessary part of oratory about a controversial figure.

[134] See below, Melanchthon, *Oration*, p. 43.

the distinction of Law and Gospel, true worship, and vocation in the world. Melanchthon points to Luther's German translation of the Bible and to his commentaries, alongside his polemical works, as well as his unwavering insistence on justification by faith, as evidence that Luther was one divinely taught.

The *Oration* then takes up the charge that Luther had been harsher than was necessary.[135] Melanchthon answers by quoting Erasmus: that the great ills of the age had led God to send Luther as a severe physician. To complain of Luther, therefore, is to protest against God. Melanchthon then elaborates on Luther's role as a divinely sent hero, echoing early humanist identification of Luther as the "German Hercules," as well as the Stoic idea of the sage whose perfect virtues could not be comprehended by ordinary ethical rules.[136]

Melanchthon then turns to the intimate side of Luther's character: his humanity and sweetness, mixed with appropriate gravity, as witnessed by his circle of friends, further showing that his harshness in dealing with opponents of the truth had been motivated by godly zeal rather than by contentiousness. Luther did not advocate sedition or seek to augment his own power; rather, he demonstrated such wisdom and virtue that they were further proof that Luther was a lofty spirit under God's guidance. Melanchthon recalled Luther's fervency in prayer, his fearlessness and penetrating judgment, his acuteness of mind, his insight into the character of others, his avid study, and his eloquence.

Although Melanchthon affirms that the loss of such a man is surely to be mourned, nonetheless he urges his hearers to rejoice in the assurance that Luther now enjoys the heavenly fellowship with Christ and all the prophets and apostles, just as he had always longed for and preached. Those who remain in the world should retain Luther's memory and teaching and imitate his virtues insofar as those who may not be heroes are able. Melanchthon concludes with a prayer for the Church and its ministry of the Gospel and a warning to his listeners that they retain and remain steadfast in God's Word, for it is with such that God dwells.

Melanchthon's Luther, therefore, is a divinely sent teacher, occupying an eminent place in a long succession and demonstrating God's miraculous

---

[135] Cf. below, Bugenhagen, *Christian Sermon*, p. 26. Luther himself had embraced the characterization of "roughness," especially in comparison with Melanchthon: see Luther, preface to Melanchthon, *Exposition of Colossians* (1529), LW 59:250. For Luther's description of "heroic" virtue, see *Commentary on Psalm 101* (1534), LW 13:154–200. Cf. Paul Althaus, *The Theology of Martin Luther*, trans. Robert C. Schultz (Philadelphia: Fortress, 1966), pp. 439–40, 441–42; Heinrich Bornkamm, *Luther and the Old Testament*, trans. Eric W. and Ruth C. Gritsch, ed. Victor I. Gruhn (Philadelphia: Fortress, 1969), p. 12.

[136] See below, Melanchthon, *Oration*, pp. 45–47. Cf. Wengert, "First Biography of Martin Luther," pp. 31, 33.

care for the Gospel and the Church. The quotations from Erasmus in praise of Luther (serving tacitly to answer Erasmus' own criticisms elsewhere) do not serve to reinterpret Luther in an Erasmian framework but to set Erasmus within a Lutheran one.[137] The effect of Melanchthon's rhetorical strategy of prolepsis is not to endorse the charge of Luther's excessive harshness but to emphasize his heroic, divinely willed role—which, to be sure, was not to be imitated in every respect by lesser spirits without such an extraordinary call.

The foregoing discussion of the structure and rhetoric of Melanchthon's *Oration* reflects the form of the text as it was printed in Leipzig in 1546 and was subsequently edited for modern publication in the *Corpus Reformatorum* edition of Melanchthon's works. In fact, however, the text of Melanchthon's funeral oration appeared in print in 1546 in two Latin versions (a shorter one originating in Wittenberg and a longer one originating in Leipzig) and in three German translations (two done outside Wittenberg corresponding to the shorter Latin text and one from Caspar Cruciger in Wittenberg mostly—but not completely—corresponding to the longer Leipzig version of the Latin). Accordingly, questions have been raised about which version corresponds most closely to what Melanchthon actually spoke in the Castle Church on February 22.

James Michael Weiss has argued that it was the short form that Melanchthon delivered orally on February 22,[138] whereas the longer form was produced afterward to polish the text for publication and, in particular, to soften the criticism of Luther's "harshness" [*asperitas*]. Siegfried Bräuer similarly concluded that the shortest form of the text was the one originally delivered in Wittenberg.[139] Because the present editor interprets the evidence as favoring the original delivery of a longer form of the Latin text paralleled (in translation) by Cruciger's German version, the arguments concerning the varying texts of the *Oration* and their transmission must be detailed here.

The dissemination of Melanchthon's *Oration* began immediately after it was delivered. A letter from Luther's student and boarder Hieronymus Besold to Veit Dietrich dated the day of the funeral was accompanied by a manuscript copy of the *Oration* and the note that a printed edition was

---

[137] See Wengert, "First Biography of Martin Luther," p. 31; Timothy J. Wengert, *Human Freedom, Christian Righteousness: Philip Melanchthon's Exegetical Dispute with Erasmus of Rotterdam* (New York: Oxford University Press, 1998), pp. 154–56; against Weiss, "Erasmus at Luther's Funeral," pp. 95–97.

[138] Weiss, "Erasmus at Luther's Funeral," pp. 91–114.

[139] Bräuer, "Die Überlieferung von Melanchthons Leichenrede."

expected "any day now" [*propediem ut puto edetur*].[140] Although it is impossible to know what version of the *Oration* Besold's manuscript conveyed, the Wittenberg edition which must have appeared about February 24 contained a short form of the Latin text, apparently (though printed without colophon) from the press of Joseph Klug (d. 1552).[141] Further editions of this text appeared in Magdeburg,[142] Marburg, and Lübeck as well.[143]

The long form of the Latin text appeared in an elegant edition from the press of Valentin Babst (d. 1556) in Leipzig, edited by the Nürnberg humanist Joachim Camerarius (1500–1574), who had been resident in Leipzig since 1541 to assist in the reorganization of the university under Lutheran auspices.[144] Melanchthon acknowledged Camerarius' work on the Leipzig edition of the *Oration* in a letter of March 11, 1546, expressing warm appreciation for his editorial changes to the text and its presentation.[145] The Leipzig edition was reproduced in a Wittenberg printing of the longer text to which Joseph Klug openly set his name.[146] An inscribed copy of this Wittenberg edition of the longer text preserved in the Gotha research library shows that Melanchthon himself gave copies of this edition to friends.[147] It was the Leipzig version of the *Oration* that was used when collections of

---

[140] See Bräuer, "Die Überlieferung von Melanchthons Leichenrede," pp. 187–88, citing *Der Briefwechsel des Justus Jonas*, ed. Gustav Kawerau, 2 vols., Geschichtsquellen der Provinz Sachsen 17 (Leipzig: Hendel, 1894–95), 2:182–84, no. 785. On Besold, see below, p. 425 n. 8. On Dietrich, see below, p. 278 n. 76.

[141] VD16 M3854. This edition has been consulted in the digitized exemplar of the Austrian National Library in Vienna. The text is edited in Bräuer, "Die Überlieferung von Melanchthons Leichenrede," pp. 210–14. On the date of its publication, see also Bräuer, "Die Überlieferung von Melanchthons Leichenrede," p. 188.

[142] VD16 M3851.

[143] VD16 lists editions from Andreas Kolbe in Marburg (M3852, with an exemplar in the Thüringer Universitäts- und Landesbibliothek, Jena) and from Johann Balhorn Sr. in Lübeck (M3850, with an exemplar in the Göttingen Staats- und Universitätsbibliothek); see the text edited in Bräuer, "Die Überlieferung von Melanchthons Leichenrede," pp. 243–52. Theresa Kilian of the Jena library kindly confirmed that the Marburg edition contains the shorter form of the text.

[144] VD16 M3849. The text is edited in Bräuer, "Die Überlieferung von Melanchthons Leichenrede," pp. 214–21. On Camerarius, see Marc R. Forster, "Camerarius, Joachim," *OER* 1:249; Rainer Kößling and Günther Wartenberg, eds., *Joachim Camerarius* (Tübingen: Narr, 2003); Frank Baron, ed., *Joachim Camerarius (1500–1574): Beiträge zur Geschichte des Humanismus im Zeitalter der Reformation* (Munich: Wilhelm Fink, 1978).

[145] Melanchthon to Joachim Camerarius, March 11, 1546, MBW T15:146–47, no. 4184 (CR 6:80). On the dating, see below, p. li.

[146] VD16 M3853, with an exemplar in the Gotha Forschungsbibliothek, Signatur Biogr 8° 01149/04. This edition includes only the Latin elegy but not the Greek poem.

[147] Gotha Forschungsbibliothek, Signatur Th 8° 00716/67 (02).

works on Luther's life including the *Oration* were published in Wittenberg—
or when Melanchthon's orations were collected and printed.[148] Whatever
else may be said for it, the version of the *Oration* edited by Camerarius was
the form in which Melanchthon himself wished to have his funeral address
for Luther published and remembered.

The appearance of German translations of the *Oration* began with
the March 13 edition by the Nürnberg preacher Johann Funck (1518–66),
based on the shorter version of the Latin text; it was followed by printings in
Augsburg and Strassburg.[149] Funck's preface, dated March 13, 1546, indicates
that he had undertaken his translation at the bidding of Friedrich Pistorius
[Hass] (1486–1553), the Lutheran abbot of St. Egidien in Nürnberg,[150] who
had supplied him with an exemplar of the Latin text.[151]

Funck acknowledged that his translation would be ill-received by some—
likely an allusion to the fact that his relationship with the Wittenbergers had
been soured because of his previous freelance editions of works of Luther
and Melanchthon, which the latter criticized as incompetent.[152] Funck may
also have been aware that a German translation of Melanchthon's *Oration*—
with which Funck's translation would be in competition—was being prepared
in Wittenberg by Cruciger. Another German translation of the shorter text
was produced in Strassburg by Caspar Hedio (1494–1552), dated March 22,
1546, and published as an appendix to Hedio's translation of Bartolomeo

---

[148] The Leipzig version of the Latin *Oration* first appeared in the 1549 Wittenberg edition
of Pollicarius' *Historia* [VD16 M3418], replacing the shorter version, taken from the Erfurt
printing, that appeared in Pollicarius' first edition. See below, p. lxiii.

[149] Johann Funck, trans., *Ein Sermon über der Leich/ des Ehrwirdigen Herrn Doctor Martin
Luthers zu Wittenberg gethon von Philip Melanthon* [sic] ([Nürnberg: Johann Petreius,
1546]) [VD16 M3868]. The text is edited in Bräuer, "Die Überlieferung von Melanchthons
Leichenrede," pp. 222–27. See also VD16 M3863 (Augsburg) and M3869 (Strassburg). Funck
was a supporter of Andreas Osiander (see below, p. 311 n. 170), followed him to Prussia in
the wake of the Interim of 1548, and eventually was executed for his zealous insistence on
Osiander's doctrine of justification: see Friedrich Wilhelm Bautz, "Funck, Johann," *BBKL*
2:154–55.

[150] Pistorius, the last abbot of the Benedictine cloister of St. Egidien, had converted the
cloister to the Reformation in 1525, turning its property over to the city to become the site
of the Nürnberg Latin school [*gymnasium*] while retaining his title. See Luther to Friedrich
Pistorius, April 22, 1527, WA Br 4:194; Luther to Wenceslaus Linck, July 5, 1527, LW 49:166
and n. 4 there. Luther dedicated his 1530 *Commentary on Psalm 118* to Pistorius: see LW 14:45.

[151] See Funck, *Sermon*, fol. a1v.

[152] See Weiss, "Erasmus at Luther's Funeral," pp. 107–8. Cf. Melanchthon to Hieronymus
Baumgartner, May 14, 1546, MBW T15:266–67, no. 4259 (CR 6:134–35).

Plantina's *Lives of the Popes*.[153] Hedio's translation did not, however, appear separately in print and enjoyed limited circulation and influence.

Meanwhile, however, Cruciger's German translation had appeared in Wittenberg.[154] The *Report* by Jonas and Coelius, published in Wittenberg shortly after March 15, indicated that a German translation (presumably Cruciger's) would appear shortly.[155] It appeared from the press of Georg Rhau in an edition that made a visual doublet with his edition of the *Report* by Jonas and Coelius, with a circular image of Melanchthon's bust on the back of the title page of the *Oration* paralleling the image of Luther appearing in the *Report*.[156] In addition to several Wittenberg reprintings in 1546, editions of Cruciger's translation appeared in Magdeburg, Zwickau, and Frankfurt am Main, as well as in Lübeck in a Low German version.[157] Like Camerarius' Latin version, Cruciger's German translation was taken into collections of material on Luther.[158] Cruciger's translation, however, is not based on Camerarius' Leipzig edition (as Bräuer assumes) but reflects a version of the text longer than the short Latin printing but not quite so long as Camerarius' Leipzig edition, pointing to the existence of a Latin text circulating in Wittenberg which provided the basis both for Cruciger's translation and for Camerarius' Latin edition.

The differences in text among the versions of Melanchthon's *Oration* chiefly involve four passages.[159] The first passage in question is a clause at the end of the first paragraph identifying Luther's doctrine as "a demonstration of the will and true worship of God, and an explanation of the Holy Scriptures, and a proclamation of the Word of God, that is, the Gospel of Jesus Christ" (see below, p. 40 and n. 6 there). The second passage is a half-line from Virgil's *Aeneid* added to a contrast between God's Word and the prophecies of the Sibyl (see below, p. 45 and n. 35 there). These two are found in Camerarius' Leipzig edition and its Latin reprintings but not in any

---

[153] Caspar Hedio, trans., *Bap.* [sic] *Platinae Historia Von der Bäpst vnd Keiser Leben* (Strassburg: Wendel Rihel, 1546) [VD16 P3271], fols. Aa2v–Aa5v, edited in Bräuer, "Die Überlieferung von Melanchthons Leichenrede," pp. 228–34.

[154] Philip Melanchthon, *Oratio Über der Leich des Ehrwirdigen herrn D. Martini Luthers*, trans. Caspar Cruciger (Wittenberg: Georg Rhau, 1546) [VD16 M3871–3873; ZV30232–30233, ZV30242]. The text is edited in Bräuer, "Die Überlieferung von Melanchthons Leichenrede," pp. 234–43.

[155] See above, p. xlvi; below, Jonas and Coelius, *Report*, p. 22.

[156] Cf. below, Jonas and Coelius, *Report*, p. 7.

[157] VD16 M3485 (Magdeburg), M3874 (Zwickau), M3864 (Frankfurt am Main), M3882 (Lübeck). The Low German text from the Lübeck edition is edited in Bräuer, "Die Überlieferung von Melanchthons Leichenrede," pp. 243–52.

[158] See Bräuer, "Die Überlieferung von Melanchthons Leichenrede," pp. 200–201.

[159] On other slight differences between the two texts, see below, p. xlix n. 164.

of the other versions. The third passage is a paragraph-length reflection on Luther's personality as witnessed by those around him (see below, p. 47 and n. 41 there). The fourth passage is a lengthy description of Luther's beatitude as a heavenly associate of the prophets and apostles (see below, pp. 48–50 and n. 51 there). These latter two passages are found both in Camerarius' Leipzig Latin edition and in Cruciger's Wittenberg German edition, but not in any of the other forms of the text. The changes which Camerarius made to the *Oration* are described in Melanchthon's letter of March 11, in which he writes:

> I am grateful to you for having seen to the publication of the funeral oration there, and for having inserted certain clauses [*membra*] which are the most outstanding ornaments of the little speech. You have also added very elegant verses; I am greatly pleased by the allusion to Luther's [identity as the] Baptist.[160]

Weiss interprets the "clauses" and "verses" as a reference to the two shorter passages, since the second of them is a half-verse from Virgil and the first passage includes a reference to Luther's "proclamation [*praeconium*] of the Word of God," which could be the "allusion to Luther's [identity as the] Baptist."[161] It is more natural, however, to understand the "added . . . verses" as a reference to the two elegiac poems that were appended to the Leipzig edition.[162] The second of these, in Greek, is cast as a dialogue between the organizer of Luther's funeral rites and a foreigner and includes a comparison of Luther and John the Baptist, playing on a fanciful Greek etymology of Luther's name—almost certainly the "allusion" to which Melanchthon refers and an explanation for why the phrase appears in Greek in Melanchthon's Latin letter:

> P[resider over the funeral rites]:   . . . Luther
> Is the Baptist. F[oreigner]: How? P[resider]: Because he brings washings.
> [As] Baptist he went before and pointed out the Lamb of God to mortals.[163]

---

[160] Melanchthon to Joachim Camerarius, March 11, 1546, MBW T15:146–47, no. 4184 (CR 6:80): "Quare tibi gratiam habeo, quod et edi apud vos curasti funebrem orationem et inseruisti membra aliquot, quae sunt praecipua ornamenta eius conciunculae. Et addidisti versus elegantissimos; valde mihi placet allusio ad βαπτιστὴν τοῦ Λοτῆρος." Weiss translates somewhat differently (see "Erasmus at Luther's Funeral," p. 106).

[161] Weiss, "Erasmus at Luther's Funeral," pp. 109, 113–14.

[162] In a letter of March 1, 1546, Melanchthon had asked Camerarius to compose an epitaph for Luther: MBW T15:128, no. 4170 (CR 6:67). See also Bräuer, "Die Überlieferung von Melanchthons Leichenrede," p. 190; and the note at MBW T15:146, no. 4184.

[163] Camerarius, ed., *Oratio*, fol. A8r, lines 21–23 of the Greek poem:
κ[οσμήτωρ τάφου].   λουτήρ
ἔστιν ὁ βαπτιστὴς. ξ[ενος]. πῶς; κ. ὅτι λοῦτρα φέρει.
βαπτιστὴς δὲ θεοῖο βροτοῖς πρόσθ' ἀμνὸν ἔδειξεν.

If the two poems are the "very elegant verses" to which Melanchthon refers, then the insertion at the end of the first paragraph and the half-verse from Virgil could be the ornamental "clauses" [*membra*], plausibly ascribed to Camerarius since they do not appear in Cruciger's Wittenberg translation. Other differences between the short Wittenberg and the Leipzig Latin editions of the *Oration* are very slight.[164]

Weiss observes that the description "clauses" [*membra*] in Melanchthon's letter to Camerarius can scarcely apply to the two long passages not found in the shorter Latin text. He argues that it is most likely, therefore, that these longer passages originated in Wittenberg before the production of the Leipzig edition (either from Melanchthon himself or from Cruciger), but that the existence of the shorter Latin text published in Wittenberg strongly suggests that they were not part of the oration as it was originally delivered.[165]

Bräuer argues that the shorter form of the Latin text circulated in manuscript, based on Melanchthon's own lost autograph, beginning with Besold's letter of February 22, and that such manuscripts furnished the basis for the translation by Funck and (perhaps) the one by Hedio. Funck's translation, if based on a copy of Melanchthon's manuscript, would show that the short version was original: "Melanchthon's short Latin version," as Bräuer calls it. Yet Besold's copy (whichever version it contained) did not reach Dietrich, who had traveled to Regensburg, until March 8 or only shortly before.[166] Any copies of the *Oration* as sent to Dietrich would have had to make their way back to Nürnberg thereafter (though Bräuer speculates that the correspondence could have been opened and copied in Nürnberg before following Dietrich to Regensburg). Surely by the first days of March copies of the Wittenberg printing of the short Latin text, produced only a day or two

---

[164] The Leipzig edition [VD16 M3849] contains the following significant differences (not including capitalization or orthography) from the "Wittenberg" printing [VD16 M3854], apart from the four passages under discussion (the Magdeburg edition [VD16 M3851] also follows all the readings of the Wittenberg edition, even the apparent typographical error): Leipzig, fol. A1v, line 14, *cogitemus* ["we may consider"] for *iuniores cogitent* ["the younger may consider"] (Wittenberg, fol. A1v, lines 18–19; see below, p. 39, line 7); Leipzig, fol. A1v, line 30, *sparsas* ["strewn"] instead of the apparent error *sparcas* (Wittenberg, fol. A2r, lines 16–17; see below, p. 40, line 6); Leipzig, fol. A2r, line 27, *decedentibus* for *cedentibus* (Wittenberg, fol. A3r, line 1; see below, p. 40, line 30); Leipzig, fol. A3r, line 1, *turbatam Ecclesiam* for *turbatam esse Ecclesiam* (Wittenberg, fol. A4r, line 4; see below, p. 43, line 7); Leipzig, fol. A4v, line 22, *Lutheri* for *Lutherum* (Wittenberg, fol. A6v, lines 14–15; see below, p. 47, line 24); Leipzig, fol. A6v, lines 5–6, *Agnoscemus eum fuisse* ["Let us recognize him to have been"] for *Sciamus fuisse eum* ["Let us be assured that he was"] (Wittenberg, fol. A7v, line 14; see below, p. 50, line 14). At most Melanchthon could have regarded these changes as an improvement in rhythm; some are deletions which could scarcely be the insertions described in Melanchthon's letter.

[165] Weiss, "Erasmus at Luther's Funeral," pp. 110–14.

[166] Bräuer, "Die Überlieferung von Melanchthons Leichenrede," pp. 192–93.

later than Besold's letter, would have arrived in Nürnberg already, even in advance of Melanchthon's surviving letter of March 1.[167] Nonetheless, Bräuer sees Funck's reference to an "exemplar" furnished by Pistorius as pointing to the use of a manuscript, since (he claims) in Luther's use "exemplar" always refers to a manuscript intended for printing rather than to a printed copy. Yet Luther's usage does not bear this out: though Luther can indeed refer to manuscripts for the printers as "exemplars," he and his correspondents most often use the term to refer to printed copies.[168] Finally, it is difficult to identify any passages in Funck's translation (or in Hedio's) which manifest divergences from the short Wittenberg Latin printing, which would hint

---

[167] Melanchthon to Veit Dietrich, March 1, 1546, MBW 4:335–36, no. 4171 (CR 6:68–69), cited in Bräuer, "Die Überlieferung von Melanchthons Leichenrede," p. 194 n. 54.

[168] Bräuer, "Die Überlieferung von Melanchthons Leichenrede," p. 194 and n. 55. Certainly Luther can use *exemplar* to refer to a manuscript copy: see *Table Talk* no. 4690 (1539), WA TR 4:431–32; Luther to Katharina Luther, September 8, 1530, WA Br 5:608 (cf. LW 48:417–18), and August 15, 1530, WA Br 5:546 (cf. LW 48:403); Luther to Wenceslaus Linck, September 12, 1530, WA Br 5:620–21, and July 13, 1530, WA Br 5:467; Luther to Martin Bucer, December 6, 1537, WA Br 8:157. Nevertheless, Luther and his correspondents most often use *exemplar* to refer to what are clearly printed copies of a text: see, e.g., Luther to Georg Wiscamp, October 20, 1528, WA Br 4:585 (referring to printed copies of the German translation of Isaiah); *Table Talk* no. 2472b (1532), WA TR 2:477 (referring to the bad paper printers are using for their "exemplars"); no. 2623a–b (1532), WA TR 2:553–54 (complaining that the greedy printers have been unwilling to provide Luther's collaborators with an "exemplar" of the translated Bible); Luther to Johann Lang, September 16, 1518, WA Br 1:203 (that "all the exemplars of the previous printing have been sold"); Luther writes to Linck that he is undertaking a revision of the German Psalter "because there are no exemplars left": January 15, 1531, WA Br 6:17; Luther to Amsdorf, August 1534?, WA Br 7:94 (complaining of other printers reprinting the Wittenberg edition of the prophets from the "finished exemplars"); Luther to the Strassburg theologians, October 1539?, WA Br 8:571 (asking that Luther's advice be printed by the Strassburg presses and exemplars be sent back to him); Luther to Gregor Brück, September 19, 1539, WA Br 8:554 (referring to the Anhalt princes' plan to have exemplars of the German Bible printed on parchment), and Luther to Linck, July 25, 1542, WA Br 10:110–11 (blaming the delay in binding the paper exemplars of the Bible because of the work on the princes' copies); cf. Luther to Linck, December 29, 1541, WA Br 9:564–65; Luther to Elector John Frederick, July 8, 1539, WA Br 8:491 (remarking that a thousand exemplars can more easily be sold at the Leipzig fair than a hundred in Wittenberg; cf. LW 50:187); Luther to Johann von Staupitz, October 3, 1519, WA Br 1:513; cf. Luther to Franz Günther, September 30, 1519, WA Br 1:511 (referring to "exemplars" of the first Galatians commentary). The correspondence among Erasmus, Wolfgang Capito, and Johann Froben refers to printed copies of Sylvester Prierias' *Replica* as "exemplars" (WA Br 1:259–60). The Basel printer Froben and Luther refer to the printed copies of Luther's work as "exemplars": see Froben to Luther, February 14, 1519, WA Br 1:332–33; Luther to Lang, April 13, 1519, WA Br 1:369–70. Bernard Edelman writes to Wilibald Pirkheimer (1470–1530) that he will send an exemplar of the Leipzig faculty's judgment as soon as it has been printed (WA Br 1:437). Stephan Roth's correspondence surrounding the 1528 *Winter Postil* clearly uses the word "exemplar" to refer to printed copies of the work (WA 21:xvi). Georg Witzel refers to "more than a thousand exemplars" of Justus Jonas' work against him in circulation, certainly referring to printed copies (WA 38:82).

at a manuscript copy rather than the printed version as the source. Funck and Hedio's German translations thus provide no evidence for any form of underlying text other than the short Wittenberg Latin edition.

Certainly Melanchthon was well-known—or infamous—for revising his work after its initial publication; his revisions to later printed editions of the Augsburg Confession, for example, would contribute to controversies among Luther's followers later in the century.[169] The differences between the short first Wittenberg printing of the *Oration*, the long Leipzig edition, and the middle form of text represented by Cruciger's translation could be accounted for by Melanchthon's revisions to the shorter text before sending the revised version to Cruciger for translation and to Camerarius (who made his own final additions, as discussed above).

Such revisions in Wittenberg (if they were made) would have had to be made quickly. In the first place, Camerarius' Leipzig edition was apparently produced several weeks closer to the date of Luther's Wittenberg funeral than Weiss realized. Melanchthon's letter to Camerarius, written upon Melanchthon's receipt of a printed copy of the Leipzig edition of his *Oration*, is dated on the "day of the [vernal] equinox" [*die aequinocti*] in the *Corpus Reformatorum* edition, which Weiss interpreted as indicating sometime between March 20 and March 25. The new edition of the letter in the *Melanchthon Briefwechsel*, however, dates the letter to March 11, based on a handwritten notation on a manuscript of the letter—and indeed March 10 or March 11 would have been the astronomical date of the vernal equinox in 1546 according to the Julian calendar.[170] The text on which the Leipzig edition was based must have reached Camerarius no later than did Melanchthon's letter of March 1.[171] Thus any Wittenberg revisions to the delivered version of the *Oration* would have had to be made within less than a week.

Yet there is evidence that the shorter text printed in Wittenberg about February 24 is in fact a truncation of a longer original, produced in haste to fit on a single folio sheet. (Weiss weighs this possibility and discounts it, but the question deserves to be reconsidered.)[172] The haste with which the printing was done is reflected, for example, in the mislabeling of folio A2v with the signature A3r, which was then repeated in its proper place on the

---

[169] On the so-called *Augustana Variata*, see below, p. lxxxv. There was also a succession of revised editions of the Apology of the Augsburg Confession in 1531: see Kolb-Wengert, pp. 108–9.

[170] See MBW T15:146–47, no. 4184.

[171] See above, p. xlv n. 145. Melanchthon's letter to Camerarius of March 1 is the first surviving letter between them after Luther's death, though it makes no explicit mention of Melanchthon's *Oration* among the texts being exchanged between the two scholars.

[172] Weiss, "Erasmus at Luther's Funeral," p. 110.

following page. Under these constraints of time and space, the excision of passages would be quite plausible.

The Wittenberg edition containing the shorter text completely fills sixteen pages in octavo format—a pamphlet that could be produced using a single folio-sized sheet of paper, using two set trays (*formes*) of type, one for each side of the folio sheet. Weiss notes that the edition was printed with space between the paragraphs which could have been closed to allow for printing at least the shorter of the two questionable passages without exceeding the page limit.[173] Yet the spaces between paragraphs that appear consistently on the first eleven pages disappear on page 12 (fol. A6v), where the first longer passage would appear, and the typography continues to be cramped through page 14 (fol. A7v), where the second longer passage would appear, until the next-to-last page (fol. A8r), where a space is again inserted before the prayer (though still omitted between other paragraphs through the end of the *Oration*). This pattern suggests that the typesetter realized on page 12 that he would run out of space for the text before the end of the available pages and decided to make cuts to keep the *Oration* to a single printed sheet.

Weiss argues that the longer passages can be explained as interpolations on the basis of their content and the surrounding rhetorical structure, reflecting an effort to temper the critical attitude toward Luther taken in the shorter version. Yet the excision of the passages can also be explained, in light of the space constraints, because of their distinctly local reference, of a kind which is mostly absent from the rest of the *Oration*. The first longer passage, on Luther's personality, appeals specifically to "those who knew him" and makes reference to "all of us as well as many persons from elsewhere."[174] Similarly, the longest questionable passage, on Luther's enjoyment of beatitude, revolves around Melanchthon's recollection of Luther's exegesis of John 1:51, appealing to "many in this assembly [who] once heard him commenting upon this verse."[175] Yet Luther's 1538 Wittenberg sermon on this passage did not appear in print until Johann Aurifaber's 1565 edition, so that the textual connection would have been inaccessible to anyone who had not heard the sermon in person.[176] If these passages were interpolated after the oral delivery of the *Oration*, the redactor was at curious pains to make them sound as if they had in fact been spoken to a Wittenberg audience. On the other hand, if the *Oration* were being printed quickly with an

---

[173] Weiss, "Erasmus at Luther's Funeral," p. 110.

[174] See below, Melanchthon, *Oration*, p. 47.

[175] See below, Melanchthon, *Oration*, p. 49.

[176] On the transmission and publication of the *Sermons on John 1–2* (1537–38/1565), see the introduction by Jaroslav Pelikan, LW 22:ix–xi.

eye to circulation outside Wittenberg, and space were short—as was evidently the case—these passages could easily have been candidates for excision. It is therefore likely that the longer form of the *Oration* was not only Melanchthon's favored version in retrospect but was also the form in which (apart from the two small additions by Camerarius) he originally delivered it in Wittenberg at Luther's funeral on February 22.

The translation in the present volume, made by the editor, reflects the long form of the text, as edited by Camerarius, but with all four passages in question marked in double brackets for ready identification. The 1546 Leipzig edition has been consulted in the digitized exemplar of the Universitäts- und Landesbibliothek Sachsen-Anhalt, alongside the edited text in the *Corpus Reformatorum*. Differences from the 1546 Wittenberg edition of the short form of the text have been indicated in the notes, with occasional reference to the German translations by Cruciger and Funck.[177]

PHILIP MELANCHTHON, PREFACE TO THE SECOND VOLUME OF THE COMPLETE EDITION OF LUTHER'S LATIN WRITINGS (1546)[178]

Within a few months after Luther's death and Wittenberg funeral, Melanchthon returned to Luther's biography in his preface to the second volume of the Wittenberg edition of Luther's Latin writings, dated June 1, 1546.[179] Although the volume itself contained material from the years 1520 to 1527, and Luther's preface for the first Wittenberg Latin volume had narrated

---

[177] See below, pp. 37–51. For previous English translations of Melanchthon's *Oration*, see Sachiko Kusukawa, ed., *Philip Melanchthon: Orations on Philosophy and Education*, trans. Christine F. Salazar (Cambridge: Cambridge University Press, 1999), pp. 256–64; Margaret L. King, ed. and trans., *Reformation Thought: An Anthology of Sources* (Indianapolis: Hackett, 2016), pp. 77–79; Kenneth R. Bartlett and Margaret McGlynn, eds., *The Renaissance and Reformation in Northern Europe* (Toronto: University of Toronto Press, 2014), pp. 110–13. A modern German translation by Siegfried Bräuer appears in *Melanchthon Deutsch*, ed. Michael Beyer, Stefan Rhein, and Günther Wartenberg (Leipzig: Evangelische Verlagsanstalt, 1997), 2:165–77.

[178] *Tomus Secundus Omnium Operum Reverendi Domini Martini Lutheri, Doctoris Theologiae, Continens monumenta, quae de multis gravissimis controversiis ab anno XX. Usque ad XXVII. Annum edita sunt* (Wittenberg: Hans Lufft, 1546) [VD16 L3414], fols. †2r–†8r, edited in MBW T15:296–311, no. 4277, and CR 6:155–70.

[179] For discussion of Melanchthon's preface, see Wengert, "First Biography of Martin Luther," pp. 23–26; Masaki, "Luther-Memoria," pp. 69–87; Franz Posset, *The Real Luther: A Friar at Erfurt and Wittenberg* (St. Louis: Concordia, 2011), pp. 43–83; Ralph Keen, "Philip Melanchthon and the Historical Luther," in *Luther's Lives: Two Contemporary Accounts of Martin Luther*, ed. and trans. Elizabeth Vandiver, Ralph Keen, and Thomas D. Frazel (Manchester, UK: Manchester University Press, 2002), pp. 12–14; Weiss, "Erasmus at Luther's Funeral," pp. 98–103.

Luther's career in the years 1517 through 1520,[180] Melanchthon chose to offer an account of the reformer's early life through about 1521 before shifting to a summary of his teaching and a reflection on his place in history, identifying Luther (as in the *Oration*) as one of the divinely sent teachers of the Church while rebutting claims that Luther (and Elector Frederick) had provoked religious disruption for their own interests.

In comparison with Melanchthon's funeral oration, the *Preface* followed much more closely the historical-biographical form recommended by Melanchthon to his students.[181] It was written in a clear but fastidious humanist Latin style—using classical words such as *academia* and *collegium* in place of medieval neologisms such as *universitas* or *monasterium*, for example—even as Melanchthon sought to place Luther not only within the world of late medieval scholastic theology but also within the Renaissance of Greek and Latin literature, a vision which included the Bible and the church fathers alongside the pagan classics. Implicitly, Melanchthon's discussion also helped to define his own role alongside Luther.

Melanchthon's decision to begin his narration at the start of Luther's life rather than with the Diet of Worms, where Luther had left off his narration in his preface to the first volume, may have been influenced by the fact that the second volume already contained so much historical material from the years it covered—including the contemporary account of Luther's stand at the Diet of Worms—whereas Luther's early years had never received a public narration. Melanchthon, who had arrived in Wittenberg as a young professor in 1518, was of course not an eyewitness to Luther's youth, career as a monk, early theological development, or even to the beginnings of the Indulgence Controversy in 1517. Yet he had long pursued a historical interest in these things, pressing Luther for biographical details at table and interviewing others. The *Preface* gives a public presentation of that research.

Melanchthon's account thus offers key testimony about many defining events in Luther's early life, sometimes confirming but sometimes also going beyond information that was recorded in the *Table Talk*. On the question of the date of Luther's birth, for example, the reformer himself had given conflicting information.[182] Melanchthon had interviewed Luther's mother

---

[180] See above, p. xxvi.

[181] According to the *Elementa Rhetorices*, pp. 130–31, the topics appropriate to an oration in praise of a person in the *genus demonstrativum* were "native land, gender, circumstances of birth, character, education, habits, teaching, deeds, rewards for deeds, departure from life, and reputation after death," to be treated in historical order.

[182] Luther's year of birth was uncertain for Luther himself, who, e.g., gave his birth year as 1484 in *Table Talk* no. 5347 (1540), WA TR 5:76–77; however, in *Table Talk* no. 5428 (1542), WA TR 5:138–39, he describes himself as sixty years old, meaning that he would have been born in 1482.

before her death in 1531 and received confirmation of the day and time, but not of the year.[183] (Part of Melanchthon's interest in the question was his desire to compute an accurate horoscope for Luther, in pursuit of his own astrological interests, which Luther himself gently mocked.)[184] It was Luther's brother Jacob who, as narrated in the *Preface*, provided Melanchthon with a family consensus that Luther had been born in 1483.[185] This is the date that has received general acceptance in historiography ever since, though the question still cannot be resolved with complete certainty.[186]

Melanchthon's account of Luther's education portrays him as an ideal student, attentive to the classics, even as it calls attention to the limitations of pre-Reformation schools. Although an interested student, Luther finds no teachers capable of imparting the humanist "gentler studies of true philosophy and a care for forming [eloquent] speech"—a characterization which understates the historical influence of humanism at the University of Erfurt while Luther was in attendance.[187] Nonetheless, it echoes some of Luther's own criticism of his education as well as his construction of Melanchthon's distinctive role in contrast to his own.[188]

Melanchthon describes Luther's entrance into the monastery as a considered academic decision, the choice of a form of life "more conducive to piety and more suitable for theological studies," as well as the result of spiritual struggles—"terrors"—at contemplating the wrath of God.[189] Melanchthon does not mention a vow made amid a thunderstorm. Unique to Melanchthon's account of Luther's spiritual development within the monastery is his detailing of the advice Luther received amid his "sorrows

---

[183] On Melanchthon's efforts to question Margaretha Luther about Luther's birth, see *Table Talk* no. 5428 (1542), WA TR 5:138–39; Melanchthon to Erasmus Ebner and to Johannes Schöner, January 1, 1531, MBW T5:30–32, nos. 1112–13; to Andreas Osiander, January 29, 1539, MBW T8:305, no. 2142 (CR 4:1053). Cf. Timothy J. Wengert, "Philip Melanchthon and Martin Luther as Partners in Evangelical Conversation," in *Lutheranism Legacy and Future: Essays in Honor of Eric W. Gritsch on the 50th Anniversary of His Ordination*, ed. Holger Roggelin and Scott Gustafson et al. (Conshohocken, PA: Infinity, 2012), pp. 59–79.

[184] See, e.g., *Table Talk* no. 2834b (1532), LW 54:172–73; no. 3520 (1537), LW 54:219–20; and Luther's preface to Lichtenberger, *Prophecy* (1527), LW 59:175–84; cf. Robin B. Barnes, *Astrology and Reformation* (Oxford: Oxford University Press, 2015), pp. 140–41.

[185] See below, Melanchthon, *Preface*, pp. 56–57.

[186] See Brecht 1:1; Scott Hendrix, *Martin Luther: Visionary Reformer* (New Haven: Yale University Press, 2017), p. 17; Jens Bulisch, "Wie alt ist Martin Luther geworden? Zum Geburtsjahr 1482 oder 1484," *LJB* 77 (2010): 29–39.

[187] See below, Melanchthon, *Preface*, p. 58. Cf. Brecht 1:38–44; Helmar Junghans, *Der junge Luther und die Humanisten* (Weimar: Böhlau, 1984).

[188] See Luther, *To the Councilmen of All Cities in Germany* (1524), LW 45:370; *Table Talk* no. 3619 (1537), LW 54:245.

[189] See below, Melanchthon, *Preface*, p. 59.

and fears" from an older monk—probably to be identified with the Erfurt master of novices Johann Greffenstein.[190] Melanchthon identifies a specific text from Bernard of Clairvaux,[191] from his sermons on the annunciation— in which the individual Christian is exhorted to believe that "your sins are forgiven you [*tibi*]" because "a man is justified freely by faith"—as crucial to Luther's spiritual and theological development.[192] From this text, Luther was led to the intensive study of Paul and then to Augustine. Alongside this humanistically shaped description of Luther's return to the sources, his studies of medieval scholastic theology are mentioned: he knew Gabriel Biel and Pierre d'Ailly practically by memory, had read Jean Gerson, and inten-sively studied Ockham in preference to Aquinas and Scotus.[193] Melanchthon characterizes these studies as a sort of sideline, which probably understates their significance for Luther.

Johann von Staupitz, in Melanchthon's account, is important to Luther's development chiefly in his administrative role: seeing Luther's talents, trans-ferring him to Wittenberg, and all but forcing him to take the doctorate in theology.[194] In the course of his narration, Melanchthon mentions Luther's travel to Rome, which he places three years after his arrival in Wittenberg (hence in 1511), with his return in the same year that he received his

---

[190] On Greffenstein, see below, p. 60 n. 34.

[191] Bernard of Clairvaux (1090–1153) was an early leader of the Cistercian order and an influential preacher and mystic whose theology, focusing on the crucified Christ, Luther highly prized. See Friedrich Wilhelm Bautz, "Bernhard von Clairvaux," *BBKL* 1:530–32; *ODCC*, 3rd ed., s.v. "Bernard." On Luther's esteem for Bernard, see Franz Posset, *Pater Bernhardus: Martin Luther and Bernard of Clairvaux*, Cistercian Studies 168 (Kalamazoo, MI: Cistercian Publications, 1999).

[192] See below, Melanchthon, *Preface*, p. 61. On this episode and its significance, see Posset, *The Real Luther*, pp. 90–99.

[193] See below, Melanchthon, *Preface*, pp. 62–63.

[194] Johann von Staupitz (ca. 1468–1524), a member of the Saxon nobility and a child-hood friend of the Saxon elector Frederick the Wise, had received his doctorate in theology in Tübingen in 1500. Having become prior of the Augustinian convent in Munich in 1502, Staupitz was elected vicar-general of the Observant Augustinian Hermits in Germany in 1503. At Frederick's invitation, Staupitz helped organize the University of Wittenberg, where he served on the faculty, recruited others to teach, and sent many friars to be educated. He would become Luther's superior in the order and his confessor, and he groomed Luther to take over his Wittenberg teaching duties. See below, Melanchthon, *Preface*, pp. 63–64; Mathesius, *History*, pp. 125–26, 128–29, 131–32, 136–37, 149–50, 446–48, 557, 579–82. On Staupitz's life and theology, see Franz Posset, *The Front-Runner of the Catholic Reformation: The Life and Works of Johann von Staupitz* (Aldershot: Ashgate, 2003). On Luther's theological relationship to Staupitz, see David C. Steinmetz, *Luther and Staupitz: An Essay in the Intellectual Origins of the Protestant Reformation* (Durham, NC: Duke University Press, 1980).

doctorate (in 1512).[195] Although Luther himself gives the date of 1510–11 for his trip, recent scholarship has inclined toward Melanchthon's dating.[196]

Melanchthon sees the fundamental themes of Luther's theology present already in his lectures on Romans (1515–16) and in the lectures on the Psalms:[197] the distinction between Law and Gospel, the rejection of merit and works-righteousness, and the free forgiveness of sins for Christ's sake through faith. It was this engagement with fundamental theological issues, joined with Luther's sanctity of life, that won him an audience—not any striving for provocation either in words or in alterations to the ceremonies of the church. Meanwhile, Melanchthon writes, an audience eager to hear something other than "the barbaric and sophistic doctrine of the monks" was being prepared through Erasmus' advocacy of study of Greek and Latin, in which Luther participated through his own study of the biblical languages.[198]

Luther had given a detailed narration of the Indulgence Controversy with Johann Tetzel in his own introduction to the first Wittenberg Latin volume as well as in *Against Hanswurst*.[199] Accordingly, Melanchthon is brief in his own relation of the affair, but he adds the first published description of the event which became iconic for the history of the Reformation:

---

[195] See below, Melanchthon, *Preface*, p. 64.

[196] Luther gives the date of his trip to Rome as 1510 in the autograph incorporated as *Table Talk* no. 5347 (1540), WA TR 5:76–77, though that document also gives his date of birth as 1484 (cf. above, p. liv n. 182). Scholars are divided on the actual dating of the trip (and, accordingly, its purpose); many hold to 1510–11, which would mean that Luther was representing the Erfurt monastery in its appeal against Staupitz's efforts to unite the Observant Augustinian Hermits with the regular Saxon province. For this view, see Brecht 1:98–105; Heiko A. Oberman, *Luther: Man between God and the Devil*, trans. Eileen Walliser-Schwarzbart (New Haven: Yale University Press, 1989), p. 141; Timothy F. Lull and Derek R. Nelson, *Resilient Reformer: The Life and Thought of Martin Luther* (Minneapolis: Fortress, 2015), pp. 27–28. However, the alternative dating attested by Melanchthon that places the trip in 1511–12 fits better with the known dates of Luther's lectures in Erfurt and Wittenberg. In this case, Luther would have been traveling to appeal on behalf of Staupitz rather than against him. For the recent defense of this later dating, see Hans Schneider, "Martin Luthers Reise nach Rom: Neu datiert und neu gedeutet," in *Studien zur Wissenschafts- und zur Religionsgeschichte*, ed. Werner Lehfeldt (Berlin: de Gruyter, 2011), pp. 1–157; Volker Leppin, *Martin Luther: Vom Mönch zum Feind des Papstes* (Darmstadt: Lambert, 2015), p. 24; Hendrix, *Luther: Visionary Reformer*, pp. 6–7.

[197] Cf. Luther's description of his engagement with Rom. 1:17 as he "returned to interpret the Psalter anew": *Preface to the Latin Writings* (1545), LW 34:336. Melanchthon probably has in mind here the second set of Psalms lectures, the *Labors on the Psalms [Operationes]* of 1518–21 (WA 5; WA Ar 2–3; LW 14:278–349; LW 64–65), rather than the first Psalms lectures of 1513–15 (WA 3–4; 55/1–2; LW 10–11), though he mentions only one series of lectures on the Psalms.

[198] See below, Melanchthon, *Preface*, p. 66.

[199] *Preface to the Latin Writings* (1545), LW 34:329–36; *Against Hanswurst* (1541), LW 41:233–35. On Tetzel, see below, p. 66 n. 71.

"[Luther] publicly affixed these [*Propositions concerning Indulgences*] to the church adjacent to the Wittenberg castle on the eve of All Saints' Day in the year 1517."[200]

Because Melanchthon could not have been an eyewitness to Wittenberg events that took place the year before his own arrival, he must again have done his own research into this period in Luther's life. His account was accepted by his contemporaries, including Georg Major, who had been a chorister at the Castle Church in 1517 and therefore a likely eyewitness.[201] Nonetheless, a sharp debate arose among twentieth-century scholars over the historical value of Melanchthon's account.[202] The negative view was argued by Erwin Iserloh in 1962, concluding that Luther had not issued the theses publicly but only circulated them in letters to Archbishop Albert of Mainz and Bishop Jerome Scultetus and to a narrow circle of friends.[203] Scholarly responses defending the historicity of Luther's public posting of the theses were made by Kurt Aland and others.[204]

The argument in favor of the posting of the theses has been strengthened by the 2006 rediscovery, by Martin Treu, of a manuscript note written at the end of a 1540 edition of the German Bible by the Wittenberg deacon Georg Rörer, Luther's longtime scribe.[205] Rörer had not been present in Wittenberg in 1517, but the note was made in the course of discussions that took place between 1541 and 1544 concerning revisions to the German Bible—discussions in which Luther, of course, took part and which Rörer was annotating in his copy of the Bible.[206] Rörer's account reads:

---

[200] See below, Melanchthon, *Preface*, p. 67.

[201] See Volker Leppin and Timothy J. Wengert, "Sources for and against the Posting of the *Ninety-Five Theses*," *LQ* 29 (2015): 374–75; Hans J. Hillerbrand, Kirsi I. Stjerna, Timothy J. Wengert, gen. eds., *The Annotated Luther* (Minneapolis: Fortress, 2015), 1:23.

[202] For summary assessments of the debate, see Leppin and Wengert, "Sources for and against the Posting of the *Ninety-Five Theses*," pp. 373–98; Joachim Ott and Martin Treu, eds., *Luthers Thesenanschlag: Faktum oder Fiktion* (Leipzig: Evangelische Verlagsanstalt, 2008); Timothy J. Wengert, introduction to "[The 95 Theses or] Disputation for Clarifying the Power of Indulgences," in *The Annotated Luther*, ed. Hans J. Hillerbrand et al. (Minneapolis: Fortress, 2015), 1:22–26. Cf. Pettegree, *Brand Luther*, p. 13.

[203] Erwin Iserloh, *The Theses Were Not Posted: Luther between Reform and Reformation*, trans. Jared Wicks (Boston: Beacon Press, 1968; from 1966 German edition); cf. Erwin Iserloh, *Luthers Thesenanschlag: Tatsache oder Legende* (Wiesbaden: Steiner, 1962). On Albert of Brandenburg, archbishop of Mainz, see below, p. 27 n. 5.

[204] Kurt Aland, ed., *Martin Luther's 95 Theses* (St. Louis: Concordia, 1967, 2004; from 1965 German edition); cf. Heinrich Bornkamm, *Thesen und Thesenanschlag Luthers: Geschehen und Bedeutung* (Berlin: Töpelmann, 1967).

[205] The notation had been published in WA 48N:116 but was taken as derivative of Melanchthon's *Preface*.

[206] See Brecht 3:105–7; and below, p. 426 n. 12, and Mathesius, *History*, pp. 475, 477.

"In the year of the Lord 1517, on the eve of the Feast of All Saints . . . the [propositions] concerning indulgences were posted [*propositae*] on the doors of the churches in Wittenberg by Dr. Martin Luther." Rörer's reference to "churches" is supported by the 1508 university statutes, which specified that theses for disputation should be posted on the doors of the Wittenberg *churches*, in the plural.[207] It may be noted in passing that neither Rörer's account nor Melanchthon's specifies the *means* by which the theses were "posted" [*propositae*] or "attached" [*affixit*] to the doors; the first descriptions that may suggest that they were attached with hammer and nails come from Ludwig Rabus' 1556 adaptation of Melanchthon's preface and Johann Mathesius' 1562 sermon on Luther's life, both of which use the German verb *anschlagen*.[208] Although neither Rabus nor Mathesius was witness to the events of 1517, both would have been familiar with the practice surrounding disputation theses in Wittenberg in the 1540s when they were studying there, and so their witness to the "nailing" cannot be dismissed out of hand.[209]

Another piece of evidence suggesting that Luther's *Propositions concerning Indulgences* were in fact posted on the doors of the Wittenberg church (or churches), like any other set of academic theses, is provided by Andrew Pettegree's analysis of early printings of the *Ninety-Five Theses*. We know, from the 1983 discovery of an edition of Luther's September 1517 theses for the *Disputation against Scholastic Theology* issued by the Wittenberg university printer Johann Rhau-Grunenberg, that it was customary to print single-sided broadsheet editions of theses for disputations in Wittenberg.[210] Yet no copy of a Wittenberg printing of the *Ninety-Five Theses* survives, only editions from Nürnberg, Basel, and Leipzig—a circumstance which seems to support the theory that Luther circulated them privately in manuscript rather than having them printed in order to post them. Yet the existence of a Wittenberg edition is mentioned by contemporaries.[211] And Pettegree has shown that the Basel and Nürnberg editions of the *Ninety-Five Theses* bear the distinctive numbering of Rhau-Grunenberg's Wittenberg thesis editions

---

[207] Walter Friedensburg, ed., *Urkundenbuch der Universität Wittenberg* (Magdeburg: Historischen Kommission, 1926), 1:33.

[208] Although *anschlagen* can have the abstract meaning of "to publicize" (see *DWB*, s.v. "anschlagen" 5) when the verb is combined with a physical prepositional object (i.e., to the church or to its doors), it seems likely that Rabus and Mathesius intended the literal, physical sense of affixing with blows, i.e., with a hammer and nails (cf. *DWB*, s.v. "anschlagen" 4).

[209] Rabus, *Historien* 4 (1557), fol. 6r (for bibliographic information, see below, p. lxiii n. 231): "Schlug die selbige offentlichen an/ an die Schloßkirch zu Wittenberg"; and below, Mathesius, *History*, p. 144: "post them on the Castle Church in Wittenberg" ["*an die Schloßkirch zu Wittenberg an jrem Kirchmeß tag anzuschlagen*"].

[210] Pettegree, *Brand Luther*, pp. 50–52.

[211] See WA 1:230.

and are therefore, presumably, based on a lost original printed in Wittenberg for public posting.[212]

Certainly Melanchthon and his first readers would have been aware that the public posting of academic theses was an everyday part of medieval and early modern university life, perhaps—as it was for Luther—not even worth mentioning in particular. What was significant about the posting of the *Ninety-Five Theses* was not the act itself or the doors of the church but the theological content of the theses and their ecclesiastical context.

In Melanchthon's narrative, it is not Luther's posting of the theses but Tetzel's outraged response that is characterized as provocative and excessive, vindicating Luther from charges—whether in 1517–18 or in the 1540s—of having acted as an *agent provocateur* in service of the political ambitions of the Wettins against the Hohenzollerns. Nor, Melanchthon argues, can Elector Frederick be charged with provocation, for he acted with all prudent deliberation, consulting Erasmus about the merit of Luther's teaching and urging Luther to moderate his pen.[213] Not Luther but his opponents made the authority of the pope an issue for debate. Luther's own fidelity to the creeds and pure doctrine, as well as his moderation in making any changes to ceremonies, is shown by the Augsburg Confession. It was Andreas Bodenstein von Karlstadt who, in Luther's absence, undertook hasty and troublesome changes, of which Luther disapproved.[214] (Melanchthon discretely passes over both his authorship of the Augsburg Confession and his involvement along with Justus Jonas and Nicolaus von Amsdorf in Karlstadt's reforms in 1521–22.)[215]

Yet even though Luther sought to avoid unnecessary conflict, Melanchthon writes, it is necessary in the Church to obey God rather than human beings [Acts 5:21], and the fault for any turmoil that results rests with those who teach errors and refuse to hear God's Word when it is preached. Luther's conflicts were for the sake of the Word; though he was fiery and passionate by nature, he refused to condone political sedition and tumult, instead teaching respect for the political order.

Melanchthon insists that the doctrine which God restored through Luther—whatever divisions it may have provoked—is nothing other than

---

[212] Pettegree, *Brand Luther*, pp. 71–77.

[213] Melanchthon's positive references to Erasmus in the *Preface* must be taken in their context in Witt Lat 2, a volume which contained not only Luther's treatise *Bondage of the Will* against Erasmus but also Luther's scathing letter of March 11, 1534, to Amsdorf in which he denounced Erasmus as an atheist: WA Br 7:27–40 (LW 74).

[214] On Karlstadt, see below, p. 154 n. 90.

[215] Cf. the letter from the University of Wittenberg to Elector Frederick, February 13, 1522, MBW T1:449, no. 212. On Jonas, see above, p. xxx. On Amsdorf, see below, p. 30 n. 15.

the "perpetual consensus of the catholic Church of God."[216] Luther belongs to the succession of faithful teachers of the Church, whom God has sent to correct errors as they have arisen. When Origen (ca. 185–253/254) and his followers corrupted the apostolic doctrine with philosophy, God sent Augustine (354–430) to correct their errors, and his influence prevailed down to Bernard. Yet afterward, Scholasticism turned theology back into philosophy again, poisoning the wellsprings of the Gospel, until God used Luther's ministry to restore the pure doctrine. For its preservation, all pious Christians should intercede with God, just as Luther did even on his deathbed.

Returning implicitly to the place of the *Preface* at the head of a volume of Luther's works, Melanchthon declares that Luther's writings in their various genres—didactic, polemical, and exegetical—stand as monuments to his faithful teaching, directing Christians back to the Scriptures themselves, from which they are drawn, and serving as encouragement to all Christians to exercise themselves in "spreading the true doctrine" and "preserving the concord of the true Church."[217] Melanchthon's preface thus claims Luther's continuity with the authentic Christian tradition reaching from the apostles through Augustine to Bernard down to Luther himself—a tradition in which Luther's readers are called to take part.

Melanchthon's *Preface* is translated here by the editor, with reference to the 2011 translation by Franz Posset.[218] The underlying original used here is the Latin text of the 1546 edition,[219] compared with the modern texts in the *Melanchthon Briefwechsel*[220] and in the *Corpus Reformatorum* (the latter of which, however, contains a number of errors of transcription).[221] The paragraph breaks in the present translation are based on the original breaks in Witt Lat 2, which differ from those in either the *Corpus Reformatorum* or the *Melanchthon Briefwechsel*. Page breaks are indicated from the *Corpus Reformatorum*, since the *Melanchthon Briefwechsel* indicates the *Corpus Reformatorum* page divisions as well.

---

[216] See below, Melanchthon, *Preface*, p. 74.

[217] See below, Melanchthon, *Preface*, p. 80.

[218] Franz Posset, "Melanchthon's Memoirs: The Preface to the Second Volume of Luther's Works (1546)," in *The Real Luther*, pp. 149–69. See also the translation by Thomas D. Frazel, "Philip Melanchthon's *History of the Life and Acts of Dr. Martin Luther*," in Elizabeth Vandiver, Ralph Keen, and Thomas D. Frazel, trans. and eds., *Luther's Lives: Two Contemporary Accounts of Martin Luther* (Manchester, UK: Manchester University Press, 2002), pp. 15–26.

[219] Witt Lat 2 (see above, p. liii n. 178), consulted in the digitized exemplar of the Universitäts- und Landesbibliothek Sachsen-Anhalt.

[220] MBW T15:296–311, no. 4277.

[221] CR 6:155–70 (cf. the editorial notes on the text in CR 20:429–38).

COLLECTIONS, CONTROVERSY, AND CONTEXT:
POLLICARIUS, RABUS, COCHLAEUS, AND SLEIDANUS

None of the texts produced in the months after Luther's death—the *Report* by Jonas and Coelius, Bugenhagen's funeral sermon, or Melanchthon's *Oration* and biographical preface—was wholly satisfactory as a complete biography or memorial. Yet in combination they were an important foundation for the memory of Martin Luther. Printers quickly recognized this and began to publish editions combining some or all of these texts. Already in 1546 there appeared booklets combining the *Report,* Bugenhagen's sermon, and Melanchthon's *Oration.*[222]

The most influential collection of texts on Luther's life and death, however, was assembled in 1547 by the Weißenfels archdeacon Johannes Pollicarius (1524–84), from Zwickau, who had studied briefly at Wittenberg in 1545. His role was that of compiler rather than that of witness or narrator. Pollicarius' Latin volume, first published in 1548 in Erfurt,[223] appeared in at least six printings in Erfurt and Wittenberg before being taken over in 1554 by the Frankfurt printer David Zöpfel (ca. 1525–after 1563), who expanded and revised the selection of material and published numerous editions in Latin as well as in German translation.[224] In addition to the texts translated in this volume, much of Pollicarius' added material is translated into English by Thomas D. Frazel in the volume *Luther's Lives.*[225]

---

[222] Such editions appeared in Magdeburg from Hans Walther [VD16 J903] and in Nürnberg from the presses of Johann Vom Berg and Ulrich Neuber [VD16 J904]. The different ordering of material (Jonas/Coelius-Bugenhagen-Melanchthon vs. Jonas/Coelius-Melanchthon-Bugenhagen) may indicate that each of these editions was independently inspired. An English translation appearing in Wesel from Dereck van der Straten [VD16 ZV25460] followed the order of the Nürnberg text. An Augsburg pamphlet offered a different selection of texts: Jonas' letter to Elector John Frederick (Schubart, *Die Berichte über Luthers Tod und Begräbnis*, no. 1, pp. 1–6; cf. above, p. xxxiii), a report on Luther's death by Count Albert's secretary Wolfgang Roth [Russ?] (Schubart, *Die Berichte über Luthers Tod und Begräbnis*, no. 18, pp. 19–22), and a description of Luther's funeral and burial in Wittenberg by an unidentified author, followed by Luther's Bible inscription on John 8 mentioned in Jonas and Coelius, *Report* (see below, pp. 15–16): *Drey Schrifften vonn des Eerwirdigen Herren Doctor Martin Luthers Christlichem abschid und Sterben/ auch Eerlichem begrebnuß* ([Augsburg: Heinrich Steiner], 1546) [VD16 ZV8746].

[223] Johannes Pollicarius, *Historia de Vita et Actis Reverendiss[imi] Viri D. Mart[ini] Lutheri, verae Theologiae Doctoris* (Erfurt: Gervasius Sturm, 1548) [VD16 M3416]. Two 1548 Erfurt editions seem to have been conflated in VD16. A second edition, digitized by the Österreichische Nationalbibliothek, is distinguished by the addition of "*denuo correcta*" at the end of the title. Pollicarius' preface is dated October 20, 1547.

[224] See Wengert, "First Biography of Martin Luther." Wengert lists the editions and their contents on pp. 40–44.

[225] Vandiver et al., *Luther's Lives*, pp. 14–37, 37–39, 353–55.

Pollicarius' collection began, after his own introductory dedication, with Melanchthon's *Preface*, slightly revised under the new title *History of the Life and Deeds of the Most Reverend Man, Dr. Martin Luther, Doctor of Purer Theology, Set Down in Writing, in Good Faith, by Philip Melanchthon.* Next came the 1521 account of Luther's dealings at the Diet of Worms[226] and a short prayer taken from the end of Luther's 1545 *Preface to the Latin Writings.*[227] Later editions added correspondence surrounding the Diet of Worms and the full text of Luther's 1545 *Preface.* Melanchthon's announcement of Luther's death to the students in Wittenberg followed.[228] Next came a series of Latin poems by Pollicarius and others summarizing Luther's life and eulogizing him. Later editions added the *Report* by Jonas and Coelius as well as Bugenhagen's funeral sermon, but all editions contained Melanchthon's *Oration* from Luther's funeral (first in the shorter form and then, beginning with the 1549 Wittenberg edition, in the longer version edited by Camerarius),[229] followed by a few more pieces of verse. Pollicarius' collection thus set Melanchthon's interpretation of Luther's life and significance at the center of Lutheran memory. Yet it also focused that memory rather unevenly across Luther's life span, emphasizing Luther's early career through the Diet of Worms, on the one hand, and his last days, death, and funeral on the other.

A decade after Luther's death, the Lutheran preacher Ludwig Rabus (1523–92) assembled a more extensive and evenly distributed biographical collection. Rabus had studied at Tübingen before taking a master's degree at Wittenberg in 1543. He served as a preacher in Strassburg, where he made a name for himself as a vigorous opponent of the Augsburg Interim,[230] before taking up the position of superintendent in Ulm in 1556. In 1552, he had begun to publish a history of the martyrs of the Church, from the earliest Christians down to his own day.[231] The fourth volume of Rabus' German martyrology, which appeared in 1556, began with a long section on Luther

---

[226] *Luther at the Diet of Worms* (1521), LW 32:105–23 (see above, p. xvii).

[227] LW 34:338.

[228] Frazel, "Melanchthon's *History of Dr. Martin Luther,*" pp. 37–39. Cf. above, p. xxxv.

[229] See above, pp. xliv–xlvi.

[230] See above, p. xxi and n. 22 there.

[231] Ludwig Rabus, *Historien der Heyligen ausserwöhlten Gottes Zeugen, Bekennern, und Martyren* . . . , 8 vols. (Strassburg: Beck, 1552; Emmel, 1554–58) [VD16 R31–50]. The fourth volume (first published in 1556) is cited here from the 1557 printing [VD16 ZV12904] in the digital exemplar of the Berlin Staatsbibliothek, fols. 1r–244v. On Rabus and his martyrology, see Kolb, *For All the Saints*, pp. 41–83. On Rabus' presentation of Luther, see Kolb, *For All the Saints*, pp. 108–15; Kolb, *Luther as Prophet, Teacher, and Hero*, p. 87.

under the title *The History of the Life, Death, and Especially of the Many-Sided Battle and Conflict which the Reverend, Highly Enlightened, and True Man of God, Dr. Martin Luther, of Blessed and Holy Memory, Steadfastly Endured for the Sake of the Confession of Evangelical Truth, through God's Gracious Assistance.* Rabus' selection of texts was more extensive than Pollicarius' had been, including, in addition to narrative biographical texts, a selection of theological and pastoral works by Luther, enriched by correspondence and other historical material that had been published in the Jena edition of Luther's works. Moreover, Rabus linked together and introduced the texts he selected with brief narrative passages of his own composition.

Rabus' account of Luther's life and career sought to present Luther as an "especially eminent witness and precious confessor of the crucified Christ,"[232] exemplifed not only by his public confession (especially at Worms) but also by his pastoral witness of Christ to individuals and communities. Rabus begins his *History* with a narration of Luther's early years, closely based on the first part of Melanchthon's preface to the second Wittenberg Latin volume of Luther's works.[233] This was followed by Georg Spalatin's account of the proceedings at Augsburg, accompanied by a number of letters from Luther, Cajetan, and Frederick the Wise.[234] Rabus then briefly narrates the negotiations with Karl von Miltitz and the Leipzig Debate.[235] He also reproduces the report by Heinrich von Zütphen and Georg Spalatin on Frederick's negotiations and conversation with Erasmus at Cologne in 1520, Luther's *Protestation*, and two reports on Luther's burning of the bull of excommunication and papal decretals.[236]

---

[232] Rabus, *Historien* 4, fol. 1v.

[233] Rabus, *Historien* 4, fols. 1r–7v (cf. below, Melanchthon, *Preface*, pp. 53–80).

[234] Spalatin's account of the proceedings at Augsburg, Rabus, *Historien* 4, fols. 8r–15r, 19v–21r (as found in Jena Ger 1 [1555], fols. 109v–114v; Witt Ger 9 [1557], fols. 35v–39v; and in part in StL 15:557–58, 561–65, different from but paralleling Luther's account translated in LW 31:259–92); Luther to "a good friend" (i.e., Karlstadt), October 14, 1518, *Historien* 4, fols. 15v–16r (WA Br 1:215–17); to Cardinal Cajetan, October 17, 1518, *Historien* 4, fols. 16v–18r (WA Br 1:220–22), and to Cajetan, October 18, 1518, *Historien* 4, fols. 18r–19v (LW 48:87–89); Cajetan to Elector Frederick, October 25, 1518, *Historien* 4, fols. 21v–24r (WA Br 1:233–35); Luther to Frederick, November [21], 1518, *Historien* 4, fols. 24v–37r (WA Br 1:236–48); Frederick, open letter to Cajetan, December 8, 1518, *Historien* 4, fols. 37v–38r.

[235] Rabus' narrative of the negotiations with Miltitz, *Historien* 4, fols. 38v–42v; account of the Leipzig Disputation, *Historien* 4, fols. 42v–44v (differing from Luther's account in LW 31:318–25); further narrative by Rabus, *Historien* 4, fols. 44v–46r.

[236] Zütphen [and Spalatin], *Account of the Dealings at Cologne* (1520), Rabus, *Historien* 4, fols. 46r–49v (StL 15:1616–17; cf. below, Mathesius, *History*, p. 162); Luther, *Protestation* [*Oblatio sive protestatio*], *Historien* 4, fols. 50v–52r (WA 6:476–83); narrative (*Historien* 4, fol. 52r–v); anon., *Why the Anti-Christian Decretals Were Burned*, *Historien* 4, fols. 52v–54r

The longest single section of Rabus' *History* deals with Luther's appearance at the Diet of Worms in 1521, including the negotiations leading up to it and its aftermath. He includes a selection of Luther's correspondence with Frederick and Spalatin in advance of the diet, copies of the letters of safe-conduct issued to Luther, and the account of Luther's dealings at Worms that was published in Wittenberg shortly after.[237] This is followed by Luther's letter to Count Albert of Mansfeld reflecting on the diet and the text of the Edict of Worms itself.[238] Luther's time in the Wartburg is reflected in a long excerpt from his exposition of Psalm 37 addressed to the congregation in Wittenberg and in his letter to Cardinal Albert of Mainz.[239] Luther's return to Wittenberg is marked by selections from his correspondence with Elector Frederick.[240]

This is followed, however, by the first sample of a genre that becomes a major focus of Rabus' collection for Luther's biography: Luther's letter of consolation to Hartmut von Cronberg (1488–1549), followed by von Cronberg's response and confession of faith.[241] After this, Rabus presents two letters in which Luther defends his harsh writing against prelates and princes, followed by documents from 1523 indicating Luther's continuing willingness to accept a peaceful resolution of his case—though the futility

---

(WA 7:183–86); Luther, *Why the Books of the Pope and His Disciples Were Burned* (1520), *Historien* 4, fols. 54v–62r (LW 31:379–95).

[237] Luther to Elector Frederick, January 25, 1521, Rabus, *Historien* 4, fols. 62v–64r (LW 48:194–97), and January 1519 (but assigned by Rabus to 1521), *Historien* 4, fols. 65r–66v (LW 48:103–6); to Spalatin, March 19, 1521, *Historien* 4, fols. 66v–67r (WA Br 2:289); safe-conduct from Emperor Charles V, *Historien* 4, fols. 57v–58r (WA Br 2:280–81); safe-conduct from Duke George of Saxony, *Historien* 4, fols. 68v–69r (WA Br 12:23–24); safe-conduct from Elector Frederick and Duke John, *Historien* 4, fols. 69r–70r (WA Br 2:286–87); "Luther at Worms," *Historien* 4, fols. 70r–89r (LW 32:105–23).

[238] Luther to Count Albert of Mansfeld, May 3, 1521, Rabus, *Historien* 4, fols. 89r–91v (WA Br 2:319–28); Edict of Worms, *Historien* 4, fols. 99v–103r (cf. *DRA* 2:640–59 [StL 15:2276–90] and the complete translation [with facsimile] in De Lamar Jensen, *Confrontation at Worms* [Provo: Brigham Young University Press, 1973], pp. 75–111).

[239] Excerpt from Psalm 37, to the congregation at Wittenberg, Rabus, *Historien* 4, fols. 104r–106v (WA 8:236–40; cf. LW 48:248–53); Luther to Cardinal Albert, December 1, 1521, *Historien* 4, fols. 107r–110r (LW 48:339–43).

[240] Luther to Elector Frederick, March 5, 1522, Rabus, *Historien* 4, fols. 112v–115r (LW 48:388–93); excerpt from Luther to Frederick, March 7–8, 1522, *Historien* 4, fol. 115v (LW 48:397–98).

[241] *Letter of Consolation to Hartmut von Cronberg* (March 26 or 27, 1522), Rabus, *Historien* 4, fols. 116r–122v (LW 43:61–70); Hartmut von Cronberg to Luther, April 14, 1522, *Historien* 4, fols. 123r–127r (WA Br 2:497–502), followed by his list of articles of faith, as in Witt Ger 6 (1553), fols. 383v–384v.

of efforts at peace is suggested by Luther's critique of the resolutions of the 1521 Diet of Worms and the 1523 Diet of Nürnberg.[242]

More consolatory letters follow, mixed with excerpts from Elector Frederick's correspondence in his last days, before Rabus gives an account of the 1529 Marburg Colloquy and the articles that were agreed on there, followed by the last section of Luther's *Confession concerning Christ's Supper*, representing Luther's definitive confession of the faith.[243] Luther's human connections are celebrated in his last letters to his father and mother.[244] The events surrounding the 1530 Diet of Augsburg are reflected indirectly in Melanchthon's 1546 preface to the new Wittenberg edition of Luther's 1530 *Warning to His Dear German People*.[245]

The 1530s are represented by a further series of Luther's consolatory writings, followed by the text of the 1536 Wittenberg Concord. The 1537 meeting at Smalcald to discuss the Lutheran position for the upcoming papal council is reflected in two of Luther's sermons delivered there and in an anecdote about Luther's response to contemporary Italian rumors of his death.[246] Rabus' survey of Luther's life concludes with more short passages of exhortation and consolation, including the hortatory (if somewhat spurious) *Preface Composed before His Passing* from the second Wittenberg

[242] Luther to Claus Sturm, June 15, 1522, Rabus, *Historien* 4, fols. 130v–131v (WA Br 2:563–64); to a friend, on his answer to Henry VIII, August 28, 1522, *Historien* 4, fols. 131v–133r (WA Br 2:593–95); "Proposal for a Peaceful Resolution of Luther's Case" (1523), *Historien* 4, fols. 134r–135r (also in Witt Ger 9 [1557], fol. 175r–v; StL 15:2191–92); Luther to Elector Frederick, May 29, 1523, *Historien* 4, fols. 135r–136v (LW 49:35–42); Luther, preface to *Two Discordant and Conflicting Imperial Mandates* (1524), *Historien* 4, fols. 137r–138v (LW 59:88–95).

[243] Luther, *Letter of Consolation to the People of Miltenberg* (1524), Rabus, *Historien* 4, fols. 139r–146r (LW 43:103–12); excerpts from letters of Elector Frederick just before his death, *Historien* 4, fols. 147v–148r (included in Witt Ger 9); Luther to Elector John, May 15, 1525, *Historien* 4, fols. 148r–149r (LSC, pp. 55–56); Marburg Colloquy, *Historien* 4, fols. 150r–152v (cf. LW 38:3–85); Marburg Articles (1529), *Historien* 4, fols. 153r–155v (LW 38:85–89); excerpt from Luther, *Confession concerning Christ's Supper* (1528), fols. 156r–163r (LW 37:361–72).

[244] Luther to his father, February 15, 1530, and to his mother, May 20, 1531, Rabus, *Historien* 4, fols. 166v–171v (LW 49:267–71; 50:17–21).

[245] Melanchthon, preface to Luther, *Warning to His Dear German People*, July 10, 1546, Rabus, *Historien* 4, fols. 172r–177v (MBW T15:357–65, no. 4319; CR 6:190–97; cf. LW 47:3–55).

[246] Luther, "Consolation to a Wittenberg Christian [Johannes Bernhardi Feldkirch, d. 1534]," Rabus, *Historien* 4, fols. 178r–185r (*Table Talk* no. 3669 [1530], WA TR 3:503–9); "Consolation in Our Last Hour," *Historien* 4, fol. 185r (*Table Talk* no. 5685 [n.d.], WA TR 5:320–21); "Comforting Writing," *Historien* 4, fols. 185v–186v (Luther to the expelled Evangelicals of Oschatz, January 20, 1533, WA Br 6:422–23; LSC, pp. 221–22); Wittenberg Concord (1536), *Historien* 4, fols. 192r–194v (see FC SD VII 12–16 [Kolb-Wengert, pp. 595–96; *Concordia*, pp. 564–65; below, p. 396 n. 9]); "Two Sermons at Smalcald" (1537), *Historien* 4, fols. 195v–213v (sermon of February 18, 1537, LW 57:253–76); Luther's response to an Italian report of his death, *Historien* 4, fols. 213v–214r (*Table Talk* no. 3595 [1537], WA TR 3:440–41).

volume of Luther's German works.[247] Rabus' *History* ends with the *Report* on Luther's last days by Jonas and Coelius and Melanchthon's funeral *Oration*.[248]

Rabus thus offered his readers a survey of Luther's life based on a broader range of texts than Pollicarius had gathered, presenting Luther as "our dear father and the prophet of the German nation," a confessor and pastoral counselor. Nevertheless, his selection was conspicuously idiosyncratic, and his framing of the texts was too sparse to provide a cohesive narrative. Embedded in Rabus' multivolume martyrology, it failed to achieve wide distribution or popularity.[249]

Meanwhile, however, the first complete narrative biography of Luther had been produced not by one of his colleagues or students but by one of his longtime opponents, the theologian Johann Cochlaeus [Dobneck von Wendelstein] (1479–1552).[250] Cochlaeus was consummately educated, with a doctorate from Ferrara and close connections with Nürnberg humanists. Beginning at the Diet of Worms, where Cochlaeus served as adviser to the papal legate Jerome Aleander, he had taken an active part in responding to Luther and the Reformation, publishing extensively against Luther and participating in diets and colloquies. Luther wrote only one work of his own in direct response—*Against the Armed Man Cochlaeus*, in 1523— though he mentioned Cochlaeus repeatedly in catalogs of his early opponents, sometimes mocking him by translating his humanist Latin name back into German as *Rotzlöffel* ["snot-spoon"].[251] Even among Cochlaeus' own

---

[247] Luther, "Exhortation," Rabus, *Historien* 4, fols. 214v–216r (i.e., preface to Adler, *Sermon on Almsgiving* [1533], LW 60:11–16); "Prophecy and Prediction of Why We in Germany Will Again Lose the Gospel," *Historien* 4, fol. 216r (the source could not be identified); "Beautiful, Comforting Saying on the Certainty of Our Salvation," *Historien* 4, fols. 216v–217r (WA 48:227); "Faithful Exhortation to True Repentance and Christian Prayer," *Historien* 4, fols. 217r–218v (WA 48:228–31); "Preface before His Parting," *Historien* 4, fols. 218v–224r (WA 54:468–77; cf. above, p. xxvi n. 45).

[248] Jonas and Coelius, *Report*, in Rabus, *Historien* 4, fols. 224v–233v (see below, pp. 5–22); Melanchthon, *Oration* (in the longer German form), fols. 234r–244v (see below, pp. 37–51; cf. above, pp. xlvi–xlvii).

[249] See Kolb, *For All the Saints*, pp. 83, 113–14; Kolb, *Luther as Prophet, Teacher, and Hero*, p. 87.

[250] On Cochlaeus, see Ralph Keen, "Cochlaeus, Johannes," *OER* 1:369–71; Keen, "Johannes Cochlaeus: An Introduction to His Life and Work," in Elizabeth Vandiver, Ralph Keen, and Thomas D. Frazel, trans. and eds., *Luther's Lives: Two Contemporary Accounts of Martin Luther* (Manchester, UK: Manchester University Press, 2002), pp. 40–52; Remigius Bäumer, *Johann Cochlaeus (1479–1552): Leben und Werk im Dienst der Katholischen Reform* (Münster: Aschendorff, 1980).

[251] WA 11:295–306 (LW 71). Cf. Luther, preface to Klingebeil, *On Clerical Marriage* (1528), LW 59:226; *On Translating* (1530), LW 35:187; *Commentary on the Alleged Imperial Edict* (1531), LW 34:95; *On the Councils and the Church* (1539), LW 41:150; *Against Hanswurst*

coreligionists his zeal provoked some dismay, and some of his anti-Lutheran treatises wound up on the *Index* of books officially prohibited by the Roman Church.[252] In 1527, Cochlaeus was appointed as chaplain to Duke George and continued his campaign against the Reformation from ducal Saxony, seeking more successfully than many of Luther's opponents to exploit the printing press and the power of popular religious propaganda. Cochlaeus' 1529 tract *Septiceps Lutherus* [The seven-headed Luther], published in German and in Latin editions, offered a memorable visual image of its title to illustrate Cochlaeus' charge of theological inconsistency made against the reformer.[253] When, after the death of Duke George in 1539, ducal Saxony itself embraced the Reformation, Cochlaeus was forced to move to Breslau (Wrocław) in Silesia, where he continued his work under adverse conditions. He welcomed the imperial victory in the Smalcaldic War, but, ironically, criticized the Augsburg Interim—which Emperor Charles imposed as a temporary settlement for the empire in religious matters—nearly as much as did the staunch Gnesio-Lutheran party, for he, too, regarded its compromises as unacceptable from the opposite side.[254]

Cochlaeus' three-decade campaign against Luther culminated in his *Commentary on the Deeds and Writings of Martin Luther from the Year of the Lord 1517 to the Year 1546 Related Chronologically to All Posterity*, published as a whole in 1549. Cochlaeus' notations in the work claim that he had completed most of it in 1534 and completed the remainder in 1546, after the dissolution of the second colloquy at Regensburg, where Cochlaeus had been appointed one of the theologians representing the imperial side,[255] the news of Luther's death having arrived in the midst of the colloquy.[256] Internal evidence suggests that Cochlaeus also made revisions to the earlier years, since his account of Luther's birth and early years (included despite a title

---

(1541), LW 41:189; preface to Melanchthon, *Response to the Clergy of Cologne* (1543), LW 60:310; *Table Talk* no. 1320 (1532), LW 54:137; no. 4543 (1539), LW 54:351.

[252] See Keen, "Johannes Cochlaeus," p. 42.

[253] Cochlaeus, *Sieben Köpffe Martini Luthers* (Leipzig: Valentin Schumann, 1529) [VD16 C4391], and *Septiceps Lutherus, ubique sibi suis scriptis contrarius* (Leipzig: Schumann, 1520) [VD16 C4386].

[254] See Keen, "Johannes Cochlaeus," pp. 47–48.

[255] See Vinzenz Pfnür, "Colloquies," *OER* 1:380.

[256] See Cochlaeus, *Deeds and Writings of Dr. Martin Luther*, in Vandiver et al., *Luther's Lives*, pp. 319, 351.

that indicates a start in 1517) seems to be derived from and responding to Melanchthon's 1546 biographical *Preface*.[257]

Cochlaeus offers a chronological narrative of Luther's life, organized year by year, based on Luther's published writings, the writings of others, Cochlaeus' own direct observation as eyewitness (to events such as the Diet of Worms), and information received from others (such as reports of Luther's demonic possession in the cloister). It is stretching the point only slightly to say that *Commentary on the Deeds and Writings of Dr. Martin Luther* is a biography of Luther in the same sense that Caesar's *Gallic War* is a biography of Vercingetorix. The reader of the *Commentary* is regularly reminded of Cochlaeus' presence (described in the third person), and the ultimate significance of Luther's acts and writings often seems to be that they elicit a conclusive response from Cochlaeus.

Cochlaeus' strategy includes ascribing diabolical influence or origins to Luther and his teaching—though the *Commentary on the Deeds and Writings of Dr. Martin Luther* does not mention charges that Cochlaeus himself had earlier brought that Luther was in fact a changeling or the product of his mother's coupling with an incubus.[258] Cochlaeus is more concerned to convict Luther out of his own writings—albeit sometimes by imposing forced interpretations or insisting on contradictions—so that, in a vicious circle, inconsistencies in Cochlaeus' portrayal of Luther become proofs of the argument against him. Just as often, however, Cochlaeus' denunciation of Luther's words and actions are made on the basis of a fundamental disjunction of values. Luther's family life, for example, which was admired and regarded as an example by his supporters, is for Cochlaeus a perpetual scandal and outrage, the manifestation of Luther's sinful lust. What Luther's supporters regarded as his courage and integrity, Cochlaeus saw as stubbornness and vainglory. Luther is charged with throwing society into turmoil, inciting sedition and disobedience not only toward the church but toward the state as well.

The last chapter of Cochlaeus' *Commentary on the Deeds and Writings of Dr. Martin Luther*, on the year 1546 and the end of Luther's life, was first published separately, in 1548, along with a Latin translation of the letters from Johann Landau and from Justus Jonas describing Luther's death.[259] The

[257] See Dierdre Hall, "Introduction," in Elizabeth Vandiver, Ralph Keen, and Thomas D. Frazel, trans. and eds., *Luther's Lives: Two Contemporary Accounts of Martin Luther* (Manchester, UK: Manchester University Press, 2002), pp. 3–4.

[258] See Ian Siggins, *Luther and His Mother* (Philadelphia: Fortress, 1981), pp. 32–39. Cochlaeus does mention the claim in his preface to his *Commentary on the Deeds and Writings of Dr. Martin Luther*, not included in the English translation by Vandiver.

[259] *Ex compendio actorum Martini Lutheri caput ultimum, et ex epistolae quadam Mansfeldensi, historica narratio: una cum annotationibus alterius epistolae, de ejusem Lutheri*

complete *Commentary* appeared in print in 1549 together with Cochlaeus' massive *History of the Hussites*.[260] Unlike much of Cochlaeus' earlier polemical work in the vernacular, the *Commentary* was issued in Latin. It proved influential on a learned Roman Catholic audience, shaping Catholic views of Luther for centuries, and provoked Lutheran response, though it enjoyed limited circulation. The work was republished on its own in 1568 and in German translation, as Cochlaeus had intended but never carried out, in 1582.[261] Cochlaeus' *Commentary* is accessible to the modern English reader in a translation by Elizabeth Vandiver, edited by Ralph Keen.[262]

If the charge of sedition was central to Cochlaeus' indictment of Luther and his movement, Johann Sleidanus (1506–56) sought to explicate the complexity of the politics surrounding Luther, his legacy, his supporters, and his opponents.[263] Sleidanus, an Alsatian diplomat and historian who had served at the French court and in Strassburg, was commissioned by the Smalcaldic League in 1545 to write an official history of the Protestant movement. Although the league's patronage was disrupted by its defeat at the hands of the emperor in the Smalcaldic War of 1546, Sleidanus continued his work on the history. He had access to the diplomatic archives of Strassburg as well as some documents from Hesse and elsewhere in the league.[264] His accounts of the imperial diets and of the Peasants' War, drawing on this material, are particularly detailed.

Sleidanus' completed work, the *Commentaries on the Condition of Religion and the State under Emperor Charles V*, appeared from the Strassburg presses in 1555, a few months before the conclusion of the Peace of

---

ultimis actis et vitae exitu (Mainz: Franz Behem, 1548). On Landau's letter (Schubart, *Die Berichte über Luthers Tod und Begräbnis*, no. 78, pp. 74–80), see above, p. xxxiii; on Jonas' letter to Elector John Frederick (Schubart, *Die Berichte über Luthers Tod und Begräbnis*, no. 1, pp. 1–10), see above, p. xxxiii.

[260] Cochlaeus, *Historiae Hussitarum Libri Duodecim . . . aedentur . . . ab eodem Cochlaeo, Commentaria De Actis & Scriptis Martini Lutheri* (Mainz: Franz Behem, 1549) [VD16 C4326/C4278].

[261] *Historia Ioannis Cochlaei de Actis et Scriptis Martini Lutheri* (Cologne: Dietrich Baum, 1568) [VD16 C4279]; *Historia Martini Lutheri*, trans. Johann Christoph Hueber (Ingolstadt: David Sartorius, 1582) [VD16 C4280].

[262] The *Commentary* is translated as *The Deeds and Writings of Dr. Martin Luther*, in Vandiver et al., *Luther's Lives*, pp. 53–351.

[263] See Alexandra Kess, *Johann Sleidan and the Protestant Vision of History* (Aldershot: Ashgate, 2008).

[264] Kess, *Sleidan and the Protestant Vision of History*, pp. 43–52, 89–104.

Augsburg.[265] Sleidanus focused on political history rather than on the intricacies of theological debates, and he strove for impartiality—Melanchthon criticized his work at first for being overly candid.[266] Nevertheless, the work was clearly Protestant and showed particular sympathy with Martin Bucer (1491–1551) and with Strassburg's mediating position in the Reformation.[267] A posthumous second edition appeared in 1558, with the addition of an appended book on the events of 1555–56, as well as Sleidanus' defense of his history against initial criticism.[268]

Sleidanus' history has Luther near the center of much of its narrative, which begins with Luther's reaction to the preaching of indulgences under Pope Leo X (r. 1513–21). Yet it is Sleidanus' vision of the Reformation as an event deeply implicated in the politics of the empire and of Europe as a whole that predominates and which influenced later biographers of Luther as well.

JOHANN WALTER, A NEW SPIRITUAL SONG ABOUT THE BLESSED, PRECIOUS, AND HIGHLY GIFTED MAN, DR. MARTIN LUTHER, THE PROPHET AND APOSTLE OF GERMANY (1564)[269]

Quite different in form from the other accounts of Luther's life translated in this volume, the *New Spiritual Song* of Johann Walter (1496–1570) is an unabashedly theological account of Luther's life and ministry. More closely associated with Luther over a longer time than any of his other biographers save Melanchthon, the musician Johann Walter [Walther] was Luther's associate and collaborator throughout most of the reformer's public life and

---

[265] *De Statu Religionis et Reipublicae, Carolo Quinto, Caesare, Commentarii* (Straßburg: Wendelin Rihel Sr., 1555) [VD16 S6668–6672].

[266] Melanchthon to Christoph Leib, May 18, 1555, MBW 7:311, no. 7492 (CR 8:483), cited in Kess, *Sleidan and the Protestant Vision of History*, pp. 76f.

[267] Kess, *Sleidan and the Protestant Vision of History*, pp. 109–16.

[268] Johannes Sleidanus, *Commentariorum de statu Religionis et Reipublicae, Carolo Quinto Caesare, Libri XXVI. Unà cum Apologia ab ipso Authore conscripta* (Straßburg: Theodosius Rihel, 1558) [VD16 ZV16828]. See Kess, *Sleidan and the Protestant Vision of History*, pp. 71–81. It is the 1558 edition of Sleidanus that is cited in this volume from the digitized exemplar of the Universitäts- und Landesbibliothek Sachsen-Anhalt.

[269] *Ein newes Geistliches Lied/ von dem Gottseligen/ thewren und hochbegnadten Manne, Doctore Martino Luthero/ Deutsches Landes Propheten und Aposteln* ([Erfurt: Georg Baumann], 1564) [VD16 ZV15419]. Exemplar in Berlin Staatsbibliothek, Sig. Hymn. 6486, with a digitized edition at http://digital.staatsbibliothek-berlin.de

became an important interpreter of his legacy after Luther's death.[270] Educated in Rochlitz and Leipzig, Walter joined the Saxon court choir as a bass singer in 1520. Walter was serving as court composer when he joined Luther in 1524 to work on the first Wittenberg collection of Lutheran vernacular hymns, in Walter's polyphonic settings, and then in 1525 to collaborate on the chant for the *German Mass* [*Deutsche Messe*].[271]

When the Saxon court choir was dissolved the year after the 1525 death of Frederick the Wise, despite protests from Luther and Melanchthon,[272] Walter became cantor at the Latin school in Torgau, with responsibilities for the choir in the town church as well as at the castle. From his new post, he remained in close contact with Luther, who in 1542 sent his son Johannes [Hans] to the Torgau school especially to be trained by Walter in music.[273] For the dedication of the Torgau castle chapel in 1544, at which Luther delivered the sermon, Walter composed a motet setting of verses from Psalm 119, with an upper part intoning the praise of Elector John Frederick and a bass line hailing Luther and Melanchthon as the restorers of Christian doctrine to the land.[274]

In addition to his musical work, Walter was also a German poet; his verse first appeared in print with his 1538 *Encomium of the Laudable Art*

---

[270] On Walter, see Carl Schalk, *Johann Walter: First Cantor of the Lutheran Church* (St. Louis: Concordia, 1992); Walter Blankenburg, *Johann Walter: Leben und Werk*, ed. Friedhelm Brusniak (Tutzing: Schneider, 1991); Friedhelm Brusniak, ed., *Johann-Walter-Studien: Tagungsbericht Torgau 1996* (Tutzing: Schneider, 1998); Joachim Stalmann, "Walter, Walther," in *Die Musik in Geschichte und Gegenwart*, 3rd ed. (Kassel: Bärenreiter, 2008), Personenteil 17:430–37. His works are edited in Johann Walter, *Sämtliche Werke*, ed. Otto Schröder et al., 6 vols. (Kassel and St. Louis: Bärenreiter and Concordia, 1953–73).

[271] On the *Geystliche gesangk Buchleyn* (1524), see Luther, *Preface to the Wittenberg Hymnal* (1524), LW 53:315–16; Walter, *Sämtliche Werke*, vols. 1–3, presenting material from the editions of 1524, 1525, 1537, 1544, and 1551. For the *German Mass and Order of Service* (1526), see LW 53:51–90, and Walter's reminiscence of his collaboration with Luther on the *German Mass* in Robin A. Leaver, *Luther's Liturgical Music: Principles and Implications* (Grand Rapids: Eerdmans, 2007), pp. 333, 336. Cf. Johannes Schilling, " 'Musicam semper amavi'—Die Musik habe ich allezeit liebgehabt: Martin Luther, Johann Walter und die Anfänge evangelischer Kirchenmusik," *Luther* 83 (2012): 133–44.

[272] See Luther to Elector John, June 20, 1526, WA Br 4:90–91; Melanchthon to Elector John, June 20, 1526, MBW T2:427–28, no. 467 (CR 1:799); Luther to Johann Walter, September 21, 1526, WA Br 4:121–22.

[273] Luther to Marcus Crodel, August 26, 1542, LW 50:230–33. Cf. Luther to Johann Walter, December 21, 1527, WA Br 4:300–301.

[274] Walter, *Psalmus CXIX*, in *Sämtliche Werke* 5:3–12. Cf. Luther, *Sermon at the Dedication of the Castle Church, Torgau* (1544/1546), LW 51:331–54. Luther last mentioned Walter in a letter written a month before his death: Luther and Bugenhagen to Elector John Frederick, January 20, 1546, WA Br 11:267.

of Music.[275] He returned to the theme in 1564 with his *Encomium of the Heavenly Art of Music.*[276] Upon Luther's death, Walter wrote and published his *Epitaph for the Reverend Father Martin Luther,* a poem of more than a hundred rhymed couplets commemorating Luther's role as God's instrument in exposing and overthrowing the tyranny of the papal antichrist and proclaiming the Gospel.[277] The *Epitaph* was a summary of Luther's theology in contrast to the doctrines of the papacy, with only a few concrete biographical references—to Luther's birth in Eisleben, for example, or to his confession before the empire at Worms in 1521. Appearing in at least seven editions across Lutheran Germany, it was a significant part of the immediate posthumous commemoration of Luther alongside the works of Melanchthon and of Jonas and Coelius.

The military and political upheaval of the Smalcaldic War which followed in the year after Luther's death dismayed Walter but also brought him new professional opportunities. Duke Maurice of Albertine Saxony (1521–53),[278] who, though Lutheran, had taken the emperor's side against the Smalcaldic League in the war, was now designated elector in the place of his deposed cousin John Frederick,[279] and in 1548 Maurice called Walter to Dresden to organize court music befitting his new dignity. Walter took up the position but soon ran afoul of Maurice's program of compromise in ceremonial matters (*adiaphora*) adopted in response to pressure from the emperor: the so-called "Leipzig Interim," which, though never endorsed by the territorial estates, was enforced selectively in Maurice's lands beginning in July 1549.[280]

Walter undertook his musical duties but refused on the basis of conscience to receive the Lord's Supper from the Dresden clergy who had accommodated themselves to the Interim. This placed Walter on the side

---

[275] Walter, *Lob und Preis der löblichen Kunst Musica,* in *Sämtliche Werke* 6:153–56; trans. in Schalk, *Johann Walter,* pp. 14–22.

[276] Walter, *Lob und Preis der himmlichen Kunst Musica,* in Walter, *Sämtliche Werke* 6:157–61.

[277] *Epitaphium des ehrwirdigen Herrn und Vaters Martini Luthers* (Wittenberg: G. Rhau, 1546), with editions that same year in Magdeburg, Lübeck, and Nürnberg [VD16 W992–996, ZV18803], edited in Walter, *Sämtliche Werke,* 6:162–64.

[278] Maurice [Moritz] of Saxony was the son of Duke Henry of Saxony (d. 1541; see below, p. 313 n. 185), who had introduced the Reformation in Albertine Saxony in 1539. Maurice, though Lutheran, refused to align with the Smalcaldic League under the leadership of Ernestine Saxony and took the side of the Hapsburg emperor. See Günther Wartenburg, "Moritz of Saxony," *OER* 3:93–94. See also below, p. 233 n. 13.

[279] See above, p. xxv n. 42.

[280] For the text of the "Leipzig Interim," see Kolb and Nestingen, *Sources and Contexts,* pp. 183–96; CR 7:258–64 (MBW no. 5387: see MBW R5:400–401); for discussion, see Arand et al., *Lutheran Confessions,* pp. 177–83.

of the Gnesio-Lutherans against the "Philippists" who, with Melanchthon, found the compromises to be acceptable.[281] Meanwhile, Walter corresponded with Gnesio-Lutheran leaders such as Nicolaus von Amsdorf and Matthias Flacius Illyricus, seeking reinforcement for his stance.[282] In 1554, after repeated conflict with the Dresden clergy, Walter retired from his court position and returned to Torgau, where he was asked to supervise music in the castle church again but to refrain from trying to "reform and criticize" the church and its preachers.[283]

The last decade and a half of Walter's life was dedicated to upholding Luther and his Reformation, as Walter personally remembered and confessed it, for a new generation. Walter pursued this goal through new publication of musical compositions—especially a six-part polyphonic setting of Luther's hymn *Erhalt uns Herr bei deinem Wort*[284]—as well as of verse: a 1554 epitaph for the deposed Elector John Frederick, hailing him (pointedly still identified as "elector") as a confessor of God's Word;[285] a 1552 adaptation [*contrafaktur*] of a seasonal folk song, *Herzlich tut mich erfreuen*, recast as a paean to the spiritual "summer" of the renewed preaching of the Gospel before the end of the world;[286] and a national call to repentance and to gratitude to God, *Wach auf, wach auf, du deutsches Land*, in 1561.[287] Although

---

[281] See Arand et al., *Lutheran Confessions*, pp. 183–89.

[282] See Armin Brinzing, "Ein neues Dokument zur theologischen Position des späten Johann Walter," in *Johann-Walter-Studien: Tagungsbericht Torgau 1996*, ed. Friedhelm Brusniak (Tutzing: Schneider, 1998), pp. 73–112. On Amsdorf, see below, p. 30 n. 15. On Flacius, see below, p. 112 n. 42.

[283] See Martin Staehelin, "Johannes Walter: Zu Leben, Werk, und Wirkung," in *Johann-Walter-Studien: Tagungsbericht Torgau 1996*, ed. Friedhelm Brusniak (Tutzing: Schneider, 1998), p. 23.

[284] *Das Christlich Kinderlied D. Martin Lutheri, 'Erhalt uns Herr'* (1566), in Walter, *Sämtliche Werke*, 6:3–82 (cf. the introduction by Joachim Stalmann, pp. xviii–xxi). See Leaver, *Luther's Liturgical Music*, pp. 203–5.

[285] *Epitaphium des durchlauchtigsten, hochgebornen Fürsten und Herrn, Herrn Johanns Friedrichen, Herzogen und Kurfürsten zu Sachsen etc.*, edited in Walter, *Sämtliche Werke*, 6:164.

[286] "Ein neuer bergreihen von dem jüngsten Tage und ewigem Leben," edited in Walter, *Sämtliche Werke*, 3:73–75, and in Wackernagel 3:187, no. 219. Selected stanzas of this song have sometimes appeared on their own as the hymn *Der Bräut'gam wird bald rufen* ("The Bridegroom Soon Will Call Us," *LSB* 514). On the use of *contrafaktur* in Reformation song, see Oettinger, *Music as Propaganda*, pp. 89–136.

[287] "Ein neues christlichs Lied, dadurch Deutschland zur Buße ermahnet," edited in Walter, *Sämtliche Werke*, 3:76–77, and in Wackernagel 3:190, no. 220. This song, at least in excerpt, has appeared frequently in German Lutheran hymnals: see, e.g., the *Evangelisches Kirchengesangbuch* (Berlin: Evangelische Verlagsanstalt, 1950), no. 390; *Evangelisch-Lutherisches Kirchengesangbuch* (Göttingen: Hubert, 1987), no. 390; *Evangelisches Gesangbuch* (Stuttgart: Bibliadruck, 1993), no. 145.

not originally intended as hymns for public use, several of these vernacular texts eventually came to be employed as such.

Walter's most concentrated theological declaration appeared in 1564 in a twenty-four-page pamphlet offering a set of three songs that, taken together, clearly delineate his Gnesio-Lutheran position in the theological disputes of his day. The second of the set was "Another new song on false prophets who teach that no human being can be saved without good works and that human beings are able to turn and orient themselves to God's grace by their natural free will": that is, against the doctrines of Majorism and Synergism.[288] The third song directed itself against "the false prophets and false Christians who, having once acknowledged the truth of the Gospel, turn again to the Antichrist and play the hypocrite for him for the sake of temporal goods": that is, against the Adiaphorists who accepted the imposition of Roman Catholic practices for the sake of the emperor's goodwill.[289] In addition to their wider resonance in intra-Lutheran debates, all of these issues had particular connections to Walter's conflict with the theologians of Albertine Saxony: the question of adiaphora had been foremost in his dealings with the Dresden clergy; the formula that "good works are necessary for salvation" had appeared in the Leipzig Interim; and the leading exponent of Synergism was Johann Pfeffinger, a theological professor at Leipzig who had helped draft the Leipzig Interim. In each theological case at issue, Walter's voice was part of the Lutheran consensus later upheld in the Formula of Concord.[290]

The polemical purpose of the first song in the collection, however, was less obvious. Walter's *New Spiritual Song about the Blessed, Precious, and Highly Gifted Man, Dr. Martin Luther, the Prophet and Apostle of Germany* instead offered a narrative of Luther's life and teaching in sixty-four stanzas.[291] Unlike Walter's 1546 *Epitaph*, the *New Spiritual Song* is biographical and largely chronological. Despite Walter's designation of the poem as a "spiritual song" and a suggestion of a hymn melody as its musical setting, it was not intended as a hymn for church use; rather, contemporaries would have received it as a kind of ballad, recounting events of religious and political significance.[292]

---

[288] Wackernagel 3:201–3, no. 223. See Arand et al., *Lutheran Confessions*, pp. 178, 191–94, 201–11.

[289] The third song is not edited in Wackernagel. On the Adiaphoristic Controversy, see Arand et al., *Lutheran Confessions*, pp. 180–83.

[290] See the Formula of Concord (Kolb-Wengert, pp. 486–660; *Concordia*, pp. 473–619).

[291] For discussion, see Kolb, *For All the Saints*, pp. 125–26.

[292] Cf. Oettinger, *Music as Propaganda*, pp. 202–3.

Walter's poem begins with a description of conditions before the Reformation ("The Age and Rule of the Antichrist"), followed by God's raising up of Luther to oppose the pope ("The Revelation and Fall of the Antichrist"); an account of Luther's teaching, controversies, and legacy to the Church follows ("God's Gracious Visitation and the Joyous Season of the Gospel; the Great Light and the Rich Knowledge of God's Word; and God's Many Other Blessings Manifested to Germany through Luther"); and, finally, Walter calls readers to thanksgiving ("An Exhortation to Thankfulness for the Great, Manifold Blessings Manifested by God and for His Gracious Visitation"). In its presentation of Luther's life and theology, however, Walter's poem emphasizes those aspects which Gnesio-Lutherans found most salient.

In Walter's poem, Luther stands as a solitary hero, prepared and supported by God alone since before his birth to do battle against the papal antichrist. Drawing on possible German meanings of Luther's name ("lute player"), Walter first depicts Luther as a musician whose playing provokes the papacy. The imagery then shifts to Luther as a warrior, standing in God's armor and wielding the sword of God's Word in opposition to the "papistic dragon's tail," even when summoned before the emperor.[293] To the image of Luther as Germanic hero, Walter adds an allusion to the biblical story of David and Goliath.

Having exposed the papacy, God pours out His truth upon Germany through Luther's teaching. Luther exposes human sinfulness and points, like John the Baptist, to Christ alone as the object of faith, whose suffering alone brings both justification and sanctification—the "chief of doctrines." Luther distinguished Law and Gospel, taught "true good works," and restored the worship of God, abolishing the Mass and returning the Lord's Supper to Christ's institution. Luther restored secular government and marriage to honor, taught Christian freedom for perplexed consciences, and freed people from the entanglement of monastic vows.

Although the specific treatises in which Luther dealt with these theological topics can sometimes be guessed, Walter gave special and explicit emphasis to the texts in which Luther communicated the Gospel to a wide popular audience: Luther's catechism, hymnal, and postils and, above all, the German translation of the Bible, with which he renewed the German language. Of Luther's theological controversies, Walter specifically mentions his opposition to the Enthusiasts and his dispute with Erasmus over the freedom of the human will. (Walter is nearly alone among Luther's early biographers in giving this episode a prominent place in the history of the

---

[293] See below, Walter, *New Spiritual Song*, p. 87, stanza 15.

Reformation.)[294] Luther is the divinely appointed champion and prophet who stood firm for God's truth throughout his life, without wavering or compromise; with his departure, no one is fit to stand as his successor.

In the final section of the poem, Walter turns to admonish Germany for its ingratitude toward God's work through Luther, citing biblical examples of God's judgment on peoples who have rejected His grace. Drawing on language that had been used by Melanchthon and Bugenhagen upon Luther's death, Walter hails Luther as the third and final Elijah, God's charioteer, whose message has, however, been lamentably perverted, leaving the chariot of the Church without a faithful driver. Walter prays for God's blessing upon Saxony (that is, Ernestine Saxony, ruled by the sons of John Frederick the Magnanimous), as well as upon the county Mansfeld, especially on Luther's birthplace of Eisleben. Mansfeld was at the time a singular haven for Gnesio-Lutherans, including numerous exiles from Albertine Saxony and the church policies of Elector Maurice; Walter's own last work, a versified table grace (the *Gratias*), was published posthumously in Eisleben.[295]

Although Walter's verse did not have the influence of Melanchthon's *Oration* or *Preface*, it stands as an important and underappreciated witness to Luther's life and influence, compact but surprisingly comprehensive, written by one of Luther's longtime collaborators and associates and from the perspective of the Gnesio-Lutheran party.

Walter's *New Spiritual Song* has been printed in modern German editions in the nineteenth-century hymn collection of Philip Wackernagel and in the twentieth-century Bärenreiter/Concordia edition of Walter's *Sämtliche Werke*, though the text of the latter is based on Wackernagel's transcription, since at the time of publication the 1564 printing had been lost.[296] Happily, a copy has since been rediscovered at the Berlin Staatsbibliothek,[297] which has been used in digitized form by the present editors to confirm the accuracy of the later editions.[298] The translation in the present volume, by Matthew Carver, is based on the German text of the 1564 printing.

---

[294] See below, Walter, *New Spiritual Song*, p. 95, stanza 44.

[295] *Das Gratias: Eine Christliche Dancksagung/ Johannis Waltheri des Eltern letztes Gedicht* (Eisleben: U. Gaubisch, 1571) [VD16 W999], edited in Walter, *Sämtliche Werke*, 6:176. On Mansfeld's role in the Gnesio-Lutheran controversies, see Christman, *Doctrinal Controversy and Lay Religiosity in the Late Reformation*; and Robert J. Christman, "Competing Clerical Efforts to Secure Lay Support in the Flacian Controversy over Original Sin," in *The Formation of Clerical and Confessional Identities in Early Modern Europe*, ed. Wim Janse and Barbara Pitkin (Leiden: Brill, 2006), pp. 225–38.

[296] Wackernagel 3:192–97, no. 221; Walter, *Sämtliche Werke*, 6:165–69.

[297] See Stalmann, in Walter, *Sämtliche Werke*, 6:xvii, xxvi; Wackernagel 3:203.

[298] On the basis of the 1564 printing, the following corrections should be made to the transcriptions in Wackernagel (W) and Walter, *Sämtliche Werke* (SW), not including variations in

The Gnesio-Lutheran interpretation of Luther's life and significance was given more expansive elucidation by the Mansfeld preacher Cyriakus Spangenberg.[299] Beginning on November 11, 1562, and continuing (usually) on the dates of Luther's birth and death every year until November 11, 1573, Spangenberg preached a series of twenty-one sermons interpreting Luther thematically: as spiritual steward, as spiritual knight, as prophet, as apostle, as evangelist, as Elijah, as Paul, as John, as theologian, as the angel of Revelation 14, as witness, as pilgrim, as priest, as laborer on the mountain of the Lord, as master miner, as excavator, as surveyor, as mining official, as spiritual judge.[300] In 1589 the collection of sermons, which had appeared separately over the years, was republished together under the title *Theander Lutherus* [Luther: Man of God].[301] Spangenberg's sermons did not form a chronological biography but emphasized Luther's unique theological authority from the perspective of the Flacian wing of the Gnesio-Lutheran party, a partisan association that seems to have reduced the appeal of the work as most Lutherans had rallied around the Formula of Concord by 1580. Even Spangenberg himself, in the later sermons of his series, drew on the series of sermons on Luther's life by the moderate Lutheran pastor Johann Mathesius, begun coincidentally on almost the same day as Spangenberg's but finished in 1564–65 and published in 1566—a biography which proved valuable to the widest range of Lutherans.[302]

---

capitalization or in modernization of spelling. The stanzas of the 1564 printing are numbered within each part rather than being numbered continuously from beginning to end as in W and SW, though continuous numbering has been retained for the present translated edition. Stanza 12 (2.4) line 2: read "sehr" (1564, W) for "gar" (SW). Stanza 13 (2.5) line 4: read "gehet-zet" (1564) for "gesetzet" (W, SW). Stanza 24 (2.16) line 6: read "auff" (1564, W) for "und" (SW). Stanza 35 (3.11) line 6: read "gesprochen" (1564, W) for "besprochen" (SW). Stanza 50 (3.26) line 6: read "Zu Christo" (1564, W) for "In Christo" (SW). Stanza 56 (4.6) line 2: read "Da sie" (1564, W) for "Daß sie" (SW).

[299] On Spangenberg, see Robert Kolb, "Spangeberg, Cyriakus," *OER* 4:99–100.

[300] On Spangenberg's Luther sermons, see Kolb, *Luther as Prophet, Teacher, and Hero*, pp. 46–55; Kolb, *For All the Saints*, pp. 120–22; Susan R. Boettcher, "Martin Luthers Leben in Predigten: Cyriakus Spangenberg und Johannes Mathesius," in *Martin Luther und der Bergbau im Mansfelder Land: Aufsätze*, ed. Rosemarie Knape (Eisleben: Stiftung Luthergedenkstätten in Sachsen-Anhalt, 2000), pp. 170–75.

[301] Cyriakus Spangenberg, *Theander Lutherus* (Oberursel: Nikolaus Heinrich, 1589) [VD16 S7690]. For the earlier separate printings of the sermons in Erfurt by Georg Baumann and Andreas Petri, see VD16 S7665–7689.

[302] On the theological positioning of Mathesius' *History*, see below, pp. lxxxv–xci.

Johann Mathesius, *History of the Origins, Doctrine, Life, and Death of the Reverend, Blessed, Precious Man of God, Dr. Martin Luther* (1562–64/1566)[303]

The most comprehensive, influential, and enduring sixteenth-century biography of Luther was produced by his former student Johann Mathesius (1504–65), preacher and pastor in the Bohemian mining town of Joachimsthal from 1545 to 1565. Mathesius' biography originated in a series of German sermons Mathesius delivered between 1562 and 1564, which appeared in print in 1566, the year after Mathesius' death. Mathesius' *History* then appeared in twelve more sixteenth-century editions and remained in print in German through the seventeenth and eighteenth centuries.[304] (Although Mathesius hoped that his colleagues and heirs would produce a Latin translation of his Luther sermons, no such edition ever saw the light of day).[305] The nineteenth century saw a fresh wave of editions of Mathesius' biography of Luther, including a first American printing under the auspices of the Ohio Synod, a condensed popular edition by the Luther scholar Georg Buchwald, and an edition by Concordia Publishing House for the Luther anniversary in 1883 which saw multiple printings.[306] Translations into Dutch and Swedish appeared.[307] A critical edition of Mathesius' Luther sermons was produced by Georg Loesche in 1898, with a revised

---

[303] *Historien/ Von des Ehrwirdigen in Gott Seligen thewren Manns Gottes/ Doctoris Martini Luthers/ anfang/ lehr/ leben vnd sterben/ Alles ordendlich der Jarzal nach/ wie sich alle sachen zu jeder zeyt haben zugetragen/ Durch den Alten Herrn M. Mathesium gestelt/ vnd alles für seinem seligen Ende verfertigt* (Nürnberg: Ulrich Neuber, 1566) [VD16 M1490], and corrected second edition (Nürnberg: Ulrich Neuber, 1567) [VD16 M1491], edited in Georg Loesche, *Luthers Leben in Predigten*, vol. 3 of *Johannes Mathesius: Ausgewählte Werke*, Bibliothek deutscher Schriftsteller aus Böhmen 9, 2nd ed. (Prague: J. G. Calve/Josef Koch, 1906; 1st ed., 1898). The two editions by Loesche are cited here as *LH* or *LH²*; the contents and pagination differ only in the notes and end matter (*LH²*, pp. 441–619).

[304] Georg Loesche, *Johannes Mathesius: Ein Lebens- und Sitten-Bild aus der Reformationszeit* (Gotha: F. A. Perthes, 1895), 2:411–16, lists editions of Mathesius' *History* through 1883. The sixteenth-century editions, all printed in Nürnberg, are cataloged in VD16 M1490–1501 and ZV10510, from which one 1568 edition and one 1570 edition are not found (or are not distinguished from others of the same year) in Loesche's list.

[305] See below, Mathesius, *History*, p. 105.

[306] *Das Leben Martin Luthers nach Johann Mathesius* (Grünsburg, PA: Jacob S. Steck, 1836); Georg Buchwald, ed., *Martin Luthers Leben in siebzehn Predigten* (Leipzig: Reclam, 1883); *Dr. Martin Luthers Leben, beschrieben von Johann Mathesius* (St. Louis: Concordia, 1883).

[307] A. G. Ziegert, trans., *Dr. M. Luthers Lefverne* (Orebro: Lindh, 1846); Willem F. Barbiers, trans., *Dr. Maarten Luther, geschetst door een tijdgenoot* (Amsterdam: P. M. van der Maade, 1858).

second edition in 1906. Although Mathesius' *History* has been superseded as an account of Luther's life by modern scholarly biographies, the outlines of Mathesius' narrative—or reactions against it—can still be discerned beneath the surface of recent works. Mathesius consolidated sixteenth-century efforts to remember Luther, producing the first sympathetic full narrative of the reformer's life, and he shaped the image of Luther for centuries to come.[308]

Mathesius was a native of Rochlitz, in Albertine Saxony, born to a family engaged—in parallel with Luther's—in the local mining industry.[309] Like Luther, he seems to have been designated for education in order to support his family's fortunes. He received an elementary education in Rochlitz and neighboring Mittweida, counting the future Mansfeld superintendent Michael Coelius among his teachers and the future cantor Johann Walter among his fellow students.[310] Mathesius was forced by his father's untimely death to seek his fortunes abroad and came to Nürnberg in 1521, where he studied in one of the Latin schools (not yet the *gymnasium* inaugurated by Melanchthon in 1526) for a year. The echoes of Luther's reformation there do not seem to have affected him, for he continued his studies at the University of Ingolstadt (1523–25), already a center of theological

---

[308] On Mathesius' Luther sermons, see Hans Volz, *Die Lutherpredigten des Johannes Mathesius: Kritische Untersuchungen zur Geschichtsschreibung im Zeitalter der Reformation*, Quellen und Forschungen zur Reformationsgeschichte 12 (Leipzig: M. Heinsius, 1930; repr., New York: Johnson, 1971); Boettcher, "Luthers Leben in Predigten," pp. 163–87; Michael Beyer, "Johannes Mathesius als Biograph Martin Luthers," in *Johannes Mathesius (1504–1565): Rezeption und Verbreitung der Wittenberger Reformation durch Predigt und Exegese*, ed. Armin Kohnle and Irene Dingel, Leucorea-Studien zur Geschichte der Reformation und der Lutherischen Orthodoxie 30 (Leipzig: Evangelische Verlagsanstalt, 2017), pp. 65–83; Armin Kohnle, "Die Reformatoren neben Luther in den Lutherpredigten des Johannes Mathesius," in *Memoria—theologische Synthese—Autoritätenkonflikt: Die Rezeption Luthers und Melanchthons in der Schülergeneration*, ed. Irene Dingel (Tübingen: Mohr Siebeck, 2016), pp. 15–44; Ernst Walter Zeeden, *The Legacy of Luther: Martin Luther and the Reformation in the Estimation of the German Lutherans from Luther's Death to the Beginning of the Age of Goethe*, trans. Ruth Mary Bethell (Westminster, MD: Newman Press, 1954), pp. 18–23; Eike Wolgast, "Biographie als Autoritätsstiftung: Die ersten evangelischen Luther-biographien," in *Biographie zwischen Renaissance und Barock, Zwölf Studien*, ed. Walter Berschin (Heidelberg: Mattes, 1993), pp. 62–66; Kolb, *Luther as Prophet, Teacher, and Hero*, pp. 86–91; Kolb, *For All the Saints*, pp. 115–20; and Irena Backus, *Life Writing in Reformation Europe: Lives of Reformers by Friends, Disciples, and Foes* (Aldershot: Ashgate, 2008), pp. 8–12.

[309] The comprehensive biography of Mathesius remains the work of Georg Loesche, *Johannes Mathesius: Ein Lebens- und Sitten-Bild aus der Reformationszeit*, 2 vols. (Gotha: F. A. Perthes, 1895). See also Christopher Boyd Brown, *Singing the Gospel: Lutheran Hymns and the Success of the Reformation*, Harvard Historical Studies 148 (Cambridge, MA: Harvard University Press, 2005), especially pp. 40–42; Robert Rosin, "Mathesius, Johannes," *OER* 3:32–33.

[310] See Loesche, *Johannes Mathesius*, 1:11; on Coelius, see above, p. xxviii n. 57; on Walter, see above, pp. lxxi–lxxii.

opposition to Luther and of persecution of his defenders.[311] After his university study, Mathesius found employment as a librarian and tutor in southern Germany, first with a member of the Bavarian ducal court in Munich (1525) and then with a noble family in Odelzhausen (1526–27), between Munich and Augsburg, where he encountered the Reformation for the first time through the tumult of Anabaptist and Sacramentarian preaching.[312] Yet it was at this point, too, in 1526, that he first encountered Luther's work in print: the 1520 *Treatise on Good Works*.[313] Reading Luther proved a conversion experience for Mathesius, and he resolved to travel to Wittenberg himself to undertake further studies there, though his plans were delayed by the temporary relocation of the university to Jena in 1528 during the plague.[314] He found support and lodging for a year with the neighboring pastor in Bruck [Fürstenfeldbruck], Zecharias Weixner, an Evangelically minded priest who helped settle questions that the local Zwinglians and Anabaptists had raised in Mathesius' mind by supplying copies of Luther's works on the Lord's Supper.[315]

In 1529, Mathesius returned to Saxony and matriculated at the University of Wittenberg, arriving at Pentecost.[316] Here Mathesius listened to sermons and lectures by Luther, Melanchthon, Bugenhagen, Justus Jonas, and other professors, as he describes in detail in the eighth sermon on Luther's history. Mathesius also formed relationships with the younger generation of Wittenberg scholars, which he would continue to cultivate throughout his life. Especially important were his connections with Caspar Cruciger, Paul Eber (1511–69), Veit Dietrich (1506–49), and Georg Major.[317] Alongside Luther himself, the "illustrious University of Wittenberg" stood in Mathesius' memory as the center of God's work of Reformation, the "water tower" of pure doctrine that was now being piped across Europe and the center of learning where Mathesius himself "first grasped the true

---

[311] Ingolstadt was the base for Johann Eck's polemic against Luther (see below, p. 154 n. 89). In 1523, the university had begun proceedings against the eighteen-year-old student Arsacius Seehofer (1503/1505–39) on charges of Lutheran heresy. See Luther, *Against the Blind and Insane Condemnation of Seventeen Articles* (1524), WA 15:94–125 (LW 71); LW 49:313 n. 11; below, Mathesius, *History*, pp. 218–19.

[312] See below, Mathesius, *History*, pp. 245–46, 382.

[313] LW 44:15–114. See below, Mathesius, *History*, p. 158.

[314] See below, Mathesius, *History*, p. 288.

[315] See below, Mathesius, *History*, pp. 242–43, 262, 292.

[316] See below, Mathesius, *History*, pp. 290–308, 593–94. See Karl Eduard Förstemann et al., eds., *Album Academiae Vitebergensis: Ältere Reihe*, vol. 1 (Leipzig: Tauchniz, 1841; repr. Aalen: Scientia, 1976), p. 135.

[317] See Loesche, *Johannes Mathesius*, 1:191–204.

religion and the liberal arts and learned to apply them properly."[318] Mathesius embodied the Wittenberg union of humanist literary and historical studies with Evangelical theology.

Thus equipped, and at Veit Dietrich's recommendation, Mathesius left Wittenberg in the summer of 1530 to take up a post as teacher at the Latin school in Altenburg, where he served for two years.[319] In March 1532, Mathesius was called to the town of Joachimsthal in the Bohemian Erzgebirge to become rector of the Latin school, a post he would occupy until 1538. Among the resources Mathesius brought with him from his time in Wittenberg was Luther's 1529 *Small Catechism*, which he introduced in his new school,[320] collaborating with the cantor Nicolaus Herman (ca. 1480–1561), also an acquaintance of Luther's, to improve the school while reinforcing the connections between Wittenberg and Joachimsthal.

Mathesius' own connection with Joachimsthal proved an enduring one. The town would become the location and focus of Mathesius' ministry for the rest of his life. Mathesius, in turn, became the town's advocate and historian, compiling a town *Chronicle* tracing the developments of the town, its mines, and its church and schools from its founding onward.[321]

Joachimsthal was a young town, having been established in 1516 ("this new city, which sprang up along with the Gospel," as Mathesius would later describe it), but a prosperous one, since its silver mines were for the moment some of the most productive in Europe. The coins minted in Joachimsthal and those modeled on them—called Joachimsthalers, Thalers, or "dollars"— became the standard currency for commerce in early modern Europe and the New World.[322] At its peak of population in 1533, Joachimsthal was the second largest town in Bohemia, next only to Prague, and about half the size of a German metropolis such as Nürnberg. Although the mines and the population of the town declined slowly thereafter, Joachimsthal remained a populous and important center. Its resources had enabled it to establish the Latin school in the very first years of the town's history and by 1537 to

---

[318] See below, Mathesius, *History*, pp. 106, 109–10, 571–97.

[319] Loesche, *Johannes Mathesius*, 1:53–57; cf. below, Mathesius, *History*, p. 354.

[320] See below, Mathesius, *History*, p. 258.

[321] The *Jochimßthalischen kurtzen Chronicken*, cited here as *Chronica*, by year, was first published as an appendix to Mathesius' *Sarepta oder Bergpostill* (Nürnberg: Ulrich Newber & Johann vom Bergs Erben, 1564; repr., in 2 vols., Prague: Národní technické muzeum, 1975) [VD16 M1557], fols. Lllr–Nn1r. The complete Joachimsthal chronicle, including its continuation through 1617 by Mathesius' successors, was reprinted by Karl Siegl, ed., *Die Joachimsthaler Chronik von 1516–1617* (Joachimsthal/Schlackenwerth: D. R. Schöniger, 1923). See also Mathesius' narrative treatment of Joachimsthal's history in the twelfth sermon of the *Sarepta* (fols. i3r–i7v).

[322] On Joachimsthal, see Brown, *Singing the Gospel*, pp. 26–42.

construct a large new church edifice, arguably the first Lutheran church to have been designed and constructed as such.

Joachimsthal and its mines were, until 1545, under the patronage of the Schlick counts, who had close connections with Wittenberg and with Luther himself and who used their power and influence to introduce or encourage the Reformation in their territories.[323] Although the progress of the Reformation in Joachimsthal through the 1520s had been tumultuous under the competing influences of Luther, Karlstadt, Thomas Münzer, and adherents of the traditional religion, by the mid-1530s Luther's version of reform had begun to take firm root.

Joachimsthal's Lutheran identity was challenged, however, by the political situation of the town, which was under the Bohemian crown, held since 1526 by the Hapsburg dynasty and assigned to Ferdinand I (1503–64), brother of Emperor Charles V and designated successor to the imperial election.[324] Ferdinand was succeeded by his son Maximilian II (1527–76), who took the Bohemian crown in 1562.[325] Joachimsthal's vulnerability had dramatically increased when in 1545 the Schlicks were deprived of their jurisdiction, leaving the mines and the town under direct Hapsburg rule. Nevertheless, though Hapsburg policy in general sought to suppress Protestantism, Ferdinand found himself obliged to tolerate Lutheranism in Joachimsthal because of the economic importance of its mines and the potential cost of any disruption.

The selection of Evangelical clergy for the Joachimsthal church was therefore a political as well as a religious challenge. Already in 1539 the Joachimsthal council proposed Mathesius as a candidate for a preaching position. He insisted, however, on his need for further theological education in Wittenberg, where he returned from 1540 to 1542, supported by the generosity of the people of Joachimsthal.[326] During his first period of study

---

[323] Cf. below, Mathesius, *History*, pp. 138–39, 208–10, 590–91.

[324] Ferdinand I (1503–64) was the brother of Emperor Charles V (r. 1519–56), holding the titles of archduke of Austria and (since 1526) king of Bohemia and Hungary. Having been named king of the Romans since 1531, Ferdinand was the designated successor to the empire after Charles' abdication in 1556. Ferdinand often served as Charles' representative at imperial diets, where he took a harder policy toward the Protestant estates than Charles himself had, though after Charles' abdication he showed somewhat more flexibility.

[325] Maximilian II, son of Emperor Ferdinand, was in 1562 elected both king of Bohemia and "Roman [or German] king," designating him as successor to Ferdinand, whom he followed as Holy Roman emperor in 1564. Compared with his predecessors, Maximilian adopted a relatively conciliatory policy toward Protestantism in the empire, with which he may have had veiled personal sympathies as well (cf. below, p. xcii and p. 562 n. 156). See Paula S. Fichtner, *Emperor Maximilian II* (New Haven: Yale University Press, 2001), pp. 32–49, 135–55.

[326] Mathesius had apparently visited Wittenberg for two weeks at some point during his time as rector, but it is unclear when. See Loesche, *Johannes Mathesius*, 1:83.

in Wittenberg, Mathesius had lodged with a fellow Rochlitzer.[327] But upon his return, Mathesius found a place at Luther's own board, supported by the mediation of Spalatin, Jonas, and Rörer. He took his place among the students who wrote down Luther's remarks at meals.[328] While studying in Wittenberg for his master's degree, Mathesius heard Luther's lectures on Genesis and witnessed the meetings for the revision of the German Bible, as well as the last stages of the Antinomian Controversy with Johann Agricola.[329]

In the spring of 1542, Mathesius accepted a call to return to Joachimsthal as preacher;[330] his ordination at the end of March was among the last that Luther performed. He served as the assistant clergyman in Joachimsthal until 1545, when Ferdinand took over rule of the town and the senior pastor departed. At that critical juncture, the town council signaled its resolution to continue with the Reformation by naming Mathesius—a Wittenberg graduate, married since 1542, who had never been ordained by papal clergy—as the new pastor, a role in which he would continue for the next twenty years. Also in 1545 Mathesius visited Luther in Wittenberg for the last time.[331]

After Luther's death, Mathesius maintained an extensive correspondence with Melanchthon, Eber, and other members of the Wittenberg circle. In turn, many Wittenberg professors visited Joachimsthal in the following decades; Melanchthon himself appeared to preside over the graduation of the Latin school students in 1552.[332] After Luther's death, however, the outbreak of the Smalcaldic War in 1546–47 brought severe troubles to both Joachimsthal and Wittenberg. When the men of Joachimsthal, under Hapsburg rule, were called to take up arms against their Saxon neighbors, Mathesius urged his congregation to refuse to take part in the persecution of the Gospel. When this report reached the court, Mathesius found himself in dire peril, summoned to Prague to answer charges of treason. Ferdinand, however, proved willing to dismiss the charges on the basis of Mathesius' promise not to mingle spiritual and secular affairs in the future—the nonnegotiable condition for Joachimsthal's toleration within Hapsburg Bohemia.[333]

---

[327] See below, Mathesius, *History*, p. 301.

[328] See below, pp. lxxxviii–lxxxix; Mathesius, *History*, pp. 424–62 (especially pp. 424–26) and p. 464.

[329] See Brecht 3:167–70; Volz, *Die Lutherpredigten des Johannes Mathesius*, pp. 190–209. Cf. below, Mathesius, *History*, pp. 412–18, 470–85.

[330] See below, Mathesius, *History*, p. 606. The call from Joachimsthal had been extended in November 1541: see Loesche, *Johannes Mathesius*, 1:93–104.

[331] See below, Mathesius, *History*, pp. 519–20, 521, 608–9.

[332] See Mathesius, *Chronica*, 1552.

[333] See Christopher Boyd Brown, "Die Lehre vom Widerstand bei Johannes Mathesius," in *Johannes Mathesius (1504–1565): Rezeption und Verbreitung der Wittenberger Reformation*

The University of Wittenberg, and Melanchthon as its leading theologian, meanwhile found themselves at the center of the maelstrom surrounding the Interims of 1547–49.[334] Mathesius, for his own part, remained firm in his personal loyalty to Melanchthon and to the university, and hostile toward Flacius and his party as ungrateful children of Wittenberg.[335] Mathesius' own theological positions, however, do not seem to have been heavily marked by "Philippist" distinctives; rather, he consistently read Melanchthon in light of Luther's teaching. If Luther was Moses, then Melanchthon, as Aaron, was his mouthpiece.[336] Mathesius emphatically condemned the so-called "crypto-Calvinists" who appealed to the Augsburg Confession while denying the "substantial presence" of Christ in the Supper, or who sought to introduce a "second Reformation" to Reformed Protestantism in their territories.[337] For Mathesius, it was the "attested Augsburg Confession" of 1530—not the so-called *Variata* of 1540—that set the standard for orthodoxy.[338]

Mathesius was a gifted and prolific preacher. More than 1,500 of his sermons appeared in print, some during his lifetime but many published posthumously by his heirs and younger clergymen. His preaching included the Sunday lectionary texts—to which a series on his own selection of Old Testament texts chosen to fit with the assigned Gospel and Epistle readings was added—and his afternoon preaching on the catechism.[339] Mathesius also preached extended series on New and Old Testament books, including 1 and 2 Corinthians, Genesis 6–7, Psalm 130, and (mentioned though not

---

durch Predigt und Exegese, ed. Armin Kohnle and Irene Dingel, Leucorea-Studien zur Geschichte der Reformation und der Lutherischen Orthodoxie 30 (Leipzig: Evangelische Verlagsanstalt, 2017), pp. 145–46; and Loesche, *Johannes Mathesius*, 1:138–72.

[334] See above, pp. xxi, lxxiii–lxxiv.

[335] See, e.g., below, Mathesius, *History*, pp. 112, 280, 308.

[336] See, e.g., below, Mathesius, *History*, pp. 325–26, 338. On Mathesius' relationship with Melanchthon, see Christine Mundhenk, "Johannes Mathesius und Philipp Melanchthon," in *Johannes Mathesius (1504–1565): Rezeption und Verbreitung der Wittenberger Reformation durch Predigt und Exegese*, ed. Armin Kohnle and Irene Dingel, Leucorea-Studien zur Geschichte der Reformation und der Lutherischen Orthodoxie 30 (Leipzig: Evangelische Verlagsanstalt, 2017), pp. 85–104.

[337] See below, Mathesius, *History*, pp. 355–56.

[338] See below, Mathesius, *History*, pp. 332–33, 355–56, 392–93.

[339] Mathesius, *Postilla: das ist/ Auslegung der Sontags und fürnemsten Fest Evangelien/ über das gantze jar. Jetzt von newem Corrigiert/ unnd gemehrt* (Nürnberg: Ulrich Neuber & Dietrich Gerlach, 1567) [VD16 M1534], with earlier editions in Nürnberg and Wittenberg, 1565 and 1566 [VD16 M1533, ZV10506]; *Postilla Prophetica* (Leipzig: Johann Beyer, 1588/1589) [VD16 M1542]; *Einfeltige Unnd kurtze Erklärung des kleinen Catechismi/ D. Martin Luthers/ für die Jugend in Lateinischer und Teutscher Schulen in S. Joachimsthal* (Nürnberg: Dietrich Gerlach, 1574) [VD16 ZV10122]; *Catechismus/ das ist/ Trostreiche und Nützliche Auslegung über die Fünff Haubtstück der christlichen Lehre* (Leipzig: Johann Beyer, 1586) [VD16 M1503].

preserved) the books of Samuel and Kings.[340] To supplement his catechism sermons, he preached a major series on the apocryphal book of Ecclesiasticus (Sirach).[341] His occasional sermons for weddings and funerals were also collected for publication, as was his preaching on the Lord's Supper.[342]

Throughout his preaching, Mathesius sought self-consciously to tie biblical texts and the structures of Wittenberg theology to the distinctive forms of life of his local community. The most distinctive of such efforts was the series published as the *Sarepta or Mining Postil*, originally preached amid the festivities of Shrove Tuesday or New Year's Day between 1552 and 1562. Here, Mathesius used biblical texts mentioning mining, minerals, and their use to explicate theology with reference to the chief economic activity of the town.[343]

It was in a similar vein, connecting Lutheranism to his parish, that Mathesius took up the task of preaching on Luther's life in the fall after the completion of the *Sarepta* sermons, beginning on the anniversary of Luther's birth in November 1562 and concluding on the anniversary of Luther's death in February 1564. (Two more sermons, one on the University of Wittenberg and one on Luther's references to mining, were delivered subsequently in March 1564 and March 1565.) Not all can be dated precisely, but the dates of the intervening sermons can be generally inferred.[344]

---

[340] Mathesius, *Homiliae Mathesii/ Das ist: Außlegung und gründliche Erklerung der Ersten und Andern Episteln des heiligen Apostels Pauli an die Corinthier* (Leipzig: Johann Beyer, 1590) [VD16 M1502]; *Diluvium Mathesii* (Leipzig: Johann Beyer, 1597) [VD16 M1468]. The sermons on Samuel are mentioned below, Mathesius, *History*, p. 104. Sermons on 2 Kings and perhaps on Exodus, as well as the surviving sermons on Genesis 6–7, are implied in Mathesius' preface to Nicolaus Herman, *Die Historien von der Sindfludt* (Wittenberg: Georg Rhau/Samuel Seelfisch, 1562) [VD16 ZV26077], fol. A4v.

[341] Mathesius, *Syrach Mathesii* (Leipzig: Johann Beyer, 1586) [VD16 B4115].

[342] Mathesius, *Vom Ehestand und Haußwesen. . . Jetzund auffs new corrigiert und gemehrt* (Nürnberg: Ulrich Neuber & Dietrich Gerlach, 1569) [VD16 M1591], with the first edition in 1563 [VD16 M1589], edited by Loesche in *Mathesius: Ausgewählte Werke*, vol. 2; *Ehespiegel Mathesii* (Leipzig: Johann Beyer, 1591) [VD16 M1469]; *Leychpredigten* (Nürnberg: Johann vom Berg & Ulrich Neuber, 1559) [VD16 M1520]; *Bekantnuß Vom Heyligen Abendmal unsers lieben Herren Jesu Christi* (Nürnberg: Dietrich Gerlach in the print shop of the late Johann vom Berg, 1567) [VD16 M1445].

[343] On the *Sarepta*, see above, p. lxxxii n. 321. A first edition had appeared in 1562 [VD16 M1556]. See Hans-Otto Schneider, "Sarepta: Die Bergpostille des Johannes Mathesius," in *Johannes Mathesius (1504–1565): Rezeption und Verbreitung der Wittenberger Reformation durch Predigt und Exegese*, ed. Armin Kohnle and Irene Dingel, Leucorea-Studien zur Geschichte der Reformation und der Lutherischen Orthodoxie 30 (Leipzig: Evangelische Verlagsanstalt, 2017), pp. 191–208.

[344] Cf. Volz, *Die Lutherpredigten des Johannes Mathesius*, pp. 9–11.

Sermon	Date	Day	Content
1	November 10, 1562	Tuesday; Luther's birthday	1483–1516
2	ca. December 10, 1562	Week of St. Joachim's Day (i.e., Dec. 6–12, 1562)	1516–19
3	January 6, 1563	Wednesday; Epiphany	1521
4	January 17, 1563	Sunday; St. Anthony	1521–22
5	Late January to early February 1563		1522–25
6	Early to middle February 1563		1525–28
7[345]	February 23, 1563	Tuesday; Shrove Tuesday	Fables [1530]
8	April 11, 1563	Sunday; Easter	1528–29
9	April to June 1563?		1530
10	ca. September 1563		1532–35
11	ca. October 1563		1536–40
12	ca. November 1563		1540
13[346]	ca. December 1563		1540–42
14	ca. January 1564		1543–46
15	Feb. 18, 1564	Friday; anniversary of Luther's death	Funeral sermon
16[347]	March 12, 1564	Sunday; school festival	Wittenberg
17[348]	March 6, 1565	Tuesday; Shrove Tuesday	Mining

By the fall of 1565, Mathesius had revised the sermons for publication through the Nürnberg publisher Ulrich Neuber, dating his preface October 5, two days before his death. Some of the sermons may have been

[345] In the 1568 edition [VD16 ZV10510] and thereafter, the sermon on Luther's fables is moved to become the ninth sermon, coming after the sermon on the 1530 Diet of Augsburg.

[346] In the 1566 first edition and 1567 second edition, the thirteenth sermon is again labeled the "twelfth," and the subsequent sermons are numbered as the thirteenth through sixteenth. See Beyer, "Mathesius als Biograph Martin Luthers," p. 80.

[347] Loesche (*LH*², p. xvi; *Johannes Mathesius*, 1:536n) argues on internal grounds that this sermon was in fact delivered on March 12, 1563, before the eighth sermon. Yet Mathesius writes to Paul Eber on May 1, 1563 (Loesche, *Mathesius: Ausgewählte Werke*, 4:588), saying that he intends to deliver a sermon in honor of the University of Wittenberg at the next school festival, i.e., in March 1564. See Volz, *Die Lutherpredigten des Johannes Mathesius*, pp. 9–11.

[348] Loesche (*LH*², p. viii) argues for a date of 1564; but as Volz points out, Shrove Tuesday would have fallen on February 15, 1564, implausibly placing this sermon before the firmly dated sermon 15. See Volz, *Die Lutherpredigten des Johannes Mathesius*, p. 11.

expanded for publication from their orally delivered forms, especially the
ninth sermon on the Augsburg Confession, though the repetitions and
recapitulations of material that seem to mark the original homiletical form
of most sermons have been preserved.[349] The first printed edition appeared
posthumously in 1566.

Mathesius' sources for his biography of Luther have been thoroughly
explored in the magisterial 1930 study by Hans Volz, whose tables serve as
the starting point for the notes in the present translated edition.[350] Mathesius
drew upon a wide range of sources, as well as his own direct observation
and experience. He drew on previous printed accounts of Luther and the
Reformation, including those of Melanchthon and Sleidanus, as well as
the *Report* of Luther's last days by Jonas and Coelius.[351] He made extensive use of the Wittenberg edition of Luther's works—both the Latin and
the German series—including the historical and contextual material that
it contained.[352] Occasionally he cited Luther's writings directly by volume
and once even by page.[353] For some things occurring in Wittenberg during
his years there, Mathesius was a direct witness.[354] For others that impinged
directly on Joachimsthal, he could find material locally.[355] Yet Mathesius had
also done his own research, drawing on his network of correspondents and
his trips to Wittenberg to acquire copies of unpublished works by Luther,
including letters, lectures, sermons, and correspondence.[356] In particular, he
exchanged manuscripts of Luther's *Table Talk*, collating the notes of others
with his own to produce the collections that are the basis of the manuscripts
cited as Math. L and Math. N in the modern Weimar edition.[357] The fact that

[349] See Volz, *Die Lutherpredigten des Johannes Mathesius*, pp. 13–19; Beyer, "Mathesius als Biograph Martin Luthers," pp. 78–79.

[350] See above, p. lxxx n. 308.

[351] For explicit reference to Sleidanus, see below, Mathesius, *History*, pp. 384, 506. Melanchthon's *Preface* and *Oration* are central sources for the first and fifteenth sermons. The *Report* by Jonas and Coelius is the basis for much of the fourteenth sermon. See Volz, *Die Lutherpredigten des Johannes Mathesius*, pp. 134–42.

[352] See Volz, *Die Lutherpredigten des Johannes Mathesius*, pp. 102–6; cf. above, pp. xxiv–xxv.

[353] See below, e.g., Mathesius, *History*, pp. 258, 270, 289, 325, 348, 365, 383–84, 402, 407, 413; Volz, *Die Lutherpredigten des Johannes Mathesius*, pp. 102, 153.

[354] See below, Mathesius, *History*, pp. 286–319, 424–504, 519–20, 608–10; Volz, *Die Lutherpredigten des Johannes Mathesius*, pp. 168–212.

[355] See below, Mathesius, *History*, pp. 210, 605.

[356] See below, Mathesius, *History*, pp. 288, 491; cf. Volz, *Die Lutherpredigten des Johannes Mathesius*, pp. 111–27; Loesche, *Johannes Mathesius*, 1:191–204.

[357] See WA TR 3:xvii–xxv; 4:xxvii–xlv; Alexander Bartmuß, "Johannes Mathesius am Tisch Martin Luthers: Ein Beitrag zur Tischredenüberlieferung," in *Johannes Mathesius (1504–1565): Rezeption und Verbreitung der Wittenberger Reformation durch Predigt und Exegese*, ed. Armin

many of the accounts related by Mathesius that are not to be found in the
Table Talk collected by him can nonetheless be corroborated by the *Table
Talk* or correspondence collected by others must increase the confidence
that Mathesius is to be trusted also in those matters for which he appears
to be the sole witness.[358] As Mathesius announced to his Joachimsthal congregation at the beginning of his first sermon on Luther's life, he desired to

> present you with an accurate and straightforward exposition of everything
> that I heard in the church and university in Wittenberg, as well as in many
> good conversations at Doctor Luther's table, and that I have read in his
> books, as well as what I have learned in truth from many good people who
> had been with him from the beginning and sat at his table.[359]

Mathesius' sermons emphasize not only Joachimsthal's theological connection with Luther but also the social connection: that Luther, too, was "a
miner's son."[360] He weaves together many of the themes that had appeared in
previous treatments of Luther, integrating them with his own emphases. For
Mathesius, as for Bugenhagen, Luther, the "man of God," was a prophet (for
Mathesius, usually the "German prophet")[361] and teacher. Yet for Mathesius
this role was bound up with Luther's public, legitimate call as a doctor of theology.[362] Mathesius' Luther does make a few predictions about the course of
the Church after his death—and Mathesius asserts that Luther had himself
been foretold by late medieval predecessors.[363] When Mathesius calls Luther

---

Kohnle and Irene Dingel, Leucorea-Studien zur Geschichte der Reformation und der
Lutherischen Orthodoxie 30 (Leipzig: Evangelische Verlagsanstalt, 2017), pp. 53–64. Math. L
was separately edited by Ernst Kroker in *Luthers Tischreden in der Mathesischen Sammlung*
(Leipzig: Teubner, 1903); Math. N was edited by Georg Loesche as *Analecta Lutherana et
Melanthoniana* (Gotha: Perthes, 1892).

[358] For example, Luther's activity as choirboy in Magdeburg (below, Mathesius, *History*,
pp. 118–19); his recollection of student depositions in Erfurt (below, Mathesius, *History*,
p. 207); the fact that Luther took the name "Junker Jörg" in the Wartburg (below, Mathesius,
History, p. 191); his oral confession concerning the Lord's Supper amid illness in his last years
(below, Mathesius, *History*, p. 396), as well as many pieces of *Table Talk* not attested in writing
elsewhere. Cf. Volz, *Die Lutherpredigten des Johannes Mathesius*, pp. 122–28.

[359] Below, Mathesius, *History*, p. 116.

[360] Below, Mathesius, *History*, pp. 138, 368, 555, 574, 582–84, 589, 598–99, 602, 610.

[361] See below, e.g., Mathesius, *History*, pp. 105, 107, 114, 147, 166, 178, 186, 197, 203, 224,
236, 362, 391, 392, 404, 406, 418, 436, 523, 535, 539, 553, 584, 589; cf. below, Bugenhagen,
Christian Sermon, pp. 26, 29, 34; Walter, *New Spiritual Song*, pp. 95 (stanza 46), 98 (stanza 59);
Volz, *Die Lutherpredigten des Johannes Mathesius*, pp. 72–76.

[362] See below, e.g., Mathesius, *History*, pp. 129–32, 143–44, 146, 164, 206, 289, 376, 545–47;
Volz, *Die Lutherpredigten des Johannes Mathesius*, pp. 52–56; Beyer, "Mathesius als Biograph
Martin Luthers," p. 72.

[363] See below, Mathesius, *History*, pp. 562–67; cf. below, *History*, pp. 120–22, 145–46,
582–89. Cf. Volz, *Die Lutherpredigten des Johannes Mathesius*, pp. 76–78, 74–76.

a *Wundermann*, he is not labeling him a miracle-worker, but identifying him with Luther's own description of *Wunderleute*—the heroic figures of world history, used by God for extraordinary tasks.[364] But Luther needs no miracles of his own—save the miracles of his bold confession and providential preservation—since his teaching is the apostolic doctrine which was already miraculously confirmed at the beginning of the Church.[365] Luther's prophetic and apostolic office, for Mathesius, is that of proclaiming the Gospel and bearing witness to Jesus Christ.[366]

Luther's reliance upon the Bible—the "writings of the prophets and apostles"—and his role in disseminating its doctrine and its text are therefore central to Mathesius' appraisal of Luther's role. He depicts Luther's early development in the monastery chiefly as a matter of discovering the Bible itself rather than as a theological breakthrough in interpretation—perhaps since, for Mathesius, Luther's reading of the Bible in terms of Law and Gospel and justification by faith had come to seem inevitable.[367] Luther's German translation of the Bible receives almost an entire sermon on its own.[368] Luther's versions of the catechism are also praised as the "layman's Bible," the foundation of religious instruction in homes and schools as well as in church, and featured by Mathesius in a set of anecdotes of Luther's own interactions that display the spiritual power conferred upon laity with even a basic grasp of the catechism.[369] With the catechism, his hymns, and his participation in the visitations of 1529, Luther is an organizer of salutary forms of church life.[370]

Luther is, for Mathesius, not only a translator and teacher but also an exemplary confessor of the Word. He stands in person before the emperor at the Diet of Worms in 1521, on what Mathesius describes as "one of the great and glorious days that was to come before the end of the world, a day on which God's Word was publicly proclaimed and confessed with Christian boldness before the Roman Imperial Majesty and the whole German

---

[364] Luther develops the idea of the "extraordinary people" [*Wunderleute*] in his *Commentary on Psalm 101* (1534), LW 13:154–63, and the idea of "salutary heroes" [*gesunden Helden*] of world history in *Disputation on Justifying Faith and Miracle-Working Faith* (1543), WA 39/2:237 (LW 73). Cf. *Sermons on Exodus* (1524–27/1564), WA 16:27 (LW 62); *Lectures on Genesis* (1535–45/1544–54), LW 2:114. See Althaus, *Theology of Martin Luther*, pp. 439–40, 441–42. Cf. Bornkamm, *Luther and the Old Testament*, p. 12.

[365] See below, Mathesius, *History*, pp. 551–52.

[366] See below, Mathesius, *History*, pp. 539–47.

[367] Cf. below, Mathesius, *History*, pp. 120, 123–25, 131–34, 136, 140–41, 144–45.

[368] See below, Mathesius, *History*, pp. 470–85; cf. *History*, p. 370.

[369] See below, Mathesius, *History*, pp. 252–58; cf. *History*, pp. 250, 442.

[370] See below, Mathesius, *History*, pp. 214–17, 249–53, 449–50.

empire."[371] Luther's boldness is extraordinary and divinely inspired,[372] a cause for wonderment and for thanksgiving to God, an inspiration, but—as in Melanchthon's appraisal of Luther's heroism—not necessarily a model for imitation by those lacking such an extraordinary gift.[373] Luther's bold confession takes place not only in person but also in his printed writings, not only against the papacy but also against the "fanatics."[374] Yet for all Luther's vehemence, his confession not only reproves the enemies of true doctrine but also draws together the faithful into unity, as in the examples of the 1537 *Smalcald Articles* and in the Wittenberg Concord.[375]

The crowning act of confession in Mathesius' narrative is both Luther's deed and a corporate act. The Augsburg Confession, whose drafting and presentation at the 1530 Diet of Augsburg occupy the entirety of the ninth sermon, is "the Christian confession of our religion, as our doctor had taught it for many years, now summarized in good order and with discretion by Master Philip," and made publicly by the "electors and princes and cities."[376] It is, in a fundamental sense, Luther who confesses by proxy. Yet Luther is accompanied by other confessors who are his "God-fearing and faithful hearers." Melanchthon is foremost among the theologians, an Elisha to Luther's Elijah, but not the only voice.[377] Indeed, the University of Wittenberg itself as an institution and collectivity becomes for Mathesius a central character in the Reformation, the reservoir of the pure doctrine of God's Word which drew students from across Germany and indeed from all of Europe.[378]

The Diet of Augsburg and its prominence in Mathesius' account illustrate another recurring theme in the *History*: that Luther's confession of the Gospel takes place within the context of the Holy Roman Empire and its politics. The imperial diets—and later the religious colloquies between the Evangelical and Catholic parties—provide a recurring structure for

---

[371] Below, Mathesius, *History*, p. 178.

[372] See below, e.g., Mathesius, *History*, pp. 178, 197, 318.

[373] See below, Mathesius, *History*, pp. 315–16, 461–62.

[374] See below, e.g., Mathesius, *History*, pp. 261–62, 363–65, 514–19, 547; cf. Volz, *Die Lutherpredigten des Johannes Mathesius*, pp. 50–52, 83–89.

[375] See below, Mathesius, *History*, pp. 354–55, 397–99, 404–6, 545–46.

[376] Below, Mathesius, *History*, pp. 329, 321; cf. *History*, pp. 335–36. On the place of the Augsburg Confession in Mathesius' *History*, see Boettcher, "Luthers Leben in Predigten," pp. 169–70; Beyer, "Mathesius als Biograph Martin Luthers," pp. 78–79.

[377] Below, Mathesius, *History*, pp. 560, 592–94. Cf. Volz, *Die Lutherpredigten des Johannes Mathesius*, p. 82.

[378] See below, e.g., Mathesius, *History*, pp. 106–7, 110–12, 145–46, 287, 304, 307–8, 563–64, 571–82, 592–95.

Mathesius' account.[379] Luther stands firm against the imposture of the papacy and before the majesty of empire, yet Luther's boldness in the face of papal imposture is not a cover for political revolution—a theme which for Mathesius is colored by his own trial before King Ferdinand.

Mathesius also takes every opportunity to emphasize signs of the emperor's sympathy with Luther or his cause.[380] Although most assessments of Charles' religious policy and sympathies would regard Mathesius' view of the emperor as unrealistic, Mathesius' strategy makes rhetorical sense in the context of Joachimsthal's political situation under Hapsburg rule. Evangelicals hoped that imperial religious policy, which had moderated under Ferdinand's rule, might become even more favorable to Protestants under Maximilian II. Providing a dynastic history to legitimate such acceptance was a shrewd approach. And, indeed, it was fair enough for Mathesius to point to Charles' historical sympathy with evangelical Catholics and their proposals for reform in order to argue that it was hypocritical to object to Lutherans for having actually made such changes.

Mathesius' biography of Luther has, of course, its limitations. Like all early modern interpreters of Luther (save for Luther himself!), Mathesius has no direct knowledge of Luther's earliest lectures, which were preserved only in manuscript and first printed centuries later, and thus he lacks sources for interpreting Luther's theological development or for reconstructing the context of Luther's own autobiographical remarks.[381] Other events and texts which have been important to modern interpretations of Luther are overlooked or pushed to the side by Mathesius: he mentions the Heidelberg Disputation only in passing and misdates it to 1521;[382] he omits any real mention of Luther's work translating the New Testament in the Wartburg;[383] and he mentions Luther's literary debate with Erasmus over the freedom

---

[379] See below, Mathesius, *History*, pp. 147–52 (Diet of Augsburg, 1518); pp. 168–82 (Diet of Worms, 1521); pp. 210–13 (Second Diet of Nürnberg, 1522–23); p. 249 (First Diet of Speyer, 1526); p. 288 (Second Diet of Speyer, 1529); pp. 320–67 (Diet of Augsburg, 1530); pp. 421, 467–70, 489–94 (colloquies of Hagenau, Worms, and Regensburg, 1540–41).

[380] See Volz, *Die Lutherpredigten des Johannes Mathesius*, pp. 97–100; below, Mathesius, *History*, p. 152 (on Maximilian I); pp. 168–69, 179–80, 322–24, 339–40, 347, 356–57, 362, 364, 558–59 (on Charles V); pp. 356–57 (on Ferdinand I).

[381] It may be that, lacking knowledge of the first Psalms lectures, Mathesius sets Luther's theological "breakthrough" in interpreting Rom. 1:17—described in the 1545 *Preface to the Latin Writings* (LW 34:336) as having taken place when Luther "returned to interpret the Psalter anew"—in the context of Luther's work with selected psalms while in the Wartburg in 1521 and his polemic *Against Latomus*, and gives it somewhat peripheral importance. See below, Mathesius, *History*, p. 189; Beyer, "Mathesius als Biograph Martin Luthers," pp. 65–66.

[382] See below, Mathesius, *History*, p. 170. Cf. LW 31:35–70. On other omissions by Mathesius, see Loesche, *LH*, pp. xi–xii.

[383] See below, Mathesius, *History*, pp. 184, 473–74.

of the will not at all.[384] Disappointingly for a biographer who had lived in Luther's home, Mathesius has relatively little to say about the reformer's family life, though there are a few vignettes.[385]

Yet Mathesius compensates for these weaknesses with his attention to Luther's later years, a period of the reformer's life that has often been neglected in modern biography. For Mathesius, Luther's last years and last works—including the Genesis lectures and his polemics against the papacy and the Jews—are among the most precious parts of his legacy, exemplifying the centrality of Scripture and of Christology for Luther's testimony.[386] Mathesius' portrait of Luther has been characterized as "static."[387] Yet if that critique is fair as applied to Mathesius' image of the younger Luther, it hardly applies to his depiction of the older reformer, as Mathesius knew him personally.

Mathesius portrays Luther not as an alabaster saint but as a human being, albeit one whose very faults and weaknesses served to magnify God's grace and work in him.[388] Mathesius (like Jonas and Coelius) sought to portray not only Luther's piety but also his sociability. He drinks with friends and is cheerful, appreciates good wine, is generous to a fault, engages in banter and jest.[389] The reformer is not only the author of hymns but also a participant in singing secular motets around the table.[390] Mathesius devoted an entire sermon to Luther's love for fables, regarded by Roman Catholic contemporaries as unspiritual and unserious.[391]

The hearers and readers of Mathesius' sermons were also reminded of the physical humanity of the reformer, not only in his participation in ordinary social life but also in his episodes of sickness. Mathesius discussed frankly the corporeal symptoms of Luther's afflictions—not only such things as vertigo, catarrh, and exhaustion but also the eleven cans of urine which Luther produced after passing kidney stones on the return from Smalcald.[392]

---

[384] Cf. *Bondage of the Will* (1525), LW 33. Mathesius does, however, mention Luther's sharply negative verdict on Erasmus: below, *History*, pp. 379–80. Compare the prominence given to Luther's *Bondage of the Will* in Walter's *New Spiritual Song*, below, p. 95, stanza 44, and in the introduction above, pp. lxxvi–lxxvii.

[385] For Mathesius' brief account of Luther's wedding, see below, *History*, p. 227; see also below, pp. 279–80, 459, 460.

[386] See below, Mathesius, *History*, pp. 523–24.

[387] Wolgast, "Biographie als Autoritätsstiftung," p. 64.

[388] See below, Mathesius, *History*, pp. 548–49; cf. below, *History*, p. 318.

[389] See below, Mathesius, *History*, pp. 451–61. Cf. Zeeden, *Legacy of Luther*, p. 20.

[390] See below, Mathesius, *History*, pp. 485–86.

[391] See below, Mathesius, *History*, pp. 266–85; for Roman Catholic criticism, see below, p. 279 n. 79.

[392] See below, Mathesius, *History*, pp. 402–3.

Such descriptions, strikingly presented from the pulpit, were a bold reminder that God's saints are not ethereal beings.[393]

Mathesius was equally frank in discussing Luther's spiritual struggles, which often became trials of faith as well—the *Anfechtungen* or temptations which Luther described in his *Preface to the German Writings*. For Mathesius, these began while Luther was in the Wartburg;[394] a particularly severe experience took place in 1527–28.[395] Although Luther is described as a model of pastoral comfort and heroic prayer in ministering to others,[396] he was also the recipient of the pastoral care and encouragement of others. Among the most striking anecdotes that Mathesius relates about Luther are ones in which Luther himself is portrayed as one whose faith is constantly in need of strengthening:

> One time a woman complained to him that she was no longer able to believe. "Can you still say the Creed?" [he asked]. "Yes," said the woman. When she had recited it devoutly, the doctor asked, "And do you regard this as true?" When the woman said, "Yes," he said, "Truly, dear woman, if you believe these words and regard them as true—as indeed they are nothing but the truth—then you believe more strongly than I. For I must also ask every day that my faith would be increased [cf. Mark 9:24]." Upon this, the woman thanked God and departed from him in peace and joy.

> Master Antonius Musa, pastor in Rochlitz, said to me that he once made a heartfelt complaint to the doctor that he was unable to believe himself what he preached to others. "God be praised and thanked," replied the doctor, "that this happens to other people too. I thought this happened to me alone." Musa was never able to forget this consolation his whole life long.[397]

Mathesius' portrayal of Luther—heroic but complex, spiritual but earthy—defied many of the expectations of medieval hagiography and defined the image of the reformer for generations of Protestants to come. It found near universal acceptance in part because Mathesius' depiction fit well into the mainstream of Lutheran orthodoxy as it took form in the decades after his death, not only in its representation of Luther as teacher and confessor of the faith but also in its interpretation of Melanchthon as a constructive contributor to Luther's legacy (rather than as either a challenger to it or an

---

[393] For a modern account similarly emphasizing Luther's physicality, see Lyndal Roper, *Martin Luther: Renegade and Prophet* (London: Bodley Head, 2016).

[394] See below, Mathesius, *History*, p. 185. Mathesius does mention once that Luther was "distressed and sad" amid the works of his early monastic life (below, *History*, p. 124).

[395] See below, Mathesius, *History*, pp. 258–60. See Brecht 2:204–11.

[396] See below, e.g., Mathesius, *History*, pp. 246–58, 350, 376–77, 419–20, 465–66, 521. Cf. Zeeden, *Legacy of Luther*, p. 20.

[397] Below, Mathesius, *History*, pp. 442–43.

adapter of it).[398] Mathesius' comprehensive biography of the reformer served as a tacit but self-conscious rejoinder to Cochlaeus' depiction of Luther as arch-heretic.[399] Yet Mathesius was also, in a fundamental way, completing the project that Luther had begun in his 1545 preface to the Latin writings, continuing the biography of Luther through his whole life span not only on the basis of contemporary sources from the years being described but also in light of Luther's own efforts to recount and interpret his life in the 1540s, of which Mathesius himself had been witness and recorder at Luther's table.

The translation in this volume has been made by Kevin Walker on the basis of Georg Loesche's text, compared as necessary with the 1566 and 1567 Nürnberg printings, and consulting the notes of Loesche's edition as well as the 1883 Concordia edition. The annotations, prepared by the editor, draw on the work of Loesche and of Hans Volz, but unlike Volz's notes, which chiefly seek to identify the sources used by Mathesius, the annotations in the present volume are intended to alert the reader to material from the full range of currently available sources that either support Mathesius' narrative or call it into question. A selection of current Luther biographies, especially the magisterial three-volume work by Martin Brecht but also the more recent works by Volker Leppin and Scott Hendrix, have also been cited in the notes to indicate parallels or divergences in modern scholarship on Luther's life.[400]

The present volume of early biographical works on Luther has involved the collaboration of many laborers, particularly the translators who have grappled with the texts in early modern German and Latin. Stephanie Woods, Eric Lundeen, Samuel Dubbelman, and Gino Marchetti served as research assistants for the editorial material. Timothy J. Wengert, Kurt Hendel, Stephen Burnett, Amy Nelson Burnett, Laura Gibbs, and Martin Damašek kindly offered comments and advice on particular questions. Dawn Mirly Weinstock has again copyedited the volume and brought it into presentable order. For the final state of the texts and the notes the editor is responsible. This volume is offered to scholars, students, and the Church on the five-hundredth anniversary of the beginning of the Reformation as a monument of the conviction of sixteenth-century Lutherans that in their days God had indeed done something extraordinary through His Word, faithfully confessed and proclaimed by Dr. Martin Luther.

Christopher Boyd Brown
October 31, 2017

---

[398] See Beyer, "Mathesius als Biograph Martin Luthers," pp. 67–68.

[399] Cf. Volz, *Die Lutherpredigten des Johannes Mathesius*, pp. 57–58.

[400] See above, pp. xi, xviii n. 8, and lv n. 186.

CATALOG OR INDEX OF ALL THE BOOKS AND WRITINGS PUBLISHED BY DR. MARTIN LUTHER, 1518–33

1533

Translated by Matthew Carver

Catalog or Index
of All the Books and Writings
Published by Dr. Martin Luther, 1518–33[1]

1533[2]

Dr. Martin Luther's Preface

Since some of my good friends have often asked to have the number or the titles of my books which have been issued since I first started writing and teaching, and since some have gathered those books in the present index, I have let myself be prevailed upon to give my consent to release this catalog or index in printed form in order to satisfy whatever desire anyone has for it. For my own part, I would not mind if they all perished,[3] since I ¦sought nothing thereby except that Holy Scripture and divine truth should come to light, and it now shines with such clarity and power in every place that my books and those like mine—and much more those unlike mine—might well be dispensed with, if the prideful desire to write many new ones did not spur us on so hard. Yet it would be beneficial for people to learn from these the history and account of how I—or, rather, the Word of God—fared: what it was forced to suffer from such numerous and notable enemies these past fifteen years before it reached full force; and how it increased; and how I, too, progressed and mounted higher in it day by day and year by year, as will be attested by contrasting the earlier books (in which I yielded a great deal—almost everything—to the papacy and honored it) with the later ones, which deal solely and purely with Christ and concede nothing to the papacy. A pious Christian will take this into account, and not (like Dr. Snot-Spoon and

---

[1] *Catalogus oder Register aller Bücher und schrifften, D. Mart. Luth. durch jn ausgelassen, vom jar. M. D. XVIII. bis jns .XXXIII. Mit einer Vorrhede* (Wittenberg: Hans Lufft, 1533), 16 leaves in octavo [VD16 L3449]. Aland 121.

[2] See the introduction above, pp. xxiii–xxiv.

[3] For this sentiment, cf. Luther, preface to Pupper of Goch, *Fragments* (1522), LW 59:15; Luther to Wolfgang Capito, July 9, 1537, WA Br 8:99; *Table Talk* no. 3797 (1538), LW 54:274–75; no. 4025 (1538), LW 54:311; no. 4691 (1539), LW 54:361; *Preface to the German Writings* (1539), LW 34:283–84; *Preface to the Latin Writings* (1545), LW 34:327.

Bishop Smith)[4] blame or condemn me for writing in contradiction to myself and for later differing from what I wrote earlier.[5] If locating contradictions were a real art, they would never ever write a single line for me, but I would catch them in a lie in their own words. I am no better than St. Augustine, who identified himself as one of those teachers who daily grow through writing and teaching;[6] I do not, like the donkey-heads Cochlöffel[7] and Smith, instantly in the first moment become more learned than St. Paul and unable ever to accept correction or to make a mistake. I thank Christ, my Lord, who has thus led and preserved me until I reached the place where I am. He will help me to a blessed departure as well. To Him be praise and glory forever with the Father and the Holy Spirit. Amen.

---

[4] *Doctor Rotzleffel und Bischoff Schmid.* "Rotzlöffel," literally, "snot-spoon," a colloquial expression for a "brat," is Luther's dismissive play on the humanist name of the Catholic controversialist Johann Cochlaeus (see the introduction above, pp. lxvii–lxviii; and below, Mathesius, *History*, p. 177). "Smith" [*Schmid*] is a play on the Latin name of Johann Fabri (1478–1541), formerly vicar-general in the diocese of Constance and since 1531 bishop of Vienna (on Fabri, see the introduction by David V. N. Bagchi, LW 59:70–71). Fabri authored the massive *Malleus in haeresim Lutheranam* (Cologne: Peter Quentel & Johann Soter, 1524) [VD16 F214], CCath 23–26. For Luther's dismissal of these two men, see *On Translating* (1530), LW 35:187; *Commentary on the Alleged Imperial Edict* (1531), LW 34:95; *On the Councils and the Church* (1539), LW 41:150–51; *Against Hanswurst* (1541), LW 41.190, preface to Melanchthon, *Response to the Clergy of Cologne* (1543), LW 60:309–10.

[5] Cochlaeus had published in 1529 both the *Septiceps Lutherus* (see the introduction above, p. lxviii) and the *Dialogus de Bello contra Turcas, in Antilogias Lutheri* [Dialogue on war against the Turk, against the contradictions of Luther] (Leipzig: Valentin Schumann, 1529) [VD16 C4290]. Fabri in 1530 published his *Antilogiarum Martini Lutheri Babylonia* [A babylon of Martin Luther's contradictions] (Augsburg: Alexander Weissenhorn, 1530) [VD16 L3460]. The woodcut of Luther with seven heads on the title page of Cochlaeus' *Septiceps Lutherus*—each head identified with a different and supposedly contradictory role—became one of the few relatively successful Roman Catholic polemical depictions of the reformer: see Robert W. Scribner, *For the Sake of the Simple Folk: Popular Propaganda for the German Reformation* (Cambridge: Cambridge University Press, 1981; repr., Oxford: Oxford University Press, 1994), pp. 232–34; Gotthelf Wiedermann, "Cochlaeus as a Polemicist," in *Seven-headed Luther*, ed. Peter Newman Brooks (Oxford: Clarendon, 1983), pp. 196–205; cf. Luther, *Table Talk* no. 2258b (1531), WA TR 2:381–82.

[6] See Augustine, Letter 143.2: "I confess that I strive to be one of those who write while making progress, and make progress by writing" (PL 33:585; WSA 2/2:302; NPNF[1] 1:490); and *Collatio cum Maximo*: "He is 'teachable' [1 Tim. 3:2] who daily both learns and makes progress by teaching better things" (PL 42:732; WSA 1/18:211). See also the newly discovered Sermon 162C.15 (WSA 3/11:176; *Vingt-six sermons au peuple d'Afrique*, ed. François Dolbeau [Paris: Institut d'Études augustiniennes, 1996], p. 56).

[7] Another play on Cochlaeus' name; here, literally, "cook-spoon."

REPORT ON THE CHRISTIAN DEPARTURE OF THE REVEREND DR. MARTIN LUTHER FROM THIS MORTAL LIFE,

Briefly Compiled by Dr. Justus Jonas, Master Michael Coelius, and Others Who Were Present

1546

Translated by Matthew Carver

REPORT ON THE CHRISTIAN DEPARTURE
OF THE REVEREND DR. MARTIN LUTHER
FROM THIS MORTAL LIFE,
BRIEFLY COMPILED
BY DR. JUSTUS JONAS,
MASTER MICHAEL COELIUS,
AND OTHERS WHO WERE PRESENT[1]

1546

ON the twenty-third day of January, at the request of the noble, wellborn counts and lords of Mansfeld,[2] the Reverend Doctor Martin Luther departed Wittenberg and stayed the first night at Bitterfeld.[3]

Now this summoning of Dr. Martin by the aforementioned counts took place because many great discords and divisions had continued among

---

[1] The end of the account attributes its authorship to Jonas, Coelius, and Johann Aurifaber (see below, p. 22). See the introduction above, pp. xxxiii–xxxiv. The image of Martin Luther from the 1546 Wittenberg printing (fol. A1v) is courtesy of Concordia Seminary Library Special Collections, St. Louis, Mo.

[2] On Luther's relationship with the counts of Mansfeld and his involvement in the negotiations among them, see the introduction above, pp. xxvii–xxix; Brecht 3:370–73.

[3] Bitterfeld, about 40 km southwest of Wittenberg, was near the western border of electoral Saxony.

their Graces for some time, from which the rulers of Mansfeld feared that all manner of difficulties would arise. For this reason, the counts jointly besought Dr. Martin, being a native of their Graces' dominion—namely, from Eisleben—to take the negotiations upon himself and to endeavor, insofar as possible, to reconcile and resolve matters. And though Dr. Martin was not accustomed to involve himself in such secular business, but attended to his own vocation at all times with the highest diligence (as is commonly known) by preaching, reading, writing, and other things, nevertheless, for the sake of his native country, in order to bring it to unity, to forestall difficulties, and to negotiate an amicable reconciliation among the counts, he was not willing to decline or to refuse this journey, notwithstanding that making a journey at such a time and taking these things upon himself was a tremendous imposition on him, as well as burdensome and contrary to his established practice. But so it was that, on the aforesaid day, he set out from Wittenberg for Eisleben in the name of the Almighty.

On the twenty-fourth of January, around eleven o'clock in the morning, he reached Halle and lodged with Dr. Jonas.[4]

On the twenty-fifth, twenty-sixth, and twenty-seventh of January, being prevented by [high] water,[5] he remained in Halle, and on the day of the twenty-sixth, which was the Tuesday after the Conversion of Paul, preached there in the Church of Our Lady a sermon on the conversion of Paul from the Acts of the Apostles.[6]

On Thursday, which was the twenty-eighth of January, he departed Halle and crossed the water in the ferry with his three sons[7] and Dr. Jonas. This he did, moreover, at some risk, so that he himself said to Dr. Jonas: "Dear Dr. Jonas, would not it give the devil great pleasure if I, Dr. Martin, with my three sons and yourself, were to drown in the water?"[8] He then set out for Eisleben.

And as he approached Eisleben, having been received at the border by one hundred and thirteen[9] horse[men], he grew rather weak in the carriage,

---

[4] On Jonas, see the introduction above, p. xxx.

[5] I.e., because of the flooding of the Saale River. Cf. Luther to Katharina Luther, January 25, 1546, LW 50:284–87.

[6] Sermon of January 26, 1546, *On the Conversion of St. Paul*, LW 58:370–84. See the introduction above, p. xxix.

[7] Johannes [Hans] Luther, Martin Luther the Younger, and Paul Luther. See the introduction above, p. xxix; cf. above, p. xxxii n. 74.

[8] On the association of the devil with streams, see Luther to Katharina Luther, January 25, 1546, LW 50:287; *Table Talk* no. 2829 (1532), LW 54:172; *Church Postil* (1540–44), sermon for Lent 3 on Luke 11:14–28, LW 76:398–99, paragraph 19.

[9] Other sources give the number of horsemen as sixty: see WA Br 11:273 n. 4.

so that there was some concern for his life.[10] Nevertheless, when he had been rubbed with warm towels in his lodgings, he ate and drank that evening and was content, making no more complaint. Yet previously in the carriage, as the illness struck him, he said, "The devil always does this to me. Whenever I have some great task ¦before me to accomplish, he first tries me in this way and attacks me with this sort of tribulation."[11]

From the twenty-ninth day of January through the seventeenth day of February, he was at Eisleben engaged in the negotiations,[12] and in addition to the negotiations he delivered four sermons,[13] received Absolution once publicly from the priest (who held Communion at the altar) and communed twice, and at the second Communion—namely, on Sunday, on Valentine's Day—he himself ordained and consecrated two priests after the apostolic usage.[14]

Moreover, from the twenty-eighth of January to the seventeenth of February, we heard a great many fine, comforting sayings from him, in which he would make frequent mention of his age, and [he would] say that when he returned to Wittenberg, he was going to lay himself to rest at home. He also expounded many weighty, comforting passages of Scripture over the table in the presence of the counts and others of us who sat at table with him, which will be published in a special anthology in due time.[15]

And in particular, every evening throughout those twenty-one days, at around eight o'clock, or frequently earlier, he would retire from the table in

---

[10] For Luther's own descriptions of this episode, see Luther's letters of February 1, 1546, to Katharina Luther, LW 50:290–91, and to Melanchthon, LW 50:294.

[11] *Tentation.* On temptation or *Anfechtung* in Luther's theology, see *Preface to the German Writings* (1539), LW 34:285–87; cf. below, p. 44 n. 32 and p. 60 n. 32; Mathesius, *History*, pp. 109, 185, 258–59, 357–58, 375–76, 377–78, 445, 449, 474 (and n. 69 there), 514, 524, 528, 548, 563; and the introduction above, p. xciv.

[12] On the progress of the negotiations, see Luther's correspondence during the period, translated in full in LW 50:290–315; cf. Brecht 3:369–74.

[13] For Luther's sermons of January 31, February 2, and February 7, 1546, see LW 58:397–459; for his sermon of February 15, 1546, see LW 51:381–92. These were published together by Johann Aurifaber in June 1546: *Vier Predigten des Ehrwirdigen Herrn D. Martini Luthers, zu Eisleben vor seinem abschied aus diesem leben gethan* (Wittenberg: Hans Lufft, 1546) [VD16 L6963]. On their dating, see above, p. xxxi n. 70.

[14] I.e., on February 14, 1546. See Brecht 3:372. These "priests" [*Priester*] were Evangelical pastors. On Evangelical ordination, see *Smalcald Articles* (1537) III X 3 (Kolb-Wengert, p. 324; *Concordia*, p. 282); *Ordination of Ministers of the Word* (1539), LW 53:122–26.

[15] This was fulfilled in Johann Aurifaber's collection of *Table Talk: Colloquia oder Tischreden Doct[or] Mart[in] Luthers* (see above, pp. xviii–xix n. 13). In this collection, some thirty pieces are specially designated as having been spoken by Luther on the final Eisleben trip. See Kroker, "Tischreden aus Johannes Aurifabers Sammlung FB," WA TR 6:xi–xv. Jonas, too, seems to have collected table talk in Eisleben, but his collection has been lost: see Kroker, "Tischreden aus Johannes Aurifabers Sammlung FB," WA TR 6:xiii.

the great hall to his room[16] and spend a good portion of the evening standing at the window and saying his prayers to God so earnestly and diligently that we—Dr. Jonas, Master Coelius,[17] [Dr. Luther's] servant Ambrose,[18] and Johann Aurifaber[19] of Weimar—once we had fallen silent, would often hear some of his words and be filled with awe. Afterward, he would turn from the window and speak happily with us, usually for another half hour, as though he had again been relieved of a burden, and then retire to bed.

However, on Wednesday, the seventeenth of February, the lords and counts, our gracious lords, themselves besought him, as did we all, not to attend the negotiations in the great hall that morning, but rather to rest. On that occasion, he lay down in his room on a leather couch, walked about the room, and prayed. Yet all the same, evening and morning, he took his seat at the table downstairs in the great hall. And it was at supper on that same day (before the day on which, shortly before three o'clock, he would make his blessed departure in God) that he spoke many weighty words and sayings concerning death and the everlasting life to come, saying, among other things: "Ah, dear God! Twenty years is a paltry span of time! Yet that short time would leave the world desolate if man and wife did not come together according to the creation and ordinance of God. What vanity creation is! [Cf. Rom. 8:20.] God is gathering a Christian Church for Himself largely from the little children. For when a one-year-old child dies, I believe that a thousand or two thousand one-year-old children die with him; but when I, sixty-three-year-old Dr. Martin, die,[20] I do not think sixty or a hundred others in the whole world will die with me, for the world does not now live to see old age. Very well! We old people must live long enough to see the devil's backside,[21] and experience so much of the world's wickedness, treachery, and misery, so that we may be witnesses that the devil was such a wicked spirit. The human race is like a fold of sheep for the slaughter."[22]

---

[16] Luther stayed in a house that had been owned by the jurist Dr. Philipp Drachstedt but was now owned by the town and occupied by the town clerk Johann Albrecht and his family: see below, p. 13. On its identification and location, see above, p. xxx n. 66. The rooms identified in Jonas and Coelius, *Report*, are the "great hall" [*grosse Stube*]; Luther's "room" [*Stüblin*], with a sofa and (or perhaps in) a window seat; and his "chamber" [*Kammer*], with a bed.

[17] On Coelius, see above, p. xxviii n. 57.

[18] Ambrosius Rutfeldt from Delitzsch was Luther's personal servant [*famulus*]; see above, p. xxix n. 63.

[19] On Aurifaber, see above, pp. xviii–xix n. 13.

[20] On the questions surrounding Luther's birthdate and age at death, see the introduction above, pp. liv–lv; and below, Melanchthon, *Preface*, pp. 56–57; Mathesius, *History*, p. 114.

[21] See Thiele no. 290, pp. 272–73.

[22] This discourse is also contained in Aurifaber's 1566 collection of *Table Talk* (see above, p. 9 n. 15): no. 6565 (n.d.), WA TR 6:45.

That same last evening, the doctor also considered this question at the table: namely, whether we will still know each other in the blessed, eternal assembly and Church that is to come. And when we pressed him for instruction, he said, "What did Adam do? He had never seen Eve all the days of his life. He lay down and slept, and when he woke, he said not 'Where did you come from? What are you?' but 'This flesh was taken from my flesh, and this bone from my bones' [Gen. 2:21–23]. How did he know that this woman had not sprung from some stone? It was because he was filled with the Holy Spirit and was abiding in the true knowledge of God. To that knowledge and image we will be restored in Christ in the life to come [cf. Col. 3:10], so that we will recognize father, mother, and one another at sight better than did Adam and Eve."[23]

Not long after saying this, he rose and went to his room, and his two little sons Martin and Paul, and Master Coelius, followed him soon after.[24] He reclined at the window in his room to pray, as was his custom. Master Coelius left, and Johann Aurifaber of Weimar came up. The doctor said, "I am again getting pain and tightness, in the chest, as before." Then Johann said, "When I was tutor to the young lords,[25] whenever they felt ill in the chest or otherwise, I observed that the countess[26] would give them some horn of unicorn.[27] If you desire some, I will fetch it." The doctor said, "Yes." Meanwhile, Johann, before going to the countess, ran down quickly and called Dr. Jonas and Master Coelius, who had not been downstairs longer than two Our Fathers and who ran up straightaway.

When we arrived upstairs, however, he complained emphatically of his chest. Immediately, according to his custom at home, we rubbed him well with warm cloths, so that he felt better and said so. Count Albert himself[28] came in haste with Master Johann, bringing the horn, and the count said, "How are you doing, my dear Doctor?" To which the doctor said, "There is no cause for concern, gracious Lord, things are beginning to mend." Then Count Albert himself grated the horn, and after the doctor felt some improvement, he departed again, leaving with him one of his councillors,

---

[23] Cf. *Lectures on Genesis* (1535–45/1544–54), LW 1:113.

[24] Cf. above, p. 8 and n. 7 there. Johannes Luther must still have been with relatives in Mansfeld, where all the boys had been from at least February 1 to February 14: see Luther to Katharina Luther, February 1, 6, and 14, 1546, LW 50:291–92, 300, 312. Johannes is next mentioned as part of the funeral procession in Wittenberg; see below, p. 20.

[25] On Aurifaber's relationship with the family of Count Albert, see above, pp. xviii–xix n. 13.

[26] On Countess Anna, see below, p. 13 n. 40.

[27] I.e., probably, the tusk of a narwhal.

[28] On Count Albert, see the introduction above, pp. xxvii–xxviii and n. 54 there.

Conrad von Wolframsdorf,[29] along with the rest of us: Dr. Jonas, Master Coelius, Johann, and Ambrose. Then, at the doctor's request, the grated horn was administered to him twice in a spoon with wine, after Conrad von Wolframsdorf himself had first taken a spoonful so that the doctor would be less hesitant.

Then, at about nine o'clock, he lay down on his couch, and said, "If I might slumber for half an hour, I would hope that all might be remedied." Then he slept in a soft and natural sleep for an hour and a half, until ten o'clock. We, Dr. Jonas and Master Michael Coelius—together with his servant, Ambrose, and his two little sons Martin and Paul—remained with him.

But when he woke at the stroke of ten o'clock, he said, "Look, you are still sitting here. Could you not lie down to bed?" We answered, "No, Doctor; we should be watching and waiting upon you now." At that he wanted to get up, and rose from his couch and went to the chamber adjoining the room, whose windows were guarded against all drafts, and though he made no complaint, yet as he passed over the sill of the chamber, he said, "In God's name I go to bed. *In manus tuas commendo spiritum meum, redimisti me, Domine, Deus veritatis* [Into Your hands I commend my spirit. You have redeemed me, O Lord, God of truth'] [Ps. 31:5]."[30]

He now went to the bed, which was well furnished with warm cushions and pillows, and as he got in, he gave us all his hand and bade us good night, saying, "Dr. Jonas and Master Coelius, and you others, pray for our Lord God and His Gospel, that it may prosper,[31] for the Council of Trent and the wretched pope are raging harshly against it."[32] Remaining with him in the chamber that night were Dr. Jonas; his two sons Martin and Paul; his servant, Ambrose; and other servants.

Throughout the twenty-one days, lights had been kept in the chamber all night, but on this night the room was kept heated as well. Then he slept well, with natural sounds of breathing, until the clock struck one. He woke up and called for his servant, Ambrose, to heat the room for him. But since it had been kept heated the whole night, as his servant, Ambrose, returned, Dr. Jonas asked him whether he was feeling weak again. He said, "Ah, Lord

---

[29] On Conrad [Kurt] von Wolframsdorf (dates uncertain), an adviser to Count Albert of Mansfeld, see WA 54:480–81, and Schubart, *Die Berichte über Luthers Tod und Begräbnis*, pp. 7, 62.

[30] In addition to its biblical source, this verse was also part of the brief responsory in the liturgy of Compline, which would have been part of Luther's daily prayer as a monk. Cf. *LSB* 255–56. See also below, pp. 13, 14.

[31] *jm wolgehe*; or: "that He may prosper."

[32] *mit jhm*; or: "against Him." Johann Cochlaeus, not appreciating Luther's sense of irony, attacked this prayer as blasphemous: see Cochlaeus, *Deeds and Writings of Dr. Martin Luther*, in Vandiver et al., *Luther's Lives*, p. 354.

God, what pain I feel! Ah, dear Dr. Jonas! I think that I am going to remain here at Eisleben where I was born and baptized." Thereupon Dr. Jonas and Ambrose the servant answered, "Ah, Reverend Father![33] God our heavenly Father will help through Christ, whom you have preached." Then without assistance or escort he passed through the chamber into the room. And as he stepped over the sill, he spoke, just as he had when he was going to bed, the words "*In manus tuas commendo spiritum meum; redimisti me, Domine, Deus veritatis*" ["Into Your hands I commend my spirit. You have redeemed me, O Lord, God of truth"] and walked back and forth in the room once or twice. He reclined again on the couch and complained that there was very intense pressure about his chest. Nonetheless, his heart was still spared.

Then, as he requested and as was his custom at Wittenberg, he was rubbed with warm towels, and some pillows and bolsters were heated for him, for he said it helped him greatly to be kept warm.[34]

Before all this, when the Doctor had just lain down on the couch, Master Coelius came rushing from his room close by ours, and Johann Aurifaber soon after him. Then his host, Johann Albrecht, the town clerk,[35] was wakened, together with his wife, as were the two physicians of the town, all of whom, since they lived nearby, came running within a quarter of an hour.

First came the host with his wife, then Master Simon Wild,[36] a physician,[37] and Dr. Ludwig,[38] a doctor of medicine,[39] and immediately after them Count Albert with his wife.[40] The countess brought with her all manner of herbs and restoratives and labored ceaselessly to reinvigorate him with all kinds of tonics. But amid all this the doctor said, "Dear God, I am in great pain and anguish. I am departing. Now I will certainly remain in Eisleben." Then Dr. Jonas and Master Coelius comforted him, saying, "Reverend Father, call upon your dear Lord Jesus Christ, our High Priest, the only Mediator! You have had a good, profuse sweat. God will grant His grace so that you will

---

[33] *Reverende Pater*, in Latin, as also hereafter.

[34] Cf. above, p. 9. For earlier applications of this treatment, cf. Brecht 3:186.

[35] See above, p. 10 n. 16.

[36] On Wild, see above, p. xxxi n. 73.

[37] *arzt*

[38] On Dr. Ludwig, see above, p. xxxi n. 73.

[39] *medicus*

[40] Countess Anna von Honstein-Klettenberg (1490–1559) was famous for accompanying her husband, Albert, on his military campaigns: see Größler, "Mansfeld, Albrecht," *ADB* 20:220–21. About February 14, she had given Luther a gift of trout in gratitude for his help, which he had conveyed to Katharina back in Wittenberg: see Luther to Katharina Luther, February 14, 1546, LW 50:312.

recover!" Then he answered, saying, "No, it is a cold sweat of death. I shall yield up my spirit, for the illness is getting worse." And then he began, saying,

> O my heavenly Father, God and Father of our Lord Jesus Christ, God of all comfort: I thank You that You have revealed to me Your beloved Son, Jesus Christ, in whom I believe, whom I have preached and confessed, whom I have loved and worshiped, whom the wretched pope and all the ungodly dishonor, persecute, and blaspheme. I beseech You, my Lord Jesus Christ, accept my little soul[41] into Your keeping. O heavenly Father, though I must leave this body and be torn away from this life, yet I know of a certainty that I will dwell with You forever, and no one can snatch me from Your hands [John 10:29].

And he continued: "*Sic Deus dilexit mundum, ut unigenitum filium suum daret, ut omnis, qui credit in eum, non pereat, sed habeat vitam aeternam*" ["God so loved the world that He gave His only-begotten Son, that whoever believes in Him should not perish but have eternal life"] [John 3:16] and the words from Psalm 68 [:20]: "*Deus noster Deus salvos faciendi, et Dominus est Dominus educendi ex morte.*"[42] That is, in German: "We have a God of salvation, and a Lord God who brings us out from the midst of death."

Meanwhile, Master [Wild] tried a very precious medicine which he always carried in his bag for an emergency, of which Doctor [Luther] tried a spoonful. But he said once more: "I am departing; I will yield up my spirit." Accordingly, he said three times in a row, very quickly: "*Pater, in manus tuas commendo spiritum meum. Redimisti me, Deus veritatis*" ["Father, into Your hands I commend my spirit. You have redeemed me, O God of truth"] [Luke 23:46; Ps. 31:5].[43] Having thus commended his spirit into the hands of God the heavenly Father, he fell silent. They again shook, rubbed, cooled, and called to him, but he shut his eyes, making no answer. Then Count Albert's wife and the physicians applied to his wrists all kinds of invigorating

---

[41] The 1546 printing contains the following marginal note: " 'little soul' [*seelichen*] is indeed what he said, no doubt to humble himself before God, as if to say, 'What a poor creature I am before You, O great and infinite eternal Majesty.' "

[42] Literally, "Our God is a God of salvation, and the Lord is the Lord who brings forth from death" [Ps. 67:21 Vg]. Luther does not give the Vulgate translation exactly, but varies in the second half of the verse. The Vulgate (LXX) reads: *Domini Domini exitus mortis* ["to the Lord GOD belongs the escape from death"].

[43] Luther assimilates the psalm verse (with the address "O Lord") with Jesus' words (with the address "Father"). Cf. above, p. 12, where the WA editors associate Luther's use of the verse with the *Admonitio morienti et de peccatis suis nimium formidanti* (PL 158:687) of Anselm of Canterbury (1033–1109), which prescribes a threefold repetition of Ps. 31:5 [Ps. 30:6 Vg; Ps. 31:6 DB] (with "O Lord"). However, the surrounding psalm verses in the *Admonitio*, as well as Anselm's invocation of the Virgin, are different.

solutions which Doctor [Luther's] wife[44] had sent and which he was accustomed to using.

But as he grew thus silent, Dr. Jonas and Master Coelius cried emphatically to him: "Reverend Father, is it your intention to die steadfast in Christ and His doctrines as you have preached them?" He said, so that he could be heard plainly: "Yes." With this he turned onto his right side and began to sleep, for almost a quarter of an hour, so that there was even hope that he would recover. But the physicians and all the rest of us said that the sleep was not to be trusted, and so we carefully lit candles to illuminate his face.

Meanwhile, Count John Henry of Schwarzburg also arrived with his spouse.[45] Soon after that, Doctor [Luther] grew very pale in his face, his feet and nose turned cold, and he drew a deep yet gentle breath with which he gave up his spirit quietly and with great patience, so that there was no more movement even in a finger or a leg. And no one could discern (this we testify before God, upon our consciences) any unrest, torment of body, or pangs of death; rather, he fell asleep in the Lord peacefully and gently, as Simeon sings [Luke 2:29].

Thus were the words of John 8 [:51] truly fulfilled in him: "Truly I say to you, whoever keeps My word will never see death eternally." And this verse from John 8 was the last inscription that he wrote, having also inscribed it for people in their Bibles as a memory verse;[46] this one he wrote on the flyleaf of a [copy of his] *House Postil*,[47] given to the Hohnstein tax official Hans Gasmann in Ellrich.[48] The most beloved father expounded the verse thus:

---

[44] *die Doctorin*. For Luther's reference to Katharina as *Frau Doctorin*, see Luther's letters of July 29, 1534; July 2 and 26, 1540; and February 10, 1546, LW 50:80, 208, 221, 305. On the traffic of medicines sent by Katharina from Wittenberg to Eisleben, cf. Luther to Melanchthon, February 14, 1546, LW 50:314.

[45] On Count John Henry of Schwarzburg (Jonas et al. give the toponymic as Schwarzenburg), one of the participants in the Mansfeld negotiations, see above, p. xxxi n. 69. His wife was Margaret of Weida.

[46] Hundreds of Luther's inscriptions made for others in Bibles and other books are preserved in the Weimar edition; collections of these were published already in 1547 by Johann Aurifaber and Georg Rörer: WA 48:1–297; WA 48N:155–56. There are seventeen inscriptions based on John 8:51: see WA 48:152–64.

[47] The *House Postil*, based largely on Luther's preaching at home for his family and students during a period of illness in 1532–34, was edited for publication in 1544 by Veit Dietrich: *Haußpostil D. Martin Luther* (Nürnberg: Berg & Neuber, 1544) [VD16 L4833], edited in WA 52; translated in Matthias Loy, ed., *Sermons on the Gospels for the Sundays and Principal Festivals of the Church Year by Dr. Martin Luther*, 2 vols. (Rock Island, IL: Augustana Book Concern, 1871) (LW 80–83).

[48] See WA 48:161–62. Ellrich was a town in the Thuringian county of Hohnstein, in the Harz Mountains.

"[*will*] *never see death*": How unbelievable this saying is, and contrary to manifest daily experience! Yet it is the truth: if anyone seriously contemplates God's Word in his heart, believes it, and falls asleep or dies in it, he slips away and departs [into the Word] before he glimpses death or becomes aware of it, and has surely made a blessed departure in that Word which he has thus believed and contemplated.

Below this was written: "Dr. Martin Luther, February 7, 1546."[49]

Now that he had departed in the Lord, Count Albert, his spouse, and the Count von Schwarzenburg and [his spouse][50] were in shock together with the rest of us and continued to cry out that they should not stop ⌐rubbing and giving him stimulants. Everything humanly possible was done; but the body only grew colder and more deathlike.[51]

And after the dead body had thus lain on the couch for about three quarters of an hour, a pile was made right next to the couch out of a number of feather beds, three mattresses, and blankets on top, onto which they lifted the body in the hope (as we all wished and prayed) that God would yet grant His grace.

Then, before daybreak, at about four o'clock, there arrived the serene, highborn prince and lord, Lord Wolf, prince of Anhalt;[52] and the noble, well-born count and lord Philip (brother of John George),[53] along with Count Vollrad, Count John [Hans], and Count Wolf,[54] also brothers, the counts and lords of Mansfeld; and other lords and persons of the nobility.

The body was left lying on the bed from four until after nine o'clock, that is, five whole hours, during which time many honorable citizens came and viewed the dead body with fervent tears and weeping. After that, it was clothed in a new white Swabian smock, and the remains[55] were laid on a

---

[49] For this particular inscription on John 8:51, see WA 48:160–62, no. 210.

[50] *etc.* Cf. above, p. 15.

[51] Among other attempts to revive Luther, the town apothecary, Johann Landau, was summoned to administer an enema. See the introduction above, pp. xxxi–xxxii; Schubart, *Die Berichte über Luthers Tod und Begräbnis*, no. 78, pp. 77–78; Brecht 3:376.

[52] On Prince Wolfgang of Anhalt-Köthen, one of the participants in the Mansfeld negotiations, see above, p. xxxi n. 68.

[53] Count Philip and Count John George were the eldest surviving sons of Ernst II (1479–1531) and had therefore succeeded to the Vorderort line of the Mansfeld nobility as the nephews of the childless Count Hoyer. See the introduction above, p. xxix.

[54] Count Vollrad, Count John [Hans], and Count Wolf[gang] (d. 1546) were sons of Count Albert of the Hinterort line. Aurifaber had served as tutor to Vollrad and John: see above, pp. xviii–xix n. 13.

[55] Here for the first time the word *die Leich* is used; to this point the word *der Leib* ["body"] has been employed.

bed and straw in the room for as long as it took to cast a pewter[56] coffin, into which he was placed. Then he was viewed lying in the coffin by a great number of the nobility, most of whom knew him, both men and women—several hundred—as well as by a very great number of the people.

On the eighteenth of February, the remains were left where [Luther] had been staying, in Dr. Drachstedt's house.[57]

On the nineteenth of February, at about two o'clock in the afternoon, according to Christian custom, the remains were carried with great honor and singing of hymns into the main parish church, St. Andreas,[58] where the princes, counts, and lords, including Count Gebhard and his two sons, Counts George and Christopher, along with the women of their households,[59] and a very large and considerable number of people, accompanied and followed.

Then, as soon as the remains had been placed in the choir of the church, Dr. Jonas delivered a sermon which is summarized here: first, concerning the person and gifts of Dr. Martin; second, on the resurrection and eternal life; third, a warning to the opponents, that this death would be followed by power against Satan's kingdom—all based on the text 1 Thessalonians 4 [:13–18].[60] Then the remains were left in the church overnight with ten of the townsfolk appointed to watch them.

Now, when, at the request of our gracious lord, the elector of Saxony, the remains were to be brought to Wittenberg[61] (with which request the counts and lords of Mansfeld, though very eager to keep the remains in their territory, nevertheless complied in order to please the elector), ¹there was another sermon on the morning of the twentieth of February, which was the Sunday after Valentine's Day, delivered by Master Michael Coelius, on the

---

[56] *ziener*, or "tin."

[57] See above, p. 10 n. 16.

[58] The *Andreaskirche* ["St. Andrew's Church"] in Eisleben was the largest church in the town and had been the location of Luther's preaching in the weeks before his death. See the introduction above, p. xxxi.

[59] Count Gebhard, his wife, Margarethe von Gleichen-Blankenhain (ca. 1480–1567), and his sons, George [Jörgen] (ca. 1514–46) and Christopher [Christoffel] (1520–91), were members of the Mittelort line of the Mansfeld nobility (see the introduction above, pp. xxvii–xxviii and n. 54 there).

[60] On Jonas' sermon, see the introduction above, p. xxxiii and n. 80 there.

[61] See Elector John Frederick to the Counts of Mansfeld, February 18, 1546, Schubart, *Die Berichte über Luthers Tod und Begräbnis*, no. 12, pp. 16–17.

words of Isaiah [57:1]:[62] *Justus perit et nemo considerat* ["The righteous man perishes and no man lays it to heart"].[63]

And subsequently, between twelve and one o'clock, he was again conducted with all honor and with Christian customs and hymns out of the town of Eisleben. Then once more the aforesaid princes, counts, and lords, and with them Count Gebhard with his two sons, Count George and Count Christoffel, also the counts and lords of Mansfeld, together with Count Gebhard's spouse, and the ladies of their household (just as they had been in attendance in the procession to the church before), as well as a great number of the people, followed with reverence and accompanied the remains to the outermost gate with many tears and much weeping. Thus he was brought to Halle by evening on this day.

In Eisleben, before all these ceremonies took place in the church, two painters had made images of his face in death: one painter from Eisleben, while the remains were still lying in the room on the bed; the other, Master Lucas Furtenagel from Halle, after he had already lain for one night in the coffin.[64]

Now, as they brought his remains out of Eisleben, bells were tolled in nearly all the villages on the way from Eisleben, and the people came out from the villages—men, women, and children—and gave signs of the earnest grief which they shared. Thus the procession arrived outside Halle after five o'clock. And as they were approaching the city, there, too, men and women of the town came out some distance to meet them along the paved highway. And when they entered the city gate with the remains, they were met by the two pastors of St. Ulrich and St. Maurice, and all the ministers of the Gospel (since the superintendent, Dr. Jonas, was riding at the rear of the funeral procession),[65] as well as the esteemed council of Halle, together with a great number of all the councilmen, as well as the entire school, the headmaster and all his pupils, with the customary funeral rites and hymns.[66] At the same time, a great multitude of people, including many honorable citizens and many matrons, ladies, and children, came to meet them at the

---

[62] The Wittenberg printing cites Isaiah 56, following the chapter divisions of Luther's German Bible (WA DB 11/1:164).

[63] On Coelius' sermon, see the introduction above, p. xxxiii and n. 80 there.

[64] On these painters, see above, pp. xxxii–xxxiii n. 79.

[65] On Jonas as superintendent of Halle, see the introduction above, p. xxx. The other Evangelical clergy in Halle were Andreas Hügel (1500–1578; see Kawerau, *Der Briefwechsel des Justus Jonas*, 2:xliii–xliv), who had accompanied Jonas from Wittenberg, the Naumburg deacon Benedict Schumann, and the 1542 Wittenberg graduate Matthias Wanckel. On Wanckel, see the introduction by Christopher Boyd Brown, LW 58:244; and Luther to Elector John Frederick, September 4, 1542, WA Br 10:144.

[66] Cf. below, p. 21 and n. 84 there.

outer gate with such loud lamentation and weeping that we heard it from the back of the procession in the hindmost carriages. And as the procession was coming up the street to the old market by the church of St. Maurice, as well as on the bridge and in the gate, there was such a great throng around the hearse and other carriages that it was often necessary to come to a halt in the streets and in the market, and [the procession] reached the church of Our Dear Lady in Halle very late, at almost half past six o'clock.

Now, the Church of Our Lady was filled in every part with people singing—or, rather, weeping—the psalm "From Depths of Woe"[67] with plaintive, broken voices. And if it had not been so late, a sermon would have been held. As it was, the remains were hurriedly borne into the sacristy and guarded overnight by several of the townsfolk.

The next morning,[68] about six o'clock, the remains were again carried out of Halle with the tolling of bells, as had also been done in every church previously, with an honorable Christian escort to the gate, as on the evening before, accompanied by the whole honorable council, all the preachers, and the schools of that place.

On that day, Sunday, the twenty-first of February, the funeral procession traveled from Halle to Bitterfeld,[69] arriving at noon. There the two counts[70] and the rest of us who were accompanying the remains were received at the border and also within the town by those appointed by our most gracious lord, the elector of Saxony—Erasmus Spiegel,[71] the captain in Wittenberg; Gangolf von Heilingen, [captain] in Düben; and Dietrich von Taubenheim, [captain] in Brehna—and were conducted that evening as far as Kemberg,[72] where the body was honorably received and accompanied with the customary Christian ceremonies, both at Bitterfeld and at Kemberg.

On Monday, the twenty-second of February, the noble and wellborn counts and lords, Count Hans and Count Hans Hoyer, counts and lords of Mansfeld, having ridden from Eisleben with approximately forty-five horse

---

[67] Luther's setting of Psalm 130, "*Aus tiefer Not schrei' ich zu dir,*" LW 53:221–24 (*LSB* 607; WA Ar 4:188–93; Wackernagel 3:7–8, no. 6)

[68] I.e., Sunday, February 21, 1546.

[69] See above, p. 7 and n. 3 there.

[70] I.e., Count John (see above, p. 16 n. 54), of the Hinterort Mansfeld line, and Count Hans Hoyer [Johann Hoyer II] (1525–85), a younger son of Count Ernst II of Mansfeld (see above, p. 16 n. 53) of the Vorderort line (see the following paragraph).

[71] Erasmus Spiegel (ca. 1480–1551) was the captain of the guard in Wittenberg. See *Table Talk* no. 4040 (1538), LW 54:313. The other captains could not be identified beyond what is in the text.

[72] Kemberg is some 14 km south of Wittenberg.

in armor, brought the remains up to the Elster Gate before Wittenberg.[73] Immediately at the gate there stood (as previously arranged at the elector's command) the rector, teachers, and doctors and the whole laudable university, together with the honorable council and the whole community and citizenry. There the ministers of the Gospel and school preceded the remains with customary Christian hymns and ceremonies the whole length of the city from the Elster Gate to the Castle Church.

In front of the remains rode the appointed captains of his most gracious lord, the elector of Saxony, as aforementioned, and the aforesaid two young counts and lords of Mansfeld,[74] with about sixty-five horse. And immediately after the hearse there came the doctor's wedded wife, the Frau Katharina,[75] along with a number of other matrons in a carriage a short distance behind. Next there followed his three sons, Hans, Martin, and Paul Luther; his brother Jacob Luther, citizen of Mansfeld;[76] his sister's sons, Georg and Cyriacus[77] Kaufmann, also citizens of Mansfeld; and others of the family. After that came the *rector magnificus*[78] of the distinguished university, with several young princes, counts, and barons residing at the University of Wittenberg on account of their studies. Then the remains were followed by Dr. Gregor

---

[73] The Elster (sometimes translated as "Magpie") Gate is the Wittenberg gate outside of which Luther had burned the papal bull threatening excommunication in 1520: see *Why the Books of the Pope and His Disciples Were Burned* (1520), LW 31:379–95.

[74] See above, p. 19.

[75] *sein ehelich gemahl, die Fraw Doctorin, Catharina Lutherin.* On Katharina Luther (née von Bora), see above, p. xxxii n. 74; Mathesius, *History*, below, p. 227.

[76] On Jacob Luther (ca. 1490–1571), see Siggins, *Luther and His Mother*, p. 14; cf. below, Melanchthon, *Preface*, pp. 56–57.

[77] *Ciliax*, a shortened form of Cyriacus. Georg and Cyriacus were the sons of Luther's sister Margarethe Luther (1485–ca. 1529) with Georg Kaufmann (d. ca. 1534). Luther and Katharina had taken in the boys after their parents' deaths. See Brecht 3:238.

[78] Augustine Schurff (1494/1495–1548), who had earned his doctorate at Wittenberg and joined the medical faculty in 1521, was a pioneer in anatomical dissection. He served as rector of the university for the third time in 1545–46, having previously served in 1525 and 1537–38. See Förstemann et al., *Album*, 1:124, 167, 228; Julius Leopold Pagel, "Schurff, Augustin," *ADB* 33:86. Cf. below, Mathesius, *History*, pp. 304, 536, 581.

Brück,[79] Dr. Philip Melanchthon,[80] Dr. Justus Jonas, Dr. Pomeranus,[81] Dr. Caspar Cruciger,[82] Dr. Hieronymus [Schurff],[83] and other senior professors of the University of Wittenberg; then all the doctors and masters and the honorable council together with the councilmen; after that, the whole great throng and splendid multitude of students; and then the citizenry, including many of the townswomen, matrons, ladies, young women, and many honorable children: the young and old, all with loud weeping and lamentation. On every street and throughout the whole market square there was such a great press and multitude of people that one could well wonder how it had assembled so quickly, and it was widely realized that nothing like it had ever been seen in Wittenberg.

When the remains were brought into the Castle Church, they were set in front of the pulpit. Then, to begin, Christian funeral hymns[84] were sung. After that, the Reverend Dr. Pomeranus ascended [the pulpit] and there, in the presence of several thousand people, delivered an altogether Christian and comforting sermon, which will also be published.[85]

After Dr. Pomeranus' sermon, Philip Melanchthon, out of his own extraordinary, heartfelt grief and for the consolation of the church, delivered

---

[79] Gregor Brück (ca. 1485–1557) was a legal scholar whom Frederick the Wise had appointed first in 1519 as one of his counselors and then as chancellor for electoral Saxony, a post he continued to hold under Elector John until 1529, when he became chancellor emeritus, delegating many practical duties to Christian Beyer (see below, p. 193 n. 53). Brück remained one of the leading political and diplomatic figures of the Reformation movement, negotiating at the Diet of Augsburg and drafting the preface to the Augsburg Confession (see Kolb-Wengert, pp. 30–35; *Concordia*, pp. 27–28), as well as leading the organization of the Smalcaldic League. After Luther's death and the transfer of the Saxon electoral title, Brück helped to organize the University of Jena. See Günther Wartenberg, "Brück, Gregor," *OER* 1:219–20; and the introduction by Gottfried G. Krodel, LW 49:51–52. Cf. below, Mathesius, *History*, pp. 335, 346, 536, 581.

[80] On Melanchthon, see the introduction above, pp. xxxix–xl.

[81] I.e., Johann Bugenhagen of Pomerania: see the introduction above, pp. xxxvi–xxxvii.

[82] On Cruciger, see above, p. xx n. 19.

[83] Hieronymus [Jerome] Schurff (1481–1554), from St. Gall in Switzerland, had studied medicine at Basel and law at Tübingen. After coming to Wittenberg in 1502 (Förstemann et al., *Album*, 1:1), he became a professor of law at the university and an electoral counselor. He served as Frederick's agent and Luther's legal adviser at Worms in 1521 and became the reformer's close friend. After Luther's death, Schurff would be forced by the Smalcaldic War to depart Wittenberg for Frankfurt an der Oder. See Andreas Otto Weber, "Schurff, Hieronymus," *NDB* 23:760–61; LW 48:219 n. 2. Cf. below, Mathesius, *History*, pp. 173, 181 n. 76, 198, 304, 446–47 n. 143, 536, 581.

[84] *funebres cantiones*. See Luther, *Preface to the Burial Hymns* (1542), LW 53:325–31. Cf. LW 53:222.

[85] For Bugenhagen's funeral sermon, see below, *Christian Sermon*, pp. 23–35. On its publication, see the introduction above, pp. xxxviii–xxxix.

a beautiful funeral oration which has already been issued in print and will also be published in German hereafter.[86]

When the oration was finished, the body was carried by a number of learned professors[87] appointed to the task, who committed it to the grave and laid it to rest. And so it was there, in the castle at Wittenberg, not far from the pulpit where, during his life, he had delivered many powerful, Christian sermons before the elector and princes of Saxony and the whole church, that the precious instrument and tool[88] of the Holy Spirit, the body of the Reverend Dr. Martin, was laid in the earth, and, as Paul says in 1 Corinthians 15 [:43], "sown in weakness," that it might rise at the Last Day in everlasting glory.

So may the eternal heavenly Father, who called the aforesaid Dr. Martin to that great work, and our Lord Jesus Christ, whom he faithfully preached and confessed, and the Holy Spirit, who by His divine power gave to him amid many profound struggles such extraordinary boldness, great courage, and heart to oppose the pope and all the gates of hell, grant us all such a Christian departure from this wretched life and bring us to that same eternal blessedness.

We, the above-named Dr. Justus Jonas and Master Michael Coelius and Johann Aurifaber of Weimar, do testify before God and upon our own final departure and conscience that we were present at the blessed end of the praiseworthy father from the start until his last breath; that we, together with the princes, counts, lords, and all who were in attendance, neither heard nor saw anything different; and that we have not recounted it otherwise than as it transpired and took place in every point. May God the Father of our Lord Jesus Christ grant His grace to us all. Amen.

---

[86] For Melanchthon's *Oration*, see below, pp. 37–51. On the publication of the *Oration* in Latin and in German translation, see the introduction above, pp. xliv–xlvii.

[87] *Magistri*

[88] *organum und werckzeug*

A CHRISTIAN SERMON
FOR THE FUNERAL
AND BURIAL
OF THE REVEREND DR.
MARTIN LUTHER
Preached by
Herr Johann Bugenhagen
of Pomerania,
Doctor and Pastor
of the Church in Wittenberg

1546

Translated by Matthew Carver

A Christian Sermon
for the Funeral and Burial
of the Reverend Dr. Martin Luther
Preached by Herr Johann Bugenhagen
of Pomerania, Doctor and Pastor
of the Church in Wittenberg

1546[1]

PAUL the holy apostle says, in 1 Thessalonians 4 [:13–14]: "But we want you, dear brethren, not to be misinformed concerning those who are asleep, that you may not grieve as the others who have no hope. For if we believe that Jesus died and rose, even so will God also, through Jesus, bring with Him those who have fallen asleep."

|Dear friends, it is my task now to preach a sermon for the burial of our dear father, the blessed Dr. Martin, and it is my eager desire to do so. But what or how shall I speak if, on account of my weeping, I cannot produce even a single word? And who shall comfort you if I, your pastor and preacher, am unable to speak? Where may I turn to escape from you? With my words I will undoubtedly cause more wailing and grief. For how should we not all grieve with heartrending mourning?—seeing that God has sent us this sorrow and taken away from us that lofty, precious man, the Reverend Dr. Martin Luther, through whom He has manifested unspeakable gifts and grace to all of us and to all the churches of Christ in German lands and in many foreign nations; and through whom He has won glorious victory throughout the world against the kingdom of Satan, against so many shameful idolatries and commandments of men [cf. Matt. 15:9; Col. 2:22]—indeed, as Paul puts it [1 Tim. 4:1], against the "doctrines of devils"—and has revealed to us in the Gospel the sublime, great, |heavenly mystery: His beloved Son, Jesus Christ (as again Paul says to the Ephesians [Eph. 3:3–9] and Colossians [Col. 1:26–27]). And through our dear father [Dr. Luther], Christ has defended His Gospel against the wretched[2] pope and numerous

---

[1] See the introduction above, pp. xxxv–xxxix.

[2] *leidige*, an epithet typically used of the devil; it could also be translated as "pernicious."

sects and tyrants—indeed, against all the gates of hell [Matt. 16:18]. He gave this dear man the Spirit of power and might [cf. Isa. 11:2], so that he recoiled before no man, no matter how great and powerful, and stood by the Gospel and pure doctrine with such boldness that it often seemed to the world that he was too severe and presumptuous in his chastening and rebuke.[3] In the same way, the Jews and Pharisees, those bitter and poisonous vipers [Matt. 3:7; 12:34; 23:33], blamed Christ because they were sorely stung and pained to be chastened by the pure truth, and yet would not accept salutary doctrine.

It is this lofty teacher and prophet, the reformer of the Church whom God sent, whom God has taken away from us. Alas! How can we cease to lament and mourn this? How can we hearken to Paul here when he says that you should not grieve for those who sleep? Yet to this he adds "as the others who have no hope." But we who believe know that those who have fallen asleep in Christ will wake again to a better life, where we will someday join them again and be together eternally.

But the world was not worthy [Heb. 11:38] to keep this dear man of God any longer in order to slander and persecute him further. And yet that same thankless world received much good through this lofty man, especially in being delivered from all the oppression and tyranny of the wretched papacy, so that many of his adversaries (those who still possessed any wisdom or sense) preferred that the dear man should have lived yet a long while.

I have said these things by way of introduction because we have, indeed, much reason to mourn with heartfelt sorrow, having lost so lofty and precious a man. And assuredly, if it is of any consolation, we are joined in our grief by Christian kings, princes, and cities, and all who have come to know the Gospel of truth; wherefore we do not grieve alone, but many thousands far and wide throughout Christendom grieve with us. Neither

---

[3] Cf. below, Melanchthon, *Oration*, pp. 45–46.

the present wretched pope[4] nor the cardinal of Mainz[5] nor Duke Henry[6] deserved to have the opportunity to rejoice over the death of this man,[7] who enraged them all by [speaking] the truth. And I trust the adversaries will not long rejoice over his death, for though his person has certainly departed in Christ, yet the mighty, blessed, and divine doctrine of this precious man lives on as powerfully as ever.

For there is no doubt that he was the angel of whom it is written in Revelation 14 [:6–8] that he was flying through the midst of the heavens, having an eternal Gospel, etc., as the text says:

> [1]And I saw an angel flying through the midst of the heavens, having an eternal Gospel to proclaim to those who reside and dwell on earth, and to all nations and tribes and languages and peoples, saying with a loud voice: "Fear God and give Him glory, for the time of His judgment has come; and worship Him who made heaven and earth, the sea and the springs of water." And another angel followed, saying, "She is fallen, she is

---

[4] Pope Paul III (r. 1534–49) was an opponent of Luther's Reformation, even as he sought to accomplish internal reforms in the Roman Church, culminating in the convocation of the long-promised Council of Trent in 1545. Luther mocked the reform proposal he had commissioned: see preface to *Counsel of a Committee of Several Cardinals* (1538), LW 34:231–67. See William V. Hudon, "Paul III," *OER* 3:228–29. At the time of Luther's death and Bugenhagen's sermon, a false but widely circulated and credited rumor claimed that Paul III had died on January 3, 1546: see Luther to Melanchthon, February 14, 1546, LW 50:315.

[5] Albert of Brandenburg (1490–1545), cardinal archbishop of Mainz, archbishop of Magdeburg, and administrator of Halberstadt, had been indirectly responsible for the start of the Indulgence Controversy, since it was under his auspices (and in view of his debts) that the preaching of indulgences by Johann Tetzel had begun (see below, pp. 137–38 n. 130). Albert was, nonetheless, a patron of the arts and of humanist studies and long gave the reformers glimmers of hope that he might become a supporter. He became increasingly firm in his opposition to the Reformation, however, as he grew older. See Bodo Nischan, "Albert of Brandenburg," *OER* 1:15–16. Albert had died in September 1545, and his successor as elector and archbishop of Mainz, Sebastian Heusenstamm (r. 1545–55), was a less prominent opponent of the Reformation and did not become a cardinal until 1550. See Friedheim Jürgensmeier, "Sebastian," *NDB* 24:108–9.

[6] Duke Henry V of Braunschweig-Lüneburg (r. 1514–68) was, in the 1540s, a vigorous opponent of the Reformation. His efforts to suppress reforms in the cities of Braunschweig (where Bugenhagen had worked in 1528 and 1529) and Goslar led to his defeat and deposition by the Smalcaldic League in 1542. Luther lampooned him in *Against Hanswurst* (1541), LW 41:179–256. At the time of Luther's death, he was a captive of Philip of Hesse (see below, p. 70 n. 96), though Henry would be restored to his duchy in 1547, after the Smalcaldic War. Henry converted to Lutheranism under the influence of his son, Julius (1528–89), at the end of his life. See Luise Schorn-Schütte, "Braunschweig," *OER* 1:210–11; Heinrich Schmidt, "Heinrich der Jüngere," *NDB* 8:351–52.

[7] Bugenhagen has in mind either previous responses to false reports or hopes of Luther's death (see the introduction above, p. xxvii) or the fact that all three of these former enemies, because of death or defeat, are unable to rejoice in Luther's passing.

fallen—Babylon the great city—for she made all the nations drink of the wine of her fornication."

This angel who says, "Fear God and give Him glory," was Dr. Martin Luther. And the words here written—"Fear God and give Him glory"— are the two parts of Dr. Martin Luther's doctrine: the Law and the Gospel, through which all of Scripture is laid open and Christ is known as our Righteousness [cf. Jer. 23:6] and eternal life. And to ¹these two parts he also added this one: "the time of His judgment has come"; and he taught about proper prayer and the invocation of God the heavenly Father in spirit and in truth [John 4:23–24], as the angel of Revelation 14 also says, "Worship Him who made heaven and earth," etc.

For after the teaching of this angel there will follow another angel who will proclaim comfort to the sorrowful and afflicted Church, but upon the adversaries the lightning and thunder of eternal judgment and damnation. As the second angel said, "She is fallen, she is fallen—Babylon the great city." Therefore, the adversaries will not long rejoice over our present sorrow. As Christ says, "Your sorrow shall be turned to joy" (John 16 [:20]). For according to Revelation, in the cited fourteenth chapter, we see that this is what happened before and still continues. If [the Book of] Revelation is to count for anything, there is no doubt the second part [joy] must follow.

But alas, how I carry on ¹in our present weeping and sorrow! Let these words suffice concerning our fitting grief. For it is indeed fitting that we should grieve that such a precious man, a true bishop and shepherd of souls [cf. 1 Pet. 2:25], has departed from us. However, in this sorrow it is also fitting that we should acknowledge God's mercy and goodness toward us, and thank God that just a hundred years after the death of St. John Hus[8] (who was slain for the truth in the year 1415) He raised up for us by His Spirit this precious Dr. Martin Luther, to oppose the anti-Christian doctrine of the wretched, satanic pope and the doctrines of devils. Even so, John Hus, before his death, had prophesied of a swan to come (for "Hus" signifies a "goose" in the Bohemian tongue): "Now you are roasting a goose," said John Hus, "but God will raise up a swan whom you will neither burn nor roast." And when the people cried against him so much that he could not answer them, he is supposed to have said, "After a hundred ¹years I will answer you." This he faithfully did by way of our dear father, Dr. Luther, beginning exactly a year after a hundred years.[9] Indeed, we ought to thank God that He sustained this precious man for us and for His Church amid severe conflict and so many bitter battles, and that for nigh upon thirty years now Christ has so

---

[8] On Hus and his prophecy, see the introduction above, pp. xxxvii–xxxviii and n. 103 there.

[9] On the dating of the start of Luther's Reformation, see below, Mathesius, *History*, p. 121.

often been victorious through him. To the Lord Christ be glory and honor forever. Amen.

However, we ought also to rejoice with our dear father, Luther, that he so faithfully carried out his mandate in the supreme office of apostle and prophet, in the course of which he has taken leave of us to go to the Lord Christ, for there the holy patriarchs, prophets, and apostles are, together with many people to whom he preached the Gospel, and all the holy angels, and Lazarus in Abraham's bosom [Luke 16:23]—which is to say, in the eternal joy of all believers. How they fare at present, until the Last Day, we will learn for ourselves [someday], as Paul says in Philippians 1 [:23]: "I have a desire to depart ¹and to be with Christ"; and as Stephen says in Acts [7:59]: "O Lord Jesus, take to Yourself my spirit"; and Christ to the thief: "Today you will be with Me in paradise" [Luke 23:43].

For there is no doubt that just as when Christ said, "Father, into Your hands I commend My spirit," etc. [Luke 23:46], His spirit was in the hands of the Father until the resurrection on Easter Day, so, too, our spirits will be in the hands of Christ until our resurrection; for such is the meaning of the words concerning Lazarus: "But now he is comforted, and you are tormented" [Luke 16:25].

Meanwhile, what manner of rest or consolation the faithful have until the Last Day, or the ungodly of unrest or torment, we cannot say so precisely on the basis of Scripture. Scripture says that they sleep, as Paul says to the Thessalonians "concerning those who are asleep" [1 Thess. 4:13]. But just as in natural sleep those who are healthy rest in sweet repose and are refreshed and made stronger and healthier by sleeping, whereas the unhealthy or troubled, and especially ¹those who are in the terror or fear of death, sleep poorly, with terrifying dreams, and restlessly, so that sleep for them is not a rest but an unrest more terrible and desolate than waking— thus there is a distinction between the sleep of the faithful and that of the ungodly. But of this we cannot speak or make conclusions beyond what the words of Scripture declare.[10]

Our dear father, Dr. Martin Luther, has now obtained what he often desired. And if he were to return to us presently, he would chastise our sorrow and perplexity with the Word of Christ: " 'If you loved Me, you would rejoice, for I am going to the Father' (John [14:28]).[11] And you would grant

---

[10] On Luther's view of the state of souls between death and the resurrection at the Last Day as a sleep, see, e.g., *Church Postil* (1540–44), sermon for Lent 5 on John 8:46–59, LW 76:412–13, paragraph 11; cf. Althaus, *Theology of Martin Luther*, pp. 411–17; Gábor Ittzés, "*The Breath Returns to God Who Gave It*": *The Doctrine of the Soul's Immortality in Sixteenth-Century German Lutheran Theology* (Th.D. diss., Harvard Divinity School, 2008).

[11] The Wittenberg printing reads: "John xvi."

me that eternal rest and joy. Christ has conquered death for us. Why, then, are we perplexed? The death of the body is the beginning of eternal life through Jesus Christ our Lord, who for us became a noble, precious sacrifice."

I still remember that when our dear father, the Reverend Dr. Martin Luther, saw certain people gently fall asleep ǀin the confession of Christ, he would say, "God grant me that I may fall asleep so sweetly in the bosom of Christ, and my body not be tortured with protracted pangs of death. Yet God's will be done."[12]

There were also previous indications that our dear father, Dr. Martin, was going to pass to a better life. He often told us during the course of the past year that he wished to move elsewhere.[13] Furthermore, he made more journeys during this year before his death than he had made for many years previously: namely, to his native city of Mansfeld,[14] to the bishop in Zeitz,[15] to Merseburg,[16] to Halle.[17] These were, so to speak, signs and prophecies that he was about to make this blessed journey to a better life. This is also why it came to pass that he departed and journeyed from this life at the home of the noble and wellborn count and lord of Mansfeld in the city of Eisleben, where he was born and baptized, not otherwise than as he had desired, except that he would no doubt rather have ǀbeen with us, his dear wife, and his children. But God ordained otherwise.

---

[12] An independent source for this remark in the *Table Talk* could not be found.

[13] On Luther's expressed desire to move from Wittenberg in 1545, see Brecht 3:262–65; and the introductions by Christopher Boyd Brown, LW 58:xx, 233.

[14] Luther traveled to Mansfeld with Melanchthon on October 3–7, 1545, and from December 25, 1545, to January 5, 1546. See Brecht 3:369–70; and the introduction by Christopher Boyd Brown, LW 58:351. For dates on all these trips, see Georg Buchwald, *Luther-Kalendarium*, 2nd ed. (Leipzig: M. Heinsius Nachfolger Eger & Sievers, 1929), pp. 157–58.

[15] I.e., Nicolaus von Amsdorf (1483–1565), a nephew of Johann von Staupitz, from a family of the minor nobility, who had been a professor of theology at Wittenberg since 1511, becoming a fervent supporter and friend of Luther's. Luther had consecrated Amsdorf as bishop of Naumburg (resident at Zeitz) in 1542. In the last year of his life, Luther had been in Zeitz from July 27 to July 30, 1545, in the course of his trip to Merseburg. No sermons from the visit are preserved. See LW 58:355 n. 2. On Amsdorf, see Robert Kolb, "Amsdorf, Nikolaus von," *OER* 1:27–28, and below, p. 182 n. 80.

[16] Luther was in Merseburg from July 30 to August 4 and again August 6–7, 1545. He installed George of Anhalt (1507–53) as Evangelical bishop on August 2; preached for the wedding of Sigismund of Lindenau on August 4; and preached on Psalm 8 on August 6. See *Sermon at Marriage of Sigismund von Lindenau* (1545), LW 51:357–67; *On Christ's Kingdom* (1545), WA 51:11–22 (LW 66); cf. Brecht 3:307.

[17] Luther was in Halle on August 5, 1545 (in the middle of his Merseburg trip) and on January 6 and 24–27, 1546 (on the journey from Wittenberg to Mansfeld). He preached in Halle on August 5, January 6, and January 26: see LW 58:242–58, 349–84; above, Jonas and Coelius, *Report*, p. 8; cf. Brecht 3:371.

Here at the university in Wittenberg there was among us a certain Master Ambrose Berndt from Jüterbog,[18] one of my dear brethren, a truly upright man who loved Christ. For some days before his end, he lay very weak and sick unto death, and yet God removed from him the sensation of illness, as though he were existing already in another life. He spoke with us about how he intended to come and see us and celebrate with us. He was completely unaware that he was so sick and on the verge of death, for which reason he was unable to be terrified at the prospect of death. Indeed, he was no longer in this life except that, whenever Christ was mentioned, he freely confessed from his heart the great grace and blessedness which come to us in Christ from the heavenly Father. For He loved Christ and was accustomed to pray eagerly, calling on God the Father in spirit and truth [John 4:23–24]. But if anyone then (thinking that he had come 'to himself) attempted immediately afterward to speak to him about his beloved wife, children, household, money, debts, etc., he was suddenly absent from himself and, as it were, in another world (yet he recognized us all and called us by name); he spoke cheerfully with laughter and pleasant wit of other subjects, so that a man who was unaware of his fantasy might think he was in full health and must just be lying in bed out of boredom, etc. But our dear Lord Jesus Christ took him out of this life to Himself in the midst of this fantasy, and yet in good confession of the Christian faith, so that he was already dead to this world several days before he died. For he knew nothing of the things of earth, to take any concern for them. Indeed, everything had been lifted from his heart so that he did not even sense his own sickness, was unconcerned by death. Indeed, he did not even see death; how, then, should he be terrified at sin and death? Thus in him we saw before our eyes the Word of Christ in John 8 [:51], which applies to all who believe in Christ: "If anyone 'will keep My Word, he will not see death eternally." For though they do not all die so easily as this Ambrose, but with great sorrows, even as the Son of God Himself died on the cross, yet when the blessed hour comes, they see life and not death, and all say, "Father, into Your hands I commend my spirit" [Luke 23:46], at which blessed last words our dear Lord Jesus Christ likewise received our beloved father, Dr. Martin, from this vale of sorrow [Ps. 83:7 Vg (Ps. 84:6)] to Himself. To God be praise and thanks forever.

---

[18] Ambrose Berndt of Jüterbog had matriculated in Wittenberg in 1520, receiving his master's degree in 1528 and returning in 1531 to become a member of the faculty: see Heinz Kathe, *Die Wittenberger Philosophische Fakultät 1501–1817* (Cologne: Böhlau, 2002), p. 95. In 1538, having been widowed twice, he married Luther's niece Magdalene Kaufmann, the orphan daughter of Luther's sister Margarethe: see *Table Talk* no. 4313a (1538), WA TR 4:214–15. Berndt died on January 12, 1542 (see WA Br 9:577 n. 10).

During Master Ambrose's sickness, when I observed that he did not sleep, I asked two physicians[19] to prepare for him a strong sleeping draught. They answered me that it would be dangerous, and they might be held responsible if it went awry. I said, "I will take responsibility for it, even if he survives it. Give it to him in God's name, as to one for whom there is no hope.[20] Who knows but that it might |help." The doctors gave him the draught, but not as potent as I requested, for they were somewhat anxious. Then sleep came upon him powerfully so that he slept two hours. When he awoke, however, he felt his pain and complained of it, and spoke lucidly with his wife about various matters of necessity. But soon thereafter, about an hour and a half having passed, he was again in good humor as he had been before, knowing nothing more of this world until, some days later, he relinquished his spirit to Christ.

This blessed and cheerful account of Master Ambrose, our dear brother, I have gladly related on this occasion for two reasons: First, that I might thereby distract you, beloved, for a while, from that wailing and weeping for which the fitting time has now come upon us. God has afflicted us; let His grace console us again. Second, because this account pertains to the subject which we presently are discussing.

|For this Master Ambrose was Doctor Martin's relative by marriage,[21] and so [Luther] often visited him in his illness. And when he spoke with him about Christ, Ambrose also spoke about Christ according to the dear Gospel, as I have said. But when he tried to speak with him about his wife, children, possessions, etc., Ambrose knew nothing of such things, but promptly fell into his blissful fantasy with words of a different kind, as stated before. In particular, he said to Doctor [Luther] with laughter and gratitude: "Good Doctor, thank you for coming to me. I will come to you in turn some evening, and we will have a good conversation together, and I will speak to you then of many happy matters." Truly, the two may be doing so even now in the life eternal, to which they have both made their journeys. In this life they were unable to keep such a meeting.

Now when Dr. Martin had left him, [he] said to me: "He is gone. He knows of no death. Whenever |we try to advise him to set his affairs in order, he knows nothing more of this world and life, but is merry, laughs, and in his joyful fantasy broaches other subjects, mocking us with such words, as if to say, 'I know nothing more on earth that I need to put in order or to be concerned with.' May God grant me in short order so quiet and blessed an hour of death! What more do I have to do on earth?"

---

[19] *Doctores Medicine*

[20] *als einem desperato*

[21] See above, p. 31 n. 18.

Not long after Master Ambrose was buried in January of the harsh winter of 1542, Dr. Martin was passing by the grave with me, when, indicating the grave with his hand, he said, "He did not know that he was sick, nor did he know that he died, and yet he was not without confession of Christ. There he lies, still not knowing that he is dead. Dear Lord Jesus Christ, take me also, even thus, from this valley of sorrow to Yourself," etc.

I often had to hear such things from my dear father [Dr. Martin]. And when he perceived my discomfort, sometimes even from my words, he would say to me: "Pray our dear Lord God to take me hence to Himself in short order. I can do nothing more on earth. I am no longer of use to you. Help me with your prayer. Do not pray that I live longer." Everyone can well imagine what answer I gave my dear father, our beloved doctor, at such words. All this shows how eagerly he wished in his final days to be free from this life of sorrow and to be with Christ. With that he sang his *Consummatum est* ["It is finished"] and commended his spirit into the hands of the heavenly Father [John 19:30; Luke 23:46].

However, that you may also have a brief account of our beloved father Dr. Martin's blessed departure, when he perceived that his hour was come, he prayed thus:[22]

O my heavenly Father, God and Father of our Lord Jesus Christ, God of all comfort: I thank You that You have revealed to me Your beloved Son, Jesus Christ, in whom I believe, whom I have preached and confessed, whom I have loved and worshiped, whom the wretched pope and all the ungodly dishonor, persecute, and blaspheme. I beseech You, my Lord Jesus Christ, accept my little soul into Your keeping. O heavenly Father, though I must leave this body and be torn away from this life, I know of a certainty that I will dwell with You forever, and no one can snatch me from Your hands [John 10:29].

After this he said three times:

Into Your hands I commend my spirit. You have redeemed me, O faithful God [Ps. 31:5].

Likewise, John 3 [:16]:

God so loved the world that He gave His only-begotten Son, so that all who believe in Him may not perish but have eternal life.

And with this he folded his hands and with perfect stillness relinquished his spirit to Christ. For this reason it is fitting that we should rejoice with him, to the extent that our grief permits.

---

[22] See above, Jonas and Coelius, *Report*, p. 14.

Here I must make mention of St. Martin, the holy bishop, whose history relates that all heretics would gasp and go pale at the sound of his name; and again, that there was great mourning and weeping by all believing and true Christians ˈat St. Martin's death; and again, that a dispute and quarrel arose among certain cities and countries about which of them were to keep the body of St. Martin and to have it buried with them.[23] All this happened in similar fashion with this holy apostle and prophet of Christ, our preacher and evangelist, in German lands;[24] yet of that I will not speak at length. God Himself holds him in honor and love, holding him in His bosom as one who in his life dearly loved us and the Church of Christ. May God reward our beloved father in the life to come, where we all trust that we, too, will come to be with him.

May God grant that the Spirit of God may be upon his successors as well, to speak a double portion of what this lofty, precious man spoke, and in the churches which the dear father planted, just as the prophet Elisha asked of Elijah when he was taken away from Elisha in a whirlwind (2 Kings 2 [:9–11]).

ˈBut if we fear or suspect that it is because of our sins and ingratitude that God has taken away this precious man, then we ought to amend our lives and call with all our hearts upon God our heavenly Father through Christ, that we may abide in the blessed and pure doctrine of faith and be defended by Christ from the sects and tyrants and from all the gates of hell [Matt. 16:18]. "Your own poor Christendom defend / That it may praise You without end."[25] "Help us, O God our Savior, and deliver us for the glory of Your name, and be merciful to our sins for Your holy name's sake" (Psalm 79 [:9]). Sustain in Your Church faithful and good preachers, give them power and might by the Holy Spirit, as Psalm 68 [:11] says: "The Lord gives the Word with great companies of those who preach good news."

The shameless, abominable, great blasphemies of the adversaries and of the stiff-necked priests and monks, as well as ˈour own ingratitude, may well now be the cause of great calamity and divine punishment in the world. But we ought to pray God the Father, in the name of the Son, our Lord Jesus Christ, that for His name's sake He would perform and fulfill and vindicate

---

[23] For the legend of Martin of Tours (ca. 336–397), see *LA* 2:292–300, no. 166. Cf. below, Mathesius, *History*, p. 117 and n. 13 there.

[24] The counts of Mansfeld had wanted to bury Luther's body in their territory, where he had died, but returned the remains to Wittenberg for burial at the request of Elector John Frederick. See above, Jonas and Coelius, *Report*, p. 17.

[25] Luther's hymn "Erhalt uns, Herr, bei deinem Wort" (1541), LW 53:305 ("Lord, Keep Us Steadfast in Your Word," *LSB* 655:2; WA Ar 4:304–5; Wackernagel 3:27, no. 46).

the truth of the epitaph and prophecy which our dear father, Dr. Martin, made for himself:

Pestis eram vivus, moriens tua mors ero Papa.[26]

That is, in German: "O pope, pope, when I lived, I was your plague. When I die, I will be bitter death for you." God be praised forever through Jesus Christ, our Lord. Amen.

Let us pray, etc.

---

[26] Literally: "Living, I was [your] plague; dying, I will be your death, O pope." Luther seems to have composed this epitaph for himself in 1537, when he feared that his death was imminent: see *Table Talk* no. 3543a–b, WA TR 3:390, 392, though it is anticipated (in German) in *Exhortation to All Clergy* (1530), LW 34:39. Cf. Cochlaeus, *Deeds and Writings of Dr. Martin Luther*, in Vandiver et al., *Luther's Lives*, p. 349.

ORATION
AT THE FUNERAL
OF DR. MARTIN LUTHER

PHILIP MELANCHTHON
1546

Translated by Christopher Boyd Brown

ORATION AT THE FUNERAL
OF DR. MARTIN LUTHER

Philip Melanchthon
February 22, 1546[1]

A LTHOUGH, amid this public mourning, my own voice is impeded by
sorrow and tears, nonetheless, in the presence of such a great gathering
of people, it is the long-standing custom that something should be said—
not, as was done by the heathen, in speaking only about the praises of the
deceased,[2] but rather in order to remind this assembly of the way in which
the Church has been marvelously governed and of the perils it has faced, so
that we may consider[3] why [its members][4] are afflicted, what they should
especially long for, and by what examples they should guide their lives. For
though godless men set in the midst of such great confusion of life judge
that everything is carried along blindly, by chance,[5] yet let us, having been
assured by many clear testimonies of God, separate the Church from the
godless multitude and lay down as a principle that it is ruled and preserved
by God. Let us rightly contemplate the constitution of the Church; let us
acknowledge those who have been its true guides and consider the course
of their lives [Heb. 13:7]; and let us choose apt leaders and teachers whom
we may in godliness imitate and revere. It will be necessary to consider and

---

[1] See the introduction above, pp. xxxix–liii. On the long Leipzig and short Wittenberg Latin texts, see the introduction above, pp. xliv–xlvii. On the translations by Cruciger and Funck, see p. xlvi n. 149 (Funck) and p. xlvii n. 154 (Cruciger).

[2] Cf. Quintilian (AD 35–96), *Institutes of Oratory* 3.7.1–6, 10–18 (Loeb 126 [2002], pp. 102–5, 106–11).

[3] The Leipzig edition reads: "that we may consider [*cogitemus*]." The short Wittenberg Latin edition reads: "that the younger ones may consider [*iuniores cogitent*]." Cruciger's translation reads: "So that Christian hearts may the more diligently contemplate and consider . . ." Funck's translation reads: "So that those of younger age may consider . . ."

[4] Melanchthon moves from the singular *Ecclesia* (or *coetum* in the previous clause) to a plural verb.

[5] *temere . . . et casu*. Cf. the criticism of Epicureanism in Cicero (106–43 BC), *On the Nature of the Gods* 2.37.94 (Loeb 268 [1933], pp. 214–15); Augustine, *Ennarationes in Psalmos* 9.2 (PL 36:112; WSA 3/15:140–41; NPNF[1] 8:33).

speak of these great matters whenever any mention is made of the Reverend Doctor Martin Luther, our dearest father and teacher. For though many godless men hated him with the most bitter hatred, let us, knowing that he was called forth by God as a minister of the Gospel, give him our love and approbation, and let us gather testimonies ᶦto show that his doctrine is not a matter of seditious opinions, strewn forth by blind impulse, as Epicurean men suppose, ⟦but a demonstration of the will and true worship of God, and an explanation of the Holy Scriptures, and a proclamation of the Word of God, that is, the Gospel of Jesus Christ.⟧[6]

For though the orations held in a situation of this kind[7] usually have a great deal to say about the admirable private qualities of those who are being praised, nevertheless I shall omit that part of the oration and speak only about the most important topic: namely, about his ecclesiastical office. For intelligent minds have always affirmed that if a man has illuminated the salutary and necessary doctrine in the Church, then thanks should be given to God, because it is He who has raised him up, and that man's labors, faith, constancy, and his other virtues should be praised, and his memory should be exceedingly dear to all good people.

Let this, therefore, be the start of our oration: The Son of God is seated, as Paul says, at the right hand of the eternal Father and bestows good things upon human beings [cf. Eph. 4:8–12]: that is, the voice of the Gospel and the Holy Spirit. And to impart these, He stirs up prophets, apostles, teachers, and pastors, and these He takes from among us, that is, from among this assembly of learners who read, hear, and love the prophetic and apostolic Scriptures. Nor does He call to this military service only those who hold authority as bishops,[8] but often He even makes war against such people by means of teachers recruited from other estates. It is a pleasant and useful spectacle to behold the Church of all ages and to consider the goodness of God in sending salutary teachers one after another in continuous succession, so that, as in the front line of battle, as previous teachers step back,[9] at once others step into their places.

The sequence of the first patriarchs is well-known: Adam, Seth, Enoch, Methuselah, Noah, Shem [Genesis 5]. While [Shem] was still alive, and

---

[6] This passage is added in the Leipzig edition (fol. A2r), probably by Joachim Camerarius (see the introduction above, p. xlv). "Jesus Christ" is printed in all capital letters for emphasis. The passage does not appear in the short Wittenberg Latin edition or in the German translations by Funck or Cruciger. See the introduction above, p. xlvii.

[7] *quae tali loco habentur*; or: "that are held in a place of this sort."

[8] *ordinariam potestatem*; or: "regular authority." In the technical language of canon law, however, the *Ordinarius* was the local bishop.

[9] *decedentibus*. The short Wittenberg Latin edition reads: *cedentibus*; Cruciger's translation reads: *hinweg komen*; Funck's translation reads: *hinweg sein*.

dwelling in the vicinity of Sodom, seeing that the nations had forgotten the doctrine of Noah and Shem and were worshiping idols in some places, Abraham [Genesis 12-20] was raised up to be a colleague to Shem and a fellow in this most excellent work of spreading the true doctrine. After him came Isaac [Genesis 21-27; 35:27-29], Jacob [Genesis 25-35, 46-50], and Joseph [Genesis 37-50], who kindled the light of the doctrine in all of Egypt, which at that time was the most prosperous kingdom in all the world. Then came Moses [Exodus 2-Deuteronomy 34], Joshua, Samuel [1 Samuel 1-12], David [1 Samuel 16-1 Kings 2], Elijah [1 Kings 17:1-2 Kings 2:12], and Elisha [1 Kings 19:16-2 Kings 13:20], whom Isaiah heard; and Isaiah was heard by Jeremiah, whom Daniel heard; and Daniel was heard by Zechariah. Then came Ezra and Onias [1 Macc. 12:1-3]. After him came the Maccabees. Then came Simeon [Luke 2:25], Zechariah [Luke 1:5-23], the Baptist [Luke 1:57-80; 3:1-20; Mark 6:14-29], Christ, the apostles [Luke 6:14-16; Acts 1:13]. This continuous line is a delight to behold and a shining testimony to the presence of God in the Church.[10]

ˈAfter the apostles, there follows a line which, though of greater frailty, was nonetheless adorned with God's witness:[11] Polycarp,[12] Irenaeus,[13]

---

[10] Cf. Luther, preface to Bibliander's edition of the Koran (1543), LW 60:292; Melanchthon, theses of February 16, 1543, for the disputation of Johann Marbach (1521-81), *On the Unity of the Church*, under Luther's presidency, Thesis 1, WA 39/2:206 (LW 73). See John M. Headley, *Luther's View of Church History* (New Haven: Yale University Press, 1963).

[11] Cf. Caspar Cruciger, dedication to the *Summer Postil* (1544), LW 77:4.

[12] Polycarp (69-155), bishop of Smyrna and martyr, was a disciple of the apostle John and the teacher of Irenaeus. See Marco Frenschkowski, "Polykarp," *BBKL* 7:809-15; *ODCC*, 3rd ed., s.v. "Polycarp."

[13] Irenaeus (140-200), a student of Polycarp and bishop of Lyons, combated Gnostic teaching. See Norbert Collmar, "Irenäus," *BBKL* 2:1315-26; *ODCC*, 3rd ed., s.v. "Irenaeus."

Gregory of Neocaesarea,[14] Basil,[15] Augustine,[16] Prosper,[17] Maximus,[18] Hugh,[19] Bernard,[20] Tauler,[21] and others elsewhere. And though this last, decrepit age has been more corrupt, nonetheless God has always preserved some remnant [Rom. 11:5]. And it is manifest that the light of the Gospel has been the more brightly kindled by the voice of Luther.

He must be added, therefore, to that most beautiful line of excellent men whom God has sent to gather and renew the Church, whom we judge to be the most outstanding flower of the human race. To be sure, Solon,[22]

---

[14] Gregory (ca. 213–ca. 270), the bishop of Neocaesarea and an effective evangelist, was remembered as "the wonder-worker" [Thaumaturgus]. He was also an important pre-Nicene Trinitarian theologian. See Friedrich Wilhelm Bautz, "Gregor Thaumaturgos," BBKL 2:338–39; ODCC, 3rd ed., s.v. "Gregory Thaumaturgus."

[15] Basil the Great (ca. 329–379), one of the Cappadocian fathers, was a bishop of Caesarea, author of an influential monastic rule, and an erudite Nicene theologian who defended the deity of the Holy Spirit. See Friedrich Wilhelm Bautz, "Basilius der Große," BBKL 1:406–9; ODCC, 3rd ed., s.v. "Basil the Great."

[16] Augustine, an African rhetorician who became the bishop of Hippo, left a monumental legacy of theological writings that served as the foundation of the subsequent Latin Christian tradition. See Friedrich Wilhelm Bautz, "Augustinus, Aurelius," BBKL 1:272–300; ODCC, 3rd ed., s.v. "Augustine of Hippo." Augustine was particularly important to Luther's theology: see above, Catalog, p. 4; and below, Melanchthon, Preface, pp. 61–62, 63, 76; Mathesius, History, p. 455; cf. below, p. 131 n. 94; Luther, preface to Augustine, On the Spirit and the Letter (1533), LW 60:35–44.

[17] Prosper of Aquitaine (ca. 390–455) was a vigorous defender of the teachings of Augustine on grace, predestination, and original sin. See Adriaan Breukelaar, "Prosper 'Tiro' von Aquitanien," BBKL 7:1002–4; ODCC, 3rd ed., s.v. "Prosper of Aquitaine."

[18] Maximus the Confessor (ca. 580–662) was an important Byzantine theologian who led the fight against Monothelitism. See Adriaan Breukelaar, "Maximus Confessor," BBKL 5:1084–93; ODCC, 3rd ed., s.v. "Maximus the Confessor."

[19] Hugh of St. Victor (d. 1141) was an Augustinian canon and theologian in Paris who advocated the historical interpretation of Scripture. See Friedrich Wilhelm Bautz, "Hugo von St. Viktor," BBKL 2:1148–51; ODCC, 3rd ed., s.v. "Hugh of St. Victor."

[20] On Bernard of Clairvaux, see above, p. lvi n. 191. On his early influence on Luther, see below, Melanchthon, Preface, p. 61.

[21] Johannes Tauler (ca. 1300–1361) was a German Dominican who taught a mystical theology centered on suffering. He was a popular preacher in his hometown of Strassburg. See ODCC, 3rd ed., s.v. "Tauler, John." On Luther's appreciation of his sermons, see below, p. 188 n. 24, and the introduction by Franz Posset, LW 59:13–14.

[22] Solon (640–558 BC), an Athenian statesman and legislator, remembered as one of the seven sages of Greece. See OCD, 4th ed., s.v. "Solon."

Themistocles,[23] Scipio,[24] Augustus,[25] and the like were great men, who either founded or ruled great empires; yet they are far inferior to our own leaders: Isaiah, the Baptist, Paul, Augustine, Luther. It is fitting that we in the Church should understand this true distinction.

What great and true things have been brought to light by Luther, then, to prove that his course of life should be praised? For many cry out that the Church has been disturbed[26] and that insoluble controversies have been spread.[27] Here I answer that this is how the [divine] government of the Church works. When the Holy Spirit reproves the world [John 16:8], divisions arise on account of the impudence of the godless. The fault lies with those who refuse to hear the Son of God, of whom the heavenly Father says, "Listen to Him" [Matt. 17:5]. Luther brought to light the true and needful doctrine. For it is manifest that the deepest shadows lay over the doctrine of penance.[28] Having discussed these, he showed what true repentance[29] is and showed what are the haven and consolation for a mind that feels the wrath of God and is terrified. He cast light upon the doctrine of Paul, which states that a man is justified by faith [Rom. 3:28]. He showed the distinction between Law and Gospel, between the righteousness of the Spirit and civil righteousness. He also showed the true invocation of God and called the whole Church back from the heathen madness that pretends to call upon God even while minds laboring under Academic doubt[30] flee from God. He ordered that we should call upon God in "faith and good conscience" [1 Tim. 1:19], and above all led us to the one Mediator, the Son of God, sitting at the right hand of the eternal Father, who is making intercession for us, and not to statues or dead human beings, as godless people, in their terrible madness, call upon statues and dead human beings.

---

[23] Themistocles (ca. 524–459 BC), a leading politician during the Persian Wars, remembered for his defeat of Xerxes in the Battle of Salamis in 480 BC and for his expansion of the Athenian naval fleet. See *OCD*, 4th ed., s.v. "Themistocles," and below, p. 46.

[24] Probably Scipio Africanus the Elder, called "The Great" (236–183 BC), a Roman statesman and general who defeated Hannibal (247–183 BC) in the Second Punic War. See *OCD*, 4th ed., s.v. "Cornelius Scipio Africanus (the elder), Publius."

[25] Augustus Caesar (63 BC–AD 14), the first Roman emperor, established peace throughout the Roman world. See *OCD*, 4th ed., s.v. "Augustus."

[26] *Clamant enim multi turbatam Ecclesiam.* The short Wittenberg Latin edition inserts *esse* before *Ecclesiam.*

[27] Cf. Erasmus, *Freedom of the Will* (1525), LCC 17:38–42, 97.

[28] See, e.g., Luther to Johann von Staupitz, May 30, 1518, LW 48:64–70, written as the preface to *Explanations of the Ninety-Five Theses* (LW 31:77–252).

[29] *poenitentia*, translated "penance" in the previous sentence.

[30] I.e., skepticism, so named from the Academy in Athens, which, though founded by Plato (ca. 428–347 BC), had become the center of skeptical philosophy by the third century BC.

He also showed that other authentic offices are pleasing to God, and he adorned and fortified civil life as no one else's writings have ever adorned and fortified it. He also separated necessary works from the childish pedagogy ¦of human ceremonies and from the rites and laws that hinder the true invocation of God. And in order that the bright heavenly doctrine might be spread among his posterity, he translated the prophetic and apostolic Scriptures into the German language with such clarity that this translation confers more enlightenment on the reader than do most commentaries.

He added many commentaries as well, which, as even Erasmus used to affirm, far excel the existing commentaries of all other authors.[31] And as is written of those working to restore Jerusalem—that they built with one hand while holding a sword in the other [Neh. 4:17]—so he, too, did battle with the enemies of the true doctrine while at the same time he constructed commentaries full of the heavenly doctrine and provided aid to the consciences of many with words of godly counsel.

Seeing that a great part of this doctrine is situated above the power of human penetration—as, for example, the doctrine of the forgiveness of sins and of faith—we must of necessity confess that he was taught by God [John 6:45]. Many of us were witnesses to his conflicts, in which he taught that it must be firmly maintained that it is by faith that we are both received and heard by God.[32]

Forever, therefore, and in all eternity, good minds shall celebrate the blessings which God has given to the Church through Luther. In the first place, they shall give thanks to God. Then they shall declare how much they owe to this man's labors, even if the atheists who mock the Church as a whole judge these κατορθώματα[33] to be a pointless game or some sort of madness.

---

[31] The apparent source of this claim is a remark attributed to Erasmus at Cologne in November 1520 at the end of a report by Spalatin printed in Witt Lat 2 (1546), fols. 121v–123r: *Brevis Commemoratio rerum Coloniae Agrippinae in Ubiis gestarum in causa Lutheri, Anno M.D.XX.* The text is reproduced in E var. arg. 5:249 and (in German translation) in StL 15:1615–16: "*Plane Lutherus tantus est, ut plus erudiar et proficiam ex lectione unius pagellae Lutheranae, quam ex toto Thoma*" ["Luther is such a manifestly great man that I learn and profit more from reading a single page of Luther than from the whole of Thomas"]. Cf. below, Mathesius, *History*, pp. 162–63, 559. Melanchthon quoted this *sententia* several times: see Veit Dietrich [Philip Melanchthon], preface to Luther, *Commentary on Micah* (October 22, 1542), MBW T11:304 (CR 4:892); Melanchthon, preface to Witt Lat 3 (before May 1, 1549), MBW 5:462, no. 5515 (CR 7:398), cited in Wengert, *Human Freedom*, p. 154; see also Melanchthon, *Oration on Erasmus of Rotterdam* (1557), CR 12:270 (in Kusukawa, *Melanchthon: Orations*, p. 253).

[32] On *Anfechtung* or "temptation" (here: *luctus*) in Luther's theology and experience, see above, Jonas and Coelius, *Report*, p. 9 and n. 11 there; and below, Melanchthon, *Preface*, p. 60 and n. 32 there. Cf. below, Mathesius, *History*, pp. 258–59.

[33] *katorthômata*; according to Stoic ethics, the perfectly virtuous deeds of the sage. See Cicero, *On Duties* 1.8 (Loeb 30 [1913], pp. 10–11).

No insoluble disputations have been stirred up, nor has an apple of discord[34] been cast in front of the Church, as some falsely say, nor is it the riddles of the Sphinx [Σφιγγός] that are being propounded. For to sound and pious arbiters, who do not pass judgment invidiously, it is a simple matter, having compared opinions, to see which are in keeping with the heavenly doctrine and which are not. Indeed, there is no question but that these controversies have now been resolved in the minds of all the godly. For since God wills that He and His will should be discerned in the prophetic and apostolic Word, in which He has revealed Himself, that Word should not be regarded as ambiguous, like the Sibyl's leaves[[, "which fly in confusion when the swift winds make sport with them"]].[35]

Yet there are some, not evil men, who have lamented that Luther was harsher than he should have been. I will not argue on either side, but give the answer that, as Erasmus often said, God gave this last age a severe physician on account of the greatness of its illnesses.[36] Since He had stirred up such an instrument against the proud and shameless enemies of the truth, as He said to Jeremiah: "Behold, I have put My Word in your mouth. You will tear down and build up" [cf. Jer. 1:9–10]; and since it was His will to confront them with this Gorgon,[37] as it were, it is in vain for them to find

---

[34] In Greek mythology, the apple which the goddess Eris (Strife or Discord) tossed among the goddesses Aphrodite, Athena, and Hera as a prize for the most beautiful; the ensuing contest and the success of Aphrodite in bribing the Trojan prince Paris as judge with the promise of Helen were the legendary provocation of the Trojan War. See Hyginus (ca. 63 BC–AD 17), *Fabulae* 92 (in R. Scott Smith and Stephen M. Trzaskoma, trans. and eds., *Apollodorus' Library and Hyginus' Fabulae: Two Handbooks of Greek Mythology* [Indianapolis: Hackett, 2007], p. 128); Augustine, *City of God* 3.25 and 18.10 (PL 41:105, 567; CCSL 47:92–93; 48:600–601; NPNF¹ 2:59, 366).

[35] *Quae turbata volant rapidis ludibria ventis*: Virgil (70–19 BC), *Aeneid* 6.76 (Loeb 63 [1918], pp. 536–37). This line seems to have been added by Camerarius in the Leipzig edition. It does not appear in the short Wittenberg Latin edition or in the German translations by Funck or Cruciger. See the introduction above, pp. xlvii, xlix. The Cumean Sibyl, as described in the Virgilian passage, customarily wrote her prophecies on leaves: see also Virgil, *Aeneid* 3.441–44 (Loeb 63 [1999], pp. 400–401); *OCD*, 4th ed., s.v. "Sibyl." For the charge that the Scriptures themselves are unclear and ambiguous, see Erasmus, *Discussion of Free Will* (CWE 76:8–9) and *Hyperaspistes* 1.64–71 (CWE 76:214–35).

[36] Erasmus, *Hyperaspistes* 1 (CWE 76:100), cited in Wengert, *Human Freedom*, pp. 154–55: "*Sic aliquando mecum cogitabam, quid si Deo visum est coruptissimis horum temporum moribus, tam saevum dare medicum, qui sectionibus et usturis sanet, quod potionibus et malagmatis non poterat*" ["Sometimes I think to myself: 'What if it has pleased God to give the utterly corrupted morals of these days a severe physician to heal with incisions and cauterization what he could not heal with medicines and salves'"]. Cf. below, Mathesius, *History*, p. 559. Melanchthon also invoked this *sententia* in his letter to Joachim Camerarius, February 9, 1544, MBW T13:80 (CR 5:310).

[37] The Gorgons, in Greek mythology, were monsters (the name means "fearsome") whose visage had the power to petrify those who looked upon it. The Gorgon's head appeared on the

fault with God. God does not rule the Church according to human counsels, nor is it His will that His instruments should all be exactly alike. Yet it
is commonly the case that men of lesser and more restrained character do
not much approve of those who are more fervent, no matter whether they
are good or bad. Aristides saw that it was by a great impulse of spirit that
Themistocles was undertaking and successfully carrying out great endeav-
ors; even though [Aristides] celebrated the success of the state, he sought to
recall that provoked spirit from its course.[38]

Nor do I deny that the more violent impulses sometimes lead to sin, for
no one in this weakness of nature is entirely without fault. But at the same
time, if there is anyone of such character that, as the ancients have said of
Hercules, Cimon, and others, he is ἄκομψος μὲν, ἄλλα τὰ μέγιστα ἀγαθός
["plain, yet good in the highest degree"], he is a good man and worthy of
praise.[39] And if, as Paul says, he does good service as a soldier in the Church,
maintaining faith and a good conscience [1 Tim 1:18–19], he is pleasing to
God and should be revered by us.

We know that Luther was such a man. For he both defended the purity
of doctrine with constancy and maintained the integrity of his conscience.

---

shield of Athena (the Aegis) as well as of a number of other gods and heroes: see, e.g., Homer
(850 BC), *Iliad* 5.733–36; 11.35–36 (Loeb 170 [1924], pp. 260–61, 494–95); [Ps.-]Hyginus,
Astronomica 2.13 (in Mary Grant, trans., *The Myths of Hyginus* [Lawrence: University of
Kansas Publications, 1960], p. 197). The intended image here, therefore, may be that of Luther
as a heroic warrior rather than as a terrible monster himself. Cf. Melanchthon, *Oration on
Erasmus of Rotterdam* (1557), CR 12:269 (in Kusukawa, *Melanchthon: Orations*, p. 253), where
Erasmus is said to have been armed by God with the Gorgon of eloquence.

[38] Themistocles (see above, p. 43 n. 23) and Aristides (d. ca. 467 BC) were political rivals
in fifth-century Athens. Themistocles urged the expansion of the Athenian navy against the
Persian invasion, leading to victory at the Battle of Salamis in 480 BC. Although Aristides
hailed the victory, he sought to prevent Themistocles from going on to secure Athenian
hegemony by destroying the fleets of the other Greek states. See Plutarch (ca. 46–ca. 120),
Life of Themistocles 20 (Loeb 47 [1914], pp. 54–57) and *Life of Aristides* 22 (Loeb 47 [1914],
pp. 280–83); *OCD*, 4th ed., s.v. "Aristides."

[39] Plutarch, *Life of Cimon* 4.4 (Loeb 47 [1914], pp. 414–15), where the line is applied to the
Athenian general Cimon (d. ca. 450 BC; see *OCD*, 4th ed., s.v. "Cimon") as quoted from the
description of Hercules in Euripides (480–406 BC), *Licymnius*, fragment 473 (Loeb 504 [2008],
pp. 562–63). The Loeb translation of the words quoted by Melanchthon reads "straightforward,
virtuous in the extreme." Although the word *akompsos* ["unadorned" or "plain"] can have a
negative meaning—such as "boorish"—the context here (after Melanchthon's earlier invocation of the Stoic *katorthômata*) suggests a positive sense, as in Marcus Aurelius (121–180),
Meditations 6.30 (Loeb 58 [1916], pp. 144–45), where it is listed as one of the virtues of a Stoic;
cf. Plutarch, *Moralia* 9 (Loeb 197 [1927], pp. 26–27). Luther had been portrayed by Hans
Holbein ("The Younger," 1497–1543) in a woodcut of 1519 as the "German Hercules" slaying
the hydra of scholastic authorities: see Christian Müller et al., *Hans Holbein the Younger: The
Basel Years, 1515–1532* (Munich: Prestel, 2006), p. 126. Cf. Luther, preface to Savonarola,
Meditation on Psalms 51 and 31 (1523), LW 59:80.

⟦And now who is there, of those who knew him, who is unaware of the great humanity with which he was endowed, or of how great was his sweetness when gathered with his household, or of how little he was given to contentiousness or quarreling? And yet all these things had an additional gravity, such as should fittingly be present in such a man, for in him there was

ἀψευδὲς ἦθος, εὐπροσήγορας στόμα
["a character without deception, and a ready mouth for speaking"].[40]

Or, rather, as Paul says, all these things were ὅσα ἀληθῆ, ὅσα σεμνά, ὅσα δίκαια, ὅσα ἀγνά, ὅσα προσφιλῆ, ὅσα εὔφημα ["whatever is true, whatever is honorable, whatever is just, whatever is pure, whatever is lovely, whatever is of good report"] [Phil. 4:8]. Thus it is evident that this harshness proceeds from zeal [ζήλου] for truth, not from ἐριθείας ["contentiousness"] or bitterness. Of this all of us as well as many persons from elsewhere are witnesses. If I were seeking to craft an encomium of the man dealing with the rest of his life, which he spent for sixty-three years in the most intensive study of all piety and good things and liberal arts, what a shining and beautiful oration I might have!⟧[41] No wanton desires were ever noticed in him, no seditious counsels; rather, he was many times the advocate for laying down arms. He did not insinuate into ecclesiastical affairs schemes for increasing his own power or those of his own people. In my judgment, his wisdom and virtue were so great that it does not seem possible that they were called forth by human diligence alone; rather, [such] minds must be under God's direction, especially those that are acute, ᶦlofty, and ardent—and the facts show that Luther's [mind] was such in every respect.[42]

What shall I say about the rest of his virtues? Often I interrupted him when he was saying his prayers, with tears, for the whole Church. Nearly every day he took a set time to read certain psalms, which he mingled with his own petitions with sighs and tears, and he often said that he was angry with those who, either out of laziness or because of their busyness, said that it was enough to pray with a single sigh. This is why, he said, that set forms have been prescribed for us by the divine counsel, so that reading them

---

[40] Euripides, *Suppliant Women* 869 (Loeb 9 [1998], pp. 100–101).

[41] This passage appears in Camerarius' Leipzig edition and in Cruciger's translation. It does not appear in the translation by Funck or in the short Wittenberg Latin edition. See the introduction above, pp. xlviii, lii.

[42] *qualem omnino Lutheri fuisse res ostendit.* The short Wittenberg Latin edition reads: *qualem omnino Lutherum fuisse res ostendit* ["and the facts show that Luther was such (read: 'a mind') in every respect"]. Cruciger's translation reads: "(as Dr. Luther was)." Funck's translation reads: "such as Luther was entirely, as the facts themselves show." The change from "*Lutherum*" to "*Lutheri*" was therefore probably made by Camerarius.

might set our minds aflame and, indeed, so that we might declare, with our voices as well, what God it is upon whom we call.[43]

Thus on the many occasions on which there were serious deliberations concerning public dangers, we noted that he had been endowed with incredible strength of mind—scarcely ψοφοδεῆ ["timorous"] nor even troubled by any fears. He relied upon the holy anchor, as it is called—that is, the help of God—nor did he suffer his faith to be shaken.

Moreover, his acuteness of mind was so great that he alone was best able to perceive in obscure affairs what was best to do. Nor was he, as many suppose, heedless in his thoughts about the state or in considering the inclinations of others, but he was well acquainted with the state and was most perceptive in discerning the capacities and inclinations of all those with whom he lived. And though the force of his intellect was sharp, without any equal, he was nonetheless most avid in reading both ancient and recent ecclesiastical writers, and all the histories, whose examples he applied with singular facility to present affairs.[44]

We have at hand the enduring monuments of his own eloquence, in which he was, without any doubt, the equal of those whose rhetorical power is considered to have been supreme.

It is fitting that we should mourn such a man—endowed with the greatest power of intellect, trained in doctrine, exercised by long practice, adorned with many excellent and heroic virtues, and chosen by God for the work of restoring the Church, and who, moreover, embraced us all with a fatherly heart—since he has now been called from our fellowship here. For we are like orphans whose excellent and faithful father has been taken away. But because it is necessary to bow to the will of God, we nevertheless shall not allow the memory of his virtues and good deeds to perish among us. ⟦And we indeed rejoice with him that he now enjoys close and sweet familiarity with God and His Son, our Lord Jesus Christ, and with the prophets and apostles, which he always looked and begged for, by faith in the Son of God. There he is not only hearing the labors which he bore for the spread of the Gospel being approved by the judgment[45] of God and the testimonies of the whole heavenly Church, ⟦but indeed he is now, having been taken from the mortal body as if from a prison and having entered a school of even greater erudition, engaged in contemplation of God's essence, and the two natures joined in the Son, and the whole plan of the founding and redemption of the Church, from close at hand.[46] And having meditated in faith on

---

[43] See, e.g., *Sermons on John 17* (1528/1530), LW 69:15-19.

[44] See, e.g., *On the Councils and the Church* (1539), LW 41:3-178.

[45] Reading *iudicio* with Camerarius' Leipzig edition for *indicio* in CR.

[46] Cf. Melanchthon's written "last words": CR 9:1098.

these great matters here, as they are set forth in brief and obscure oracles, he now sees them openly and is overcome with the deepest joy, and, his mind all aflame, he gives thanks to God for this great blessing.

He is learning why the Son of God is called λόγος καὶ εἰκὼν ["word and image"] of the eternal Father [John 1:1; Col. 1:15] and how the Holy Spirit is the bond of mutual love not only between the eternal Father and Son but also between Them and the Church.[47] He had learned the first principles and rudiments of this doctrine in this mortal life, and he used to discourse with great wisdom about these most sublime matters: distinguishing between true and false worship, about the true knowledge of God in view of the divine revelations, and discerning the true God from false deities.

Many in this assembly once heard him commenting upon this verse: "You will see heaven opened, and the angels of God ascending and descending upon the Son of Man" [John 1:51].[48] He first urged his hearers to fix this exceeding consolation in their minds: the affirmation that heaven is open, that is, that our access to God lies open; that the divine wrath which barred the way has been moved aside for all those who flee for refuge to the Son; that God is now close at hand, working among us; and that those who call upon Him are received, governed, and preserved by Him.

This decree of God, which atheistic men[49] denounce as a fable, he used to admonish us to set against human doubt and the fears which deter recoiling minds from daring to call upon God or resting in His will.

Then he said that the angels ascending and descending upon the body of Christ were the ministers of the Gospel, who first, being led by Christ, ascend to God and receive the light of the Gospel and the Holy Spirit from Him. But then they descend; that is, they exercise the office of teaching among human beings.

And he added this interpretation: that even those heavenly spirits themselves, whom we are accustomed to call angels, as they gaze upon the Son, are enlightened and rejoice in the marvelous conjunction of the two natures, and since they are soldiers of this Lord in the defense of the Church, they are governed, as it were, by His own hand.

He is now beholding these sublime things, and just as formerly he used to ascend and descend among the ministers of the Gospel, led by Christ, so now he perceives the angels being sent by Him, and together with them he enjoys meditating upon the divine wisdom and divine works.

---

[47] Cf. Augustine, *On the Trinity* 15.5 and [17].27 (PL 42:1080; WSA 1/5:418; NPNF¹ 3:215).

[48] See *Sermons on John 1–2* (1537–38/1565), LW 22:200–211, based on Luther's sermon of February 9, 1538.

[49] *homines* ἄθεοι; i.e., those who deny God's involvement in the world.

We remember with what great delight he used to recount the government, advice, perils, and deliverance of the prophets and with what erudition he used to compare all the ages of the Church, thereby indicating that he was aflame with an extraordinary desire [to meet] those exceptional men.[50]

He is now embracing them and rejoicing to hear their living voices and to respond in turn. They greet him with joy as their own συμφοιτητήν ["schoolfellow"], and united they give thanks to God, who gathers and preserves the Church.

Concerning Luther himself, let us have no doubt that he is blessèd. We are in anguish because we have been orphaned. Since we, too, must bow to the will of God now that He has called him from here, let us know that this also is what God wills: that we should retain the memory of this man's virtues and of the blessings we have received from him. Let us now fulfill that duty.]][51] Let us recognize him to have been[52] a salutary instrument of God and diligently learn his doctrine. Let us also imitate the virtues which we urgently need, in proportion to our moderate capacity: the fear of God, faith and fervency in calling upon Him, integrity in ministry, decency, care to avoid seditious counsels, a desire to learn. Just as we often reflect deeply upon the other pious governors of the Church whose histories survive—on Jeremiah, on the Baptist, on Paul[53]—even so let us meditate upon the doctrine and course of life of this man, and add thanksgiving and prayer thereto, just as should be done now at the present time in this gathering. Therefore, say together with me, in true piety of mind:[54]

"We give thanks to You, almighty God, the eternal Father of our Lord Jesus Christ, who are the founder of Your Church together with Your coeternal Son, our Lord Jesus Christ, and the Holy Spirit: You are wise, good, merciful, a truthful judge, mighty, and supremely free, for You gather from the human race an inheritance for Your Son, and preserve the ministry of the Gospel, and have even now renewed it through Luther. And we pray with fervent petitions that You will henceforth both preserve and govern

---

[50] Cf. Melanchthon, *De Luthero et aetatibus Ecclesiae* (1548), CR 11:783–88.

[51] This passage appears in Camerarius' Leipzig edition and in Cruciger's translation. It does not appear in the translation by Funck or in the short Wittenberg Latin edition. See the introduction above, pp. xlvii, liii.

[52] *Agnoscamus eum fuisse.* The short Wittenberg Latin edition reads: *Sciamus fuisse eum* ["Let us be assured that he was . . ."]. Cruciger's and Funck's translations (*erkennen* and *wissen*) reflect the Leipzig and short Wittenberg versions respectively.

[53] See, e.g., Melanchthon, *De Paulo Apostolo* (1543), CR 11:618–30.

[54] On Melanchthon's prayers, see Martin Jung, *Frömmigkeit et Theologie bei Philipp Melanchthon: Das Gebet im Leben und in der Lehre des Reformators* (Tübingen: Mohr Siebeck, 1998).

Your Church, and seal upon us the true doctrine, as Isaiah prays for his own disciples [Isa. 8:16], and set our minds afire by Your Holy Spirit, that we may call upon You aright and govern our behavior in godliness."

Furthermore, since the death of great rulers often threatens impending punishment for their posterity, we and all those to whom the office of teaching has been committed beseech you all to take thought for the perils to which the world is prey. In one place the Turks are on the move;[55] elsewhere other enemies threaten domestic wars;[56] in some places the impudence of clever persons is so great that, especially now that they no longer fear Luther's censure, they will seek with all the more insolence to corrupt the doctrine that was correctly passed down.[57]

That God may avert these evils, let us be the more diligent in governing our behavior and our studies and ever retain this saying fixed in our minds: that so long as we shall retain the pure doctrine of the Gospel, hear it, learn it, and love it, we shall be the dwelling place and Church of God, as the Son of God says, "If anyone loves Me, he will keep My Word, and My Father will love him, and We will come to him and make Our home with him" [John 14:23]. May we be enkindled by this exceedingly great promise to learn the heavenly doctrine, knowing that it is for the sake of the Church that the human race and governments are preserved, and let us keep our gaze in our minds upon the eternity to come to which God has called us. For it is not in vain that He has revealed Himself through such splendid testimonies, nor has He sent the Son in vain, but He truly loves and cares for those who magnify these blessings. I have spoken.[58]

---

[55] The Ottoman Turks were consolidating their power in Hungary, having captured Esztergom in 1543 and forcing the Hapsburgs to recognize Ottoman control in the Truce of Adrianople in 1547. See Stephen A. Fischer-Galati, *Ottoman Imperialism and German Protestantism, 1521–1555* (Cambridge, MA: Harvard University Press, 1959), pp. 88–97.

[56] The Smalcaldic War (see the introduction above, pp. lxxiii, lxxxiv; and below, p. 233 n. 13; cf. below, Mathesius, *History*, p. 562) between Emperor Charles V and the Lutherans of the Smalcaldic League would break out in July 1546.

[57] Perhaps a reference to Luther's Protestant opponents such as Caspar von Schwenkfeld: see below, Mathesius, *History*, pp. 259–60 (and n. 166 there).

[58] *Dixi*, a customary formula for ending an oration.

PREFACE
TO THE SECOND VOLUME
OF THE COMPLETE EDITION
OF LUTHER'S
LATIN WRITINGS

PHILIP MELANCHTHON
1546

Translated by Christopher Boyd Brown

Preface to the Second Volume of the Complete Edition of Luther's Latin Writings

Philip Melanchthon
June 1, 1546[1]

PHILIP Melanchthon to the pious reader, greeting:

The Reverend Martin Luther had given us hope that in the preface to this volume of his works he would relate both the course of his life and the occasions of his conflicts;[2] and he would have done so, if it had not happened that, before the printer had completed work on this volume, the author was called from this mortal life into everlasting fellowship with God and the heavenly Church.[3] Indeed, a lucidly written reflection upon his private life would have been useful—being full of examples that would have served to strengthen devotion in good minds—[1]as well as a narrative of the things that took place, which could have served to inform posterity about the many events and would also have refuted the slanders of those who spread the fiction that he was incited by political leaders or others to undermine the dignity of the bishops, or that he was inflamed by private lust to break the bonds of monastic servitude.[4]

---

[1] Translated from CR 6:155–70 (cf. CR 20:429–38), checked against the text edited in MBW T15:296–311, no. 4277, and the original publication in Witt Lat 2 (1546), fols. †2r–†8r: *Tomus Secundus Omnium Operum Reverendi Domini Martini Lutheri, Doctoris Theologiae, Continens monumenta, quae de multis gravissimis controversiis ab anno XX. Usque ad XXVII. Annum edita sunt* (Wittenberg: Hans Lufft, 1546) [VD16 L3414]. The paragraph divisions in the present translation are based upon the divisions in Witt Lat 2, which differ from both CR and MBW. See the introduction above, pp. liii–lxi.

[2] See Luther's promise to compose additional prefaces for the volumes of his works in *Preface to the Latin Writings* (1545), LW 34:338.

[3] Luther died on February 18, 1546, three and a half months before the composition of Melanchthon's preface.

[4] On the accusation that Luther was "incited by political leaders," see Luther's letter to Spalatin, February 22, 1518, LW 48:56, and below, pp. 71–72. The charge that Luther was "inflamed by private lust" was a common one among Luther's opponents in the 1520s: see Thomas Fudge, "Incest and Lust in Luther's Marriage: Theology and Morality in Reformation Polemics," *SCJ* 34, no. 2 (2003): 334–44; cf. the 1539 *Monachopornomachia* of Simon Lemnius

It would have been helpful to have these things set forth and recalled in their entirety and at length by the man himself. For even if the ill-disposed would have objected with the common saying, Αὐτὸς αὐτὸν αὐλεῖ ["He toots his own horn"],[5] we know nevertheless that he was a man possessed of such seriousness that he would have narrated the history with the utmost fidelity. And many good and wise men are still living who (as he knew) were aware of the sequence of these events and would have found it ridiculous if some other story had been mixed in, as sometimes happens in poems. But because the day of his death came before the publication of this volume, we shall offer a good-faith account ourselves, dealing with the matters which we have in part heard from him and have in part witnessed ourselves.

His is an old and widely propagated family, of people of middling station, in the domain of the illustrious counts of Mansfeld. Martin Luther's parents first made their home in the town of Eisleben, where he was born, and then moved to the town of Mansfeld, where his father, Hans Luther, held offices and was, because of his integrity, well esteemed by all good people.[6]

In his mother, Margaretha, the wife of Hans Luther, there existed all the virtues befitting an honorable matron, but her modesty, reverence for God, and prayer shone forth especially brightly, and the other honorable women looked to her as a model of virtues.[7] When I asked her on several occasions about the time of her son's birth, she answered me that she remembered the day and hour exactly, but was uncertain of the year.[8] However, she affirmed that he was born the night of November the tenth after eleven o'clock, and that the name Martin was given to the infant because the next day, on which the infant was grafted into the Church of God through Baptism, had been St. Martin's Day.[9] His brother Jacob, an honest and upright man, said that the

---

(see below, Mathesius, *History*, pp. 410–11); Cochlaeus, *Deeds and Writings of Dr. Martin Luther*, in Vandiver et al., *Luther's Lives*, p. 130.

[5] Erasmus, *Adages* 2.5.86 (CWE 33:279).

[6] Luther's father, Hans Luder (1459–1530), was born a peasant farmer but became the owner of a mine and gained higher status as a result; he held office supervising the local mines on behalf of the counts of Mansfeld: see *Table Talk* no. 5362 (1540), WA TR 5:95; Hendrix, *Luther: Visionary Reformer*, p. 19. On the varying spellings of Luther's name, see below, Mathesius, *History*, p. 114 and n. 2 there.

[7] Luther's mother, Margaretha Luder, née Lindemann (ca. 1459–1531), was from a family of burghers originating in Neustadt an der Saale, in Bavaria, who had settled in Eisenach at least by the time of Margaretha's childhood (cf. below, p. 58). On Luther's mother and the debate over her maiden name, see Siggins, *Luther and His Mother*.

[8] See the introduction above, pp. liv–lv.

[9] On Martin of Tours, whose feast day was November 11, see above, p. 34 n. 23; and below, p. 117 n. 13.

family's opinion of his brother's age was that he had been born in the year 1483 after Christ's birth.[10]

Once he had reached an age capable of being taught, his parents diligently accustomed their son Martin to the knowledge and fear of God and to the practice of the other virtues through their household instruction; and, as is the custom of honorable people, they saw to it that he learned to read and write. ¹Since he was still a little boy, the father of Georg Aemilius carried him to school—and this man, since he is still living, can testify to the truth of this account.[11]

Now, at that time the grammar schools in the towns of Saxony[12] were enjoying something of a renaissance.[13] Therefore, when Martin reached his fourteenth year, he was sent to Magdeburg together with Johann Reinecke, who was later a man of outstanding virtue and enjoyed in these regions the great authority born of such virtue.[14] There was always the greatest goodwill between these two men, Luther and Reinecke, whether by some natural sympathy or arising from their companionship during their childhood studies. Nevertheless, Luther did not remain in Magdeburg longer than a year.

He next studied in the school at Eisenach for four years with an instructor who taught grammar more correctly and skillfully than others elsewhere,

---

[10] On Jacob Luther, see Siggins, *Luther and His Mother*, p. 14. On Luther's date of birth, see the introduction above, pp. liv–lv and nn. 182–83 there.

[11] Nicholas Oemler (ca. 1475–1555) would have been a schoolboy a few years older than Luther and eventually came to be related to the reformer somehow through marriage, though the point of connection is uncertain: see Luther, inscription no. 189 (1544), WA 48:144–45. Oemler's son Georg (1517–69), from his marriage to Anna Reinecke (the sister of Johann Reinecke: see below, n. 14), had (at the time of the composition of Melanchthon's preface) recently studied in Wittenberg, adopting the humanist name Aemilius (Ämylius: see MBW T7:84–88, no. 1717) and obtaining his master's degree in 1537 before taking up a position as rector of the Latin school in Siegen in 1540: see Luther to Joachim of Anhalt, May 20, 1539, and April 13, 1540, WA Br 8:430–33; Melanchthon to Nicholas Öhmler, January 4, 1537, and October 7, 1537, MBW T7:323, 528–29. On Georg Oemler, see Friedrich Wilhelm Bautz, "Aemilius, Georg," *BBKL* 1:47; Joachim Kirchner, "Aemilius, Georg," *NDB* 1:90–91. On the school in Mansfeld, see below, p. 117 n. 15.

[12] I.e., the larger historical region of Saxony, of which Magdeburg was a part, not the territory of the Saxon duchies as they existed at the end of the fifteenth century.

[13] *Florebant . . . mediocriter.* Reading *florebant* with MBW and Witt Lat 2 for CR *florebunt.*

[14] Johann [Hans] Reinecke (ca. 1483–1538), the son of a Mansfeld smeltermaster, was a close childhood friend of Luther. He eventually took over Hans Luther's business and office under the Mansfeld counts. Luther and Reinecke remained friends; it was Reinecke who informed Luther of his father's death in 1530. Cf. LW 49:318–19 n. 16; Luther to Melanchthon, June 5, 1530, LW 49:316–19; Veit Dietrich to Katharina Luther, June 19, 1530, WA Br 5:379; Luther to Philipp Gluenspiess, September 1, 1538, WA Br 8:280. Luther and Melanchthon sent Reinecke a joint letter of consolation upon the death of his wife: April 19, 1536, WA Br 7:399–400.

for I remember that Luther praised[15] his intelligence.[16] He was sent to that city because his mother had been born in that region of a respectable and old family.[17] Here he completed his elementary studies.[18] Since he had an exceedingly sharp intellect and a special aptitude for eloquence, he quickly surpassed his peers. He readily excelled the rest of the youth who were studying with him at the time, not only in his vocabulary and richness of expression in speaking but also in writing both prose and verse.

Therefore, having tasted the sweetness of literature, and being ardent by nature with the desire for learning, he sought out the university,[19] as the fountain of all teaching. His great power of intellect would have been capable of grasping all the arts in proper order, if only he had found suitable teachers. And perhaps the gentler studies of true philosophy and a care for forming [eloquent] speech[20] would have helped to temper the fervency of his nature. But what he encountered at Erfurt in that era was a rather thorny instruction in dialectics. He took it in quickly, since with his penetrating intellect he discerned the causes and sources of the precepts better than the other students.

Since his mind, being eager to learn, was always seeking out more and better things, he read on his own[21] most of the writings of the ancient Latin writers: Cicero, Virgil, Livy, and others.[22] He would read them not as boys do, picking out the words only, but as lessons for human life. Therefore, he was more concerned to examine the advice and the ideas of these writers, and because he had a reliable and good memory, most of the things he had read or heard [he retained] as if they were lying open before his eyes. Thus,

---

[15] In later collected editions of Melanchthon's works: "spoke favorably of [*probari*]."

[16] The Eisenach teacher praised by Luther was Wigand Güldenapf. See Luther to Duke John Frederick, May 14, 1526, WA Br 4:74–75; Brecht 1:19–20.

[17] See above, p. 56 n. 7.

[18] *grammaticum studium*

[19] *academiam*

[20] I.e., the humanist studies [*studia humaniora*] of ethics and rhetoric. On humanist instruction at Erfurt, see below, Mathesius, *History*, pp. 119–20.

[21] *ipse*

[22] Luther later complained that he had not read more of the classical poets and historians: see *To the Councilmen of All Cities in Germany* (1524), LW 45:370, though in *Table Talk* no. 116 (1531), LW 54:14, he mentions having brought copies of Plautus (ca. 254–184 BC) and Virgil into the Augustinian cloister with him. For a survey of Luther's familiarity with classical authors, see Carl P. E. Springer, *Luther's Aesop* (Kirksville, MO: Truman State University Press, 2011), pp. 12–15.

in his youth, Luther was so outstanding that his intelligence was cause for amazement by the entire university.[23]

Therefore, having been awarded the degree of master of philosophy, he began the study of law at the age of twenty, on the advice of his relatives, who thought that so great a power of intelligence and such eloquence should be brought forth into the light for the benefit of the state. However, a short time later, at the age of twenty-one, against the wishes of his parents and friends,[24] he suddenly went to the convent[25] of Augustinian monks[26] at Erfurt and petitioned to be received. Once he had been received, he not only devoted himself with the keenest interest to learning the Church's doctrine but also gained self-mastery by the strictest discipline, and in all the exercises of reading, disputing,[27] fasting, and praying he by far surpassed the others. Now, he was by nature moderate in his need for food and drink, at which I often marveled, seeing that he was neither slight nor feeble in body. I saw him, even when he was in good health, taking no food or drink for four days straight. Otherwise I often saw him content for many days with a tiny bit of bread and a herring each day.

The occasion for his entrance into this kind of life, which he deemed more conducive to piety and more suitable for theological studies, was the following, as he himself recounted and as many are aware: Often, when he was attentively contemplating the wrath of God or singular examples of [divine] punishments, he was suddenly so deeply troubled by great terrors that he nearly died. I myself once observed him, stretched to the limit by exertion in the midst of a certain disputation over doctrine, going into the nearby room to lie down on the bed, where he mixed the following verse, frequently repeated, into his prayer: "For God has concluded all in disobedience, that He might have mercy upon all" [Rom. 11:32]. He felt those terrors

---

[23] Luther ranked second in his class for the master's degree: see Brecht 1:33–34.

[24] *propinquorum*; or: "relatives." Other accounts mention the opposition of Luther's father and his university friends: see *Table Talk* no. 4707 (1539), WA TR 4:440; Brecht 1:50.

[25] Reading *collegium* with MBW T15:300 and Witt Lat 2 for CR *colloquium* ["conversation"]. Melanchthon is probably using the word *collegium* as a classical Latin term for a monastic community (see, e.g., DuCange 2:407a) rather than in the later medieval academic sense of "college," though the Augustinian houses at Erfurt and Wittenberg were both enmeshed with the universities there.

[26] *Monachorum*, used as a general term, though, technically speaking, the Augustinian Hermits were not monks but mendicant friars.

[27] *exercitiis ... disputationum*, possibly in a classical Latin sense of "meditation[s]," but more likely a reference to the practice of academic disputation in the universities.

either for the first time or most sharply in that year, when he lost a companion—I do not know the circumstances.[28]

Therefore, it was not poverty but zeal for piety that led him into this kind of monastic life. Although he was daily engaged there in learning the customary doctrine of the schools and in reading the commentators on the *Sentences*,[29] in skillfully untangling labyrinths no others could escape in public disputations, to the admiration of many, nevertheless, since he was not seeking in that kind of life to win a reputation for cleverness but to nourish piety, he treated these studies as a side pursuit, quickly picking up those scholastic methods. Meanwhile, on his own[30] he was avidly reading the sources of the heavenly doctrine, namely, the writings of the prophets and the apostles, in order to inform his mind about the will of God and to nourish his reverence[31] and faith with firm testimonies. His sorrows and fears[32] moved him to pursue this study all the more.

He used to recount that he was often strengthened by the words of an old man in the Augustinian convent[33] at Erfurt.[34] When he laid out his troubles to this man, he heard him talk a great deal about faith and said that he was led to the Creed, in which is said, "I believe in . . . the remission of

---

[28] On the crisis of the year 1505, see Brecht 1:46–48. On the death of one of Luther's fellows at the university, see below, Mathesius, *History*, p. 122 and n. 45 there.

[29] The *Sentences* by Peter Lombard (ca. 1095–1160), a professor in the schools of Paris (and later bishop of Paris), surveyed questions in Christian theology, collating the opinions [*sententiae*] of the church fathers and passages of Scripture to explore apparent tensions or contradictions in order to arrive at a well-supported synthetic resolution. See PL 192; *The Sentences*, trans. Giulio Silano, 4 vols. (Toronto: Pontifical Institute of Medieval Studies, 2007–10). Lombard's *Sentences* became the basic theological textbook for the rest of the Middle Ages and were lectured on by virtually all later teachers of theology. Luther gave lectures on the *Sentences* in 1509–10 and again in 1511: see the preserved notes in WA 9:29–94 (LW 70). Luther's mature opinion of Lombard was critical but not altogether dismissive: see *Table Talk* no. 192 (1532), LW 54:26; no. 3698 (1538), LW 54:260–61. On the medieval commentators on the *Sentences* whom Luther read, see below, pp. 62–63.

[30] *ipse*

[31] *timor*

[32] *doloribus et pavoribus*. Probably a circumlocution for *Anfechtung*: see above, Jonas and Coelius, *Report*, p. 9; Melanchthon, *Oration*, p. 44; and below, Mathesius, *History*, pp. 258–59.

[33] *Collegio*; see above, p. 59 n. 25.

[34] The old friar who served as Luther's confessor was Johann Greffenstein [Grevenstein], the master of the novices at Erfurt, for whom Luther often expressed his appreciation. See *On Eck's New Bull and Lies* (1520), WA 6:591 (LW 71); *Table Talk* no. 461 (1533), LW 54:74–77 (cf. WA TR 1:200–201); letter to Elector John Frederick, June 10, 1540, *LSC*, pp. 288–91 (cf. WA Br 9:133–34); Brecht 1:57, 59–61. Cf. below, Mathesius, *History*, pp. 124–25. On this episode, see Posset, *The Real Luther*, pp. 90–99.

sins."[35] The old man interpreted this article to mean that it was not only to be believed in general that some people are forgiven, just as "even the demons believe" [James 2:19] that David or Peter had been forgiven, but that it was God's commandment that each of us human beings individually should believe that our sins are forgiven. And [Luther] said[36] that this interpretation was confirmed by a saying of Bernard,[37] and that [he] was shown the passage in a sermon on the annunciation where these words are found: "But add thereto that you believe this as well: that through Him your sins are forgiven YOU.[38] This is the testimony that the Holy Spirit bears in your heart [Rom. 8:16], saying, 'Your sins are forgiven you' [1 John 2:12; Matt. 9:5]. For thus the apostle concludes that 'a man is justified freely by faith' [Rom. 3:24, 28]."[39]

Luther said that he was not only strengthened by these words[40] but also moved to consider the whole meaning of St. Paul, who so often inculcates this maxim: "By faith we are justified" [Rom. 3:26–30; 5:1; 10:4; Gal. 2:16; 3:24; Phil. 3:9]. [Luther said that], having read many expositions of this [maxim], he began, on the basis both of this man's words and of the comfort he found for his own mind, to discern the emptiness[41] of the interpretations that enjoyed currency at that time. Little by little, as he read and compared the sayings and examples which are recorded in the prophets and apostles, and as he kindled his faith in daily prayer, he gained more light.

Then he also began to read the works of Augustine, where he found many clear statements, both in the *Explanations of the Psalms* and in *On the Spirit and the Letter*,[42] which confirmed this doctrine concerning faith and

---

[35] Apostles' Creed (Kolb-Wengert, p. 22; *Concordia*, p. 16).

[36] *dicebat*, an imperfect verb like *narrabat* ("used to recount") which introduces Luther's account, unlike the perfect tenses that describe the old friar's actions.

[37] Bernard of Clairvaux, whose theology Luther highly prized; see above, p. lvi n. 191.

[38] In Witt Lat 2 (1546), fol. †3v, as in CR, the word "you" [*TIBI*] is given in all capital letters for emphasis.

[39] Bernard of Clairvaux, *Sermo in Festo Annunciationis Beatae Mariae Virginis* 1.3 (PL 183:384; CF 52:64). Cf. below, Mathesius, *History*, pp. 124–25.

[40] *hac voce*

[41] *vanitatem*

[42] Augustine, *Explanations of the Psalms* (PL 36–37; WSA 3/14–17; cf. NPNF[1] 8:1–683); *On the Spirit and the Letter* (PL 44:199–246; WSA 1/23:140–202; NPNF[1] 5:80–114; LCC 8:182–250). For Luther's appreciation and use of *On the Spirit and the Letter*, see his preface to Augustine, *On the Spirit and the Letter* (1533?), LW 60:35–44; letter to Spalatin, October 19, 1516, LW 48:24; to Johann Lang, May 18, 1517, LW 48:42; the section "Concerning the Letter and the Spirit" in *Answer to Emser* (1521), LW 39:175–203; *Preface to the Latin Writings* (1545), LW 34:337; and *Lectures on Romans* (1515–16/1938–39), LW 25 (WA 56–57). Luther's use of Augustine's *Explanations* is evident throughout *First Lectures on the Psalms*

the consolation that had been kindled in his own heart. Nevertheless, he did not completely abandon the commentators on the *Sentences*.[43] He was able to quote Gabriel[44] and the [bishop of] Cambrai by heart, almost word for word.[45] He long devoted himself to intensive reading of the writings of Ockham,[46] whose acuity he preferred to Thomas[47] and Scotus.[48] He had

---

(1513–15/1743–1876): see the annotations in WA 55/1–2; cf. LW 10–11 (though the LW notes do not track the influence of Augustine until vol. 11). On a similar claim about Luther's reading of Augustine's *On the Trinity* (PL 42; CCSL 50A; WSA 1/5; NPNF¹ 3), see Lohrmann, "Newly Discovered Report of Luther's Reformation Breakthrough," pp. 324–30.

[43] See above, p. 60.

[44] The Tübingen theologian Gabriel Biel (ca. 1410–95; see Siegfried Hoyer, "Biel, Gabriel," *OER* 1:172–73) had composed a commentary on the *Sentences* based on the work of William of Ockham (below, n. 46): *Collectorium circa quattuor libros Sententiarum* (1501) (ed. Hans Rückert et al., 4 vols. in 5 [Tübingen: Mohr Siebeck, 1973–92]). Luther was also deeply familiar with Biel's theological commentary on the Canon of the Mass: *Canonis Misse expositio* (ed. Heiko A. Oberman and William J. Courtenay, 4 vols. [Wiesbaden: Steiner, 1963–67]). Cf. Luther, *Table Talk* no. 3722 (1538), LW 54:264. See Heiko A. Oberman, *The Harvest of Medieval Theology: Gabriel Biel and Late Medieval Nominalism* (Cambridge, MA: Harvard University Press, 1963).

[45] I.e., Pierre d'Ailly (ca. 1350–1420), cardinal bishop of Cambrai and rector of the University of Paris, who took an important role in the conciliar movement to end the papal schism of the fourteenth century. See *ODCC*, 3rd ed., s.v. "d'Ailly, Pierre." For d'Ailly's commentary on Lombard's *Sentences*, see *Petri de Alliaco Questiones super primum, tertium et quartum librum Sententiarum* (ed. Monica Brinzei, CCCM 258 [Turnhout: Brepols, 2013], and other volumes forthcoming). For Luther's use of d'Ailly, see *Babylonian Captivity* (1520), LW 36:28–29.

[46] William of Ockham (ca. 1285–ca. 1348) was a Franciscan theologian who taught at Oxford and Paris and was the leading theologian of the Nominalist school or *via moderna*, to which Biel and d'Ailly later belonged. See Edward A. Synan, "Ockhamism," *OER* 3:167–68. Luther hailed him as "my dear master" even as he sharply criticized his soteriology: see *Exhortation to All Clergy* (1530), LW 34:27. Ockham's lectures on the *Sentences* are preserved as the *Ordinatio* or *Scriptum* on the first book of the *Sentences* and the *Reportatio* on books 2–4: see Gedeon Gál et al., eds., *Guillelmi de Ockham opera theologica*, vols. 1–7 (St. Bonaventure, NY: Franciscan Institute, 1967–86).

[47] Thomas Aquinas (ca. 1225–74), a Dominican who taught at the University of Paris, was an important theologian within his own order but not regarded in this period as a universal and normative authority. See Bernd Kettern, "Thomas von Aquin," *BBKL* 11:1324–70; *ODCC*, 3rd ed., s.v. "Thomas Aquinas." Luther's opinion of Thomas was almost entirely negative: see, e.g., *Against Latomus* (1521), LW 32:257–58; *Against King Henry of England* (1522), WA 10/2:180–222 (LW 61); *Wider den neuen Abgott* (1524), WA 15:184. Cf. Dennis Janz, *Luther on Thomas Aquinas* (Stuttgart: Steiner, 1989).

[48] John Duns Scotus (ca. 1265–1308) was a Franciscan theologian who taught at Oxford, Paris, and Cologne. See *ODCC*, 3rd ed., s.v. "Duns Scotus, Johannes." His most complete commentary on the *Sentences* is the *Ordinatio* based on his Paris lectures: see Carolus Balić, ed., *Ioannis Duns Scoti opera omnia*, vols. 1–15 (Vatican City: Typis polyglottis, 1950–2004); Scotus' older Oxford lectures on the *Sentences* are found in vols. 16–21. Cf. Allan B. Wolter and Oleg Bychkov, trans., *The Examined Report of the Paris Lecture, Reportatio I-A*, 2 vols. (St. Bonaventure, NY: Franciscan Institute, 2004–8). Together with Aquinas, Scotus

carefully read Gerson as well.[49] But all the works of Augustine he not only read frequently but also remembered best.

He began this intensive study at Erfurt, where he stayed for four years in the Augustinian convent.[50]

|At this time, the Reverend Staupitz,[51] who had helped with the founding of the University of Wittenberg,[52] was eager to promote the study of theology in the new university, and in consideration of Luther's intelligence and learning, he transferred him to Wittenberg, in 1508, at the age of twenty-six. Here, amid the daily exercises of the school and of preaching, his native intelligence began to shine forth even more. Whenever wise men, such as Doctor Martin [Pollich von] Mellerstadt[53] and others, would listen to him attentively, Mellerstadt often said that there was so great an intellectual power in

represented the *via antiqua* of theologians embracing metaphysical realism who were opposed by the Nominalists of the *via moderna*. Luther's opinion of Scotus was mixed, criticizing him for teaching that human beings were able to love God by their natural powers, though he preferred Scotus to Thomas: see *Table Talk* no. 280 (1532), LW 54:38–39; *Explanations of the Theses Debated at Leipzig* (1519), WA 2:403 (LW 71); *Table Talk* no. 1745 (1532), WA TR 2:202; no. 4807 (1542), WA TR 4:526.

[49] Jean Gerson (1363–1429), a student of d'Ailly (see above, p. 62 n. 45) and later chancellor of the University of Paris and a participant in the conciliar movement, advocated a union of mystical theology with scholasticism. See *ODCC*, 3rd ed., s.v. "Gerson, Jean le Charlier de." For his work, see Steven E. Ozment, ed. and trans., *Jean Gerson: Selections from A Deo exivit, Contra curiositatem studentium and De mystica theologia speculativa* (Leiden: Brill, 1969). Luther's later opinion of him was generally good: see *Table Talk* no. 5523 (1542–43), LW 54:443; *Commentary on Psalm 90* (1534–35/1541), LW 13:113; and *Lectures on Galatians* (1531/1535), LW 27:81. Cf. Steven E. Ozment, *Homo Spiritualis: A Comparative Study of the Anthropology of Johannes Tauler, Jean Gerson, and Martin Luther (1509–16) in the Context of Their Theological Thought* (Leiden: Brill, 1969). Ockham, d'Ailly, Gerson, and Biel may be grouped together as Nominalists, or representatives of the *via moderna*: see below, Mathesius, *History*, p. 135; cf. below, *History*, pp. 126, 456–57, 520. For this whole catalog of Luther's early theological reading and his criticism and appreciation of the scholastic theologians, see *Table Talk* no. 3722 (1538), LW 54:264; cf. the *Disputation against Scholastic Theology* (1517), LW 31:3–16.

[50] *In cuius urbis collegio Augustiniania*; see above, p. 59 n. 25. On Luther's time in Erfurt, see below, Mathesius, *History*, pp. 122–25.

[51] On Staupitz, see above, p. lvi n. 194.

[52] See below, Mathesius, *History*, pp. 125–26.

[53] Martin Pollich von Mellerstadt (ca. 1455–1513) was a polymath doctor who began serving as Elector Frederick's personal physician in 1492 and accompanied him to the Holy Land the following year. He was the first rector of the University of Wittenberg and a supporter of humanism. See Maria Grossmann, *Humanism in Wittenberg, 1485–1517* (Nieuwkoop: de Graaf, 1975), pp. 41–47; Ernest Schwiebert, *The Reformation*, 2 vols. (Minneapolis: Fortress, 1997), 2:220–21; Theodor Grüneberg, "Martin Pollich von Mellerstadt, der erste Rektor der Wittenberger Universität," in *450 Jahre Martin-Luther-Universität Halle-Wittenberg* (Halle: Universität Halle-Wittenberg, 1952), 1:87–91; Helmut Schlereth, "Pollich, Martin," *NDB* 20:605–6. Cf. below, Mathesius, *History*, pp. 125, 127, 577–80.

that man that he clearly foresaw that he would change the traditional form of teaching, which was the only one being conveyed in the schools at that time.

Here [in Wittenberg] he lectured first on Aristotle's dialectics and physics,[54] yet all the while he did not abandon his aforementioned zeal for reading theological writings.[55] After three years he made a trip to Rome, on account of controversies among the monks.[56] In the same year that he returned, he was adorned with his doctoral degree, as we say, at the expense of Duke Frederick, the elector of Saxony.[57] He had heard Luther preach and had marveled at the power of his intellect, the vigor of his speech, and the excellence of his explications in preaching. And so that you may see that the doctor's degree was awarded to him for maturity [not of years but] of judgment,[58] you should know that this was in the thirtieth year of Luther's life. He told us that he was ordered by Staupitz to allow himself to be awarded this degree, though he himself was quite reluctant. Staupitz jokingly said that God would have a great deal of business to take care of in the Church, for which he would make use of [Luther's] help. This statement, even though it was uttered in jest at that time, corresponded to the ensuing events, even as many signs [usually] anticipate changes[59] to come.[60]

Afterward, he began to comment on the Epistle to the Romans, and then on the Psalms.[61] He clarified these writings in such a way that it seemed

---

[54] I.e., Aristotle's (384–322 BC) works on logic (the "Organon," Loeb 325, 391) and *Physics* (Loeb 228, 255). In fact, Luther's earliest lectures in 1508–9 seem to have been on Aristotle's *Nicomachean Ethics* (Loeb 73). See below, Mathesius, *History*, p. 126 and n. 69 there. Luther did at least prepare notes on Aristotle's *Physics* in 1517, as he writes in his letter to Johann Lang, February 8, 1517, LW 48:36–38.

[55] Cf. Luther to Johann Braun, March 17, 1509, WA Br 1:16–17.

[56] On the debate over the dating and purpose of Luther's trip to Rome, see above, p. lvii n. 196; cf. below, Mathesius, *History*, pp. 127–28. Melanchthon's description here of a trip beginning three years after the start of Luther's lecturing and ending in the same year he received his doctorate supports a date of 1511–12 for the trip to Rome.

[57] Luther received his doctorate on October 18, 1512: see below, Mathesius, *History*, pp. 128–29.

[58] *Quadam quasi maturitate iudicii.* Thirty was relatively young, though not unheard of, for promotion to the doctorate.

[59] *ut multa praecedunt mutationes praesagia.* On *mutationes*, see below, p. 71 n. 102, p. 74 n. 118, p. 77 n. 136.

[60] On this exchange with Staupitz, see below, Mathesius, *History*, pp. 128–29. For other *praesagia* of Luther's significance, see below, Mathesius, *History*, pp. 120–22, 145–46, 554–58, 582–89, 599.

[61] *Postea enarrare epistolam ad Romanos coepit, deinde Psalmos.* On the exegetical meaning of *enarratio*, see Kenneth Hagen, "Commentary as 'Enarratio,'" in *Luther's Approach to Scripture as Seen in His "Commentaries" on Galatians 1519–1538* (Tübingen: Mohr, 1993), pp. 49–66. For Luther's *Lectures on Romans* (1515–16/1938–39), see LW 25 (WA 56). Melanchthon

in the judgment of all the pious and wise that a new light of doctrine was rising after a long, dark night. Here he pointed out the essential difference between Law and Gospel; here he refuted the error which was prevalent at that time in the schools and in the pulpits, which teaches that human beings merit forgiveness of sins by their own works and that human beings are righteous before God by virtue of keeping a particular mode of life,[62] as the Pharisees taught [cf. Matt. 15:1–9]. Luther thus summoned people's minds back to the Son of God, ¹and, like the Baptist,[63] he pointed to the Lamb of God, who takes away our sins [John 1:29]. He showed that sins are forgiven freely, for the sake of the Son of God, and that this favor must be received by faith. He clarified the other parts of the Church's doctrine as well.

Having begun in this way, dealing with the most important themes, he came to be endowed with great authority, particularly since his character agreed with his speech as a teacher, and his speech seemed to be born not from his lips, but from his heart. Admiration for his life produced great sympathy toward him in the minds of his hearers, as the ancient authors, too, have said, "Moral character, so to speak, constitutes the most effective means of proof."[64] That is why, later, when he introduced changes in certain received ceremonies, honorable men who were acquainted with him did not stand in such vehement opposition because of the authority which he had previously acquired by the way he had clarified important matters and by the sanctity of his character. They agreed with him in the very positions by which they saw, with great sadness, that the world was being divided.

At that time, however, Luther made no changes in the ceremonies, being, instead, a strict guardian of discipline within his own [order];[65] neither did he mingle any shocking opinions [into his teaching]. Instead, he clarified more and more for everyone the universal and absolutely necessary doctrine: concerning penance, the remission of sins, faith, and the true consolations [to be found] in the cross. All the pious were wholly captivated by the sweetness of this doctrine, and the learned were pleased that Christ, the prophets, and the apostles were being (so to speak) led out of darkness,

---

apparently omits mention of Luther's *First Lectures on the Psalms* (1513–15/1743–1876), LW 10–11 (WA 55/1–2). Luther's second set of lectures on the Psalms, the *Labors on the Psalms* [*Operationes in Psalmos*], were given in 1518–21: WA 5 (LW 64–65); WA Ar 1–3 (cf. LW 14:279–349).

[62] *disciplina*; or: "custom."

[63] Cf. the introduction above, p. xlviii; below, Walter, *New Spiritual Song*, p. 91, stanza 29.

[64] σχεδὸν ὡς εἰπεῖν κυριωτάτην ἔχει πίστιν τὸ ἦθος: Aristotle, *Art of Rhetoric* 1, 1356a (Loeb 193 [1926], pp. 16–17).

[65] *inter suos*. In 1515, Luther was elected provincial vicar of the Observant Augustinians in Meissen and Thuringia. See Brecht 1:156–60; Hendrix, *Luther: Visionary Reformer*, pp. 45–46.

prison, and squalor; that the distinction between Law and Gospel, between the promises of the Law and the promise of the Gospel, between philosophy and the Gospel,[66] and between spiritual righteousness and [righteousness] in political matters[67] were being brought to light—something certainly not present in Thomas, Scotus, and others like them.

In addition to this, Erasmus[68] had in his writings attracted many young people to the study of Latin and Greek.[69] Many of them who were endowed with good and free minds, having been shown the sweeter kind of doctrine, began to abhor the barbaric and sophistic doctrine of the monks.

Luther also began to dedicate himself to the study of Greek and Hebrew, so that having learned the character of [each] language and its diction, he might also be able to form a more accurate judgment of the doctrine he had drawn from these sources.[70]

While Luther was engaged in this course, indulgences were being circulated for sale in these regions by the Dominican Tetzel,[71] an utterly shameless

---

[66] See, e.g., *Disputation against Scholastic Theology* (1517), especially Theses 39–53, LW 31:11–13; *Heidelberg Disputation* (1518), LW 31:39–70.

[67] Political or civil righteousness is the righteousness by which human beings deserve praise or condemnation in their society with one another, yet it is not (according to Luther) the righteousness that avails before God. See *Lectures on Isaiah* (1527–30/1532–34), LW 17:63; *Lectures on Galatians* (1531/1535), LW 26:183; *Disputation concerning Justification* (1536), LW 34:184, 196; also Melanchthon, Ap II 12, 43; IV 22–24; XVIII 4 [70] (Kolb-Wengert, pp. 114, 118–19, 124, 233–34; *Concordia*, pp. 77–78, 80–81, 86, 197–98).

[68] On Erasmus, see above, p. xix n. 16.

[69] Cf. Erasmus, *Enchiridion* (CWE 66:127); Erasmus to Martin Dorp, CWE 3:130.

[70] On Luther's own early study and use of Greek and Hebrew, see Brecht 1:42–43, 47–48, 82–90. Luther joined the call for study of the biblical languages as the foundation of theological education: see *To the Councilmen of All Cities in Germany* (1524), LW 45:339–78, though he insisted that linguistic knowledge was not enough without faithful theology, as the examples of Jerome (ca. 345–420) and Augustine showed: see Luther to Spalatin, October 19, 1516, LW 48:24–25; and to Johann Lang, March 1, 1517, LW 48:39–41.

[71] Johann Tetzel (1465–1519) was a Dominican who had studied theology at Leipzig and at Frankfurt an der Oder, where he would be awarded the doctorate in 1518. He taught at the Dominican *studium* in Leipzig. After working successfully as an inquisitor and indulgence preacher across central Europe, he was appointed indulgence commissioner by Albert of Brandenburg in 1516. After Luther's publication of the *Ninety-Five Theses* (see below, p. 67), Tetzel sought to defend the established theology and practice of indulgences in both academic and popular forums. He died of the plague at Leipzig in 1519. See Jeff Bach, "Tetzel, Johann," *OER* 4:149; Pettegree, *Brand Luther*, pp. 77–83; David V. N. Bagchi, *Luther's Earliest Opponents: Catholic Controversialists, 1518–1525* (Minneapolis: Fortress, 1991), pp. 17–35. For Tetzel's own writing, see Peter Fabisch and Erwin Iserloh, eds., *Dokumente zur Causa Lutheri (1517–1521)* (Münster: Aschendorff, 1988), 1:310–75; Dewey Kramer, ed. and trans., *Johann Tetzel's Rebuttal against Luther's Sermon on Indulgences and Grace* (Atlanta: Pitts Theology Library, 2012).

trickster.[72] His impious and abominable sermons provoked Luther, who was burning with zeal for piety, to issue his *Propositions ⌐concerning Indulgences*, which are to be found in the first volume of his [Latin] writings.[73] And he publicly affixed these to the church[74] adjacent to the Wittenberg castle on the eve of All Saints' Day in the year 1517.[75] At this, Tetzel, true to his own character and also hoping to obtain favor for himself with the Roman pontiff, summons his own council[76]—that is, a few friars and theologians who were at least lightly tinged with his sophistry—and he ordered them to put together something against Luther. Meanwhile, Tetzel himself, not wanting to be a silent bystander,[77] now flings not just sermons but thunderbolts against Luther: he cries out everywhere that this heretic must be burned. He even publicly hurls Luther's *Propositions* and the *Sermon on Indulgence* into the flames.[78] It was these ravings of Tetzel and his cronies that made it necessary for Luther to undertake a more expansive discussion of these matters and to defend the truth.[79]

These were the beginnings of this controversy, in which Luther had not the slightest thought or dream of any future change in ceremonies; indeed, he did not even reject indulgences completely, but only urged moderation![80] It is false, therefore, when people accuse him of having begun under a laudable pretext so that afterward he could bring about a revolution in the state

---

[72] *sycophanta*

[73] *Ninety-Five Theses* (1517), LW 31:17–33, included in Witt Lat 1 (1545), fols. 51r–53r.

[74] *templo*

[75] On the question of how Luther made the *Ninety-Five Theses* public, see the introduction above, pp. lvii–lx; cf. below, Mathesius, *History*, pp. 143–46.

[76] *senatum*, a word that could also refer to the assembled faculty of a university. Tetzel held his own public disputation in opposition to Luther's *Ninety-Five Theses* in January 1518 at the Dominican chapter at the University of Frankfurt an der Oder. The theses were prepared by the scholastic theologian Conrad Wimpina (1460–1531), and a verdict in Tetzel's favor was rendered by the university theological faculty. See Pettegree, *Brand Luther*, p. 78; Fabisch and Iserloh, *Dokumente zur Causa Lutheri*, 1:310–37.

[77] κωφὸν πρόσωπον; literally: "a silent mask," a technical term in ancient Greek theater for an actor without a speaking part. See Erasmus, *Adages* 1.10.78 (CWE 32:270).

[78] I.e., the *Ninety-Five Theses* (see above, n. 73) and Luther's *Sermon on Indulgence and Grace* (1517), WA 1:243–46 (LW 70; Hillerbrand et al., *Annotated Luther*, 1:57–66). For Tetzel's threat to consign Luther himself to the flames, see *Table Talk* no. 3846 (1538), WA TR 3:656. The report that Tetzel burned Luther's theses is difficult to confirm. Students in Wittenberg did burn the printing of Tetzel's countertheses: see Pettegree, *Brand Luther*, p. 79.

[79] See Luther, *Explanations of the Ninety-Five Theses* (1518), LW 31:77–252.

[80] See, e.g., *Against Hanswurst* (1541), LW 41:231–32; see also *Sermo de indulgentiis pridie Dedicationis*, January 16 or 17, 1517(?), WA 1:94–99 and 4:670–74 (on dating, see Timothy J. Wengert, "Martin Luther's Preaching an Indulgence in January 1517," *LQ* 29 [2015]: 62–75); *Sermon for St. [Matthias'] Day* (February 24, 1517), LW 51:26–31. Cf. below, p. 142 n. 17.

and seek power either for himself or for others. And it is completely untrue that he was suborned and incited by people at the court, as the duke of Braunschweig wrote,[81] so that even Duke Frederick [the Wise][82] had regretted setting the conflicts in motion, foreseeing that eventually, even though things had taken their origin from a praiseworthy concern, nonetheless little by little this fire would spread more widely, as is said in Homer about Eris: "small at first out of fear, but quickly rising up to the skies."[83]

Frederick was, of all the princes of our age, the one most devoted to public tranquility and the least concerned with his own advantage;[84] and it was his particular habit to refer his plans to the common welfare of the whole world, as can be discerned from many of his undertakings. He neither incited nor applauded Luther, and he frequently gave expression to the concerns which he daily bore, fearing greater dissensions.

Being a wise man, he did not merely follow worldly judgments, which bid that even the tender beginnings of any changes should be suppressed as quickly as possible, but in forming his counsels he also applied the divine standard, which bids that the Gospel should be heard, forbids opposition to the known truth, and which denounces as blasphemy subject to God's terrible condemnation all stubborn resistance to the truth. Therefore, this man did what many other pious and wise men did: he yielded to God; ʰe carefully read the things that were written, and those things he judged to be true he refused to do away with.

I happen to know that [Frederick] often requested the opinions of learned and wise people about these matters. At the diet which Emperor Charles V held in Cologne after his coronation,[85] [Frederick] amicably

---

[81] On Duke Henry of Braunschweig-Wolfenbüttel, see above, p. 27 n. 6. For his accusations about Luther's motives, and Luther's response, see *Against Hanswurst* (1541), LW 41:229-35; cf. Mark Edwards, *Luther's Last Battles: Politics and Polemics, 1531-46* (Ithaca, NY: Cornell University Press, 1983), pp. 143-62. For the accusation, see also above, p. 55.

[82] Frederick III, "The Wise," elector of Saxony (r. 1486-1525), one of the most powerful princes in the Holy Roman Empire, was the founder and patron of the University of Wittenberg and Luther's prince and protector. See Ingetraut Ludolphy, "Frederick III of Saxony," *OER* 2:138-40.

[83] Virgil, *Aeneid* 4.176 (Loeb 63 [1916], pp. 434-35), imitating Homer, *Iliad* 4.440-443 (Loeb 170 [1924], pp. 196-97). Melanchthon gives the name of the goddess Eris ["strife"] in its Latin form [*Lis*].

[84] πλεονεκτικὸς. See Georg Spalatin, *Friedrichs des Weisen: Leben und Zeitgeschichte*, ed. Christian Neudecker and Ludwig Preller (Jena: Mauke: 1851), pp. 24-25.

[85] Charles was crowned as German king in Aachen on October 23, 1520, making him the elected Holy Roman emperor. His papal coronation as emperor would not take place until 1530, in Bologna. See Karl Brandi, *Emperor Charles V*, trans. C. V. Wedgwood (London: Jonathan Cape, 1965), pp. 121-24; cf. below, p. 288 n. 14.

requested Erasmus of Rotterdam[86] to tell him frankly whether he judged that Luther had erred in the controversial matters which he had discussed most.[87] On that occasion Erasmus plainly said that Luther's opinions were correct, but that he wished that there were more gentleness in him.[88] Duke Frederick afterward wrote a very serious letter to Luther about this matter and strongly admonished him to moderate the harshness of his pen.[89]

It is commonly known that Luther promised Cardinal Cajetan that he would remain silent, if [Cajetan] would enjoin silence on his opponents as well.[90] From this it clearly can be seen that, at least at that time, he had no intention of going on to provoke other conflicts but desired tranquility. Instead, he was dragged little by little into other subjects by the uneducated authors who were challenging him from all sides.

Accordingly, there then followed arguments concerning the distinction of divine and human laws and concerning the abominable profanation of the Lord's Supper when it was sold and applied to others.[91] Here a full account of the meaning of sacrifice had to be given and the [proper] use of the Sacraments had to be made plain. And when pious men in the monasteries now heard that [such] idolatry should be shunned, they began to turn away from their impious servitude.

Therefore, Luther added to his explanation of the doctrine of penance, remission of sins, faith, and indulgences the following matters as well: the

---

[86] On Erasmus, see above, p. 66.

[87] The discussion between Frederick and Erasmus took place on November 5, 1520. It is described in Spalatin, *Friedrichs des Weisen*, p. 164; and Luther, *Table Talk* no. 131 (1531), LW 54:19; no. 4899 (1540), WA TR 4:573–74. See Brecht 1:417; cf. below, Mathesius, *History*, p. 133. For the summary opinion ascribed to Erasmus here, see Erasmus, *Minute Composed by a Person Who Seriously Wishes Provisions to Be Made for the Reputation of the Roman Pontiff and the Peace of the Church*, CWE 71:108–12, which was included in Witt Lat 2. Cf. Erasmus to Johannes Reuchlin, November 8, 1520 (in *Opus epistolarum Des. Erasmi Roterdami: Complete Letters of Erasmus*, ed. P. S. Allen [Oxford: Oxford University Press, 1992], 4:370–72, no. 1155).

[88] *Ibi Erasmus plane dixit recte sentire Lutherum, sed lenitatem se in eo desiderare.*

[89] No such letter from Frederick survives; but for the sentiment, cf. Erasmus to Melanchthon, before June 21, 1520 (Allen, *Complete Letters of Erasmus*, 4:287, no. 1113; MBW T1:216–18, no. 97), which Melanchthon forwarded to Spalatin on July 14 (MBW T1:220–21, no. 100); see also Erasmus to Spalatin, July 6, 1520 (Allen, *Complete Letters of Erasmus*, 4:298, no. 1119).

[90] On Tommaso de Vio, Cardinal Cajetan, the papal legate at the Diet of Augsburg in 1518, see below, p. 148 n. 47. On Luther's offer of silence, see Luther to Cajetan, October 17, 1518, WA Br 1:220–22; *Freedom of a Christian* (1520), "Open Letter to Pope Leo X," LW 31:339 (contained in Witt Lat 2).

[91] See, e.g., *Babylonian Captivity* (1520), LW 36:3–126; *Misuse of the Mass* (1521), LW 36:127–230; *Defense and Explanation of All the Articles* (1521), LW 32:3–99; *Abomination of the Secret Mass* (1525, but given as 1523 in Witt Lat 2, fol. 419r), LW 36:307–28, all appearing in their Latin versions in Witt Lat 2.

distinction between divine and human laws, the doctrine of the use of the Lord's Supper and the other sacraments, and of vows.[92] These were the chief points of contention. But Eck raised the issue of the power of the Roman bishop for no other reason than to enkindle the animosity of the pontiff and of the kings against [Luther].[93]

In fact, [Luther] retained the Apostolic, Nicene, and Athanasian Creeds in all their purity;[94] moreover, he fully explained in numerous writings what changes in ceremonies and human traditions needed to be made and why. And what things that he wanted retained as well as the form of doctrine and of the administration of the sacraments that he approved are all clearly apparent from the Confession which Duke John, the elector of Saxony,[95] and Prince Philip, landgrave of Hesse,[96] and others presented to Emperor Charles V in 1530 at the Diet of Augsburg.[97] It is also clearly apparent from the very manner in which the ceremonies of the church are conducted in this city[98] and from the doctrine to which our church gives voice, of which the Augsburg Confession contains a lucid summary. I make mention of this not only so that pious people may think of the errors that Luther rebuked and of the idols he removed, but so that they may also know that he embraced the entirety of doctrine that is necessary for the Church and that he restored purity to the ceremonies and gave pious people examples of how to renew the churches. Thus it is useful for posterity to know about the things to which Luther gave his approval.

---

[92] See, e.g., *Babylonian Captivity* (1520), LW 36:3–126; *Judgment on Monastic Vows* (1521), LW 44:243–400. Both of these were contained in Witt Lat 2.

[93] On the Ingolstadt theologian Johann Eck and the Leipzig Disputation of 1519 (LW 31:307–25), see below, Mathesius, *History*, pp. 154–56.

[94] For these creeds, see the *Book of Concord* (Kolb-Wengert, pp. 21–25; *Concordia*, pp. 16–18). Cf. Luther, *The Three Symbols* (1538), LW 34:197–229.

[95] John the Steadfast, the younger brother of Frederick the Wise, became elector in 1525 and proved a staunch supporter of Luther's Reformation. See Gunda Wittich, "Johann I., der Beständige," *BBKL* 3:174–75.

[96] Landgrave Philip of Hesse (r. 1509–67) became one of the most important lay defenders of Protestantism and a leading organizer of the Smalcaldic League. While supporting Luther, he sought to achieve theological and political reconciliation among different Evangelical factions, as at the Marburg Colloquy in 1529, and between Evangelicals and Catholics, as at the Regensburg Colloquy of 1541 (see below, Mathesius, *History*, pp. 309–13 [Marburg], pp. 491–94 [Regensburg]). Philip's 1540 bigamy, however, compromised his leadership. See William J. Wright, "Philipp of Hesse," *OER* 3:262–63; Hans J. Hillerbrand, *Landgrave Phillip of Hesse, 1504–1567: Religion and Politics in the Reformation* (St. Louis: Foundation for Reformation Research, 1967).

[97] I.e., the Augsburg Confession (1530) (Kolb-Wengert, pp. 27–105; *Concordia*, pp. 27–63).

[98] Probably Wittenberg rather than Augsburg. On the appeal to ceremonies as a witness to doctrine, cf. AC XXIV 1–9 (Kolb-Wengert, pp. 68–69; *Concordia*, pp. 47–48).

At this point I do not want to mention who the people were who first publicly offered the Lord's Supper under both kinds, or who first ceased to hold private Masses, or where monasteries were first abandoned.[99] Luther did not dispute much about these matters prior to the diet that was held in the city of Worms in 1521. He himself did not change the ceremonies; it was Karlstadt and others who changed the ceremonies in his absence.[100] And since Karlstadt had caused more trouble than necessary in doing some of these things, Luther, when he returned, made a declaration of what things he approved and of what he disapproved by publishing clear testimonies of his own opinion.[101]

We know that statesmen vehemently detest all upheavals,[102] and it must be admitted that even those dissensions that are set into motion by the most just causes come to be mingled with some kind of evil amid this sad disorder of human life. Nevertheless, in the Church it is necessary that the commandment of God should be preferred to all human considerations [cf. Acts 5:29]. This is the declaration that the eternal Father has made concerning His Son: "This is My beloved Son; listen to Him" [Mark 9:7].[103] And He threatens eternal wrath against blasphemers, that is, against those who strive to blot out the acknowledged truth. It was thus Luther's pious and necessary duty, especially since he was engaged in teaching the Church of God, to rebuke the pernicious errors which Epicurean men were piling up with unprecedented shamelessness.[104] Moreover, it was incumbent upon his hearers to assent to what he was teaching correctly. Now, if upheaval is odious, if there are many misfortunes in turmoil—as we see with great sadness that there are—then

---

[99] On these developments in Wittenberg in 1521, see below, Mathesius, *History*, pp. 193–200. Melanchthon was, in fact, among the first of those who received the Sacrament in both kinds in Wittenberg, and he, Justus Jonas, and Amsdorf supported the change, along with the Augustinian Gabriel Zwilling (1487–1558): see Brecht 2:26–40. The recommendations of the university committee delegated to consider the change were contained in Witt Lat 2 (1546), fols. 373r–379r.

[100] On Karlstadt, see below, p. 154 n. 90.

[101] See Luther's *Invocavit* sermons of March 1522, LW 51:67–100; also *Sincere Admonition* (1522), LW 45:51–74; and *Concerning the Order of Public Worship* (1523), LW 53:7–14, the last of which appeared in Latin in Witt Lat 2.

[102] *mutationes*; or: "changes," probably here in its political sense. Cf. above, p. 64 n. 59, and below, p. 74 n. 118, and p. 77 n. 136. Cf. Sallust (86–34 BC), *Bellum Jurguthinum* 3.2 (Loeb 116 [2013], pp. 170–71).

[103] Cf. Luther, *Avoiding the Doctrines of Men* (1522), LW 35:135, contained in Witt Lat 2; also *On the Councils and the Church* (1539), LW 41:129–30.

[104] On "Epicurean" as an epithet of theological abuse, see above, Melanchthon, *Oration*, pp. 39–40 and n. 5 there.

it is those who first spread the errors who are to be blamed, as well as those who are now defending those errors with diabolical hatred.

I make mention of these things not only in order to defend Luther and his hearers but also so that pious minds may contemplate, at the present time and hereafter, how the Church of God is and always has been governed: how God by the voice of the Gospel gathers for Himself an eternal Church ᶦfrom that sinful mass,[105] that is, from the great cesspit of humanity, in the midst of which the Gospel shines forth like a spark in the darkness. Just as in the time of the Pharisees there were still Zechariah, Elizabeth, Mary, and many others who preserved the true doctrine, so also in the age preceding our own there were those who called upon God aright and held fast the doctrine of the Gospel, some more clearly and some less so.[106] Such a one was that old man of whom I have spoken, the one who so often lifted Luther up when he was struggling with his fears and at least in some way pointed him toward the doctrine about faith.[107] Therefore, let us pray with fervent pleas that God would preserve the light of the Gospel among many, as Isaiah prays for his listeners: "Seal the Law among my disciples" [Isa. 8:16]. Moreover, this discussion shows that fictive superstitions do not endure but are rooted out by divine power. Since this is what causes upheavals, care must be taken that no errors are taught in the Church.

But I return to Luther. Just as at the start he entered upon this cause without self-serving motivation, so in the same way, despite being by nature fiery and passionate, he remained always mindful of his office and waged his battles only by teaching; he forbade the taking up of arms. Wisely he distinguished between offices utterly different in kind: that of a bishop teaching the Church of God and that of magistrates who restrain the multitude in particular places by the sword.[108]

When at times the devil, who is eager to use scandals to scatter the Church and to bring reproach upon God and who, as one who is ἐπιχαιρέκακος,[109] takes pleasure from the errors and downfall of wretched human beings, inflamed seditious minds to stir up tumult, as he did with Münzer and his

---

[105] *massa peccati*, an Augustinian epithet: see, e.g., Augustine, *De diversis quaestionibus ad Simplicanum* 1.2.16 (PL 40:121; WSA 1/12:198).

[106] On Melanchthon's historical argument for the preservation of the Gospel, see Peter Fraenkel, *Testimonia Patrum: The Function of the Patristic Argument in the Theology of Philip Melanchthon* (Geneva: Droz, 1961).

[107] See above, pp. 60–61.

[108] See Luther, *Temporal Authority* (1523), LW 45:75–129. Cf. AC XXVIII 1–29 (Kolb-Wengert, pp. 90–95; *Concordia*, pp. 58–59).

[109] One who rejoices over another's misfortune. Cf. Aristotle, *Nicomachean Ethics* 2.7.15 (1108b) (Loeb 73 [1926], pp. 104–5).

ilk,[110] then [Luther], accordingly, condemned such raging with the greatest severity.[111] He not only adorned the dignity of the political order but even fortified all its bonds.[112] When I ponder how often many great men in the Church have fallen into delusions in this matter, I come to the conclusion that, manifestly, his heart must have been governed not merely by human diligence but by divine light itself in order for him to have remained with such constancy within the boundaries of his office.

Consequently, he execrated not only the seditious teachers of his time, Münzer and the Anabaptists,[113] but also the bishops of the city of Rome who in the decrees they have issued have claimed with the most brazen shamelessness that Peter was given not only the office of teaching the Gospel but also imperial political authority.[114]

In short, [Luther] exhorted everyone to give to God the things of God, to Caesar the things of Caesar [Matt. 22:21]: that is, that they should worship God with true repentance, with the acknowledgment and propagation of the true doctrine, with true invocation, and with the offices of a good conscience; ʲand that with respect to government each person should reverently, for God's sake, obey his own in all matters of civic duty. And indeed Luther himself was such a man: he gave to God the things of God; he taught properly; he called on God aright. He also possessed the other virtues required in a person who is pleasing to God. Furthermore, in political affairs he shunned all seditious counsels with absolute consistency. I judge these virtues to be of such great dignity that there are none greater that could be desired in this life.

Yet though the virtue of this man, who made reverent use of the gifts of God, is surely worthy of praise, nonetheless we must above all give thanks to God that through him He has restored the light of the Gospel to us, and we must retain and propagate the memory of his teaching. I am not disturbed by the shouts of Epicureans or hypocrites who either ridicule or condemn the manifest truth; rather, I am convinced that the proclamation of doctrine[115]

---

[110] On Thomas Münzer, see below, Mathesius, *History*, pp. 217–26.

[111] See below, Mathesius, *History*, p. 220.

[112] See, e.g., *Temporal Authority* (1523), LW 45:75–129.

[113] On the Anabaptists, see below, Mathesius, *History*, pp. 195–96, 209, 245–47, 380–93.

[114] See Gratian (fl. 1140), *Decretum* dist. 22, c. 1 (Friedberg 1:73; translated in Brian Tierney, *The Crisis of Church and State, 1050–1300* [Englewood Cliffs, NJ: Prentice-Hall, 1964; repr., Toronto: University of Toronto Press, 1988], p. 119). Among Luther's works included in Witt Lat 2, see *Response to Catharinus* (1521), WA 7:705–78 (LW 71), where the passage from the *Decretum* is cited at WA 7:775. Luther's *Explanation of the Thirteenth Thesis on the Authority of the Pope* (1519), WA 2:183–240 (see p. 204) (LW 71), had appeared in Witt Lat 1.

[115] *doctrinae vocem*

that sounds forth in our churches is nothing other than the perpetual consensus of the catholic Church of God,[116] and that the recognition of this teaching must necessarily determine our worship[117] and life. In short, this is the very doctrine of which the Son of God says, "Whoever loves Me will keep My Word, and My Father will love him, and We will come to him and make Our dwelling with him" [John 14:23]. I am speaking of the sum of doctrine as it is understood and explained by the pious and learned in our churches. For though some people explain something more or less properly and elegantly than others at times, or one speaks more roughly than another, there is nevertheless a consensus on the whole in these matters among the pious and learned.

As I have reflected long and deeply upon the [history of] doctrine in all ages since the time of the apostles, it seems to me that after the original state of purity there have followed four notable mutations[118] in doctrine. In the age of Origen[119]—even though there were some who thought in the right way, such as I judge Methodius to have been,[120] who condemned Origen's delusions—nonetheless, in the minds of the multitude, the Gospel was twisted into philosophy. That is, [Origen] spread the idea that a moderate discipline according to reason merited the remission of sins and that this was the righteousness of which it is said, "The righteous shall live by his faith" [Rom. 1:17]. This age almost completely lost the distinction of Law

[116] The 1554 translation into German has *"All gemeyne Kirche Gottes"* ["universal Church of God"]. Cf. AC XXI (Conclusion or Summary) 1 (Kolb-Wengert, pp. 58–61; *Concordia*, pp. 44–45).

[117] *invocationem*

[118] *mutationes*; or: "changes" or "upheavals" (cf. above, p. 64 n. 59, p. 71 n. 102; and below, p. 77 n. 136).

[119] Origen of Alexandria was a prolific but controversial biblical scholar who promoted the allegorical interpretation of the Scriptures as well as a Platonizing speculative approach to theology. See Eusebius (ca. 263–339), *Ecclesiastical History* 6.1–39 (PG 20:519–602; FC 29:3–67; NPNF² 1:249–81; *ODCC*, 3rd ed., s.v. "Origen." For Luther's criticism of Origen, see, e.g., *Babylonian Captivity* (1520), LW 36:30; *Answer to Emser* (1521), LW 39:175; preface to Menius, *Commentary on 1 Samuel* (1532), LW 60:9; *Lectures on Genesis* (1535–45/1544–54), LW 2:150–64.

[120] Methodius of Olympus (d. ca. 311), bishop of Lycia, was one of the first opponents of Origen. See *ODCC*, 3rd ed., s.v. "Methodius of Olympus." His works (PG 18) were not published until the seventeenth century, but Melanchthon would have known of him from Jerome, *De viris illustribus* 83 (PL 23:691–92; NPNF² 3:378–79). Cf. Luther, WA DB 4:356. Melanchthon also knew of a seventh-century commentary on Revelation circulating under Methodius' name, of which Luther also was aware: see Timothy J. Wengert, "Philip Melanchthon and the Jews: A Reappraisal," in *Jews, Judaism, and the Reformation in Sixteenth-Century Germany*, ed. Dean Phillip Bell and Stephen G. Burnett (Leiden: Brill, 2006), pp. 105–35.

and Gospel and unlearned[121] the apostolic Word. For it did not retain the original meaning of the words "letter," "spirit," "righteousness," "faith." And once the proper meaning of a word is lost, ˡsince words serve to designate things, it is necessary to make up other things.[122] It is from those seeds that Pelagius' error arose, which spread so widely.[123] Thus whereas the apostles had given to the Church the pure doctrine, the clear and most salutary well-springs, Origen poured much filth into them.[124]

To correct the errors of that age, at least in part, God raised up Augustine.[125] This man cleaned the springs again to some extent, and I have no doubt that, if this man were judge over the controversies of the present age, we would have him completely on our side.[126] Certainly he is in explicit agreement with us regarding the gratuitous remission [of sins], justification by faith, the use of the Sacraments, and *adiaphora*.[127] Although in some places he explained what he meant more clearly or accurately than in others, nevertheless a reader who brings candor and skill to evaluating him would acknowledge that he thinks as we do. For when our adversaries sometimes cite opinions picked out from [Augustine] against us, and appeal to the fathers with a great clamor, it is not out of zeal for the truth and for

---

[121] *dedidicit*; or "forgot," but the word is an unusual one in Latin as well.

[122] *alias confingi res necesse est*

[123] Pelagius (ca. 354–ca. 418) taught that human beings were born innocent, without original sin, and were able to keep God's Law by their own free will. Augustine opposed him in the fifth century, and Luther regarded the scholastic soteriology of the medieval church as being essentially Pelagian: see, e.g., *Disputation against Scholastic Theology* (1517), LW 31:9, 11; *Heidelberg Disputation* (1518), LW 31:67–68; preface to Augustine, *On the Spirit and the Letter* (1533?), LW 60:43.

[124] On the importance of the definition of central theological terms against their corruption through misuse of philosophy under Origen and others, see Melanchthon, *Commonplaces: Loci Communes (1521)*, pp. 19–25 (cf. LCC 19:19–22). Cf. Timothy J. Wengert, "Famous Last Words: The Final Epistolary Exchange between Erasmus of Rotterdam and Philip Melanchthon in 1536," *Erasmus of Rotterdam Society Yearbook* 25 (2005): 18–38.

[125] Augustine's theology of sin and grace and his denunciation of Pelagius' insistence on the salvific power of human free will were fundamental influences on Luther (see above, p. 42 n. 16).

[126] ὁμόψηφον; literally: "voting together with [us]."

[127] I.e., "things indifferent," neither prohibited nor commanded, such as external ceremonies in the church. The question of the character of *adiaphora* and the propriety of making changes in church ceremonies in response to political coercion by religious enemies would become a controversial question among Lutherans after the military defeat of the Smalcaldic League in 1547 and the imposition of the Augsburg Interim in 1548: see above, p. xxi n. 22. Melanchthon would encounter heavy opposition from within the Lutheran camp for his willingness to accept compromises in external matters under these circumstances. See Kolb and Nestingen, *Sources and Contexts*, pp. 144–96; FC SD X (Kolb-Wengert, pp. 635–40; *Concordia*, pp. 597–602).

antiquity that they do this. Rather, they are deceitfully seeking to cover the present-day idols with the authority of the ancients, to whom the idols of the recent age were still unknown.

It is apparent, however, that the seeds of superstition were already in existence during the age of the fathers. Thus Augustine also laid down certain arrangements concerning vows, though here, too, he spoke less uncouthly about them than others did.[128] The pollutions of a given age always spatter even good people with something of its follies, for just as we are well-disposed toward our homeland, so are we toward the contemporary rites with which we grew up. Most true is Euripides' saying: "Everything familiar is pleasant."[129] If only all those who continually boast that they are following Augustine would repeat his unvarying meaning—and, so to speak, the heart of Augustine—and not merely twist certain mutilated sayings slanderously to fit their own opinions.

And the light restored by the writings of Augustine was of great benefit to posterity. For thereafter Prosper, Maximus, Hugh,[130] and others like them who shaped the study [of theology] down to the age of Bernard[131] were virtually following Augustine as their standard. Meanwhile, however, as the realms and the riches of the bishops grew, there followed, as it were, the age of the Titans.[132] Worldly and uneducated men reigned in the church, some of whom had training [only] in the arts of the Roman Curia or in legal instruction.

Therefore, the Dominicans and Franciscans arose, who, seeing the extravagance and wealth of the bishops and despising their worldly way of living, established a more modest way of life and shut themselves up, as it were, in prisons of [monastic] discipline.[133] However, their lack of

---

[128] See, e.g., Augustine, Letter 211 (PL 33:958–65; WSA 2/4:19–28; NPNF[1] 1:563–68), which was later adapted to become the "Rule of St. Augustine." See Augustine, *The Monastic Rules*, trans. Agatha Mary and Gerald Bonner, ed. Boniface Ramsey (Hyde Park, NY: New City Press, 2004).

[129] Πᾶν σύντροφον γλυκύ. Cf. Euripides, *Dramatic Fragments* 1046 (Stobaeus 3.39.4) (Loeb 506 [2009], pp. 588–89). For similar proverbs, cf. Luther, *Preface to the Latin Writings* (1545), LW 34:334.

[130] Prosper of Aquitaine (see above, p. 42 n. 17) advocated Augustine's anti-Pelagian cause in Gaul in the following generation. Maximus the Confessor (see above, p. 42 n. 18) advocated a Chalcedonian Christology of two natures and two wills in opposition to Monothelite Christology. Hugh of St. Victor (see above, p. 42 n. 19) drew on Augustine in his exegesis of Genesis and advocacy of the liberal arts as a support for theology.

[131] On Bernard of Clairvaux, see above, p. lvi n. 191.

[132] Cf. Ovid (43 BC–AD 17), *Metamorphoses* 1.151–62 (Loeb 42 [1916], pp. 12–13).

[133] Along with the Carmelites, the Servites, and the Augustinian Hermits (to which order Luther belonged), the Dominicans and Franciscans were mendicant orders that originally renounced all possessions and begged for necessities. Dominic de Guzmán (ca. 1170–1221)

knowledge, first of all, increased the superstitions. Moreover, when they saw that the studies of people in the schools were being turned solely toward legal instruction—for litigation at Rome increased the power and wealth of many—they tried to call people back to theological studies; but they lacked good judgment. Albertus[134] and those like him, who were devoted to the doctrine of Aristotle, began to transform the doctrine of the Church into a philosophy. And this fourth age [of the Church] poured into the evangelical springs not only filth but also poison—that is, opinions approving of manifest idolatry. There are so many great labyrinths and false opinions in Thomas, Scotus, and their ilk[135] that the sounder theologians always longed for a different kind of doctrine, one plainer and more pure.

It is only with extraordinary shamelessness that one can claim that there was no need for a change[136] of this doctrine, since it is evident that a great part of the sophistry in those disputations is not understood even by those who have grown old in this kind of doctrine. Besides that, their mania for idols[137] is openly confirmed: when they teach the efficaciousness of sacrifice *ex opere operato*,[138] when they excuse the invocation of statues, when they deny that sins are freely forgiven by faith, when they make a torture for consciences out of human ceremonies. In short, there are still many other things still more hideous and slanderous[139] which make my whole body shudder when I think about them.[140]

Therefore, let us give thanks to God, the eternal Father of our Lord Jesus Christ [cf. Rom. 15:6], whose will it was that the filth and poisons should again be removed from the wellsprings of the Gospel by the ministry of Martin Luther, and who has restored the pure doctrine to the Church. It is fitting that all pious people throughout the whole world should, in

---

founded the Order of Preachers (the Dominicans); and Francis of Assisi (ca. 1181–1226) established the Franciscans.

[134] Albertus Magnus ("The Great," ca. 1200–1280) was the Dominican teacher of Thomas Aquinas and a pioneer in the thoroughgoing use of Aristotle in Christian theology. See *ODCC*, 3rd ed., s.v. "Albertus Magnus."

[135] See above, pp. 62–63 nn. 47–48.

[136] *mutatione*; see above, p. 64 n. 59, p. 71 n. 102, p. 74 n. 118.

[137] εἰδωλομανίαι

[138] I.e., "by the [mere] performance of the work," the scholastic doctrine that the sacraments were efficacious not only regardless of the faith or merit of the minister but also regardless of the faith or preparation of the recipient, provided only that the minister intended to perform a sacrament of the church and that the recipient did not willfully impose an obstacle to the sacrament. See Oberman, *Harvest of Medieval Theology*, pp. 146–60, 467. Cf. AC XIII (Kolb-Wengert, pp. 46–47; *Concordia*, p. 38).

[139] δύσφημα

[140] Cf. Cicero, *Divinatio in Caecilium* 13.41 (Loeb 221 [1928], pp. 36–37).

contemplating this, join their voices and sighs and beg with ardent hearts that God would strengthen what He has worked within us, for the sake of His holy temple [cf. Ps. 68:29–31]: "O living and true God, the eternal Father of our Lord Jesus Christ [cf. Col. 1:3] and Creator of all things and of the Church, this is Your word and promise: 'For the sake of My name' I shall have mercy upon you, 'for My own sake, for My own sake I shall do it, that I may not be blasphemed' [Isa. 48:9, 11]. I ask You with my whole heart, for the sake of Your glory and that of Your Son, that by the Word of Your Gospel You would ever gather to Yourself the eternal Church even from among us; ʲand that for the sake of Your Son, our Lord Jesus Christ, crucified for us and raised again, the Mediator [1 Tim. 2:5] and Supplicator [cf. Heb. 5:7],[141] You would rule our hearts through the Holy Spirit, that we may truly call upon You and fulfill those duties which are pleasing to You.

"Direct also the studies of doctrine, and govern and preserve these governments and their discipline, for they are the inns in which Your Church and these studies are dwelling.[142] Since You created the human race in order that You might be known and invoked by human beings, and for that reason also You have made Yourself known by splendid testimonies, do not permit these ranks among whom Your doctrine is sounding forth to be blotted out. And since Your Son, our Lord Jesus Christ, as He was about to undergo His agony, prayed for us: 'Father, sanctify them in the truth; Your Word is truth' [John 17:17], we join our petitions to the prayer of this our Priest, and together with Him we ask that Your doctrine may always shine forth in the human race and govern us." We heard Luther, too, daily praying for these things, and it was during such petitions that his soul was peacefully called from his mortal body, in the midst of his sixty-third year.[143]

Posterity is endowed with many monuments of this man's doctrine and piety. He published didactic[144] writings in which he set forth the doctrine that is salutary and necessary for all people, which instructs good minds about repentance, faith, the true fruits of faith, the use of the Sacraments, the distinction of Law and Gospel, the distinction of Gospel and philosophy, the dignity of the political estate—in short, the principal articles of doctrine

---

[141] μεσίτην καὶ ἱκέτην

[142] *Quae sunt hospicia tuae ecclesiae et studiorum*

[143] See above, Jonas and Coelius, *Report*, pp. 12–14.

[144] διδασκαλικά, i.e., writings providing instruction. Among examples in Witt Lat 2, see *Freedom of a Christian* (1520), LW 31:327–77; *Fourteen Consolations* (1520), LW 42:117–66; *How Confession Should Be Made* (1520), LW 39:23–47; *Babylonian Captivity* (1520), LW 36:3–126; *Concerning the Ministry* (1523), LW 40:3–44; *That a Christian Assembly Has the Right to Judge All Teaching* (1523), LW 39:301–14; *Order of Mass and Communion* (1523), LW 53:15–40.

which must necessarily exist in the Church. Next he added polemical writings[145] in which he refuted many errors that are harmful to the people. He also published exegetical writings,[146] that is, many commentaries on the prophetic and apostolic writings. In this genre of writing, even his opponents admit that he surpasses all the extant commentaries.[147] All pious minds understand that these [writings] have deserved great [praise]. But assuredly these works are equaled both in usefulness and in the labor he expended on them by the translation of the Old and New Testaments, in which there is such great perspicuity that the reading of the German itself can serve in place of a commentary. It is not only the bare text, but includes exceedingly learned annotations and summaries of the arguments of the individual sections. These point out the most important parts of the heavenly doctrine and instruct the reader about the character of the discourse,[148] enabling any good mind to draw solid testimonies of the doctrine from the very sources themselves.[149]

ǀFor Luther did not want to hold people back in his own writings, but rather to lead all people's minds back to the sources.[150] He wanted us to hear the very voice of God, and through it he wanted true faith and prayer to be kindled in many, so that God might be truly worshiped and many be made heirs of eternal life [Titus 3:7]. This intention of his and his great labors deserve to be proclaimed with thankful hearts and to be remembered as an

---

[145] ἐλεγκτικά. Witt Lat 2 contained Luther's *Bondage of the Will* (1525), LW 33, as well as a number of early polemical works, including *Response to the Faculties of Louvain and Cologne* (1520), WA 6:174–95 (LW 71); *Adversus execrabilem Antichristi Bullam* (1520), WA 6:597–612; *Vindication of All the Articles of Luther* (1520), WA 7:94–151 (LW 71); *Response to Catharinus* (1521), WA 7:705–78 (LW 71); *Against Latomus* (1521), LW 32:133–260; *Misuse of the Mass* (1521), LW 36:127–230; *Judgment on Monastic Vows* (1521), LW 44:243–400; *Against the Spiritual Estate of the Pope and the Bishops* (1522), LW 39:239–99; *Against King Henry of England* (1522), WA 10/2:180–222 (LW 61); *Against the Armed Man Cochlaeus* (1523), WA 11:295–306 (LW 71).

[146] ἐξηγητικά. Although Witt Lat 2 contained no independent exegetical works, Witt Ger 1 had presented Luther's exegesis of the New Testament Epistles, including *Lectures on Galatians* (1531/1535), LW 26–27, as well as a number of sermons on the Epistles.

[147] See above, Melanchthon, *Oration*, p. 44, where the sentiment is ascribed to Erasmus. Cf. Erasmus to Luther, May 30, 1519, WA Br 1:413.

[148] *de genere sermonis;* or: "about the genre of literature."

[149] For Luther's German Bible translation, including marginal notes and other paratextual elements, see WA DB 6–12. For Luther's Bible prefaces, see LW 35.

[150] *Ad fontes* ["to the sources" or "wellsprings"] was the humanist watchword, referring both to classical and to biblical texts: see, e.g., Erasmus, *On the Method of Study* (CWE 24:673); Melanchthon, *De corrigendis adulescentiae studiis* (CR 11:23; MSA 3:40; translated in Kusukawa, *Melanchthon: Orations*, p. 30); Luther to Spalatin, December 9, 1518, LW 48:95–96; preface to *Annotations on Matthew 1–18* (1534–35/1538), LW 67:3. Cf. Wengert, *Melanchthon's 'Annotationes in Johannem' of 1523*, pp. 26–27.

example, so that we, too, each in proportion to his own capacity, may seek to adorn the Church. For the whole of life and all our studies and plans in life must be referred to these two ends: first, that we make known the glory of God; second, that we may be of use to the Church. About the first, Paul says, "Do everything for the glory of God" [1 Cor. 10:31]. About the other, Psalm 122 [:6–7] [says], "Pray for the peace of Jerusalem," and in the same verse this supremely sweet promise is added: that those who love the Church will be happy and blessed.[151] May these heavenly commands and these promises induce everyone to learn the doctrine of the Church aright, to love the ministers of the Gospel and salutary teachers, and to direct their own zeal and labor to spreading the true doctrine and to preserving the concord of the true Church.

Farewell, dear reader. Wittenberg, on the first day of June, in the year of the Lord 1546.

---

[151] "Jerusalem" is taken as a figure for the Church. Cf. Luther, *First Lectures on the Psalms* (1513–15/1743–1876), scholia on Psalm 121 (Vg), WA 55/2:1024 (LW 11:540), where Luther's application of Psalm 122 to the Church on earth (*ecclesia militans*) rather than to the heavenly Church (*ecclesia triumphans*) seems to be an innovation in the tradition.

A NEW SPIRITUAL SONG
ABOUT THE BLESSED, PRECIOUS,
AND HIGHLY GIFTED MAN,
DR. MARTIN LUTHER,
THE PROPHET AND APOSTLE
OF GERMANY

JOHANN WALTER
1564

Translated by Matthew Carver

A New Spiritual Song
about the Blessed, Precious, and Highly Gifted Man, Dr. Martin Luther, the Prophet and Apostle of Germany

Johann Walter
1564[1]

To the tune: O HERRE GOTT dein Göttlichs Wort, etc.[2]

Part 1: The Age and Rule of the Antichrist

1   O Lord my God, to You I pray;
    Your grace from heaven lend me!
    Lord Jesus Christ, hear what I say;
    Your Holy Spirit send me.
    Grant wisdom, let my lips intone
    To praise Your Word undying,
    Which You to German lands made known,
    Proof of Your love supplying.

---

[1] See the introduction above, pp. lxxi–lxxviii.

[2] "O God, Our Lord, Thy Holy Word" (*TLH* 266; *Lutheran Worship* [St. Louis: Concordia, 1982], 341), a text by Anarg von Wildenfels (1555–1602) set to an anonymous melody, first published in the Erfurt *Enchiridion* (1527). See Fred L. Precht, *Lutheran Worship: Hymnal Companion* (St. Louis: Concordia, 1992), pp. 359–61.

2   O God, how many a weary day
      The Antichrist[3] has ruled us,
      And mercilessly led astray
      Your lowly Church and fooled us
      Through doctrines false and lies immense
      That twist Your Word's rare treasure,
      With man's decrees heaped up offense
      On Christians without measure!

3   He multiplied idolatry
      And Christ humiliated,
      With poison and hypocrisy
      Blind reprobates created.
      He twisted words which God had said,
      Made many a false believer.
      The people with his filth he fed,
      Of soul and flesh deceiver.

4   He claimed as his the Maker's stead,
      Spurned not men's adoration;
      Beneath his feet he deigned to tread
      Christ's suff'ring, blood, and Passion.
      His feet men kissed,[4] his body bore
      As if some holy relic.
      His stench they would not dare deplore,
      But praised it as angelic.

5   "Most Holy" he his title claimed—
      Christ's vicar and successor;[5]
      The Church's head himself he named,
      Of God's domain possessor.
      St. Peter gave him (so he says)
      The Keys to life and heaven

---

[3] On the papacy as Antichrist, see below, pp. 87–88 n. 12.

[4] By the sixth century, it was customary for the emperor to kiss the pope's feet when they met. Later this tradition expanded and prescribed that cardinals kiss the pope's feet upon his election and that individuals given a private audience with the pope greet him in this way. By the early eleventh century, the custom of foot-kissing had become an established ritual in the ceremony for the papal coronation of emperors. Cf. Luther's preface to Barnes, *How Popes Adrian IV and Alexander III Showed Good Faith to Emperor Barbarossa* (1545), LW 60:347–51.

[5] The bull of Boniface VIII (r. 1294–1303), *Unam sanctam* (1302), asserted that the pope is the vicar of Christ and that all authority, temporal and spiritual, has been entrusted to him. See Tanner 1:640–45.

As Christ those Keys in ancient days
Had first to Peter given.[6]

6   The whole wide world, to its great pain,
    Believed his words fallacious
    And flocked in haste by wealth to gain
    The pope's indulgence gracious.
    Unnumbered were the cunning sins
    His godless mind invented.
    He sat and flayed our German skins
    And laughed as we lamented.

7   With blindness and with gloom of night
    He kept the world astounded.
    ¦The light of truth was snuffed from sight;
    His lies alone resounded.
    Against him no man dared to spread
    One word of condemnation;
    All men must bow to him or dread
    Their excommunication.

8   Thus did the Child of Sin[7] subdue
    Beneath him all creation,
    And many thousand souls he threw
    To fires of condemnation.
    It was God's wrath that wrought this purge,
    Whose gracious love was slighted;
    God hid His Word and light—the scourge
    We thankless men invited.

PART 2: THE REVELATION AND FALL
OF THE ANTICHRIST

9   Yet God His great displeasure turned
    And pitied the offender;
    Love of His Son our mercy earned,
    His heart made soft and tender.
    And in His counsel He decreed
    By godly pow'r unfailing

---

[6] See Matt. 16:18–19.

[7] See 2 Thess. 2:3.

To crush the Antichrist indeed,
His wickedness curtailing.

10 God for His glorious work on earth
Chose out this man and claimed him—
In Eisleben he had his birth,
They Martin Luther[8] named him.
This precious man God then bestowed
As Mansfeld's rarest treasure,
Which fair domain is famed abroad
And honored without measure.

11 Much love God on this Luther spent
Ere from the womb He brought him;
That he might be His instrument
With heav'nly sense He taught him.
And gave him pow'r, and boldness too,
With mighty talents graced him;
He stripped him of all papal hue
And in th' arena placed him.

12 God richly crowned this doctor, prized
With graces of His Spirit,
To know His holy Word of Christ,
To own it and revere it.
God in His Scripture made him wise,
To teach with mind insightful,
And th' Antichrist to recognize,
Who claimed God's worship rightful.

13 Thus did God rouse this man aright
And as His mouth ordain him.
On th' Antichrist he set his sight,
To challenge and arraign him.
By wondrous ways did God advance
The papacy's confounding:
He made the pope to hear the dance
That Luther's flute was sounding.

---

[8] Walter uses different spellings of Luther's name at various points in the poem. Here and in the next stanza he spells it "Lauter," with allusion to the German words for "lute" and for "pure." Cf. above, p. 56 n. 6; and below, p. 114 n. 2.

14   He played him an "indulgent" air,[9]
    And little did he like it,
    Which very song, though sounding fair,
    Stirred up the pope to strike it.
    He tried that hour to grind by force
    Both dance and pipe to powder,
    But Luther firmly held his course
    And only played the louder.

15   That piping brought the pope to dance
    So that he started leaping:
    With tricks he jumped at ev'ry chance
    Some vict'ry to be reaping.
    The whole papistic dragon's tail[10]
    On Luther was descending;
    All their intention, without fail,
    Was Luther's mortal ending.

16   But Luther by God's armor fine
    On ev'ry side was shielded;
    At ev'ry turn the sword divine[11]
    With utmost skill he wielded.
    Whene'er the anti-Christian horde
    Believed to have him buried,
    He struck them down with one accord;
    Their ev'ry stroke he parried.

17   By Holy Scripture Luther fought,
    The papacy decrying
    For tyranny and falsehoods taught,
    But Jesus glorifying.
    The pope he named the Antichrist[12]

---

[9] I.e., *Ninety-Five Theses* (1517), LW 31:17–33.

[10] The "dragon's tail" in the *Smalcald Articles* (1537) II II 11 is the Mass, which produces "idolatries" such as purgatory, pilgrimages, vigils, fraternities, relics, and indulgences (Kolb-Wengert, pp. 303–5; *Concordia*, pp. 265–66); cf. *The Keys* (1530), LW 40:376. Elsewhere, however, Luther interprets the "devil's scales" as "the pope and the bishops" (*Lectures on Galatians* [1531/1535], LW 26:97) or as "pope, bishops, tyrants" (*Commentary on Psalm 110* [1535/1539], LW 13:246).

[11] Cf. Heb. 4:12; Eph. 6:17.

[12] For Luther's identification of the papacy as the Antichrist, see *On the Papacy in Rome* (1520), LW 39:49–104; *Smalcald Articles* (1537) II IV 10 (Kolb-Wengert, p. 309; *Concordia*, p. 269). See also David M. Whitford, "The Papal Antichrist: Martin Luther and the

From Scripture's basis solid,
Exposing from God's Word his lies,
Disgrace, and vices squalid.

18 The pope still waged his vicious war
And with all vigor jousted,
That Luther, whom he hated sore,
Might be accursed and ousted.
The emp'ror to his aid he gained,
This "heretic" to banish;
But God His snow-white swan[13] sustained
And would not let him vanish.

19 Then Luther, called before the crown,
Came, humble and obedient.[14]
The pope, to bring this Luther down,
Tried ev'ry art expedient,
That Luther might put down his shield
And so renounce his writing.
But not an inch would Luther yield
Nor take their bait inviting.

20 ¹The emperor and pope, distraught,
To ban and curse resorted,[15]
But God their counsel put to naught
And all their purpose thwarted.[16]
He turned the tables on their game
And ran it to His liking.
He put the foes to utter shame,
Their hordes to ruin striking.

21 For Christ arose with force to smite
And crush the false god neatly;
Thus Luther gained from God the might

Underappreciated Influence of Lorenzo Valla," *Renaissance Quarterly* 61, no. 1 (2008): 26–52; Scott H. Hendrix, *Luther and the Papacy: Stages in a Reformation Conflict* (Philadelphia: Fortress, 1981), pp. 97–117, 150–52; see below, p. 109 n. 28.

[13] On Luther as "swan," see the introduction above, pp. xxxvii–xxxviii; Bugenhagen, *Christian Sermon*, p. 28; and below, Mathesius, *History*, p. 121.

[14] I.e., to the Diet of Worms in 1521: see below, Mathesius, *History*, pp. 168–78.

[15] The papal bulls *Exsurge Domine* (1520) and *Decet Romanum Pontificem* (1521) and the imperial Edict of Worms: see below, Mathesius, *History*, pp. 158, 160, 180.

[16] See Isa. 8:10; Neh. 4:15.

To pluck the pope completely:
He pulled his feathers like a grouse—
His fame in which he boasted—
And cast him from God's holy house
Where long in pride he roosted.

22 With God to lead him, Luther came
And battled with the giant:
He ventured forth with sling to tame
Goliath all defiant.[17]
The lowly little monk brought down
The idol God detested,
Who brashly claimed the highest crown,
From ev'ry emp'ror wrested.

23 Thus God the Antichrist revealed,
His deeds to us exposing;
His throne o'erturned, his pow'r repealed,
His kingdom brought to closing.
God put his crown to utter shame,
Unveiled his gross perversions,
Till all men, pointing, mocked his name
And show'red him with aspersions.

24 'Twas Christ who carried out this plan,
As Paul had first predicted,[18]
By both His Spirit and God's man—
Who, specially selected,
Rode forth with God to meet the ranks
And fought the host assembled,
Securing victory and thanks
Where all men else had trembled.

---

[17] 1 Samuel 17.

[18] See 2 Thess. 2:8. Cf. below, Mathesius, *History*, pp. 147, 152, 330, 381, 473, 518, 520.

PART 3: GOD'S GRACIOUS VISITATION AND THE JOYOUS SEASON OF THE GOSPEL; THE GREAT LIGHT AND THE RICH KNOWLEDGE OF GOD'S WORD; AND GOD'S MANY OTHER BLESSINGS MANIFESTED TO GERMANY THROUGH LUTHER

25 Now when the pope, that rogue uncouth,
From off God's throne was driven,
God poured His grace, the light of truth,
In torrents down from heaven
And visited the German shores,
His knowledge plainly showing,
Enlight'ning by His Word with force,
As 'twere a flood o'erflowing.

26 God called a golden jubilee[19]
Of grace and love unbounded;
His Word, so clear, it seemed to be
With heav'nly flow'rs surrounded:
O happy day, O blest event,
All Christians' joy and gladness!—
When Christ, by Luther's doctrine, sent
His sun to chase all sadness!

27 For by this Luther God made known
To us His grace and favor,
And showed the treasure of the Son
Who is our Life forever.
All Christian doctrines in this way
Through him God so expounded,
That since the apostolic day
They ne'er so clear resounded.

28 He first revealed in manner plain
The depth of our transgression,
And how our nature seeks in vain
To work its own salvation,
By which false ground a man would fain

---

[19] A reference both to the biblical jubilee (Lev. 25:8–55) and to the papal jubilees, or "golden years," associated with papal indulgences since the first jubilee declared under Boniface VIII in 1300: see LW 60:127 n. 21 and *Smalcald Articles* (1537) III III 25 (Kolb-Wengert, p. 316; *Concordia*, pp. 274–75).

Be just and earn God's favor,
And that we no right standing gain
Through any works whatever.

29 He pointed, like St. John before,
To Christ, God's Lamb victorious,
Who all the world's transgressions bore
And stilled God's anger for us.[20]
He praised God's grace in Christ, His Son—
Before all glorified Him.
Directing saving faith alone
To Christ and none beside Him.

30 Through Scripture clearest proof he gave
That Christ's own body riven
And blood alone our life could save
And make us heirs of heaven;
And that by Him alone are we
Both justified and sainted.
None else can e'er our Savior be:
This is the truth untainted.

31 This chief of doctrines he proclaimed
With care and dedication;[21]
In all his writings ever framed
And proved its firm foundation;
In earnest charged us all on earth
To keep this prize well guarded;
And with it on his lips went forth
And finally departed.[22]

32 The Law and Gospel did he preach,
The twain divided nicely;
The pow'r, effect, and form of each
Explained with words precisely.[23]
Of true good works he Christians taught,

---

[20] See John 1:29; cf. Paul Speratus (1484–1551), *Es ist das Heil* ("Salvation unto Us Has Come," *LSB* 555:5; Wackernagel 3:31–32, no. 55).

[21] Cf. *Smalcald Articles* (1537) II I (Kolb-Wengert, pp. 300–301; *Concordia*, p. 263).

[22] Cf. above, Jonas and Coelius, *Report*, pp. 14–15.

[23] See, e.g., *Freedom of a Christian* (1520), LW 31:327–77; *Against Latomus* (1521), LW 32:133–260.

False, human works uprooted,[24]
And into church true worship brought
As God had instituted.

33 The popish Mass deposing quite
    With all its profiteering,
    He purged away and put to flight
    All fraud thereto adhering.[25]
    He brought the Supper of the Lord,
    Thus by the pope polluted,
    Into agreement with God's Word,
    As Christ had instituted.[26]

34 By Scripture he restored the crown
    And worldly pow'rs respected
    Which papal clerics had thrust down
    And to their feet subjected.[27]
    True marriage (which the pope did hate)
    He praised, and well enriched it,
    Acclaiming it a high estate,
    And so he ever preached it.[28]

35 What Christian freedom is he taught
    And from God's Word attested,
    And many consciences distraught
    From popish chains he wrested.[29]
    From monkish vows he set men free,
    As things which little mattered;
    The cloisters' foul hypocrisy
    By God's true Word he shattered.[30]

---

[24] See *Treatise on Good Works* (1520), LW 44:15–114.

[25] See *Misuse of the Mass* (1521), LW 36:127–230.

[26] See *The Blessed Sacrament and the Brotherhoods* (1519), LW 35:45–73; *Treatise on the New Testament* (1520), LW 35:75–111; *Babylonian Captivity* (1520), LW 36:3–57; see also *Receiving Both Kinds in the Sacrament* (1522), LW 36:231–67; *Adoration of the Sacrament* (1523), LW 36:269–305; and *Abomination of the Secret Mass* (1525), LW 36:307–28.

[27] See *To the Christian Nobility* (1520), LW 44:115–217; *Temporal Authority* (1523), LW 45:75–129. Cf. above, p. 84 n. 4.

[28] See *Sermon on the Estate of Marriage* (1519), LW 44:3–14; *Babylonian Captivity* (1520), LW 36:92–102; *Sermon on Married Life (Estate of Marriage)* (1522), LW 45:11–49.

[29] See *Freedom of a Christian* (1520), LW 31:327–77.

[30] See *Judgment on Monastic Vows* (1521), LW 44:243–400.

36 He put into the German tongue
    The Word of God unfailing;
    For which work thanks and praise be sung
    To God, who, thus unveiling
    So gloriously in clarity
    His Word, a mighty saber,[31]
    Had saved for Luther specially
    This gift and glorious labor.[32]

37 No tongue of man will ever tell
    The worth of this great treasure:
    For faith it glows and profits well—
    His writings in like measure—
    For God His Spirit did impart
    And by His pow'r did steer them;
    Their strength and life can strike the heart
    Of all who hear or read them.

38 The catechism he composed
    In questions pure and stirring;
    Within that golden book enclosed
    Is balm for doctrines erring.
    For in it he, with spirit free,
    True Christian doctrine grounding,
    Gives Christians an anthology
    Of sustenance abounding.[33]

39 The German Psalter[34] testifies
    How lofty are his talents.
    His hymnals o'er men's praises rise

---

[31] Cf. above, p. 87 n. 11.

[32] On Luther's German Bible translation, cf. *Preface to the New Testament* (1546, 1522), LW 35:357–62, and the other Bible prefaces in LW 35; and *On Translating* (1530), LW 35:175–202; WA DB 1–12.

[33] *Small Catechism* (1529) (Kolb-Wengert, pp. 345–75; *Concordia*, pp. 309–48).

[34] I.e., Luther's metrical hymn versions of the psalms and by extension all his hymns: see, e.g., "Ach, Gott vom Himmel, sieh darein" (Psalm 12), LW 53:225–28 ("O Lord, Look Down from Heaven, Behold," *TLH* 260; WA Ar 4:175–79; Wackernagel 3:6, no. 3); "Ein feste Burg ist unser Gott" (Psalm 46), LW 53:283–85 ("A Mighty Fortress Is Our God," *LSB* 656–657; *TLH* 262; WA Ar 4:247–49; Wackernagel 3:19–20, nos. 32–33); "Es wollt uns Gott uns genädig sein" (Psalm 67), LW 53:232–34 ("May God Bestow on Us His Grace," *LSB* 823–824; *TLH* 500; WA Ar 4:184–87; Wackernagel 3:8, no. 7); "Wär Gott nicht mit uns diese Zeit" (Psalm 124), LW 53:245–46 ("If God Had Not Been on Our Side," *TLH* 267; WA Ar 4:232–35; Wackernagel 3:17–18, no. 27); "Aus tiefer Not schrei ich zu dir" (Psalm 130), LW 53:221–24 ("From Depths

When set upon the balance;
His songs with spirit rich—indeed,
With truth and consolation—
Can comfort Christians in their need,
In any situation.

40 He who would all his writings praise—
(Which were a thing worth trying,
For they are filled in every phrase
With doctrines edifying)—
That man would find the skill and word
Are not in his possession,
For, but the postils to regard,
Their worth defies expression.[35]

41 All things for which a Christian looks
Regarding God and neighbor
Are richly treated in these books,
Whate'er one's place or labor.
Whatever Christians seek to know
When grief or ill they suffer,
These writings do the answer show,
And help and counsel offer.

42 For all who on God's kingdom wait,
For wisdom God imploring,
He, like a father, fills their plate,
His heav'nly bread outpouring.
Those who like not this wholesome food
Or cast it out untaken,
They have, one clearly must conclude,
The doctrine pure forsaken.

43 Enthusiasts he overcame
By Scripture's firm foundation,

---

of Woe I Cry to Thee," *LSB* 607; *TLH* 329; WA Ar 4:188–93; Wackernagel 3:7–8, nos. 5–6). On Luther's hymns and hymnals in general, see Leaver, *Luther's Liturgical Music.*

[35] A postil is a collection of sermons published as examples for preaching or for devotional use. Luther is associated with the *Church Postil,* which the reformer began assembling at the Wartburg (see below, Mathesius, *History,* p. 188 and nn. 24–26 there) (LW 75–79); and the *House Postil,* based on notes on Luther's preaching at home during illnesses, which appeared in an edition of 1544 edited by Veit Dietrich (see Loy 1–2 [LW 80–82]) and a posthumous 1559 edition edited by the Erfurt pastor Andreas Poach (1515–85) (see Klug 1–3).

Put factious spirits all to shame,
Though great their generation.
In public view their lies absurd
He manifested wholly,
And by the Spirit, with God's Word
He silenced all their folly.[36]

44 He with Erasmus, highly famed,
Victoriously contended.
The notion of free will was shamed,
And as a wreck descended;
It was in Luther's day laid low
And in disgrace was banished.
Now many a knight seeks high and low
To find where it has vanished.[37]

45 ꞮThe German tongue he wrought anew
And did the language render
As fitting, lucid, clear, and true
And pure, pristine, and tender.
All who God-fearing are confess
That, more than any other
And to God's praise, this Luther is
The German tongue's dear father.

46 Of Germany the prophet he,
Whom God at last had sent us;
Elijah-like he downward cast
The Baal that did torment us,
Restored the people to the way,
And to right faith converted
All those in darkness gone astray,[38]
Who had God's truth deserted.

47 His faith in God was firm and fast,
Availing, his petition;
He always sought whate'er was best
And helped the Church's mission.

---

[36] See *Against the Heavenly Prophets* (1525), LW 40:73–223; *The Sacrament of the Body and Blood of Christ* (1526), LW 36:329–61. See also below, p. 139 n. 137 and p. 195 n. 61.

[37] See *Bondage of the Will* (1525), LW 33.

[38] Cf. Isa. 52:7; 53:6.

He was a blessing and, no doubt,
A source of hope illustrious,
An iron wall, a pillar stout,
In godly faith industrious.

48 He was no fickle weathercock
That winds of fashion favored;
His road was straight, his ground a Rock,
He was no reed that wavered.[39]
The world's goodwill he cast away
Nor let his courage falter;
The threats which led so many astray
Could not his actions alter.

49 Where may his equal now be found—
A champion so redoubted?
For ev'ry man is worldly bound
And, yielding, soon is routed;
In things divine the world they heed,
And skillfully can flatter.
If there be some God-pleasing deed,
How quickly they will scatter!

50 In all these matters Luther strove
With conduct ever valiant;
The truth he neither cut nor clove,
But stood with heart resilient.
Now, having gone to blessed sleep,
With Christ he is residing.[40]
May God his doctrine stainless keep
Within the Church abiding!

PART 4: AN EXHORTATION TO THANKFULNESS FOR THE GREAT, MANIFOLD BLESSINGS MANIFESTED BY GOD AND FOR HIS GRACIOUS VISITATION

51 To what extent the German lands
Have grasped these fruits supernal

---

[39] Cf. Isa. 42:3; Matt. 11:7.

[40] Cf. Job 3:11–13; Dan. 12:2; Matt. 27:52; John 11:11–14; 1 Cor. 15:20; 1 Thess. 4:13–15; Luther, "In Peace and Joy I Now Depart," LW 53:247–48 (*LSB* 938; *TLH* 137; Wackernagel 3:17, no. 25).

And turned with faithful hearts and hands
To their own good eternal
Is shown this day by young and old,
In sin so rife and jaded;
Belief and love have all grown cold,
And faithfulness has faded.

52　No human could the height have guessed
　　To which these wrongs have mounted;
　　The world, it seems, has been possessed
　　By devil-hordes uncounted.
　　So rank and foul with sin it stinks,
　　It must by wrath be followed.
　　'Twill be no wonder if it sinks
　　And in the ground is swallowed!

53　There must some mighty purpose be
　　Why God so greatly tarries—
　　God in His suff'ring long and free
　　Some greater chast'ning carries.
　　For full and lofty is His grace
　　His hand to us has given,
　　And yet all men His Word efface
　　And curse His name to heaven.

54　Woe unto you, Chorazin![41] Woe,
　　To you, O German cities,
　　Which scorn the grace of God to know,
　　Who much the sinner pities.
　　For Tyre and Sidon would have praised
　　With thanks and fruit that favor,
　　Repented, turned, and soon embraced
　　God's light and grace forever.

55　And woe to you, Capernaum,
　　So highly elevated!
　　You will be cast down soon, and come
　　To hell, humiliated.
　　More bearable will be that day
　　The word on Sodom spoken—

[41] Matt. 11:21–24.

More hot the wrath your thankless way
Will in God's heart have woken.

56 God shattered Jewry when they spurned
And thrust away His favor,
And Sodom all to ashes burned,
For they abused it ever.
In wrath He made the world to drown
When Noah they derided,
And countless kingdoms tumbled down
When God their fate decided.

57 This fate may Germans, too, betide;
God will repay th' ungrateful.
It cannot long this way abide;
Soon comes that judgment fateful.
For Luther often this foretold
Before to sleep he laid him:
God sharply will the Germans scold
Who thanklessly have paid Him.

58 'The light of truth, dear Luther said,
May well from us be taken,
For thanklessness is widely spread
And truth for lies forsaken.
For many now maliciously
Have Luther's books distorted,
And wittingly with falsity
Vile things of him reported.

59 O Luther, you we hold and own
God's prophet true elected,
The third Elijah, whereof none
Hereafter is expected![42]
The father, Israel's charioteer,[43]
Her knight and rider dauntless,
Like Samuel true to God you were,[44]
Yet are our failings countless.

---

[42] Cf. Matt. 17:11; Rev. 11:3. See below, Mathesius, *History*, pp. 555, 574, 583, 592.

[43] See 2 Kings 13:14. See the introduction above, p. xxxv; and below, Mathesius, *History*, pp. 560, 592.

[44] See 1 Samuel 1–25.

60 O God, how ill the chariot turns
    No man need ask or wonder!
    Each Christian knows its state and mourns
    To see it rent asunder!
    The wheel has none by whom it might
    Be guided and directed,
    No man to help in fall or fright,
    No charioteer detected.

61 Therefore, O Jesus Christ, our Lord,
    With Your relief attend us!
    Vain is the help that men afford;
    Alone Your comforts mend us.
    Come, Lord our God, with mighty pow'r
    Your own high cause defending.
    Grant us to watch until Your hour[45]
    While in the faith contending.

62 O God, we pray especially
    In peace to nurture ever
    The noble house of Saxony,
    Illumined by Your favor.
    Your Holy Word keep free from stain;
    From ev'ry lie defend us.
    Your Spirit in Your Church maintain
    With succor to attend us.

63 Help Mansfeld's county too, we pray,
    Lord God, by Your providing,
    Within Your peace and rest to stay,
    In Luth'ran truth abiding.
    Since Luther there was born and died
    In blessing undisputed,[46]
    So let Your Word in her reside,
    Christ Jesus, unpolluted.

64 He who this song has sought to chant
    To honor Christ, His Savior,
    Implores the Lord hereby to grant

---

[45] See Matt. 25:13.

[46] See the introduction above, pp. xxvii–xxviii; Jonas and Coelius, *Report*, pp. 8, 13; Bugenhagen, *Christian Sermon*, p. 30; Melanchthon, *Preface*, p. 56; below, Mathesius, *History*, pp. 114, 538.

His faith to flourish ever,
And by His blood and death to turn
All those to error tending,
And to give all the heaven-born
By grace a blessed ending.

HISTORY OF THE ORIGINS, DOCTRINE, LIFE, AND DEATH OF THE REVEREND, BLESSED, PRECIOUS MAN OF GOD, DR. MARTIN LUTHER,

All Arranged in Order by Year,
as All the Events Took Place
at Their Respective Times,
by the Aged Master Mathesius,
and Edited in Its Entirety
before His Blessed Death.

PSALM 112 [:6]
"THE RIGHTEOUS SHALL NEVER BE FORGOTTEN"

1524–64 / 1566

Translated by Kevin G. Walker

HISTORY
OF THE ORIGINS, DOCTRINE, LIFE, AND DEATH
OF THE REVEREND, BLESSED,
PRECIOUS MAN OF GOD,
DR. MARTIN LUTHER,
ALL ARRANGED IN ORDER BY YEAR,
AS ALL THE EVENTS TOOK PLACE
AT THEIR RESPECTIVE TIMES,
BY THE AGED MASTER MATHESIUS,
AND EDITED IN ITS ENTIRETY
BEFORE HIS BLESSED DEATH.

Psalm 112 [:6]
"The righteous shall never be forgotten"
1566[1]

PREFACE
TO THE HISTORY[2] OF DR. MARTIN LUTHER

To the illustrious, reverend, honorable, most learned and erudite lords, the rector, pastor, dean, doctors, professors, and masters of the Christian church and highly praiseworthy university in the electoral city of Wittenberg, my most benevolent and beloved lord preceptors and friends:[3]

Grace and peace through Jesus Christ! Amen.

---

[1] See the introduction above, pp. lxxix–xcv.

[2] Here, as in the title of the work, Mathesius uses the plural *Historien*, which might also be translated "accounts."

[3] In 1565, the higher offices in Wittenberg mentioned by Mathesius were held by Baron Sigismund Ludwig von Polheim (1545–76, rector), Mathesius' close friend Paul Eber (pastor and superintendent), and his friend and teacher Georg Major (dean). On Polheim, see Förstemann et al., *Album*, 2:82; on Eber, see below, p. 300 n. 89; on Major, see below, p. 300 n. 88; on the relationship of both Eber and Major to Mathesius, see Loesche, *Johannes Mathesius*, 1:50, 93.

Having preached with God's help these twenty-four years not only on the Sunday Gospels, the catechism, the prophet Samuel, and some of David's psalms and St. Paul's Epistles but also, by way of occasional preaching,[4] my *Sarepta* or *Mining Postil* and many wedding sermons for my beloved parishioners,[5] I wanted in my old age[6] also, in due course, to preach publicly to my little lambs on the beautiful and true history of the doctrine, life, and death of the Reverend Herr Doctor Luther, of blessed memory.

For seeing that the eternal Son of God, the supreme Archbishop of our souls [1 Pet. 2:25], has used this extraordinary man[7] to free us from the abominable kingdom and doctrine of the Antichrist[8] and to rekindle the Gospel, which had been obscured, and fan it into flame, and seeing that many people living today do not know the state of things fifty years ago in the oppressed and captive Church, and many are lacking in any gratitude for this great man ˡand want to forget his faithful zeal and labor altogether, I have considered it advisable and useful to give the church entrusted to me a thorough account of all this in order to glorify God as well as to laud and praise this blessed instrument of God, and as a true testimony for young people how God used one man to inaugurate this final reformation, graciously delivering us from the Babylonian captivity and its abomination and idolatry in this end time before the Last Day and bringing us back to the pure fountain of Israel, the writings of the prophets and apostles. And I would furthermore remind and exhort my listeners to abide steadfast and undaunted in [the teaching][9] of this German prophet and blessed expositor of Holy Scripture.

Good people of great merit, through whom our God makes provision for the world, are nonetheless soon forgotten in this wicked world. Neither does the crafty old serpent rest, who from the beginning has pierced Christ in His heel (the office of preaching) [cf. Gen. 3:15][10] and contaminated the

---

[4] *extraordinarie*

[5] On Mathesius' preaching activity and its publication, see the introduction above, pp. lxxxv–lxxxviii.

[6] Mathesius was sixty-one years old in 1565.

[7] *Wundermann.* See the introduction above, pp. lxxxix–xc.

[8] On the papacy as the Antichrist, see above, pp. 87–88 n. 12.

[9] The word *Lehr* seems to have been dropped by a printer's error: see Volz, *Die Lutherpredigten des Johannes Mathesius*, p. 157 n. 7.

[10] For this interpretation of Christ's "heel" as the preaching office, see below, Mathesius, *History*, pp. 116, 194, 229, 265, 352, 370, 388, 568. Cf. Luther, *Lectures on Genesis* (1535–45/1544–54), LW 1:252–53; *Church Postil* (1540–44), sermon for Sunday after Ascension on John 15:26–16:4, LW 77:317; cf. *Sermons on John 3–4* (1538–40/1847), LW 22:470; sermon on the Festival of St. Michael and All Angels, September 29, 1544, LW 58:185–86.

pure doctrine by mixing in his leaven [cf. Matt. 16:6; 1 Cor. 5:7–8], dregs, chaff, and evil dross.

Now, because I, as a native German, preached about this estimable German prophet, whom God finally sent as a gift to us Japhethites[11] and to the holy German Empire,[12] to my dear German parishioners in my native tongue, in accord with my office, I have decided after due consideration to have these German sermons printed in the German language in order to glorify God and the blessed German theology. In this way, moreover, everyone in Germany may be reminded of how this blessed German church, located in the kingdom of Bohemia,[13] has esteemed the teaching of this great German prophet, and how it has firmly and faithfully stood by and upheld the Confession of Wittenberg and Augsburg down to the present hour here in the Ore Mountains.[14] |Meanwhile, if it should be God's will and seem good to the church, it is my hope that my sons and sons-in-law or my dear friends and students will translate these German accounts into Latin as they have opportunity.[15]

Furthermore, I am confident that I will find general pardon for having at times departed from the standard form and pattern that are customary in historical narratives. For as the regular pastor and preacher, I was preaching to young and old, to the laity and the simpleminded. Therefore, I had to adapt these accounts to the market and my listeners; I accommodated myself and sometimes tried to insert useful commonplaces of doctrine so

[11] According to long-established interpretation of Genesis 10, Noah's son Japheth was regarded as the progenitor of the peoples of Europe. See *Lectures on Genesis* (1535–45/1544–54), LW 2:187–93, and below, Mathesius, *History*, pp. 119, 147, 167, 338, 561, 585–87; cf. below, p. 470 n. 43.

[12] I.e., the Holy Roman Empire, officially known (since the 1512 Diet of Cologne) as the Holy Roman Empire of the German Nation.

[13] On Joachimsthal and its situation, see the introduction above, pp. lxxxii–lxxxiii.

[14] *disem Sudetischen gebirge.* Sixteenth-century geographers took classical references to the *Sudeti montes* as applying to the Erzgebirge or Ore Mountains between Saxony and Bohemia, where Joachimsthal was located. In modern nomenclature the Sudetes are to the northeast of the Erzgebirge, between the Czech Republic and Poland.

[15] Although Mathesius' biographical sermons on Luther were sometimes cited under the Latin title *Vita Lutheri*, no Latin translation such as the one envisioned here was ever made. Mathesius' sons were Johannes (1544–1607), Paul (1548–84), Eutyches (1552–65), and Caspar (1553–70); his sons-in-law were Felix Zimmerman (1536–1610), who married Sibylla Mathesius in the spring of 1565, and Johann Franck (dates uncertain, one of six sons of Caspar Franck Sr. [1520–78]), though his marriage to Christine Mathesius did not take place until 1568. Zimmerman and Franck, alongside Johannes and Paul Mathesius and their descendants, took roles in the posthumous publication of many of Mathesius' other sermons. See Loesche, *Johannes Mathesius*, 1:211–17; cf. Hans Lorenz, *Bilder aus Alt-Joachimsthal: Umrisse einer Kulturgeschichte einer erzgebirgischen Bergstadt im 16. Jahrhundert* (Joachimsthal: Verlag der Stadtgemeinde, 1925), pp. 161–62.

that you might have not only a bare historical account but consolation, doctrine, admonition, and blessed examples as well, for all the various sorts of circumstances that arise in the church. "Preaching to scholars is easy";[16] they determine for themselves what to take and note from these accounts. With the laity and the simple one should and must lay things out a little more plainly and simply, and at times also in greater detail. Let that suffice as an explanation of why I am having these histories published in German in this form.

Now, while I, as a called preacher, with good intention and due deliberation, was undertaking the preparation of these German sermons and ecclesiastical histories of our religion for the press, I realized how highly and greatly God has magnified the illustrious church and university[17] in Wittenberg with rich blessings, great people, and outstanding gifts, even as He has shown me great kindness and goodwill as a true citizen of this laudable church and a member of this renowned university, since, in addition to the enjoyment of good peace and civil protection, it was here that I first grasped the true religion and the liberal arts and learned to apply them properly. |Accordingly, I resolved to dedicate these ecclesiastical histories of the sainted Herr Doctor Luther to my esteemed preceptors and friends as a way of manifesting my thanks.

And it is my duty, as far as I am able, to demonstrate my gratitude to this church, university, and city community,[18] and especially to the laudable house and electorate of Saxony, my beloved fatherland.[19] For while I was in this church, university, and city under the most gracious protection and at the expense of the laudable electorate, I experienced so much good and kindness that I am unable to repay it with all the days of my life.[20] As a grateful student, it is my duty and desire to speak of this place and its eminent people and patrons with honor and a thankful heart, not only on this little globe but also, God willing, in the other life that is to come, before the face of God, in the great congregation of Jesus Christ in the presence of all the

---

[16] A proverb, similar to "a word to the wise is sufficient": see Wander 1:1532, "Gelehrter" no. 3.

[17] *Schule*, "school," often translated here as "university" in context.

[18] *gemeinder Statt*

[19] Mathesius had been born in Rochlitz, in Ernestine Saxony; see the introduction above, p. lxxx.

[20] The University of Wittenberg had been founded in 1502 by the Saxon elector Frederick the Wise, and he and his successors—his younger brother John and John's son, John Frederick—made the university the special object of their patronage: see below, Mathesius, *History*, pp. 576–80. Mathesius' 1540–41 study in Wittenberg was supported by the mediation of the electoral counselor Georg Spalatin; see Mathesius to Spalatin, June 19, 1540, in Loesche, *Johannes Mathesius*, 2:231–32. On Spalatin, see below, p. 136 n. 121.

saints and angels, [and] for all eternity to proclaim the praise and honor of the German prophet and his faithful colleagues, the professors and learned men, the patrons and blessed persons who have contributed to supporting and sustaining this city, church, and university, according as my faithful God and His beloved Son enable me so to do.

For the present I must move beyond expressing [my own] thanks and paying my tuition and must help [others] to honor these people and this place, which our God has honored and blessed above many other people and universities with pious and learned people, as well as faithful and God-fearing patrons.

Let this be an eternal and blessed boast: that our God has, through the house of Saxony, established on the Elbe River a church and university and has caused it to be adorned with great and illustrious people, through whom He has rescued His captive and exiled Christendom from the Babylonian captivity and its abominations. They have reformed the greater part of churches and schools in the German and neighboring kingdoms and brought them to the saving knowledge of the Lord Christ, and of how man is justified before God and saved, as well as to the skillful application of reason and the proper use of the liberal arts. And [let it be boasted] that God has awoken such rulers in this place that they have not only founded this university and honorably supported it but also protected the pure doctrine, which God sent to the banks of the Elbe, against all the gates of hell. They have publicly confessed it, firmly and steadfastly professed it, along with their land and people, and helped to spread God's Word almost to the ends of the earth.

Our God sent His Son from His bosom [John 1:18] and heart and ordained Him to be the eternal preacher and interpreter, to proclaim His will, counsel, and statutes, and to prophesy to Adam in the beginning after the fall.[21] The eternal Son of God preserved this grace and blessed word among Adam and his pious heirs down to Enoch [Gen. 5:24] and Noah [Gen. 6:8]. Noah's descendants also safeguarded the treasure entrusted to them down to Abraham [Genesis 12], Isaac [Gen. 17:21], Jacob [Genesis 27], Joseph [Genesis 39–46], and Moses [Exodus 2ff.]. It was at this time that the Son of God established and instituted the first university[22] with the tabernacle and His covenant [Exod. 27:21, etc.]. He Himself was the true Rector

---

[21] See *Table Talk* no. 5800 (n.d.), WA TR 5:361. On the agency of the Second Person of the Trinity in the Old Testament, cf. Luther, *On the Last Words of David* (1543), LW 15:313–14; Melanchthon, *Chronicon Carionis* (1558), CR 12:750, 769. See Bornkamm, *Luther and the Old Testament*, pp. 200–207. See below, Mathesius, *History*, pp. 230, 253.

[22] *hohe Schule*

and Professor;²³ He Himself orally explained the will and counsel of God and guided the blessed rivers of eternal wisdom—which were in Him and the Holy Spirit essentially, from eternity, from the Father's heart—into the blessed streams and cisterns²⁴ of Israel, as David later calls them [cf. Ps. 65:9].

For as many great and illustrious prophets and kings as existed in Israel, they were all, by virtue of their office, filled from this living fountain, from which blessed waters spring forth to eternal life [John 4:14]. Such salvific streams not only watered and irrigated the precious Promised Land but also entered over time into the neighboring kingdoms and monarchies.

Through Elijah the Tishbite, the Son of God led this blessed stream into Syria [1 Kings 17–19], just as it was through the prophet Jonah that the blessed conduit was extended to Nineveh in Assyria [Jonah 3]. It was through Daniel, the dear man, full of grace and wisdom [Dan. 6:25–27; 10:11], that this blessed water of God's Word entered Babylon and all of Chaldea. Mordecai and Ezra also distributed this blessed water in the Persian and Median kingdom [Esth. 3:2f.; Ezra 7–10].

In sum, what the Son of God with His Spirit has received from the Father's heart and poured out into His chosen tools and vessels, the eternal Son of God continues to preserve against Satan and the wicked world, which was complicit in the ancient serpent's lying and murdering, even down to the blessed time at which the eternal and essential Word became flesh [John 1:14] and visibly revealed the counsel and will of His Father.

In the days of His flesh [Heb. 5:7], the incarnate Son of God again appointed twelve new and blessed fountains, the holy apostles [Matt. 10:1–4], even as He Himself along with John the Baptist were [Matthew 3]. Later the twelve apostles and their disciples and hearers established their Christian academies²⁵ in Asia and Greece, and some of the disciples and students came to us Germans in Europe.²⁶

---

²³ *ordinarius*, an "ordinary" or "full" professor in the university.

²⁴ *theyler = Wasserteiler.* Mathesius' extended image of cisterns, pipes, and water towers is drawn from the apparatus used in mining, which would have been familiar to his congregation in Joachimsthal. The use of hydraulic engineering in mining is described and illustrated in the Joachimsthal town physician Georg Agricola's (1494–1555) *De re metallica*, trans. Herbert Clark Hoover (New York: Dover Publications, 1950). On the sophisticated use of water towers and conduits in sixteenth-century German cities, see, e.g., B. Ann Tlusty, *Bacchus and Civic Order: The Culture of Drink in Early Modern Germany* (Charlottesville: University of Virginia Press, 2001), pp. 22–23.

²⁵ *hohe und Christliche Schulen hielten*

²⁶ The most famous Christian schools of the ancient world were the catechetical academy in Alexandria and the competing school in Antioch. Mathesius may be thinking of earlier, less formal activities associated with Ephesus (where the students of John the apostle and his successors included Irenaeus, who became bishop of Lyons in Gaul) and with Athens (where Dionysius the Areopagite, converted by Paul, was supposed to have become a Christian

Now, whenever Satan, since the beginning, obstructed this fountain and sought to contaminate and fill the blessed conduits with impure and poisonous water along with his frogs and toads, the eternal Son of God in due time sent His spiritual master pipemen, who cleaned out the fountains and conduits which had been filled and obstructed and made the water clean again. Or, as the prophets say, they were to smelt and purge away the evil dross and contaminants which had been mixed in with the pure silver [cf. Isa. 1:22, 25; Mal. 3:3]. And so 'it is that God's Word never advances without tribulation.

When our dear Lord Jesus Christ had brought this wellspring of salvation not only into Greece, Italy, and France but into Germany as well, the archenemy of Jesus Christ finally awakened Arius and Mohammed[27] in the East and the Antichrist in the West.[28] They split open and bored into the blessed conduits of God and dumped in their poisonous and contaminated water in many places, with the final result that now, for many hundred years, the entire East has not had a wholesome drink and pure water about God and His gracious will and beloved only-begotten Son.

Likewise in the West—although the disciples of the apostles and the early church set up many beautiful and blessed water towers where it was still possible to enjoy the pure water in Rome, Paris, Fulda, and Westphalia[29]— in the end the blessed fountains were all stopped up like Isaac's wells [Gen. 26:15, 18], the cisterns were broken down [cf. Jer. 2:13], and the conduits were filled with strange and unhealthy water and doctrine. Eventually

---

theologian before traveling to Paris, where he was venerated as St. Denis). In Germany itself, there were Christian congregations at Roman colonies such as Trier and Cologne as early as the second century.

[27] The teaching of the Alexandrian presbyter Arius (ca. 280–336), that Christ was only the highest creature and not true God, was condemned at the Council of Nicaea in 325. Mohammed (d. 632), the founder of Islam, rejected the divinity of Christ as well as the reality of His crucifixion.

[28] That is, the papacy. Luther set the historical origins of the universal claims of the papacy and the beginning of its role as Antichrist in the period after Gregory the Great (r. 590–604), specifically in the pontificate of Boniface III (r. 607), who received confirmation of his claims from the emperor (or usurper) Phocas (r. 602–610). See *On the Councils and the Church* (1539), LW 41:90; and above, pp. 87–88 n. 12.

[29] Rome was an early center of the Western Church. Paris became the seat of one of the oldest and most respected universities (with a history projected back before its twelfth-century origins; see, e.g., above, n. 26 on Dionysius the Areopagite). Fulda was the center of St. Boniface's mission to the Saxons and the home of a renowned monastic school (cf. below, Mathesius, *History*, p. 437). In "Westphalia," Mathesius may have in mind the important archbishopric of Cologne, an early center of Christianity in Germany (see above, n. 26) whose medieval university was associated with Albertus Magnus (see above, p. 77 n. 134), or Charlemagne's (ca. 742–814) capital at Aachen (with its associated church and school).

the water from the conduits was so overgrown with weeds[30] that the heavenly and fresh water was scarcely to be found in all of Europe.

Now while poor, captive Christendom was suffering greatly for want of fresh and pure water, it grieved the chief conduit-Master, the blessed and living Fountain. He fashioned a water tower in this kingdom of Bohemia and again laid two blessed conduits[31] through which He had His salutary water sent to the places in the north. But the Philistine water thieves[32] [cf. Gen. 26:15–21], the archenemies of Jacob and his descendants, smashed and burned these cisterns; they split open and stopped up the conduits which God had used to give drink to the hungry souls and to refresh them.

At last, the Lord Christ had the university and church established and founded in Wittenberg, where God placed a new water tower and cistern, and laid down new and blessed conduits, ⌐and gave His holy, living Word in abundance, with great hosts of evangelists [Ps. 68:11]. And though the devil and his Antichrist have rushed in against these water towers and conduits with great power and vicious guile, the Tower remained above all human thoughts and drew His salvific water from the cistern into nearly all of the Roman Empire, so that now there is no proper church or school that has not partaken of the Wittenberg fountain. And—not to speak of other places for the moment—we in Joachimsthal confess it to be true that all we know of God's Word and possess of good skills has been drawn here from the cistern in Wittenberg. The conduits for church and school were bored out in Wittenberg and laid down to this valley.

May the eternal Son of God maintain this blessed water tower and heavenly cistern along with all of the conduits tapping into this tower down to this present hour, and may He protect all of the conduits in which the Wittenberg water is being conveyed against any kind of muddy, impure, poisonous, turbid, or putrid water, of the sort that many wicked people would like to dump into the conduits. May He also cleanse and purge the conduits of all kinds of growth and weeds,[33] with which Satan would like to see this pipework overgrown, so that these conduits may not be stopped up by any frog or toad. And may He Himself remove and throw away any [conduit] that is rotten, foul, or ruptured. This is what I wish from the bottom of my heart for this blessed water tower and all the conduits.

Now since the eternal and blessed Wellspring of living water has provided this pure stream in our days under the House of Saxony and has preserved

---

[30] *nixflachs*; literally: "frogbit."

[31] I.e., John Hus and Jerome of Prague. On both men, see the introduction above, pp. xxxvii–xxxviii; and below, Mathesius, *History*, p. 121.

[32] *wiesenwesserer*

[33] *nixflachse*; see above, n. 30.

it these past fifty years,[34] appointing blessed people for that purpose, from whose diligence and labor we continue to benefit down to the present hour, it is my intention that these sermons of mine about Herr Doctor Martin should call to remembrance the durable and sturdy pinewood conduits by dedicating these sermons to the highly praiseworthy university and church in Wittenberg, so that under their name they might be conveyed to other people. I trust with all well-meaning and dutiful confidence that my beloved lords and preceptors, my old masters and friends, my students, and posterity will graciously be pleased by my expression of thanks and goodwill, and that they will help maintain this blessed water and old pipework so that this blessed water may continue flowing onward steadily and without hindrance and may spring into eternal life [John 4:14].

This will eternally please the Lord Jesus Christ, the true and living Fountain and supreme master pipeman, as well as His faithful servants, who from the beginning have supplied this water in church, school, and government. Our dear God has supplied this water through these servants and (God be praised) has furthered and preserved it now for fifty years with their great care, toil, diligence, and labor.

As for my person (since I unabashedly, until I am laid in my grave, confess myself to be a citizen of the Wittenberg church and a member and student of the university there and an obedient subject of the House of Saxony,[35] and entrust my children[36] and any grandchildren God may grant me to the university in Wittenberg, even as I have my dear son[37] under the discipline of Master Christoph Pezel[38] at this moment), I most sincerely commend myself, my sons, and my future heirs to this Christian church and university.[39] I also

---

[34] Since Mathesius' preface is dated 1565, he may be speaking in round numbers of the years since 1517. Cf. below, Mathesius, *History*, p. 236.

[35] Mathesius, as a native of Rochlitz, was born a Saxon subject, though he had spent his career as pastor in Joachimsthal, in Bohemia, under Hapsburg rule, where his obedience to the Roman Catholic king and emperor had been called into question. His self-identification as a Saxon subject here is thus somewhat provocative.

[36] On Mathesius' sons, see above, p. 105 n. 15.

[37] Paul Mathesius had matriculated at the University of Wittenberg in May 1561: Förstemann et al., *Album*, 2:20.

[38] Christoph Pezel (1539–1604) had received his master's degree and become an instructor in Wittenberg in 1564. Later, in 1576, he would be expelled from Saxony under suspicion of crypto-Calvinist teaching. He went on to help introduce Reformed confessions in Nassau and Bremen. See Luther D. Peterson, "Philippists," *OER* 3:260; Helmar Junghans, "Wittenberg, University of," *OER* 4:285; and Ilonka Egert, "Bremen," *OER* 1:213.

[39] Mathesius' oldest son, Johannes, had matriculated at Wittenberg in 1551 (Förstemann et al., *Album*, 1:274). In 1578, having received his doctorate in medicine, he was elected rector of the university: Förstemann et al., *Album*, 2:278; cf. Lorenz, *Bilder aus Alt-Joachimsthal*, pp. 118, 161–62.

hereby give my most cordial thanks for the manifold kindness which the church, university, and authorities very graciously showed me during three years[40] there, and then in Altenburg during my period of schoolteaching, as well as to my son and all the children of my parishioners and colleagues over the past three years[41] and which they will continue to show, if it be God's will. It is my humble intention to do this in due obedience, love, fidelity, and steadfast friendship as long as I live and thereafter to |all eternity in order to repay your excellence and worthiness and for the sake of my children and grandchildren, as well as for my dear parishioners and their heirs, to render my acknowledgment and laud herewith.

For since I have entered into a blessed friendship with the aforementioned university and church, based on the knowledge and confession of the Lord Jesus Christ, no slanderer, apostate, or ungrateful cuckoo[42] and despiser of the Gospel shall deny me this. *Est pietas vere nervus amicitiae* ["Piety is truly the sinew of friendship"].[43] To this end, may our eternal Lord and Savior Jesus Christ help me and those in my care and all who in love and simplicity remain steadfast with the Lord Jesus Christ, His Word and Sacraments.

May the laudable church, university, and government hereby be commended at all times to His protection and defense and to His Word of grace. Dated on October 5, 1565,[44] in St. Joachimsthal, whose church abides with

---

[40] Mathesius studied for the first degree in theology in Wittenberg from 1529 to 1530 and then served as a teacher in Altenburg from 1530 to 1532. See Loesche, *Johannes Mathesius*, 1:39–57.

[41] In the period from January 1560 to October 1565, twenty-three students from Joachimsthal, including Paul Mathesius, are listed in the Wittenberg album, and one is listed as a scholarship student (*gratis inscriptus*): Förstemann et al., *Album*, 1:369–72; 2:1–92. See Lorenz, *Bilder aus Alt-Joachimsthal*, pp. 117–18.

[42] The "cuckoo" was identified with the theologian Matthias Flacius in a satirical poem (*Synodus Avium* or "The Synod of the Birds") written by Mathesius' former Joachimsthal student Johann Major (1533–1600): *Synodus avium depingens miseram faciae ecclesiae propter certamina quorvndam qui de primatu contendunt, cum oppresione recte meritorum* (Wittenberg: Veit Kreutzer, 1557) [VD16 M348]. Flacius was a vocal critic of Melanchthon's participation in the religious settlements (the "Interims" of 1548) imposed on the Lutherans after the imperial victory in the Smalcaldic War, and he became a leader of the "Gnesio-Lutheran" party opposed to the "Philippist" supporters of Melanchthon. See Oliver Olson, *Matthias Flacius and the Survival of Luther's Reform* (Wiesbaden: Harrassowiz, 2002). Mathesius' attitude toward Flacius is consistently negative: see below, *History*, pp. 291–92, 308; and the introduction above, p. lxxxv.

[43] This Latin verse, whose source could not be otherwise identified, also appears in Mathesius' *Trostpredigt* (Nürnberg: U. Neuber, 1565) [VD16 ZV10505], fol. C3r, where he cites a longer version: *Crescit amor verus vera pietate fideque/ Est pietas verae* [sic] *nervus amicitiae.*

[44] Mathesius died two days later, a few hours after preaching the *Trostpredigt* (see the previous note), on October 7, 1565.

Christian steadfastness in Doctor Martin Luther's doctrine and the Augsburg Confession and intends to stand firm thereby.

Johann Mathesius, a citizen of the Church of God and member of the illustrious university in Wittenberg, pastor in St. Joachimsthal, under our most gracious lord Emperor Maximilian II.[45]

---

[45] On the succession of Hapsburg rulers and Mathesius' attitude toward them, see the introduction above, pp. lxxxiv, xcii.

THE FIRST SERMON
ON THE HISTORY
OF HERR DR. MARTIN LUTHER,
OF BLESSED MEMORY,
BY JOHANN MATHESIUS,
PASTOR IN ST. JOACHIMSTHAL
[ON THE YEARS 1483 TO 1516]

[November 10, 1562]

BELOVED in the Lord! Today, on the eve of St. Martin's Day—on the tenth of November, in the one-thousand, four-hundred, and eighty-third year after the birth of Christ our Savior[1]—Martin Luther, the great and worthy prophet of Germany, was born in the territory of the counts of Mansfeld, in Eisleben by the Harz Mountains, to Hans Luder, a miner, and Margaretha, Luder's wife.[2] On this day, in St. Peter's Church,[3] he received Christian Baptism in the name of the Holy Trinity and was named Martin, in the same year that the blessed martyr Girolamo Savonarola was burned in Florence for his Christian confession.[4]

---

[1] On the year of Luther's birth, see the introduction above, pp. liv–lv; Jonas and Coelius, *Report*, p. 10; Melanchthon, *Preface*, pp. 56–57.

[2] On Hans Luther (Luder), see above, p. 56 n. 6; on Margaretha (née Lindemann), see above, p. 56 n. 7. Luther began using the spelling "Ludher" at Erfurt in 1501 and began using the spelling "Luther" consistently in 1517 with his letter to Cardinal Albert (see below, Mathesius, *History*, p. 146). See Oberman, *Luther*, p. 86; James Nestingen, *Martin Luther: A Life* (Minneapolis: Fortress, 2003), p. 37; and Bernd Moeller and Karl Stackmann, *Luder-Luther-Eleutherius: Erwägungen zu Luther Namen* (Göttingen: Vandenhoeck & Ruprecht, 1981).

[3] Luther was baptized on St. Martin's Day itself (November 11) in Eisleben, at the parish church of SS. Peter and Paul (the *Petrikirche*). Because the church was being renovated, Luther was probably baptized in the tower chapel. Cf. above, Melanchthon, *Preface*, p. 56; Brecht 1:1–3; Volz, *Die Lutherpredigten des Johannes Mathesius*, p. 157. Cf. Luther's account of his birth, Baptism, and early life in his letter to Spalatin, January 14, 1520, LW 48:145–46.

[4] Girolamo Savonarola (1452–98) was, in fact, executed as a heretic in 1498. A Dominican friar, Savonarola was a popular preacher in the northern Italian city of Florence who urged repentance, prophesied of the city's republican glory, and denounced the state of the papacy until he was excommunicated and imprisoned in 1497. See Lauro Martines, *Scourge and Fire:*

Since this day calls to our minds the great and extraordinary man[5] through whom the Lord Christ rescued us from the Babylonian captivity,[6] rekindled the blessed truth of the holy Gospel, and restored to the pulpit and homes the article[s] [of faith] concerning true repentance, acknowledgment of sins, faith in Jesus Christ, good works, and the proper use of the holy Sacraments and of marriage and government, therefore, in the name of God, the supreme Head of Christendom, who sent us this prophet, and for His eternal glory and to render Him due thanks, we intend to preach for a time about how God inaugurated this reformation of the church, also as a testimony and affirmation of our true Christian religion and as a commemoration of this outstanding prophet, |as well as to teach, comfort, and remind the multitude of young people [how God has done this].

It is the Lord Christ who for our sakes raised up this man as a chosen instrument [cf. Acts 9:15] and before the end of this world, by means of His Word, rescued His oppressed Church from lamentable blindness, abominations, idolatry, and false understanding of Holy Scripture. Surely He has well deserved that we should here publicly and honorably commemorate His marvelous kindness and this deliverance, as well as His faithful servant and steadfast confessor of His Word. For—praise and thanks be to God!— what all upright preachers know, teach, and write today, what all believers in Christ believe with the heart unto righteousness [Rom. 10:10] and confess with their mouth unto salvation, all that is what the Spirit of Jesus Christ has proclaimed and taught to us through this esteemed doctor and through his friends in the laudable University of Wittenberg who steadfastly and publicly taught and wrote in accord with him.

Now, you young people ought to listen attentively and retain this history of the Herr Doctor, from his childhood to his grave, in order that you may be made aware of the situation in which Christendom found itself fifty years ago as well as about the person from whom your pastors, authorities, schoolmasters, and parents have received this doctrine, which is taught and defended here in its simplicity.

Savonarola and Renaissance Florence (London: Jonathan Cape, 2006). Luther published a 1523 edition of Savonarola's *Meditation on Psalms 51 and 31* in which he hailed the friar as an opponent of the papal Antichrist and a preacher of faith in God's mercy proclaimed in the Word (LW 59:77–81). Other sixteenth-century Evangelicals continued to identify Savonarola as a forerunner of the Protestant Reformation. See Bruce Gordon, "'This Worthy Witness of Christ': Protestant Uses of Savonarola in the Sixteenth Century," in vol. 1 of *Protestant History and Identity in Sixteenth-Century Europe*, ed. Bruce Gordon (Aldershot: Scolar Press, 1996), pp. 93–107. On Savonarola, see also below, Mathesius, *History*, pp. 169, 317.

[5] *Wundermann.* See the introduction above, pp. lxxxix–xc and n. 364 there.

[6] An allusion to Luther's *Babylonian Captivity of the Church* (1520), LW 36:3–126. See below, Mathesius, *History*, pp. 156–57, 159.

For Satan not only bites the Lord Christ in the heel [Gen. 3:15],[7] seeking to tear His holy Word out of our churches and hearts or to distort and misapply it with new interpretations, but he would also like to bring this salutary instrument under suspicion within Christendom and to blot out or utterly to uproot the memory of him, so that [Satan] may once again be able to sow his tares and 'to bewitch the people by means of false little cunning glosses and to lead them away from the acknowledged truth.

Holy people and blessed servants of the Church of Christ should not be quickly forgotten, for though it is in the heart that they believe in the Son of God unto righteousness for themselves, they also make a glorious confession and testimony with their mouth about their hope and comfort, to make their own calling sure and certain [2 Pet. 1:10] and thereby to strengthen and comfort other people. And though weakness and frailty accompany them throughout their life (as all saints on earth, still in our own times, have been made acceptable, pleasing, blessed, and righteous before God freely, without any righteousness or merit of their own, solely by confessing and relying on the blood and sacrifice of Jesus Christ), nevertheless much great spiritual virtue shines forth in those who believe in Jesus Christ without any hypocrisy and have been made partakers of His Holy Spirit.

This man had a humble heart and keen awareness of his sins, and a living faith, and confidence in Christ, whom he praised and extolled, by God's grace, with true and constant invocation and courageous confession of the Gospel along with his holy and fervent zeal against all ungodliness (as you will hear in the following sermons, God willing). You should, therefore, listen very attentively to this doctor's teaching, confession, faith, virtue, suffering, and the entire course of his life, and also help me pray in Christ's name that I may present you with an accurate and straightforward exposition of everything that I heard in the church and university in Wittenberg, as well as in many good conversations at Doctor Luther's table, and that I have read in his books, as well as what I have learned in truth from many good people who had been with him from the beginning and sat at his table.[8]

'It is the truth that I will make known to you, showing partiality or prejudice to no one. So help me, the eternal and true Son of God, before whose face I shall give a proper answer and response for these sermons of mine, God willing, to every man who questions me and calls me to account for them! Help me pray with a devout Our Father, in the name of Jesus Christ.

---

[7] See above, p. 104 n. 10.

[8] On Mathesius' time in Wittenberg and his sources for Luther's biography, see the introduction above, pp. lxxxviii–lxxxix.

It was on this day, seventy-nine[9] years ago, dear friends, as I mentioned at the outset, that Martin Luther was born in the region of the Harz Mountains to an honorable miner or slate quarrier[10] who had moved to Eisleben from the village Möhra by Smalcald.[11] And [I told] how, on the eve of St. Martin's Day,[12] this little child was sprinkled with the blood of Jesus Christ in holy Baptism and was accepted as a child and heir of God by sheer grace, and received Martin as his baptismal name, as a blessed attestation and confession of this blessed "covenant of a good conscience" [1 Pet. 3:21 DB]. He, too, bore and upheld this baptismal name with Christian honor throughout his life as a blessed champion and knight of the Lord Christ.[13]

Now when our generous and rich God blessed the mining work of this child's father, providing him with two furnaces or smelteries in Mansfeld, then Hans Luther, as a true Zarephathite,[14] honorably brought up his baptized son in the fear of God, using the honest income from the mines. And when his son had reached the age of discretion, he sent him to Latin school with a heartfelt prayer,[15] and there this little boy diligently and readily learned the Ten Commandments, children's Creed,[16] and the Lord's Prayer in addition to the *Donat*,[17] children's grammar, *Cisiojanus*,[18] and Christian hymns and chants. For though the truth was obscured under the Antichrist, God nevertheless wonderfully preserved the holy catechism in the schools

---

[9] I.e., from 1483 (see above, p. 114 and n. 1 there) to 1562.

[10] I.e., Hans Luther; see above, p. 114 and n. 2 there.

[11] In fact, Salzungen is the closest large town, but Smalcald [Schmalkalden], though more distant, was more important in the later history of the Reformation as the location of the formation of the Smalcaldic League (1531) and of the 1537 conference for which Luther drafted the *Smalcald Articles*. See below, Mathesius, *History*, pp. 356, 397–402.

[12] On the correct date of Luther's Baptism, on St. Martin's Day itself (November 11), see above, p. 114 n. 3.

[13] St. Martin of Tours was remembered in the later Middle Ages as a soldier-saint, a Roman officer who had become a "soldier of Christ." His name, derived from the Roman god of war, carried a military connotation. See *LA* 2:292–300, no. 166.

[14] See below, p. 138 and n. 133 there.

[15] The Latin school in Mansfeld, located next to St. George's Church, was financially supported by the local counts. Luther probably began attending on March 12, 1491. See Brecht 1:12–13.

[16] I.e., the Apostles' Creed.

[17] The elementary Latin grammar, popularly named after its author Aelius Donatus (fl. ca. 354). See *The Ars Minor of Donatus*, trans. Wayland Johnson Chase (Madison: University of Wisconsin, 1926).

[18] The *Cisiojanus* was a mnemonic poem for remembering the calendar of fixed festivals and saints' days. See Karl Pickel, ed., *Das heilige Namenbuch von Konrad Dangkrotzheim, herausgegeben mit einer Untersuchung über die Cisio-Jani* (Strassburg: K. J. Trübner, 1878).

alongside the most precious Baptism of children ¦in the parish churches, for which we older people have our God and the old schools to thank.[19]

For though Satan despised and scorned the schools, those who served in them, and those who were sent there, nevertheless whatever great and excellent people there were to hold spiritual and secular offices received their education in the court schools and in other ordinary elementary schools and universities.

Then, when this boy turned fourteen, his father sent him to school in Magdeburg in the company of Johann Reinecke.[20] At the time the school had a better reputation than did many others.[21] It was there that this boy, like many the child of an honorable and affluent man, went begging for bread and bawled his *"Panem propter Deum!"*[22] Great things start small,[23] and if a child is pampered and indulged from the beginning, it will hurt him for his whole life.

In the following year, with the knowledge and command of his parents, this boy transferred to Eisenach, where his mother had kin.[24] After having sung for his bread from door to door for a time there as well, a devout

---

[19] On the preservation of the catechism in medieval schools, see *Table Talk* no. 5557 (1542–43), LW 54:452; and below, Mathesius, *History*, pp. 256–58, 437.

[20] On Reinecke, see above, p. 57 n. 14. On Luther's year in Magdeburg, see Luther to Georg Spalatin, January 14, 1520, LW 48:146; *Table Talk* no. 5347 (1540), WA TR 5:76; and above, Melanchthon, *Preface*, p. 57.

[21] During Luther's stay in Magdeburg, he apparently attended the cathedral school while lodging with the Brethren of the Common Life, the lay branch of the *Devotio Moderna*. See Luther to Claus Storm, June 15, 1522, WA Br 2:563. See Oberman, *Luther*, 96–99; Brecht 1:15–17; Hendrix, *Luther: Visionary Reformer*, p. 23. On the Brethren of the Common Life, see John H. Van Engen, *Sisters and Brothers of the Common Life: The Devotio Moderna and the World of the Later Middle Ages* (Philadelphia: University of Pennsylvania Press, 2008).

[22] I.e., "Bread for the sake of God," a cry of beggars in the Middle Ages. It was customary for schoolboys, regardless of their means, to be organized to beg for alms [*Parteken*]—money or sweets—sometimes while singing, as Mathesius mentions taking place in Eisenach (see the next paragraph). Cf. *Sermon on Keeping Children in School* (1530), LW 46:250–51.

[23] A proverb: see Wander 2:146, "Gross" no. 45.

[24] On Luther's family connections to Eisenach (through his mother), see Luther to Spalatin, January 14, 1520, LW 48:145; and above, Melanchthon, *Preface*, p. 58. Cf. Oberman, *Luther*, p. 90; Siggins, *Luther and His Mother*, pp. 45–52.

matron[25] took him in to board, since she had become quite taken with the boy because of his singing and his heartfelt praying in the church.[26]

In 1501[27] this young fellow's dear parents sent him to the university in Erfurt and supported him from the success of their honorable property in the mines. It was God's intention to use the descendants of Japheth [Gen. 5:32; 10:1-5] and Tubal [Gen. 10:2],[28] the German Zarephathites and miners, to reform His Church at the end of the world and to send the contaminated doctrine and scrap silver of the Levites and clergy into the fire or furnace to smelt it and produce pure silver again, just as the prophets speak and prophesy [Mal. 3:3; Isa. 1:22-25]. It was necessary, therefore, that this spiritual smelter be born in an honorable mining city from good miners and be supported from their honorable property in the mines.

It was at this university that this student began with great zeal and diligence to study his old logic and the other liberal arts and the arts of rhetoric, to the extent that these were being taught at that time, just as he also applied himself to the study of law for a while.[29] Although by nature he was a spirited

---

[25] This "matron" came to be identified as Ursula Cotta, though the tradition is late and has been questioned: see Siggins, *Luther and His Mother*, pp. 49-50; Oberman, *Luther*, pp. 99-100. Luther himself speaks fondly of his Eisenach hostess without naming her (*Table Talk* no. 6910 (n.d.), WA TR 6:265) but identifies his host in Eisenach as Heinrich Schalbe (*Randbemerkungen zu Melanchthons Apologia*, WA 30/3:491; cf. *Table Talk* no. 5362 [1540], WA TR 5:95). Cf. Volz, *Die Lutherpredigten des Johannes Mathesius*, pp. 161-62. The traditions are reconciled in Brecht's reconstruction with Ursula Cotta as the daughter of Heinrich, living with her husband, Kunz Cotta, in the same house: Brecht 1:18-19.

[26] Luther's period in Eisenach lasted from 1498 (or possibly 1497) to 1501. He attended the parish school of St. George. Luther remembered his instruction in Eisenach favorably: see above, Melanchthon, *Preface*, pp. 57-58; Brecht 1:17-21; Oberman, *Luther*, pp. 99-102.

[27] Luther arrived in Erfurt in April or May 1501. See Brecht 1:29. Cf. below, Mathesius, *History*, pp. 589, 598-99.

[28] Japheth was commonly regarded as the ancestor of the European peoples (see above, p. 105 n. 11). Luther himself associates the German people not with Japheth's son Tubal, but with his son Gomer and grandson Ashkenaz (*Lectures on Genesis* [1535-45/1544-54], LW 2:189-93), as does Mathesius, below, *History*, pp. 585-87. Perhaps Tubal is mentioned here by conflation with Tubal-cain, who is described as "an artisan in every kind of skillful work of bronze and iron" (Gen. 4:22).

[29] Luther studied in the arts faculty at Erfurt, earning his baccalaureate degree in September 1502 (and the master's degree in 1505, as Mathesius notes below, p. 122). Luther studied law in Erfurt for only a few weeks, in the summer of 1505, before abandoning it to enter the Order of Hermits of St. Augustine. The description of Luther's studies as "*seine alte Loiken und ander freye Schul unnd redekünst*" may reflect the presence at Erfurt of humanist instruction in rhetoric [*Redekunst*] alongside the traditional scholastic instruction in the trivium with its emphasis on logic (the "old logic" consisted of the logical works of Aristotle known already in Latin Europe before the twelfth century: the *Categories*, *On Interpretation*, and their commentary by Porphyry [ca 234-ca. 305]). See Brecht 1:23-44; Junghans, *Der junge Luther*. Cf. above, Melanchthon, *Preface*, p. 58.

and cheerful young fellow, he began his studies every morning with fervent prayer and attendance at church, for he held to the maxim "Diligent prayer is more than half of study."[30] He never slept through or skipped a lecture, he liked to ask questions of his preceptors and conversed with them respectfully, often studied with his friends, and whenever no public lecture was being held, he always spent his time in the university library.[31]

Once, when he was looking through the books one after another, in order to become acquainted with the good ones, he came across the Latin Bible, which he had never before seen in all his life. He realized with great astonishment that it contained many more texts, Epistles and Gospels, than what was customarily expounded in the common postils and from the pulpit in church. As he looked through the Old Testament, he came across the story of Samuel and his mother, Hannah [1 Sam. 1:1–2:21]. He quickly read through it with fervent desire and joy, and since this was all new to him, he began to wish from the bottom of his heart that one day our faithful God would grant him his own copy of this book, a wish and sigh that was richly fulfilled.[32]

Not long afterward, when he had fallen so seriously ill that he despaired of his life, an old priest visited him.[33] He consoled him, saying, "Take comfort, my bachelor,[34] you will not die in this bed. Our God will make you into a great man yet, who will in turn comfort many people. For when God loves someone and wants to draw something salutary from him, He lays the holy cross upon him for a time, and in this school of the cross, patient people learn a great deal."

This is the first prophecy which the doctor heard, and it touched his heart, for he often mentioned this consolation and prophecy. For rarely does our God accomplish something extraordinary and wonderful without first having it proclaimed and revealed, as He says in the prophet [Amos 3:7].

---

[30] *Fleissig gebet ist uber die helff studirt.* See Wander 1:342, "Beten" no. 31. The proverb does not seem to appear in Luther's own writings or *Table Talk.*

[31] In fact, the statutes for students at Erfurt at the time would not have allowed regular access to the library. See Volz, *Die Lutherpredigten des Johannes Mathesius*, pp. 163–64.

[32] See *Table Talk* no. 116 (1531), LW 54:13–14; no. 3593 (1537), WA TR 3:438–40; no. 3767 (1538), WA TR 3:598–99; no. 5346 (1540), WA TR 5:75–76. Cf. Brecht 1:85.

[33] For similar though not identical accounts, see *Table Talk* no. 223 (1532), LW 54:29 (cf. WA TR 1:95); no. 1368 (1532), WA TR 2:74; and no. 2520 (1532), WA TR 2:501. See Volz, *Die Lutherpredigten des Johannes Mathesius*, p. 217 on *LH* 18–19. The illness mentioned here may possibly be identified with the accidental wound which Luther sustained while on his way home to Mansfeld at Easter in 1503 or 1504. See *Table Talk* no. 119 (1531), LW 54:14–15; no. 6428 (n.d.), WA TR 5:657; Brecht 1:46–47; Oberman, *Luther*, p. 125.

[34] I.e., someone who had received the bachelor's degree. Luther received his in September 1502, as quickly as was possible under the university regulations.

The precious martyr from Bohemia, Master John Hus,[35] also prophesied of this doctor a hundred years beforehand, and even named the year in which he would arise and sing the Roman Church a valediction. "Today you roast a goose," said Master Goose[36] in the year 1415, when the Council of Constance intended to burn him, "but in a hundred years," that is, in 1516, as men reckon, "a pure[37] swan will come, who will sing you another swan song"[38]—just as came to pass, praise God! For it was in 1516 that Dr. Luther began disputing against indulgences.[39]

Similarly, there was a pious old monk in the cloister in Eisenach who was being held captive by his brothers, whom the deacon of this church, Herr Bartold Gruntzebach,[40] when he was a young monk in the aforementioned cloister, served as personal attendant. In his prison, this man, Johann

---

[35] On Hus and his reception in the sixteenth-century Reformation, see above, pp. xxxvii–xxxviii n. 103.

[36] "Hus" in Czech means "goose."

[37] *lauterer*, in German, a play on the name "Luther."

[38] Luther himself cited this prophecy in his *Commentary on the Alleged Imperial Edict* (1531), LW 34:104 (cf. WA 30/3:387). Haberkern (*Patron Saint and Prophet*, p. 189) notes that this prophecy is apocryphal, drawn from a letter written after Hus' 1412 exile from Prague and from the final words of Jerome of Prague, who was also condemned and burned at the Council of Constance. On the reception of Hus' prophecy, see Robert Scribner, "Incombustible Luther: The Image of the Reformer in Early Modern Germany," *Past and Present* 110 (1986): 38–68, especially pp. 41–42. Cf. above, Bugenhagen, *Christian Sermon*, p. 28, and below, Mathesius, *History*, pp. 556–57.

[39] As is apparent at the beginning of the second sermon (below, *History*, pp. 141–44), Mathesius knew that the *Ninety-Five Theses* were posted on October 31, 1517. However, he saw the famous theses as the culmination of Luther's activities in the previous year, such as Luther's disputation "against [Scholastic] sophistry" (the *Disputation on the Powers and Will of Man apart from Grace*, September 25, 1516, WA 1:145–51 [LW 72]; cf. below, pp. 135–36). See also Luther's reference to his disputations of 1516 and his beginning to write against the papacy in *Table Talk* no. 5346 (1540), WA TR 5:76; no. 884 (1530), WA TR 1:441; no. 2250 (1531), WA TR 2:376. Luther's first preaching against indulgences seems to have taken place in January 1517: see Wengert, "Luther's Preaching an Indulgence in January 1517," pp. 62–75, which translates and redates sermons preserved in WA 1:94–99 and 4:670–74.

[40] On Gruntzebach, who was deacon in Joachimsthal until 1548, see Loesche, *Johannes Mathesius*, 1:276, 288, 542.

Hilten,[41] called to himself his superior,[42] who sharply rebuked and reproved him. "Very well," said the captive man (at about the time when Doctor Luther was born), "in 1516 one will come who will reform you and make my prophecy against you come true." I mention these three prophecies here as a testimony and confession concerning our dear doctor. For people keep talking about a thing until God one day makes it come true.[43]

|At the beginning of the year 1505,[44] Martin Luther received the master's degree in Erfurt, where he ably studied the liberal arts, as they were taught in schools at that time. At the end of the same year, when a good friend of his had been stabbed[45] and a great storm and horrifying thunderclap had severely frightened him, and he was sincerely terrified of God's wrath and Day of Judgment, he resolved and vowed to enter the monastery,[46] to serve God there and propitiate Him by holding Mass, and to earn eternal salvation with monastic holiness—for this was in fact the teaching and view of the most pious monks and nuns. Therefore, it was not out of laziness, lack

---

[41] Johann Hilten (ca. 1425–ca. 1500; spelled "Hielten" by Mathesius) became a Franciscan monk after studying in Erfurt. Because of his accusations and apocalyptic denunciations against the Church and the order, he was kept under guard. He wrote commentaries on Daniel and Revelation during his confinement. Although he died without revoking his accusations of abuses in the Church or his prophecies, he was provided with the sacraments before his death. See Friedrich Wilhelm Bautz, "Hilten, Johann," *BBKL* 2:870–71; Hans Volz, "Hilten, Johann," *NDB* 9:164–65. See also below, Mathesius, *History*, p. 557. The story of Hilten's prophecy is also recounted by Melanchthon in Ap XXVII 1–3 (Kolb-Wengert, pp. 277–78; *Concordia*, p. 237), where Luther commented on it in the margin of his own copy, noting that Hilten had been part of Heinrich Schalbe's (see above, p. 119 n. 25) acquaintance in Eisenach: WA 30/3:491; see also *On the Councils and the Church* (1539), LW 41:116.

[42] *Gardian*; i.e., the *custos*, the title given by Franciscans to the superior over the local community of friars. The *custos* in Eisenach would have been Heinrich Kühne: see Volz, *Die Lutherpredigten des Johannes Mathesius*, p. 218 on *LH* 19. He is mentioned in Luther, *Die kleine Antwort auf Herzog Georgs nächstes Buch* (1533), WA 38:148–49.

[43] Cf. Wander 3:1833, "Sagen" no. 69, but with "until it comes to pass."

[44] I.e., January 1505. See *Table Talk* no. 5347 (1540), WA TR 5:76.

[45] The death of a friend of Luther is mentioned by Melanchthon (see above, *Preface*, p. 60) and by Cochlaeus (*Deeds and Writings of Dr. Martin Luther*, in Vandiver et al., *Luther's Lives*, p. 55). Only Mathesius specifies the cause of death as a stabbing [*erstochen*]. Some of Luther's associates at Erfurt are known to have died of the plague in 1505: see Brecht 1:47.

[46] For Luther's own report of his 1505 vow to become a monk, made to St. Anne amid a thunderstorm on July 2, 1505, see *Table Talk* no. 4707 (1539), WA TR 4:440; no. 5373 (1540), WA TR 5:99. Cf. *Table Talk* no. 623 (1533), LW 54:109; Luther to Hans Luther, November 21, 1521, LW 48:332 (preface to *Judgment on Monastic Vows* [1521], LW 44:243–400); *Table Talk* no. 4414 (1539), LW 54:337–38; and see Brecht 1:48–49. Melanchthon (above, *Preface*, pp. 59–60) does not mention the storm or the vow. Because St. Anne is first connected to the vow in Luther's report of 1539, the historicity of this element in the account is questioned by Angelika Dörfler-Dierken, "Luther und die heilige Anna: Zum Gelübde vom Stotternheim," *LJB* 64 (1997): 19–46; and Leppin, *Martin Luther*, pp. 29–31.

of talent, or poverty that he became an Augustinian monk in Erfurt,[47] yet he did so without the approval or knowledge of his dear father, who was deeply dismayed at this and said two things to his son: "See to it that your terror was not a diabolical deception. In any case, a person should obey his parents for the sake of God's Word [Exod. 20:12; Matt. 15:4] and not undertake anything without their knowledge and counsel." This later caused the doctor constant regret, until he took off his cowl again, as we can clearly see in the preface [dedicated] to his father for the book *On Monastic Vows*.[48]

Before he made his profession of vows in the monastery, at his request the chapter[49] gave him a Latin Bible, which he read through with the greatest of zeal and prayer and learned much of it by heart.[50] The monks, however, greatly disdained him and tied him to many duties, so that he had to serve as janitor and sexton and clean out the filthiest latrines. They also paired him with a mendicant friar and brazenly said, *"Cum sacco per civitatem!"* ["Through the city with your sack!"]; [in other words], "Begging, not studying, is the way to serve and enrich the monasteries."[51]

Since, however, he was a respected member of the university in Erfurt and had received his master's degree,[52] |the laudable university interceded for one of its members and on his behalf petitioned his prior and chapter so that they were obliged to spare him in part from this repugnant burden.

---

[47] Cf. above, Melanchthon, *Preface*, p. 60. Luther entered the "Black Monastery" (so named from the habit of the friars) of the Observant Hermits of St. Augustine in Erfurt on July 17, 1505 (Brecht 1:58). Strictly speaking, the Augustinian Hermits were mendicant friars and not monks, but Luther and his contemporaries were scarcely ever careful to observe the nice distinction in language, at least in German. (Mathesius does refer to Luther as a "friar" using the Latin title *Frater*, below, *History*, pp. 125–26, 128, 129, 582.) See Brecht 1:23–32, 55–57; Oberman, *Luther*, pp. 124–29. On the Augustinian Hermits and the Observantine reform, see Eric L. Saak, *High Way to Heaven: The Augustinian Platform between Reform and Reformation, 1292–1524*, Studies in Medieval and Reformation Thought 89 (Leiden: Brill, 2002).

[48] LW 44:243–400. The sentiments of Luther's father reported here come from Luther's preface, LW 48:330–36, especially p. 332. Luther ceased wearing the monastic habit in 1523. Cf. *Table Talk* no. 3556a (1537), WA TR 3:410–11; no. 4414 (1539), LW 54:338–39; no. 5034 (1540), WA TR 4:624; no. 6430 (n.d.), WA TR 5:657.

[49] *Convent*; i.e., the assembly of the monastic community to discuss business.

[50] On Luther's receipt of a Bible from the community, see *Table Talk* no. 116 (1531), LW 54:14; no. 5346 (1540), WA TR 5:75.

[51] Mathesius' description of Luther's monastic life here is paralleled in Luther's *Table Talk* no. 5375 (1540), WA TR 5:99–100. Begging was a standard part of the life of the mendicant orders and not a surprising activity for Luther as a novice. Nonetheless, there may have been some special desire to exercise Luther in humility in light of his prior academic degrees and perceived scholarly interests: see Brecht 1:90–91; *Table Talk* no. 6039 (n.d.), WA TR 5:452–43; cf. Oberman, *Luther*, p. 136.

[52] *ein promovirter Magister ware*

Having professed his vows and donned the cowl,[53] he then became a priest in the year 1507, as shown by the letter in which he extended an invitation to his first Mass.[54] His brothers took the Bible away from him again and put the sophistry of their Scholastics into his hands, which out of obedience he diligently and thoroughly read, but whenever he had a chance, he hid in the monastery library and constantly and faithfully kept to his beloved Bible.[55] Alongside this, as a pious monk, he read his Mass with the deepest devotion for fifteen years;[56] afterward, when he had come to the knowledge of the truth, he regarded this for the rest of his life as his most abominable sin, with which he had angered his faithful God and desecrated the one, perfect sacrifice of the innocent and precious blood of Jesus Christ [Heb. 10:12–14].

Now since he was engaged in study and prayer day and night in the monastery in addition to chastising and enervating himself with fasting and keeping vigil, he was always distressed and sad. None of his celebrations of Mass would give him any consolation, so God sent to him as father confessor an old brother in the monastery,[57] who gave him profound comfort, pointing him to the gracious forgiveness of sins in the Apostles' Creed[58] and teaching him from the sermons of St. Bernard[59] that he, too, had to believe for himself that God the merciful Father had won for him the forgiveness of sins through the one sacrifice and blood of His obedient Son, and had

---

[53] The required period of novitiate was a year and a day, so Luther's solemn vows would have taken place after July 17, 1506.

[54] Luther to Johann Braun, April 22, 1507, LW 48:3–5. Luther was ordained a priest on April 3, 1507, and celebrated his first Mass shortly thereafter on May 2. See Brecht 1:72.

[55] *Table Talk* no. 5346 (1540), WA TR 5:75.

[56] *biß inn fünfftzehen jar*. Probably not "until 1515" (so *LH²*, p. 462 on 21.13). Dating from 1507, "for fifteen years" would extend through 1521, when Luther ceased to read private Masses in the fall. Thereafter, Luther made his first concrete proposals for the revision of the liturgy of the Mass in 1523 with *Concerning the Order of Public Worship* and *Order of Mass and Communion*, LW 53:7–14, 15–40. For Luther's own statements about his "fifteen years" saying Mass, see *Table Talk* no. 5589 (1543), LW 54:461–62; *Confession concerning Christ's Supper* (1528), LW 37:370–71; *Church Postil* (1540–44), sermon for Pentecost Monday on John 3:16–21, LW 77:371, paragraph 21; *The Private Mass* (1533), LW 38:149; *Sermon for the Rededication of the Church of St. Paul in Leipzig* (1545), LW 58:272–73; cf. *Sermons on Holy Baptism* (1534), LW 57:177; *Sermon at the Dedication of the Castle Church, Torgau* (1544/1546), LW 51:345; *Table Talk* no. 5499 (1542), LW 54:433.

[57] The "old brother" who served as Luther's confessor was Johann Greffenstein: see above, Melanchthon, Preface, p. 60 and n. 34 there. Later, Johann von Staupitz would serve as Luther's confessor: see below, Mathesius, *History*, pp. 446–47; cf. above, p. lvi n. 194.

[58] Apostles' Creed 3 (Kolb-Wengert, p. 22; *Concordia*, p. 16).

[59] On Bernard of Clairvaux, see above, p. lvi n. 191. For this account, see above, Melanchthon, *Preface*, p. 61. For the passage from Bernard, see above, p. 61 n. 39.

caused this to be proclaimed in the apostolic church through the Holy Spirit by means of the word of Absolution. This was a living and powerful consolation in our doctor's heart. Later he recalled this for his comfort, as he sang the verse in the sequence for Christmas: "*O beata culpa quae talem meruisti redemptorem*" ["O blessed fault which has deserved such a ¹Redeemer"].[60] He often mentioned this father confessor of his with great respect and expressed his profound thanks.[61]

Not long before this time, at the instigation of his brother, the bishop of Magdeburg,[62] the highly praiseworthy elector, Duke Frederick of Saxony,[63] caused the university in Wittenberg to be founded[64] by Dr. Martin [Pollich von] Mellerstadt[65] and Dr. Johann Staupitz, who at this time was vicar or superintendent over forty Augustinian monasteries in Meissen and Thuringia.[66] And since Staupitz, who had been commissioned, among other things, to look for scholars and call them to come to Wittenberg, saw extraordinary ability and earnest piety in this man, he brought Friar[67] Martin to the

---

[60] Mathesius seems to conflate the Christmas sequence *Eia recolamus laudibus* with its line *O culpa nimium beata qua redempta est natura* ["O fault exceedingly blessèd, by which nature has been redeemed"] (PL 131:1005) and the Easter *Exsultet*, which reads: *O felix culpa, quae talem ac tantum meruit habere redemptorem* ["O happy fault, which deserved to have such a great Redeemer"] (PL 72:364). On the *O culpa nimium*, see *Table Talk* no. 428 (1532), WA TR 1:185. On the *O felix culpa*, see Luther, sermon of December 25, 1537, WA 45:349 (with allusion to the *O culpa nimium* as well); preface to Rhegius, *Exposition of Psalm 52* (1541), LW 60:243; *Lectures on Genesis* (1535–45/1544–54), LW 2:154.

[61] Cf. *Table Talk* no. 122 (1531), WA 1:147; no. 518 (1533), LW 54:93–95; preface to Bugenhagen's edition of Athanasius, *Against the Idolatry of the Gentiles* (1532), LW 59:346; Luther to Elector John Frederick, June 10, 1540, WA Br 9:130.

[62] Ernest II of Saxony (1464–1513), the younger brother of Frederick the Wise, was confirmed as archbishop of Magdeburg by papal dispensation in 1478. His role in the founding of the university at Wittenberg (emphasized by Mathesius again below, *History*, p. 577) is difficult to trace. In 1504, he did mediate the controversy over the relative positions of poetry and theology between Conrad Wimpina (see above, p. 67 n. 76) and Martin Pollich von Mellerstadt (see above, p. 63 n. 53; and below, p. 127). See below, Mathesius, *History*, p. 579; and Grossman, *Humanism in Wittenberg*, pp. 43–44.

[63] On Frederick III of Saxony, see above, p. 68 n. 82.

[64] Frederick obtained imperial privileges for the founding of the University of Wittenberg from Emperor Maximilian (r. 1493–1519) on July 6, 1502. Papal confirmation of the university was given later in 1507. See Grossman, *Humanism in Wittenberg*, pp. 36–54; Schwiebert, *The Reformation*, chapter 17, 2:220–31.

[65] On Mellerstadt, see above, p. 63 n. 53.

[66] On Staupitz, see above, p. lvi n. 194.

[67] *Frater*; or, simply, "Brother," but the Latin suggests that the technical title of a mendicant is meant. Cf. above, p. 123 n. 47.

monastery in Wittenberg in 1508, the university having been founded there six years before.[68]

Here our Friar Martin assiduously devoted himself to Holy Scripture and began disputing against sophistry in the university.[69] At this time sophistry was prevalent everywhere, and since the foundation of Christianity at that time was being laid in all the universities, monasteries, and pulpits on the basis of the master of the sublime *Sentences*[70] as well as from Thomas Aquinas, Scotus, and Albertus,[71] our Friar Martin started disputing against their first principles and inquired after the true and sure foundation of our salvation. He held the Scripture of the prophets and apostles, which has come forth from the mouth of God [Matt. 4:4], to be higher, firmer, and more certain than all sophistry and scholastic theology, which was already at that time a source of great consternation to good people.

---

[68] Luther's initial teaching activity in Wittenberg was as temporary replacement for Wolfgang Ostermayr [Cäppelmair] (d. 1546; Georg Westermayer, "Cäppelmair, Wolfgang," *ADB* 3:776) as an instructor in philosophy during the winter term of 1508-9. After receiving his first theological degree (*baccalaureus biblicus*) in Wittenberg on March 9, 1509, and completing requirements for the second degree (*baccalaureus Sententiarius*), Luther returned to the cloister and university in Erfurt where he was awarded the latter degree in the fall of 1509. See Brecht 1:90-98. Mathesius, following his sources, is silent about Luther's return to Erfurt: see Volz, *Die Lutherpredigten des Johannes Mathesius*, p. 155 n. 3; Luther, *Table Talk* no. 5347 (1540), WA TR 5:76-77; above, Melanchthon, *Preface*, p. 64. Luther returned to Wittenberg after his trip to Rome, in 1511 or 1512 (see below, pp. 127-28).

[69] In fact, Luther's assignment during his 1508-9 stay in Wittenberg was to lecture on Aristotle's *Nicomachean Ethics* while Staupitz lectured on the Bible, though Luther would rather have been teaching theology himself. See Luther to Johann Braun, March 17, 1509, WA Br 1:16-17. Cf. Brecht 1:92-93. Disputation was a standard part of scholastic practice in the universities, not evidence of any special quarrelsomeness on Luther's part. Cf. Luther's description of his career at this point in *Table Talk* no. 5346 (1540), WA TR 5:75. On Luther's engagement with scholastic theology, cf. above, Melanchthon, *Preface*, pp. 60, 62-63.

[70] *Auß dem Meister von hohen sinnen*, a German rendering of Peter Lombard's Latin epithet *Magister Sententiarum*, from his theological textbook, *The Sentences*. On Peter Lombard and *The Sentences* and Luther's relationship with this material, see above, p. 60 n. 29.

[71] The theologians listed were regarded as the founders of schools of thought within Scholasticism. On Thomas Aquinas, see above, p. 62 n. 47. His teacher Albertus Magnus ("The Great," see above, p. 77 n. 134) continued to have followers who opposed Thomists, especially at Cologne. Although he could be critical of him, Luther preferred John Duns Scotus (see above, pp. 62-63 n. 48) to Thomas. Collectively, Aquinas, Albertus, and Scotus and their followers were identified with the *Via Antiqua*, sharing a realist metaphysics. Curiously, Mathesius does not here mention the theologians of the *Via Moderna*, or Nominalists, such as Gabriel Biel and William of Ockham (see above, p. 62 nn. 44 and 46), the school that most influenced Luther's theological education and against which he chiefly reacted. See Oberman, *Harvest of Medieval Theology*. Mathesius does mention Ockham and Biel later: see below, *History*, pp. 135, 456-57. In the early years, the Wittenberg theological faculty consisted primarily of Thomists and Scotists: see Brecht 1:120.

Dr. Mellerstadt, who in his day was a *lux mundi* ["light of the world"],[72] a doctor of medicine, of jurisprudence, and of monastic sophistry,[73] could not forget the arguments and explanations of this monk even when he sat at table. "This monk," he often said—as I heard from the mouth of his brother, Herr Valten,[74] many times—"this monk will confound all the doctors ¹and introduce a new doctrine and reform the whole Roman Church. For he relies on the Scripture of the prophets and apostles and stands upon the Word of Jesus Christ, which no philosophy or sophistry, Scotism, Albertism, Thomism, or the whole [work of] Tartaretus[75] is able to topple or refute."

In 1510, as shown by his own handwriting, his chapter sent him on to Rome on behalf of the monastery.[76] There he saw the most holy father, the pope,[77] and his gilded religion and wanton courtesans and courtiers, which later gave him strength when he was writing so intently against the Roman abomination and idolatry.[78] As he was often heard to say at his table, he

---

[72] Mellerstadt was given the epithet *lux mundi* by his humanist friends.

[73] Mellerstadt had a master's degree in arts and a doctorate in medicine, received from Leipzig in 1486. He received his doctorate in theology ("monastic sophistry") in Wittenberg in 1503. Despite having published a little in the field, he does not seem to have held a doctorate in law: see Volz, *Die Lutherpredigten des Johannes Mathesius*, p. 13; and below, Mathesius, *History*, pp. 578–79.

[74] Valentin [Valten] Pollich von Mellerstadt (d. after 1552), the younger brother of Martin, matriculated at Wittenberg in 1502 and remained around Wittenberg and in association with Luther in the following decades, when Mathesius must have made his acquaintance. On Valentin Mellerstadt, see WA Br 3:243 n. 2 and Luther's *Testament* of 1542, WA Br 9:583, where he is named as a creditor; see also below, Mathesius, *History*, p. 302.

[75] *Tardaret*; i.e., Petrus Tartaretus (d. ca. 1522) was a Franciscan master at Paris who published commentaries on Aristotle, Porphry, Petrus Hispanus, and Scotus. His work was printed at Wittenberg in 1504 [VD16 J654]. See Sachiko Kusukawa, *The Transformation of Natural Philosophy: The Case of Philip Melanchthon* (Cambridge: Cambridge University Press, 1995), pp. 14–21.

[76] On the debate concerning the date of and the reasons for Luther's trip to Rome, see the introduction above, pp. lvi–lvii and n. 196 there. If the trip in fact occurred in 1511–12 rather than in 1510–11, then Luther would have left for Rome from Wittenberg on behalf of Staupitz, rather than from Erfurt on behalf of the monastery there. For the dating to 1510 "in his own handwriting," see *Table Talk* no. 5347 (1540), WA TR 5:76–77.

[77] There is no other evidence that Luther saw the pope himself (Julius II, r. 1503–13) while in Rome: see Hendrix, *Luther and the Papacy*, p. 10; Brecht 1:102. If Luther's visit took place in 1501–11, Julius would have been away from Rome, in the field with his armies at Bologna. In 1511–12, Julius would have been in Rome, preparing for the Fifth Lateran Council, which opened in May 1512: see Christine Shaw, *Julius II: The Warrior Pope* (Oxford: Blackwell, 1993), pp. 261, 285, 287–99.

[78] For Luther's own descriptions of his trip to Rome, see *Against the Roman Papacy* (1545), LW 41:278–79; *Instructions for the Visitors [in Naumburg]* (1545), WA 26:198; *Brief Confession* (1544), LW 38:318; *Lectures on Genesis* (1535–45/1544–54), LW 3:254; *Defense of the Sermon on Papal Indulgence and Grace* (1518), WA 1:390 (LW 70); sermon of November 15, 1545,

would not trade having seen Rome for a thousand gulden.[79] For when he was there and wanted to release his friends from purgatory with his sacrifice of the Mass, as everyone at that time believed, and was saying his Mass very devoutly and slowly, at the altar next to him seven Masses were said before he had finished even one. The Roman servants of the Mass said to him: "*Passa passa*," "Get going, get going! Get her Son back home to our Lady quickly." Others divulged at table the words some Romanists used when they consecrated and censed their bread and wine: "*Panis es et panis manebis, vinum es et vinum manebis*" ["Bread you are, and bread you will remain; wine you are, and wine you will remain"].[80] Having returned to Wittenberg and his monastery by the help of God, he continued studying and engaging in disputations.[81]

In the year of our Lord 1512, as shown by his own published open letter in which he invited the [Augustinians] of Erfurt to come to [the conferral of] his doctorate,[82] his vicar[-general] as his superior,[83] along with the chapter,[84] resolved that Friar Martin should become a doctor of Holy Scripture. Doctor Staupitz presented this resolution to him under a tree in the monastery in Wittenberg, which he himself once showed me and others. But when Friar Martin ǀmost humbly excused himself, putting forward, among many others, the argument he was a weak and sick friar who had not long to live and that they should look for someone more capable and healthy, Doctor Staupitz gave an answer, in jest, only to this last argument: "It appears that our God will soon have a great deal of business to accomplish in heaven and on earth for which He will need many

---

LW 58:337; *Table Talk* no. 3582a (1537), LW 54:237; no. 3930 (1538), LW 54:296; cf. *Table Talk* nos. 3478, 3479a (1536), LW 54:208–9, as well as the specific citations below, n. 80.

[79] See, e.g., *Table Talk* no. 5484 (1542), LW 54:427. A gulden was the most valuable gold coin in common circulation. By way of comparison, Luther's annual salary as a full professor from 1525 onward was 200 gulden.

[80] For Luther's account of these episodes from his time in Rome, see *Commentary on Psalm 117* (1530), LW 14:6; *The Private Mass* (1533), LW 38:166; *Table Talk* no. 3428 (n.d.), WA TR 3:313. See also Brecht 1:98–105; Oberman, *Luther*, pp. 146–50.

[81] If Luther traveled to Rome in 1510–11, he would in fact have first returned to the Augustinians in Erfurt before moving to Wittenberg. If the trip was in 1511–12, he would have returned directly to Wittenberg, as Mathesius suggests here. The first evidence of Luther's residence in Wittenberg comes from 1512: Luther to the Augustinians at Erfurt, September 22, 1512, LW 48:5–7.

[82] Luther to the Augustinians at Erfurt, September 22, 1512, LW 48:5–7.

[83] I.e., Johann von Staupitz, who was vicar-general of the Observant Augustinian Hermits in Germany (as well as prior of the Saxon province) and hence Luther's monastic superior.

[84] Here, the chapter not simply of the local cloister but of the German congregations of the Augustinian Hermits as a whole, held in Cologne on May 5, 1512: see Brecht 1:126.

young and industrious doctors through whom He can conduct His affairs. Whether you live now or you die, God has need of you in His council. Therefore, accept the charge your chapter is laying upon you, even as you are obligated, according to your vows, to obey me and the chapter.[85] As far as the expenses are concerned, our most gracious elector, Duke Frederick, will most graciously pay for these from his treasury to support God, this university, and this monastery"—as indeed came to pass.

Then Friar Martin was sent off to Leipzig to receive this money from the electoral chamberlain.[86] In keeping with the way things have always been done at court, they kept him waiting so long that he was even willing to leave without the money, if his monastic obedience had not compelled him to wait for it to be made ready. For though lords are often gracious in opening their hands, much depends on those who are to execute the lords' commands and put them into effect. Thus at the command of his vicar and chapter, and at the expense of the estimable elector of Saxony, and on the basis of the privileges and authority of Roman Emperor Maximilian and the see of Rome, which ten years earlier had established the university *iure humano* ["by human right"], Friar Martin received his doctorate of Holy Scripture on St. Lucy's Day in Wittenberg.[87] There he took a solemn oath to Holy Scripture, promising to spend his life studying and preaching it and defending the Christian faith with disputations and writings in opposition to all heretics, so help him God.[88]

ᴵWith this legitimate[89] and public call—which was committed to him by an established and laudable university, in the name and by the order of his High Imperial Majesty and the see of Rome, according to the counsel

---

[85] See *Table Talk* no. 2255a (1531), WA TR 2:379; no. 3143a–b (1532), WA TR 3:187–88; no. 5371 (1540), WA TR 5:98; no. 6422 (n.d.), WA TR 5:654–55. Cf. above, Melanchthon, *Preface*, p. 64.

[86] Frederick's chamberlain [*Cammerer*] was Degenhard Pfeffinger (1471–1519). The receipt for Frederick's gift of 50 gulden for the expenses of Luther's doctorate, dated October 9, 1512, is preserved in WA 12:405.

[87] Luther's letter of September 22 (LW 48:6) says that the doctoral promotion was to take place on St. Luke's Day (October 18). Mathesius' dating to St. Lucy's Day (December 13) is probably a one-letter error either of reading or of printing (*Luciae* for *Lucae*). See Volz, *Die Lutherpredigten des Johannes Mathesius*, p. 157. Andreas Bodenstein von Karlstadt, as dean of the theological faculty, presided over the conferral of the doctorate (on Karlstadt, see below, p. 154 n. 90).

[88] On Luther's doctoral oath, see Brecht 1:126; Obermann, *Luther*, p. 22; and Siegfried Freiherr von Scheurl, "Martin Luther's Doktoreid," *Zeitschrift für bayerische Kirchengeschichte* 32 (1963): 46–52. Cf. Luther, *Commentary on the Alleged Imperial Edict* (1531), LW 34:103. For the text of the oath administered at Wittenberg, see Friedensburg, *Urkundenbuch der Universität Wittenberg*, 1:35–36.

[89] *ordenlichen*

and decree of his preceptors and the spiritual authorities set over him, by means of his elector's most gracious aid and contribution, and upon his solemn oath, which he made to God, Holy Scripture, and the university in Wittenberg—he often comforted and sustained himself in dire straits and struggles, whenever the devil and world sought to make him afraid and anxious by asking who had commanded him to do this and how he would answer for having caused such a commotion in the whole of Christendom. Then, I say, he would recall and take comfort in his legitimate doctorate and public mandate and solemn oath, on the basis of which he advanced his causes (in fact, God's own) in Christ's name, without fear, honorably and for the salvation of many people, and valiantly carried them to completion with the help of God.[90]

Alas, few people these days believe that a proper call is so very important, whether it be a public doctorate and general call[91] or the office of a parish pastor and deacon in a particular and individual city. For a steadfast doctor [of theology] and preacher must be certain of his calling and mandate and must also base all of his teaching and writing on God's Word firmly and without wavering if he wants to fulfill his office and persevere steadfast in his calling. How on earth will they answer for themselves in conscience before God, those who appoint themselves to the doctoral office without any warrant or who force themselves upon a church or write in other people's parish registers[92] or displace legitimate teachers or wantonly abandon their own call? May God in heaven have mercy!

⌐I have to mention this here in connection with the doctor's legitimate doctorate and call, on the basis of which, with God's help, he accomplished things far beyond what he or any human being had imagined. It is indeed true what Emperor Frederick [III] says in his [acrostic] vowels: "*Aquila electa iuste omnia vincit*" ["The chosen eagle conquers all by right"],[93] and a

---

[90] For Luther's appeal to his doctorate, see, e.g., *Why the Books of the Pope and His Disciples Were Burned* (1520), LW 31:383; *Commentary on the Alleged Imperial Edict* (1531), LW 34:67; *To the Christian Nobility* (1520), LW 44:124, 204.

[91] The university doctorate was in principle the "right to teach anywhere" [*ius ubique docendi* or *licentia ubique docendi*]. See Hilde de Ridder-Symoens, ed., *Universities in the Middle Ages*, vol. 1 of *A History of the University in Europe*, ed. Walter Rüegg et al. (New York: Cambridge University Press, 1992), p. 21. On the importance of a call, cf. Luther, *Infiltrating and Clandestine Preachers* (1532), LW 40:387–88.

[92] *inn frembde Kirchen bücher schreiben*; i.e., performing the kind of pastoral acts that were recorded in the parish register (e.g., Baptisms, weddings, funerals) without a call to that parish. Or, if one follows Latin rather than German idiom: "who write books against other people's churches."

[93] Austrian Archduke Frederick III (1415–93), who was elected the first Holy Roman emperor of the Hapsburg dynasty in 1452, employed the vowels of the Latin alphabet as an acrostic motto capable of multiple German and Latin renderings, e.g., the more common

teacher who enters his office and estate with God and a good conscience and perseveres in this, basing all of his teaching upon Holy Scripture, cannot be thwarted or overcome by all the gates of hell [Matt. 16:18]. This can be seen in all the prophets, apostles, and godly bishops—and in this doctor of ours.

Now since this man was a legitimate and called doctor of Sacred Scripture, he occupied himself seriously with God's holy Bible and read through it again with the greatest diligence while taking counsel from the ancient fathers and doctors of the Church about how to understand and thus expound the texts of Scripture in such a way that they might be in proportion and accord with faith in Christ and with the apostolic rule and standard [Rom. 12:6] and might cast light on Christ.[94] He also began at the order of his superior to lecture, preach, and engage in disputations. He wrote at this time many letters of consolation to troubled consciences, in which he faithfully exhorts them to Holy Scripture, since it is only from the words of the prophets and apostles that we can come to know Jesus Christ as our only righteousness.[95] For example, among his letters that have been printed there is a Christian letter to an afflicted brother in the monastery in Memmingen [in which he says] that Christ and His righteousness are ours, and our sins are His, for which He has paid and made satisfaction by means of His one sacrifice on the holy cross.[96]

For after the conferral of his doctorate and on into 1516, when he began disputing against the Roman indulgences, as a legitimate doctor of Sacred Scripture he occupied himself in earnest with the holy Bible, upon which he had sworn and to which he had committed himself[97] He also began lecturing on the Epistles of St. Paul and the Psalter.[98] Likewise, at the same time

---

"*Alles Erdreich ist Österreich untertan*": "The whole earth is subject to Austria." For other renderings of the motto, see Katherine Arens, *Vienna's Dreams of Europe: Culture and Identity beyond the Nation-State* (New York: Bloomsbury Academic, 2015), p. 25.

[94] During this period, Luther read through the entire Bible twice a year and most frequently consulted the commentary of traditional authorities such as Jerome, Nicholas of Lyra (ca. 1270–1349), John Chrysostom (ca. 347–407), and, above all, Augustine. See Oberman, *Luther*, p. 173; Brecht 1:129–30. Cf. Luther, *Table Talk* no. 5346 (1540), WA TR 5:75–76; above, Melanchthon, *Preface*, pp. 64–66. On the principle of "cast[ing] light on Christ" [*Christum erklären*], cf. Luther's definition of the apostolic Word as "*was Christum treibet*" ["what inculcates Christ"]: *Preface to James and Jude* (1522, 1546), LW 35:396.

[95] See Brecht 1:156–61, which cites many of Luther's letters of counsel from these years. See, e.g., Luther to Georg Leiffer, April 15, 1516, WA Br 1:37–38; to Johann Lang, May 29, 1516, LW 48:14–16; to Michael Dressel, June 23, 1516, WA Br 1:46–4, and September 25, 1516, LW 48:20–23.

[96] Luther to George Spenlein, April 8, 1516, LW 48:11–14.

[97] See *Table Talk* no. 5346 (1540), WA TR 5:75–76.

[98] Luther lectured at Wittenberg on the Psalms from 1513 to 1515 (*First Lectures on the Psalms* [published 1743–1876], LW 10–11) and on Romans in 1515–16 (*Lectures on Romans*

Doctor Staupitz, by virtue of his office, abolished reading from the books of St. Augustine and others at table and appointed the holy Bible to be used instead in all of his monasteries.[99]

At this time the excellent man Dr. Johann Reuchlin[100] spoke up: as a Christian Hebraist, he was unable to concur or consent with the agitation of Pfefferkorn, the baptized Jew (later burned as a devil),[101] and of the inquisitors in Cologne that the Hebrew books of the Jews should be burned. For we in Christendom, if we were to gain the proper and salutary understanding of the prophets, could by no means dispense with the Hebrew books and language. Luther supported this excellent man and his cause when a good

---

[published 1938–39], LW 25), followed by Galatians in 1516–17 (*[First] Lectures on Galatians* [published 1519], LW 27:151–410). Thereafter he lectured on Hebrews in 1517–18 (*Lectures on Hebrews* [published 1929], LW 29:107–241) and then again on the Psalms (*Labors on the Psalms* [published 1519–21], WA 5 and WA Ar 1–2 [LW 64; cf. LW 14:287–349) between 1518 and 1521. See Brecht 1:129, 286–97. The order given by Mathesius here may reflect Melanchthon's report that the lectures on Romans had come before the lectures on the Psalter: see above, *Preface*, pp. 64–65.

[99] See *Table Talk* no. 5346 (1540), WA TR 5:75–76. The change made by Staupitz as vicar-general that is described here involved the monastic practice of having one brother read out loud from the writings of the church fathers or from the Bible in the refectory during meals [*zu tische zu lesen*] (*The Rule of Saint Augustine*, trans. Raymond Canning [Kalamazoo, MI: Cistercian Publications, 1996], 3.2, p. 14). This was not a change in the Wittenberg university theological curriculum, where the role of Augustine was being deliberately expanded at the expense of scholastic authors: see Luther to Johann Lang, May 18, 1517, LW 48:41–42.

[100] Johann Reuchlin (1455–1522), the granduncle of Philip Melanchthon, was a distinguished Christian Hebraist with particular interest in the Jewish mysticism known as the *Kabbalah*. He wrote an influential Hebrew grammar used by Luther, the *Rudimenta Hebraica*. On the work of Reuchlin, see David Price, *Johannes Reuchlin and the Campaign to Destroy Jewish Books* (New York: Oxford University Press, 2011); Jerome Friedman, *The Most Ancient Testimony: Sixteenth-Century Christian-Hebraica in the Age of Renaissance Nostalgia* (Athens, OH: Ohio University Press, 1983), ch. 4.

[101] Johannes Pfefferkorn (1469–1522), a Jewish convert to Christianity, worked since 1504 in concert with the Dominicans for the conversion of other Jews and called for the destruction of all Hebrew books except for the Bible. See *The Jews' Mirror (Der Juden Spiegel)*, trans. Ruth I. Cape (Tempe, AZ: Arizona Center for Medieval and Renaissance Studies, 2011); Avner Shamir, *Christian Conceptions of Jewish Books: The Pfefferkorn Affair* (Copenhagen: Museum Tusculanum Press, 2011). Reuchlin protested in his *Augenspiegel* of 1511: see Daniel O'Callaghan, ed. and trans., *The Preservation of Jewish Religious Books in Sixteenth-Century Germany: Johannes Reuchlin's Augenspiegel* (Leiden: Brill, 2013). The expanding public controversy set Pfefferkorn and his Dominican patrons at odds with the German humanists, who collaborated in the satiric *Epistolae obscurorum virorum*: see Francis Griffin Stokes, trans., *Letters of Obscure Men*, ed. Hajo Holborn (Philadelphia: University of Pennsylvania Press, 1972). On the (false) report of Pfefferkorn's execution at the stake, see Luther, *The Private Mass* (1533), LW 38:168 and n. 16; it seems to be founded on a confusion of Reuchlin's opponent with another Jew named Pfefferkorn who was executed in 1514: see Volz, *Die Lutherpredigten des Johannes Mathesius*, p. 157.

friend asked him to do so.[102] Erasmus of Rotterdam, who had spent some time in Rome with the cardinals and experienced their depravity for himself, came forward with his dialogue about Pope Julius,[103] who came to St. Peter at the gates of heaven, and with other writings in which he attacked the gray-haired schoolboys[104] and the schools of the sophists as well as the unspiritual life and conduct of the clergy.[105] In addition, he helped to reestablish the languages and the liberal arts.[106] Initially he, too, was pleased by Dr. Luther's books, as he made clear when Duke Frederick, elector of Saxony, put the question to him in Cologne concerning Dr. Luther's doctrine. He said that Dr. Luther had committed two grave sins: he had laid hands on the threefold crown of the pope[107] and on the potbellies and victuals of the monks; nevertheless, Dr. Luther's doctrine was true and in accordance with Scripture; and, that though he might carry on rather vehemently and intemperately, nevertheless roast wolf requires a spicy sauce.[108]

---

[102] See Luther to Spalatin, February 1514, WA Br 1:23–24, and August 5, 1514, LW 48:8–11.

[103] *Julius Excluded from Heaven: A Dialogue* [*Dialogus Julius exclusus e coelis*] (CWE 27:155–97; *Erasmi Opuscula: A Supplement to the Opera Omnia*, ed. Wallace K. Ferguson [The Hague: Nijhoff, 1933], pp. 65–124). Although the authorship of the *Julius exclusus* has been debated, most scholars now ascribe the work to Erasmus based on internal and external evidence. Erasmus was in Rome in 1508–9: see James D. Tracy, *Erasmus: The Growth of a Mind* (Geneva: Droz, 1972), p. 112. For Luther's comments on the *Julius exclusus* and Erasmus' stay in Rome, see *Table Talk* no. 4902 (1540), WA TR 4:574; no. 5535 (1542–43), WA TR 5:220.

[104] *alte Bachanten*; i.e., mature men whose understanding remains at the level of a beginning student. A *Bachant* was a schoolboy who had completed his most elementary education but was not yet ready for university study. The word comes from the Latin *vagari* ["to wander"] combined with *bacchari* ["to revel"]. See *DWB*, s.v. "Bachant." For Erasmus' criticism of the scholastic theologians and the clergy, see, e.g., *Praise of Folly* (CWE 27:77–153; ASD 4/3:72–194).

[105] *der geystlichen ungeystlich wesen unnd leben*

[106] Erasmus positioned himself as the leading humanist scholar of his day, advocating study of the humanities and languages. See Rummel, *Erasmus*; Lisa Jardine, *Erasmus, Man of Letters: The Construction of Charisma in Print*, 2nd ed. (Princeton, NJ: Princeton University Press, 2015). Luther made extensive use of his Greek New Testament of 1516. See Brecht 1:163–64; cf. above, Melanchthon, *Preface*, p. 66.

[107] The papal tiara had three tiers, interpreted as signifying papal authority over heaven, earth, and purgatory.

[108] The discussion between Frederick and Erasmus took place on November 5, 1520. See Brecht 1:417; *Table Talk* no. 4899 (1540), WA TR 4:573–74. *Table Talk* no. 131 (1531), LW 54:19, reports Erasmus' witticism about the "two sins"; Melanchthon (above, *Preface*, p. 69) reports Erasmus' judgment that Luther was "correct." The remark about the roast wolf and its sauce seems to be proverbial; cf. Wander 5:1043, "Braten" no. 47 (with citation of Mathesius' *Leichpredigten*) and no. 48. See also below, Mathesius, *History*, p. 559. On later conflict between Luther and Erasmus, see above, Walter, *New Spiritual Song*, p. 95, stanza 44; and below, Mathesius, *History*, pp. 379–80; cf. the introduction above, pp. lxxvi–lxxvii, xcii–xciii.

Meanwhile, Dr. Luther continued on, by virtue of his solemn doctoral oath, ˡand in all of his lectures and disputations he dealt primarily with this question or article: whether the true faith and how to live as a Christian and die a blessed death is something we should or can learn from Holy Scripture or from the godless heathen Aristotle, from whose works the Scholastics wanted to uphold the Roman Church and the doctrine of the cloisters.

This is the first conflict between Dr. Luther and the sophists.[109] As an elected doctor of Sacred Scripture, Luther says that he is baptized in the name of Jesus Christ and has sworn and promised to abide with the universal Christian Church, with feet firmly planted and a steadfast heart and a bold confession until his end. This universal Christendom is built and founded upon the writings of the prophets and apostles, as the holy Nicene Creed, which at that time was sung in all churches, clearly confesses and as the words of our children's Creed declare: "I believe there is one holy or universal Christian Church."[110] For the Nicene Creed says clearly that the Holy Spirit, whom Christ has gained for us and has given to us by grace, spoke through the prophets and apostles, which is why we call the Church or the followers of Jesus Christ an "apostolic Church." Upon the words of these prophets, which were written by inspiration of the Holy Spirit for our instruction [2 Pet. 1:21; Rom. 15:4], and upon the voice of Jesus Christ, which He, as the eternal Interpreter and Orator, brought forth from His Father's heart and revealed and gave to His dear friends, the apostles, which is now called the holy and divine Scripture—upon this, the young Doctor Luther says that he had sworn a binding, public, formal oath to God in all solemnity that he would abide with the blessed and sure Scripture.[111] Thus in matters of faith and conscience it is always more fitting to search divine Scripture [John 5:39] and remain with it—which has been brought forth ˡfrom God the Father's heart by the eternal and essential Word and Orator; and which has been attested and confirmed by the Holy Spirit from the beginning of the world through the ancient fathers, prophets, kings, apostles, holy bishops, and ancient creeds, along with the blood of many holy martyrs; and which is known to all good Christians who have entered their blessed rest—than for us to hazard soul and conscience on the uncertain

---

[109] The word "sophist"—originally used to designate Socrates' (ca. 470–399 BC) opponents, who claimed to be able to teach wisdom [*sophia*] for a fee—was often used by humanist and Protestant critics as a derogatory name for Scholastics, especially the Scholastic theologians.

[110] For the Nicene Creed and Apostles' (here, "children's") Creed, see Kolb-Wengert, pp. 22–23; *Concordia*, p. 16. Cf. Luther, *The Three Symbols* (1538), LW 34:197–229.

[111] On Luther's doctoral oath, see above, p. 129 and n. 88 there.

dreams and opinions of the obscure[112] Scotus and foolish[113] Albertus and doubtful[114] Thomas Aquinas, or of the Moderns or Occamists,[115] or of the Master of the sublime, keen *Sentences*[116] and [all] the godless and quarrelsome sophists. For we shall come before the strict Judge of all flesh, who will place to His right all those who have come to know Him from His Word and served people in His name [Matt. 25:33–40].

This, dear friends, is Doctor Luther's first [point of] disputation, which he vehemently emphasized and affirmed in his lectures and disputations, even before he began to battle indulgences.[117] Already at that time he was decried as a heretic for this and condemned by many, since he turned his back on all the universities and scholars and regarded nothing but the Word of our Lord Jesus Christ, recorded by the prophets and apostles, as necessary for faith and a good conscience and as the source from which we can teach and learn how to live as a Christian, die blessedly, and come with joy before the judgment seat of Jesus Christ.[118]

Although his fellow friars[119] and the members of other orders disputed against this, they were unable to bring forward or maintain anything that could stand in opposition to him and his firm principles.[120] He cut through

---

[112] Σκότος in Greek means "darkness."

[113] *Albern* in German means "foolish."

[114] For "doubting Thomas," see John 20:24–29.

[115] The "Moderns" (followers of the *Via Moderna*) or Nominalists were followers of William of Ockham (see above, p. 62 n. 46), who was the major influence on Luther in his years at Erfurt, and Luther initially held his teachings in high regard. See Brecht 1:34, 36; Oberman, *Luther*, pp. 118–20.

[116] I.e., Peter Lombard: see above, p. 126 and n. 70 there.

[117] Luther's earliest preserved disputation is the September 25, 1516, *Disputation on the Powers and Will of Man apart from Grace* (see above, p. 121 n. 39), followed by the 1517 *Disputation against Scholastic Theology*, LW 31:3–16. The 1538 collection of Luther's theses for disputation, in which these appeared first, claimed to begin "with the beginning of the business surrounding the Gospel" [*ab initio negocii Evangelici*]: see WA 1:143. On the next major disputation, *Against Scholastic Theology*, see below, Mathesius, *History*, p. 141. On Luther's early lectures, see above, pp. 131–32 n. 98. Cf. Brecht 1:164–74.

[118] Mathesius' account here of Luther's early development is elaborated from Luther's own summary in *Table Talk* no. 5346 (1540), WA TR 5:75–76. For modern discussion, see Althaus, *Theology of Martin Luther*; Gerhard Ebeling, *Luther: An Introduction to His Thought*, trans. R. A. Wilson (London: Collins, 1970); Bernhard Lohse, *Martin Luther's Theology: Its Historical and Systematic Development*, trans. and ed. Roy A. Harrisville (Minneapolis: Fortress, 1999).

[119] *seine Brüder*; perhaps simply "his brothers" in the more general sense of "colleagues."

[120] Luther's public disputations within his order and with others came slightly later, after the Indulgence Controversy: the Heidelberg Disputation, at the chapter of the Augustinian Hermits in 1518 (LW 31:35–70); a disputation with the Wittenberg Franciscans took place in 1519 (WA 59:678–97). The first theologians to challenge Luther's teaching (many of whom

with Holy Scripture, and all the sophists and Scotists had to yield to the Holy Scripture upon which Dr. Luther relied and had to let him prevail with the doctrine of the prophets and apostles.

|As Luther was learning to read the holy Bible letter by letter in this way, Dr. Staupitz and Herr Spalatin[121] and many good people helped put in a good word with their elector in favor of the beautiful languages and liberal arts, and these beautiful languages together with fervent prayer, the holy cross, and earnest contemplation are the most beautiful commentary on and interpreters of the Word of God.[122] That is why the text in the Bible is becoming clearer and more familiar day by day. For even as the pope was once a schoolboy, so also Dr. Luther had to learn the ABCs of the Bible from day to day, an education in which his opponents were of considerable service and help, both at that time and afterward.

At about this time the elector of Saxony, who had previously traveled to the Holy Land,[123] founded a new collegiate church in the name of All Saints in his castle in Wittenberg, in which he collected all kinds of relics.[124]

---

would later become Luther's supporters) were other members of the Wittenberg theological faculty: see Brecht 1:167–74. It was Andreas Bodenstein von Karlstadt, the dean of the Wittenberg theological faculty, who threatened to denounce Luther as a heretic for questioning the papal privileges of the All Saints' Church: Brecht 1:168.

[121] Georg Spalatin [Burckhardt] (1484–1545) was a German humanist who had studied theology and law in Erfurt and Wittenberg and was ordained a priest before entering the court of Frederick the Wise in 1508 as tutor to the young duke John Frederick, the future elector. In the following years he was appointed to became the elector's chaplain, secretary, and adviser as well. Spalatin was thus the chief intermediary between Frederick and Luther and a principal agent in the elector's diplomacy surrounding Luther's trial, serving also at times as censor of Luther's works for political reasons. Spalatin continued as an adviser to Frederick's successors alongside duties as superintendent in Altenburg from 1528 on. He was also a historian both in public works and in his private memoir on Frederick's life: Spalatin, *Friedrichs des Weisen* (see above, p. 68 n. 84). Luther's professional and personal relationship with Spalatin is reflected in the more than eight hundred letters to Spalatin that survive. See also Luther, preface to Spalatin, *Marvelously Comforting Examples and Sayings* (1544), LW 60:324–29; Noel C. LeRoque, *Martin Luther's Friends* (Franklin, TN: Providence House Publishers, 1997), pp. 159–88; Irmgard Höß, "Spalatin, Georg," *OER* 4:96–99; Irmgard Höß, *Georg Spalatin: Ein Leben in der Zeit des Humanismus und der Reformation*, 2nd ed. (Weimar: Böhlau, 1989).

[122] Cf. Luther's declaration that prayer, meditation, and temptation [*oratio, meditatio, tentatio*] are the key to understanding the Scriptures: *Preface to the German Writings* (1539), LW 34:285–87; see also below, Mathesius, *History*, p. 445.

[123] Frederick made a pilgrimage to Jerusalem in 1493. See Ingetraut Ludolphy, *Friedrich der Weise: Kurfürst von Sachsen, 1463–1525* (Göttingen: Vandenhoeck & Ruprecht, 1984; repr., Leipzig: Leipziger Universitätsverlag, 2006), pp. 351–54.

[124] Frederick began construction of a new castle in Wittenberg, with an attached church, in 1490. The church, completed in 1509, was much larger than a typical chapel because Frederick intended it to serve a variety of purposes. First, it was the collegiate church [*Stiftkirche*] for the All Saints' Foundation [*Allerheiligenstift*], founded in 1338, a "chapter" of clergy supported

Then Dr. Staupitz was dispatched to the Netherlands to bring back relics from a monastery.[125] Meanwhile, Dr. Martin was entrusted with the office of vicar,[126] for the visitation of the Augustinian monasteries. And so for a time he traveled from one monastery to another, helping to establish schools and exhorting all of the members of his vicariate to hold fast to the Bible and also to lead a holy, peaceful, and chaste life.[127]

This took place in 1516, at the time when indulgence peddler Johann Tetzel[128] (for whom Elector Frederick of Saxony had interceded in Innsbruck to save him from the sack where Emperor Maximilian wanted to have him put on a charge of adultery)[129] sold Roman indulgences and grace for money in Germany at the behest of certain bishops who wanted to gain their palliums in Rome from the indulgence money.[130] This is also when Joachimsthal

---

by an endowment to say Masses. Second, the church also served the university, after its 1507 union with the All Saints' Foundation—which also provided a source of support for faculty (such as Karlstadt). Third, the Castle Church housed the vast collection of relics which Frederick had assiduously gathered—in 1520 there were some 18,970 relics cataloged, one of the largest collections in Europe. See Sibylle Harksen, *Die Schlosskirche zu Wittenberg* (Berlin: Untion Verlag, 1966).

[125] Staupitz made numerous trips to the Netherlands in his quest for monastic reform. On a trip in 1509, Staupitz examined a potential bride for Elector Frederick, though it is unclear from other sources that the acquisition of relics was part of his commission. See Posset, *Front-Runner of the Catholic Reformation*, pp. 69–120. Luther mentions a 1516 trip in which Staupitz was engaged in acquiring relics for Frederick: see Luther to Spalatin, December 14, 1516, LW 48:33–34.

[126] At the chapter of the Augustinian Hermits in Gotha in spring 1515, Luther was elected to a three-year term as district vicar over Meissen and Thuringia, where there were ten monasteries. See Brecht 1:156.

[127] Luther traveled to visit the monasteries of his district from late April to early June 1516. See Brecht 1:157; Luther to Johann Lang, May 29, 1516, LW 48:14–16, and June 30, 1516, WA Br 1:48–49; to Michael Dressel, September 25, 1516, LW 48:20–23.

[128] On Tetzel, see above, p. 66 n. 71.

[129] This dubious story about Tetzel's conviction and Frederick's intercession is found in Luther, *Against Hanswurst* (1541), LW 41:231. In Roman law, the *Codex Theodosianus* (11.36.4) prescribed the *poena cullei*—being sewn in a sack, sometimes with an assortment of live animals—for parricide and sometimes for adultery. In Germany, the punishment was extended to other offenses, including adultery, but was usually applied to women: see Mitchel P. Roth, *An Eye for an Eye: A Global History of Crime and Punishment* (London: Reaktion, 2014), p. 117.

[130] Albert of Brandenburg, who had become archbishop of Magdeburg and administrator of the diocese of Halberstadt in 1513, secured election as archbishop-elector of Mainz in 1514. Because it was against canon law to hold more than one diocese simultaneously (plurality) and because Albert, at the age of 24, was below the canonical age for election as bishop, he had to pay for papal dispensation from the irregularities as well as the fees for conferral of the pallium by Pope Leo X. Albert secured a loan for 10,000 gulden from the Fugger bank in Augsburg under an arrangement with the pope for the proclamation of a special plenary indulgence to

began and was built[131] so that[132] poor members of monastic orders, persons able to write, many of whom left the monasteries for reasons of conscience, might have their livelihood here in these mountains, even as many of you started making a living here at the windlass and on the rock face and in the clerk's office.

¦For as our God used a miner's son to reopen the mines of His Christendom and put the impure doctrine through the furnace again to eliminate the idolatry, as Malachi [3:3] had prophesied, so He also caused these laudable mines to be started and this Christian mining town to be built so that the Gospel could be richly preached here at His own expense and from His stipend, which He generously gave from His hand by means of the mines, as you have often heard in your *Sarepta*.[133] With this we bring to a close the accounts of 1516 for this time and carve our mark here.[134] Next time we will take up our picks again here and give a complete report on the miner's son, who split the rock covering the Bible and five Books of Moses[135] and produced a favorable yield, and who throughout his life loved and supported miners and their children.

We thank the eternal Son of God, who sent this doctor out into this land in advance of His appearing and final judgment and has brought His doctrine into this valley by means of Count Stephan Schlick[136] and preserved

---

be preached in Albert's territories: half of the funds collected would go to the construction of the new St. Peter's Basilica in Rome, and the other half would go toward repayment of the loan. Tetzel was named as indulgence commissioner. Luther's account of the economics of Tetzel's preaching of indulgences and Cardinal Albert's involvement is given in *Against Hanswurst* (1541), LW 41:232–33.

[131] See, e.g., Mathesius, *Sarepta*, fols. 1r–v, 311v. On the founding of Joachimsthal, see Brown, *Singing the Gospel*, p. 16.

[132] Mathesius' interpretation here of the purpose of the founding of the town is a providential rather than a historical one.

[133] On Mathesius' *Sarepta*, see above, p. lxxxvi (for bibliographic information, see above, p. lxxxii n. 321). *Sarepta* is the Latin name of Zarephath, the Phoenician mining town mentioned in 1 Kings 17:9–10; Obadiah 20; and Luke 4:26. In Mathesius' preaching, the biblical town and its name became a proxy for Joachimsthal. Cf. above, pp. 117, 119.

[134] *ein stuffe allhie schlagen*

[135] There was, in fact, a Joachimsthal mine named the "Five Books of Moses" which had been opened in 1559. See Mathesius, *Sarepta*, fol. Mm6r.

[136] Count Stephan Schlick (1487–1526), patron of the founding of Joachimsthal, was the eldest scion of a Bohemian noble family with close ties to Wittenberg. Although other branches of the Schlick family were active in introducing the Reformation into their lands, Stephan took a more indirect approach, giving or obtaining for the new town council authority to introduce religious reforms at its own initiative. After his death at the Battle of Mohács, his brothers Lorenz and Hieronymus became more active as patrons of Lutheranism in the town. See Luther to Lorenz and Hieronymus Schlick, October 9, 1532, WA Br 6:373. On Stephan Schlick and the founding of Joachimsthal, see Brown, *Singing the Gospel*, p. 32.

it to this day. We also ask [God], on the ground of His gracious oath and promise, that He would preserve us and our kin henceforth in pure doctrine and holy living and Christian obedience, and graciously through His Son preserve us from the deceptive glimmer of the Enthusiasts'[137] white mica and their worthless gangue.[138] Amen.

---

[137] The "Enthusiasts" were those who insisted on the direct action of the Holy Spirit, not mediated by the external Word or Sacraments. See LW 60:332 n. 11; above, p. 95 n. 36; and below, p. 195 n. 61.

[138] *Katzensilberblende und tauber Bergart*; i.e., the glittering mica that gave the appearance of silver and the worthless rock that contained no ore (see *DWB*, s.v. "Bergart").

THE SECOND SERMON,
ON THE YEARS 1516, 1517, 1518, AND 1519

[Between December 6 and 12, 1562]

BELOVED friends in the Lord! *Ecce florent valles cum Evangelio*. ["Behold! The valleys are in bloom with the Gospel!"][1] Since St. Joachim's Day[2] has traditionally been celebrated this week, and Joachimsthal, this "valley of St. Joachim," arose at the same time as the Gospel, as the Roman numerals in this saying of ours indicate,[3] we want to continue with the accounts of Doctor Luther, to the glory of the Lord Christ, the grandson of our patron St. Joachim, and of His Gospel, to see what other precious lodes can be mined further down this vein.[4]

Doctor Luther, as a baptized member of holy Christendom, had a heartfelt desire and longing for the holy Bible from his youth on. In the monastery, he came upon it by God's grace and was often heard reading from it,[5] on account of which he was solemnly appointed in due order to be a doctor of

---

[1] This verse, apparently composed by Mathesius, served as a kind of motto for Joachimsthal, associating its "valley" with the Gospel of the Reformation. See Mathesius, *Chronica* (in *Sarepta*, fol. 317r).

[2] Joachim was, according to extrabiblical tradition, the father (with St. Anne) of the Virgin Mary, and hence the grandfather of Jesus. See *LA* 2:150–52, no. 131. The date of St. Joachim's Day, a late addition to the calendar, was not universally set (as March 20) until 1584; in Joachimsthal, an older custom associating St. Joachim's Day with the feast of Mary's immaculate conception (December 9) was observed. December 9 would have fallen on Wednesday in 1562. See Mathesius, *Postilla* (Nürnberg: Gerlach, 1584) [VD16 M1539], fols. 12v–20v; Volz, *Die Lutherpredigten des Johannes Mathesius*, p. 9, contra *LH*², p. 468 n. 32.6.

[3] This is a chronogram, in which the letters that are also Roman numerals are to be added up: eCCe fLorent VaLLes CVM eVangeLIo = 100+100+50+5+50+50+100+5+1000+5+50+1 = 1516. On the date 1516, see above, Mathesius, *History*, pp. 121, 137. On this kind of numerology, pioneered by Luther's friend Michael Stifel (see above, p. xxxvii n. 101) and later systematized by Melanchthon's student Sigismund Schwabe [Suevus] (1526–96) in his *Arithmetica historia* (1593), see Robin Bruce Barnes, *Prophecy and Gnosis: Apocalypticism in the Wake of the Lutheran Reformation* (Stanford: Stanford University Press, 1988), pp. 195–96, especially p. 196 n. 29 on Mathesius' origination of the Joachimsthal chronogram. For another example, see below, p. 145 and n. 32 there.

[4] For the metaphor, see above, Mathesius, *History*, p. 138.

[5] See above, Mathesius, *History*, pp. 120, 123–24.

Sacred Scripture. Accordingly, by virtue of his calling and office, he began to expound Holy Scripture in his monastery and to dispute against sophistry, driving back the Scholastics with their new four ways or sects,[6] down to the year of our Lord 1516, as you heard in the previous sermon.

Now as he was laying down new and firm principles and foundations for our Christian faith from God's Word and publicly testifying that Holy Scripture alone shows us the way to heaven, it happened that the indulgence peddler Johann Tetzel[7] was displaying his indulgences for sale in Jüterbog,[8] about twenty ‖miles[9] away from Wittenberg. He was a real incendiary and confidence man and made grandiloquent protestations on behalf of this worthless Roman gangue.[10] Namely,[11] he said that his red cross with the papal coat of arms was just as powerful as the cross of Jesus Christ. Again, [he said that] he would not trade places with St. Peter in heaven, for with his indulgences he had redeemed more souls than St. Peter with his Gospel. Again, that the grace granted by an indulgence was the very grace by which human beings are reconciled with God.[12] Again, that there was no need to have repentance, sorrow, or contrition for sins if you bought grace and

---

[6] I.e., the schools [*viae*] of the Albertists, Thomists, Scotists, and Occamists; see above, Mathesius, *History*, p. 126 and n. 71 there. Luther presided over the *Disputation against Scholastic Theology* (1517), LW 31:3–16, on October 4, 1517.

[7] On Tetzel, see above, Mathesius, *History*, p. 137.

[8] Although Tetzel was prohibited from preaching in electoral Saxony, Jüterbog was an exclave of the archdiocese of Magdeburg. Tetzel preached there on Good Friday, April 10, 1517, the closest he came to Wittenberg. See Brecht 1:183, 188.

[9] *vier meyl.* The "mile" [*Meil*] in electoral Saxony was about 9 km or 5.6 English miles. Jüterbog and Wittenberg are about 34 km distant as the crow flies.

[10] Cf. above, p. 139 and n. 138 there.

[11] For the following account of Tetzel's preaching and Luther's response, see *Table Talk* no. 5346 (1540), WA TR 5:75–76; no. 5349 (1540), WA TR 5:77–80. Luther gives his fullest summary of Tetzel's claims in *Against Hanswurst* (1541), LW 41:231–33, which is Mathesius' primary source here, though Mathesius rearranges the order. Luther also enumerates some of Tetzel's pronouncements in his letter to Cardinal Albert, October 31, 1517, LW 48:47, and in the *Ninety-Five Theses* (1517) themselves, LW 31:25–33. Behind these claims is Albert's *Instructio Summaria* for the indulgence preachers in *Instructiones Confessorum* (Mainz: J. Schöffer, 1516) [VD16 ZV27163], edited in Fabisch and Iserloh, *Dokumenta zur Causa Lutheri*, 1:229–93; and in part in Walther Köhler, ed., *Dokumente zum Ablassstreit von 1517* (Tübingen: Mohr, 1902), pp. 104–24, which is translated in excerpt in Henry Bettenson and Chris Maunder, eds., *Documents of the Christian Church*, 4th ed. (Oxford: Oxford University Press, 2011), pp. 195–97; cf. LW 48:47 n. 16.

[12] See also *Ninety-Five Theses* (1517), Thesis 33, LW 31:28; Albert, *Instructio summaria*, in Köhler, *Dokumente zum Ablassstreit*, p. 110; Fabisch and Iserloh, *Dokumenta zur Causa Lutheri*, 1:264.

letters of assurance from him and the pope.[13] "For as soon as the penny in the coffer rings, the soul from purgatory toward heaven springs."[14] Such great grace and power had been imparted to him in Rome, [that] even if someone assaulted Mary, the mother of God, he was able to forgive that as well as future sins, if the person placed the proper amount in the coffer.[15]

As Tetzel was thus extolling his Roman baubles[16] and fraud beyond all measure, many people came running to this indulgence fair wanting to buy grace and eternal life with their money. Then Doctor Luther in his monastery began to warn the listeners against this kind of indulgence in exchange for money. At first he taught very discreetly that it would be better to give poor people alms in accordance with Christ's command than to buy such uncertain grace with money.[17] Anyone who repents his whole life long and turns to God with his whole heart will receive the generous and heavenly grace and forgiveness of all sins which the Lord Christ acquired for us by means of His one sacrifice and His blood [Heb. 10:12], which He offers purely out of grace, without money, and sells without price, as it is clearly written in Isaiah [52:3; 55:1]. At the same time he also began asking questions and

---

[13] See also Luther to Cardinal Albert, October 31, 1517, LW 48:47; *Ninety-Five Theses* (1517), Thesis 35, LW 31:28. This is perhaps the most controversial claim, since the official teaching was that indulgences were for the benefit of the *contritis et confessis*: those who were contrite and had made sacramental confession (see below, Mathesius, *History*, p. 187). Albert's *Instructio summaria*, however, declared that contrition and confession, though generally necessary for indulgences (Köhler, *Dokumente zum Ablassstreit*, p. 111; Fabisch and Iserloh, *Dokumenta zur Causa Lutheri*, 1:264), were both unnecessary for those who obtained indulgences on behalf of souls in purgatory and that at least confession was unnecessary to obtain the graces of the confessional letters as a whole (Köhler, *Dokumente zum Ablassstreit*, p. 116; Fabisch and Iserloh, *Dokumenta zur Causa Lutheri*, 1:269). The marginal heading at this point in the *Instructio summaria* made the full claim that "neither contrition nor confession is required to purchase confessional letters or for the consequent participation of this kind."

[14] See *Ninety-Five Theses* (1517), Thesis 27, LW 31:27–28. Luther also refers to Tetzel's jingle in *Exhortation to All Clergy* (1530), LW 34:17; *Against Hanswurst* (1541), LW 41:232; and afterword to Hus, *Three Letters* (1536/1537), LW 60:128.

[15] See *Ninety-Five Theses* (1517), Thesis 75, LW 31:32; Luther to Cardinal Albert, October 31, 1517, LW 48:46; *Explanations of the Ninety-Five Theses* (1518), LW 31:240–41; *Exhortation to All Clergy* (1530), LW 34:17; *Against Hanswurst* (1541), LW 41:232.

[16] *getetzlich*; a play in German on Tetzel's name. Literally, the word denotes ornamental cuffs.

[17] Cf. *Ninety-Five Theses* (1517), Thesis 43, LW 31:29. On Luther's preaching on indulgences before the *Ninety-Five Theses* (though primarily in the Wittenberg parish context rather than "in his monastery"), see *Against Hanswurst* (1541), LW 41:231–32; Brecht 1:183–90; Wengert, "Luther's Preaching an Indulgence in January 1517," pp. 70–73; and above, Melanchthon, *Preface*, p. 67 and n. 80 there.

disputing these matters in his monastery and university.[18] And since he was a doctor of Sacred Scripture, he always grounded his cause on the words of the prophets and apostles.

ⁱWhen news of this reached the indulgence swindler, who was exchanging Roman letters, wax, and lead[19] for good Schreckenberger [*groschen*], Spitzgröschel, and gold gulden,[20] Tetzel began to curse and swear, condemning Doctor Luther as an arch-heretic.[21] Thus with his immoderate rhetoric and horrible slanders this indulgence peddler drove Doctor Luther to take up spiritual arms—namely, David's sling [1 Sam. 17:50] and the spiritual sword [Eph. 6:17], which is fervent prayer and the pure Word of God—in defense. By virtue of his doctoral office and oath he attacked Tetzel and his Roman indulgence in God's name and confidently taught that such indulgences are a perilous deception. Thus began the dispute between Doctor Luther and Tetzel concerning papal indulgences. At first, to be sure, Dr. Luther did not attack [the doctrine of indulgence] itself, but sought only to have people speak of this matter more circumspectly, to prevent the great name of His Holiness the Pope, under which such indulgences were being doled out, from being defamed. For at this time the good monk was still concerned about preserving the reputation and dignity of the Roman head [of the Church].[22]

Now since Tetzel and his entourage sought to defend their trumpery with the authority of Rome and of the episcopacy and with the Keys of the Church,[23] Dr. Luther was compelled by his oath and doctoral office to

---

[18] Cf. above, Mathesius, *History*, pp. 135–36. For this version of events, including the association of Luther's early teaching with the Scriptures, see *Table Talk* no. 5346 (1540), WA TR 5:75–76.

[19] I.e., the papal letters of indulgence, sealed in wax, and the bull authorizing them, sealed in lead [*bulla*].

[20] These were coins of good reputation and wide circulation: silver coins from Annaberg and Zwickau worth respectively 1/7 and 1/21 the value of a gulden or florin, the standard gold coin of late medieval and early modern Europe.

[21] There is no evidence elsewhere that Tetzel became aware of Luther's theology or criticism of indulgences until after the publication of the *Ninety-Five Theses*: see Brecht 1:183. Volz suggests (*Die Lutherpredigten des Johannes Mathesius*, p. 222 on *LH* 34) that Mathesius may have misconstrued Luther's recollection that in the years before 1517 he was regarded as a heretic in Wittenberg for his insistence on the Scriptures: see *Table Talk* no. 5346 (1540), WA TR 5:76.

[22] See, e.g., *Ninety-Five Theses* (1517), Theses 26, 48, 50, 51, 55, LW 31:27–30; *Table Talk* no. 5346 (1540), WA TR 5:75–76; *Preface to the Latin Writings* (1545), LW 34:329; Luther to Pope Leo X, January 5 or 6, 1519, LW 48:100–102.

[23] I.e., both by theological appeal to the authority of the pope and the bishops and their exercise of the Keys to bind and loose sins and their punishment and by the threat of discipline by pope and bishops using their power of excommunication.

formulate theses and arguments[24] against Johann Tetzel and all those in his camp and to post them on the Castle Church in Wittenberg on the annual festival of its dedication[25] and to have them printed, which happened on the last day of October in the year 1517.[26] They begin as follows: "Our Lord and Master Jesus Christ, says, 'Repent, for the kingdom of heaven is at hand' [Matt. 3:2], etc."[27] Now, our doctor's first question concerning Roman indulgences was whether such purchased indulgences pardon all punishment and sin and redeem souls from purgatory, ¹or whether this happens through genuine Christian repentance and conversion to God, when one feels heartfelt sorrow for sin throughout his life and believes the holy Absolution, namely, that solely for the sake of the blood of Jesus Christ alone, purely by grace, all his inborn and actual sin is pardoned and forgiven, insofar as one has the good intention of avoiding sin henceforth as much as humanly possible by the power of the Holy Spirit and of embarking upon a new and holy life.

For that is the authentic doctrine of true and Christian repentance, as Dr. Luther and later Herr Melanchthon faithfully and steadfastly taught, proclaimed, and confessed this doctrine until their end.

Now, it is true that, having been mired deep in the papacy and its abominable idolatry for some time, Dr. Luther spoke somewhat obscurely about this article at first, but afterward, day by day, it became ever more plain and clear from Scripture and under the cross.[28] Note this well, dear friends: Our doctor at the outset attacked the Roman indulgence and alongside that he began to testify of and preach the true and heavenly indulgence, which is the gracious forgiveness of sins through the blood of Christ, as he clearly teaches and confesses in his other theses.[29] In sum of all, he says, the righteous lives

---

[24] *positiones und gründe*; i.e., *Ninety-Five Theses* (1517), LW 31:25–33, perhaps considered together with the *Explanations of the Ninety-Five Theses* (1518), LW 31:77–252.

[25] The Castle Church in Wittenberg was named the Church of All Saints, and All Saints' Day, together with its eve, All Souls' Day, was observed as an annual festival, including the exposition of its collection of relics. However, the formal dedication had been performed by the papal legate and indulgence commissary Raymond Peraudi (1435–1505) on January 17, 1503, and January 17 was in fact observed as the anniversary of the dedication: see Wengert, "Luther's Preaching an Indulgence in January 1517," p. 71.

[26] On the debate over the posting of the *Ninety-Five Theses*, see the introduction above, pp. lvii–lx.

[27] An abbreviated quotation of Thesis 1, which reads in full: "When our Lord and Master Jesus Christ said, 'Repent,' He willed the entire life of believers to be one of repentance" (*Ninety-Five Theses* [1517], LW 31:25).

[28] Cf. *Preface to the Latin Writings* (1545), LW 34:328–34.

[29] See *Ninety-Five Theses* (1517), Thesis 62: "The true treasure of the church is the most holy gospel of the glory and grace of God" (LW 31:31); explanation of Thesis 7 in *Explanations*

not by his works or by the Law, much less by Roman indulgence, but through faith in Jesus Christ, Romans 1 [:17; cf. 3:20–28; 9:32].

This year had been proclaimed by Christendom for a long time beforehand in St. Ambrose's hymn of praise, though in a hidden kabbalah,[30] when in all the churches[31] they sang this verse from the Te Deum laudamus with resounding joy: *Tibi Cherubin & Seraphin incessabili voce proclamant* ["To You cherubim and seraphim cry out with unceasing voice"]. For the number of this year is contained in the Roman numerals here.[32]

ᴵNow after the doctor's first disputation had been issued in print, it reached Rome and all the universities and monasteries within a month's time.[33] All the pious monks who thought they would be saved in their monasteries, and who still had the business at Constance[34] always on their minds as a discreditable affair, received this brief writing with joy. Such is the story told about the good monk Doctor Fleck,[35] who helped dedicate the University of Wittenberg with his preaching and, it is said, also prophesied that the whole world would gain wisdom from this "white mountain" (he meant Wittenberg).[36] This monk (I say), who never celebrated a Mass in his life and who already before that time had ridiculed the reform of his fellow

---

of the Ninety-Five Theses (1518), LW 31:100–107; and deduction from Thesis 5, *Explanations of the Ninety-Five Theses* (1518), LW 31:95–97.

[30] Kabbalah was a type of Jewish mysticism, advocated by some Christian Hebraists such as Johann Reuchlin (see above, p. 132 n. 100), which included numerological readings of the letters of Scripture. See Friedman, *Most Ancient Testimony*, pp. 75ff.

[31] *in allen Stifften.* See below, p. 159 n. 114.

[32] I.e., by adding the values of the Roman numerals of the Latin verse: *tIbI CherVbIn & seraphIn InCessabILI VoCe proCLaMant*—1+1+100+5+1+1+1+100+1+50+1+5+100+100+50+1000 = 1517. On this form of chronogram, see above, p. 140 n. 3. The transliteration of "cherubim" and "seraphim" with a final "n" was not uncommon.

[33] Although Luther's theses spread quickly throughout Germany, they do not seem to have reached Rome until Cardinal Albert of Mainz (see above, p. 27 n. 5) forwarded them to the Curia in December. See Brecht 1:205–7; Oberman, *Luther*, pp. 192–93; Pettegree, *Brand Luther*, pp. 74–77, 89–90.

[34] I.e., the Council of Constance (1414–18), where the papal schism that had begun in 1378 was ended and John Hus was condemned (see the introduction above, pp. xxxvii–xxxviii.

[35] Johann Fleck (fl. ca. 1500) was prior of the Franciscan monastery in Steinlausig near Bitterfeld in electoral Saxony, where he had become notorious for his refusal to say Mass. In Mathesius' account (though its historical accuracy is doubtful), Fleck had preached at the dedication of the new university in Wittenberg on October 18, 1502 (see below, Mathesius, *History*, pp. 572, 579). See Brecht 1:205; *Table Talk* no. 5480 (1542), WA TR 5:177; LW 60:278 n. 22. See also below, Mathesius, *History*, pp. 287, 457, 557; Mathesius, *Sarepta*, fol. 130v. The story of Fleck's response to the *Ninety-Five Theses* was narrated in Matthias Flacius, *Catalogus testium veritatis* (Basel: Oporinus, 1562) [VD16 F1294], p. 573.

[36] *von diesem Weissenberge.* A play on words, resting on the similarity of the German adjectives *weis* ["wise"] and *weiß* ["white," in dialect *witt*].

barefoot friars[37] in a fine courteous way—like Elijah [1 Kings 18:27]—found these theses posted in his refectory in Steinlausig. And once he had read a little from them, he cried out for joy "Ho, ho!" and said, "This one will do it. The one we have so long awaited is coming." He also wrote a very comforting letter about this to Dr. Luther and exhorted him to carry on with confidence, for he was on the right path, and the prayers of all the captives in the Roman Babylon would be with him.[38]

Many others, who had tormented themselves nearly to death with prayer and fasting in monasteries, thanked our dear God that they were able to hear the singing of this swan, of whom Master John Hus had prophesied.[39] Those, however, who had entered the monastery and taken up religion for the sake of their stomach, good days, and honor and esteem, and who bore the Roman mark and sign [cf. Rev. 14:9], began condemning Dr. Luther and writing against him.

When our doctor saw and heard that people were intending to defend Tetzel's indulgences and also to attack and defame true repentance and the gracious forgiveness of sins, ⌐he wrote first, on the day when his theses were printed, to the bishop of Mainz,[40] who had sent out such indulgence peddlers, and as a legitimate doctor of Sacred Scripture he most humbly petitioned him to do away with this scandalous trade and these dangerous words, lest they cause great detriment to His Holiness the Pope and his episcopal primacy. Likewise, our doctor also wrote to his ordinary, the bishop of Brandenburg,[41] to whose diocese the university, church, and monastery in Wittenberg still belonged at that time, and to both of them he sent along his printed theses. However, this produced little response. He was advised that he should keep silent, for this was a great matter.

---

[37] The Franciscan movement as a whole underwent successive waves of division and reform of their observance, one of the points of contention being the permissibility of wearing sandals as opposed to going barefoot as St. Francis' original rule had stipulated. Perhaps the recent conflicts between conventual and observant Franciscans of the Saxon province during the term of Matthias Döring (1427–61) as provincial are in view here. See Petra Weigel, *Ordensreform und Konziliarismus: Der Franziskanerprovinzial Matthias Döring* (Frankfurt a.M.: Peter Lang, 2005). *LH²*, p. 470, attributes the reform to Johann Busch (1399–1479/1480) instead.

[38] Luther describes this correspondence and laments his loss of Fleck's original letter itself in *Table Talk* no. 5480 (1542), WA TR 5:177. See Brecht 1:205.

[39] See above, Mathesius, *History*, p. 121.

[40] Luther to Cardinal Albert, October 31, 1517, LW 48:43–49.

[41] Luther's letter of 1517 to Jerome Scultetus [Schultz], bishop of Brandenburg, whose diocese included Wittenberg, is lost: see Brecht 1:192; WA Br 1:113–14. Cf. the letter of Luther to Scultetus, February 13, 1518, WA Br 1:135–40, accompanying a copy of the *Explanations of the Ninety-Five Theses*. It was Scultetus who advised Luther to keep silent. For Luther's later comments on this episode, see *Against Hanswurst* (1541), LW 41:233–34; *Preface to the Latin Writings* (1545), LW 34:329; *Commentary on Psalm 51* (1532/1538), LW 12:387.

But since God had, at the end of the world, granted the imperial majesty, crown, and scepter to the illustrious German land, to the true Japhethites,[42] and was now sending them a German prophet as well, Dr. Luther arose and preached and wrote against indulgences publicly, as a German prophet, and taught what true Christian and blessed repentance is, through which we are made righteous before God and eternally saved. In God's name he published these sermons, along with an explanation of the Ten Commandments,[43] and thereby set all the Rhine, Oder, Danube, and Tiber ablaze, and brought down upon himself all who at that time thought themselves great, wise, holy, and learned in the monasteries and throughout the world.

He always founded his cause on God's Word and shielded himself against his opponents with nothing but Scripture, along with fervent prayer in which he constantly commended this sublime cause to his faithful God, [praying that] He would graciously visit Germany before the Last Day to reveal and slay the Antichrist, the child of sin, by the mouth of His Spirit [cf. 2 Thess. 2:3–8].[44] Thus God's Word and the prayer of wretched and oppressed Christendom are breaking through, and the truth is again in the ascendant, so that many great, excellent, and learned people are upholding this divine doctrine and helping promote it by teaching, writing, and praying.

In the year 1518, Emperor Maximilian[45] held an imperial diet in Augsburg,[46] which Cardinal Cajetan attended as well, in place of His Holiness

---

[42] On Japheth as the progenitor of the European peoples, see above, p. 105 n. 11.

[43] Mathesius probably has in mind the *Sermon on Indulgence and Grace* (1517), WA 1:243–46 (LW 70); the *Sermon on Penance* (1518), WA 1:319–24 (LW 70); and one (or both) of the following: *Eine kurze Erklarung der 10 Gebote* (1518), WA 1:250–56 (later incorporated in the *Personal Prayer Book* [1522], LW 43:13–24), and *The Ten Commandments, Preached to the People of Wittenberg* (1516–17/1518), WA 1:398–521 (LW 70).

[44] "By the mouth of His Spirit" is an inversion of 2 Thess. 2:8 which Luther occasionally made in citation of this verse as well as of the parallel in Ps. 33:6. See *Sincere Admonition* (1522), LW 45:67; *Last Words of David* (1543), WA 54:57 (not reflected in the translation in LW 15:301). Mathesius consistently cites it in this form: see below, *History*, pp. 152, 330, 381, 473, 518, 520; cf. above, Walter, *New Spiritual Song*, p. 89, stanza 24.

[45] Maximilian I was active in consolidating the position of the Hapsburg dynasty, a patron of humanists, and a supporter of church reforms in opposition to Pope Julius II, including an unsuccessful effort to secure his own election as pope. See Paula Sutter Fichtner, "Maximilian I," *OER* 3:35–36. Luther had a generally high opinion of Maximilian and regarded him as sympathetic with reform: see, e.g., *Table Talk* no. 4369 (1539), WA TR 4:264–65; no. 4785 (1530s), WA TR 4:502–3; no. 5343 (1540), WA TR 5:74; no. 5583 (1543), WA TR 5:262.

[46] The Augsburg Diet of 1518 began in July and ended on September 22. Luther's chief accounts of his encounter at Augsburg in 1518 are found in *Proceedings at Augsburg* (1518), LW 31:253–92, and *Preface to the Latin Writings* (1545), LW 34:330–31, as well as in his correspondence from the period (especially his letters to Spalatin, August 8 and 28 and October 10 and 14, 1518, LW 48:70–76, WA Br 1:209–10, and LW 48:83–87; and to Elector Frederick,

the Pope.[47] Cajetan wanted to have Dr. Luther sent to Rome so that his heretical doctrine could be judged and condemned there. But the very wise Duke Frederick, elector of Saxony, undertook negotiations with the papal legate there: Since the path is long and the trip to Rome is dangerous, and many good people have gone there whereas few have returned, Dr. Martin should be examined in Augsburg; he would have him brought in at the end of the imperial diet. This was granted. Thus Luther went to Augsburg by foot, in a cowl borrowed from Dr. Wenceslaus Linck[48] and with a letter of commendation from the elector of Saxony to good friends, who bade him stay in the monastery where he had stopped[49] until they secured safe-conduct for him from the emperor.

Meanwhile, the papal legate called Dr. Luther to himself by means of an ambassador,[50] but [Luther] heeded the command he had received [already] and waited for [the emperor's] decision. When he finally told this to the ambassador, who had come back again several times to call on him, the ambassador replied, "Do you think that princes and lords will take up your cause or defend you against the power of the Roman see? Where do you think you can stay and remain safe?" The doctor gave him a brief and bold reply: "Under heaven," he said. Soon thereafter his escort came.

November [21], 1518, WA Br 1:237) and his later *Table Talk*: see no. 509 (1533), WA TR 1:233; no. 3857 (1538), LW 54:285–87; and no. 5349 (1540), WA TR 5:77–80.

[47] Tommaso de Vio, Cardinal Cajetan (1469–1534), was an influential Dominican theologian and master-general of the order from 1508 to 1518. He had been made a cardinal in 1517. He had originally been sent to Augsburg to gain financial support for a crusade against the Turks sponsored by the papacy, but in the event, he was ordered to deal with Luther as well. See Jared Wicks, "Cajetan," *OER* 1:233–34; Jared Wicks, "Introduction," in *Cajetan Responds: A Reader in Reformation Controversy*, ed. and trans. Jared Wicks (Washington, DC: Catholic University of America Press, 1978), pp. 1–46. For Luther's later opinion on Cajetan (who was himself eventually denounced for heresy by the Sorbonne), see afterword to *Letter Censuring Cajetan* (1534), LW 60:45–56.

[48] Wenceslaus Linck (1482–1574) was Luther's fellow Augustinian and former prior and professor in Wittenberg. Since 1517 he had been preacher for the Augustinians in Nürnberg, where he joined Luther for the trip to Augsburg in 1518. See Charles E. Daniel Jr., "Linck, Wenceslaus," *OER* 2:425.

[49] I.e., the Carmelite monastery, now the St. Anna-Kirche, in Augsburg. See Luther to Cardinal Cajetan, October 18, 1518, LW 48:87–89. Elector Frederick had secured this lodging for Luther by promising the Carmelite prior, Johann Frosch (ca. 1480–1533), a subsidy for his doctoral promotion at Wittenberg: Luther to Spalatin, October 31, 1518, LW 48:92–93. Luther himself later misremembered that he had stayed with the Augustinians: *Table Talk* no. 5349 (1540), WA TR 5:79.

[50] Urban von Serralonga, ambassador [*orator*] of Margrave William IX of Montferrat to the imperial court, was also an agent of Frederick the Wise. See Luther to Spalatin, October 10, 1518, WA Br 1:209–10; to Elector Frederick, November [21], 1518, WA Br 1:237; *Table Talk* no. 5349 (1540), WA TR 5:79; Walter Delius, "Urbanus von Serralonga und der Prozeß Luthers," *ARG* 52 (1961): 29–48.

And so he appeared before the cardinal in all humility and reverence, as his friends had previously instructed him. Doctor Staupitz and Doctor Wenceslaus Linck stood beside him, along with some electoral counselors[51] and Doctor Peutinger,[52] just as the men from Chlum[53] stood beside John Hus at Constance.[54]

ᵢThe papal legate spoke with friendly words and offered Dr. Martin the favor of the Roman [see] and its mighty patronage, if only he would repeat three syllables—"*Re-vo-co*"[55]—and recant all that he had said in disputations, had written, and had preached concerning Roman indulgences and true repentance.[56]

Doctor Luther humbly replied that he would gladly and sincerely do this and more, insofar as he were convinced of having taught incorrectly by God's Word in addition to the pope's decretals and the ancient doctors.[57] Upon this the legate set before him an *Extravagant*,[58] that is, a canon from the pope's law, on the basis of which he intended to convince him that he had taught heretically and contrary to the Roman decretals. But since Dr. Luther explained the pope's words correctly and showed that the legate was applying and interpreting them improperly, they were at loggerheads for a few days straight.[59]

---

[51] Dr. Johann Rühel (fl. 1505–39), adviser to Count Albert of Mansfeld, and Philipp von Feilitzsch (before 1473–after 1532). Cf. Luther to Spalatin, October 14, 1518, LW 48:85.

[52] Conrad Peutinger (1465–1547) was a German humanist who had served as city secretary of Augsburg since 1492 and later became a syndic of the city. As a supporter of Reuchlin, he hosted Luther when he came to Augsburg in 1518, but he believed the proper avenue for church reform was an ecumenical council and thus stood apart from Luther as matters progressed. See Lewis W. Spitz, "Peutinger, Conrad," *OER* 3:252.

[53] John of Chlum (d. ca. 1425), along with Wenzel of Duba, are mentioned as Hus' companions in Luther's edition of Hus' letters from Constance: WA 50:26; see Luther's preface, LW 60:122–33. See Thomas A. Fudge, *Jan Hus between Time and Eternity: Reconsidering a Medieval Heretic* (Lanham: Lexington Books, 2015), pp. 118–23; Matthew Spinka, *John Hus: A Biography* (Princeton: Princeton University Press, 1968), pp. 228–32.

[54] On Hus, cf. above, Mathesius, *History*, p. 121.

[55] I.e., "I recant," in Latin.

[56] For Luther's account of this event, see *Table Talk* no. 5349 (1540), WA TR 5:77–80.

[57] Decretals were official papal decisions, which were gathered together to form the chief basis of canon law. The authoritative collection, issued under Pope Gregory IX (r. 1227–41) in 1234, was itself known as the *Decretals* [*Decretales*].

[58] I.e., the *Unigenitus* of Clement VI (r. 1342–52), promulgated January 27, 1343: *Extravagantes Communes* 5.9.2 (Friedberg 2:1304–6; Denzinger, nos. 550–52). The *Extravagantes* were so called because they were papal documents "wandering outside" the earlier official collections of canon law.

[59] Luther's interview with Cardinal Cajetan lasted from October 12 to October 14. Mathesius' account conflates the meetings and those who were present at different points in

Cajetan accused Dr. Luther of teaching two notorious heresies: by attacking the pope's indulgences and grace as well as by asserting among his propositions that it is impossible to receive the holy Sacraments in a salutary way apart from personal faith.[60] Therefore, he should sing *"Revoco,"* ["I recant"] disclaim all this, and swallow it all back down again. Dr. Luther was neither willing nor able to do so, because his doctrine had a good and sure foundation from God's Word and the testimony of the holy fathers, as he indicated in a personal statement on behalf of his faith and assertion, which he drafted in a few days upon consultation with Doctor Staupitz and with the legate's consent.[61]

However, since this did not at all satisfy the legate, who was instead provoked and commanded Dr. Luther to depart from him, Dr. Luther withdrew for a few days, during which Doctor Staupitz released him from the monastic vow of obedience he had made to him and the convent.[62] Then, when Doctor Staupitz also took leave, Dr. Luther left Augsburg after having publicly and solemnly appealed from Cajetan to Pope Leo X.[63]

Thus our dear God helped Dr. Luther arrive back home in Wittenberg on the last day of October.[64] However, since he had remained steadfast in God's Word in Augsburg and was unable to recant his doctrine against the Roman indulgences, Pope Leo in Rome prepared a new decree in November in which he confirmed his indulgences and commanded that they should be regarded as the greatest treasure in Christendom.[65] This document was sent to Emperor Maximilian.

When Dr. Luther realized that Pope Leo was defending indulgences, contrary to God's Word, and wanted them to be considered an article of faith, and that he had already been condemned as a heretic in Rome and had been summoned to appear there in person before several bishops, he

---

the proceedings. Linck was present at the first session; Staupitz, Peutinger, and von Feilitzsch at the second; and Rühel and von Feilitzsch at the third. See Brecht 1:252–57.

[60] *Explanations of the Ninety-Five Theses* (1518), especially Thesis 7 and Thesis 38, LW 31:98–107, 191–96.

[61] Luther submitted this statement to Cardinal Cajetan on October 14. It is reproduced in *Proceedings at Augsburg* (1518), LW 31:264–75.

[62] See *Table Talk* no. 225 (1532), LW 54:30; no. 884 (1530s), WA TR 1:441–42.

[63] For Luther's appeal from Cardinal Cajetan to Pope Leo X, see *Appellatio ML a Caietano ad Papam* (1518), WA 2:27–33. Staupitz had left several days before Luther. Luther left in haste and in secret on the night of October 20, fearing his imminent arrest. Cf. *Table Talk*, no. 1203 (1530s), WA TR 1:597–98; Brecht 1:258, 260.

[64] For the date, see Luther to Spalatin, October 31, 1518, LW 48:90–93, against *Table Talk* no. 5349 (1540), WA TR 5:78, which gives November 1 as the date, and *LH²*, p. 471, which gives October 30. Cf. Brecht 1:260.

[65] Leo X, *Cum postquam*, promulgated November 9, 1518 (Denzinger, no. 740).

appealed on November 28, 1518, from the Roman see to a free, general, Christian council.[66] In addition, he continued preaching, writing, and lecturing in God's name.[67] Thus it was at this time that he lectured on St. Paul's Epistle to the Galatians, which he published and dedicated to the laudable university in Wittenberg,[68] giving no heed to the fact that many neighboring and foreign universities and monasteries were writing against him and condemning and burning his books.[69]

In view of the incessant denunciations and condemnations from the Roman court, and because the elector of Saxony had an ambassador[70] dispatched to the emperor at the time, petition was made for his most gracious written intercession and mediation so that Luther's case might be adjudicated in German territory,[71] since [Luther] was happy to accept certain bishops[72] and any of the universities (with the exception of three

---

[66] For the breve of August 23, revealing that Luther had already been condemned as a heretic and summoned to appear before Bishop Jerome of Ascoli, see *Proceedings at Augsburg* (1518), LW 31:286–89; for Luther's appeal to a council, see WA 2:34–40. Cf. Luther to Spalatin, October 31, 1518, LW 48:90.

[67] See Brecht 1:286–97.

[68] *[First] Lectures on Galatians* (1516–17/1519), LW 27:151–410. Luther had lectured on Galatians from October 27, 1516, until March 13, 1517, though he did not revise and publish these lectures until 1519. See Brecht 1:129 and the introduction by Jaroslav Pelikan, LW 27:ix–x. Luther's dedication (to Petrus Lupinus [d. 1521] and Andreas Bodenstein von Karlstadt, of the Wittenberg faculty) is found in LW 27:153–60. In 1518, Luther finished lecturing on Hebrews (LW 29:107–241) and began his second set of lectures on the Psalms (*Labors on the Psalms* [published 1519–21], WA 5; WA Ar 1–2 [LW 64; cf. LW 14:279–349]).

[69] The University of Frankfurt an der Oder supported Tetzel, conferring a doctorate on him in 1518 and hosting a disputation in which Tetzel defended 106 theses, drafted by the theologian Conrad Wimpina, against Luther's *Ninety-Five Theses*: see Fabisch and Iserloh, *Dokumenta Causa zur Lutheri*, 1:310–36. At the University of Ingolstadt, the theologian Johann Eck composed his *Obelisci* against the *Ninety-Five Theses* in March 1518: see *Asterisci Lutheri adversus obeliscos Eccii*, WA 1:281–314. The Dominicans in general rallied behind Tetzel against Luther: see Klaus-Bernward Springer, *Die deutschen Dominikaner in Widerstand und Anpassung während der Reformationszeit* (Berlin: Akademie, 1999). A little later, in 1519, the Franciscan monasteries in Jüterbog and Wittenberg attacked Luther's teaching, leading to a disputation at the meeting of the Franciscan provincial chapter in Wittenberg in October 1519: see *Franziskanerdisputation*, WA 59:606–97. Cf. below, p. 152 n. 73.

[70] Degenhard Pfeffinger, chamberlain to Frederick the Wise; see above, p. 129 n. 86.

[71] See Elector Frederick to Degenhard Pfeffinger, November 19, 1518, StL 15:665–67; Frederick to Cardinal Cajetan, November 1518, WA Br 1:250–51.

[72] Bishops mentioned in Saxon sources as favorable or at least neutral judges include Lawrence von Bibra (ca. 1456–1519), bishop of Würzburg (see also below, p. 169 n. 19); Philipp of the Palatinate (1480–1541), bishop of Freising and Naumburg; Richard von Greiffenklau (1467–1531), archbishop of Trier; Matthäus Lang von Wellenburg (1468–1540), archbishop of Salzburg. See Luther to Elector Frederick, January 13 and 19, 1519, LW 48:103–6; Brecht 1:249, 268–73.

which had already made themselves suspect)[73] as commissaries and media-tors. But nothing could be accomplished with the Roman Curia. After this another imperial diet was scheduled for the following year, which Emperor Maximilian would personally visit at Epiphany, that is, on Three Kings' Day.[74]

I have heard from a great man that the emperor was heard to say in passing, in audience with the elector's ambassador, Degenhard Pfeffinger:[75] "Tell our dear uncle[76] to protect this monk Luther for us with diligence, for an occasion in which we have need of him may soon arise."[77] For Emperor Maximilian was aware of many schemes within his government on the part of the Roman Curia, and so he was reported to have been waiting and looking for opportunity to avenge himself on the enemies and oppressors of the imperial majesty and crown. Yet the crown and power of the pope are not to be overthrown by human might, but by the mouth of God's Spirit [cf. 2 Thess. 2:8][78] and with Holy Scripture. In accordance with his own prophecy, therefore, the good emperor, who at this time had also read and praised the doctor's propositions,[79] set out on Epiphany and came to his blessed end.

Now as Emperor Maximilian entered his blessed rest at the beginning of 1519[80] and the Roman court stood rigidly opposed to our doctor's bold and steadfast teaching, though unable to suppress it by the power of the sword and illegitimate legal proceedings, Leo X dispatched his chamber-lain, Karl von Miltitz,[81] to the praiseworthy elector of Saxony and his chief

---

[73] Cf. Brecht 1:249, where the Universities of Erfurt, Leipzig, and Frankfurt an der Oder are excluded, citing Spalatin to Hans Renner, StL 15:550.

[74] Cf. Christoph Scheurl to Luther, December 20, 1518, WA Br 1:279. Scheurl (1481–1542) reports that Maximilian planned a diet for Easter 1519 in Worms or Frankfurt, but planned to visit Augsburg at Epiphany, where Luther should meet the papal legate. But according to the account in Spalatin, *Friedrichs des Weisen*, p. 51, Pfeffinger had been told that Frederick should plan to attend an imperial diet in Frankfurt at Epiphany, where the emperor would come: see WA Br 1:279 n. 9. In fact, the next imperial diet was held in 1521, under Maximilian's succes-sor, Charles V, at Worms (see below, Mathesius, *History*, pp. 172–78).

[75] See above, p. 151 n. 70.

[76] "Uncle" was the common form of address by the imperial chancellery for imperial princes; according to genealogy, Frederick the Wise would have been a cousin-nephew (first cousin once removed) of Maximilian. See *LH²*, p. 472 on 41.7.

[77] On Maximilian's views of the Roman Church, see above, p. 147 n. 45.

[78] Cf. above, p. 147 n. 44.

[79] See *Table Talk* no. 5343 (1540), WA TR 5:74.

[80] Maximilian died in Wels, in Austria, on January 12, 1519, though Luther, *Preface to the Latin Writings* (1545), LW 34:332, places his death in February.

[81] Karl von Miltitz (ca. 1490–1529) was a Saxon nobleman, a canon of Mainz, Trier, and Meissen, and from 1514 a junior member of the Roman Curia. He was sent as papal nuncio in

counselors and secretaries, sending with him a Golden Rose which the pope himself had blessed in Rome on Laetare Sunday,[82] along with some letters in which he requested that the elector send Dr. Luther to Rome or cease to allow him to remain in his electoral territory. For Miltitz had both the commission and the papal breves[83] to bring Dr. Luther from Germany to Rome by force, but the Roman crown, Keys,[84] rose, and letters ⏐had already lost their reputation and esteem among the Germans on account of God's Word. Therefore, Miltitz accomplished little and did not dare to attempt to lay hands on Luther.

He received permission to conduct a dialogue with Luther in Altenburg; here Luther consented to abstain from writing henceforth, as long as his opponents were obligated to the same condition.[85] He also wanted to have his hearing in Germany before certain bishops and in accordance with God's Word. However, the time was at hand in which the Antichrist and his foolishness would be made manifest; therefore, negotiations in good faith would no longer be of any help in the matter, though Miltitz enjoined Tetzel to refrain from holding his indulgence fairs any longer.[86] Dr. Luther is supposed to have said that had Miltitz's advice been taken at the start, the matter could have been resolved. For when the papacy was on the rise and waxing, no human power or wisdom was able to subdue it. Now that it was falling and waning, no power or counsel on earth could prop it up again.[87]

1518 to bring the Golden Rose to Frederick the Wise, to interview Luther, and to investigate charges against Tetzel. See Beitenholz and Deutscher, *Contemporaries of Erasmus*, 2:444–45.

[82] The Golden Rose was a finely crafted token of papal goodwill, blessed in Rome on the Fourth Sunday in Lent as described by Mathesius. At this time it was usually conferred on secular rulers; it may have been intended to appeal to Frederick's passion for collecting relics. See Brecht 1:265–66.

[83] *breuia*; i.e., official papal letters. For these texts, see StL 15:666–79.

[84] See above, p. 143 and n. 23 there.

[85] Luther's negotiations with Miltitz took place at Spalatin's house in Altenburg, January 4–6, 1519. See Brecht 1:267–68.

[86] Miltitz met with Tetzel shortly after his meetings with Luther, around January 20, 1519. See Brecht 1:267.

[87] On Luther's encounter with Miltitz, see *Preface to the Latin Writings* (1545), LW 34:332, 334–36; *Freedom of a Christian* (1520), LW 31:339–41; *Table Talk* no. 156 (1532), WA TR 1:74; no. 1203 (1530s), WA TR 1:598; no. 3413 (1530s), WA TR 3:308; no. 5375c (1540), WA TR 5:102–3; and Luther's correspondence from 1519–20, especially to Elector Frederick and to Pope Leo X, January 5 or 6, 1519, LW 48:96–102; to Johann von Staupitz, February 20, 1519, LW 48:108–9; to Georg Spalatin, October 12, 1520, LW 48:179–81. For the judgment that Miltitz's advice should have been followed, see *Preface to the Latin Writings* (1545), LW 34:336; on the papacy, cf. *Table Talk* no. 5079 (1540), WA TR 4:646.

Now, while Dr. Luther earnestly continued teaching, lecturing, preaching, and writing in Christ's name and in His Word,[88] Doctor Johann Eck[89] stepped forward, desiring to disprove Doctor Martin's doctrine of true Christian repentance and to defend the indulgences and primacy of the pope in Rome—that the pope is the supreme head of the universal Christian Church according to Christ's Word and institution. He arranged a disputation in Leipzig on these topics with Karlstadt,[90] and then with Luther, for whom he himself obtained a safe-conduct.[91]

Doctor Luther held fast to the Word of the prophets and apostles, in which there is not so much as a word that hints at Roman indulgences, and he publicly testified that Jesus Christ is the only and highest Head of the holy Christian Church since the time of Adam, and will remain so to the Last Day, even as St. Paul ¦in Colossians 2 clearly calls the Lord Christ the Head of the Christian Church and Lord over everything in heaven, earth, and hell [cf. Col. 2:10; 1:18; Eph. 1:20–23]. In the same way, Dr. Luther used God's Word to explain the article concerning true repentance and conversion to God: that the only true penitent is one who recognizes his sins through the Law and is

---

[88] Cf. *Preface to the Latin Writings* (1545), LW 34:336. For Luther's lecturing activity in 1519, see above, p. 151 n. 68; p. 126 nn. 68–69, pp. 131–32 n. 98.

[89] Eck (1486–1543; see Walter L. Moore, "Eck, Johann," *OER* 2:17–18) was a leading theologian at the University of Ingolstadt. He was drawn into the controversy by his bishop, for whom Eck drafted the *Obelisci* criticizing Luther's *Ninety-Five Theses* (see above, p. 151 n. 69); Luther responded privately with his *Asterisci* (1518), WA 1:281 314, while Karlstadt made a public attack in his own series of theses against Eck. Eck challenged the Wittenberg faculty to a debate in 1519, with the University of Leipzig as a neutral forum. Eck subsequently made a career out of opposing the Reformation, assisting with the preparation of the papal bull condemning Luther—*Exsurge Domine* (1520)—and publishing extensively in defense of the papacy, providing an influential controversial manual (his *Enchiridion* of 1525) while engaging directly with Evangelical theologians in discussions at Augsburg (1530), Worms (1540), and Regensburg (1541). See below, *History*, p. 160, 306–7, 337–40, 343–44, 491–94.

[90] Andreas Bodenstein von Karlstadt (1486–1541) was Luther's senior in the Wittenberg theological faculty, over which he frequently served as dean, and had conferred the doctorate on Luther in 1512. Although Karlstadt—trained as a Thomist and Scotist with a doctorate in theology in addition to doctorates in both canon and civil law—was initially strongly hostile to Luther's teaching, his reading of Augustine upon Luther's challenge had turned him into an avid supporter by 1517. Later, after Karlstadt's introduction of changes in Wittenberg during Luther's exile in the Wartburg—reforms which Luther regarded as precipitous—the two theologians had a permanent falling out over issues such as iconoclasm and the doctrine of the Lord's Supper. See below, Mathesius, *History*, pp. 194–99, 213–18, 238–40, 260–62. See Ronald J. Sider, *Andreas Bodenstein von Karlstadt: The Development of His Thought, 1517–1525* (Leiden: Brill, 1974); Ulrich Bubenheimer, "Bodenstein von Karlstadt, Andreas," *OER* 1:178–80.

[91] Duke George of Albertine Saxony (1471–1539), in whose territory Leipzig was located, had initially refused to grant a safe-conduct to Luther. See *Preface to the Latin Writings* (1545), LW 34:333. Eck debated with Karlstadt June 27–28, 1519, and June 30–July 3, then with Luther July 4–13, and again with Karlstadt July 14–15. See Brecht 1:316.

contrite from the heart; who acknowledges the blood, sacrifice, and inter-cession of Jesus Christ to be the sole payment and satisfaction for our sins and the sins of the whole world [cf. 1 John 2:2]; and that such a justified, reconciled, and accepted sinner, having been blessed by the grace of the Holy Spirit, is obligated to enter upon a new and holy life, to glorify God, and will-ingly to do many good works in accordance with God's Word, as a sacrifice of praise and thanksgiving. All this can be discerned at length in the acts of the Leipzig Disputation,[92] which began on June [2]7[93] in the year 1519.

As scholastic theology—the sophistry of the schools—had already been driven to the ground by the Word of God, so now the primacy and preeminence of the pope with his decretals and bulls also began to taper off and come to an end after the Leipzig Disputation. For Dr. Luther, as the true Samson [cf. Judg. 16:28–31], tore down the pillars upon which the Romanists had built the pope's preeeminence. For the text upon which Eck was relying—"You are Peter, and on this rock I will build My Church" [Matt. 16:18][94]—does not refer to St. Peter, much less to his successors and supposed heirs to the see, but rather to the Lord Jesus Christ, who is the true Rock and Foundation, as St. Paul calls Him [1 Cor. 3:11; 10:4], upon which Christendom, having been baptized in His name and established upon His Word, shall withstand all the gates of hell.[95]

Now since, in light of the disputation in Leipzig and the treatise that followed,[96] many people began to lose respect for the pope's triple tiara and

---

[92] Luther's theses for the disputation are printed in *Leipzig Debate* (1519), LW 31:307–25, along with his letter of July 20 to Spalatin describing the debate. The acts of the disputation itself as printed while the decision of the university was still pending are in WA 2:254–83; a version derived from the official notary protocols is edited in WA 59:433–605. Luther's first twelve theses deal with sin, penance, and purgatory; the thirteenth thesis, which became the center of Eck's attack, deals with the primacy of the Roman Church.

[93] The text of Mathesius' sermon gives the erroneous date of "June 17," which may have appeared, however, on the title page of the printing of the disputation used by Mathesius (not found in VD16). See Volz, *Die Lutherpredigten des Johannes Mathesius*, pp. 104, 155. On the correct dating to June 27, see Brecht 1:312.

[94] See Luther to Spalatin, July 20, 1519, LW 31:321. Both Luther and Eck also preached on Matthew 16, the appointed Gospel for the Feast of SS. Peter and Paul, on June 29, 1519. See Luther to Spalatin, July 20, 1519, LW 31:324; *Sermon Preached in the Castle at Leipzig* (1519), LW 51:53–60; Brecht 1:317–19.

[95] See *Contra Malignum Eccii Iudicium* (1519), WA 2:628–42. For Luther's explanation of this position after the pope had condemned it in *Exsurge Domine* (see below, Mathesius, *History*, p. 160), see *Defense and Explanation of All the Articles* (1521), LW 32:67–74.

[96] Luther published two written defenses of his Leipzig theses: a detailed argument against papal primacy in the *Explanation of the Thirteenth Thesis on the Authority of the Pope* (1519), WA 2:183–240 (LW 71), which appeared in a first edition before the debate and in an expanded second edition afterward; and a defense of all the theses, published after the

the fabricated authority of which he boasted,[97] which he had usurped based on a false interpretation of God's Word, ¹many German and Roman writers stepped forward alongside Eck, seeking to support and defend the pope's authority and preeminence by means of the ancient teachers, or, as they put it, with the long spear and the short dagger of ancient custom.[98] Some secular princes also lent their support to this endeavor.[99]

Whereas Dr. Luther previously had done nothing more than to engage in disputations and pose questions about papal preeminence and would gladly have let it remain and helped reform it, now the clear Word of God instructed and convinced him that the pope in Rome, who had been regarded by all as an earthly god and the most holy, was, in fact, the true and arch-Antichrist and the opponent of God, who had elevated himself above Jesus Christ and true worship [cf. 2 Thess. 2:3–4] and subjugated all of Christendom with his

---

debate: *Explanations of the Theses Debated at Leipzig* (1519), WA 2:391–435 (LW 71). See Brecht 1:307, 325.

[97] On the papal tiara, see above, p. 133 n. 107.

[98] Jerome Emser (1478–1527), a theologian in the service of Duke George of Saxony, attended the Leipzig Disputation and began to write against Luther frequently thereafter. In his *Wider das unchristenliche Buch Martini Luthers Augustiners an den Tewtschen Adel außgangen* [Against the unchristian book of the Augustinian Martin Luther addressed to the German nobility] (1520), Emser described his weapons as the "spear" of ecclesiastical traditions and the "dagger" of patristic biblical interpretation, alongside the "sword" of God's Word. See the introduction by Eric W. Gritsch, LW 39:139. Among Luther's replies to Emser, see *To the Goat in Leipzig* (1521), LW 39:105–115; *Concerning the Answer of the Goat in Leipzig* (1521), LW 39:117–35; *Answer to Emser* (1521), LW 39:137–224; *Retraction of the Error Forced by Emser* (1521), LW 39:225–38; *To Emser the Goat* (1519), WA 2:658–79 (LW 71). Other opponents of Luther in the wake of the Leipzig Disputation included the Leipzig theologian Hieronymus Dungersheim (1465–1540) (see LW 40:230 n. 3; LW 48:145 n. 6; Dungersheim to Luther, October 7, 1519, WA Br 1:518–22; December 1519, WA Br 1:574–94; January 1520, WA Br 2:2–22; Luther to Dungersheim, December 1519, WA Br 1:567; 1:601–3; May 1520, WA Br 2:113); Augustin von Alveldt (1480–1535), a Franciscan (see *On the Papacy in Rome* [1520], LW 39:49–104); and the Strassburg Franciscan Thomas Murner (1475–1537) (see *Answer to Emser* [1521], LW 39:137–224; Luther to Johann von Staupitz, January 14, 1521, LW 48:194; to Melanchthon, May 26, 1521, LW 48:234). From Rome itself, the Dominican Thomist Sylvester Prierias (1456–1523) had written against Luther's *Ninety-Five Theses* in early 1518 and continued with responses until 1520 (see *Explanations of the Ninety-Five Theses* [1518], LW 31:77–252); Eck traveled to Rome after the debate to aid in drafting the 1520 bull condemning Luther (see below, p. 160); and the Cremona Dominican theologian Isidor Isolani (1480–1528) published a *Revocation* calling Luther back to obedience to the papacy (see the introduction by Abdel Ross Wentz, LW 36:6; WA 6:397). See Bagchi, *Luther's Earliest Opponents*; Brecht 1:330–48.

[99] In particular, Duke George of Saxony patronized many of the Leipzig writers, and, after the University of Erfurt failed to render a verdict on the Leipzig Disputation, he demanded that the University of Paris condemn Luther's writings in November 1520. See Brecht 1:338.

murder and lies.[100] In 1520, therefore, with great resolve and zeal in accordance with God's Word, Dr. Luther attacked the pope's preeminence and crown and the horrible power of excommunication which he exercised[101] and began, as the true Samson, to free the good old Germans from Roman and Babylonian captivity.[102] Soon thereafter he also began attacking the whole fabricated Roman religion by means of God's Word: its worship, monastic vows, clerical celibacy, and especially the strong fortress of the Roman Church, the private Masses, and he dashed them to the ground.[103] For he did not teach and write in a corner, as the sneaks do nowadays, shunning the light and a public hearing and disseminating their little books under false or fabricated names and selling them in clandestine stalls. Instead, he wrote to Pope Leo the blessed book on Christian freedom,[104] in which he confidently showed from God's Word that the natural man [1 Cor. 2:14] is ¦bound and obliged to render humble obedience to the authorities and all secular ordinances which are legitimately placed over land and people, life and property, in accordance with reason and equity, for the sake of the Lord Jesus Christ, who Himself confirmed secular authority with His Word and honored it with His obedience, and also for the sake of conscience. Every rebel and seditionary gravely sins against conscience by wantonly and impudently opposing the legitimate authorities, to whom he is bound by oath and duty to be subject. Again, [one is bound and obliged] on account of the certain punishment which will surely come upon all the disobedient and their heirs and descendants according to God's judgment. In the same vein, Dr. Luther later published a separate Christian treatise on secular authority.[105]

Above and beyond such physical subjection, which God imposed on fallen Adam and his descendants as punishment for his sin and so that we might better tame our stubborn and rebellious flesh and hold it in check in order to maintain outward discipline and obedience, there is the inner and

---

[100] On Luther's earlier conciliatory attitude toward the papacy, see above, p. 143. Luther's public critique of the papacy, in which he began to propose conditionally that the papacy might be the Antichrist, began with his reply to Alveldt: *On the Papacy in Rome* (1520), LW 39:49–104, and continued with the works that followed. See Hendrix, *Luther and the Papacy*, pp. 95–120.

[101] *Sermon on the Ban* (1520), LW 39:3–22. See also below, p. 159.

[102] Mathesius probably has in mind *To the Christian Nobility* (1520), LW 44:115–217, as well as *Babylonian Captivity* (1520), LW 36:3–126; see also below, p. 159.

[103] Luther's systematic critique of the sacramental system continued in his works of the following year: *Von der Beichte, ob der Papst macht habe zu gebieten* (1521), WA 8:140–85; *Against Latomus* (1521), LW 32:133–260; and *Judgment on Monastic Vows* (1521), LW 44:243–400.

[104] *Freedom of a Christian* (1520), LW 31:327–77. The dedicatory letter to Pope Leo X is LW 31:334–43.

[105] *Temporal Authority* (1523), LW 45:75–129.

new man, born again from the Word and Spirit of God in holy Baptism, received as a child and heir of God, who is a free and unfettered person, whose heart, soul, and conscience no human order, law, or regulation can bind and fetter in opposition to God's Word. For Christ our Lord, who liberates and frees us from death, sin, and hell, also frees the heart and conscience of the baptized believers so that they are not obliged to obey any human tradition by means of which some attempt to set up a form of worship of God or articles of faith and to help souls obtain eternal life. For as a member of the body politic and the secular kingdom swears and pledges upon his hope of salvation that he will obey the authorities and their representatives and secular orders, laws, and mandates, so also everyone being baptized pledges and swears to God the Father and His Son and Holy Spirit to obey nothing but the Word and command of the Holy Trinity in matters of religion and faith. This is the wellspring from which Christian freedom flows, so that a baptized member of Jesus Christ is not obliged or bound to obey any human ordinance that opposes the clear Word of God. Indeed, if anyone obeys the command of his earthly lord or bishop when it is diametrically opposed to Christ's Word and command, he is unworthy of Christ and all His treasures and forfeits his place in heaven.

In April[106] Dr. Luther wrote to Pope Leo concerning these two articles in a remarkable preface,[107] in which he offered to perform obediently everything that the pope would impose upon him, save that he would not recant his doctrine, which he had confirmed with the Word of Jesus Christ, and [wrote] that no one was able to interpret or judge this Word by means of the wisdom of reason and human understanding, much less to condemn it.

Also published in this year [1520] was the Christian book concerning good works,[108] from which I first learned the rudiments of Christianity, praise God, in the year 1526, in Bavaria at Odelzhausen Castle, where I instructed the children of the Christian matron Sabine Auer, née Stettner.[109]

---

[106] In fact, Luther's letter to Pope Leo X was dated September 6, 1520, the date on which Luther agreed to write the letter, though it was not drafted until October; the earlier dating was retained to situate the letter before the arrival in Wittenberg of the papal bull *Exsurge Domine* condemning Luther: Brecht 1:404–5. In the Wittenberg edition of Luther's Latin works, however (followed by the Jena edition), the date of the letter was given as April 6: see WA 7:49 n. 4.

[107] "Open Letter to Pope Leo X," LW 31:334–43. Although the letter to Pope Leo served as the preface to Luther's Latin version of *Freedom of a Christian*, the German translation of the letter was published separately, and the treatise and letter were printed separately in the Wittenberg edition of Luther's works as well. See WA 7:1–3.

[108] *Treatise on Good Works*, published in June 1520, LW 44:15–114; see Brecht 1:365–68.

[109] The *Treatise on Good Works* was Mathesius' first exposure to Luther and the beginning of his conversion to Lutheranism. See the introduction above, p. lxxxi; Loesche, *Johann Mathesius*, 1:28–33.

Meanwhile, Dr. Eck, with his baseless disputations and scurrilous books,[110] was helping Dr. Luther confirm that the Roman Curia is the true Babylon, in which the true Antichrist was holding dear Christendom captive with his decretals, idolatrous worship, and [monastic] orders, as Dr. Luther was writing concerning the ban and Babylonian captivity,[111] attacking all the innovations of the Roman religion and its forms of worship invented by human beings. He also taught that Jesus Christ instituted the Supper in its entirety, and made the Christian request that the Bride of Jesus Christ again be allowed the whole Supper of the Lord's true body and blood and that ¦a true Christian Mass along with the distribution of the Lord's Supper be reestablished.[112]

With these writings Dr. Luther ignited a new fire—for the Elbe, Elster, Mulde,[113] and many rushing waters came together in an effort to extinguish this blaze, which was helping to consume and burn up all the monasteries, chapters,[114] and all the trafficking of the Roman Mass. The man from Stolpen[115] also stumbled[116] over God's Word, which is the Rock of offense [Isa. 8:14; Rom. 9:33; 1 Pet. 2:8], seeking by means of his assistant and his assistant's assistants to deploy public edicts in defense of the public robbing of the Church—that one kind [the cup] was hidden away and withdrawn from the baptized laity.

---

[110] See above, p. 154 n. 89.

[111] *Sermon on the Ban* (1520), LW 39:3–22; *Babylonian Captivity* (1520), LW 36:3–126. Cf. above, pp. 156–57.

[112] According to medieval practice (codified at the Council of Constance in 1415), the laity were allowed to receive the body and blood of Christ under only one "species" or "kind," i.e., the form of bread and not the cup in Communion. The followers of John Hus, as well as the Lutherans a century later, insisted that both species should be administered to the laity. See Luther, *Babylonian Captivity* (1520), LW 36:12–28; anticipated more circumspectly in *The Blessed Sacrament and the Brotherhoods* (1519), LW 35:49–50.

[113] Wittenberg is on the Elbe River; the Mulde and Black Elster are tributaries of the Elbe. The image seems to be that of water (i.e., opposition) converging on Wittenberg from across Germany. Cf. above, p. 147.

[114] *Stifft*; an association of clergy (such as the canons of a cathedral chapter) endowed with corporate identity, property, and rights under church law.

[115] Bishop Johann von Schleinitz of Meissen (ca. 1470–1537) had issued a mandate condemning Luther's defense of lay reception of the Lord's Supper in both kinds. See StL 19:460–63. The mandate appeared under the seal of the bishop's judicial vicar [*Officialis*] whose chancellory was at Stolpen. Luther responded immediately with his *Antwort auf die Zettel, so unter des Officials zu Stolpen Siegel* (1520), WA 6:137–41. See Brecht 1:363–65.

[116] A play on words in German: *Der von Stolpen stolpert*. It is possible that in Mathesius' printed text the word *Official* ["vicar-general"] from Luther's title has dropped out by a slip of the pen or printer's error: see Volz, *Die Lutherpredigten des Johannes Mathesius*, pp. 157, 225.

Dr. Luther, however, armed himself with the clear Word of Jesus Christ and drove back all his enemies and the opponents of God. For since Christ commands all of His disciples to drink from His cup the true blood of the new testament [Matt. 26:27], not even all the popes, councils, bishops, officials, universities, scholars, monks, chapters, or old custom are able to prohibit the reception of both kinds in accordance with Christ's institution. This strong Word of the Lord Christ has prevailed to such an extent that now the pope himself and many scholars are beginning to yield[117] in this article, provided that it be sought solely from the Roman see, with humble obedience. For the Word of Christ, the Son of God and our only High Priest, must not be valid—so the wisdom of the world claims—unless it first be permitted and approved by the anti-Christian see in Rome.

While God's Word was making such a clamor in the Roman Church by means of Luther's tongue and pen, overturning the tables of the money changers [Matt. 21:12] and the Mass tables and driving them out of many parishes and hearts where the clergy had been playing games with the blood, possessions, and souls of the poor laity, Dr. Eck joined with the Roman see and produced an abominable papal bull and mandate in which Christ and His eternal Word are blasphemed and condemned.[118]

|As soon as this bull arrived in Germany, the doctor defended the clear articles which, contrary to God's Word, were condemned as heresy in it[119]

---

[117] The pope at the time of this sermon was Pius IV (r. 1559–65), who in 1562 reconvened the Council of Trent, which had been suspended in 1552. In January 1562, Emperor Ferdinand I submitted to the Council of Trent proposals which included permitting the chalice to the laity. Many bishops voted in favor and decided to permit it, at least as an exception; this reform was published in Vienna on June 18, 1564, later in Salzburg, Passau, Mainz, and Prague, but then quickly annulled. See Michael Mullett, *Historical Dictionary of the Reformation and Counter-Reformation* (Lanham: Scarecrow Press, 2010), p. 288, s.v. "Laity."

[118] The bull *Exsurge Domine* of June 15, 1520, listed and condemned (without any explicit refutation) forty-one statements from Luther's writings, calling upon Luther to cease and recant or else be condemned as a heretic and excommunicated. For the text of the bull, see Carl Mirbt and Kurt Aland, eds., *Quellen zur Geschichte des Papsttums und des römischen Katholizismus* (Tübingen: Mohr Siebeck, 1967), 1:504–13, translated in *The Reformation: A Narrative History Related by Contemporary Observers and Participants*, ed. Hans J. Hillerbrand (New York: Harper & Row, 1964), pp. 80–84. On the bull and Eck's role, see Brecht 1:389–95.

[119] The bull arrived in Wittenberg on September 10, 1520. See Luther to Spalatin, October 11, 1520, WA Br 2:195. Luther responded in print with *On Eck's New Bull and Lies* (1520), WA 6:576–94 (LW 71), and *Adversus execrabilem Antichrsti bullam* (1520), WA 6:597–612, followed by a German edition, WA 6:613–29. In fact, Luther's *Freedom of a Christian* (1520) and letter to Pope Leo X belong here chronologically as well (see above, p. 158 and n. 106 there), though they were dated to appear as if they had been issued before the delivery of the bull.

and denounced the pope's hot air[120] or counsel, in light of which even many papal bishops began to feel ashamed of the pope's letter. Von Hutten also expressed himself with such martial vigor in his postil[121] that many of them wished the bull had never bellowed[122] like this in Germany.

Since Dr. Luther's Christian doctrine was being attacked from all sides by means of cunning and force, and since the most praiseworthy king of Spain, Charles,[123] had recently been duly elected as Roman emperor, Dr. Luther wrote to this man of noble blood, toward whom he always had a cordial and trusting attitude,[124] with a most humble petition that he would not allow Luther's doctrine, which he had drawn from God's Word, to be condemned without due process at the instigation of insolent people. Whoever acts and teaches rightly does not flee nor shun the light and is glad to give account of his faith if he is required to do so in proper order [cf. 1 Pet. 3:15]. It was also in this year, 1520, that the beautiful little book of consolation entitled *Tesseradecas* was published—a consolatory writing whose like had never before been drafted in the German language.[125]

When the Roman crowd insinuated its way into many rulers' courts, however, seeking aid in suppressing Luther's doctrine, the doctor was induced to repeat his previous appeal,[126] in which he had appealed from the

---

[120] *blase*; literally, "bubble," a play on the literal meaning of the word "bull" [*bulla*], so named from the bubble-shaped lead seal attached to the document.

[121] Ulrich von Hutten (1488–1523) was an imperial knight and a humanist who had defended the Hebraist Johann Reuchlin and contributed to the satirical *Letters of Obscure Men* attacking his monastic critics (see above, p. 132 n. 100). After the Leipzig debate, Hutten began to take up Luther's cause as well. He published an edition of *Exsurge Domine* with his own mocking glosses in the *Bulla Decimi Leonis* ([Strassburg: Schott, 1520]) [VD16 K277], edited in E var. arg. 4:261–304, and he called for a military uprising to liberate Germany from the pope in the *Dialogi Huttenici Novi* ([Strassburg: Schott, 1521]) [VD16 H6311]. See Brecht 1:370–71, 419–20; Eckhard Bernstein, "Hutten, Ulrich von," *OER* 2:281–82.

[122] Another play on words: *Bulle . . . geprüllet.*

[123] Charles V (1500–1558), the grandson of Maximilian I, was king of Spain from 1516 to 1556 and Holy Roman emperor from 1519 to 1556. He had been elected, with the support of Frederick the Wise and against the wishes of Pope Leo X, on June 28, 1519. See Peter O'M. Pierson, "Charles V," *OER* 1:304–7.

[124] Luther to Emperor Charles V, August 30, 1520, LW 48:175–79. On Luther's guarded attitude toward Charles, see, e.g., *Warning to His Dear German People* (1531), LW 47:30–34.

[125] *Fourteen Consolations* (1520), LW 42:117–66, written for Frederick the Wise during his illness in the fall of 1519 as a replacement for the "Fourteen Holy Helpers," a catalog of saints whose devotion was specially cultivated in late medieval Germany. Luther in fact wrote the booklet in Latin, and it was translated into German by Spalatin. Erasmus praised Luther's *Fourteen Consolations* and commended the work to others: see Erasmus to Christoph von Utenheim, early January 1523, Ep. 1332 (CWE 9:231); to Johann von Botzheim, January 30, 1523, Ep. 1341A (CWE 9:343).

[126] See above, pp. 150–51.

pope's unjust condemnation to a free and Christian council, expanding it with a section addressed to all secular authorities, which was notarized on November 17, 1520.[127]

Meanwhile, Marinus and Aleander (whom many people regarded as an unbaptized Jew), came to Cologne with Roman breves,[128] in which the pope again besought the elector of Saxony, Duke Frederick, to burn Luther's books, arrest him, and 'send him to the pope in Rome. But the laudable elector met the pope's legates with a clever and well-grounded answer, to which they could not make any objection.[129] Therefore, they stayed at the imperial court and sought to win over the noble emperor and to induce him to take action to suppress and stamp out Dr. Luther's doctrine by force, without a hearing.

By God's gracious providence, however, Emperor Charles, who had been elected to the imperial eminence by common consent and with the special support of the elector of Saxony, gave the papal legates the answer that he would first like to speak with his kinsman, the elector of Saxony, before answering the pope. Upon this, the pope's emissary offered Erasmus of Rotterdam a major bishopric if he would take up the pen against Doctor Luther. But Erasmus refused this at this time, also confessing that a little

---

[127] *Appellatio D. M. Lutheri ad concilium a Leone X denuo repetita et innovata* (1520), WA 7:74–82, followed by a German edition, WA 7:83–90. Luther's expanded appeal to the secular authorities is found in WA 7:80–82. See Brecht 1:414–15.

[128] Marino Caracciolo (ca. 1469–1538) had served already as papal nuncio to the imperial court under Maximilian I (Bietenholz and Deutscher, *Contemporaries of Erasmus*, 1:264–65); Jerome Aleander (1480–1542) was a doctor of theology, humanist scholar, and Pope Leo's Vatican librarian (Bietenholz and Deutscher, *Contemporaries of Erasmus*, 1:28–32). Caracciolo and Aleander first presented themselves to Emperor Charles in the Netherlands, where they presided over the burning of Luther's books at Louvain on October 8. They then followed the emperor to Cologne, arriving on October 29, where he was joined by Elector Frederick. The false rumor that Aleander was not a baptized Christian but a Jew seems to have been spread by Erasmus himself: see Bietenholz and Deutscher, *Contemporaries of Erasmus*, 1:28; and Erasmus to a patron, December 1520, Ep. 1166 (CWE 8:105–8); to Mathias Kretz, December 22, 1530, Ep. 2414 (Allen, *Complete Letters of Erasmus*, 9:395); to Erasmus Schetz, 1532, Ep. 2578 (Allen, *Complete Letters of Erasmus*, 9:395); cf. Wolfgang Capito to Luther, December 4, 1520, WA Br 2:223. It was repeated in the satirical *Acta Academiae Lovaniensis contra Lutherum* of 1520 [VD16 A137–139], which was included in the Wittenberg and Jena editions of Luther's works (E var. arg. 4:304).

[129] A description of the negotiations between the papal nuncios and the elector by Heinrich von Zütphen (see below, p. 163 n. 133) and Georg Spalatin was included in both the Wittenberg and Jena editions (see E var. arg. 5:243–48; StL 15:1612–17). On November 6, 1520, Frederick the Wise gave the nuncios a reply (E var. arg. 5:244–47; StL15:1612–15) in which he expressed disapproval if Luther had indeed written unfairly against the pope, but in which he also called for a convincing refutation of Luther's writings before a council of educated judges—something that had not yet been done. See Brecht 1:418–19.

piece written by Luther was more instructive for him than the whole of Thomas along with all of his caperers[130] and sophists.[131]

Here I must also mention the courteous response of Lady Margaret,[132] which she is supposed to have given the sophists and monks in Louvain in the Netherlands, as described by the excellent martyr Heinrich von Zütphen, who confirmed Doctor Luther's doctrine with his blood.[133] For since the sophists claimed that Luther was leading astray the whole of Christendom, Maximilian's daughter is supposed to have asked who this Luther was. When the denouncers accused him of being an unlearned monk, she said, "If you learned monks write against one unlearned, surely the world will give more credence to many learned men than to one who is unlearned."

Now since those from Louvain as well as other universities, monasteries, and bishops were attacking Luther's books with blazing fire,[134] even as the pope in Rome had stirred up the fire and |was now fanning the flames with his bellowing, the Spirit of God came upon this second Samson also [cf. Judg. 14:6, 19], and on December 10, in front of the Elster Gate in Wittenberg,[135] he had another great fire kindled. Into it he himself cast the pope's Koran—the *Decretals*—along with Leo X's bull, with these words: "Because you, unholy book, have troubled or slandered the Lord's Holy One, may the eternal fire trouble and consume you."[136]

---

[130] *Capreolen*; a play on the name of John Capreolus (ca. 1380-1444), a leading late medieval Thomist: see *ODCC*, 3rd ed., s.v. "Capreolus, John."

[131] For Erasmus' remark, see above, Melanchthon, *Oration*, p. 44 and n. 31 there; cf. below, Mathesius, *History*, p. 559.

[132] Margaret of Austria (1480-1530) was daughter of Maximilian, aunt of Charles V, and regent of the Netherlands. She was a skillful politician who labored especially for the expansion of the house of Hapsburg, a patron of northern humanists, and an opponent of the Reformation. See Bietenholz and Deutscher, *Contemporaries of Erasmus*, 1:388-89.

[133] Heinrich von Zütphen (b. 1488/1489) was a Dutch Augustinian and adherent of Luther who was executed in 1524, becoming one of the first Evangelical martyrs. See Luther, *The Burning of Brother Henry* (1525), LW 32:261-86. For Zütphen's report of Margaret's remark, see E var. arg. 5:250 (StL 15:1616-17), though it is found in the portion of the report for which Spalatin was responsible.

[134] Cf. above, p. 162 n. 128. The bull *Exsurge Domine* called for the burning of Luther's books, and such actions had also taken place at Cologne and Mainz. See *Why the Books of the Pope and His Disciples Were Burned* (1520), LW 31:384; Luther to Spalatin, December 10, 1520, LW 48:186-87; to Johann von Staupitz, January 14, 1521, LW 48:191-94; to Spalatin, February 17, 1521, WA Br 2:265, and February 27, 1521, WA Br 2:270; and to Johann Lang, March 6, 1521, WA Br 2:276.

[135] The burning took place at the charnel pit by the Chapel of the Holy Cross, just outside the Elster Gate. See Brecht 1:423.

[136] Luther's words are reported in the *Exustionis Antichristianorum decretalium acta*, incorporated in the Wittenberg and Jena editions of Luther's works: WA 7:184, though Mathesius seems to be aware of variants in other reports. See Brecht 1:424. Cf. Ps. 21:9 [20:10 Vg].

The next day, Dr. Luther admonished his listeners to beware and guard against the books and religion of the Roman Curia as those of the true Antichrist and to abide in the Gospel and Word of Jesus Christ, the Son of God and of Mary, steadfastly in faith and with a good conscience. Then he published an open statement in which he indicated the reason and cause for his public burning of the pope's decretals.[137] To wit: that in St. Paul's day godless books were also burned, as can be seen in the Acts of the Apostles, chapter 19 [Acts 19:19]; that he is a baptized Christian and a legitimate doctor, sworn upon Holy Scripture, and a called preacher, therefore he is compelled by his Christian faith, baptismal vow, doctorate, oath, office, and conscience to assist in blotting out or at least opposing and obstructing ungodly and heretical doctrine and books.[138]

In the pope's book[139] there are abominable blasphemies against Jesus Christ, the true Son of God, and His saving Gospel, as well as against all the obedience which is due the secular authorities according to God's Word.

For example,[140] [it is claimed that] the pope and his men are not required to render humble obedience to the Commandments of God.[141]

Again, that it is not a commandment but a free counsel[142] in St. Peter that all people are to obey kings [1 Pet. 2:13].[143]

Again, the pope has in the shrine of his heart full power over all written laws.[144]

---

[137] *Why the Books of the Pope and His Disciples Were Burned* (1520), LW 31:379–95.

[138] *Why the Books of the Pope and His Disciples Were Burned* (1520), LW 31:383–84.

[139] I.e., canon law.

[140] These and the following statements from canon law are excerpted from *Why the Books of the Pope and His Disciples Were Burned* (1520), LW 31:383–95, though not always in the order of Luther's text.

[141] *Why the Books of the Pope and His Disciples Were Burned* (1520), LW 31:385, no. 1. See *Decretales* 1.33.6 (Friedberg 2:196–98).

[142] On the scholastic distinction between Commandments, binding on all people for obtaining eternal life, and "counsels of perfection," which human beings were free to choose to observe to obtain greater merit, see Luther's critique in *Explanations of the Ninety-Five Theses* (1518), LW 31:235; *Temporal Authority* (1523), LW 45:81, 87–92, 101–2; *Sermons on John 18–20* (1528–29/1557), LW 69:190–93; *Sermon on the Mount* (1530–32/1532), LW 21:3–4, 70, 74.

[143] *Why the Books of the Pope and His Disciples Were Burned* (1520), LW 31:385, no. 2. See *Decretales* 1.33.6 (Friedberg 2:197).

[144] *Why the Books of the Pope and His Disciples Were Burned* (1520), LW 31:385, no. 5. See Boniface VIII, *Liber Sextus* 1.2.1 (Friedberg 2:937).

Again, even if the pope is careless and leads countless souls into the fire of hell along with himself, no one has a right to rebuke him for this.[145]

Again, no one on earth has a right to judge the pope and his ordinances, but he judges all the world.[146]

Again, that, with St. Peter's Keys in Matthew, chapter 16 [Matt. 16:19], the pope has received authority over the heavenly as well as all worldly kingdoms and lordships; therefore, he can set up or depose emperors and kings as he pleases and tread them underfoot.[147]

Again, that no good husband or wife is able to serve God in the estate of marriage.[148]

Again, that the pope does not possess his power and dignity from Holy Scripture, but Holy Scripture from the pope.[149]

In summary, the canon law which Dr. Luther burned teaches that the pope is the earthly god above all heavenly, earthly, spiritual, and temporal things, to whom no one is allowed to say, "What are you doing?"[150]

This is an extract from the works of Dr. Luther, [explaining] why he condemned the canon law, the pope's book, to the fire and burned it. Later, as can be read at length in his books, he defended this action in powerful writings against a Papist who wrote against him on this account.[151]

---

[145] *Why the Books of the Pope and His Disciples Were Burned* (1520), LW 31:386, no. 8. See Gratian, *Decretum* 1 D. 40 c. 6 (Friedberg 1:146).

[146] *Why the Books of the Pope and His Disciples Were Burned* (1520), LW 31:387–87, no. 10. Gratian, *Decretum* 2 C. 9 q. 3 c. 17 (Friedberg 1:612).

[147] *Why the Books of the Pope and His Disciples Were Burned* (1520), LW 31:390–91, nos. 19 and 23. See Gratian, *Decretum* 1 D. 22 c. 1 (Friedberg 1:73); and the *Dictatus Papae* of Gregory VII (r. 1073–85), nos. 12 and 27 (in Tierney, *Crisis of Church and State*, pp. 49–50).

[148] *Why the Books of the Pope and His Disciples Were Burned* (1520), LW 31:391, no. 27. For canon law on clerical celibacy, see, e.g., *Decretales* 3.3.1–10 (Friedberg 2:457–60), 4.6.1–7 (Friedberg 2:684–87). Cf. Helen Parish, *Clerical Celibacy in the West, c. 1100–1700* (Farnham: Ashgate, 2010).

[149] *Why the Books of the Pope and His Disciples Were Burned* (1520), LW 31:392, no. 30. This claim had been made explicitly by the papal theologian Sylvester Prierias as the third thesis ("*fundamentum*") of his *Dialogus* against Luther's *Ninety-Five Theses*. Prierias appealed to *Decretum* 1 D. 22 c. 1 (Friedberg 1:73) and *Decretales* 5.7.9 (Friedberg 2:780). See Fabisch and Iserloh, *Dokumente zur Causa Lutheri*, 1:55, 180–81; Luther, preface, notes, and afterword to Prierias, *Response* (1520), WA 6:341 (LW 71). For similar claims in canon law, see also *Decretum* 2 C. 9 q. 3 c. 17 (Friedberg 1:611); *Dictatus Papae*, no. 17 (in Tierney, *Crisis of Church and State*, p. 50).

[150] *Why the Books of the Pope and His Disciples Were Burned* (1520), LW 31:393. On the epithet "earthly god" for the pope, see LW 69:291–92 n. 24.

[151] Luther, *Response to Catharinus* (1521), WA 7:705–78 (LW 71), written in response to the Dominican Ambrosius Catharinus Politus (see below, Mathesius, *History*, p. 186 and nn. 17–18 there.

After this conflict, the Emperor Charles called for the first Diet of Worms, to which Dr. Luther was summoned and of which we will speak, God willing, at another time.[152] With this we conclude for today the history from the year 1516 through 1520 and thank our Lord Christ from the bottom of our heart for having sent us from His right hand a ¹German prophet, causing him to arise in the electorate of Saxony and wondrously preserving him there for forty years, and through him attacking the anti-Christian papacy and tearing and driving it out of many peoples' hearts, churches, and schools. Let us also ask Him, our High Priest [Heb. 6:20] and the only and faithful Pastor of our souls, Jesus Christ [cf. 1 Pet. 2:25], that He would graciously continue to preserve His dear Christian Church— including this church in St. Joachimsthal, which arose at the same time as the doctor's teaching—in His Gospel and laudable peace, as He has hitherto, under the protection and shield of our gracious lord, the emperor, and of Maximilian, the newly elected and crowned Roman king.[153] And hereby, as most humble Christians obedient to his Majesty, we wish from the bottom of our heart that, in addition to the honor and crown he has from our God, who distributes kingdoms on earth, he would have happiness, health, and a blessed reign, and that his crown and majesty would serve to honor God and spread His precious Word and bring prosperity to the Holy Roman Empire, to the praiseworthy German nation, and to this crown of Bohemia, including our Joachimsthal mines, town, school, and church. May the Father of Jesus Christ, whom we have learned to know and to call upon again in faith through Doctor Martin's doctrine, grant us this. May He be highly exalted forever! Amen!

---

[152] See below, Mathesius, *History*, pp. 172–78.

[153] On Emperor Ferdinand I and his son Maximilian II, who had been elected king of Bohemia and Roman [or German] king in 1562, see above, p. lxxxiii.

THE THIRD SERMON,
ON THE YEAR 1521

[Epiphany, January 6, 1563]

BELOVED friends in the Lord! Today the dear Christian Church celebrates the feast of the holy three kings or Wise Men from the East who visited the newborn Child. Having been enlightened by Daniel's prophecy[1] and led by the new star to Jerusalem, they found Him in Bethlehem and honored Him in true faith with their gifts [Matt. 2:1–11]. They also freely confessed Him with their mouths before Herod [Matt. 2:2], declaring to us poor Japhethites[2] and assuring us that we uncircumcised heathen also belong to the Church, people, descendants, and heirs of the blessed Shem[3] [Gen. 10:21; 9:26–27] and his dear Son, Jesus Christ.

Now, since our dear God also has His little flock of people and wise men in the west and the north, from among whom He has gathered for Himself an eternal Church and through whom He has had the Gospel of His Son proclaimed and brought forth in our days, we want to continue with the history of Doctor Luther at this hour and to speak of the wise men of the west and north, who with Christian boldness opposed the blasphemers in the east and the antichrists in the south,[4] and by whose efforts God's Word is being confessed and, praise God, is increasing and advancing in these lands with rich blessing.

O Lord Jesus, the eternal and substantial Wisdom, You make the Persians in the east and the Germans in the north wise and learned in Your Word[5] and Spirit. Help us to speak wisely and comfortingly of this whole history, to the glory of Your divine wisdom, that we may be able to praise You, who ¹alone are wise with Your Word, today and in all eternity.

---

[1] Perhaps a reference to Dan. 7:13 or a confusion with Num. 24:17.

[2] I.e., the peoples of Europe. See above, p. 105 n. 11.

[3] I.e., the progenitor of the Jews and therefore of Christ.

[4] I.e., the Turk in the east and the pope in the south. On the papacy as the Antichrist, see above, pp. 87–88 n. 12.

[5] I.e., in this context, Holy Scripture.

My dear friends! After the blessed departure of good Emperor Maximilian,[6] and once Charles, the king of Spain, the old emperor's grandson, had been legitimately elected and confirmed as the Roman emperor,[7] the papal courtiers and legates incessantly solicited and pressed the new emperor to condemn Dr. Luther's doctrine forthwith and to eradicate it by force.[8] So the most wise elector of Saxony strove to pursue this course: that Luther should first be given a hearing in person before the whole Roman Empire and that [his] doctrine should be judged by prudent and impartial men of wisdom in accordance with God's Word.[9]

Although Emperor Charles, being a wise young ruler, was inclined to do so, this laudable counsel was nonetheless hindered and delayed for a time.[10] Finally, however, at the persistent insistence and supplication of several electors and princes, consent was given to have Luther appear in person before Emperor Charles and the whole Roman Empire at Worms.[11] As he had confidently expressed it beforehand, at the request of the wise elector of Saxony, in a letter to Spalatin:[12] they should trust him to do whatever was expected of him, save for flight or recantation; he intended to stand and confess in God's name; he was unable to flee or to recant; let it befall him on that account as God wills.

After extensive consultation, Emperor Charles summoned Dr. Luther to appear before His Majesty in Worms with an imperial safe-conduct, which

---

[6] See above, p. 152 n. 80.

[7] Charles' election had taken place in June 1519; his coronation at Aachen and confirmation of his title by Pope Leo X took place in October 1520. See above, Mathesius, *History*, pp. 161–62.

[8] See *Table Talk* no. 5350 (1540), WA TR 5:80–81; and Luther to Johann Lang, March 6, 1521, WA Br 2:277. The papal bull *Decet Romanum Pontificem*, confirming Luther's condemnation and excommunication as threatened in *Exsurge Domine*, was issued on January 3, 1521: see E. G. Rupp and Benjamin Drewery, eds., *Martin Luther* (New York: St. Martin's, 1970), pp. 62–67.

[9] See above, Mathesius, *History*, pp. 160–63, as well as Brecht 1:434; cf. Luther to Johann von Staupitz, February 9, 1521, WA Br 2:263–64, and the correspondence of November 1520 between the papal legates and Elector Frederick edited in StL 15:1612–17 (previously reproduced in the Wittenberg and Jena editions).

[10] See Luther to Johann von Staupitz, January 14, 1521, LW 48:191–94; to Wenceslaus Linck, January 14, 1521, WA Br 2:247; to Spalatin, January 16, 1521, WA Br 2:248–50; to Staupitz, February 9, 1521, WA Br 2:262–65; to Linck, March 7, 1521, WA Br 2:281–82; to Johann Lang, March 6, 1521, WA Br 2:276–77; and to Elector Frederick, January 25, 1521, LW 48:194–97.

[11] See the answer of the estates of February 19, 1521, and the emperor's responses of March 1–2, 1521, DRA 2:515–26 (cf. StL 15:1729–30).

[12] Luther to Spalatin, December 29, 1520, LW 48:188–91. See Brecht 1:422–23.

was issued on March 6, 1521,[13] when the imperial herald Caspar Sturm[14] was ordered to accompany Dr. Luther to Worms and return him to safe quarters. With such an imperial summons and safe-conduct, Dr. Luther set out in God's name,[15] |everywhere commending himself to the prayers of good people. On the way there he became a little weak and indisposed, but traveled on.[16]

A priest from Naumburg, who had endeavored his whole life to collect antiquities, sent him along the way an image of the pious Christian Savonarola[17] and exhorted him to stand firm upon the acknowledged truth, for his God would be with him once more and would firmly stand by and uphold him.[18]

[Lawrence] von Bibra,[19] the wise bishop of Würzburg and loyal friend of the house of Saxony, received the doctor with joy and showed him nothing but goodwill, even as he commended him to Elector Frederick with a Christian witness after he had made his confession. For God's Word had already taken root in the hearts of many great men, who, like kindhearted Nicodemuses [cf. John 3:1–21], confessed it as God's eternal truth and gave it their patronage.

When the report reached Worms that Luther was on his way and intended obediently to appear and be heard, his opponents became apprehensive, for they realized that Luther would greatly advance his cause if he were to receive a public hearing. Therefore, the Romanists sought [new] strategies and had Luther's doctrine condemned without a hearing and his

---

[13] Charles V to Luther, March 6, 1521, WA Br 2:278–81 (*DRA* 2:526–27). Luther probably received the summons and safe-conduct on March 29. See Brecht 1:445, 448.

[14] Caspar Sturm (1475–1552) from Oppenheim was a German imperial herald. A sketch by Albrecht Dürer (1471–1528), dated 1520, is preserved in the Musée Condé at Chantilly. Throughout the following decade, Sturm began to write and publish in German on military and political subjects: see VD16 S10009–10023. For the identification of Sturm as Luther's courier to Worms, see *Luther at the Diet of Worms* (1521), LW 32:106.

[15] Luther set out for Worms in early April 1521, possibly April 2. See Brecht 1:448.

[16] Luther to Spalatin, April 14, 1521, LW 54:197–98.

[17] On Savonarola, see above, pp. 114–15 n. 4.

[18] Mathesius is the sole source for this account. Luther did stay in Naumburg on his way to Worms. See Volz, *Die Lutherpredigten des Johannes Mathesius*, p. 127; Brecht 1:448.

[19] Lawrence [Lorenz] von Bibra (Mathesius gives the toponym "von Biberach"), prince-bishop of Würzburg (r. 1495–1519), was a moderate ecclesiastical reformer, humanist, and patron of the arts. Luther's encounter with von Bibra in fact took place on his way to Augsburg via Heidelberg in 1518 rather than on the way to Worms in 1521, by which time the bishop had died (cf. below, p. 170 n. 21). See Brecht 1:215; Luther to Spalatin, April 19, 1518, WA Br 1:168; *Table Talk* no. 5375a (1540), WA TR 5:100. For the account of von Bibra's letter commending Luther to Elector Frederick, see Spalatin, *Friedrichs des Weisen*, p. 161. On von Bibra, see Alfred Wendehorst, "Lorenz von Bibra," *NDB* 15:169.

books [ordered to be] burned again. They also had the emperor's edict published in order to put some fear and dread into Dr. Luther and give him pause, but our doctor continued on as a fearless and bold teacher of the truth, regardless of the fact that his doctrine and books had at that time been condemned already.[20]

On this trip he also came to Heidelberg;[21] there he participated in a public disputation, much as John Hus proposed disputations in all the towns on his way to Constance, wanting to give everyone a full account of his doctrine.[22]

Now, since Doctor [Luther] refused to be frightened and continued on his way to Worms, his opponents began pursuing other strategems. For the papal nuncios stated publicly that a safe-conduct for a heretic must not be honored.[23] Some secular [rulers] are supposed to have approved such Roman designs as well. But the wise and peaceful elector on the Rhine, Count Palatine Louis, with whom the peace and tranquility of Germany was buried, refused, as an honorable and praiseworthy German, to allow his signature and seal to be violated.[24] For it had not yet been forgotten, he said,

---

[20] Although the imperial estates had approved Luther's summons to Worms, they repeatedly refused to issue a new mandate against Luther. Emperor Charles was therefore forced to issue the mandate of March 10 (*DRA* 2:529–33) in his own name. It condemned Luther's books, requiring that they be sequestered and not circulated further, but it did not, despite Aleander's protest, demand that they be burned (though in Luther's reports concerning the mandate, it did). The emperor's mandate was not published until the end of March; Luther first learned of it in Weimar. See Brecht 1:444–46, 448; Luther to Melanchthon, April 7, 1521, WA Br 2:296; *Table Talk* no. 3357a (1533), WA TR 3:281–84; no. 5107 (1540), WA TR 4:666–67; no. 5123 (1540), WA TR 4:672–73; no. 5342a–b (1540), WA TR 5:65–73.

[21] As with the encounter with Lawrence von Bibra (see above, p. 169 n. 19), Mathesius has transposed the Heidelberg disputation of April 19–21, 1518—which took place on Luther's journey to Augsburg—to his 1521 journey to Worms. For the *Heidelberg Disputation* (1518), see LW 31:35–70.

[22] On Hus, see the introduction above, pp. xxxvii–xxxviii and n. 103 there; Mathesius, *History*, p. 121. As Hus traveled from Prague and across Germany to Constance, he posted notices inviting locals to question him; more formal disputations took place in at least two cities: Nürnberg and Biberach. See Spinka, *Hus*, pp. 229–30; Peter of Mladonovice (ca. 1370–1451), *An Account of the Trial and Condemnation of Master John Hus in Constance*, in Matthew Spinka, trans. and ed., *John Hus at the Council of Constance* (New York: Columbia University Press, 1965), pp. 98–100. Luther engaged in preaching rather than disputations on the way to Worms, preaching in Erfurt, Gotha, and Eisenach. His Erfurt sermon is preserved and translated in LW 51:60–66.

[23] Canon law stipulated that promises made to heretics were invalid: see *Decretales* 5.7.16 and 5.7.13 (Friedberg 2:789–90, 788).

[24] Elector Louis [Ludwig] V, "The Pacific," Count Palatine (r. 1508–44), had served along with Frederick the Wise as regent during the interregnum between Maximilian and Charles and had cooperated in securing protection for Luther in the deliberations at Worms (thus his signature and seal were at stake). As a territorial prince, he was relatively tolerant of the

that [the safe-conduct] for the noble martyr John Hus had not been honored either, and on that account those who had given their consent ceased to enjoy either victory or prosperity any longer themselves.[25]

Now, as this issue was beginning to cause trouble, Dr. Luther was warned of the concern that his safe-conduct might not be upheld for him as a condemned heretic. Upon this he wrote to Spalatin,[26] as I later heard him say in these words at his table, that since he was summoned, therefore he would appear, even if there were as many devils in Worms as there are tiles on the rooftops.[27] If the cause is good, the heart swells in the chest,[28] giving strength and courage to preachers and soldiers.

Now, since this Christian Saxon refused to be frightened, the great and clever people, who had been appointed for the time being by the papal delegation to go set the church clock,[29] tried another strategem and sent word to Luther that he should go to the Ebernburg[30] and have a friendly discussion about urgent and weighty matters with Glapion,[31] the emperor's father confessor, and the monk Bucer.[32] But God directed Luther, who did not

Reformation (cf. below, Mathesius, *History*, p. 362), though he remained Catholic himself, serving repeatedly as a mediator between Emperor Charles and the Protestant estates in the following decades. Soon after his death, the Smalcaldic War broke out, in 1546. See Charles D. Gunnoe Jr., "Palatinate," *OER* 3:196.

[25] On Louis' defense of Luther's safe-conduct, cf. *Table Talk* no. 5342a–b (1540), WA TR 5:65–73; no. 5350 (1540), WA TR 5:80–81; no. 5375b (1540), WA TR 5:100–102, though the remark about Hus is not found in any of these. On Hus and the breach of his safe-conduct, see below, p. 179.

[26] Luther to Spalatin, April 14, 1521, LW 48:197–98.

[27] For this statement, see Luther to Elector Frederick, March 5, 1522, LW 48:390; *Table Talk* no. 5342a–b (1540), WA TR 5:65–69.

[28] Wander 3:1797, "Sache" no. 225.

[29] *zum Seyger stellen angeschifftet.* This expression perhaps means simply "to do its dirty work" or perhaps has more specific reference to "running out the clock" on Luther's safe-conduct. Behind the plan would have been the papal nuncio Aleander (see above, p. 162 and n. 128 there); the imperial chamberlain Paul von Armerstorff and the emperor's confessor Jean Glapion (see below, n. 31) were the agents sent to carry it out.

[30] Mathesius reads "Pocksberg," as does *Table Talk* no. 5107 (1540), WA TR 4:666–67, cf. p. 667 n. 1: probably a false back translation of Ebernburg via the Latin *Porciburgum*. The Ebernburg was the castle of the knight Franz von Sickingen (1481–1523; see Ulman Weiss, "Sickingen, Franz von," *OER* 4:55), a friend and supporter of Ulrich von Hutten (see above, p. 161 n. 121). Cf. *Table Talk* no. 5342b (1540), WA TR 5:69.

[31] Jean Glapion (d. 1522), a French Franciscan, had served as Emperor Charles' confessor since 1520. His own motivations in the Luther affair may have included at least limited sympathy for some of Luther's proposed reforms. See Brecht 1:450; Bietenholz and Deutscher, *Contemporaries of Erasmus*, 2:103–5.

[32] Martin Bucer, a Dominican, was chaplain to Sickingen at the time. He had heard and favored Luther at the Heidelberg Disputation in 1518 and later became the influential

perceive the stratagems at the time, so that he went straight to Worms, for the appointed ¹time within which he was to appear under the imperial safe-conduct was a rather short twenty-one days.³³

Then Dr. Luther, along with several who had been assigned to him in Wittenberg,³⁴ arrived in Worms on the Tuesday after *Misericordias Domini*³⁵ and was assigned quarters, along with his people, in the house of the German Order.³⁶ On Wednesday, the next day, at four in the afternoon, there was a hearing for him, at which he appeared with fitting reverence and defer-ence, with due obedience and Christian boldness. Here, at the behest of His Imperial Majesty, the imperial speaker, Doctor Johann [von der] Ecken,³⁷ vicar-general of the archbishop of Trier,³⁸ presented the following, first in Latin, then in German: that His Imperial Majesty, upon the deliberation and counsel of all the estates of the Holy Roman Empire, had summoned him to appear before His Imperial Majesty and to be questioned concerning these two charges,³⁹ whether he would confess that these books (which were there, bound together, and shown to him) were his own, and whether he would

---

reformer of Strassburg, mediating between Wittenberg and the Swiss reformers. See Martin Greschat, "Bucer, Martin," *OER* 1:221–24; and below, Mathesius, *History*, pp. 243–44, 353–54. Bucer brought the invitation to Luther in Oppenheim (about 25 km north of Worms) on April 15. See Brecht 1:450.

³³ Since Luther had received the safe-conduct about March 29 (see above, p. 169 n. 13), he would have been due in Worms by April 19, a deadline that would have been in jeopardy if, on April 15 or 16, he had returned with Bucer from Oppenheim to the Ebernburg, a distance of some 50 km. See Charles V to Luther, March 6, 1521, WA Br 2:280–81.

³⁴ When Luther left Wittenberg, he was accompanied by his fellow Augustinian Johann Petzensteiner, according to the rule that the friars were to travel in pairs; Nicolaus von Amsdorf, from the Wittenberg faculty (see also below, p. 182 n. 80); and Petrus von Suaven (1496–1552), a student from the Pomeranian nobility. Justus Jonas joined the Wittenbergers at Erfurt. On Jonas, see the introduction above, pp. xxix–xxx; on Luther's journey, see Brecht 1:448.

³⁵ I.e., April 16, 1521, the Tuesday after the Second Sunday of Easter. For the account of Luther in Worms, see *Luther at the Diet of Worms* (1521), LW 32:101–31.

³⁶ In fact, Luther and his party stayed not in the house of the Order of German Knights but with another crusading order, the Knights of St. John or the Knights of Rhodes. See Brecht 1:451. The version of Luther's acts at Worms published in the Wittenberg and Jena editions, however, designate the German Order as Luther's hosts: see WA 7:826 n. 6; Volz, *Die Lutherpredigten des Johannes Mathesius*, p. 155.

³⁷ This Johann von der Ecken (d. 1524), in the service of the archbishop of Trier, is not to be confused with the Ingolstadt theologian Johann Eck who had debated with Luther at Leipzig in 1520 (see above, pp. 154–56). Von der Ecken is here given the title *orator*, not in the sense of an ambassador (cf. above, p. 148 n. 50) but in the sense of a representative appointed ad hoc. On von der Ecken, see Erwin Iserloh, "Eck, Johann von," *NDB* 4:277.

³⁸ I.e., Richard von Greiffenklau (r. 1511–31): see above, p. 151 n. 72.

³⁹ *Artickel*

recant them and their contents or would persist in and stand by what he had written. Before Dr. Martin had answered, Dr. Hieronymus Schurff,[40] whom the elector had appointed for him, called out with a loud voice and said, "Let the titles of the books be read." When this had been done, Dr. Martin gave a brief answer in Latin and German:[41] that he acknowledged the books before him as his own and would never deny them; however, as to immediately declaring whether he would defend or recant these things, since this question concerned faith, the soul's salvation, and God's Word, it would be arrogant and reprehensible for him to make a declaration without consideration. Therefore, he requested His Imperial Majesty to grant him time for deliberation, that he might offer a proper response.

Upon this, thanks to the native clemency of His Imperial Majesty, Dr. Martin was granted one day for deliberation, on condition that he present his response not in writing but orally. Then he was led back to his quarters by the herald.

On the next day, the doctor again appeared as required, and when the imperial speaker repeated his case, Dr. Luther, as a most humble subject, gave this answer in Latin and in German,[42] with great modesty and discretion, in Christian boldness and steadfastness: He confessed once again that the books were his. However, they were not all of the same kind, for in some he had taught God's Word in sincerity and purity; in others he had attacked the false doctrine of the Roman Church; in the remainder, he had written against certain private individuals who sought to protect and defend the papal tyranny. There he may have been more sharp and severe than was fitting for his status as a monk and professor,[43] since he, too, was no living saint.

Now, he did not know how he could deny the books in which God's Word is taught and expounded, lest Christ also deny him before His Father [Matt. 10:33].

---

[40] Schurff (see above, p. 21 n. 83), a Wittenberg professor of law, had been sent to Worms two months previously to act on behalf of Frederick the Wise and was now appointed Luther's counsel at the hearing.

[41] According to the earliest text of *Luther at the Diet Worms* (LW 32:106), the order of the languages was the reverse; however, Mathesius is following the order given in the Wittenberg and Jena editions: see WA 7:829 n. 1.

[42] Here Mathesius follows the order given in all the editions of *Luther at the Diet Worms* (LW 32:108; cf. WA 7:831), but, in fact, Luther may have spoken first in German: see Brecht 1:456.

[43] *nach gelegenheit der Religion und profession* (WA 7:434: *quam pro religione aut professione*); cf. Brecht 1:458. The whole expression may, however, refer solely to Luther's status as a religious, i.e., someone who has professed vows of religion.

Likewise, he was also unable to contradict what he had written upon a firm basis against the pope's idolatry and tyranny, lest he help to strengthen and enforce the pope's godlessness and tyranny and become guilty of the perdition of the poor souls in Christendom whom the pope has deceived.

In the third place, it would also be inappropriate for him to recant the books in which he attacked the pope's advocates and defenders, lest he give them an excuse for defending every kind of godlessness henceforth and for setting up new abominations and insanity.

Therefore, insofar as he was not convinced of having erred with the prophetic and apostolic Scriptures, which are and remain the pure Word of God, he did not know how to deny or contradict God's truth. He asked, therefore, that these great and important matters be given further wise consideration, lest the wrath of God be brought down upon the Roman Empire and the German nation, for He brings to a sudden and terrible end all those who set themselves up against God and His Word, such as Pharaoh [Exod. 14:28] and many godless kings of Israel, etc. [e.g., 1 Kings 11–13, 16–20].

Upon this the imperial speaker indicated that Doctor Luther had not answered the posed question plainly and directly, and so he should give a simple and unambiguous[44] answer: Would he renounce and recant his books or not? To this Dr. Luther replied and confessed: that unless he were to be persuaded and convinced by the testimony of Holy Scripture or by plain and clear arguments (for he would give credence neither to the pope nor to the councils, since it is manifest and evident that they have often erred and contradicted themselves), he could not and would not recant anything, for it was neither safe nor advisable to do anything against conscience. "Here I stand. I cannot do otherwise. God help me! Amen."[45]

The imperial speaker responded, after the [estates of the] empire had deliberated, that the doctor had given an impertinent answer because he had condemned the councils and contradicted the sense of the Church. He should have given a plain and direct answer: "No" or "Yes." The doctor stood by his confession and offered to prove that the councils had erred many times. Thereafter, since it was also getting dark, everyone went home.

---

[44] *runde antwort*; cf. WA 7:837: "*non cornutum responsum*," i.e., "an answer without horns."

[45] Mathesius gives Luther's answer as it appears in the Wittenberg and Jena editions. The words "Here I stand. I cannot do otherwise" are found in contemporary reports only in the 1521 Wittenberg printing by Johann Rhau-Grunenberg (d. after 1522) [VD16 L3650], in inverted sequence. See Brecht 1:460 n. 24. Timothy Lull and Derek Nelson defend the authenticity of the longer version as it is given by Mathesius, arguing that it was excised from the earlier printings because of Luther's brazenness toward the emperor: Lull and Nelson, *Resilient Reformer*, p. 130.

On the Friday[46] after *Misericordias Domini*, this matter was taken up by the imperial estates, on the basis of the emperor's proposal,[47] and deliberated for two days. On the Monday[48] after *Jubilate*, the archbishop of Trier[49] had announced to Dr. Martin that he should appear before him and certain princes and bishops on the coming Wednesday,[50] since, out of Christian love and the special favor of the Imperial Majesty, they had obtained [permission] to admonish him in a friendly and brotherly manner.

The doctor obediently appeared, along with his companions and the imperial herald. Then Doctor Vehus,[51] the chancellor of the margrave of Baden, began to exhort Doctor Luther with many words of friendship as well as of threat. He should consider respectability, honor, [the public] welfare, good law, justice and order, his conscience, the common good of the empire, and now especially the danger that could befall him if he were to bring the ruling authorities down upon himself. Therefore, he should carefully consider and weigh the exhortation and earnest admonition which these princes were giving out of goodwill and special favor.[52]

Doctor Martin himself later praised this artful and adroit speech, though he was astonished that such a great and revered lawyer should, in the presence of a doctor of Holy Scripture, utter not even a single syllable about the

---

[46] I.e., April 19.

[47] Charles sent a written statement declaring his resolve to "pursue Martin himself and his adherents with excommunication," following in the example of his ancestors as an obedient defender of the Roman Church (*DRA* 2:594–96, no. 82). See *Luther at the Diet of Worms* (1521), LW 32:114–15.

[48] I.e., April 22, the Monday after the Third Sunday of Easter.

[49] I.e., Greiffenklau (see above, p. 172 and n. 38 there).

[50] I.e., April 24.

[51] Jerome Vehus (1484–1543/1544) was a humanist who had taught at the University of Freiburg and in 1517 became chancellor to Margrave Philip of Baden (r. 1515–33). Vehus participated in the negotiations at Worms as well as at the Diets of Nürnberg (1524) and Augsburg (1530). See Franz Wöhrer, "Behus, Hieronymus," *BBKL* 17:1456–57.

[52] The group consisted of Elector-Archbishop Greiffenklau of Trier, Elector Joachim I of Brandenburg (r. 1499–1535; cf. below, p. 346 n. 140), Bishop Jerome Scultetus of Brandenburg (see above, p. 146 n. 41), Bishop Christoph von Stadion (1478–1543) of Augsburg, Duke George of Saxony (see above, p. 154 n. 91), Count George of Wertheim (d. 1530), and Dietrich von Cleen (1455–1531), the master of the German Order (see above, p. 172 n. 36), as well as two representatives of free imperial cities: Dr. Conrad Peutinger (see above, p. 149 n. 52) from Augsburg and Dr. Hans Bock from Strassburg. See *Luther at the Diet of Worms* (1521), LW 32:116; Luther to Emperor Charles V, April 28, 1521, LW 48:205; Brecht 1:464. A full summary of Vehus' address and Luther's response is given in *Luther at the Diet of Worms* (1521), LW 32:116–19.

Word of God and of His Son, Jesus Christ, and of the prophets and apostles.[53] At the time, however, Doctor Luther thanked the princes as a Christian subject. He mentioned in particular how the Council of Constance had condemned an article of our faith.[54] He would also be obliged and willing to obey the secular rulers and authorities in all that was honorable and just. In this matter, however, which concerns the eternal and immutable Word of almighty God and His only-begotten Son, he and everyone else who wants to be saved must, in accordance with the express words of St. Peter, obey God more than men [Acts 5:29].

Now whether or not this would cause offense, it was nonetheless certain that the Gospel of Jesus Christ could not ¹be taught or confessed without offense, for in fact Christ with His Gospel is a Rock of offense [Isa. 8:14; Rom. 9:33; 1 Pet. 2:8]. Therefore, he could not stand down from the Word of the Lord Christ on account of offense or danger, much less be persuaded or compelled to deny the Word of God, which is the sole and supreme truth.

Then the princes who were present held a discussion, after which the chancellor repeated his earlier speech with the additional exhortation that Dr. Luther should submit his writings and affairs to the judgment of His Imperial Majesty and the empire. Dr. Martin's humble reply to this was that he would not like it said of him that he had scorned or fled the judgment and decision of His Imperial Majesty and the empire. Accordingly, he would willingly and gladly allow his books to be most carefully examined and evaluated, except that the judgment must be made by God's Word in accordance with Holy Scripture. For God's Word is the highest and most certain truth, which is above all the wisdom and authority of the world. This same true Word needs only to be believed and obeyed. Other books need to be tested and judged by God's Word, for in matters concerning God and faith, human wisdom is unable to render a proper and Christian judgment apart from God's Word. Therefore, he humbly requested that they not burden his conscience, which is bound and held captive by God's Word and Holy Scripture, by pressing him to deny his doctrine or to submit it to human judgment, since apart from God's Word no human being knows anything salutary about God and Jesus Christ [and] can do nothing but misjudge and err. This is why human beings cannot be set as judges over God's Word.

---

[53] For Luther's subsequent positive assessment—at least of the rhetorical skill of Vehus' oration—see *Table Talk* no. 3357a (1533), WA TR 3:283; and Luther to Count Albert of Mansfield, May 3, 1521, WA Br 2:322.

[54] Although the issue is surprisingly not mentioned in Mathesius' summary just above, Vehus had devoted much of his oration to defending the councils of the Church. Luther argued that the Council of Constance, in condemning Hus' definition of the Church as the "community of the elect," had thus condemned the Third Article of the Apostles' Creed: "I believe there is one holy catholic Church." See *Luther at the Diet of Worms* (1521), LW 32:116–18.

When he had spoken this with Christian discretion, one of the electors from their midst[55] asked him whether he would refuse to yield unless he were convinced by Holy Scripture. ｜Dr. Martin replied, "Yes, most gracious lord, or by clear and manifest reasons and arguments." Upon this the discussion came to an end. The archbishop, however, asked Dr. Luther and his companions into his private chamber, along with the chancellor from Baden and Cochlaeus,[56] on their own. There all kinds of speeches were given. But Dr. Martin stood firm as a rock upon the true rock of the Word of the Lord Jesus Christ, and so once again they parted ways. Then, on this evening, Dr. Luther's imperial safe-conduct was extended two days, during which time this wise archbishop saw that Luther was dealt with graciously, finally discussing with him privately how and by what means this matter could finally be brought to a favorable conclusion. Dr. Martin responded: "There is no better counsel or aid than what Gamaliel gave, as St. Luke shows in Acts 5 [:38–39]: 'If this counsel or work is of men, it will soon fail, but if it is of God, you will be unable to overthrow it.' That is what His Imperial Majesty, the electors, princes, and estates of the empire may write to the pope." He knew for certain that if this plan and deed were not of God, it would fail within three—or, indeed, within two—years of its own accord. Then the archbishop asked what he would do if the articles that were to be submitted to the council were drawn from his books. Dr. Luther replied, "If only it is not the ones which were condemned by the Council of Constance." The archbishop said, "Those are the very ones they will be, I fear." Luther said, "Then I cannot and will not keep silent, for God's Word is condemned there. Therefore, I should rather forfeit life and limb on this account than betray the clear and true Word of God."[57]

After that, this wise bishop let him depart in good grace and, at the doctor's request, helped him obtain permission to depart on favorable terms. Not long afterward, Dr. Martin received his decision: ｜that by order of His Imperial Majesty he might travel within twenty days[58] from there back to safe quarters under a public safe-conduct, and that his liberty was to be maintained, but with the condition that he not stir up the people along the

---

[55] I.e., Elector Joachim of Brandenburg: see *Luther at the Diet of Worms* (1521), LW 32:119.

[56] Although Cochlaeus was initially favorable to Luther, after Worms he became on ardent opponent and polemicist; see the introduction above, pp. lxvii–lxix. Also present at this private conversation was Johann von der Ecken, as the archbishop's vicar-general. See Brecht 1:466.

[57] Mathesius follows the order of the conversation given in *Luther at the Diet of Worms* (1521), LW 32:121–22. In fact, the order of discussion of Gamaliel and the Council of Constance may have been reversed. See Brecht 1:468–70.

[58] *Luther at the Diet of Worms* (1521), LW 32:122, indicates twenty-one days of safe-conduct, but reckoned from the date of the imperial resolution [*Abschied*] rather than from the start of Luther's travel.

way by preaching and writing. At this, Dr. Luther said with great and heart-felt zeal: "As it has pleased the Lord, so it has come to pass. Blessed be the name of the Lord!" And when he had thanked His Imperial Majesty and all the estates of the empire as a most humble and obedient subject and had most humbly commended himself to all of them and given his friends a blessing, he set off again with the imperial herald and his companions on the next day, the Friday[59] after *Jubilate*.

Along the way, he wrote back from Friedberg to His Imperial Majesty and the estates of the empire and excused himself for having been unable to submit God's Word to the judgment of the imperial authority.[60]

This is one of the great and glorious days that was to come before the end of the world, a day on which God's Word was publicly proclaimed and confessed with Christian boldness before the Roman Imperial Majesty and the whole German empire. For this, we today give heartfelt thanks to our dear God, who raised up a chosen instrument [cf. Acts 9:15] for His precious Word and fortified him with His bold and fearless Spirit, so that he freely and confidently made his steadfast Christian confession and dared to contradict the pope in Rome, his so-called councils, and his decretals and statutes. Surely this man's doctrine must have possessed a firmer foundation and more power than many people at that time could have foreseen.[61]

O Lord Jesus, the eternal and substantial Wisdom, preserve Germany and this Church in the doctrine and testimony of this wise confessor and prophet, since they are founded upon the Scripture of the holy prophets and apostles of God and on the testimony and confession of Your martyrs, and were freely and openly ¦proclaimed and confessed before the greatest leaders. For he publicly and boldly attacked the abomination and idolatry of the Antichrist, mightily casting them down in many hearts and lands!

And since we are speaking at this time about the wise men in the west and the north,[62] today we also thank our faithful God and His Son, the eternal defender of His precious Christendom, for having used the counsel, aid, and support of wise people to bring this religious matter before our highly laudable emperor and the whole Roman Empire. Likewise, to the honor of the noble line from Austria[63] and to the eternal praise of God, we

---

[59] I.e., April 26.

[60] Luther to Emperor Charles V, April 28, 1521, LW 48:203–9. It appears that, in absence of a courier, the letter was never actually delivered to Charles. However, it was published almost immediately both in Latin and in a German version addressed to the estates. See Brecht 1:471.

[61] A version of this remark is attributed to Emperor Charles V at the Diet of Augsburg in 1530: see below, Mathesius, *History*, pp. 347, 558–59.

[62] See above, p. 167.

[63] I.e., the house of Hapsburg.

ought also to extol here the fact that, as a good and true lord, His Imperial Majesty constantly, firmly, and steadfastly upheld the safe-conduct he had granted to one single man who was opposed by the entire Roman Church, and out of his native clemency extended it until Doctor Luther could return to safe quarters.

If anyone keeps faith and his promises, God in turn protects that person and blesses and prospers the government of people such as this. Or there is the case of Emperor Sigismund:[64] he let the trouble-making clergy persuade him that one is not obligated to uphold a safe-conduct for heretics,[65] and thereafter he was severely afflicted. Alas! clergy in secular councils and dogs in the church have never been much use, as the wise and true old German proverb testifies.[66] So King Władysław would have to confess as well, for he followed the advice of Cardinal Julian and turned against the Turk, with whom Hunyadi had made peace, attacking to his unspeakable harm.[67]

Today, therefore, it is fitting that we thank our dear God, who kept the hearts of Emperor Charles and some of the German princes on the side of the unchanging truth against the strategems of many wicked and ill-natured people. For though a severe edict was issued soon after, once Dr. Luther had departed, it was easy to see that the Papists and their dear children had

---

[64] Sigismund of Luxemburg (1368–1437) was crowned Holy Roman emperor in 1410 and was a major figure at the Council of Constance (1414–18). He had promised John Hus safe-conduct to Constance but allowed the Bohemian reformer's martyrdom, which led to the ensuing Hussite Wars (1419–34). See Robert E. Bjork, ed., *The Oxford Dictionary of the Middle Ages* (New York: Oxford University Press, 2010), 11:287.

[65] See above, p. 170 n. 23.

[66] See Wander 3:705, "Mönch" no. 191 (cf. Wander 3:1231, "Pfaffe" no. 170, but with "in the kitchen [*Küche*]" rather than "in the church [*Kirche*]").

[67] Władysław [Vladislav, Ladlislaus] III (1424–44) was king of Poland (r. 1434–44) and Hungary (r. 1440–44). With his armies under the command of János [John] Hunyadi [Corvinus] (ca. 1407–56), he had enjoyed military success against the Ottoman Turks, and in June 1444 a peace treaty was negotiated by Cardinal Julian [Giuliano] Cesarini (1398–1444). By the fall, however, the cardinal, encouraged by Pope Eugenius IV (r. 1431–47), persuaded the king to break the treaty and begin a new crusade in the Balkans against the Turks. At the Battle of Varna in November 1444, the Ottoman sultan Murad [Amurad] II (r. 1421–51), returning unexpectedly from short-lived retirement in Anatolia, defeated the Hungarian army. Cesarini and Władysław were both killed on the battlefield; King Władysław's body was never found, though the Ottomans displayed his head as a trophy. The Turkish victory cleared the path for subsequent Ottoman expansion into southeastern Europe. See Bjork, *Dictionary of the Middle Ages*, 2:828–29; 3:652; 6:347, 363–64; 8:536–37; 9:727. For Luther's references to these events, see *To the Christian Nobility* (1520), LW 44:194–95; *Defense and Explanation of All the Articles* (1521), LW 32:90; *Table Talk* no. 3522 (1537), LW 54:220.

extorted this edict under the pretext of maintaining peace and quiet in the German kingdom, for it was never seriously enforced subsequently.[68]

Haman, the Gentile, also proclaimed a proscription and greater proscription[69] against God's poor little people in Persian captivity [Esth. 3:8–15], but our God graciously foiled this strict mandate by means of wise Mordecai and his blessed cousin, the king's wife, and He steered and guided the king's disposition (since He has the heart of kings in His hands [Prov. 21:1]) so that the wicked counsel which Haman had offered out of envy came down upon his own neck when he was lifted up for all to see, with eternal disgrace, on the gallows he had set up in the open at his house [Esth. 7:9–10].

Now, since Dr. Luther had been both proscribed by the emperor and placed under the ban by the pope as an arch-heretic, our God, from whom all good counsels, deeds, and ideas proceed,[70] inspired the most wise elector of Saxony to issue an order through trusted and discreet people to take the proscribed and excommunicated Dr. Luther for a time, just as God's pious servant Obadiah, the governor of King Ahab's house, hid two hundred priests[71] in a cave and fed them for a time, because the wicked Queen Jezebel was seeking their lives [1 Kings 18:4]. The aforementioned elector, however, did not even want to know himself where his captive was going to be taken, so that, in the event that he were to be asked, he could excuse himself with plausible truth. For he would encounter great difficulty in safeguarding and defending one person from powerful rulers and the whole empire, on account of the edict that had been published. Meanwhile, he hoped that God would take the cause of His Word and of His confessor

---

[68] The Edict of Worms had been composed by Aleander, the papal nuncio, on May 8, but it was not submitted to the estates until after the close of the diet, on May 25, when many had departed already, though the original dating was retained. It enforced Luther's excommunication by placing him under imperial proscription, forbade anyone to give him shelter or aid, and threatened all who did help or continue to support him with the same penalties. The circulation of Luther's books was prohibited. For the text of the edict, see *DRA* 2:640–59 (StL 15:2276–90) and the complete translation (with facsimile) in Jensen, *Confrontation at Worms*, pp. 75–111. Charles was unable to enforce the edict strictly, even exempting Frederick from serving Luther with it, but this had more to do with political constraints than with personal reluctance or sympathy on the part of the emperor. Mathesius is following, however, Luther's own favorable portrayal of Charles (see above, p. 161 n. 124). The enforcement, or nonenforcement, of the Edict of Worms became a perennial topic of debate at imperial diets throughout the 1520s. See Brecht 1:473–76; Luther, preface and afterword to *Two Discordant and Conflicting Imperial Mandates* (1524), LW 59:88–96.

[69] *acht unnd uberacht*; i.e., the technical terms for the proscription or ban under which Luther had been placed by the Edict of Worms. See Dorothee Mussgnug, *Acht und Bann im 15. und 16. Jahrhundert* (Berlin: Duncker & Humblot, 2016).

[70] Cf. the Collect for Peace, originally from the *Gelasian Sacramentary*, translated by Luther, LW 53:138.

[71] The biblical text says one hundred priests.

into His own hands, as indeed came to pass, and would provide further counsel and aid in this matter.[72]

Our doctor was not particularly pleased with this business of hiding or being taken, ¦since he would willingly and gladly have shed his blood as a testimony to the truth, but he consented to this wise counsel at the zealous insistence of good people.[73] For the holy apostle St. Paul also permitted his brethren in Damascus to lower him over the wall [Acts 9:25], and our faithful God sent His holy angel to warn the Wise Men of the East and prevent them from walking into the cunning snare of that court fox Herod [Matt. 2:12; cf. Luke 13:32].

Accordingly, after Dr. Luther had dismissed the imperial herald from Oppenheim,[74] he traveled peacefully through Hesse with the landgrave's safe-conduct[75] and arrived at the Harz Mountains. From there, he had to travel through the forest to get to Waltershausen, so he dismissed some of the companions who were escorting him through the forest, and the others he sent on ahead to arrange lodging.[76] Meanwhile,[77] he came to a place near Altenstein where there was a narrow pass, where two noblemen, von Steinburg[78] and Captain Berlepsch,[79] charged in on horse with two servants. And when one of them had gotten a response from the wagon driver, they commanded him to stop, seized Dr. Luther with feigned roughness, and pulled him out of his wagon. One servant struck the wagon driver and

---

[72] On Luther's staged abduction to the Wartburg, see Luther to Spalatin, May 14, 1521, LW 54:222–28; *Table Talk* no. 5353 (1540), WA TR 5:82; Volz, *Die Lutherpredigten des Johannes Mathesius*, pp. 138–40; Brecht 1:472.

[73] Luther to Lucas Cranach, April 28, 1521, LW 48:201.

[74] I.e., Caspar Sturm, who was dismissed at Friedberg on April 28. See above, p. 169 n. 14.

[75] I.e., Philip of Hesse: see above, p. 70 n. 96. His safe-conduct for Luther is dated April 26. See WA Br 12:26–27.

[76] Schurff, Jonas, and Suaven (see above, p. 172 n. 34 and p. 173 n. 40) had accompanied Luther to this point, leaving Amsdorf and (though unmentioned by Mathesius) the friar Petzensteiner (see above, p. 172 n. 34).

[77] On May 4, 1521. See Brecht 1:472.

[78] Probably the knight Burkhard Hund von Wenkheim, to whom the Altenstein Castle (the "Steinburg") belonged (so *LH²*, p. 483); otherwise Hans von Sternberg (d. 1532), who later became the custodian of the Coburg castle: see *Table Talk* no. 5353 (1540), WA TR 5:82 n. 34, where the orthography of the name varies among the different sources.

[79] Hans von Berlepsch (1480–1533), captain of the Wartburg castle. Mathesius' German text gives his name in the form "Prelops." See again *Table Talk* no. 5353 (1540), WA TR 5:82, where the orthography of the name also varies.

chased him away, and Herr Amsdorf[80] drove on while they put a riding coat over the captive and helped him onto a horse. They led him along the riding path in the forest for a few hours until night fell upon them. They also bound someone on horseback, so that they would be bringing a prisoner with them. Thus they arrived at the Wartburg castle near Eisenach at nearly midnight,[81] sometime during Rogationtide.[82] There they kept the prisoner so well and decently that even the steward was amazed at this. Dr. Luther remained there in his chamber, just as the captive St. Paul remained in his room in Rome [Acts 28:16, 30–31]. And though he would rather have been in Wittenberg and attended to his teaching office and would have lain on red-hot coals to glorify God and confirm His Word, 'as he wrote to a good friend soon thereafter,[83] he endured it obediently for a time, in order to prevent greater danger from breaking upon the land and people of his dear elector.

Now, since our doctor is weary and weak from the trip, as he complained in a letter,[84] because the riders led him around in the forest so long that they were surrounded by dark in the dead of night, we will let him rest a little and recover.

Next we will continue, in God's name, and hear what he did in his captivity and why he voluntarily returned to Wittenberg to his [professor's] chair[85] and pulpit.

To God be laud, glory, and praise for this and all His blessings. May He be highly exalted forever! Amen.

---

[80] On Amsdorf's travel with Luther, see below, p. 192 n. 47. Amsdorf also attended the conference in Smalcald (see below, p. 397 n. 16) and the colloqies in Hagenau and Worms (see below, p. 467 n. 27 and p. 489 n. 159). See Robert Kolb, "Amsdorf, Nikolaus von," OER 1:27–28.

[81] The time is given in Luther's letter to Amsdorf, May, 12, 1521, LW 48:219.

[82] ungeferlich in der Creutzwochen. The Kreuzwoche, or Rogationtide, was the week of Ascension Day. Luther arrived at the Wartburg on May 4. See Brecht 1:472.

[83] Luther to Melanchthon, May 26, 1521, LW 48:232.

[84] Luther to Amsdorf, May 12, 1521, LW 48:219.

[85] Cathedra unnd Predigstuel

THE FOURTH SERMON,
ON THE YEARS 1521 AND 1522

[Sunday, January 17, 1563]

BELOVED friends in the Lord! In the papacy it is customary on this day[1] to sing and preach of St. Anthony the Hermit and his companion St. Paul:[2] about how they wove baskets and panniers and ate dried fruit, roots, and pea pods in their deserts and cells, and how they led an austere and hard monastic life, maintaining Pythagorean silence.[3] But their baskets, fasting, and silence combined with all of their merits and intercessions are worthless to us and do us no good whatsoever, since we, in all boldness, confidently rely on nothing but the sole merit and intercession of our eternal Priest and Savior Jesus Christ.

But someone who sincerely believes in Jesus Christ and is righteous on that basis alone, and confesses and bears witness to this eternal Redeemer with his mouth and pen—such a person serves us and helps us unto salvation, which we receive and have solely through the knowledge of Jesus. For Christ's merit and intercession, grasped by means of sincere faith in the Word, is our righteousness before God. The testimony and confession of the saints serves us believers unto salvation (Romans 10 [:1–4]).

---

[1] I.e., January 17, which fell on a Sunday in 1563. It was the traditional feast day of St. Anthony of Egypt (ca. 251–356), the hermit who is regarded as the founder of monasticism: see Athanasius (ca. 296–373), *Vita beati Antonii Abbatis* (PL 73:125–67; NPNF[2] 4:188–221). Jerome discusses Anthony in his *Vita Pauli* (PL 23:17–28; FC 100:12–14; NPNF[2] 3:362–63) and in *De viris illustribus* (PL 23:693). Cf. *LA* 1:93–96, no. 21.

[2] St. Paul here is probably not the hermit Paul of Thebes (d. ca. 340: see *LA* 1:84–85, no. 15) but the contemporary Paul the Simple (d. ca. 339), a disciple of Anthony, whose discipline included weaving and unweaving baskets as well as silence. For Anthony as a basket weaver, see Athanasius, *Vita beati Antonii* 53 (PL 73:164; NPNF[2] 4:210); on Paul the Simple's weaving and unweaving of baskets, see *Historia Monachorum* 31 (in *Vitae Patrum* 2) (PL 21:457–59) and *Historia Lausiaca* 28 (in *Vitae Patrum* 8) (PL 73:1126–30).

[3] One part of the asceticism practiced by the followers of the Greek philosopher and mathematician Pythagoras (ca. 570–ca. 495 BC) was a discipline of silence. See Erasmus, *Adages* 4.3.72 (CWE 36:44).

Now, since our doctor faithfully served us and all of Christendom with his blessed labor and witness in his Patmos[4] [Rev. 1:9] and captivity, we will hear at this time what good this hermit accomplished in his desert, as well as when and why he left his captivity.[5]

Because Dr. Luther faithfully bore witness to You, Lord Christ, throughout his life, ⌐help us, Lord Jesus, to elucidate well the testimony and declaration of Your confessor and take comfort in Your blood and eternal collect prayers[6] alone, rather than in the merits and intercessions of the departed saints. So will we be righteous and acceptable in the presence of Your Father in the knowledge of You, and will confess You again, then blessedly fall asleep and rest in peace, and will joyfully rise again and worthily appear before Your judgment seat, to be and abide with You eternally, in honor, as Your dear brethren, in perfect wisdom, righteousness, holiness, and immortality. Amen.

Listen now to what the doctor accomplished in his Patmos, as well as when and why he returned from it. Although Doctor Luther kept close silence in the Wartburg castle,[7] he was not idle, but daily attended to his studies and prayer, applied himself to the Greek and Hebrew Bible,[8] and wrote many good and comforting letters to his good friends.[9] On festival days he preached to his host and trusted people and earnestly exhorted them to prayer.[10]

---

[4] I.e., the Wartburg, which Luther called his "Patmos" in allusion to St. John's exile, and so dated his letters from the Wartburg. See, e.g., Luther to Franz von Sickingen, June 1, 1521, LW 48:246–47.

[5] For Luther's own description of himself in the Wartburg as "a hermit, an anchorite, and truly a monk," see Luther to Melanchthon, May 26, 1521, LW 48:234; cf. Luther to Spalatin, July 15, 1521, LW 48:270.

[6] An allusion to the traditional short prayers (collects) used in the liturgy. See LW 53:127–46.

[7] Cf. Luther to Melanchthon, circa May 8, 1521, LW 48:213.

[8] Remarkably, this is the closest Mathesius comes to mentioning Luther's work translating the New Testament from Greek into German during his time in the Wartburg (see Brecht 2:46–56). Cf. below, History, p. 473, where Mathesius refers to the work of translation as having begun "in Wittenberg."

[9] Many of the letters from the Wartburg period (March 4, 1521, to early May 1522) can be found in LW 48:210–393. The "good friends" include Spalatin, Melanchthon, Amsdorf, Wenceslaus Linck, Johann Lang (ca. 1488–1548), and Johann Agricola, in addition to Luther's letters to Elector Frederick.

[10] In his correspondence from the Wartburg, Luther complains of being "excluded" from the "exposition of the Word" (to Melanchthon, May 26, 1521, LW 48:232), though this may refer primarily to his lecturing responsibilities. There was a priest at the Wartburg who said Mass daily; Luther complained about his lack of concern for proclaiming the Word: see Luther to Spalatin, October 7, 1521, LW 48:317. The claim that Luther preached while in the Wartburg

But since the power of God's Word cannot be recognized apart from the holy cross, and flesh and blood cannot be subdued and stilled apart from God's rod, God sent our hermit many kinds of crosses, for which he expressed heartfelt and sincere thanks to his God in a letter to a good friend.[11] For he had fallen into severe and dangerous physical illness, which even caused him to despair of his life.[12] In this way, the devil tormented him severely with oppressive thoughts, seeking to deceive him with all kinds of apparitions and poltergeists.[13] Amid this tribulation and testing, God's Word, together with his ardent sighs and the sincere intercession of his brethren, was a comforting rod and staff [Ps. 23:4], upon which he leaned while he patiently waited for God.

So far as was humanly possible for him, however, and with God's help and strength, he attended to his calling and the work he had begun; he worked and wrote against the wicked papacy; he comforted and exhorted the scholars in Wittenberg that they should confidently put their hand to the plow [cf. Luke 9:62] and continue lecturing and preaching in the name of Christ; if by the counsel and good-pleasure of God he did not return to them, nevertheless God's Word and Christendom would not perish. God could awaken teachers even from stones [cf. Matt. 3:9].[14] For God will

---

may be based on a letter from Luther to the Basel humanist Konrad Pellikan in which Luther mentions having to preach twice each day. Although in its Latin original it is signed from Wittenberg, and dated by the Weimar editors to the end of February 1521, before the Diet of Worms and Luther's stay in the Wartburg (WA Br 2:272-74), in the translation that appeared in Witt Ger 3 (1550), fols. 275v-276r, it is signed "from Patmos" [*ex Pathmo*], i.e., from the Wartburg. See Volz, *Die Lutherpredigten des Johannes Mathesius*, p. 141; *LH²*, pp. 484-85. However, Mathesius' claim, which is specific to "festival days" [*Feyertagen*] rather than daily preaching, may instead be based on the assumption that Luther must have not only written but also preached the postil sermons for the Christmas season which he composed during his stay in the Wartburg (LW 52; see Gottfried Krodel's discussion of the composition of the *Christmas Postil* in LW 48:237-43; cf. Brecht 2:6). Luther did engage in theological conversations with the castellan Hans von Berplesch (see above, p. 181 n. 79), to whom he proposed dedicating his 1522 treatise on *Avoiding the Doctrines of Men*, LW 35:125-53 (see the introduction by E. Theodore Bachmann, LW 35:127).

[11] Luther to Spalatin, June 10, 1521, LW 48:253-56; cf. Luther to Spalatin, September 9, 1521, LW 48:307.

[12] Luther suffered in the Wartburg from severe constipation: in addition to the previous citation, see Luther to Melanchthon, May 12, 1521, LW 48:217; to Amsdorf, LW 48:219; Brecht 2:2.

[13] See Luther to Spalatin, November 1, 1521, LW 48:324; *Table Talk* no. 2885 (1533), WA TR 3:50; no. 3814 (1538), LW 54:279-80; no. 5358b (1540), WA TR 5:87; no. 6816 (n.d.), WA TR 6:209. See below, Mathesius, *History*, p. 551.

[14] See, e.g., Luther to Melanchthon, May 26, 1521, LW 48:232-36, and May 12, 1521, LW 48:216; to Johann Agricola, May 12, 1521, LW 48:221. Among Luther's exhortations was that Melanchthon himself, though not ordained, should begin preaching publicly, a counsel

vindicate Himself in the whole world before His final coming by revealing the Gospel. And since the Antichrist's measure and leaden bushel [cf. Zech. 5:6–7] are full, God will completely and utterly knock out the bottom from the cask[15] by the Spirit of His mouth [2 Thess. 2:8].

Alongside such prophetic and comforting exhortations which he wrote to good friends individually, he did not rest, but prepared for the press many good books in which he forcefully attacks the papacy and battles against his opponents as a pious teacher, driving them back with Scripture, and instructs and comforts deceived and confused consciences with strong arguments from God's Word. He himself enumerated the books he wrote in his captivity [in a letter] to a well-disposed lawyer.[16]

First, the book on the antichrist,[17] which he wrote against the Italian Catharinus,[18] in which he forcefully proves that the pope in Rome is the true Antichrist, who is sitting in the temple and Church of God and who exalts and elevates himself above all that is called God [2 Thess. 2:4], condemns God's Word, fills his cup with the blood of the saints [Rev. 17:6], is at enmity with honorable married love [cf. Dan. 11:37], and wallows in the unclean filth of Satan.

He also published a German sermon, as the German prophet, about true Christian confession,[19] ¡in which he reproaches the harsh torture of souls which confessors inflict on consciences. He also reproved their efforts to compel the people to recount to the confessor all of their sins together

---

at which Melanchthon demurred: Luther to Spalatin, September 9, 1521, LW 48:308–9; to Nicolaus von Amsdorf, September 9, 1521, LW 48:311–12.

[15] I.e., bring things to an end. For the proverb, see Thiele no. 335, pp. 305–6; Wander 1:933–34, "Fass" nos. 109, 122.

[16] Luther to Nicolaus Gerbel, November 1, 1521, LW 48:317–22. Gerbel (ca. 1485–1560) was a humanist scholar who served as lawyer for the Strassburg cathedral chapter, becoming Luther's literary agent in Strassburg and lifelong friend. He served as godfather to Luther's son Johannes [Hans]. On Gerbel, see the introduction by Gottfried Krodel, LW 48:317–18; the introduction by Timothy J. Wengert, LW 59:43–45; Karin Brinkmann Brown, "Gerbelius, Nikolaus," OER 2:167–68.

[17] *Response to Catharinus* (1521), WA 7:705–78 (LW 71). Luther had in fact completed writing this book in April, before the Diet of Worms, but it was not printed until June 1521, during his Wartburg captivity. See Brecht 1:430–32.

[18] Ambrosius Catharinus Politus (1484–1553) of Siena was a Dominican and Thomist who attacked Luther and defended his fellow Dominican Sylvester Prierias (see above, p. 156 n. 98) in his *Apologia pro veritate catholicae et apostolicae fidei ac doctrinae adversus impia ac valde pestifera Martini Lutheri dogmata* (Florence, 1520). See LW 48:291 n. 10; Bietenholz and Deutscher, *Contemporaries of Erasmus*, 3:105–6; Jared Wicks, "Prierias, Sylvester Mazzolini," OER 3:290–91.

[19] *Von der Beichte, ob die der Bapst macht habe zu gebieten* (1521), WA 8:140–85; see the dedicatory letter to Franz von Sickingen, LW 48:244–47.

with all of their circumstances, and their poisoning of innocent ears with the shameless questions of their sophistic angel.[20] Moreover, they directed penitents to their own contrition and satisfaction, absolved on the basis of the merits and intercessions of the saints, and imposed penance or satisfaction on them as payment for their sins, thus scorning and belittling the innocent redeeming blood and perfect sacrifice of the Lord Jesus Christ, which alone cleanses us of all our sins [1 John 1:7], so long as we confess that we are poor sinners and offer up all of our transgressions upon the saving wounds of the Son of God with a contrite spirit [Ps. 51:17] and, by the power of the Holy Spirit, believe the sure and certain words of holy Absolution, in which the blessed treasures or gracious remission which flowed from Christ's wounds are distributed and applied to us freely, without any worthiness of our own.

Dr. Luther was attacking the abuse of papistic auricular confession—not the true Christian confession in which penitents confess their sins and ask for absolution. For this kind of confession has remained in its proper and blessed use in the church in Wittenberg from the time when this purified doctrine began down to the present day.

Our doctor also interpreted Psalm 68,[21] concerning the suffering of Jesus Christ, for at that time preaching dealt only with the suffering of Mary and the saints. For this reason he advised that, in accordance with Scripture, one should think on the Lord Christ and proclaim and contemplate His death and suffering.

He also published the song of Mary, the Magnificat [Luke 1:46-55],[22] with a beautiful exposition, as a warning to all who trust in their own piety, strength, and skill ¹and set themselves against God's Word and the Seed of the woman who has now been sent [Gen. 3:15], and also as comfort for all the humble and afflicted who have had their contrite hearts sprinkled with the blood of Jesus Christ in the Word of grace.

---

[20] Perhaps a reference to Thomas Aquinas as "Angelic Doctor," but more likely a reference to the casuistic manual of Angelus de Clavasio (Angelus de Chiavasso Carletus, 1411–95), the *Summa Angelica de Casibus Conscientiae*. Luther had burned a copy of the *Summa Angelica* along with the canon law in 1520 (see above, Mathesius, *History*, p. 163): see Luther to Spalatin, December 10, 1520, LW 48:186–87. Neither scholastic theologian is explicitly mentioned in *Von der Beichte*.

[21] In Mathesius' text, "Psalm 67," following the Vg numeration. See Luther, *Commentary on Psalm 68* (1521), LW 13:1–37.

[22] *The Magnificat* (1521), LW 21:295–355. Luther had begun this work in 1520, and printing had started in Wittenberg, but he did not finish writing it until June 1521 at the Wartburg. The printing was not completed until August: see Luther to Spalatin, May 14, 1521, LW 48:22; June 10, 1521, LW 48:254; August 15, 1521, LW 48:296; and the introduction by Jaroslav Pelikan, LW 21:xvii–xix.

And since in the papacy the Sunday Gospel was often omitted entirely in favor of [saints'] legends,[23] and there were, apart from Tauler's,[24] few postils available from which one could give children and simple laity plain and correct instruction in how to live as a Christian and die a blessed death, Dr. Luther wrote the German *Church Postil*,[25] in which he interprets the Sunday Epistle and Gospel readings; faithfully exhorts to saving faith and brotherly love, to patience under the cross and Christian obedience as subjects; and earnestly warns against idolatry and human wares. Doctor Cruciger later abridged these sermons with the counsel and approval of the master.[26]

Furthermore: In this wilderness of his, he also published the learned book against Master Latomus[27] from Louvain, in which he discusses letter and spirit, Law and Gospel, the office of Moses and of Jesus Christ, as well as what sin and grace are and how we are justified and saved before God by

---

[23] *Legenda*—meaning literally: "[words] to be read"—was the technical name for the stories of the saints read as part of the liturgy.

[24] On Tauler, see above, p. 42 n. 21. Luther read Tauler's sermons in 1516 and commended them to Spalatin in a letter of December 14, 1516, LW 48:35–36. Luther's early annotations on Tauler's sermons are edited in WA 9:97–104 (LW 70). In December 1521, Luther asked his Wittenberg colleagues to send him a copy of Tauler's sermons to use in preparing his own postil: see WA 10/1.2:lxv–lxvi and Melanchthon to Spalatin, December 26–27, 1521, MBW 1:414–15, no. 191. Tauler's sermons had just been reprinted in a new Basel edition: *Joannis Tauleri des heiligen lerers Predig* (Basel: Adam Petri, 1521) [VD16 J784]. For a modern edition, see Ferdinand Vetter, ed., *Die Predigten Taulers* (Berlin: Weidmann, 1910; repr., 1968), with selections available in English in Josef Schmidt, ed., *Johannes Tauler: Sermons,* trans. Maria Shrady (New York: Paulist Press, 1985).

[25] In the late medieval church, a postil (Latin *postilla*, from the phrase *post illa verba*) was a collection of sermons on the appointed Gospel and Epistle texts for the Sundays and festivals of the church year. In the Wartburg, Luther wrote sermons for the Christmas season, and then for Advent (LW 52; cf. LW 75), as the beginning of an envisioned project to produce a complete Evangelical postil. On Luther's activity in the Wartburg, see the excursus by Gottfried Krodel, LW 48:237–43. On the gradual assembly of the complete set, eventually known as Luther's *Church Postil*, see the introduction by Benjamin T. G. Mayes, LW 75:xiii–xxxi, and the translation of the whole series in LW 75–79 and Lenker 1–8.

[26] Luther entrusted the final revision of the *Church Postil* (the summer portion) to Caspar Cruciger. His work appeared at the end of 1543 (dated 1544). See the introduction by Benjamin T. G. Mayes, LW 75:xxii–xxiv; Cruciger's dedication of the *Summer Postil*, LW 77:3–6; and Luther's preface to the *Summer Postil*, LW 77:7–11. On Cruciger, see above, p. xx n. 19; below, p. 298 n. 81. On Cruciger's role editing Luther's sermons and lectures for publication, see the introduction by Christopher Boyd Brown, LW 69:4–5; and below, Mathesius, *History*, pp. 249, 292, 373, 374 n. 37, 408, 514–15, 525. Cruciger had visited Mathesius in Joachimsthal in 1545: see Loesche, *Johannes Mathesius,* 1:193.

[27] *Against Latomus* (1521), LW 32:133–260. See Luther to Melanchthon, May 26, 1521, LW 48:229; Brecht 2:7–9. Jacques Masson, called Latomus (ca. 1475–1544), was a professor and canon in Louvain. He wrote extensively against both Luther and Erasmus. See Bietenholz and Deutscher, *Contemporaries of Erasmus,* 2:304–6; and the introduction by George W. Forell, LW 32:135–36.

faith in Christ alone. He treats this all so thoroughly that, for all that I understand of Christianity, I have read nothing more correct and fundamental, alongside his second exposition of the Epistle to the Galatians[28] and Master Philip's [exposition] of the Epistle to the Romans[29] and his *Loci communes*.[30] Latomus was a learnèd man—the doctor himself confessed that he had no opponent more clever[31]—and he attempted to refute our doctor's teaching with Scripture, which none of the Roman writers had done before, citing the interpretations of the ancient teachers. In this way, he wanted to put in a word in defense of scholastic theology and its principles and foundations, and of human piety and righteousness in opposition to the sacrifice and obedience of Jesus Christ.

|But our hermit broke through with the text from St. Paul[32] and upheld the certain and blessed doctrine that the righteous lives by his faith alone [Rom. 1:17; cf. Gal. 3:11], when Christ's blood and redemption are reckoned to him by grace through faith. And so, throughout his life, then, he took this passage of St. Paul, drawn from the prophet Habakkuk [2:4], as his motto, holding it up boldly in the face of the Roman idolatry and his conscience, which accused him, and all the gates of hell.[33]

---

[28] *Lectures on Galatians* (1531/1535), LW 26; 27:1–149.

[29] The 1540 edition of Melanchthon's Romans commentary, edited in CR 15:493–796, is translated in Melanchthon, *Commentary on Romans*, trans. Fred Kramer (St. Louis: Concordia, 1992; 2nd ed., 2010). The first edition had appeared in 1522: see Luther, preface to Melanchthon, *Annotations on Romans and Corinthians* (1522), LW 59:18–22, and the introduction by Timothy J. Wengert there. The edition of 1530 is edited in CR 15:441–92; the 1532 edition is edited in MSA 5. The final edition of 1556 is edited in CR 15:797–1052.

[30] Melanchthon's *Loci communes* was first published in 1521 and subsequently revised and expanded in Latin editions of 1535, 1543, and 1559. The 1521 edition, edited in MSA 2/1:15–185 and CR 21:59–228, is translated in Wilhelm Pauck, ed., *Melanchthon and Bucer*, LCC 19 (Philadelphia: Westminster Press, 1969), pp. 1–152; and in *Commonplaces: Loci Communes 1521*, trans. Christian A. Preus (St. Louis: Concordia, 2014). The 1535 edition is edited in CR 21:229–560. The 1555 German edition is translated in Clyde Leonard Manschreck, ed., *Melanchthon on Christian Doctrine: Loci communes, 1555* (New York: Oxford University Press, 1965). The 1559 edition is edited in MSA 2/1:186–388, 2/2, and CR 21:561–1106, and is translated in *The Chief Theological Topics: Loci praecipui theologici 1559*, trans. J. A. O. Preus (St. Louis: Concordia, 2011). The readings of the 1543 edition are reflected in the notes to the 1559 edition in CR and MSA. See the introduction by Benjamin T. G. Mayes, in *Chief Theological Topics*, pp. xiii–xv.

[31] See *Table Talk*, no. 5345 (1540), WA TR 5:75; see also *Table Talk* no. 463 (1533), LW 54:77; no. 1709 (1532), WA TR 2:189; no. 4119 (1538), WA TR 4:145–46.

[32] See, e.g., Luther's appeal to Rom. 3:21, 28, and Rom. 5:1 in *Against Latomus* (1521), LW 32:227.

[33] Although Luther does not refer explicitly to Rom. 1:17 or Hab. 2:4 in *Against Latomus*, the Pauline text figures prominently elsewhere: see, e.g., *Judgment on Monastic Vows* (1521), LW 44:287, 295 (described by Mathesius immediately below); *Preface to the Latin Writings*

Now, since God's Word had not gone forth in vain and without fruit [Isa. 55:10–11], many kindhearted men and pious women resolved to leave the godless life of the cloister. Our doctor, therefore, as a bishop, following the command of St. Paul [Rom. 14:1], took thought for the fallen and distressed consciences and wrote instruction and comfort for them in the little book about monastic vows.[34] In this book, he demonstrated thoroughly and rightly that vows taken apart from and contrary to God's command, and which are impossible in and of themselves, cannot bind or hold captive the heart of one who is baptized. Again: that no one who is baptized and has taken a vow to the Holy Trinity with the covenant of a good conscience [1 Pet. 3:21] and bound himself by oath to God's Word and the universal apostolic Church can swear or vow anything to anyone else in matters of religion and conscience without prejudice to and annullment of the first faith and baptismal vow. For our soul is bound by oath and sworn to Jesus Christ and His Word in Baptism. Therefore, if someone has taken an impossible and unchristian vow because of ignorance and deception, the eternal Son of God frees him and by grace joyfully receives whoever returns to Him and adheres to the first vow.

This book loosed many bonds and freed many captive hearts, though some who had run into the monastery for the sake of their belly [cf. Rom. 16:18] ¹thoughtlessly leaped out again and shamefully abused both the first and the second vow and their faith. Our doctor dedicated this book to his dear father, who had always borne a paternal animus against his life in the cloister, and yielded himself once more to obedience to him, having lapsed from it many years before.[35]

Now as our doctor continued studying and writing in his cell like this, it made him weak, so that good friends advised him to go for walks and get fresh air and move around for the sake of his health.[36] Accordingly, he was taken along on hunts;[37] sometimes he went into the strawberry patch on the

---

(1545), LW 34:336–37; *Lectures on Genesis* (1535–45/1544–54), LW 5:158. On the passage as Luther's "motto," see WA 48:286.

[34] *Judgment on Monastic Vows* (1521), LW 44:243–400.

[35] See Luther to Hans Luther, November 21, 1521, LW 48:329–36.

[36] Most of the correspondence addressed to Luther in the Wartburg has not been preserved, though it is clear from repeated mentions in Luther's letters that his friends were concerned about his health: see, e.g., Luther to Melanchthon, August 3, 1521, LW 48:288.

[37] See Luther to Spalatin, August 15, 1521, LW 48:295.

castle hill.[38] At length he was given an honorable servant,[39] a discreet cavalryman, whose loyalty and spirited interjections and admonitions he often praised later. For example, he forbade him to put aside his sword when he entered his lodgings and to start poring over the books straightaway, lest he be marked as a clerk. This is how Dr. Luther entered some monasteries and yet was not recognized.[40]

He went to his friends in [Martschall],[41] but they failed to recognize Squire George[42] (which is the name the cavalryman gave him). A lay brother recognized him in Reinhardsbrunn;[43] when his steward noticed this, he reminded his "squire" that he had an appointment to keep in the evening, and so he quickly set out again.[44]

However, because his church and pulpit in Wittenberg were always on his mind—once while sitting at table deep in thought he suddenly exclaimed: "Ah, if only I were in Wittenberg!"[45]—he undertook a journey, arriving in

---

[38] See *Table Talk* no. 5353 (1540), WA TR 5:82. Although the edited text of this *Table Talk* seems to place Luther's strawberry-picking in his youth (*adulescens*), while he was in school in Eisenach (see above, Mathesius, *History*, pp. 118–19), the variant texts omit the adjective and associate the strawberry-picking with Luther's hunting excursions (*venationes*), as Mathesius does. See Volz, *Die Lutherpredigten des Johannes Mathesius*, p. 139 n. 1.

[39] Luther mentions being attended by servants during his time in the Wartburg in *Table Talk* no. 5353 (1540), WA TR 5:82—though the textual variant of this piece which Mathesius follows (above, *History*, pp. 181–82) in his narrative of Luther's capture assigns the two servants to the noblemen who took him to the Wartburg—and in *Table Talk* no. 5375d (1540), WA TR 5:103.

[40] Luther mentions a visit to a Franciscan monastery (presumably in Eisenach) in *Table Talk* no. 5353 (1540), WA TR 5:82, where he was not recognized thanks to the "discretion of the cavalrymen." *Table Talk* no. 5375d (1540), WA TR 5:103, recounts a visit to the Augustinian cloister in Erfurt (see below, n. 44). See Brecht 2:1.

[41] Mathesius' text reads *Wartsal*, which cannot be identified. An inversion of the first letter could give the reading of either "Martschall," north of Eisenach (so *LH²*, p. 486), or "Marksuhl," southwest of Eisenach.

[42] *Juncker Georgen*. Luther describes his disguise as a knight in his letter to Spalatin, May 14, 1521, LW 48:228, and to Melanchthon, May 26, 1521, LW 48:234. He was painted by Lucas Cranach under this disguise: Max J. Friedländer and Jakob Rosenberg, *The Paintings of Lucas Cranach* (Amsterdam: Meulenhoff, 1979), nos. 148–49. Mathesius seems, however, to be the primary source for the alias "Junker Jörg" under which Luther was known during his time in the Wartburg.

[43] In Mathesius' text: *Reinhartsborn*. Reinhardsbrunn, southwest of Gotha, was home to an old Benedictine abbey.

[44] Compare *Table Talk* no. 5375d (1540), WA TR 5:103, which gives a very similar account but places it in a cloister in Erfurt, identifies the man who recognizes Luther as a monk rather than a lay brother [*Convers*], and pairs Luther with his servant rather than with the "steward" [*Hofmeister*], which might refer either to Hans von Berlepsch as castellan of the Wartburg (see above, p. 181 n. 79) or to the cavalryman in his feigned relation to "Junker Jörg."

[45] Mathesius is the source for this anecdote.

Wittenberg in about November,[46] and stayed with his traveling companion[47] Herr Nicolaus [von] Amsdorf, having informed several of his good friends.[48] After conversing with them and enjoying their company for several days, he secretly returned to the Wartburg.[49] Meanwhile, [word] slipped out through a chancery clerk; accordingly, a prince and several important women sought him but were unable to catch sight of him.[50]

Shortly before this he learned of how his brethren, the Augustinians in Wittenberg, had ceased to hold daily private Masses.[51] But since this was one of the greatest pillars upon which the papacy rests, and this impurity was so deeply rooted in the hearts of many people and regarded as the highest worship on earth, he wrote to his brethren and instructed and comforted them concerning this article.[52]

---

[46] In fact, the visit took place about December 2–12, 1521. See Brecht 2:29–30. On Mathesius' misdating of the visit, see below, n. 49.

[47] In addition to accompanying Luther to and from the Diet of Worms (thus being present at the time of Luther's capture), Amsdorf had traveled with Luther to Leipzig (1519): see above, p. 30 n. 15, p. 172 n. 34, p. 181 n. 76.

[48] Luther's contacts in Wittenberg during his visit, in addition to Amsdorf, were Melanchthon, the painter Lucas Cranach, and the goldsmith Christian Döring (alias Düring or Aurifaber, ca. 1490–1533); the latter two were members of the town council as well as printers. See Brecht 2:29.

[49] For Luther's description of this visit, on which Mathesius' account is based, see Luther to Spalatin, ca. December 5, 1521, LW 48:350–52, which is dated from Amsdorf's house. Brecht 2:29 places Luther with Melanchthon. Mathesius' dating of the visit to late November was likely prompted by the arrangement of this undated letter in the earliest editions of Luther's correspondence: *Epistolarum Reverendi Patris Domini D. Martini Lutheri, Tomus Primus* (Jena: Rödinger, 1556) [VD16 L4649], fols. 365v–367v, placed immediately after Luther's letter to Spalatin of November 22 (LW 48:337–38).

[50] The rumor of Luther's location in the Wartburg is mentioned in a letter to Amsdorf, ca. July 15, 1521, LW 48:264, and a letter to Spalatin, July 15, 1521, LW 48:269, mentioning that the secretary of Duke John of Saxony had disclosed his location to "a woman in Torgau." Luther to Spalatin, September 9, 1521, LW 48:307, indicates that the castellan Hans von Berlepsch had just revealed Luther's location to Duke John himself. *Table Talk* no. 6816 (n.d.), WA TR 6:209, describes the efforts of the wife of Hans von Berlepsch to catch a glimpse of Luther in the Wartburg. On Duke John, the younger brother of Frederick the Wise, see above, p. 70 n. 95.

[51] On October 6, the Augustinian preacher Gabriel Zwilling preached in the Wittenberg cloister against holding private Masses; under his leadership, the Wittenberg Augustinians ceased celebrating the Mass on October 13. See Brecht 2:26; on Zwilling, see Siegfried Hoyer, "Zwilling, Gabriel," *OER* 4:319–20.

[52] Luther wrote the Latin treatise *De abroganda missa privata Martini Lutheri sententia* in early November 1521 (WA 8:411–76), with a dedication to the Wittenberg Augustinians (see the introduction by Gottfried Krodel, LW 48:324–25), and he prepared a German translation by the end of the month: *Misuse of the Mass* (1521), LW 36:127–230. However, Spalatin delayed the publication of both works because of their provocative nature, so that neither appeared in print in Wittenberg until January 1522.

The New Testament knows of only one Priest, who offered Himself up to His Father as an acceptable sacrifice on the tree and high altar of the cross one time to reconcile mankind and gain complete forgiveness of sins for the whole world. Thus the holy Sacrament, which believers eat and drink in accordance with Christ's command, thereby commemorating His death, cannot and must not be a sacrifice and satisfaction for the sins of the living, much less for the dead in purgatory—or for the benefit of the hunters and hawkers who for the sake of their mercenary Mass have set up the sacrifical Masses of the monks. In accordance with Scripture, therefore, we can and should discontinue the daily sacrifice of the Mass.

In addition to this, however, he admonished his brothers not to presume to change or abandon anything without good counsel and consideration, until it has been decided with common consent by those who bear responsibility. Idolatry is to be abolished, yet it should happen by common counsel and consent, as when King Joash tore down the altar of Baal and abolished his sacrifices [2 Kings 11:17-21] and Hezekiah destroyed the bronze serpent with which the people practiced idolatry [2 Kings 18:1-4].

Not long after this, the Augustinians submitted their defense and explanation for having discontinued the private Mass; by order of the elector, the laudable university in Wittenberg consulted over it and sent their opinion to their territorial prince. Upon this, the electoral chancellor, Doctor Christian Beyer,[53] was sent to those from Wittenberg with an instruction, and this matter was weighed in a Christian and requisite manner according to God's Word, resulting in this unanimous decision:[54] Because the private Masses have been instituted by human beings apart from and contrary to God's

---

[53] Christian Beyer [Beier, Bayer, Peyer, Bowarius] (ca. 1482-1535), who in 1528 became chancellor to Elector John the Steadfast, was from 1511 to 1528 a member of the Wittenberg law faculty. On Beyer, see Bietenholz and Deutscher, *Contemporaries of Erasmus*, 1:144; below, Mathesius, *History*, p. 329.

[54] The Wittenberg faculty submitted its opinion on October 20; the electoral instruction, which refused to authorize changes in the Mass, was issued on October 25, 1521. The texts on which Mathesius bases this account—the opinion of the Wittenberg faculty, the electoral instruction, and the response of the Wittenberg faculty on December 12 (in which, in fact, not all the members agreed)—were included in the Wittenberg Latin and German editions of Luther's works: Witt Lat 1 (1545), fols. 201v-204r; Witt Lat 2 (1551), fols. 345r-351r; Witt Ger 9 (1557), fols. 133r-143r (cf. StL 15:1948-49, 1952-65). In Witt Ger 9 (1557), fols. 134r-v and 134v-136r, a set of resolutions including abolition of votive Masses, which in fact derive from the chapter of the Augustinians held at Epiphany 1522, is printed before the October 20, 1521, opinion of the faculty, creating the impression that they sparked the response that follows. A modern edition of these texts is provided in Nikolaus Müller, *Die Wittenberger Bewegung, 1521 und 1522: Die Vorgänge in und um Wittenberg während Luthers Wartburgaufenthalt* (Leipzig: Heinsius, 1911), pp. 35-40, 50-52, 84-90, 149-51. See Brecht 2:27; James S. Preus, *Carlstadt's Ordinaciones and Luther's Liberty* (Cambridge, MA: Harvard University Press, 1974), pp. 13-50; Roper, *Luther*, pp. 209-15.

Word, as a daily sacrifice and payment for the sins of the world, detracting from and denying the sole and eternal sacrifice of Jesus Christ; and because the Lord's Supper is being celebrated in isolation, without proclaiming the death of Christ; and because this has caused a great deal of abominable offense and idolatry, through which it drains away the property and money of the whole world, this idolatry should be abolished and discontinued in God's name, in accordance with the Scriptures, regardless of the great danger and offense which this may provoke in the godless world. For in matters concerning God, one must do what is right according to God's Word, even if it means that the whole world and every foundation for saying Mass will be destroyed on that account. Christ lives and rules; He will know how to defend and preserve His Word and order and His Church, which conforms to His command.

Upon this, the abominable sacrifice of the Mass fell into complete desuetude—first, in the monastery, then in the parish [church], and, finally, after multiple discussions, also in the Castle Church in Wittenberg[55] and in many other places where divine worship was established in accordance with God's Word.[56]

Now, even as Dr. Luther in his wilderness did not rest, but instead attended to the Church of God and poor consciences in a Christian manner as a true bishop and pastor of souls, so also the ancient serpent, who bit into Christ's heel [Gen. 3:15] and preaching office from the beginning,[57] did not rest. And because this ancient serpent could not suppress the rising truth by means of lies and force, ¹there arose all kinds of unrest and offense from among Dr. Martin's listeners.[58] For after the private, secret Mass had fallen away in Wittenberg, through God's Word and Christian deliberation and counsel, and the proper use of the Lord's Supper had been established in

---

[55] Whereas private Masses and Communion in one kind were abolished in the Augustinian cloister in 1521–22, the first Communion in both kinds in the Wittenberg parish church took place under Andreas Bodenstein von Karlstadt's leadership at Christmas 1521. Luther did not begin to adopt the change until March 1522 and did not apply it universally until January 1523: see Brecht 2:122; cf. *Order of Mass and Communion* (1523), LW 53:15–40. The celebration of Mass in the Castle Church was not reformed until Christmas 1524: see Luther to the All Saints' Foundation, November 17, 1524, WA Br 3:376–77; Brecht 2:127–29; and below, Mathesius, *History*, p. 226.

[56] See, e.g., *Concerning the Order of Public Worship* (1523), LW 53:7–14, and *Concerning Public Worship and Concord* (1525), LW 53:41–50, in which Luther advises the churches in Leisnig and Dorpat, respectively, about the reform of the liturgy.

[57] See above, p. 104 n. 10.

[58] On the Wittenberg unrest of 1521–22, see Mark U. Edwards Jr., *Luther and the False Brethren* (Stanford: Stanford University Press, 1974), chapter 1, pp. 6–33; Müller, *Die Wittenberger Bewegung 1521 und 1522*.

accordance with Christ's institution,[59] Karlstadt,[60] the father of all fanatics and agitators[61] in our times, took it upon himself without due order, out of his own wanton presumption, to attack the images and cast them out of the churches;[62] he set up a scandalous liberty, so that the people took the Supper from the altar themselves, unworthily, without any preceding contrition, and impudently devoured eggs and meat.[63] Karlstadt's comrades also began to disparage and slander the schools and all liberal arts, as well as the laudable customs according to which public [academic] titles and attestations are conferred on capable people.[64] For if only you had the Spirit and the impulse from within, [they claimed,] you had no need of any of the [liberal] arts or any Scripture.[65] Then Christian schools went into decline, and many people fell away from their studies, eventually becoming Enthusiasts,

---

[59] Mathesius overstates the progress of reforms in Wittenberg by the end of 1521. Although the private Mass had been largely suppressed outside of the All Saints' Foundation (the Castle Church), and both kinds had been distributed at the Augustinian cloister and privately among some of the university faculty (including Melanchthon) and students, it was Karlstadt who celebrated the first public Mass with lay Communion in both kinds in the Wittenberg parish church (St. Mary's) on Christmas Day 1521. See Brecht 2:26–34.

[60] On Karlstadt, see above, p. 154 n. 90; and below, Mathesius, *History*, pp. 238–40. Luther gives an extended account of Karlstadt's activities in *Against the Heavenly Prophets* (1525), LW 40:73–223, and in the version of the 1521 *Invocavit Sermons* printed in the postils and early collected editions of Luther's works: see WA 10/3:lviii–lxiii, especially p. lix; cf. LW 51:67–100.

[61] *Schwermer* [or "Enthusiasts"] *und stürmer* [the root used in the word "iconoclast," *Bilderstürmer*]. *Schwärmer* was Luther's favored German term—parallel to the Greek/Latin *enthusiastici*—for describing those who rejected the external Word or the Sacraments: see *Smalcald Articles* (1537) III VIII 3–13 (Kolb-Wengert, pp. 322–23; *Concordia*, pp. 280–81); *Against the Heavenly Prophets* (1525), LW 40:146–48. See also above, p. 95 n. 36 and p. 139 n. 137.

[62] On January 26, 1522, Karlstadt preached a sermon "On the Abolition of Images and That There Should Be No Beggars among Christians," in which he advocated the speedy removal of images. For the published version of the sermon, see E. J. Furcha, ed. and trans., *The Essential Carlstadt: Fifteen Tracts* (Waterloo, ON: Herald, 1995), pp. 100–128. See Brecht 2:39–40.

[63] At his celebration of the Lord's Supper, Karlstadt encouraged the congregation to commune without having made confession or fasting and to receive the elements in their own hands. He also criticized fasting more generally. See *Invocavit Sermons* (1521), WA 10/3:lix; Hieronymus Schurff to Elector Frederick, March 9, 1522, StL 15:1995–98; Karlstadt, *On the Reception of the Holy Sacrament* (1522), in Amy Nelson Burnett, ed. and trans., *The Eucharistic Pamphlets of Andreas Bodenstein von Karlstadt*, Early Modern Studies 6 (Kirksville, MO: Truman State University Press, 2011), pp. 79–88.

[64] Karlstadt rejected the use of academic titles (including his own) among Christians: see *Table Talk* no. 361 (1532), LW 54:54; *Against the Heavenly Prophets* (1525), LW 40:162; Karlstadt, *The Meaning of the Term 'Gelassen'* (1523), in Furcha, *Essential Carlstadt*, pp. 161–62.

[65] Or "writing." Cf. *Table Talk* no. 406 (1532), LW 54:64–65; no. 4081 (1538), LW 54:318; Karlstadt, *The Meaning of the Term 'Gelassen'* (1523), in Furcha, *Essential Carlstadt*, p. 153.

heavenly prophets, and Anabaptists themselves.[66] For example, Neighbor Andy[67] stabbed the university in the belly[68] and became a peasant farmer,[69] both before and later running away from his calling,[70] as an inconstant man. Afterward, he spent his life not only slandering the precious Supper but also engaging in and stirring up all kinds of mischief.[71]

For once Satan has lifted someone from his place and station and started him rolling, he is unable to remain at rest in any place or upon any doctrine.[72]

Now when news of the innovations, unrest, and offense that were being stirred up by false brethren in Wittenberg reached our doctor by means of well-disposed people[73]—in keeping with the example of Chloe's servants, who also wrote to St. Paul that the false brethren in Corinth were wantonly making one division and change after another (1 Corinthians 1 [:11–17])—it was unthinkable to our doctor that he should remain hidden. In God's name, therefore, he decided to return to Wittenberg, to his church and pulpit, regardless of whether he was under the pope's ban and the proscription and greater proscription of the secular authorities,[74] and regardless of whether this would incur the terrible displeasure of his territorial prince.

---

[66] On Karlstadt's relation to other movements in the radical Reformation, see Calvin Augustine Pater, *Karlstadt as Father of the Baptist Movements* (Toronto: University of Toronto Press, 1984). The Anabaptist leader Melchior Hoffman (d. 1543) was particularly influenced by Karlstadt: see Rollin S. Armour Sr., "Hoffman, Melchior," *OER* 2:240–43. On Enthusiasts, see above, p. 95 n. 36, p. 139 n. 137, and p. 195 n. 61.

[67] *Neber Enders.* This was the nickname Karlstadt assumed when he rejected his academic titles and took up peasant life. See *Against the Heavenly Prophets* (1525), LW 40:162.

[68] A vivid expression for definitively abandoning something. See Wander 1:251, "Bauch" no. 163.

[69] In 1523, Karlstadt, feeling increasingly isolated in Wittenberg, bought a farm in Orlamünde, resigned his positions in the university and All Saints' Foundation, and then, in May, attempted to take charge of the parish there on the basis of his tenure of the benefice. See *Against the Heavenly Prophets* (1525), LW 40:117; Brecht 2:157–58.

[70] Cf. *Table Talk* no. 483 (1533), LW 54:80–81.

[71] On Karlstadt's later criticism of Luther's doctrine of the Lord's Supper and Luther's suspicion of his involvement in the Peasants' War, see below, Mathesius, *History*, pp. 216–17, 238–40, 260–62; cf. below, p. 217 n. 99. By 1534, Karlstadt had again, despite his earlier denunciation of academic life, taken up a university position in Basel.

[72] Cf. Wander 4:1097, "Teufel" no. 897.

[73] Although Mathesius names only Karlstadt, the so-called "Zwickau prophets," who arrived in Wittenberg in late December 1521, were also causing unrest in the town. For correspondence to Luther about the disturbances, see Luther to Amsdorf, January 13, 1522, LW48:364; to Melanchthon, January 13, 1522, LW 48:365–72; and the letters to Elector Frederick cited below, p. 197 n. 75.

[74] See above, Mathesius, *History*, p. 180.

For as his letters[75] to the elector about his return attest, the reasons that in fact drove and compelled him to leave his safe haven were that the whole church in Wittenberg had called him again and summoned him in writing with great pleas and petitions.[76] It was this call, therefore, in addition to his conscience and Christian love, which compelled him to feed his parishioners [John 21:16–17] and to give his life for his parishioners [John 10:11], in accordance with Scripture.

Second: Because Satan had attacked his sheepfold and used those who had eaten bread with him [Ps. 41:9] to disseminate all kinds of unrest and scandal in his church, he could not suppress this diabolical arrogance through writings while absent, but had to be present in person.

Third: He could discern, as one who knew Satan's tricks, that because Satan was unable to destroy the pure doctrine of Jesus Christ by means of lies and condemnations, he would produce turmoil by means of false brethren and seditious people. For most people were taking his spiritual doctrine of inward liberty in a carnal sense and seeking only physical and external freedom. As far as he was able, therefore, he was obliged to serve the God of peace and the peaceable Gospel, as a preacher of inward and external peace, and to help bring all the unrest to a stop in due time.

These and other reasons caused and impelled him to lift up his voice again in public. He did not do this to despise the high authorities or to bring disturbance to the land he was entering. He was, [he said,] the servant of the eternal Son of God ʾand was preaching the true Gospel; [the Son] had enough angels in His kingdom still to be able to intervene on behalf of one doctor, together with his prince, against all the gates of hell [Matt. 16:18].

It is for these reasons, which he made known with great boldness as a prophet and extraordinary man of God,[77] and which he in the same way valiantly carried out, with God's help, that he departed from the Wartburg.[78] In the course of his journey, he wrote to the elector from Borna on Ash Wednesday,[79] and on the next day, on Thursday, he arrived in Wittenberg on horseback.[80]

---

[75] Luther to Elector Frederick, ca. February 22, 1522, LW 48:386–88; March 5, 1522, LW 48:388–93; March 7 or 8, 1522, LW 48:393–99 (cf. WA Br 2:459–62, and the letter to Frederick, March 12, 1522, WA Br 2:467–70).

[76] The three reasons elucidated here by Mathesius are taken directly from Luther's letter to Elector Frederick, March 7, 1522, LW 48:393–99.

[77] *wundermann Gottes.* See the introduction above, pp. lxxxix–xc and n. 364 there.

[78] Luther left on March 1, 1522. See Brecht 2:42.

[79] I.e., March 5, 1522. See Luther to Elector Frederick, March 5, 1522, LW 48:388–93.

[80] I.e., on March 6, 1522. See Brecht 2:59.

Soon thereafter, at the mediation of Dr. Hieronymus Schurff,[81] he wrote a letter to the elector, which was moderated and softened with his permission.[82] The good elector sent this letter to many princes to maintain his honor and supply an appropriate exculpation: it was without the knowledge, consent, counsel, permission, or support of the elector, of his own accord and at his own risk and peril, in the name of Jesus Christ, that Dr. Luther had returned to Wittenberg.

In addition to Dr. Luther's letter, I must also recall the good and well-considered answer of the Christian and prudent lawyer Hieronymus Schurff, electoral counselor and highly renowned professor in Wittenberg.[83]

For when he dealt with Dr. Luther at the elector's behest, he helped defend his arrival with sound arguments, along with the Christian hope that the almighty and gracious God would grant Doctor Martin His grace and mercy, so that by means of his preaching, by the power of the Holy Spirit, he might bring a blessed end to the present offenses, godlessness, and scandal that Karlstadt and his archangel[84] had stirred up, and cause them to be torn out of the hearts of the people. The agitators and seditious preachers who had infiltrated themselves without any call, however, were no longer to be permitted to teach. The advice and prophecy of this blessed and very wise lawyer were, praise be to God, richly fulfilled by the presence of Dr. Martin.

For this is how the church in Wittenberg was liberated from its false brethren: Some of them hoisted anchor on their own[85] and snuck into other parishes[86] and held their secret conventicles, wanting to dispense with God and His saving Word and all secular authority, law, and good order; others crawled to the cross[87] and confessed that they had been misled and foolish. After Doctor Martin's death, however, they started to rage like fanatics again with what were obviously quibbles against the surplice and other inoffensive

---

[81] On Schurff, see above, p. 21 n. 83; and above, Mathesius, *History*, p. 173.

[82] Luther's letter to the elector (LW 48:393–99) was written on March 8 (though backdated to March 7) after meeting with Schurff. For the dating of this letter, see the introduction by Gottfried Krodel, LW 48:394, and LW 48:398 n. 17. The "softened" and "milder" version to which Mathesius refers was a revision of the letter by Spalatin approved and signed by Luther on March 12. See LW 48:398 n. 19 and WA Br 2:467–70.

[83] Schurff to Elector Frederick, March 9, 1522, WA Br 2:462–65. See also Frederick to Schurff, March 11, 1522, WA Br 2:465–66.

[84] I.e., the Augustinian preacher Gabriel Zwilling: see above, p. 192 n. 51. Although he had supported Karlstadt during Luther's absence, Zwilling reconciled with Luther upon his return to Wittenberg: see Luther to Wenceslaus Linck, March 19, 1522, WA Br 2:478.

[85] *Sich . . . aus dem staub machten*; see Wander 4:785, "Staub" no. 35.

[86] Perhaps a reference to Karlstadt's departure for the parish of Orlamünde: see above, p. 196 and n. 69 there.

[87] See Wander 2:1611, "Kreuz" no. 184.

ecclesiastical customs and ceremonies, and continued until they came to their graves.[88]

Of course, it is true, as even reasonable pagans say, that as much as peace is better than war and unrest, so much is sedition worse and more pernicious than legitimate war which is to be conducted outside of one's own land, against public enemies.[89] Thus all the Papists with their slander and condemnation did not cause so much harm to our doctor and his Gospel or detriment to God's Word as what was done by his own students, the false brethren, who had often sat at table with him. *Qui ex nobis abierunt* ["Those who went out from us . . ."] [1 John 2:19], the fanatics[90] and perjured Mamelukes,[91] cast offenses and stumbling blocks in the way of the Gospel, over which many ignorant and simpleminded people fell, and many a good heart among people elsewhere stumbled over these things. As Dr. Luther himself wrote in his letter to the elector sent from Borna: "Everything done to hurt me in this cause to date has been a joke and nothing." What Neighbor Andrew[92] and his fanatical rebels had done in his absence, however, "that we cannot answer for, neither before God nor before the world."[93]

But though the Lord Jesus Christ's "woe" [Matt. 18:17] later befell these scandalous preachers and impudent listeners more severely than we could have wished, the pure doctrine of our faithful doctor has nevertheless remained. As he openly confesses in his letter, along with St. Paul [Gal. 1:12], he has this doctrine not from men, but solely from heaven,

---

[88] Mathesius is making a polemical connection between the participants in the Wittenberg unrest of 1521–22 and the later Gnesio-Lutheran party that criticized Melanchthon and his followers for accepting the reintroduction of the surplice and other liturgical vestments where they had fallen out of use. These changes to ecclesiastical customs were part of the Augsburg (and so-called Leipzig) Interims of 1548–49. Mathesius probably has in mind Gabriel Zwilling in particular (see above, p. 198 n. 84), who took the Gnesio-Lutheran side in opposition to the introduction of the Leipzig Interim in Albertine Saxony in 1548–49. On Mathesius' position in the inter-Lutheran conflicts after Luther's death, see the introduction above, pp. lxxxiv–lxxxv.

[89] Herodotus (ca. 484–ca. 430 BC), *Histories* 8.3 (Loeb 120 [1925], pp. 4–5).

[90] Cf. *Table Talk* no. 5667 (1544), WA TR 5:309.

[91] Although originally slaves, the Mamelukes became the military class of the Muslim world of the Middle East and had established themselves as sultans of Egypt from 1250 until their defeat by the Ottoman Turks in 1517. "Mamelukes" came to be used as a derogatory term in Christian Europe, used either to imply slavish devotion to a ruler (such as the pope) or, as here, as a term for "apostates" or "unbelievers": cf., e.g., *Table Talk* no. 6145 (n.d.), WA TR 5:511; and frequently in Aurifaber's edition of the *Table Talk*, e.g., no. 3301 (1533), WA TR 3:260; no. 4086 (1538), WA TR 4:127; etc.

[92] See above, p. 196 and n. 67 there.

[93] Mathesius is adapting Luther's text, inserting the specific derogatory reference to Karlstadt. See Luther to Elector Frederick, March 5, 1522, LW 48:389–90.

through Jesus Christ and His Word.[94] Moreover, many popes, bishops, papistic writers, and tyrants, along with fanatics, rebels, and false brethren, have been brought low in terror, as were Pharaoh [Exod. 14:24] and the vile[95] Korah [Numbers 16]. After they had been suppressed in these lands, they were obliged to let the Gospel remain in the reformed churches against their will, together with the ring on the church [door],[96] which they had already knocked on so hard and violently.[97]

God lives, and Christ is sitting and ruling at the right hand of the Father, giving and preserving good gifts from heaven, over which He sets His little angels to watch, as He did with Elisha, the good pastor [2 Kings 6:17], and He encamps with His protection around those who hear and keep His Word [Ps. 34:7], driving out the devils so that they dash into the sea with their swine and are destroyed [Matt. 8:30–32]. Therefore, when shepherds and sheep perish, it is not a question of wolves [Matt. 7:15; 10:16; Acts 20:29], or of hirelings [John 10:12], or of faithless and lazy dogs—as we (praise God!) have clearly come to realize over these past fifty years, in fact and in daily experience. But you will hear more about the false brethren, iconoclasts, and fanatics at another time.[98]

Now we will conclude for the present time concerning Dr. Martin's Patmos and his return to Wittenberg. Next, God willing, we will hear more about how the doctor dealt with his public enemies and persecutors and the false friends who wickedly and murderously stirred up scandal and sedition, to the detriment of the peaceful kingdom of Jesus Christ.

We thank our Lord and Savior Jesus Christ, who has visited us in these lands with His Gospel; and has provided and preserved us down to the present day with faithful teachers, as well as with blessed nurturers and confessors of the pure doctrine; and has protected this valley from monasteries and graciously has turned away from us many kinds of fanaticism and rebellion. May He continue to help us in the future, that we ministers of His Word may teach pure doctrine in simplicity and may faithfully exhort those under our care to the true faith, good conscience, Christian endurance, and due obedience as subjects while bringing them up to the glory of God, that we may rejoice in them here and in all eternity. Amen! Our only Lord and Savior Jesus Christ, highly exalted! Amen!

---

[94] Cf. Luther to Elector Frederick, March 5, 1522, LW 48:390.

[95] *kale*; the first printing has *kalte*, "cold."

[96] Cf. Wander 3:1690, "Ring" no. 39: i.e., to leave empty-handed after knocking at the door in vain. Cf. below, Mathesius, *History*, p. 264.

[97] For the image of the enemy having to leave the ring on the door while Christ remains, cf. *Table Talk* no. 4944 (1540), WA TR 4:589.

[98] See below, Mathesius, *History*, pp. 201–2, 213–18, 237–47, 259–62, 380–92, 410–19.

THE FIFTH SERMON,
ON THE YEARS 1522, 1523, 1524, AND 1525

[Late January–Early February 1563][1]

BELOVED friends in the Lord! There once was a Jew who wanted to be baptized and asked where he could encounter the God of Christians. He was directed to Rome, to his vicar.[2] When the Jew had looked around there for a while, he said, "Surely the true God, of whom all our prophets testify, who alone is gracious, kind, merciful, and very patient and long-suffering [cf. Ps. 86:15], must live here. For no other God could look upon such sin, disgrace, idolatry, unrighteousness, and fornication and endure it for so long." Then he is said to have been baptized.[3]

This most gracious God, who loved the world and gave His Son into death for its sins [John 3:16], and who in the first [age of the] world held back His righteous and severe wrath with great patience for 120 years [Gen. 6:3] before sending the flood—it was to this God that our doctor, whose history you have now heard down to the year 1522, bore witness and whom he confessed. In addition to this confession, he rebuked the wickedness and unbending impurity of the Roman Curia, and particularly the abominable doctrine, life, and conduct of the spiritual estate, falsely so called.[4]

For he returned to Wittenberg from his safe quarters at his own risk and preached against Karlstadt's fanaticism, engaged in disputations, instructed perplexed consciences with God's Word, comforted those who had been caused to stumble, and testified of the mercy of God that shines forth in the blood of Jesus Christ. |He faithfully taught and admonished that we should tear the idolatrous images out of our hearts and serve

---

[1] Since the fourth sermon was preached on Sunday, January 17 (see above, p. 183 and n. 1 there) and the seventh sermon was preached on Shrove Tuesday, February 23, 1563 (see below, p. 266), the fifth and sixth sermons must have been preached in the intervening weeks.

[2] I.e., the pope.

[3] For this anecdote, cf. *Table Talk* no. 3479 (1536), LW 54:208–9. The original source of the story is Giovanni Boccaccio (1313–75), *The Decameron*, trans. and ed. Wayne A. Rebhorn (New York: W. W. Norton, 2013), day 1, story 2, pp. 28–30.

[4] See below, p. 202 n. 6.

our neighbor in brotherly love and, for the sake of those who are weak [Rom. 14:1; 1 Corinthians 8] and have a milk-faith [1 Cor. 3:2; Heb. 5:12], should tolerate and bear with things that are not directly opposed to God's Word.[5] As a called doctor of Holy Scripture, he also began to write in vehement earnest against what is falsely called the spiritual estate, rebuking them summarily for their decadence, false doctrine, and abominably dissolute lifestyle, and calling them to true penitence and genuine repentance toward God.[6] Meanwhile,[7] he began to give clear instruction from Holy Scripture about who stands in the real spiritual estate, namely, those who have been sprinkled with the blood of Jesus Christ [1 Pet. 1:2] in holy Baptism, sanctified by the Holy Spirit, consecrated as royal priests [1 Pet. 2:9; Rev. 1:6], and elected and accepted as children and heirs of God by grace, solely through faith in Jesus Christ, so that they may praise their God here and each one may proclaim His grace and power to those in his own house and estate.

It is this common Christian estate—which, as the holy martyr John Hus rightly teaches,[8] also includes all popes, bishops, abbots, and priests, insofar as they wish to be sanctified by the Most Holy Lord Christ for [membership in] Christendom and inheritance of eternal salvation—through and from which[9] our eternal High Priest [Heb. 6:20] calls and sends forth prophets and apostles on earth, whom He specially and extraordinarily clothes and invests from on high and adorns and arrays with the gifts of His Spirit, placing His Word in their mouth. Thus St. Paul truthfully relates that he had learned nothing from human beings, but learned his Gospel in the third heaven from the Son of God [cf. Gal. 1:11–12; 2 Cor. 12:2]. Accordingly, through His Spirit, who is mighty in the Word and Church, the Son of God has suitable people set apart for Himself, who are consecrated, instructed, and ordained and confirmed in the congregation of God with laying on of hands and prayer by the elders [cf. 1 Tim. 4:14]. These, then, do blessed service for the lambs of Christ [John 10:1–18; 21:15–17] by teaching, baptizing, absolving, and distributing the Supper, and they win many souls for our God through the Word and prayer, and help save the people by means of

---

[5] See the series of sermons which Luther preached immediately after his return to Wittenberg, from Invocavit Sunday, March 9, to Reminiscere Sunday, March 16, 1522: *Eight Sermons at Wittenberg* (1522), LW 51:67–100.

[6] *Against the Spiritual Estate of the Pope and the Bishops Falsely So-Called* (1522), LW 39:239–99.

[7] The topics of the rest of this paragraph and the one following are further developed in Luther's works of 1523: *That a Christian Assembly Has the Right to Judge All Teaching*, LW 39:301–14, and *Concerning the Ministry*, LW 40:3–44.

[8] See John Hus, *The Church*, ed. and trans. David S. Schaff (New York: Scribner's, 1915). On Hus, see the introduction above, pp. xxxvii–xxxviii; and Mathesius, *History*, p. 121.

[9] *Über solchen gemeinen Christenstand . . . darauß beruffe*

Christian doctrine and the gracious distribution of Christ's treasures. Our doctor's book on the spiritual estate treats these topics in detail.[10]

But our doctor—having a clear command as a prophet of God and called doctor of Holy Scripture to warn the clergy of the godless and unspiritual "spiritual" estate[11] against ruin and to tell them to desist from their abominable teaching and devilishness—did not want to be numbered among the accursed himself or to go about God's work half-heartedly and speciously. Instead, he vehemently and sharply attacked the godlessness and unrighteousness and sinful living along with the devilish idolatry that was cloaked and covered with their vestments and monk's cowls as if with Adam's fig leaves [Gen. 3:7], just as Jeremiah [Jeremiah 23] and Ezekiel [Ezekiel 13] used forceful and severe words in their days to attack the false shepherds and whoever was involved in priapic[12] sin and shame. Likewise, John the Baptist and the Lord Christ Himself and St. Peter and St. Paul did not mince words[13] when they reproached the Pharisees and their own false brethren as adulterous and spiritual whores, thieves, robbers, murderers, evildoers, dogs, and fools [cf. Matt. 3:7; Matthew 23; 1 Cor. 6:9–10].

One who takes things seriously cannot make jokes[14]—not if he is judging the lies, murders, and impurity of the devil—and a gnarled and knotted log requires a steel wedge and heavy hammer.[15] One must admit that our doctor does indeed take a hard and sharp tone and uses forceful words, but they are drawn for the most part from the Bible, and he speaks quite clearly and understandably about wicked matters. How can one spin fine thread from coarse flax?[16] The abomination and impiety of the "spiritual" monks and nuns, falsely so called, was an infernal cesspool in which the worst sin and disgrace flowed together.

For example, St. Ulrich, bishop in Augsburg, wrote that the skulls of three thousand children were found in a pond near St. Gregory's nunnery

---

[10] In fact, these arguments are drawn from a number of Luther's works of 1522–23. See above, p. 202 nn. 5–7.

[11] *die Gotlosen vermeinten und ungeystlichen Geystlichen*

[12] For Luther's association of the immorality and idolatry of the clergy with the ancient Greek worship of the ithyphallic idol Priapus, see *Against the Spiritual Estate of the Pope and the Bishops* (1523), LW 39:261, cf. pp. 264–65.

[13] *kein blat fürm mund namen*; literally, "did not put a leaf over their mouths." For the expression, see *DWB*, "Blatt" no. 2.

[14] For the expression, see also below, Mathesius, *History*, p. 461.

[15] Cf. *Table Talk* no. 5089 (1540), LW 54:387 (no. 5091 in WA TR 4:653); no. 5054 (1540), WA TR 4:637; Wander 2:1237, "Keil" no. 1; 4:126, "Scheit" no. 1.

[16] Wander 1:1044, "Flachs" no. 1.

in Rome.[17] The shameful world helps to cover up [such things]; the bishops, too, smear it over with their buckets of grease and their chrism.[18] The Italians make excuses for it. But experience shows that Baal's procession,[19] the worship in Lampsacus,[20] the Eleusinian rites in Greece,[21] and the Bacchanalia in Rome[22] were all secretly being practiced in the monasteries and cathedral chapters,[23] and this foolishness and unchastity has now been revealed, though only in part. On the Last Day, however, when all the devilry and secret "spirituality" of the monks and nuns will be plain as day and stand written on the forehead of each [cf. Rev. 20:4], then it will be evident that one of their Caiaphases made a true prophecy [cf. John 11:49–51]: "Priests have never been good"[24]—neither have the decency, purity, devotion, chastity, and holiness of cardinals, canons, and cloisters. Indeed, upon discovering unspeakable things in a cloister, the good Emperor Frederick

---

[17] Ulrich of Augsburg (890–973) was a reforming bishop under Emperor Otto I (r. 962–973). Ulrich became the patron saint of Augsburg in 993. Luther published an annotated edition of a letter ascribed to him (actually an eleventh-century composition) which describes the discovery of the skulls of more than 6,000 infants by Pope Gregory I. See Luther, preface to [Ps.]-Ulrich of Augsburg, *Letter against Clerical Celibacy* (1520), LW 59:1–5; see also *Lectures on Genesis* (1535–45/1544–54), LW 1:238. The passage is found in *Epistola Divi Hulderichi* (Wittenberg: [Lotter, 1520]) [VD16 U10], fol. A3r.

[18] I.e., the oil used in ordinations of clergy.

[19] On the worship of Baal as an occasion for sexual debauchery, see, e.g., Num. 25:1–5 (cf. *Against the Spiritual Estate of the Popes and the Bishops* [1523], LW 39:260–61). Elsewhere Baal is also associated with child sacrifice: Jer. 19:5.

[20] Lampsacus, a Greek city on the Hellespont in Asia Minor, was the original center for the worship of the male fertility god Priapus (see above, p. 203 n. 12).

[21] The Eleusinian mysteries were strictly secret rites conducted by the Athenians in honor of the goddesses Ceres and Demeter. Although the rites included obscene jokes, their secrecy is probably the chief point of comparison here. See "Eleusis and the Eleusinian Mysteries," *The Oxford Encyclopedia of Ancient Greece and Rome*, ed. Michael Gagarin (New York: Oxford University Press, 2010), 3:38–41. Cf. Erasmus, *Adages* 2.5.66 (CWE 33:207).

[22] The Bacchanalia were secret rites in honor of the Roman god of wine, suppressed by the Roman senate in 186 BC for their debauchery and disorder: see Livy (59 BC–AD 17), *History of Rome* 39.8–18 (Loeb 313 [1936], pp. 240–73); *OCD*, 3rd ed., s.v. "Bacchanalia."

[23] See above, p. 159 n. 114.

[24] The saying *Pfaffen sind nie gut gewesen* (Wander 3:1227, "Pfaffe" no. 77) was ascribed by Luther to Cardinal Matthäus Lang von Wellenburg, archbishop of Salzburg (see above, p. 151 n. 72): see *Warning to His Dear German People* (1531), LW 47:32, 45; *Commentary on the Alleged Imperial Edict* (1531), LW 34:86, 89; *Table Talk* no. 5513 (1542–43), LW 54:441–42, which also compares Lang to Caiaphas; see also *Table Talk* no. 5681 (n.d.), WA TR 5:319; no. 6489 (n.d.), WA TR 5:692; no. 6940 (n.d.), WA TR 6:283. Cf. below, Mathesius, *History*, pp. 233, 343–44, 469. Initially Lang had been considered fair-minded enough by Luther and the Saxon court to be approved as a potential judge in Luther's case, though he became a fierce opponent of the Lutheran Reformation. See Bietenholz and Deutscher, *Contemporaries of Erasmus*, 2:289. See also *Table Talk* no. 5681 (n.d.), WA TR 5:319.

said: *Intret monasterium qui vult cognoscere mundum* ["Go into a monastery if you want to know the world"]![25]

Now, since it was our God's will to reproach this infernal scum by means of His Moses[26] and to have the worst people on earth called to repentance, who is there that will dare to put the worst construction on the harsh words of His servant? God preserve us from this archdevilry! Harsh words from a gentle heart are readily justified before God and honorable people.

Not long afterward, our doctor published the useful treatise on *Avoiding the Doctrines of Men*.[27] In the beginning he had fought against the foundation and first principles of the sophists, ¹and then the pope's decretals and the canons of the councils.[28] However, since some of the pope's advocates relied on sayings of the ancient fathers and doctors to defend the Roman Church's idolatry, worship, chapters, and monasteries, our doctor wrote this treatise, just as he had previously often taught that no one but God and His Son has the authority and right to speak for troubled consciences in the Church and to reproach ungodliness and unrighteousness. Additionally, no human being could or should institute any worship, estate, or order, since God alone is able to ordain true forms of worship and blessed estates and to bless the creatures with His Word [1 Tim. 4:5]. Therefore, our doctor also took up the negative and proved with clear passages from the Old and New Testaments that no person, angel, saint—much less any pope or council—had the command and authority to institute any worship or estate.

For Moses forbade anyone to add to or to take away from God's Word [Deut. 4:2]. In the same way Christ Himself teaches in Matthew 15 [:9] that people worship God in vain with human traditions and trifles. For doctrines of men by which people intend to save souls are doctrines of the devil, having been fabricated and dreamed up apart from and contrary to God's Word. So, because the consciences of many people had been firmly bound and bewitched by these, it was God's will to release and liberate these bound and captive hearts by the power of His Word, as then came to pass, praise God, by the power of the Gospel, as believers tore free from all papal canons and monastic rules as if through a spiderweb.

---

[25] Emperor Frederick III. For the saying, cf. *Table Talk* no. 1073 (1530), WA TR 1:545.

[26] I.e., Luther. On Luther as Moses, see the introduction above, p. lxxxv; and below, Mathesius, *History*, pp. 229–30, 236–37, 244, 262–65, 325–26, 347, 349.

[27] *Avoiding the Doctrines of Men* (1522), LW 35:125–53. In fact, this work was published in late May 1522, before *Against the Spiritual Estate of the Pope and the Bishops*, but in Witt Ger 7 (1554), fols. 329v–354v, the order of these two works was reversed, as Mathesius has it. See Volz, *Die Lutherpredigten des Johannes Mathesius*, p. 156.

[28] See above, Mathesius, *History*, pp. 126, 155–57, 159–60, 163–64.

Now, since the Roman faction had been unable to patch up this tear by help of its writers, for their cause was coming apart at the seams, the pope prompted the king of England to help mend and repair St. Peter's net again [cf. John 21:11].[29] ʜThis new king-turned-author began the battle and sharpened his quill using the penknife (as was supposed) of the monk Lee,[30] attacking Doctor Luther's book on the *Babylonian Captivity*, intending to produce a living exposition of Psalm 2[31] by defending the sacrilege committed by the Roman Church against what Christ had instituted and ordained, as well as their recently invented sacraments—confirmation and [extreme] unction—together with their [doctrines of] sacramental character[32] and the sacrifice of the Mass.

At this point, our doctor had no other fitting choice, by virtue of his doctorate, than to defend God's Word, upon which he had based his book. Therefore, he repeated his previous arguments concerning both kinds in the Lord's Supper and spoke in defense of Jesus Christ, to whom he had made a promise in holy Baptism and his doctoral oath, against the unbelieving

---

[29] King Henry VIII of England (r. 1509–47) published his *Defense of the Seven Sacraments* in Latin in 1521 in response to Luther's *Babylonian Captivity* (1520), LW 36:3–126, perhaps at the prompting of Cardinal Thomas Wolsey (ca. 1474–1530) as papal legate; Pope Leo X subsequently conferred on Henry the honorific title *Fidei defensor*, or "Defender of the Faith," in recognition of this work. See the English translation edited by Louis O'Donovan (New York: Benziger Brothers, 1908), and by Pierre Fraenkel, ed., *Assertio Septem Sacramentorum* (Münster: Aschendorff, 1992). On Henry, see Clifford S. L. Davies, "Henry VIII of England," *OER* 2:227–33. "St. Peter's net" was an established image for the church under the pope.

[30] Edward Lee (ca. 1482–1544) was not a monk but an English doctor of theology who later became archbishop of York (1531–44). He was famous for his 1517–20 polemics against Erasmus. See Bietenholz and Deutscher, *Contemporaries of Erasmus*, 2:311–14. Luther suspected Lee's involvement in Henry's book (see *Against King Henry of England* [1522], WA 10/2:183 [LW 61]); others thought it likely that Bishop John Fisher (ca. 1469–1535) or Thomas More (1478–1535) or even Erasmus were involved. However, current consensus is that the work was in fact largely Henry's own, though Lee may have influenced certain passages and More made stylistic revisions to the finished whole. See Fraenkel, *Assertio Septem Sacramentorum*, pp. 17–23; Neelak Serawlook Tjernagel, *Henry VIII and the Lutherans: A Study in Anglo-Lutheran Relations from 1521 to 1547* (St. Louis: Concordia, 1965), p. 10.

[31] I.e., by exemplifying the attack of the kings of the earth against the Lord which is described in Psalm 2.

[32] *Weih character*. Medieval theology proposed that certain sacraments—namely, Baptism, confirmation, and holy orders—imprinted an "indelible" character on the soul. See Aquinas, *ST*, 3 q. 63 (Blackfriars 56:76–99). Particularly at stake in the polemic against Luther was his rejection of the indelible character of clerical ordination: see *Babylonian Captivity* (1520), LW 36:110–11, 117.

Thomists,[33] so that everyone who could understand perceived that the new patron of the Roman see had gotten smeared with soot.[34]

But because the king was occupied with English affairs and had not delved very deeply into Holy Scripture, our doctor fairly excoriated[35] this English author, just as he had seen in Erfurt during his years as a student, when they would excoriate and "depose" doctoral candidates after Vespers on the evening before receiving the doctorate, so that they would learn to accustom themselves to being patient and put to the test.[36] In the event, it became evident that this seraphic doctor[37] was not really concerned with religion after all.

Of course, it is true what the wise old Germans say in their proverb: "If anyone is able to forget his previous wife quickly, he will not love the new one for long."[38] Likewise, therefore, if anyone has never taken his first religion seriously, the one in which he was nursed and cradled, neither will he remain steadfast in a new religion, even if he adopts a new creed every year. How often in our days this proverb has proven to be very true! The Holy Spirit knows best how he should speak of everyone.

So it usually happens if someone abandons his calling and wants to mingle in unfamiliar affairs. Secular lords should protect and defend land and people, maintain law and justice, be gracious and benevolent. The Lord Christ says, *Vos non sic* ["Not so with you"] [Luke 22:26]. Apostles and pastors, who have the mandate to do so, are to devote themselves to the Word and prayer, as St. Peter says [Acts 6:4], write books, explain Scripture, be forceful in driving their teaching home to their opponents and in shutting up their snouts, as Christ does with the Epicurean Sadducees [cf. Matt. 22:23–33].[39]

Vos etiam non sic ["Not so with you either"], said Dr. Luther when a ruler sent him a book in which he catechized him up and down about faith

---

[33] Cf. above, Mathesius, *History*, p. 135.

[34] *Against King Henry of England* (1522), WA 10/2:180–222 (LW 61), and in German, WA 10/2:227–62. Luther's dedication is dated July 15, 1522. Cf. LW 35:128 n. 7.

[35] *vesperiert . . . auß*, a verb derived from the academic ceremony described below.

[36] In the evening ceremony of "deposition" [*depositio/deponierung*], the professors confronted the doctoral candidate in theology with his faults and failures. See *DWB*, s.v. "vesperieren." This recollection of Luther's student days in Erfurt seems to be preserved uniquely by Mathesius. Cf. *Table Talk* no. 4714 (1539), LW 54:362–63; no. 5024 (1540), WA TR 4:619; no. 7033 (n.d.), WA TR 6:347 (on depositions in Wittenberg).

[37] "Seraphic doctor" was usually the honorific for Bonaventure (see below, p. 456 n. 204); here it may be used with mocking reference to the older Henry's physiognomy.

[38] For the proverb, see Loesche, *Mathesius: Ausgewählte Werke*, 1:91.

[39] Both the Sadducees and the Epicureans denied life after death. Cf. Luther, *On the Jews and Their Lies* (1543), LW 47:227.

and good works. For as Christ says of His preachers, "You are not to be like rulers," so also the opposite applies to rulers: "You are not to be like preachers." Each is to do and perform what God has laid upon him: Preachers are to teach and pray; rulers are to defend and protect; the common man is to attend to his trade, business, mining, and farming and diligently go to [hear] God's Word, as well as confessing it when asked. Rulers help to nurse and nourish church and school with their breasts [Isa. 49:23].[40] Thus everyone has his hands full of things to do, and at the same time each one can be saved through faith in Jesus Christ.

Our doctor dedicated this book of his against King Henry to Count Sebastian Schlick[41] because this noble opponent of his and many others relentlessly called Dr. Luther a Bohemian or Wycliffite[42] heretic and could only imagine that, in the end, he would seek his refuge in this kingdom[43] and rekindle his condemned and burned heresy from the drenched ashes of John Hus.[44]

|But because Dr. Luther was certain that Hus' doctrine had been unjustly condemned and that our noble Bohemians, who remained steadfast in the doctrine of Hus, had been unfairly declared heretics by the Roman

---

[40] For this long-established application of Isa. 49:23 to the protection of the church by kings, see, e.g., *Lectures on Genesis* (1535–45/1544–54), LW 8:63; *Lectures on Psalm 45* (1532/1533–34), LW 12:290; *Table Talk* no. 4007 (1538), LW 54:309.

[41] Count Sebastian Schlick (1470–1527), of the Elbogen line of Schlicks, was a cousin of Stephan Schlick of the Schlackenwerth line (see above, p. 138 n. 136), who was the founding patron of Joachimsthal. On the genealogy of the Schlick family, see Karl Siegl, "Zur Geschichte der 'Thalergroschen': Ein Beitrag zur Historiographie des St. Joachimstaler Bergwerks- und Münzwesens," *Mitteilungen des Vereines für Geschichte der Deutschen in Böhmen* 50 (1911/12): 198–228, the family tree after p. 220; and Brown, *Singing the Gospel*, pp. 32, 218. Since the end of the fifteenth century, the Schlick family had been divided into three branches, centered in the Bohemian towns of Elbogen, Schlackenwerth, and Falkenau. Sebastian, whom Luther addressed in the preface as the "most Christian layman" (WA 10/2:182), had installed a Lutheran preacher and instituted an Evangelical church order already in 1521. A month prior to Luther's dedicatory letter of July 15, in June 1522, King Louis II of Bohemia (r. 1506–26) had held an assembly considering ecclesiastical reunion with Rome. Luther likely hoped to fortify the Bohemians against this. See Brecht 2:72–74. See also below, Mathesius, *History*, p. 604.

[42] That is, a follower of John Hus (see the introduction above, pp. xxxvii–xxxviii and n. 103 there) or John Wycliffe: see Fraenkel, ed., *Assertio Septem Sacramentorum*, pp. 107, 109, 237. Wycliffe (ca. 1320–84) was an English theologian who taught that the true Church consisted only of the number of the predestined, denied transubstantiation, and insisted on the sole authority of the Bible in matters of doctrine. His works were an influence on Hus. Wycliffe was posthumously condemned by the Council of Constance together with Hus in 1415. See *ODCC*, 3rd ed., s.v. "Wycliffe, John."

[43] Fraenkel, *Assertio Septem Sacramentorum*, pp. 136, 237.

[44] Hus' ashes were scattered in the Rhine. On Henry's Hussite accusations against Luther, see Haberkern, *Patron Saint and Prophet*, pp. 164–65; for Henry's speculation that Luther would flee to Bohemia, see Fraenkel, *Assertio Septem Sacramentorum*, p. 136.

crowd, and because there were many well-disposed lords in this land who
sought counsel and consolation from him, he sent his book to Elbogen. In
like manner, he later (in the same year that I came to Joachimsthal) sent
a reassuring message to Count Hieronymus and Lorenz Schlick:[45] that
the Sacramentarians and Anabaptists who wanted to sneak into this new
mining town and make their nest here should not be tolerated.[46] I saw in our
old church the public mandate issued by the two Lords Schlick against the
fanatics[47] and have recently seen Dr. Martin's own autograph letter in which
the Christian count, the sainted Lord Stephan Schlick, is also mentioned
with high esteem.[48]

Some years later the treatise against the Sabbatarians and mamelukes[49]
who let themselves be circumcised by the Jews was published.[50] The treatise
is addressed to Count Wolf Schlick of Falkenau[51] under the name of a "good
friend," as I have ascertained from three fine letters in the doctor's handwriting, in the keeping of the aforementioned lord.[52]

---

[45] Hieronymus and Lorenz Schlick were the younger brothers of Stephan Schlick (see
above, p. 138 n. 136 and p. 208 n. 41) in the Schlackenwerth line. After Stephan's death at the
Battle of Mohačs in 1526, Hieronymus and Lorenz ruled Joachimsthal jointly, in alternating
years.

[46] Luther to Counts Hieronymus and Lorenz Schlick, October 9, 1532, WA Br 6:372–73.

[47] The older church in Joachimsthal had been built in 1516; after the dedication of the
new church in 1537, it became the chapel for the cemetery and hospital. On the Joachimsthal
mandate against the Sacramentarians and Anabaptists, see Mathesius, *Chronica*, 1531 (where
the date is probably in error); Brown, *Singing the Gospel*, p. 35.

[48] On Stephan Schlick, see above, p. 138 n. 136. The oldest form of Luther's 1532 letter to
Hieronymus and Lorenz Schlick available to the Weimar editors was a copy in the Zwickau
Ratsschulbibliothek; the autograph seen by Mathesius may have been kept in the Joachimsthal
castle Burg Freudenstein, which was destroyed during the Thirty Years' War, or it may have
been among the three manuscript letters shown to Mathesius by Count Wolfgang Schlick (see
below, n. 52).

[49] See above, p. 199 n. 91.

[50] *Against the Sabbatarians* (1538), LW 47:57–98.

[51] Wolfgang Schlick (ca. 1500–1556), of the Falkenau line, was a cousin of Sebastian,
Hieronymus, and Lorenz Schlick. His brother Christoph had served as rector of the University
of Wittenberg in 1520–21: see Brown, *Singing the Gospel*, p. 32.

[52] *wie ich bey genantem Herrn drey gute brieff Doctors handschrifft darvon gesehen habe.*
Mathesius' account here (and below, *History*, p. 605) is the source identifying Wolfgang Schlick
as the addressee of *Against the Sabbatarians* (see LW 47:59; WA 50:310). Which three letters
from Luther Mathesius was shown by Count Wolfgang is uncertain. That one of them was an
autograph of *Against the Sabbatarians* is strongly implied here; Loesche suggests that the other
letters were autographs of the 1522 dedicatory epistle for *Against Henry of England* addressed
to Sebastian Schlick and of the 1532 letter on the Anabaptists to Hieronymus and Lorenz,
which would exhaust Luther's public and private correspondence to the Schlicks as it survives
(see *LH²*, p. 492). However, Mathesius elsewhere (see below, *History*, pp. 604–5) distinguishes

It was God's will to build in these Bohemian mountains a special city for His Gospel, under the Schlick lords. Satan would have liked to prevent this by means of monks, fanatics, wandering and infiltrating preachers, rebels, and evil books, and would have brought the blessed and peaceful doctrine into suspicion among prominent people, but our God has preserved His Word here along with good civil discipline and good ordinances, down to the present day, with the support and good testimony of Dr. Luther.[53] I make mention of this in honor both of this valley and of our old Schlick lords[54] and of this laudable kingdom of Bohemia, for they have helped promote the doctor's teaching with many good books from the library of the von Hassensteins[55] and from [other] good people, and have confessed the doctrine of Hus, and helped deflect the title of "heretic" onto the godless crowd of Roman courtiers.

Meanwhile, when King Henry had put his quill away again and was gradually beginning to think about other ways he might defend his new

---

the 1532 letter from the three in Wolfgang's possession. Also possible, then, would be an autograph of Luther's 1523 treatise *Concerning the Ministry*, addressed as an open letter to the Bohemian estates and dated the same day as the letter to Sebastian (see WA 10/2:171 and below, p. 215 and n. 88 there). Perhaps most likely (especially if *darvon* is to be translated as "on the same subject") would be Luther's treatise *On the Jews and Their Lies* (1543), LW 47:121–306, which is framed as a letter to an anonymous "Dear sir" (or "lord") "and good friend" (LW 47:137, 305), just as in the case of *Against the Sabbatarians*, and was prompted once again by Wolfgang's reports of Jewish proselytizing in Bohemia: cf. *Table Talk* no. 4795 (1541), WA TR 4:517; the introduction by Franklin Sherman, LW 47:133; and the introduction by Ferdinand Cohrs and Oskar Brenner, WA 53:412–14. Later in the series of sermons, however, when Mathesius discusses *On the Jews and Their Lies* (below, *History*, pp. 507–8, he connects it with *Against the Sabbatarians* as having been provoked by Jewish books sent to Luther by "a count in this land" but does not name Wolfgang Schlick or claim to have seen Luther's autograph. A final possibility would be additional correspondence from Luther dealing with Wolfgang's reports that did not survive for incorporation in sixteenth-century or modern printed editions.

[53] In addition to Luther's 1532 letter to Hieronymus and Lorenz Schlick, see the catalog of Luther's connections with Joachimsthal below, *History*, pp. 603–8.

[54] In 1545 the Schlicks had been stripped of their rights in Joachimsthal by the Hapsburg Ferdinand I, as king of Bohemia: see *Table Talk* no. 6310 (1545), WA TR 5:595; Brown, *Singing the Gospel*, p. 40.

[55] The Bohemian nobleman Bohleslaw Felix von Hassenstein (1517–83), of Hussite background, was appointed to administer Joachimsthal's mines after the removal of the Schlicks. He and his wife, Margaretha von Plauen (d. 1555), were patrons of the Lutheran church in Joachimsthal. Among other benefactions, Margaretha contributed the works of Luther to the town library, and Mathesius was allowed to consult texts, including Hussite manuscripts, in the Hassenstein library. See Brown, *Singing the Gospel*, pp. 45–46, 117, 227 n. 27, and 264 n. 66. Mathesius' funeral sermon for Margaretha von Hassenstein is edited in Loesche, *Mathesius: Ausgewählte Werke*, 4:21–41; cf. the encomium in his preface to the *De Profundis*: Loesche, *Mathesius: Ausgewählte Werke*, 4:663.

title while also taking revenge on the pope,[56] the empire held a diet in Nürnberg in the absence of Emperor Charles, who had business to take care of in his hereditary lands and with his neighbors.[57] In the end, they underscored in red the verse in Psalm 68: *Dispergit Deus qui bella volunt* ["God scatters those who desire war"] [Ps. 68:30].[58] Here the pope waited for his chance and sent his legate *a latere* to the diet.[59] He solicited many princes and cities with his letters, struck some good chords,[60] and spoke flattering words.[61] He strongly urged them to concern themselves with the Knights of Rhodes[62] and the kingdom of Hungary,[63] which were being sorely pressed and besieged by the Turks at this time. In addition to these things, he did not want the German Empire to allow the resolution and edict of its great leaders [at the Diet of Worms] to be forgotten, but to help

---

[56] Henry was increasingly preoccupied with securing the annulment of his marriage to Catherine of Aragon, though the case was not formally advanced until 1527. His pursuit of an annulment put him at odds with the papacy, which had originally granted a dispensation for the marriage because Catherine was the widow of his older brother, Arthur. In any event, the writing of a response on Henry's behalf to Luther's *Against King Henry of England* was delegated to Thomas More, whose *Responsio ad Lutherum* appeared in 1523: see John M. Headley, ed., *The Yale Edition of the Complete Works of Thomas More*, trans. Sister Scholastica Mandeville (New Haven, CT: Yale University Press, 1969), vol. 5.

[57] The so-called Second Diet of Nürnberg, held from November 1522 to February 1523. Brecht 2:109.

[58] Charles had returned to Spain from the summer of 1522 until 1529. He was engaged in war with France over holdings in northern Italy, culminating in his victory over King Francis I (r. 1515–47) at Pavia in 1525. See Brandi, *Emperor Charles V*, book 2, chapter 1, pp. 181–236; and Sleidanus, *De statu religionis* (1558), book 3, p. 69.

[59] Cardinal Francesco Chieregati (1479–1539) had been sent to the Diet of Nürnberg as plenipotentiary legate by Pope Adrian VI (r. 1522–23). See Bietenholz and Deutscher, *Contemporaries of Erasmus*, 1:301.

[60] *zeucht gute seyten auff*; literally: "strung good strings."

[61] A copy of the papal letter (breve) to the Bamberg city council was diverted to Luther in Wittenberg, where he published it with his own mocking afterword: see afterword to Chieregati and Pope Adrian VI, *Papal Breve against Luther* (1523), LW 59:37–42, and the introduction by Benjamin T. G. Mayes there.

[62] The Knights of St. John or Knights Hospitaller had established themselves in Rhodes since the fourteenth century. Under siege at the time of the opening of the diet, by December 1522 they had been forced to surrender Rhodes to the Ottoman sultan Suleiman the Magnificent (r. 1520–66). Cf. LW 59:143 n. 27.

[63] Belgrade had fallen in August 1521, and Hungary lay exposed to the Ottoman advance.

suppress and stamp out Luther's doctrine.[64] However, the holy empire had learned its lesson in Worms[65] and now knew how to discern the Roman ruses and tricks, so they gave the pope's legate a fitting response.[66] Among other things, they reiterated (as had already been discussed at Worms)[67] that the pope should consent to have the annates and some lapsed benefices return to the empire[68] in order to muster resources against the archenemy of the Roman Empire and make it possible to declare war against the Turk and carry it out successfully in the long term. Likewise, the empire put eighty-eight[69] articles into writing, which were later published with a foreword by Dr. Luther.[70] There the German princes themselves deliver quite a good sermon, preaching Law to the pope and his clergy. They complain in earnest about many manifest and proven burdens and ask that His Holiness the Pope would look into these matters with fatherly goodwill, so that the churches and pulpits might be better supplied, and dangerous abuses and ceremonies abolished, and so that mendicant priories, indulgence peddlers, and members of the Curia, along with [their] simony[71] and unchastity, could be abolished by a Christian reformation or free council.

Reasonable and urgent entreaties such as these should certainly not be allowed to die down, because they redound to the great and eternal honor of

---

[64] On January 3, 1523, the papal legate Chieregati presented Pope Adrian VI's demand that the empire implement the Edict of Worms. See Sleidanus, *De statu religionis* (1558), books 3–4, pp. 69–72, 75–78, 86–87, 89–95. Brecht 2:109–10.

[65] Literally, "had heard a good sermon."

[66] The complete acts of the diet are edited in *DRA* 3:214–938.

[67] I.e, in the *Gravamina* ["burdens"] of Worms, a list of 104 complaints, chiefly against the papacy, which were approved even by Luther's firmest opponents at Worms in 1521. See *DRA* 2:661–704; Gerald Strauss, ed. and trans., *Manifestations of Discontent in Germany on the Eve of the Reformation: A Collection of Documents* (Bloomington: Indiana University Press, 1985), pp. 52–63. On the *Gravamina* of the diets throughout the 1520s, see also Rosemarie Aulinger and Annelies Grundmann, eds., *Die Beschwerden der deutschen Nation auf den Reichstagen der Reformationszeit (1521–1530)*, *DRA* 21.

[68] Annates were the income of the entire first year of an ecclesiastical benefice, to be presented by the newly installed cleric to his superior (here, annates due from bishops to the pope); lapsed benefices were ecclesiastical positions which, having remained vacant for a period of time, had come, together with their income, under papal control.

[69] In fact, seventy-four articles, as numbered in the modern edition, differing only slightly from the *Gravamina* of Worms. See *DRA* 3:645–88. Several of the *gravamina* on which Luther made specific comment are translated in LW 60:185–201.

[70] See Luther, preface, marginal glosses, and afterword to *Legation of Pope Adrian VI* (1538), LW 60:185–201, and the introduction by Timothy Maschke there.

[71] The sin of simony, named after Simon Magus' attempt to purchase the Holy Spirit from the apostles (Acts 8:18), was defined under canon law as the attempt to obtain or confer spiritual goods or (clerical) office for payment; see, e.g., Denzinger, nos. 354, 358, 359, 364, 400.

the Holy German Empire, now and on the Last Day, and help to confirm Dr. Luther's books against the spiritual estate falsely so called.[72]

The manifold business of this imperial diet extended into the year 1523, when a recess was finally adopted and came to Doctor Luther in Wittenberg.[73] He obediently accepted the recess and helped explain it correctly in opposition to its false interpreters.[74] He was cautiously content with it, because this recess postponed the controversial discussion about religious matters to a future Christian and free council in Germany, and at the same time expressly stated that the Gospel of Jesus Christ should be preached by competent and duly called people in accordance with Holy Scripture and the writings of the pure fathers.

Seeing that the laudable German Empire meeting at the imperial diet had dealt so well with this business and had presented its petitions on many subjects of practical importance to the pope, in seriousness and with all dutiful submission, and had also put the brakes on[75] the previous edicts, Dr. Luther was resolved faithfully to attend to his pulpit and professor's chair[76] at home in peace, as a Christian doctor and duly appointed professor and interpreter in the laudable university, and as a called ecclesiast[77] and preacher of the church in Wittenberg. He called the people to true repentance, taught what sin is and the wages of sin, testified that the blood of Jesus Christ is the only cleansing and payment for the sin of the whole world, exhorted and urged them to a good conscience and true faith, which is active in love

---

[72] See above, p. 202 n. 6.

[73] The final resolution (called a "recess" [*Abschied*]) of the diet was adopted on February 9, 1523: *DRA* 3:736–59. The third article, responding to the pope on religious matters (pp. 745–48), instead of reaffirming the Edict of Worms (see above, p. 180 n. 68), stipulated that the pope should summon a free Christian council on German soil within a year's time and that meanwhile nothing new should be published by Luther or his adherents, that preaching should be restricted to the "pure Gospel in accordance with the writings approved by the Church," and that those abandoning vows of celibacy should not be subject to secular punishment. See the introduction by Timothy Maschke, LW 60:186–87; Brecht 2:110. Luther received the text of the recess by March 8: see Luther to Spalatin, March 8, 1523, WA Br 3:41.

[74] See *Against the Corrupters and Falsifiers of the Imperial Mandate* (1523), LW 59:53–64, which includes summaries of the chief points of the recess, and the introduction by Benjamin T. G. Mayes there for a full discussion of the 1522–23 Diet of Nürnberg.

[75] *ein hemschuch angeleget*

[76] *Cathedren*; cf. above, Mathesius, *History*, p. 182.

[77] *Ecclesiastes*. Luther had adopted this title, in lieu of the traditional ones that had been officially stripped from him by the papal bulls and imperial edict, at the beginning of *Against the Spiritual Estate of the Pope and the Bishops* (1523), LW 39:247. He also used it, e.g., in his *Ordinance of a Common Chest* (1523), LW 45:169, and *Letter of Consolation to the People of Miltenberg* (1524), LW 43:103.

[Gal. 5:6] and makes itself visible and perceptible.[78] Again: he admonished them to obedience as subjects and warned against the false doctrine of the monks and of the infiltrators who had fallen away from the spoken Word and appealed to their own spirit and dreams. Again: he warned against the iconoclasts and patrons of carnal freedom, some of whom attacked and nullified all secular law and outward discipline in the state and the churches. Some even wanted to reestablish the civil law of Moses and the Jews.[79] He also instructed[80] the people and used God's Word to urge them toward the entire Supper,[81] teaching them to receive it often with contrite and believing hearts.[82] Similarly, this year he also preached on the Epistles of St. Peter,[83] besides publishing the good book *That Jesus Christ Was Born a Jew*—of the tribe of Judah and David, from a chaste and holy virgin.[84] Additionally, he helped to reestablish the proper distribution of the Supper and to supply his church with competent people, who helped him preach, administer the Sacrament and absolve the people, and visit and comfort the sick.[85] Likewise, he helped reestablish singing by students and laity with his fine hymns from

---

[78] Mathesius is summarizing Luther's preaching and publishing activity from 1522 to 1525, surveying both works which he has already mentioned specifically as well as those which he is about to discuss in the remainder of the sermon. See *Eight Sermons at Wittenberg* (1522), LW 51:67–100; *Sincere Admonition* (1522), LW 45:51–74; *Temporal Authority* (1523), LW 45:75–129; *Avoiding the Doctrines of Men* (1522), LW 35:125–53; *Letter to the Princes of Saxony* (1524), LW 40:45–59; *Open Letter to the Town of Mühlhausen* (1524), WA 15:238–40.

[79] Karlstadt, in addition to opposing images partly on the basis of an appeal to the Mosaic Law, also advocated restoring the Christian observance of the Sabbath: see Karlstadt, "On the Sabbath," in Furcha, *Essential Carlstadt*, pp. 317–38. Cf. Luther, *Against the Heavenly Prophets* (1525), LW 40:92–98; *How Christians Should Regard Moses* (1525), LW 35:155–74; Luther to Spalatin, March 14, 1524, LW 49:72–74.

[80] *Bericht*; or: "administered the Sacrament to."

[81] I.e., in both kinds. See above, Mathesius, *History*, pp. 159–60, 206.

[82] See *Receiving Both Kinds in the Sacrament* (1522), LW 36:231–67; *Ein Sermon am Gründonnerstag* (1523), WA 12:476–93 (Lenker 2:223–37); *Order of Mass and Communion* (1523), LW 53:15–40. See Brecht 2:123–24.

[83] *Sermons on 1 Peter* (1522), LW 30:1–145; *Sermons on 2 Peter* (1523/1524), LW 30:147–99; on the dating of these sermons, see the introduction by Jaroslav Pelikan, LW 30:ix–x.

[84] *That Jesus Christ Was Born a Jew* (1523), LW 45:195–229.

[85] In addition to responding to a large number of requests for Evangelical preachers beyond Wittenberg, Luther saw Bugenhagen (see the introduction above, pp. xxxvi–xxxvii) called as pastor of the Wittenberg town church in the fall of 1523. In May 1525, Luther ordained Georg Rörer (see above, p. xx n. 20) as an assistant clergyman ("deacon") for the Wittenberg church, the first new ordination in Wittenberg since the break with Rome. See Brecht 2:284.

Holy Scripture, in German and in Latin.[86] Many neighboring churches were very pleased by this and followed this Christian example.

Certain people from this kingdom of Bohemia also desired instruction about how they should supply their church with clergy.[87] So the doctor wrote a letter to the council in Prague,[88] in which he exhorts the whole world to beware of the pope's [indelible] character, chrism, and mark,[89] and that no one should consent to be ensnared or bound in any way to holding daily Masses or impossible celibacy, even if the clergy granted a dispensation to administer both kinds [in the Supper] to the laity.

Truly, dear friends, at this time Germany enjoyed a fine new beginning. For the writings and dealings of the Romanists had little weight, since no foundation in God's Word or [evidence of] episcopal care for souls could be found in them.

However, since Satan was unable to achieve anything by means of papistic murder and lies and was being daily driven out and overcome by the finger and power of God [Luke 11:20], he crept into desolate places and sought a place of refuge [cf. Matt. 12:43–45]. He employed more clever devils and entered into the new monks, who presented themselves in angelic holiness, without a cowl or tonsure, and passed themselves off as heavenly prophets.[90] They hypocritically boasted of having God's Spirit, relying on their dreams and secret revelations while mockingly and scornfully despising the spoken and written word of the prophets and apostles. They were especially hostile to the church and university in Wittenberg and babbled against them

---

[86] Luther's Latin *Order of Mass and Communion* (1523) called for vernacular singing (LW 53:36), and Luther began composing German hymns in the fall of 1523 and encouraging others to do so: see Luther to Spalatin, December 1523, LW 49:68–70. After appearing singly on broadsheets, the hymns were gathered into collections by printers in Nürnberg and Erfurt before the appearance of the first Wittenberg collection, the *Geystlich Gesangkbuchlin* of 1524, which included Latin hymns as well as German ones. See *Preface to the Wittenberg Hymnal* (1524), LW 53:315–16; Brecht 2:129–35; Robin Leaver, *The Whole Church Sings: Congregational Singing in Luther's Wittenberg* (Grand Rapids: Eerdmans, 2017).

[87] Since the pope had refused to approve an Utraquist archbishop of Prague, the see had been vacant since 1421, so that the Utraquist Bohemians had adopted the expedient of sending pastoral candidates to Italy to be ordained by bishops approved by the papacy. The Utraquist priest Gallus Cahera had come to Wittenberg in 1523 and prompted Luther to write his advice (see the next note and the introduction by Conrad Bergendoff, LW 40:5).

[88] *Concerning the Ministry* (1523), LW 40:3–44, dated November 13, 1523.

[89] On the *character indelibilis*, see above, p. 206 n. 32. On chrism, see above, p. 204 n. 18.

[90] "New monks" was a term Luther used for the Enthusiasts and Anabaptists: see *Sermon on the Mount* (1530–32/1532), LW 21:5, 259; *Lectures on Galatians* (1531/1535), LW 26:28; *Lectures on Psalm 45* (1532/1533–34), LW 12:274; *Against the Heavenly Prophets* (1525), LW 40:81, 205. "Heavenly prophets" was Luther's epithet for Karlstadt and his followers in particular (as in the title of his 1525 treatise), but Mathesius' description is probably intended to include the earlier "Zwickau prophets" of 1521–22 as well. See Brecht 2:158, 293–94.

in their corners. By means of these fanatics, these corner-preachers, these scorners and slanderers of the public preaching office and of all secular law, discipline, and order, and by means of secret agitators, Satan stirred up such great scandal and tumult that many people fell away from the Word. Other good hearts took serious offense at this dissension and unrest and came to regard the doctor's doctrine as suspicious.

The doctor, however, complained most vehemently about these instigators and false brethren and warned his territorial prince[91] and many cities[92] against their efforts to sneak in. He also published a public warning to all good Christians that they should be on guard against these seditious preachers and the devil's revolt, because God had earnestly commanded obedience as subjects.[93] Also, no one drawing the sword without command and wantonly attacking his authorities and the ordinance of God [Rom. 13:2] could preserve faith and good conscience [1 Tim. 1:19].

Our doctor was well acquainted with Satan's lies and murder [John 8:44] from Scripture and daily experience. Therefore, when he learned that the false brethren from every quarter wanted to make nests with their seditious doctrine on the Saale River and in the Harz Mountains,[94] and that Karlstadt would tolerate no criticism, shunned the light, and wantonly abandoned his call without any cause and had taken over the parish in Orlamünde[95] so that he would be able to pour out his embittered heart in a corner and take vengeance on the church in Wittenberg, Doctor Luther was sent to Jena at the prince's command, along with Master Wolfgang Stein,[96] court preacher

[91] See Luther to Spalatin, June 18, 1524, WA Br 3:304–5; *Letter to the Princes of Saxony* (1524), LW 40:45–59.

[92] *Open Letter to the Town of Mühlhausen* (1524), WA 15:238–40; *Letter to the Christians at Strassburg* (1524), LW 40:61–71.

[93] *Sincere Admonition* (1522), LW 45:51–74, which, however, was written at the end of 1522, before the appearance even of the "Zwickau prophets." In the first edition of Witt Ger 2 (1548), fols. 66v–71v, however, it appears between the *Open Letter to the Town of Mühlhausen* (1524) and the *Admonition to Peace* (1525) (LW 46:3–43). The 1551 and later editions of Witt Ger 2 rearrange the material in more nearly chronological order: see Aland, *Hilfsbuch*, p. 552.

[94] I.e., Karlstadt's parish at Orlamünde on the Saale and Thomas Münzer's (see below, p. 217 n. 98) parish at Allstedt in the Harz.

[95] On Karlstadt, see above, p. 154 n. 90.

[96] Wolfgang Stein was the court chaplain to Duke John (the future elector of Saxony: see below, pp. 225–26) in Weimar and spent time with Luther in Wittenberg in 1522. Cf. LW 49:15 n. 11; 40:107 n. 40. Luther carried on an extensive correspondence with him from late 1522 through 1524: see letters of December 11, 1522, WA Br 2:619–24; December 20, 1522, WA Br 2:638; March 2, 1523, WA Br 3:38–39; April 16, 1523, WA Br 3:60; May 17, 1523, WA Br 3:69; January 14, 1524, WA Br 3:233–34; March 9, 1524, WA Br 3:252–53; beginning of September 1524, LW 49:83–85; September 10, 1524, WA Br 3:344; October 11, 1524, WA Br 3:356.

in Weimar, to warn the people about these wandering corner-preachers and seditious spirits.[97]

Karlstadt was present at the doctor's sermon there, after which he had a conversation with Doctor Luther and took the sermon against the Allstedt[98] spirit as directed against himself.[99] But once the doctor had clarified his meaning, whereas Karlstadt gave obscure and inconsistent answers about his doctrine and intentions, then, after a far-ranging discussion, the doctor proposed to Karlstadt that he should put his case for iconoclasm into writing, as well as what he thought and taught about the Supper, or even, if he so pleased, to have them printed. Then he would counter with a proper answer, so that everyone would be able to tell and to judge what is the doctrine of Doctor Luther and what are the claims, dreams, and vacuous glosses of Karlstadt. Karlstadt agreed to this and later published his book, in which he attacked the presence of the Lord Christ in the Supper and interpreted the Lord's words maliciously and falsely.[100]

In response to this slanderous writing, the doctor published his treatise against Karlstadt and the heavenly prophets, who wanted to show that they were Christians by means of iconoclasm and the burning of images as well as with scorn for the spoken Word and the holy Sacrament.[101]

---

[97] Luther's sermon in Jena and subsequent conversation with Karlstadt took place on August 22, 1524. See *Wes sich Doctor Andreas Bodenstein von Karlstadt mit Doctor Martino Luther beredet zu Jena* (1524), WA 15:334–47, which seems to be Mathesius' primary source; see also *Against the Heavenly Prophets* (1525), LW 40:106–7.

[98] I.e., Thomas Münzer (ca. 1489–1525), who had been preacher in Allstedt, in the Harz Mountains, since 1523. In his previous ministry in Zwickau in 1520–21, he had been associated with the "Zwickau prophets," though he later distanced himself from them. Münzer preached that God's elect should extirpate the enemies of the Gospel and establish God's kingdom. In 1525, he assumed leadership of the militant peasants but was captured and executed after their defeat at Frankenhausen (see below, pp. 223–24). Luther was wary of Münzer from 1523 onward and regarded him as a "heavenly prophet" and "fanatic." See Ulrich Bubenheimer, "Müntzer, Thomas," *OER* 3:99–102. See also below, pp. 221–25; cf. Mathesius, *History*, pp. 238, 245.

[99] Luther's sermon had named the "spirit of Allstedt" (i.e., Münzer) as the author of sedition and murder, but identified the destruction of images, associated with Karlstadt, as one of the fruits of this spirit. See Brecht 2:159–60; Burnett, *Eucharistic Pamphlets of Andreas Bodenstein von Karlstadt*, p. 11. Despite real theological similarities between Karlstadt and Münzer, Karlstadt and his congregation in Orlamünde would explicitly reject Münzer's call for violence: see *The Statement of the People of Orlamünde to Those of Allstedt on the Christian Way to Fight* (1524), in Peter Matheson, ed. and trans., *The Collected Works of Thomas Müntzer* (Edinburgh: T&T Clark, 1988), pp. 93–94.

[100] Karlstadt in fact rapidly published several works, but Mathesius probably refers to the *Dialogue on the Horrible and Idolatrous Misuse of the Most Worthy Sacrament*: Burnett, *Eucharistic Pamphlets of Andreas Bodenstein von Karlstadt*, pp. 163–204. See also the introduction by Conrad Bergendoff, LW 40:75–76.

[101] *Against the Heavenly Prophets* (1525), LW 40:73–223.

But when Dr. Martin went to Orlamünde upon invitation[102] |and had a short conversation with the council and congregation there concerning their writing, the spirit of Allstedt and Karlstadt spoke up with very unseemly and impertinent words. They said that they had been well within their rights to take Karlstadt and had good warrant and right according to Scripture [cf. Exod. 20:4; Deut. 5:8] to tear the images out of the church. Dr. Luther rightfully contested Karlstadt's call and demonstrated that according to Scripture there was a distinction: Moses commanded the rejection only of those images to which God's name and authority had been attached and which the people were glorifying and calling upon as if they were God. Nonetheless, a cobbler came forward from the crowd and wagered that he could prove from Moses that all images were to be torn away. Dr. Luther wanted to hear this, so the cobbler replied, "God says, 'I want My bride to be naked and do not permit her to wear a nightgown.'"[103] When the doctor heard this and many other insane and fanatical kinds of talk, he took his leave. For he realized that the people had been bewitched and blinded by the fanatical spirits and that God's Word and all discipline had been lost among them.

I heard from the doctor himself that he was supposed to preach at that time in Kahla.[104] As it happened, these spirits had broken a crucifix to pieces and strewn it upon the pulpit. When the doctor discovered this, he was provoked at first, yet he mounted the pulpit nonetheless, scraped the pieces into a pile, and delivered an edifying sermon and faithful warning that they should preserve faith and good conscience in all subjection. He did not mention a single word about the shameless wantonness which they had shown him. For even on the devil one can inflict burning pain by scorning him at the opportune time.

After this our doctor hurried back to his church and defended the articles of Master Arsacius Seehofer from Munich, which had been condemned by the university in Ingolstadt.[105] |In addition, he wrote about both

---

[102] I.e., on August 24, 1524. "Upon invitation" may refer either to the commission from the elector to investigate (cf. above, p. 216) or to the letter which the Orlamünde congregation had sent to Luther while he was in Jena: see Brecht 2:160.

[103] According to Luther, *Against the Heavenly* Prophets (1525), LW 40:100–101, the cobbler based this claim on the words of Jesus in the Gospel. The cobbler's idea reflected Karlstadt's teaching that the soul had to come naked (i.e., without mediation of any external things) to be united with Christ. See Brecht 2:161.

[104] Luther preached at Kahla on August 23, 1524, the day before his arrival in Orlamünde: Brecht 2:160. See *Table Talk* no. 97 (1531), WA TR 1:37; no. 2051 (1531), WA TR 2:304.

[105] Arsacius Seehofer had studied with Melanchthon in Wittenberg in 1521. Returning to the University of Ingolstadt, he began using Melanchthon's materials in his lectures there. Seehofer was condemned by the university for heresy in September 1523 on the basis of

the papistic Canon and the secret Mass, in which they sacrifice even their unconsecrated bread and wine to our God, intending to reconcile the dead and the living with God.[106]

In the fall of the same year, 1524, the peasants revolted at Lake Constance; this rebellion was suppressed.[107] Not until the following year did the dreadful revolt of the peasants in Swabia, Lotharingia, and Franconia took place. A seditious doctor[108] had drafted twelve articles for them, which Dr. Luther refuted, with solid grounds from God's Word, while warning those who had been deceived against ruin.[109] For things have never turned out well for any rebel who has forgotten his obligation and oath to the authorities over him. God confirmed the authorities with the Word and obedient submission of His Son [e.g., Matt. 17:24–27; 22:21]; He also commanded every person to render obedience to the authorities over them with their body and property, for the sake of God's ordinance, their conscience, and punishment [cf. Romans 13].

In addition, [Luther] admonished the authorities not to lay false hands on God's Word, but rather to let themselves be chastened by it, as King David preaches in Psalm 2 [:10–12], and to deal reasonably with those who

---

seventeen theses drawn from his writings and was imprisoned in a cloister. His condemnation attracted the response of numerous Evangelical writers, including the Bavarian noblewoman Argula von Grumbach (ca. 1492–ca. 1554) as well as Luther's *Against the Blind and Insane Condemnation of Seventeen Articles* (1524), WA 15:95–140 (LW 71). See Brecht 2:88–89; Martin Brecht, "Seehofer, Arsacius," *BBKL* 15:1275–78; and (on Argula von Grumbach and Seehofer) Peter Matheson, ed., *Argula von Grumbach: A Woman's Voice in the Reformation* (Edinburgh: T&T Clark, 1995), introduction and pp. 56–95.

[106] *Abomination of the Secret Mass* (1525), LW 36:307–28. Mathesius (and Luther, LW 36:315) refer to "unconsecrated" bread and wine because the Canon of the Mass uses sacrificial language already before the consecration of the elements with the Words of Institution.

[107] Unrest began in 1524 in the territory of the counts of Lupfen, northwest of Lake Constance. Peasants used rent strikes to fight against serfdom and heavy taxation, showing their disdain for their subjugation under the feudal system as a whole. Peter Blickle, *The Revolution of 1525: The German Peasants' War from a New Perspective*, trans. Thomas A. Brady Jr. and H. C. Erik Midelfort (Baltimore: The Johns Hopkins University Press, 1981), pp. xiv–xv, 66. Here and throughout his account of the Peasants' War, Mathesius draws on the account in Sleidanus, *De statu religionis* (1558), book 4, pp. 107–8, 112–16, and book 5, pp. 117–24.

[108] Mathesius probably has in mind Balthasar Hubmaier (ca. 1485–1528; see below, p. 246 n. 84), an Ingolstadt doctor of theology who, after a period of sympathy with Ulrich Zwingli (1484–1531), became an Anabaptist leader. Although the *Twelve Articles* were sometimes ascribed to him by contemporaries, their primary author seems to have been the furrier Sebastian Lotzer (ca. 1490–ca. 1525). See Blickle, *Revolution of 1525*, p. 25. In fact, the articles strove for moderation and appealed explicitly to Luther and Melanchthon as judges. See LW 46:8–16; Brecht 2:174.

[109] *Admonition to Peace* (1525), LW 46:3–43. In fact, Luther acknowledged most of the complaints of the peasants to be just.

had been deceived, letting benevolence and mercy be mingled together, lest God in His wrath forcefully cut them off as well and devour them as tyrants. For there is no judge on earth so great that he cannot be judged by one who is higher.

But the peasants had stopped up their ears and pushed forward with diabolical audacity, yet still under the name and pretext of the Gospel. They attacked not only monasteries and clergymen but also the secular authorities over them. They made a count run a gauntlet of spears;[110] they burned and plundered the castles of noblemen. Because of this, Dr. Luther was moved to defend God's ordinance and the estate of governing authority and to condemn the peasants' wanton and bloodthirsty enterprise with ˡa very harsh book,[111] exhorting the daunted authorities that they should and could subdue and suppress such pernicious conflagration with the power of the sword.

Doctor [Luther] was severely reproached by the peasants and their ringleaders, and seditious preachers severely reproached the doctor on account of this, and many others were displeased by this vehemence and severity.

Afterward, however, the doctor offered a well-founded explanation of what had driven him to write this vehement and severe book.[112] Indeed, the outcome and experience helped provide testimony and confirmation that books of this kind are necessary against people like this who forget their oath and duty and turn against their authorities, are unable to do anything but steal and rob, and moreover want to use the Gospel to cover up and excuse their godless impertinence. God also took part in seeing the matter to a just conclusion, and watched over His representatives, so that the Swabian League quelled this revolt in Swabia, Franconia, and around Salzburg, and many fell in God's vengeance [Rom. 13:4]. Many sensible lords quelled their errant subjects with clemency and discretion.[113]

---

[110] Count Ludwig von Helfenstein (1493–1525), who led a force against the peasants at Weinsberg, was captured and forced to "run the gauntlet" of peasants' spears before being killed. The incident is related in Sleidanus, *De statu religionis* (1558), book 4, p. 114. See Tom Scott and Robert W. Scribner, eds. and trans., *The German Peasants' War: A History in Documents* (Atlantic Highlands, NJ: Humanities Press, 1991), p. 158.

[111] *Against the Robbing and Murdering Hordes of Peasants* (1525), LW 46:45–55.

[112] *Open Letter on the Harsh Book against the Peasants* (1525), LW 46:57–85. See Brecht 2:185–89.

[113] See *Vertrag zwischen dem löblichen Bund zu Schwaben und den zwei Haufen der Bauern vom Bodensee und Allgäu, mit Vorrede und Vermahnung* (1525), WA 18:335–43. The Swabian League was a peacekeeping federation in Upper Swabia that mediated disputes between peasants and lords. Although willing to use force if necessary, the league had proven willing to make concessions to peasants in the past. See Thomas F. Sea, "The Swabian League and Peasant Disobedience before the German Peasants' War of 1525," *SCJ* 30, no. 1 (Spring 1999): 89–111.

Our lord, the emperor, who was at the time archduke of Austria, was riding among his disobedient subjects in the mountains around Salzburg on a white horse, which was letting out one cry after another. When one of the rebels cried out that someone should keep the horse quiet until they had made their request, Archduke Ferdinand said, "When my horse makes itself heard, it is far more fitting that you should keep quiet."[114]

Elector Frederick of Saxony also used good and princely words to quell his subjects whom the spirit of Allstedt[115] had stirred up against him, and he brought them back to their [proper] station. Likewise, in some of his letters written shortly before his death, which are still extant, he wrote in a princely and Christian manner to his brother, Duke John, admonishing him to exercise leniency and discretion and giving him a brotherly reminder not to become tangled up with the clergy, who had little goodwill toward either of them.[116] Then, after *Misericordia Domini*,[117] in Lochau,[118] the aforementioned elector took his blessed departure from this poor world in true invocation and confession of the Lord Christ.[119]

It is well said, "Great people, great virtue."[120] Gracious and kind words are able to pacify and remove much wrath and indignation; they show that by grace our God adorns great people with special gifts. For example, it is said of Emperor Frederick III that he always commanded his judges and jurors to mingle in mercy whenever they had to deliberate on capital punishment.

After the death of this precious and most wise elector, the seditious and mendacious spirit of the heavenly prophets broke out in Thuringia. For in Zwickau, Thomas Münzer,[121] alongside and in opposition to Egranus, was

---

[114] The peasants and miners around Salzburg had taken control of the city from the archbishop Matthäus Lang (see above, p. 151 n. 72) in June 1525 with the goal of transforming the territorial government. Despite multiple attempts at truces with Lang, only the military intervention of the Swabian League was able to end the rebellion. See Blickle, *Revolution of 1525*, pp. 101–5. This story about Ferdinand and his horse also appears in Mathesius' funeral sermon for Ferdinand: Loesche, *Mathesius: Ausgewählte Werke*, 4:371.

[115] I.e., Thomas Münzer. See above, p. 217 n. 98.

[116] These letters were included in Witt Ger 9 (1557), fol. 216r–v. The letter quoted by Mathesius is Elector Frederick to Duke John of Saxony, April 14, 1525: see StL 16:111.

[117] *Misericordia Domini*, the Second Sunday of Easter, fell on April 30; Frederick died on the following Friday, May 5, 1525.

[118] Lochau Castle, renamed Annaburg in 1573, is situated 35 km southeast of Wittenberg.

[119] Frederick died shortly after receiving the Lord's Supper in both kinds for the first time. See Brecht 2:183. On Luther's funeral preaching for Frederick, see below, p. 225 and n. 146 there.

[120] Wander 3:76, "Leute" no. 695.

[121] On Münzer, see above, p. 217 n. 98. On his role in the Peasants' War, see Hans-Jürgen Goertz, *Thomas Müntzer: Apocalyptic Mystic and Revolutionary*, trans. Jocelyn Jaquiery,

ventilating his opinions in the pulpit without any discretion.[122] Finding the light too bright for his eyes, he set off (as people tend to do) in search of a corner and followers.[123] And when he was next driven out from Allstedt, he secretly crept into Nürnberg to make his nest there, but this cocoon of his was also destroyed, so he returned to his old haven, like the unclean spirit in Luke 11 [:24].[124] At the instigation of certain rebellious citizens with whom he had previously colluded, he made his way to Mühlhausen,[125] rebuking at the same time both the pope in Rome and the Wittenbergers.[126] He abandoned the Word, and together with his adherents he appealed to his revelations and spiritual dreams, expected signs from heaven, claimed a new holiness consisting of "refining" and mortification of the flesh;[127] he

---

ed. Peter Matheson (Edinburgh: T&T Clark, 1993). After Münzer's defeat, Luther published a selection of his correspondence with Luther's own preface, afterword, and notes: *Terrifying Story of Münzer* (1525), LW 59:120–26 (see the introduction by Carolyn Schneider there). Münzer's involvement in the Peasants' War is also narrated in Sleidanus, *De statu religionis* (1558), book 5, pp. 117–24, and by Melanchthon in *Die Historia Thome Müntzers*, included in Witt Ger 2 (1548), fols. 98r–104r: see Ludwig Fischer, ed., *Die Lutherischen Pamphlete gegen Thomas Müntzer* (Tübingen: Niemeyer, 1976), pp. 27–42.

[122] Johannes Wildenauer of Eger, called Sylvius Egranus (ca. 1485–1535), was a preacher of Erasmian humanist sympathies serving in Zwickau from 1517 to 1520; during his absence to visit Wittenberg, among other places, in 1520, Münzer was installed in Zwickau as interim replacement on Luther's recommendation. As a result of Münzer's open attacks, Egranus left Zwickau to become pastor in Joachimsthal from 1521–23, returning again the year before his death (1534–35). On Egranus, see Brecht 2:35–36; Bietenholz and Deutscher, *Contemporaries of Erasmus*, 1:425; Harry Vredeveld, "Egranus, Sylvius," OER 2:31; and Münzer's own sarcastic *Propositions Attributed to Egranus*, in Matheson, *Collected Works of Thomas Müntzer*, pp. 380–83. Münzer was dismissed by the Zwickau city council in April 1521.

[123] Münzer traveled to Prague from Zwickau, seeking to attract support there (see *Prague Manifesto*, in Matheson, *Collected Works of Thomas Müntzer*, pp. 352–79). By 1523, after further travels, Münzer was called to Allstedt, where he remained until August 1524.

[124] After leaving Allstedt, Münzer stayed briefly in Mühlhausen (until he was expelled at the end of September 1524), and then, after a short sojourn in Nürnberg (see Goertz, *Thomas Müntzer*, pp. 165–68), Münzer returned to his native Thuringia.

[125] Returning to Mühlhausen in the early spring of 1525, Münzer was supported by the preacher Henry Pfeiffer (see below, p. 223 n. 130) and a group of citizens who sought to transform the town into a theocracy: see the *Mühlhausen Articles* of September 1524 and Münzer's letter to the church in Mühlhausen, September 22, 1524, in Matheson, *Collected Works of Thomas Müntzer*, pp. 455–59 and 132–34; and Luther, *Open Letter to the Town of Mühlhausen* (1524), WA 15:238–40.

[126] See, e.g., Münzer's *Protestation or Proposition* (1523) and his *Vindication and Refutation* (1524), directed against the "unspiritual, soft-living flesh in Wittenberg," in Matheson, *Collected Works of Thomas Müntzer*, pp. 183–209, 324–50.

[127] *entgröbung und tödtung des fleisches*. By *entgröbung*, Münzer meant the removal of "coarse" [*grob*] external sins: see Luther, *Letter to the Christians at Strassburg* (1524), LW 40:70; *Lectures on Genesis* (1535–45/1544–54), LW 6:261; *Table Talk* no. 1204 (1530), WA TR

burned images, stormed and plundered the monasteries, attracted a following, formed a seditious union,[128] deposed the old council, chose others, plopped himself down with them on their cushion, pronounced judgment, and proclaimed as a heavenly prophet that they should 'attack the godless. He courted the support of the miners in Mansfeld and called them to arms, and having armed himself with the peasants' swine goads, threshing flails, and pitchforks, he went to Frankenhausen and took the field with the peasants.[129] His companion, Pfeiffer,[130] piped for the common man to dance and sounded the attack. The neighboring princes, whose responsibility it was to punish such rebels, entered the field and sought peaceful ways of calling back and pacifying the deceived peasants.[131]

But Münzer and his false god hardened their hearts and closed their ears with their heavenly consolation as he rode around his company: The enemy's cannonballs would be turned aside, and some of them he would catch in his sleeve.[132] God would be with them and send them fortune and victory from heaven; therefore, He was causing a rainbow to shine for them even now.[133] Then, contrary to the law of nations and all the laws of war, he seized the young boy of noble birth sent as messenger and had him miserably killed.[134] Upon this, the landgrave of Hesse exhorted his people with a princely and comforting address and charged against weaponry and host

---

1:598–600; Münzer, *Deutsch-Evangelische Messe*, in *Schriften und Briefe*, ed. Günther Franz (Gütersloh: Gütersloher G. Mohn, 1968), p. 162.

[128] *Gewerckschaft*; a technical term for a union of miners.

[129] Münzer arrived at Frankenhausen on May 12, 1525: Goertz, *Thomas Müntzer*, p. 181. For more on Münzer's involvement at Frankenhausen, see Goertz, *Thomas Müntzer*, pp. 181–86.

[130] Henry Pfeiffer ["Piper"] was a former Cistercian monk who preached sermons in Mühlhausen highly critical of the church. He was banished along with Münzer and thereafter followed him to Nürnberg, back to Mühlhausen, and finally to Frankenhausen, where he was executed following the battle. See Brecht 2:155–57. For his relationship with Münzer, see Abraham Friesen, *Thomas Muentzer, a Destroyer of the Godless: The Making of a Sixteenth-Century Religious Revolutionary* (Berkeley: University of California Press, 1990), pp. 239–42.

[131] Count Albert of Mansfield (see above, p. xxviii n. 54), a Lutheran, had written to the peasants offering to hear their grievances, and the peasants responded positively until Münzer demanded Count Albert's public humiliation. Münzer's letter was included in Luther's *Terrifying Story of Münzer* (1525). See the introduction by Carolyn Schneider, LW 59:122–23.

[132] See Luther, afterword to *Terrifying Story of Münzer* (1525), LW 59:125; Friesen, *Thomas Muentzer*, pp. 213–14, 261.

[133] The claim of catching projectiles and the rainbow appear in the account of Münzer's sermon to the peasants in Sleidanus, *De statu religionis* (1558), book 5, p. 121. Under the rainbow on Münzer's banner were written the words "This is the sign of God's eternal covenant [cf. Gen. 9:12–17]; those who wish to join this covenant must step under it." See Friesen, *Thomas Muentzer*, p. 260; Goertz, *Thomas Müntzer*, pp. 174, 186.

[134] Sleidanus, *De statu religionis* (1558), book 5, p. 122.

of the heavenly prophets at Frankenhausen, about five thousand of whom were slain, and many of whom were captured.[135] Münzer turned tail like a rabbit[136] and fled into the city; a nobleman found him lying in bed as if sick with a fever and identified him from several letters he found in Münzer's bags. Thus the agitator and captain of the peasants was captured, taken to Heldrungen,[137] and interrogated. Afterward, when he had confessed his sins and pleaded for those whom he had deceived, he was beheaded, along with his seditious Pfeiffer and some other wanton people.[138]

I have to mention another story in connection with this. When the captured rebels had been wretchedly and piteously bound together, a well-known, great lord saw a sturdy little peasant in the crowd. "Little man," he said, "which government do you like best now, that of the peasants or of the princes?" The poor man spoke with deep emotion, with a deep sigh: "My dear lord! No knife cuts more sharply than when one peasant becomes lord of another.[139] May God preserve our children, so that they may never give credence to renegade priests but may bless all princely governments their whole life long." These words pleased the lord, so he had them conveyed to the princes who were present and by his petition obtained the freedom of this peasant.

That is to say: A good word serves in good stead[140] and is like golden apples in a silver bowl if spoken at the right time [Prov. 25:11]. Thus the revolt was suppressed, though not without much bloodshed, serving as a testimony and eternal reminder that no one should hack away at what is above him, stir up rebellion, and become involved with rebels. For the [wood] chips fly back into the face of such people,[141] and they must die with bloody heads in accordance with God's ordinance, even as our doctor, as a true prophet of God, had prophesied to these and many other people and their agitators.

Now if anyone would like to put himself forward as a preacher in a salutary way, preserving his faith and conscience, let him wait for a legitimate

---

[135] Philip of Hesse's address, his charge, the aftermath of the battle, and Münzer's capture and interrogation are recounted in Sleidanus, *De statu religionis* (1558), book 5, pp. 122–24. Other accounts of the battle give the number of peasants killed variously between 4,000 and 6,000, with about 600 taken captive. See Friesen, *Thomas Muentzer*, p. 262.

[136] *wirffts Hasenpanier auff*; Wander 2:380, "Hasenpanier" no. 1.

[137] The castle at Heldrungen had previously been besieged by Münzer.

[138] See Münzer's *Vindication and Refutation* (1524), in Matheson, *Collected Works of Thomas Müntzer*, pp. 324–50. The executions took place on May 27, 1525.

[139] See Wander 3:642, "Messer" no. 43.

[140] *Ein gut wort findt ein gute stad*; Wander 5:403, "Wort" no. 122.

[141] Thiele no. 29, p. 56.

call. Once he has entered in the right way, let him abide in the name of Christ, devote himself to the Word, tend his flock, and teach in a simple way what promotes peace. He is not to seek a foothold in the city hall, but should let those to whom it has been committed govern, not trying to carve out his own jurisdiction or attract his own following (if it gets big, it will break the trees).[142] He should not let people tattletale to him, except when a grieved heart wants to disclose and accuse itself. In this way, says our doctor, one can win many souls for Christ and help bring peace and quiet and save oneself and others (as St. Paul writes to Timothy [1 Tim. 4:16]).

For in Münzer we surely see the true characteristics of a false teacher. They come trotting along without being called, or even if they are legitimately installed, if a little dark cloud begins to appear, they tie up their pack like any other ᐟfair-weather peddler and spread it out again somewhere else. They always want to have their hand in the stew[143] and in the government, but in the end they fall away from the Word. They boast of the Spirit and seek new and subtle interpretations, maligning and slandering salutary and peaceful teachers in order to gain popularity among the mob—as has all been demonstrated in our own times by countless examples.

So now the Thuringian revolt had been suppressed with legitimate force, on the basis of Doctor Martin's book,[144] and the pious and Christian Duke John[145] had become the elector of Saxony. The doctor continued to devote himself to God's Word, his pulpit, and the university; he lectured and wrote, preached two funeral sermons for the laudable elector,[146] exhorted to peace, comforted the distressed,[147] helped set his and the neighboring

---

[142] *mache jm kein stab unnd anhang/ wenn der groß wird/ so zubricht er die beume.* See Wander 1:90, "Anhang": "*Je grosser der Anhang ist, je eher bricht der Baum.*" The sentence depends on the range of literal and figurative meanings of several German words: *Stab* is literally a (wooden) "staff" but also refers figuratively to the judicial and other offices for which a staff is part of the regalia. *Anhang* means literally "something suspended from [something else]" but means figuratively a group of followers or "hangers-on."

[143] Wander 4:591, "Sode" no. 1.

[144] See above, p. 220 n. 111.

[145] On John the Steadfast, see above, p. 70 n. 95.

[146] *Two Sermons for the Burial of Elector Frederick the Wise* (May 10 and 11, 1525), WA 17/1:196–227 (LW 56). See Brecht 2:183.

[147] See, e.g., *Christian Letter of Consolation to the People of Miltenberg* (1524), LW 43:97–112; *The Burning of Brother Henry* (1525), LW 32:261–86; *Open Letter to Bartholomew von Staremberg* (1524), WA 18:5–7 (*LSC*, pp. 53–55); *Letter of Comfort to the Christians in Augsburg* (1523), WA 12:224–27; Luther to Lambert Thorn, January 19, 1524, WA Br 3:237–39 (*LSC*, pp. 197–99); to Elector John, May 15, 1525, WA Br 3:496–97 (*LSC*, pp. 55–56); to Duke John Frederick, May 15, 1525, WA Br 3:497–98.

churches in order,[148] and warned many other places[149] of the infiltrators who were insinuating their way into many large towns, as can be seen at length in his works.[150]

Doctor Luther had given the two pillars[151] [Judg. 16:29–31] of the papal church a powerful push and blow with the finger of God [Luke 11:20]. The private sacrifice of the Mass had now ceased even in the Wittenberg Castle Church,[152] as well as in many other places that were no longer toeing the line or keeping Roman time. Likewise, the celibacy of the clergy and monks had been brought to an end with God's Word and become something suspicious and foul to all sensible people. Many people of good heart had been thoroughly instructed from the clear words of St. Paul [1 Tim. 3:2] that a Christian bishop or pastor or a deacon may be the husband of one wife, without any burden of conscience, insofar as he was unable to receive the word concerning voluntary celibacy [Matt. 19:12] and preserve himself from devilish fornication and impurity.[153] The priests in the Old Testament, some apostles, and the bishops in the first church had their wives for a long time, even as the Greek and German pastors later did.[154] Under the Gospel, too, some entered the estate of marriage in God's name, such as Herr Bartholomaeus Bernhardi,[155] the provost in Kemberg, who had the first priest's wedding in Luther's times, and then later the pastor of Hersfeld.[156] Accordingly, Doctor Luther also wanted to help confirm God's Word and holy ordinance and the laudable estate of married priests with his

---

[148] See, e.g., *German Mass and Order of Service* (1526), LW 53:51–90; Luther to Elector John, October 31, 1525, and November 30, 1525, LW 49:130–39. Cf. Brecht 2:251–59, 259–66.

[149] See, e.g., *Open Letter to the Town of Mühlhausen* (1524), WA 15:238–40; *Letter to the Christians at Strassburg* (1524), LW 40:61–71; *Open Letter to the Christians of Antwerp* (1525), WA 18:547–50; *Infiltrating and Clandestine Preachers* (1532), LW 40:379–94.

[150] I.e., the Wittenberg edition of Luther's works. See the introduction above, pp. xxiv–xxv.

[151] I.e., the Mass and clerical celibacy.

[152] As of Christmas 1524. See Brecht 2:129 and above, pp. 193–94.

[153] See *Answer to Several Questions on Monastic Vows* (1526), LW 46:139–54.

[154] Cf. *Table Talk* no. 5300 (1540), LW 54:407.

[155] Bartholomaeus Bernhardi (1487–1551) had taught in Wittenberg since 1512 and served as rector, defending Luther in the early stages of his trial, before becoming provost at Kemberg in 1518. He was married in 1521. See Luther to Melanchthon, May 26, 1521, LW 48:231. On Bernhardi, see LW 48:115 n. 21; Julius August Wagenmann, "Bernhardi, Bartholomäus," *ADB* 2:459–60. For his status as the vanguard of clerical marriage in the Reformation, see Marjorie Elizabeth Plummer, *From Priest's Whore to Pastor's Wife: Clerical Marriage and the Process of Reform in the Early German Reformation* (Farnham: Ashgate, 2012), pp. 51–52.

[156] The pastor in Hersfeld was Henry Fuchs; Luther mentions his marriage in the same May 26, 1521, letter to Melanchthon: LW 48:235. See Plummer, *From Priest's Whore to Pastor's Wife*, pp. 57–58.

own Christian example, in accordance with Scripture and the laudable and blessed custom of the early church.

For this reason he chose a nun, Katy von Bora,[157] to whom he pledged a righteous and Christian marriage in the name of the Holy Trinity. He was betrothed to her on [the Tuesday after] Trinity Sunday in 1525 in the name of Jesus Christ and in accordance with His Word, in the presence of good people in Wittenberg.[158] Soon afterward he had a public procession to church and celebrated a proper wedding with her.[159]

Once, for a monk to take a nun as his wife in God's name and in accordance with God's institution and ordinance was one of the greatest sins according to the judgment of the worldly-wise. On the Last Day, however, we will see this married couple with their Christian descendants, as well as many Christian husbands and wives—who have been saved in bearing children, as St. Paul says [1 Tim. 2:15], insofar as they have persevered in faith in Jesus Christ in Christian love and married chastity—standing at the right hand of Christ [Matt. 25:33], the just Judge, and lauding and praising our God throughout eternity together with their baptized offspring, while they see the Sodomites [Jude 6–7] and adulterers, who wallow and soil themselves in all kinds of sin, both secret and open, standing on the left side with the ancient Beelzebub [1 Kings 1:2; Matt. 12:24] among the unchaste buck and doe goats, and departing with all unclean spirits into the fire of hell.

Now if you believe that God, who is pure [James 3:17], graciously takes delight in pure and Christian spouses, and that all the lewdness stirred up by the devil is one of the worst abominations before God, and that the eternal Son of God will judge and pronounce sentence in accordance with His Word at the last judgment, then surely you will be unable to reproach godly and chaste marital life or to condemn anyone who has entered the blessed estate of marriage in order to avoid fornication and licentiousness [1 Corinthians 7].

---

[157] On Katharina von Bora, see above, p. xxxii n. 74.

[158] Both the betrothal and the immediately subsequent marriage vows were exchanged in the former Augustinian cloister on the evening of Tuesday, June 13, in the presence of Justus Jonas, the jurist Johann Apel (1486–1536), Lucas Cranach and his wife, and Bugenhagen, who performed the ceremony. See Brecht 2:198. Mathesius' error as to the date (placing the betrothal and vows on Trinity Sunday, June 11, rather than on the following Tuesday) is based on the uncertain dating of Luther's letter to Michael Stifel of June 10 or 17, 1525, WA Br 3:535–36. See the editorial notes there (p. 535) and Volz, *Die Lutherpredigten des Johannes Mathesius*, p. 155 n. 8.

[159] The public procession to church for the blessing and marriage feast took place on June 27, 1525. See Luther to Spalatin, June 21, 1525, LW 49:115–16.

May God preserve all pious spouses and bless their children, so that they may appear before the judgment seat of Christ with honor and joy. May He destroy all estates and houses in which all chastity and honor have been lost.

With this we will conclude the history of Doctor Luther from the year 1525, rendering heartfelt thanks to our God, who caused the marriage of priests to be reestablished, in accordance with His Word and the example of the ancients. May He be highly exalted forever! Amen!

The Sixth Sermon,
on the Events That Took Place in the Year 1525

[February 1563][1]

D EAR friends in the Lord! We believers have one sole eternal King, Jesus
Christ, who is with the Father from eternity [John 1:2], who, as the true
Immanuel, has been concerned for His Church and people on earth from
the beginning, and who still today cares for us as a faithful priest.

Our Lord Christ, together with His little flock on earth, also has an
adversary and archenemy, who from the beginning has pierced Christ's heel
[Gen. 3:15][2] with his evil spirits, tyrants, heretics, and hypocrites. He assails
the holy Gospel with lies, murder, and cunning and wants to bring it under
suspicion by means of abominable scandals. Therefore, it is rightly said that
the affairs of Christendom are all alike from the beginning,[3] because there
is an intractable enmity between Christ and Lucifer [Isa. 14:12; 2 Cor. 6:15].
The people through whom Christ attacks His enemy, and the tyrants, heretics, and hypocrites through whom Satan attacks Christ and His Word, will
keep changing until the Last Day. For just as Satan caused much pain and
great distress for Moses, the prophet of God, by means of tyrants, sorcerers, false brethren, and ungrateful people, when he was leading the seed
of Abraham out of the iron house of bondage, out of Egypt [Exod. 13:3;
Deut. 4:20], so it has also happened in our times, when our Lord Christ was
leading His people out of the Babylonian captivity,[4] out of the papal doctrine and hypocrisy. For in both exoduses God's strong hand and gracious
help can be seen, 'as well as the devil's rage and murder. Therefore, before

---

[1] The sixth sermon covers the years 1525 (beginning after the Peasants' War and Luther's
marriage) to 1528. The sermon must have been delivered in February 1563, since the following (seventh) sermon is firmly dated to February 23, Shrove Tuesday (see below, p. 266).

[2] See above, p. 104 n. 10.

[3] *Die hendel der Christenheyt von anfang sind einerley.* Cf. below, p. 236. The proverb also
appears, e.g., in Zacharias Theobald, *Widertaufferischer Geist* (Nürnberg: Halbmayern, 1623),
fol. (:)3r, but its original source could not be determined.

[4] Cf. Luther, *Babylonian Captivity* (1520), LW 36:3–126.

I continue with the history of Dr. Luther, I want to speak to you by way of introduction about the exodus of the children of Israel from Egypt as well as how Moses fared, that holy and wise prophet of God.[5]

When Abraham's seed was being held captive in Egypt, abused and sorely oppressed by Pharaoh and his taskmasters [Exod. 1:11], the Son of God called Moses out of the wilderness to lead his people out of Egypt with his staff and God's strong hand. But when Pharaoh, hardened by the devil, violently opposed God's ambassador and his people by means of his noblemen and clergy (or sorcerers), Moses pressed on with his mighty wonders, at God's command, and led the Israelites out of their harsh captivity and brought them to the Sea of Reeds.[6]

When Pharaoh, spurred by the devil, under the providence of God, pursued Moses, the Son of God surrounded His people with the pillars of cloud and fire; He made a path through the Red Sea for them and led Moses and his people through on dry land, but drowned Pharaoh with all his horsemen and the sorcerers who had helped him persecute God's people, so that not one escaped [Exod. 14:28]. Whoever refuses to believe God and His Word, but insists on rebelling against them, must ultimately learn, by ruin and eternal perdition, that God alone is Lord, and His Word is true, and His people cannot be overcome.

Now when Moses and his people had been gloriously rescued from the Egyptian tyrants and sorcerers by the Son of God[7] and had come to Mount Sinai in the wilderness, the neighboring princes and kings tried to destroy God's faithful servant and His people. But to those who enjoy God's goodwill, no one can do evil.[8] The Lord Christ, ʼwho with His angels camped around Abraham's seed day and night [Deut. 23:14; Ps. 34:7], protected His people and cleared away all who set themselves against His inheritance and congregation.

Since the abominable opponent, Satan, was unable to accomplish anything against the seed of Christ and Abraham by means of the violence and malice of others, he provoked many abominable offenses and rebellions

---

[5] Luther occasionally drew parallels between his own ministry and that of Moses: see *Von heimlichen und gestohlenen Briefen* (1529), WA 30/2:44; *Table Talk* no. 6063 (n.d.), WA TR 5:468–69. The thoroughgoing exploration of the parallel, however, is one of Mathesius' contributions to Luther's biographical tradition: see Volz, *Die Lutherpredigten des Johannes Mathesius*, pp. 69–70.

[6] Luther translated the Hebrew סוּף יַם [*yam suph*] as *Schlifmeer*, "Sea of Reeds," where the Septuagint and Vg had the equivalent of "Red Sea."

[7] On the identification of the agent in these and other Old Testament histories as the preincarnate Second Person of the Trinity, see Mathesius, *History*, above, pp. 107–10, and below, p. 254.

[8] *Wem Gott wol will/ dem mag niemand übel.* Wander 2:76, "Gott" no. 1867.

among Moses' own parishioners. Thus the name of the Lord was horribly blasphemed on account of the sins and misdeeds of His people, and Moses, as Scripture says, was the most wretched and afflicted man [Num. 11:11–15] on account of his own people. For once God's glorious and mighty hand had led Moses' listeners out of their house of iron and through the Red Sea, they immediately began to grumble and murmur against their leader and thought back to their fleshpots in Egypt [Exod. 16:3]. Moses communicated their need to his God, who supernaturally provided bread for them and fed them from heaven.

Soon this miracle, too, was forgotten. When there was a little shortage of fresh water to drink, they raised such a great outcry against Moses that he feared they would stone him [Exod. 17:1–7; Num. 20:2–13]. Although Moses here faltered hard, nonetheless, since great and holy prophets are also human and are saved solely by grace through the forgiveness of sins, the Son of God remembered the covenant He had established with Abraham [Gen. 17:1–14] and created fresh drinking water from the rock for His restless and doubting people. Likewise, soon afterward, through the mighty prayer of Moses, who had laid his hands on the Rock, who was Christ [1 Cor. 10:4], they were saved from the evil neighboring [king] Amalek, whom He blotted out and extirpated along with all of his descendants [Exod. 17:8–16].

Now that Moses' people had received the needed peace and provisions from heaven and had miraculously acquired drinking water from a hard rock, the Son of God gave him His Law on the mountain [Exod. 20:1–17], established a particular worship for them, and set in order their government, something which no other nation on earth had ever experienced [Ps. 147:20].

But when Moses had been called onto the holy mountain to converse with the Son of God, and tarried there for forty days and nights without food, his own brother, Aaron, meanwhile set up an abominable idolatry, calf-Mass, and church dance [Exodus 32];[9] he fashioned a golden calf, with which he intended to worship the God of Israel, apart from and contrary to God's Word. Although God was ready to smite Moses' brother and people and to create another congregation for Himself, nevertheless at the intercession of Moses He was reconciled and accepted Aaron again, by grace, [even though] he had released Moses' people from God's Word. Great people truly fall into no small foolishness[10] once they abandon God's Word and try to

---

[9] *Kelbermeß und Kirchentanz.* Mathesius is playing on the late medieval institution of the *Kirchmeß* or *Kirmes*, the annual festival in each parish held in connection with the festival of its patron saint, which was an occasion for dancing and became notorious for debauchery. For the comparison of the *Kirmes* with Exodus 32, cf. *Table Talk* no. 1157 (1530), WA TR 1:572–73.

[10] Cf. Wander 3:75, "Leute" no. 689.

help the Church of God with their own counsel. For example, the natural children of the great man Aaron later set up another abominable offense with their strange fire [Lev. 10:1], on account of which they were suddenly and dreadfully consumed and killed because of their forbidden worship. God has bound His ministers and Church to His Spirit's Word; if anyone falls away from the Word, he has lost God and wanders in the Egyptian darkness [Exod. 10:22] and sets up nothing but heresy.

But there was no gratitude to be earned with Moses' students, those stiff-necked and stubborn people [Exod. 32:9]. They forgot all of the trouble and want they had suffered in Egypt and all the heavenly and miraculous blessings that the Son of God had shown them for the sake of His covenant.

Not long afterward the mob again began to lust and yearn for the Egyptian cucumbers, melons, leeks, onions, garlic, and meat [Num. 11:4–6], on account of which they became very impatient and found much to complain about concerning Moses and his God.

Since God could accomplish very little with this ungrateful people by doing good, He became angry against them and caused His fire to burst forth from the earth and strike them [Num. 11:1], so that the rabble-rousers and blasphemers met a terrible destruction. Yet as soon as they came to themselves and confessed their sins and cried to the eternal Mediator, things went better for them, except that a great plague came among them, and many of them were killed by fire at Kibroth-hattaavah [Num. 11:33–34].[11]

When this conflict had scarcely been settled, Aaron and Miriam began a new revolt against their own brother. They took as their pretext that he had married a Cushite woman, the daughter of the priest of Midian [Num. 12:1], but in fact they were irritated because God spoke with them only through Moses, and because they had to follow their brother Moses. The Son of God promptly took up the cause of His loyal and afflicted servant [Num. 12:5–9]; He became angry against this insolent woman, who wanted to preach and to criticize God and His Word, and made her become leprous [Num. 12:10]. Moses, however, as the better one, pleaded with the Son of God on her behalf upon Aaron's report, and after seven days He cleansed her again and restored her to health by grace.

But when the eternal Messiah had scouts sent out to spy on the Promised Land, all of them, save Joshua and Caleb, advised against obeying God [Numbers 13]. They made the people rebellious, so that they grumbled hard against Moses and Aaron, thought back to their old papacy again, and wanted to stone to death all who raised any objection to them.

---

[11] Mathesius, following Luther's German Bible, gives the place-name in translation as *Lustergrebern*, "the graves of craving."

Moses did not make this stubborn and rebellious people pay the price, but faithfully interceded for them with the Son of God; upon Moses' petition He relented from His steadfast wrath, yet on the condition that of these unbelieving Israelites, none would cross into or take possession of the Promised Land except for Joshua and Caleb, who believed and were steadfast. And on that very day, the scouts who had spied out the land died [Num. 14:1–38].

Now, even though the common man had witnessed God's wrath, some of them, out of arrogance and presumptuousness, dared to act contrary to God's will and command and attacked the enemy to capture the land of Canaan by military force, despite the fact that Moses had forbidden them and forewarned them of ruin [Num. 14:41–45]. Since they were so blinded and stubborn as to go to battle without command or sufficient cause, and to tempt God, they were struck down by the Canaanites, just as the Ephraimites were, who also arrogantly and presumptuously sought to capture the Promised Land by force of sword at the wrong time and were driven back hard [cf. Judg. 12:5–6].[12] Refusing to fight when you have the command of God and your authorities, and willfully undertaking your own war or being incited to do so without such a command, both have the same fate and outcome, as we have experienced in our own times, to our ruin.[13]

Now when this rebellion had been suppressed as well, Moses was severely grieved by someone who despised the preaching office, acted contrary to the established ceremonies, and gathered wood on the Sabbath. By God's judgment, therefore, this man was stoned by the congregation on account of his presumptuousness [Num. 15:32–36].

Not long afterward, the clergy, who indeed never have been good,[14] raised a terrible uproar and attracted as followers the children of [Jacob's] firstborn Reuben, as well as some councillors and respectable people; they opposed Moses and Aaron and instigated a rebellion against God, His Word,

---

[12] The reference may also be to 1 Chron. 7:21 or to Num. 14:41–45, though that passage does not specifically mention the Ephramites. See also below, pp. 262–63.

[13] As examples, Mathesius may have in mind the 1542 occupation of Braunschweig by the Smalcaldic League (see Brecht 3:320–23) and the ensuing Smalcaldic War between the league and the emperor in 1546–47, in which the Lutheran Duke Maurice of Saxony (see above, p. lxxiii n. 278) refused to support the league, resulting in the disastrous defeat of the Saxon Elector John Frederick and the ensuing imperial efforts to regulate or suppress Protestantism (the Interims): see John F. Guilmartin Jr., "Schmalkald War," *OER* 4:15–16. In Joachimsthal itself, Mathesius advised his parishioners not to take up arms for the Hapsburgs against their Saxon fellow-Evangelicals, for which he was summoned to Prague to answer charges of treason: see Loesche, *Johannes Mathesius*, 1:138–72; Brown, *Singing the Gospel*, p. 40. More distant from Joachimsthal, the French wars of religion had recently broken out in 1562–63 after the Massacre of Wassy [Vassy]; see J. H. M. Salmon, "Wassy, Massacre of," *OER* 4:264.

[14] Here in the context of Numbers, a reference to the Levites. For the proverb, see above, p. 204 n. 24.

and worship. Moses laid out the matter in the presence of his Messiah and summoned the instigators and agitators to a hearing. Dathan and Abiram, however, refused to appear; they had brazen and insolent words relayed to Moses, ridiculed God's promise, defended their rebellious peasants,[15] and refused to acknowledge the faithful servant of God as their prophet and leader any longer [Numbers 16].

At this, Moses became very angry, and in his mighty zeal prayed against the fanatics,[16] appealing against the congregation on the basis of his own conscience and innocence. He set God as judge between himself and the rebellious teachers[17] who were slandering God's Word and servant: Each was to take his censer and incense before the tent of meeting and stand before the whole congregation. Then the Son of God appeared, and, upon the zealous petition of Moses, He commanded the congregation to step away from the accused. And immediately the earth beneath Korah, Dathan, and Abiram opened up and swallowed them, because they had committed abominable blasphemy against the Lord and slandered His Word, ordinance, and servant.

But since the rebellious congregation was grumbling against Moses [Num. 16:41] and wanted to avenge and defend the Korahites and Dathanites, God sent a dreadful plague among the congregation, so that more than fourteen thousand of them died [Num. 16:49]. After this punishment had been lifted because of the intercession of Moses and Aaron, Moses' students and colleagues in office began stirring up another dissension at the waters of Meribah [Num. 20:2–13]. Once again they made trouble, because the rebellious Levites and their company had been killed, and they yearned again for the Roman pomegranates, monks' figs, and the holy water. At this point Moses asked the Son of God for counsel and struck the rock in error, because his faith faltered and failed. When he had taken heart, however, he confidently struck again, and fresh water sprang forth from the solid rock.[18]

Our God was continuously manifesting Himself visibly among His people through His great grace, rich blessing, and extraordinary kindness; He conquered their neighboring enemies, who would have liked to gobble them down with mustard![19] Nonetheless the people forgot all of these blessings and spoke with stubbornness, arrogance, and bitterness against Jesus Christ and His faithful servant and prophet, who had delivered them from the Egyptian papacy. They despised and profaned the heavenly fare and

---

[15] A reference to the Peasants' War of 1525. See above, Mathesius, *History*, pp. 219–24.

[16] *Schwermer*; see above, p. 195 n. 61.

[17] Cf. *Table Talk* no. 5096 (1540), LW 54:389; cf. WA TR 4:657 and n. 11.

[18] Compare Luther's interpretation of Moses' failure of faith in his sermon of June 28, 1528, on Numbers 20, WA 25:471–74 (LW 63).

[19] A colorful German expression: see Wander 4:541, "Senf" no. 13.

became sick of the two kinds of food from heaven [Num. 21:5].[20] Then the righteous wrath of God was kindled against His own people, and in Arabia, He caused fiery and poisonous snakes to come among them, which killed many of them, until in true contrition they entreated Moses to intercede for them [Num. 21:6–9]. At God's command, he depicted the Son of God for them in the form of a bronze serpent, in order that all who looked upon Him in faith [John 3:14–15] would be saved from their snakebites and wounds, as well as from sin and death, out of pure grace.

At this time the neighboring kings and lords took up arms against this witness of the living Son of God. The Israelites had requested peaceful passage and transit through their land, but when this request for peaceful passage was denied, they struck Sihon, king of the Amorites, and Og, the king of Bashan, with the edge of the sword and took possession of their land and cities [Num. 21:21–35].

When Balak, king of the Moabites, became afraid of Moses' people, he summoned Balaam, the prophet of the God of Jacob, and won over this greedy person [2 Pet. 2:15] with great gifts, so that he gave the impious king advice about how to defeat God's people [Numbers 22–24]. Then [Balak] invited the Israelites to his Venusberg,[21] to the vile sacrifices of the abominable and naked Priapus [cf. Numbers 25; Rev. 2:14].[22] Because of this, at God's command, Moses had the princes among the people of God who had committed fornication with heathen women hanged from the gallows for all to see [Num. 25:4]. In his zeal, Phinehas, the priest's son, also pierced one such clod, who shamelessly lay with a Moabitess [Num. 25:7–8]. Balaam, who gave evil counsel, was also slain in the war in the end [Num. 31:8]. This is the history of how Moses fared among foes and friends when he led Abraham's seed out of Egypt, through the Red Sea, and into the Promised Land, on the basis of God's Word.

Here, there is no doubt that this was the people of God and that Moses was God's servant. The Son of God also frequently made Himself visible in the pillar of cloud and fire and let Himself be heard. He spoke with Moses personally and repeatedly displayed His wonders and His wrath, and yet Moses could earn no thanks from his own people, even though God had

---

[20] *an beyden Himmelbroden*; i.e., the manna and the quail (Num. 11:9, 31).

[21] The Venusberg, in German legend, was a mountain in whose caverns the goddess Venus was supposed to hold court. In the sixteenth-century *Lied von dem Danheüser*, the knight Tannhäuser is lured there to a life of sensuality at the cost of his salvation. See J. W. Thomas, *Tannhäuser: Poet and Legend*, University of North Carolina Studies in the Germanic Languages and Literatures 77 (Chapel Hill: University of North Carolina Press, 1974), pp. 184–91. For Luther's use of the Venusberg legend, see *Warning to His Dear German People* (1531), LW 47:27.

[22] On Priapus, see above, p. 203 n. 12.

routed their enemies. His own parishioners, friends, and colleagues in ministry, who were supposed to help him teach and govern, all turned against him, but God protected His faithful servant and was a fiery wall around him [Zech. 2:5]. He also remained healthy and strong in his office until a ripe old age, when God finally took him to Himself [Deuteronomy 34], as He did with the pious Enoch [Gen. 5:24], and paid him with rich grace for all his faithful service.

Someone might ask, "What is your point with this long preface?" *Res sunt eaedem, personae mutantur* ["The issues at stake are the same; only the people are changed"]—so say the wise about civic affairs.[23] Even as the Lord Christ called Moses and was with His people at all times, so also in our times He has rescued His beloved Christendom, which had been baptized in His name, blood, and merits under the papacy, from its own house of iron. Fifty years ago[24] it lay captive under the pharaoh in Rome and his sorcerers and taskmasters, in universities, collegiate churches, and monasteries where the clergy had permitted themselves to be bound and taken in by the mark, vow, and anointing of the Babylonian whore [Rev. 16:2; 17:1],[25] all of which then ensnared the baptized children in Roman idolatry and heresy.

But when our God heard the heartfelt sigh of His oppressed people, as in Psalm 12, and wanted to avenge the blood of Master John Hus[26] and to rescue His people from this Babylonian captivity and Egyptian darkness, He awakened Dr. Luther, to whom He entrusted His Word, in order that he should set himself against the Roman pharaoh and call Christendom to the Word and fear of God.

Pharaoh and all who had committed fornication with the scarlet whore [Rev. 17:4], along with all of their sorcerers and conjurers, wanted to stop the Son of God and His faithful counselor and cut off their every path. But our prophet pressed on, for the Son of God, our eternal Immanuel, was with him and gave power to his thunder and word, so that the pope and his abominable idolatry and heretical hypocrisy became manifest and fell farther into contempt every day.

Although this pharaoh and his horsemen and sorcerers are continuously being driven back, the Red Sea will not come crashing down upon them until the Last Day, when the prophet in the East and the abominable

---

[23] Cf. above, p. 229. A classical source for the proverb could not be found; cf., however, Wander 2:331, "Händel" no. 9: *Die Hendel bleiben, die Leut vergehen.*

[24] Perhaps a vague reference; this sermon was preached in 1563 and printed in 1566, so fifty years before would have been either 1513 or 1516.

[25] Mathesius here and elswhere uses the euphemism *Braut* ["bride"] instead of the word *Hure* ["whore"] found in the biblical text.

[26] On Hus, see the introduction above, pp. xxxvii–xxxviii, and Mathesius, *History*, p. 121.

beast in the West will be cast into the lake of fire [Rev. 19:20; 20:10].[27] In like manner, from day to day our God is always removing one godless person after another and clearing good paths for His Word and people, so that nearly the entire German Empire and some neighboring kings, as true Gibeonites [Josh. 9:3], have joined in fellowship with God's Word on friendly terms.[28]

Now that foreign and neighboring opponents were beginning to yield to the mighty arm of God, and the dear Christians among our neighbors began to hear Jesus Christ and His faithful prophet, as well as other babes and sucklings [Matt. 21:16], Satan did not rest, but stirred up false prophets in Thuringia.[29] These set themselves up in their corners against God's Word and our doctor's teaching; with appalling violence they rebuked our Moses and incited the common man to rebel against lawful authority and Mount Lebanon,[30] upon which God made Himself heard, as you have heard at length in the last sermon.[31] But He who preserved His Word and faithful servant in the Arabian wilderness against the rebels and agitators also caused the heavenly prophets[32] with their rebellious disciples to be taken away in His wrath, so that more than a hundred thousand rebels met a dreadful death in 1525.[33]

When this appalling uprising had been suppressed by the spiritual and secular sword—though it caused much offense and many reasonable people began to hesitate and to view the divine doctrine with suspicion—nonetheless the course of the Gospel was unhindered. For God protected Wittenberg and other places where the heavenly infiltrators were not allowed to make their nests. Thus it was possible to advance God's Word in relative peace through preaching, lecturing, and writing, and by establishing churches, schools, and ceremonies, accompanied by Christian admonitions and warnings to be on careful guard against the unbidden infiltrators who have

---

[27] I.e., Mohammed and the pope.

[28] On the political position of Lutheranism in the 1560s, see Thomas A. Brady Jr., "Settlements: The Holy Roman Empire," in *Handbook of European History, 1400–1600*, ed. Thomas A. Brady Jr., Heiko A. Oberman, and James D. Tracy (Grand Rapids: Eerdmans, 1996), 2:349–83.

[29] A reference to Thomas Münzer and the Peasants' War of 1525. See above, Mathesius, *History*, pp. 217, 219–24.

[30] "Lebanon" means "white" or "snowy" mountain, here in a play on the German meaning of "Wittenberg": see below, Mathesius, *History*, pp. 307, 567, 575–76, 602; contrast, p. 287. Cf. Luther, *De abroganda missa privata* (1521), WA 8:476; *Misuse of the Mass* (1521/1522), LW 36:229.

[31] On the Peasants' War, see above, Mathesius, *History*, pp. 219–24.

[32] See above, p. 215 n. 90.

[33] Modern scholars estimate that about 100,000 peasants died in the war. See Carter Lindberg, *The European Reformations* (Cambridge, MA: Blackwell, 1996), p. 165. Cf. Sleidanus, *De statu religionis* (1558), book 4, p. 115.

come running without a call and forced their way into other churches. For example, many beautiful [expositions of] psalms were published in 1526,[34] and commentaries on the prophets Jonah[35] and Habakkuk,[36] as well as beautiful admonitions, particularly the one to Herr Eberhard von der Tannen.[37] If you compare ancient and recent history, you will find that the ancient devil always practices his old tricks using new people. The Word of God, meanwhile, always remains under the cross, as do those who firmly and steadfastly rely on it and cling to it.

Karlstadt, the restless fanatic who had previously withdrawn from Wittenberg and illegitimately forced his way into Orlamünde,[38] had united with the heavenly prophets and attacked the Lord's Supper in published writings.[39] When Münzer had been beheaded, Karlstadt, like Cain [Gen. 4:12–14], feared for his life and fled.[40] In his fear and terror, he had

---

[34] *Commentary on Psalm 112* (1526), LW 13:389–420; *Four Psalms of Comfort* (Psalms 37, 62, 94, 109) (1526), LW 14:207–77; cf. below, p. 248.

[35] *Lectures on Jonah [German]* (1525), LW 19:33–104. These lectures, like those on Habakkuk, were delivered in Latin in 1525 but edited by Luther for publication in German in 1526.

[36] *Lectures on Habbakuk [German]* (1525), LW 19:149–237.

[37] Eberhard von der Tannen [Tann] (1495–1574) was appointed electoral counselor and chief magistrate [*Amtmann*] of the Wartburg in 1527. See Georg Müller, "Tann, Eberhard von der," *ADB* 37:372–73. Luther's 1532 treatise *Infiltrating and Clandestine Preachers* (1532), LW 40:379–94, is addressed to him. Either Mathesius is in error about the date, or he is confusing Eberhard von der Tannen with the knight Assa von Kram (ca. 1490–1528), to whom Luther's 1526 treatise *Whether Soldiers, Too, Can Be Saved* (1526), LW 46:87–137, was addressed. Other works of admonition or advice from 1526 include *Advice on the Establishment of an Enduring Order in a Christian Community* (1526), WA 19:440–46 (LW 61); *Answer to Several Questions on Monastic Vows* (1526), LW 46:139–54; *Response to the Christians in Reutlingen* (1526), WA 19:118–25; *Grund und Ursache, daß Marquard Schuldorp seiner Schwester Tochter zur Ehe genommen hat* (1526), WA Br 4:966; see also below, pp. 247–49.

[38] Karlstadt had gone to Orlamünde in the summer of 1523. See above, pp. 196, 198; Luther, *Table Talk* no. 90 (1531), WA TR 1:34.

[39] See, e.g., Karlstadt, *Against the Old and the New Papistical Mass* (1524) and *Dialogue or Gesprächbüchlein on the Abominable and Idolatrous Misuse of the Most Revered Sacrament of Jesus Christ* (1524), in Burnett, *Eucharistic Pamphlets of Andreas Bodenstein von Karlstadt*, pp. 110–15, 163–204. See Brecht 2:166–67. For this entire episode, see Amy Nelson Burnett, *Karlstadt and the Origins of the Eucharistic Controversy: A Study in the Circulation of Ideas* (New York: Oxford University Press, 2011); Burnett, *Eucharistic Pamphlets of Andreas Bodenstein von Karlstadt*. Mathesius' contemporary source, in addition to Karlstadt's writings and Luther's prefaces (see below, p. 239 nn. 44 and 46), may have been Erasmus Alberus, *Widder die verfluchte lere der Carlstader* (Neubrandenburg: Brenner, 1556) [VD16 A1562], fols. 1 2v–3v and V 3v–4r: see Volz, *Die Lutherpredigten des Johannes Mathesius*, pp. 106–7 and 237.

[40] Karlstadt had left Orlamünde after being expelled from Saxony in September 1524. From late 1524 through the spring of 1525, he traveled to Strassburg, Zurich, and Basel, and then

no idea where he could be safe, for he was under the severe disfavor of the prince of Saxony and in great danger from him.[41] Therefore, he decided to crawl back to the cross;[42] he prevailed upon Dr. Luther to become his patron[43] and excused his blasphemy against the Sacrament by saying that he had merely disputed and posed questions about this matter, without asserting or concluding anything.[44] Thus he asked for forgiveness, said he wanted to reform and be converted, just like the captured wolf in its pit.[45]

Dr. Luther, being a merciful man, believed his good words, took him in and secretly harbored him, [though] not without concern, excused him in published writings, and even regained the favor of the good Christian elector for him.[46] Then [Karlstadt] stuck a stake through his own doctorate and theology[47] and became a peasant near Kemberg; he drove pigs to market as old Neighbor Andy.[48]

---

to Rothenburg, where he was when the Peasants' War broke out. He fled from Rothenburg in June 1525; Münzer had been beheaded shortly before, on May 27. See Brecht 2:169–70; Bietenholz and Deutscher, *Contemporaries of Erasmus*, 2:254–55.

[41] Karlstadt to Luther, February 18, 1525, WA Br 3:441–42. Because of the tension between him and Luther, Karlstadt fled Wittenberg in 1523 to Orlamünde, where he had held the sinecure of the parish in his position as a canon of the All Saints' Foundation. Karlstadt requested Duke John's permission to assume pastoral duties in Orlamünde, but problems with the transfer, including Karlstadt's obligation as an archdeacon to lecture at the university and financial issues within the Orlamünde pastorate, led to conflict between Karlstadt and Duke John. Karlstadt spent 1523–24 between Wittenberg and Orlamünde until, because of the problems at Orlamünde and his disagreements with Luther, Karlstadt was banished from Saxony on September 18, 1524. See Sider, *Andreas Bodenstein von Karlstadt*, pp. 181–97.

[42] On this expression, see above, p. 198 n. 87.

[43] Karlstadt to Luther, June 12, 1525, WA Br 3:529.

[44] See Karlstadt, *Declaration of How Karlstadt Regards His Teaching about the Venerable Sacrament*, in Burnett, *Eucharistic Pamphlets of Andreas Bodenstein von Karlstadt*, pp. 258–70; and Luther's 1525 preface, LW 59:134–37. Cf. above, Mathesius, *History*, p. 217.

[45] Cf. Wander 5:350, "Wolf" no. 4: "When the wolf lay in the pit, he wanted to become a holy monk."

[46] Luther secretly harbored Karlstadt for more than eight weeks, beginning June 27, 1525. See Brecht 2:17. Luther sponsored the publication of two public statements by Karlstadt, and supplied them with his own prefaces: one on the Lord's Supper (see above, n. 44) and the other on Karlstadt's relation to Münzer and the Peasants' War: *Defense against the False Charge of Rebellion*, in Furcha, *Essential Carlstadt*, pp. 378–86; for Luther's 1525 preface, see LW 59:127–33 (also Furcha, *Essential Carlstadt*, pp. 395–98).

[47] *sticht er ein Spieß durch sein Doctorat und Theologia*. Wander 5:1741, "Spiess" no. 55.

[48] After leaving Wittenberg, Karlstadt, thanks to Luther's support with the elector, was allowed to reside in electoral Saxony, moving from village to village in the vicinity of Wittenberg before settling as a farmer in Kemberg in late 1526. Karlstadt had been dressing as a layman and referring to himself as "Brother Andrew [Andreas]" since 1522 or 1523. Brecht 2:171–72. On the nickname "Brother [Neighbor] Andy," see above, p. 196 n. 67.

At this time Zwingli, the self-made doctor in Switzerland,[49] also began to fanaticize against the holy Supper. Although he did not endorse the arguments and reasons with which Karlstadt attempted to prove that there is nothing but bread and wine in the Supper, he upheld the heresy that Karlstadt had recanted[50] and dug around in the words of Jesus Christ until he was instructed in a dream that "is" in the Supper means "signifies":[51] therefore, Christ is not present substantially in the Supper; rather, it only signifies the true body and blood of Jesus Christ.

The world likes what is new; therefore, some audacious disputers came to agree with Zwingli's misinterpretation, though they were not without apprehension until Oecolampadius, who had been a learned monk in Altomünster in Bavaria, helped to defend and spread the fanaticism of Karlstadt and Zwingli in Basel.[52] He interpreted the word "body" to mean "figure of the body."[53]

---

[49] Zwingli had no advanced theological degree, only a master's degree in arts. For the criticism, cf. Luther, *Confession concerning Christ's Supper* (1528), LW 37:271; Alberus, *Widder die verfluchte Lehre*, fols. E3v, H2v; Volz, *Die Lutherpredigten des Johannes Mathesius*, p. 87.

[50] For Luther's view of the connections among Karlstadt, Zwingli, and the other Sacramentarians, see, e.g., preface to Brenz, *Swabian Syngramma* (1526), LW 59:156–61; *That These Words of Christ* (1527), LW 37:38–41.

[51] Zwingli, *Subsidium sive coronis de eucharistia* (1525), CR 91:483–84. For an English translation of Zwingli's account of his dream, see Bruce Gordon, "'It Is the Lord's Passover': History, Theology and Memory in the Liturgy of the Lord's Supper in Reformation Zurich," in *Liturgy's Imagined Past/s: Methodologies and Materials in the Writing of Liturgy History Today*, ed. Teresa Berger and Bryan D. Spinks (Collegeville, MN: Liturgical Press, 2016), p. 188.

[52] Johann Heußgen (1482–1531), called Oecolampadius ["house lamp"] in a German pun translated into Greek, was trained both as a humanist and as a doctor of theology. He had been a preacher in Basel and Augsburg from 1515 to 1520 before becoming attracted by Luther's writings and entering the Bridgittine cloister in Altomünster for a period of reflection. In 1522, as a convinced Evangelical, he sought refuge with Franz von Sickingen in the Ebernburg, together with Martin Bucer (see above, Mathesius, *History*, p. 171), before returning to Basel, where he became its leading reformer. Luther originally had a very high opinion of him: see Luther to Oecolampadius, June 20, 1523, LW 49:42–45; preface to Melanchthon, *Annotations on John* (1523), LW 59:47 and n. 22 there. In the matter of the Lord's Supper, however, Oecolampadius declared his own distinctive position in *De genuina verborum Domini, hoc est corpus meum, iuxta vetustissimos authores expositione* (Basel 1525) [VD16 O331]. See E. Gordon Rupp, *Patterns of Reformation* (London: Epworth Press, 1969), pp. 16–17. On Oecolampdius, see Rupp, *Patterns of Reformation*, pp. 3–46; Diane Poythress, *Reformer of Basel: The Life, Thought, and Influence of Johannes Oecolampadius* (Grand Rapids: Reformation Heritage Books, 2011); Jeff Fisher, *A Christoscopic Reading of Scripture: Johannes Oecolampadius on Hebrews* (Göttingen: Vandenhoeck & Ruprecht, 2016), pp. 13–27.

[53] Oecolampadius, *De genuina*, fol. C5v. For this passage, see Bryan D. Spinks, *Do This in Remembrance of Me: The Eucharist from the Early Church to the Present Day* (London: SCM Press, 2013), p. 284. Cf. Luther, *The Sacrament of the Body and Blood of Christ* (1526), LW 36:346; *That These Words of Christ* (1527), LW 37:30, 34, 40, 45, 49–50; *Confession concerning Christ's Supper* (1528), LW 37:255; *Brief Confession* (1544), LW 38:297.

All of the Sacramentarians[54] had a common heresy, as they still do, but each one adduces his own proof on the basis of a forced and uncertain interpretation of the clear words of Jesus Christ. However, since they themselves sensed that their dreams, specious glosses, forced interpretations, *alloeoses*, and *metalepses*[55] would not hold firm in their own consciences or among godly and reliable people, they searched Scripture and dragged in many passages by the hair[56] to support their opinion, but they missed the mark here as well and finally gave up the attempt.

ᶦIn the end they grabbed hold of Jacob's wooden ladder [Gen. 28:12],[57] climbed into heaven, and based their fluttering thoughts on the articles of our children's Creed:[58] the Son of God ascended into heaven with His human body and sits at the right hand of His Father with His physical members in a particular location; therefore, He cannot come down to be present with His true body at the distribution of the Supper. This is what they insist upon, contrary to the express command and institution of the Lord Christ, thereby robbing us of the firm consolation of Christ, our Immanuel [Isa. 7:14],[59] who dwells among us here in this valley[60] with His Word and the [Sacraments]

---

[54] Luther's term for those who attacked the correct doctrine of the Lord's Supper: see Luther to Spalatin, March 27, 1526, LW 49:146; *That These Words of Christ* (1527), LW 37:150.

[55] Zwingli defines *alloeosis* as "an expression taking a leap" or "a trope by which an interchange takes place between members of a category or scheme of things where, namely, on account of some affinity in the grammatical phenomena, a leap or interchange is made from one to the other": Huldrych Zwingli, *Amica Exegesis* (1527), in H. Wayne Pipkin, trans., *Huldrych Zwingli: Writings* (Allison Park, PA: Pickwick Press, 1984), 2:319 (CR 92:679). In application to Christology, Zwingli uses the figure to mean "an exchange or interchange of the two natures which are in one person, by which in naming one nature we mean the other, or name them both but mean only the one." *Metalepsis* is a figure in which something is referred to by means of something connected to it but not really the same, as in the expression "this man has become God": Zwingli, *Daß diese Worte: "Das ist mein Leib"* (1527), CR 92:925–27; cf. Zwingli, *Commentary on True and False Religion* (1525), ed. Samuel Macauley Jackson and Clarence Nevin Heller (Durham, NC: Labyrinth Press, 1981), p. 226 (CR 90:797). See W. P. Stephens, *Zwingli: An Introduction to His Thought* (New York: Oxford University Press, 1992), p. 101; Stephens, *The Theology of Huldrych Zwingli* (Oxford: Clarendon Press, 1986), pp. 112–17. Cf. Luther, *That These Words of Christ* (1527), LW 37:34, 41; *Confession concerning Christ's Supper* (1528), LW 37:213–14, 231–32, 235–36.

[56] For the expression, see Thiele p. 59, no. 32; Luther, *Misuse of the Mass* (1521), LW 36:181; *Answer to Emser* (1521), LW 39:156.

[57] Cf., e.g., Luther, *Sermons on Matthew 18–24* (1537–40/1796–1847), LW 68:155.

[58] I.e., the Apostles' Creed. Cf. Luther, *That These Words of Christ* (1527), LW 37:60–63.

[59] I.e., "God with us."

[60] Probably a reference both to Joachimsthal and to the traditional characterization of mortal life in the fallen world as a "vale of tears": cf. above, Bugenhagen, *Christian Sermon*, pp. 31, 33; and below, Mathesius, *History*, pp. 435, 530. Cf. *Small Catechism* (1529) III 7 (Kolb-Wengert, p. 358; *Concordia*, p. 338).

He has instituted. They do not direct their feet down the path lit by the lamp and eternal light of God's Word, but instead by this house lamp,[61] which leads them astray from the Word of God, which is the only lamp and light to our feet in this dark world [Ps. 119:105].

In the pope's book[62] they also found a passage from St. Augustine, which was their strongest defense and weapon: that Jesus Christ's true body must and can be in only one place.[63] When I was still in Bavaria on the Glonn River,[64] three fanatics earnestly pressed upon me the article on the ascension and this passage from canon law; the third portrayed Dr. Luther as a real Saul,[65] who had indeed begun in the Spirit and won some battles and skirmishes against the pope, but now that he was urging that the rebels be struck dead, the Spirit had departed from him as from Saul, who in his hypocritical mercy refused to obey God's command to shed the blood of the condemned [1 Samuel 15].

Upon my oath, as I am accountable to God on the basis of my baptismal vow, the words of these three fanatics would have made their nest in my heart. However, since I pressed upon God in prayer and leaned on Christ's Word, God led me into His school of the cross and severe tribulation, in which I learned and perceived from Dr. Luther's books that the four words[66] which are so despised by Zwingli and all the fanatics are a real spear piercing the heart. Then a Christian pastor living by the Ammer River comforted me;[67] he had the doctor's two books on the Supper[68] sent to me, for which I

---

[61] I.e., Oecolampadius. On his name, see above, p. 240 n. 52.

[62] I.e., the books of canon law.

[63] Augustine, *Tractates on John* 30.1 (PL 35:1632; NPNF[1] 7:186), incorporated in altered form in Gratian, *Decretum*, 3, *de consecratione* D. 2 c. 44 (Friedberg 1:1330): "For the body of the Lord, in which He rose again from the dead, can be only in one place; but His truth is everywhere diffused." See Luther, *That These Words of Christ* (1527), LW 37:55–57, 63.

[64] At Odelzhausen, near Augsburg, where Mathesius worked as a tutor from 1526 to 1527. See above, Mathesius, *History*, p. 158; Loesche, *Johannes Mathesius*, 1:28–38.

[65] Oecolampadius accused Luther of being abandoned by the Spirit in his *Billiche Antwort* (Basel: Wolff, 1526) [VD16 O295], fol. C4r. Cf. *Table Talk* no. 5122 (1540), WA TR 4:672 (with comparison to Saul); *That These Words of Christ* (1527), LW 37:21, and, with the evidence of Luther's writing against the peasants adduced, LW 37:149–50; *Auf des Königs zu England Lästerschrift Titel Martin Luthers Antwort* (1527), WA 23:35.

[66] "This is My body" (Matt. 26:26; Mark 14:22; Luke 22:19; 1 Cor. 11:24).

[67] In 1528, Mathesius stayed with Zecharias Weixner, an Evangelically inclined pastor in Bruck by Fürstenfeld, while he waited for the University of Wittenberg to return from Jena, where many of the faculty and students had moved during the plague (see below, *History*, p. 288). See Loesche, *Johannes Mathesius*, 1:38–39.

[68] Luther's "two books on the Supper" here are probably *The Sacrament of the Body and Blood of Christ* (1526), LW 36:329–61, and *That These Words of Christ* (1527), LW 37:3–150.

want to thank the Lord Christ and my dear Herr Zachariah and Dr. Luther now and for all eternity.

At that time, Doctor Luther was earnestly defending the Supper, along with the pious twelve preachers in Swabia.[69] As Herr Melanchthon writes of him: *Magno animo bella pro pietate ciebat* ["With a great spirit he was rousing wars on behalf of piety"].[70] He opposed the inapplicable and ill-construed arguments of the fanatics, and with his steadfast witness he explained and confirmed the Lord Christ's words concerning the Supper. Moreover, he confessed his faith for posterity; in his sermons and lectures at home, he warned against the cunning and deceitful poison of the opponents, which had seeped into the hearts of many people then, or at least was not felt without inner battle and conflict.

It is true that in his good books the doctor expressed himself vehemently, severely, and derisively, like Elijah [1 Kings 18:21–29], which was deeply hurtful to the Sacramentarians. "St. Arbogast" raised complaints about this rather strenuously against "St. Sebald" in a dialogue by the grecizing cat—as if a few lines of Elijah's mockery were supposed to excuse whole pages full of derisive words and old priests' tales concerning the Papists' consecration.[71]

Later, when this man, [Bucer,] had been sent to Wittenberg by good people as a mediator, and had a friendly colloquy with Doctor Luther and the whole faculty of theologians there, the good man let himself be corrected graciously, and he then drafted the agreement concerning the Supper in Wittenberg on his own behalf and also personally accepted what all the

---

Luther's *Confession concerning Christ's Supper* (1528), LW 37:151–372, which appeared in the spring of 1528, is also a possibility. See below, p. 261.

[69] In fact, there were fourteen Swabian pastors behind the *Swabian Syngramma*, drafted by Johann Brenz in response to Oecolampadius and published in two German translations with prefaces by Luther: see prefaces to Brenz, *Swabian Syngramma* (1526), LW 59:150–62, and the introduction by Amy Nelson Burnett there. The text of the *Syngramma* is edited in Brenz, *Werke: Eine Studienausgabe*, vol. 1: *Frühschriften*, ed. Martin Brecht et al. (Tübingen: Mohr Siebeck, 1970), pp. 234–78.

[70] The source in Melanchthon could not be identified. Cf. Virgil, *Aeneid* 1.541 and 6.820f. (Loeb 63 [1916], pp. 298–99, 590–91).

[71] Martin Bucer (who sometimes published under the Greek and Latin pseudonym "Aretius Felinus") issued a response to Luther's *Confession concerning Christ's Supper* in the form of a dialogue between "St. Arbogast" (bishop of Strassburg, ca. 650–678), representing Bucer's position, and St. Sebald (d. 770, the patron saint of Nürnberg), representing the Lutheran position: *Vergleichung D. Luthers unnd seines gegentheyls vom Abentmal Christi. Dialogus, das ist, ein freundlich Gespräch. Gar nahe alles, so D. Luther in seinem letzten Buch, Bekenntniß genannt, fürbracht hat, wurde hierinn gehandelt, wie das zu erkenntnüß der Warheyt und christlichen frid dienet* (Strassburg: Capito, 1528) [VD16 B8932]. The complaint cited by Mathesius appears on fol. H5r. On Bucer's *Dialogus*, see Martin Greschat, *Martin Bucer: A Reformer and His Times*, trans. Stephen E. Buckwalter (Louisville, KY: Westminster John Knox, 2004), pp. 76–77.

theologians had drawn up, ꞌapproved it, and signed it with his own hand.[72] One who has never fallen has no occasion to stand upright.[73] Blessed is he who has confessed his error and given clear testimony to the truth.

This division in religion and this opposition to the Lord's institution and our faithful Moses by the second Korah and Dathan (this is what the doctor, in his prophetic spirit, called the leaders among the Sacramentarians)[74] caused terribly dangerous and harmful scandals. The pope's writers, and those who protected and defended him, filled all their chapels and books with [reports of] the division and opposition of the Evangelical scholars and concluded with utmost certainty (yes, the Papists, who always waver in their eroded and seared consciences and prompt others to doubt and be uncertain)[75] that Doctor Luther's doctrine was incorrect because it did nothing but cause turmoil and uproar for governments and tumult in churches. This accusation and others like it are all bundled up together in the dreadful preface to Emser's New Testament.[76]

Nevertheless, our doctor and his little flock adhered to the straightforward text and the clear Word of Christ. He wrote, preached, lectured, and prayed against the false brethren who were roused against Christ's Word, truth, and omnipotence by the ancient serpent and their own arrogance. He also had to endure the incrimination, provoked sedition, fanaticism, and disunity; and the scandals that had been stirred up he had to commend to God, who alone is the just Judge and understands what is right, to whom vengeance belongs [Deut. 32:35; Ps. 94:1; Rom. 12:19], and from whom counsel is to be found. Finally, as we will hear, He did intervene in this matter and

---

[72] For the text of the Wittenberg Concord of 1536, see CR 3:75–81; FC SD VII 13–16 (Kolb-Wengert, pp. 595–96; *Concordia*, pp. 564–65). See below, Mathesius, *History*, pp. 313, 404–5. On Bucer's involvement in and the theology of the Concord, see Greschat, *Bucer*, pp. 132–41; Herman Sasse, *This Is My Body*, rev. ed. (Adelaide: Lutheran Publishing House/Openbook, 1977), pp. 244–52.

[73] *Wer nie fiel, der stund nie auff.* See Wander 1:923, "Fallen" no. 56.

[74] Luther, *Confession concerning Christ's Supper* (1528), LW 37:173, refers to Zwingli in passing as "a second Korah" and Oecolampadius as "a new Abiram." Cf. Volz, *Die Lutherpredigten des Johannes Mathesius*, p. 87.

[75] Cf. Luther's attack on the *monstrum incertitudinis* in *Lectures on Galatians* (1531/1535), LW 26:385–88.

[76] In 1527, Jerome Emser (see above, p. 156 n. 98) published a German edition of the New Testament (largely an emendation of Luther's own translation, which Emser had sharply criticized in 1523). Duke George supplied the preface for Emser's New Testament: StL 19:494–503; Felician Gess, ed., *Akten und Briefe zur Kirchenpolitik Herzog Georgs von Sachsen* (Leipzig: Teubner, 1905–17; repr., Cologne: Böhlau, 1985–2012), 2:775–80; cf. Luther to Jonas, December 10, 1527, LW 49:183. See Kenneth A. Strand, *Reformation Bibles in the Crossfire: The Story of Jerome Emser, His Anti-Lutheran Critique, and His Catholic Bible Version* (Ann Arbor, MI: Ann Arbor Publishers, 1961).

quelled the strife and division that had been awakened in the government and church, and suddenly and fearfully took away the instigators and agitators of this sacramentarianism, even as He did with the vile old Korah and Dathan.[77] Whoever is able to offer everything up to God will surely find justice, vindication, and aid from Him early and at the proper time.

After the Zwinglians and their adherents had abominably and blasphemously maligned, ridiculed, and slandered the Lord Christ's Supper and His true and substantial presence at the distribution of the Supper, twisting and forcing many beautiful texts to defend their warped dreams, the devil also stirred up their godless and rebellious kin as well, the pernicious and delirious Anabaptists. They, too, scorn the spoken Word of God and the holy Baptism of children, support the Sacramentarians, deny the true humanity of Jesus Christ, despise the Absolution, and want to abolish all [secular] authorities.[78] Moreover, since many rebellious peasants and some feathers from the spirit of Allstedt[79] were buried in their hearts, they wanted to have everything in common [Acts 2:44].[80] Their doctrine and intentions came out later in Münster in Westphalia, which we will speak of more when we come to the time of Jan of Leiden, the king of the Anabaptists, who was hung up on display.[81]

O God! Hear the lament over the desolation caused by these fanatical spirits in all the world, particularly under the papacy, since [the Papists] do not refute their preachers and there was no real pastor capable of warning the people against them. I saw and heard this wretchedness in the Lechrain[82] and by the Glonn [River],[83] where hordes of people let themselves be

---

[77] On the deaths of Zwingli, Oecolampadius, and Karlstadt, see below, pp. 261, 314.

[78] Although "Anabaptist" groups (a name given by their opponents) shared a common rejection of infant Baptism, and generally rejected both the medieval doctrine of transubstantiation and Luther's doctrine of the Lord's Supper, the other positions mentioned varied among different Anabaptist teachers and communities. See George H. Williams, *The Radical Reformation*, 3rd ed. (Kirksville, MO: Sixteenth Century Journal Publishers, 1992). Cf. below, Mathesius, *History*, pp. 380–93.

[79] A reference to the Peasants' War and Thomas Münzer: see above, p. 217 n. 98. On the "feathers" of the radical reformers, cf. Luther, *Against the Heavenly Prophets* (1525), LW 40:83.

[80] Community of goods was taught in varying forms in several strains of Anabaptism. See Williams, *Radical Reformation*, 3rd ed., pp. 351–54, 637–57.

[81] On the Anabaptist revolution in the town of Münster in 1534–35, and its king, Jan of Leiden (Jan Bockelson), see below, Mathesius, *History*, pp. 380–92. Jan's corpse was hung in a cage from the tower of St. Lambert's Church after his execution.

[82] That is, the region between Swabia and Bavaria along the right bank of the Lech River between Augsburg and the Alps, where Mathesius was working in 1526–27. See Loesche, *Johannes Mathesius*, 1:28–38.

[83] See above, p. 242.

rebaptized and immersed in water, as people who had been driven out of their senses and bewitched. Balthasar Hubmaier,[84] Denck,[85] Doltzk,[86] and Hätzer[87] (the abominable heretic who also wrote a book against the divinity of Christ) were the authors of this desolation in Upper Germany and finally also exported it to Thuringia. For this reason, in addition to the corporal punishment that befell almost all of them, they will find themselves in dire straits, along with the prophets from Münster, at the last judgment. May God preserve all churches from this savage[88] and diabolical madness!

|Dear friends, I am narrating for you the offenses and tumult that Satan stirred up beginning in 1524 and on into 1529, and indeed right up to the fall

---

[84] For the list of Anabaptist leaders, cf. Luther, *Table Talk* no. 100 (1531), WA TR 1:38 (Doltz/Kautz is not mentioned there). The Ingolstadt doctor of theology Balthasar Hubmaier, a native of Friedberg, near Augsburg and Odelzhausen, was a popular preacher who became the leading theologian of early Anabaptism in Germany after his adult baptism in 1525 (see also above, p. 219 n. 108). He was burned at the stake in Vienna in 1528. See James M. Stayer, "Hubmaier, Balthasar," *OER* 2:260–63; Torsten Bergsten, *Balthasar Hubmaier: Anabaptist Theologian and Martyr,* ed. William R. Estep (Valley Forge, PA: Judson Press, 1978); Williams, *Radical Reformation,* 3rd ed., pp. 224–43.

[85] Hans Denck (ca. 1500–1527) was a former Latin school rector in Nürnberg, Augsburg, and elsewhere who became an influential early theologian of south German Anabaptism, combining German mysticism with the sacramentarian theology of figures such as Karlstadt. See Patrick Hayden-Roy, "Denck, Hans," *OER* 1:469–70; Williams, *Radical Reformation,* 3rd ed., pp. 248–63.

[86] No Anabaptist leader named "Doltz[k]" (mentioned also below, Mathesius, *History,* p. 380) can be identified. Loesche suggests that the name is a mistake for Jacob Kautz [Cucius] (see *LH²,* p. 503; Volz, *Die Lutherpredigten des Johannes Mathesius,* p. 158 n. 1). Kautz (ca. 1500– after 1532) was a student in Wittenberg in 1524 and then a preacher in Worms, where he came into contact with Denck and Hätzer and participated with them in a German translation of the Old Testament prophets published in the composite Worms Bible of 1529 [VD16 B2681]. In 1527, he publicly declared himself against infant Baptism, resulting in his expulsion from Worms; he then traveled in Anabaptist circles before taking refuge in Strassburg, until he was expelled again in 1529 and probably died in exile thereafter. See Christian Hege, "Kautz, Jakob," in H. S. Bender et al., eds., *The Mennonite Encyclopedia* (Scottdale, PA: Mennonite Publishing, 1957), 3:159–60; Williams, *Radical Reformation,* 3rd ed., pp. 262–63.

[87] Ludwig Hätzer (ca. 1500–1529) was a Swiss priest who came to Zurich in 1523 as a supporter of Zwingli, but Hätzer came to reject infant Baptism by 1525, though he was not himself rebaptized. He found refuge in Strassburg with Wolfgang Capito before traveling to Worms with Denck, where he met Kautz as well. After a stay in Augsburg, he seems to have returned to his Swiss home (in the diocese of Constance), where he was prosecuted by the bishop on charges of adultery and executed in 1529. His book against the divinity of Christ remained unpublished, though it is mentioned by contemporaries: see, e.g., Melanchthon to Duke Henry [IV] of Saxony, October 16/17, 1529, CR 1:1103 (StL 17:1947); MBW T3:623–24, no. 832. See Walter Klaassen, "Hätzer, Ludwig," *OER* 2:213–14.

[88] *Türckischen*; literally, "Turkish." For Luther's association of Anabaptists and Turks, see Luther to Lazarus Spengler, February 4, 1525, LW 49:99; preface to *New Report on the Anabaptists at Münster* (1535), LW 60:93–95.

of the king in Münster [in 1534], so that you may see that the ancient devil is living still and continues stirring up sedition and offense in opposition to Christ, giving His Gospel a bad name and bringing it into discredit. He did the same in the days of Moses, of David, of Paul, and of Athanasius.[89] The heathen and Papists have not been nearly as bloodthirsty and hell-bent on opposing the Lord Christ and His servants as were Moses' assistants in the church [Numbers 16] and Christ's kinsmen and disciples, or their children, who later gnashed their teeth at Stephen [Acts 6–7] and St. Paul [cf. Acts 14:19; 2 Cor 11:22–25] many times; or, in our own days, the false brethren, fanatics, and mamelukes[90] who have joined the fight against the Gospel with lies and murder in the name of Christ, of His Gospel, and of feigned enmity toward monks and priests. David and Christ say, "He who eats my bread" [Ps. 41:9; John 13:18], and St. John says, "Those who have gone out from us" [1 John 2:19];[91] and in his book against the Englishman, Dr. Luther writes: "Those whom I have taught at my table and in my university and who have been freed from the papacy through me are unfortunately treading me underfoot."[92]

Although the holy spirit in Dr. Luther was deeply distressed and enflamed with great zeal until 1528, when his great confession concerning the Lord's Supper was published,[93] he still tended diligently to the Church

---

[89] Athanasius of Alexandria defended the Trinitarian orthodoxy of the Council of Nicaea against the Arianism (or Semi-Arianism) of the emperors who ruled after Constantine and of most of the rest of the bishops of the Roman world. See Angelo Di Berardino, ed., *Encyclopedia of the Early Church*, trans. Adrian Walford (New York: Oxford University Press, 1992), 1:93–95.

[90] See above, p. 199 n. 91.

[91] For Luther's use of these two verses, see *Auf des Königs zu England Lästerschrift Titel Martin Luthers Antwort* (1527), WA 23:35; *Table Talk* no. 5667 (1544), WA TR 5:309; no. 69 (1531), WA TR 1:24; Luther to Johann Brießmann, July 31, 1529, WA Br 5:125; to Anthony Lauterbach, February 9, 1544, WA Br 10:527. See also Mathesius, *History*, above, pp. 197, 199; and below, pp. 413–14.

[92] I.e., in Luther's third work addressed to King Henry VIII of England, *Auf des Königs zu England Lästerschrift Titel Martin Luthers Antwort* (1527), WA 23:35. After Henry's 1521 *Assertio septem sacramentorum* and Luther's sharply worded 1522 *Against King Henry of England* (described above, Mathesius, *History*, pp. 206–8), Henry had delegated the continuation of his polemic to Thomas More (see above, p. 211 n. 56). However, upon receiving news that Henry was becoming more favorably inclined toward the Reformation, Luther wrote a letter of apology: Luther to Henry VIII of England, September 1, 1525, WA Br 3:563–64. Henry, however, responded with renewed hostility: Henry to Luther, [March–August 1526], WA Br 12:74–93, and Luther published an equally sharp reply in his third work addressed to King Henry VIII of England: *Auf des Königs zu England Lästerschrift* (1527), WA 23:17–37. For this entire episode, see Brecht 2:346–49.

[93] *Confession concerning Christ's Supper* (1528), LW 37:151–372. On Luther's other writing on the Supper in this period, see above, pp. 242–43 n. 68.

of God and gave counsel to all who sought his instruction and advice and wanted to listen to him—or, rather, to the Holy Spirit and the written Word. This is evident from the numerous letters of consolation and admonition to many Christians lords and cities during these three years, in addition to the publication of many other good books.[94] For in 1526 Dr. Luther wrote [commentaries on] four psalms,[95] along with a letter of consolation to the pious widow queen of Hungary, who lost her dearest lord in the war against the Turks.[96] Also published at that time were the [commentary on] Psalm 112;[97] the [sermon on the] magnificent testimony concerning Jesus Christ in chapter 23 [:5–8] of Jeremiah;[98] whether one may flee from the plague without burdening one's conscience;[99] and whether soldiers, too, were among the saved.[100] And in 1527 he published the beautiful *Account of Herr Leonhard Kaiser*,[101] whom the Bavarian bishops and theologians had burned at the stake in Schärding on account of his confession of Jesus Christ and His

---

[94] In addition to the works already mentioned or enumerated just below, see *Letter of Consolation to the Christians at Halle* (1527), LW 43:139–65; *Report to a Good Friend concerning Both Kinds in the Sacrament* (1528), WA 26:560–618 (LW 61).

[95] *Four Psalms of Comfort* (1526). LW 14:207–77. This work was already alluded to above, p. 238.

[96] Queen Mary of Hungary (1505–58) was the sister of Charles V and Ferdinand I. Born archduchess of Austria, she married the young Louis II in 1515, who had been made king of Hungary and Bohemia in 1508–9. Louis died in August 1526 while retreating from the victorious Ottoman army at Mohács. Mary seems to have been sympathetic to Lutheranism and corresponded with Luther by proxy (see Luther to Mary of Hungary, [September] 1531, WA Br 6:194–97). Nonetheless, her own religious inclinations did not affect her service to the house of Hapsburg, including her tenure as regent of the Netherlands (1531–55). On Mary, see Gernot Heiss, "Mary of Hungary and Bohemia," OER 3:28–29; on Louis II, see Bietenholz and Deutscher, *Contemporaries of Erasmus*, 2:352–53. Luther's dedicatory letter to Mary is translated in LW 14:209–10.

[97] *Commentary on Psalm 112* (1526), LW 13:389–420. Cf. above, p. 238.

[98] *Sermon on Jeremiah 23:5–8* (1526), WA 20:549–80 (LW 56).

[99] *Whether One May Flee from a Deadly Plague* (1527), LW 43:113–38. Note that the date of this work is 1527 rather than 1526.

[100] *Whether Soldiers, Too, Can Be Saved* (1526), LW 46:87–137.

[101] Leonhard Kaiser (ca. 1480–1527) was a native of Raab, in Austria, serving as a priest in the diocese of Passau. After study in Wittenberg beginning in 1525, Kaiser returned to Raab in 1527 to visit his dying father. He came under suspicion for Lutheran teachings and was arrested, accused of heresy, and burned on August 16. Luther wrote him a letter of comfort in his imprisonment (dated May 20, 1527); this was published along with Luther's preface and accounts of Kaiser's interrogation, confession of faith, and martyrdom in preface, letter accompanying, and afterword to *Blessed Account of Leonhard Kaiser* (1527), LW 59:194–202. The primary materials published along with Luther's contributions are edited in WA 23:453–72. See Brecht 2:349–50. On Kaiser, see also below, Mathesius, *History*, pp. 303, 559.

Gospel. Around this time [the sermons on] the first book of Moses,[102] which the doctor had expounded in the pulpit, were compiled by Dr. Cruciger for the salutary instruction and consolation of many people.[103]

While the Emperor Charles of blessed memory, whose public and secret enemies God brought into check for him in these years, was burdened by great affairs in his hereditary lands and therefore absent, the German Empire held several imperial diets to consider common peace and the Turk.[104] At these diets it was decided and decreed[105] that each person might act in matters of religion as he is able to answer for himself with firm grounds and a good conscience before God and the Roman emperor, which is what Dr. Luther had called for many times in opposition to his adversaries.[106]

Following this, at the Christian petition and proposal of Dr. Luther, the elector of Saxony was asked to carry out an inspection and visitation of the churches in his land.[107] This fine and useful work of the Christian authorities, under whose auspices and protection our God had committed His Son's Church, was honorably and productively undertaken for the ordering and preservation of many churches and as a good example for pious neighbors. Towns and villages were visited, and competent people were appointed for them; the old and weak [pastors], who were not accustomed to preaching and providing pastoral care because they had started under the papacy, were provided with sufficient provision and support.[108] Moreover, [the

---

[102] *Predigten über das 1. Buch Mose* (1523–24/1527), WA 24:1–710 (the published version; cf. the notes on the sermons as preached in WA 14:97–488).

[103] On Cruciger, see above, p. xx n. 19.

[104] On Charles' absence in Spain from 1522 to 1529, see above, Mathesius, *History*, p. 211; Sleidanus, *De statu religionis* (1558), book 6, pp. 146–47; Brandi, *Emperor Charles V*, pp. 195–274. During his absence, the second and third diets at Nürnberg (1522–23, 1524) and the first and second diets at Speyer (1526 and 1529) were held.

[105] The recess of the first diet at Speyer in 1526 declared that every estate was responsible, with respect to the strictures of the 1521 Edict of Worms (see above, p. 180 n. 68), "so to live, govern, and carry himself as he hopes and trusts to answer it to God and His Imperial Majesty" (B. J. Kidd, *Documents of the Continental Reformation* [Oxford: Clarendon, 1911], no. 90, p. 185). See Sleidanus, *De statu religionis* (1558), book 6, p. 150; Brandi, *Emperor Charles V*, p. 246. Luther quotes the recess in *Von Heimlich und gestohlenen Briefen* (1529), WA 30/2:34 and 43, applying it to himself and "every person," as Mathesius does.

[106] See, e.g., *Luther at the Diet of Worms* (1521), LW 32:112–13, 119; preface and afterword to *Two Discordant and Conflicting Imperial Mandates* (1524), LW 59:88–96.

[107] Luther to Elector John, November 30, 1525, LW 49:137–39, and November 22, 1526, WA Br 4:133–34.

[108] After a disorganized attempt at visitations in Saxony in 1526–27, Melanchthon drew up detailed instructions and standards for evaluation during the visitation, which were published with Luther's approval and preface in 1528: *Instructions for the Visitors* (1528), LW 40:263–320. On the visitations and provisions for the pensioning-off of unsatisfactory clergy, see Susan

visitation] provided for the ᴵestablishment of Latin and German schools so that the youth might grow up in salutary doctrine, liberal arts, and laudable discipline, and so that Christian singing and ceremonies might be established and preserved in the churches.[109] This necessary and truly episcopal undertaking was carried out with the most gracious support and generous expenditure of the good and Christian elector,[110] who is highly praised here and for all eternity among all the good-hearted who by means of this came to the true knowledge of the Son of God, and he will receive his reward and thanks on the Last Day.

Alongside many other great noblemen and scholars, Dr. Luther himself was ready to help in this salutary and episcopal work,[111] and he listened to the poor peasants at prayer, carefully examined their knowledge of the catechism, and patiently instructed them. He once told me a fine story about this: A poor Saxon peasant was supposed to recite the Apostles' Creed[112] in his own language and said, "Ah b'lieve in Gawd awl-maightee."[113] The doctor asked what "awl-maightee" meant, and the good man answered, "I dunno."[114] "Yes, my man," said the doctor, "neither do I and all the scholars know what God's power and omnipotence is. But you should simply believe that God is your dear and faithful Father. He wants to help you, your wife, and your children in every need, and, as the wisest lord, He also knows how and is able to do so."

As to how the visitation was carried out and how it dealt with the doctrine and the preservation of the faithful pastors and diligent teachers, that can be clearly seen in the little book on the instruction of the visitors for the pastors in the electorate of Saxony, which was first published in Wittenberg in 1528[115] with a beautiful foreword that laudably praises this holy and

---

Karant-Nunn, *Luther's Pastors: The Reformation in the Ernestine Countryside*, Transactions of the American Philosophical Society 69.8 (Philadelphia: American Philosophical Society, 1979), pp. 21–27; Brecht 2:259–73.

[109] See *Instructions for the Visitors* (1528), LW 40:306–10, 314–20.

[110] I.e., Elector John the Steadfast: see above, p. 70 n. 95.

[111] Luther himself personally participated in the visitations from October 1528 through January 1529 and again in April 1529 and January 1530. The visitors regularly included members of the university faculty as well as representatives of the electoral and town government. See Brecht 2:262–63, 271–72; *Instructions for the Visitors* (1528), LW 40:272.

[112] *Kinderglauben*; see above, p. 117 n. 16, p. 134 n. 110, p. 241 n. 58.

[113] *Ich glöue inn Gat allmächteigen.* Mathesius' spelling reproduces a strongly accented dialect of German. For the story, compare *Table Talk* no. 5332 (1540), LW 54:409. Mathesius recounts the same anecdote in *Sarepta*, fol. 55r (also in Loesche, *Mathesius: Ausgewählte Werke*, 4:217).

[114] *Ick wes nicht*

[115] See above, pp. 249–50 n. 108.

Christian work from Scripture and passionately bewails the papacy, which had utterly neglected such visitation.[116] Although from ancient times the archpriests held their synods, councils, and convocations,[117] which were appointed for the benefit of the churches and in order to calculate the calendar for movable feasts in the church year,[118] these meetings survived in some lands only in abuse, as occasions to engage in crapulence and licentiousness. As an old pastor in Bavaria said to me, "Long ago the old archpriests would call together all the priests in their deaneries and circuits every year for the calculation and organization of the calendar; now we come with our cooks for dancing and compotation."[119]

Pious bishops also used to send learned and competent people for visitations, and themselves went along, to listen to and to examine pastors and laity alike. Afterward, however, only unlearned and dissolute vicars-general came,[120] who on the day of examination were only seeking money, [the payment of] penance and penalties; in addition to the restoration fee,[121] they exacted the "honor" tax,[122] which the unmarried and dissolute priests had to give their pandering[123] bishops annually *pro dispensatione* or *permissione* ["for dispensation or permission"] on account of their dissolute bedroom-cooks.[124] It finally became so bad that pious priests who were gladly living chastely had to pay this mistress tax even if they kept house with their mother or a female relative. Once, when such a chaste curate wanted to excuse himself and said, "*Propriam sororem habeo, non coquam* ['I have my own sister, not a cook']," the vicar replied, "*Sive habeas sive non habeas,*

---

[116] On visitations, synods, and the vicar-general [*officialis*] in medieval dioceses, see Margaret Deanesly, *A History of the Medieval Church: 590–1500,* 9th ed. (London: Routledge, 1969), pp. 181–85.

[117] *Synodos, send und caland.* Cf. *DWB,* s.v. "Send."

[118] I.e, in order to communicate the schedule of festivals depending on the changing date of Easter.

[119] A play on the Latin words *calculatio* and *compotatio.*

[120] *Offiziel;* see above, n. 116.

[121] *Restaur*

[122] *ehrzins;* also known as the *Hurenzins,* or "whore tax." For the custom and its critique, cf. WA 30/2:254, and the 1523 *Gravamina* of Nürnberg in some German versions and the Latin translation: see *DRA* 3:686 note (m) and Kidd, *Documents of the Continental Reformation,* p. 120.

[123] *rifianischen*

[124] *Betköchin*

Episcopus vult habere pecuniam ['Whether you have one or not, the bishop wants money'].”[125]

I am mentioning these old convocations and visitations in the papal church so that we may sincerely thank God for this holy work which was set up in the electorate at the Christian advice of Dr. Luther. Many German princes and cities have blessedly followed suit and taken up this beautiful work to the glory of God and for the edification of the Church.[126]

The experience gained from such examinations ⏐and in Christian confession revealed, however, that few pastors knew the catechism and that many laity were unable to pray properly, much less to understand the six parts of the catechism.[127] Therefore, the doctor published his *Large Catechism*,[128] in which he very skillfully summarized, arranged, and explained the catechism (the Ten Commandments, the Creed, the Our Father, Baptism, Absolution, and the Supper), so that it could be taught to the youth and ordinary people in all simplicity, and so that it could be heard back from the people again, in keeping with the meaning of the word “catechism.”[129] The useful practice of discussing this catechism for two weeks four times a year has continued to this day in Wittenberg and many other churches; children, servants, and craftsmen meet in large numbers for this.[130] Many pastors also discuss the catechism on Sunday before and along with the Gospel and call the children

---

[125] A parallel transmission of the story, attributed to Mathesius, is found in a manuscript of Luther's *Table Talk* recorded by Conrad Cordatus: WA TR 4:xliii. Loesche (*LH²*, p. 506) points out a similar anecdote in the satire *De fide concubinarum in Sacerdotes*, fol. b1r, attributed to Paul Olearius (i.e., Jacob Wimpfeling, 1450–1528) and first printed about 1500 [VD16 O660], though Volz (*Die Lutherpredigten des Johannes Mathesius*, pp. 239–40) questions the direct dependence of Mathesius' story on this version.

[126] Visitations became a standard practice of Lutheran territories. See Gerald Strauss, *Luther's House of Learning: Indoctrination of the Young in the German Reformation* (Baltimore: The Johns Hopkins University Press, 1978), pp. 249–67.

[127] The parts of the Lutheran catechism were variously numbered as six (as given by Mathesius) or five (not including Absolution as a separate part). Cf. Luther, *Small Catechism* (1529), Pref. 3, 7–8 (Kolb-Wengert, pp. 347, 348; *Concordia*, p. 313); *Large Catechism* (1529) Short Pref. 24 (Kolb-Wengert, p. 386; *Concordia*, p. 358). See Otto Albrecht, “Borbemerkungen zu beiden Katechismen,” WA 30/1:440–45, and Albrecht Peters, *Confession and Christian Life*, trans. Thomas H. Trapp, Commentary on Luther's Catechisms 5 (St. Louis: Concordia, 2013), pp. 3–30.

[128] *Large Catechism* (1529) (Kolb-Wengert, pp. 377–480; *Concordia*, pp. 351–440).

[129] I.e., the components of the Greek word κατηχισμός can be taken to mean, literally, “to sound back,” i.e., to echo or repeat, though already in classical Greek the word had the sense of “instruction.” See the introduction, Kolb-Wengert, p. 345.

[130] Regular catechetical preaching was recommended in the *Instructions for the Visitors* (1528); LW 40:308. Cf. the Wittenberg church order of 1533, Sehling 1:700–701.

together in the summer to explain the catechism and hear them recite it, which, thanks be to God, is also customary among us now.[131]

In order to help the catechists and catechumens easily to retain, understand, and recite this teaching, our doctor composed a concise version of it and had this *Small Catechism* published in questions and answers.[132] Thanks be to God, it is said that more than a hundred thousand have been printed in our days; it has been translated into all kinds of languages and brought abundantly into foreign lands as well as into all Latin and German schools.[133]

Surely this layman's Bible[134] and children's book has accomplished a great deal. From the beginning God had a large Bible put into writing, through Moses, the prophets, evangelists, and apostles, by special inspiration of the Holy Spirit, and had it brought to us. From this the bishops and teachers have summarized the fundamentals of Christianity in their entirety and have drawn positive and negative examples for those who keep and transgress God's Commandments and for the strengthening and comfort of believers. Since this large book was too lofty and difficult for the children and laity, He Himself, through the eternal Mediator, took all the Commandments which teach us what is ungodly and unrighteous and show us what pertains to true worship of God, brotherly love, secular obedience, Christian discipline, and a good conscience and summarized them in ten brief statements on two stone tablets [Exod. 20:1–17]. In addition to this, He had the holy apostles summarize in three brief paragraphs all the articles of the salutary Christian creed:[135] namely, that God alone is our Father, Christ

---

[131] Mathesius had introduced Luther's *Small Catechism* in Joachimsthal at the beginning of his rectorate there in 1532. During his pastorate, the Joachimsthal clergy held preaching on the catechism every Sunday afternoon and examined the children on Wednesdays during the summer months. See Loesche, *Johannes Mathesius*, 1:312–13; Brown, *Singing the Gospel*, pp. 56, 91–92. For references to Mathesius' own catechism preaching, see below, p. 258.

[132] The first three parts of the *Small Catechism* were published on separate broadsheets in January 1529. The whole *Small Catechism*, including sections on Baptism and the Lord's Supper, appeared in booklet form in May. See the introductions in Kolb-Wengert, p. 346, and in *Concordia*, pp. 310–11. For the text of the *Small Catechism* (1529), see Kolb-Wengert, pp. 345–75; *Concordia*, pp. 309–48.

[133] On the use of the catechism in Lutheran schools, see Strauss, *Luther's House of Learning*, pp. 188–90, 199–202. On the practice in Joachimsthal, see Brown, *Singing the Gospel*, pp. 56–59. Through the year 1563, when this sermon was preached, at least sixty-eight editions of the *Small Catechism* had been published in Germany, and the *Small Catechism* had been translated into Latin, Low German, Greek, Danish, Finnish, Italian, Slovenian, Dutch, Polish, and Old Prussian. See Otto Albrecht and Johannes Luther, "Bibliographie zum Kleinen Katechismus," WA 30/1:688–93, 698–720, 782–800, 825–26.

[134] Luther refers to the catechism as the "the laymen's Bible" in *Table Talk* no. 6288 (n.d.), WA TR 5:581.

[135] Before Luther, the Apostles' Creed had usually been divided into twelve statements, each of which was traditionally ascribed to one of the apostles. Luther advocated the division into

alone is our Mediator and High Priest, the Holy Spirit is our only Teacher, who uses the spoken or written Word to teach us about the Father's gracious love and the blood, death, reconciliation, intercession, and merit of God's Son. The Holy Spirit also bears witness and confirms that we have the gracious forgiveness of all punishment and guilt[136] by the blood of Jesus Christ alone, completely freely, without any merit and righteousness of our own. And though we must decay here and turn back into ash and dust on account of our lingering sin and wicked desire, which remain clinging in the blood even of believers and the righteous until death, nevertheless, in Christ, for His sake, and through Him, we will rise again at the end of the world with new bodies, and after the judgment we will enter into eternal life with glory and joy and will remain and abide with the Lord forever [1 Thess. 4:16–17].

Beyond the Ten Commandments and the Apostles' Creed, the eternal Son of God, our only High Priest [Heb. 4:14] and the Bishop of our poor souls [1 Pet. 2:25], Himself fashioned a prayer and thereby taught us to call upon His Father alone, in faith and sure confidence, because of His own merit and intercession [Rom. 8:34; Heb. 7:25]; He also taught us that all our needs concerning our body, soul, house, land, and government should be commended to [the Father] [Matt. 6:9–13; Luke 11:2–4].[137]

|Again, Christendom also had to have its own ceremonies once the liturgies[138] of Moses had been abolished; in His own clear words, therefore, the Son of God instituted His three holy Sacraments for the whole of Christendom: namely, Baptism, Absolution, and the Supper.[139] In these Sacraments, in His Word along with the external signs, He distributes to us His treasures and merit, which He earned and acquired for us with His unique sacrifice on the tree of the cross and His eternal and unending

---

three articles, dealing respectively with the Father, Son, and Holy Spirit, or creation, redemption, and sanctification. See *Large Catechism* (1529) II 4–6 (Kolb-Wengert, pp. 431–32; *Concordia*, p. 399); *Personal Prayer Book* (1522), LW 43:24 (cf. WA 7:214).

[136] An allusion to the medieval theology of penance (and indulgences), which asserted that the guilt of sin was removed through the sacraments whereas the penalty due for sin was transformed from an eternal punishment to a temporal one to be paid through suffering in the present life or in purgatory (and which might be reduced by an indulgence). Cf. the introduction by Christopher Boyd Brown, LW 69:315–16; *Smalcald Articles* (1537) III III 25 (Kolb-Wengert, p. 316; *Concordia*, pp. 274–75).

[137] Cf. *Small Catechism* (1529) III 14 (Kolb-Wengert, p. 357; *Concordia*, p. 335).

[138] *Kirchenweyse*

[139] Luther (and Melanchthon) could give the number of "sacraments" as either three or two, depending on the definition of the term as requiring a visible sign or not; they were much more concerned with upholding the divine power of the Word operating in Baptism, in the Supper, and in Absolution. See *Babylonian Captivity* (1520), LW 36:81–91, 123–24; *Large Catechism* (1529) IV 74 (Kolb-Wengert, pp. 465–66; *Concordia*, p. 430); Melanchthon, Ap XIII 2–4 (Kolb-Wengert, p. 219; *Concordia*, p. 184).

intercession; He applies these to the believers, unites us in one body with Him, and makes us brothers and heirs.

Those are the six parts of the laymen's or children's Bible,[140] which God Himself caused to be set in writing and explained for us through His Son and apostles, even as the entire holy Bible is nothing other than a foundation, witness, and solid explanation of the holy catechism, from which all sermons are drawn and to which they lead back.

Of course, it is true that the Ten Commandments of God are *scientia scientiarum*, a knowledge above the knowledge of all wise people, about true virtues.[141] And the Apostles' Creed, the children's Creed, is a history above all histories, which bears clear witness to the most eminent persons and to the greatest events: the creation and preservation of the world, the redemption and restoration of the human race, the kingdom and eternal rule of Jesus Christ at the right hand of the Father, as well as what has happened from the beginning of the world until now, what will continue on until the Last Day, and what will be throughout all of eternity. Likewise, the Our Father is a prayer above all prayers in all the world. Baptism, Absolution, and the Supper, along with the public preaching which, in accordance with Christ's command, takes place when the true body and blood of the Lord are distributed [cf. 1 Cor. 11:26] and will continue to take place until the end of the world, also transcend all the ceremonies, forms of worship, and liturgies of Moses and the whole world, not to mention the canons and rules of Mohammed, the pope, and monks, as well as their new articles of faith, their prayers, and their self-devised ceremonies [cf. Col. 2:23] and diabolical worship.

For it is with this lofty name[142] that Dr. Luther calls, honors, and attests the catechism for all pastors[143] and for everyone who wishes to be saved. Likewise, Dr. Bugenhagen always had the catechism on his person and spoke harshly to the ordinands who disregarded this book,[144] which God had restored to our churches and schools, for which we heartily thank You, Lord Christ, with the heartfelt wish that You would graciously preserve this catechism in our pulpits and schools. And if the manifest light of Your Word should be hidden under Zechariah's ephah [Zech. 5:8] before the Last Day on account of our ingratitude, may the holy catechism with the Wittenberg

---

[140] On the numbering of the "six parts," see above, p. 252 n. 127. On the expression "laymen's Bible" [*Laienbibel*], see above, p. 253 n. 134.

[141] Cf. *Table Talk* no. 757 (1530), WA TR 1:360; no. 6288 (n.d.), WA TR 5:581–82.

[142] I.e., "the laymen's Bible."

[143] *Seelsorgern*

[144] Perhaps at Mathesius' own ordination on March 29, 1542: see Volz, *Die Lutherpredigten des Johannes Mathesius*, p. 207. On Bugenhagen, see the introduction above, pp. xxxvi–xxxvii.

explanation be preserved in the homes and hearts of pious fathers as well as in the hearts of their children, and may it graciously be preserved from vain new patches [cf. Matt. 9:16]. For if anyone guards and seals his children's catechism in his heart, he will know how to lead a Christian life and die a blessed death, even if he were stuck in the midst of the papacy or of the Turks, as in the case of the boy who was captured and taken to Turkey during the first siege of Vienna.[145] During the second siege,[146] he sent his parents a letter (thrown by a Turk over the wall into the city), in which the captive boy confessed his Christian faith and promised his parents that in his physical captivity he would remain steadfast with Jesus Christ the crucified in the hope of eternal life.[147]

Children were properly baptized under the papacy and received the sure covenant of a good conscience [1 Pet. 3:21] for the sake of Christ's blood. As the Son of God wondrously preserved His baptized under the papacy, so also He preserved ¦some parts of the catechism for them in homes and schools. For parents and headmasters taught their children the Ten Commandments, Creed, and Our Father, even as I learned these parts in schools during my childhood and often recited them in front of other children according to the old school practice.[148]

The devil slipped the *Adiutorium*[149] into the old primers, corrupted with papistic doctrine, in order to turn baptized children into acolytes who would

---

[145] The first siege of Vienna by the Ottomans took place in September–October 1529; the "second" siege mentioned by Mathesius may be the unsuccessful Ottoman campaign of 1532. For more on the Hapsburg-Ottoman conflict, see Thomas A. Brady Jr., *German Histories in the Age of Reformations, 1400–1650* (Cambridge: Cambridge University Press, 2009), pp. 349–64.

[146] See below, Mathesius, *History*, p. 365.

[147] Urban Sagstetter (ca. 1529–73) was captured as a young child in 1529 and lived for years as an Ottoman slave, yet later became bishop of Gurk (1556–73), administrator of the see of Vienna (1563–68), and court preacher to Emperor Ferdinand I. See Brady, *German Histories in the Age of Reformations*, p. 361.

[148] Knowledge of the Apostles' Creed and the Lord's Prayer had been the basic standard for lay Christians in the medieval West since Carolingian times; in the late Middle Ages, the Ten Commandments were sometimes added, or some other systematic analysis of sins and good works (such as the seven deadly sins and seven corporal and spiritual works of mercy). See John Bossy, "Moral Arithmetic: Seven Sins into Ten Commandments," in *Conscience and Casuistry in Early Modern Europe*, ed. Edmund Leites (New York: Cambridge University Press, 1988), pp. 214–34. On Luther's perception of the preservation of the catechism in the medieval church, cf. above, Mathesius, *History*, pp. 117–18.

[149] A reference to one of two psalm texts used liturgically: either Ps. 70:1 [Ps. 69:2 Vg]: "*Deus in adiutorium meum intende*" ["Make haste, O God, to deliver me"]; or Ps. 124:8 [Ps. 123:8 Vg]: "*Adiutorium nostrum in nomine Domini*" ["Our help is in the name of the Lord"]. Ps. 70:1 was used at the beginning of the monastic offices (Matins, Vespers, etc.) but also at the beginning of the "Little Hours of the Virgin," a Marian devotion which became a staple in the primers used by late medieval laity. Ps. 124:8 was used as a versicle before

serve the papistic Mass at the altar, even as he interpolated the idolatrous *Salve Regina*[150] into the schoolbooks to detract from the one Mediator and Intercessor, Jesus Christ.

I cannot recall ever having heard [preaching about] the Ten Commandments, the Creed, the Our Father, or [the doctrine of] Baptism from the pulpit in my youth, having been lamentably captive in the papacy until the age of twenty-five.[151] In school during Lent, we read about confession and one kind [in the Lord's Supper].[152] As for the Absolution and comfort that are imparted through receiving the body and blood of Christ in faith—to my knowledge, never in my life did I hear so much as a word about that in church or in school until I came to Wittenberg. Likewise, I cannot recall ever having seen a printed or handwritten explanation of the catechism in the papacy,[153] though from my youth on I read all the legends and Birgitta prayers,[154] especially while I was in Munich with my

---

the priest's confession at the beginning of the Mass. On primers and the "Little Hours," see Eamon Duffy, *The Stripping of the Altars: Traditional Religion in England, c. 1400–c. 1580* (New Haven: Yale University Press, 1992), pp. 233–65; for the use of the *Adiutorium nostrum*, see Bard Thompson, *Liturgies of the Western Church* (Philadelphia: Fortress, 1961), pp. 56–57. Cf. Luther, *Ten Sermons on the Catechism* (1528), LW 51:171.

[150] The *Salve Regina* ["Hail, Queen"] is an eleventh-century Marian hymn, sung at Compline during the Trinity season and incorporated in prayer books (books of hours) for the laity. See Duffy, *Stripping of the Altars*, pp. 257, 265; John Harper, *The Forms and Orders of Western Liturgy from the Tenth to the Eighteenth Century* (Oxford: Clarendon, 2001), pp. 131–32. Cf. Luther, *Sermon on the Nativity of Mary* (September 8, 1522), WA 17/2:481; 10/3:321–22 (Baseley 2:156–65).

[151] On the obscuring of the content of the catechism in the medieval church, cf. Luther, preface to Cruciger's edition of the *Summer Postil* (1544), LW 77:7–8.

[152] On Communion in one kind [*sub una specie*], see above, p. 159 n. 112.

[153] Although there were certainly late medieval catechisms, catechetical instruction tended to focus on strategies for preparation for confession rather than on the "chief parts" as Luther and Mathesius regarded them. See, e.g., Dietrich Kolde, *Mirror for Christians*, in *Three Reformation Catechisms: Catholic, Anabaptist, Lutheran*, ed. Denis Janz (Toronto: Edwin Mellen Press, 1982), pp. 29–130.

[154] The most popular late medieval collection of saints' legends (so called because they were assigned to be read, *legenda*, at the appropriate festivals) was the *Legenda Aurea* [*Golden Legend*] of the Dominican Jacobus de Voragine (ca. 1230–ca. 1298): see LA 1–2. St. Birgitta of Sweden (ca. 1303–73), founder of the Bridgettine order, was associated with a cycle of fifteen prayers (the "Fifteen Oes") to which indulgences and other promises were attached; they became vastly popular in lay devotion in the late Middle Ages. See Duffy, *Stripping of the Altars*, pp. 249–54. Cf. Luther, *Personal Prayer Book* (1522), LW 43:12; *Exhortation to All Clergy* (1530), LW 34:25. On medieval lay prayer books as a whole, see also the introduction by Gustav K. Wiencke, LW 43:5–6.

lord, who had a very extensive German library, where I read through these for a whole year.[155]

Dear friends, I am mentioning this in the history of our doctor in order to honor this blessed treasure, the holy catechism, which I brought from Wittenberg and Altenburg[156] into this valley, and, by God's grace, from my school into the homes of many people, and, finally, into the church and pulpit—to God be glory and praise!—and ʼwhich I have often explained and taught over these thirty years.[157] Even if Dr. Luther had instituted and accomplished nothing good in his life aside from having brought back into homes, schools, and the pulpit the catechism, as well as the prayer before and after meals and before going to bed and upon rising, the whole world could never thank him enough or adequately repay him.[158]

At this time Doctor Martin fell into severe tribulation;[159] he had often had to endure a beating from the devil, but now he experienced physical and spiritual anxiety and distress so great that he despaired of his life.[160] Dr. Bugenhagen and Dr. Justus Jonas[161] witnessed his anxiety, deep sighs, and tears of pain, as well as his glorious confession and fatherly concern for the afflicted Christian Church, as they attended to him; they recorded these things at length, and they were included in the volumes [of Luther's works].[162] When the inward grief and hellish tribulation of the patriarchs and all the saints is revealed on the Last Day along with their great comfort and deliverance from all their tribulations, then we will see what great martyrs God

---

[155] In 1525, Mathesius apparently was employed by a Herr Kasimir living at the ducal court in Munich. See Loesche, *Johannes Mathesius*, 1:26–28.

[156] On Mathesius' first period as a student in Wittenberg and his subsequent teaching post in Altenburg, see above, Mathesius, *History*, pp. 111–12.

[157] See above, p. lxxxv n. 339 for two collections of Mathesius' own sermons and lessons on the catechism. In addition, see Mathesius, *Kurze Außlegung der Sontags Evangelion, und Catechismi* (Nürnberg: Berg & Neuber, 1558) [VD16 M1505]. For more information on his catechism preaching and teaching, see Loesche, *Johannes Mathesius*, 1:553–74. Cf above, pp. 252–53 and nn. 130–31 there.

[158] Luther appended the mentioned prayers to his *Small Catechism* already in 1529: see WA 30/1:260–63 (Kolb-Wengert, pp. 363–64; *Concordia*, pp. 344–45).

[159] *Anfechtung*; see above, Jonas and Coelius, *Report*, p. 9; Melanchthon, *Preface*, pp. 59–60.

[160] This episode took place on July 6, 1527, with difficulties continuing into August. See Luther to Spalatin, July 10, 1527, WA Br 4:221; to Melanchthon, August 2, 1527, WA Br 4:226–27. A report on Luther's *Anfechtungen* by Bugenhagen and Jonas included in the Wittenberg and Jena editions was probably Mathesius' source (see the next sentence and Volz, *Die Lutherpredigten des Johannes Mathesius*, p. 241). Their report is reproduced (in German translation) in StL 21a:985–96 and in *Table Talk* no. 2922b (1533), WA TR 3:81–90. See Brecht 2:205–7 and cf. below, Mathesius, *History*, p. 551.

[161] On Jonas, see above, p. xxx.

[162] See above, n. 160.

had on the earth. Some examples of this kind of mortal agony are recorded in order to furnish patience, comfort, and refreshment for the afflicted, that in the midst of their own fear of hell and the pangs of death they may be instructed by and take heart from the bloody sweat of Jesus Christ and His struggle for life and death. For in these, holy people sip from God's cup the drink He has poured for His own house, and they taste what His wrath and the fear of hell are [cf. Ps. 75:8; Matt. 26:39; Luke 22:42]. But the Son of God intercedes for them, delivers them, and helps them to endure this through His power. The godless, however, who ridicule such wretched people, just as they did Christ on the cross [Luke 23:35], will one day find themselves drinking up the dregs [Ps. 75:8] for all of eternity in the eternal fire of hell, along with their torturers, the horrible devils, and suffering from an eternally afflicted heart ¦in the unquenchable flames of hell. That is what they chose, because they would not be gathered under the shadow of Christ's wings [Matt. 23:37; Ps. 91:1] by the words of the catechism during the time of grace.

Among other wonderful words that the doctor uttered from his depths of woe[163] [Ps. 130:1] and Peter's sieve [Luke 22:31],[164] he also said that he would gladly have shed his blood for the glory of Christ and His Gospel, but he comforted himself with the fact that St. John the Evangelist also fell asleep without having shed his blood. Thus he was satisfied that he was absolved with Christ's words by his pastor[165] and was assuredly fed with the true body and blood of Jesus Christ to strengthen his faith and make it certain. Moreover, it cut him to the heart that the devil would take conscience-stricken spirits and dying people and snatch away this comfort through the Sacramentarians and followers of Stenkfeld,[166] who, as mentioned before, were fanaticizing in large numbers against Christ's institution.

---

[163] *inn seim Deprofundis*, from the first words of Psalm 130 in the Vg.

[164] Cf. Luther to Amsdorf, November 1, 1527, WA Br 4:274–75.

[165] I.e., Johann Bugenhagen. Cf. above, p. 258.

[166] "Stenck[e]feld" (literally, "stink-field") was a pejorative nickname coined by Luther (see *Brief Confession* [1544], LW 38:288) for the Silesian nobleman Caspar von Schwenkfeld [von Ossig] (1489–1561), who, after early sympathy with Luther and success in planting the Reformation in Silesia, moved in an increasingly Spiritualist direction, visiting Luther in late 1525 to present his new theology of the Supper as a feeding on the "spiritual food" of Christ's heavenly body; Zwingli and Oecolampadius demonstrated their recognition of Schwenkfeld by publishing some of his treatises themselves. Luther rejected Schwenkfeld's theology in a letter addressed to him (April 14, 1526, LW 49:148–50) and then (not always by name) in his printed works on the Supper (e.g., *That These Words of Christ* [1527], LW 37:41; *Confession concerning Christ's Supper* [1528], LW 37:288–94, 321). Schwenkfeld's other emphases included insistence on the ethical fruits of justification, the inner Word, and a Christology asserting that Christ's human nature, including His body, was not earthly or creaturely but a heavenly and divine thing: see Luther, *Disputation on the Divinity and Humanity of*

Once God had brought Doctor Luther back out of this hell through the help and intercession of Jesus Christ—who alone can help in such adversities and deliver us from hell and death—he comforted and strengthened his brethren [cf. Luke 22:32]. And since Karlstadt, though reconciled, kept stabbing [at Luther] from behind the fence[167] and was colluding now with Zwingli, now with Stenkfeld and Krautwald,[168] the Silesian fanatics, and because (contrary to his promise) he was secretly disseminating his poison again through his writings and trying to intrude his uncertain opinion into the electoral court,[169] Doctor Luther refuted Karlstadt's trumpery with a learned treatise,[170] which also displeased Karlstadt's fellow sectarians.

Now since this inconstant and restless man could find no peace in either his old position or in his new life as a peasant, and since, as is characteristic of those with a wicked nature, he would not allow himself to be overcome by any kindness, he secretly crept off again and joined those who justified and defended his recanted fanaticism in their own corners.[171] Thus he proved and confirmed Doctor Luther's rule that arch-heretics rarely turn back to God and His truth with their hearts.[172]

Christ (1540), WA 39/2:93–121 (LW 73). After residence in Strassburg from 1529 to 1534, Schwenkfeld lived a peripatetic existence until settling with supporters in Ulm shortly before his death. See R. Emmet McLaughlin, "Schwenckfeld, Kaspar von," OER 4:21–23; David C. Steinmetz, "Caspar Schwenckfeld (1489–1561): The Renunciation of Structure," in Reformers in the Wings (New York: Oxford University Press, 2001), pp. 131–37; R. Emmet McLaughlin, Caspar Schwenckfeld, Reluctant Radical: His Life to 1540 (New Haven: Yale University Press, 1986). On his theology of the Lord's Supper, see Schwenkfeld, A Letter to Luther's Malediction (1544), LCC 25:161–81.

[167] durch den zaun stach; literally, "stabbed through the fence." See Wander 5:511, "Zaun" no. 90. On Karlstadt's "reconciliation," see above, pp. 238–39.

[168] Valentin Crautwald (1465?–1545), a cathedral canon in Liegnitz from 1524 to 1537, was a humanist and spiritualist who collaborated with Schwenkfeld, supporting his theology with his visions. On his works during the controversy over the Supper, see the introduction by Robert H. Fischer, LW 37:11. See Douglas H. Shantz, "Crautwald, Valentin," OER 1:451–52. Karlstadt's letter of May 17, 1528, to Schwenkfeld and Krautwald was intercepted by the elector's agents; it is described by Luther in a letter to Gregor Brück of September 24, 1528, WA Br 4:568–73, which includes Karlstad's letter as an appendix. On Karlstadt's relation with Zwingli, see Burnett, Karlstadt and the Origins of the Eucharistic Controversy, pp. 91–114.

[169] Karlstadt, Explanation of 1 Corinthians 10 (1525), On the New and Old Testament (1525), A Declaration of How Karlstadt Regards His Teaching about the Venerable Sacrament (1525), in Burnett, Eucharistic Pamphlets of Andreas Bodenstein von Karlstadt, pp. 205–69.

[170] That These Words of Christ (1527), LW 37:3–150.

[171] Karlstadt served as a deacon in the Zurich Grossmünster from 1530 to 1534, and then as a professor of Old Testament at the University of Basel until his death in 1541. Ulrich Bubenheimer, "Bodenstein von Karlstadt, Andreas," OER 1:179–80.

[172] See That These Words of Christ (1527), LW 37:19–21; Confession concerning Christ's Supper (1528), LW 37:162; Lectures on Malachi (1526/1554), LW 18:394; Lectures on 1 John (1527/1708),

As for what Karlstadt did in those places, and how before his end he was terrified by seeing an evil spirit with his own eyes while in the pulpit,[173] these things are attested in the writings of Herr Melanchthon,[174] who faithfully warned everyone of this man's fanaticism in his good *Passages concerning the Lord's Supper.*[175]

But since Karlstadt's students and fellow sectarians took strength from his arrival[176] and without any call[177] started pouring out the slops of their uncertain doctrine among the people and into other churches by means of many heated treatises,[178] Dr. Luther was compelled, alongside his other admonitory treatises, to put his confession of the Lord's Supper into writing.[179] In this confession he forcefully opposed the Sacramentarians' empty and worthless thoughts, seven-cleft glosses,[180] false interpretations, and twisted sayings;

WA 20:795 (cf. LW 30:324–25), where Rörer's text (not used for LW 30) reads: "I have often said that it is not easy to find a case in which the author of a heresy has been converted." On Mathesius' possession of this text in manuscript, see below, *History,* p. 288.

[173] Cf. below, Mathesius, *History,* p. 546.

[174] Karlstadt died in Basel on December 24, 1541. A letter on Karlstadt's death, from Johannes Oporinus (1507–68) to Joachim Camerarius, is included in Melanchthon's works, CR 4:784, which, however, speaks of an apparition *after* Karlstadt's death, a story reflected also in Luther to Jonas, February 16, 1542, LW 50:225–30. The story as reported by Mathesius is found in Oswald Myconius to Luther, March 17, 1542, WA Br 10:13, and Veit Dietrich to Luther, March 1542, WA Br 10:27; this account is passed on by Luther to Amsdorf, April 7, 1542, WA Br 10:29. These letters are reproduced, without the names of their authors, in Alberus, *Widder die verfluchte lere der Carlstader,* fol. m1a–b. See Volz, *Die Lutherpredigten des Johannes Mathesius,* p. 107 n. 1. On the various accounts of Karlstadt's death—friendly as well as hostile—see Bruce Gordon, "Malevolent Ghosts and Ministering Angels: Apparitions and Pastoral Care in the Swiss Reformation," in *The Place of the Dead: Death and Remembrance in Late Medieval and Early Modern Europe,* ed. Bruce Gordon and Peter Marshall (New York: Cambridge University Press, 2000), pp. 87–89.

[175] Melanchthon, *Sententiae veterum aliquot scriptorum de Coena Domini* (1530), CR 23:727–52, translated into German as *Vom Abendmahl des Herrn, Etliche sprüche der alten Veter* (1532): see CR 23:729–32. See the attack on Karlstadt in Melanchthon's dedicatory letter, CR 2:31; MBW T4/1:48–49. On the *Sententiae,* cf. below, Mathesius, *History,* pp. 310, 356.

[176] Fleeing from Saxony in 1529, Karlstadt traveled to Holstein and East Frisia, where he stayed with the Anabaptist Melchior Hoffman before finding refuge in Zurich with Zwingli in 1530.

[177] *one befelh*

[178] See the introduction by Robert H. Fischer, LW 37:8–11, for a list of treatises against Luther's theology of the Lord's Supper.

[179] *Confession concerning Christ's Supper* (1528), LW 37:151–372. The other "admonitory writings" [*Warnungschriften*] probably include *Warning to Guard against Public Errors on the Sacrament* (1527), WA Br 3:599–611.

[180] On the seven "heads" [cf. Rev. 13:1]—i.e., varying exegetical and theological positions— of the Sacramentarian movement, see Luther, first preface to Brenz, *Swabian Syngramma* (1526), LW 59:157–58; *That These Words of Christ* (1527), LW 37:41–42.

he thoroughly expounded and proved his faith on the basis of the words of Jesus Christ and the evangelists while also presenting a full confession of his faith concerning all the articles. This book was responsible for bringing many people who had been shamefully led astray back to the right path, even as this book served to renew my own strength when I was in Bavaria and stirred in me the desire to see and hear the man the following year.[181]

Dr. Luther's books from this time testify to what was going on among the Papists and wicked neighbors, as well as how Dr. Luther joined battle with those who challenged him. For although our God wanted to use him as a Moses to lead the captive Christian Church out of the Babylonian captivity by the power of the Gospel, this Moses of ours, as we heard at the beginning, encountered many obstacles placed in his way by his own people, who wanted to preach the Gospel alongside him. Likewise his neighbors refused to give the Gospel safe passage and were continually blocking its way as well as persecuting and maligning his assistants. However, even as the spiritual pharaoh and his monastic taskmasters and whoever else entered their consecrated service were unable to force our Moses to yield much, such also was the outcome with Dr. Luther's Korah, Dathan, Abiram, the wicked sons of Aaron, Balaam, and all those who opposed the staff of Moses and the rod of Aaron.

Jannes and Jambres, whom St. Paul mentions [2 Tim. 3:8; cf. Exod. 7:11, 22], also helped attack the afflicted Moses, but they have been forgotten by the pious along with the [other] godless people like the coppersmith and goldsmith [2 Tim. 4:14; Acts 19:24], whom St. Paul also mentions, as well as Pilate [Acts 13:28; 1 Tim. 6:13]. The godly must suffer tribulation, but the remembrance of Moses and God's servants remains while the heretics and tyrants are brought low. That is why Amalek, Sihon, the great Og of Bashan, Ammon, and Moab (all of whom wanted to suppress or at least to hinder God's witnesses, and therefore gathered many violent confederates and used force to oppress and torment their own subjects) along with Balak (who won over friend and foe from among the scholars[182] and filled their mouths [with his own words])—none of these, I say, was able to accomplish anything or prevail against the little flock of Jesus Christ and His faithful servants, who adhered to the strong Word of God and prayed patiently and waited with long-suffering, until God Himself intervened and took away one after the other [Num. 21:21–24:25]. The Ephraimites, too, wanted to go to battle too

---

[181] See above, pp. 257–58. Mathesius came to Wittenberg in 1529. See Loesche, *Johannes Mathesius*, 1:39.

[182] I.e., the prophet Balaam [Numbers 22].

soon and sweep out the Canaanites, against the counsel and faithful warning of Moses [Num. 14:41–45], but all they won in the end was a sore neck.[183]

At the prompting of good people, Doctor Luther endeavored at that time with kindness and gentleness to restore peace and friendly relations with wicked neighbors,[184] |but the people's ears had been stuffed with the Levitical frogs that had been spewed forth from the great dragon [Rev. 12:3; 16:13], as we see in the preface to the Revelation of John,[185] and their hearts had been bewitched, so that they scorned good counsel and faithful admonition, and soon thereafter they and those with them were destroyed amid terror and tumult.[186]

Truly, dear friends, many gentle writings were also published at that time,[187] in which peace and concord were sought, and people who had been oppressed or who had suffered injury were counseled simply to bear it patiently and kindly while committing and commending their cause to God, who is faithful, and while remaining obedient as subjects in the body, to confess God's Word and what preserves a good conscience. If they suffered violence on that account, they were to bite the sour apple[188] until God awoke [cf. Ps. 44:23]. Or in the meantime, they could defend and preserve themselves using their due legal rights. God would surely care for those who are His at the proper time, as indeed happened a few years later.[189]

---

[183] *sie gewannen entlich das krimmen im nacken.* Cf. Wander 2:1634, "Krimmen" no. 1; *DWB*, 4:6023.

[184] In 1528–29, Luther, though sharply denouncing Duke George of Saxony's efforts to enforce Communion in one kind (see above, p. 159 n. 112) in ducal Saxony, advised his subjects to remain as obedient as possible without violating conscience and, though Luther gave credence to what were in fact forged reports that Duke George had entered a military alliance for the destruction of the Evangelicals, he nonetheless urged against preemptive war. See Brecht 2:351–52, 355–58. See Luther to Nicholas Hausmann, March 29, 1527, LW 49:161–64; to Elector John, May 1 or 2, 1528, LW 49:189–95; to the Christians at Halle, April 26, 1528, WA Br 4:444–45; to Heinrich von Einsiedel, January 24, 1528, WA Br 4:356–60.

[185] *Preface to Revelation* (1530), LW 35:407–8, where "the frogs are the sophists, such as Faber, Eck, Emser, etc."

[186] Jerome Emser, who attacked Luther under the patronage of Duke George, died suddenly in November 1527. On Emser, see above, p. 156 n. 98; below, p. 482 n. 115; and above, p. 244.

[187] See *Letter of Consolation to the Christians at Halle* (1527), LW 43:139–65; *Report to a Good Friend concerning Both Kinds in the Sacrament* (1528), WA 26:560–618 (LW 61).

[188] *in ein sauren apffel bissen*; Wander 2:1663, "Kugel" nos. 12–13.

[189] I.e., when the Reformation finally prevailed in Albertine (ducal) Saxony in 1539 (see below, Mathesius, *History*, p. 421; cf. p. 313 n. 185) and in Halle in 1541 (see the introduction above, p. xxx; below, Mathesius, *History*, p. 408). See *Sermon Preached in Castle Pleissenburg, Leipzig* (1539), LW 51:301–12; *Sermon on John 5:39–43* (1545), delivered in Halle, LW 58:242–58; *Sermon for the Rededication of the Church of St. Paul in Leipzig* (1545), LW 58:259–80; *Sermons for Epiphany and the Conversion of St. Paul* (1546), delivered in Halle, LW 58:349–84. See Brecht 3:297–300.

Moses with his staff, and those who leaned upon it, prevailed; no matter how hard the lords in the wilderness tried, they had to go away empty-handed.[190] And good counsel did come with the new day:[191] those who had been oppressed and driven out arose again and went in while the others went out. This is what will finally happen with God's Word and all those who hold fast to it and possess their souls in patience [Luke 21:19].

Who trusts in God, will surely be
A man of all corruption free.
Death, devil, world rage violently;
Christ gives His own the victory.[192]

With this, dear friends, we will close the year 1528 in Dr. Luther's history and give thanks to God, who has freed us from the Egyptian darkness and Babylonian captivity and has led us through the wilderness, wicked neighbors, ¦diabolical sorcerers, and false brethren to the promised land, protecting us along the way and removing many stumbling blocks. We ask, moreover, that He would abide with us hereafter, for the night is drawing near [Luke 24:29],[193] and that He would be our leader and guide,[194] and strengthen us through His Word and Spirit, that we may take offense neither at Him [Matt. 11:6] nor at the seditious people and false brethren, nor blame the holy Gospel for provoking any revolt or strife, but instead take comfort from the history of Moses. Although his office of teaching and governing[195] also had to endure many assaults from rebels and fanatics, the Son of God was with him and made Himself seen and heard and manifest in His deeds; He protected the godly who held fast to the Word and stood firmly by Moses with steadfast hearts, and gave a good thrashing to those who wanted to reject, scorn, and overthrow Moses.

---

[190] *den ring inn der thür lassen*; literally, "to leave the ring in the door": see Wander 3:1689, "Ring" no. 39. Cf. above, Mathesius, *History*, p. 200.

[191] *Es kam auch mit dem tag guter rath*; cf. Wander 3:1474, "Rath" no. 169.

[192] A version of these verses by Luther (not published until 1728) appears as an inscription under Lucas Cranach's portrait of John the Steadfast: see WA 35:590; Friedländer and Rosenberg, *Paintings of Lucas Cranach*, no. 338B, pp. 135–36. The first two lines appear as a proverb in Wander 2:89, "Gott" no. 2167. The last two lines vary between the Cranach portrait and Mathesius' version or versions (see below, *History*, p. 347; *Sarepta*, fol. 287r [Loesche, *Mathesius: Ausgewählte Werke*, 4:273–74]). Both Luther and Mathesius may have independently adapted an established bit of popular verse: see Volz, *Die Lutherpredigten des Johannes Mathesius*, pp. 113–14 n. 8.

[193] Cf. Melanchthon's Latin couplet based on Luke 24:29: CR 23:723.

[194] Cf. the hymn by Nicolaus Herman, "*In Gottes Namen fahren wir*," Wackernagel 3:1229–30, no. 1436. Cf. "Lord Jesus Christ, with Us Abide," *LSB* 585, stanza 1.

[195] *lehr und wehrampt*

So, then, if anyone objects today also that much strife and fanaticism have been stirred up during the time of the Gospel, let him refer to the story of Moses: he was truly a faithful servant in the house of God [Heb. 3:2] and was close to Christ and His Word; nevertheless, the ancient serpent never rests, but has bitten into Christ's heel and the preaching office from the beginning [Gen. 3:15],[196] and during the ages of all the prophets he has sown his tares and cockles amid the holy seeds of God's Church [Matt. 13:25] and has befouled the true Church of God with terrible offenses and dissension.

For it does not hold true what some claim: "Many Evangelicals lead wicked lives; therefore, it is a doctrine of the devil."[197] Rather, this stands firm: The Papists and fanatics teach apart from and contrary to God's Word. Therefore, their see and schools, doctrine and office, glosses and interpretations—even their discipline and sanctimonious lives—cannot be right in any way, even if they possess these in abundance.

If anyone is of God, he hears God's Word [John 8:47] and distinguishes offenses and abuses from it, preserving faith and a good conscience [1 Tim. 1:19]. If anyone stirs up heresy, idolatry, factions, sects, and schism, he will not escape the devil, even if he is sometimes able to evade the executioner and temporal punishment until his time comes.

Glory and praise be to God, who cares for His little flock and faithful servants as a father, from now on and into all eternity! And though He leads them in fearsome ways [cf. Isa. 29:14], still He does not reject them, but preserves them to His glory and through them gathers an eternal Church for Himself. As He says, "Fear not, little flock, for it is God's good-pleasure to give you His eternal kingdom" [Luke 12:32]. Amen!

---

[196] See above, p. 104 n. 10.

[197] The charge that the Reformation had failed to produce moral improvement among its adherents was a stumbling block for Caspar von Schwenkfeld, among others. See, e.g., Schwenkfeld's 1524 *Admonition* [VD16 S4914]; Erasmus, letter to Martin Bucer, November 11, 1527, CWE 13:428–30, no. 1901. See Luther's response in *Table Talk* no. 624 (1533), LW 54:110.

The Seventh[1] Sermon,
on Jotham's Fable, Judges 9

Shrove Tuesday, [February 23,] 1563

BELOVED friends in the Lord! Having held the mining sermons for some years now at this miners' festival of yours,[2] today we will continue with the history of Doctor Luther and pay the occasion its due.[3] In order that we may take up something amusing and delightful, and so that we may all the more appropriately discuss the doctor's [edition of] Aesop['s fables],[4] you shall hear, by way of introduction, an ancient fable that the Holy Spirit had recorded in His holy Bible and handed down to us.

When Jotham, the son of Gideon or Jerubbaal, wanted to punish the Jews for having so quickly forgotten his father, their faithful judge [Judg. 8:33–35], having so savagely attacked his sixty-nine sons and having set up a wicked man as ruler [Judg. 9:5–6], he told them this fable, which has been recorded by the Holy Spirit in chapter 9 [:7–20] of the Book of Judges.

Jotham said, "Listen, men of Shechem, that God may listen to you again. The trees wanted to anoint a king over themselves and said to the olive tree: 'Be our king.' But he answered, 'Shall I leave my fatness, which is praised by God and men alike, and rule over the trees?' Since the olive tree declined in this manner, they directed their request to the fig tree, who also refused to acquiesce to the ungrateful trees: 'Shall I leave my sweetness and good

---

[1] Some later editions of Mathesius' sermons place this sermon as the ninth, after the sermon on the Diet of Augsburg, in closer chronological sequence, since Luther worked on his translation of Aesop (ca. 620–564 BC) while he was in the Coburg in 1530. See below, Mathesius, *History*, p. 350. On the sequence of the sermons, see the introduction above, p. lxxxvii.

[2] Mathesius' sixteen mining sermons, delivered on Shrove Tuesdays and some New Year's days between 1552 and 1562, were published in the *Sarepta oder Bergpostill* (see above, p. lxxxii n. 321). See Loesche, *Johannes Mathesius*, 1:490–521; Brown, *Singing the Gospel*, p. 27.

[3] *der zeyt jr recht thun*; Wander 5:541, "Zeit" no. 403.

[4] Luther began preparing a German version of Aesop in 1530 (and his original manuscript still survives in the Vatican Library), but completed only thirteen fables and a preface. The unfinished work was not published until after his death, when it appeared in 1557 in Jena Ger 5, fols. 285v–290r, and in Witt Ger 9, fols. 454v–458r, as *Selected Fables of Aesop*, WA 50:432–60 (LW 61); Springer, *Luther's Aesop* (see above, p. 58 n. 22).

fruit and reign over the trees?' Then the trees said to the vine: 'You be our king.' He answered, 'Shall I leave my wine, which cheers God and men, and be a ruler over you? That is no good counsel.' Therefore, the trees chose the bramble. 'If it is true, and you really want me to be your master,' said the prickly ruler, 'then all of you come and entrust yourselves to my shade. If not, let fire come out of the bramble and devour the cedars of Lebanon.'"

This is the fable of Jotham, the wise man and great ruler and physical savior in Israel, the son of Gideon. I am relating this to you so that you may see that the Holy Spirit is also pleased by this manner of speaking, when wise people use veiled and obscure language to preach to ungrateful and coarse people and that the wisest men on earth, among both Jews and heathen, as well as within Christendom, are very fond of employing this manner of speaking, couching the loftiest wisdom according to God's Word in these images and likenesses of irrational creatures and beasts and presenting them to the people.

Therefore, I hope that you will also excuse me today for calling to mind on Shrove Tuesday the doctor's [version of] Aesop and how much care he devoted to these wise and prudent fables.

For since, as you have heard, our doctor had now spent many years in severe conflict against the monks and fanatics and had worked himself weary with preaching and translating the holy Bible, and [now] began to suffer from vertigo, as he wrote from the Coburg as he began this work, he therefore also wished to refresh and entertain himself a little, as great people are wont to do.[5] He had observed that the Holy Spirit had caused prudent and wise fables to be set down in His Bible and that the ancients had delighted in ᶥcloaking and veiling such truth and wisdom with animal skins and proverbs.[6] Wise people had put together their own book of fables with great insight, but now it had been tainted by coarse and ignorant people mixing their muddled and indecent discourses and fables.[7] Accordingly, he used the time after meals in the Coburg[8] to take up the old German Aesop in order to purify it and adorn it with good, strong German words

---

[5] See Luther to Melanchthon, April 24, 1530, LW 49:287–91, and May 12, 1530, WA Br 5:316–17, which mentions tinnitus and fainting spells; to Wenceslaus Linck, May 8, 1530, WA Br 5:309. Cf. Brecht 2:374–75.

[6] Aesop's fables (at least all of those translated by Luther) had animals as main characters and used their actions to convey pithy moral lessons.

[7] Cf. Luther, preface to *Selected Fables of Aesop* (1530/1557), WA 50:454 (LW 61); Springer, *Luther's Aesop*, pp. 83–86.

[8] Mathesius may have received a detailed report on Luther's activity from Veit Dietrich: see below, *History*, p. 354; Volz, *Die Lutherpredigten des Johannes Mathesius*, p. 124.

and beautiful explanations or moral instruction.[9] He made sixteen[10] splendid fables packed full of wisdom, good instruction, and astute admonition, containing excellent images and illustrations *de casibus mundi* ["about the affairs of the world"], showing how things typically go in the world, both in governments and in domestic affairs here on earth.

Having begun this delightful and useful work, he also furnished it with a preface,[11] in which he confesses that, after Holy Scripture, the world's finest wisdom is to be found in prudent fables, if only one were to contemplate them carefully.[12] For beneath the animals and trees, one can find the true little pearl of the world's wisdom, just as the rooster found a precious little gem in the dung.[13] Blessed are those who know this and are able

---

[9] By "the old German Aesop" is meant Heinrich Steinhöwel, [*Fabulae*] (Ulm: J. Zainer der Ä., ca. 1476), cited here in the edition of Hermann Oesterley, ed., *Steinhöwels Äsop*, Bibliothek des literarischen Vereins in Stuttgart 117 (Tübingen: L. F. Fues, 1873). Steinhöwel's edition of Aesop presented an adaptation of the Latin verse fables by Phaedrus (fl. first century) (see Babrius and Phaedrus, *Fables*, ed. Ben Edwin Perry [Loeb 436 (1965)]) and those in Latin prose by "Romulus" (see Georg Thiele, ed., *Der lateinische Aesop des Romulus und die Prosa-Fassungen des Phaedrus* [Heidelberg: Winter, 1910; repr., Hildesheim: Olms, 1985]) alongside Steinhöwel's German translation. For modern English readers, versions of Aesop's fables are available in the facing text of the Loeb edition of Phaedrus, as well as in Laura Gibbs, trans. and ed., *Aesop's Fables* (Oxford: Oxford University Press, 2002). The appendix of Loeb 436 gives a nearly complete numbered list of Aesopic fables compiled by the editor; these are cited as Perry by number.

[10] In fact, there are thirteen fables in the printed version of Luther's Aesop. Luther's manuscript had contained fourteen numbered items, of which no. 11 was not a fable but a contemporary anecdote about the late jurist Dr. Mogenhofer (d. 1510): see WA 50:446–47; Springer, *Luther's Aesop*, pp. 160–61. This was omitted in the printed versions of the fables, but the numbering of the remaining fables was maintained (skipping from no. 10 to no. 12). Finally, the Roman numeral for the last fable in both the Wittenberg and the Jena editions was transposed from XIV to XVI, so that a quick check of the last number suggested that there were sixteen fables. See WA 50:438; Volz, *Die Lutherpredigten des Johannes Mathesius*, pp. 155, 242, on *LH* 139.9.

[11] For Luther's preface, see WA 50:452–55 (LW 61); Springer, *Luther's Aesop*, pp. 82–87. The exact date of Luther's composition of the preface (not present in Luther's 1530 manuscript) is unknown, but it is mentioned as complete in *Table Talk* no. 4085 (1538), WA TR 4:126. Mathesius possessed a manuscript copy of Luther's preface: see Mathesius to Paul Eber, May 7, 1557, in Loesche, *Mathesius: Ausgewählte Werke*, 4:569; Volz, *Die Lutherpredigten des Johannes Mathesius*, p. 113.

[12] Cf. Luther's comments in the *Table Talk*: "In short, next to the Bible the writings of Cato and Aesop are in my opinion the best, better than the mangled utterances of all the philosophers and jurists" (LW 54:211).

[13] "The Rooster and the Pearl" was the first fable in Luther's collection: WA 50:455 (LW 61); Springer, *Luther's Aesop*, p. 104; Phaedrus, *Fables* 3.12 (Loeb 436 [1965], pp. 278–79; Perry no. 503); Thiele, *Der lateinische Aesop des Romulus*, no. 1, pp. 8–11; Gibbs, *Aesop's Fables*, no. 403, p. 188.

skillfully to make proper and fitting use of them at the right time and in appropriate places.

As the royal prophet David lauded his Psalter in the first psalm, which is the preface to the Book of Psalms,[14] so also the masters who compiled the fables praised this book in the first fable, commending it to the people. Although peasants and the simple pay no heed to the wisdom hidden in the fables, regarding it as worthless, it still is and remains a noble little pearl and wise little book containing much good instruction, faithful admonition, and astute warning. For even though the worldly-wise portray Aesop as a Carnival bogeyman or hobgoblin for the sake of the children and the simple,[15] this book was in fact put together not by any fool or person lacking wisdom, but by some of the most intelligent people on earth. For it was not only the ancient Latins and Greeks, but the noblest Jews, who always possessed the true religion, also devoted themselves to the wisdom of fables.

Thus the first wise authors of fables were not in Phrygia[16] or Greece, but among the Jews long before, as is clearly proved, for example, by Jotham's fable, which was already old in the three-thousandth year [of the world], before the birth of Christ.[17] What if Asaph[18] the choirmaster, who composed many fine psalms, were the true Aesop, the first to compile the fables, as other people compiled Solomon's proverbs? After all, their names are nearly identical.

Now since this is one of the most clever and subtle ways for great people to convey the bitter truth and harsh reality (which otherwise would be odious and unpleasant) even to children, just like sugar-coated bitter medicine,[19]

---

[14] On Psalm 1 as preface to the Psalter, see [Ps.]-Jerome, *Breviarium in Psalmos* (PL 26:832); Peter Lombard, *In Psalmos Davidicos Comentarii* (PL 191:60); *Glossa ordinaria*, Ps. 1:1, "Psalmus iste primus," in *Biblia Latina cum Glossa Ordinaria: Facsimile Reprint of the Editio Princeps Adolph Rusch of Strassburg 1480/81*, ed. Karlfried Froehlich and Margaret T. Gibson (Turnhout: Brepols, 1992), fol. 458v.

[15] Grotesque and frightening masks were a feature of Carnival celebrations. Aesop was depicted as deformed and frightening in appearance by classical sources (see Gibbs, *Aesop's Fables*, p. ix) such as the first-century *Life of Aesop*, included in Oesterley, *Steinhöwels Äsop*, p. 6, a tradition reflected in the woodcut frontispiece of the original Ulm edition and many others.

[16] Phrygia, in Asia Minor, was traditionally identified as Aesop's homeland, at least in the *Life of Aesop* prefixed to Steinhöwel: see Gibbs, *Aesop's Fables*, p. ix.

[17] According to Luther's chronology in the *Supputatio annorum mundi* (1541, 1545), WA 53:75, the usurpation of Abimelech took place in the year 2693 after the creation of the world, or 1267 BC. Aesop would have been born around the year 3340 after creation according to this reckoning (ca. 620 BC).

[18] On Asaph, see 1 Chron. 16:5, 7; Psalms 50, 73–83, especially Ps. 78:2.

[19] *überzuckerten Wurmsamen unnd Kellerhals*; i.e., absinthe and spurge laurel (whose berries were used as a purgative). Cf. Luther, *Lectures on Galatians* (1531/1535), LW 26:417.

and since illustrious people have often accomplished great things with rulers, subjects, children, and servants by means of such fables, our doctor decided to devote his effort and work to the old, corrupted [edition of] Aesop and to prepare for his Germans a renewed and purified book of fables. Many good people at that time were delighted by this book; when Herr Philip saw our doctor's preface and the fables, he asked him to go on and complete this book and said that he would procure a thousand gulden[20] for him from a great lord, to whom he should dedicate it.[21]

However, since this precious man was laboring on [translating] the Bible in addition to much preaching and writing, this work that he had begun remained unfinished. Master Georg Rörer later included what had been started in the ninth part of Luther's German works.[22] Although this useful [edition of] Aesop was not completed,[23] nonetheless Doctor Luther was fond, both before and after [working on it], of using the ancient fables and the prudent proverbs that have come into the German language from the fables, especially when speaking of the government and court life at table and in his books.[24]

In [his exposition of] the beautiful court psalm, Psalm 101,[25] regarded by Doctor Cruciger as the most learned and wisest work in the German language, Doctor [Luther] mentions the ape that wanted to split wood: having forgotten to pound in a wedge, when he pulled the ax out of the wood he

[20] See above, p. 128 n. 79.

[21] This account rests on Mathesius' testimony. On Melanchthon's support for the translation of Aesop's fables and their use in the schools, see Springer, *Luther's Aesop*, pp. 188–89. In 1526, Melanchthon had written a treatise *De utilitate fabularum* [On the usefulness of fables], CR 11:116–20, and in 1545 he supplied a preface, dated March 17 or 18, for Joachim Camerarius, *Fabulae Aesopicae Quaedam Notiores* (Leipzig: V. Babst, 1545) [VD16 A500]: see MBW T14:207–10, no. 3850 (CR 7:561–64).

[22] On Rörer, see above, p. xx n. 20. Mathesius' description here of the publication of Luther's version of Aesop is misleading. Rörer was in fact by 1557 working on the Jena edition rather than the Wittenberg edition of Luther's works, and the first publication of Luther's version of Aesop appeared in Jena Ger 5 on March 1, 1557, shortly before Rörer's death on April 24; Witt Ger 9, which appeared in August 1557, offered a copy of the Jena text (see above, p. 266 n. 4). See the introduction by Ernst Thiele and Oskar Brenner, WA 50:438.

[23] See above, p. 266 n. 4.

[24] See, e.g., *Table Talk* no. 3663 (1530), WA TR 3:499–500; no. 3997 (1538), WA TR 4:64; and no. 3490 (1536), LW 54:210–13, where Luther recounts five more fables. For a survey of Luther's use of Aesop's fables in his own writing, see Springer, *Luther's Aesop*, pp. 35–73.

[25] *Commentary on Psalm 101* (1534/1535), LW 13:143–224. It is a "court psalm" because Luther applies it to elucidate the office of rulers. The report of Caspar Cruciger's opinion apparently rests upon Mathesius' direct acquaintance; on Mathesius' friendship with Cruciger, see below, *History*, p. 375; Loesche, *Johannes Mathesius*, 1:93; Volz, *Die Lutherpredigten des Johannes Mathesius*, p. 79n.

was hurt.[26] For if someone presumes to engage in unfamiliar work, which he has not learned, he seldom walks away unharmed. He also mentions the frog that sat on a penny[27] and boasted that the money brought him honor.[28] Likewise, he ridicules the fanatics who engaged in vain boasting with the ancient proverb: "Extol yourself, little caterpillar, for your father was a cabbage worm."[29]

I heard several good fables and proverbs from him at table.[30] For example, there is the one about the crow who reproached some monkeys for wanting to blow fire from a little glowworm and lost its head in the process.[31] That is what happens to those who try to object to other people who have no sense. Monkeys and priests will not brook reproach,[32] as I have come to know from extensive experience. Again, when mention was made of someone who presented himself very hypocritically as a mild-mannered person, [Luther] recalled the splendid proverb that has been spun from the fable of the old mouse and her little daughter, which saw a noisy rooster and a stealthy cat and was very amazed at its silent tread. "Beware of the stealthy ones," said the mother mouse. "The noisy ones will do you no harm."[33]

Again, when someone reported that some hornets[34] had appropriated a great deal of cloister property and given it out to lackeys from the court, he said, "Aesop teaches that when someone snatches a roast from the altar,

---

[26] *Commentary on Psalm 101* (1534/1535), LW 13:162. This fable apparently comes from the Sanskrit *Panchatantra*, by way of late medieval translations into Latin (John of Capua [fl. 1262–69], *Directorum humanae vitae*) and German (*Das Buch der Weisheit*): see Springer, *Luther's Aesop*, p. 176; Patrick Olivelle, trans. and ed., *The Pañcatantra: The Book of India's Folk Wisdom* (Oxford: Oxford University Press, 1997), p. 8 (1.1).

[27] *Heller*, a coin of proverbially low value and quality, less than a standard silver penny.

[28] Luther, *On the Last Words of David* (1543), LW 15:340; for the saying, see Wander 1:1480, "Geld" no. 242.

[29] *Against the Heavenly Prophets* (1525), WA 18:194 and LW 40:204 (where the English translation paraphrases the German translated literally above as "for a nobody you boast pretty loftily"). See Thiele no. 162, pp. 171–72; cf. *Table Talk* no. 5434 (1542), WA TR 5:150–51; Mathesius, *History*, above, p. 223, and below, p. 381, where Enthusiasts are compared with caterpillars.

[30] See above, p. 270 and n. 24 there. For the collection of *Table Talk* from the year 1540 recorded by Mathesius, see LW 54:365–409; WA TR 4:559–705.

[31] This report appears only here in Mathesius. See Olivelle, *Pañcatantra*, p. 60 (1.9); Springer, *Luther's Aesop*, p. 176.

[32] *Affen und Pfaffen lassen sich nicht straffen*. See Wander 1:34, "Affe" no. 9.

[33] This report appears only here in Mathesius. For the fable, see Babrius and Phaedrus, *Fables* (Loeb 436 [1965]), pp. 606–7; Perry no. 716); cf. Springer, *Luther's Aesop*, p. 72. For the concluding proverb, see Wander 4:233, "Schleicher" no. 6.

[34] *Hurneusel*

there is usually a little burning coal still stuck to it, which will burn both nest and nestlings, as happened to the eagle."[35]

I have also seen the doctor take the Saxon version of Reynard the Fox along with him to the table and read in it during the meal.[36] He also assigned some German fables for his son to translate into Latin as an exercise, one of which I will return to later.[37]

Great people have always been fond of using such veiled and cloaked sayings; sometimes in their orations they incorporated entire fables, or brilliant proverbs derived from them, not just in jest or for entertainment but also in important matters. The Son of God and His prophets and apostles also liked to open their mouths in brilliant parables [Matt. 13:35; Ps. 78:2], using the imagery of animals to depict great wisdom for Christians. Christ directs us to the sparrow [Matt. 10:29, 31], the mother hen [Matt. 23:37], the flowers of the field [Matt. 6:28–29], snakes and doves [Matt. 10:16], and calls Herod a fox [Luke 13:32]. St. Paul calls Nero a lion [cf. 2 Tim. 4:17], and the preachers who pull out each other's hair like street brawlers[38] he calls dogs [Phil. 3:2]; heretics, who hypocritically adorn themselves with God's Word and in Christ's sheepskin, he calls ravening wolves [Acts 20:29]. Solomon directs us to the little ant [Prov. 6:6; 30:25], Jotham portrays good government in his fable [Judges 9], even as the Son of God[39] depicted the Babylonian emperor as a beautiful tree under which the little animals sit in the shade [Dan. 4:10–12], before which it is fitting to bow[40] rather than to strike at it or rub against it like a sow. Our Jotham also portrays a wicked ruler with his bramble [Judg. 9:14–15], even as the Lord Christ uses one to

---

[35] *Table Talk* no. 5375u (1540), WA TR 5:108–9; cf. *Table Talk* no. 4978 (1540), WA TR 4:597–98. For the fable, see Phaedrus, *Fables* 1.28 (Loeb 436 [1965], pp. 224–25; Perry no. 1); Gibbs, *Aesop's Fables*, no. 155, pp. 80–81; Oesterly, *Steinhöwels Äsop* 1.13, p. 95. Cf. below, Mathesius, *History*, p. 402.

[36] The tales of Reynard [Reineke] the Fox had been published in Low German in 1498: see Hoffmann von Fallersleben, ed., *Reineke Vos nach der Lübecker Ausgabe vom Jahre 1498*, 2nd ed., 2 vols. (Breslau: Grass, Barth & Co., 1852). For an English translation of the tales, see Donald B. Sands, ed., *The History of Reynard the Fox, Translated and Printed by William Caxton in 1481* (Cambridge, MA: Harvard University Press, 1960). On Luther's use of the book, see Luther to George of Anhalt, January 2, 1539, WA Br 8:350–51; cf. *Table Talk* no. 7024 (n.d.), WA TR 6:334 (LW 58:70 n. 46); see Volz, *Die Lutherpredigten des Johannes Mathesius*, p. 202 n. 1.

[37] *Argument*; i.e., a school exercise in paraphrase. Below, p. 279, the son is identified as Johannes [Hans] Luther.

[38] *Kelbertreiber*; strictly, a reference to the participants in a kind of traditional mob justice: see *DWB*, s.v. "Kühtreiben" and "Halberfeldtreiben."

[39] I.e., as the agent in the Old Testament; cf. above, p. 107 and n. 21 there.

[40] Cf. Thiele no. 291, pp. 273–74: "It is fitting to bow before the tree from which one gets shade."

depict a false prophet [Matt. 7:16]. And David portrays his Jews as thorny thistles or eryngo [2 Sam. 23:6] while in Psalm 22 he depicts Christ as a hart without horns, Judas as a bloodhound, and the priest's servants as tracking dogs and greyhounds [cf. Ps. 22:16, 20].[41]

When the plebeians in Rome rose up in revolt, a wise man persuaded the agitated and obstinate crowd to return by telling them the fable about the hands and feet which refused to give any credit to the head and belly, thinking they were idle and gluttonous, as a result of which they withered and died.[42] A wise man in Greece persuaded his citizens not to hand the sheepdogs over to the tyrant, for afterward the wolves would have their way with the whole herd.[43] Because of his foolish desire, the lion who gained the love of the shepherd's daughter let himself be persuaded by the maiden's father that his teeth should be knocked out and his claws extracted; once he was defenseless, he had to pay with his hide.[44] Christendom's white teeth, claws, defense, and weapon is the strong Word of God as written down by the prophets and apostles;[45] if we hand that over to the would-be shepherd and his hirelings in the council,[46] Christendom will be defenseless and unable to stand against the devil's murdering and lying. For this reason, our doctor refused throughout his life to abandon Scripture and the oral Word or to let any man stand in judgment over his doctrine without a clear scriptural text. Lord Jesus, You who are the strong Lion from the tribe of Judah [Rev. 5:5]; do not let Your claws, the Ten Commandments, and Your white teeth, Your holy Gospel, be taken from us!

Now, in order to consider further the wisdom of the Germans and how they make such artful use of the fables, here I will also note what Emperor Rudolf answered when asked why he would not allow himself to be crowned

---

[41] The reference to the "hart" comes in the superscription for Psalm 22: "according to the hind of the dawn." For the interpretation, see Luther, *Auslegung der ersten 25 Psalmen auf der Coburg* (1530/1559), WA 31/1:353, 359–60.

[42] The oration by Menenius Agrippa (d. 493 BC) is related in Livy, *History of Rome* 2.32 (Loeb 114 [1919], pp. 322–25).

[43] Plutarch, *Life of Demosthenes* 23.4 (Loeb 99 [1919], pp. 56–57).

[44] For the fable, see Babrius (fl. first century), *Fables* 98 (Loeb 436 [1965], pp. 126–27; Perry no. 140), and Diodorus Siculus (ca. 80–20 BC), *Library of History* 19.25.5–6 (Loeb 377 [1947], pp. 296–99; cf. Gibbs, *Aesop's Fables*, no. 355, p. 168). It appears in a letter from Luther, Jonas, Bugenhagen, and Melanchthon to the Nürnberg clergy, ca. February 12, 1540, WA Br 9:57. Cf. Volz, *Die Lutherpredigten des Johannes Mathesius*, p. 243.

[45] Cf. Eph. 6:17.

[46] I.e., the pope and the Council of Trent (1545–63), which was in its final session as Mathesius preached this sermon.

in Rome:[47] "Many emperors travel from Germany to Rome, but few return. 'Therefore, I shudder,' said the fox to the lion."[48] When speaking with an Evangelical, a great bishop told him not to think of the pope and bishops with such hostility. [The Evangelical responded:] " 'Let neither of us tread on the other,' said the rooster to the horse,[49] 'until we have ¡grown as high as your head and our feet are clad in iron.' " In our own days, when someone was trying to pass off false reports about a great truce, a prince made very fine use of the proverb spoken by the fox to the rooster:[50] "It may well be that a general peace has been declared, but not everyone has yet received the announcement."

The wise also say, "How quickly the decision and resolution are made, but who will bell the cat and carry it out?"—as the old mouse said when her little ones proposed that someone should put a bell on the cat.[51] When speaking to the sick lion, a wolf accused the fox of being an agitator. Upon learning this, the fox came and apologized for his absence, saying that he had been delayed speaking with the doctors on behalf of the king's health; they advised him to lay a warm wolfskin on his heart. No time was wasted in skinning the wolf.[52] Thus the one who digs a pit for someone else usually ends up falling in himself [cf. Ps. 7:15].[53]

Again, an old herding dog that faithfully kept watch over its master's cattle went out in the evening. Although little lapdogs in the street were barking at him, he ambled straight on without looking around; when he found himself before the slaughtering yard, the butcher's dog asked him how

[47] Rudolf I (r. 1273–91), the first German king of the Hapsburg dynasty. Although he received papal blessing in 1275, he refused to travel to Rome for a coronation and was placed under papal excommunication from 1275 to 1278. See *HRED*, pp. 392–84. Cf. Luther, *Against the Roman Papacy* (1545), LW 41:376.

[48] Babrius, *Fables* 103 (Loeb 436 [1965], pp. 130–33; Perry, no. 142); Oesterley, *Steinhöwels Äsop*, no. 72, p. 185; Gibbs, *Aesop's Fables*, no. 18, p. 12; Horace (65–8 BC), *Epistles* 1.1.73–75 (Loeb 194 [1926], pp. 256–57). Cf. above, Mathesius, *History*, p. 148. The anecdote is also recounted in Mathesius, *Hüldigungs-Predigt*, in Loesche, *Mathesius: Ausgewählte Werke*, 4:342–43; Mathesius, *Sarepta*, fol. 123r.

[49] Thiele no. 370, pp. 336–37.

[50] *Table Talk* no. 7053 (n.d.), WA TR 6:361. For the fable, see Babrius and Phaedrus, *Fables* (Loeb 436 [1965], p. 472; Perry no. 252); see also Oesterly, *Steinhöwels Äsop*, no. 164, p. 351; Gibbs, *Aesop's Fables*, no. 149, p. 77.

[51] Babrius and Phaedrus, *Fables* (Loeb 436 [1965], p. 545; Perry, no. 613); Gibbs, *Aesop's Fables*, no. 250, p. 123; cf. Wander 2:1185, 1195, 1199, 1208, "Katze" nos. 402, 599, 705, and 928. Cf. Luther, *Sermons on John 14–16* (1533–34/1538–39), LW 24:134; *Against Hanswurst* (1541), LW 41:234.

[52] Babrius and Phaedrus, *Fables* (Loeb 436 [1965], pp. 473–74; Perry no. 258); Oesterley, *Steinhöwels Äsop*, no. 89, pp. 208–14; Gibbs, *Aesop's Fables*, no. 17, p. 12.

[53] Wander 2:153, "Grube" no. 6.

he could put up with these yappers and why he did not take one by the scruff of the neck. "No," said the herding dog, "none of them snaps at me or bites me. I have to save my teeth for the wolves."[54] Likewise, the lion refused to take revenge on the little mouse. In the end, this was richly repaid him when the mouse freed him from his bonds.[55]

Ah, if only people were able to ignore things at times and not respond to everything; if they left the swords of Peter [John 18:10] and Roland[56] in their sheaths, they would remain unscathed for a long time and achieve reconciliation in many situations.

The great King Alexander also said, "It is the part of a prince to serve the people and to receive wicked words and ingratitude in return."[57] And when people spoke ill of him, Emperor Augustus justified himself in this way: "I am content that the people cannot harm me with their wicked words."[58] A good conscience outweighs and makes peace with many calumnies and insolent utterances.

Again, there once was an owner of a mine who bought out the other miners, wanting to have the profit all to himself. When this was mentioned at table, the doctor said, "The same was done in Aesop by the peasant whose goose laid a golden egg for him every three months. Being overcome by greed, he cut open the goose, thus cutting off his supply of gold as well.[59] This is what happens when people are dissatisfied with the fortune that God has bestowed on them in due course, or when the hunter denies his hounds and sparrow hawks their share of the game. Peasants are supposed to plow and thresh; lords are supposed to take care of the taxes, tithes, and revenues as well as to protect their poor people; pastors are supposed to teach and

---

[54] No source for this fable could be identified.

[55] Babrius, *Fables* 107 (Loeb 436 [1965], pp. 136–39; Perry no. 150); Oesterley, *Steinhöwels Äsop*, no. 18, p. 102; Gibbs, *Aesop's Fables*, no. 70, p. 37.

[56] The story of Roland (d. 778), one of Charlemagne's paladins, and his famous sword Durandal is immortalized in the eleventh-century epic the *Song of Roland*. See Dorothy L. Sayers, trans., *The Song of Roland* (New York: Penguin, 1957).

[57] Alexander the Great (356–323 BC), the Greek king of Macedonia who united Greece and conquered much of the Mediterranean world, including the Persian Empire. *OCD*, 4th ed., s.v. "Alexander the Great." For the saying, see Plutarch, *Life of Alexander* 41.1 (Loeb 99 [1919], pp. 344–45).

[58] On Augustus, see above, p. 43 n. 25. For this anecdote, see Suetonius (ca. 69/75–after 130), *Augustus* 51 (Loeb 31.3 [1914], pp. 230–31); Erasmus, *Apophthegmata* 4.194 (CWE 37:399).

[59] The specific circumstances here seem to be reported only by Mathesius, though Luther cites the fable in *Table Talk* no. 5375v (1540), WA TR 5:109–10, and in his letter to Count Albert of Mansfield, February 23, 1542, WA Br 9:629. For the fable, see Babrius, *Fables* 123 (Loeb 436 [1965], pp. 158–61; Perry no. 87); Oesterley, *Steinhöwels Äsop*, no. 138, p. 288; Gibbs, *Aesop's Fables*, no. 434, p. 201. See also Springer, *Luther's Aesop*, p. 70.

pray," says Dr. Martin Luther. "Thus every one does his part, and God gives His blessing to it."

Again, a great lord looked out the window and saw one of the court lackeys approaching the yard. "What a big thief he is," he said to a counselor standing beside him, who replied, "Do you tolerate such people in your service?" "What did the fox say to the hedgehog?" answered the lord. " 'Let the well-fed flies sit on me; if the hungry ones come, they will bite and drink up [my blood] even harder.' "[60] A master has to see and hear many things while managing a household with many people; now and then you will find one that wrings out a sponging courtier, like a sponge full of water, and hangs him out in the sun, as Ahasuerus did to his unfaithful Haman [Esth. 7:10]. Some even place the noose around their own necks, as in the case of Ahithophel [2 Sam. 17:23]. For faithless service is a blow against one's own lord,[61] and if [punishment] is slow in coming, then the heirs will pay in the end.[62]

Thus, I say, we Germans need many good fables, ˈas well as proverbs of a few words, which nonetheless give you much to think about, and stick and stay with you a long time, coursing through your veins and beating in your heart and ringing in your ears.[63]

Since our Jotham also wanted to gain a hearing among wild and coarse people, he invented a well-made fable in which he adroitly represents the faithful service and countless benefactions of Moses, Joshua, and his dear father, Gideon, as the three fruitful trees and masterfully and artfully depicts the new and illegitimate ruler as the bramble, the son of a maidservant [Judg. 9:18]. For when God provides good rulers, an entire land has shade. Indeed, they please God when they provide for the Church and schools and accept the true religion; then God provides sweetness and joy for their subjects.

If, however, a land and city forgets about its good governors and repays their heirs with no thanks but the devil's,[64] rarely will a better master come afterward. Instead, croaking and ungrateful frogs must have a stork that

---

[60] For the fable of the fox and the hedgehog, see Aristotle, *Rhetoric* 2.20.6 (Loeb 193 [1926], pp. 276–77); cf. Loeb 436 [1965], p. 504; Perry no. 427); Gibbs, *Aesop's Fables*, no. 29, p. 18. See Luther, *Whether Soldiers, Too, Can Be Saved* (1526), LW 46:111. Cf. Wander 1:1066, "Fliege" no. 60.

[61] Wander 4:1485, "Untreue (die)" no. 12.

[62] Cf. Wander 1:828, "Erbe (das)" no. 13.

[63] *als wenn man einem ein floch ins ohr setzet*; literally, "as when someone puts a flea in your ear," but the German idiom lacks the implication of rebuke that the English expression conveys. See Wander 1:1076, "Floh" no. 57.

[64] Wander 4:1130, "Teufelsdank" no. 2. See below, p. 281.

flays them and gobbles them up.[65] Or they must suffer under a bramble, where hedgehogs, mice, snakes, and toads are breeding, scratching the land to pieces and scraping everything away. Ultimately, a fire breaks out that consumes both land and people, as also happened here to the ungrateful Shechemites, who not only forgot about their old judge but also helped their thornbush murderously and tyrannically execute sixty-nine of Gideon's children upon a stone [Judg. 8:30–9:5].

Through such ingratitude and infidelity, these subjects and their descendants tied a broom and bramble around their own body.[66] Their new judge gave them a good thrashing about their heads and struck them dead, just as he, too, was also overthrown in the end by a woman [Judg. 9:53–54]. *Aquila electa iuste omnia vincit* ["The chosen eagle conquers all by right"], said Emperor Frederick III.[67] Whoever comes to power as a bramble, uninvited and uncultivated, is able only to scratch and stab and fleece the sheep and usually leaves with a bloody or burning head. And on account of the people's sin, ingratitude, and wickedness, God often sends a thornbush and worldly thistleheads.

I mention these things concerning Jotham's fable and our doctor's edition of Aesop and the tales of many wise people, a number of which have also been compiled in the works of the ancient sages, because great and noble people, whether in government or in the schools and churches, who have worn themselves out with their service, must also have honorable diversions with which to refresh, amuse, and enjoy themselves. As the holy apostle and evangelist St. John said when some accused him of keeping birds and partridges and sometimes shooting at targets with his companions:[68] "A bow that is always drawn tight grows slack and becomes no good in the end."[69]

---

[65] For the fable, see Phaedrus, *Fables*, 1.2 (Loeb 436 [1965], pp. 193–94; Perry no. 44) (these earlier versions of the fable involve a water snake rather than a stork; for the stork, see the German version: Oesterley, *Steinhöwels Äsop*, no. 21, pp. 110–11). Luther makes frequent reference to this fable (with the stork as king): see *Praelectio in librum Judicum* (1516–17), WA 4:573 (of questionable authenticity: see Brecht 1:129); *Temporal Authority* (1523), LW 45:114; *Whether Soldiers, Too, Can Be Saved* (1526), LW 46:112; *Wochenpredigten über das 5. Buch Mose* (1529/1564), WA 28:644; *Table Talk* no. 2294 (1531), WA TR 2:409; *Sermons on John 14–16* (1533–34/1538–39), LW 24:270–71; Luther to Gabriel Zwilling, September 30, 1535, WA Br 7:280; cf. Springer, *Luther's Aesop*, pp. 41, 49, 50, 53–54, 55, 58.

[66] Cf. Wander 5:966, "Besen" no. 78: "To bind a broom over one's own back."

[67] On Emperor Frederick III, "The Peaceful," of the Hapsburg dynasty, and the acronym, see above, Mathesius, *History*, p. 130; *HRED*, pp. 149–53.

[68] Cf. *LA* 1:54, no. 9.

[69] Cf. Wander 1:423, "Bogen" no. 5.

Emperor Charles the First[70] and Maximilian[71] took pleasure in hunting. St. Mark sometimes painted to pass the time.[72] Cyrus the Elder[73] and the holy patriarch Abraham built pleasure gardens and planted trees [Gen. 21:33]. Solomon discussed all kinds of herbs and trees on occasion [1 Kings 4:33]. Elector Frederick of Saxony had his lathe,[74] with which he made smooth shafts for crossbow bolts, which he feathered and were often shot by other people. Emperor Augustus sometimes composed verse; one time, his Ajax killed himself with a sponge, as Suetonius writes.[75] Doctor Martin told many good proverbs and cheerful stories at table; for example, when in Coburg with Master Veit Dietrich,[76] he was shooting at a target and once pulled a bat's heart out with his bolt when he pulled it from the hole.[77]

So, now, if the scholars can take wise Homer's fantastical tale about the fearsome battle of the frogs and mice in good part,[78] how can anyone take it ill that our doctor and others mention the fables for entertainment and

---

[70] I.e., Charlemagne: see Einhard (775–840), *Life of Charlemagne* 23.22, in David Ganz, trans. and ed., *Two Lives of Charlemagne* (London: Penguin, 2008), p. 34.

[71] On Emperor Maximilian I, the grandfather of Charles V, see above, pp. 137, 152–53, and p. 147 n. 45. He was famous for his love of hunting: see, e.g., the *Theuerdank*, a romanticized account of his marriage to Mary of Burgundy (1457–82): *Die geverlicheiten und einsteils der geschichten des loblichen streytparen vnd hochberümbten helds und ritters herr Tewrdannckhs* (Nürnberg: H. Schönsperger, 1517) [VD16 M1649], fol. D6r.

[72] Among the evangelists, St. Luke was identified as a painter in a tradition which, originating in the East in the eighth century, passed into wide circulation in the West comparatively late. It is not reflected in the thirteenth-century *Golden Legend* (*LA* 2:247–54, no. 156) but appears in the late fourteenth-century collection by Petrus de Natalibus (d. ca. 1400), *Catalogus Sanctorum* (Lyon), fol. 184v. Mathesius, apparently by confusion, associates this tradition with Mark.

[73] On the gardens of Cyrus the Great (r. 559–530 BC) at Pasargadae, see Xenophon (ca. 430–354 BC), *Anabasis* 1.2.7 (Loeb 90 [1998], pp. 56–57); Arrian (92–175), *Anabasis of Alexander* 6.29.4 (Loeb 269 [1983], pp. 192–93).

[74] See Spalatin, *Friedrichs des Weisen*, pp. 52–53.

[75] I.e., Augustus had erased his account of Ajax using a sponge. Suetonius, *Lives of the Caesars* 2.85 (Loeb 31 [1914], pp. 274–75); Erasmus, *Apophthegmata* 4.146 (CWE 37:382). Cf. Erasmus, *Adages* 1.5.58 (CWE 31:437).

[76] Veit Dietrich, from Nürnberg, came to Wittenberg in 1522 and served as Luther's secretary from 1527 to 1535. He accompanied Luther to Marburg in 1529 as well as to the Coburg in 1530. He collected and edited a number of Luther's sermons for publication, especially the *House Postil* of 1544. He made the first collections of Luther's *Table Talk* (see LW 54:3–113; WA TR 1:3–308) and was a friend of Mathesius (Loesche, *Johannes Mathesius*, 1:53; cf. below, Mathesius, *History*, p. 354). See Jeffrey P. Jaynes, "Dietrich, Veit," *OER* 1:485; Brecht 2:374.

[77] See below, Mathesius, *History*, p. 354. Cf. Brecht 2:373–74.

[78] The *Batrachomyomachia* [*The Battle of Frogs and Mice*], a satirical mock epic, was attributed to Homer: Loeb 496 (2003), pp. 262–93.

amusement and write and preach about them, particularly since they speak of useful and erudite matters?[79]

In order for us to finish observing this Shrove Tuesday now in keeping with the occasion, I will conclude this sermon of Jotham and Aesop not with rabbinic[80] or Mohammedan or ancient monkish examples or with old wives' tales [1 Tim. 4:7], but instead with two or three sharp and pointed fables—and let burrs be cast into many a beard, or a stake be driven into many a heart, by means of the crab, fox, and sparrow. But I ask and admonish you not to apply these to yourself if you are innocent; if anyone cries out, we must suppose that he has been hit.[81]

Our doctor once wrote this fable for his little son Johannes:[82] A crab wanted to take a trip across the country. Along the way he met a snake who became his traveling companion. The snake slithered off in her winding way, wriggling this way and that. The crab, who was not so nimble on his many legs, ran out of breath trying to follow his twisted and crooked fellow traveler; he grew tired and wore himself out on this hard journey. When evening fell, the two turned in under a bush. The snake coiled up and started to sleep and snore. The crab was tired, but he could not fall asleep; the snoring and hissing bothered him so much that he poked the snake to make her be quiet. When she reared up to defend herself, he grabbed her by the head with his claw and squeezed hard, until her breath was gone. Then she stretched out all the way and laid there lifeless, nice and straight. "Well," said the crab, "if you had gone straight like that today, I would have been able to follow better."

Oh, how hard and deadly bitter it is for someone to have to travel overland with crooked, twisted, slippery, bent, double-tongued, false, and venomous people, or who has to take counsel or deal with them in government, or with false preachers and colleagues, or to manage a household with an unfaithful wife and servants. Therefore, Dr. Luther concluded the fable thus: "Dear son, it is a beautiful treasure not only to have a good neighbor but also when God grants good and straight people to accompany you overland and in your office. With those who are twisted and false, it is difficult to make

---

[79] The Roman Catholic polemicist Johann Nas (1534–90; see Richard Ernest Walker, "Nas, Johannes," *OER* 3:129–30) attacked Luther's use of fables, on the basis of Mathesius' sermon, in his *Sextae Centuriae Prodromus* (Ingolstadt: Weißenhorn, 1569) [VD16 N101], fols. 29r–30v. See Volz, *Die Lutherpredigten des Johannes Mathesius*, pp. 24–25.

[80] For the negative comparison of rabbinic texts with Aesop, see Luther, *On the Jews and Their Lies* (1543), LW 47:228; cf. Springer, *Luther's Aesop*, p. 71.

[81] Cf. Wander 4:1302, "Treffen" nos. 34–35.

[82] I.e., Hans. See above, p. 272. For the fable, see *Table Talk* no. 4890 (1540), WA TR 4:571; Babrius and Phaedrus, *Fables* (Loeb 436 [1965], pp. 458–59; Perry no. 196); Gibbs, *Aesop's Fables*, no. 141, p. 73.

any progress and will become bitter for you. For a crooked and deceitful friend is far worse than an open and angry enemy."

Listen to another, though the hourglass has run out.[83] When I and other good friends escorted Herr Philip from here, he told us this fable while we were at table in Wiesental[84] (for he, too, was burdened with perilous companions):[85] A large snake fell into a pit and proceeded to cry out piteously. A peasant came to the opening and asked who was there. The snake begged him to help her get out. "Certainly not," said the man. "No good is to be expected from vile animals. I might as well bring up a snake in my bosom."[86] The snake persisted and promised the peasant that from her god, who once spoke through her,[87] she would acquire for him the best reward the world is known to give. Rewards, presents, and great promises make fools even of the wise.[88] The peasant helped the wicked and cunning snake out of the pit, whereupon she meant to devour him as his reward. "Is that what I have earned from you? Is that in keeping with your promise?" said the peasant. "I am double-tongued," said the snake. "The world rewards no differently. If you plead to set someone free from the gallows, he will usually bring you straight back there himself."[89]

While the peasant stood there in fear, the snake said, "Since you will not believe me, let us leave it up to the next two who come upon us; whatever they say will decide this matter for us, for good or for ill." Soon an old horse came along, and they explained the situation to him. Their arbiter said, "I have served my wagoner for fifteen years, and tomorrow he is going to give me to the knacker. The world gives no other reward." Likewise, the old dog,

---

[83] I.e., the hourglass kept in the pulpit to time the sermon. Cf. LW 69:200 n. 203.

[84] Melanchthon visited Joachimsthal in March 1552: see Loesche, *Johannes Mathesius*, 1:192. Melanchthon's fable has parallels with the version in the Low German *Reineke Vos* 3.4 (ed. Hoffmann von Fallersleben, 1:102–7; English translation in Sands, *History of Reynard the Fox*, no. 30, pp. 132–38; cf. Babrius and Phaedrus, *Fables* (Loeb 436 [1965]), pp. 558–60; Perry no. 640). Melanchthon told the parable on several occasions: see Luther, *Table Talk* no. 3281 (1538), WA TR 3:638–39; Wolfgang Musculus (see below, pp. 490–91 n. 163), "Itinerary," May 1536, in Theodor Kolde, ed., *Analecta Lutherana* (Gotha: Perthes, 1883), p. 219; Melanchthon, sermon for Trinity 14 (CR 25:451). See Volz, *Die Lutherpredigten des Johannes Mathesius*, p. 211.

[85] I.e., Melanchthon's Lutheran theological opponents such as Matthias Flacius (see the introduction above, pp. xxi, lxxxv; Mathesius, *History*, p. 112 and n. 42 there, and below, p. 308 and n. 153 there) and Andreas Osiander (see below, p. 311 n. 170, p. 391 n. 112, p. 485 n. 133, p. 561 n. 150, p. 563 n. 163, p. 592 n. 168).

[86] Wander 4:225, "Schlange" no. 82.

[87] Probably a reference both to Genesis 3, in which the devil is understood to be speaking through the serpent, and to the oracle of Apollo at Delphi, associated with the python.

[88] Cf. Wander 1:1312, "Gabe" no. 24.

[89] Cf. Wander 1:1318, "Galgen" no. 46.

on whom they also agreed, said, "For ten years, day and night, I helped my squire hunt and catch many foxes and rabbits. Now he has told his huntsman to hang me from a willow tree. That is the world's reward." The peasant was becoming frightened, but then a little fox came wandering along. The peasant explained his situation to the fox as well and promised to give him all of his hens, if only he would help him get away from this evil snake. The fox agreed to undertake the business; he convinced the snake to show him the pit and the danger she had been in and what the peasant's service was. When they came to the hole, the fox jumped in, and the snake followed after to show him all the circumstances. As she did, the fox sprang back out, and before the snake could turn around, as arranged with the fox, the peasant threw a big board over the opening.

Now that the peasant was free, the fox demanded that he leave the henhouse open for him that evening. The peasant returned home and gave his wife a full account of all that had happened and what he had promised the fox for his services as judge. His wife answered that the hens and geese were hers; he had none to give away to the fox. The peasant, however, wanted to keep his word, so he left the gate to the hens open for the fox. When his wife became aware of this, she laid in wait for the fox with the farmhand that night. When the fox approached in *bona fiducia* ["good faith"], they ran out, blocking the gate, and lunged at him until they finally got hold of him. "Alas!" said the fox. "If this is justice and the world's highest reward for the greatest good deed, then I, poor knave, confirm this worldly justice today with my life and pelt."

Indeed, it does not happen otherwise on earth. Anyone who ǀserves the world not only loses his good deed but eventually gets the devil's thanks as a reward as well. Yet everything must be repaid in the end. Having said this, the good Herr Melanchthon smiled, for he himself had received a large share of such thanks from his own camp.[90] The moral of the story is this: Do not undertake anything for the sake of the world's reward or thanks, and do not leave anything undone for the sake of its ingratitude or faithlessness! The Lord lives and reigns at the right hand of His Father; He will honorably and richly reward all faithful service and good deeds, and at the proper time He will reveal the righteousness of each individual. Of Him alone King David sings: *Qui custodit veritatem in saeculum* ["Who keeps truth forever"] [Ps. 146:6]; the world does not keep it.

---

[90] See above, p. 280 n. 85.

In conclusion, listen to my sparrow as well,[91] for mouse droppings and husks must always get mixed in with the pepper.[92] A sparrow had four nestlings in a swallow's nest; when they were fledged, some naughty boys came and knocked down the nest, but all the fledglings were able to escape in a gust of wind. Their old father was sad now, because his sons had gone out into the world before he had been able to forewarn them of all its dangers and to prepare them with some good lessons.

In autumn, many sparrows gathered in a wheat field, and there the father was reunited with his four sons, and he joyfully led them back home. "Oh, my dear sons, how worried I was about you all summer long, since you were carried away from me by the wind without having received my instruction. Listen to my words now, follow your father, and be on your guard. Little birds must endure many great dangers." Then he asked the eldest where he had spent the summer and how he had made his living. "I stayed in a garden and looked for caterpillars and worms until the cherries were ripe." "Ah, my son," said the father, "that kind of food for birds is not bad, but it comes with great danger; therefore, be on your guard from now on, and especially when people are walking around in the garden carrying long green poles that are hollow and have a little opening on top." "Yes, father, but what if there is a little green leaf stuck to the edge of the opening with wax?" asked the son.[93] "Where did you see that?" "In a merchant's garden," replied the son. "Oh, my son," said the father, "merchants are crafty people.[94] If you have been around these children of the world, you have gained enough worldly experience. See that you make good and proper use of it and do not become overconfident."

Then he asked the second: "Where have you been living?" "In a court," answered the son. "Sparrows and other plain little birds are of no service in that place, where there is a lot of gold, velvet, silk, weaponry, armor, sparrow hawks, owls, and falcons. Stay in the horse stable where the oats are tossed or threshing is done. With some luck, then, you can receive your daily grain in peace." "Yes, father," said this son, "but when the stableboys use berries to

---

[91] This fable is Mathesius' own composition; he had sent a copy in his letter to Paul Eber, May 7, 1557, in Loesche, *Mathesius: Ausgewählte Werke*, 4:569. It was later incorporated in the *Kinder- und Hausmärchen* of the Brothers Grimm, no. 157. See Kurt Ranke et al., eds., *Enzyklopädie des Märchens*, 15 vols. (Berlin: de Gruyter, 1977–2015), 5:580–81.

[92] Cf. Thiele no. 371, pp. 337–38. Luther was fond of the expression: see, e.g., *Preface to the Wittenberg Hymnal* (1529), LW 53:318 (called *Preface to the Weiss Hymnal* [1528] in LW 53); *Sermons on Matthew 18–24* (1537–40/1796–1847), LW 67:364; *On the Councils and the Church* (1539), LW 41:56. Luther also used it (as Mathesius does here) in self-deprecation: see *Preface to the German Writings* (1539), LW 34:287; *Wider den Bischoff zu Magdeburg, Albrecht Cardinal* (1539), WA 50:404.

[93] I.e., apparently, as a means of disguising the apparatus for trapping small birds.

[94] Wander 2:1226, "Kaufleute" no. 10.

make traps and rig their gins and snares in the straw, many wind up stuck hanging there." "Where have you seen that?" asked the father. "At court where the stableboys are." "Oh, my son, court boys are bad boys![95] If you have been at court and around the lords without losing any feathers there, you have learned rather well. You will probably know how to get out of a pinch in the world.[96] But make sure you look around and up. Even smart little dogs are often devoured by the wolves."[97]

Then the father turned to his third son: "Where have you tried your luck?" "I have mined[98] the roads and highways and sometimes found some nuggets: a bit of grain or spelt." "That is good food," said the father, "but be sure also to watch your back and be on guard. Especially if someone stoops down to pick up a stone, be quick to leave." "This is true," said the son, "but what if someone already has a sample rock or stone[99] at hand or in a pocket?" "Where have you seen this?" "Among the miners, dear father. When they leave the mine, they usually carry some stones with them." "Miners and workmen are clever people.[100] If you have been around mining folk, you have seen and learned something. Go forth and likewise be very careful in what you do. Miners' boys have killed many a sparrow with cobalt."[101]

Finally, the father came to his youngest son: "You, my dear and littlest hatchling, you were always the simplest and weakest. Stay with me, for the world has many coarse and wicked birds with hooked beaks and long talons who are just waiting for poor little birds to catch and devour. Stay among your own kind and feed on the little spiders and grubs from the trees and houses. Then you will remain content for a long time." "My dear father, those who make a living without causing harm to others will go far, and no sparrow hawk, kestrel, eagle, or falcon will harm him, particularly if, every morning and evening,[102] he faithfully commends himself and his honorable means of subsistence to God, the Creator and Preserver of all the

---

[95] Wander 2:711, "Hofbube."

[96] *dich . . . wol wissen außzueysen*; literally, "know how to free yourself from ice."

[97] Thiele no. 60, pp. 83–84.

[98] *kübel und seyl eingeworffen*; literally, "thrown in basket and rope," i.e., to lower a miner into a shaft for further excavation. See *LH²*, p. 514 on 152.27.

[99] *wand oder handstein*; a sample of particularly beautiful or interesting stone from the mines.

[100] Cf. Wander 1:317, "Bergleute" no. 2, which, however, has "distinguished [*ansehnliche*] people" instead of Mathesius' "clever [*anschlegige*] people."

[101] I.e., probably, with thrown stones of cobalt ore, which was commonly mined in the Erzgebirge, rather than by means of cobalt ore (which contains arsenic) used as a poison.

[102] Cf. Luther, *Small Catechism* (1529), Morning and Evening Prayers (Kolb-Wengert, pp. 363–64; *Concordia*, p. 344).

birds in the forests and villages, who also hears the cries and prayers of the young ravens [Ps. 147:9]. For not even a sparrow or little wren falls to the ground apart from His will [Matt. 10:29]." "Where have you learned this?" The son answered, "When the great gust of wind carried me away from you, I came into a church. There I fed on flies and spiders from the windows in the summer and heard these things being preached. The Father of all sparrows provided me with food throughout the summer and protected me from all misfortune and vicious birds." "By all means, my dear son, fly back to the church and help get rid of the spiders and buzzing flies, and chirp to God like the young ravens, and commend yourself to the eternal Creator. In doing so you will continue to be well, even if the whole world be filled with wild and wily birds."

> Commend yourself to God each day.
> Be still, endure and wait and pray—
> Discreet ʲand gentle on your way.
> Keep faith and conscience ever free,
> Then God your help and shield will be.[103]

This saying of the littlest sparrow[104] and his father are my gift to you, dear friends, on this Shrove Tuesday. The children of this world are wiser and shrewder in their own way than the children of the light [Luke 16:8], and the wolf does often devour clever little dogs,[105] but God takes the shrewd in their wickedness [cf. Job 5:13; 1 Cor. 3:19], and all the sly foxes wind up in the furrier's lye together. However, the one who trusts in God has built well[106] [Matt. 7:24] and will be sustained in this wicked world and delivered out of all misfortune with glory in the end, when the conduct and righteousness of each person will come to light and, standing before the judgment seat of Jesus Christ, all will receive in their bodies the good or evil they have done in their life [cf. 2 Cor. 5:10].[107] For we have not been created, redeemed by Christ's blood, and blessed by His Spirit for this life [only], like the poor little birds, but rather so that we may believe and preserve a good conscience and hope and wait patiently for the eternal life to come. Come, Lord Jesus, and show Yourself on the judgment seat; deliver and renew us, who bear the heat and burden of the long day here [Matt. 20:12]. And in the meantime, clear

---

[103] No outside source for this verse could be identified. It also appears in Mathesius' *Postilla Symbolica* (Leipzig: Beyer, 1588), fol. 247r [VD16 ZV10518], and may be his own composition. See Volz, *Die Lutherpredigten des Johannes Mathesius*, p. 114 n. 8.

[104] *Abärschel*; a diminutive parallel to "Cinderella" [*Aschenbrödel*].

[105] See above, p. 283 and n. 97.

[106] Cf. Wander 2:2, "Gott" no. 32.

[107] Cf. Athanasian Creed 38–39 (Kolb-Wengert, p. 25; *Concordia*, p. 18).

away all the buzzing and droning flies which murmur in the Church and seek to hinder the preaching. Amen, Lord Jesus Christ, Amen. For You also point us to the poor sparrows in Your Word [Matt. 10:29–31] and set them before us as professors and teachers. Amen!

The Eighth Sermon,
on the History of Doctor Luther
in the Years 1528 and 1529[1]

[Easter Sunday, April 11, 1563]

BELOVED friends in the Lord! It used to be the custom at this time to preach Easter fables and funny stories so that the absurd and idle talk would cheer and comfort the people, who had been so afflicted by their penitence during Lent and had suffered along with the Lord Christ during Holy Week.[2] In my youth I heard some Easter tales of this sort. For example, when the Son of God came to the gates of hell and touched them with His cross, two devils stretched forth their long noses to serve as bars for the gate. When Christ pounded, however, then the door and its hinges burst open, breaking off the two devils' noses.[3] The scholars of that time called such stories *risus paschales* ["Easter laughter"].[4] In past years at this time, we, too, followed the example of great people and dealt with allegories and amusing subjects—such as the cave of Machpelah [Gen. 23:9], which Abraham bought for the burial of his wife, Sarah, and Joseph's dungeon [Gen. 40:3], in which we portrayed for you the resurrection of the Lord Christ and of the faithful and the godless; or again, Ezekiel's bones [Ezekiel 37] and Daniel's pit and den [Dan. 6:16–24], in which we explained and depicted articles

---

[1] In some later editions of Mathesius' sermons, this sermon is numbered as the seventh sermon, and the seventh sermon in the earlier editions is moved to be the ninth. See above, p. 266 n. 1, and the introduction above, p. lxxxvii.

[2] On the emphasis on participation in Christ's suffering in late medieval Passion devotion, see the introduction by Christopher Boyd Brown, LW 69:123–40.

[3] Cf. Luther's discussion of physical descriptions of Jesus' descent into hell in *Sermon about Jesus Christ* (1533), LW 57:127–33.

[4] On the *risus paschales* or *Ostergelächter* in late medieval Easter preaching, see LW 76:386 n. 7. For Luther's criticism of the practice, see *Church Postil* (1540–44), sermon for Lent 3 on Eph. 5:1–9, LW 76:386–87, paragraph 11; *Lectures on Titus* (1527/1902), LW 29:59 and n. 12 there. Cf. Mathesius, *Postilla: Das ist/ Außlegung der Sontags unnd fürnemesten Fest Evangelien* (Nürnberg: K. Gerlach, 1584) [VD16 M1539], vol. 4, fols. 19v–20r.

of Christian comfort[5]—but this time we will continue in the history of Doctor Luther and speak both of his blessed work and of the laudable and most illustrious university in Wittenberg. I will speak about the state of the university and church there at the time when God brought me there from Bavaria, about the excellent people who were there, and about what they lectured and preached, and how they educated the youth there at that time.[6]

It is not only about His only-begotten Son that our God has willed to have written in His holy Bible—for the Old and New Testaments are, properly speaking, a book about the Lord Jesus Christ, who has led His kingdom by means of His Word from the beginning and in the fullness of time became a man—but He also mentions His holy patriarchs, prophets, kings, teachers, and students with great honor. Likewise, in addition to Jerusalem, the chief university of His people, He also speaks honorably of the schools of Elijah and Elisha in Jericho and Gilgal [cf. 2 Kings 2:5; 4:38]. For we Christians also ought to know when and through whom God has revealed and proclaimed to us the pure teaching of the Gospel, in order that we learn to guard against the corner-preachers and infiltrators who come unbidden and sneak their way in, and that we may abide in the blessed doctrine that we have heard and learned and which has been entrusted to us in due order with the laying on of hands and the prayers of holy teachers, just as St. Paul writes to his beloved student in 2 Timothy 3 [:14] that he should not forget from whom he has learned his theology.

In our days, God has chosen for Himself this new university[7] and blessed it with excellent people, through whom all schools and pulpits where something pure and useful is taught have been reformed and purified. For heavenly wisdom has entered the whole Roman Empire from this "wise mountain"[8] (in accordance with the prophecy of Dr. Fleck)[9] and has been received by us; and even though the evil spirit tries all his tricks against this man and university, yet he has not had much success thus far.

---

[5] Many of these passages appear in the Easter sermon in Mathesius, *Postilla* (1584), vol. 4, fols. 2r–6v, along with an Easter fable based on Samson (Judges 14), fols. 11r–15v.

[6] Mathesius arrived in Wittenberg on May 21, 1529 (see below, p. 292, and Volz, *Die Lutherpredigten des Johannes Mathesius*, p. 168). He left in the fall of 1530 to take up a teaching position in Altenburg. On his 1529 stay, see Loesche, *Johannes Mathesius*, 1:39–53.

[7] The University of Wittenberg was founded in 1502. See above, p. 106 n. 20; Mathesius, *History*, above, p. 125; and below, pp. 577–81.

[8] *Weisenberge*; a play on the name of Wittenberg: see above, Mathesius, *History*, pp. 145, 237.

[9] On Fleck and this prophecy, see above, Mathesius, *History*, pp. 145–46.

When Satan blew pestilential air into in the region around the Elbe River in 1528[10] and 'the university, at the counsel of good people, was moved to Jena for the sake of the youth, our doctor remained in his calling and with his little flock; he preached, lectured, and continuously served the people. He also did not hesitate to enter pestilential and putrid houses, as he was invited, to teach and to comfort those entrusted to his care.[11] For the students who remained with him during this time, he lectured on John's [First] Epistle,[12] which Master Georg Rörer[13] later gave me to transcribe. Meanwhile, there was an imperial diet in Speyer, which Herr Melanchthon attended with his elector and at which a new and dangerous resolution was passed, which was protested by a number of Christian princes and cities; the decision was also made to send an ambassador to the emperor in Bologna.[14]

When by God's grace and the service of His dear angels the air had been purified and the university was again meeting in Wittenberg, the Turk advanced on Germany and laid siege to Vienna in Austria.[15] This provided the doctor with opportunity, at the request and insistence of good people, to write not only about war against the Turk but also about Mohammed's blasphemous religion, warning good people against it.[16] He also set forth a

---

[10] In fact, an outbreak of plague had forced the university to move from Wittenberg to Jena on August 15, 1527. It then moved closer, to Schieben, on September 15 as the plague eased. The university remained there until April 13, 1528. See Brecht 2:248; the introduction by Gustav K. Wiencke, LW 43:115–18.

[11] Despite Elector John's order to leave Wittenberg with Melanchthon and the rest of the faculty (Elector John to Luther, August 10, 1527, WA Br 4:227–28), Luther remained with Bugenhagen in Wittenberg to provide pastoral care. See Luther's description of his activity in *Whether One May Flee from a Deadly Plague* (1527), LW 43:113–38.

[12] *Lectures on 1 John* (1527/1708), LW 30:217–327.

[13] On Rörer, see above, p. xx n. 20, and the introduction above, p. lxxxiv.

[14] The Second Diet of Speyer took place from March to April 1529. The resolution [*Abschied*] passed by the majority at the diet demanded the enforcement of the 1521 Edict of Worms (see above, p. 180 n. 68) against Luther, his writings, and his adherents, without the exception for conscience affirmed at the 1526 First Diet of Speyer (see above, p. 249 and n. 105 there). The Evangelical estates (six princes and fourteen imperial cities) submitted a formal protestation of this decision—the origin of the term "Protestant." See DRA 7/2:1296–314 (cf. 1142), 1260–65, 1273–88, 1345–56. Cf. Sleidanus, *De statu religionis* (1558), book 6, pp. 171–73; Wolgast, "Speyer, Protestation of," OER 4:103–5. On the Protestant embassy, see Sleidanus, *De statu religionis* (1558), book 6, p. 173, and book 7, p. 177. Charles was in fact in Placentia at the time of the diet, though he came to Bologna in 1530 to be crowned by the pope (having previously been crowned by the archbishop of Cologne in 1520): see above, Melanchthon, *Preface*, p. 68; below, Mathesius, *History*, pp. 322–23; and Brandi, *Emperor Charles V*, pp. 297–303.

[15] The first (and unsuccessful) Ottoman siege of Vienna took place from September to October 14, 1529. See above, Mathesius, *History*, p. 256.

[16] Cf. preface to [George of Hungary], *On the Ceremonies and Customs of the Turks* (1530), LW 59:255–62.

form and pattern for doing battle[17] and for praying against the Turk.[18] This same year he also published a muster sermon[19] and translated into German the refutation of the Turkish Koran that had previously been written in Latin by Brother Richard;[20] this he adorned with a splendid preface about the chapters in Ezekiel concerning Gog and Magog.[21] These books have been collected in good order in the second volume of the German series [of Luther's works].[22]

Now because our doctor had received a legitimate call in his doctorate to be a faithful servant of the Lord Christ and His Church; and because the Turk was not only intent on defending Mohammed's blasphemy and heresy in his land but also on eradicating the Christian faith by the power of the sword and intruding his own diabolical religion into another empire, and ⌐on claiming that Mohammed was the final prophet while suppressing and supplanting the divinity and salvific office of Jesus Christ, weakening lawful government, and wiping out all discipline and decency, together with the holy estate of marriage and Christian schools; and because many people were astonished at the Turk's great victory and success and began to suffer from dark thoughts—our doctor wanted to put in his own word for his Lord and Savior Jesus Christ against the Mohammedan devilry, to defend Christ's name, person, and office, as well as to warn everyone against the calumniator who speaks abominable things against the Most High, as Daniel prophesies [Dan. 11:36]. In addition, he wanted to instruct the Christian authorities as to how preparation could be made with a contrite heart, true faith, a good conscience, and powerful prayer for entering the field for the necessary defense against the devil's murderers and the infernal lying mouths.

For alongside the pope's idolatry, Mohammed's abomination and blasphemy are indeed the devil's final wrath for assailing the dear Christian Church and devouring it entirely, if only he could. On account of our sin and ingratitude, God has merely watched this for a time to let this abominable beast and this false prophet [Rev. 16:13][23] truly fill up their measure

---

[17] *On War against the Turk* (1529), LW 46:155–205.

[18] *Appeal for Prayer against the Turks* (1541), LW 43:213–41. Note that this work dates from a later period: see Volz, *Die Lutherpredigten des Johannes Mathesius*, p. 156.

[19] *Muster-Sermon against the Turks* (1529), WA 30/2:160–97 (LW 56).

[20] Preface and afterword to Brother Richard, *Refutation of the Koran* (1542), LW 60:251–66. Note that this work also belongs to a later period.

[21] Preface to *Ezekiel [38–39]* (1530), LW 59:277–84. Luther's preface, drawing on Rev. 20:8–9 as well as Ezekiel, identifies "Gog" with the Turks.

[22] See Witt Ger 2 (1557), fols. 417v–478r, where these works are grouped together thematically, accounting for Mathesius' apparent confusion about their dating.

[23] I.e., Mohammed and the pope respectively.

[1 Thess. 2:16] and finally receive the wages they have earned. First, their foolishness and devilry had to be reproved and revealed by the mouth of God and be slain in the hearts of many people and swept away. And when the Lord Christ appears, both [the beast and prophet] will be cast alive into the lake of fire, which will burn with pitch and sulfur for eternity [Rev. 19:20; 20:10].

Indeed, dear friends, the pope in Rome did sometimes send his cardinals and bishops out on the campaigns against the Turks and collected a great deal of money from Germany for the war against the Mohammedans; he also gave his *cruciata* and indulgence letters to those who served against the enemy,[24] who was taking such deadly and dreadful aim at Christendom and kept striking off one horn and kingdom after another from the Roman Empire [cf. Daniel 7–8].[25] But in all the papacy there was no one, apart from Brother Richard, who defended the honor, person, blood, and sacrifice of Jesus Christ against the horrid calumniator or who opposed and exposed this crass heresy and deception.[26] Therefore, we Germans truly owe our dear God many thanks for this salutary instrument, who revealed to us Mohammed's abomination and infernal dregs[27] by means of blessed and well-founded writings, and who faithfully warned us against the diabolical and mendacious religion of the Turks and so fervently and zealously helped people to pray against it in his own day.

It was at this very time, when the Turk had laid siege to Vienna, that I first came from Bavaria to Wittenberg, where I heard in the sermons and lectures so much bountiful and excellent consolation, fervent sighs, powerful prayers, and faithful admonition.[28] For example, that though hell's dragon was at that time directing all of his power and might against Germany, nonetheless the Turk, pope, and all their helpers' helpers would be unsaddled before the gates of Christendom, and the Son of God would surely remain at the right hand of His Father, a Deliverer and Savior of all who trust in Him and keep His Word; all the baptized children whom the Turk had speared through or hung on a fence or woefully slain by hacking with a saber would appear in glory and joy together with the children of Bethlehem [Matt. 2:16] on the Last Day before the face of Jesus Christ, upon whose blood they have

---

[24] *Bulla cruciata* were the papal declaration indulgences and dispensations for those taking part in a crusade. See *On War against the Turk* (1529), LW 46:186.

[25] The fourth kingdom of Daniel 7 was traditionally identified with the Roman Empire. See *Muster-Sermon against the Turks* (1529), WA 30/2:166 (LW 56); *Preface to Daniel* (1530), LW 35:294–316 (especially pp. 295–96, 300, 314).

[26] See above, p. 289.

[27] Cf. *On War against the Turk* (1529), LW 46:184.

[28] See above, p. 287 and n. 6 there.

been baptized [cf. Rom. 6:3], and they will again trample underfoot all Turks and enemies of Jesus Christ.[29]

We do not yet know even now who was the true wall protecting Germany or the true soldier and commander at that time against the murder and heresy of the Turk.[30] When everything comes to light, we will recognize not only the fervent praying of the Our Father by many |good people but also the power and protection of our Lord Christ, who is able to set a ring in the nose of Sennacherib [2 Kings 19:28; Isa. 37:29] and the great Leviathan [cf. Job 41:2], to cut their sinews and to stop and destroy their wickedness utterly.

And while I am recalling here what I personally heard in Wittenberg, it would also behoove me, as a student and member of this laudable university, to mention alongside the history of Dr. Luther and of this university also the other sermons, lectures, and good people that I found there and saw and heard at that time. Surely, if God wills, I will recall such things on the Last Day, to the eternal praise of this university and its good people.[31]

And yet, dear friends, at this time people were often obliged to hear and read about what wicked and fabricated lies Egranus[32] and other mamelukes[33] and ungrateful students (just like those of Damascene[34] and Cassian[35]) were circulating in their blather, along with other godless people, against

---

[29] Cf. *Muster-Sermon against the Turks* (1529), WA 30/2:162, 177, 182 (LW 56).

[30] Although the commanders of Vienna during the siege were Wilhelm von Roggendorf (1481–1541) and Nicholas of Salm (1459–1530), Luther ascribed the lifting of the siege to God's intervention. See Luther to Amsdorf, October 27, 1529, LW 49:239–43.

[31] On Mathesius' 1529–30 stay in Wittenberg, see Loesche, *Johannes Mathesius*, 1:39–53; Volz, *Die Lutherpredigten des Johannes Mathesius*, pp. 168–90.

[32] Although initially sympathetic toward Luther and his reforms, Egranus (i.e., Johannes Wildenauer of Eger; see above, p. 222 n. 122) became increasingly critical of disruptive changes in religious life and of Luther's doctrine of justification. See Egranus, *Ein Christlicher unterricht von der gerechtigkeit des glaubens/ und von guten wercken* (Leipzig: Michael Blum, 1534); Brown, *Singing the Gospel*, p. 38.

[33] See above, p. 199 n. 91.

[34] John of Damascus (ca. 675–ca. 750) was a Greek theologian and hymnographer living under Muslim rule who defended icons against the iconoclast policy of the Byzantine emperors. According to the hagiographic tradition in the Greek *Vita Joannis Damasceni* (PG 94:452–60), the emperor is supposed to have obtained a sample of John's own handwriting, presumably from some of his students, on the basis of which he had a treasonous letter forged and sent to the caliph, resulting in John's punishment by amputation of his hand, which was then miraculously restored by the Virgin Mary. See Andrew Louth, *St. John Damascene: Tradition and Originality in Byzantine Theology* (New York: Oxford University Press, 2002), pp. 16–19. On John, see *ODCC*, 3rd ed., s.v. "John of Damascus."

[35] The fourth-century Christian schoolmaster Cassian of Imola was killed by his own students after he refused to sacrifice to the gods. See Prudentius (b. 348), *Crowns of Martyrdom* 9 (Loeb 398 [1953], pp. 220–29).

this illustrious and Christian university.[36] I know that you will be glad and pleased to hear about the city and the people from which God sent out His Word and truth into this land, and in which all of your ministers and school-teachers and the children of many good people have received a fine and salutary education in the knowledge of Christ and in the liberal arts.[37]

My dear friend Herr Zecharias Weixner, pastor in Bruck on the Ammer River by Fürstenfeld,[38] provided me with room and board and very good books for a whole year, until the university returned from Jena to Wittenberg. Then, on the Friday after Pentecost in 1529,[39] I arrived there for the first time. On the Saturday following, at Vespers, I heard the great man Doctor Luther preach.[40] He expounded the words of St. Peter in Acts 2 concerning the nature and power of holy Baptism, for which I have to thank our God all the days of my pilgrimage here and for all eternity. At that time, I was about to turn twenty-five years old; I had listened to many mendicant and secular priests in the papacy, but never before in my life had I heard mention of holy Baptism, aside from occasionally hearing the Anabaptists and fanatics in Bavaria babble very scandalously about Baptism and the Lord's Supper. Therefore, it was for me a profound delight, in the depths of my heart [Prov. 22:18], to hear salutary Christian instruction concerning this highly necessary and comforting article right at the start. Afterward as well, when other sermons of the doctor concerning holy Baptism were diligently and skillfully prepared for publication by Doctor Cruciger in 1535,[41] that was always one of my favorite books next to the Bible and the catechism. For my own consolation and in order to impress it firmly upon myself, I translated this book into Latin when I was schoolmaster.[42]

---

[36] In addition to Egranus, Mathesius likely has in mind Georg Witzel, a priest who had embraced Lutheranism in 1524 but in 1527 began to criticize the Wittenberg Reformation and returned to Roman Catholicism in 1531. See John M. Dolan, "Witzel, Georg," *OER* 4:287–88.

[37] On Joachimsthal's connections with Wittenberg, see the introduction above, pp. lxxxii–lxxxv; and Mathesius, *History*, above, pp. 110; and below, pp. 590–91, 596, 603–8.

[38] See the introduction above, p. lxxxi; and Mathesius, *History*, above, pp. 242–43; and below, p. 353.

[39] I.e., May 21, 1529.

[40] Luther's afternoon sermon of Saturday, May 22, 1529, on Acts 2, is edited in WA 29:382–84 (LW 56); the material on Baptism, however, is chiefly found in Luther's continued exegesis of the text in his sermon for Vespers on the next day, Trinity Sunday, May 23, WA 29:388–90 (LW 56). See Volz, *Die Lutherpredigten des Johannes Mathesius*, pp. 168–69; Loesche, *Johannes Mathesius*, 2:356–57.

[41] *Sermons on Holy Baptism* (1534), LW 57:139–89. On Cruciger's role as editor, see above, p. 188 n. 26.

[42] I.e., as rector in Joachimsthal in 1532: see Loesche, *Johannes Mathesius*, 1:34, 82.

I neither can nor want to nor shall forget this salutary first sermon on Baptism, so long as there is breath within me. For it is through Baptism that we enter Christendom; in Baptism we are sprinkled with Christ's blood and His Spirit, which is the holy chrism[43] and the true divine anointing which consecrates and seals us as royal priests. In this Baptism, God makes the covenant of a good conscience with us [1 Pet. 3:21], and we are buried in Christ's death [Rom. 6:4], made one body with Him [1 Cor. 12:12–13], incorporated into God's Church [Eph. 2:14–19], and clothed with the garment of imputed righteousness [Gal. 3:27] and of the hope of salvation [cf. 1 Thess. 5:8]. This covenant of salt [2 Chron. 13:5] stands firm and endures throughout our lives until our last breath; upon it we can live confidently and die with joy. God is our Father, who receives us as His children and heirs in the name of and by the merit of the blood and intercession of His Son. He drowns all of our sin and death in this blessed sea and crimson flood, colored by Christ's blood,[44] |and brings us into the communion and eternal brotherhood of the saints and inscribes our names in His heavenly register. On this foundation, we may live blessedly in the power of the Holy Spirit and with confidence await the dissolution [cf. 1 Cor. 15:52] at any hour or moment. For that is what it really means to be baptized in the name of the Father, Son, and Holy Spirit, and, having been reborn by water and the Word, to have become God's child, righteous and saved, and to receive forgiveness of all sins freely, out of pure grace, solely for the sake of faith in Jesus Christ. Whoever received the mark and brand of the red whore of Babylon [Rev. 13:16; 17:3–6] under the papacy rejected Baptism once again, for the pope and monks considered their monastic rules, anointing, and vows to be higher than the Baptism of Jesus Christ;[45] therefore, they also rejected their original baptismal names and received a new name, consecration, anointing, and sanctification.[46]

These things from the first sermon to which I came in Wittenberg, by God's grace, I recall with joy. Throughout the whole year following, I heard (God be praised) many more such edifying and comforting sermons and lectures in both churches[47] and in the university. For since Doctor Johann

[43] On chrism, see above, p. 204 n. 18.

[44] Cf. Luther's hymn "To Jordan When Our Lord Had Gone" (1541), LW 53:301, stanza 7 (*LSB* 406:7; Wackernagel 3:25–26, no. 43; WA Ar 4:301).

[45] A charge frequently made by Luther on the basis of scholastic texts such as Thomas Aquinas, *ST*, 2–2, q. 189 a. 3 ad 3 (Blackfriars 47:241): see, e.g., Luther, *To the Christian Nobility* (1520), LW 44:174; *Judgment on Monastic Vows* (1521), LW 44:318; *Against Hanswurst* (1541), LW 41:199–200; *Against the Roman Papacy* (1545), LW 41:336.

[46] A reference to the practice whereby those professing religious vows took a new "name in religion," as did a pope upon his election. Cf. Luther, *Lectures on Genesis* (1535–45/1544–54), LW 6:286.

[47] I.e., in the town church of St. Mary's and in the castle church of All Saints'.

Bugenhagen,[48] pastor in Wittenberg, was absent at this time, having been duly called to set in order the churches and schools in the land of [lower] Saxony,[49] our doctor preached three or four sermons every week, in which he provided a Christian and wise exposition of the Sunday Gospel readings,[50] St. John the Evangelist,[51] and Exodus chapters 19 and 20.[52] Then, on St. James' Day, he also made a fine application of the legend of St. Christopher[53] to all preachers and Christian laity who carried Jesus Christ in their heart and arms, preserved their consciences, helped people, and in return earned nothing but ingratitude from the world and the false brethren.[54]

It was this year also that I first heard the catechism, in addition to many other comforting doctrines, expounded by Doctor Justus Jonas[55] in the Castle

---

[48] On Bugenhagen, see the introduction above, pp. xxxvi–xxxvii.

[49] Bugenhagen was in Braunschweig and then Hamburg in Lower Saxony, organizing the Reformation there from May 1528 to June 1529. See Brecht 2:284–85; the introduction by Christopher Boyd Brown, LW 69:3.

[50] For Luther's Sunday preaching in 1528 during Bugenhagen's absence, see WA 27:129–540; 29:1–443. Only one of these sermons (from July 12, 1528) seems to have been published: WA 22:74–92. Luther also preached on Matthew 11–15 on Wednesdays, though most of the notes on the Matthew sermons are lost: see WA 28:4–30; 52:828–39; cf. the introduction by Christopher Boyd Brown, LW 67:xx.

[51] *Sermons on John 16* (1528–29), WA 28:43–69; *Sermons on John 17* (1528/1530), LW 69:1–119; *Sermons on John 18–20* (1528–29/1557), LW 69:121–310.

[52] Although a set of Luther's sermons on Exodus 19–20 was published in 1528 as *Auslegung der Zehn Gebote*, he had preached the sermons in 1525: see Aland, *Hilfsbuch*, p. 130, no. 520 (Pr 531–38); WA 16:394–528 (LW 62). In 1529, however, Luther was preaching on Deuteronomy: see WA 28:509–750. Mathesius must have heard the sermons on Deuteronomy 4–5, including the Ten Commandments (parallel to Exodus 19–20), which were delivered between June 20 and August 29, 1529, accounting for the confusion here. See Volz, *Die Lutherpredigten des Johannes Mathesius*, pp. 169–70.

[53] For the legend of the giant St. Christopher, who carried the child Christ across a river, see *LA* 2:10–14, no. 100.

[54] *Legend of St. Christopher* (1529), WA 29:498–505 (LW 56); cf. *Table Talk* no. 6990 (1529), WA TR 6:308–9; WA 48:678.

[55] On Jonas, see the introduction above, p. xxx; in 1529, Jonas was provost of the All Saints' chapter and dean of the theological faculty.

[Church] and by the three deacons: Master Georg Rörer,[56] Johann Mantel,[57] and Master Sebastian Fröschel.[58] Thus the parish and castle churches at that time were very well staffed, and the Word of Christ was taught wisely and in full harmony and produced much fruit; in the same way, the university at that time also enjoyed the highest reputation.[59]

From Doctor [Luther] himself, I got to hear for about forty weeks the exposition of the last twenty-two chapters of the prophet Isaiah;[60] often I went home from this lecture full of comfort and joy.

---

[56] On Rörer, see above, p. xx n. 20 and p. 270 n. 22. On the three Wittenberg deacons at this time, see Volz, *Die Lutherpredigten des Johannes Mathesius*, p. 174. A slightly earlier set of catechism sermons by the three Wittenberg deacons (from February 1529, before Mathesius' arrival) has been preserved: see Georg Buchwald, "Die letzten Wittenberger Katechismuspredigten vor dem Erscheinen des kleinen Katechismus Luthers," in *Beiträge zur Reformationsgeschichte: Herrn Oberkonsistorialrat Professor D. Köstlin . . . eherbietigst gewidmet*, ed. Otto Albrecht et al. (Gotha: Perthes, 1896), pp. 49–59.

[57] Johann Mantel (ca. 1495–1542/1543) had been prior of the Celestine cloister at Königstein near Pirna in ducal Saxony but abandoned monastic life to come to Wittenberg in 1523. He served as deacon in Wittenberg and in Mühlhausen before returning to Wittenberg in 1528. He served as archdeacon in his native Cottbus, in Brandenburg, from 1537 to the end of his life. Cf. Luther to Mantel, November 10, 1539, WA Br 8:596–97. See Seidemann, "Mantel, Johann," *ADB* 20:250–51.

[58] Sebastian Fröschel (1497–1570) had witnessed the 1519 Leipzig Disputation (see above, pp. 154–55) while a student there and came to Wittenberg in 1522. After stints preaching in (and being expelled from) the anti-Lutheran centers of Leipzig and Halle, he became a deacon in the Wittenberg church in 1528, then served as archdeacon from 1542 to the end of his life. Bugenhagen commended his catechism preaching, which later appeared in print: *Catechismus* (Wittenberg, 1559) [VD16 F3089]. See Friedrich Wilhelm Bautz, "Fröschel, Sebastian," *BBKL* 2:139–40. Mathesius seems to have been relatively close to him: see Mathesius to Paul Eber, September 5, 1564, in Loesche, *Mathesius: Ausgewählte Werke*, 4:597; Loesche, *Johannes Mathesius*, 2:267.

[59] For what follows concerning teachers and faculty in Wittenberg, see Volz, *Die Lutherpredigten des Johannes Mathesius*, pp. 174–82; Walter Friedensburg, *Geschichte der Universität Wittenberg* (Halle [Saale]: Niemeyer, 1917); Friedensburg, *Urkundenbuch der Universität Wittenberg*; Armin Kohnle and Beate Kusche, eds., *Professorenbuch der Theologischen Fakultät der Universität Wittenberg, 1502 bis 1815/17* (Leipzig: Evangelische Verlagsanstalt, 2016); Heinz Kathe, *Die Wittenberger Philosophische Fakultät*; Ernest G. Schwiebert, *The Reformation as a University Movement*, vol. 2 of *The Reformation* (Minneapolis: Fortress, 1996). Schwiebert, *Reformation as a University Movement*, p. 486, lists the teaching responsibilities of the Wittenberg faculty as of the reorganization of the university in 1536, overlapping to a large extent with what Mathesius reports from 1529. On Mathesius' 1529–30 stay at the university, see also below, Mathesius, *History*, pp. 593–94.

[60] Luther would have been lecturing on Isaiah 44 at the end of May 1529 and finished his lectures on Isaiah on February 22, 1530. See *Lectures on Isaiah* (1527–30/1532–34), LW 17:1–416; Volz, *Die Lutherpredigten des Johannes Mathesius*, p. 170.

From Master Philip, the faithful and diligent professor,[61] I was able to hear during this short time part of Cicero's [De] Oratore[62] and the beautiful Latin oration Pro Archia,[63] and over the course of the year his entire Dialectics,[64] which he dictated to us anew, along with the Rhetoric.[65] In the morning, this great man would explain the Epistle to the Romans;[66] Wednesdays he lectured on honorable discipline and virtue from Aristotle's Ethics.[67] In addition to this, disputations or declamations were held every week.[68]

---

[61] On Melanchthon's activity as professor, see Irene Dingel, Robert Kolb, et al., eds., Philip Melanchthon: Theologian in Classroom, Confession, and Controversy (Göttingen: Vandenhoeck & Ruprecht, 2012), pp. 17–76.

[62] ein stück von Ciceronis oratorn. Probably a reference to Cicero's On the Orator (Loeb 348 [1942], pp. 1–479; Loeb 349 [1942], pp. 1–185) rather than to one of his other works with similar names or alternate titles: Orator (Loeb 342 [1939], pp. 295–509); the Brutus or De claris oratoribus (Loeb 342 [1939], pp. 1–293); or the De optimo genere oratorum [The Best Kind of Orator] (Loeb 386 [1949], pp. 347–73). Melanchthon's commentary on De Oratore, based on his classroom lectures, first printed in 1524, was published in a new edition in 1530 [VD16 C3405]: see CR 16:685–766. Melanchthon's commentary on the Orator was first published in 1534: see CR 16:767–804.

[63] Cicero, Pro Archia (Loeb 158 [1923], pp. 6–41); see CR 16:889–920.

[64] See Melanchthon, Erotemata Dialectices, CR 13:507–760. The first edition of the Dialectic had been published in 1520; revised editions appeared in 1528 and in 1547. See Karin Maag, ed., Melanchthon in Europe: His Work and Influence beyond Wittenberg (Grand Rapids: Baker Books, 1999), pp. 93–95.

[65] Melanchthon had published his De rhetorica in 1519 [VD16 M4179ff.] and allowed the publication of notes from his lectures as Institutiones rhetoricae in 1521 [VD16 M3514ff.]. In 1531, he published a new rhetorical textbook, Elementa rhetorices, which was probably antici-pated in the lectures Mathesius heard in 1529–30: CR 13:413–506 (see above, p. xli n. 127; English translation by Mary Joan La Fontaine, "A Critical Translation of Philip Melanchthon's Elementorum rhetorices libri duo" [PhD diss., University of Michigan, 1979]).

[66] Cf. Melanchthon, Commentary on Romans (see above, p. 189 n. 29), CR 15:497–795. On Melanchthon's 1529 lectures, see Luther to Spalatin, May 28, 1529, WA Br 5:85.

[67] See Melanchthon, Enarrationes in aliquot librorum ethicorum Aristotelis, CR 16:277–416, interpreting Aristotle, Nicomachean Ethics (Loeb 73). Melanchthon's commentary was first published in 1529 but revised numerous times thereafter.

[68] On the use of declamations and disputations in Wittenberg, see Schwiebert, Reformation as a University Movement, pp. 338–39, 454, 485–86; Friedensburg, Geschichte der Universität Wittenberg, pp. 160–64, 191–93. Since public doctoral disputations had fallen into abey-ance at Wittenberg between about 1525 and 1532–33, Mathesius must be referring to the weekly disputations held in the student Aula. See Volz, Die Lutherpredigten des Johannes Mathesius, pp. 172–73, and Melanchthon's own statutes for the university in Karl Hartfelder, Melanchthoniana paedagogica (Leipzig: Teubner, 1892), p. 83. For Melanchthon's own decla-mations (often written to be delivered by others), see CR 11; 12:5–398; Karl Hartfelder, ed., Philippus Melanchthon Declamationes, 2 vols. (Berlin: Weidmann, 1891–94).

Johann Bugenhagen interpreted the Epistles to the Corinthians,[69] and Doctor Jonas, some psalms.[70] Aurogallus[71] taught his Hebrew grammar and lectured on Psalm 119. Master Franz[72] from Weimar taught Greek; Tulich[73] lectured on the *De Officiis*[74] of Cicero; Master Vach[75] lectured on Virgil;[76] old

---

[69] On Bugenhagen, cf. above, pp. 293–94. He had returned to Wittenberg from Hamburg on June 24, 1529. See *Commentarius in quatuor capita prioris Epistolae ad Corinthios* (Wittenberg: H. Lufft, 1530) [VD16 B9293].

[70] On Jonas, cf. above, pp. 294–95. These lectures apparently were never published.

[71] Matthaeus Aurogallus [Goldhahn] (ca. 1490–1543) had come to Wittenberg in 1519 and became professor of Hebrew in 1521. He worked with Luther on translations of the Old Testament, authored a Hebrew grammar, and in 1542 became rector of the University of Wittenberg. Aurogallus' Hebrew grammar, *Compendium Hebraeae Grammatices*, was published in Wittenberg in 1523 [VD16 G2550] and often reprinted thereafter. His lectures on Psalm 119 do not seem to have been published. See Schwiebert, *Reformation as a University Movement*, pp. 479–80; Kathe, *Die Wittenberger Philosophische Fakultät*, pp. 68, 112–13; Friedensburg, *Geschichte der Universität Wittenberg*, pp. 125–26; Hermann Wendorf, "Aurogallus, Matthäus," *NDB* 1:457; Friedrich Wilhelm Bautz, "Aurogallus (Goldhahn), Matthäus," *BBKL* 1:304.

[72] Franz [Franciscus] Burchart [Burkhard] (ca. 1503–60), a favorite student of Melanchthon, received his master's degree in Wittenberg in 1524 and then taught Greek there from 1526 until 1535, when he was summoned to the electoral court to become vice chancellor. See Fabian Ekkehart, "Burchart, Franz," *NDB* 3:33; Kathe, *Die Wittenberger Philosophische Fakultät*, p. 60; Friedensburg, *Geschichte der Universität Wittenberg*, pp. 219–20.

[73] Hermann Tulich [Tulken or Tulichius] (1486–1540) from Steinheim, a 1511 Wittenberg baccalaureate, was a German humanist who worked for a time in Leipzig (ca. 1512–19) as an editor of classical texts for the printer Michael Lotter (ca. 1490–after 1544) before coming to Wittenberg, where he became a member of the philosophical faculty in 1522. He lectured primarily on classical authors, including Virgil, Horace, Ovid, and Cicero. From 1532 on he was rector of the Latin school in Lüneburg. See Kathe, *Die Wittenberger Philosophische Fakultät*, pp. 58, 75–76; Felix Dahn, "Tulichius, Hermann," *ADB* 38:777–81; Friedensburg, *Geschichte der Universität Wittenberg*, pp. 132, 161; Stephan Waldhoff, "Tulichius, Hermann," *BBKL* 17:1393–97.

[74] Cicero, *De Officiis* [*On Duties*] (Loeb 30 [1913], pp. 2–403). Tulich's lectures on the *De Officiis* do not seem to have been published.

[75] Balthasar Fabricius from Vacha (hence Vach or Fach) (ca. 1480–1541) received his master's degree in Wittenberg in 1507, after which he lectured on Latin poetry. His death is mentioned by Luther in a letter to Elector John Frederick, July 10, 1541, WA Br 9:468–69. See Kathe, *Die Wittenberger Philosophische Fakultät*, pp. 22, 39, 42; Friedensburg, *Geschichte der Universität Wittenberg*, p. 222; Conrad Bursian, "Fabricius, Balthasar," *ADB* 6:505; Olaf Ditzel, "Fabricius Phacchus (Vach), Balthasar," *BBKL* 25:408–9.

[76] See the poems of Virgil—the *Eclogues*, the *Georgics*, and the *Aeneid*— in Loeb 63–64.

Master Volmar[77] lectured on the *Theorica Planetarum*;[78] and Master Milich[79] lectured on the *Sphaera*.[80] Master Caspar Cruciger taught Terence to the young students at this time as a pedagogue.[81] Likewise, the private schools[82]

---

[77] Johannes Volmar of Villingen (d. 1536) taught mathematics at Wittenberg after receiving his master's degree there in 1515, having previously studied in Cracow: see Schwiebert, *Reformation as a University Movement*, p. 486; Kathe, *Die Wittenberger Philosophische Fakultät*, pp. 69, 114; Friedensburg, *Geschichte der Universität Wittenberg*, pp. 134–35.

[78] Probably the thirteenth-century *Theorica Planetarum* sometimes attributed to Gerard of Cremona (1114–87), though by the mid-1530s the later *Theoricae Novae Planetarum* of Georg von Peuerbach (1423–61) was in use in Wittenberg: see Katherine Anne Tredwell, "The Exact Sciences in Lutheran Germany and Tudor England" (PhD diss., University of Oklahoma, 2005), pp. 34–36, 40–52, 120–37.

[79] Jacob Milich (1501–59) was born in Freiberg (Breisgau), where he received bachelor's and master's degrees in 1520 before continuing with medical study in Vienna. The reputation of Melanchthon drew him to Wittenberg in 1524, where he taught mathematics and astronomy in the arts faculty in addition to teaching in medicine. He visited Joachimsthal in 1549 (*Chronica*): see Loesche, *Johannes Mathesius*, 1:193. On Milich, see Schwiebert, *Reformation as a University Movement*, p. 486; Kathe, *Die Wittenberger Philosophische Fakultät*, pp. 97, 114–16; Friedensburg, *Geschichte der Universität Wittenberg*, pp. 211–12; Jakob Franck, "Milich, Jakob," *ADB* 21:745.

[80] *die Speram*; i.e., the *Tractatus de Sphaera* by John de Sacrobosco (ca. 1195–ca. 1256), the most widely read introduction to Ptolomaic astronomy in late medieval universities. See Lynn Thorndike, *The Sphere of Sacrobosco and Its Commentators* (Chicago: University of Chicago Press, 1949). For its use in the Wittenberg curriculum, see Tredwell, "Exact Sciences in Lutheran Germany," pp. 48–49; and Melanchthon, preface to Sacrobosco, *De Sphaera*, CR 11:430–37 (in Kusukawa, *Melanchthon: Orations*, pp. 105–12).

[81] Caspar Cruciger Sr., who would receive his doctorate in 1533 and become a member of the theological faculty, was in 1529 serving as a pedagogue who was assigned to tutor newly matriculated beginning students, including work in such basic Latin texts as the comic playwright Terence (ca. 195–159 BC; Loeb 22–23). On Cruciger's work as Luther's editor, see the introduction above, p. xx and n. 19 there; and p. 188 n. 26. He was among Mathesius' close friends and correspondents; Mathesius' 1542 farewell dinner in Wittenberg was held in Cruciger's house, and Cruciger visited Joachimsthal in person together with Paul Eber in 1545 (*Chronica*): see Loesche, *Johannes Mathesius*, 1:103, 193. See Robert Rosin, "Cruciger, Caspar," *OER* 1:456–57; Friedensburg, *Geschichte der Universität Wittenberg*, p. 162; Kathe, *Die Wittenberger Philosophische Fakultät*, pp. 94–99; Kohnle and Kusche, *Professorenbuch*, pp. 45–47.

[82] Many of the Wittenberg faculty took on boarders in their houses, whom they also instructed. Cf. Kathe, *Die Wittenberger Philosophische Fakultät*, p. 73; Friedensburg, *Geschichte der Universität Wittenberg*, p. 162 n. 3. Melanchthon, e.g., maintained a model private school in his home for ten years, beginning in 1519, in which students learned and performed Greek plays and literature: see Glenn Ehrstine, *Theater, Culture, and Community in Reformation Bern, 1523–1555* (Leiden: Brill, 2002), pp. 136–37.

were also excellently staffed: Masters Winsheim,[83] Kilian,[84] Ammerbach,[85] and Erasmus Reinhold[86] kept their students in good discipline and diligently

---

[83] Veit Oertel from Winsheim had come to Wittenberg in 1523 and earned the master's degree in 1528. He became an assistant to Melanchthon, teaching rhetoric and Greek in the arts faculty before obtaining a medical degree in 1550. See Kathe, *Die Wittenberger Philosophische Fakultät*, pp. 93–96; Friedensburg, *Geschichte der Universität Wittenberg*, p. 220; Karl Hartfelder, "Winsheimer, Veit," *ADB* 43:462–63.

[84] Kilian Goldstein the Elder (1499–1568), from Kitzingen, came to Wittenberg in 1520 and earned his master's degree in 1526 and his law degree in 1536. He joined the arts faculty in 1528, serving briefly as rector in 1541 before leaving to advance the Reformation in Halle (see the introduction above, pp. xxix–xxx), where until his death he served as general counsel and syndic. See Friedensburg, *Geschichte der Universität Wittenberg*, pp. 162, 205 n. 5; Hans Volz, "Goldstein, Kilian der Ältere," *NDB* 6:622–23. See also *Table Talk* no. 4716 (1539), LW 54:364; Luther to Jonas, February 16, 1542, LW 50:225–30.

[85] Veit Amerbach [Trolmann] (1503–57) studied at Ingolstadt and taught at the grammar school in Eisleben, earning his master's degree at Wittenberg in 1529. From 1530 to 1543, he taught in the arts faculty at Wittenberg. He left after coming into conflict with the leaders over Melanchthon's *De Anima* and Luther's understanding of justification, converted to Roman Catholicism, and became a professor of rhetoric at Ingolstadt for the remainder of his life. See Kathe, *Die Wittenberger Philosophische Fakultät*, pp. 101–2, 115; Friedensburg, *Geschichte der Universität Wittenberg*, pp. 225–26; Friedrich Wilhelm Bautz, "Amerbach, Veit," *BBKL* 1:144–45.

[86] Erasmus Reinhold (1511–53), from Thuringia, was an astronomer and mathematician at Wittenberg, studying under Jacob Milich (see above, p. 298 n. 79) and becoming a professor in 1536. Reinhold became an important student of Copernican theory, and in his 1551 *Tabulae Prutenicae* (VD16 R964), Reinhold was the first to develop astronomical tables based on the ideas of Copernicus (1473–1543). See Andreas Kühne, "Reinhold, Erasmus," *NDB* 21:367–68; Kathe, *Die Wittenberger Philosophische Fakultät*, pp. 116–18; Friedensburg, *Geschichte der Universität Wittenberg*, pp. 232–34; Owen Gingerich, *The Eye of Heaven* (New York: American Institute of Physics, 1993), pp. 205–51.

taught and tutored, and soon thereafter Master Marcellus,[87] Herr Georg Major,[88] and Master Eber[89] did so as well.

ᴵThere was also good peace and harmony between the students and townsmen. One time the nobility—or, rather, some of the nobles—kicked up a row and commotion with the children of a burgher in a burgher's house, on account of which they were given a sound thrashing about the head by the deputies of the citizenry[90] and were stuck in the tower overnight until the next morning. However, when some of them, after the matter had been settled, came to the town judge's house and broke his windows, our doctor publicly spoke out in the pulpit, to the effect that by the reasonable provision and law of the laudable electors, God had granted this university a quiet and peaceful existence thus far, but now there were people present who would not be content with equal rights and who committed all kinds of

---

[87] Johannes Marcellus (1510–52), from Franconia, earned his master's degree at Wittenberg in 1534, eventually being appointed to the professorship in Latin grammar in 1537 and the professorship in Latin poetry in 1541, as successor to Balthasar Fabricius (see above, p. 297 n. 75). See Kathe, *Die Wittenberger Philosophische Fakultät*, pp. 94–95; Friedensburg, *Geschichte der Universität Wittenberg*, pp. 222–23.

[88] Georg Major, from Nürnberg, had come to Wittenberg as a boy in 1511 and earned his master's degree in 1523. From 1529 to 1537 he was rector of the Latin school in Magdeburg. Upon returning to Wittenberg, he became preacher at the Castle Church and earned a doctorate in theology in 1544 (see his doctoral disputation, *On the Mystery of the Holy Trinity and the Incarnation of the Son, and on the Law*, WA 39/2:287–336 [LW 73]), joining the theological faculty thereafter. He later served as its dean and helped to edit the Wittenberg edition of Luther's works. He became the center of a controversy in the 1550s with his proposition that "good works are necessary for salvation," later addressed in FC SD IV (Kolb-Wengert, pp. 574–81; *Concordia*, pp. 546–52; see also Arand et al., *Lutheran Confessions*, pp. 191–94). Major visited Joachimsthal in 1546 (*Chronica*) and later commended Mathesius' Evangelical preaching in his *Enarratio epistolae . . . ad Philippenses* (Wittenberg: H. Lufft, 1554) [VD16 M2025], fols. A3v–A4r, dedicated to the Joachimsthal town council: see *LH²*, p. 456; Mathesius, *Chronica*, 1546. At the time of Mathesius' 1529–30 stay in Wittenberg, however, beginning the Friday after Pentecost, Major would have been absent, since his tenure as Magdeburg rector had begun at Easter. See Robert Kolb, "Major, Georg," *OER* 2:501–2; Kohnle and Kusche, *Professorenbuch*, pp. 134–37; Kathe, *Die Wittenberger Philosophische Fakultät*, pp. 130–35; Friedensburg, *Geschichte der Universität Wittenberg*, pp. 197–99; cf. Luther, preface to Major, *Lives of the Fathers* (1544), LW 60:315–23.

[89] Paul Eber, from Franconia, began his studies at Wittenberg in 1532 and joined the faculty in 1537 after earning his master's degree. Eber became professor of Latin in 1541, professor of Hebrew and preacher at the city church in 1557, and pastor of the city church and superintendent in 1558. He earned his doctorate in theology in 1559 and joined the theological faculty. He was a close friend and regular correspondent of Mathesius and visited Joachimsthal in 1545 (*Chronica*). See Marilyn J. Harran, "Eber, Paul," *OER* 2:17; Loesche, *Johannes Mathesius*, 1:193; Kohnle and Kusche, *Professorenbuch*, pp. 45–47; Mundhenk, "Mathesius und Philipp Melanchthon," pp. 99–101.

[90] *von ordentlicher Burgerschafft*

violence and wantonness under cover of darkness,[91] who provoked people and unjustly violated the sanctity of their homes. "I am," said the doctor from the pulpit, "a member of the clergy.[92] [But] if such a disturber of the peace came up to my house, I would rush out to him with my kitchen spit[93] and defend my home's peace and privacy, as is lawful for and behooves the man of the house. If with my spit I were to run through such a disturber of the peace, I would stop and cry out: 'This is the right granted by God and the emperor,' before both of whom I would give a Christian and lawful answer for myself, with honor and a good conscience, for defending myself and my house."[94]

Once our doctor, as a lover of civil peace and unity, had expressed himself in this way, things turned out for the best, and there was quiet and peace in all the city. God also pronounced His blessing at that time on the supply of food, despite the very wet, cold, and unfruitful summer that had fallen upon us. Several times the Elbe poured through the city wall through the loopholes, and the unhealthy air and turbulent time stirred up the dangerous illness known as the English sweating sickness, with which I and others lay sick.[95] |Nevertheless, food was rather inexpensive at this time. At the home of my host and fellow countryman Wolf Jahn of Rochlitz,[96] I boarded very well for five silver groschen [per week], not including drink, in the company of old, learned, honorable, and good table companions, who showed me (poor fellow that I was) nothing but goodwill, so I mention them here to

---

[91] *bey nacht und nebel*

[92] *ein geystlich Mann*; or, literally, "a spiritual man" (1 Cor 2:15).

[93] *Haußspieß*

[94] This exhortation is not preserved in the notes on Luther's sermons from the period (Rörer customarily did not include such topical exhortations, delivered from the pulpit after the sermon proper, in his notes). On Luther's admonitions from the pulpit in general, see the introduction by Christopher Boyd Brown, LW 58:xix–xx and n. 25 there, which lists the admonitions preserved from 1528–32. Cf. the introduction by Paul Pietsch, WA 32:xxi; Volz, *Die Lutherpredigten des Johannes Mathesius*, p. 170.

[95] For the "English sweating sickness" and its effects in Wittenberg in the summer of 1529, see Brecht 2:210–11. Cf. Luther to Johann Briesmann, July 31, 1529, WA Br 5:124–26; and to Nicholas Hausmann, August 27, 1529, WA Br 5:138–39.

[96] Wolf Jahn was a butcher by trade. See Loesche, *Johannes Mathesius*, 1:41; Volz, *Die Lutherpredigten des Johannes Mathesius*, p. 183. On Mathesius' origins in Rochlitz, see the introduction above, p. lxxx.

honor them:[97] Licentiate[98] Zülsdorf;[99] Master Staffelstein[100] (a former professor); Herr Valentin Mellerstadt[101] (Doctor Mellerstadt's brother) and his nephew Master Martin;[102] Johann Figulus[103] from Nürnberg; Hieronymus von Glauburg;[104] Herr Clam from Frankfurt;[105] Master Franz Gross[106] from

---

[97] See the identification of Mathesius' table companions in Volz, *Die Lutherpredigten des Johannes Mathesius*, pp. 183–88.

[98] The licentiate was a stage preliminary to the doctorate in late medieval universities, though it fell out of formal use in Wittenberg by the 1530s. See Thomas Albert Howard, *Protestant Theology and the Making of the Modern German University* (Oxford: Oxford University Press, 2006), pp. 57–58, 65.

[99] Andreas Zülsdorf was apparently the son of the elder Andreas Zülsdorf (d. before 1518) who served as mayor of Wittenberg from 1474 to 1509. The younger Zülsdorf matriculated at Wittenberg in 1502, earned his licentiate in law in 1508, and became the university rector in 1517. See Volz, *Die Lutherpredigten des Johannes Mathesius*, p. 183.

[100] Georg Elner (ca. 1473–1543), from Staffelstein in Upper Franconia, earned his master's degree in Wittenberg in 1505 and joined the arts faculty in 1509. In 1522, he became part of the theological faculty but was at first part of the resistance to Luther, becoming a supporter only in 1524. See Volz, *Die Lutherpredigten des Johannes Mathesius*, p. 178; Kathe, *Die Wittenberger Philosophische Fakultät*, pp. 27, 72; Günter Dippold, "Georg Elner (†1543): Professor an der Universität Wittenberg," in *Staffelsteiner Lebensbilder*, ed. Günter Dippold and Alfred Meixner (Staffelstein: Verlag für Staffelsteiner Schriften, 2000), pp. 39–40.

[101] On Valentin [Valten] Pollich von Mellerstadt, see above, p. 127 n. 74; and Volz, *Die Lutherpredigten des Johannes Mathesius*, p. 183.

[102] Martin was the son of Dr. Martin Pollich von Mellerstadt (on whom see above, p. 63 n. 53, p. 127 nn. 72–73). He matriculated at Wittenberg in the winter semester of 1502/1503. See Kohnle and Kusche, *Professorenbuch*, p. 169.

[103] Johann Figulus (d. 1565), from Nürnberg, matriculated at Wittenberg in 1520 and (according to his university obituary) became one of Luther's domestic assistants. He studied law before turning to theology as well and taught jurisprudence as a private lecturer in Silesia and in Wittenberg. See Volz, *Die Lutherpredigten des Johannes Mathesius*, pp. 184–85.

[104] Hieronymus von Glauburg (1510–74) was a jurist who matriculated at Wittenberg in 1527 and later studied in Bologna and Pavia before becoming a syndic in Frankfurt. See Volz, *Die Lutherpredigten des Johannes Mathesius*, pp. 138–39; and Franz Lerner, "Glauburg, Johann von" (Hieronymus' brother), *NDB* 6:438–39, which diverge radically in characterizing Hieronymus either as a Gnesio-Lutheran friend of Cyriakus Spangenberg (Volz) or as an adherent of the traditional religion (Lerner).

[105] Johann Clam, from Frankfurt am Main, had apparently studied previously in Wittenberg in 1525, though he does not appear in Förstemann et al., *Album*. See Volz, *Die Lutherpredigten des Johannes Mathesius*, p. 186.

[106] Franz Gross matriculated at Wittenberg in 1528 after studies in Leipzig. In 1540, Melanchthon recommended him to the council in Mittweida, where he served from 1541 to 1555 as a deacon, and then became pastor in 1555. While Mathesius was in Wittenberg, Gross tutored him in Hebrew: see Volz, *Die Lutherpredigten des Johannes Mathesius*, p. 186; Loesche, *Mathesius: Ausgewählte Werke*, 2:40, 44.

Oschatz; Andreas Forberger from Mittweida;[107] Master Peter from Zerbst;[108] Carl Drachstädt from Halle and his tutor, Bernhard Zettler[109] from Ulm; the excellent martyr Mr. Leonhard Kaiser, who was burned [at the stake] for the sake of the Gospel in Bavaria;[110] and many other great people also used to sit at this table.

At that time there was no dissension among the scholars, and so no perilous disputations arose at table.[111] We were all joyful and in good spirits, [gathered] in love and friendship. We all sang in harmony,[112] and alongside that, the elder [table companions], whom we younger ones held in sincere awe and reverence, let fall many good discourses and stories, which I have diligently retained in my memory. And since Master Philip was lecturing then on the *Dialectics*,[113] from one lecture or another there arose many good discussions on questions and statements. Neither was there any excessive or inappropriate feasting or banqueting; everyone attended to his studies, which were the reason why he had come to this place. Thus God educated many good and great people at this table, some of whom are still alive and laudably and honorably serving churches, princes, lords, and cities. God willing, on the Last Day we will also bring this kind of friendship with one another at table and in studies before God's countenance and preserve it throughout eternity.

ᴵAmong the precious and renowned people in other faculties at that time, I knew the following illustrious men:[114] my rector, Doctor Caspar

---

[107] Andreas Forberger (d. after 1568) was probably one of the sons of the Mittweida councilman Blasius Forberger. Andreas' name does not appear in Förstemann et al., *Album*, but he served as a city clerk in Wittenberg until 1540, when he left to serve in Spandau, where he later became mayor.

[108] Probably Peter Sonnenwalde from Zerbst, who had matriculated at Wittenberg in 1525 after studies in Leipzig. He received his master's degree in August 1529.

[109] Carl Drachstädt and his tutor, Bernhard Zettler (d. 1552), had come to Wittenberg in 1527 and returned after a brief stay in Leipzig. According to *Table Talk* no. 5186 (1540), WA TR 4:704, Zettler had impaired sight; later Mathesius, Luther, and Melanchthon sought to secure him a teaching position (see Volz, *Die Lutherpredigten des Johannes Mathesius*, pp. 187–88).

[110] On Kaiser, see above, Mathesius, *History*, pp. 248–49 and n. 101 there.

[111] In contrast with the later divisions between Philippists and Gnesio-Lutherans: see the introduction above, pp. xxi, lxxiii–lxxxv, lxxviii, and Mathesius, *History*, above, pp. 198–99 (and n. 88 there); and below, pp. 594–95.

[112] *hatten unser Canterey*. Likely a literal description of singing at table as well as a figurative description of harmony. See, e.g., below, Mathesius, *History*, pp. 485–86.

[113] See above, p. 296.

[114] See the identification of these members of other faculties in Volz, *Die Lutherpredigten des Johannes Mathesius*, p. 182.

Dietleben;[115] Doctor Hieronymus Schurff;[116] Dr. Benedikt Pauli;[117] Dr. Augustine Schurff;[118] and Licentiate Melchior Vend,[119] who educated many excellent people, princes, lords, and cities, some of whom are still helping serve both governments[120] faithfully in word and deed. For one must and should concede this praise to this university: that there the rod of Aaron has budded abundantly and blossomed very beautifully and borne much good fruit [Num. 17:8], so that today there are few schools and princes' courts where the fruits of this rod are not to be found.

God wanted to adorn His Word with the praiseworthy liberal arts, and so He created many good people and great artists at this place, so that this university is held in high regard and has a well-deserved reputation in foreign lands for having thoroughly and wisely explained the best books from the Greeks and Latins and having put them in the public square for proper use.[121] For before that time, as is unfortunately still the case in some places, the scholars only sat in Plato's cave or pit; they saw only the shadow of art and had to make do with husks and hulls.[122] But in this place,[123] God provided people who were able to speak of the earth and the grain and could properly show the young people the end which the liberal arts serve and how they could make proper and skillful use of them, along with the languages, in Holy Scripture, law, and medicine.[124]

A great man in Vienna, as I heard here from a student of his, openly confessed when lecturing on Peter of Spain[125] that he and all his colleagues had not known what the middle term in the syllogism was until he had seen

---

[115] Caspar Dietleben [Teutleben] earned his doctorate in law in Wittenberg and joined the faculty in the spring of 1529, serving as rector of the university beginning that summer. Mathesius would have matriculated under Dietleben.

[116] On Hieronymus Schurff, see above, p. 21 n. 83.

[117] Benedikt Pauli (1490–1552) earned his law degree in 1529 and served on the faculty following graduation. He also served as mayor of Wittenberg in 1529, 1532, and 1535.

[118] On Augustine Schurff, see above, p. 20 n. 78.

[119] Melchior Vend [Fendt] (1486–1564) joined the Wittenberg arts faculty in 1523, earned his doctorate in medicine in 1543, and became a professor of medicine in 1545.

[120] I.e., the state and the Church. On Luther's distinction between the two governments or kingdoms, see *Temporal Authority* (1523), LW 45:77–129.

[121] *fein zu marckt oder rechtem brauch gericht wurden.* Cf. Wander 3:468, "Markt" no. 110.

[122] See Plato, *Republic* 7 (Loeb 276 [2013], pp. 106–17).

[123] *Ort.* Loesche (*LH²*, p. 521) suggests that the word here is a mining term referring to the working face of a horizontal excavation, though that meaning seems unnecessary in this context.

[124] I.e., in the three higher faculties of the medieval university: theology, law, and medicine.

[125] Petrus Hispanus was a thirteenth-century logician who wrote the *Tractatus* or *Summulae Logicales*, which became a standard university textbook for dialectic. See Brian P. Copenhaver,

Melanchthon's *Dialectics*.[126] Likewise, at that time this precious and great philologist's ¦grammar book taught the children in nearly all schools in Germany how to decline and conjugate words.[127]

Afterward the egg became wiser than the old hen,[128] and every pedant came up with a new dialectic, just as practically everyone tried to make his own catechism and postil, so that there are now almost as many different schoolbooks as schoolmasters and students. *Grammatici certant et adhuc,* "The grammarians are vying with each other still, [yet no verdict has been handed down in the case],"[129] says the *Synod of the Birds*.[130] Therefore, the youth become confused and are quickly brought up to quarrel and wrangle. Recently, Master Philip's *Dialectics* was published in Italy, though his examples were apparently left out entirely;[131] it was for those good examples that a young monk in Venice sincerely thanked God and a German physician with these words: "If it were not for this book, I would not know how I was to be saved, poor wretch that I am. Oh, my God, bestow upon me more such books."[132] In that same place our doctor's [exposition of the] Our Father was translated into Italian.[133] When the local bishop[134] saw this publication without the name of the author, he said, "Blessed is the one who produced this exposition of the Our Father and whoever shall print it or read it."[135]

Calvin G. Normore, and Terence Parsons, eds., *Peter of Spain: Summaries of Logic* (Oxford: Oxford University Press, 2014).

[126] See above, p. 296 n. 64.

[127] I.e., Melanchthon, *Grammatica Graeca*, CR 20:3–180.

[128] Wander 1:752, "Ei" nos. 33, 41.

[129] Horace, *Ars Poetica*, line 78 (Loeb 194 [1926], pp. 456–57).

[130] A reference to Johann Major's satirical poem: see above, p. 112 n. 42. Cf. CR 20:767–76, here p. 773 line 27.

[131] *Dialecticae Philippi Melanchthonis libri tres* (Venice, 1535) [USTC 841945], and *Dialecticae Philippi Melanchthonis libri quatuor* (Venice, 1545) [USTC 841950]. Cf. above, p. 296 n. 64.

[132] A previous source for this anecdote could not be identified.

[133] In 1525, in Venice, an Italian translation was published, without Luther's name, of the 1520 *Brief Form of the Ten Commandments, Brief Form of the Creed, and Brief Form of the Lord's Prayer* (WA 7:204–29), in the form that these texts had been incorporated in the *Personal Prayer Book* of 1522 (LW 43:13–38): *Uno libretto volgare, con la dechiaratione de li dieci comandamenti: del credo: del Pater noster* (Venice: Niccolò Zoppino, 1525). Subsequent reprintings followed in 1526, 1540, and 1543. See Massimo Firpo, *Juan de Valdés and the Italian Reformation* (Farnham: Ashgate, 2015), p. 67.

[134] *Ordinarius*; presumably Girolamo Querini, patriarch of Venice from 1524 to 1554.

[135] Mathesius may have heard this anecdote while in Wittenberg in 1529. Cf. Luther to Gabriel Zwilling, March 7, 1528, WA Br 4:404–5, where Luther rejoices in a report that the Venetians "have received the Word of God."

When Bishop Lang[136] in Salzburg, if I am not mistaken, saw the second book of Pliny with the precious Wittenberg exposition and some tables of the course of the heavens,[137] this wise man of the world said, "There are indeed adventurous scholars[138] in Wittenberg. If we want to prevail against them, we are also going to have to give some attention to good schools. I fear that we will not suppress them with sword and might."

Likewise, Cardinal Cajetan[139] is supposed to have said at the public imperial diet in Regensburg: "We will have to focus our attention on the people and on good schools; the Lutherans are far ahead of us in this. We find [our] people in Germany to be incompetent." Our king bore witness to this same charge when he spoke Latin with a Bohemian abbot who was unable to answer anything but *sic* and *ita* ["yes" and "even so"]: "Ah, what unlearned people are in these monasteries."[140]

While at table with the doctor, I heard from him that Duke George of Saxony had asked Erasmus for counsel in spiritual matters by means of a letter.[141] When the slippery man gave an ambiguous and twisted answer that was neither cold nor hot, the wise prince is supposed to have said, "Dear Erasmus, wash my fur, but don't get it wet.[142] I laud those from Wittenberg despite everything. They are not mealymouthed,[143] but boldly say straight out what they think."

When Doctor Cruciger was the secretary for our side at the colloquy in Worms[144] and not only recorded all the words of Herr Philip and of Herr

---

[136] On Bishop Matthäus Lang, see above, p. 151 n. 72. For the anecdote, see *Table Talk* no. 4877 (1540), WA TR 4:566.

[137] *Liber Secundus C. Plinii de Mundi Historia*, ed. Jacob Milich (Hagenau: Peter Braubach, 1535). On Milich, see above, p. 298 n. 79. On the role of Pliny (AD 23–79) in the Wittenberg curriculum, see Kusukawa, *Transformation of Natural Philosophy*.

[138] *gelerte ebenthewer*

[139] Probably a confusion between Cardinal Cajetan (d. 1534), who was present at the Diet of Augsburg in 1518 (see above, Mathesius, *History*, pp. 147–50), and Cardinal Contarini (see below, p. 492 n. 170), who was present at the Diet of Regensburg (see below, Mathesius, *History*, pp. 493–96).

[140] For this anecdote about Ferdinand I, see Mathesius, *Leichenrede auf Ferdinand I*, in Loesche, *Mathesius: Ausgewählte Werke*, 4:367.

[141] See *Table Talk* no. 4899 (1540), WA TR 4:573–74.

[142] Wander 3:1206, "Pelz" no. 28; cf. *Table Talk* no. 155 (1532), WA TR 1:73; no. 1721 (1532), WA TR 2:192–93.

[143] Wander 3:561, "Mehl" no. 61; cf. Thiele no. 135, p. 150. See *Table Talk* no. 4899 (1540), WA TR 4:573.

[144] The colloquy at Worms took place from November 1540 to January 1541. Melanchthon and Johann Eck (see above, p. 154 n. 89) were chosen as the representatives of the respective parties. See Vinzenz Pfnür, "Colloquies," *OER* 1:377. Cf. below, Mathesius, *History*, pp. 489–90.

Eck but also reminded him which of Eck's sophisms remained to be refuted, Granvelle, who was presiding, said, "The Lutherans have a secretary who is more learned than all our Papists."[145]

Again, some young jurists from Wittenberg went to Ingolstadt[146] to hear the famous Italian jurist Dr. Curtius.[147] In the course of a regular disputation, however, when they couched their arguments in lapidary form within the bounds of a sleek and lean syllogism and resolutely stood by their position, other scholars, who were accustomed to opposing and defending in a clumsy and bombastic manner, began to heap scorn on the subtle and pointed way in which the Wittenbergers disputed. But the aforementioned Dr. Curtius is supposed to have said, "That is the correct Aristotelian method and manner, which is in proper accord with reason, even if nothing like it has been heard before in Europe. Therefore, it behooves the unlearned to gather around the learned, and the bad should yield to the good." Thus far Curtius.[148]

Dear friends, I repeat these testimonies from great people from elsewhere in honor of this laudable university, since truth, honor, and my duty will permit me to do no less than I have done. In the last days God has caused a school to be erected for Himself by the House of Saxony on the white mountain or mountain of life;[149] He has adorned and exalted it to such an extent that any friend or foe who has even a spark of human reason remaining within him could not help but be amazed and astonished, even as local and foreign Jews and proselytes were bewildered at the twelve apostles on the great day of Pentecost [Acts 2:1–11]. Therefore, many good people from throughout the entire Roman Empire and from everywhere under heaven also gathered at this academy so that they might hear the Wittenberg wisdom, obtain it, and carry it home, like Candace's eunuch [Acts 8:27–39],

---

[145] Nicolaus Perrenot de Granvelle (1486–1550) was counselor for Charles V and represented the emperor at religious discussions at Augsburg (1530), Worms (1540–41), and Regensburg (1541) and in negotiating for the Council of Trent. See Maurenbrecher, "Granvelle, Nicolaus Perrenot von," *ADB* 9:580–84. For Granvelle's remark on Cruciger, see *Table Talk* no. 5452 (1542), WA TR 5:162; Volz, *Die Lutherpredigten des Johannes Mathesius*, p. 246.

[146] The University of Ingolstadt, where Johann Eck (see above, p. 154 n. 89) was professor, quickly became a leading opponent of Luther and the Reformation. Cf. above, Mathesius, *History*, pp. 218–19.

[147] Probably Marcus Antonius Caymus from Milan, who taught in Ingolstadt from 1538 to 1540: see Carl Prantl, *Geschichte der Ludwig-Maximilians-Universität in Ingolstadt* (Munich: Kaiser, 1872), 1:196 (*LH²*, p. 593). On Mathesius' error in giving Caymus' name, see Volz, *Die Lutherpredigten des Johannes Mathesius*, p. 158 n. 1.

[148] *Haec ille.*

[149] Translations of Wittenberg, taking "witt" as either a form of the German *weiss* ["white"] or of the Latin *vita* ["life"]. See Mathesius, *History*, above, pp. 145, 237; and below, pp. 572–73, 579.

from this Mount Lebanon.[150] For not to mention German neighbors from Meissen, Saxony, Rhineland, Franconia, Swabia, Bavaria, Austria, Silesia, Hesse, the Mark [Brandenburg], and Pomerania who frequently sent their children and teachers there, I also saw there people from Russia, Prussia, Holland, Denmark, Sweden, Lithuania, Bohemia, Poland, Hungary, Lusatia, Slovenia, Transylvania, Wallachia, France, Spain, Scotland, England, and Greece,[151] though probably not all of them were staying there for the sake of learning. For Judas, too, was in the Lord Christ's school, until the ravens promoted him to rabbi on the gallows [Matt. 27:5].

I allow all other universities the dignity and honor they deserve; I am a student of Wittenberg, a member of this university, a citizen of its church, and a disciple of these blessed Christian people. Many of them afterward took me into their friendship, in which God has preserved me from that time for thirty-four years now, honorably and steadfastly, as befits a good and thankful student. Therefore, I bear witness to my university, where God enabled me to study not only the liberal arts but also how I—with God and a good conscience, to the glory of Christ—should believe, live, teach, suffer, and take a blessed departure from this world to join my dear friends and preceptors. Let someone else, as an honorable disciple, praise his own university and teachers as well. Faithful fathers and teachers such as these are worthy of great thanks and all honor here and in eternity, and they will hear the endless laud and praise of their well-taught and thankful students in the eternal university of heaven. When Judas takes his own professorial chair next to all the students of Cassian and Damascene, and those like Nero,[152] it will be plain as day how they are all of a piece with those who at the present time have likewise come to the Mount of Olives by night with lanterns and torches [John 18:3] and have said to their teachers: "Woe to you, rabbi" (as one old parson read Iscariot's greeting in the Passion [Matt. 26:49]).[153]

But to return to our theme—our doctor, along with other Christian and peace-loving scholars, spent the whole summer engaged in preaching, lecturing, writing, and giving counsel to many neighboring and foreign lands

[150] "Lebanon" is derived from לְבָן, the Hebrew word for "white." Cf. above, Mathesius, *History*, p. 237.

[151] Mathesius' description of the international student body at Wittenberg is borne out by the lists of matriculated students with their places of origin in Förstemann et al., *Album*.

[152] On the students of Cassian and Damascene, see above, p. 291. The Roman emperor Nero (r. 54–68) forced his teacher, the philosopher Seneca (ca. 4 BC–AD 65), to commit suicide. See Suetonius, *Lives* 35.5 (Loeb 38 [1914], pp. 144–45); Tacitus (ca. 56–ca. 120), *Annals* 15.40–44 (Loeb 322 [1937], pp. 310–19).

[153] The Vg of Matt. 26:49 reads: "*Ave Rabbi*," which the pastor interpreted as the German "*auweh*." For Mathesius' critique of former Wittenberg students (such as Matthias Flacius) who later criticized Melanchthon, see above, Mathesius, *History*, pp. 112, 291–92.

which were inquring here after divine Law and instruction in cases of conscience.[154] When the rumor began to circulate that Emperor Charles was supposed to return to Germany the following year,[155] good people would have gladly seen the dissension between the Saxons and the churches of upper Germany and Switzerland concerning the Lord's Supper[156] reconciled, resolved, and settled in an agreeable and peaceful way. For in the most recent imperial diets this matter had also divided and splintered the secular [estates]. Therefore, the landgrave of Hesse sent a request to Dr. Martin that he and others would give their consent to the meeting to be held in Marburg and would attend.[157]

ᴵLuther could have little interest in such a colloquy or hope for it, as can be seen from his reply to the landgrave,[158] noting moreover, by God's Spirit, that it would not only bear little fruit but even have a prejudicial outcome—and his prophecy and apprehension have seldom been mistaken.[159] Nonetheless, he was moved to attend the meeting that had been arranged, for the sake of goodwill and brotherly love. In advance of the meeting, he held a public disputation on the precious Supper[160] in which Master Veit Dietrich[161] and Bonnus[162] from Lübeck, if I remember correctly, as well as students of Herr Philip, disputed against the doctor's propositions, syllogisms, and confession

---

[154] Luther primarily preached on the Gospels in the summer of 1529, with most of his focus on Luke. Other notable sermons from this period include a sermon on the catechism and a sermon on St. Christopher: *Catechism Sermon on the Creed* (1529), WA 29:471–73 (LW 56); *Legend of St. Christopher* (1529), WA 29:497–505 (LW 56). See also Luther to Thomas Löscher, August 26, 1529, LW 49:232–34.

[155] I.e., in 1530. See below, pp. 320–67.

[156] See above, Mathesius, *History*, pp. 240–46.

[157] In the wake of the renewed call for enforcement of the Edict of Worms at the Second Diet of Speyer in 1529 (see above, p. 288), Philip of Hesse took the lead in seeking the formation of a united Evangelical theological and defensive front, for which the colloquy at Marburg was supposed to prepare the way. See Landgrave Philip of Hesse to Luther and Melanchthon, July 1, 1529, WA Br 5:107–8; Brecht 2:325.

[158] Luther to Landgrave Philip of Hesse, June 23, 1529, LW 49:228–31.

[159] On Luther's prophecies, cf. below, Mathesius, *History*, pp. 562–67; Volz, *Die Lutherpredigten des Johannes Mathesius*, pp. 76–77.

[160] No other record of this disputation survives. See Volz, *Die Lutherpredigten des Johannes Mathesius*, pp. 172–73.

[161] On Dietrich, see above, p. 278 n. 76.

[162] Hermann Bonnus (1504–48) had studied in Wittenberg since 1523, then at Greifswald, but had gone to Denmark in 1528 to serve as tutor to the prince. It is unlikely that he was in Wittenberg in 1529 to take part in this disputation. He became superintendent in Lübeck in 1531 and composed a church order for Osnabrück in 1543. See Friedrich Wilhelm Bautz, "Bonnus (Bonn), Hermann," *BBKL* 2:696; Volz, *Die Lutherpredigten des Johannes Mathesius*, p. 173.

for the sake of learning to pose questions, in accordance with the university's laudable practice.[163] Not much that was new was presented, however, that had not already been publicly refuted in Luther's books. Karlstadt's sophistry about when the body of Christ is present and regarding the composition and division of both kinds[164] were brought into the debate,[165] in addition to St. Augustine's statement that Christ's true body must be substantially and corporeally present at only one particular location,[166] all of which the doctor readily refuted, solved, and explained with solid grounds from Scripture.

To wit: that one should simply and straightforwardly cling to the clear and true words of the Lord in faithful candor, and that in divine matters and articles of faith all reason and sophistry should and must be taken captive. For God's Word was recorded in God's power by the Holy Spirit; therefore, fallen human reason and cleverness are incapable of fathoming its depths. All who keep and obey the Word in faithful simplicity walk most truly and surely. Even if the good fathers and doctors of the Church sometimes expressed themselves dangerously, one must let Scripture be and remain the only rule and norm, by which alone the old and new teachers and the decrees of all councils must be judged. The following year, in his little book on the sayings of the fathers concerning the Lord's Supper, Herr Melanchthon provided a fine Christian and comforting explanation of this statement from Augustine, on which many people still heavily rely and to which they still appeal.[167]

Around the time of Michaelmas, Dr. Luther, Herr Philip, and Dr. Jonas departed for Marburg;[168] the teachers from southern Germany also went,

---

[163] Cf. above, p. 296.

[164] *de compositione et divisione beyder gestalt*

[165] Perhaps a reference to Karlstadt's treatise *Whether One Can Prove from Holy Scripture That Christ Is in the Sacrament* (1524), in Burnett, *Eucharistic Pamphlets of Andreas Bodenstein von Karlstadt*, pp. 116–42, and to his idea that the bread and wine were associated with different and distinct promises: see Karlstadt, *On Both Forms in the Holy Mass* (1521), in Burnett, *Eucharistic Pamphlets of Andreas Bodenstein von Karlstadt*, pp. 49–77.

[166] See Augustine to Dardanus, Ep. 187 (PL 33:832–48; *Augustine of Hippo: Selected Writings*, trans. Mary T. Clark [New York: Paulist Press, 1984], pp. 403–25). See Burnett, *Karlstadt and the Origins of the Eucharistic Controversy*, pp. 81, 87. On Augustine of Hippo, see above, p. 42 n. 16.

[167] *Sententiae veterum aliquot scriptorum de coena domini*, CR 23:745–52, esp. pp. 745–47. Cf. above, Mathesius, *History*, p. 261; Luther and Melanchthon to Landgrave Philip of Hesse, October 5, 1529, WA Br 5:155–56. Cf. p. 261 n. 175.

[168] The Wittenbergers had gathered at the Saxon court in Torgau to discuss their own articles of faith, formulated in what came to be known as the Schwabach Articles (see Kolb and Nestingen, *Sources and Contexts*, pp. 83–87; WA 30/3:81–91). They departed from Torgau on September 17 and arrived in Marburg on September 30 (Michaelmas is September 29). Also

along with Herr Brenz,[169] Osiander,[170] and Dr. Stephan Agricola.[171] Dr. Luther engaged in discussion with Oecolampadius;[172] Herr Philip, with Zwingli.[173] Seeing that the Upper German teachers at that time had been speaking and writing in a dangerous and offensive way concerning other articles as well, from which further error was to be feared, Dr. Luther presented these articles to his colloquist, as Philip also did to Zwingli. Once they had both sufficiently clarified, declared, and confessed that they taught concerning original sin and the ministry of the Word and Sacraments just as was taught in Wittenberg,[174] and once Zwingli had appealed to the Nicene Creed concerning Christ's divinity[175] and repudiated Hätzer's book

---

accompanying those named by Mathesius were Caspar Cruciger and Georg Rörer. See Brecht 2:327.

[169] Johann Brenz (1499–1570), the reformer of Schwäbisch Hall and later of Württemberg, was a leading defender of Luther's doctrine of the Lord's Supper in southern Germany, having drafted the 1525 *Swabian Syngramma* against the teachings of Oecolampadius and Zwingli (see above, Mathesius, *History*, p. 243 and n. 69 there). Brenz also wrote a catechism and church orders, helped with the reorganization of the University of Tübingen, and participated in the Diet of Augsburg. Luther contributed prefaces to a number of his writings: the *Swabian Syngramma* (1526), LW 59:150–62; *Exposition of Ecclesiastes* (1528), LW 59:216–19; *Exposition of Amos* (1530), LW 59:285–89; *On the Christian Conduct of Marriage Cases* (1531), LW 59:335–41; and *Twenty-Two Sermons* (1532), LW 60:1–6. See James M. Estes, "Brenz, Johannes," *OER* 1:214–15.

[170] Andreas Osiander (ca. 1496–1552) had served as preacher at St. Lorenz in Nürnberg since 1522 and became that city's leading Evangelical reformer. Generally aligned with Luther and the Wittenberg theology (as he was at Marburg in 1529, the Diet of Augsburg in 1530, and the Smalcald conference of 1537), he came into conflict with the Wittenbergers over the doctrine of the Keys and Absolution and over the character of justification, which he later, as preacher and professor in Königsberg from 1549, described as a participation in the divine righteousness of Christ (cf. FC SD X, on adiaphora [Kolb-Wengert, pp. 635–40, *Concordia*, pp. 597–602]; FC SD III 1–17, on justification [Kolb-Wengert, pp. 562–65, *Concordia*, pp. 536–39]). On Osiander, see Gottfried Seebaß, "Osiander, Andreas," *OER* 3:183–85.

[171] Stephan Augsburg [Kastenbauer] Agricola (ca. 1491–1547) was a former Augustinian who came to Augsburg in 1524 and worked as a reformer under Urbanus Rhegius (see below, p. 357 n. 203) (see *LH*, p. 213). He represented Rhegius and Augsburg at Marburg. In the last years of his life, Agricola was pastor in Eisleben. See Gustav Hammann, "Agricola, Stephan der Ältere," *NDB* 1:104–5; Karin Brinkmann Brown, "Agricola, Stephan," *OER* 1:12.

[172] On Oecolampadius, see above, p. 240 n. 52.

[173] There are a variety of reports of the colloquy. See the harmonization by Herman Sasse, *This Is My Body*, pp. 215–72; *Marburg Colloquy* (1529), LW 39:3–85; and Melanchthon's reporting (cited by Mathesius: see below, p. 313), CR 1:1098–106. See also Luther, *Brief Confession* (1544), LW 38:288–89.

[174] See Melanchthon to Elector John, October 5, 1529, CR 1:1099; to Duke Henry [IV] of Saxony, October 5, 1529, CR 1:1103; *Marburg Articles* (1529), LW 38:87; Sasse, *This Is My Body*, pp. 225–29.

[175] *Marburg Colloquy* (1529), LW 38:43; Melanchthon's report, CR 1:1103. On the Nicene Creed, see above, Mathesius, *History*, p. 134.

against Christ's divinity,[176] the others were satisfied with them concerning these points.[177]

Finally, they took up the article of the Lord's Supper. Dr. Luther openly protested that he neither could nor would deviate from his writings, because they were true and based on God's Word.[178] His counterparts relied upon the passage in John 6 [:63]—"the flesh is of no help"—and claimed that a natural body could not be present in many places at one time and that the sacraments are signs, and so they merely signify the body of Christ. Accordingly, the Lord Christ's true body and blood are not with the bread or in the distribution of the Lord's Supper.[179]

Dr. Luther refuted this as follows: The text "the flesh is of no help" is not speaking of the flesh of Jesus Christ, which ᴵbrings and gives life, but rather of the carnal natural understanding. Again, one neither can nor should think or speak of Christ's glorified body—which is united with the divine nature in an undivided person, has ascended into heaven, and everywhere rules and and is active at the right hand of His Father—in the way that we think and speak of our natural human body. For God has given the Lord Jesus a name and authority above all names and power [Phil. 2:9]. Therefore, even though reason thinks of this as impossible and illogical, God can nevertheless do all that He says. Now, here stand the clear and true words of Christ: "This is My body; this is My blood" [Matt. 26:26–28; Mark 14:22–24; Luke 22:19–20; 1 Cor. 11:24–25]. No one ought to shorten God's hand in this [Num. 11:23], for with Him, as the Virgin Mary says, nothing is impossible [cf. Luke 1:37].[180]

Since they so stubbornly insisted on the article of the ascension into heaven,[181] the words of the Creed can bear being interpreted and explained according to Scripture better than the words of the Supper, which the evangelists and St. Paul faithfully repeated many years after one another without alteration. For "heaven" in the Scriptures is a single word with many and varied meanings. Therefore, the word "heaven" should not and cannot be

---

[176] On Hätzer and his book on the divinity of Christ, see above, Mathesius, *History*, p. 246 and n. 87 there.

[177] The agreement between the parties is expressed in the *Marburg Articles* (1529), LW 38:85–89; Kolb and Nestingen, *Sources and Contexts*, pp. 88–92.

[178] Sasse, *This Is My Body*, pp. 231–36; *Marburg Colloquy* (1529), LW 38:75–76.

[179] *Marburg Colloquy* (1529), LW 38:20–21, 31, 37–38, 47; Melanchthon's report, CR 1:1100, 1104; Sasse, *This Is My Body*, p. 232.

[180] *Marburg Colloquy* (1529), LW 38:31–32, 45; Sasse, *This Is My Body*, pp. 239–40, 255; Melanchthon's report, CR 1:1100, 1104.

[181] I.e., in the Apostles' Creed (Kolb-Wengert, p. 22; *Concordia*, p. 16); Sasse, *This Is My Body*, p. 248; Melanchthon's report, CR 1:1104; *Marburg Colloquy* (1529), LW 38:26–27.

understood as meaning a circumscribed or separate location in the empyrean heaven.[182]

As to the interpretation of the Sacraments: it is true that they are signs, but they are not to be interpreted otherwise than as Christ Himself explains them with His Word. Namely, they point us to the promise in which Christ's blessing and treasure are presented to us and applied and apprehended in faith. So that we may be confirmed and made certain in this article—that Christ's body and blood have been [given and] shed for us for the forgiveness of sins [Matt. 26:28],[183] and that through this we partake in both the inheritance and the likeness of Christ's body, by grace, and will be like Him in radiance, glory, ¹and immortality through all eternity [cf. Rom. 8:29; Phil. 3:21]—He gives us His true and substantial body and blood to eat and drink in the power of His Word. Therefore, we should and must let Christ and His Word explain and interpret the Sacraments rather than dreaming up and inventing explanations and empty glosses ourselves, without a sure [passage of] Scripture.[184]

This is about the sum of the colloquy held in Marburg, as Herr Melanchthon himself recorded it, dedicating it to Duke Henry of Saxony.[185]

The good people had driven their cart too far into [the mud].[186] Therefore, even though in the other articles they yielded entirely and followed Dr. Luther, they held out in comparative hope for their article on the Lord's Supper. Martin Bucer[187] and others later allowed themselves to be corrected and undertook many discussions with their own people in order to establish peace and unity and come to the support of the Wittenbergers.[188]

---

[182] *im fewrigen Himmel.* See Sasse, *This Is My Body*, pp. 248–49; *Marburg Colloquy* (1529), LW 38:43.

[183] *Small Catechism* (1529) VI 5–8 (Kolb-Wengert, pp. 362–63; *Concordia*, p. 343).

[184] Sasse, *This Is My Body*, pp. 249, 262; *Marburg Colloquy* (1529), LW 38:45.

[185] Melanchthon to Elector John, October 5, 1529, CR 1:1098–102; to Duke Henry [IV] of Saxony, October 5, 1529, CR 1:1102–6. Henry was the younger brother of Duke George of Albertine Saxony (see above, p. 154 n. 91). Henry, however, was a convinced Lutheran, who introduced the Reformation in his own seat at Freiberg in 1537 and in all of ducal Saxony when he succeeded the childless Duke George in 1539. See Günther Wartenberg, *Landesherrschaft und Reformation: Mortiz von Sachsen und die albertinische Kirchenpolitik bis 1546* (Gütersloh: G. Mohn, 1988).

[186] Wander 2:1146, "Karren" no. 21.

[187] On Bucer, see above, Mathesius, *History*, pp. 243–44 and pp. 171–72 n. 32.

[188] On Bucer's role in the Wittenberg Concord of 1536, see Mathesius, *History*, above, pp. 243–44; and below, pp. 395–96.

I have heard from Peter Plateanus,[189] your old school rector, about what he witnessed at the Hessian court. The landgrave is supposed to have taken great pains to hold separate conversations with Oecolampadius about these matters.[190] Among the things he is supposed to have said was: "My good doctor, those from Wittenberg at least stand upon a solid text [of Scripture], but all you have are glosses and explanations.[191] The one surely has more weight than the other. Why do you incriminate yourselves?" Dr. Oecolampadius is supposed to have responded with a sigh: "Gracious prince and lord, I would rather have had this fist of mine cut off than to have written a single letter about this."

Without a doubt, conscience and Dr. Luther's prophecy were already being felt in the heart of this poor and uncertain man, as indeed a few years later Dr. Luther's prophecy about Zwingli and Oecolampadius came true.

"Ah, gentlemen, be very careful," said Luther. ["I fear that within three years you will have clasped your hands over your heads."[192] *Et factum est ita* ["And so it came to pass"] [Gen. 1:7, 11, 15, 30]. Before that time had passed, Zwingli was killed in battle,[193] and the evil news terrified and overwhelmed Oecolampadius at night on his bed.[194] The prayer and prophecy of Moses against his Korah, Dathan, and Abiram did not fall back to earth in vain. Who knows what end may befall those who since Zwingli's death have tried to rekindle the extinguished fire and have again tried to peddle the

[189] Peter Plateanus (d. 1551) was rector in Joachimsthal from 1525 to 1531, and then in Zwickau from 1535 to 1546, before becoming superintendent in Oelsnitz. Cf. Zwickau Council to Luther, March 15, 1537, WA Br 8:58. See Otto Kaemmel, "Plateanus, Petrus," ABD 26:241–43; Bietenholz and Deutscher, *Contemporaries of Erasmus*, 1:99–100. Mathesius is the source for this anecdote.

[190] On the efforts of Philip of Hesse to negotiate with Oecolampadius, see David M. Whitford, *A Reformation Life: The European Reformation through the Eyes of Philipp of Hesse* (Santa Barbara, CA: Praeger, 2015), pp. 74–75.

[191] Oecolampadius appealed extensively to the church fathers in the eucharistic controversies, sometimes also relying on logic and philosophy, to the neglect of the text of Scripture. See Irena Backus, *The Disputations of Baden, 1526, and Berne, 1528: Neutralizing the Early Church* (Princeton, NJ: Princeton Theological Seminary, 1993), ch. 2.

[192] Wander 2:318, "Hand" no. 605. Mathesius is the only source for this prophecy of Luther's: see Volz, *Die Lutherpredigten des Johannes Mathesius*, p. 247.

[193] Zwingli was killed while serving as chaplain to the Zürich troops in the battle at Kappel on October 11, 1531. For Luther's references to his death, see *Table Talk* no. 1232 (1531), WA TR 2:3; no. 1451 (1532), LW 54:152; no. 1793 (1532), WA TR 2:216; no. 2692 (1532), WA TR 2:602–3; no. 3372b (1533), WA TR 3:295; and the citations on Oecolampadius in the following annotation.

[194] Oecolampadius died the night of November 23–24, 1531. For Luther's interpretation of the deaths of Zwingli and Oecolampadius, see *Table Talk* no. 5322 (1540), WA TR 5:58; *The Private Mass* (1533), LW 38:157; *Brief Confession* (1544), LW 38:289. Cf. below, Mathesius, *History*, pp. 394–95, 430–31, 515, 546, 563.

arguments and rationalizations of those poor people concerning the nature of the true God and the human body for their own wicked schemes while deceiving many poor people with a specious display of scholarship.[195]

Now when our doctor and his companions returned home, he again continued with lecturing, writing, and preaching. Early in the year 1530 his jealousy was kindled against his own parishioners, and he delivered a harsh penitential sermon to them, almost like the Lord Christ with His cries of woe against the people of Capernaum and Bethsaida [Matt. 11:21–24]. For the Word of God was threatening to become a reproach and derision for him, as the prophet Jeremiah lamentably complains about his listeners in chapter 20 [Jer. 20:7–13] when he, too, decided that he would no longer preach in God's name. So, likewise, at this time the doctor also publicly said that he would no longer preach, and he did refrain for a time, until his anger had cooled—or, rather, his calling burned in his heart—so that he took to the pulpit again.[196]

Great people also have lofty thoughts[197] and their own particular tribulations, which we simple folk cannot always follow. Moses in his anger cast down the two tablets, upon which were written the Ten Commandments [Exod. 32:19]. Phinehas in his zeal pierced the licentious Israelite through [Num. 25:7–8]. Samuel condemned the king [1 Sam. 28:19] because Saul had spared [the Amalekites] with great hypocrisy, contrary to God's Word [1 Samuel 15]. St. Paul delivered the incestuous Corinthian man to the devil [1 Cor. 5:5]. God and His people also have their hot zeal and burning wrath.[198] Our doctor, too, was often so pained in heart on this account that his writings hail down like a cloudburst.[199] Many times he wished that he could rain as gently and pleasantly as Herr Philip and Herr Brenz,[200] but the single Spirit works in manifold ways [cf. 1 Cor. 12:4–11]. We who travel on the highway or common path neither can nor should follow those who

---

[195] *mit scheinlicher kunst und farben*

[196] At the end of his *Sermon for the Circumcision of Christ* on January 1, 1530 (WA 32:4 [LW 56]), Luther told the congregation that he was going to cease from preaching because of their disobedience and ingratitude; cf. Volz, *Die Lutherpredigten des Johannes Mathesius*, p. 170, and below, Mathesius, *History*, p. 522. Although Luther was forced to preach several times in the following months because of Bugenhagen's absence, he maintained this stance for some time, declaring repeatedly that he would not preach to the Wittenberg congregation any longer: see Brecht 2:288; *Exhortation to All Clergy* (1530), LW 34:50. He resumed regular preaching in September 1530.

[197] Wander 3:75, "Leute" no. 686.

[198] Cf. below, Mathesius, *History*, pp. 461–62, 517–18.

[199] *rauchen wie die platzregen*

[200] See Luther's preface to Melanchthon, *Exposition of Colossians* (1529), LW 59:249–50; to Brenz, *Exposition of Amos* (1530), LW 59:287–88; *Table Talk* nos. 347–48 (1532), LW 54:49–50; no. 397 (1532), LW 54:62–63; no. 5054 (1540), WA TR 4:637; no. 5091 (1540), WA TR 4:653.

leave the wagon road and beaten path and instead make their way through marshland, water, forests, mountains, and valleys. Much less should we be quick to judge the seriousness, ardor, zeal, and vehemence of great people; they have their own surveyor and charioteer[201] within their own hearts, who often comes upon them and stirs them up, drives them onward, and often leads them where they did not imagine. God also pronounces His favor and blessing upon their paths and wondrously brings their journey to completion, giving everyone cause to cross himself [in astonishment].

In 1541, when the doctor was lecturing on Rebekah (Genesis 27), who slipped her younger son, Jacob, in against the will and command of her husband, I heard these words from him:[202] "Rebekah began the undertaking in an improper way, but she carried it out. Likewise, I also have often departed from the highway after preparing the way with a strong Our Father or using it to clear a path.[203] I found my way out with God's help, but I don't advise this to any of you. Stay on the beaten path and act in accordance with the rule; then no one will bar your way."

Many a person in our days has wanted to follow after this chariot and horseman of Israel [2 Kings 2:12] but has wound up stranded.[204] Therefore, let us act in accordance with the rule. If there are some who have stepped away from the rule and yet have accomplished something, let us marvel at such great and extraordinary people and thank God for their heroic courage instead of maligning, slandering, and defaming their extraordinary deeds. Great deeds are not accomplished without danger.[205] Cursed be those who do the work of God with slackness, says the prophet [Jer. 48:10]. There is a time and occasion to be mild and temperate, but sometimes one also needs a downpour and gale to blow away the old snow.[206]

Let us now also recall here how the doctor employed both down feathers and pinions [to write] at this and other times, depending on what was

---

[201] *Seygersteller und Schirrmeister.* Loesche (*LH²*, p. 525) suggests that *Seygersteller* is used here not in the usual sense of "one who maintains a clock" but as a mining term referring to the one who uses a plumb line (*Seiger*) to direct the excavation of a shaft.

[202] In fact, Luther lectured on Genesis 27 in the spring of 1542 (see Volz, *Die Lutherpredigten des Johannes Mathesius*, p. 200). On Mathesius' attendance at the Genesis lectures, see below, *History*, pp. 522–26. Mathesius quotes Luther's remark from his own recollection; for parallels in the published text, see *Lectures on Genesis* (1535–45/1544–54), LW 5:117–19.

[203] *zu brucken gebraucht*

[204] For the identification of Luther as the "chariot of Israel and its horsemen," see Melanchthon, *On the Death of Luther*, in Vandiver et al., *Luther's Lives*, p. 100; and below, Mathesius, *History*, p. 560. Cf. below, Mathesius, *History*, pp. 560–61, 592–93; above, Walter, *New Spiritual Song*, p. 98, stanza 59.

[205] *Grosse werck gehen nicht one gfahr abe.* Cf. Wander 5:197, "Werk" no. 51.

[206] Cf. *Table Talk* no. 397 (1532), LW 54:62–63.

appropriate for the situation.[207] Sometimes the man's quills would crackle and spatter, yet he continued to use common ink instead of writing with either red ink or the pope's rubrics or red blood.[208] Instead, his quills gave Christian counsel for peace and obedience as subjects, which, God be praised, has not caused or resulted in any injury to Christ and His Word. For until the day he died, he used his sharp and crackling quills in such a way, in tranquility together with public peace and quiet conduct, that he had no need to make the confession Savonarola made at his end.[209] Herr Melanchthon, the excellent man, was particularly astonished at this extraordinary man, among other things, for constantly advising for public peace and admonishing to obedience as subjects; his whole life long he never helped sound a call to arms.[210]

His writings and prayers[211] comforted and quieted the consciences of many people; he also answered many angry people in a way that moved them to sheathe their sword and quills. His life ended on the day of Concord, after which a dangerous and vexatious feast of discord has unfortunately been observed down to the present day in many lands, churches, and schools.[212] God help all peaceable rulers and teachers that they may depart this life in peace, as did Simeon [Luke 2:29], instead of preparing and bequeathing to their posterity unrest and danger under the pretext and cover of the unity of the territory and the Church.[213]

---

[207] I.e., soft quills for writing pastoral counsel and stiff quills for polemical treatises.

[208] Cf. *Wider den Meuchler zu Dresden* (1531), WA 30/3:450; *Table Talk* no. 6997 (n.d.), WA TR 6:313.

[209] Savonarola was forced under torture to confess that he had fabricated his prophecies and visions in order to secure power. He then retracted this statement, then confessed it again. See Roberto Ridolfi, *The Life of Girolamo Savonarola*, trans. Cecil Grayson (New York: Knopf, 1959), pp. 252–55. See also above, pp. 114–15 n. 4.

[210] See above, Melanchthon, *Oration*, pp. 45–47; Melanchthon, *Preface*, p. 73.

[211] Literally, "Our Father," but Luther's prayers in general rather than a particular prayer or exposition of the Lord's Prayer seem to be meant.

[212] Luther died on February 18, 1546. February 18 was observed in Germany as the feast of St. Concordia of Rome, nursemaid of St. Hippolytus. See *LA* 2:75, no. 118, and Mathesius' sermon for St. Concordia's Day in *Postilla* (1584), 2:122v–127v; cf. below, Mathesius, *History*, p. 535. Mathesius' reference to a "feast of discord" seems to be an allusion to the doctrinal debates among Lutherans after Luther's death.

[213] After his accession in 1559, Elector Frederick III (1515–76) of the Palatinate sought to replace Lutheranism with a "second Reformation" in his territories, dismissing Lutheran pastors and professors in order to replace them with Reformed personnel, adopting the Heidelberg Catechism in 1563 and a new church order based on models from Geneva and Zurich. German Lutherans demanded at the Diet of Augsburg in 1566 that all such Calvinist innovations be revoked. See Andrew Pettegree, ed., *The Reformation World* (New York: Routledge, 2000), pp. 392–93.

Let that be enough concerning Doctor Luther's extraordinary spirit, boldness, salutary and admirable vehemence, and his godly zeal which was blessedly enkindled against the abominable papacy and poisonous ¹and false brethren and violent neighbors, for the honor of God and to spread the holy Gospel. Whatever shortcoming or weakness of flesh and blood was to be found mingled with this noble nature has been forgiven him and graciously covered by the blood of Jesus Christ, with which he was often sprinkled in holy Absolution. Who are we, then, to blame or find fault with a faithful servant of God, to denigrate and belittle the holy preaching office by reproving or exposing him? The two good sons of Noah concealed and covered over their father's error when he had faltered and stumbled [Gen. 9:20–23]; in doing so, they accomplished far more than Ham and his son, who laughed in their sleeves and not only shamed and exposed their father but also mocked the promised highly exalted Messiah in their father's loins [Gen. 9:22, 25; cf. Heb. 7:10]. Ishmael likewise laughed at the Son of God in Isaac's thigh [Gen. 21:9]. God and His servants will not be mocked. It took the descendants of Canaan a long time to pay for their father, the mocker and maligner of Jesus Christ, in accordance with the prophecy concerning Shem [Gen. 9:26].

Verily, dear friends, let us not sit with the mockers and Epicureans,[214] who slander God and His members and expose His servants or trumpet their errors and maliciously lay them bare. When parting from his faithful disciple and successor Elisha, the great prophet Elijah, who also had his flaws[215] and blunders (seeing that all men are sinners, and all the saints pray for forgiveness and are saved by the blood of Christ alone), left him his cloak [2 Kings 2:13], that he might cover and help excuse his (Elijah's) deficiencies and faults and the failings of all faithful teachers. In the same way, the Emperor Constantine in his day also wanted to cover the transgressions of his bishops with his purple cloak.[216]

¹Christian hearts and godly listeners and grateful students and obedient subjects will help to conceal and excuse the failings of their authorities, parents, teachers, and friends. Godless, rebellious, hateful knaves are

---

[214] The ancient Greek philosopher Epicurus (341–270 BC) and his followers were notorious for their mockery of traditional religion and piety and their dismissal of the idea of life after death. The epithet was used loosely to associate contemporaries with any combination of these positions. See above, Mathesius, *History*, p. 207.

[215] *Pfabenfuß*; literally, "peacock's foot," which was proverbially ugly as compared with its beautiful plumage. See Wander 3:1253, "Pfau" no. 9; cf. below, Mathesius, *History*, p. 466.

[216] Cf. the account of Emperor Constantine (ca. 272–337) taking the complaints that the bishops at Nicaea brought against each other and hiding them unread in the fold of his cloak: Rufinus (ca. 345–410), *Historia Ecclesiastica* 10.2 (GCS 9/2:961; trans. Philip R. Amidon, *The Church History of Rufinus of Aquileia* [Oxford: Oxford University Press, 1997], pp. 9–10).

and remain Epicurean sows,[217] who pass by the vegetable garden and do not see or recognize the faithful work and great beneficence of honorable people. Therefore, they stick their snout into sheer filth and wallow in it, making themselves reek and others with them. May God preserve us from such company and all those who want to grab the deceased hero Ajax by the beard[218] and make themselves knights by [fighting against] the deceased.

With this we conclude the year 1529 and the beginning of 1530. O Lord Jesus, help and preserve the laudable Christian university in Wittenberg and its nourishers and patrons, that they may endure with unanimity in the pure doctrine which our God there had purified and brought forth through this prophet, and let us not forget the service and beneficence of faithful teachers and patrons nor participate in denigrating it, for You are a God who desires gratitude and reverence, You who are highly praised with Your Father, the Spirit, and all Your prophets, apostles, and faithful preachers through all eternity! Amen!

---

[217] Cf. Horace, *Epistles* 1.4.16 (Loeb 194 [1926] pp. 276–77).

[218] Ajax was one of the foremost Greek heroes in the *Iliad*. Zwingli refered to Luther as an "Ajax" in 1527 in his *Daß diese Worte: "Das ist Mein Leib" usw.* (1527), CR 92:824: see Edwards, *Luther and the False Brethren*, p. 100 and n. 71. Although the expression sounds proverbial, no source could be identified.

THE NINTH SERMON,[1]
ON THE CONFESSION OF THE GOSPEL
AT AUGSBURG
BEFORE HIS IMPERIAL MAJESTY
AND THE ENTIRE EMPIRE,
MADE WITH CHRISTIAN BOLDNESS
BY THE ELECTOR OF SAXONY
AND HIS ASSOCIATES,
AND WHAT OUR DOCTOR SOUGHT TO DO
DURING THIS IMPERIAL DIET,
IN THE YEAR OF OUR LORD 1530[2]

[Spring 1563][3]

BELOVED friends in the Lord! Once, a doctor [of theology] posed from the pulpit the question of whether princes could also be saved. He then gave an answer himself: "Yes, if they die in the cradle. For if they make it

---

[1] Some later editions of Mathesius' *History* number this sermon as the eighth because of the relocation of the original seventh sermon (see above, p. 266 n. 1, and the introduction, p. lxxxvii).

[2] For modern accounts of the genesis and presentation of the Augsburg Confession, see Wilhelm Maurer, *Historical Commentary on the Augsburg Confession*, trans. H. George Anderson (Philadelphia: Fortress, 1986); and Arand et al., *Lutheran Confessions*, pp. 87–105 (on the Augsburg Confession) and pp. 107–38 (on the Apology). The critical edition of the proceedings of Augsburg in the *DRA*, edited by Alfred Kohler and Martina Fuchs, is forthcoming.

[3] The date of Mathesius' preaching of this sermon cannot be determined with certainty; probably it was delivered not long after the eighth sermon (see above, *History*, p. 286), which was preached on Easter Sunday, April 11, 1563. The tenth sermon (see below, *History*, p. 368), also undated, indicates that some time had elapsed between the ninth and tenth sermons. Although it would be tempting to place the ninth sermon on June 25, 1563, the anniversary of the presentation of the Augsburg Confession, Mathesius does not here acknowledge any connection of the date of preaching with the events he is narrating as he does elsewhere (see *History*, above, pp. 114–15; and below, p. 538), so presumably sermon nine was preached before the date of the anniversary. The next sermon that can be dated with certainty is the fifteenth, preached on February 18, 1564, the anniversary of Luther's death.

onto a horse, they usually gallop straight to hell."[4] This answer is not so good, for the men of former days who had been consecrated with the pope's spirit and chrism[5] did not always speak very well of the dear authorities and would have liked to trample on their head or to persuade them to enter their monastery.

But (praise God!) since our doctor has written about secular authorities and soldiers on the basis of God's Word,[6] and his quill has freed many of them from the pope's feet[7] and murderous power and has magnificently adorned the estate of rulers with God's Word and instructed their consciences in such a fine and salutary way—namely, that in their estate they should serve our God as Christians, call upon Christ, and could finally be saved in doing so, if they abide in their Baptism, believe in Christ, |honor and boldly confess His Word, help to nourish and protect God's Church and Christian schools, and steadfastly, in patience and humility, preserve their faith and good conscience to the end—therefore, we are able to give a more certain and comforting answer to the question of whether princes, too, can be saved.

Now, since the order of our history reminds us to speak about the blessed confession of numerous electors and princes and cities,[8] who truthfully, as God-fearing and faithful hearers of our doctor, confessed the pure doctrine of the Gospel in Augsburg with great boldness and steadfastness, we want in all simplicity to report the conclusion that not only baptized princes in their cribs but also aged emperors, kings, and lords may attain a

---

[4] Cf. Wander 1:1288, "Fürst" no. 130.

[5] See above, p. 204 n. 18.

[6] See, e.g., *To the Christian Nobility* (1520), LW 44:115–217; *Temporal Authority* (1523), LW 45:75–129; *Letter to the Princes of Saxony* (1524), LW 40:45–59; *Whether Soldiers, Too, Can Be Saved* (1526), LW 46:87–137.

[7] A reference to the custom of kissing the pope's feet (see also above, p. 84 n. 4) as well as to reports that popes claimed figurative and literal authority to trample rulers underfoot: see Luther, *Against the Roman Papacy* (1545), LW 41:297, 332; preface to Barnes, *How Popes Adrian IV and Alexander III Showed Good Faith to Emperor Barbarossa* (1545), LW 60:347–51.

[8] *etliche Chur und Fürsten und Stedte*. Although John the Steadfast was the only elector to sign the Augsburg Confession, his son John Frederick, who succeeded him as elector in 1532, also signed the Augsburg Confession in his role as duke of Saxony: see the list of signatories (Kolb-Wengert, pp. 104–5; *Concordia*, p. 63).

blessed end and join the ancient Christian[9] potentates David,[10] Hezekiah,[11] Cyrus,[12] Ahasuerus,[13] Constantine,[14] Theodosius,[15] Arcadius,[16] Charles I,[17] Louis [IV] of Bavaria,[18] Electors Frederick and John,[19] and Charles V[20] with honor and joy on the Day of Judgment.

For once Emperor Charles of laudable memory had arranged his affairs in his hereditary kingdom in a praiseworthy way, with God's help, and was intending to travel back to Germany, he left Spain and went to Italy so that

---

[9] I.e., as believers in Christ either before or after the incarnation or apparently as those who served as providential protectors of believers.

[10] David (r. 1009–970 BC) was second king of the United Kingdom of Israel. Record of his reign is found in 1–2 Samuel, 1 Kings, and 1 Chronicles.

[11] Hezekiah (r. 715–686 BC) was thirteenth king of Judah. His reign is recorded in 2 Kings 18–20 and 2 Chronicles 29–32.

[12] Cyrus the Great was the king of Persia who gave the Jews permission to return to Jerusalem from their captivity in Babylon. See Isa. 44:28; 45:1; 2 Chron. 36:22–23; Ezra 1–6.

[13] Ahasuerus (r. 486–465 BC), also known as Xerxes the Great, was the king of Persia who married Esther and protected the Jews from Haman's genocidal plot. See Esther 1–10.

[14] The Roman emperor Constantine the Great (r. 306–337) declared toleration for Christianity in 313, becoming the first Christian emperor and a patron of the Church. He summoned the Council of Nicaea in 325 against the Arian heresy (see above, Mathesius, *History*, p. 109). See *ODCC*, 3rd ed., s.v. "Constantine the Great."

[15] The Roman emperor Theodosius I (r. 379–395) supported Nicene Christianity, summoned the First Council of Constantinople in 381, and outlawed pagan sacrifice. Despite numerous conflicts, Theodosius was strongly influenced by Bishop Ambrose of Milan (r. 374–397), and their relationship became a model for ecclesial authority in the Middle Ages. See *ODCC*. 3rd ed., s.v. "Ambrose."

[16] Arcadius (r. 395–408) was the eldest son of Theodosius I, with authority over the Eastern empire. He enforced the orthodoxy defined under his predecessor. See Michael P. McHugh, "Arcadius," in Everett Ferguson et al., *Encyclopedia of Early Christianity*, 2nd ed. (New York: Garland, 1997), 1:99–100.

[17] Charles I, also known as Charlemagne, was crowned Holy Roman emperor in 800. He regarded himself as "rector of the Christian people" and took an active role in theological and ecclesiastical matters. See *ODCC*, 3rd ed., s.v. "Charlemagne."

[18] Louis IV of Bavaria was elected German king [*Rex Romanorum*] in 1314 and crowned Holy Roman emperor by the captain of the Roman commune (rather than by the pope) in 1328. He had been excommunicated by Pope John XXII (r. 1316–34) in 1324, but declared the pope himself deposed in 1328 and asserted his legitimacy on the basis of the imperial election itself. His court in Munich became a refuge for antipapal theologians, including the Franciscans William of Ockham (see above, p. 62 n. 46) and Michael of Cesena (d. 1342). On Louis IV, see *HRED*, pp. 283–87.

[19] Frederick the Wise (see above, p. 68 n. 82) and his brother John the Steadfast (see above, p. 70 n. 95), electors of Saxony.

[20] Holy Roman emperor Charles V (see above, p. 161 n. 123). On Mathesius' favorable portrayal of Charles, see Mathesius, *History*, above, pp. 161, 168, 179–80; and below, pp. 341–42, 362, 364, 493, 558–59.

he could receive the imperial crown in Bologna by virtue of the Golden Bull[21] and might put a proper and fitting end to every kind of dissension.[22]

However, when Pope Clement[23] most vehemently insisted that the emperor use the power of the sword to suppress and obliterate the new doctrine from German lands, this laudable emperor gave answer in council through his chancellor Mercurino[24] that there were two possible paths for establishing peace and unity in Christendom: either to punish the stubborn by the power of the sword or to employ peaceable and gracious means and ways. Now, not all of those who had intervened in such cases by the power of the sword had enjoyed good fortune, as was attested by the history of Emperor Sigismund.[25] Therefore, said Mercurino, His Majesty was inclined to employ friendly means and to attempt to have the scholars settle and eliminate the errors and divisions that had arisen in religious matters.

As the emperor's chancellor was saying this, Pope Clement interrupted his speech, claiming that he was making these proposals without any commission to do so. Then Emperor Charles himself began to assert the same position with great seriousness. Although this peaceful course displeased the bloodthirsty people, Emperor Charles nonetheless decided to undertake this high matter in an amicable way.

---

[21] The Golden Bull of 1356, issued under Emperor Charles IV (r. 1355–78), codified the procedure for the election of the emperor by the prince-electors and his coronation, stipulating that (as Louis IV of Bavaria had claimed, see above, p. 322 n. 18) he possessed all imperial rights after his election even without papal coronation. See *HRED*, pp. 183–86. Charles V was crowned by the archbishop of Cologne in Aachen on October 23, 1520 (see above, p. 168 n. 7), but did not receive papal coronation until February 24, 1530. See P. N. Bebb, "Golden Bull," *HRED*, pp. 183–86; Jonathan W. Zophy, "Electors," *OER* 2:31–32.

[22] On Charles' progress from Spain to Italy and his coronation, see Sleidanus, *De statu religionis* (1558), book 6, pp. 174, 176; book 7, pp. 181–82; Brandi, *Emperor Charles V*, pp. 282–91.

[23] I.e., Clement VII (r. 1523–34; see William V. Hudon, "Clement VII," *OER* 1:362–63) had insisted in the negotations for the Treaty of Barcelona in 1528 that Charles and Ferdinand use force against the Protestant heretics: see Brandi, *Emperor Charles V*, pp. 276–77. On the exchange at Bologna related by Mathesius here, see Melanchthon, *De congressu Bononiensi* (1559), CR 12:307–15; Luther, *Warning to His Dear German People* (1531), LW 47:24; cf. Volz, *Die Lutherpredigten des Johannes Mathesius*, pp. 98–99.

[24] Mercurino Arborio di Gattinara (1465–1530) was a prominent legal scholar and had served as grand chancellor to Charles as Spanish king since 1518. He died on June 5, 1530, en route to the Diet of Augsburg. See John M. Headley, "Gattinara, Mercurino Arborio di," *OER* 2:159–60.

[25] Emperor Sigismund (see above, p. 179 n. 64) violated John Hus' safe-conduct to the Council of Constance and was thereafter inundated by the Hussite wars: see above, Mathesius, *History*, p. 179.

Accordingly, the magnificent imperial diet in Augsburg was announced in writing, to be held in May of the year 1530;[26] Emperor Charles would attend in person in order to ensure faithful dealing, both in matters concerning religious contention and with regard to long-term aid against the Turk.

The imperial diet having been scheduled, everyone, especially the clerics and their confederates, awaited the emperor and their day of redemption with ineffable hope and joy; many began to imagine that the protesting [estates] adhering to Luther's doctrine in their lands and cities would completely lose their heart and courage and would flee from the light or crawl back to the cross without being heard.[27] Thus Elector John took counsel with his scholars and with those who together with him confessed this doctrine before the whole world and all potentates, and they unanimously decided in the name of Jesus Christ on the basis of timely and Christian counsel that they would attend this imperial diet. As they firmly and steadfastly in their hearts believed this doctrine unto justification, so also they desired to make a steadfast public confession, to the honor of God, as a testimony of their faith and for the consolation and salvation of many people. Accordingly, the aforementioned elector prepared himself for this blessed trip before all the others, shielding himself with the precious words of Jesus Christ in Matthew 10 [:32]: "Whoever confesses Me before men, I also will confess before My Father who is in heaven and all angels."

During Passion Week, Doctor Martin, Master Philip, and Doctor Jonas set off for Torgau and a few days later traveled to Coburg.[28] On account of great and weighty considerations, Doctor Luther was left at this castle,[29] so that his presence might not further embitter the opponents and aggravate the main issue. For since this imperial diet had been proclaimed primarily on account of religion, and certain princes had taken up the cause of the Word of God, as befits Christians, the imperial rescript summoned to Augsburg the adherents of all religions from among the princes, lords, and estates.

Although our doctor, in keeping with the judicious counsel and command of his own governing authorities as well as the Christian concerns

---

[26] See Sleidanus, *De statu religionis* (1558), book 7, p. 181, where, however, the date announced is given as April 8. The opening of the diet was postponed several times until the eventual opening on June 20, 1530.

[27] Luther, *Warning to His Dear German People* (1531), LW 47:23.

[28] See Elector John to Luther, Jonas, Bugenhagen, and Melanchthon, March 14, 1530, WA Br 5:263–65. The party, including Luther, left Wittenberg on April 3, 1530, and arrived at Coburg on April 15: see Brecht 2:371–72.

[29] Luther had not only been excommunicated, but also, since he had been placed under imperial proscription by the Edict of Worms, his life and safety were forefeit, and he was safe only in the territory of his own prince or other allies. The Coburg fortress was the most convenient place within electoral Saxony that was close to Augsburg.

of his friends and brethren, stayed in his safe haven alone, nevertheless the protesting estates did not undertake anything in religious matters without his judgment, counsel, and approval, as can be seen from his writings and advice as collected in the ninth volume [of his works].[30] Before they made ready to leave Torgau, he had composed seventeen concise and pointed articles,[31] from which the Augsburg Confession[32] and its Apology[33] were later derived.

Now since there is one Spirit but a variety of gifts and working [1 Cor. 12:4], and our God had blessed Herr Melanchthon with the particular skill for this task, ¹God set Melanchthon at our doctor's side, even as the Son of God gave His prophet Moses in Egypt the eloquent Aaron as colleague [Exod. 4:15–16]. For as Aaron served as his brother's mouth and orator, and Moses was his brother's prophet and prince and filled or directed the tongues of both of them to speak God's Word before Pharaoh, so also our faithful God provided and appointed for our doctor his Aaron, Hur,

---

[30] Cf. Sleidanus, *De statu religionis* (1558), book 7, pp. 201–3; Brecht 2:384–405. Thirty letters written by and to Luther in the Coburg are included in Witt Ger 9. For Luther's correspondence from Coburg, from April 18 to October 4, 1530, see LW 49:280–429; WA Br 5:275–649. Also included in Witt Ger 9 were his *Theses against the Whole Synagogue of Satan* (1530), WA 30/2:420–27 (LW 72); *That a Christian Should Bear His Cross with Patience* (1530), LW 43:179–86; *Sayings in Which Luther Found Comfort* (1530/1550), LW 43:167–77. Luther's *Exhortation to All Clergy* (1530), LW 34:3–61, had been included in Witt Ger 7. See Aland, *Hilfsbuch*, pp. 555–59.

[31] In fact, the Wittenberg theologians had met in Torgau in March to prepare for the diet. See Brecht 2:370–71. On the "Torgau Articles," which originate in this work, see Kolb and Nestingen, *Sources and Contexts*, pp. 93–104, though the text there consists of only ten articles. What Mathesius has in mind is apparently the seventeen articles offered in *Ein Bekenntnis christlicher Lehre und christlichen Glaubens* (1530), WA 30/3:178–82, published without official approval by an enterprising printer; cf. Luther, *Auf das Schreien etlicher Papisten über die 17 Artikel* (1530), WA 30/3:186–97. These seventeen articles were, in fact, an adaptation of the Schwabach Articles of 1529 (see above, pp. 310–11 n. 168; Kolb and Nestingen, *Sources and Contexts*, pp. 83–87).

[32] On the sources for the Augsburg Confession (including the Schwabach Articles, the Marburg Articles [Kolb and Nestingen, *Sources and Contexts*, pp. 88–92], and the Torgau Articles) and its composition, see Arand et al., *Lutheran Confessions*, pp. 92–104; Maurer, *Historical Commentary on the Augsburg Confession*, pp. 3–57; Kolb-Wengert, pp. 27–28; *Concordia*, pp. 22–23, 25. Cf. Elector John to Luther, May 11, 1530, WA Br 5:311; Helmar Junghans, "Augsburg Confession," OER 1:93–97. For the Augsburg Confession itself, see Kolb-Wengert, pp. 30–105; *Concordia*, pp. 31–63.

[33] The Apology of the Augsburg Confession was drafted by Melanchthon in August and September and was submitted to the emperor on September 22, 1530, though Charles refused to allow it to be read. See Kolb-Wengert, pp. 107–8; *Concordia*, pp. 69–70; Arand et al., *Lutheran Confessions*, pp. 107–38. See below, p. 342. For the Apology itself, see Kolb-Wengert, pp. 109–294; *Concordia*, pp. 73–251.

Joshua, and Caleb [Exod. 17:12; Numbers 13–14], who helped to promote and advance the work of God.

Our doctor acknowledged and praised this great grace and gift in his colleague, as he made clear in writing to his elector[34] when he received Herr Melanchthon's confession and apologia,[35] saying that he was very pleased by it and knew of nothing to improve or change in it; he also openly admitted in that same letter that he would not have been able to tread so softly and quietly. But we will say more later about the Confession and what our doctor accomplished in his Patmos [Rev. 1:9][36] by giving counsel, writing, translating, exhorting, and praying.

Now, once the doctor had been stationed on the border of [the elector's] territory,[37] so that he could be quickly reached in case of emergency, the pious elector of Saxony went on in God's name and was the first of those summoned to arrive in Augsburg. There he let his preachers openly and publicly preach God's Word, even though this displeased some people.[38]

Meanwhile, Emperor Charles set out from Innsbruck, traveled through Bavaria, and arrived in Augsburg with great pomp and grandeur on the eve of Corpus Christi.[39] For in addition to the pope's plenipotentiary legate Cardinal Campeggio,[40] many emissaries of princes, lords, and great potentates had come, in addition to all the princes and bishops of the empire who had come to meet His Imperial Majesty.

---

[34] Luther to Elector John, May 15, 1530, LW 49:295–99.

[35] Mathesius is referring to the Augsburg Confession with both of these terms (as both Melanchthon and Luther did at the time) rather than making reference to Melanchthon's later Apology. See, e.g., Melanchthon to Luther, May 11, 1530, MBW T4/1:164–66, no. 905 (WA Br 5:314; CR 2:45–46; cf. LW 49:296); Luther to Elector John, May 15, 1530, LW 49:297. Cf. Kolb-Wengert, p. 28; Brecht 2:387–88.

[36] Mathesius uses the biblical place-name to refer to the Coburg, as Luther himself had in 1521–22 in referring to the Wartburg; see above, Mathesius, *History*, p. 184.

[37] I.e., at the Coburg (see above, p. 324).

[38] The Saxon electoral party arrived in Augsburg on May 2. On imperial efforts to restrict Evangelical preaching, see Elector John to Luther, June 1, 1530, WA Br 5:344; Brecht 2:387–88.

[39] The feast of Corpus Christi, instituted in the thirteenth century to be observed on the Thursday after Pentecost, celebrated the presence of the body of Christ in the Eucharist. In 1530, Corpus Christi fell on June 15. On the imperial entrance into Augsburg, see Jonas to Luther, June 18, 1530, WA Br 5:367–69.

[40] Cardinal Lorenzo Campeggio (1474–1539) was a seasoned papal diplomat, having served under Popes Julius II, Leo X, and Clement VII on missions to England as well as throughout the Roman Empire. In 1530, Campeggio accompanied Charles from Bologna to Germany as *legatus a latere*. See Nelson H. Minnich, "Campeggio, Lorenzo," OER 1:250–52.

ⁱOn that same evening, His Imperial Majesty called for the elector and his associates to cease their preaching.[41] Although they most humbly petitioned several times that evening and on the following morning, and Margrave George[42] publicly stated that he would kneel down before His Imperial Majesty and have his head chopped off sooner than deny God and His Gospel, nevertheless, after long negotiating which drew on nearly until noon, the protesting estates finally consented in this matter. Since Augsburg was an imperial city, and the resolution from Speyer[43] granted each governing authority the right to act according to his conscience before God and His Imperial Majesty in religious matters, no one could impose a condition on the emperor in his own imperial city. (Doctor Luther's counsel, which he had addressed to the elector at his request beforehand, on the Sunday *Cantate*, also regarded this as best.)[44] For since the emperor is our lord, and the city and everything is his, each governing authority is to provide order in its territories, which the subjects should not oppose with force if they cannot find or carry out good and proper ways and means to exempt themselves.

After these negotiations were held, Emperor Charles personally, together with all the princes and lords, processed around the city with the consecrated bread and his clergy.[45] In a humble and Christian manner, the elector of Saxony, Margrave George of Brandenburg, the landgrave of Hesse, the

---

[41] The emperor finally commanded that both sides should refrain from preaching, only reading the bare Gospel text. See Jonas to Luther, June 18, 1530, WA Br 5:368–69; Melanchthon to Luther, June 19, 1530, MBW T4/1:253–55 (WA Br 5:371; CR 2:118–19); Brecht 2:390.

[42] George "The Pious" of Brandenburg-Ansbach (1484–1543) had corresponded with Luther since 1523 and introduced the Reformation into his territories while encouraging other Hohenzollern princes to do the same. He sought to maintain scrupulous loyalty to the emperor even while upholding the Evangelical faith and confession. See Günter Vogler, "George of Brandenburg-Ansbach," *OER* 2:166–67. The account of his offer to kneel and be beheaded is found in the report on the events at Augsburg printed in Witt Ger 9 (1557), fols. 409v–410v, under the title *Schrifft aus Augsburg* (here fol. 409v) and reproduced in StL 16:736. This text may be the report drafted by Spalatin promised in the letter from Jonas to Luther, June 18, 1530, WA Br 5:369.

[43] On the First Diet of Speyer in 1526, see above, Mathesius, *History*, p. 249 and n. 105 there.

[44] *Cantate* Sunday in 1530 was May 15. For Luther's advice, see his letter to Elector John, May 15, 1530, LW 49:298–99, in answer to Elector John to Luther, May 11, 1530, WA Br 5:311.

[45] Such a eucharistic procession was a central part of the celebration of Corpus Christi. On the procession and the abstention of the Evangelical princes, see Jonas to Luther, June 18, 1530, WA Br 5:368, and StL 16:736–37; Sleidanus, *De statu religionis* (1558), book 7, p. 183.

two brother dukes of Lüneburg,[46] and Prince Wolfgang of Anhalt[47] requested that His Imperial Majesty would graciously excuse them in this case, which was directly contradictory to God's Word and their religion.

On the following Saturday, His Imperial Majesty ʰhad his herald announce, accompanied by two trumpets, that no one in Augsburg was to preach, on penalty of corporal punishment;[48] he also ordered that the papal clergy were simply to recite the text of the Epistle and Gospel, without any interpretation, alongside the public confession of sins.[49]

On this day, His Imperial Majesty also received a gift from the cathedral chapter in Augsburg[50] and gave them a personal audience. In return, he ordered that these words be given them in answer: "His Majesty requests, along with his lord brother, that they would beseech God Almighty for them as poor sinners that He would send them His Holy Spirit to instruct them, so that they might establish a common Christian order in this great matter rather than provoke God to anger." Upon this, His Majesty's eyes are said to have overflowed.

On the following Monday, as advised by his theologians,[51] the elector of Saxony dutifully performed his appointed office as imperial marshal by helping celebrate the imperial festivities in the cathedral, in honor of the Imperial Majesty,[52] even as Naaman, the great general of the king of Syria,

---

[46] Duke Ernest "The Confessor" (1497–1546) and Duke Francis (1508–49) of Braunschweig-Lüneburg ruled jointly after the abdication of their brother Otto in 1527. They were cousins of Elector John of Saxony and had all studied in Wittenberg; the Reformation had been formally introduced in their territories in 1527. See Sauer, "Ernst," *ADB* 6:260.

[47] Prince Wolfgang of Anhalt had heard Luther at the Diet of Worms and became a zealous supporter of the Reformation. He was present in Eisleben at Luther's death: see the introduction above, pp. xxx–xxxi; Jonas and Coelius, *Report*, p. 16.

[48] I.e., June 18, 1530. See Jonas to Luther, June 18, 1530, WA Br 5:369 (where Jonas mentions four trumpets), and June 25, 1530, WA Br 5:391; Elector John to Luther, June 25, 1525, WA Br 5:394–95 (where two trumpets are mentioned). Cf. StL 16:737 (with "some trumpets").

[49] I.e., the general confession, such as the *Confiteor* (see *LSB* 254).

[50] For this episode, see the report *Schrifft aus Augsburg*, in Witt Ger 9 (1557), fol. 410r–v (StL 16:768–69; cf. above, p. 327 n. 42). The cathedral chapter in Augsburg was a generally conservative force, even as the town government moved toward support of the Reformation. In 1537, the bishop and the chapter would be expelled from Augsburg and would relocate to Dillingen. See Herbert Immenkötter, "Augsburg," *OER* 1:88–90; J. Jeffrey Tyler, *Lord of the Sacred City: The Episcopus Exclusus in Late Medieval and Early Modern Germany* (Leiden: Brill, 1999), pp. 184–85.

[51] I.e., June 20, 1530. See Elector John to Luther, May 11, 1530, WA Br 5:313–14; cf. Sleidanus, *De statu religionis* (1558), book 7, p. 183.

[52] The office of imperial archmarshal was permanently assigned to the elector of Saxony by the Golden Bull (see above, p. 323 n. 21). Among the ceremonial duties of the office was the bearing of the imperial sword. See *HRED*, p. 185, s.v. "Golden Bull."

also went into the idol's temple with his lord and yet honored, invoked, and confessed the one God of Israel [2 Kings 5:17–19].

On June 25, which was the Saturday after [the Nativity] of John the Baptist, after much negotiation,[53] the Christian confession of our religion, as our doctor had taught it for many years, now summarized in good order and with discretion by Master Philip, was read forth publicly in the court of the bishop of Augsburg to the Emperor Charles and King Ferdinand, along with the whole Roman Empire, by Dr. Christian Beyer,[54] in the name of the elector of Saxony, Margrave George of Brandenburg, Duke John Frederick of Saxony, Duke Ernest of Braunschweig[-Lüneberg], Landgrave Philip of Hesse, Duke Francis of Lüneburg, Prince Wolfgang of Anhalt, and the two Christian cities of Nürnberg ¹and Reutlingen, and, after being read aloud in German, it was submitted to the emperor in Latin and in German.[55]

Therein these Christian witnesses and confessors openly confessed their faith and religion before everyone, as if on the real Feast of Trumpets [Num. 29:1; Lev. 23:24], as it was taught by Doctor Luther from God's Word and as they had allowed it to be preached freely in their lands and cities; they gave a good and proper account of and showed the ground for their faith and hope, in the fear of God and with a good conscience, meekness, and modesty in accordance with the doctrine of Christ and St. Peter [1 Pet. 3:15].

No greater and higher work has been done since the time of the apostles, no more precious or glorious confession has been made, than this one in Augsburg before the entire [Holy] Roman Empire. In Jerusalem, the twelve apostles, poor fishermen, confessed and proclaimed the name of Jesus Christ, even with great boldness of the Spirit, before the high priests, scribes, council, and captains of the temple; the apostles also rebuked them for having crucified and killed the King of glory, Jesus Christ, the incarnate Son of God. And this took place on the great day of Pentecost [cf. Acts 2–5] and was, to be sure, the greatest work of Christendom to take place since the world began.

Now, when the would-be heir to St. Peter's see had exalted himself in opposition to God [2 Thess. 2:4] and His Anointed [Ps. 2:2] and over the preached Christ and His Word [cf. 2 Thess. 2:4],[56] and as the scarlet whore[57]

---

[53] Cf. Elector John to Luther, June 25, 1530, WA Br 5:394–95.

[54] On the Saxon chancellor Christian Beyer, see above, Mathesius, *History*, p. 193 and n. 53 there.

[55] The reading of the Confession was moved to the episcopal court so that there would be no room for a public audience, but Beyer is supposed to have read so clearly that it could be heard outside. See Jonas to Luther, ca. June 30, 1530, WA Br 5:427–28; cf. below, p. 335.

[56] Cf. *Bondage of the Will* (1525), LW 33:139.

[57] Literally, "bride"; see above, Mathesius, *History*, p. 236 and n. 25 there.

of Babylon he had deceived and blinded nearly all of Christendom with his cup [Rev. 17:4–5] and bound the people to her idolatry with oaths, it was God's will to begin liberating His captive Christendom from the Babylonian captivity once again by means of the Word of His Spirit [cf. 2 Thess. 2:8]. And so this Word and work of God were not in vain [cf. Isa. 55:11] but accomplished a great deal, and God drew a number of great Christian lords and cities to Himself through His Gospel;⁵⁸ in the power of the Spirit they recognized on the basis of the writings of the prophets and apostles that the great Babylon is the mother of all unchastity and abomination on earth, who has become drunk with the blood of the holy martyrs and witnesses of Jesus Christ [Rev. 17:5–6], and that the Son of God is the only High Priest, Head, and Savior of the whole world. Therefore, as blessed instruments of God, true members of Jesus Christ, and sincere hearers and lovers of the living Word, filled with genuine and living faith, these lords and cities boldly and fearlessly confessed their faith and what they had learned and maintained out of Doctor Luther's books and sermons: the following articles, in para-phrase, as they are listed in the Augsburg Confession.⁵⁹

Namely,⁶⁰ that there is a single eternal divine essence: the almighty Father, who from eternity begat a substantial Son, from both of whom the essential Holy Spirit proceeds or is sent forth from eternity, a single, undi-vided God, three distinct and subsistent persons.

Again,⁶¹ the Second Person, the only-begotten and true Son of God, who is truly equal to the Father in essence and eternity, has been ordained from eternity by God's oath to be the eternal Priest, Head, and Defender of Christendom, who in the fullness of time took upon Himself human nature, without sin or disorder, and through His obedience, blood, and death He has suffered, paid for, and taken away the sins of the whole world, killed death, trampled the head of the devil [Gen. 3:15], and restores and bestows righteousness and life to all believers purely out of grace, in the Word and the Spirit.

Again,⁶² that through Adam's disobedience and trespass the devil, the ancient serpent, has brought sin and death in and from Adam upon all human

---

⁵⁸ The four free imperial cities of Weissenburg, Heilbronn, Kempten, and Winsheim attached themselves to the Augsburg Confession at the diet: see Helmar Junghans, "Augsburg Confession," *OER* 1:97.

⁵⁹ *ungefehrlich dise Artickel/ wie sie inn der Augspurgischen Confession verzeichnet.* The fol-lowing list (through p. 335) is a paraphrase of the articles of the first part of the Augsburg Confession, shortened by the omission of the anathemas of rejected doctrines.

⁶⁰ AC I: "God" (Kolb-Wengert, pp. 36–37; *Concordia*, p. 31).

⁶¹ AC III: "The Son of God" (Kolb-Wengert, pp. 38–39; *Concordia*, p. 32).

⁶² AC II: "Original Sin" (Kolb-Wengert, pp. 36–39; *Concordia*, pp. 31–32).

beings born of father and 'mother. Therefore, all natural children, from the womb on, are born in sin and under God's wrath for eternal death and the eternal fire of hell. They would have to remain damned if they were not reborn by the Gospel and the Holy Spirit in holy Baptism and faith in Christ.

Again,[63] no person on earth is able to free himself from sin, death, and God's wrath by his own power or piety. Therefore, God the Father, out of His great mercy and ineffable love, made His Son to be wisdom, righteousness, sanctification, and redemption for us [1 Cor. 1:30]; He had Him die on the cross for our sins and kill death and destroy the gates of hell for our benefit, so that we might be reconciled to God, be righteous and pleasing before Him, and be won again in Christ's resurrection to live eternally—out of pure grace and goodness, without cost, solely by the heartfelt acknowledgment of and reliance on the merit, blood, and intercession of Jesus Christ. For only faith and trust in the precious blood and intercession of Jesus Christ makes us righteous, saves us, and cleanses us from all our sins [1 John 1:7].

Again,[64] the treasure, benediction, and blessing which our merciful God has prepared and accomplished for us, through pure grace, in Christ's cross and blood, the Son of God has caused to be offered and presented to us through His Spirit in the office of preaching and the Word of the Gospel and reconciliation, as it has been written down by the prophets and apostles, and through holy Baptism, Absolution, and the Supper, so that all who lay hold of Christ with His treasures by means of the spoken and preached Word and Sacraments, and who apply and appropriate these to themselves through their own faith, in the power of the Holy Spirit, will not perish or be lost in sins, but 'instead will be truly righteous, pleasing to God, and saved through pure grace and an alien goodness and righteousness.[65]

Again,[66] though God requires of His creatures, His redeemed and sanctified children, a new obedience and blessed Christian life and genuine good works, and though believers are obligated to begin a new life in accordance with the will and Law of God and to become rich in good works [1 Tim. 6:18] and to preserve a good and unstained conscience [1 Tim. 1:19] throughout their lives—nevertheless, so far as our new obedience and inchoate love and suffering are concerned, we are and remain unworthy servants [Luke 17:10]

---

[63] AC IV: "Justification" (Kolb-Wengert, pp. 38–41; *Concordia*, pp. 32–33).

[64] AC V: "The Ministry" (Kolb-Wengert, pp. 40–41; *Concordia*, p. 33).

[65] On Christ's righteousness as an "alien" [*frembder*] righteousness received by believers, see Luther, *Two Kinds of Righteousness* (1519), LW 31:297–300; *Disputation concerning Justification* (1536), LW 34:153, Thesis 27.

[66] AC VI: "New Obedience" (Kolb-Wengert, pp. 40–41; *Concordia*, pp. 33–34). Here, rather than simply paraphrasing and condensing, Mathesius makes significant elaborations to the text of the Augsburg Confession.

as long as we are active in this sinful body, and we are unable, even with all of our works, to stand before God's strict judgment. Rather, all of our confidence and boldness consists solely in the knowledge and assurance of the precious blood of propitiation [Rom. 3:24–25], only redemption, and perfect and blessed sacrifice of the Lamb, Jesus Christ [John 1:29], who was sacrificed and shed His blood on the holy cross once as a perfect payment and satisfaction for our sins and the sins of the whole world [1 John 2:2; Heb. 2:17], so that we might inherit a sure salvation through the name, merit, and good work of this only High Priest [cf. Heb. 9:25–28].

Again,[67] that from the beginning of the world the Son of God has used His Word and seal of grace to call and elect for Himself an eternal Church from the human race, to be His holy people and bride, whom He sprinkles with His blood in the Word and Sacraments and seals and confirms them with His Holy Spirit, so that by grace they might be children of God and heirs of all heavenly riches and might live and rule with Christ in eternity when, having passed through death, they are awakened to eternal glory in the resurrection of the flesh.

Again,[68] that many hypocrites and false Christians belong to the outward fellowship of the Church on earth, allowing themselves to be numbered and named among true members of Christ, even though they live without faith and a good conscience. However, when such people distribute Christ's Word and Sacraments in an office within the Church, their service, in and of itself, is good and efficacious, even though the person, in himself, remains unbelieving and reprobate.

Again,[69] that the Baptism of children, administered according to God's Word, is right, and that God incorporates us into Jesus Christ in holy Baptism and gives birth to us again through water and the Spirit to be new creatures.

Again,[70] that the true body and blood of Christ are truly and substantially distributed and received with bread and wine in the Supper under the Lord Christ's clear and true Word. And that all who eat and drink of this worthily, with a penitent heart and in faith in Christ's Word and with good intention, thereby remember and proclaim Christ's death [1 Cor. 11:26]

---

[67] AC VII: "The Church" (Kolb-Wengert, pp. 44–45; *Concordia*, p. 34).

[68] AC VIII: "What the Church Is" (Kolb-Wengert, pp. 42–43; *Concordia*, p. 34).

[69] AC IX: "Baptism" (Kolb-Wengert, pp. 42–43; *Concordia*, p. 35).

[70] AC X: "The Lord's Supper" (Kolb-Wengert, pp. 44–45; *Concordia*, p. 35). Although combining elements of both, Mathesius' summary here is closer to the original 1530 text of the Augsburg Confession ("that the body and blood of Christ are truly present and distributed to those who eat the Lord's Supper" [*Concordia*, p. 35]) than to Melanchthon's 1540 "Variata," which said merely that "with the bread and the wine the body and blood of Christ are truly exhibited to those who eat in the Lord's Supper" (Arand et al., *Lutheran Confessions*, pp. 174–75; cf. Sasse, *This Is My Body*, pp. 257–58).

[and] are strengthened in heart and reassured that through such faithful use they apply and appropriate to themselves Christ's blood, which was shed for them once on the cross.

Again,[71] that Christian confession of sins is to be retained in the Church for the sake of the holy Absolution, even though it is neither necessary nor possible to recount all one's sins and the attending circumstances. And all who firmly believe and hold fast to the Absolution spoken by Christ through the mouth of His servant have been accredited[72] and assured that they have certain forgiveness of all sins. Not on account of their repentance, contrition, and sorrow, but solely for the sake of the merit, sacrifice, and promise of Jesus Christ, who alone is able to forgive and extinguish sin.

Again,[73] that those who have fallen after Baptism can return to the forgiveness of sins, provided that they truly turn back to God, not concealing their sin, and rely on Christ's blood and gracious promise, and sincerely pledge with good intent to mend their ways.

Again,[74] concerning the government of the Church, they teach that no one should publicly teach, preach, or administer Sacraments in the Church without a regular call.

Again,[75] concerning ecclesiastical ordinances established by human beings, they teach that those which are conducive to peace and good order in the Church are to be retained, yet in a way that does not ensnare consciences, as if these were necessary acts of divine worship for removing sin. However, anything that is directly opposed to God's Word and takes consciences captive can be omitted, as a human tradition [Matt. 15:3], without any burden to conscience.

Concerning civil polities and secular government,[76] they teach that all authority in the world and appointed governments, along with their laws and good order, have been instituted by God [Rom. 13:1]; and that Christians may serve without sin in [a position of] authority or in judicial office, that they may judge and deliver verdicts in accordance with the imperial code and other customary laws, punish convicted offenders with the sword, wage just wars, fight, buy and sell, swear an oath when it is required of them, have

---

[71] AC XI: "Confession" (Kolb-Wengert, pp. 44–45; *Concordia*, pp. 35–37).

[72] *verbriefft*; an ironic allusion (not found in the Augsburg Confession itself) to letters [*Briefe*] of indulgence.

[73] AC XII: "Repentance" (Kolb-Wengert, pp. 44–47; *Concordia*, pp. 37–38).

[74] AC XIV: "Order in the Church" (Kolb-Wengert, pp. 46–47; *Concordia*, pp. 38–39). Mathesius here omits Article XIII: "The Use of the Sacraments" (Kolb-Wengert, pp. 46–47; *Concordia*, p. 38).

[75] AC XV: "Church Ceremonies" (Kolb-Wengert, pp. 48–49; *Concordia*, p. 39).

[76] AC XVI: "Civil Government" (Kolb-Wengert, pp. 48–51; *Concordia*, pp. 39–40).

possessions, be married, etc. Therefore, Christian subjects ought to obey the commands and laws of their authorities in all that can be done without sin [1 Pet. 2:13–14]. For if the authorities were to command something contrary to God, we must obey God rather than men, Acts 4 [:19; 5:29].

Among us it is also[77] taught in accordance with Scripture that our Lord Jesus Christ will come on the Last Day to judge all people, awaken the dead, and grant eternal life to the elect and righteous but condemn godless people and the devils to hell and eternal punishment.

Again,[78] concerning free will, it is taught that in outward virtue human beings have some degree of free will to lead a good and chaste life and to choose between things that reason can grasp. But without the grace, help, and working of the Holy Spirit, a human being is incapable of becoming pleasing to God or of wholeheartedly fearing, loving, or believing in Him, or of casting the inborn lust out of the heart. Rather, all those things happen through the Holy Spirit, who is given through the Word. For St. Paul says in 1 Corinthians 2 [:14]: "The natural man does not understand anything of the Spirit of God."

Again,[79] concerning the cause of sin, it is taught that, though God the Almighty has created and preserves nature, the perverted will in all who are wicked and despise God is in fact the cause of sin when it turns to forbidden things and follows the devil, who speaks lies from his own [nature] and instigates murder [John 8:44].

Again,[80] they also confess how they teach concerning faith and good works, namely, that whereas we become righteous and pleasing before God's judgment solely through faith in Christ and not from the merit and worthiness of our own preceding or subsequent good works, nevertheless, those who are justified by pure grace remain obliged to live according to God's Law [Eph. 2:8–10]. Likewise, the Holy Spirit, who is given to believers by grace, in and with the Word, when they are graciously accepted, initiates in believers a new desire and obedience for holy living. Because of the sin and evil desire that linger in believers, however, this new obedience remains impure and imperfect as long as they carry the old Adam around their necks. But in the resurrection, this inchoate obedience and holiness will at last be made entirely perfect, when our body, soul, and spirit are made entirely new and sanctified completely. Meanwhile, our confidence and hope rests and is founded solely upon the precious blood of Jesus Christ, which is the

---

[77] AC XVII: "Christ's Return for Judgment" (Kolb-Wengert, pp. 50–51; *Concordia*, p. 40).

[78] AC XVIII: "Free Will" (Kolb-Wengert, pp. 50–53; *Concordia*, pp. 40–41).

[79] AC XIX: "The Cause of Sin" (Kolb-Wengert, pp. 52–53; *Concordia*, p. 41).

[80] AC XX: "Good Works" (Kolb-Wengert, pp. 52–57; *Concordia*, pp. 41–44).

only cause and worthiness of the righteousness and salvation of all believers [1 John 1:7].

¹Again, what these Christian witnesses publicly confessed and then submitted to His Imperial Majesty in their Confession concerning the cult of the saints, both kinds [in the Sacrament], the marriage of priests, the papal Mass, Roman confession, distinction of foods, monastic vows, and the power of bishops everyone can and should read in the Latin and German Confession,[81] to which we refer you herewith. For it was not really our intention to repeat the whole Confession word for word at the present time, but only to present a brief overview and faithfully to exhort you to read the originals.

Now when this Confession had been openly and publicly read before the emperor and whole empire, Dr. Brück[82] handed the Latin and German Confession[83] over to the emperor's secretaries[84] to pass on to the archbishop of Mainz.[85] But Emperor Charles himself reached for these and took them for himself, most graciously proposing that he would consider the matter further.

This is the Christian and well-founded Confession which pious and obedient electors and princes[86] of the Roman Empire and two Christian imperial cities subscribed and publicly submitted at that time. These lords and cities, among others who committed themselves to this Confession at this imperial diet and afterward and became fellow confessors, have also remained steadfast in it to this day in their lands and cities. For this reason, among all who are pious and believe in Christ they have and retain due renown here on earth as steadfast confessors and representatives of the truth

---

[81] Mathesius gives only the titles of Articles XXI–XXVIII, the second part of the Augsburg Confession, "Concerning Abuses." See Kolb-Wengert, pp. 58–103; *Concordia*, pp. 44–62.

[82] On Brück, chancellor for electoral Saxony, see above, p. 21 n. 79.

[83] Cf. above, p. 329.

[84] According to the narrative in Georg Spalatin, *Annales Reformationis* (ed. Ernst Salomon Cyprian [Leipzig: Gleditsch, 1718]), p. 139, excerpted in Witt Ger 9 (1557), fol. 412v (see StL 16:878), the secretary involved here was Alexander Schweiß (d. by 1536; see Friedrich Otto, "Schweiß, Alexander von," *ADB* 33:365–66), who had been one of Charles' privy secretaries since 1523. Other secretaries who may have been involved were Alfonso de Valdés (ca. 1490–1532) (see below, pp. 336–37), successor to Gattinara as Charles' chancellor (see above, p. 323), and Cornelius von Schepper (1502–55), a Flemish imperial counselor: see *LH²*, p. 531 on p. 194; Franz von Krones, "Schepper, Cornel Duplicius von," *ADB* 31:93–97.

[85] Under the Golden Bull (see above, p. 323 n. 21), the archbishop of Mainz served as imperial archchancellor for Germany and was thus in charge of the imperial archives: see *HRED*, p. 185, s.v "Golden Bull." Cardinal Albert was the incumbent in 1530 (see above, p. 27 n. 5). The original copies submitted at Augsburg were lost or destroyed by the end of the sixteenth century: see *BSLK*, 13th ed., p. xviii; *BSELK*, p. 69.

[86] See above, p. 321 n. 8, p. 329; and below, p. 336 n. 88.

of Jesus Christ. They also have and retain their crown [cf. Rev. 2:10], attestation of honor, and heavenly reward before the face of God for all eternity, because they acted on behalf of the Lord Christ and His eternal truth by defending His honor and name before men and by speaking against the Antichrist's doctrine, which was full of lies, heresy, idolatry, murder, and bloodshed, and faithfully warning everyone against it, and because with their blessed testimony and steadfast confession they have done a Christian service for the salvation of many lands and people.

May the Almighty richly repay the descendants, lands, people, and cities of these confessors and preserve them henceforth in this Confession, which is founded on the prophets, apostles, holy Creed, and the ancient, true Christian witness. It also received the attestation and approbation of many good people, both at that time and afterward, and has firmly stood and been preserved to this day against all the gates of hell and tribulation as well as against all their collaborators who have sought to overturn this Confession or to help falsify or adulterate it with their lies and malicious or cunning interpretations. And, if God wills, it will remain standing until the revelation of Jesus Christ on the Last Day. Before His heavenly Father and all the elect and the holy angels, He in turn will confess and honor these martyrs and witnesses[87] and all who have in sincerity persevered in this Confession through good and ill, and for all eternity He will praise and reward this great work which took place in Augsburg.

For myself and on behalf of the church duly commended to my care, I hereby honor these seven Christian electors and princes together with the two laudable imperial cities, for they did not let fear or shame prevent them from bearing public witness to the evangelical truth, and under their protection I received blessed instruction in Nürnberg and Wittenberg concerning this doctrine.[88]

As soon as this Confession had been read aloud and submitted, many good and honorable statements were received from all nations. For though the truth does not remain unopposed, at times there are nevertheless also to be found those who approve of it. Doctor Luther's doctrine was falsely incriminated and maliciously reported among many great people by wicked father confessors and hypocrites at court. For example, Alfonso,[89] Emperor

---

[87] I.e., "martyr" in the original Greek sense of "witness."

[88] The seven electors and princes who signed the Augsburg Confession were John, elector and duke of Saxony; George, margrave of Brandenburg; Ernest and Francis, dukes of Lüneberg; Philip, landgrave of Hesse; John Frederick, duke of Saxony; and Wolfgang, prince of Anhalt. In addition, the mayors and councils of the two imperial cities, Nürnberg and Reutlingen, also signed the document. See Kolb-Wengert, pp. 104–5; *Concordia*, p. 63; and above, p. 329.

[89] Alfonso de Valdés, secretary to Mercurino Arborio di Gattinara (see above, p. 323 n. 24). Valdés took the role of mediator at the Diet of Augsburg after the death of Gattinara. He also

Charles' imperial chancellor, was heard to say unabashedly in a friendly conversation in Master Philip's presence that the Spaniards had been convinced by their clergy that the Lutherans did not believe in God, rejected the Holy Trinity, and had no respect for Christ and Mary;[90] likewise, many German monks accused our people of having no respect for authority, private property, the estate of marriage, and the liberal arts.[91]

Now when some of the opponents heard this Confession[92] of the faith as taught in Wittenberg and elsewhere in schools and churches, some great princes ordered their scholars to discuss it. Afterward, Duke William of Bavaria is supposed to have said to his Doctor Eck[93] that this is not what he had been told before about this cause and doctrine.[94] And afterward, when the twenty papal doctors were asked by their own people whether they were able also to refute the Confession and doctrine of the [elector] of Saxony and his associates with solid grounds, the doctors unanimously replied that they knew of no way to refute the Confession as it had been read by using the writings of the prophets and apostles, but only with the ancient fathers and councils.[95]

---

translated the Augsburg Confession into Spanish. See A. Gordon Kinder, "Valdés, Juan de," *OER* 4:212.

[90] This anecdote is contained in the *Schrifft aus Augsburg*, printed in Witt Ger 9 (1557), fol. 410r–v, and StL 16:769 (see above, p. 327 n. 42).

[91] Cf. the attacks on Luther and his adherents surveyed in Bagchi, *Luther's Earliest Opponents*, e.g., pp. 86, 89, 151, 168–69, as well as the *404 Articles* by Johann Eck (though Eck himself was not a monk), especially nos. 280–93 [281–94] (on marriage), nos. 333–59 [334–60] (on authority), nos. 386–87 and 389–91 [387–88 and 389–91] (on property), in Kolb and Nestingen, *Sources and Contexts*, pp. 66–68, 73–76, 79–80. For criticism that the Reformation destroyed the liberal arts, see Erika Rummel, *The Confessionalization of Humanism in Reformation Germany* (Oxford: Oxford University Press, 2), pp. 30–49.

[92] *dise Confession und bekenntnus des glaubens*

[93] Duke William IV of Bavaria (r. 1508–50), a staunch opponent of the Reformation, ruled jointly with his brother Louis X until Louis' death in 1545. Leonhard von Eck (1480–1550), the Bavarian chancellor—not to be confused with the theologian Johann Eck (see above, p. 154 n. 89) or the imperial orator Johann von der Ecken (see above, p. 172 n. 37)—strongly opposed representative bodies and consequently regarded the Lutheran movement as a threat to the state. See Gerald Strauss, "Bavaria," *OER* 1:129–31.

[94] This account of William of Bavaria's exchange with Leonhard von Eck (and the following exchange) comes from the *Etliche Historica* by Georg Spalatin, as printed in Witt Ger 9 (1557), fol. 413r, based partly on Spalatin, *Annales*, p. 140. The text is edited in StL 21b:3267–82, with portions excerpted in StL 16: see StL 16:879–80; 21b:3267, 3272. Cf. Volz, *Die Lutherpredigten des Johannes Mathesius*, p. 249 on *LH* 196.14–23.

[95] In addition to the *Etliche Historica* by Spalatin, Witt Ger 9 (1557), fols. 414v–415r (StL 21b:3272; 16:880), see Luther, *Table Talk* no. 4409 (1539), WA TR 4:299 (Aurifaber's version). But the question and response in these sources involve only William of Bavaria and the Ingolstadt theologian Johann Eck, who was the leader of some twenty-six Catholic

Sometimes Caiaphas and his clergy must also let slip a word in confirmation of the truth [John 11:51]. God the Father from heaven on high commands us to hear His Son [Mark 9:7; Matt. 17:5]; and this chief and most holy Bishop sends His apostles into all the world to preach the Gospel of the crucified Messiah and to teach all the heathen what He had commanded them [Matt. 28:19–20]. He also gave them and the whole apostolic Church His Holy Spirit, the Spirit of truth, who will bring to remembrance and explain to us the powerful and true Word of Christ and will guide us into all blessed truth [John 14:26; 15:26; 16:13] through the words of the prophets and apostles. The Son of God also sanctified and instructed St. Paul in the third heaven with such words as no one but the eternal Interpreter could utter [2 Cor. 12:2–4], about what and how he was to teach the poor Japhethites.[96] For these six thousand years[97] He has given and preserved for us the Old Testament and the New Testament, establishing His holy Church on the foundation of the prophets and apostles, and testifying that it is through the word of the apostles that people can believe in Him and be saved [John 17:20–21].

And the twenty elders[98] of the Roman see assembled in Augsburg in opposition to Christ freely and openly confessed that they did not know how to refute God's Word as put forward by Doctor Luther, well summarized by Master Philip, and confessed by the laudable elector and his fellow witnesses before the Roman emperor and all his members as well as before the legates of the Antichrist and consecrated clergy, at least not by using Scripture, which is the living and certain Word of God; instead, they wanted to [defend][99] their corrupt and uncertain idolatry and monastic abominations with the

---

theologians engaged in drafting the Roman Catholic response (the *Confutation*) to the Augsburg Confession: see Kolb and Nestingen, *Sources and Contexts*, p. 105. A list of twenty theologians—from Spalatin's *Annales*—was included in Witt Ger 9: see StL 21b:3269–70; 16:887. See also Luther, *Against the Roman Papacy* (1545), LW 41:362–63; *Table Talk* no. 2639a (1532), WA TR 2:570; no. 5513 (1542), LW 54:441–42 (where the subsequent comparison with Caiaphas is made); cf. *Warning to His Dear German People* (1531), LW 47:20–21; Jonas to Luther, June 30, 1530, WA Br 5:427.13–15; Luther to Nicholas Hausmann, July 6, 1530, LW 49:348–52; to Jonas, February (?), 1534, WA Br 7:18.

[96] I.e., the Gentiles of Europe; see above, p. 119 n. 28.

[97] I.e., the expected duration of the created world: see Luther, *Supputatio annorum mundi* (1541, 1545), WA 53:22. Cf. below, Mathesius, *History*, pp. 427, 435.

[98] An allusion to the elders of the Sanhedrin who sat in judgment on Jesus (Mark 14:53–65; Matt. 26:57–68; Luke 22:66–71; John 18:12–24), here referring to the theologians charged with drafting the Roman *Confutation*. See above, p. 337; and below, pp. 339–40.

[99] Mathesius repeats the verb "refute" [*widerlegen*], which seems to be a slip of the tongue. Otherwise, the sense could be ironic: "They [seemed] intent on refuting their own corrupt and uncertain idolatry and monastic abominations with the discordant fathers and contradictory councils."

discordant fathers and contradictory councils. If those are not the true doves of the Roman Church[100] and the ancient ravens who abandon Noah's ark [Gen. 8:7–12] to help devour the dead in purgatory, who die in their own sins, then I do not know how else to call or depict them.[101]

Keep listening, dear friends, so that you may become even better acquainted with the defenders and teachers of the Roman Church and learn to esteem the Augsburg Confession more highly and adhere to it more confidently. The good emperor, for his person, sought to promote the cause of religion; he was dissatisfied with the monks in Spain[102] and dismissed them from his wife,[103] who was at death's door, because they wanted to recite to her so many [stories] about the saints, and he commanded his son's tutor[104] to speak about Christ. He gave the Confession which we have now frequently mentioned to the doctors of the Roman Church ¦and their patrons; they sat over it for a whole month and made such an outlandish response that even some of their own party had great reservations about their counsels.[105] It is said that, in the end, even the emperor himself was very displeased with

---

[100] *columbae Romanae ecclesiae*

[101] Noah's ark, and the raven and doves which he sent out in Genesis 8, had long been the objects of allegorical interpretation. See *Glossa ordinaria*, Gen. 8:7–8; Luther, *Lectures on Genesis* (1535–45/1544–54), LW 2:108–11, 157–64. According to the *Glossa*, the raven and the doves represented wicked people and the good within the Church respectively. Mathesius' point may be that in the Roman Church there is no discernible difference.

[102] On Charles' sometimes contentious relationship with monastic and episcopal structures in Spain, see Sean T. Perrone, *Charles V and the Castilian Assembly of the Clergy* (Leiden: Brill, 2008).

[103] Isabella of Portugal, the wife of Emperor Charles V, died in 1539: see Peter O'M. Pierson, "Charles V," *OER* 1:304–7. The story about her spiritual care on her deathbed is related by Melanchthon, *Historiae Quaedam Recitatae inter Publicas Lectiones* (CR 20:522 no. 7).

[104] Dr. Wolfgang Schiefer, also know as Wolf Severus, from Austria, had studied in Wittenberg in 1523 before returning to Austria to serve as a tutor in the Hapsburg court, eventually teaching the children of Ferdinand. He was dismissed in 1539 because of his Lutheranism and returned to Wittenberg, where he was a prominent table companion of Luther during Mathesius' stay, apparently leaving Wittenberg again by the fall of 1540: see below, Mathesius, *History*, pp. 431, 461, 561. See the following from 1540: *Table Talk* no. 4978, WA TR 4:598 (Aurifaber's version); no. 5341, WA TR 5:64. Cf. these table talks recorded by Mathesius in 1540: no. 4917, LW 54:371–72; no. 4922, LW 54:372; no. 4991, LW 54:373–75; no. 5005, LW 54:376, no. 5010, LW 54:377, no. 5015, LW 54:377–78; no. 5038, LW 54:379–82. For a biography of Schiefer, see LW 50:211–12 n. 35 (cf. the introduction by Ernst Kroker, WA TR 4:xxxii–xxxiv). Since he composed an epitaph for Luther, which Mathesius quotes below (*History*, p. 561), Schiefer must have lived at least to 1546.

[105] On the objections raised by the other Catholic princes and the emperor to the first drafts of the *Confutation*, and the ensuing delay, see Sleidanus, *De statu religionis* (1558), book 7, p. 187, and Spalatin, *Annales*, StL 21b:3272–75; cf. Brecht 2:398–405. On the *Confutation* and its development, see Kolb and Nestingen, *Sources and Contexts*, pp. 105–6; Arand et al., *Lutheran Confessions*, pp. 118–21; Vincenz Pfnür, "Confutation," *OER* 1:408–9; and Herbert

their vehemence and severity and earnestly directed them to frame it more mildly in order to facilitate peaceable discussion. How true it is that those who are in an unfavorable position employ deception or malicious words and shy away from making a direct answer out of shame.

It was reported from Augsburg at that time that many pious Nicodemuses [cf. John 3:1–21; 7:50; 19:39],[106] who could not condemn the innocent Lord Christ, were dismissed from the opponents' counsel and assembly. For any who were not quick to cry "Crucify!" over Christ and His Word were of no help whatsoever to the anti-Christian people.

Finally, after much insistent pressure, the twenty doctors[107] were at last finished and submitted their document to the emperor on the twelfth of July, along with a great heap of libels that they and their coreligionists had pieced together from Doctor Luther's writings.[108] It is said that it must have come to nearly three hundred pages.[109] Bad carpenters make a lot of chips and ruin a lot of good wood,[110] even as godless writers befoul a lot of good paper.[111]

When this confutation of the Papists had been publicly read,[112] the adherents of the [Augsburg] Confession requested a copy, as is customary, even as they had provided a copy of their own Confession. At first they were refused, and in the end they were put off by conditions and means so prejudicial that they no longer wanted a copy.[113]

Immenkötter, *Die Confutatio der Confessio Augustana vom 3. August 1530*, CCath 33 (Münster: Aschendorff, 1979), pp. 15–36.

[106] In the wake of the Reformation, the figure of Nicodemus, the member of the Sanhedrin who came to Jesus secretly, "by night" (John 3:1–21), came to be associated with those "Nicodemites" who secretly acknowledged the truth of the Gospel as confessed by the reformers but still maintained outward conformity to the (Roman Catholic) religious establishment. On the dismissal of some members of the Catholic party from deliberations, see Spalatin, *Annales*, StL 21b:3272–74, 3275.

[107] Cf. above, p. 338. The leading writers in the group were Johann Eck (see above, p. 154 n. 89) and Bishop Johann Fabri (see above, p. 4 n. 4). See Arand et al., *Lutheran Confessions*, pp. 108–10.

[108] E.g., Johann Eck's *Four Hundred Four Articles for the Imperial Diet at Augsburg*, in Kolb and Nestingen, *Sources and Contexts*, pp. 31–82. Spalatin, *Annales*, pp. 144–46 (StL 21b:3274–75, 3278–79), gives a list of collections of Lutheran "errors" drafted by the theologians at Augsburg.

[109] Spalatin, *Annales*, p. 146 (StL 21b:3279), estimates that this draft was 260 pages.

[110] Wander 5:586, "Zimmerleute" nos. 1–2. Mathesius combines the two proverbs.

[111] Wander 4:337, "Schrieber" no. 2 (cf. no. 8).

[112] For the publicly read version of the *Confutation of the Augsburg Confession*, see Kolb and Nestingen, *Sources and Contexts*, pp. 105–39.

[113] The Lutheran estates and theologians were told they could have a copy of the *Confutation* only on condition that they agree to accept it and not to circulate it further or to make any

How much truth and sound reason was hiding under this cover and snare, however, as well as what kind of people these were—who, ˡwhen receiving their doctorates, had sworn a solemn oath to advocate for the truth publicly before all the world and to oppose all heresy—can be discerned easily from the words of our Lord Jesus Christ in John 3 [:20]. He who is in the wrong or doing wrong shuns the light, sneaks around, and flies by night, like any other night owl or bat.[114]

Dear friends in the Lord, is this not an astonishing thing? Whereas after numerous negotiations and humble petitions with solemn entreaties the adherents of the Confession were scarcely able to secure permission to read their confession of faith publicly, these people, upon whom the Roman Church rests, like the world upon the tail of the great Hildebrand,[115] shun and flee the light, they feel ashamed of their faith, even as there have been very few to this day who have come forward to express an opinion concerning the Roman creed or catechism.

At this most laudable imperial diet, God established for His Gospel and Doctor Luther's doctrine a festival and third Feast of Trumpets,[116] at which Jesus Christ and His precious blood were to be preached and trumpeted before the highest-ranking people, as also happened with St. John [the Baptist], who likewise celebrated this Feast of Trumpets at the Jordan [John 1:19–36]. Therefore, the anti-Christian crowd, who deny the blood, intercession, and Word of Jesus Christ, just as St. Peter prophesies concerning them [2 Pet. 2:1], had to keep their silence at this time and give place to God's Word, so that not only those who were summoned to Augsburg at that time for this great preaching but also many other rulers and nations might not be hindered by the Papists' leaven and dregs, but be enabled to ponder this blessed Confession with all diligence.

Indeed, this Christian preaching bore fruit, and afterward many people came to regard it more favorably. In a few years, not only the heirs of many princes who ˡwere in Augsburg then but even their Imperial and Royal

---

public response. See Sleidanus, *De statu religionis* (1558), book 7, p. 188; Melanchthon to Luther, August 6, 1530, MBW T4/2:522–25, no. 1014 (WA Br 5:536–38); cf. Luther, *Warning to His Dear German People* (1531), LW 47:24–25; for Melanchthon's description of the conditions, see Ap Pref. 1–4 (Kolb-Wengert, pp. 109–10; *Concordia*, p. 73).

[114] Cf. below, Mathesius, *History*, pp. 386, 412, 490.

[115] "Kunz Hildebrand" was a vernacular name playing on the word "concelebrant," i.e., a priest assisting at the celebration of the Mass, which was used as the epithet for the giant fish or serpent (like the biblical Leviathan) imagined to encircle or carry the world. Cf. Luther, *Commentary on Psalm 82* (1530), LW 13:56; *Church Postil* (1540–44), sermon for Epiphany on Matt. 2:1–12, LW 76:110, paragraph 122 (cf. LW 52:205).

[116] See above, p. 329.

Majesties themselves gave permission for this Confession,[117] and, as great people have claimed in writing, [the Emperor Charles] finally on his death-bed is supposed to have approved of and accepted this Confession, where-upon he blessedly fell asleep in the name of Jesus Christ.[118] The truth must be proven right in the end, and falsehood be put to shame;[119] God still brings both of these things to pass every day.

Now when the adherents of the Confession had offered a well-grounded refutation of the confutation that the opponents had pulled back and with-held [from them], based on what they had been able to catch of it out of the air and jot down [as it was read],[120] then, at the suggestion of some wise and irenic people from Spain and Germany, who spoke in the presence of the emperor like reasonable Gamaliels [Acts 5:34], a committee including both parties was appointed to mediate the issues, dig into the questions raised, and set things on a path to reconcilation.[121] For the good emperor heard the heavy tread of the Roman clergy and is supposed to have said, "If the priests were more pious, they would have no need of a Luther."[122] Therefore, this precious hero's heart was always longing for peace and unity,[123] especially since he had listened in person to two very good and edifying sermons: one before in Worms[124] and now again in Augsburg.

Thus this discussion between certain princes and scholars of the two parties was organized. They were to reconcile the truth and lies, Christ and

---

[117] In addition to the many princes who later (or whose heirs later) accepted the Augsburg Confession, Charles and Ferdinand accepted its offical toleration in the Peace of Augsburg of 1555. See Helmar Junghans, "Augsburg Confession," *OER* 1:91–93.

[118] The story that Charles on his deathbed acknowledged the Lutheran doctrine of justi-fication is found in Melanchthon, *Annales ad annum 1558*, CR 9:717; cf. below, Mathesius, *History*, p. 562.

[119] Cf. Wander 4:1758, "Wahrheit" no. 298.

[120] Melanchthon's Apology of the Augsburg Confession was drafted for presentation at the diet in September 1530, but the emperor refused permission to read it publicly. Melanchthon reworked it for publication in the spring of 1531 (the quarto edition), and then in a revised (octavo) edition in September 1531. See Kolb-Wengert, pp. 107–8; *Concordia*, pp. 69–70; Arand et al., *Lutheran Confessions*, pp. 107–38.

[121] On the formation of a "committee of fourteen" on August 14 and the subsequent negoti-ations, see Pfnür, "Confutation," *OER* 1:408–9; Arand et al., *Lutheran Confessions*, pp. 121–23. According to Spalatin's report (StL 16:1079), Cardinal Albert of Mainz was among those urging continued discussion; Luther had appealed to Albert to serve as a Gamaliel in his *Brief an den Kardinal Erzbischof zu Mainz* (1530), WA 30/2:402.

[122] See Luther, *Warning to His Dear German People* (1531), LW 47:32; cf. below, Mathesius, *History*, p. 559.

[123] On Mathesius' perception of Charles' stance toward the Reformation, see the introduc-tion above, p. xcii; cf. Mathesius, *History*, above, pp. 179–80; and below, pp. 362, 364, 558–59.

[124] See above, Mathesius, *History*, pp. 172–74.

the devil, the Gospel and the pope, Doctor Luther's doctrine and the doctrine of the twenty scholars, speaking with another as if with good friends.

Although with Doctor Luther's counsel and consent some of our party were willing to yield and grant something with respect to outward ceremonies and episcopal power and jurisdiction for the sake of peace and unity, without injury to conscience or prejudice to the Gospel,[125] which could well have been allowed for the sake of peace and harmony, yet they were not able at this time to reconcile Christ and Belial [2 Cor. 6:15], or those who limped or hopped on one or both legs [1 Kings 18:21] with those who walked upright and straight. This is because the Papists were never willing to have the water troubled [John 5:4] and insisted on being right on every question, though they would permit the adherents of the Confession [to receive the Lord's Supper in] both kinds, as the kingdom of Bohemia,[126] and would allow the married priests their wife and children on the condition that their one kind along with their sacrifice of the Mass and celibacy should be regarded as correct or left unchallenged.[127]

Doctor Eck[128] nevertheless stood quite firmly upon his opinion that Christ had instituted both kinds not for the laity but only for the ordained priests. When in the course of this same discussion a great prince held the word *Omnes* ["all"] before his nose and insisted that Christ had instituted both kinds for all of His disciples [Matt. 26:27], just as the church in Corinth afterward received the Lord's bread and cup from St. Paul [1 Cor. 11:23], Doctor Eck is supposed to have applied the word "all" to the ordained Roman priests alone. "If 'all' means 'an ordained priest' in the Gospel," replied the prince, "then surely this text applies to you priests alone as well: 'You are clean, but not all' [John 13:10].[129] Therefore, you must never have been good, as your great bishop testifies of your entire sect: 'Priests have never been

---

[125] See Sleidanus, *De statu religionis* (1558), book 7, p. 190; Luther to Melanchthon, August 26, 1530, WA Br 5:577–78; to Elector John, August 26, 1530, LW 49:403–12, especially pp. 411–12. Documents from the negotiations were incorporated in Witt Ger 9 (1557), fols. 393v–395v, 432v–433v, 442v–450v: see StL 16:1348–485.

[126] Under the *Compactata* of 1433, approved by the Council of Basel, the Bohemian Utraquists were allowed to receive the Eucharist in both kinds. See Bjork, *Oxford Dictionary of the Middle Ages*, 1:275–76, s.v. "Bohemia."

[127] Cf. Melanchthon to Luther, August 25, 1530, MBW T4/2:591–93, no. 1041 (WA Br 5:563–64); and August 29, 1530, MBW T4/2:614–17, no. 1050 (WA Br 5:597–99; CR 2:327–28).

[128] I.e., the Ingolstadt theologian Johann Eck.

[129] See Luther, *Table Talk* no. 5375t (1540), WA TR 5:108 (WA 48:600); cf. *Table Talk* no. 2710b (1532), WA TR 2:610; no. 6773 (n.d.), WA TR 6:180 (WA 48:658). Only Mathesius places the exchange at Augsburg. *Table Talk* no. 5375t (from the Leipzig manuscript "Mem.," cataloged by the WA editors among "*Table Talk* from the year 1540 which were probably not copied by Mathesius") identifies Duke John Frederick and Elector John of Saxony as Eck's interlocutors but sets the exchange at the Diet of Worms, which is difficult to sustain.

good,'[130] therefore they neither allow themselves to be reformed nor let their doctrine be opposed with God's Word."

Now when this amicable negotiation produced no fruit, Belial [2 Cor. 6:15] tried again with the old methods which he employed against Christ in the wilderness [Matt. 4:1-11], albeit to no avail.[131] He would have liked to drive a wedge between the different adherents of the Confession and make the imperial cities change with the weather, so he roared out with menacing threats.[132] Many of them had been heard to say they would stand by the old religion and oppose the Lutherans with body, blood, and possessions. The poor adherents of the Confession, having now been led into the wilderness, held fast to the Word to which Doctor Luther had faithfully directed them from his Patmos, as you are about to hear.

Since Belial was unable to accomplish anything with his snarling, snorting, blustering, swaggering, and threatening, he took some and set them on the pinnacle of the temple [cf. Matt. 4:5; Luke 4:9] with flattery, telling them that they were divine scholars and very learned people in God's own vineyard [Matt. 20:1], men who had great renown and on whom God was especially keeping an eye, together with His angels. They should help negotiate amicable agreements, conceding and overlooking some things for the sake of peace, and that would redound to their honor and good reputation.[133]

The good people standing on the pinnacle at that time did not yield to this insinuation that they should undertake something new without any command, apart from and contrary to God's Word—though, to tell the truth, some were unable to follow this path at that time only on account of the steadfast confessors of God's Word, and something from the wicked, cunning serpent still clung to them and stirred in not a few of them twenty

---

[130] For this remark, attributed to Bishop Lang of Salzburg, see above, Mathesius, *History*, p. 204. Cf. above, Mathesius, *History*, p. 233

[131] On the failure of the negotiations of the committee of fourteen, see Melanchthon to Luther, August 22, 1530, MBW T4/2:578-80, no. 1036 (WA Br 5:554-56; CR 2:299-300). On the identification of the temptations to compromise at Augsburg as "Belial," see Luther to Spalatin, August 26, 1530. LW 49:413; *Table Talk* no. 5312 (1540), WA TR 5:54-55.

[132] On the threats made by the emperor and the papal party, see Sleidanus, *De statu religionis* (1558), book 7, pp. 195-96; Melanchthon to Luther, August 26, 1530, MBW T4/2:600-602, no. 1046 (WA Br 5:580-81; CR 2:314). The imperial cities were more insistent on opposing any restoration of episcopal jurisdiction, and this threatened to become a wedge between them and Melanchthon, who was inclined to be more flexible.

[133] On August 23, the committee of fourteen had been replaced by a smaller group of six, among whom Melanchthon was the only Evangelical theologian, placing him under a great deal of pressure from both sides. See Brecht 2:404-5. For the flattery of Melanchthon by representatives of the papal party, see, e.g., the letter from Otto Beckmann (ca. 1476-1556; see Klemens Honselman, "Beckmann, Otto," *NDB* 1:729), on behalf of the chancellor of the bishop of Liège, September 4, 1530, MBW T4/2:641-43, no. 1063 (CR 2:341-43).

years later, when they were again set on the pinnacle to negotiate a temporary settlement between the two religions.[134]

When Belial did not succeed in this opportunity either, he took a few[135] up high and slippery mountains on their own, and showed them the majesty and titles of the world and of the empire [cf. Matt. 4:8], and offered a vast guardianship and the hope of a notable inheritance to come.[136] Or, again, some he offered tranquil possession, not only a handbreadth but even an entire square cubit,[137] if only they would fall down before him and worship his vicar and administrator. But the evil serpent was rebuffed; God strengthened and secured the heart of the confessors with His Spirit's Word and Doctor Luther's ardent writings[138] and ¹fervent prayers, so that all of them stood steadfastly by God's Word, as it was taught by Doctor Luther and summarized by Master Philip in the Confession, even as the apostles in Jerusalem stood before the high priests [Acts 4:19–20].

Now when none of these paths served to advance toward this perilous unification, attention was turned to the recess of the diet in order to bring

---

[134] Johann Agricola, who was in Augsburg as preacher for the electoral Saxon delegation, had a definitive falling-out with Luther and Melanchthon in the late 1530s over the theological role of the Law (the Antinomian Controversy) and left Wittenberg in 1540 to become general superintendent in Brandenburg. In 1548, he was appointed to the commission working on the Augsburg Interim (i.e., a "temporary settlement"), which sought to impose a number of controversial theological and ceremonial compromises on the Lutherans in the wake of the defeat of the Smalcaldic League. See Steffen Kjeldgaard-Pedersen, "Agricola, Johann," *OER* 1:10–11; Friedrich Wilhelm Bautz, "Agricola, Johann," *BBKL* 1:57–59; Timothy J. Wengert, *Law and Gospel: Philip Melanchthon's Debate with John Agricola of Eisleben over Poenitentia* (Grand Rapids: Baker, 1997); Günther Wartenberg, "Interims," *OER* 2:319–21. See also above, p. xxi n. 22.

[135] On these negotiations, see Sleidanus, *De statu religionis* (1558), book 7, p. 190.

[136] The emperor threatened to withhold the investiture of Elector John as duke of Saxony and to strip Margrave George of Brandenburg of the guardianship of his nephews, the sons of his older brother, Casimir (r. 1515–27).

[137] The emperor promised Landgrave Philip of Hesse to resolve in his favor his dispute with the counts of Nassau over the county of Katzenelnbogen (literally, "cat's elbow" or "cat's cubit"). Cf. Luther, *Table Talk* no. 5038 (1540), LW 54:380.

[138] See Luther's letters from the Coburg to his colleagues in Augsburg between the end of April and the beginning of October 1530: LW 49:287–424; WA Br 5:285–646.

about the final resolution of the matter.[139] The good emperor's orator put it forward, sketching it out in the following harsh terms:[140]

> [That] since the Confession of the elector of Saxony and his associates had been sufficiently refuted with Holy Scripture by the scholars of the Roman Church, and since they willfully persisted in adhering to it nonetheless, His Imperial Majesty and the Empire were justified in punishing this contumacy with utmost severity.

Reports from Augsburg indicated that some ambassadors of absent princes publicly protested against this resolution, since they had not consented to it; for this reason, a clarification and explanation followed not long afterward that was somewhat milder and more tolerable.[141]

After taking counsel, however, the elector and his associates decided in God's name to express themselves in a clear and direct answer. For a straight path makes good runners.[142] Then Doctor Brück responded [to the emperor] that in the response which had been withheld by the other party,[143] there was to be found no solid refutation on the basis of God's Word; therefore, they did not know how they could retreat from the clear Scripture of the prophets and apostles. Whatever might result of this, [they prayed that] it might come to pass in accord with the gracious will of God, to which they committed and commended all matters, making another appeal to a general, free, Christian council in Germany as well.

---

[139] The first draft of the Recess [*Abschied*] of the Diet of Augsburg, declaring the Augsburg Confession conclusively refuted and ordering all the estates to implement the Edict of Worms by April 15, 1531, was presented on September 22, 1530. See Witt Ger 9 (1557), fols. 450v–451v (StL 16:1531–34); Johann Michael Reu, *The Augsburg Confession: A Collection of Sources with a Historical Introduction* (Chicago: Wartburg, 1930; repr., St. Louis: Concordia, 2005), pp. 390–92. On the version of the recess finally approved, see the next paragraph and below, n. 141.

[140] Elector Joachim Nestor of Brandenburg (see also above, p. 175 n. 52), brother of Cardinal Albert of Mainz and a bitter opponent of the Reformation, spoke on behalf of the emperor. See Bodo Nischan, "Brandenburg," *OER* 1:207–8. For Joachim's address on September 23, 1530, and the response from the Lutheran estates, delivered by the Saxon chancellor Gregor Brück, see StL 16:1545–50 and the narrative in Sleidanus, *De statu religionis* (1558), book 7, pp. 195–96.

[141] Cf. Sleidanus, *De statu religionis* (1558), book 7, p. 197; "Bericht der chursächsischen Gesandten," September 24, 1530, StL 16:1559–60. The archbishops of Mainz and Trier and the Count Palatine disavowed their intention to pledge their help and fortunes to suppress Lutheranism, as Elector Joachim's oration had threatened. Cf. Landgrave Philip of Hesse to Luther, October 21, 1530, WA Br 5:654–55. In part because of criticism from these princes as well as from the Evangelical estates, a second version of the Recess of Augsburg was issued on November 19, 1530, published as *Abschiedt des Reichßtags zu Augsburg Anno M.D.xxx. gehalten* (Mainz: Johann Schöffer, 1531) [VD16 R781]: see StL 16:1596–616.

[142] Wander 1:1561, "Geradezu" no. 4.

[143] I.e., the *Confutation of the Augsburg Confession*: see above, p. 340.

In response, the excellent emperor, who was deliberating with many people at the time, is supposed to have said wistfully: "This doctrine must have a better foundation than anyone has been able to imagine."[144] That is why this gracious lord even afterward refused to be drawn into sniping and persecuting, on account of which his own people complained most bitterly.

Although court letters and edicts were issued, these were not only not enacted but even mitigated and restricted within a few years while the Christian elector [John the Steadfast] was still alive.[145]

The wise say that one should neither be too greatly frightened if the lords show themselves severe or ungracious nor come to rely on it too much if they are indulgent and show much grace and kindness. Both can change in an instant. Only keep God and a good conscience above all. For our God has the hearts of kings in His hands and can turn and steer them wherever He wills [Prov. 21:1].

> Who trusts his cause to God, will be
> A man of all corruption free.
> A good cause he shall vindicate;
> Bad causes topple home and state.[146]

With this we conclude the imperial diet in Augsburg and return to our doctor, who was not idle in his safe haven but raised his holy hands as the true Moses, and, when he became weary, he rested on Christ, the true Rock [1 Cor. 10:4], having with him his people of his own who strengthened and consoled him [Exod. 17:11–12]. For since this imperial diet had been convened chiefly to oppose Doctor Luther's own doctrine as well as those who helped preach this doctrine and upheld it as correct in their lands and cities—as the books submitted by the Roman doctors clearly demonstrate— our doctor did not rest either, but was like Moses who sent his faithful servant Joshua into the field against King Amalek with many good people armed for battle [Exod. 17:9]. For Doctor Luther also held God's staff and rod in his hand; he came before God's face, and in the knowledge of the Lord Christ he lifted his holy and heavy hands with which he had hard pressed and severely

---

[144] Mathesius' source for this report on Emperor Charles cannot be identified. See Volz, *Die Lutherpredigten des Johannes Mathesius*, p. 99; cf. Mathesius, *History*, above, p. 178; and below, pp. 558–59.

[145] In July 1532, the Peace of Nürnberg (the so-called "Nürnberg Standstill") suspended the Recess of Augsburg, a few weeks before the death of Elector John on August 6, 1532. See Sleidanus, *De statu religionis* (1558), book 8, p. 227; Günther Vogler, "Nuremberg, Peace of," *OER* 3:162–63; and below, Mathesius, *History*, pp. 362, 364–65, 369, 398.

[146] *Wer nur Gott sein sachen vertrawen kan, / der bleibt ein unverdorben Mann / Unnd fürt sein sach mit ehren hinauß, / Böß sachen fellen Land, Leut und Hauß.* This is another adaptation of an epitaph for Elector John the Steadfast: see above, Mathesius, *History*, p. 264.

weakened the papacy; he cried out day and night to God, that He would preserve the honor of His name [Ps. 66:2], the holy Gospel, and His kingdom
and would keep the true followers of Joshua and German knights[147] in the
true faith and pure doctrine as they battled alongside His angels against the
antichrist in Augsburg, and that He would strengthen and console them
with His Spirit and guard and protect them with His angels. Indeed, all true
Christians in the whole of the Roman Empire at that time, in all schools
and churches, were helping Doctor Luther and his fellows with their faithful cries and sighing. And Christ, the eternal Protector and Guardian of His
Church, upon whose Word, blood, merit, and oath Doctor Luther laid his
hands and on which he founded and offered up his prayers, also gave His
aid with His continual and ineffable sighing [cf. Rom. 8:26] before His God
and Father, repeating His eternal prayer: "Ah, Father, preserve the authors
and confessors of the Confession in Augsburg in Your truth; Your Word is
truth [John 17:17]." This prayer of the supreme Church Father and of all His
brethren was certainly not in vain or lacking in notable fruit.

In the ninth part [of the Wittenberg edition of Luther's German works]
there is a letter to Herr Melanchthon from the Coburg, dated July 30,[148]
written by Master Veit Dietrich,[149] who was waiting on the doctor in his
Patmos at this time. In this letter, the honorable man reports that he could
not marvel enough at Doctor Luther's extraordinary steadfastness, joy, faith,
and hope amid these dismal and dangerous times, as well as at his daily
meditation and exercise in God's Word. For he would not let any day go by
without taking three hours of the time most conducive for studying to use
for prayer.

He [Dietrich] also had the good fortune to hear him praying once,
speaking with his God in the same spirit, faith, wholehearted confidence,
and bold insistence as does a child with its dear father,[150] and he knew he
could not forget this for the rest of his life. "I know," Doctor Luther prayed
then, "that You are our dear God and Father; therefore, I am certain that You
will blot out those who are persecuting Your Church. If You do not, You will
stand with us in the same danger; the cause is Yours; it is the enemies of the

---

[147] *Josuiten unnd deutschen Ritter*; i.e., the true followers of Jesus ("Joshua" in Hebrew). This
is probably also a play on the names of religious orders: the Jesuits (founded in 1534) and the
Teutonic Knights.

[148] The date is given as July in Witt Ger 9 (1567), fol. 430r. The correct dating is June 30,
1530: see CR 2:158–60, MBW T4/1:298–304, no. 949.

[149] On Veit Dietrich, see above, p. 278 and n. 76 there. On Dietrich's observations of Luther
in the Coburg, see Brecht 2:39.

[150] Cf. *Small Catechism* (1529) III 2 (Kolb-Wengert, p. 356; *Concordia*, p. 331).

cross of Christ who beset us; therefore, it touches Your own name and honor to protect Your confessors in Augsburg."

Additionally, Master Veit wrote of how he [Luther] insisted upon God's promise with an ardent spirit, holding up the Psalms before God: "Nevertheless, You have promised this and are able to keep this promise, as You have done from the beginning. Therefore, let Your help be seen now in the present extremity as well."

These were Doctor Luther's sighs and cries, which Master Veit dutifully held up before our dear preceptor, Master Philip, in his melancholy and doubt,[151] alongside the Christian exhortation that in this case he would let go of his useless worries and anxieties and faithfully follow the doctor's example, relying upon almighty God and His Son, who will be a wall of fire [Zech. 2:5] around all His followers who trust in His goodness and boldly confess His name before men. Was that not the prayer of a Moses for God's witness and warrior, who had taken the field in Augsburg for battle against Satan? It was with these Paternoster beads[152] which were then cast as stones that the great Goliath, Satan himself, and all the infernal helpers were driven back as with a sling.

Alongside such fervent daily prayer, the doctor also wrote many excellent, spirit-filled, and peaceable counsels and letters to his elector and the ambassadors of the Lord Christ in Augsburg.[153] God had entrusted His paradise, His beloved Christendom, along with His Word, to this pious ruler, in his territory and under his protection, where young and old were crying out to God on his behalf day and night, and the baptized youth prayed a collect for the prince of their land with their innocent lips. This is the kind of prayer that is effective and penetrates all the way into heaven, bringing counsel and preserving those who confess the Gospel, that they might again laud and confess the Son of God in the presence of His Father for all eternity. Ample testimony of this confident hope, firm exhortation, and spiritual counsel and instruction can be seen in the letters Doctor Luther wrote at that time from the Coburg to the elector and scholars,[154] particularly when the adversaries were frightening some of our people with threats and thundering, making them faint of heart, and were proposing strange courses of action.

---

[151] In addition to Veit Dietrich to Melanchthon, June 30, 1530, WA Br 5:420, see Luther to Melanchthon, June 27, 1530, WA Br 5:398–400, and June 29, 1530, LW 49:331–32; to Johann Agricola, June 30, 1530, LW 49:340–41; to Melanchthon, June 30, 1530, WA Br 5:411–13. Cf. Brecht 2:390, 396.

[152] *Pater noster steinen*; a reference to stone beads used in prayer, such as, but not confined to, the sequence known as the rosary.

[153] The following is a summary of Luther's May 20, 1530, letter to Elector John of Saxony, LW 49:305–11.

[154] Cf. above, p. 345 n. 138.

The doctor held firm; in a most comforting way and with the most beautiful passages [of Scripture] he exhorted them simply to abide with God in the truth which they had confessed and not to be frightened, but to be confident and undaunted and to undertake nothing based on the human counsels, wisdom of reason, and ungodly concessions with which [others] sought to advance God's lofty cause, for Christ was with them; He had become Head over all the gates of hell [Matt. 16:18] and was at work abolishing the devil's lies and murder and crushing his head underfoot [Gen. 3:15]. Christ would go far beyond what anyone imagined and not fall short, and He would vindicate His own cause—His own and no one else's—with honor and victory, even if the whole world were to collapse under its weight and on its account. For, praise God, Doctor Luther's consolation bore fruit, and the cause of the Gospel continued to advance from day to day and year to year, receiving ever more approval from good people down to the present day. For this we want from our hearts to thank and praise God eternally, and His Son, the true Bishop [1 Pet. 2:25] and sole Protector of His Church.

In addition to such steadfast prayer and abundant good counsel and consolation, which our doctor shared with the confessors in his letters, on a daily basis he devoted himself to the Word, studied, translated the prophets, and worked on the Psalter,[155] and when he became weak he also entertained himself with the wise fables of Aesop, which he took up as he had opportunity, as you heard on Shrove Tuesday;[156] and he mentioned this work in his letters to Master Philip.[157] Besides this, he published many good and comforting books. For in this year he wrote his *Recantation of Purgatory*,[158] in which he masterfully portrays the snares and deceptions of the monks. Again, he wrote the good book *On the Keys*,[159] in which he puts in a word for the holy and comforting Absolution and scours and purifies the Roman Church's skeleton key and falsified absolution.

Again, he wrote from the Coburg to the cardinal of Mainz [a commentary on] Psalm 2,[160] including a Christian admonition that he, as the

---

[155] On Luther's literary activity at the Coburg, see Brecht 2:379–84. Luther worked on the translations of Jeremiah, Ezekiel, and Hosea while there: see WA DB 2, especially pp. xii–xiii; and the preface to *Ezekiel [38–39]* (1530), LW 59:277–84. He also composed his *Auslegung der ersten 25 Psalmen* [Psalms 1–25] (1530), WA 31/1:258–383.

[156] See above, Mathesius, *History*, pp. 266–85.

[157] Luther to Melanchthon, April 24, 1530, LW 49:287–91, mentions these three categories of work. See also Luther to Melanchthon, May 12, 1530, WA Br 5:316–17; and August 15, 1530, WA Br 5:547–48.

[158] *A Recantation of Purgatory* (1530), WA 30/2:367–90 (LW 61).

[159] *The Keys* (1530), LW 40:321–77.

[160] *Ein Brief an den Kardinal-Erzbischof zu Mainz*, July 6, 1530, WA 30/2:397–412.

primate of Germany,[161] might help Christ advance His kingdom and cause and, falling upon his knees, might render blessed homage to the Son of God before His wrath were kindled along the way and He were suddenly to blot out and remove His adversaries. Our doctor likewise composed in great seriousness a forceful *Exhortation* to the clergy assembled at the imperial diet; in this he painted the Roman and monastic religion for them in all its colors and urged them with God's Word to repent and mend their ways.[162] Young people who have never been under the papacy or seen the tomfoolery of the monks should diligently read this book, so that they may see what the pope's religion was before God cleansed many churches and pulpits with His Gospel or refined them of dross by putting them through the furnace, and so that they may hold the true religion, which is purely taught among us, all the more dear. For if anyone has been stuck in the papacy and oppressed and tortured in the monasteries; or has happened to read the monastic books, legends,[163] agendas,[164] the *Rationale of the Divine [Offices]*,[165] Summarists,[166] or seen something of them in Doctor Luther's books, where the abominations and human trifles of the monks' synagogue are attacked—he will treasure the purified doctrine a thousand times more. He will also be all the more faithfully on guard against both the old monkery and the new fanaticism, both of which attack and slander Doctor Luther's well-sifted and firmly grounded doctrine, and avoid them, lest the devil catch him again unawares and once again rent out a little chamber in him, leaving him worse off than before [Matt. 12:43–45; Luke 11:24–26]. Experience shows that many return to devour the popery they have vomited out, like St. Peter's dog [2 Pet. 2:22], and after being purified with the Gospel through the blood of Christ, they soiled themselves again in the filth of the fanatics, Anabaptists, Sacramentarians, and Schwenkfelders, and many became more hell-bent and enraged against the pure doctrine than they had been before.

---

[161] The archbishop of Mainz, by long-standing tradition, held primacy over the other German bishops.

[162] *Exhortation to All Clergy* (1530), LW 34:3–61.

[163] I.e., readings on the lives of the saints, incorporated in the liturgy of the hours on the saints' days or compiled in works such as the *Golden Legend* of Jacobus de Voragine (see above, p. 257 n. 154) or the *Catalogus Sanctorum* of Petrus de Natalibus (see above, p. 278 n. 72).

[164] I.e., liturgical orders.

[165] William Durandus (ca. 1230–ca. 1296), *Rationale divinorum officium* (CCCM 140B), an explication of the liturgical year, the liturgy, and its related apparatus.

[166] I.e., the scholastic theologians in general who composed *summae* of theology (such as Thomas Aquinas' *Summa theologiae* and *Summa contra Gentiles*), but especially the casuists who composed *summae* for the use of confessors (such as the *Summa Angelica* of Angelus de Clavasio: see above, p. 187 n. 20).

Satan used to make himself heard with hissing, rumbling, and stomping,[167] when he held most of the world in his clutches, but now he seeks to rip and throw away the Scriptures of the prophets and apostles by means of the Papists, or else give them perilous interpretations and expositions by means of his infernal scholars, in the name of the true religion, so that he can bring to fruition the first prophecy about the promised Seed of the woman by biting Jesus Christ's heel or foot [Gen. 3:15],[168] attacking the blessed ambassadors of the Son of God, and tearing the Word and Sacraments out of the newly consecrated churches and from cleansed and adorned hearts by cunning and force.

In this year the beautiful *Confitemini* was published as well:[169] that psalm of comfort, the staff and rod to which Doctor Luther clung in his adversities and deep waters and to which he, as an experienced student in the school of the cross under Jesus Christ, brought other people who were suffering under affliction and tribulation. For when Satan and most of the world were seeking after his body, life, and soul, he grasped hold of this beautiful verse with the confidence of faith: *Non moriar, sed vivam et narrabo opera Domini* ["I shall not die, but I shall live, and recount the deeds of the Lord"] [Ps. 118:17]. And in the power of the Spirit he was most certain from God's Word that in Augsburg the right hand of the Lord [Ps. 118:15–16] would surely gain the victory against all the gates of hell. Even if he and his brethren were to be severely chastened, they would abide in Christ and continue to proclaim the work of the Lord in the Gospel: that He has removed death and sin, restored righteousness and life through His blood, and that out of pure grace He offers us these treasures in the Word, which He applies and makes our own through true faith.

With his own hand he wrote this beautiful verse on every wall,[170] and often sang it with the antiphon[171] *In pace in idipsum* ["In peace I will both (lie down and sleep)"] [Ps. 4:8]. In addition, he asked Ludwig Senfl,[172] the widely

---

[167] I.e., as a poltergeist; see above, Mathesius, *History*, p. 185.

[168] See above, p. 104 n. 10.

[169] *Commentary on Psalm 118* (1530), LW 14:41–106. "*Confitemini*" is the first word of the Latin Vulgate text of the psalm. See Brecht 2:391–93.

[170] The physician Matthias Ratzenberger (1501–59) visited the Coburg in 1550 and copied Luther's inscriptions, including his notation of the verse *Non moriar sed vivam*: see "I Shall Not Die, But Live" (1545), LW 53:335–41. The collection of Coburg inscriptions was published posthumously by Matthias Flacius. See *Sayings in Which Luther Found Comfort* (1530/1550), LW 43:167–77; WA 48:324–32. See Brecht 2:372.

[171] An antiphon is a verse (from the same psalm or elsewhere) sung before and after a psalm (or portion thereof) in liturgical use, varying depending on the day, season, or circumstances.

[172] Luther to Ludwig Senfl, October 4, 1530, LW 49:426–29. Senfl (ca. 1489–1543) had been court composer and director of the imperial chorus under Maximilian I; he and Luther may

renowned Christian composer from Bavaria, to consent to adorn these two chants with multiple voices, because sweet music is able, with and alongside God's Word, to chase away the devil and his deceptions as well as to refresh and to comfort a troubled heart. This is why, alongside theology, the ancient prophets principally devoted themselves to pure and blessed music and were glad to have spiritual musicians and choirmasters like this around them and to have God's teaching set in psalms and spiritual songs.[173]

My good friend Senfl,[174] who sent me many fine psalms by way of the pastor in Bruck,[175] was glad to carry out Doctor Luther's wish and sent him the beautiful motets: the [psalm] *Non moriar* [Ps. 118:17; 117:17 Vg] and the responsory *In pace in id ipsum* [Ps. 4:8; 4:9 Vg].[176] These, along with his artful *Ecce quam bonum* [Ps. 133:1; 132:1 Vg],[177] which he published for the imperial diet as an exhortation when the emperor arrived,[178] |frequently gladdened me and my fellow singers in our hearts, along with his *Nunc dimittis* [Luke 2:29].[179] Beautiful motets or artful melodies, which have a soul, life, and a good text, are worthy of all honor as precious gifts of God.

Besides such daily reading, writing, and giving of consolation and counsel, the doctor also sent off many emissaries and good friends every day. Since the adherents of the Confession would not accept the Zwinglian confession about their Supper as being covered by their Confession or allow it to be included, whereas some were inclined to follow the Swiss, Martin

---

have encountered each other at Augsburg in 1518. After Maximilian's death, Senfl took up a position as composer at the ducal court in Munich, where Mathesius made his acquaintance (see above). Senfl was at Augsburg again in 1530 with the Bavarian court. See Leaver, *Luther's Liturgical Music*, pp. 49–54; Brecht 2:376. Luther's letter of October 4 asks only for a setting of *In pace in id ipsum*. The dating of Luther's letter to Senfl is questionable and may have been October 1: see WA Br 5:637 and Luther to Hieronymus Baumgartner, October 1, 1530, WA Br 5:640–41.

[173] This characterization of music is a summary of Luther's letter to Senfl. See also *Concerning Music* (1530), WA 30/2:696 (LW 61); Leaver, *Luther's Liturgical Music*, pp. 85–97.

[174] On Mathesius' friendship with Senfl, apparently dating to Mathesius' 1525 stay in München (see above, Mathesius, *History*, pp. 257–58), see Loesche, *Johannes Mathesius*, 1:28.

[175] Zecharias Weixner; see above, Mathesius, *History*, p. 292.

[176] The motets *Non moriar sed vivam* and *In pace in id ipsum* are edited in Ole Kongsted, *Motetter af Ludwig Senfl/Motetten von Ludwig Senfl/Motets by Ludwig Senfl*, Capella Hafniensis Editions A1 (Copenhagen: Royal Library, 2001).

[177] *Ecce quam bonum*, in Ludwig Senfl, *Sämtliche Werke*, ed. Landesinstitut für Musikforschung Kiel et al., 11 vols. (Wolfenbüttel: Möseler, 1937–74), 3:32–42.

[178] I.e., for Emperor Charles' arrival in Augsburg in 1530: see above, p. 326.

[179] Senfl's setting of the *Nunc dimittis* has not appeared in a recent edition but is included in Friedrich Rochlitz, *Sammlung vorzüglichen Gesangstücke*, 2 vols. (Mainz: B. Schotts Söhnen, 1838–40), 1:36. Cf. Johannes Hoyer, *Die mehrstimmigen Nunc dimittis Vertonungen vom 15. bis zum frühen 17. Jahrhundert* (Augsburg: Wissner, 1992), p. 30.

Bucer was sent to Coburg with the elector's permission to negotiate an agreement in this article with Doctor Luther.[180] He arrived the day after the evening when Dr. Luther had shot a bat in the heart, which came out of the body with the arrow when he pulled it from the target.[181] This story I heard from my old friend Master Veit Dietrich at the school in Altenburg with my dear friend Herr Andreas Misenius.[182]

When, however, Dr. Luther made clear in a Christian and friendly manner that they would find in him no lack of love or willingness to agree, if only the Zwinglians would express themselves properly in accordance with God's Word and would abandon their pedantic and uncertain glosses, Bucer amicably took his leave and relayed this to his associates. After the demise of the leaders,[183] Bucer again served several times as mediator in these negotiations. Finally, in 153[6],[184] he willingly committed to a Christian confession for himself and his fellow emissaries, yet contingent upon the agreement of his associates.[185] He and many others, including Dr. Martin, Dr. Bugenhagen, Dr. Jonas, Dr. Cruciger, and Master Melanchthon, signed this confession voluntarily, with their own hands, and to this day in the church in Wittenberg it is esteemed as a solid Christian confession.[186] This year it was printed by Master Paul Eber, duly called pastor and doctor and professor

---

[180] See Martin Bucer to Luther August 25, 1530, WA Br 5:566–72; 12:126–32; Sleidanus, *De statu religionis* (1558), book 7, p. 203. Bucer visited Luther in Coburg, September 26–27, 1530. On this meeting, see Brecht 2:409–10; cf. Luther, *Table Talk* no. 1549 (1532), WA TR 2:128; Luther to Johann Briessmann, November 7, 1530, WA Br 5:678; to Elector John, ca. January 16, 1531, LW 50:3–6; to Jacob Sturm et al., September 30, 1530, in Reinhold Friedrich et al., eds., *Martin Bucer Briefwechsel: Correspondance* (Leiden: Brill, 2004), 5:1–10.

[181] See above, Mathesius, *History*, p. 278.

[182] Mathesius was brought to Altenburg by Veit Dietrich in the fall of 1530 to serve as a teacher under the rector Andreas Meisner [Misenius] (d. 1571). See Loesche, *Johannes Mathesius*, 1:55. On Meisner, see Luther, *Table Talk* no. 5238 (1540), WA TR 5:22; no. 5252 (1540), WA TR 5:27; Luther to Elector John Frederick, April 10, 1541, WA Br 9:362.

[183] On the deaths of Zwingli on October 11, 1531, and of Oecolampadius on the night of November 23–24, 1531, see above, Mathesius, *History*, p. 314.

[184] The early printings of Mathesius' history give the year as 1537, though in the eleventh sermon below (*History*, pp. 395, 404), Mathesius sets the Wittenberg Concord correctly in the year 1536 with its signing on May 29.

[185] Bucer was present in Wittenberg with his Strassburg colleague Wolfgang Capito, the Augsburg preacher Bonifacius Wolfhart [Lycosthenes] (ca. 1490–1543), Gervasius Schuler (ca. 1495–1563) of Memmingen, and Martin Frecht (1494–1556) from Ulm. On the Wittenberg Concord, see Mathesius, *History*, above, pp. 243–45, and the full narration in chronological sequence below, *History*, pp. 394–96; William R. Russell, "Wittenberg Concord," *OER* 4:286–87.

[186] The esteem in which the Wittenberg Concord was held among Lutherans is shown by its incorporation (at least of the portion concerning the Supper) into the Formula of Concord: FC SD VII 12–16 (Kolb-Wengert, pp. 595–96; *Concordia*, pp. 564–65).

of theology, in his confession of the holy Supper,[187] and from [the Concord] the sixty preachers in Ulm also drew their brief and well-founded confession on the Supper.[188]

It is not without cause that I mention these accounts; there are some people today who speak deceitfully about the holy Supper and attack the churches in these lands on account of the Lord Christ's substantial presence, and yet like to appeal to the Augsburg Confession.[189] They would like thereby to put a good face on their uncertain sophistries and defend them in order to assure us, even though the article on the Lord's Supper is concisely framed in the Confession and explained at greater length in the Apology[190] in such a way that the doctor saw nothing lacking or in error at that time, nor did any of the adherents of the Confession. Their witness is to be well noted, for they regarded the opponents' confession[191] regarding the

---

[187] Although Mathesius' sermon was preached in 1563, Eber's work had first been published in 1562, though Mathesius may have encountered it in one of the 1563 editions printed in Wittenberg, Strassburg, and Frankfurt am Main: *Vom heiligen Sakrament des Leibes und Blutes unseres Herrn Jesu Christi* (Wittenberg: G. Rhau Erben, 1562) [VD16 E64], fols. b7r–b8v [cf. VD16 E66–67, ZV22527, and E65]. Cf. Volz, *Die Lutherpredigten des Johannes Mathesius*, pp. 11–12 n. 5. On Eber, see above, p. 300 n. 89.

[188] Although Martin Frecht (see Friedrich Wilhelm Bautz, "Frecht, Martin," *BBKL* 2:115–16) subscribed the Wittenberg Concord as Ulm's representative, the city council resisted officially adopting the document until October 30, 1536, when it did so with qualifications. See Council of Ulm to Luther, October 30, 1536, WA Br 7:572–73. The clergy of Ulm wrote their own more positive letter, accepting the concord on October 31, 1536, WA Br 7:574–78, though there are only forty-four signatories listed or mentioned there. The Wittenberg Concord became the basis of conflict between Frecht along with most of the other Ulm clergy and the spiritualist Caspar von Schwenkfeld, who was at the time also a pastor in Ulm. See McLaughlin, *Caspar Schwenckfeld*, pp. 190–99.

[189] German princes, such as Frederick III of the Palatinate, who were attempting to replace Lutheranism in their territories with a Reformed version of Protestantism (thus altering the doctrine of the Lord's Supper in particular), sought to lay claim to the Augsburg Confession (especially the 1540 *Variata*, on which see the introduction above, p. lxxxv, and, p. 332 n. 70), in part because under the 1555 Peace of Augsburg (see the introduction above, p. lxxxv, and p. 342 n. 117) only those Protestants who adhered to the Augsburg Confession were officially recognized in the Holy Roman Empire. See Charles D. Gunnoe Jr., "Palatinate," *OER* 3:196.

[190] On the Augsburg Confession and its Apology, see above, pp. 332–33 and n. 70 there, p. 342 and n. 120 there.

[191] The *Confessio Tetrapolitana*, composed by Capito and Bucer, was presented to Charles V at the Diet of Augsburg on behalf of the cities of Strassburg, Constance, Memmingen, and Lindau. It describes the Lord's Supper as a spiritual eating beneficial only for the faithful. See Robert Stupperich, ed., *Martini Buceri Opera Omnia: Deutsche Schriften* (Gütersloh: G. Mohn, 1960–), 3:13–185; translation in Arthur C. Cochrane, ed., *Reformed Confessions of the Sixteenth Century* (Louisville: Westminster John Knox, 2003), pp. 51–88 (chapter 18, "Of the Eucharist," pp. 75–76); James M. Kittelson, "Tetrapolitan Confession," *OER* 4:148–49.

Lord's Supper as unchristian and did not allow the Zwinglian cities[192] to sign Melanchthon's public Confession.[193] This is also attested by Master Philip's Apology as well as by the second confession[194] drafted for the council [in Mantua], along with [Melanchthon's] own signature, with which he, along with the entire University of Wittenberg,[195] voluntarily subscribed to this article; and by the outstanding, beautiful little treatise on the sayings of the fathers,[196] all showing that the laudable Augsburg Confession would give no support to the Sacramentarians. That is why the Christian elector, too, would not enter any agreement with the upper Germans thereafter, on account of this division, even though some pressed hard for one and would have liked to expand the number of adherents, in human terms, with people of all sorts. And again, afterward, at the great meeting in Smalcald in 1537, where Doctor Luther was present and participating, the scholars of the protesting estates unanimously subscribed to this article on the Lord's Supper and others, in addition to the Confession.[197]

ⁱAlthough we will say nothing here of the concurring testimony of the Roman scholars, who found no deficiency in this article on the Lord's Supper,[198] I must include the testimony of the emperor,[199] who always exonerated the adherents of the Confession in this article and regarded them

---

[192] Here referring to the signatories of the Tetrapolitan Confession, though strictly they were not "Zwinglian," since Zwingli had submitted his own, separate confession at the Diet of Augsburg, the *Fidei Ratio*: see CR 93(Z 6/2):753–817, translated in *The Latin Works and the Correspondence of Huldreich Zwingli, Together with Selections from His German Works*, ed. Samuel Macauley Jackson, trans. Henry Preble, 3 vols. (New York: Putnam, 1912–29), 2:33–61.

[193] On the exclusion of Strassburg and its allies from the Augsburg Confession, see Brecht 2:409.

[194] I.e., the *Smalcald Articles* (1537), particularly SA III III VI "The Sacrament of the Altar" (Kolb-Wengert, pp. 320–21; *Concordia*, p. 279). For Mathesius' treatment of the conference at Smalcald in chronological sequence, see below, Mathesius, *History*, pp. 397–403.

[195] Luther's articles were signed at Smalcald as a private matter by the theologians, including Melanchthon as well as other members of the Wittenberg theological faculty: see Kolb-Wengert, pp. 326–28; *Concordia*, pp. 284–85.

[196] Melanchthon, *Sententiae veterum aliquot scriptorum de Coena Domini* (1530), CR 23:727–52. See above, Mathesius, *History*, p. 261.

[197] See Brecht 3:178–84. On the signing of the Augsburg Confession and its Apology by the theologians at Smalcald in February 1537, see "Doctors and Preachers Who Subscribed to the Augsburg Confession and Apology, 1537" (Kolb-Wengert, pp. 343–44; *Concordia*, pp. 305–6; cf. Arand et al., *Lutheran Confessions*, p. 152).

[198] See *Confutation* 10, in Kolb and Nestingen, *Sources and Contexts*, p. 112.

[199] I.e., Charles V; see above, p. 342.

as correct; likewise, our lord the current emperor,[200] as he traveled from the election in Frankfurt to Nördlingen, is supposed to have said frankly and openly over supper: "If I were to depart from my old religion, I would become Lutheran, for they retain the German Mass and believe correctly regarding the Sacrament."[201]

I call this to mind to honor and exonerate the Augsburg Confession and to confirm the blessed article of the substantial and true presence of the body and blood of Jesus Christ in the distribution and use[202] of the blessed Supper of our Lord and Savior. The church in Wittenberg and many Saxon churches, along with all those who believe in and praise Christ's truth and omnipotence, remain steadfastly with this article in its purity down to this moment, praise be to God, and day by day many churches that had been led astray are joyfully receiving it again.

Doctor Urbanus Rhegius,[203] who at that time moved from Augsburg to the prince in Lüneburg, also sought the counsel of our doctor when passing through Coburg and received much good instruction and comfort from this conversation, as can be seen in the two beautiful testimonials he wrote about Luther afterward, which can be read in his Latin works.[204] He had diligently read the excellent man's books beforehand with much gratitude and had learned much from them. Now, however, he had seen and heard the great prophet himself—praise God—and would never forget it for the rest of his life.

Here I should also say a few words about how our doctor in his Patmos[205] and tribulation often asked for holy Absolution from the local pastor Johann

---

[200] I.e., Ferdinand I, the brother of Emperor Charles, who became king of Hungary and Bohemia in 1526, was elected German king [*Rex Romanorum*] in 1531 and Holy Roman emperor in 1558.

[201] Mathesius places this anecdote in the wake of the Diet of Frankfurt in 1556, where Ferdinand was elected emperor. Other sources set it in 1564, the year of his death. See Volz, *Die Lutherpredigten des Johannes Mathesius*, pp. 252–53 on *LH* 213.6–10.

[202] *bey der außtheylung und geniessung des seligen Abendmals.* For the language, cf. FC SD VII 86 (Kolb-Wengert, p. 608; *Concordia*, p. 576).

[203] Urbanus Rhegius (1489–1541) was the Evangelical superintendent in Augsburg in 1530 when he was invited to Lüneberg by Duke Ernest (see above, p. 328 n. 46) to consolidate the Reformation there. See Scott H. Hendrix, "Rhegius, Urbanus," *OER* 3:429–30. For Luther's appreciation of his co-worker, see his preface to Rhegius, *Prophecies of the Old Testament concerning Christ* (1542), LW 60:267–73.

[204] Urbanus Rhegius, "Iudicium D. Urbani Regii de D. Martino Luthero ... Anno MDXXXIII," in *Opera Urbani Regii*, 2 vols. (Nürnberg: J. Berg & U. Neuber, 1562) [VD16 R1723], 2:80.

[205] See above, p. 326.

Karg[206] and received heartfelt consolation from the holy Supper, as he often told his father confessor, through whose words the Lord Christ greatly refreshed him. The tribulations of great people are not small;[207] they inwardly bear and feel their lingering sin and frailty, and so they do not despise the ordinance and institution of God but go often to receive Absolution and the Supper to strengthen their faith. Alas, how sad and inexplicable it is that members of Christendom abstain from the Supper or receive it unworthily and heedlessly, soon forgetting about Communion and speaking of it deceitfully and carelessly, for the master of a thousand tricks[208] is hard at work here. For even as he drew Eve away from the simple meaning of God's Word so that she ate the forbidden food and brought eternal death upon herself and her descendants, so also today there are many who fast to death, not wanting to follow the Son of God's command to eat and drink of this bread and wine, and who do not discern the body of Christ [1 Cor. 11:29], but instead constantly blaspheme against it.

Now when the elector of Saxony left the imperial diet and came to Coburg,[209] he took Dr. Luther, together with other scholars, through Altenburg (where for the first time I saw this excellent elector during the sermon)[210] and then back to Torgau and Wittenberg.[211] However, the imperial diet in Augsburg was to be followed immediately by another in Cologne, at which Emperor Charles wanted to have the king of Hungary and Bohemia

---

[206] The person in view here as pastor in Coburg in 1530 cannot be Johann Karg [Parsimonius] (1525–88; Julius August Wagenmann, "Karg, Johannes," *ADB* 15:120–21), but must have been Johann Grosch, a native of Kassel, the former guardian [*custos*] of the Franciscan monastery in Coburg who had matriculated at Wittenberg in 1520 and then became Evangelical pastor in Coburg. Veit Dietrich later published a collection of Grosch's words of comfort drawn from Scripture, in the preface to which Dietrich identifed Grosch as Luther's confessor in the Coburg: *Trost Sprüche* (Nürnberg: J. Heller, 1560) [VD16 ZV30422], fols. A2v–A3r. See Brecht 2:374; WA 48:326; Luther to Johann Fesel, April 29, 1531, WA Br 6:84 and n. 5; to Spalatin, July 14, 1531, WA Br 6:151. Cf. Volz, *Die Lutherpredigten des Johannes Mathesius*, p. 125; *LH²*, p. 538.

[207] See above, Mathesius, *History*, p. 315.

[208] I.e., the devil; cf. Wander 4:1068, "Teufel" no. 218. Luther frequently used the epithet *Tausendkünstler* or *mille artifex*: see, e.g., *That These Words of Christ* (1527), LW 37:13; *Large Catechism* (1529) Pref. 12–13 (Kolb-Wengert, pp. 381–82; *Concordia*, p. 354).

[209] Elector John departed the Diet of Augsburg on September 23, 1530, and arrived at Coburg on October 1. The Saxons departed Coburg on October 4. See Brecht 2:406–7.

[210] On Luther's sermon of October 9, 1530, in Altenburg, which has not been preserved, and on the dating of the stages of the journey from Coburg to Wittenberg, see the introduction by Paul Pietsch, WA 32:xviii–xix; cf. below, Mathesius, *History*, pp. 454, 566. On Mathesius' tenure as a teacher in Altenburg from 1530 to 1532, see *History*, above, pp. 112, 258, 287, 354; and below, p. 453.

[211] Luther arrived in Wittenberg on either October 11 or October 13: see Brecht 2:407.

elected as Roman king,[212] so that in his absence the German Empire would have its own head;[213] moreover, all kinds of harsh and disquieting talk was circulating about the recess of Augsburg with respect to its implementation.[214] Therefore, the elector spent a few days with his associates [to consider] what was the right and most defensible course of action in both cases.

|The matters of what was negotiated and decided concerning the election of the Roman king, and of how the old elector dispatched his son Duke John Frederick to Cologne and protested the rigged election at the counsel of his legal experts on the basis of the Golden Bull,[215] are not topics for theologians or the pulpit. For it is perilous for preachers to study the Golden Bull, as can be clearly perceived from Balaam [Numbers 22] and Judas [Matt. 10:4; 26:14–56; 27:3–10] and the supposed vicar of St. Peter.[216]

The same applies to the other question and counsel about whether princes and cities may form a league and, in a case of emergency, if they are being attacked on account of their religion, unite for the sake of defense against their own superior authorities—to whom they are bound by oath and God's Word to render obedience—and thus take steps to ensure their security with God's favor and a good conscience. When this question came before Doctor Luther, he expressed his position both orally and in writing: that he, as a theologian and preacher of the Gospel, could not advise the formation of a league in this spiritual case, because he could not look into anyone's heart and see why they were undertaking such a thing.[217] The prophets in the Old Testament had preached harshly against leagues, especially those established with foreigners [cf. Isa 30:1; 31:1; 2 Chron. 20:37; Hosea 10:6;

---

[212] Charles' brother Ferdinand had become king of Hungary and Bohemia in 1526. The title of "Roman King" [*Rex Romanorum*] had traditionally been ascribed to the king of Germany upon his election by the princes before he was crowned as emperor by the pope, though since Maximilian the title "emperor elect" [*electus imperator*] had begun to be used in this situation. The title "King of the Romans" had also been used, as Charles sought to do here, for the designated heir, elected king in anticipation of his future election as emperor upon the death of the incumbent; after Charles, this was the sole use of the title. See Bjork, *Oxford Dictionary of the Middle Ages*, 4:1430.

[213] On the Diet of Cologne, held from December 24, 1530, to January 5, 1531, see Sleidanus, *De statu religionis* (1558), book 7, pp. 203–7; Brandi, *Emperor Charles V*, pp. 317–18.

[214] On the final recess of the Diet of Augsburg, see above, p. 346 and n. 141 there.

[215] Cf. Luther, *Table Talk* no. 2860b (1532–33), WA TR 3:31–32; Luther to Elector John, December 12, 1530, WA Br 5:697–99. On the Golden Bull, which prohibited the election of a Roman king while the emperor was still living, see above, p. 323 n. 21. In the end, Ferdinand was elected king on January 5, 1531, with the vote of all the electors except for Saxony.

[216] I.e., the pope (cf. Matt. 16:16–19).

[217] For Luther's opinion on alliances and the right of resistance against the emperor, see his letters to Lazarus Spengler, January 15, 1531, WA Br 6:16–17, and March 18, 1531, WA Br 6:55–57, from which Mathesius quotes here.

Josh. 9:3–15; 1 Kings 3:1]. Seldom is anything good accomplished by placing our hope and confidence in man.

Evangelical causes must be commended with sincere trust to the Lord of the Gospel, the true Defender of precious Christendom, and they must be upheld with strong prayer and fervent sighs. God knows how to represent His own cause without any uncertain human counsels or perilous and inconstant help, as He has richly and mightily demonstrated from the beginning. However, the question of whether a Christian may make an alliance not as a believer in Christ, but as a citizen and member of the body politic,[218] and oppose the authorities over him in accordance with ancient imperial law and its interpretation by the jurists, to which some wanted to appeal, that is something he and his fellow preachers were obliged to allow. He and his associates were speaking about the members of Christ and the body of the Church; they can, without any burden to conscience, wield the sword and exercise secular office against their equals and those who are incited against them. Therefore, he shifted the question to the authorities and their conscience and directed them to the jurists, as seen in the Christian and peaceful counsels of the doctor and Master Philip.[219] Some of these counsels were published at that time, having previously been brought to the opponents by agitators wanting to incite their own party to war, since the doctor was advising his own followers against taking up arms in defense.[220]

Now the jurists and the worldly-wise wrote a great deal and offered much advice on this question, for which they will have to answer at the appropriate time. Nürnberg and some other [cities] followed these Christian counsels and held steadfastly to the Augsburg Confession; they took care of their churches and sought peace, which they also obtained from the legitimate authorities over them. In like manner, our peacemaking God granted the pious and obedient Elector Duke John and his churches protection and peace throughout his life. For whoever delights in war always fights in order to fight more and, finally, wins the least, because our God scatters all who delight in illegitimate wars [Ps. 68:30]. "We will seek peace and henceforth

---

[218] *membrum corporis politici*

[219] See the advice of the Wittenberg theologians from March 1530: Luther to Elector John, March 6, 1530, LW 49:272–80 (WA Br 5:249–61); Melanchthon to Elector John, March 6, 1530, MBW T4/1:66–71, no. 872. Cf. Luther to the Electoral Saxon Government, ca. October 27, 1530, LW 49:429–33; to Landgrave Philip of Hesse, October 28, 1530, LW 49:433–37, where Luther is willing to allow a right of armed resistance if the jurists are able to prove it on the basis of imperial law.

[220] Luther's March 1530 advice to Elector John was published in 1531 by his Roman Catholic opponent Johann Cochlaeus (see the introduction above, pp. lxvii–lxviii), together with other documents from the Diet of Augsburg and Cochlaeus' own criticism of the Lutheran position: Cochlaeus, *Ein Auszug des Kaiserlichen Abschieds* (Dresden: Stöckel, 1531) [VD16 C4263].

serve that end with faithful counsel, pursuing unity in a Christian way. God, who has the hearts of our opponents in His hands and who with His eyes looks upon the just and the peacemakers and listens to their cries, will be and remain our wall and mighty fortress,[221] and we will be and be called God's obedient children [Matt. 5:9]"—this is what the good and peaceable elector is supposed to have said.[222]

ⁱI speak this for the sake of the truth, to the glory of the God of peace and His peaceful Gospel and of Dr. Luther's peacemaking doctrine, and in honor of his obedient listeners and peace lovers. I mention it also as a salutary instruction and reminder for us preachers that we should not pass judgment lightly and rashly in unknown matters or in the business of others, and should steer away from secular matters, diligently tend to our own spiritual office, and devote ourselves to the Word and prayer, as St. Peter says in Acts [6:4]. For it is just as great a wisdom to leave alone matters that are not our concern as it is wisely and without pride to carry out the things that are entrusted to our care. Again, let them not help sound the war trumpets or wield the spear in one hand and the Bible in the other, as did those who worked at rebuilding the temple [Neh. 2:8; 4:13–23] or those in our days who drummed up the troops, designated a place for muster, helped put people under arrest, and went along on the watch.[223]

On the Mount of Olives, the Son of God commanded Peter to sheathe his sword, even though he wanted to defend Him against godless and wicked people [Matt. 26:52; John 18:10–11]. Likewise, the chosen and anointed King David, when he was driven from his kingdom and had to flee, did not want to lay a hand on his hereditary lord and king, the anointed of the supreme Messiah, even though his counselors and scribes advised with sublime reason in favor of preemptive resistance [1 Samuel 24]; instead, he commended the whole affair and vengeance to God, who arranged things far better than he ever could have wished.

We preachers ought to proclaim inward peace through the Word and knowledge of Christ and counsel to outward peace where we can; we ought also to exhort to obedience while not forgetting the grievous errors of

---

[221] Cf. Luther, "Our God Is a Castle Strong [*Ein feste Burg*]" (1527 or 1528), LW 53:283–85 (*LSB* 656–57; *TLH* 262; WA Ar 4:247–49; Wackernagel 3:19–20, nos. 32–33).

[222] Cf. Luther to Elector John, December 31, 1528, WA Br 4:629–30, and June 29, 1532, LW 50:56–60. Melanchthon's funeral oration for Elector John, *Oratio funebre in mortem Ioannis Ducis Saxoniae*, CR 11:223–27, emphasizes this leader's unwavering commitment to peace.

[223] Apparently an allusion to Zwingli, who died, sword in hand, as chaplain to the troops defending Zurich. See above, Mathesius, *History*, p. 314 and n. 193 there.

Savonarola[224] and other people. Military men and jurists counsel and write much on the management of external affairs; they will have to answer for that themselves, even as did the orators in Greece.

Now when our doctor had faithfully advised for peace and obedience as subjects ᶦin accordance with God's Word, along with Master Philip and the others, nevertheless a harsh edict was issued in the emperor's name that put many good people in danger.[225] So our German doctor, as the German prophet, published his *Warning to His Dear Germans*[226] along with a counterstatement against the imperial edict,[227] in which he very respectfully exculpated the good emperor as a gracious, highly intelligent, and illustrious man, saying that he was for the time being beset and surrounded by all kinds of people who had never had much desire or inclination for peace and who would rather have been serving other people.[228] And this is no wonder, for Haman was able single-handedly to provoke and incite his good king against the innocent people of God in Persia [Esth. 3:1–15]. What kind of provocation and incitation will be beyond this multitude of wicked serpents, who are people's clients, adherents, dear relatives, and protectors, and who have trodden upon the head of many a good German emperor and plucked many feathers from the Roman eagle.

That this was never the good emperor's earnest intention is evident and apparent from the fact that Emperor Charles never enforced the edict,[229] no matter how vehemently certain troublemakers insisted upon it and scolded the excellent man for this as if he were a dead falcon.[230] Again, within two years, through the negotiations of the two peace-loving electors of the Palatinate and Mainz,[231] the irenic hero had graciously granted and issued an empire-wide truce for the protesting estates and those who were united with them in religious matters.[232]

---

[224] On Girolamo Savonarola, who came to dominate Florentine politics during his period of influence there, see above, pp. 114–15 n. 4.

[225] I.e., the recesses of the Diet of Augsburg: see above, p. 346.

[226] *Warning to His Dear German People* (1531), LW 47:3–55.

[227] *Commentary on the Alleged Imperial Edict* (1531), LW 34:63–104.

[228] *Warning to His Dear German People* (1531), LW 47:30–34.

[229] See above, p. 347.

[230] I.e., without any respect. See Wander 1:920, "Falke" no. 28; cf. Luther, *An Kurfürsten zu Sachsen und Landgrafen zu Hessen von dem gefangenen Herzog zu Braunschweig* (1545), WA 54:393–94.

[231] Count Palatine Louis V (see above, pp. 170–71 n. 24) and Cardinal Albert of Mainz (see above, p. 27 n. 5).

[232] The Peace of Nürnberg (1532) had been negotiated by Electors Albert and Louis. See above, p. 347 n. 145.

However, since the clergy had interpolated their own concerns into the imperial edict and forged and welded them into place, and used the name and seal of the good man to condemn the pure and incontrovertible truth which is founded upon the Scriptures of the prophets and apostles and in the ancient creeds, our doctor honorably and fearlessly put in a word for the Son of God and His ˈGospel in opposition to the devil's lies and abominations, as was only fitting for an evangelical doctor to do, and repeated his unrefuted doctrine as found in the Augsburg Confession, and particularly the article concerning the justification of man or how a poor sinner becomes righteous, saved, and pleasing to God alone through faith and confidence in the blood, merit, and intercession of Jesus Christ.[233] The edict decried and condemned as heretical this article that faith in Christ alone justifies us, without any works; Dr. Luther said that "the Roman emperor, the Turkish emperor, the Tartar emperor,[234] the Persian emperor, the pope, all cardinals, bishops, priests, monks, nuns, kings, princes, lords, and the whole world together with all devils, false brethren, and fanatics will have to let this article stand and remain for me, no thanks to them."[235] You can read for yourselves the doctor's own words and his inspiration from the Holy Spirit in the sixth volume of his German books.[236]

And now, as the doctrine of the holy Gospel was making its way into many other lands and Christian hearts, our doctor gave a warning to his own parishioners, the dear and noble Germans, whom the old popes had often freed from their obligations and oaths by virtue of the Roman skeleton key, agitating and inciting them against their own emperor; he warned them not to oppose or help suppress the pure doctrine of the holy Gospel, so that they would not become guilty of all the abominations and blasphemies which the pope, his monks, and "spiritual" clergy, falsely so called, had for so long forced and finagled, by lies and murder, into God's temple, dear Christendom.[237]

Teach and preach—that is what a public doctor of Holy Scripture should do, even as he has been appointed and sworn through imperial and papal

---

[233] Luther was engaged at the time in preparations for a treatise *On Justification* (1530), which was never completed, though his outline and notes were preserved by Veit Dietrich: *Outline for a Book on the Article of Justification* (1530), WA 30/2:652–76 (LW 61). See Brecht 2:384.

[234] The Tartars were a Central Asian people, identified in the medieval European mind with the thirteenth-century Mongol conquests.

[235] *Commentary on the Alleged Imperial Edict* (1531), LW 34:91.

[236] *Commentary on the Alleged Imperial Edict* is found in Witt Ger 6 (1558), fols. 153v–164v.

[237] *Commentary on the Alleged Imperial Edict* (1531), LW 34:98–102.

authority to be a public and legitimate²³⁸ preacher, ⁱin order that he should, at his own risk and responsibility, use God's Word to warn and admonish everyone against the antichrist, worship of devils, and ruin of body and soul, so that the baptized may not break the covenant God made with them (and they in turn with God) in Baptism for a good conscience nor act against God and the honor of His name by word or deed at the illegitimate behest of any human being.²³⁹

The ancient Christians also worked and prayed [1 Tim. 2:1–2] to help the sensible heathen emperors battle and fight against the enemies of the emperor and empire.²⁴⁰ King Saul's soldiers, however, refused in the name of their Messiah to lay a hand on the innocent priests in Nob; only Doeg consented to carry out the command for his own profit and gain [1 Sam. 22:17–19]. Not long after, however, master and servant alike received their baleful visitation and recompence, as both impaled themselves on their own cold iron [1 Sam. 31:4–6].

The great warrior Valentinian surely was not attempting to help defend idolatry, even though, as an honorable Christian, he most faithfully rendered his liege service to Julian the Apostate against the enemy of the empire, for which God later honored the good prince with the imperial crown and scepter.²⁴¹ For if anyone honors God and His Word, God will bring that one to honor in his turn [1 Sam. 2:30].

Now when our doctor had bidden his associates to remain still, in accordance with his peaceable Gospel, and to defend God's spiritual cause with spiritual weapons—genuine trust and prayer—in obedience as subjects in everything that belongs to Caesar [Matt. 22:21], and when he had reminded the leaders and soldiers of the opposing party of their status as Christians and warned them against the abominable papacy with solid reasons from God's Word, his writing did not remain without notable fruit. Emperor Charles, the noble German, acted circumspectly ⁱand engaged in negotiations toward the council for which Dr. Luther's people had constantly pressed.²⁴² And when, in addition to the aforementioned two electors,²⁴³ other good people seeking general peace in the emperor's beloved fatherland diligently worked

---

²³⁸ *gemeiner und ordenlicher*

²³⁹ See *Commentary on the Alleged Imperial Edict* (1531), LW 34:95–96.

²⁴⁰ See, e.g., Tertullian (ca. 160–220), *Apology* 30–42 (PL 1:440–95; ANF 3:42–49).

²⁴¹ Valentinian I (321–375), a Christian, served as a commander under the pagan Julian (Western Caesar, r. 355–361; emperor, r. 361–63) before becoming emperor himself in 364. See Socrates Scholasticus (380–440), *Ecclesiastical History* 4.1 (PG 67:463–64; NPNF² 2:96).

²⁴² See Mathesius, *History*, above, pp. 150–51, 161–62, 213, 346; and below, pp. 397–98. Cf. Mathesius, *History*, above, p. 212; and below, p. 407.

²⁴³ Electors Albert of Mainz and Louis V of the Palatinate. See above, p. 362.

and strove for the establishment of an armistice, and the pious elector also spoke in a Christian manner in favor of peaceful negotiation, God granted His grace and blessing to these efforts toward peace. Thus after much negotiation and Dr. Luther's faithful perseverance, a laudable general truce was decreed on the twenty-third of July in the year 1532; the empire agreed by common consent to provide ongoing aid against the Turk, who had laid siege to Vienna this year for the second time,[244] and allowed the Evangelical churches to continue proclaiming and teaching God's Word and the liberal arts in peace and harmony. For this praiseworthy German peace we should duly and heartily thank our dear God and the Roman emperor, also the [electors of the] Palatinate and Mainz as faithful and diligent negotiators, as well as the elector of Saxony and Doctor Luther.[245]

In preaching about this history, I must for the present pass over the efforts and diligence of the others and speak in particular about our doctor, who, in addition to his fervent prayers, earnestly sought as a Christian to promote this peace, which is evident from the three letters he wrote during those negotiations to Duke John Frederick and his father, Elector John,[246] which are included in the ninth volume of his German works on page 472 of the Wittenberg printing,[247] as an eternal testimony to the peaceful Gospel and its peace-loving servant, and as a good example for all Christian court preachers and pastors. In these letters, he strongly exhorted his elector and territorial prince to accept the peace with which God and the good emperor were approaching them ¹and most graciously presenting. As a wise doctor, he also pointed out with good reason that such an offer of peace ought not to be rejected for the sake of a political matter that still needs to be disputed. Things must turn out for peace in the end, he wrote, and now we are far nearer to it than if peace were to have to be negotiated one day on the battlefield or in the midst of war.[248]

Our doctor also prudently reminded both his most gracious and his gracious lord[249] that they should not rely too heavily on an alliance. When things came to a head, it might happen that not a single townsman or city would risk his own life or possessions for the sake of a prince. Again, in the second letter to Elector John, he clearly stated that both the principals and

---

[244] Cf. above, Mathesius, *History*, p. 256.

[245] On the Peace of Nürnberg, see above, p. 347 and n. 145 there.

[246] Luther to Elector John, ca. February 12, 1532, LW 50:41–47; to Duke John Frederick, February 12, 1532, WA Br 6:262–64; to Elector John, June 29, 1532, WA Br 6:324–27.

[247] Witt Ger 9 (1569), fols. 471v–473v.

[248] A summary of the letters of February 12, 1532: see LW 50:44; WA Br 6:263.

[249] *beyde seine gnedigste unnd gnedige Herrn*; i.e., Elector John and his son and heir apparent, Duke John Frederick.

the negotiators should have true resolve and proper intent and that it was of great significance that they had received from the emperor such a broad and far-reaching commission to negotiate. In the same way, he exhorted his lord the elector to prevent his own emissaries whom he was dispatching for the peace negotiation from making a fine point of everything and from pressing too hard out of excessive cleverness for an unconditional peace. In negotiations one must believe the people involved instead of setting everything down so exactly and unambiguously. A blade that has been sharpened too much is bound to break;[250] and if one does not thank God, who is letting us receive these overtures of peace, the chance is lost, and rarely does anything good come along afterward. Therefore, they should not let the proposed peace, with tolerable means and ways, that was being suggested to them slip through their hands. Regardless of what might be behind this, God will make everything work out for the best [cf. Rom. 8:28] and bring forth His Gospel into times of peace.[251]

What use is good counsel and wise judgment that no one follows? But Elector John took to heart and followed the judgment and admonition of this man of God, and soon thereafter, in good peace and in true knowledge and invocation of the eternal Savior, the elector met his last hour in the presence of Doctor Luther and was gathered to be with all believers and his Lord Christ when he fell asleep in Christ in Schweinitz on August 16, 1532, and God caused a comet to illuminate the burial of this excellent elector.[252]

All who desire peace and pursue it [Ps. 34:14; 1 Pet. 3:11], who love it and delight in it, and sacrifice and yield something of their own for the sake of general peace, who follow peaceable counsels and accomodating people, to them God grants twofold peace: both in the world and in their hearts; they preserve their conscience and leave their posterity a good name and a state of peace. Those who accept no counsel cannot be helped.[253] Yet good counsels must receive the praise and thanks they deserve in the end, as the precious elector is supposed to have confessed openly before his young lords

---

[250] Wander 4:103, "Scharf" nos. 2, 8.

[251] From Luther to Elector John, June 29, 1532, WA Br 6:324–27.

[252] Elector John's funeral was held on August 18, 1532. See Luther, *Two Sermons at the Funeral of Elector Duke John*, August 18 and 22, 1532, WA 36:237–70; Melanchthon, *Oratio funebris in mortem Ioannis Ducis Saxoniae*, CR 11:223–27. The comet of 1532 appeared a month after the electoral funeral, in September–December 1532. See Johannes Cario, *Vom Cometen den man newlich im M.D.XXXII. jar gesehen hat / iudicium* (Wittenberg: G. Rhau, 1533) [VD16 C1036]; cf. Luther to Gerhard Wiskamp, October 19, 1532, WA Br 6:380–81; *Table Talk* no. 3711 (1538), WA TR 3:554–55.

[253] Cf. Wander 3:1481–82, "Rath" 348, 380.

shortly before he died:[254] Not all those who have handed out letters with their seals and signature in abundance will endure in times of need.[255] The Son of God alone endures, as the psalm sings: "Who keeps truth" [Ps. 146:6]. God grant that we may desire and faithfully pray for peace and advise for it throughout our life; then the spires both of princes' houses and of Christian churches will be preserved.

With this we conclude the history of the Confession in Augsburg and the other things that befell Doctor Luther in the same year, and we thank our dear God for the excellent Christian elector who provided protection and room for the Gospel of the Son of God in his electorate as well as publicly confessing it with boldness and at great risk, ¦peacefully persevering in the same until his end with steadfastness and utmost patience as a Christian while also most graciously safeguarding the university in Wittenberg. May God bless his heirs and lands for this and grant him new joy and glory in the life to come. Amen, dear Lord Jesus, Amen!

---

[254] The "young lords" were Elector John's sons John Frederick (1503–54), who would succeed his father as elector of Saxony, and his younger brother John Ernest (1521–53), duke of Saxe-Coburg.

[255] Cf. Luther to Elector John, June 29, 1532, LW 50:58.

THE TENTH SERMON[1]
ABOUT DOCTOR MARTIN LUTHER,
ON THE YEAR 1532 AND FOLLOWING
[THROUGH 1535]

[Fall 1563][2]

BELOVED friends in the Lord! We have set aside our picks for a while,[3] but now we will resume in God's name and continue with the history of Doctor Luther, of blessed memory. May our dear God help, through your devout prayers, that good ore may be found on this miner's son's claim[4] and that today I may be able to show you beautiful samples[5] of it. For this man—through whose teaching the Lord Jesus delivered us from the trumpery of the monks and brought us back to the blessed fountain of Israel [Ps. 68:26] and the salutary doctrine—is worthy of having his course of life, his salutary labor and difficult struggles, commemorated with honor, for the sake of posterity.

Good people and their service and good deeds are soon forgotten in this ungrateful world. There will always be children of Envy[6] and glory-seeking teachers who would gladly find fault with the labor and salutary work of their predecessors and suppress it, so that they alone might have the praise and thanks and gain a great name among their presumptuous listeners. It is surely true what the wise say: nothing gets old so quickly or is forgotten so readily as one who has rendered the highest service to the people.[7] Since we, however, still benefit from and make use of this man in our churches

---

[1] Some later editions of the *History* move Mathesius' seventh sermon (see above, p. 266 n. 1) to this position, after the sermon on the Diet of Augsburg.

[2] The date of Mathesius' preaching of this sermon cannot be determined with certainty. The opening of the sermon indicates that some time has elapsed since the previous sermon (see the first sentence), which would probably have been preached in the late spring.

[3] *ein zeytlang auffgesetzt*

[4] On Luther as a miner's son, see above, Mathesius, *History*, p. 114.

[5] *schöne Handstein*; cf. above, Mathesius, *History*, p. 283 and n. 99 there.

[6] *neidhartskinder*; Neidhart is a Germanic personification of envy.

[7] Cf. Wander 4:1527, "Veralten" no. 2; 4:1546, "Vergessen" no. 11; Pindar (ca. 518–438 BC), *Isthmian Odes* 7.16–17 (Loeb 485 [1997], pp. 200–201).

today, who can hold it against us or speak evil of us that we commemorate this illuminated man, through whom our God has in these last days of the world manifested His exceedingly great and excellent salvation to those who recognize and receive it.

Therefore, beloved in the Lord, since you have heard in the previous sermons the accounts about our dear doctor up to this point, and about the firmly grounded Confession in Augsburg and its confessors, up to the year 1532, when the laudable elector of Saxony made his blessed departure,[8] continue listening now to what happened in matters of religion and with our doctor's teaching in the years following the deaths of the two wise and pious electors of Saxony.[9]

While Duke John, elector of Saxony, and the fellow adherents of the Augsburg Confession were steadfastly confessing the doctrine of Dr. Luther and Herr Melanchthon, firmly persevering in it and enduring in the acknowledged and confessed truth with fervent prayer, blessed patience, and Christian obedience, and when God had granted a gracious truce to these peaceable people through the emperor's clemency and the negotiations of peace-loving princes,[10] the beautiful work of translating the Bible was progressing day by day.[11]

The *Summaries on the Psalter* were also published in 1532.[12] The doctor finished this fine and useful little book in four days, writing each day for four hours: two before and two after eating.[13] He also commonly preached twice on festival days, sometimes even three times when he was younger; on

---

[8] See above, Mathesius, *History*, pp. 366–67.

[9] I.e., Elector Frederick the Wise (d. 1525) and Elector John the Steadfast (d. 1532) considered together, presumably, because they were brothers; the succession of John Frederick, John's son, marked a change in generations.

[10] I.e., the Peace of Nürnberg: see above, Mathesius, *History*, pp. 347, 362.

[11] Although the first edition of Luther's translation of the New Testament was published in Wittenberg in 1522 and additional sections of the Old Testament, prepared by Luther in consultation with his Wittenberg colleagues, appeared serially thereafter, the whole Bible was not published together until 1534. For the translation of the 1522 New Testament at the Wartburg, see Brecht 2:46–56; for the completion of the entire Bible, see Brecht 3:95–113.

[12] The *Summaries of the Psalms* (WA 38:17–69 [LW 65]), published together with *Defense of the Translation of the Psalms* (LW 35:203–23), bore the date 1531 on the title page and 1533 in the colophon; in fact, the printing seems to have been completed at the end of the calendar year 1532. See the introduction by Gustav Koffmane and Oskar Brenner, WA 38:1–4. For an English translation of the *Summaries*, see *Reading the Psalms with Luther*, trans. Bruce A. Cameron (St. Louis: Concordia, 1993, 2007), pp. 16–356.

[13] For this description of Luther's composition of most of the *Summaries* between November 27 and November 30, 1532, see *Table Talk* no. 404 (1532), WA TR 1:175. Cf. Brecht 3:104. In fact, Luther had begun work on the *Summaries* as early as 1531, and then (according to *Table Talk* no. 404) finished the first three signatures in the summer of 1532 before finally

one Sunday he preached four times.[14] Furthermore, during the week he lectured two or three times—or four, if he was healthy—and often participated in disputations and persisted in the great labor of translating the Bible and correcting this translation, along with his assistants. Even though he helped abolish the superfluous festivals by means of God's Word, the man did not rest.[15] Instead, when hard at work writing, he often forgot to eat, drink, and take his sleep.

I commend these *Summaries*, along with the Holy Spirit's Psalter, to you, my parishioners, for, alongside the exposition by Herr Philip,[16] they provide an excellent and correct guide for finding Christ and much blessed consolation in the Psalms. Also published this year, besides this good little book, was the beautiful sermon about the Christian's armor and weaponry from St. Paul's Epistle to the Ephesians [6:10–17], in which our doctor equips his followers against the attacks of the cunning and murderous devil, who, along with his infernal gates, is ever and always seeking to bite the Lord Christ in His heel [Gen. 3:15] and preaching office,[17] to wipe out His Word and kingdom, and to cause them to be mingled with worldly kingdoms.[18]

This year, therefore, our doctor was moved to preach many beautiful sermons from the prophet Micah concerning the King Christ and His

---

completing the last five signatures in the intensive work of November. See the introduction by Gustav Koffmane and Oskar Brenner, WA 38:1–3.

[14] See *Table Talk* no. 4916 (1540), WA TR 4:579; no. 5372 (1540), WA TR 5:99; Volz, *Die Lutherpredigten des Johannes Mathesius*, pp. 171–72. Mathesius' report likely reflects a slightly earlier period of Luther's activity; in 1531–32, Luther himself reports preaching four times a week and lecturing only twice: *Table Talk* no. 154 (1532), LW 54:22–23. See also Brecht 2:433–39; 2:57–72; 3:249–53. Cf. above, pp. 184–85 n. 10.

[15] In German, a play on words: *Feyertag* ["festival day"] and *gefeyert* ["rested"]. For Luther's changes to the church calendar, see *Concerning the Order of Public Worship* (1523), LW 53:14.

[16] Melanchthon, *Commentarii in Psalmos* (1547–48/1562), CR 13:1017–472, though the material from column 1245 onward in fact originates with Caspar Cruciger. The edition of Melanchthon's works edited by Caspar Peucer (1525–1602), vol. 2 (1562), put the material together under Melanchthon's name. On the dating and contents of Melanchthon's psalm commentary, see Timothy J. Wengert, "The Biblical Commentaries of Philip Melanchthon," in *Philip Melanchthon (1497–1560) and the Commentary*, ed. Timothy J. Wengert and M. Patrick Graham (Sheffield: Sheffield Academic Press, 1997), pp. 119–21; Wengert, "Caspar Cruciger," pp. 422, 427. An earlier set of Melanchthon's comments on selected psalms had also appeared in 1528: *In Psalmos aliquot Davidicos enarrationes doctissimae* (Hagenau: J. Setzer, 1528) [VD16 M3468].

[17] See above, p. 104 n. 10.

[18] *On the Christian's Armor and Weapons* (1531/1533), sermon of October 29, 1531, WA 34/2:371–406, incorporated in the *Church Postil* (1540–44), sermon for Trinity 21, LW 79:224, 353–88.

eternal and spiritual kingdom.[19] These sermons were also published this year, in addition to the blessed sermons preached in Torgau about the Lord Jesus Christ from the Second Article of the Apostles' Creed.[20] What else does a Christian doctor and pastor have to preach about all his life if not about his Lord, the King of glory [Ps. 24:7–10], our Savior Jesus Christ, and about His benefits, which He, as an eternal Priest and Mediator, presents to His little flock with eternal intercession and temporal suffering and the sending out of His Word and the pouring out of His Father's Spirit?

Turks preach about their Mohammed,[21] Romanists about their pope,[22] the monks about their Francis,[23] the idolaters about their uncertain saints,[24] the Arians about their idol Arius,[25] and the fanatics about their arch-heretics. Others sing the tune of those whose bread and water they enjoy;[26] ¦many scratch the [itching] ears of their surfeited and lustful listeners [cf. 2 Tim. 4:3] and chide the monks and priests in all their sermons to

---

[19] Luther regularly preached on Mic. 5:2 as quoted in Matt. 2:6, which was part of the Gospel reading for Epiphany. In 1532, Luther preached twice on January 6, and these sermons were published later the same year together with one of his sermons from January 1: see *How Law and Gospel Are to Be Thoroughly Distinguished* (afternoon of January 1, 1532), LW 57:61–76; *What Christ and His Kingdom Are* (morning and afternoon of January 6, 1532), WA 36:43–64. The January 6 sermons were incorporated in the 1559 Rörer/Poach edition of the *House Postil* as the first and second sermons for Epiphany, Klug 1:196–215 (StL 13:1550–73), where the second sermon (Klug 1:208–15, StL 13:1564–73) is based on Mic. 5:2. Cf. the introduction by Georg Buchwald and Oskar Brenner, WA 36:xiii–xvi.

[20] *Sermon about Jesus Christ* (April 16–17, 1533), LW 57:90–138.

[21] Cf. Luther, preface and afterword to Brother Richard, *Refutation of the Koran* (1542), LW 60:251–66; preface to Bibliander's edition of the Koran (1543), LW 60:286–94.

[22] Cf., e.g., Luther, *To the Christian Nobility* (1520), LW 44:168; *The Private Mass* (1533), LW 38:189–92.

[23] On Francis of Assisi, the founder of the Franciscan order, see *LA* 2:220–30, no. 149; cf. Luther, preface to Alber, *The "Eulenspiegel" and Koran of the Barefoot Monks* (1542), LW 60:274–80.

[24] "Uncertain" in the sense that not only their power to respond to petitions but also the accounts of their lives and even their historical existence is in doubt. See, e.g., Luther, preface to Spengler, *Confession* (1535), LW 60:72.

[25] On Arius, see above, p. 109 n. 27.

[26] See Wander 3:181, 183, "Lied" nos. 7 and 45; 1:472, 480, "Brot" nos. 92 and 303.

please them,[27] or they are and remain Thersites,[28] Marcolph,[29] and Zoilus[30] and disparage the authorities and ridicule and criticize useful doctrine, writings, and sermons.

On the other hand, doctors and preachers who are sound and virtuous bear witness to the King and High Priest Jesus Christ, following the example of the good king and prophet David, who also sings in his Psalm 146: "Praise the Lord, O my soul. I will praise the Lord Christ as long as I live and sing praise to my God as long as I am on the earth" [Ps. 146:1–2]. Our doctor recited this verse many times when he began expounding the Pentateuch, the prophets, and the psalms.[31]

Our Preacher-King, who alone is worthy of all glory and praise in the Church, earnestly commanded His apostles and all preachers after His resurrection to preach repentance and the forgiveness of sins in His name [Luke 24:47], so that people would be brought to the knowledge of their sins and to a blessed sorrow [2 Cor. 7:10], would learn obediently to meditate upon the Word of grace and reconciliation, and would preserve a good conscience in a holy, new, inchoate obedience, in order that they might learn to recognize the blessed doctrine of the gracious forgiveness of sins in the blood of Jesus Christ and to grasp this with their own faith and preserve it. Many foolish and unlearned Evangelical preachers neglected the preaching of repentance and spoke indiscreetly about faith and perilously about leading a holy life, good works, and brotherly love—which, in fact, belongs to the preaching of repentance, assures us in our calling, alongside the Spirit of God, and is a strong sign and testimony that we are Christ's disciples and God's children and heirs solely through faith, as Christ says in Luke 6 [:27–36] and John 13 [:35].[32] That is why this year our doctor preached the fine sermons

---

[27] Cf. below, Mathesius, *History*, pp. 406, 417, 438–39.

[28] Thersites was a Greek soldier in the Trojan War who publicly reviled his king, Agamemnon: Homer, *Iliad* 2.211–77 (Loeb 170 [1924], pp. 78–81); cf. Luther, *Commentary on Psalm 101* (1534/1535), LW 13:202.

[29] Marcolf, according to medieval legend, was the jester in the court of King Solomon. See Jan Ziolkowski, trans., *Solomon and Marcolf*, Harvard Studies in Medieval Latin 1 (Cambridge, MA: Harvard University Press, 2008). For Luther's references to Marcolf, see LW 58:268 n. 57; 69:303 n. 47.

[30] Zoilus (ca. 400–320 BC) was notorious as a harsh critic of Homer's poems. See, e.g., Ovid, *Remedies for Love* 365–366 (Loeb 232 [1929], pp. 202–3); *OCD*, 3rd ed., s.v. "Zoilus." Cf. Luther, *Notes on Ecclesiastes* (1526/1532), LW 15:186. For the three proverbial critics together, cf. Mathesius to Paul Eber, June 6, 1559, in Loesche, *Mathesius: Ausgewählte Werke*, 4:572.

[31] See, e.g., Luther, preface to *Lectures on Genesis* (1543), WA 42:1 (LW 62).

[32] Probably a reference to the controversy which had begun in 1527 between Luther's longtime associate Johann Agricola (see above, p. 345 n. 134) and Melanchthon over the place of repentance in Christian preaching—whether on the basis of the Law and fear of God, as preliminary to faith, as Melanchthon and Luther taught, or on the basis of the Gospel and love of

from the [First] Epistle of St. John regarding Christian brotherly love, which Doctor Caspar Cruciger transcribed as our doctor spoke and most diligently prepared them for publication.[33]

In these sermons, our doctor teaches very clearly from St. John's text that a believer is obliged to demonstrate his faith and calling in Christian love and that everyone needs to remain confident and keep a good conscience toward all, if he wants to remain standing in God's strict judgment, trusting in the blood and intercession of God's Son as his chief confidence. It is true that only faith and trust in the grace of God, which shines in the blood and death of the one Mediator, make us acceptable to God, righteous, and saved, through pure grace, without any merit, glory, or worthiness from our own love and good works. However, when a heart does not sense this confidence and good conscience which springs forth from love, but instead feels an evil conscience, devoid of good intentions, Christ with His blood of propitiation has not been grasped. Neither is the testifying Holy Spirit [cf. Rom. 8:16] within the hearts of these people, who, with an evil conscience, do not earnestly pursue love and peace.

Dear friends, I ask that you would read these sermons about love frequently and diligently and that you would remind yourselves of the passage from St. Paul which they include and I have now assigned as a memory verse and Sunday homework:[34] "Preserve faith and a good conscience" [1 Tim. 1:19]. For where there is no good intention and good conscience toward your neighbor, there also is no Holy Spirit. It is the Holy Spirit who shows us the wounds of Christ by means of the Word and bears witness to us that we enjoy God's grace solely for the sake of Christ's sacrifice and intercession, and who helps us to groan with groaning too deep for words [Rom. 8:26], and who sighs for the gracious forgiveness of sins. Without the Holy Spirit, there is no blessed, true, and living knowledge of our Savior Jesus Christ.

We are glad to give and render glory and praise to the Son of God, for it is solely through Christ's name, holy blood, and merit that we have the gracious forgiveness of sins and a blessed confidence, fearless heart, and sure conscience in the face of the wrath of God, and that the righteous shall live by his faith alone [Hab. 2:4; Rom. 1:17; Gal. 3:11; Heb. 10:38]. According to Scripture and Doctor Luther's doctrine, we confess that a believer must

---

God, in consequence of faith, as Agricola argued. See Luther and Melanchthon, *Instructions for the Visitors* (1528), LW 40:293–96; Wengert, *Law and Gospel*. By 1537, the dispute, called the Antinomian Controversy, would break out again: see below, Mathesius, *History*, pp. 412–14.

[33] Luther's series of five sermons on 1 John 4:16–21, preached on June 9, 16, and 30, and July 21 and 28, 1532, were published in 1533 as *Several Beautiful Sermons from 1 John, on Love* (1532), LW 78:363–405. On Caspar Cruciger, see the introduction above, p. xx n. 19 and p. 298 n. 81.

[34] *zum Symbolo und Sontags latein*

also have this confidence from love on the Day of Judgment, as the words of John clearly state, John 4 [1 John 4:17]. Not as if he makes himself worthy of righteousness or earns forgiveness of sins with his new obedience, but rather that he thereby demonstrates his faith and that he is a true disciple of Christ and makes his calling sure [2 Pet. 1:10].

For such confidence and good conscience, or new obedience, is not the merit, price, or cause of our righteousness and being children of God; rather, it is a sure sign and testimony that we have properly and truly grasped Christ with a living and saving idea of faith. Our doctor also treated this very article in Dessau,[35] before the good princes of Anhalt,[36] when he preached on St. Paul's passage in 1 Timothy 1 [:5–7][37] concerning the sum of the commandment, that is, concerning Christian penitence, which comprises love from a pure heart, a good conscience, and an unfeigned faith. For this is how to preach properly about conversion in accordance with Christ's command: We are to reveal sin through the Law and admonish to brotherly love, a good conscience, and genuine, Christian obedience while urging to faith in Jesus Christ. This comprises the three parts of true conversion: contrition, faith, and new obedience.[38]

Such repentant, contrite, believing, loving ʲhearts receive the gracious forgiveness of sins and imputed righteousness through grace, freely, through the pure mercy of God, solely for the sake of the one Mediator's merit, blood, and intercession, not for the sake of their contrition, confession, faith, or good conscience—all of which, on our part, is incomplete and imperfect and an impure thing, and which still needs the perfect and imputed obedience of Jesus Christ. For just as our contrition and new obedience are neither perfect nor pure in this life, so also our knowledge and faith in Him, as much as they are a work of God's Spirit in our hearts, in us they are something partial and fallible. Therefore, we properly teach according to Scripture that we are and remain righteous solely through the forgiveness of sins, not of

---

[35] In fact, the sermon was preached in Wörlitz (see the introduction by Georg Buchwald and Oskar Brenner, WA 36:xxvii–xxx), but Witt Ger 1/2 [1539], fol. 128r, gave the place as Dessau.

[36] I.e., Princes John (1504–51), Joachim (1509–61), and George III (see above, p. 30 n. 16) of Anhalt-Dessau, who had ruled jointly since 1516. After the 1530 Diet of Augsburg, they had begun to introduce the Reformation into their territories, influenced by their cousin Wolfgang of Anhalt-Köthen (see above, p. xxxi n. 68): see above, Mathesius, *History*, p. 328. See Luther's correspondence with the brothers, cited below, p. 378 n. 52. See Brecht 3:25–28.

[37] *Sermon on the Sum of the Christian Life* (November 24, 1532), LW 51:257–87, edited by Cruciger for publication in December 1532.

[38] See AC XII 3–6 (Kolb-Wengert, pp. 44–45; *Concordia*, p. 38); Melanchthon, *Elementa Rhetorices* (ed. Volkhard Wels, pp. 46–47; CR 13:425).

ourselves and not through our repentance and conversion, inchoate faith, and received gifts.

My dear master and friend, Doctor Caspar Cruciger,[39] later instructed me about this when he showed me this article in Doctor Luther's *Church Postil*, in the exposition of the Epistle for Christmas Day. Here Doctor Luther writes: "Our faith and what we have from God is not enough, nor is it spotless, but Christ satisfies God's righteousness for us. He gives us grace and salvation, not for the sake of our faith, but through pure grace."[40] Again, on the Gospel for St. Stephen, the doctor writes: "It is not enough for one who is to stand before God's judgment to say, 'I believe and have grace,' for all that is within him is not enough to protect him; but let him oppose this judgment with Christ's own righteousness; this is what he must allow to deal with God's judgment and what will stand in all glory before Him forever."[41] And as he continues: "Thus one is preserved not because of one's self or because of such faith, but for the sake of Christ's righteousness, under which he takes refuge."[42] Thus far Luther.[43] For when we were lying in ungodliness and unrighteousness, and God had mercy on us, He made His Son to be wisdom, righteousness, sanctification, and redemption for us [1 Cor. 1:30]. He has this proclaimed to us through His Spirit in the Word of the Gospel while calling for repentance, so that, acknowledging our sin and having a good intention, we may with believing hearts grasp hold of and apply these treasures prepared for us—as St. Paul says to the Philippians: that we should allow ourselves to be taken hold of and nurtured by the Word and sprinkled with the blood and Spirit of Christ [Phil. 2:10; 3:12; cf. 1 Pet. 1:2].

Amid the pangs of death and severe tribulations, sometimes neither contrition nor sorrow, neither faith nor a good conscience can be felt—when sin awakens in earnest, when God's wrath is pressing down upon us, and we would like simply to disappear. Therefore, we must seek our confidence and boldness outside of ourselves, our conversion, and our gifts; we have to seek them in Christ and let ourselves be grasped hold of by Him [Phil. 3:12]. For that is what it means to be made righteous and saved through grace, freely,

---

[39] On Cruciger and Mathesius' friendship with him, see above, p. 298 n. 81. Luther entrusted Cruciger with the last round of revisions to the *Church Postil*: see the introduction by Benjamin T. G. Mayes, LW 75:xxii–xxiv.

[40] *Church Postil* (1540–44), sermon for Second Day of Christmas on Titus 3:4–8, LW 75:230–47, here p. 246, paraphrased.

[41] *Church Postil* (1540–44), sermon for St. Stephen's Day on Matt. 23:34–39, LW 75:330–41, here pp. 336–37 (cf. LW 52:89–101, here p. 96).

[42] *Church Postil* (1540–44), sermon for St. Stephen's Day on Matt. 23:34–39, LW 75:337 (cf. LW 52:96).

[43] *Haec ille.*

not from ourselves or for the sake of our preceding or concurrent contrition and faith, nor on the basis of subsequent love, good works, good intention and conscience, and renewal of the gifts of the indwelling Spirit.

Our doctor speaks and writes about these articles correctly, making the proper distinctions. Since the people possessed the Gospel and yet began living coarsely—and a few years later many false brethren sprang up who wanted to relegate the Law and preaching of repentance together with the necessary new obedience from the Church of Christ to the city hall[44]—he earnestly admonished them to lead a life of repentance and good works, yet with a proper distinction, as you will hear more extensively later, when we speak about the enemies of the Law of God.[45]

However, the blessed teaching of the Lord Jesus Christ was ringing out among the neighboring territories and in many lands, and through God's Word, Spirit, and the steadfast confession of Christian martyrs, the people were convinced that Christ alone makes us righteous and saves us through His blood, and that, as the High Priest and sole Head of Christendom, the Son of God alone has the power to institute divine worship and Sacraments, and that the Antichrist in Rome had presumptuously and arbitrarily changed God's institution and stolen the blood of Christ from the laity. Thus many people resolved to adhere to the institution and ordinance of Christ and to use both kinds (that is, the whole of the Lord's Supper as it was instituted) in their neighboring churches, which provoked many questions and great persecution.[46]

Now, since good-hearted people wanted to preserve their consciences, they addressed our doctor with the following question: Could they receive the Sacrament in one kind at the command of their secular authorities with a good conscience? Our doctor, who by virtue of his doctorate had a universal call to instruct anyone who asked him what is right and Christian according to Scripture, gave his neighbors this reply: Anyone who has been instructed in his heart by God's Word and who holds the conviction in conscience that [receiving in] both kinds is correct according to God's Word and ordinance should by no means act contrary to his conscience—or, rather, contrary to God Himself—but should instead risk his body and soul upon Christ and His Word in bold confession.[47]

---

[44] See below, Mathesius, *History*, pp. 411–12.

[45] I.e., the Antinomians. See below, Mathesius, *History*, pp. 412–14.

[46] On the situation in ducal (Albertine) Saxony, where Duke George remained a steadfast opponent of Luther and the Reformation (e.g., see above, p. 154 n. 91 and p. 156 n. 99), see Brecht 3:65–70.

[47] Luther to the Evangelicals in Leipzig, April 11, 1533, WA Br 6:448–52 (*LSC*, pp. 223–24).

Many good people took this Christian and faithful counsel in full earnest and sought to follow it, which put them, too, in danger. With a fine letter of consolation, our doctor comforted all who were unjustly exiled for receiving both kinds; he also gave an answer for himself to the kind of talk which imposed a pernicious interpretation on his counsels and letters of consolation;[48] and since he had been denounced as a false, perjured, and seditious teacher, he responded quite vehemently, as a true Elijah. For as we see in 1 Kings 18 (where the godless King Ahab, who promoted the idolatry of his wicked Jezebel and drove the prophets of God from his kingdom, denounced the great prophet Elijah as a rebel and troubler of Israel [v. 17]), this holy prophet defended himself just as boldly and fiercely: "I am not the one troubling and disrupting the kingdom," says Elijah, "but you and your people, who follow after the Baals and idols and persecute the Word of the Lord of hosts" [cf. 1 Kings 18:18].

Christians should make their confession of faith with patience and mildness and suffer injustice on this account. Prophets and bishops, too, should not fail to do anything on behalf of God and His Word. But this harsh preaching worked on Ahab: he repented and grieved and found grace [1 Kings 21:25–29]. May God help all who are opposed to His Word and servants so that they, too, may come to their senses instead of kicking against the goads [Acts 26:14]. For the grace of God is great and limitless; He even saved many of the priests who helped put His Son, the Lord of glory, on the cross but afterward confessed their sin and let themselves be sprinkled with the innocent blood of Jesus Christ [Acts 6:7]. Manasseh, who had the prophet Isaiah sawed apart [Heb. 11:37], also crawled to the cross in the end and was saved through grace [2 Chron. 33:12–13],[49] through the promised and blessed Seed of the woman [Gen. 3:15]. Blessed are they who seek and desire the forgiveness of all their sins in the time of grace, relying on the precious blood of Jesus Christ. For God's goodness and Christ's blood are far greater than the whole world's sin and transgression.

---

[48] Luther, *Verantwortung der aufgelegten Aufruhr von Herzog Georg samt einem Trostbrief an die Christen, von ihm aus Leipzig unschuldig verjagt* (1533), WA 38:96–127; see also Luther, *Kleine Antwort auf Herzog Georgen nächstes Buch* (1533), WA 38:141–52.

[49] See also the Prayer of Manasseh in the Apocrypha, which Luther treasured: *How Confession Should Be Made* (1520), LW 39:29, 46–47; and the introduction by Gustav K. Wiencke, LW 43:8, which lists the contents of Luther's *Personal Prayer Book* (1529), including this prayer. The account of Isaiah being sawn in two at King Manasseh's behest is found in the pseudopigraphal *Martyrdom and Ascension of Isaiah*: see the translation by M. A. Knibb in *The Old Testament Pseudepigrapha*, ed. James H. Charlesworth (New York: Doubleday, 1985), 2:143–76.

The Word of truth must be accompanied by tribulation;[50] those who teach and receive it will not walk on roses here.[51] Yet in the end this Word of the cross brings glory and joy to all who patiently endure their cross, relying on the cross of Jesus Christ. Both of these things will be made visible at the last judgment: If anyone has innocently suffered here with Christ and been denounced, exiled, or killed for His sake and His Gospel's, they will receive their reward in the regeneration [Matt. 19:28–29] and wear their crowns for eternity. Those who have been unwilling to risk or suffer anything for the sake of the Word of Life, but have instead taken part in tormenting and exiling servants and lovers of the holy Gospel, and have persisted with deliberate and wanton zeal in doing so until their life's end, are unworthy of the Lord Christ and of the glory and joy of His kingdom. They will find their tormentor and their torture more severe than anyone would ever wish them. Let that be enough of this matter for the present.

There is still one thing I must mention: When some who had been deprived of their possessions on account of their religion sought counsel from Doctor Luther regarding whether they could make use of their rights and take legal action with good conscience against their hostile ruling authorities, our doctor gave fitting and prudent counsel.[52] The injured parties ought to exercise Christian patience in confident hope and should commend their cause and rights to God with a humble Our Father. What is right is and remains right[53] with the righteous God, who finally looks upon the righteous at the right time and repays the unjust sevenfold upon their heads for their presumption [cf. Ps. 79:12]. Even if [God] is very patient in watching the unjust for a time, one must not seek to take away the holy cross from its place next to the Gospel. If someone is able to use the help found in the jurists' laws to retain or regain something with good right from his duly appointed ruling authorities, [Luther] must also permit that course of action, since he defends the dear authorities and their laws alongside his Gospel.

---

[50] *anfechtung.* See above, p. 44 n. 32.

[51] An allusion to the legend of St. Tibertius (d. 286), *LA* 1:23, no. 23: see LW 58:450 n. 18.

[52] The source behind Mathesius' report of this advice could not be identified: see Volz, *Die Lutherpredigten des Johannes Mathesius*, p. 256. The letter cited by Loesche (*LH²*, p. 542, Luther to Princes John and Joachim of Anhalt, October 15, 1533, WA Br 6:536–37) is not parallel to Mathesius' description here. Luther's counsel is parallel in structure to his advice on making use of imperial law in resistance to the emperor (see above, Mathesius, *History*, p. 360): Luther to the Electoral Saxon Government, ca. October 27, 1530, LW 49:429–33; to Lazarus Spengler, February 15, 1531, LW 50:9–12.

[53] Cf. Wander 3:1529, "Recht (Subst.)" no. 220.

Meanwhile, our doctor continued with his work: he faithfully preached, diligently lectured at the university,[54] expounded many beautiful psalms,[55] and comforted many afflicted lords and cities.[56] |He also expressed his opinion of the exposition of the Creed set forth by Erasmus of Rotterdam[57]

---

[54] Luther finished his lectures on the Song of Songs in June 1531 (1530–31/1539, LW 15:189–264) and then turned to Galatians for the rest of the year (1531/1535, LW 26–27). In 1532, he began lecturing on selected psalms: Psalm 2 (1532/1546, LW 12:1–93), Psalm 51 (1532/1538, LW 12:301–410), Psalm 45 (1532/1533–34, LW 12:195–300), and then on the Psalms of Degrees (Psalms 120–134) until the fall of 1533 (1532–33/1540, WA 40/3:9–475 [LW 66]). In the fall of 1534, he lectured on Psalm 90 (1534–35/1541, LW 13:73–141), finishing in the spring of 1535 before beginning his monumental series on Genesis (1535–45/1544–54, LW 1–8) in the summer.

[55] In addition to the lectures on the psalms cited in the previous note, some of which (Psalms 128 and 129) were adapted for separate publication in vernacular editions, see *Commentary on Psalm 147* (1531/1532), LW 14:107–35; *Commentary on Psalm 101* (1534/1535), LW 13:143–224; *Sermon on Psalm 65* (July 16–18, 1534), WA 37:425–50 (LW 66).

[56] See Luther, to an anonymous city magistrate, August 19, 1532, WA Br 6:349–51; to Martin Lodinger, councilman in Gastein, August 27, 1532, WA Br 6:352–53; to Johann Riedesel, former Saxon chancellor, September 7 and ca. December 3, 1532, WA Br 6:353–54, 391–92 (*LSC*, p. 160); to King Christian II of Denmark, September 28, 1532, WA Br 6:366–68 (*LSC*, pp. 216–18); to Jonas von Stockhausen, city captain in Nordhausen, and his wife, November 27, 1532, WA Br 6:386–89 (*LSC*, pp. 88–91); to Counts Hieronymus and Lorenz Schlick, October 9, 1532, WA Br 6:372–73; to Lorenz Zoch, chancellor in Magdeburg, November 3 and December 7, 1532, WA Br 6:382–83, 392–93 (*LSC*, pp. 65–67); *Letter to the Christians in Frankfurt am Main*, December 1, 1532, WA 30/3:558–71; to the Council of Soest, December 21, 1532, WA Br 6:397–98; to the Council of Münster, December 21, 1532, WA Br 6:398–401; Luther, Jonas, and Melanchthon, to an unknown nobleman, ca. 1532, WA Br 6:405–6; Luther, to the Evangelicals expelled from Oschatz, January 20, 1533, WA Br 6:422–23 (*LSC*, pp. 221–22); to the mayor and Council of Rothenburg on the Tauber, January 26, 1533, WA Br 6:423–24; Luther et al., to the Council of Bremen, February 27, 1533, WA Br 6:428–31; Luther, to George of Anhalt, March 28, 1533, WA Br 6:440–41 (*LSC*, pp. 162–63); to John of Anhalt, March 28, 1533, WA Br 6:441–42 (*LSC*, pp. 163–64); to Dr. Georg Curio, May 13, 1533, WA Br 6:464–67; to Joachim of Anhalt, June 19, 1533, WA Br 6:491–92; to an anonymous nobleman, summer 1533, WA Br 7:275–76; Luther et al., to Heinrich and Abraham von Einsiedler, March 3, 1534, WA Br 7:22–23; Luther, to John, George, and Joachim of Anhalt, April 5–6, 1534, WA Br 7:55–57; Luther, to Joachim of Anhalt, May 23, June 9, 23, and 26, 1534, WA Br 7:65–67, 70, 76–78 (*LSC*, pp. 92–95); to Anna von der Dahme, November 13, 1534, WA Br 7:115–17; to Caspar Müller, chancellor in Mansfeld, November 24, 1534, WA Br 7:117–18 (*LSC*, pp. 38–40); to Joachim of Anhalt, December 25, 1535, WA Br 7:335–36 (*LSC*, p. 98); to Lorenz Kastner, February 11, 1536, WA Br 7:365–67.

[57] Erasmus, *An Explanation of the Apostles' Creed* (1533), CWE 70:231–387. Erasmus had published an earlier exposition of the Creed in *An Examination concerning the Faith* (1524), CWE 39:419–47. See also Erasmus, *On Mending the Peace of the Church* (1533), CWE 65:125–216, and Luther's preface to Corvinus, *How Far Erasmus' "Mending the Peace" Should Be Followed* (1534), LW 60:57–65.

and warned everyone against the writings of this untrustworthy and dangerous man, as his letter to Herr Amsdorf clearly demonstrates.[58]

I will also mention the *Simple Way to Pray*, which our doctor prepared
for Master Peter the Barber and often recalled afterward, because it is such a
necessary and comforting little book for the laity and a fine, brief exposition
and application of the precious catechism.[59] Polemical books of all kinds
are of no help for common pastors, simple laity, and young schoolchildren
to read; therefore, one must maintain a distinction among his books (in
keeping with his own good advice) and treasure this writing about how to
pray from the catechism.[60]

Certain people, having been instructed from God's Word, were now
publishing their own confessions in print, and Dr. Luther wrote many prefaces and forewords this year, which were later collected separately in his
books,[61] along with his expositions of biblical verses,[62] which he had written
by hand for many people in their Bibles and other books. Finally, when this
was threatening to become too much, and he complained in one foreword
that people were trying to turn him into nothing but a writer of prefaces in
his old age, some took the hint and left our doctor in peace, so that he could
attend to his preaching and the translation of the Bible.[63]

Since, after the imperial diet in Augsburg, God's Word had opened a
wide door in Germany [cf. 1 Cor. 16:9], and the Confession was resounding and being received even in foreign lands, the devil now sought to bring
the Gospel into disrepute once again and stirred up the Anabaptists in
many places. They had been driven out of Switzerland; Hubmaier, Denck,
and Doltzk,[64] who were their instigators and who, in addition to their false

---

[58] Luther to Amsdorf, ca. March 11, 1534, WA Br 7:27–40 (LW 74), with criticism of
Erasmus' *Explanation of the Apostles' Creed* on pp. 30–31. Luther's letter was quickly published
as an open denunciation of Erasmus. See Brecht 3:78–84.

[59] *Simple Way to Pray* (1535), LW 43:187–211. See Brecht 3:14. On Peter the Barber, see the
introduction by Gustav K. Wiencke, LW 43:187–91.

[60] For Luther's distinctions among his books, see, e.g., *Luther at the Diet of Worms* (1521),
LW 32:109–11; *Preface to the Catalog of All the Books and Writings* (1533), above, pp. 3–4;
Preface to the German Writings (1539), LW 34:283–85; *Preface to the Latin Writings* (1545),
LW 34:327–28; *Table Talk* no. 3493 (1536), LW 54:213; no. 5511 (1542–43), LW 54:439–40.

[61] Luther's prefaces were gathered posthumously in Witt Ger 9 and 12. See LW 59–60.

[62] *Auslegung vieler schöner Sprüche aus göttlicher Schrift, welche D.M. Luther vielen in ihre
Bibeln geschrieben* (1547), WA 48:1–297. These were published in Witt Ger 9.

[63] Luther, preface to Kymaeus, *Ancient Christian Council in Gangra* (1536), LW 60:136. On
Luther's prefaces written for the works of others, see the introduction by Christopher Boyd
Brown, LW 59:xvii–xl.

[64] On these Anabaptist leaders, see above, Mathesius, *History*, p. 246. "Doltzk" (here spelled
"Doltzs") seems to be Mathesius' error for Jacob Kautz. See LH², p. 503; cf. below, p. 474 n. 67.

doctrine, stirred up rebellion and much abominable mischief, found their way to the hangman's ¹noose, even as their seditious brethren were executed in many lands in accordance with secular law.[65]

When Christian authorities together with their scholars did not allow such people to enter and multiply in the places where the holy Gospel was being preached purely according to the writings of the prophets and apostles and the Augsburg Confession, the exiles secretly crept into the lands of lords and bishops where the pure doctrine was not tolerated, and there they excreted their filth just like filthy worms. Many simple people, who would have liked to learn God's Word and were not hearing anything better in the territory or diocese of their lord, were lured and bewitched by these apostles of the devil; they gathered secretly in gardens[66] and meadows, even by night, and carried on in an abominable and wild way. For the bishops and their scholars and everyone else on the side of the Antichrist were much too weak and ignorant to succeed in opposing Anabaptism with solid Scripture and in showing the people the right way. Some of the papistic teachers themselves had even ordered the rebaptism of children who had been baptized in German under the Gospel according to Christ's command.[67]

But because the foolishness of the pope and his clergy had now been revealed through the mouth of the Spirit [cf. 2 Thess. 2:8], and even the children playing in the streets knew that there was nothing to be found in the monasteries but deceit, the Anabaptists decked out their lies by saying they were opposing the pope and by boasting remarkable things about the heavenly Father and His Spirit, with great hypocrisy and monkish sanctimoniousness. Thus the poor common man naively supported these bewitchers and infiltrators, many examples of which I experienced by the Lech River.[68]

---

[65] The first execution of an Anabaptist (Felix Manz) took place in Zurich at the beginning of 1527, and the execution of Michael Sattler in Rottenburg under imperial auspices followed later the same year. An imperial mandate imposing the death penalty for rebaptism, based on the sixth-century *Codex of Justinian*, was issued at the Diet of Speyer in 1528 and incorporated into the imperial criminal code, the *Constitutio Carolina*, in 1532. On persecution of Anabaptists, see Claus Peter Clasen, *Anabaptism: A Social History, 1525–1618* (Ithaca, NY: Cornell University Press, 1972), pp. 358–422.

[66] On the designation of Anabaptists as "hedge preachers" or "garden brethren," see Clasen, *Anabaptism*, pp. 13–14.

[67] On Roman Catholic clergy who (contrary to canon law) required the rebaptism of children who had received Evangelical baptism in the vernacular, see Luther, *Concerning Rebaptism* (1528), LW 40:230–31.

[68] See above, Mathesius, *History*, p. 245.

When these apostles of the devil directed their efforts toward suppressing not only the pope but also Dr. Luther's doctrine and all governing authorities, and to establishing an abominable Turkish[69] |order and a new kingdom of their own before the Last Day, and having slain all authorities and teachers, they sought space where they could make their nests and sow their blasphemy and sedition and defend it in strong fortresses by power of the sword, advancing and maintaining it just like Mohammed.

They settled on the town of Münster as best for their purpose, because the people there were weary of the papistic doctrine, and there was no one there who was capable of refuting their lies.[70] Therefore, the ancient serpent sent certain persons to Münster in Westphalia, who crept into houses here and there and spewed out their poison among the people, convincing them to be rebaptized. Bernhard Rothmann,[71] who had previously preached outside the city and now entered the city without a regular call, warned against rebaptism at first. In the end, however, hoping to rise in the world and to take the bishop's place, he helped defend the Anabaptists' heresy with word and deed.

---

[69] "Turkish" in the sense of allowing polygamy and using the power of the sword to establish a new religion. Cf. above, Mathesius, *History*, p. 246.

[70] On the history of the Anabaptist kingdom at Münster in 1534–35, see Sleidanus, *De statu religionis* (1558), book 10, pp. 267–83; Heinrich Dorp, *Warhafftige historie/ wie das Evangelium zu Münster angefangen/ und darnach durch die Widderteuffer verstöret/ widder auffgehört hat* (Wittenberg: G. Rhau, 1536) [VD16 D2434], included in Witt Ger 2 and edited in Robert Stupperich, *Schriften von evangelischer Seite gegen die Täufer*, Die Schriften der münsterischen Täufer und ihrer Gegner 3 (Münster: Aschendorff, 1983), pp. 220–45. For modern discussion of the Münster episode, see Williams, *Radical Reformation*, 3rd ed., pp. 553–88; James M. Stayer, *Anabaptists and the Sword* (Lawrence, KS: Coronado, 1972), pp. 211–305; Sigrun Haude, *In the Shadow of "Savage Wolves": Anabaptist Münster and the German Reformation during the 1530s* (Leiden: Brill, 2000).

[71] Bernhard Rothmann (1495–1535), a native of the diocese of Münster, was a Catholic priest who, after contacts with Wittenberg and Strassburg, began to protest the preaching and practice of the diocesan clergy, resulting in a ban on his own preaching in Münster until the city council decided in his favor in 1532 and allowed him to reform the city parishes according to a Lutheran model. Rothmann himself, however, moved away from Luther toward Zwingli's eucharistic theology and then, by 1533, to an Anabaptist doctrine of Baptism. Embracing the apocalyptic prophecies of Melchior Hoffman (see above, p. 196 n. 66), Rothmann became the leading theologian of the Münster Anabaptist regime. See Karl-Heinz Kirchhoff, "Rothmann, Bernhard," *OER* 3:451–52; Robert Stupperich, ed., *Die Schriften Bernhard Rothmanns*, Die Schriften der münsterischen Täufer und ihrer Gegner 1 (Münster: Aschendorff, 1970).

When the Anabaptists gained control, they ousted the council and formed a new government,[72] elected their own king,[73] crafted a new Koran,[74] reapportioned the land, closed access to the city, committed mayhem and murder, and fomented an abominable, diabolical devilish state of affairs, the likes of which I have never, to my knowledge, heard nor read about.

The besieged city of Jerusalem had more people and more division, but in this place they not only roasted children, but they also slaughtered many people and salted and smoked them, since there were too few dogs, mice, and cats in the city.[75] In Corinth there was an abominable Venusberg[76] and unheard of fornication, for they regarded the abominations and devilry of Baal-peor and Priapus[77] as their greatest worship. Even more dreadful were the Bacchanalia in Rome, which consisted of nothing but murder and Sodom and Gomorrah.[78] All this infernal sewage flowed together into a cesspool in Münster.[79] |The abomination of this charnel house is described

---

[72] In February 1534, the supporters of Rothmann prevailed in the new elections for the Münster town council and recognized the Dutch Anabaptist Jan Matthijs (ca. 1500–1534) as prophet. Under his rule, the land records were destroyed and a form of communism was introduced. See Hans J. Hillerbrand, "Matthijs, Jan," *OER* 3:33–34; Williams, *Radical Reformation*, 3rd ed., pp. 563–66.

[73] Matthijs perished in action against the besieging forces of the prince-bishop of Münster in April 1534 on the day on which he had prophesied the end of the world. His follower Jan Bockelson (1509–36) of Leiden, a former tailor and innkeeper with ties to Münster on his mother's side, succeeded him as the charismatic leader of the Münsterites. Bockelson replaced the government of the town council with twelve "elders of Israel" of his own appointment. In September he was crowned as a new King David. See James M. Stayer, "John of Leiden," *OER* 2:350–51.

[74] A reference to the claims of prophetic status by the leaders of the Münster Anabaptists, expressed also in publications by Rothmann such as the *Bekenntnis des Glaubens und Lebens der Gemeinde Christi zu Münster* (1534), the *Restitution rechter und gesunder christlicher Lehre* (1534), and *Von der Verborgenheit der Schrift des Reiches Christi* (1535), in Stupperich, *Die Schriften Bernhard Rothmanns*, pp. 195–208, 208–84, and 298–372.

[75] See Josephus (ca. 37–ca. 101), *Jewish War* 5.10, 6.3.3–5 (Loeb 210 [1928], pp. 134–41, 234–41). For reports of cannibalism in Münster, see the pamphlet *Des Münsterischen Künigreichs und Widertauffs an und abgang/ Bluthandel unnd End* (Augsburg: Steiner, 1536) [VD16 M6732], incorporated in Witt Ger 2 (1557), fol. 401r–v.

[76] Corinth was the location of a temple of Aphrodite (Venus) and the associated cultic prostitution, proverbial in the ancient world for sexual immorality: see *OCD*, 3rd ed., s.v. "Corinth." On the Venusberg in German legend, see above, p. 235 n. 21.

[77] On these deities, associated with sexual debauchery, see above, p. 203 n. 12, p. 204 n. 19.

[78] On the Bacchanalia, see above, p. 204 n. 22.

[79] Among the revivals of Old Testament practice in Münster under Jan Bockelson was the introduction of polygamy. Bockelson himself is supposed to have had as many as nineteen concubines, and Rothmann, nine wives. See Dorp, *Warhafftige historia*, in Stupperich, *Schriften von evangelischer Seite gegen die Täufer*, pp. 238, 242; Williams, *Radical Reformation*, 3rd ed., pp. 568–70, 577–78.

in the second volume of Dr. Luther's German books[80] and in Sleidanus,[81] so that henceforth everyone may be on guard against these hell-bent knaves and their horrible blasphemy and abomination.

When neighboring Christian princes and cities and their scholars were unable to find a remedy or defense against this infernal blaze, in the end they were forced to confine these seditious fanatics with wooden fortifications[82] and let them waste away together from hunger, until finally they stormed the city by night and slew the rebels. The instigators were dolefully torn apart with tongs and hung up in iron cages as a dreadful reminder and a warning to everyone.[83]

Now since these blinded and bloodthirsty people wanted to defend their diabolical ambition with their books, the Hessian preachers,[84] along with

---

[80] Material about Münster, by Luther and his associates, fills almost the whole of Witt Ger 2. See above, p. 382 n. 70, p. 383 n. 75; and below, n. 84, p. 385 nn. 85–86, 90.

[81] See above, p. 382 n. 70.

[82] See Sleidanus, *De statu religionis* (1558), book 10, p. 272; Luther, *Table Talk* no. 5088 (1540), WA TR 4:650 and n. 11.

[83] Sleidanus, *De statu religionis* (1558), book 10, pp. 281–83. The city was taken on June 24, 1535, when Rothmann perished in the fighting. Bockelson and two of his lieutenants were tortured and executed on January 22, 1536.

[84] Antonius Corvinus, *Antwort der hessischen Prediger auf Rothmanns Buch "Von der Verborgenheit der Schrift"* (1535), in Stupperich, *Schriften von evangelischer Seite gegen die Täufer*, pp. 184–206. This work was drafted by Corvinus (1501–53) but issued in the name of the preachers Johannes de Campis (d. 1536), Johann Fontius (d. 1539), Johann Kymaeus (1498–1552), and Johann Lening (1491–1566) as well. It was included in Witt Ger 2. On Corvinus, see Luther's prefaces for Corvinus, *Postils* (1535, 1537), LW 60:103–10, and the introduction by Anna Marie Johnson there.

Doctor Urbanus Rhegius,[85] Justus Menius,[86] and Myconius,[87] took great pains in this affair, trying to save at least some of them [1 Cor. 9:22].[88] Earlier our Dr. Luther himself had written an excellent book against the Anabaptists to two preachers who sought his advice.[89] Likewise, Herr Melanchthon fought against this heresy with solid arguments and warned everyone against their blasphemy and rebellion.[90]

Because the evil spirit in Münster had manifested himself only as a simple schoolboy devil[91]—in such a coarse and foolish way that he made it easy for him to be generally recognized as an indubitable and unclean archliar and murderer [cf. John 8:44]—accordingly, Dr. Luther did not want to engage in writing against the rebels in Münster apart from praising and

---

[85] Urbanus Rhegius, *Refutation of the Confession of the New Valentinians and Donatists at Münster* (1535), in Stupperich, *Schriften von evangelischer Seite gegen die Täufer*, pp. 82–137 (see also Luther's preface for this work, LW 60:82–90); and Rhegius, *De restitutione regni Israelitici* (1536), in Stupperich, *Schriften von evangelischer Seite gegen die Täufer*, pp. 137–58. Rhegius' *Refutation* was included in Witt Ger 2. On Rhegius, see above, p. 357 n. 203.

[86] Justus Menius (1499–1558), from Fulda, studied in Wittenberg and worked as teacher and preacher in Erfurt (1525–28) before becoming superintendent in Eisenach (1529–47) and later in Gotha (1547–56), ending his career in Leipzig. Deeply involved as superintendent in opposing Anabaptism in Thuringia, Menius wrote extensively against the movement: *Doctrine and Secret of the Anabaptists* (1530) [VD16 M4603] (see Luther's preface, LW 59:263–71); *How Every Christian Should Conduct Himself* (1538) [VD16 M4601] (see Luther's preface, LW 60:209–13); *On the Spirit of the Anabaptists* (1544) [VD16 M4587], excerpted in Stupperich, *Schriften von evangelischer Seite gegen die Täufer*, pp. 245–48 (see Luther's preface, LW 60:330–35). Only the last of these works dealt directly with the Münster uprising; all three were included in Witt Ger 2. On Menius, see the article by Luther D. Peterson, *OER* 3:49–50, and the introductions by Carol Geisler and Robert Kolb for Luther's prefaces to his works in LW 59–60.

[87] Friedrich Myconius (1490–1546), a former Franciscan, became a Lutheran pastor (1524–29) and then superintendent in Gotha (1529–46). As Menius' colleague there, he was involved in the early planning of the *Doctrine and Secret of the Anabaptists*, though Menius seems to have completed the work on his own: see LW 59:265 n. 8 and Luther to Menius and Myconius, February 1530, WA Br 5:244. On Myconius, see the article by Robert Rosin, *OER* 3:117–18; Luther, preface to Myconius, *How Ordinary Folk Should Be Instructed in Christianity* (1539), LW 60:220–22, and the introduction by William R. Russell there.

[88] Cf. Sleidanus, *De statu religionis* (1558), book 10, p. 274.

[89] Luther, *Concerning Rebaptism* (1528), LW 40:225–62.

[90] Melanchthon, *De deliriis et furoribus anabaptistarum* (1535); *Propositiones wider die lehre der Wiedertäufer* (1535); *Wider das gotslesterliche und schentliche buch* (1535), in Stupperich, *Schriften von evangelischer Seite gegen die Täufer*, pp. 55–59, 59–62, 62–68. Also *Verlegung etlicher unchristlichen Artickel* (1535 or 1536), CR 3:28–34; StL 20:1706–22; *That Secular Authority Is Obligated to Defend against the Anabaptists with Physical Punishment* (1536), CR 3:195–201; WA 50:6–15. All of these were included in Witt Ger 2. On the Lutheran literary campaign against the Anabaptists, see John S. Oyer, *Lutheran Reformers against Anabaptists: Luther, Melanchthon and Menius and the Anabaptists of Central Germany* (The Hague: Nijhoff, 1964).

[91] For the "schoolboy devil" at Münster, see Luther, preface to *New Report on the Anabaptists at Münster* (1535), LW 60:94–95.

confirming the good and useful writings of other people with his forewords and testimonies,[92] and he warned everyone against their flittering bats and secret infiltrators,[93] who have still not all been cleared away.

|For though the devil is repeatedly put to shame and his murder and lies are revealed and he is driven out by the power of God's Word, he nonetheless returns, well-armed, with fellow [devils] even more crafty, and tries new strategies to see whether he can storm, conquer, and make his habitation in God's Church and purified hearts once again [cf. Luke 11:24–26].

That I might now warn my own little flock and our children, students, and descendants against the doctrine and sedition of the Anabaptists, I will briefly relate to you from the books of the Herr Doctor[94]—and of Melanchthon, Urbanus, Menius, and other good people[95]—what the abominable lies, heresy, and the murderous, rebellious, and disgraceful licentiousness of this crazed and bewitched people were.

Their chief article was that they despised the written Word, the holy Bible, and had very little place or none at all for Jesus Christ, the eternal Son of God.[96] For their confession, creed, and worship were directed only to the Father and His Spirit; about the Son of God they knew, maintained, and testified very little or nothing whatsoever. Now it is certain that whoever does not have the Son and denies His blood does not know or have the Father either [1 John 2:23], even if he constantly speaks about the Father and His mercy; likewise, Turks, Jews, and monks who reject the person and office of

---

[92] In addition to Luther's prefaces named with the works above (see above, pp. 384–85 nn. 84–87), see also Luther, preface to *New Report on the Anabaptists at Münster* (1535), LW 60:91–98.

[93] Cf. Luther, *Infiltrating and Clandestine Preachers* (1532), LW 40:379–94; cf. above, p. 381.

[94] In addition to *Concerning Rebaptism* and the prefaces to the works of other authors cited above (pp. 384–85 nn. 84–87, and n. 92 above), see also *Sermons on Holy Baptism* (1534), LW 57:139–89; cf. *Table Talk* no. 5232a–b (1540), WA TR 5:19–20.

[95] See above, pp. 384–85 nn. 84–87, and above n. 92.

[96] Melanchthon analyzed the root of the Münster Anabaptist heresy as a spiritualism that rejected the external Word: see *Verlegung etlicher unchristlichen Artikel*, StL 20:1710, 1723. Cf. Oyer, *Lutheran Reformers against Anabaptists*, pp. 225–30. The charge that the Münster Anabaptists had little place for Christ reflects Lutheran suspicion that the patently novel doctrine of the heavenly flesh of Christ (see below, p. 387 n. 98) concealed even more extensive Christological heresy (see Melanchthon, *De deliriis*, in Stupperich, *Schriften von evangelischer Seite gegen die Täufer*, p. 58) and that Anabaptist soteriology marginalized Christ as Savior with its emphasis on the holiness and good works required of believers (see below, p. 387 n. 100). Rothmann, *Bekenntnis*, in Stupperich, *Schriften Bernhard Rothmanns*, p. 198, rejects the charge that the Münster Anabaptists "give no heed to Christ [*halten von Christo nichts*]," but goes on to assert sharp differences with both Lutherans and Catholics in Christology and soteriology. Certainly the Münster Anabaptists claimed ongoing prophecy beyond the written Scriptures; Rothmann claimed that the hidden understanding of the Bible had been restored.

Christ are fundamentally ignorant of the one true God.[97] For whoever denies that Christ is the eternal, sole, only-begotten, substantial, self-subsisting Son of God also denies the one, eternal, and indivisible divine essence, which is God the Father, God the Son, God the Holy Spirit. Again, whoever denies the tender humanity of the substantial Word of God, refuses to concede that the worthy Virgin Mary is Jesus Christ's physical and true mother, and denies that Christ assumed real and natural flesh and blood, ʹwithout the help of a man, from the seed of Mary, also denies the person of Jesus Christ.[98] Likewise, all who lay hands on Christ, dividing His person or mingling His two natures, or who teach that the humanity of Christ has vanished into the divinity after His ascension or that it is now locked up and confined in some separate and circumscribed place.[99]

Those who propose their own worship and sacrifice and insist on saving themselves by their own holiness, cross, and obedience—as do the Jews and the false and fictitious christs [cf. Matt. 24:24]—also deny Jesus Christ, who redeemed and won us with His precious blood and single sacrifice.[100]

Now the Anabaptists are very careless in speaking about the divinity of Jesus Christ, even as they deny His humanity, as if it were not produced from the blood and seed of Mary and united with the divine nature, and they do not cry out to their Father in Christ's name and on the basis of His merit and intercession. Therefore, the devil caused the doctrine of the Jews, Turks,

---

[97] Cf. Luther, *Sermons on John 17* (1528/1530), LW 69:27.

[98] Rothmann taught that Christ did not derive his human nature from Mary but brought it from heaven. See Rothmann, *Bekenntnis*, in Stupperich, *Schriften Bernhard Rothmanns*, pp. 199–200; and Rothmann, *Restitution*, in Stupperich, *Schriften Bernhard Rothmanns*, pp. 226–30; cf. Williams, *Radical Reformation*, 3rd ed., p. 577. For the Lutheran response, see especially Rhegius, *Refutation*, in Stupperich, *Schriften von evangelischer Seite gegen die Täufer*, pp. 88–118, and Luther, preface to *New Report on the Anabaptists at Münster* (1535), LW 60:96.

[99] Cf. Luther, *Confession concerning Christ's Supper* (1528), LW 37:151–372, especially pp. 204–6, 209–15; FC SD VIII (Kolb-Wengert, pp. 616–34; *Concordia*, pp. 581–96).

[100] Rothmann condemned the Lutherans for emphasizing faith at the expense of works: see *Bekenntnis*, in Stupperich, *Schriften Bernhard Rothmanns*, pp. 200–202. Lutheran theologians accused the Münster Anabaptists of denying Christ's power to save and of falling into the heresy of Pelagianism: see Rhegius, *Refutation*, in Stupperich, *Schriften von evangelischer Seite gegen die Täufer*, pp. 117, 123–24.

Samosatenes,[101] monks, Servetans,[102] and many other fanatics and heretics to be stirred up again and set in motion by these new baptists.

Since no one had seen the Father in His splendor because no one was able to approach Him [John 1:18; 1 Tim. 6:16], the eternal Father therefore had His heart, counsel, and decree uttered and proclaimed to us through the eternal Mediator, Chancellor, and Interpreter, His substantial Word. The Holy Spirit heard and received this Word from the Son and had it written down and preached by duly called prophets and apostles. Christ testifies to all of this in the Supper and directs us to the testimony of the Holy Spirit [John 16–17]. The Anabaptists, however, reject the writings of the prophets and apostles, upon which Christendom is based and through which ¹the Spirit of God speaks.[103] Thus they reject the sublime office of the Holy Spirit together with the holy Gospel and rob Christendom of the greatest treasure that we possess on this earth.

If the leaders of the blind [Matt. 15:14] had any esteem for the spoken and written Word, which truly is God's Word (1 Thessalonians 2 [:13]) and the voice of Jesus Christ and the testimony and proclamation of the Holy Spirit, why do they only appeal to and cast themselves solely upon their dreams and concocted stories? Therefore, dear friends, beware of their deceptive dreams, visions, revelation, inspiration, and "refinement,"[104] with which they reject the Holy Spirit's speaking office along with the Word of grace and reconciliation, and through the inspiration of their own spirit they bite Christ's heel [Gen. 3:15] and public office of preaching[105] and insolently set themselves against the Holy Spirit.

Whoever denies or contradicts the Holy Spirit's Word and Scripture also denies the Holy Spirit, who testifies in the Scriptures about the person, blood, merit, and intercession of Jesus Christ. Whoever does not listen to the Holy Spirit and His testimony surely knows nothing of Christ's blood, wounds, eternal reconciliation, and His righteousness that is imputed to us. If anyone is not directed to Christ's wounds by the Holy Spirit through the Word, how can he see or recognize the Father's heart, love, fidelity, and sheer mercy?

---

[101] Paul of Samosata, bishop of Antioch (r. 260–268/272), held that the Word was the power of the Father (rather than a distinct person) that had descended upon the man Jesus at His Baptism. He was condemned as a heretic by other bishops and declared deposed in 268. See *ODCC*, 3rd ed., s.v. "Paul of Samosata." Cf. AC I 6 (Kolb-Wengert, pp. 36–37; *Concordia*, p. 31).

[102] The Spanish physician Michael Servetus (1511–53) openly rejected the doctrine of the Trinity beginning with his *De Trinitatis erroribus* of 1531 and was executed as a heretic in Calvin's Geneva. See Jerome Friedman, "Servetus, Michael," *OER* 4:48–49.

[103] See above, p. 104 n. 10.

[104] *entgröbung*; literally, "decoarsening." See above, Mathesius, *History*, p. 222.

[105] Cf. above, p. 370.

The invisible and hidden God, who has been unknown and hidden to the whole world [cf. Isa. 45:15], sends His substantial Son out of His own bosom and heart, clothes Him with the holy flesh and blood of the Virgin, and allows His heart to be opened on the cross, so that in these wounds we might see and recognize the Father. He also places His Word and counsel in the mouth of His dear Son, from ⌐whom the Holy Spirit receives it, so that from these two true and divine witnesses we might receive the certain news that the only God is our dear Father, through pure grace, and we are His beloved adopted or elected children, and that together with His only Son, our dear fellow heir, we, too, have become heirs of all heavenly treasures and riches [Eph. 1:3–14].

Now, since the Anabaptists set Christ's blood and wounds out of sight, and plug their ears against the preached testimony and confirmed Scriptures of the Holy Spirit, and do not let themselves be directed to the open wounds of God's Son by the Word of the prophets and apostles, how can they possibly call the invisible God their God and Father?

Again, since the wicked, diabolical serpents have no regard for the wounds of Jesus Christ and cast the heavenly testimony of the Holy Spirit to the wind, what can they possibly have to say with any certainty and constancy about the article of justification or about any particle of comfort and certain joy?

If anyone does not believe that the Father has made His Son to be wisdom, righteousness, holiness, and redemption for us through pure grace [1 Cor. 1:30], and that we wretched, great sinners become reconciled and acceptable to God and become His children and heirs through this one Mediator's alien, imputed righteousness and obedience [Rom. 8:14–16], how can he comfort and encourage a troubled heart and contrite spirit so that it can stand and endure against sin, a bad conscience, God's Law, death, the devil, and all the gates of hell?

As the Anabaptists rob us of Christ's blood and His Spirit's Word, so also they contest and condemn Christ's institution and ordinance, for He instituted the holy Sacraments for us as seals of righteousness [Rom. 4:11], which ⌐assure us and attest that we become children and heirs of God through pure grace.

For as the Holy Spirit assures us of this and confirms it through the written and spoken Word of the prophets and apostles, so also the water alongside the Absolution and the flesh and blood in the Supper alongside the gracious promise in the Word provide a sure testimony, living power, and mighty comfort that the blood of Jesus Christ was shed on the cross for every single person, because in holy Baptism we are sprinkled with it, and thus are blessed with the gifts of the Holy Spirit and born again from above as children of God.

The holy Absolution, in which Christ causes everyone who is truly penitent to be sprinkled individually with the power of His blood, is utterly and entirely rejected by the Anabaptists in their diabolical assemblies. For they do not retain any kind of confession, private correction, recollection or acknowledgment of sins, even as in a particular case they do not seek individual counsel or consolation according to the command and institution of the Lord. These stiff-necked people go their way without acknowledging their sins and consider themselves righteous and holy because some of them preserve outward decency and pass themselves off as true penitents in their gray garments.[106]

As for what they think of the holy Supper, however, you can tell that they are one with the Sacramentarians in this article and distribute their bread and wine with horribly great disorder, speaking of it not only unworthily but also blasphemously.[107] Here, in the presence of innocent ears, I cannot repeat the horrible blasphemy that one of these Münster prophets used in their diabolical congregation when the bread fell from his hand to the ground.[108]

Among these people, one can discern sheer diabolical lies and 'heresy against the Holy Trinity, the entire office of preaching and the public call and ordination, and the venerable Sacraments. Likewise, their idol's murder [cf. John 8:44] and impurity can be seen clearly in Anabaptists in Münster and in others. They do not hold any catechism, and so they do not publicly rebuke any sin from the Ten Commandments; they teach no truly good work, aside from prohibiting personal possessions and the wearing of velvet and silk. In addition to this, they slander and defame the authorities instituted by God [Rom. 13:1] and set themselves up as those whom God has ordained to wipe out all the godless on earth and to establish their own spiritual kingdom before the Last Day; they take up arms themselves, stir up rebellion, commit mayhem and murder, tear apart the holy estate of marriage, and each takes as many wives as he wants,[109] like real Mohammedans. They take and rob everyone's property, acknowledge no law or court, and dispense promises and punishments in all matters according to the inspiration

---

[106] The Anabaptists indeed generally rejected private confession and absolution, but usually placed great emphasis on public discipline in their communities. See Williams, *Radical Reformation*, 3rd ed., pp. 621–23, and Luther's association of Enthusiasm with the rejection of Absolution in *Smalcald Articles* (1537) III III VIII (Kolb-Wengert, pp. 321–23; *Concordia*, pp. 279–81); cf. FC SD XII, especially 14, 20, 31, 32, 34 (Kolb-Wengert, pp. 657–59; *Concordia*, pp. 616–17).

[107] See Luther, preface to Menius, *On the Spirit of the Anabaptists* (1544), LW 60:334. Cf. Rothmann, *Restitution*, ch. 13, in Stupperich, *Die Schriften Bernhard Rothmanns*, pp. 256–68.

[108] According to Dorp, *Warhafftige historia*, in Stupperich, *Schriften von evangelischer Seite gegen die Täufer*, p. 232, Rothmann once took a piece of the eucharistic bread, broke it, threw it to the ground, and said, "Look, where is the flesh and blood here? If that were God, He would surely pick Himself up off the ground and put Himself back on the altar. Therefore, you should be certain that neither the body nor the blood of Christ is in the Sacrament." Cf. Williams, *Radical Reformation*, 3rd ed., p. 559.

[109] See above, p. 383 n. 79.

of their spirit.[110] They have given sufficient proof of their Christian conduct and of the work of their spirit in Münster, concerning which true accounts have been issued in print by credible people, as an eternal testimony and reminder of their diabolical wantonness.[111]

I mention all of this here in the history of Doctor Luther for the sake of our children and posterity, in case the devil, who is not given to resting, would eventually begin to stir again in his instruments, in order that we may steadfastly endure in the simple teaching of the holy Gospel and not forget the writings and testimony against this devil's sect from the German prophet and from other good people who have recorded their godless and infernal doctrine and behavior.

For many people, the Anabaptists' name has become obnoxious. But their heresy, lies, murder, and rebellion still have not been put to rest among all of those who indeed also take the name "Evangelical." ¹Christ and His blood are already being challenged among many people, because some of them teach that this precious and unique sacrifice is only a beginning and preparation for true righteousness.[112] Many fanatics, indeed, are opposing the preaching office as well as the spoken and written Word of God. They want to direct us, according to the teaching of the Anabaptists, to their spirit and its hidden and internal inspiration, apart from and contrary to the Word.[113] The Council [of Trent] likewise sought to make the holy Bible unreliable and shaky, so that we would attend solely to their decisions and explanations.[114]

---

[110] The doctrinal positions enumerated here, particularly Trinitarian heresy, were embraced by some but by no means all Anabaptists. See above, Mathesius, *History*, p. 246 and n. 87 there; cf. Menius, *Doctrine and Secret of the Anabaptists* (1530), and Luther's preface, LW 59:263–71; FC SD XII (Kolb-Wengert, pp. 657–59; *Concordia*, pp. 616–17). For Rothmann's critique of Trinitarian doctrine on behalf of the Münster Anabaptists, see *Von Verborgenheit der Schrift*, in Stupperich, *Schriften Bernhard Rothmans*, p. 330.

[111] See above, pp. 384–86.

[112] Mathesius likely has in mind several of the heresies that arose among Evangelicals after Luther's death: Andreas Osiander's teaching that justifying righteousness consisted not in Christ's sacrifice on the cross but in the indwelling of His divine nature and the infusion of virtues (see FC SD III 62–63 [Kolb-Wengert, p. 573; *Concordia*, p. 545]); the Synergist teaching that the human will was a necessary cause of conversion and not only the Holy Spirit and the Word as His instrument (see FC SD II 77–90 [Kolb-Wengert, pp. 559–62; *Concordia*, pp. 533–36]); and the similar Anabaptist teaching that Christian righteousness had to be completed with new obedience (see FC SD XII 10 [Kolb-Wengert, p. 657; *Concordia*, p. 617]).

[113] See *Smalcald Articles* (1537) III VIII 3–13 (Kolb-Wengert, pp. 322–23; *Concordia*, pp. 280–81).

[114] See the Council of Trent, session 4, "Decree on the Canonical Scriptures" (Denzinger, no. 783), which declares that unwritten traditions are to be received with the same reverence as the Scriptures.

Many worldly people, even in those places where the Gospel is being preached, no longer want to tolerate the useful [practice of] confession and individual absolution because it has a papistic appearance, even as some preachers do not include the Absolution among the parts which are necessary and useful for catechesis.[115] As for the ways in which the mendacious devil is attacking the Lord's Supper under the pretext of the Gospel and of the greatest hostility against the papacy, wanting to defend his seditious doctrine in the Anabaptist fashion, with sword and musket—that daily experience shows, and much abominable bloodshed.[116]

Therefore, though the ancient devil is clothing himself with new and more subtle names and cloaking himself with spiritual zeal, the Anabaptists' lies, murder, and impurity can be clearly seen. And if many groups had a fortified Münster and a strong following, we would soon find out whether the Anabaptists' spirit is totally dead or has arisen from the iron cage.[117] Therefore, it will surely be most necessary that we warn our children diligently against these serpents and their murderous spirit.

The world is weary of the pure doctrine. Some preachers and rulers— and even parents with their children—speak quite scornfully about religion, the ministers of the Church, and their authorities. The devil keeps slipping in bad books along with the others, and we hear many evil examples of how certain people in churches and schools have stirred up strife and contention with others. Therefore, we must surely beware and take heed, lest the devil suddenly set a game in motion[118] on account of which church, school, government, all discipline, and honorable domestic decency may go to wrack and ruin.

Our dear prophet and doctor faithfully pursued his course for thirty years with teaching, comfort, and admonition for everyone. In the eighteen years since his death,[119] other good people have also admonished us to remain steadfast in the catechism in simplicity, and to persevere simply and sincerely in the attested Augsburg Confession,[120] and in true faith and a good conscience, without any new digging around or useless disputation. But the one who refuses to be admonished—that is, the tender world—nonetheless

---

[115] On different enumerations of the parts of the catechism, see above, p. 252 n. 127.

[116] On the efforts of certain Protestant rulers to introduce a Calvinist version of reform (particularly in the doctrine of the Lord's Supper but also in abolishing private absolution), making use of the power of the state, see above, Mathesius, *History*, p. 355.

[117] See above, p. 384.

[118] Cf. Wander 4:703, "Spiel" no. 222.

[119] I.e., from February 1546 to the fall of 1563, almost eighteen years.

[120] On the difference between the original text of the Augsburg Confession and the so-called *Variata*, see the introduction above, p. lxxxv, and above, p. 332 n. 70.

seeks to excuse herself with the Gospel and to conceal the wantonness of her heart. Nevertheless, one who heeds advice will see his house stand longest,[121] but one who will not heed counsel, and who will neither listen nor be persuaded, cannot be helped.[122] Our God preserves His little flock in humility and simplicity in the refined doctrine, pure as gold [cf. Ps. 12:6], which He had reformed and purified for us by our doctor, and correctly and fittingly summarized for us by Herr Melanchthon, and confessed for us by the precious people at Augsburg[123] and Smalcald.[124]

If anyone casts a faithful admonition to the wind and mocks God's messengers, as those from Judah and Israel did when Jeremiah and others preached to them about the first destruction of Jerusalem [Mic. 3:12; Jer. 5:1–14; cf. Dan. 9:2], let him also wait for the Lord's wrath: either the Turk or general devastation and the Last Day. At least then good counsel and faithful admonition will finally be praised, when the godless are clasping their hands over their heads and will utter an eternal cry of woe and gnashing of teeth, with the worm that does not die and the fire that is not quenched [cf. Matt. 13:42, 50; Mark 9:44, 46, 48] for all eternity among all the devils, heretics, rebels, and unchaste people.

With this we now conclude the years 1534 and 1535 in the history of our doctor. O Lord Jesus, the eternal Protector and Shield of Your poor Christendom, help and protect us in these lands from the Anabaptists[125] and all the lies and sedition of their confederates, and from all who oppose Your holy Bible and the precious office of preaching along with Your Sacraments, who want to tear the Word of the blessed truth out of our mouths and hearts or who maliciously and craftily seek to muddle, misconstrue, and distort it. For You alone are able to trample the devil's head [Gen. 3:15], and to protect us from his heresy and his murderous and filthy works and practices, and to preserve us in the simplicity of Your true Word and Holy Spirit. May You be highly exalted, with Your Father and Holy Spirit, forever and ever! Amen!

---

[121] *Dennoch wird warners hauß am lengsten bestehen.* See Wander 4:1787, "Warner" no. 2.

[122] Cf. Wander 3:1481, "Rath" no. 348. Mathesius here gives the proverb in negative form.

[123] See above, Mathesius, *History*, pp. 320–67.

[124] See below, Mathesius, *History*, pp. 396–402.

[125] Mathesius' *Chronica* records a public mandate against Anabaptists by the Counts Schlick in 1532 (erroneously entered under 1531) and the expulsion of an Anabaptist from Joachimsthal in 1535: see *Sarepta*, fols. Ll4v, Ll5v; Luther to Counts Hieronymus and Lorenz Schlick, October 9, 1532, WA Br 6:372–73, and above, Mathesius, *History*, p. 209.

The Eleventh Sermon,
on the Years 1536 to 1540
in the History of the Herr Doctor

[Fall 1563][1]

BELOVED friends in the Lord! Psalm 112 [:6] says, "The righteous shall never be forgotten." Now, you know that all those are righteous who trust in Jesus Christ, the only righteous one, or those to whom the true righteousness of the Son of God has been imputed by grace through faith and who praise and proclaim this gracious and freely given righteousness in the congregation of the righteous and believers [Ps. 1:5; 89:5; 111:1; 149:1], and through their confession help others to be saved.

Now, since our doctor was justified in his heart through his own faith in the crucified Lord Christ and confessed his heartfelt confidence and hope in the blood and wounds of Christ throughout the course of his life with great boldness and power, both in writing and in speaking, and remained steadfast in this confession until his end, it is fitting that we should laud him, in truth, as a righteous and blessed preacher of the righteousness of Jesus Christ. We do rightly not to forget his faith and steadfast confession here in this laudable church, so that we may praise our God for this blessed instrument and preacher of His gracious righteousness and point our people and descendants to this doctor's righteous witness, exposition [of Scripture], and Christian example.

Therefore, we intend, in God's name, to continue with his history and speak to you about what he taught, wrote, and did, to the glory of God and His Gospel, from the year 1536 to the year 1540. May the Lord Christ grant us His grace and Holy Spirit thereto! Amen.

Now when the teaching and the murderous character of the Anabaptists had been revealed in Münster and had been suppressed by means of writings and secular punishment, and Zwingli, Oecolampadius, and others had been

---

[1] On the dating of this sermon, see above, p. 368 n. 2; and the introduction above, p. lxxxvii.

taken away in a terrible end,[2] many good people in the churches of upper Germany discerned God's judgment on those who had wantonly attacked the Lord's Supper and holy Baptism. Herr Martin Bucer,[3] among other teachers, stepped forward and sought to find ways to resolve the issues in contention concerning the Supper and to bring the erring back onto the right path. Then a colloquy was arranged in Strassburg,[4] where, along with Herr Capito,[5] many learned people and delegates from some cantons[6] in Switzerland attended and dispatched Herr Bucer and Lycosthenes[7] to Wittenberg.[8]

After the delegates had given the confession of their own preachers and others a public airing—Bucer even preached a public sermon in Wittenberg on this subject—the scholars in Wittenberg were satisfied with this confession, because it was in conformity and accordance with the institution and words of Christ and it acknowledged, with a clear explanation, the presence of the blood and flesh of Jesus Christ in the distribution of the bread and wine. Therefore, this was set down on paper with the knowledge and consent of both parties and accepted at that time by the theologians

---

[2] See Mathesius, *History*, above, pp. 244–45, 382–91 (on the Münster Anabaptists in 1534–35), 261 n. 174, 314–15; and below, pp. 515, 546, 563 (on the 1531 deaths of Zwingli and Oecolampadius).

[3] On Bucer, see above, pp. 171–72 n. 32. On the negotiations that led to the Wittenberg Concord, see above, Mathesius, *History*, pp. 243–44 and n. 72 there, pp. 353–56.

[4] Mathesius seems to conflate two meetings with which Bucer was involved before the Wittenberg Concord. On June 3–14, 1533, a synod was held in Strassburg in response to the spread of Anabaptist preaching there, for which Bucer composed sixteen doctrinal articles (Stupperich, *Buceri Opera Omnia: Deutsche Schriften*, 5:388–92). On April 13, 1534, the Strassburg council issued a decree requiring all Anabaptists to agree to Bucer's sixteen articles or leave the city. On February 1, 1536, representatives of the Reformed churches in the Swiss cantons met in Basel along with Bucer and Wolfgang Capito, producing the First Helvetic Confession: see Philip Schaff, *The Creeds of Christendom* (New York: Harper, 1919), 3:211–31. See Greschat, *Bucer*, pp. 121–23, 135–36.

[5] Wolfgang Capito was a humanist and theologian who became a prominent reformer alongside Martin Bucer in the city of Strassburg. He supported Luther but remained flexible on the question of the Lord's Supper and in his relationship to Anabaptist and Spiritualist leaders. See James M. Kittelson, "Capito, Wolfgang," *OER* 1:259–60.

[6] *orten*

[7] Bonifacius Wolfhart, called Lycosthenes, was a preacher in Augsburg. See Heinz-Peter Mielke, "Wolfhart, Bonifatius (Lycosthenes)," *BBKL* 29:1575.

[8] The colloquy in Wittenberg leading to the agreement known as the Wittenberg Concord took place May 22–29, 1536. See Brecht 3:39–59; Sasse, *This Is My Body*, pp. 244–52; James M. Kittelson and Ken Schurb, "The Curious Histories of the Wittenberg Concord," *CTQ* 50, no. 2 (1986): 119–37; Edwards, *Luther and the False Brethren*, pp. 127–55. Cf. above, Mathesius, *History*, pp. 243–44, 353–56; Volz, *Die Lutherpredigten des Johannes Mathesius*, pp. 238, 252. On Mathesius' sixteenth-century sources for the history of the Wittenberg Concord, see Volz, *Die Lutherpredigten des Johannes Mathesius*, p. 257.

in Wittenberg; it was also signed by our Dr. Luther, Dr. Caspar Cruciger, Dr. Johann [Bugenhagen] of Pomerania, and Herr Philip Melanchthon with their own hands, even as Herr Martin Bucer confirmed this concordat and his confession with his own hand, and later many others approved and accepted it with their signatures.[9] |For what is true and right according to God's Word remains true, and those who are truthful and upright approve of it, even though troublemaking and presumptuous people are always eager to defile the truth and put forward something new.

Dr. Luther remained steadfast and firm in his own confession. With regard to this article, for example, he once had all the theologians and ministers of the church in Wittenberg summoned to him in his illness; he testified and confessed boldly and in full knowledge that he could not deviate in any way from the simplicity of the clear words of Jesus Christ in the Supper, but intended to stand fast and persevere in them, even if people were to make and establish a different, dangerous agreement behind his back or if they were to make up a different story about him at some future time.[10]

Now, Dr. Luther had, in the presence of Cajetan,[11] appealed to a council for protection, just as he had also offered at Worms in 1521 to submit his doctrine for judgment to a Christian council in which God's Word would be the judge.[12] In 1530, it had finally been worked out that the religious question should be discussed by a free and general Christian council, and Emperor Charles gave the protesting estates assurance of this in the following year.[13]

---

[9] For the text of the Wittenberg Concord, see WA Br 12:206–11; MBW T7:131–48 (CR 3:75–81), quoted (in part) in FC SD VII 12–16 (Kolb-Wengert, pp. 595–96; Concordia, pp. 564–65). On the efforts by Bucer and Luther to secure official public acceptance of the concord in the south German cities and (unsuccessfully) in Switzerland, see Brecht 3:51–59; cf. WA Br 12:203.

[10] The date of this episode, for which Mathesius appears to be the principal source, is uncertain. The sentiments here were reflected in Luther's 1544 Brief Confession, LW 38:279–320. In the context of Mathesius' preaching in the 1560s, the anecdote serves to counter rumors spread in places such as Heidelberg that were undertaking a "second Reformation" in the direction of Calvinism (see above, Mathesius, History, pp. 317, 355, 392) to the effect that Luther had come by the end of his life to regret his teaching on the Lord's Supper and privately advised his associates to moderate it after his death—the so-called Heidelberger Landlüge. See Mörlin, Wider die Landlügen der Heidelbergischen Theologen; FC SD VII 28–33 (Kolb-Wengert, pp. 597–98; Concordia, pp. 566–68).

[11] See above, Mathesius, History, pp. 150–51.

[12] See Brecht 1:468–69; cf. above, Mathesius, History, pp. 176–77.

[13] The recess of the 1530 Diet of Augsburg, though it rejected the Augsburg Confession and threatened the Protestant estates with punishment if they did not conform within a year's time, concluded with the emperor's promise to secure the convocation of a "free, general Christian council" (Kidd, Documents Illustrative of the Continental Reformation, p. 300; cf. the introduction by Franklin Sherman, LW 47:5; the introduction by Lewis W. Spitz, LW 34:65). Further assurances about the emperor's advocacy for a council were given to the Protestant estates in late

Over time, he was tireless in constantly urging the pope and other rulers that this plan should be moved forward, and Pope Paul III finally consented and undertook to hold a council in Mantua.[14] At this development, a great deal of discussion took place in the German Empire as to whether they should attend [a council held] at suspect locations in Italy, which was not in keeping with the previous assurances and resolutions.[15] Accordingly, the protesting estates held a large conference in Smalcald, and because they were primarily going to deliberate about the council, the electors, princes, lords, and cities adhering to the Augsburg 'Confession brought with them their most renowned scholars.[16] Thus Doctor Martin also personally attended this conference for the last time, as you shall hear.[17]

As for the secular business dealt with there[18]—concerning the Chamber Court,[19] ecclesiastical fiefs,[20] and the members who had joined the league of

---

1531 in the course of Charles' negotiations for support for the election of his brother Ferdinand as king of the Romans. See Luther to Elector John, ca. February 12, 1532, LW 50:41–47.

[14] See above, Mathesius, *History*, p. 356.

[15] The resolutions (recesses) of imperial diets since the Diet of Nürnberg in 1522–23 had regularly called for a free Christian council to be held on German soil. See above, Mathesius, *History*, p. 212. On the Catholic plans for a council and the Smalcald Assembly, see Brecht 3:173–93.

[16] The conference in Smalcald was summoned for February 7, 1537, and met from February 9 to February 28. In addition to Luther, Melanchthon, and Bugenhagen from Wittenberg—joined along the way by Georg Spalatin (see above, p. 136 n. 121) after Justus Jonas (see the introduction above, p. xxx) had to turn back—the conference was attended by the Nürnberg reformers Andreas Osiander (see above, p. 311 n. 170) and Veit Dietrich (see above, p. 278 n. 76), Johann Brenz from Schwäbisch Hall (see above, p. 311 n. 169), Nicolaus von Amsdorf from Magdeburg (see above, p. 30 n. 15), Urbanus Rhegius from Lüneburg (see above, p. 357 n. 203), Johann Lang from Erfurt, Johannes Aepinus (1499–1553) from Hamburg, Erhard Schnepf (1495–1558) from Württemberg, Martin Bucer from Strassburg, and Ambrosius Blaurer (1492–1564) from Constance. See Brecht 3:183 and the signatures to the *Smalcald Articles* and the *Treatise on the Power and Primacy of the Pope* (Kolb-Wengert, pp. 326–28, 344; *Concordia*, pp. 284–85, 306).

[17] That is to say, the conference at Smalcald was the last public religious consultation in which Luther took part. On the later colloquies, attended by other members of the Wittenberg faculty, see below, p. 422 n. 177.

[18] See Sleidanus, *De statu religionis* (1558), book 11, pp. 296–320, where the secular business is discussed; cf. Brandi, *Emperor Charles V*, pp. 396–405.

[19] The Imperial Chamber Court functioned as the court of final appeal for cases under imperial law: see *HRED*, pp. 232–34. Under the 1532 Peace of Nürnberg, the emperor had agreed that it would have no jurisdiction over religious controversies; however, the application of this principle to cases of partly religious nature was controverted. See Thomas A. Brady Jr., *Protestant Politics: Jacob Sturm (1489–1553) and the German Reformation* (Atlantic Highlands, NJ: Humanities Press, 1995), pp. 162–69.

[20] I.e., the question of the legal status of feudal holdings belonging to bishoprics or abbeys that had been converted to the Evangelical faith.

the protesting estates after the Nürnberg pact,[21] as well as the emperor's war against the French[22]—none of that pertained to the theologians.

About the Augsburg Confession and the council, and what should be discussed there, they engaged in urgent and helpful discussions, as well as about how the ecclesiastical property in the territories of the protesting lands and cities could and should be employed for pious purposes[23] and be used to make provision for churches and schools and for the support of aged and infirm ministers of the Church and their legitimate wives and children.[24] In religious matters, much good was accomplished and set in order at this conference. For after the Evangelical preachers had expressed themselves publicly and in one accord from the pulpit at this conference,[25] and all had subscribed and confirmed the Confession submitted to the emperor in Augsburg, as can be seen in the [published] volume,[26] then they also set forth very fine and sound counsels regarding what was necessary for a council to be Christian and free and why one should not attend the council convoked by the pope and scheduled to be held in perilous locations in Italy with suspect and biased judges and counselors, contrary to the prior resolutions and assurances.[27]

---

[21] The 1532 Peace of Nürnberg (the so-called "Nürnberg Standstill": see above, p. 347 n. 145) had listed the Protestant estates included in the peace by name; therefore, the question arose concerning its application to those who subsequently joined the Smalcaldic League. On the expansion of the league during the 1530s, see Brady, *Protestant Politics*, pp. 143–44.

[22] Although the Smalcaldic League had intermittently sought and sometimes received the support of the French king against the emperor, its members agreed at Smalcald to suspend such negotiations and to support Charles in his war against France: see Brandi, *Emperor Charles V*, pp. 398, 400–401; Brady, *Protestant Politics*, pp. 155–61.

[23] *ad pios usus*

[24] I.e., the question of how the property and income of churches now under Evangelical control should be used: see below, Mathesius, *History*, pp. 401–2; Brady, *Protestant Politics*, pp. 170–74; and the petition of the assembled preachers to the princes at Smalcald, February 24, 1537, CR 3:288–90.

[25] Luther himself preached in Smalcald on February 9, 11, and 18: see LW 57:242–76; cf. below, Mathesius, *History*, p. 484. According to Luther's report, Spalatin preached on February 8 (Luther to Jonas, February 9, 1537, WA Br 8:40). Not all preaching was harmonious, however: see Brecht 3:184; *Table Talk* no. 5047 (1540), LW 54:382–84.

[26] I.e., in Wit Ger 12 (1559), fols. 289r–290r, in a report by Johann Brenz appended to the German translation of the *Treatise on the Power and Primacy of the Pope*. See Melanchthon, Tr (Kolb-Wengert, pp. 343–44; *Concordia*, pp. 305–6) Cf. CR 3:286–87. At Augsburg, the Confession had been signed by princes and the representatives of the cities (see above, p. 336 n. 88); now, at Smalcald, the theologians were asked to subscribe in their own names.

[27] Although the other theologians indeed came to the consensus sought by the princes—that the papal invitation to the council should be rejected on good grounds—Luther himself advised that the Evangelicals should not refuse outright. See *Luthers Bedenken über die Beschickung des Konzils*, February 8 or 9, 1537, WA Br 8:35–38; Brecht 3:183–84.

Dr. Martin also set down on paper some articles[28] which ought properly to be discussed according to God's Word at the council; and in the year following, many good opinions and writings of all sorts were issued against the so-called and deceitful councils.[29] Finally, in 1539, Dr. Martin published his excellent book *On the Councils and the Church,* |in which he very correctly and credibly summarized the whole matter on the basis of Scripture and trustworthy histories.[30]

[He showed] that a council does not have authority to make new articles of faith contrary to God's Word or to establish any idolatry or false worship; rather, [a council] is when pious people are gathered in an orderly way in the Holy Spirit, like the apostles in Jerusalem, or when pious bishops are called together by the Christian authorities, as at the Council of Nicaea, which Emperor Constantine convoked and personally attended. Only such a Christian assembly of clergy and prudent laymen had the authority, according to Christ's Word, to judge false doctrines and to condemn them, as well as to attest and confirm Christian articles [of faith] with God's Word on the basis of the prophetic and apostolic Scriptures, as happened in Jerusalem and Nicaea, when the apostles concluded on the basis of God's Word that no one should burden the Gentiles with the Levitical law, ceremonies, and circumcision [Acts 15:6–29], and, again, that a person becomes righteous and pleasing in God's sight only through faith in Jesus Christ, without any performance of or merit from the Law. Likewise, in Nicaea, the heresy of Arius, which denied that Jesus Christ is God's substantial and natural Son, was condemned based on the Scriptures;[31] at the same time, it was attested that Jesus Christ is the only-begotten and true Son of God, God of God, Light of Light, one substance with His Father, yet in His own person and hypostasis,[32] as the Nicene Creed expresses it, in accordance with Scripture.[33]

For Church and council are called by God's Word and born to be God's Bride, and the Holy Spirit is and remains with the Scriptures of the prophets and apostles, reminding us and testifying to us from the Word

---

[28] I.e., the *Smalcald Articles* (1537) (Kolb-Wengert, pp. 295–328; *Concordia*, pp. 253–85). See also Brecht 3:178–85 and above, Mathesius, *History*, p. 398. The *Smalcald Articles* were subscribed individually by most of the theologians at Smalcald, but not officially adopted by the league (see above, p. 397 n. 16).

[29] For Mathesius' catalog of writings from 1537 to 1539 against the councils, see below, *History*, pp. 408–9.

[30] *On the Councils and the Church* (1539), LW 41:3–178. See Brecht 3:193–98.

[31] Cf. above, p. 109 n. 27.

[32] *in einer eignen person und selbstendigkeyt*

[33] See the Nicene Creed (Kolb-Wengert, pp. 22–23; *Concordia*, p. 16).

[cf. John 14:26], which is the only impartial judge over all disputed articles in the Christian religion, even as Christendom is the sole and sure expositor, the real and true grammarian and interpreter of the divine Scriptures.

However, the anti-Christian sect, the Roman Babylon, has exalted itself above God and His written Word, has changed much of what God has instituted and ordained, has set up abominable idolatry, which it still justifies and defends with falsehood, blood, sword, and fire. But in these articles, all this has been indicted with clear and solid Scripture and finally convicted, so that the whole world recognizes their foolishness—as well as on the basis of their own abominations and books. Therefore, it is impossible for this anti-Christian sect to summon and hold a Christian council, much less to judge God's Word or to bear witness to Christian doctrine, because the Romanists have been indicted by the true and apostolic Church with the prophetic and apostolic Scriptures, and their manifest heresies and false worship have been convicted. Moreover, these Italian and papal councils are not in accordance with the resolutions of the emperor and the empire, which assure the German nation of a free, general, Christian council, to which also Dr. Luther and the protesting estates have always made their appeal.

Dr. Luther discusses these and similar principles and arguments in his book *On the Councils*, and all the proposals upon which the adherents of the Augsburg Confession have taken their stand down to the present hour appeal to them, and therefore—with God, a good conscience, and invincible truth—they have been unable to participate in the so-called, worthless councils or to accept their perilous and uncertain resolutions and decrees.

Noble Christendom must have a better and firmer foundation than a Roman council if it is to withstand all the gates of hell [Matt. 16:18] and to pass through the terrors of death and hell with peace and joy and enter into eternal life. That is why God did not found His Church and her faith on an earthly head or a throng of bishops, who themselves show little regard for Christ and Saints Peter and Paul, but instead upon His Son, the true Rock [Matt. 16:18], and on the Scriptures of the prophets and apostles, upon which the Church of God and the true faith are founded and fortified (Ephesians 2 [:19–21]).

Ah, God! The whole world understands and perceives what the corrupt, hypocritical, and wicked principles and the uncertain religion of the Romanists really are, and how they have deceived and hoodwinked everyone, even the great rulers, by means of their councils. That is why they themselves constantly delayed and postponed councils that had been scheduled. For example, Paul III wanted to move the council set for Mantua and to hold it in Vicenza after All Saints'.[34] When this news reached our doctor, he politely said, "I have long thought so privately that before All Saints' Day[35] there would be no true council, because Christ Himself must be present."[36]

I mention this in connection with the conference in Smalcald, at which the Evangelical preachers unanimously received and subscribed the Augsburg Confession, engaging in much salutary consultation and formulating articles which the adherents of the Confession had to maintain in religious matters, in a Christian manner and with a good conscience, for the protection and confirmation of the truth. It is on the basis of these principles that they have recused themselves and refused to this day (praise God!) to attend all illegitimate, suspicious, and partisan assemblies and sectarian gatherings organized by consecrated Roman cardinals, bishops, abbots, and prelates.

At this time they also deliberated in a Christian manner regarding the ordinances for maintaining schools and churches, ʲand these were duly put into effect by many good-hearted rulers.[37] Although it was impossible to turn all the false ecclesiastical property[38] to pious use[39] for the benefit of God and His Church, it nevertheless holds true that the property of priests is plunder,[40] and this mammon of iniquity, laden with idolatry and false worship, is difficult to put to proper use, in order to make friends everywhere with it [cf. Luke 16:9], by providing for Christian schools, parishes, churches, and poor people. The secular [authorities], who are supposed to serve the Church with counsel and protection, are reluctant to guard the holy sepulcher for nothing,[41] and this sweet bread of Christ is quite tasty to

---

[34] Pope Paul III first (on April 20, 1537) delayed the announced council until November 1 without setting a place; on October 8, he announced its relocation to Vicenza and another delay, to May 1, 1538. The opening of the council was then repeatedly delayed until it was finally begun in Trent in December 1545. See Hubert Jedin, *A History of the Council of Trent*, trans. Ernest Graf (London: Thomas Nelson & Sons, 1957), 1:288–354. Cf. Sleidanus, *De statu religionis* (1558), book 11, p. 320; book 12, p. 329.

[35] I.e., the last judgment.

[36] See *Table Talk* no. 6993 (n.d), WA TR 6:310; nos. 6993, 6993a, WA 48:679.

[37] See Sleidanus, *De statu religionis* (1558), book 11, p. 314.

[38] *ungeistliche güter*

[39] *ad pios usus*

[40] *Pfaffen gut raffen gut ist.* See Wander 3:1240, "Pfaffengut" nos. 7 and 9; Luther, *Table Talk* no. 4978 (1540), WA TR 4:597. Cf. below, Mathesius, *History*, p. 498.

[41] Wander 2:177, "Grab" no. 7. Cf. Matt. 27:64.

many of the courtiers. May God repay it to them and to their children, as the saying goes.[42]

Poor churches and schools should thank God that Christ still has a little chamber [cf. 2 Kings 4:10] for the present time and that His servants are being supported frugally and thriftily. If anyone serves the heavenly and spiritual Lord, let him be satisfied with true spiritual goods, with which the soul is fed, and look forward to the heavenly crown and eternal life [cf. Rev. 2:10]. If anyone serves the world, the world rewards him,[43] or he takes what he can while he can.[44] But the little coal still clinging to the sacrificial roast set fire to the eagle's nest.[45] It is also rare for monastic estates to bring much fortune or blessing to the family line; some lands have yielded strong evidence of this, as the parish property of empty churches reverts to the collators,[46] and yet at the same time children remain unbaptized and the elderly die without the Sacrament and without consolation.

At the conference, our doctor was overwhelmed by a serious illness, as his age began to burden him, and he was severely tormented by the stone, so that he was blocked for eleven days in a row.[47] Because of this, he himself and many other good people utterly despaired of him. When the illness gained the upper hand, he asked to be taken from Smalcald. ˈThen he commended himself to the prayer of the Church and made his brief and Christian confession: that he would abide with the Lord Christ and His Word, and knows of no other righteousness in his heart but the precious blood of Jesus Christ, which cleanses him and all who believe this from all sins through pure grace, just as his books and the Augsburg Confession openly confess. He also prepared his last will and testament there on the wagon;[48] to his preacher

---

[42] Mathesius is likely alluding to proverbial sayings to the effect that ill-gotten gains will not be passed down as far as the third generation of heirs: see, e.g., Wander 2:198, "Gut (Subst.)" no. 291.

[43] Wander 5:177, "Welt" no. 499.

[44] *er schneidet jm selber ein riemen, weyl jm die haut eingereumpt*; literally, "he cuts himself a belt while the leather allows." Cf. Wander 2:1872, "Leder," nos. 3, 5, and 17.

[45] See above, Mathesius, *History*, pp. 271–72.

[46] I.e., the patrons who have the right to nominate clergy to the post but fail to do so in order to claim the property for themselves.

[47] See Brecht 3:185–87; Luther, *Table Talk* no. 5368 (1540), WA TR 5:96–97; no. 3553 (1537), LW 54:232; Luther to Melanchthon, February 27, 1537, WA Br 8:48–50; to Katharina Luther, February 27, 1537, LW 50:165–69.

[48] See Bugenhagen's reduction to writing of Luther's testament, delivered orally in Gotha (not, apparently, "on the wagon") on February 27: WA Br 8:54–56; cf. *Table Talk* no. 4991 (1540), LW 54:373–75. See Brecht 3:187; Harry Gerald Haile, *Luther: An Experiment in Biography* (Princeton: Princeton University Press, 1983), pp. 219–20. Mathesius transposes this episode before the loosing of the blockage (below, p. 403).

friends he left and bequeathed the *Odium in Papam* ["hatred against the pope"]:[49] that is, that they would not only remain untroubled by the pope's doctrine but also would be and remain steadfast as public enemies of its idolatry until their end.

For God had already condemned the Antichrist, and from now on no one would be able to reestablish or defend his abominations, either through writings or through use of force. Since God was graciously taking him home already, his death would surely be the death and demise of the papacy.[50] [Thus far Luther.][51] The pope's legate,[52] who was present at that time on account of the council, would have liked to have seen the ill Dr. Luther, but this was not permitted. Then, the ill man started on his way; he was accompanied by people and a whole wagon full of [medical] instruments and coal, so that he could be treated with heat and warmed while on the way.[53]

As our doctor came to Tambach[54] on the same day, our God gave His blessing to the medicine and the movement [of the wagon]; He heard the heartfelt sighs and tears of the pious and reopened the ill man's passageways overnight, so that with joy he started to be relieved of his pain and burden, which he had borne as the pangs of death for eleven whole days, as he wrote about this to Master Philip that very night[55] and thanked his dear God, who had comforted him, visited him with grace, helped him, and brought him out of the Smalcaldic pit, as he phrased it, 'onto level ground. Next to the date in his letter he called this village *locum benedictionis suae* ["the place of his blessing"], where God blessed and delivered him, appearing to him with help as he did to the patriarch Jacob at Peniel [in] Genesis 32 [:30].

In his letter, the doctor also mentioned that out of joy he himself measured the volume of his urine, and, as I heard from him, this night it filled up nearly eleven cans.[56] Here I should also mention the salutation of his

---

[49] See *Table Talk* no. 3543a (1537), LW 54:228: "*Impleat vos Dominus benedictione sua et odio papae*" ["May God fill you with His blessing and with hatred of the pope"]; cf. *Table Talk* no. 6974 (n.d.), WA TR 6:302; no. 5310 (1540), WA TR 5:53.

[50] Cf. below, Mathesius, *History*, pp. 566.

[51] In the German, the use of the subjunctive indicates an indirect quotation of Luther's "testament" to this point.

[52] The papal nuncio was Peter van der Vorst (1500–1548), bishop of Acqui and auditor of the Roman Rota. On his rebuff at Smalcald, see *Table Talk* no. 3545 (1537), LW 54:228.

[53] *Table Talk* no. 5368 (1540), WA TR 5:96–97.

[54] Present-day Tambach-Dietharz, about 20 km northeast of Smalcald. Cf. *Table Talk* no. 3553 (1537), LW 54:232.

[55] Luther to Melanchthon, February 27, 1537, WA Br 8:48–50. That night Luther also wrote to Katharina Luther, LW 50:165–69.

[56] *kanden.* Depending on which local measure was involved, the quantity reported by Mathesius would have been just under two gallons. In the letter to Melanchthon, Luther

letter, from which you can see the heartfelt and trusted friendship between him and the one with whom he shared this joyful message. For this is what he wrote: "To my most heartily beloved Master Philip Melanchthon in Smalcald." Great people have great virtue[57] and maintain good and solid friendships. So, likewise, it is beloved children who need the rod of discipline [cf. Heb. 12:6–8]; this can be observed not only from all the saints and this German prophet but also from the Son of God, upon whom His Father laid a far heavier burden and cross than Abraham laid upon his most beloved son on Mount Moriah [Gen. 22:6].

God leads His people in strange ways and plunges them deep into all kinds of misery, and yet He Himself helps them bear the cross, alleviates the burden, and by means of His gracious and salutary rod, He brings to pass much good, both in the case of His only-begotten Son and with His adopted and elected children, rescuing them in the end from all misfortune with honor and joy, and redeeming the believers from sin and death through Christ's cross and making them deserve eternal righteousness and life. The others, who take comfort in the cross of Jesus Christ in blessed patience, He chastens and purifies; He teaches them through experience to believe, hope, and pray more strongly, and He subdues and kills the old Adam and plants new virtue and obedience in them. Then they can provide other people with more salutary comfort and can more willingly renounce this miserable life and the whole wicked world.

‡Now, when our doctor continued on his journey and came to Gotha on the Thursday after *Reminiscere*,[58] he was followed there by Herr Bucer and Lycosthenes,[59] who had been sent to Smalcald by the churches of upper Germany to promote the concord agreed upon in Wittenberg the year before.[60] They also brought along respectful letters from six cantons[61] in Switzerland and from the mayor in Basel, who had personally signed with

---

gives the volume of urine as "more than a full gallon" [*plus quam cantharum plenum*]; in his letter to Katharina, he reports the volume in German as "about a gallon" [*wohl ein Stübigen*] (see WA Br 8:51 n. 4). Cf. Brecht 3:187; James M. Kittelson and Hans Wiersma, *Luther the Reformer*, 2nd ed. (Minneapolis: Fortress, 2016), p. 223.

[57] Wander 3:76, "Leute" no. 695.

[58] I.e., March 1, 1537. Luther had arrived already on February 27, but the conference took place on March 1.

[59] See above, p. 395; cf. above, Mathesius, *History*, pp. 353–54.

[60] Cf. above, Mathesius, *History*, pp. 353–54. See Brecht 3:187–88. On Mathesius' sources, see Volz, *Die Lutherpredigten des Johannes Mathesius*, pp. 119–21.

[61] *orten*; Zürich, Bern, Schaffhausen, St. Gallen, Mülhausen, and Biel.

these words: "Your venerable, ever obedient son and servant Jacob Meyer, mayor in Basel."[62]

Although Dr. Luther was still somewhat ill in Gotha, he admitted the emissaries, listened to them, and answered them in a friendly manner, and their conversation was written down by good people.[63] He asked that the emissaries and their people abroad,[64] particularly the Swiss confederates who had written to him, would always believe that he was sincere in speaking the things he said to them and that they would be assured that he was dealing with them in the matter of the Supper without any deception. Neither did he think ill of them for being unable so suddenly to disentangle and tear themselves free of a matter in which they were so deeply stuck. Neither was he able to keep all his own people under full control or keep them in check, so that they would always take [the Swiss] in good part, seeing that they continued to write books in which they claimed that neither side had properly understood the other.[65]

Then he continued by saying that the best thing for this matter would be that they should hold their peace henceforth, to teach rightly, and freely and clearly to confess: "'Dear friends, God has let us fall; we have erred. Let us take heed now and teach rightly.' For nothing can be accomplished by covering things up, neither can one put the people's consciences at ease by beating around the bush. God will also demand a strict accounting with respect to doctrine; therefore, we dare not do anything in our office that derogates from the honor of God.

"Your people in foreign lands speak in a patois of dark and obscure words. Even Karlstadt, who promoted me to doctor,[66] is incapable of setting forth and teaching anything correctly, even if he once possessed some knowledge.

"The common man must not be taught with lofty, difficult, and obscure words, because he cannot understand them. There are little children, maids, and old men and women who go to church; sublime teaching is of no use to them, neither do they grasp any of it. Even if they say, 'What wonderful things he has said!' if you ask them what was said, they say, 'I don't know.'

---

[62] Jacob Meyer zum Hirzen (d. 1541) to Luther, October 7, 1536, WA Br 7:556–58. A letter from the six cantons is inferred from Luther's reply to the cities of Switzerland, December 1, 1537, WA Br 8:149–53.

[63] The record of the conversation by Anton Lauterbach (1502–69) and Hieronymus Weller (1499–1572) is preserved in *Table Talk* no. 3544 (1537), WA TR 3:394–98.

[64] *draussen*

[65] On Luther's insistence that the disagreement over the doctrine of the Lord's Supper should not be characterized as a misunderstanding, despite Bucer's efforts to use such an interpretation to ease achievement of a consensus, cf. Luther's instructions to Melanchthon, December 17, 1534, WA Br 12:157; Brecht 3:44–45.

[66] See above, Mathesius, *History*, p. 129 and n. 87 there.

We have to tell the poor people: '*Scapha scapha, ficus ficus*' ['A boat is a boat; a fig is a fig']⁶⁷—and yet they barely grasp this.

"Oh, how our dear Lord Christ strove to teach simply! He used parables about agriculture—the harvest [Matt. 13:24–30; Luke 13:6–9], the vine [John 15:1–11], and the sheep [Matt. 10:16; 12:11–12; 15:24; 18:12–14; 25:32–33; Luke 15:4–7; John 10:1–18]—all so that the people would be able to understand, grasp, and retain them. You have among you populous congregations, for whom you must give account to God. Therefore, strive to teach them simply, faithfully, and clearly. If I die, then refer to the letter I wrote to the mayor of Basel.⁶⁸ But if I live, and our dear God, to whom I have commended myself, gives me strength, then I will gladly serve those who so kindly wrote to me by likewise writing most sincerely and kindly."

Our doctor spoke these and similar words to the emissaries, which I gladly mention to you, because they testify to us that this excellent prophet always and at all times faithfully stood by his doctrine of the Supper, and that he was able to demonstrate his graciousness and gentleness, using the friendliest words, with those who had fallen and were likewise most friendly and kind toward him. ᴵHe was sharp in response to those who were sharp, and people found him in whatever way they sought him. But those who were around him and heard his consolation, graciousness, and prayer can truthfully bear witness that his spirit was a gentle and modest spirit.

Also, dear friends, do not forget here the fine admonition in which our doctor exhorted not only these emissaries but also all Evangelical preachers: to plain simplicity. He, for himself, was also a plain and gracious teacher when he spoke with his dutiful parishioners and listeners. More than once while at table I heard from his mouth: "Schools are oriented toward holding disputations and training [students] to say something sharp to confute their opponents. In the pulpit, the best preachers are those who speak *pueriliter, trivialiter, populariter,* and *simplicissime*: ['like children, in ordinary language, like the common people, and in the simplest way'];⁶⁹ who do not bring in and refute all sorts of extraneous questions and the arguments of the adversaries; and who do not rebuke absent authorities or monks and priests, or revile and upbraid their opponents or enemies." In churches one

---

⁶⁷ In English idiom, "call a spade a spade." For the thought on teaching, cf. *Table Talk* no. 6800 (n.d.), WA TR 6:198 (WA 48:661). For the expression, cf. Luther, *Lectures on Genesis* (1535–45/1544–54), LW 1:5.

⁶⁸ Luther to Jacob Meyer, mayor of Basel, February 17, 1537, WA Br 8:43–45.

⁶⁹ See *Table Talk* no. 5047 (1540), LW 54:382–84, see especially p. 384; cf. *Table Talk* no. 5200 (1540), WA TR 5:6.

speaks to those who are present; in schools one used to call [the names of] those who were absent.[70]

As our doctor expounded John 17 from the pulpit, which later appeared in print, he spoke these words: "I say it upon my soul, from all that I have seen and experienced, that those at present who would and should be the best preachers and writers know (with but few exceptions) absolutely nothing about this article" (that only the knowledge of Christ and His Father is eternal life and that everything is dependent on the Word). "And even though they once in a while make a guess and hit the mark, it is like something spoken or heard in a dream. They are all capable enough of criticizing the pope, monks, and clerics, but they know little, in truth, about the proper and necessary basis for overturning the papacy and every kind of false doctrine."[71] |Thus far Dr. Luther on John 17, in sexternion S in quarto.[72] More than once at table he also said that he had not heard more than three people who were able to explain Christ and His office thoroughly and simply.[73] But more about this later.[74] Let that be enough about the conference in Smalcald and the conversation in Gotha.

When Dr. Luther had returned home from Smalcald and the Anabaptists in Westphalia had been suppressed,[75] the churches of upper Germany expressed themselves somewhat more mildly, and the Papists who did not dare to publicize their doctrine at Augsburg sheepishly fell silent.[76] The pope's thunderbolts also grew somewhat weaker, and Emperor Charles faithfully pressed for a common Christian council while the Romanists quite foolishly made it known that they had little desire or inclination for a council themselves. The protesting estates relied upon the resolutions of the general imperial diet whereas the neighbors were unable to accomplish much with their snorts of defiance. The churches in Saxony had been supplied in a Christian manner with the catechism and schools during the

---

[70] *In Kirchen gibt man presentes, in Schulen lase man etwan absentes.*

[71] See *Sermons on John 17* (1528/1530), LW 69:107.

[72] *im sechstern S in quarto.* The citation matches the 1538 edition (except that only the last gathering, V, is a sexternion): *Das siebenzehend Capitel S. Johannis/ von dem Gebete Christi* (Wittenberg: Joseph Klug, 1538) [VD16 L6692], fols. S1v–S2r. See Volz, *Die Lutherpredigten des Johannes Mathesius*, pp. 104–5.

[73] This saying could not be located elsewhere in the *Table Talk*. Cf., however, *Table Talk* no. 868 (1530), WA TR 1:433, where someone else at Luther's table (Forstemius) names Luther, Conrad Cordatus, and Georg Rörer as the only three preachers able to move their hearers.

[74] See below, Mathesius, *History*, p. 436 and nn. 69–70 there.

[75] On the Anabaptist uprising in Münster, in Westphalia, see above, Mathesius, *History*, pp. 380–84.

[76] On the refusal of the Roman party to publish its *Confutation*, see above, Mathesius, *History*, p. 340.

visitation,[77] and one city and territory after another came to the Gospel.[78] Our doctor enjoyed considerable peace from his foreign adversaries, whose mouths had been shut rather well in Augsburg,[79] and he attended to his prayer, studying, lecturing, and preaching. In addition, he wrote a great deal of fine instruction and good counsel to those who requested it from him,[80] and he continued his Genesis [lectures], which he had begun in 1536 and did not complete until as late as 1545.[81]

From the pulpit he also expounded the Lord Christ's final sermon during the [Last] Supper [John 14–17]; these sermons were transcribed by Dr. Caspar Cruciger and later published.[82] The Herr Doctor very often took this book to church with him and liked to read in it. As I and others heard from his own mouth at table, this was the best book he had written, "though I did not write it," he said, "but Dr. Caspar Cruciger showed his deep understanding and great diligence in [editing] it. After the holy Bible, this should be [esteemed as] my most worthy and precious book."[83]

In these years, because the question concerning the council was foremost at all the diets of the empire and the [Smalcaldic] League,[84] Dr. Luther and Herr Philip wrote a number of books: *Articles which Should Be Taken*

---

[77] See above, Mathesius, *History*, pp. 249–50.

[78] Ducal (Albertine) Saxony and the Mark Brandenburg embraced the Reformation in 1539; the city of Halle, in 1541. See Brecht 3:287–18.

[79] I.e., by the Augsburg Confession of 1530: see above, Mathesius, *History*, pp. 320–65.

[80] Mathesius may have in mind a letter to an anonymous recipient printed in Witt Ger 12 (fol. 168) under the erroneous date of May 21, 1537. This was, in fact, Luther's letter of encouragement to the Eisleben girls' schoolteacher Elisabeth Agricola, written on June 10, 1527. See WA Br 4:210–11.

[81] *Lectures on Genesis* (1535–45/1544–54), LW 1–8. Note that Luther in fact began lecturing on Genesis in June 1535, though the lectures were interrupted by the outbreak of plague in Wittenberg in July and were not resumed until January 1536. See Brecht 3:134–41.

[82] *Sermons on John 14–16* (1533–34/1538–39), LW 24; *Sermons on John 17* (1528/1530), LW 69:1–119. In fact, the sermons on John 14–16 had been preached in 1533–34 and not in 1536–37: see the introduction by Christopher Boyd Brown, LW 69:xvi; and Johannes Schilling, "Auslegung des XIV., XV. und XVI. Kapitels S. Johannis (1533–1534/1538 und 1539) nebst weiteren Nachträgen zu Luthers Predigttätigkeit in den Jahren 1533–1535 und 1544 auf Grund von Georg Helts Predigttagebuch," WA 59:242–310. On Cruciger, see above, p. xx n. 19.

[83] Cf. *Table Talk* no. 5275 (1540), WA TR 5:41.

[84] Cf. above, pp. 396–97. From Melanchthon, in addition to the *Treatise on the Power and Primacy of the Pope* (Kolb-Wengert, pp. 329–44; *Concordia*, pp. 289–306), see also *Causae quare Synodum indictam a Romano Pontifice recusarint Principes, Status, et Civitates imperii, profitentes puram et Catholicam Evangelii Doctrinam* (Wittenberg: Georg Rhau, 1537) [VD16 M2658], CR 3:313–25.

Up and Considered at the Council in Mantua[85] and *Concerning the Donation of Constantine.*[86] The *Lie[-gend] of St. John Chrysostom* was also glossed.[87] So was the treatment of Emperor Frederick Barbarossa by Popes Adrian IV and Alexander III.[88] The *Counsel of Several Cardinals* was also glossed and published with Dr. Luther's foreword,[89] in addition to several acts and letters of John Hus from the Council in Constance.[90]

In addition to this, as mentioned earlier, Dr. Luther's instructive and thorough book *On the Councils and the Church* was published,[91] which is very necessary and useful to read. For because many people set their hopes on the council and great people thought that it could serve to resolve and remedy the religious division, this book set forth the good things that were discussed and decided, since the time of Christ's ascension, in the apostles' [council] and thereafter in the four chief councils in Nicaea, Constantinople, Chalcedon, and others,[92] as well as the evil that was later discussed, decided, and, through their spiritual hypocrisy and scheming, put into effect to the eternal and manifest detriment of both the Church of God and the Holy Roman Empire, by God's permission. At the same time, work continued on translating and correcting the German Bible, which you will hear about at another time.[93]

Now, though the churches in Saxony enjoyed considerable peace from their foreign adversaries and the correct doctrine was making fine and peaceful progress in churches and schools, ¹the lying and murderous Satan stirred up many secret divisions and perilous offenses by means of false brethren and those who are Christians in word only, both at the university in Wittenberg and in neighboring churches, on account of which our doctor had to bear much trouble and many cries of woe.

---

[85] This is the title under which the *Smalcald Articles* were published in 1538, with some revisions to the articles themselves and with Luther's preface. See the introduction in Kolb-Wengert, pp. 295–97.

[86] Preface, marginal glosses, and afterword to the *Donation of Constantine* (1537), LW 60:158–84.

[87] *Die Lügend von S. Johanne Chrysostomo* (1537), WA 50:52–64.

[88] Preface to Barnes, *How Popes Adrian IV and Alexander III Showed Good Faith to Emperor Barbarossa* (1545), LW 60:347–51. Emperor Frederick I (Barbarossa) ruled the Holy Roman Empire from 1155 to 1190 during the papacies of Adrian IV (r. 1154–59) and Alexander III (r. 1159–81).

[89] *Counsel of a Committee of Several Cardinals* (1538), LW 34:231–67.

[90] Preface and afterword to Hus, *Three Letters* (1536/1537), LW 60:122–33.

[91] See above, p. 399.

[92] I.e., the Councils of Nicaea (325), Constantinople I (381), Ephesus (431), and Chalcedon (451), discussed in part 2 of *On the Councils and the Church* (1539): see LW 41:54–142.

[93] See below, Mathesius, *History*, pp. 470–85.

In 1538, a poetaster called Simon Lemchen[94] came forward; he began to slander many good people with scandalous and shameful verses, as well as to praise the great persecutors of the Gospel with his poetry.[95] He also mocked our doctor in his illness,[96] and the relatives[97] of great people helped him see to it that these slanderous writings were published and secretly distributed. This Lemnius later published a lewd[98] and appalling libel that he

---

[94] Simon Lemnius Emporicus from Graubünden (ca. 1511–50), called here (and by Luther) with the derogatory diminutive "Lemchen," had been a humanist student at Wittenberg since 1534. For Lemnius and his satiric poetry, see Lothar Mundt, *Lemnius und Luther: Studien und Texte zur Geschichte und Nachwirkung ihres Konflikts (1538/39)*, 2 vols. (Bern: P. Lang, 1983); H. W. Hawkins, ed. and trans., *The Poems of Simon Lemnius*, vol. 1: *Luther's Whorely War, The Epigrams, and A Grievance to the Prince* (Manquin, VA: Uppingham House, 2009), and the introduction there, pp. 1–55. On this episode, see Brecht 3:87–89.

[95] Lemnius' two books of *Epigrammata*, published in Wittenberg at Pentecost, June 9, 1538 (VD16 L1134), included Lemnius' (scarcely concealed) description of a claimed affair with the wife of the Hebraist Matthaeus Aurogallus [Goldhahn] (see above, p. 297 n. 71; *Epigrammata* 2.13, 46, 76 [Hawkins, *Poems of Simon Lemnius*, 1:146–47, 166–67, 190–91]); disparaging remarks about other Wittenberg women (e.g., Anna Globick: *Epigrammata* 2.77 [Hawkins, *Poems of Simon Lemnius*, 1:190–91]); and satirical attacks on Wittenberg figures such as the printer Hans Lufft (*Epigrammata* 1.39, 2.54 [Hawkins, *Poems of Simon Lemnius*, 1:104–5, 172–73]), the city treasurer Matthias Meier (d. 1564; *Epigrammata* 2.69 and 78 [Hawkins, *Poems of Simon Lemnius*, 1:186–87, 192–93]), the theologian and mathematician Michael Stifel (see above, p. xxxvii n. 101; *Epigrammata* 1.40 [Hawkins, *Poems of Simon Lemnius*, 1:106–7]), the jurist and theologian Justus Jonas (see the introduction above, p. xxx; *Epigrammata* 1.73 [Hawkins, *Poems of Simon Lemnius*, 1:132–33]), the poet Johannes Tirolff (d. after 1541; *Epigrammata* 2.19 [Hawkins, *Poems of Simon Lemnius*, 1:152–53]), the Greek professor Veit Oertel from Winsheim (see above, p. 299 n. 83; *Epigrammata* 2.63 [Hawkins, *Poems of Simon Lemnius*, 1:182–83]), the astronomers Johannes Regiomontanus (1436–76; *Epigrammata* 2.60 [Hawkins, *Poems of Simon Lemnius*, 1:180–81]) and Erasmus Reinhold (see above, p. 299 n. 86; *Epigrammata* 2.62 [Hawkins, *Poems of Simon Lemnius*, 1:182–83]), the chancellor Gregor Brück (see above, p. 21 n. 79; *Epigrammata* 2.51 [Hawkins, *Poems of Simon Lemnius*, 1:172–73]), and even Elector John Frederick himself (see above, p. xxv n. 42; *Epigrammata* 1.20 [Hawkins, *Poems of Simon Lemnius*, 1:82–83]). Lemnius dedicated his verse to Cardinal Albert of Mainz (see above, p. 27 n. 5; *Epigrammata* 1.1 [Hawkins, *Poems of Simon Lemnius*, 1:58–59]), on whose hostility to the Reformation see above, Bugenhagen, *Christian Sermon*, p. 27. In his 1539 *Apologia*, Lemnius rather disingenuously denied ever having had these people in mind: see Mundt, *Lemnius und Luther*, 2:173–255, especially pp. 206–33.

[96] At the time, Luther was suffering from dysentery. It was Lemnius' third book of *Epigrammata* (VD16 L1133), published in September 1538 after his expulsion from the university, that included attacks on Luther (*Epigrammata* 3.7, 16, 23, 32, 42, 47, 51, 57, 63 [Hawkins, *Poems of Simon Lemnius*, 1:228–29, 240–41, 248–49, 256–57, 266–67, 272–73, 276–77, 284–85, 294–95]; the last of these is the verse mocking Luther's dysentery). Among Luther's responses was his own scatalogical Latin epigram: *Table Talk* no. 4032 (1538), WA TR 4:89–90.

[97] Melanchthon's son-in-law, Georg Sabinus, had helped Lemnius publish the *Epigrammata* with the Wittenberg printer Nicholas [Nickel] Schirlentz (d. 1547). See Hawkins, *Poems of Simon Lemnius*, 1:9.

[98] *Risianische*; see above, Mathesius, *History*, p. 251.

called *The Whorely War* to dishonor the holy estate of marriage, the marriage of ministers of the Church, and many honorable women.[99]

Accordingly, the aforementioned versifier was officially summoned to appear before court by the rector;[100] however, because he secretly left, contrary to the oath he had previously given, and failed to present himself, he was relegated and expelled from the University of Wittenberg for life for his slander and contumacy.[101] Dr. Martin also publicly warned everyone against these calumnies and slanderous verses and asked all the pious to cast them into the fire, for the glory of God and His Word.[102] Among the heathen, it was regarded as an abomination when someone applied beautiful gifts and the liberal arts—in which God wishes to be made known and perceived, and which He gives to prosper general peace and honorable discipline—and maliciously used them to derogate from God's honor and from virtue and to destroy the honor and reputation of good people.[103]

Now it is surely also lamentable when venomous people employ poetry—in which the holy prophets, inspired by the Holy Spirit, have artfully and felicitously couched the pure doctrine of God and His Son, even as the honorable and virtuous heathen poets have done likewise with fine rules of virtue and discipline and the biographies of many great people—to denigrate and disparage our God and His Word and servants, as well as their reputation, and to praise and exalt godless doctrine and people. And yet this is what happens: God's precious name and His noble gifts are misused. Therefore, everyone who has been blessed with skills, talents, and special abilities above other people will have to render a strict account. Judas, the traitor, and the students of Cassian and Damascene[104] must have their companions in the fires of hell, where their ingratitude and wickedness against the eternal God and His faithful servants are punished for all eternity. May God preserve all clever heads so that they may not allow themselves to be driven, deceived, or stirred up by the diabolical spirit and wicked enemy.

When these writings were suppressed, other false brethren and ungrateful students came forward with their insidious, devious doctrines, seeking

---

[99] Lemnius published the *[Monacho]pornomachia*—literally, "Battle of the Monks and Whores"—in 1539 (VD16 L1136). See Hawkins, *Poems of Simon Lemnius*, 1:322–91; cf. Luther, *Table Talk* no. 4592 (1539), WA TR 4:393.

[100] Melanchthon was rector of the university at the time. Lemnius was summoned on June 11, 1538, to appear on June 18. See Melanchthon's announcements to the university, CR 3:543–44, nos. 1688–89.

[101] See Melanchthon, July 4, 1538, CR 3:549–50, no. 1693.

[102] *Erklärung gegen Simon Lemnius* (June 16, 1538), WA 50:348–51.

[103] See, e.g., Cicero, *On Invention* 1.1 (Loeb 386 [1949], pp. 2–5).

[104] See above, Mathesius, *History*, p. 291.

to relegate the Law of God from the church to the town hall and the public gallows while drawing the people to true repentance and knowledge of their sins through the preaching of the crucified Lord Christ.[105] When the conclusions they [drew from this] and their [character as] bats [who shun the light][106] finally became apparent, our doctor organized a public disputation against the enemies of God's Law and battled against this new and dangerous heresy.[107]

Now when the initiators of this new heresy would not let themselves be pinned down, the doctor publicly challenged one by name to stand and defend his bats and secret writings in front of everyone.[108] But false doctrine creeps around in the darkness, shuns the light, and seeks only hidden corners, and so these people did not step out into the public square.[109] When they were pressed to explain themselves, the initiator confessed that this kind of

---

[105] I.e., the Antinomians, who taught that the Law had no role to play in teaching Christians and that Christian repentance should therefore be taught on the basis of Christ's suffering. Cf. above, Mathesius, *History*, pp. 375–76. The leading proponent of this view was Johann Agricola (see above, p. 345 n. 134), who at first circulated his views anonymously: see *Response of Dr. Martin Luther to the Theses of a Certain Unknown Author* (1539), WA 39/1:342–45 (LW 72); *Against the Antinomians* (1539), LW 47:99–119. Agricola, a native of Eisleben, had come to Wittenberg as a student in 1515 and received his master's degree in arts and the bachelor's degree in theology. He became part of Luther's circle, attending him as secretary at the Leipzig Disputation in 1519 and lecturing privately in Wittenberg before returning to Eisleben as preacher and rector of the Latin school in 1525. Agricola remained involved in Saxony, however, both as occasional preacher to the electors and, by 1527, as a critic of Melanchthon's teaching about the Law and repentance, though Luther was able to mediate the dispute surrounding the publication of the *Instructions for the Visitors* (1528), LW 40:263–320. In 1536, Agricola came back to Wittenberg and was employed as Luther's substitute during the meeting of the Smalcaldic League. Upon Luther's return, however, the reformer became concerned about reports on Agricola's preaching, as well as about the anonymously circulated theses. On the Antinomian Controversy, see Brecht 3:156–71.

[106] This language about bats is found in Luther in reference to the supporters of the papacy: see *Warning to His Dear German People* (1531), LW 47:21, 25; *Commmentary on the Alleged Imperial Edict* (1531), LW 34:72; preface to *Exposition of Psalm 37* (1521), LW 48:250; afterword to *The Papacy with Its Members* (1526), LW 59:149.

[107] The first Antinomian disputation took place on December 18, 1537, though Agricola failed to attend. See *Theses against the Antinomians*, WA 39/1:345–47, 360–417 (LW 73). Luther eventually prepared five more sets of theses against the Antinomians, though protocols for only three of these disputations survive: the second Antinomian disputation of January 12, 1538 (with Agricola present), WA 39/1:347–50, 419–85; the third and fourth sets of theses, also dating from early 1538, WA 39/1:352–57; the fifth disputation of September 13, 1538, for the doctorate of Cyriacus Gericke (d. 1551), WA 39/1:350–52, 489–584; and the sixth disputation of September 10, 1540, for the doctorate of Joachim Mörlin (1514–71), WA 39/1:358, 39/2:124–44, all to be translated in LW 73.

[108] I.e., Agricola. Cf. *Table Talk* no. 3650a (1537), LW 54:248; no. 3650c (1537), WA TR 3:483.

[109] Agricola did not attend the first disputation.

ⁱantinomianism was not right.[110] At the same time, however, they kept attacking secretly from behind the fence[111] and sought to withdraw so they might the more easily sow their thistles and set up a hedge around them.

Meanwhile, the division was becoming deeper and deeper—for rarely does an arch-heretic return to the right path, or even if he is convinced by solid arguments or corrects himself out of fear, he nevertheless is unable to let go of his error entirely. Our doctor was so greatly grieved by these fellow countrymen,[112] friends, students, and those who had eaten his bread many a time [cf. Ps. 41:9]—and whom he had also helped [earn] honorable [degrees] and [find] good, eminent positions—that he despaired of his own life, because his own people had stirred up such a division and offense in his own parish, and he was forced in the end to despair of their salvation and welfare. Therefore, he was forced to take action against some of them in writing and to refute their insidious and dangerous deception. These writings of his against Johann [Agricola of] Eisleben have been placed in volume 12 [of the Wittenberg German edition].[113]

Now when the antinomian had oversalted his porridge,[114] and he was put under arrest and subject to confiscation *re et corpore* ["in property and body"] on this account, and he could find no way to defend his false doctrine either by writing or through patronage, he broke free and violated his arrest and custody, forgot his vow, and made off secretly through the stable

---

[110] On Agricola's various concessions, see Brecht 3:160–64, 169–70.

[111] For the expression *durch den Zaun stechen* (Wander 5:511, "Zaun" no. 90), cf. Luther, *Table Talk* no. 817 (1530), WA TR 1:397, where it is applied to Erasmus.

[112] Agricola, like Luther, was a native of Eisleben in the county of Mansfeld.

[113] Witt Ger 12 (1559), fols. 228r–239r, including the theses against the Antinomians (see above, p. 412 n. 107) and *Against Johann Agricola of Eisleben* (1540/1549), WA 51:429–44 (LW 61). *Against the Antinomians* (1539), LW 47:99–119, had appeared in Witt Ger 6 (1553), fols. 458r–461v.

[114] *sein muß versalzen*; i.e., gone too far: see *Table Talk* no. 4954 (1540), WA TR 4:592. Cf. Wander 1:458, "Brei" no. 39.

window,[115] seeking a place of refuge.[116] As for what he accomplished there afterward, that will one day be made clear in his funeral sermon.[117]

O God! What heartfelt sighing I saw and what words of lamentation I heard from Dr. Luther during this affair, because he had to bear this faithlessness and pernicious mischief from his dear friend, the one to whom he had commended his church, school, wife, child, and house as his closest, most trusted colleague when he went to Smalcald.[118] "But," said the doctor, "I, too, must have a teacher and instructor to explain to me the verse in the psalm: *Qui edit panem mecum, sustulit adversus me calcaneum suum* ['The one who has eaten my bread has lifted up his heel against me'] [Ps. 41:9].[119]

"For my part, I would gladly keep quiet and forget," he often said with bitter tears, "except that he has fallen away from the recognized truth and is willfully and maliciously kicking against the goads [Acts 9:5]. God must have mercy in eternity if I have to see my dearest friend sitting in the fire of hell. Christ, my Lord, is used to having had people pierce His heel and lift their heels against Him from the beginning [Gen. 3:15; John 13:18]. O Lord Jesus, protect all godly students from falling into this invincible confusion, for in such a case all aid and counsel is of no avail, and there is no help for those who profane the Holy Spirit and His Word [Matt. 12:31]."

---

[115] *raumet heimlich des Küfensters*. The stable window was apparently a favorite path of thieves. See *DWB*, s.v. "Kuhfenster."

[116] Cf. *Table Talk* no. 5273 (1540), WA TR 5:40. Elector John Frederick had forbidden Agricola to leave Wittenberg while his complaint with Luther was pending a hearing. In August 1540, Agricola nonetheless fled Wittenberg to take up a call as court preacher for Elector Joachim II of Brandenburg (r. 1535–71). See Luther to Gregor Solinus, September 13, 1540, WA Br 9:232.

[117] Agricola died in Berlin in 1566, two or three years after this sermon by Mathesius, which was delivered in the middle of 1563. Mathesius may be alluding critically to Agricola's role in helping draft the Augsburg Interim of 1548 (see above, p. 345 n. 134) or to his continuing attacks on Melanchthon.

[118] For Luther's complaint concerning Agricola, see *Table Talk* no. 4960 (1540), WA TR 4:593.

[119] Cf. *Table Talk* no. 4968 (1540), WA TR 4:595.

Now while the poets[120] and recorders of proverbs[121] and young court preachers[122] were lashing out in every direction in secret, like poisonous scorpions, pouring all kinds of venom and poison into their books and seeking to draw the people to themselves—and to speak the truth before God, I myself was given some of their writings—there were secret gatherings always taking place, an amalgam of people of all sorts,[123] some of whom, at the beginning, slipped in past our doctor without being noticed and helped defame and disparage eminent and good people in the university and church.

One member[124] of this antinomian sect disparaged nearly every doctor and teacher in Wittenberg, assigning each of them some tag: one baked

---

[120] In addition to the satirical poet Simon Lemnius (see above, p. 410), the epithet applies to Agricola, who was a writer of hymns that had appeared in Wittenberg hymnals since 1524: see Wackernagel 3:51–55. Mathesius may also be thinking of Agricola's followers Heinrich Hamm, a poet and preacher in Königsberg, and Caspar Adler [Aquila] (1488–1560), a hymn writer and the superintendent in Saalfeld: see *Table Talk* nos. 4724 and 4790 (1539), WA TR 4:451, 512–13; Wackernagel 3:1013–14. On Hamm, see WA Br 8:380 n. 7, and Kurt Hannemann, "Unbekannte Melanchthonbriefe in badischem Bibliotheksbesitz an den Pfarrer Heinrich Ham(me) in der Neumark," *Zeitschrift für die Geschichte des Oberrheins* n.s. 62 (1953): 353–412; n.s. 63 (1954): 449–574. On Adler, see Luther, preface to Adler, *Sermon on Almsgiving* (1533), LW 60:11–16, and the introduction by Neil Leroux; Wackernagel 3:1013 no. 1190. Volz, *Die Lutherpredigten des Johannes Mathesius*, p. 260 ad loc., suggests that the reference to "Hams" [*Hammen*] in Luther, preface to Freder, *Dialogue in Honor of Matrimony* (1545), LW 60:346, is a reference to Heinrich Hamm rather than to the son of Noah (Gen. 9:22).

[121] Agricola's full collection of 750 proverbs appeared in 1534: *Sybenhundert und Fünfftzig Teütscher Sprichwörter* (Hagenau: Peter Braubach, 1534) [VD16 A962], combining two 1529 editions containing 300 and 450 proverbs respectively [VD16 A956, A957]. Among Luther's other opponents, the spiritualist Sebastian Franck (see below, p. 440 n. 100) was also a prominent collector of proverbs, which he published in 1541: *Sprichwörter/ Schöne/ Weise/ Herrliche Clůgreden/ unnd Hoff sprüch* (Frankfurt a.M: Christian Egenolff, 1541) [VD16 F2122]. See Luther, preface to Freder, *Dialogue in Honor of Matrimony* (1545), LW 60:336–46.

[122] In addition to Agricola's service as court preacher in Brandenburg, Mathesius may have in mind Jacob Schenk (ca. 1508–46), regarded by Luther as an antinomian, who after receiving his doctorate in Wittenberg served as court preacher first to Duke Henry IV of Saxony in Freiburg, from 1536 to 1538, then to Elector John Frederick in Weimar from 1538 to 1540, and later to Elector Joachim II of Brandenburg in Berlin in 1544. On Schenk, see Brecht 3:152–56; Robert Stupperich, ed., *Reformatorenlexikon* (Gütersloh: G. Mohn, 1984), p. 187; Georg Müller, "Schenk, Jakob," *ADB* 31:49–51.

[123] *samelt sich jmmer fein heimlich zusamen allerley Glockenspeyse*; literally, "all sorts of metals for casting bells were always gathering quite secretly." See *DWB*, s.v. "Glockenspeise" 3; Thiele no. 125, p. 136; cf. below, Mathesius, *History*, p. 499. Luther used the expression in reference to Agricola and his mix of good-hearted and evil-minded hearers in the discussion of Deuteronomy 29 amid the Bible revisions of 1539–41 (see below, Mathesius, *History*, pp. 477–78): WA DB :333–34.

[124] I.e., Agricola. For the identification of the epithets with particular figures, compare *LH²*, p. 551, and Volz, *Die Lutherpredigten des Johannes Mathesius*, p. 152 n. 1.

a little cake[125] in the pulpit; another was incapable of stopping;[126] another taught and lectured only what others had shown him how to play and had chewed for him beforehand;[127] yet another always fiddled on the same string and always taught only one thing: if you were to read one of his books, you would know what was in all of them.[128] Moreover, this poet and ˈfarmer[129] gave everyone a special nickname: one had acquired his knowledge in the tavern kitchen,[130] another was a Westphalian peasant,[131] but the "*baccalaureus* from Kemberg"[132] had particularly offended many of them; the majority attacked him. Some dragged him to the court and defamed him;[133] others kindled [trouble] for him with our doctor.[134] This kind of secretive beginning to the later divisions and all the offenses that were

---

[125] It is uncertain to which person this characterization should be assigned. The expression might refer to the use of awkward gesticulations in the pulpit or to a propensity for preaching what people wanted to hear (in German idiom: *jemandem ein Küchlein backen*): see *DWB*, s.v. "Küchlein" 2.g.

[126] Probably Bugenhagen (see the introduction above, p. xxxvi), whose long sermons were notorious: see *Table Talk* nos. 2643a–b (1532), WA TR 2:574; no. 2898 (1533), WA TR 3:60; no. 4956 (1540), WA TR 4:592; no. 5171b (1540), LW 54:393; no. 6400 (n.d.), WA TR 5:642.

[127] Probably Caspar Cruciger (see above, p. 298 n. 81), who was accused by Conrad Cordatus (see above, p. xl n. 121) of reading his lectures from notes prepared by Melanchthon: see Wengert, "Caspar Cruciger"; cf. WA 40/1:9. The charge could also apply to Hieronymus Weller, who was so timid, despite his doctorate in theology, that he refused to preach unless someone else had written a sermon for him. Luther's *Annotations on Matthew 1–18* (1534–35/1538) were written for Weller's use. See LW 67, especially the introduction by Christopher Boyd Brown, pp. xxx–xxxiv.

[128] A reference to Melanchthon: see *Table Talk* no. 4923 (1540), WA TR 4:582.

[129] *Agricola* means "farmer" or "peasant" in Latin.

[130] *Der het sein kunst inn der Jarkuch [Garküche] gelerntz*; a reference to Justus Jonas (see the introduction above, p. xxx), whose German family name was Koch (i.e., "Cook").

[131] Perhaps Hermann Tulich from Steinheim in Westphalia (see above, p. 297 n. 73), though he had left Wittenberg in 1532; or Johannes Turstenius [Gölen] from Dorsten, who had matriculated at Wittenberg in 1529 and was present at Luther's table in 1540: see Förstemann et al., *Album*, 1:134; and *Table Talk* no. 4996 (1540), WA TR 4:604 and n. 8.

[132] A nickname Agricola coined for Melanchthon, perhaps intended to remind him that the two men had both been awarded the baccalaureate in theology at the same time, in 1519. Kemberg was a small town some 15 km south of Wittenberg. See *Table Talk* no. 4923 (1540), WA TR 4:582.

[133] The questions Jacob Schenk raised over Melanchthon's advice on permitting Communion in one kind resulted in a case against Melanchthon before the elector in 1537: see Brecht 3:153. Agricola's own charges were directed against Luther himself: see Brecht 3:167–68.

[134] In addition to the trouble between Melanchthon and Luther caused by Schenk's case, the charges brought by Conrad Cordatus against both Cruciger and Melanchthon for teaching that good works were a *sine qua non* of justification also stirred conflict with Luther. See Brecht 3:148–52; Wengert, *Law and Gospel*, pp. 206–10.

stirred up caused our doctor great sorrow; he barred the door and faithfully made a stand; he also provided his faithful helpers with defense and refuge for as long as he lived.

Our God also took an interest in this matter, for these slanderers and agitators kept slipping away, one after the other, like the Pharisees who accused the public adulteress to the Lord Christ in John [8:9]. Some ate up their undigested vomit again, like St. Peter's dog [2 Pet. 2:22]; the others cloaked and whitewashed their malicious tricks and traps with disingenuous courtesy,[135] although in the end their dishonesty could not remain fully concealed, and they kept seeking new places of refuge and retreat until finally they were tracked down and driven out in disgrace, like unlicensed tradesmen.[136] Now unemployed or without a call, with tottering consciences, they gnashed their teeth together and clasped their heads in their hands.[137] In short, our God carried out the first psalm upon these people who walked in the counsel of the ungodly, tread the path of scoundrels, and took their seat among the scoffers and Epicureans, so that they were scattered like chaff and driven out of the congregation of the righteous and believers [Ps. 1:1, 4–5].

In addition to this, many others from among our people also stirred up wicked offenses with their shameless lives and inept teaching. For having been freed from the pope's tyranny by the Gospel, they abused their Christian freedom, caroused, lived in debauchery, started one dispute after another, devoted themselves to nothing but defamation and slander, disparaged the authorities, and passed judgment only on monks and nuns—all of which the common man liked to hear. Many of them had little respect for their own preceptors, who from time to time reproved their wickedness and indiscretion and exhorted them to moderation and discretion.

Once I was standing with the doctor in his garden, and he said that his own people were going to force and compel him to apply to the elector for a priests' tower, where such wild and savage people could be put, as in a prison.[138] For there were many of them who no longer wanted to be drawn by the Gospel. He also used to say that all those who had run to enter a monastery in order to have a full belly and enjoy good days were now jumping

---

[135] *hofschmincke*

[136] *Störer*

[137] Schenk is supposed to have starved to death after losing his position in Berlin and being unable to find a new one. See Georg Müller, "Schenk, Jakob," *ADB* 31:51; Stupperich, *Reformatorenlexikon*, p. 187.

[138] See *Table Talk* no. 3710 (1538), WA TR 3:553–54; no. 5020 (1540), WA TR 4:618.

out again for the sake of carnal freedom: only a minority of those with whom he was acquainted had left their monk behind in the monastery.[139]

Satan also stirred up great scandals among the noble patrons and the hearers of the new teaching; the common man became wild and secure and began to regard the ministers of the Church as low and unworthy; many of them refused ever to listen to reproof or admonition. "Now Lord Everyman[140] is learning how to gnaw at the leather leash,"[141] said the doctor, "and in time we shall see what shall befall the faithful and zealous ministers of the Church."[142]

Our doctor had to endure this in his old age—as did the aged St. Polycarp,[143] whom he mentioned in an open letter[144]—when he publicly posted a serious public complaint against the Midianite [Num. 25:6] licentiousness that had crept in, against the wicked prostitutes who had been arrested in his district.[145] Truly, truly, the soul of this pious old man was severely tormented from day to day by unrighteous works, since he was forced to see and hear almost as much as did pious Lot in Sodom [Genesis 19]. But what more or what else could he have done? He continued rebuking and exhorting, in season and out of season [1 Tim. 4:13; 2 Tim. 4:2], and threatened them with the coming wrath of God, against which he had sincerely and fervently prayed throughout his life. He was holding back the rod of God, as he wrote, as a prophet, to Prince George of Anhalt: that so long as he was alive, there would be no change or destruction.[146]

---

[139] Mathesius is the source for this saying, which is apparently not otherwise attested in Luther's *Table Talk*.

[140] *Er Omnes*. For the expression, cf. *Sermon on the Mount* (1530–32/1532), LW 21:224; *Answer to Emser* (1521), LW 39:219; *Sincere Admonition* (1522), LW 45:63; *Sermons on John 18–20* (1528–29/1557), LW 69:171.

[141] An allusion to the proverb "Dogs learn to chew leather starting with their leashes" (Wander 3:1683, "Riemen" no. 1); i.e., a small misbehavior, if tolerated, will become the basis of serious transgressions.

[142] Mathesius appears to be the source for this saying. Cf., however, *Table Talk* no. 3726 (1538), in the version by Johann Aurifaber, WA TR 3:569–70.

[143] Polycarp, bishop of Smyrna, was probably martyred in AD 155 or 156 at about the age of 86. See above, p. 41 n. 12.

[144] *Admonition of Dr. Martin Luther, in the Absence of Dr. Pomeranus* (1542), WA 53:209–12, here, p. 212 (LW 61).

[145] *Warning against Prostitutes* [*Wider die Speck- und Huren-Studenten*] (May 13, 1543), WA 49:278–79 (*LSC*, pp. 292–94).

[146] Luther spoke these words in the presence of Prince George of Anhalt (see above, p. 30 n. 16) and others, but they were later published in Georg Rörer's 1549 collection of Luther's Bible inscriptions: see WA 48:230, 228–33; *Table Talk* no. 5375k (1545?), WA TR 5:106. Cf. below, Mathesius, *History*, pp. 499, 564; Mathesius, *Diluvium* (1587), fol. 34v.

He also prophesied openly that this state of affairs could not long endure and that after his death God would carry out the Magnificat [Luke 1:51] upon many of them and punish the ungrateful world. Many dangerous forms of enthusiasm would also arise, and many from his own university and church would step forward and violently assail those who remained in steadfast simplicity in the pure and peaceful doctrine. As he said to me at table: "Mathesius, you will see the kind of people who will be stirred up against this university and church and will write against them. But as much as our people persevere in the true doctrine, so will the others become great heretics and pernicious Enthusiasts."[147]

In addition to this, he prayed unceasingly (because the weakness of his body would not let him do much studying) that God would seal the hearts of his students and listeners with the Holy Spirit [Eph. 1:13] and preserve them in the Word of grace and the simple doctrine. He also stood confidently in the hope that things would not yet become dire while the people who had heard him were still alive: Doctor Bugenhagen, Doctor Caspar Cruciger, and Herr Philip.[148] When these had all been taken away, however, then one would have to be vigilant. For it was to be feared that soon afterward the pure doctrine of the catechism would only barely survive, within the four walls of pious fathers, as when [Elijah] departed [1 Kings 19].[149] To the extent possible given his physical weakness, through the grace and power of God, he continued teaching and lecturing even in his old age. In 1539 he expounded Psalm 110, "The Lord said to my Lord," which is also one of his very excellent and comforting works.[150]

In addition, he continued his [lectures on] Genesis, in which he clearly points us to the speaking Son of God, of whom Moses wrote, as Christ Himself testified in John [5:46].[151] He also shows us how to wield the Books of Moses against all the gates of hell [Matt. 16:18] and how we should use them to defend and protect ourselves. Likewise, [he shows us] how teachers and parents can use the Word of God and the examples and severe tribulations of the patriarchs to comfort, encourage, and accustom themselves to

---

[147] Cf. *Table Talk* no. 5296 (1540), WA TR 5:49–50; no. 5126 (1540), LW 54:391; *Church Postil* (1540–44), sermon for Trinity 8 on Matt. 7:15–23, LW 78:280, paragraph 5. See below, Mathesius, *History*, pp. 563–64, 595.

[148] Cf. *Table Talk* no. 3589 (1537), WA TR 3:435–36.

[149] The 1566 and 1567 printings read *Esaias* ["Isaiah"] instead of *Elias* ["Elijah"], probably a typographic error. For the thought, see *Preface to Daniel 12*, WA DB 11/2:123 (LW 63). Cf. below, Mathesius, *History*, p. 435; *LH²*, p. 552.

[150] *Commentary on Psalm 110* (1535/1539), LW 13:225–348.

[151] Cf. above, p. 408.

patience and long-suffering under the cross of their teaching office and of their household. But more about this book later in the year 1545.[152]

In these years, German translations of the three creeds were also published, with a very fine exposition in which he concisely treats the articles of the Holy Trinity and, in particular, of the divinity of Jesus Christ.[153] He treated these more fully later in the four books against the Jews,[154] and, in particular, when, as a conclusion, he wrote about the *Last Words of David*.[155]

For this chosen instrument could neither rest nor be idle. For example, he often entered the pulpit while he was quite weak, and several times, due to growing weakness, he had to step down before the sermon was finished.[156] Again, rarely did he fail to respond to good people or to those who had written about an urgent matter. He was especially inclined to answer people who were troubled and afflicted. Some of his letters on doctrinal matters and his letters of consolation have been included in the volumes [of his works], and more of them, God willing, will eventually be published.[157]

And so our doctor persisted in the Word, in prayer, and endured in patience with utmost resolve and diligence, attending to the church and university commended to him as a faithful doctor. He waged a good warfare, guarding the faith and a good conscience [1 Tim. 1:18–19], stood as defender of the pure doctrine, and zealously prayed against both of the enemies of the cross of Christ. For Satan, the archenemy of the Son of God, not only stirred up heretics and false brethren who assaulted the Church with infernal lies but also roused wrathful people, who would gladly have taken violent action against God's congregation, if the good and irenic emperor had given his consent or simply been willing to turn a blind eye to it. The pope made quite a nuisance of himself, expressing himself in true papal fashion against the Emperor Charles.[158] Therefore, many of these people in Germany were only waiting for a call to arms, as can be clearly discerned from certain people's

---

[152] See below, Mathesius, *History*, pp. 515–16.

[153] *The Three Symbols* (1538), LW 34:197–229. See Brecht 3:190.

[154] See below, Mathesius, *History*, pp. 507–9.

[155] *On the Last Words of David* (1543), LW 15:265–352. See below, Mathesius, *History*, pp. 514–15.

[156] See Brecht 3:229–30. E.g., on Palm Sunday 1539 Luther had to stop preaching because of vertigo: see Luther to Melanchthon, March 2, 1539, WA Br 8:379; *Table Talk* no. 4454 (1539), WA TR 4:321; no. 4479 (1539), LW 54:346.

[157] On the publication of Luther's letters, including Johann Aurifaber's efforts to assemble a complete edition, see the introduction above, p. xxi. Witt Ger 12 in particular contained an extensive selection of Luther's correspondence.

[158] Cf. the 1537 bulls of Paul III, which Luther published with his prefaces and glosses: *Bulla Prorogationis*, WA 50:92–95; *Bulla de indulgentiis*, WA 50:111–16.

secret correspondence.[159] The pope's legates tried to insist that the protesting estates should be suppressed by force and utterly extirpated. For since he had been unable to accomplish anything with the skeleton key[160] of his St. Peter, he wanted to use the sword of St. Paul [Rom. 13:4].[161] Throughout these years, therefore, one conference after another was always being scheduled,[162] and, finally, in Frankfurt,[163] imperial ambassadors engaged in negotiations with the protesting estates about how the religious questions could be resolved without use of the sword, by lawful means and ways, either through a general, free, or national council or through friendly colloquy and negotiation. Although many people were inclined to hostility, God heard the prayer of the peacemakers, so that at this time all considerations were conducive to peace and, following that, to a candid discussion.[164]

After negotiation of an armistice, Duke George of Saxony died this year in April,[165] which gave many people palpitations, and Duke Henry of Saxony received the territory.[166] Then Dr. Luther's prophecy was fulfilled once again,[167] for he |publicly appeared a second time in Leipzig and gave a glorious testimony to his Lord Jesus Christ and the Gospel,[168] just as he had done twenty years before during the disputation in Leipzig.[169]

---

[159] On secret letters, see Sleidanus, *De statu religionis* (1558), book 12, pp. 339–40.

[160] For Luther's dismissive characterization of papal authority (symbolized by the keys of St. Peter) as a mere "skeleton key"—i.e., a thieves' tool or counterfeit—see, e.g., *On the Councils and the Church* (1539), LW 41:153; *Against Hanswurst* (1541), LW 41:202.

[161] The keys and the sword were the traditional attributes of SS. Peter and Paul, respectively, in Western iconography. Although Paul's sword was traditionally associated with the "sword of the Spirit" in Eph. 6:17, Mathesius is likely referring here to Rom. 13:4 and the popes' resort to political power. See *Table Talk* no. 3628 (1537), WA TR 3:467. Cf. below, Mathesius, *History*, pp. 493–94.

[162] Loesche reads *angesagt* ["announced"], but the 1566 edition has *angesatzt*.

[163] The negotiations at Frankfurt am Main in 1539 resulted in the so-called "Truce of Frankfurt," which extended protections accorded to adherents of the Augsburg Confession. See Sleidanus, *De statu religionis* (1558), book 12, p. 341; Brandi, *Emperor Charles V*, p. 420; Brecht 3:203–5.

[164] On the colloquies of 1540–41, see below, p. 422 n. 177.

[165] Duke George of Saxony died on April 24, 1539; his death and Henry's succession are recounted in Sleidanus, *De statu religionis* (1558), book 12, pp. 343–44. George had been a steadfast opponent of Luther since the early days of the Reformation and a chief leader of Catholic political resistance.

[166] On Duke Henry the Pious, see above, p. 313 n. 185.

[167] This prediction was apparently made in 1537. See Volz, *Die Lutherpredigten des Johannes Mathesius*, p. 75 n. 1.

[168] *Sermon in Castle Pleissenburg, Leipzig* (1539/1618), LW 51:301–12.

[169] See above, Mathesius, *History*, pp. 154–55; Luther, *Sermon Preached in the Castle at Leipzig* (June 29, 1519), LW 51:53–60.

Now, when no one attended the out-of-the-way council in Vicenza, the pope canceled it and took counsel as to how he might stir up a blood-bath in Germany.[170] For after Emperor Charles' great disputes in Spain and Italy had been quelled,[171] and peace had also been established with France,[172] those from Ghent[173] rose in revolt against him; he journeyed through France and arrived in Paris on New Year's Day,[174] then entered the Netherlands,[175] and later, after numerous negotiations in Smalcald[176] and the colloquies in Hagenau and Worms,[177] he arrived at the imperial diet in Regensburg,[178] which is described at length in other historical accounts.[179]

Also at about this time, Dr. "Anthony" Barnes[180] was burned at the stake in England as a heretic on account of the truth of the Gospel, along with

---

[170] On the postponement of the council, see Sleidanus, *De statu religionis* (1558), book 12, pp. 329, 332, 344; and above, p. 401 n. 34.

[171] Charles had secured the situation in Spain enough to leave his 12-year-old son Philip as regent in Spain in 1539; Charles had been in Italy in 1535–36. See Brandi, *Emperor Charles V*, pp. 421–24, 368–81.

[172] In June 1538, Charles and Francis I negotiated a ten-year armistice. See Sleidanus, *De statu religionis* (1558), book 12, p. 331; Brandi, *Emperor Charles V*, pp. 388–89.

[173] The city of Ghent, in Flanders, had declared its independence in August 1539. Charles suppressed the rebellion in February 1540. See Sleidanus, *De statu religionis* (1558), book 12, p. 346; book 13, p. 361; Brandi, *Emperor Charles V*, pp. 426–30.

[174] Charles arrived in Paris at the beginning of 1540. See Sleidanus, *De statu religionis* (1558), book 12, p. 347; Brandi, *Emperor Charles V*, pp. 424–45.

[175] After putting down the revolt of Ghent, Charles then sought to resolve the succession in Cleves: see Brandi, *Emperor Charles V*, pp. 432–35; Sleidanus, *De statu religionis* (1558), book 13, p. 366.

[176] I.e., not the 1537 assembly at Smalcald, but the assembly of the league in March 1540: see Sleidanus, *De statu religionis* (1558), book 12, pp. 351–52.

[177] Colloquies between the Evangelical and Roman parties took place under the emperor's aegis at Hagenau in the summer of 1540, at Worms from November 1540 to January 1541, and at Regensburg, during the diet, from April to June 1541. See Brecht 3:215–28; Sleidanus, *De statu religionis* (1558), book 14, pp. 382–89.

[178] The 1541 Diet of Regensburg was held from April to July. Its recess extended the Peace of Nürnberg (see above, p. 347 n. 145). See Brandi, *Emperor Charles V*, pp. 444–53.

[179] See Sleidanus, *De statu religionis* (1558), book 11, pp. 291–93, 321; book 12, pp. 331, 346–48; book 13, pp. 361, 374; book 14, p. 389.

[180] Robert Barnes (1495–1540), an English Augustinian and early adherent of Luther, had visited Wittenberg under the pseudonym "English Anthony" [*Antonius Anglus*] while fleeing arrest in 1528 (see LW 60:230 n. 9). He returned in 1535 as King Henry VIII's ambassador to the Smaldaldic League. When Henry's religious policy again took a more traditional turn, Barnes was burned at the stake in 1540 along with two other English Evangelicals (and three Catholic deniers of Henry's supremacy over the Church). See James Edward McGoldrick, "Barnes, Robert," *OER* 1:122; Luther, preface to Barnes, *Lives of the Roman Pontiffs* (1536), LW 60:111–16; preface to Barnes, *Confession* (1540), LW 60:228–33; Brecht 3:59–64.

others who were unable to condone and approve of all that was going on in that country. The history of this good martyr has been diligently set down by Dr. Luther.[181]

Thus we will conclude this sermon, in God's name, at the beginning of the year 1541.[182] In the next sermon, since I returned to Wittenberg that year to study and sat at the doctor's table, I will recount to you what I experienced, saw, and heard there myself from Doctor Luther, of blessed memory, my dear preceptor and host.

We thank our dear God, who for the last days of this world has sent His Word and faithful teachers into this land, has given the Roman Empire a peace-loving and wise emperor, ʲand has warded and restrained the murder and lies of the devil and wicked people—for the eternal glory of His name, for the blessed consolation of many people, and for the fall of the Roman idolatry, hypocrisy, and unchastity. May God continue to preserve pure doctrine and general peace for us, as well as for our most gracious [imperial] authorities and our gracious and benevolent [royal] authorities![183] Amen!

---

[181] Luther, preface to Barnes, *Confession* (1540), LW 60:228–33. Cf. below, Mathesius, *History*, p. 431.

[182] The next sermon, however, continues with the year 1540: see below, Mathesius, *History*, p. 424.

[183] I.e., in 1563, Emperor Ferdinand I and his son, Maximilian II, the king of Bohemia.

THE TWELFTH SERMON,
ON THE HISTORY OF DOCTOR LUTHER
FROM THE YEAR 1540

[Fall 1563]

BELOVED friends in the Lord! We have (praise God!) reached the year 1540 in the history of our doctor. Now may God help us—and your faithful prayers—so that we may continue felicitously and tell you something useful about his life, his household, and his good words at table. For even as his ministry and his doctrine were holy and comforting, so, too, in his life there were many fine and great virtues to be seen, and those who were around him heard many good words and stories, and he also explained many a beautiful and precious text [of Scripture] at table, and gave many good replies when someone took opportunity to ask about something in Scripture. In this year, [1540,] our God sent me to Doctor Luther's table through the support of Doctor Justus Jonas and Master Georg Rörer, for which I owe thanks to my God and my patrons for the rest of my life.[1] I diligently took note of what I heard and saw there.[2] Likewise, through the help of industrious people, God provided me with many good colloquia and conversations[3] that had been written down previously by Master Veit Dietrich[4] from Nürnberg;

---

[1] See Loesche, *Johannes Mathesius*, 1:94. Mathesius elsewhere mentions the patronage of Georg Spalatin: see Mathesius to Spalatin, June 19, 1540, in Loesche, *Johannes Mathesius*, 2:231. Cf. Brecht 3:245. On Jonas, see the introduction above, p. xxx; on Rörer, see above, p. xx n. 20. On the dating of this sermon to fall 1563, see the introduction above, p. lxxxvii.

[2] Luther's table conversations recorded by Mathesius himself are edited in *Table Talk* nos. 4858–5341 (1540), WA TR 4:559–705; 5:1–64. Another group, *Table Talk* nos. 5342–78 (1540), WA TR 5:65–113, is appended by the Weimar editors as "probably not written down by Mathesius"; it may be connected with Georg Plato (see below, p. 425 n. 9). See the introductions by Ernst Kroker in WA TR 4:xxvii–xlv; 5:xi–xxi. A few of the talks recorded by Mathesius are translated in LW 54:365–409.

[3] On Mathesius' collection of *Table Talk* from these sources, see the introduction above, pp. lxxxviii–lxxxix.

[4] For Dietrich's *Table Talk*, see nos. 1–656 (1529–35), WA TR 1:3–308 (LW 54:3–114), and the introduction by Ernst Kroker, WA TR 1: xxvi–xxxvi. On Dietrich, see above, p. 278 n. 76.

Doctor Weller[5] from Freiberg; Master Anthony Lauterbach[6] from Pirna; and afterward by Master Caspar Heidenreich,[7] superintendent in Torgau; Master Jerome Besold[8] from Nürnberg; Master Plato;[9] and others of the doctor's

---

[5] For Hieronymus Weller's *Table Talk* (or, rather, *Table Talk* ascribed to Weller and Lauterbach), see nos. 3465–659 (1536–37), WA TR 3:335–496 (LW 54:201–49), and the introduction by Ernst Kroker, WA TR 3:xi–xxv. On Weller, see above, p. 416 n. 127.

[6] For Lauterbach's *Table Talk*, see the previous footnote (with Weller) and nos. 3683–4719 (1538–39), WA TR 3:527–695; 4:1–448 (LW 54:249–364), and the introduction by Ernst Kroker, WA TR 3:xxvii–xliv. Anton [Anthony] Lauterbach was a student in Wittenberg from 1529 until 1533, when he became a deacon in Leisnig on Luther's recommendation. He returned to Wittenberg in 1537 to serve as second deacon for two years until his departure to Pirna in 1539. During this second stay in Wittenberg, Lauterbach kept a diary which includes his *Table Talk*. He later made his own collection drawing on material collected by others (WA TR 5:427–701). See Michael Welte, "Lauterbach, Anton," *BBKL* 4:1254–55; Stupperich, *Reformatorenlexikon*, p. 129.

[7] For Heidenreich's (sometimes "Heyderich," as Mathesius gives it) *Table Talk*, see nos. 5379–603 (1542–43), WA TR 5:117–274 (LW 54:411–64), and the introduction by Ernst Kroker, WA TR 5:xxii–xxix. Heidenreich (ca. 1510–86) first studied in Wittenberg from 1528 to 1529; he briefly succeeded Mathesius as rector of the Joachimsthal Latin school in 1540 but soon followed him to Wittenberg, where Heidenreich also boarded at Luther's table and received his master's degree in 1541. He then served as court preacher to Catherine of Mecklenburg (1487–1561), the widowed duchess of Saxony, until 1553, when he became superintendent in Torgau. See Stupperich, *Reformatorenlexikon*, p. 101.

[8] For Besold's *Table Talk*, see nos. 5659–75 (1544), WA TR 5:299–314 (LW 54:465–76), and the introduction by Ernst Kroker, WA TR 5:xxii–xxiii and xxxii. Jerome [Hieronymus] Besold (1522–62) was the son-in-law of the Nürnberg reformer Andreas Osiander and studied at Wittenberg from 1537 to 1544, during which time he recorded table talks. He was later involved in the publication of Luther's *Table Talk* and Genesis lectures. See Karl Schornbaum, "Besold, Hieronymus," *NDB* 2:179.

[9] Georg Plato (sometimes "Placo") of Hamburg was in Luther's household from 1540 to at least 1542. The *Table Talk* that he recorded or copied and that he collected in a manuscript titled *Memorabilia dicta et facta Lutheri* is found in the WA appendix to the Khummer collection of *Table Talk* (see WA TR 4:xxvi and *Table Talk* nos. 4857k–p [1540], WA TR 4:551–55) and mixed with Mathesius' collection (see WA TR 4:xxxviii–xxxvi and *Table Talk* no. 5375a–z, WA TR 5:100–111). On Plato, see *Table Talk* no. 2332b (1540), WA TR 2:422; 5:xiv.

table companions.[10] Ferdinand à Maugis[11] from Austria also noted in his Bible many interpretations of various passages. Master Georg Rörer very diligently collected many precious things from letters and counsels, and especially what was spoken during the work of translating the Bible.[12]

Drawing from these writings, the doctor's books, and the reports and accounts of many good people, we now intend, in God's name, to speak about his household, virtues, and fine discourses, which are seasoned with the true salt of wisdom [Col. 4:6] and contain much good teaching, useful instruction, blessed consolation, and good admonition.[13]

It is a good thing, truly, to take note of a fine or wise saying from a great and holy man; the examples of holy people also furnish teaching, comfort, and admonition, and make a most pleasant adornment for a sermon.

---

[10] Other collectors of Luther's *Table Talk* included Conrad Cordatus (see above, p. xl n. 121): *Table Talk* nos. 1950–3416 (1531–34), WA TR 2:273–672; 3:1–308 (LW 54:167–200). Johann Schlaginhaufen (ca. 1498–1560), who had matriculated at Wittenberg in 1520, served briefly as a pastor in Joachimsthal, and returned to Wittenberg by 1531 before taking up a position in nearby Anhalt-Köthen, where he eventually became superintendent (see Franz Kindscher, "Schlaginhaufen, Johannes," *ADB* 31:329–36; Brown, *Singing the Gospel*, pp. 34–35): *Table Talk* nos. 1232–889 (1531–34), WA TR 2:2–249 (LW 54:123–65). Ludwig Rabe, who matriculated at Wittenberg in 1517 but boarded at Luther's table while he completed his study of law in the early 1530s, then returning to his native Halle where he ran afoul of Cardinal Albert and fled back to Wittenberg until being named chancellor to Prince Wolfgang of Anhalt in 1538 (see WA TR 2:xviii–xx): *Table Talk* nos. 1890–949 (1530), WA TR 2:253–72. Johann Aurifaber (see above, pp. xviii–xix n. 13), WA TR 6. Cf. the introduction by Theodore G. Tappert, LW 54:xiii.

[11] For collections of Bible inscriptions made by Luther, see WA 48, though the collection made by the Austrian nobleman Ferdinand à Maugis (1520–after 1546) has apparently been lost: see WA 48:xiii n. 1. Some of the *Table Talk* found elsewhere was likely originally recorded by him: see *Table Talk* no. 4857a (1545), WA TR 4:549; no. 5375k (1545), WA TR 5:106; the introductions by Ernst Kroker, WA TR 4:xxv; 5:xxxiv (cf. the introduction by Theodore G. Tappert, LW 54:xiii). On Maugis, who lodged and traveled with Luther in 1545, see WA BR 11:149 n. 2; the introduction by Ernst Kroker, WA TR 4:xxv; and the introduction by Gottfried G. Krodel to Luther's letter to Katharina, July 28, 1545, LW 50:273.

[12] Georg Rörer (see above, p. xx n. 20) published a compilation of Luther's Bible inscriptions in 1547 (see Otto Albrecht, "Einleitung zu den Bibel- und Bucheinzeichnungen Luthers," WA 48:xvii–xxii, xliii–xlviii, xlix–l; and Hans Volz, WA 48N:15–22), and in 1554 he published a compilation of consolatory material drawn from Luther's letters of spiritual counsel (expanded from a collection of 1544 edited by Caspar Cruciger), which is probably what Mathesius has in mind here (cf. Kolb, *Luther as Prophet, Teacher, and Hero*, p. 166). For Rörer's minutes (protocols) of the meetings of the "Wittenberg Sanhedrin" for revision of the German Bible, see WA DB 3 and the introduction by Otto Reichert there, pp. xv–xvii; cf. below, Mathesius, *History*, pp. 475, 477. Rörer did record *Table Talk* as well, edited in nos. 5342–75 (various dates, 1530–44), WA TR 5:65–111, and nos. 657–684 (1530), WA TR 1:309–30 (see LW 54:115–21), as well as copying and collecting material from others: see the introductions by Ernst Kroker, WA TR 1:xv, xxii; 6:xvi–xvii.

[13] On Luther's personal affairs and family life during this time, see Brecht 3:229–47; see also Brecht 2:195–211, 429–33.

The saying of St. Bartholomew[14]—"The Gospel is long yet short"—is very fruitful to consider: how in the Word of God, brief as it is, such rich and great wisdom is revealed. Similarly, the saying of St. Andrew that is mentioned in his legend truly provides a good lesson:[15] the common man should not disturb the peace of the Gospel or bring it under suspicion by unrest and riot. St. Augustine's response to the question of what God was doing before He made heaven and earth is sharp and good: God was making a hell for impertinent teachers who were not content with His Word.[16] Likewise, St. Luke recorded a beautiful maxim of the Lord for us: "It is better to give than to receive" [Acts 20:35], said Christ.

Would God that diligent students had been more faithful in writing down their teachers' sayings and ideas, seeing that the Holy Spirit is never at rest in His instruments! Then we would not need to bring in so much material from other people[17] in our sermons. Whoever collected the wise proverbs of the great King Solomon [cf. 1 Kings 4:32] has truly done Christendom no little service. Likewise, whoever recorded the saying from the house of Elijah[18] that the world would stand for six thousand years: For two thousand years it would be empty and deserted; for two thousand, the Law of Moses will hold sway; and the final, yet abbreviated, two thousand will belong to the Lord Christ, the Messiah. After these six days of work, the eternal Sabbath day and rest day will begin—the day of refreshment, on which everything will be made right, and an eternal year of liberty and jubilee [cf. Leviticus 25]. Alas, how few precious little pearls like this are to be found in the dung piles of the old legends and hermits, which Satan once piled upon Christendom.

Since you are now rather well acquainted with our doctor's teaching and faith, today you shall hear about what he spoke at home as well, and

---

[14] See *LA* 2:110, no. 123. The saying is originally attributed to St. Bartholomew in Ps.-Dionysius, *Mystical Theology* 1.3 (PG 3:1000; translated in Colm Luibheid, Paul Rorem, et al., eds., *Pseudo-Dionysius: The Complete Works* [Mahwah, NJ: Paulist Press, 1987], p. 136).

[15] See *LA* 1:17, no. 2.

[16] Augustine, *Confessions* 11.12.14 (PL 32:815; Loeb 27 [2016], pp. 212–13). Augustine, however, recounts the response as having been given by someone else and disapproves of it himself. Cf. Luther, *Table Talk* no. 5010 (1540), LW 54:377; *Lectures on Genesis* (1535–45/1544–54), LW 1:10.

[17] *so vil frembdes dinges*; or: "so much extraneous material."

[18] This saying and its attribution to "a Jew of the house of Elijah" are found in Johann Carion's *Chronicle*, drawing on Paul of Burgos' (ca. 1351–1435) *Scrutinium Scripturarum* (see below p. 509 n. 31). From Carion (1499–1537), the saying found its way into the first edition of Luther's *Supputatio annorum mundi* (1541) (see below, p. 429), though in the second edition (1545) Luther withdrew the association with Elijah: WA 53:22. In fact, the original form of the chronology is found in the Talmud. See *Supputatio annorum mundi* (1541), WA 53:11–13.

about his Christian example. For this will provide a good testimony of his true doctrine and show that he faithfully distributed the mysteries of God with his right hand without taking anything away from his listeners with his left hand (that is, bad example or tasteless speech). For though one's life and good example do not make the doctrine better, it is proper and promotes the doctrine if the preachers lead a Christian and prudent life and let their light shine [Matt. 5:16] at table and in the discipline of their household, or let their church bell ring[19] so that they, like devout wives [1 Pet. 3:1], may win over many people for our God with their words and good conduct rather than frightening the converts away from the truth with dissolute behavior and making them worse.

Now, our doctor had reached his fifty-eighth year, and all kinds of physical ailments had come upon him with age, so that he was forced to give up a great deal of his preaching, lecturing, and traveling because of his illness.[20] He remained at home, therefore, just as he had several years before, when he had expounded the Gospel in a plain and simple way for his whole household on Sundays; these household sermons were gathered with faithful diligence by Master Veit Dietrich in the doctor's *House Postil.*[21]

The man was unable to cease from labor, even though his catarrh, vertigo, and weakness caused him much suffering.[22] All morning and evening, and often during supper, he said his prayers as he had been accustomed to do in the monastery since his youth. In addition, he recited his

---

[19] *jre kirchenglöcklein klingen*; the expression sounds proverbial, but no source could be identified.

[20] Forty sermons by Luther from the year 1540 are preserved (Aland Pr 1799–1802, 1856–58, 1898–1930). Although the precise internal chronology of Luther's delivery of his Genesis lectures is uncertain, a break between May 1540 and the summer of 1541 would, however, fit the suggestive evidence pointed out by Jaroslav Pelikan in the middle of the lectures on Genesis 24: see the introduction, LW 4:x. Cf. below, p. 430. On Mathesius' presence in Wittenberg in 1540, see the introduction above, pp. lxxxiii–lxxxiv.

[21] In 1532, Luther preached at home nineteen times (WA 36); in 1533, forty times (WA 37); and in 1534, thirty times (WA 37). Many of these sermons were adapted from Georg Rörer's notes to form the *House Postil*, first by Veit Dietrich in 1544: WA 52 (translated in Loy; in a new edition, LW 81–83). In 1559, an edition of the *House Postil* was published by Andreas Poach based on a fresh examination of Rörer's manuscripts: see StL 13b (translated in Klug 1–3). On Poach, see the introduction by Christopher Boyd Brown, LW 58:xxvi; Reinhold Jauernig, "Andreas Poach," in *Luther in Thüringen* (Berlin: Evangelische Verlagsanstalt, [1952]), pp. 198–206.

[22] On Luther's illnesses during these years, see Brecht 3:229–35.

Small Catechism like any schoolboy[23] and continued reading constantly.[24] His little Psalter was his prayer book,[25] and the catechism was his household account book;[26] he taught, comforted, and admonished himself from this. And since he was now correcting and reviewing his German Bible for the last time, he applied extraordinary diligence to make sure that he was rendering the simple and correct sense with clear words; he asked [others] for advice and often began a disputation at table about how a Hebrew word or passage should be rendered in good, understandable German, as we intend to discuss at another time.[27]

In the previous year, our doctor had also prepared a chronology[28] of the years since the beginning of the world, setting the biblical stories in proper order, which is one of his greatest and most valuable efforts, with which he rendered an outstanding service to many readers of the Bible.

And because usury[29] was a general plague on the whole country, ruining and sucking dry the upper and lower classes alike, our doctor at this time published his book on usury addressed to the pastors.[30] At table he said, "My book will trouble the conscience of little usurers, who take five or six [percent] with permission from the authorities, but the big thieves in the banks,[31] who flay and fleece the whole land, will laugh in their sleeves at me.[32] For example, one of the biggest usurers was recently heard to say that until now he had regarded me as a wise man, but I give no sign of that in this book, because I attempt to write about matters in which I have no

---

[23] Cf. *Large Catechism* (1529) Pref. 7 (Kolb-Wengert, p. 380; *Concordia*, p. 353). On Luther's catechisms, see above, Mathesius, *History*, pp. 252–53.

[24] *hielt immer an im lesen*; probably referring here to private reading rather than to public lecturing. See below, p. 430.

[25] Probably a specific reference to the small Psalter which Luther kept with him and made notes in, which he had with him at the time of his death. See WA 48:266–68 and below, p. 448.

[26] *haußbuch*; i.e., a book kept ready at hand of which he made daily use.

[27] See below, Mathesius, *History*, pp. 476–85.

[28] *Supputatio annorum mundi* (1541, 1545), WA 53:1–184. See Brecht 3:138. Having started work on the chronology in 1536, Luther completed his work on it in 1540: see WA 53:6–8; cf. *Lectures on Genesis* (1535–45/1544–54), LW 1:334.

[29] The sin of usury, for Luther and the preceding Christian tradition, was any lending of money at interest (cf. Ps. 15:5; Luke 6:35).

[30] *To Pastors, That They Should Preach against Usury* (1540), WA 51:331–424 (LW 61). See Brecht 3:258–62.

[31] *Stulrauber*; see *Large Catechism* (1529) I 229 (Kolb-Wengert, p. 417; *Concordia*, p. 385); *Sermons on Matthew 18–24* (1537–40/1796–1847), LW 68:199.

[32] Cf. Wander 1:946, "Faust" no. 32, and *DWB*, s.v. "Faust."

experience. He ᴵwould be better able to write about the subject, because he has had many dealings in this kind of business with great princes and lords."³³

This year the doctor also wrote the account about "Dr. Anthony,"³⁴ who was burned at the stake in London in England on account of the true religion; this was included in volume 6 [of the German works]. Then it became apparent what the English Gospel really was. As Dr. Johann Bugenhagen said at table:³⁵ "Now I realize that the Holy Spirit knows how to speak better than we. I often spoke in defense of the king with many good people and asked our doctor not to call him King Harry.³⁶ But I realize that whomever the Holy Spirit calls 'Harry' is and remains so."

In addition to this work, our doctor also preached and lectured at times, when he had the strength, although in the two years following, he expounded only three chapters in his [lectures on] Genesis³⁷ and rarely preached, on account of his vertigo and headaches. He also rarely came to the table without bringing along a book.³⁸ One time he had Oecolampadius' book³⁹ with him and was looking at it; then he began reading out, in good German words: "If my intent is dishonest or I am seeking something in this

---

³³ These remarks by the Nürnberg banker Bonaventura Furtenberg, who was involved in lending to Cardinal Albert, are reported in *Table Talk* no. 4805 (1542), WA TR 4:523–25; no. 4863 (1540), WA TR 4:560. See also *Appeal for Prayer against the Turks* (1541), LW 43:221; and Melanchthon, *Historiae quaedam recitatae inter publicas lectiones*, CR 20:525, no. 18.

³⁴ On Barnes, see above, Mathesius, *History*, pp. 422–23 and n. 180 there. Luther's German edition of Barnes' *Confession*, with Luther's preface (1540), LW 60:228–33, was included in Witt Ger 6 (1553), fols. 417r–420r.

³⁵ See *Table Talk* no. 5068 (1540), WA TR 4:641.

³⁶ See above, Mathesius, *History*, pp. 206–8. *Heinz* was the German diminutive of the name Heinrich [Henry], but also the stock German name for a "fool," and hence a pointedly dismissive epithet. See LW 60:230 n. 12 and below, p. 465 n. 11, p. 494 n. 186. Luther also applied it to Duke Henry of Braunschweig: *Against Hanswurst* (1541), LW 41:179–256.

³⁷ Luther lectured on Genesis 22–24 in 1540. Cf. above, Mathesius, *History*, p. 408; *Table Talk* no. 4959 (1540), WA TR 4:4959; and below, p. 432. See *Lectures on Genesis* (1535–45/1544–54), LW 4:91–299.

³⁸ Cf. above, Mathesius, *History*, p. 272; *Table Talk* no. 3502 (1536), LW 54:215; no. 3588a (1537), WA TR 3:435; no. 3654 (1537), WA TR 3:489–90; no. 4127 (1538), WA TR 4:153; no. 4374 (1539), WA TR 4:268–69; no. 4879 (1540), WA TR 4:566–67. See Volz, *Die Lutherpredigten des Johannes Mathesius*, p. 202 and n. 1.

³⁹ *Ioannis Oecolampadii ad Billibaldum Pyrkaimerum de re Eucharistiae responsio* (Zürich: Christoph Froschauer, 1526) [VD16 O281], fol. d1r. Cf. Oecolampadius, *Apologetica. De dignatato eucharistiae sermones 2. Ad Theobaldum Billicanum, quinam in verbis caenae alienum sensum inferant. Ad ecclesiastas Svevos antisvngramma* (Zürich: Christoph Froschauer, 1526), fol. h3b. On Oecolampadius, see above, p. 240 n. 52.

other than God's glory and what is best for the Church, God will punish me for it and suddenly dispose of me."[40]

"Ah, you poor man!" said our doctor. "You were indeed your own prophet.[41] May God forgive you, if that is still possible." Someone at the table said, "I wouldn't have thought that the man could write so well in German." But the book was in Latin. Another time the doctor brought along the Saxon [version of] Reynard the Fox,[42] which he praised as a masterful poem and vivid representation of court life.

Our doctor often came to the table with weighty and deep thoughts, sometimes ᶦmaintaining his old cloistered silence for the entire meal, so that not a word was spoken at the table, but when the time was right he provided very stimulating conversation. These talks we usually referred to as *condimenta mensae* ["seasonings for the table"], which we liked more than all the spices and delectable foods.

When he wanted to get us to talk, he would usually prompt us: "What news have you heard?" We would let this first encouragement pass. If he pressed again: "You prelates, what news is there in the land?" then the older ones[43] at the table would start talking. Doctor Wolf Severus,[44] who had been the tutor for His Majesty, the Roman king, sat by the head of the table. He would start up with something if there was no one from abroad present, such as a traveling member of the court.

Once the conversation was under way, others would also chime in at times, but of course with due decorum and reverence, until someone got the doctor to start talking. Often good questions were posed from Scripture, which he answered clearly and concisely. And if anyone contradicted him, he could also bear with this and give a deft response in rebuttal. Distinguished people from the university,[45] as well as from foreign places,[46] often came to the table; then there were very fine talks and stories. I would like to mention some of them here briefly. Perhaps they can all be collected some day; it

---

[40] *Table Talk* no. 5322 (1540), WA TR 5:58.

[41] Cf. above, Mathesius, *History*, p. 314.

[42] See above, Mathesius, *History*, p. 272.

[43] Mathesius himself would have been 36 years old in 1540.

[44] On Wolf Severus [Wolfgang Schiefer], who had until 1539 been employed by King Ferdinand (see above, p. lxxxiii n. 324) as tutor for his son Maximilian (see above, p. lxxxiii n. 325): see above, Mathesius, *History*, p. 339 and n. 104 there.

[45] E.g., Melanchthon, Bugenhagen, Cruciger, Jonas, and Georg Major. See Brecht 3:245.

[46] In addition to the English reformer Robert ["Anthony"] Barnes (see above, p. 422 n. 180), a steady stream of visitors from across Europe passed through Luther's house: see Brecht 3:318–20, 239–40.

would truly be a fine and useful labor to write *Elbian Nights and Days*[47] or *Miscellanea of Dr. Luther*.[48]

A certain bishop wanted to know what the Lord Christ did in His youth.[49] He dreamed that he saw a little boy collecting wood and chips, and when lunch had been prepared, he called His father to the table and said, "Mother, should I call the other man too?"[50] At this the bishop was frightened and woke up. "I also believe," said the doctor, "that dear little Jesus helped His mother with the house chores as an obedient child and sometimes went to get water, perhaps also on occasion bringing along wine. Therefore, when there was a shortage of wine at the wedding in Cana [John 2:1–12], His mother was addressing Him based on prior experience. So far as the book about the Lord's youth is concerned, it is much too trivial a thing, which is why the ancient decrees reject it as a useless book."[51]

One time when his dog was begging at the table, someone asked if there would be irrational animals after the resurrection, in the new world. "By all means," he said. "For the new heaven and earth will not be empty or desolate, but full of beautiful creatures. Every little dog will have a golden collar with precious stones and a little pearl on every little hair. For the splendor and jewelry of this world will be only for irrational animals then; blessed human beings will be adorned with the substantial and perfect wisdom, righteousness, clarity, and glory of the Lord Christ, which no eye has seen, no ear has heard, and no heart has yet imagined" [1 Cor. 2:9; Isa. 64:4].[52]

---

[47] *Noctes & dies Albiacas*, a title recalling Aulus Gellius (ca. 123–170 BC), *Noctes Atticas* [Attic nights] (Loeb 195 [1927], pp. 200, 212).

[48] The first printed collection of Luther's *Table Talk* was published in 1566 by Johann Aurifaber under the title *Tischreden oder Colloquia Doctor Martin Luthers* (see above, pp. xviii–xix n. 13).

[49] *Table Talk* no. 5360 (1540), WA TR 5:89–94. The *Table Talk* identifies the bishop as "Solynus" or "Solinus," who is difficult to identify further.

[50] I.e., the bishop, who was apparently visible to the child Jesus in the vision.

[51] The stories of Jesus' childhood found in the *Infancy Gospel of Thomas* (*De infantia Iesu euangelium Thomae graece*, ed. Tony Burke, Corpus Christianorum Series Apocryphorum 17 [Turnhout: Brepols. 2010]; ANF 8:395–404) and the *Protoevangelium of James* (Ronald Hock, *The Infancy Gospels of James and Thomas* [Santa Rosa, CA: Polebridge Press, 1996], pp. 2–81; ANF 8:361–67) were combined in the Latin *Gospel of Pseudo-Matthew* [*Liber de infantia Mariae et Christi Salvatoris*]: see Constantin von Tischendorf, ed., *Evangelia Apocrypha* (Leipzig: Avenarius & Mendelssohn, 1853; repr., Hildesheim: Olms, 1966), pp. 50–105 (ANF 8:368–83). For an account of the boy Jesus fetching water for Mary, see *Infancy Gospel of Thomas* 10 (11).1–2 (Corpus Christianorum Series Apocryphorum 17:324–25; ANF 8:397, 399, 402); *Gospel of Pseudo-Matthew* 33 (Tischendorf, *Evangelia Apocrypha*, p. 97; ANF 8:380). Gratian, *Decretum* 1 D 15 c. 3 (Friedberg 1:38) lists the *Liber de infantia Salvatoris* (i.e., *Gospel of Pseudo-Matthew*) among works rejected as heretical or schismatic.

[52] *Table Talk* no. 1150 (1530), WA TR 1:567–68.

In addition, he mentioned the Seven Sleepers [of Ephesus][53] and the person who wanted to see the smallest joy in heaven: He went into the forest and heard a little bird singing, and at this he fell asleep for two hundred years[54] (perhaps it was Johannes de Temporibus,[55] who also is supposed to have lived three hundred years [beginning] in the time of Emperor Charles I). When he awoke, thinking he had slept hardly an hour, he found that his monastery and the city had been destroyed meanwhile, and a different house was there instead.

"Yes, dear friends," said our doctor, "it will be a joy different from what the Jews hope with their *shor-habor*[56] and from what the Turks hope according to their Koran, or from what the world in general hopes. The world also says, 'A fresh drink and a raw egg after a bath are equal to the smallest joy in the kingdom of heaven.'[57] |Then we will behold God in eternal righteousness and be wholly filled and satisfied and will have abundant pleasures and perfect joy, as Psalm 16 [:11] and 17 [:15] say."[58] The man was able to accommodate and apply his stories and conversation well, so that his listeners received joy and consolation from them.

Someone else asked whether we would also recognize each other after the resurrection.[59] "By all means," he said. "For if Adam knew his Eve, who was made from his rib while he slept, even though he had never seen her before [Gen. 2:22–23], how much more shall we in our new righteousness and perfection recognize those with whom we were associated on earth.

---

[53] The legend of the Seven Sleepers of Ephesus recounts that seven Christian men from Ephesus were fleeing the Decian persecution (AD 251) when they entered a cave and fell asleep for two hundred years, waking up in the reign of Theodosius II (r. 408–450). See *LA* 2:15–18, no. 101.

[54] This story is told both of St. Virilia, abbot of the monastery of Leyre, in Navarre, and of a monk from the Cistercian monastery of Heisterbach, in the Siebengebirge. See Kurt Rössler, *Der Mönch von Heisterbach zu Zeit und Ewigkeit* (Königswinter: Stiftung Abtei Heisterbach, 2003).

[55] According to Johannes Nauclerus (d. 1510), *Chronica* (Cologne: Peter Quentel, 1544) [VD16 N168], fol. 753, Johannes de Temporibus was a knight under Charlemagne who lived for 361 years and died in 1139. These anecdotes are not found in Luther's *Table Talk* recorded elsewhere.

[56] The *shor-habor* in rabbinic tradition was the wild ox, in battle with Leviathan, on which the pious would feast at the coming of the Messiah: see Leviticus Rabbah 13:3, in Jacob Neusner, *Judaism and Scripture* (Chicago: University of Chicago Press, 1986), pp. 294–95. Cf. Luther, *Table Talk* no. 232 (1532), WA TR 1:98; and *Lectures on Genesis* (1535–45/1544–54), LW 8:225, which also comments on Muslim hopes for the next world.

[57] Wander 1:1343, "Trunk" no. 25; 1:755, "Ei" no. 92.

[58] This material is not found elsewhere in the records of Luther's *Table Talk.*

[59] For this conversation, which took place on Luther's final trip to Eisleben in 1546, see above, Jonas and Coelius, *Report,* p. 11.

And since we, as adopted children of God, shall be like the Lord Christ and conformed to Him through the communicated divinity [2 Pet. 1:4], we will also know all believers from the beginning of the world. After all, Mary Magdalene recognized the Lord Christ by His speech, which He brought with Him from the grave [John 20:16]. And the disciples recognized the glorified Moses and Elijah on the holy mountain, when they appeared in order to comfort Christ [Matt. 17:1–4; Luke 9:28–33]. In the same way, the people recognized the saints who rose from their graves with Christ on Easter Day [Matt. 27:52–53].

"I also maintain," said the doctor, "because the rich man in his hell sees and recognizes Abraham and Lazarus [Luke 16:23], that the godless[60] will not only recognize each other but will also see the believers in heaven, whom they tormented and persecuted, and this will cause them great anguish; they will be grieved and tormented by this, much as the pious here at times experience tribulation and are impatient even now when things go so well for the godless (Psalm 37 [:1])."

One time when someone mentioned the calculations of people who were naming a definite year and day for the Last Day,[61] the doctor said, "No, no! The text in Matthew is too clear: 'Concerning the day and the hour no one knows, not even the angels in heaven, but only My Father' [Matt. 24:36]. Therefore, neither I nor any man or angel can name the day or hour. I believe, however, that all the signs which are to precede the Last Day have already happened. The Gospel is being preached in all the world [Matt. 24:14]; the son of perdition has been revealed and killed in the hearts of many people [2 Thess. 2:3]. The Roman Empire is being laid low in death; all the elements and creatures are stirring and waning. There is no more love and faith on earth [cf. Matt. 24:12; Luke 18:8]. Let Christ come when He wills; He will find a small flock of believers. Gluttony, drunkenness, usury, worry, greed, [ostentatious] dress and building, and all kinds of immorality are just as prevalent as in the days of Noah [Matt. 24:37–39; cf. Luke 17:26–30]. That

[60] For the thought, see the sermon for Trinity 2, June 6, 1535, WA 41:298; and in Dietrich's 1544 edition of the *House Postil*, WA 52:371 [LW 81] (translated under Trinity 1 in Loy 2:243–44; cf. Klug 2:235); cf. *Table Talk* no. 3904 (1538), WA TR 3:696–97.

[61] Those who attempted such calculations included Michael Stifel, a talented mathematician who left the Augustinan cloister in Esslingen in 1522 to become one of Luther's early followers and a friend (see above, p. xxxvii n. 101). In 1532, as pastor in Lochau, Stifel announced the end of the world for the following year. When Luther reproached him, Stifel became embittered against Luther, though the two were reconciled after the failure of Stifel's predictions, and Stifel returned to Wittenberg for further study in 1541. See Brecht 3:8–9; Luther to Stifel, June 24, 1533, WA Br 6:495–96. The discourse reported by Mathesius here does not appear elsewhere in the *Table Talk*, but cf. *Table Talk* 3360a (1533), WA TR 3:290; no. 5488 (1542), LW 54:427–28. Other contemporary chiliasts included the Augsburg Anabaptist Augustin Bader (d. 1530): see Friedrich Wilhelm Bautz, "Bader, Augustin," *BBKL* 1:332.

is why I think the signs before the Last Day have been fulfilled. In addition to the papacy, Gog and Magog[62] [Ezek. 38:2; Rev. 20:8] have yet to be suppressed and destroyed at the appointed time beforehand, and perhaps unusual supernatural eclipses of the sun and moon will occur [Matt. 24:29], as at the time of Christ's suffering [Matt. 27:45]. Meanwhile, the Gospel will be driven out of every church, school, and pulpit before the Last Day and remain only with pious parents and their households within their own four walls, as during the time of Elijah [1 Kings 19:19],[63] as seems about to be the case. Otherwise everything that is to take place before the Last Day has come to pass.

"I think Christ our Lord is already sounding a call to arms in heaven,[64] and the angels [Matt. 16:27] are mightily arming themselves for the campaign. And because all of the great signs during these six thousand years, of which Elijah prophesied,[65] have taken place during spring and at Easter,[66] I hope that Christ will also appear at Easter and make His voice heard with thunder in a morning storm, followed by the sudden destruction of heaven and earth, and in an instant and the blink of an eye 'the living will be transformed and the dead will awaken, the new heaven and earth will be created, and He will hold judgment in the clouds [Luke 21:27; 1 Cor. 15:52; 1 Thess. 4:16–17; 2 Pet. 3:10–13]. And Scripture, along with His third 'It is finished' [cf. Gen. 2:1–3; John 19:30], will be fully and completely fulfilled. That is what we hope for.

"For in this valley of tears[67] we surely have little life, joy, and comfort left, except insofar as we listen to, contemplate, believe, and preserve the precious Word of God. Grant this Word to us, O Lord Jesus, eternal Word; then we will be and remain alive, and we will prevail and finally triumph over death, the devil, and all the gates of hell. I undertook my cause on the basis of the spoken and written Word, and to this day I have carried on by the power of God, upon and with the Word. With the Word I have overcome all my foes. I still stand and rely upon the Word; relying upon this Word, I will pass through death and go to my dear Lord and Savior. Therefore, anyone

---

[62] Luther identified these figures in biblical prophecy with the contemporary activity of the Turkish Empire. See Luther, preface to *Ezekiel [38–39]* (1530), LW 59:277–84. Cf. above, Mathesius, *History*, p. 289.

[63] Cf. above, Mathesius, *History*, p. 419.

[64] *Table Talk* no. 5337 (1540), WA TR 5:63.

[65] See above, p. 427.

[66] I.e., the creation of the world, the flood, the exodus from Egypt, the annunciation, and Christ's resurrection. See *Lectures on Genesis* (1535–45/1544–54), LW 1:37–38; 2:92–93; *Table Talk* no. 5237 (1540), WA TR 5:21–22; cf. *LA* 1:200–201, no. 51.

[67] On the expression, see above, p. 241 n. 60.

who wants to risk everything on this Word along with me—indeed, along with Christ—is welcome to do so. I know of nothing more reliable or certain than the Word of God recorded in the prophets and apostles."[68]

These are the kinds of talks that our dear prophet was accustomed to hold during and after meals with those in his house; I cannot recount all of them here. He discussed all sorts of [preachers], and particularly the Evangelical preachers, giving a good account of the special gifts and graces each had compared to the others and, again, of the shortcomings and flaws that many of them brought into the pulpit. One he praised for his simple manner of speaking; another, for his skillful and apposite parables. He praised them for organizing their material well and for speaking correctly and with good German words.[69]

He also particularly praised someone who based his sermon on a single passage, remained with it, and clearly and comprehensibly explained the words and topics of the appointed text, often repeating and reiterating things for the common man, and favorably concluded by applying and addressing it well to his listeners. "Those are the preachers," he said, "who humble themselves and think about to whom they are preaching."[70]

He compared three preachers to a full keg from which someone had pulled out the tap; they flowed continuously so long as there was something inside, but now and then some mold and yeast came out too.[71] He also praised those who began speaking in the pulpit and stopped when the time was right.[72] He gave me this rule when I asked him to teach me what behooves a young preacher: "When you see that the people are listening very

---

[68] *Table Talk* no. 480 (1533), WA TR 1:210–11. See also below, Mathesius, *History*, pp. 517, 544.

[69] Cf. *Table Talk* 2580 (1532), WA TR 2:531; no. 5047 (1540), LW 54:382–84; no. 5469 (1542), WA TR 5:169–70.

[70] See *Table Talk* no. 5489 (1542), LW 54:428; no. 3579 (1537), WA TR 3:427–28; no. 3612 (1537), WA TR 3:454–55. Cf. *Table Talk* no. 1005 (1530), WA TR 1:505; no. 4719 (1539), WA TR 4:446–48.

[71] See *Table Talk* no. 5199 (1540), LW 54:396. The three preachers were Joachim Mörlin, who served briefly as a Wittenberg deacon before receiving his doctorate in 1540 (see above, p. 412 n. 107; Sigrid Looß, "Mörlin, Joachim," *OER* 3:94–95); Nicholas Medler (1502–51), who had preached in Wittenberg during his advanced studies from 1531 to 1535 before becoming superintendent in Naumburg in 1536 (see Inge Mager, "Medler, Nikolaus," *BBKL* 5:1151–53); and Jacob Schenk, who after completing his Wittenberg doctorate served as court preacher to the dukes of Saxony (see above, p. 415 n. 122; cf. *Table Talk* no. 4884 (1540), WA TR 4:568).

[72] *Table Talk* no. 5171a, (1540), WA TR 4:692; no. 5171b (1540), LW 54:393; no. 2580 (1532), WA TR 2:531; *Sermon on the Mount* (1530–32/1532), LW 21:7; *Sermons on John 6–8* (1530–32/1565), LW 23:227.

attentively and are interested, then stop. Next time the people will be that much more inclined to return."[73]

One time a pastor got stuck on a nail in the pulpit and tore his robe on it. When the doctor heard of this, he said, "I was thinking that he must have been nailed down, because he couldn't stop."[74] He also warned us very often against inept methods of teaching.[75] "My friend," he said, "do not take up and explain all the passages that you can think of. Do justice to one of them; that is as much as the common man and layman can retain."[76] He also often said jokingly that preachers should not take these three contentious little hounds with them into the pulpit: pride, greed, and envy.[77] For they lead many a preacher astray and cause him to forget the words before him.

Frequently he made very favorable mention of the schools. "In them," he said, "there is still something good left in the papacy, for they still retain the Our Father, the Creed, and the Ten Commandments, and by virtue of these things they provide the Church with people.[78] The ancient emperors devoted many resources to the schools; Charlemagne, for example, supported thirty teachers in Fulda ¦and himself made appointments to his bishoprics and other offices from there.[79] But the bumblebees drove the honeybees out of this hive,[80] and the monks and canons[81] who lounged around in the schools shared with the poor schoolmasters and grammar teachers the way the peasant shared with Mercury: having asked and promised to give the church half of whatever he granted him, he gave the outside of the nuts and the inside of the dates for pious uses—the rest he gobbled up on his own.[82]

---

[73] Cf. *Table Talk* no. 3422 (n.d.), WA TR 3:311.

[74] The anecdote almost certainly refers to Bugenhagen, whose long sermons were a frequent object of Luther's jest: see parallels in *Table Talk* no. 2643a (1532), WA TR 2:574; no. 2898 (1533), LW 54:179; no. 4956 (1540), WA TR 4:592; no. 6400 (n.d.), WA TR 5:642.

[75] *ungeschickligkeyt im leren*

[76] Cf. *Table Talk* no. 5489 (1542), LW 54:428.

[77] Cf. *Table Talk* no. 5022 (1540), WA TR 4:618.

[78] See above, Mathesius, *History*, pp. 117–18.

[79] On Charlemagne's patronage of Fulda as a center of learning, see his *Epistola de litteris colendis*, in Luitpold Wallach, *Alcuin and Charlemagne: Studies in Carolingian History and Literature* (Ithaca: Cornell University Press, 1959), pp. 198–226. Cf. *Table Talk* no. 5126/FB 4:548 (1540), WA TR 4:675.

[80] Cf. Wander 5:990, "Biene" no. 70: "Hardworking bees make honey; lazy bumblebees eat it up."

[81] "Canons" were priests who had vowed to follow a form of monastic rule, particularly the clergy of the cathedral chapter who possessed the right to elect the bishop and exercised considerable control over the property of the diocese.

[82] See *Table Talk* no. 954 (1530), WA TR 1:482, translated in Springer, *Luther's Aesop*, p. 71.

"If it were my place to set things in order, I would favor choosing no one to be deacon or pastor unless he had already spent a year or three in schools teaching the children not only the liberal arts but also the catechism, and diligently drilling them in it.[83] Schools, too, are temples of God, where students are taught and learn what ministers of the Church need to know. That is why the ancient prophets were both pastors and teachers, as is still said to be the case now for the Christians under the Turk."

When great jurists and people from court and his close friends were around him and spoke and had discussions about the courts and ministers of great rulers, he expressed himself very prudently, as a man of experience. He also used to say—in jest, of course: "It is up to us to help reform heaven and earth. For the great reformation, for which the popes have so long made the pious emperors and kings wait with gaping mouths, is now surely about to commence. The great prelates are seizing the Lord Christ by the beard and are about to get themselves dirty.[84] Faith and fidelity are becoming a rare commodity at court. Fraudulent dealing[85] is prevalent everywhere. Wicked rascals are promoted while good men are made to stand in back. Indecency is gaining the upper hand. And those who are the best in their own estimation attack our Gospel and refuse to open their door and gate, parish and church for Christ. Therefore, Christ is now laughing at the great prelates and will soon carry out Psalm 2 and the Magnificat [Luke 1:51–53] with them;[86] He will come knocking and burst open their doors and gates [cf. Ps. 24:7], and their bastions and ramparts will lie in a heap on the ground. Many are even good evangelical people—so long as there are still chalices, monstrances, and cloister property [to plunder]. But before long it will become evident who has adhered to the Gospel in earnest. God will not be deceived. No one can blind Him; He sees into the heart.

"I worry that there will yet be many who have held to our doctrine who will suffer a shipwreck of faith [1 Tim. 1:19]. Yet I am also of the hope that there will yet be many of those who now oppose us with ardent resolve and pure papistic zeal who will accept the holy Gospel. For there is far more hope for a pious Papist, who earnestly keeps his religion and thinks he will be saved by his works, than for the others who denounce and accuse the pope and help to pluck out his pinions for the sake of carnal liberty and wantonness and like listening only to preachers who throw down slanderous and

[83] See *Table Talk* no. 5252 (1540), WA TR 5:27–28; no. 4701 (1539), WA TR 4:438; and no. 6248, WA TR 5:557; Luther to Elector John Frederick of Saxony, March 20, 1545, WA Br 11:56–57.

[84] *unnd wöllen rham fangen*; or: "and want to smear [Him] with soot."

[85] *finantz*

[86] See above, Mathesius, *History*, p. 418.

derisive cards[87] against the abbots, canons, and their opponents. Manasseh [2 Kings 21:1–18; 2 Chron. 33:1–20][88] and St. Paul [Acts 9:1] were full of zeal; St. Paul also bore witness that his brethren had great zeal, but not according to knowledge [Rom. 10:2]. And yet such people can be converted on any day, at any hour. Those who adhere to our religion out of hypocrisy or for personal gain, or because it conceals their hatred and depravity, will continue to do so only as long as they can draw benefit from it. Saul and Julian do not last for long, as experience shows.[89]

"The papacy has as many people who do not take the pope's religion seriously as we do of people who ought to take the Gospel seriously. For the courts are full of Eceboliuses[90] and inconstant people. If only some sovereign ¦were to make a proclamation in his court as Constantine did, we would soon see who would [still] kiss the pope's feet.[91] And when persecution begins, we will see who will persevere.

"We thank God that we still have a pious lord. God preserve him! I worry for him only on account of wicked people who would like to lead him astray. But we intend to pray [for him], as we ought to do, as long as we live."[92]

Regarding the estate of marriage he often delivered very commendable and good talks.[93] Seeing that he was a chaste husband and spoke honorably of wives and maidens, he was inimical toward licentiousness and shameful speech.[94] In all the time I was around him, I never once heard an indecent word come out of his mouth. When people occasionally brought up such stories, he was able to make subtle changes for the sake of decency, as he also

---

[87] *böse und spitzige karten außwerffen*. See Wander 2:1151, "Karte" no. 40.

[88] See also the apocryphal *Prayer of Manasseh*, which Luther treasured, including it in his *Personal Prayer Book* (1522), LW 43:8 (cf. Mathesius, *History*, above, p. 377) . See also *To the Saxon Princes* (1545), LW 43:272; *Lectures on Genesis* (1535–45/1544–54), LW 1:296; *Commentary on Psalm 90* (1534–35/1541), LW 13:92.

[89] On Saul and his fall, see 1 Samuel 8–15. Emperor Julian (called "the Apostate"), though raised as a Christian, announced his embrace of paganism ("Hellenism") upon his accession to the throne and sought to suppress Christianity, though he soon died on campaign against the Persians. See *ODCC*, 3rd ed., s.v. "Julian the Apostate."

[90] The fourth-century sophist Ecebolius [Eubolus] of Constantinople is supposed to have acted like a zealous Christian during the reign of Constantine and as a pagan during the reign of Julian: see Socrates, *Ecclesiastical History* 3.13, in Cassiodorus (ca. 485–ca. 580), *Historia Tripartita* 6.38 (PL 69:1055–56; NPNF[2] 2:85).

[91] See above, p. 84 n. 4 and p. 321 n. 7.

[92] I.e, John Frederick the Magnanimous (see above, p. xxv n. 42). See *Table Talk* no. 5137 (1540), WA TR 4:680–81.

[93] See, e.g., *Table Talk* no. 185 (1532), LW 54:25–26; no. 233 (1532), LW 54:31; no. 1659 (1532), LW 54:161; no. 2867b (1533), LW 54:177–78; no. 3528 (1537), LW 54:222–23; no. 4408 (1539), LW 54:337; no. 4873 (1540), WA TR 4:565; and nos. 6903–41 (n.d.), WA TR 6:260–84.

[94] See, e.g., *Table Talk* no. 3523 (1537), LW 54:221.

did with the proverbs[95] which, in the German style, sound rather coarse. One time he said from the pulpit: "A broad posterior and ready excrement are soon parted."[96] And once when a word in the old verse "*Ut corpus redimas,*"[97] etc., led him off track in the midst of preaching, he became alarmed and retracted it three times: "Not so!"

Oh, how often I heard him speak in great earnest against the licentiousness of the cathedral canons, as well as against their brood, the crude choirboys,[98] who imposed a very impious and foul interpretation and exposition on many fine passages. "The devil has smeared his filth on many fine texts,"[99] [he said,] which the clergy used to employ for their gratification and amusement. He was very angry at Sebastian Franck[100] as well, whom he called a Latin "art" fly[101] in his writings, because he printed many shameful

---

[95] *Table Talk* no. 5335 (1540), WA TR 5:62–63.

[96] *Ein weyter leyb und zeytiger mist ist gut zu scheyden*, a modification of the proverb *Ein weiter Arschloch und reiffer Mist ist gut zu scheiden* ["A wide asshole and a ripe turd are soon parted"] (for variations, see Wander 3:6, "Leib" no. 40; 5:1700, "Scheiden" no. 21; 4:1427, "Unflat" no. 2). Although Luther's version may seem no less offensive to modern sensibilities (cf. Hartmann Grisar, *Martin Luther: His Life and Work*, trans. Frank J. Eble, ed. Arthur Preuss [Westminster, MD: Newman Press, 1953], p. 259), what Mathesius sees as problematic is not the scatology as such but the language in which it is expressed. Although the expression cannot be found in the surviving records of Luther's preaching, see Luther to Anton Lauterbach, November 3, 1543, WA Br 10:440–41; *Table Talk* no. 2616a–b (1532), WA TR 2:547–48.

[97] Ovid, *Remedia Amoris* 229 (Loeb 232 [1929], pp 192–93): "*Ut corpus redimas, ferrum patieris et ignis*" ["To restore the body, you will endure iron and fire"]. The expression cannot be found in the surviving records of Luther's preaching, but appears in *Table Talk* no. 5161 (1540), WA TR 4:687 (LW 54:392): "To restore the body, you would sell off shoes, clothes, hose, everything!" The verse was also written on the back leaf of Luther's copy of Jacques Lefevre d'Étaples (1455–1536), *Psalterium Quincumplex*: see WA 4:464.

[98] *Table Talk* no. 5341 (1540), WA TR 5:64.

[99] See also *Table Talk* no. 5335 (1540), WA TR 5:62–63.

[100] Sebastian Franck (1499–1542) had supported Luther as a preacher near Nürnberg in the mid-1520s but became increasingly inclined to spiritualism and abandoned his preaching position. Distancing himself from all of the organized religious groups of the sixteenth century, Franck expressed his own views indirectly through historical works such as his 1531 *Chronica* and his 1541 collection of proverbs, to which Mathesius refers here (see above, p. 415 n. 121, edited in Franck, *Sämtliche Werke: Kritische Ausgabe mit Kommentar*, ed. Peter Klaus Knauer, vol. 11 [Bern: P. Lang, 1992–]). For Luther's judgment on Franck, see preface to Freder, *Dialogue in Honor of Matrimony* (1545), LW 60:336–46; *Table Talk* no. 4966 (1540), WA TR 4:594–95.

[101] *ein Lateinische kunsthummel*; that is, an outhouse fly or "arse-fly," since "art" [German *Kunst*] in Latin is *ars*, a near homophone with the German word *Arsch* (cf. *Table Talk* no. 2953b [1533], WA TR 3:114). In his preface to Freder, *Dialogue in Honor of Matrimony* (1545), Luther wrote the word in a composite of Latin and German orthography, as *Arshummel*: LW 60:345 and n. 36 there.

proverbs that dishonor the estate of marriage and the female sex. [Luther] said, "Anyone who speaks wicked or foul things about wives, maidens, governing authorities, and the clergy is not worthy of honor."[102]

According to God's Word, the world has no treasure on earth more lovely or amiable than the holy estate of marriage, ʰwhich He Himself established, preserves, and has adorned and blessed more than all estates. From this [estate] were born not only all emperors, kings, and saints but also the eternal Son of God, though in a different, unique way. Therefore, anyone who is against the estate of marriage and speaks ill of it is certainly of the devil.[103] The doctor said, "God help poor Jerome.[104] I hope that, before his end, he regretted having glorified the celibate life and having spoken so poorly of the estate of marriage."

All honorable trade guilds and associations have excluded illegitimately born and unchaste people from their association. Neither does God, therefore, want to have any fornicators, adulterers, or bastards in His kingdom or any children born out of wedlock[105] in His tabernacle [Deut. 23:2]. Only the pope, who is the enemy of chaste married love, as Daniel says [Dan. 11:37],[106] has spoken in defense of concubinage[107] and what is conceived therein and has made it a part of his religion. That is why the world is filling up with bastards and illegitimate offspring, so that the devil may expect all the more guests. "I praise the holy estate of marriage, will continue to do so, and shall die doing so," said the doctor.[108]

And thus on any subject, wise discourses of every kind took place as occasion arose. The man was full of grace and the Holy Spirit, and so all who sought counsel from him, as from a prophet of God, found what they desired.

Once someone asked, "Is it a true marriage if a young man marries an old and feeble hag who, like the aged Sarah, is no longer in the way [of women] [Gen. 18:11]?"[109] "We must let that slide by," he said, "for the sake of the honor of the estate of marriage; [but] neither of them will get much joy or good in life from it. I am not inclined to make an ordinance, but if

---

[102] See *Table Talk* no. 3664 (1530), WA TR 3:500–501; no. 3523 (1537), LW 54:221.

[103] *Table Talk* no. 5282 (1540), WA TR 5:42–43.

[104] Jerome was, in addition to his study of Hebrew and translation of the Bible into Latin (the Vulgate [Vg]), one of the most vocal advocates of celibacy: see Jerome to Eustochium, *Letter 22* (PL 22:394–424; NPNF² 6:22–42). See *Table Talk* no. 445 (1533), LW 54:72; cf. *Table Talk* no. 824 (1530), WA TR 1:399; no. 5316 (1540), WA TR 5:56–57.

[105] *unehelichen*

[106] Cf. *Table Talk* no. 755 (1530), WA TR 1:359–60; *Preface to Daniel* (1530), LW 35:313.

[107] *Unehe*; "celibacy" and "common-law marriage" are also possible translations of the word.

[108] Cf. *Table Talk* no. 974 (1530), WA TR 1:493.

[109] *Table Talk* no. 5212 (1540), LW 54:397.

I did, I would dictate that the words 'Be fruitful and multiply!' [Gen. 1:28] should not be spoken over her in the wedding.[110] For one should ¹not misuse the name and Word of God." Then he cited the verse from Philo[musus]: "*Arvinam quaerunt multi in podice porci*" ["Many try to get lard from a hog's anus"].[111]

Since he was experiencing extreme vertigo and loud, prolonged ringing and roaring in his ears at this time, he began to think that a stroke would follow. Being unable to rid himself of this thought for some time, finally he said, "Strike, dear Lord Jesus, strike at will! I am ready, because I have been absolved upon Your Word and fed with Your flesh and blood. Come, *in nomine Domini!* ['in the name of the Lord!']. After all, Your dear disciple St. John[112] and our good elector[113] were also called out of this misery in such a manner." And in this way his heavy thoughts departed from him.[114]

One time a woman[115] complained to him that she was no longer able to believe. "Can you still say the Creed?" [he asked]. "Yes," said the woman. When she had recited it devoutly, the doctor asked, "And do you regard this as true?" When the woman said, "Yes," he said, "Truly, dear woman, if you believe these words and regard them as true—as indeed they are nothing but the truth—then you believe more strongly than I. For I must also ask every day that my faith[116] would be increased [cf. Mark 9:24]." Upon this, the woman thanked God and departed from him in peace and joy.

Master Antonius Musa,[117] pastor in Rochlitz, said to me that he once made a heartfelt complaint to the doctor that he was unable to believe

---

[110] *Table Talk* no. 5212 (1540), WA TR 5:10 (cf. LW 54:397).

[111] This verse (originally *Arvinam multi quaerunt in podice aselli*, "from the anus of an ass") appears in Sebastian Brant's (1458–1521) *Narrenschiff* [*Ship of Fools*], in the section on "marrying for the sake of wealth" in the 1497 Latin translation which Brant prepared with Jacob Locher (1471–1528), who was known as Philomusus Suevus (hence "Philo" in Mathesius' reference): *Stultifera Navis* (Basel, 1497), § 60, [p. 119]. (In the German, the equivalent passage is § 52.) See Michael Rupp, *Narrenschiff und Stultifera navis: Deutsche und lateinische Moralsatire von Sebastian Brant und Jakob Locher in Basel 1494–1498* (New York: Waxmann, 2002).

[112] See *LA* 1:55, no. 9.

[113] I.e., John the Steadfast, who died of a stroke: see above, Mathesius, *History*, p. 366.

[114] Cf. *Table Talk* no. 5364 (1540), WA TR 5:95.

[115] See *Table Talk* no. 5562 (1542), LW 54:453; *Lectures on Genesis* (1535–45/1544–54), LW 5:46; cf. *Table Talk* no. 5658a (n.d.), WA TR 5:294–95. Mathesius may have been present to hear the anecdote in the Genesis lectures: see Volz, *Die Lutherpredigten des Johannes Mathesius*, p. 200 n. 4.

[116] The 1566 edition has *unglaubens* ["unbelief"], probably a confusion based on Mark 9:24; Loesche corrects to *glaubens* ["faith"]: see *LH²*, p. 559 on p. 289.21.

[117] Anton Musa (ca. 1485–1547) studied in Erfurt and Jena and worked as pastor and then superintendent in these towns, supporting the Reformation with one of the earliest Evangelical hymnals, the 1524 Erfurt *Enchiridion* [VD16 E1151]. He became the first Lutheran

himself what he preached to others. "God be praised and thanked," replied the doctor, "that this happens to other people too. I thought this happened to me alone."[118] Musa was never able to forget this consolation his whole life long.

Now, I must also mention some table talks that took place at other times.[119] A rich townsman bequeathed him a goblet because he had hosted his son at his table.[120] The executors notified the doctor and requested a certificate of receipt, for which they sent him a form, with the request that he have it sealed with the signet of a trustworthy man. Upon this the doctor said with a laugh: "Where shall I find a man who can notarize this for me? What nice people these are! I have well-nigh written the world full of books, and they still want me to fill out the form for a certificate of receipt. I will comply." Not long afterward the goblet arrived.

Although this man was able to speak well and present his message in ornate and rich language, as he demonstrates in his books, especially in the court psalm[121] and his writings on the Jews,[122] he liked listening to people speaking in clear and concise language. Once, when a renowned city requested a preacher from him through its chief clerk, and the man proceeded with a mouthful of grand titles and made a long, windy, ornate, and intricate speech using sesquipedalian words, the doctor listened with displeasure and vexation. When the orator finally finished, the doctor said, "Dear friend, what do your lords request?" "A Christian preacher," said the emissary. "That, I understand; and I will see to it that they are supplied."[123] Great people prefer to express their message with a few clear words; they do not like listening to long and diffuse orations, neither do they care to read overloaded letters.

---

superintendent in Mathesius' Saxon hometown of Rochlitz in 1536, moving to Merseburg as visitor and superintendent in 1544. See Loesche, *Johannes Mathesius*, 1:15–16; Susanne Siebert, "Musa, Anton," *BBKL* 6:370–72.

[118] For the thought, cf. *Lectures on Isaiah* (1527–30/1532–34), LW 17:222; *Table Talk* no. 4864 (1540), WA TR 4:560–62; no. 2658a–b (1532), WA TR 2:587–89.

[119] I.e., not during Mathesius' own stay at Luther's table in 1540.

[120] The cup was a bequest from the Augsburg burgher Hans Honold (d. 1540), whose son Hans had matriculated at Wittenberg in 1534–35. See *Table Talk* no. 4872 (1540), WA TR 4:564 and below, p. 500 n. 233. Mathesius is the primary source for the anecdote about Luther's response.

[121] See above, Mathesius, *History*, p. 270.

[122] See below, Mathesius, *History*, pp. 507–9, 514–15.

[123] Mathesius is the source for this anecdote, which could not be found elsewhere in Luther's *Table Talk*.

Master Philip thanked the guests at the end of Dr. Paul Eber's[124] wedding festivities; he began by telling a story about a deacon in Tübingen who started his sermon thus: "People do not like listening to me, and I do not like preaching; and so I will not keep you long." "*Magnifice domine Rector,*"[125] he [then] said in Latin, "the bridegroom offers his thanks and asks you to be content with that and return in the evening."

One time a city clerk wanted to be ordained as a minister of the Church.[126] Master Philip asked him how a person becomes righteous in God's eyes and is saved. "O scholar most revered in God, gracious sir, preceptor exceedingly dear!" said the orator. "According to my own simple understanding, which God has graciously imparted to me, it seems to me that in response to this Christian and highly important question it would, in my candid and extemporaneous opinion, be fitting at this time," and so forth. But before he could get his speech fully shored up and nailed down, the good man interrupted his speaking: "Answer the question. There is no need for you to keep giving a speech! You must leave that for the one who comes after you and learn now how to speak simply, rightly, and plainly about the Lord Christ and what pertains to Him."

It would also be profitable to consider the short and fine sayings that were spoken at table, which he often used in his books, if it weren't that it would make [this sermon] too long. Nonetheless, we will mention a few. An old preacher was reading the doctor's book at the table; upon noticing this, [Luther] said, "The [German] Bible is done now, God be praised! Therefore, no one has need for my books any longer. They are a preparation for Holy Scripture. An old preacher should have only one book, namely, the Bible, for that is the wellspring; all other books are just little streams.[127] Upon the Bible you can stand secure and certain; with the Bible you can drive away devils and heretics. Doctor Karlstadt feared me because, as he said, I had read the prophets and apostles ten years before he had. Therefore, he would have no advantage against me."[128]

---

[124] On Eber, see above, p. 300 n. 89. He was married to Helene Kuffner in Leipzig on September 13, 1541, though it is unclear whether these festivities took place in Leipzig or in Wittenberg. Mathesius, a close friend of Eber, could well have been an eyewitness.

[125] The rector of the University of Wittenberg in September 1541 would have been Kilian Goldstein (see above, p. 299 n. 84): see Förstemann et al., *Album,* 1:188. In Leipzig, the rector was Henning Pyrogallus [Feuerhahn]: see E. G. von Gersdorf, *Beitrag zur Geschichte der Universität Leipzig: Die Rectoren der Universität Leipzig* (Leipzig: Weigel, 1869), p. 37.

[126] This anecdote about an ordination exam presumably came from Melanchthon himself: see Volz, *Die Lutherpredigten des Johannes Mathesius,* p. 124 n. 7.

[127] For Luther's thoughts here, cf. *Table Talk* no. 6442 (n.d.), WA TR 5:662–65.

[128] For the anecdote about Karlstadt, see *Table Talk* no. 2512a–b, (1532), WA TR 2:499; no. 5030 (1540), WA TR 4:622.

Once [Luther] also said, "The Bible is a beautiful forest, in which there is no tree that I have not clapped with my own hand."[129] Again: "The finest exposition of Moses, the prophets, and the Psalms is the New Testament, especially St. John and Paul, even as the Old Testament is the foundation of the New Testament. If I were younger, I would look for all the words of the New Testament in Moses and the prophets. Comparing the languages and texts with one another is a great and wonderful help in explaining the Scripture."[130]

Again: "A preacher should do three things: ⌐read the Bible diligently, pray fervently, and remain a disciple and student; then he is a great doctor."[131]

Again: "Three things make a theologian: *meditatio, oratio, et tentatio* ["meditation, prayer, and tribulation"].[132] One must think and meditate on the words of Scripture and fervently ask the Lord of the Bible for His Spirit, who is the gatekeeper to God's library. One must also be tried and have gained some experience in the school of the cross, even as Christ Himself was led into the wilderness by the Spirit and tempted by the devil before He began His public ministry at the age of thirty" [Matt. 4:1–11, 17].

He also liked to use the following words when he spoke of righteousness: "There is *passiva* and *activa iustitia* [a 'passive' and an 'active righteousness'].[133] One kind happens to us,[134] when God imputes to us the obedience and righteousness of His Son, freely, through faith alone, as with Abraham [Gen. 15:6; Romans 4; Galatians 3]; we do nothing in this case but to keep our hearts open and receive it in the Word. The other is called 'activa,' which the Holy Spirit, who was given to us in the rebirth [of Baptism], works within us; this is and remains imperfect for as long as we live. And we can do no better than to desire, pray, and yearn to be good and, like St. Paul in Romans 7 [:18–25], lament that we are unable to be good. *Velle esse iustum, est summa iustitia* ['To want to be righteous is the highest righteousness'] that we are able to accomplish."

---

[129] See *Table Talk* no. 674 (1530), LW 54:121; cf. *Table Talk* no. 1877 (1532) LW 54:165; no. 5355 (1540), WA TR 5:84.

[130] See *Table Talk* no. 1097 (1530), WA TR 1:550; no. 4116 (1538), WA TR 4:144; no. 5585 (1543), WA TR 5:262. The closest parallel is reported in Jerome Besold (see above, p. 425 n. 8), preface to the fourth volume of the *Lectures on Genesis*, WA 44:xxxii–xxxiii.

[131] Mathesius appears to be the source for this saying.

[132] Cf. *Preface to the German Writings* (1539), LW 34:285–87, and the manuscript note edited in WA 48:276.

[133] Cf. *Table Talk* no. 141 (1531), WA TR 1:63–64; no. 1584 (1532), WA TR 2:141; *Preface to the Latin Writings* (1545), LW 34:336–37; *Lectures on Galatians* (1531/1535), LW 26:4–12.

[134] *Eine die wir leiden;* literally, "one that we suffer."

He gave many fine and comforting talks at table concerning the holy cross of Christians: *"Melius est tentari quam inflari* ["It is better to be tempted than to become puffed up"].¹³⁵ After the cross of Christ, the greatest treasure on earth is the holy cross in the house of God. For it clarifies Scripture for us and strengthens our faith, teaches us to pray rightly and in earnest, suppresses our sinful flesh, and makes God's Word sweet for us; it is by this means that God plants great virtues in us."¹³⁶ Again: "Anyone who flees the cross loses the path to eternal life."¹³⁷ Again: "Our Lord God has a Hebrew way of speaking; His counsel and will are not recognized until the end."¹³⁸ Again: "The ʲdevil hands out heaven to those who are secure before they acknowledge their sin, but Christ gives comfort to believers after they acknowledge their sins."¹³⁹ Again: "Before the deed is done, the devil makes the sin look small and insignificant, but great and serious after the deed."¹⁴⁰

He also often recalled good sayings of Dr. Staupitz.¹⁴¹ For example: "If you are set on disputing about eternal predestination," Dr. Staupitz said, "then hold up the wounds of Jesus Christ. Then the devil will leave and the evil thoughts will subside."¹⁴²

Again, Doctor Staupitz often mentioned Doctor Summe[n]hart, a teacher in Tübingen who dealt in the old scholastic theology and teachings of the sophists.¹⁴³ He is said to have often uttered the heartfelt lament: *"Quis me liberabit ab ista rixosa theologia?* [cf. Rom. 7:24]? O dear God,

---

¹³⁵ Cf. *Lectures on Genesis* (1535–45/1544–54), LW 5:255 (WA 43:605).

¹³⁶ Cf. *Table Talk* no. 141 (1532), WA TR 1:65 (Aurifaber); no. 1012 (1530), WA TR 1:511; no. 1950b (1531), WA TR 2:275 (Aurifaber); no. 1753 (1532), WA TR 2:206–7; no. 3135 (n.d.), WA TR 3:183.

¹³⁷ Cf. *Table Talk* no. 6287 (n.d.), WA TR 5:577; no. 759 (1530), WA TR 1:361; no. 6516 (n.d.), WA TR 6:11.

¹³⁸ Probably a joke referring to the writing of Hebrew from right to left. Mathesius appears to be the only source for this saying.

¹³⁹ *Table Talk* no. 1202 (1530), WA TR 1:597.

¹⁴⁰ Cf. *Table Talk* no. 141 (1531), WA TR 1:62; no. 6629 (n.d.), WA TR 6:88.

¹⁴¹ On Johann von Staupitz, see the introduction above, p. lvi and n. 194 there. For Luther's references in the *Table Talk*, see no. 141 (1531), WA TR 1:62, whose contents have been frequently involved in this series of citations by Mathesius; the passages cited in the following footnote; and the indexes of the *Table Talk*: WA TR 6:676 and LW 54:483.

¹⁴² See *Table Talk* no. 1017 (1530), WA TR 1:512–13; no. 1820 (1532), WA TR 2:227–28; cf. *Table Talk* no. 1490 (1532), WA TR 2:111–13; no. 2654a–b (1532), WA TR 2:582–83; no. 5658a (n.d.), WA TR 5:295; *Lectures on Genesis* (1535–45/1544–54), LW 5:47.

¹⁴³ Konrad Summenhart (ca. 1458–1502) (Mathesius gives the name as "Summerhart") was a German theologian and canonist at the University of Tübingen, a Scotist who criticized some practices of the late medieval church. He taught the future Wittenberg jurist Hieronymus Schurff (see above, p. 21 n. 83). See Heiko A. Oberman, *Masters of the Reformation: The Emergence of a New Intellectual Climate in Europe* (Cambridge: Cambridge University Press,

who will save me and us poor theologians from this contentious sophistry?"[144] "It is Christ!" said Dr. Luther. "He has done it (praise God!) through His holy Word. Few of the young preachers who are unfamiliar with monkery, papistry, and sophistry will thank Him for this, and so they will establish a new contentious theology soon after we are gone. They will let Christ and His Word slip out of sight and out of mind and will propose perilous disputations and unanswerable questions over unnecessary and uncertain matters, setting the clergy against each other tooth and nail.[145] *A doctore glorioso, et pastore contentioso, et inutilibus quaestionibus, liberet suam ecclesiam Christus Dominus* ['May the Lord Christ free His Church from vainglorious doctors, contentious pastors, and useless questions']!"[146]

Doctor Luther also frequently mentioned this preceptor of his with great honor[147] and always called him "my Staupitz,"[148] even though the terrible downfall of the rulers of the temple[149] and of the tyranny of the Roman bishops frightened him greatly.[150] "He was an excellent man," said the doctor, "who not only made his voice heard in universities and churches as

---

1981), pp. 28–29, 61–63, 116–24, 134–37; Melanchthon, *Oratio de vita Hieronymi Schurfii* (1554), CR 12:90; Helmut Feld, "Summenhart, Konard," *BBKL* 11:260–62.

[144] *Table Talk* no. 5374 (1540), WA TR 5:99.

[145] *schedlich Pfaffengebeiß . . . fürgeben*

[146] Mathesius is the source for the material following the quotation from Summenhart.

[147] See, e.g., in addition to the other citations here, *Table Talk* no. 4868 (1540), WA TR 4:563; no. 173 (1532), WA TR 1:80.

[148] *suum Staupicium.* On the phrase "my Staupitz" [*meus Stupitcius*], see *Table Talk* no. 445 (1533), LW 54:72; no. 526 (1533), LW 54:97; no. 1490 (1532), WA TR 2:112; Luther to Spalatin, August 21, 1544, WA Br 10:638–40.

[149] *Tempelherrn*; probably not a reference to the Knights Templar, the crusading order disbanded in 1312, but to the leaders of the temple in Jesus' day, used here to denote the medieval ecclesiastical hierarchy.

[150] Staupitz, as Luther's monastic superior (see the introduction above, p. lvi and n. 194 there), supported Luther in his early career and through his public trials in 1517–19 (see above, Melanchthon, *Preface*, p. 64; Mathesius, *History*, pp. 125–26, 128–29, 149–50). However, Staupitz came under increasingly severe pressure to renounce Luther and his teaching and to submit himself unconditionally to the papacy, despite the fact that Staupitz had released Luther from obedience to the Observant Augustinian Hermits in 1518 and had himself resigned as vicar-general of the German congregation in the summer of 1520. Staupitz continued in monastic life as abbot of the Benedictine monastery in Salzburg, where he served from 1521 until his death in 1524. Luther regarded Staupitz as having accommodated himself to the ecclesiastical powers that be. See Luther to Wenceslaus Linck, August 19, 1520, LW 48:169–71; to Staupitz, January 14, 1521, LW 48:191–94, and June 27, 1522, LW 49:10–13; Staupitz to Luther, April 1, 1524, WA Br 3:263–64. Posset, *Front-Runner of the Catholic Reformation*, pp. 264–345, offers a more positive interpretation of Staupitz's relation to Luther in these last years.

a scholar but |also was a man of good standing in the world, at court, and among great people."[151]

Once Doctor Staupitz was trying to recite the text of genealogy of Jesus Christ in Matthew 1 from memory, as was the custom then, but he got mixed up in the fourteen princes from the tribe of Judah that are enumerated after the Babylonian Captivity. "God punishes pride," he said, then read from the written text and began expounding it. Both of the former electors of Saxony[152] who were present during the sermon had him invited to dinner. At table Duke John began by saying, "Doctor, what happened to you during the Gospel reading today?" "Gracious prince," said Staupitz, "I had three kinds of lords in my Gospel reading. The patriarchs were godly people; you could get along with them. Likewise, the ancient kings, who permitted you to speak with them and about them. But when I got to the princes—those were difficult people; they caused me confusion during the Gospel reading." "Does your grace have anything more to ask?" said Elector Frederick. "You will never catch Dr. Staupitz without an answer!"[153] Let us return to our doctor.

"In case of bad and gloomy thoughts, what you need is a good and joyful song and friendly conversation," he often said.[154]

He also liked saying good German rhymes at table and in the pulpit. I copied down a few from his little Psalter:[155] "If you know something, keep your peace. Are things well? Then let them be. If you have something, hold it fast; ill fortune soon will come to blast."[156]

Again: "Eat what is cooked, drink what is clear, speak what is true."[157]

---

[151] See *Table Talk* no. 3143a (1532), WA TR 3:187; no. 5374 (1540), WA TR 5:99; cf. *Table Talk* no. 4708 (1539), WA TR 4:440; no. 2797b (1532), WA TR 2:666.

[152] I.e., Frederick the Wise (see above, p. 68 n. 82) and his brother and successor, John the Steadfast (see above, p. 70 n. 95).

[153] Mathesius appears to be the source for this anecdote.

[154] See, e.g., *Table Talk* no. 194 (1532), WA TR 1:86; no. 968 (1530), WA TR 1:490; no. 1300 (1532), WA TR 2:33; no. 2632 (1532), WA TR 2:434; no. 2545a (1532), WA TR 2:518; no. 3470 (1536), LW 54:206; no. 7034 (n.d.), WA TR 6:348; Luther to Joachim of Anhalt, June 26, 1534, WA Br 7:78–79 (*LSC*, p. 94); to Matthias Weller, October 7, 1534, WA Br 7:104–6 (*LSC*, pp. 96–97); *Table Talk* no. 491 (1533), LW 54:82–83.

[155] On Luther's custom of keeping a small Psalter for his personal use and annotation, see above, p. 429.

[156] *Weistu was, so schweig. Ist dir wol, so bleyb. Hastu was, so halt; Unglück mit seinem breyten Fuß kombt bald.* See *Table Talk* no. 7048 (n.d.), WA TR 6:358; Wander 5:299, "Wissen" no. 237; cf. Wander 5:301, "Wissen" no. 304; cf. Thiele p. 177, no. 169.

[157] *Iß, was gar ist, Trinck, was klar ist, Red, was war ist.* See the introduction by Ernst Kroker, WA TR 4:xli; Wander 1:893, "Essen" no. 90.

Again: "Keep silent, endure, turn aside, and come to terms; let no one hear you complain; of God do not despair; your help will come daily."[158]

Truly, many good discourses took place that later often instructed and comforted me when questions and disputations of all kinds arose.[159]

Someone asked whether a father confessor, too, would be obligated to report to the authorities what he heard in private confession, so that the judge could preserve his conscience and deliver a verdict. "By no means!" he replied. "The penitent does not confess to me, but to my Lord Jesus Christ; therefore, I have nothing to repeat."[160]

He spoke judiciously concerning honorable ecclesiastical ceremonies. For example, with regard to the princes of Anhalt, he said that he would have gladly and joyfully listened to their old Passion chants[161] during Passion Week, and he approved of their retaining the elevation in their churches along with the Latin hymns.[162] "Those who attack only the ceremonies," he said, "truly have no proper understanding of the papacy; they are trying to confirm their Gospel by rejecting harmless ecclesiastical customs."

---

[158] *Schweig, leyd, meyd und vertrag, dein not niemand klag, An Gott nicht verzag, dein hülff kombt alle tag. Table Talk* no. 5375q (1540), WA TR 5:107–8; Wander 4:437–38, "Schweigen" nos. 52, 73–74.

[159] Cf. the similar sentiment of Jerome Besold in his preface to the fourth volume of the Genesis lectures, quoted in WA 38:719.

[160] *Table Talk* no. 5178 (1540), LW 54:395; cf. *Table Talk* no. 5176 (1540), LW 54:394; no. 5459 (1542), WA TR 5:165–66.

[161] For Luther's fondness for the traditional chants of Passion Week, see *Table Talk* no. 4975 (1540), WA TR 4:596. On the princes of Anhalt, see above, p. 374 n. 36.

[162] See *Table Talk* no. 5665 (1544), WA TR 5:308; Luther to George of Anhalt, June 26, 1542, WA Br 10:85–86, and July 10, 1545, WA Br 11:132–34; July 22, 1545, WA Br 11:145–46. In Wittenberg, many Latin chants and hymns were retained alongside German hymns; the elevation of the host had finally ceased in 1542: see *Table Talk* no. 5589 (1543), LW 54:461–62; *Brief Confession* (1544), LW 38:313–19; and the Wittenberg consistorial constitution of 1542 and church order of 1545 in Sehling 1/1:202–3, 212–14. The church in Joachimsthal, like the church in Anhalt, retained the elevation, as well as many Latin hymns: see Mathesius, "Ein kurtzer bericht/ von der Lehr und Ceremonien/ der Christlichen Kirchen inn Sanct Joachims Thal," in *Postilla* (1593) [VD16 M1540], vol. 4, fol. Rr3r. For the Anhalt church order of 1545, see Sehling 2/2:549–53, especially p. 551; cf. the 1538 order (p. 546) and mention of the elevation in the order of 1568 (p. 570). George of Anhalt was also responsible for the Celle church order of 1545 (Sehling 1/1:291–304, where the use of Latin and the elevation are mentioned on pp. 300–301).

One time he came to the church in Eisenberg at Easter.[163] When the Introit[164] was sung in German to the Latin notes, he winced hard. When he came home and sat at table, his host asked him what had happened to him. He answered, "I thought I was going to have an attack of the stone[165] on account of their inept chanting. If you want to sing in German, then sing good German songs; if you want to sing in Latin, as schoolboys should, then keep the old melodies and texts and purge them of what is impure. No one will do better than that." And he concluded, "I am opposed to those people who are always introducing one novelty after another in ceremonies. They are the ones who will eventually do the same to the doctrine. In Latin schools, one should sing in Latin; in German churches, one should sing in German. That is the proper way."[166]

Let us make an end, for the present, [of these sayings]. Some day God will awaken someone who will collect this excellent man's sayings, parables, proverbs, rhymes, stories, and other ideas and good statements.[167] That would be a very fine book for the Germans, especially if the wise and prudent sayings of our emperors, kings, princes, and lords were included.

Now, I would like briefly to tell the young people about his daily life and conduct, for the example and life of great and holy men provides good teaching and instruction for the young. Although he often had to stay home in his old age because of illness and vertigo, he did not cease from labor. During and after meals, he often wrote material for his companions who

---

[163] Luther is known to have passed through Eisenberg, in Thuringia, in August 1524, in April 1528, in April 1530, and in February 1537: see Buchwald, *Luther-Kalendarium*, pp. 36, 58, 71, 111. Only on the 1528 or 1530 trips would he have been present in Eisenberg around Easter, on April 27, 1528 (the Monday after the Second Sunday of Easter)—though on this visit Luther was only passing through—or April 6, 1530 (the Wednesday before Palm Sunday), when Luther stayed in Eisenberg. By Good Friday 1530, Luther had reached his destination at the Coburg (see above, p. 324). See Brecht 2:372; WA Br 5:274 n. 7. The 1530 date is thus, perhaps, the most likely. Mathesius appears to be the earliest written source for this anecdote, which he may have heard from Veit Dietrich, Luther's attendant in the Coburg (cf. above, p. 348). Loesche (*LH²*, p. 561) endorses the 1530 dating; Volz, *Die Lutherpredigten des Johannes Mathesius*, p. 206 and n. 7, suggests a date in the mid-1520s.

[164] I.e., the appointed psalm beginning the Mass. If this incident took place when Luther was present in Eisenberg on Wednesday, April 6, 1530, the preaching service would presumably have been Matins or Vespers, which also began with psalmody but not with an Introit strictly speaking: see *Instructions for the Visitors* (1528), LW 40:306–9.

[165] *es würde mich die kalten pese ankommen*; i.e., *die kalten pisse*, meaning stranguria or dysuria.

[166] Luther wanted both Latin and German singing to be used in the church, but insisted that the music employed had to be adapted to the different character of each language: see the introduction by Ulrich S. Leupold, LW 53:54; cf. below, Mathesius, *History*, p. 484.

[167] See the introduction above, pp. xviii–xx and n. 13 there.

were going to preach. For example, he wrote his fine book on Matthew[168] for his table companion Dr. Weller after meals and [his commentary] on the Twenty-Third Psalm[169] during meals. Likewise, he often had to make corrections [to manuscripts] after the meal.[170] Aside from this, he liked going to church and always carried a book with him. For, as he said, it was much easier for him to pray in the congregation than at home. His seat was by the high altar, but for the sermon he went to the university seats and listened attentively and devoutly.[171]

One time he was traveling on a Sunday, and when the church in a village rang the bell for preaching, he and his companions dismounted, went to the church, and listened to the whole sermon. When they were on their way again, they discussed the sermon, and someone said, "The pastor could have explained the Gospel more correctly." But [Luther] said, "If a teacher can preach Christ simply from the catechism, he is a blessed preacher.[172] In Moses' tabernacle there were not only vessels of gold and silver but also those of copper and iron [cf. Exodus 26–27, 35–36, 38–39; Josh. 6:19; 1 Chron. 29:2], and yet they all serve the eternal Son of God."

Moreover, he also went frequently to confession and the holy Supper, taking great comfort from his Absolution in the midst of tribulation. ¹He also always stayed in church until everything was finished. Although he had a rather stout body, he ate and drank little—and rarely any delicacies—being content with common food. At night, when he could not sleep well, he had to drink a little sleeping draught, for which he often made an apology: "You

---

[168] See the *Annotations on Matthew 1–18* (1534–35/1538), LW 67:1–328, written to support Weller's Wednesday preaching in the Castle Church. See also the twenty-two surviving sermon outlines [*Conciunculae*] which Luther prepared to support Weller's Sunday preaching, WA 45:421–64 (cf. LW 69:418–23). See *Table Talk* no. 5169 (1540), WA TR 4:691. On Weller, see above, p. 416 n. 127.

[169] *Commentary on Psalm 23* (1535–36/1536), LW 12:145–79.

[170] It is difficult to find other references in the *Table Talk* attesting Luther's correction of texts at table. See, however, *Table Talk* no. 3945 (1538), WA TR 4:25.

[171] In the Wittenberg town church, the pulpit in Luther's day was located in the middle of the north wall of the nave (in the Castle Church it was located in the middle of the south wall), with the students seated close to the pulpit in either case, far from the seats for university faculty in the chancel. See Helmar Junghans, *Wittenberg als Lutherstadt* (Göttingen: Vandenhoeck & Ruprecht, 1979), pp. 40 and 60 and plate 23.

[172] For the thought, cf. *Table Talk* no. 2554a–b (1532), WA TR 2:522; no. 3143a–b (1532), WA TR 3:187–88; no. 3421 (n.d.), WA TR 3:310–11; no. 3573 (1537), LW 54:235–36. Mathesius seems to be the source for this particular anecdote.

young fellows will have to allow our elector[173] and me, old man that I am, a stronger little drink. We have to seek our cushion and pillow in our mug."[174]

Occasionally he also went to suppers at the houses of good people elsewhere and, in keeping with the occasion, was of good cheer and engaged in good conversation during the meal. Once, when someone mentioned the small and weak voice of St. Paul [cf. 2 Cor. 10:10], he said, "I, too, have a small and weak voice." "And yet you are heard very far away," said Master Philip.[175]

A professor in Wittenberg invited him and others as guests. Since he came to the table with heavy thoughts, everyone was quiet. When they had finished eating, Master Philip, who was quite good at understanding the doctor's manner, wanted to make their departure. The host asked them to spend another hour with him. Meanwhile, someone else had moved the bench. Since our doctor agreed to stay, the host started to sit down again and fell flat on his back, which resulted in good, polite laughter. The doctor said, "We have an ungracious host—he serves the best dish last."[176] Upon this, everyone became cheerful and happy and remained together for a good while longer in convivial spirits.[177]

One time the legate of a great ruler came to the elector in Wittenberg.[178] The doctor was also invited to his lodgings. The legate wanted to get him to talk. "My dear doctor," he said in the courtly manner, "what do you think of the priests who distribute one kind and both kinds at the same altar?" "Gracious lord," said the doctor, "they are knaves." A short while later, the doctor in turn asked a question of the legate: "Gracious lord, what does Your Grace think of those who banish or imprison people on account of both

---

[173] John Frederick the Magnanimous (see above, p. xxv n. 42), who was known for his drinking: see, e.g., *Table Talk* no. 3468 (1536), LW 54:205–6; no. 3514 (1536), LW 54:218–19; *Against Hanswurst* (1541), LW 41:237–38.

[174] See *Table Talk* no. 122 (1531, WA TR 1:52 (Aurifaber) (cf. LW 54:18); cf. *Table Talk* no. 139 (1531), LW 54:20; no. 5173 (1540), WA TR 4:693.

[175] Mathesius appears to be the source for this anecdote. Luther's voice may be characterized here as it was amid illness; other observers described him (as a younger man) as having a "high, clear voice": see Brecht 1:313.

[176] Cf. Thiele no. 248, p. 238.

[177] *in bona charitate*

[178] Hans Ungnad von Sonnegg (1493–1564), an Austrian lord who was sympathetic to the Reformation, came in September 1536 to the Saxon electoral court in Torgau (where this episode would in fact have taken place) as legate of King Ferdinand (see the introduction above, p. lxxxiii). Sonnegg later severed himself from service to the Hapsburgs after the Peace of Augsburg in 1555 and became a leading patron of the publication of Bibles and other Lutheran literature in Slovenian, Croat, and Serbian. On Ungnad, see Oskar Sakrausky, "Ungnad von Sonnegg, Hans," OER 4:196; *Table Talk* no. 3469 (1536), WA TR 3:338–39. For an account of the episode narrated by Mathesius, see *Table Talk* no. 6768 (n.d.), WA TR 6:176–77.

kinds?" Since he had no commission to answer this question, the legate turned[179] to a prince at the table and said, "Lord, Your Grace must be quite old now. We have known each other for quite a long time." Upon this, the elector, the host, said, "That lord is a real cavalier. He knows how to turn the cheek!"[180] For according to the prudent fashion observed at court, not all questions are to be answered. "Fortunate is the man who can hold his ground or get out of a bind politely," as the wise say.[181]

He also came home from a dinner and greeted his own guest with a good toast: "I should and must be joyful today, for I have heard bad news.[182] Nothing counters that better than a strong Our Father and good courage. It vexes the melancholic devil when we insist on being joyful nonetheless."

I heard from his prior, Master Eberhard,[183] preacher in Altenburg, about the time when the extremely disturbing news of the pope's excommunication and the imperial ban came to the monastery.[184] On hearing it, the doctor was singing joyfully in the garden. "Doctor," said the prior, "haven't you heard the news?" "That is of no concern to me," replied the doctor, "but rather to our Lord Christ. If He wants to step down from the right hand of His Father and allow His Church to be conquered, let Him see to it. I am much too weak to defend Him and His cause against the prince of this world [John 12:31] and his comrades."

---

[179] According to *Table Talk* no. 6768 (n.d.), WA TR 6:176–77, it was Andreas Pflugk zu Knauthain (1480–1542; see Institute für Sächsische Geschichte und Volkskunde, *Sächsische Biographie*, http://www.isgv.de/saebi/), counselor to Duke George of Saxony, who interrupted the exchange between Luther and Ungnad by posing this question to Duke Philip I of Braunschweig-Grubenhagen (1476–1551; Paul Zimmermann, "Philipp I," *ADB* 25:762–64).

[180] *ein backen werfen*. This remark by Elector John Frederick is not found in the parallel account in *Table Talk* no. 6768 (n.d.), WA TR 6:176–77.

[181] *Wol dem der sich mit gelimpff auffhalten oder außeysen kan, sagen die weysen*. Cf. Wander 1:1724 "Glimpf" no. 4.

[182] Cf. *Table Talk* no. 5284 (1540), LW 54:405.

[183] Eberhard Brisger (ca. 1490–1545), an Augustinian Hermit who had studied at Wittenberg and at Cologne, returned to Wittenberg in 1519 and became the (last) prior of the Augustinian cloister in 1522, remaining there with Luther until it was transferred to the elector in 1525. Brisger then became a preacher in Altenburg under Spalatin's superintendency, where Mathesius met him in 1530–32 (see the introduction above, p. lxxxii). On Brisger, see Ernst Kähler, "Brisger, Eberhard," *NDB* 2:618.

[184] Presumably this episode took place in the spring of 1521, when news of the bull *Decet Romanum Pontificem*, promulgated in January, was making its way to Wittenberg and Luther's summons to the Diet of Worms was being negotiated. Note that the Wittenberg prior at this time would not yet have been Brisger, but still Conrad Helt. See Brecht 1:426–48; Volz, *Die Lutherpredigten des Johannes Mathesius*, p. 122 n. 4. Cf. *Commentary on Psalm 118* (1530), LW 14:67.

When he left the Coburg to return home and stopped with his companions at Master Spalatin's house,[185] and Master Philip was constantly preoccupied with the Apology[186] and was writing during the meal, he stood up and took away his pen. "One can serve God not only with work but also with resting. That is why He gave the Third Commandment and commanded the Sabbath [Exod. 20:8–11]."[187]

Sometimes during and after meals the doctor also sang, being a lutenist as well. I sang with him, and he wove good remarks in between songs. "Josquin," he said, "is the master of the notes—they had to do as he willed; the other choirmasters have to do as the notes will.[188] Of course, this composer also had his good spirit, as did Bezalel [Exod. 31:2], especially since he masterfully and elegantly arranged the *Haec dicit Dominus* [Hosea 13:14] and the *Circumdederunt me gemitus mortis* [Ps. 18:5; Ps. 17:5 Vg] together."[189]

---

[185] Luther departed the Coburg on October 4, 1530, stopping first at Altenburg (see above, Mathesius, *History*, p. 358). On Spalatin, who had been superintendent in Altenburg since 1525, see above, p. 136 n. 121. Mathesius himself was present in Altenburg at this time and heard Luther preach, though he likely heard the details of this exchange from his friend Spalatin: see Volz, *Die Lutherpredigten des Johannes Mathesius*, p. 124.

[186] Melanchthon continued working on revisions to the Apology of the Augsburg Confession (see above, Mathesius, *History*, pp. 325–26) after its submission to the emperor (and his rejection of it) on September 22, 1530. See Arand et al., *Lutheran Confessions*, pp. 124–25.

[187] See *Table Talk* no. 5124 (1540), LW 54:390–91; cf. *Table Talk* no. 4907 (1540), WA TR 4:576; Luther to Melanchthon, May 12, 1530, WA Br 5:316–17.

[188] Josquin Desprez (ca. 1450–1521) was a Franco-Flemish composer whose masterful command of the resources of Renaissance polyphony gave him a lasting reputation after a career working in Italy, the Low Countries, and France. On Josquin, see Stanley Sadie, ed., *New Grove Dictionary of Music and Musicians*, 2nd ed. (New York: Grove, 2002), 13:220–66; David Fallows, *Josquin* (Turnhout: Brepols, 2009).

[189] In this motet, two voices sing *Circumdederunt me* ("The groans of death have surrounded me; the sorrows of hell have surrounded me") in canon while four sing *Haec dicit Dominus* ("Thus says the Lord: I shall deliver [My] people from the hand of death until I redeem them. I will be your death, O death; I will be your sting, O hell") in free counterpoint. Although the music is by Josquin (originally with a French secular text), the Latin biblical text had been added in *contrafactum* by the Saxon court composer Conrad Rupsch (ca. 1475–1530), published in 1537 by the Nürnberg bookseller Hans Ott (d. 1546) as *Novum et insigne opus musicum* [VD16 ZV12076]: see Leaver, *Luther's Liturgical Music*, pp. 54–56. For Luther's comments on Josquin, cf. *Table Talk* no. 1258 (1531), LW 54:129–30; no. 1563 (1532), WA TR 2:134–35; no. 3516 (1537), WA TR 3:371–72. Cf. Eyolf Østrem, "Luther, Josquin and *des fincken gesang*," in *The Arts and the Cultural Heritage of Martin Luther* (Copenhagen: Museum Tusculanum Press, 2003), pp. 51–79. For Josquin's music, see Willem Elders, ed., *New Josquin Edition* (Utrecht: Vereniging voor Nederlandse Muziekgeschiedenis, 1987–2015), 30:7–10, no. 6; 30:59–85, esp. pp. 80–82. The Wittenberg *contrafactum* is edited in Hans Joachim Moser, *Die Kantorei der Spätgotik* (Berlin: Sulzbach, 1928), pp. 22–23.

One of his table companions once gave him a hundred beautiful oranges. "O Lord God!" he said. "What will You some day give Your dear children, who love and honor You and Your dear Son, especially since You now let so much beautiful fruit grow for the cardinals and courtiers, who mock and slander You? Let us, dear children, persevere with our good God; He preserves our portion for us and will give us something better."[190]

One time he had as guests several people from Joachimsthal who were having their children go through the deposition.[191] The doctor himself matriculated them[192] and said, among many other fine things: "This is only a children's deposition. When you are grown and serve people in churches, schools, and governments, then your parishioners, students, and citizens will put you through a real deposition and vex you. But this vexation is necessary, so that children become accustomed to enduring it from their youth on. Anyone who cannot endure or ignore something is not fit to be a preacher or ruler."

Doctor Georg Major, who was rector at that time,[193] visited him after a meal. Upon the doctor's advice, he was engaged in reading all the way through the books of St. Augustine for himself. ["Rector," [Dr. Luther] said, "have you finished with your Augustine? Keep on reading. Old preachers who have to deal with the Papists also have to read and know the ancient teachers and fathers."[194] Then he turned to us and said, "Read Philip's *Loci communes*.[195] Next to the Bible it is the finest book, in which pure theology is summarized correctly and in an orderly fashion. Augustine accomplished something because the heretics provoked him to take up arms.[196]

---

[190] See *Table Talk* no. 5340 (1540), WA TR 5:64.

[191] *deponieren*; from the medieval Latin *depositio*, denoting a ritual on the occasion of moving upward in academic status in which each candidate was reproached with his faults and failings. Cf. above, Mathesius, *History*, p. 207. Here, young students [*Bachanten*; see above, p. 133 n. 104] were being advanced from preparatory work to university study. For this anecdote, cf. *Table Talk* no. 5024 (1540), WA TR 4:619; no. 7033 (n.d.), WA TR 6:347; see also below, Mathesius, *History*, p. 606.

[192] *absolvirt*

[193] On Major, see above, p. 300 n. 88. He was rector of the University of Wittenberg in the winter semester of 1540: see Förstemann et al., *Album*, 1:184.

[194] See *Table Talk* no. 5787 (n.d.), WA TR 5:352. Cf. Luther, preface to Augustine, *On the Spirit and the Letter* (1533?), LW 60:43.

[195] For the commendation of Melanchthon's *Loci communes* (see above, p. xl n. 117) after the Bible but above the patristic and medieval theologians, see, e.g., *Table Talk* no. 5787 (n.d.), WA TR 5:352; no. 5511 (1542–43), LW 54:439–40; no. 5647, WA TR 5:291. Cf. above, Mathesius, *History*, p. 189.

[196] On Augustine, see above, p. 42 n. 16. For the thought, cf. *Table Talk* no. 3984 (1538), WA TR 4:55–56; no. 51 (1531), LW 54:8; Luther, preface to Augustine, *On the Spirit and the Letter* (1533), LW 60:44; *Table Talk* no. 4412 (1539), LW 54:337.

Bernard also speaks well in his sermons concerning the Lord Christ and the gracious forgiveness of sins; he is no good at disputing.[197] Chrysostom is a prattler.[198] Jerome is good at praising monks and nuns but has little understanding of Christianity.[199] Ambrose has good sayings.[200] If Peter Lombard had made any headway with the Bible, he would have surpassed all the monks.[201] Read the *Glossa ordinaria*[202] and Lyra[203] for the sake of the grammar and the comparison of the accounts. Bonaventure[204] and Gabriel

---

[197] On Bernard of Clairvaux, see the introduction above, p. lvi n. 191; Melanchthon, *Preface*, p. 61; below, Mathesius, *History*, p. 529. For the thought, see *Table Talk* no. 584 (1533), LW 54:105; no. 872 (1530), WA TR 1:435–36.

[198] John Chrysostom, bishop of Constantinople, received the epithet "golden-mouthed" for his oratorical skill, though Luther found much of the content of his preaching to be theologically dubious moralism. See *ODCC*, 3rd ed., s.v. "Chrysostom, John"; *Table Talk* no. 252 (1532), LW 54:33–34; no. 5089 (1540), WA TR 4:652; no. 2544b (1532), WA TR 2:516.

[199] On Jerome and Luther's attitude toward him, see above, p. 441.

[200] Ambrose, bishop of Milan, was a notable preacher, exegete, and hymn writer who influenced and baptized Augustine. See *ODCC*, 3rd ed., s.v. "Ambrose"; *Table Talk* no. 51 (1531), LW 54:8; no. 252 (1532), LW 54:34; no. 1968 (1531), WA TR 2:283.

[201] On Lombard, author of the *Sentences*, see above, Melanchthon, *Preface*, p. 60 and n. 29 there. For the thought, see *Table Talk* no. 192 (1532), LW 54:26; no. 2544a (1532), WA TR 2:515–16.

[202] The *Glossa ordinaria* was the standard set of marginal notes on the biblical text, compiled from patristic sources by Anselm of Laon (ca. 1050–1117; *ODCC*, 3rd ed., s.v. "Anselm of Laon"), with the addition of interlinear commentary. Since the late fifteenth century, the *Glossa* had been ascribed to Walafrid Strabo (ca. 808–849; *ODCC*, 3rd ed., "Walafrid Strabo"), and Luther connected it with Lombard and Aquinas (see *Table Talk* no. 7118 [n.d.], WA 48:691). The incunabular edition is reproduced in *Biblia Latina* (see above, p. 269 n. 14). The *Patrologia latina* (PL 113:67–1316; 114:9–752) offers a defective edition of the marginal glosses. On the history of the *Glossa*, see Lesley Smith, *The "Glossa Ordinaria": The Making of a Medieval Bible Commentary* (Leiden: Brill, 2009). On Luther's evaluation and use of the *Glossa*, see Karlfried Froehlich, "Martin Luther and the *Glossa Ordinaria*," LQ 23 (2009): 29–48; *Table Talk* no. 116 (1531), LW 54:14.

[203] Nicholas of Lyra was a Franciscan friar and biblical scholar notable for his emphasis on the literal meaning of the Bible, drawing on his knowledge of Hebrew and of rabbinic interpretation: Nicholas of Lyra, *Postilla super totam Bibliam*, 4 vols. (Strassburg, 1492; repr., Frankfurt am Main: Minerva, 1971). For Luther's critical evaluation of Lyra, especially as a commentator on the Old Testament, see, e.g., *On the Last Words of David* (1543), LW 15:269; *Lectures on Genesis* (1535–45/1544–54), LW 3:26 and passim (cf. the introduction by Jaroslav Pelikan, LW 1:xi); *Table Talk* no. 7118 (n.d.), WA 48:691; no. 3271a–b (1532), WA TR 3:243. See *ODCC*, 3rd ed., s.v. "Nicholas of Lyre."

[204] Bonaventure (1221–74), known as the "Seraphic Doctor," was an eminent Franciscan theologian who served as general of the order. He was contemporary with Thomas Aquinas at the University of Paris and cultivated mystical theology as well as scholastic forms of argument. See *ODCC*, 3rd ed. s.v. "Bonaventure." For Luther's evaluation, cf. *Table Talk* no. 683 (1530), WA TR 1:330; no. 3370b (1533), WA TR 3:295.

Biel[205] were good people. Likewise, after the time of Hus,[206] something of the pure doctrine was maintained and put forward by Gerson,[207] Dorsten,[208] Proles,[209] Staupitz,[210] Wesel,[211] and Fleck.[212] Our Master Philip, however, can explain Scripture, reflect on its substance, and do a fine job of summarizing it briefly. He learned to pray amid the cross and tribulation, has conversed with the greatest and most learned opponents, and takes his theology seriously. Therefore, young fellows, diligently read his *Loci* and [*Commentary on the Epistle*] *to the Romans*.[213] If anyone cares to use my [commentaries

---

[205] On Biel, see above, Melanchthon, *Preface*, p. 62 and n. 44 there. For Luther's evaluation, cf. *Table Talk* no. 3722 (1538), LW 54:264.

[206] On John Hus, and Luther's evaluation of him, see the introduction above, pp. xxxvii–xxxviii and p. 121 n. 38. For the following list of late medieval theologians, cf. below, Mathesius, *History*, p. 520, and Flacius, *Catalogus* (see above, p. 145 n. 35), which includes all of the figures named except for Dorsten and Gabriel Biel.

[207] On Gerson, see above, Melanchthon, *Preface*, p. 63 and n. 49 there. For Luther's judgment, see *Table Talk* no. 2544a (1532), WA TR 2:516; no. 5523 (1542–43), LW 54:443–44; no. 1340 (1532), WA TR 2:56; no. 5711 (n.d.), WA TR 5:327; no. 5743 (n.d.), WA TR 5:339; no. 6760 (n.d.), WA TR 6:170; no. 2457a (1532), WA TR 2:468; no. 1492 (1532), WA TR 2:114.

[208] Johannes [Bauer] von Dorsten (ca. 1435–81) was an Augustinian Hermit who taught theology at the University of Erfurt and served as provincial of the order. He protested against the incursion of the canon lawyers into the province of theology and criticized certain forms of popular devotion to miracles. See Erich Kleineidam, "Johannes von Dorsten," *NDB* 10:548; Berndt Hamm, *Frömmigkeitstheologie am Anfang des 16. Jahrhunderts: Studien zu Johannes von Paltz und seinem Umkreis* (Tübingen: Mohr Siebeck, 1982), pp. 60–62, 308–13. There does not appear to be any reference by Luther to Dorsten apart from this passage in Mathesius; neither is he included in Flacius, *Catalogus*.

[209] Andreas Proles (1429–1503) was Johann von Staupitz's predecessor as vicar-general for the Observant Augustinian congregations in Saxony. He expressed sympathy for Hus' cause and criticized Jerome. See Karl Janicke, "Proles, Andreas," *ADB* 26:661–63; Adolar Zumkeller, "Proles, Andreas," *BBKL* 7:998–99. For Luther's judgment, see his afterword to Hus, *Three Letters* (1536/1537), LW 60:130–31; *Table Talk* no. 445 (1533), LW 54:72; no. 6991 (n.d.), WA TR 6:309. Cf. below, Mathesius, *History*, p. 582.

[210] On Johann von Staupitz, see the introduction above, p. lvi and n. 194.

[211] *Wesalia*; probably Johann Ruch[e]rath von Wesel (d. 1481), an Erfurt doctor of theology and then cathedral preacher in Worms, who was known for his connections to the Hussites and his criticism of established ecclesiastical doctrines and practices, including indulgences. He was tried for heresy at Mainz in 1479 and sentenced to life imprisonment in the Augustinian cloister there. See *ODCC*, 3rd ed., s.v. "John of Wesel." For Luther's remarks on him, see *On the Councils and the Church* (1539), LW 41:115; *Explanations of the Ninety-Five Theses* (1518), LW 31:157. Less probably, the reference could be to the Dutch theologian Johannes Wessel Gansfort (ca. 1419–89): see Luther, preface to Gansfort, *Letters* (1522), LW 59:6–11.

[212] On the Franciscan prior Johann Fleck, see Mathesius, *History*, above, p. 145 and n. 35 there; and below, p. 557.

[213] On Melanchthon's *Loci communes* and *Commentary on Romans*, see above, Mathesius, *History*, p. 189.

on] Deuteronomy[214] and Galatians,[215] he will be able to develop his preaching better and more richly."[216]

A learned and excellent young man[217] wrote some letters to our doctor in Greek. The doctor asked and admonished that such letters not be written to him, since they were too learned for him. When another one came, the doctor responded and wrote in Latin, along with this old bit of patched-together doggerel[218] in ⌐Hebrew letters: *Mer Dauid satis, lis faden ab do die nat ist.*[219]

Many of these words sound as if they are good Hebrew words; therefore, the Greek scholar researched the words and consulted some Hebraists. Finally, he went to Augsburg, to the scholars at the imperial diet, whom the doctor had already informed about how he had gotten back at his Greek scholar.

Among his other great virtues was that he was easily pleased and very generous. When Elector John gave him a new garment, he wrote back that he had done too much for him. If he were recompensed for everything now, what could he expect in the next life?[220] Elector John Frederick offered him a share[221] in the Fürstenvertrag [mine] on the Schneeberg,[222] but he did not want it. "The devil is my enemy," he said. "He says that all the treasures in the earth are his [Matt. 4:9]; he might cut off the ore on my account, and

---

[214] Probably the *Lectures on Deuteronomy* (1523–25), LW 9, which Luther prepared for publication, rather than the *Wochenpredigten über das 5. Buch Mose* (1529/1564), WA 28:509–763, which had appeared only in a partial edition during Luther's lifetime.

[215] Probably the 1531 *Lectures on Galatians* (LW 26; 27:1–149) published in 1535, rather than the 1516–17 *Lectures on Galatians* (LW 27:151–410), which were published in 1519 and 1523 (cf. the introduction by Jaroslav Pelikan, LW 27:ix).

[216] For these recommendations, see *Table Talk* no. 5511 (1542–43), LW 54:439–40.

[217] This was Melanchthon's friend and correspondent Joachim Camerarius (see the introduction above, p. xlv and n. 144 there). See Camerarius to Luther, May [6]. 1530, WA Br 5:307–8. The second Greek letter of Camerarius and Luther's reply are not preserved, but see Luther to Melanchthon, May 12, 1530, WA Br 5:317; 13:133; cf. WA Br 18:195 n. 1. See Volz, *Die Lutherpredigten des Johannes Mathesius*, pp. 124, 149 n. 5.

[218] *den alten unnd schneyder Knüttelvers*; or "wretched old bit of doggerel."

[219] I.e., *Wer daut, sat ist; lies Faden ab, da die Naht ist* ["One who is digesting is full; gather the thread where the seam is"] (see *LH²*, p. 565)—perhaps intended, in its German meaning, to admonish Camerarius that he has written enough Greek already. Michael Beyer ("Johannes Mathesius als Biograph," p. 78 n. 54), however, suggests a different reading, translated as "David is sufficient for me; when sewing, he concentrated on the seam."

[220] See Luther to Elector John, August 17, 1529, WA Br 5:134.

[221] *Kux.* See *Table Talk* no. 3471 (1536), WA TR 3:341; no. 6374 (n.d.), WA TR 5:630. Cf. *Table Talk* no. 4617 (1539), WA TR 4:404; no. 5675 (1544), WA TR 5:314.

[222] The Schneeberg is a mountain in the Saxon Erzgebirge which gives its name to the silver mining town founded in 1471.

then the other shareholders would be on the hook because of me. It would be much more fitting for me to pay my assessment[223] with an Our Father so that the ore may remain in good supply and the profit be put to good use."

The opponents also attested this [virtue] of his when one said, "Someone ought to stuff a few hundred gulden down his throat." "That wouldn't help with him," said another. "The German beast has no regard for money and won't accept any even if it is offered."[224] Honorable and grateful people occasionally honored him with gifts, but he gave most of them away. One time a poor man lamented to him about his great extremity, and, since he had no ready cash, he went to his wife, who was in confinement after childbirth, and got the money that had been given by the godparents and brought it to the man in need. When someone reproached him, he said, "God is rich, and He will give in a different way."[225]

At the beginning, many vagabonds and runaway monks were able to swindle him into providing cloth for [new] clothing.[226] He also used to intercede willingly for the thieves who were arrested. Finally, he confessed, "I thought that all who made an appeal to me and invoked the Gospel were devout, but wicked scoundrels have made me wiser. The best place for a fish is in water and for a thief, on the gallows."[227] Thus Scripture says that one should provide for his own house before giving to a stranger [1 Tim. 5:4, 8; 2 Cor. 8:13–14]."

At table, there was a discussion over the claim that it was possible to read a person's palm and that one could see from that whether the person is generous. "I believe it," said the doctor, "because if someone wants to give, he has to use own his hands or other people's to do so."[228]

In addition to his contented heart and generous hands, he had a mouth that was truthful and disciplined. If he made a promise, he always kept it

---

[223] *Zubuß gebe*; a technical term for additional payments by shareholders for the maintenance of the mine.

[224] *Table Talk* no. 2499a–b (1532), WA TR 2:493 and WA 48:495.

[225] Cf. *Table Talk* no. 3360b (1533), WA TR 3:290; no. 2922a (1533), WA TR 3:81. The *Patengeld* was the customary gift given by the godparents for the benefit of the child. Luther's third son, Paul, had been born on January 28, 1533. His godparents included Duke John Ernest, son of the late Elector John of Saxony from his second marriage: see Brecht 3:20.

[226] See *Table Talk* no. 5201 (1540), WA TR 5:6. In 1541, Luther was host to a supposed former nun calling herself Rosina von Truchsess, who turned out to be a swindler and thief: see Luther to Jonas, August 30, 1541, WA Br 9:505; to Anton Lauterbach, November 10, 1542, WA Br 10:176; to Johann Göritz, January 29, 1544, WA Br 10:519–20; to Katharina Luther, July 28, 1545, LW 50:273–81. See Brecht 3:239–40.

[227] Wander 1:587, "Dieb" no. 85; 1:1028, "Fische" no. 22. See *Table Talk* no. 976 (1530), WA TR 1:493.

[228] See *Table Talk* no. 5421 (1542), WA TR 5:132.

without wavering. Nor did he speak ill of people. Likewise, he was opposed to those who made disparaging mention of others in their absence. "Those are real sows," he often said, "who pay no attention to the roses and violets in the garden but only stick their snouts in the dirt. That is what slanderers do as well. They overlook the virtues of great people, and when they notice that one has a failing or some blemish, it is their habit to broadcast it or to gorge themselves on it."[229]

So far as the conduct of his household was concerned, he engaged a private tutor[230] for his children, had them pray and read something aloud before a meal, and he himself often gave them assignments.[231] He admonished those in his house not to create any scandals for him there. "The devil is keeping a sharp eye on me, hoping to bring my teaching under suspicion or to bring me into disrepute some day."[232]

By nature the doctor was possessed of a manly heart and courage, although he was the humblest of men, who gladly followed the good advice of his friends. For example, during this year [1540] he let himself be persuaded to seek out Agricola in order to make peace. "But fortunately for me," he said at table, "I did not find him at home, otherwise the little man would have had that to boast about for the rest of his life."[233]

Master Philip established it as a custom that all the students in the auditorium would rise when the doctor came to lecture.[234] Even though this is an old and honorable discipline in the schools, the humble doctor was not happy with it and said, "I wish that Master Philip would not bother with his ordinance. On account of this standing up, I am forced to pray the Our Father a few more times, and, if I dared, I would sometimes walk away without lecturing. But as a pious old monk said when Satan was tickling his [vanity] in the pulpit at the sight of a great crowd of listeners and he wanted to step down again: 'We are neither to begin nor to leave on that account.' *Doxa,*

---

[229] Cf. *Sermons on Leviticus and Numbers* (1527–28), WA 25:427 (LW 63).

[230] The private tutors hired by Luther for his children included Hieronymus Weller (ca. 1530; see above, p. 416 n. 127), Hans Fuchs (ca. 1535; see WA 48:60–61), Georg Schnell (ca. 1536; see WA DB 12:534), Franz Bock from Flanders (ca. 1541; see WA Br 8:384–85) (this "Franciscus" has sometimes been confused with Franz Gross from Oschatz: see above, p. 302 n. 106, and Volz, *Die Lutherpredigten des Johannes Mathesius*, pp. 87–88 n. 2), and Ambrosius Rutfeldt [Rudtfeld] (ca. 1545; see above, p. 10 n. 18).

[231] Cf. above, Mathesius, *History*, pp. 272, 279.

[232] Cf. *Table Talk* no. 5050 (1540), WA TR 4:636.

[233] *Table Talk* no. 5195 (1540), WA TR 5:4.

[234] This seems indeed to have been a matter of "custom," rather than an official regulation, since it is not reflected in the university statutes in Friedensburg, *Urkundenbuch der Universität Wittenberg*.

doxa est magna noxa ['Glory, glory is a great harm'].[235] Whoever chases after glory does not obtain it, or if he does get some, it comes with great danger. Herr Severus,[236] your verse is true: '*Gloria philosopho, sed Christi discipulo crux*' ['Glory is for the philosopher, but the cross for the disciple of Christ']. God will not give His people the true glory or the heavenly liripipe[237] until they are in heaven. Here on earth we theologians should let ourselves be excoriated, as they do to the young doctors in Erfurt on the day before they receive their degree."[238]

He was also deadly serious in his sermons at times and spoke with a severe tone if someone had made him angry.[239] Great people have great virtues[240]—they also have lofty and great zeal. *Et faciles motus mens generosa capit* ["The nobler the mind, the more readily it is stirred"].[241] If you take something seriously, you cannot always be joking around, let alone be tepid or tread too lightly. Christ Himself, who was without any sin or depravity, had His anger kindled against death [cf. John 11:33, 38 DB] and against the Pharisees [Mark 3:5]. And the prophets, who were driven and governed by the Holy Spirit, also frequently burned against the godless. Phinehas in his anger and zeal stabbed a fornicator to death [Num. 25:7–8]. Elijah had the prophets of Baal slain [1 Kings 18:40]. Samuel laid his own hands on the captive king [1 Sam. 15:33]. Paul often curses the false teachers [Gal. 1:8–9]. Moses in his wrath threw down the two tablets when Aaron set his people free from the Law of God through idolatry [Exod. 32:19]. God frequently leads His great saints in astonishing ways [Ps. 4:3 DB] and vindicates their cause.

As our doctor liked to say about Herr Brenz and Philip: "We need not only gentle rain and soft breezes but also stormy winds and pouring rain if the leaves and grass, trees and stalks are to bud and sprout."[242]

Those of us who are weak and fainthearted instruments in God's tabernacle, we who are little lights and lanterns, have to interpret the blazing

---

[235] Cf. *Table Talk* no. 4971 (1540), WA TR 4:596 n. 2.

[236] I.e., Dr. Wolfgang Schiefer [Severus]: see above, p. 339 n. 104. For the verse, cf. Mathesius, *Homiliae* (1590), fol. 140r, and *Syrach* (1586), fol. 150r; Otto Clemen, "Zu Caspar Brusch," *Mitteilungen des Vereines für Geschichte der Deutschen in Böhmen* 42 (1903): 106.

[237] *liripipium*; the tail of the hood on an academic gown, especially a doctoral gown.

[238] See above, Mathesius, *History*, p. 207.

[239] On Luther's anger, cf. above, Mathesius, *History*, pp. 315–16.

[240] Cf. above, Mathesius, *History*, p. 404.

[241] Ovid, *Tristia* 3.5.32 (Loeb 151 [1924], pp. 122–23).

[242] See above, Mathesius, *History*, p. 315.

flames of the great torches[243] and lamps in the best way and help to make them bearable. For God has made greater and lesser lights in the firmament [Gen. 1:14–18]; and fire, hail, mist, and stormy winds also fulfill His word and command [Ps. 148:8]. Although our doctor's downpours and cloudbursts sometimes wash out the path of the monks, fanatics, tyrants, false brethren, and worldly-wise, and he sometimes distresses them in his zeal, as Christ did to the Pharisees, scribes, and teachers of the Law, take it as the hand of God and of Gideon [Judg. 7:20], as the mouth of Moses and Elijah. If something [ill] is mingled in at times—even as all saints have had their flaws and imperfections and received forgiveness of sins only through grace—it belongs in the Lord's Prayer and under Elijah's mantle, which he left on earth for his disciple to help cover up the times when occasionally too much or too little was done [cf. 2 Kings 2:13].

It is just as much gross malfeasance in an office to act with excessive mildness and leniency as it is to act with burning zeal and violence, as we observe in Saul [1 Sam. 15:9] and Aaron [Exodus 32]. More than once I heard the doctor warn that we should keep on the main road and proceed according to the rule instead of being ready to cut across the field—that is something for exceptional horsemen.[244]

ᴵWith that I will now conclude this apologia and defense, in the Christian hope that I shall give an honorable answer for it before the Lord Christ. When there is a need, may God grant His Church people who do not carry out their office deceitfully[245] [Jer. 48:10], and may He preserve us poor pastors in moderation and discretion, so that each one may carry out his office as he is prepared to answer for it with God and a good conscience on the Last Day before the Supreme Judge! Amen!

---

[243] *kertzen*; an emendation suggested by Loesche (*LH²*, p. 566 on 305.11) for *herzen* ["hearts"] in the printed texts.

[244] Cf. above, Mathesius, *History*, pp. 315–16.

[245] *fraudulenter*

The Thirteenth Sermon,[1]
on the Year 1540 [Down to the Year 1542]
in the History of Doctor Luther

[Late 1563]

BELOVED friends in the Lord! Last time we began with the year 1540 in our history and told you about the doctor's conduct, life, and some of his good sayings and stories, as many as occurred to us quickly. Now we are still in the year 1540, so this time we will say something about his other talks which took place at meals at that time as the time and events gave occasion. If we have time remaining, we intend to discuss the translation of the Holy Bible, to the glory of God and of His Word, and the other things that happened in this year.

When an excellent man speaks a word at the proper time, it is surely like a golden apple or a beautiful orange and citron in a silver bowl, as the wise King Solomon says [cf. Prov. 25:11], and will scarcely be forgotten by good people. Likewise, it is fitting that the deeds of honorable people should be extolled forever by their posterity. May the Son of God, therefore, help us now with His Spirit that I, as a grateful student, may speak something useful and pleasant[2] about the good sayings and blessed deeds of my dear preceptor.

While the good Emperor Charles was delayed in the Netherlands,[3] there were all kinds of strange dealings in the empire, and many people began to snort and snarl, hoping to stir up some trouble, so that good people were worried and 'in danger, but the Son of God maintained a continuous watch over His Gospel, which kept its course, and He opened one door after another for it. For the foolishness and wantonness of the adversaries became more apparent with every passing day. One after another, Christ gradually cleared away those who opposed His Word and servants.

---

[1] In the 1566 first edition, fol. 156r (and still in the 1567 second edition), this sermon is numbered (again) as the twelfth, both in the title and in the page headings, and the following sermons are numbered in sequence as the thirteenth, etc. On the numbering of the sermon and its dating, see the introduction above, p. lxxxvii and n. 346 there.

[2] *nützlichs und lustigs*; cf. Horace, *Ars Poetica* 343 (Loeb 194 [1926], p. 478).

[3] See above, Mathesius, *History*, p. 422.

In those days, as I said last time, I sat along with other good people at the doctor's table, where good and instructive talks took place. Since there was a very beautiful spring that year, in which everything was blossoming and turning green, the doctor said to Justus Jonas: "If only sin and death were gone, we would be satisfied with a paradise like this. But it will become much more beautiful when the old world and the old skin are made entirely new, and an eternal spring begins and will last forever."[4]

This year at Pentecost, while at table, the doctor recounted for us the whole story of how he traveled to Worms in 1521, stood before the emperor, confessed his doctrine, and answered for his books.[5] You heard a good report about that at the appropriate time.[6] In all my days I have never heard anything sweeter and more delightful. Someone who has personally been involved in a certain business and has been directly affected by it is able to speak vividly of what took place. Most people talk based on hearsay.

Around this time there were all sorts of rumors about arsonists and people who were allegedly poisoning food and drink in many places.[7] For example, Einbeck[8] and many other places burned during the summer, and many people were tortured and sentenced to horrible deaths.[9] In Wittenberg itself, four people were smoked to death by being chained to oak posts and then lamentably asphyxiated and baked dry by fire, as if they were tiles for the roof. This gave rise to all kinds of discussions at table. The doctor laid blame primarily on the evil ¹spirits, who wanted to destroy the Church and Word of God with lies and murder, because their end was near, when they would be bound with eternal chains in the fire of hell [cf. 2 Pet 2:4; Jude 6; Rev. 20:1-3]. They wanted to make a display of their envy and rage beforehand.

---

[4] Cf. *Table Talk* no. 4949 (1540), WA TR 4:590 (MathL); Mathesius, *Leychpredigten*, fol. s4v.

[5] See *Table Talk* no. 5342a-b (1540), WA TR 5:65-74; no. 5107 (1540), WA TR 4:666-67; no. 5375b (1540), WA TR 5:100-102.

[6] See above, Mathesius, *History*, pp. 167-82.

[7] See, e.g., *Table Talk* no. 5231 (1540), WA TR 5:19; no. 5131 (1540), WA TR 4:678; no. 5160 (1540), WA TR 4:687-88; no. 5253 (1540), WA TR 5:28-29, where Luther and his companions engage in speculation about the role of Anabaptists, the Franciscans and other monks, and the papacy itself. On these episodes, see Volz, *Die Lutherpredigten des Johannes Mathesius*, pp. 208-9.

[8] Einbeck was a town belonging to the Hanseatic League in the duchy of Braunschweig-Grubenhagen, which had joined the Smalcaldic League in 1536. Einbeck burned almost completely to the ground on July 26, 1540. Several other Evangelical cities reported fires as well; the contributions of environmental factors (a long drought) and political and religious conflict were unclear. See Bob Scribner, "The *Mordbrenner* Fear in Sixteenth-Century Germany," in *The German Underworld*, ed. Richard J. Evans (London: Routledge, 1988), pp. 29-56.

[9] Cf. *Table Talk* no. 5271 (1540), WA TR 5:39; Luther to Melanchthon, December 7, 1540, WA Br 9:289. Executions of four persons took place on June 29, 1540.

Although some confessions came to light in which certain persons were accused of having allegedly instigated and paid these arsonists,[10] the doctor said, "It takes a great deal to convict powerful people and wicked men publicly. The one for whom they are now stoking a fire and rendering their services will find them and their associates when the time is right and be able to pay them back the wages they have earned.[11] If the evildoers received all the proper wages and punishment they have earned here, our Lord Christ would not need to hold any Day of Judgment or take up all the cases again.[12] Great and small [matters] will be revealed before the judgment seat of Christ [cf. Rev. 20:12], and each will be punished eternally for what he has done during his life in the body, according to his desert" [cf. 2 Cor. 5:10].[13]

This summer Herr Melanchthon went to Weimar, where he became very ill, so that everyone feared for his life. Our doctor was hastily summoned, and he consoled and encouraged him.[14] As he said afterward, "I have rescued our Philip and my Kate[15] and Herr Myconius[16] from death through prayer"[17]—and in the end Myconius even asked the doctor to stop crying out on his behalf!

---

[10] Several of the suspected arsonists confessed under torture that they had been hired by Duke Henry of Braunschweig-Wolfenbüttel (see above, p. 27 n. 6), who was publicly accused of inciting arson at the Diet of Regensburg in 1541. See Sleidanus, *De statu religionis* (1558), book 13, pp. 370, 378.

[11] Cf. Luther's satirical "hymn" "O villainous Harry [*Ach du armer Heinze*]": in *Against Hanswurst* (1541), LW 41:255–56.

[12] Cf. Augustine, *City of God* 1.8.2 (PL 41:20; CCSL 47:7; NPNF¹ 2:5–6).

[13] Cf. *Table Talk* no. 5284 (1540), LW 54:405–6; no. 5154 (1540), WA TR 4:686.

[14] Melanchthon traveled to Weimar on his way to the colloquy in Hagenau (see below, p. 467), but had to stop there because of the onset of a severe fever and his increasing depression over the scandal caused by Philip of Hesse's bigamy, undertaken with the advice of Luther, Melanchthon, and Bucer (see Brecht 3:205–9)—a development which Mathesius never mentions except by allusion here. At Elector John Frederick's request, Luther came to Weimar on June 23 to attend Melanchthon, who had begun to improve in physical and mental health by July 10. See Brecht 3:209–10. For Luther's report on his prayers and admonitions, see Luther to Katharina Luther, July 2, 1540, LW 50:207–12; *Table Talk* no. 5088b (1540), WA TR 4:651–52; no. 5096 (1540), LW 54:387–90.

[15] Katharina was in peril of her life after a miscarriage in late January 1540. See Luther to Hieronymus Weller, March 16, 1540, WA Br 9:73; *Table Talk* no. 4991 (1540), LW 54:373–75; Brecht 3:235.

[16] Friedrich Myconius (see above, p. 385 n. 87) was seriously ill at the beginning of 1541. For Luther's prayer on his behalf, see Luther to Myconius, January 9, 1541, WA Br 9:302–3; and April 5, 1543, WA Br 10:287.

[17] Luther mentions the power of prayer in restoring Melanchthon and Katharina in *Table Talk* no. 5565 (1543), LW 54:453–54; no. 4885 (1540), LW 54:369; no. 5407 (1542), WA TR 5:129; no. 6751 (n.d.), WA TR 6:162–63, though none of these mentions Myconius.

In those days, Herr Philip was stuck in severe and deep tribulation. But God, who also graciously heard the prayer of Moses when he fervently prayed for his fallen brother Aaron [Exod. 32:11–14, 31–33; Num. 12:11–14], demonstrated and magnified His kindness this time as well, and heard the sighs of the faithful, and preserved for us this excellent man, who accomplished many good things the following year in colloquies and imperial diets and who faithfully cared for the true Church and the pure doctrine and steadfastly defended them.[18] |When God wants to bring His servants into great honor, He first allows them to sink into weakness or to stumble and to learn that they, too, are only human, so that henceforth they may battle the enemies of Christendom by the power and wisdom of God alone.

I heard many good talks at this time as well. For example, Doctor Bugenhagen mentioned this verse in Luther's house: *Omnia vincit amor et nos cedamus amori* ["Love conquers all; let us, too, yield to love"].[19] "*O Domine pastor*," said Herr Philip, "leave that verse and your Our Father to me. I need them both." Likewise, one time when this failing[20] was mentioned, the doctor quoted Terence: "'And does this please you?' 'No, but because I cannot alter it, I have to be content with it.'[21] It would have been better if this course had not been pursued from the beginning.[22] But who knows what God will make of it? He can make everything turn out for the best. David also caused a severe offense; because of it he had to endure severe adversity and flee his land[23] [2 Sam. 12:7–12; 15:14–19:10]. Yet his fall serves as a consolation for many even until the Last Day. One who has never fallen has no occasion to stand upright.[24] All of the saints have had to bear their flaws on earth,[25] in order that they might receive the gracious forgiveness of sins and eternal life solely through Christ's blood and

---

[18] On Mathesius' appreciation of Melanchthon, see the introdution above, p. lxxxv.

[19] See *Table Talk* no. 5142 (1540), WA TR 4:682 and WA 48:283; Virgil, *Eclogues* 10.69 (Loeb 63 [1916], pp. 94–95).

[20] *schwachheyt*; or "weakness" or "illness," but here probably a reference to the advice on Philip of Hesse's bigamy (see above, p. 465 n. 14). Cf. Volz, *Die Lutherpredigten des Johannes Mathesius*, p. 60.

[21] *Table Talk* no. 5096 (1540), LW 54:387–90; Terence, *Adelphoe* ll.737–38 (Loeb 23 [2001], pp. 336–37).

[22] For Luther's comments in the aftermath of Philip of Hesse's bigamy, see, e.g., *Table Talk* no. 5038 (1540), LW 54:380; no. 5046 (1540), LW 54:382; Luther to Elector John Frederick, June 10, 1540, WA Br 9:133 (*LSC*, p. 290).

[23] *sein land mit dem rucken ansehen*; literally, "look upon his land with his back." See Wander 3:1755, "Rücken (Subst.)" no. 83.

[24] Cf. above, Mathesius, *History*, p. 244.

[25] *jr Pfabenfüß auff erden tragen müssen*; see above, Mathesius, *History*, p. 318.

obedience, and thus be able to bear witness to this article all the more stead-fastly. Furthermore, the faults and stumbles of the faithful accomplish far more good within Christendom than do the holy, austere, and invented sanctity of all monks and hypocrites."[26]

Since Herr Philip was ill, Doctor Caspar Cruciger and others were sent to the colloquy at Hagenau.[27] What was accomplished there is summarized in a separate booklet, which consists of little more than a title.[28] However, another colloquy was scheduled for Worms,[29] where the scholars from both parties were to hold a discussion and reach agreement, so that the negotia-tion at the coming imperial |diet, which was scheduled for the following year in Regensburg,[30] would move forward that much more quickly and directly, and so that the controversy in religious matters could be the more swiftly resolved.

The scheduled colloquy provided many occasions for good discussions at the table.[31] "Until now," said our doctor, "they have wanted to tackle these matters with force and have sought eradication, but the truth always rises higher [cf. 1 Esdras 4:41] and shines on the eyes of many good-hearted

---

[26] It is uncertain where the end of the quotation from Luther should be placed. The end of the paragraph may be intended as Mathesius' exposition.

[27] The Hagenau colloquy (relocated from Speyer because of plague) took place in June and early July 1540. Because of Melanchthon's illness, the elector sent Cruciger (see above, p. xx n. 19) and Myconius, along with Nicolaus von Amsdorf (see above, p. 30 n. 15): see Luther to Katharina Luther, June 16, 1540 LW 50:218–20. On the colloquy, see Sleidanus, *De statu religionis* (1558), book 13, pp. 366–69; Alois Schmid, "Hagenau, Colloquy of," *OER* 2:208; the discussion by Gottfried Krodel in LW 50:219 n. 17; and the acts edited by Klaus Ganzer and Karl-Heinz zur Mühlen, *Das Hagenauer Religionsgespräch (1540)*, ADRRG 1/1–2. For Luther's dismissal of the results of the colloquy, see his letter to Katharina Luther, July 26, 1540, LW 50:221–22; see also Brecht 3:215–17.

[28] *das nur ein blossen tittel hat.* The imperial recess of the Diet of Hagenau, printed in Wilhelm H. Neuser, ed., *Die Vorbereitung der Religionsgespräche von Worms und Regensburg 1540/41*, Texte zur Geschichte der Evangelischen Theologie 4 (Neukirchen-Vluyn: Neukirchner, 1974), pp. 96–107, announces the convocation of another colloquy in Worms for the fall of 1540. However, this text does not seem to have been printed in the sixteenth century. Mathesius may, therefore, have in mind the dismissive booklet published by Martin Bucer under the pseudonym Waremund Luitholden: *Vom Tag zu Hagenaw und wer verhinderet hab, das kein gesprech von vergleichung der Religion daselbst fürgangen ist* (Strasbourg: Johann Prüß, 1540) [VD16 B8937], 62 pages in quarto.

[29] See below, pp. 490–91.

[30] See below, pp. 491–94.

[31] See., e.g., *Table Talk* no. 5310 (1540), WA TR 5:53; no. 5312 (1540), WA TR 5:54–55, no. 5365 (1540), WA TR 5:95. What follows here, however, is chiefly dependent on Mathesius' own witness.

and honorable people. The wise Emperor Charles[32] has certainly noticed this. Therefore, his thoughts are simply and sincerely directed, in keeping with his imperial disposition, to seeing that these matters might be resolved peacefully and be mediated and arbitrated in a conciliatory way.

"Surely they see that the ideas of the clever bishop of Salzburg[33] cannot be put into effect. The opponents do not accept our doctrine; likewise, God will protect us from having to go back and affirm the idolatry of the Papists. Our people do not hope to overcome the other side, which, I am afraid, would hardly happen even if it were attempted. Likewise, the adversaries realize that their plans and intentions also fall far short, just like new fabric that has shrunk.[34] God will not let His Word be overthrown by force—just let anyone who is unable to keep his hands off give it a try." Now, since Bishop Lang's methods would not work, some clever people resolved to see if the matter could be arbitrated in such a way that each party would concede and yield and let their positions be cobbled together and united. "I am inclined to think," said Dr. Luther, "that Emperor Charles, our prudent lord, means this sincerely; but the majority of those advocating this are acting underhandedly, intending to present us with a dilemma by means of which they might be able to outwit our people and catch them by the ear.[35] For the wicked devil, too, is able to set forth his wickedness with good words and a beautiful appearance, even as he enticed Eve with sweet promises ¹and led her around the tree[36] with plausible and erudite words [Gen. 3:1–5].

"For the sake of politeness, one cannot refuse to engage in discussion and peaceful negotiation. Neither will any negotiation be without fruit if we

---

[32] Cf. above, Mathesius, *History*, pp. 179–80, 342, 343. On Mathesius' attitude toward the Hapsburg emperors, see the introduction above, p. lxxxiv.

[33] On the Salzburg bishop Matthäus Lang, see above, p. 151 n. 72; cf. p. 204 n. 24; and above, Mathesius, *History*, p. 306. The approach ascribed to Lang here may be that of personal friendly approach to individual Evangelical theologians while conceding the need for moral reforms of the clergy in the Roman Church, as Lang had dealt with Melanchthon at Augsburg: see *Table Talk* no. 5681 (n.d.), WA TR 5:319; cf. above, Mathesius, *History*, p. 344.

[34] *an jren gedancken unnd anschlegen auch vil abgehet, wie an gespantem tuch*; i.e., like cloth once removed from the tenterhooks on which it was stretched. See Thiele no. 185, p. 188; *Large Catechism* (1529) Pref. 19 (Kolb-Wengert, p. 382; *Concordia*, p. 356); *Sermons on John 6–8* (1530–32/1565), LW 23:253, 255, 258; and Wander 1:1352, 1354 "Tuch" nos. 5, 44. Cf. *On the Councils and the Church* (1539), LW 41:63, 161; preface to Alber, *The "Eulenspiegel" and Koran of the Barefoot Monks* (1542), LW 60:278.

[35] Cf. Wander 5:1541, "Lauern" no. 21.

[36] *das helmlein durch jren mund zog unnd sie. . . umb die fichte fürete*; literally, "pulled the straw through her mouth and led her around the spruce," here likely with an allusion to the tree of the knowledge of good and evil (Gen. 3:1–6). See Wander 2:279, "Hälmlein" nos. 1 and 3; cf. Wander 1:1009, "Fichte" no. 4.

but confess the truth simply and sincerely. But matters will not be settled. For in Paradise the Son of God Himself announced this war and strife between the Seed of the woman and the serpent [Gen. 3:15], which will not be put to rest or buried until He makes Himself seen and heard once again upon the rainbow [Rev. 4:3]; He will judge the case rightly once and for all. In the meantime, no one will reconcile our Lord Christ and Belial [2 Cor. 6:15], even if all reasonable and peaceable people here were to strive together. Christ has a good cause and an upright scepter; therefore, He cannot and will not back down; neither will He yield or concede anything to His enemies. Likewise, Belial will not admit to having done wrong, nor will he yield to anyone until he must do so on the Last Day.

"In the beginning there were only three men: a father with two sons. Adam and Abel, as the holy and redeemed seed, stood with the Seed of the woman and His revealed Word. Cain, having been born from the corrupted flesh and blood of believers, defended the serpent's cause, as one coming from evil [cf. 1 John 3:12].[37] The good and grieved father was unable to reconcile his two sons in the matter of religion. How, then, can anyone today expect to bring the evil world, which is entirely immersed in the devil and wickedness, as St. John says [1 John 5:19;], into accord with the holy seed of Jesus Christ, which cleaves to the Word?

"One of the greatest examples of the wise and clever world's foolishness is that it wants to unite the members of Christ with the associates of the devil. You, too, will come to see that this will accomplish nothing. We must wait patiently for the supreme Judge and His sentence. He will bring this case to an end and 'fulfill the words of the bishop of Salzburg:[38] he will condemn one party and cast them into the infernal fires; then the case will be arbitrated and resolved. Meanwhile, if you wish to lead a Christian life, meet a blessed end, enter your rest in peace, sleep sweetly, stand worthily before the judgment seat of Christ with honor and joy in expectation of the final verdict and the awaited redemption and promise, and remain with your Lord forever, then humbly adhere to the Word of the Gospel; believe and confess it when questioned; preserve your conscience; be rich in good works; let your love shine in patience, in all modesty and decency. Then you can be sure and confident and wait for the matter to be brought to its conclusion."

After the colloquy held in Hagenau, Herr Philip returned to Wittenberg in good health and good cheer,[39] along with Dr. Caspar Cruciger, who then

---

[37] Cf. *Lectures on Genesis* (1535–45/1544–54), LW 1:252–55.

[38] On Bishop Lang and his "prophecy"—that "priests have never been good"—see above, p. 204 n. 24.

[39] Luther and Melanchthon returned to Wittenberg at the beginning of August 1540.

began his lectures on John.[40] Dr. Luther, to the extent permitted by his weakness, continued with [his lectures on] Genesis.[41] In addition, the important and blessed work of translating the Bible made good progress; this year the large Bible was published.[42]

One of the greatest wondrous works [cf. Ps. 105:5] that our God accomplished through Dr. Luther before the end of the world is that He caused him to prepare an exceedingly lovely German Bible for the children of the firstborn Japhethite [Gen. 10:2],[43] having also honored us with the highest crown and scepter on earth;[44] He spoke to us and explained what His eternal, divine being and gracious will are, using good, sound, and understandable German words. Even people from other lands say that inhabitants of Meissen speak a good kind of German, once they have traveled among other people and shed their particular dialect.[45] Therefore, the Son of God raised

---

[40] Cruciger's lectures on John, which continued at least through 1542, were published in 1546: *In Evangelium Johannis Apostoli Enarratio* (Strasbourg: Kraft Müller, 1546) [VD16 C5855]. These lectures were incorporated into editions of Melanchthon's works beginning in the sixteenth century and are printed in CR 15:1–440 under the questionable assumption that they were in fact prepared by Melanchthon. On Cruciger, see above, p. xx n. 19, p. 298 n. 81, and Mathesius, *History*, pp. 306–7, 375; on his lectures on John, see Volz, *Die Lutherpredigten des Johannes Mathesius*, p. 208; Timothy J. Wengert, "Caspar Cruciger Sr.'s 1546 'Enarratio' on John's Gospel: An Experiment in Ecclesiological Exegesis," *Church History* 61, no. 1 (1992): 60–74; Wengert, "Caspar Cruciger," especially pp. 422–29.

[41] See above, Mathesius, *History*, p. 408. In December 1541, Luther began lecturing on chapter 26, and his comments about political events within the commentary on chapters 27–30 suggest that he delivered the material no later than early 1542: see the introduction by Jaroslav Pelikan, LW 5:ix–xi.

[42] Luther's German translation of the New Testament was first published in 1522; the books of the Old Testament appeared individually or in groupings over the following years until the first complete version of Luther's German Bible (including Old Testament, New Testament, and Apocrypha) appeared in 1534. Mathesius appears to be conflating the (partial) revision of the complete Bible—the printing of which was completed in 1541 (though some of its parts bore the date 1540) and was the first to have the indication "newly edited" [*auffs new zugericht*] on the title page—and the larger format (median folio) edition of 1541 which contained a more complete set of revisions: WA DB 2:634–40, no. 68 [VD16 ZV1473] and no. 69 [VD16 B2712]. See Volz, *Die Lutherpredigten des Johannes Mathesius*, p. 269 on *LH* 313.19f.

[43] Japheth's firstborn son was Gomer, regarded as the ancestor of the Germanic peoples: see Mathesius, *History*, above, p. 119; and below, p. 585; Luther, *Lectures on Genesis* (1535–45/1544–54), LW 2:190.

[44] I.e., the Holy Roman Empire.

[45] *wenn sie untern leuten gewesen/ und jrs Landsmans vergessen.* On the proverbial purity of the Meissen dialect, see Wander 3:578–79, "Meissner."

up a German from Saxony who had traveled, and He brought God's Bible into the language of Meissen.[46]

This sublime work deserves a sermon of its own. ʹThe good Doctor Johann Bugenhagen, pastor in Wittenberg, established a special festival in his house in honor of the translation of the Bible,[47] which he celebrated annually,[48] and together with his children and friends thanked God for this excellent and blessed treasure of the Bible translated into German. Since the birth of Christ, many translations have come into Christendom. Both Chaldean [translations][49] are worthy of all respect, for in many places they call the Son of God, the Messiah of the Jews, "the eternal Word," and they were highly esteemed by the ancient Jews.[50] The Greek translation, which is said to have been translated by seventy Jews because of the resolution of and at the expense of Ptolemy Philadelphus, the king of Egypt, is also renowned.[51] However, these translators often speak rather carelessly about the Son of God and frequently omit whole [parts of the] text, as can be seen in Isaiah 9 [:6].[52]

---

[46] The language of Luther's German Bible was based on the German used in the Saxon chancery, drawn from the Meissen dialect but adapted for the greatest possible understanding across Germany. See *Table Talk* no. 1040 (1530), WA TR 1:524–25 (Aurifaber); Brecht 2:48.

[47] *Translationis Bibliorum*; perhaps with an implied parody of medieval church festivals commemorating the "translation" (i.e., the transfer) of saints' relics from one church to another.

[48] This celebration (apparently a private, domestic affair rather than a public liturgical observance) may have been held on September 21, commemorating the publication of Luther's German New Testament in 1522. See Volz, *Die Lutherpredigten des Johannes Mathesius*, p. 207 and n. 1.

[49] I.e., the two principal Jewish Aramaic paraphrases of the Hebrew Bible—the Targum Onkelos and Targum Jonathan; probably not the Peshitta translation used by the Syriac Church, since Mathesius describes these as "esteemed by the ancient Jews." See *ODCC*, 3rd ed., s.vv. "Targum" and "Peshitta." The various historical dialects of Aramaic were referred to as "Chaldean" by early modern Western authors.

[50] The Targums often use the Aramaic *memra* ["Word"] to refer to God: see *ODCC*, 3rd ed., s.v. "Memra."

[51] The Septuagint (LXX) is a Greek translation of the Hebrew Bible, including also works originally composed in Greek (the Apocrypha and deuterocanonical books). The translation was begun in Alexandria in the third century BC under the Hellenistic ruler Ptolemy Philadelphus (r. 285–246 BC). According to the account transmitted in the later pseudepigraphic *Letter of Aristeas*, the LXX was produced by the cooperative work of seventy-two translators; still later versions of the legend recount that each translator produced his own translation of the whole Bible, but that all were miraculously found to be identical. See *ODCC*, 3rd ed., s.vv. "Septuagint" and "Aristeas, Letter of." For the Septuagint text, see Alfred Rahlfs and Robert Hanhart, eds., *Septuaginta*, 2nd ed. (Stuttgart: Deutsche Bibelgesellschaft, 2006).

[52] See *Table Talk* no. 4896 (1540), WA TR 4:572, where Luther criticizes the LXX translations of the titles in Isa. 9:6 (9:5 LXX). Cf. *Commentary on Isaiah 9* (1544/1546), WA 40/3:597–682 (LW 63), especially pp. 663–64, where Luther weighs the Hebrew, Aramaic, Latin, and Greek texts. For Luther's further criticism of the LXX, see *Table Talk* no. 3271a (1532), WA TR 3:243; no. 5001 (1540), WA TR 4:607–8.

We also thank God for the Latin Bible, which remained in the Roman Church, whether Jerome made it or someone else, even though it is rather obscure in many places and does not always do justice to the Hebrew text.[53] According to the church histories, Ulfilas, bishop in Hungary, is supposed to have been the first to translate the Greek Bible into German,[54] in the days when the ancient warriors, the Cimbri,[55] still lived alongside the Greeks.

In my youth, I also saw an un-German German Bible, no doubt translated from the Latin, that was obscure and difficult to understand.[56] For at that time the scholars did not place much value on the Bible.[57] My father had a German postil, in which the Sunday Gospel readings as well as some passages from the Old Testament were expounded.[58] I often read to him

---

[53] The Vulgate (Vg), which became the standard Latin translation of the Bible for the Western Church, originated in the efforts of Jerome (see above, p. 441 n. 104) to revise existing translations of the Old Testament by reference to the Hebrew text. The revision of other portions of the Bible may have been carried out by others. See *ODCC*, 3rd ed., s.v. "Vulgate." For the Vulgate text, see Robert Weber et al., eds., *Biblia Sacra Vulgata*, 5th ed. (Stuttgart: Deutsche Bibelgesellschaft, 2007). For Luther's appraisal of the Vulgate translation, see, e.g., *Table Talk* no. 961 (1530), WA TR 1:486–87; no. 1040 (1530), WA TR 1:525; *On Translating* (1530), LW 35:183–84 (with relatively positive assessments); also *Defense of the Translation of the Psalms* (1531), LW 35:221–22; *Lectures on Zephaniah* (1526/1552), LW 18:361–62; *Lectures on Deuteronomy* (1523–25/1524–25), LW 9:167 (with negative judgments).

[54] Ulfilas [Ulphilas] (ca. 310–383) was a missionary to the Goths in Moesia Inferior (part of Hungary in the sixteenth century) who had been consecrated by the Arian bishop Eusebius of Nicomedia (d. 341) in Constantinople. As part of his work among the Goths, Ulfilas translated the Bible (with the exception of some of the historical books, which he considered too bellicose for his audience) into the East German Gothic language. See *ODCC*, 3rd ed., s.v. "Ulphilas." His story is narrated in the *Historia Tripartita* 8.13 (PL 69:1118–19): see Socrates, *Ecclesiastical History* 4.33 (NPNF² 2:115); Sozomen (ca. 400–ca. 450), *Ecclesiastical History* 6.37 (NPNF² 2:373); Theodoret (ca. 393–ca. 460), *Ecclesiastical History* 4.33 (NPNF² 3:131). For the surviving text, see Wilhelm Streitberg, ed., *Die gotische Bibel*, vol. 1 (Heidelberg: Carl Winter, 1910; 7th ed., 2000); cf. PL 18:497–867.

[55] The Cimbri had in fact been nearly wiped out by the Romans near Vercellae in 101 BC (see *OCD*, 4th ed., s.v. "Cimbri"), but the account of the Roman victory over the Goths at Pollentia in 402 by the poet Claudian conflates the two geographically proximate but historically distant victories and Germanic tribes: *Gothic War* ll.635–47 (Loeb 136 [1922], pp. 172–73), which may account for Mathesius' confusion.

[56] The first printed German translation of the Bible, based on the Vulgate, was published in 1466 by Louis Mentelin in Strassburg and was followed by thirteen more High German editions and four in Low German before the appearance of Luther's German New Testament. See John L. Flood, "Martin Luther's Bible Translation in Its German and European Context," in *The Bible in the Renaissance*, ed. Richard Griffiths (Aldershot: Ashgate, 2001), pp. 46–48.

[57] Cf. above, Mathesius, *History*, pp. 111, 131–33, 352, 391–92, 400.

[58] On the postil genre, see above, Mathesius, *History*, p. 188 and n. 25 there. On pre-Reformation postils, see John M. Frymire, *The Primacy of the Postils: Catholics, Protestants, and the Dissemination of Ideas in Early Modern Germany*, Studies in Medieval and Reformation Traditions 147 (Leiden: Brill, 2010), pp. 12–14.

from that with joy. "How I yearn," my father said, "to see an entire Bible in German." Likewise, Dr. Martin, when he was in the library in Erfurt reading the stories about Hannah, Samuel's mother, desired with all his heart that God would one day grant him such a book.[59]

ⁱIn his book against Pfefferkorn, the baptized Jew who advised burning all the books of the Jews, Dr. Johann Reuchlin, who was the first to bring the Hebrew language to Germany, writes that there were once seventeen translations;[60] Galatinus likewise mentions several translations in the good book which he dedicated to Emperor Maximilian in 1515.[61]

Now, since it was God's will to cast down the Antichrist through the mouth of His Spirit [cf. 2 Thess. 2:8][62] and the Word of the prophets and apostles, and to reform His Church before His Son's bodily appearance for the last judgment, and to have His Gospel printed, written, and preached as a brightly shining testimony for all the world, He raised up Dr. Luther with his assistants, whom He adorned with great gifts of His Spirit and understanding of the languages. This important and blessed work began in Wittenberg, first with the New Testament,[63] which had been worked on in Latin some time before by Laurentius Valla and later by Erasmus of Rotterdam.[64] This

---

[59] See above, Mathesius, *History*, p. 120.

[60] On Pfefferkorn and Reuchlin, see above, Mathesius, *History*, pp. 132–33. Reuchlin published the first Christian textbook for the study of Hebrew, the *Rudimenta Hebraica*. In his *Augenspiegel* (Tübingen: Thomas Anshelm, 1511) [VD16 R1306], fol. 16v, he lists ten translations of the Bible made into Aramaic, Greek, and Latin, down to Jerome's revision of the Latin Bible.

[61] Petrus Galatinus (ca. 1460–1539/1540), a Franciscan friar who served as a papal penitentiary under Leo X, came to the defense of Reuchlin with his *Opus toti christianae Reipublicae maxime utile, de arcanis catholicae veritatis, contra obstinatissimam Iudaeorum nostrae tempestatis perfidiam ex Talmud, aliis hebraicis libris nuper excerptum; et quadruplici linguarum genere eleganter congestum* (Ortona: Girolamo Soncino, 1518); the commendatory epistle from Maximilian (fol. a2r), which is immediately followed by Galatinus' dedication, is indeed dated 1515. Galatinus discusses ancient translations of the Hebrew Bible on fols. 13v–14v and fol. 3v. On Galatinus, see Bietenholz and Deutscher, *Contemporaries of Erasmus*, 2:72.

[62] On Mathesius' inversion of the phrase, see above, p. 147 n. 44.

[63] Luther's German translation of the Greek New Testament was in fact undertaken while he was in seclusion in the Wartburg in late 1521 and early 1522 and was published in Wittenberg in September 1522: *Das Newe Testament Deutsch* (Wittenberg: Melchior Lotter Jr., 1522) [VD16 B4318]. See Brecht 2:46–56; WA DB 6–7.

[64] On Erasmus, see above, p. xix n. 16. His 1516 *Novum Instrumentum* (Basel: Johann Froben, 1516) was the first printed edition of the Greek New Testament, accompanied by his own new Latin translation: see ASD 6/1–4. In the previous century, the Italian humanist Lorenzo Valla (1405–57), most famous for his critique of the *Donation of Constantine*, had also criticized the Vulgate translation of the New Testament in his *Collatio Novi Testamenti*, which was first printed in Erasmus' edition of 1505: *In Latinam Novi testamenti interpretationem ex*

book was very welcome among pious Germans, and many hundred thousand copies of it are supposed to have been printed in the German language, even though this greatly pained the devil and his helpers.[65]

Afterward, when many other scholars began expounding Moses and the prophets in universities and preaching them from the pulpit, people also gained the Old Testament. In 1529, the prophet Isaiah was first published in Wittenberg,[66] although before this all of the prophets had been [published] in Worms, with the involvement of Jews, as the doctor mentions in his book on translation.[67] When Dr. Luther was in his Patmos in the Coburg, he worked on the prophet Ezekiel, as can be seen in his letters.[68]

Now, when the entire German Bible had been published for the first time, since *dies diem docet* ["one day teaches another"] [cf. Ps. 19:2 (18:3 Vg)]—along with tribulation [cf. Isa. 28:19 DB][69]—the doctor took up the Bible again from the beginning |with great zeal, diligence, and prayer, and thoroughly revised it.[70] And because the Son of God had promised

---

collatione Grecorum exemplarium Adnotationes apprime utiles (Paris: Josse Bade/Jean Petit, 1505). See Valla, *Collatio Novi Testamenti*, ed. Alessandro Perosa (Florence: Sansoni, 1970).

[65] On the early printing of Luther's German New Testament, see Mark U. Edwards Jr., *Printing, Propaganda, and Martin Luther* (Berkeley, CA: University of California Press, 1994; repr., Minneapolis: Fortress, 2004), pp. 123–26.

[66] Luther's German translation of Isaiah first appeared in 1528: *Der Prophet Jesaia Deutsch* (Wittenberg, 1528) [VD16 B3773]; see WA DB 2:439, no. 30. Luther's translation of the Pentateuch had appeared already in 1523, the historical books and the writings in 1524, and the minor prophets beginning in 1526: see WA DB 2:201ff.

[67] A German translation from the Hebrew of the prophetic books of the Old Testament appeared in Worms in 1527, the so-called "Worms Prophets": *Alle Propheten nach hebraischer sprach verteütschet* (Worms: Peter Schöffer, 1527) [VD16 B3720]. It was the work of the anti-trinitarian Anabaptists Hans Denck and Ludwig Hätzer (see above, p. 246 nn. 85 and 87; Bender, *Mennonite Encyclopedia*, 4:983–84). Luther's judgment may reflect Hätzer and Denck's collaboration with Jewish teachers in Worms or may be an extrapolation from the antitrinitarian theology reflected in the translation. See *On Translating* (1530), LW 35:194–95.

[68] See above, Mathesius, *History*, p. 350; Luther to Melanchthon, August 15, 1530, WA Br 5:547–48.

[69] See Wander 4:995, "Tag" no. 103; Pubilius Syrus (fl. ca. 45 BC), *Sententiae* 146 (Loeb 284 [1934], pp. 34–35). On "tribulation" [*Anfechtung*], cf. Luther's translation of Isa. 28:19 ("Only tribulation teaches [us] to pay heed to the Word") and above, p. 9 n. 11.

[70] The complete German Bible had appeared in 1534 (see above, p. 470 and n. 42 there); intensive committee work on a thorough new revision of the Old Testament began in 1539 and culminated in the edition of 1541/1542 (see below, p. 478 and n. 93 there). See Brecht 3:105–7. Although Mathesius does not mention it, Luther had already used a similar approach for revisions to the Psalter in 1531 and in preparation for the 1534 revision itself; further revisions on the New Testament translation would take place in 1544: see Brecht 3:103–7. On the 1539–41 revisions, see Stefan Michel, "'Luthers Sanhedrin': Helfer und Mitarbeiter an der Lutherbibel," in Margot Käßmann and Martin Rösel, eds., *Die Bibel Martin Luthers: Ein Buch und seine Geschichte* (Leipzig: Evangelische Verlagsanstalt, 2016), pp. 117–35.

to be in the midst of those who gathered in His name and asked for His Spirit [cf. Matt. 18:20; Luke 11:13], Dr. Luther right away appointed his own Sanhedrin,[71] consisting of the best people there at the time, who gathered for several hours every week before supper in the doctor's monastery,[72] namely: Dr. Johann Bugenhagen, Dr. Justus Jonas, Dr. Cruciger, Master Philip, Matthew Aurogallus.[73] Master Georg Rörer, the corrector, also attended;[74] doctors and scholars from elsewhere often came to this important work, such as Dr. Bernhard Ziegler[75] and Dr. Forster.[76]

---

[71] The Sanhedrin was the Jewish council at Jerusalem at the time of the New Testament (see, e.g., Matt. 26:59; Acts 5:21). See *ODCC*, 3rd ed., s.v. "Sanhedrin."

[72] I.e., the former Augustinian cloister which Elector John had given to Luther and his heirs in perpetuity in 1532, formalizing an earlier arrangement under Frederick or John from 1524 or 1525 (for which documentation no longer survives) in which Luther had been given use of the property: see Elector John to Luther, February 4, 1532, WA Br 6:257–58; cf. Luther to Elector Frederick, November 1523?, LW 49:57–59. See Ernst Schwiebert, *Luther and His Times* (St. Louis: Concordia, 1950), pp. 226–27.

[73] On Bugenhagen, see the introduction above, pp. xxxvi–xxxvii; on Jonas, see the introduction above, p. xxx (he would have been present in Wittenberg until his departure for Halle in April 1541); on Cruciger, see above, p. xx n. 19 and p. 188 n. 26; on Melanchthon, see the introduction above, pp. xxxix–xl; on Matthaeus Aurogallus [Goldhahn], see above, p. 297 n. 71.

[74] On Rörer, see above, p. xx n. 20. He was responsible for taking notes on the deliberations and marking the final corrections to the translation: see below, Mathesius, *History*, p. 477.

[75] Bernhard Ziegler (1496–1552) had studied Hebrew under the Jewish convert Anton Margaritha (ca. 1500–after 1537; see below, p. 509 n. 32) in the Cistercian cloister at Altenzeller. Ziegler became a supporter of the Reformation by the mid-1520s. At the recommendation of Luther and Melanchthon, he moved to Leipzig to become professor of Hebrew in 1540, though he traveled periodically to Wittenberg, as for the doctoral disputation of Heinrich Schmedenstede (d. 1554) on July 7, 1542 (see the introduction by Lewis W. Spitz, LW 34:301). He was one of Mathesius' circle of friends (Loesche, *Johannes Mathesius*, 1:134). On Ziegler, see Stephen G. Burnett, "Reassessing the 'Basel-Wittenberg Conflict,'" in *Hebraica Veritas? Christian Hebraists and the Study of Judaism in Early Modern Europe*, ed. Allison Coudert and Jeffrey S. Shoulson (Philadelphia: University of Pennsylvania Press, 2004), pp. 181–201, here pp. 183, 196–97; Irene Dingel, ed., *Controversia et Confessio Digital*, s.v. Ziegler, Bernard, http://www.controversia-et-confessio.de/ On Ziegler's connection with Margaritha, see Michael T. Walton, *Anthonius Margaritha and the Jewish Faith* (Detroit: Wayne State University Press, 2012), p. 70. For Luther's praise of Ziegler and appeal to his judgment, see Luther to Georg Vogler, July 18, 1529, WA Br 5:118–19; *Lectures on Genesis* (1535–45/1544–54), LW 8:241; *On the Last Words of David* (1543), LW 15:286; *On the Shem Hamphoras and on the Lineage of Christ* (1543), WA 53:647 (LW 61), note on Isa. 25:8, WA 48:99 and 48N:69; *Table Talk* no. 5001 (1540), WA TR 4:607–8; no. 5533 (1542), LW 54:446; no. 7176 (n.d.), WA 48:702; cf. also below, p. 479.

[76] Johann Forster [Forstemius] (1496–1558) was a Christian Hebraist who had studied under Johann Reuchlin at Ingolstadt and then came to Wittenberg to study (and boarded at Luther's table) from 1530 to 1535. He served as preacher in Augsburg from 1535 to 1538, and then as professor of Hebrew at Tübingen from 1539 to 1541, being finally dismissed from each of these positions because of his firm anti-Zwinglian teaching. He seems to have been present

Now when the doctor had made a preliminary examination of the Bible as it had been published, and had sought information from Jews and linguists from elsewhere,[77] and had asked old Germans about good words (as, for example, when he had some sheep slaughtered so that a German butcher could teach him what all the parts of a sheep are called),[78] the doctor entered the consistory[79] with his old Latin and new German Bible; he also always had the Hebrew text along.[80] Master Philip brought the Greek text

---

in Wittenberg in 1541 and 1542 (see LW 5:x; Volz, *Die Lutherpredigten des Johannes Mathesius*, pp. 193–95) before being appointed to a new position as dean of St. Lorenz in Nürnberg, where the town council allowed him leave to organize the Reformation in Regensburg and in the county of Henneberg. Eventually he would return to Wittenberg as professor of Hebrew in 1549. His life's work as a Hebraist was the *Dictionarium Hebraicum Novum* (Basel: Froben, 1557) [VD16 F1901] (see below, p. 480). On Forster, see Friedrich Wilhelm Bautz, "Forster, Johann," *BBKL* 2:72; Burnett, "Reassessing the 'Basel-Wittenberg Conflict,'" pp. 183, 186, 196. For Luther's praise of Forstemius and appeal to his judgment, see *Table Talk* no. 961 (1530), WA TR 1:467 and WA 48:448; no. 1040 (1530), WA TR 1:525; no. 2844b (1533), WA TR 3:23; no. 3271b (1532), WA TR 3:243–44; no. 3391b (1533), WA TR 3:302; no. 3697 (1538), WA TR 4:39–42; no. 5001 (1540), WA TR 4:607–8; no. 5002 (1540), LW 54:375–76; no. 5533 (1542–43), LW 54:446; Luther to Georg Rörer, June 30, 1540, WA Br 9:166–67.

[77] In 1536, Luther had spoken about the translation of the Hebrew Bible with three rabbis who had come to Wittenberg: see *Table Talk* no. 5026 (1540), WA TR 4:619–20; no. 3512 (1536), WA TR 3:369–70; cf. Brecht 3:336–37. On the restriction of Jewish residence and travel in Saxony in this period, see Stefan Litt, *Juden in Thüringen in der Frühen Neuzeit (1520–1650)* (Cologne: Böhlau, 2003), pp. 150–51, 156–58.

[78] Mathesius appears to be the source for this anecdote. Cf. Luther to Spalatin, March 30, 1522, LW 49:4, where Luther asks Spalatin for assistance identifying proper German words for the Bible translation, but the specific reference is to the precious gems of Rev. 21:19.

[79] The term *consistorium* could be used for a number of formal imperial or episcopal assemblies, including the formal meeting of the pope with the cardinals, which may be in view here, in a facetious hyperbole like the description above of the gathered biblical scholars as a "Sanhedrin." See *ODCC*, 3rd ed., s.v. "consistory."

[80] I.e., the Vulgate (see above, p. 472 n. 53) and the latest printed edition of the German Bible (see above, p. 474 n. 70). Luther made annotations in a 1538–39 edition of the Old Testament and a 1540 edition of the New Testament: see the introduction by Karl Drescher, WA DB 3:vii. On the printed copies of the Vulgate known to have been used by Luther, see WA DB 5:xvii–xviii. Luther's primary copy of the Hebrew Bible was the quarto 1494 edition published in Brescia by Gerschom Soncino [USTC 760506]: see WA 60:240–307; and Stephen G. Burnett, "Luthers hebräische Bibel (Brescia, 1494)—ihre Bedeutung für die Reformation," trans. Henning Jürgens, in *Meilensteine der Reformation: Schlüsseldokumente der frühen Wirksamkeit Martin Luthers*, ed. Irene Dingel and Henning P. Jürgens (Gütersloh: Gütersloher, 2014), pp. 62–69. Luther may also have possessed a copy of Daniel Bomberg's *Biblia Rabbinica*, used by Cruciger (see below, p. 477 n. 82); Bomberg (d. 1549) met several of the Wittenberg theologians in Augsburg in 1530 while Luther was in the Coburg (see above, Mathesius, *History*, p. 324), and Jonas' letter describing the visit mentions Luther's familiarity with his published Bibles: see Jonas to Luther, June 12, 1530, WA Br 5:358; WA DB 9/1:xiii; cf. Burnett, "Reassessing the 'Basel-Wittenberg Conflict,'" pp. 187, 188.

with him.[81] Dr. Cruciger brought the Chaldean Bible alongside the Hebrew.[82] The professors had their rabbis with them.[83] Dr. Pommer[84] also had a Latin text before him, in which he was very well-versed.[85] Everyone had prepared ahead of time for the text over which they were to deliberate and had read through Greek and Latin as well as Jewish expositors. Then [Luther] as presider proposed a translation, let the others vote in turn, and listened to what each had to say about it based on the nature of the language or the exposition from the old doctors.

Marvelously fine and instructive discussions must have taken place during this work, some of which Master Georg [Rörer] recorded[86] |and were later printed in the margins of the text as short glosses and explanations.[87]

---

[81] I.e., the Septuagint (see above, p. 471 n. 51). Melanchthon provided the preface for the 1545 edition of the Septuagint published by Johann Herwagen (1497–1557/1558) in Basel [VD16 B2576]: see MBW T13:516–20, no. 3741; CR 5:535–40.

[82] Cruciger probably had on hand the *Biblia Rabbinica* published in Venice by Daniel Bomberg in 1523–24, which included the Aramaic ("Chaldean") Targums (see above, p. 471 n. 49) alongside the Hebrew biblical text, in addition to other forms of rabbinic commentary. See Stephen G. Burnett, "The Strange Career of the *Biblia Rabbinica* among Christian Hebraists, 1517–1620," in *Shaping the Bible in the Reformation*, ed. Bruce Gordon and Matthew McLean (Leiden: Brill, 2012), pp. 68–83; Burnett, "Reassessing the 'Basel-Wittenberg Conflict,'" p. 187; and Stephen G. Burnett, "Christian Aramaism: The Birth and Growth of Aramaic Scholarship in the Sixteenth Century," in *Seeking out the Wisdom of the Ancients*, ed. Ronald L. Troxel et al. (Winona Lake, IN: Eisenbrauns, 2005), pp. 421–36, especially p. 433.

[83] I.e., rabbinic interpretations of the biblical text, not Jewish rabbis in person. Compendia of such rabbinic material were published by Sebastian Münster (1488–1552) in his *Hebraica Biblia*, 2 vols. (Basel: Froben, 1535) [VD16 B2881], as well as in the *Biblia Rabbinica* (see the previous note), of which at least Melanchthon owned a personal copy as well (Burnett, "Reassessing the 'Basel-Wittenberg Conflict,'" p. 187). See Volz, *Die Lutherpredigten des Johannes Mathesius*, pp. 196–97 n. 6.

[84] I.e., Bugenhagen.

[85] This may be a reference to the Vulgate, perhaps in the 1529 Wittenberg revision (see WA DB 5). Bugenhagen had conducted an intensive and detailed critique of the Vulgate translation in his *In Librum Psalmorum Interpretatio* (Basel: Adam Petri, 1524) [VD16 B3137]. Other possibilities would include Sebastian Münster's 1535 Latin translation of the Hebrew text in his *Hebraica Biblia* or the 1527 Latin translation by Santes Pagnino (see below, p. 481 n. 107), both cited in the revision protocols (see WA DB 9/1:xxvii) and discussed critically by Luther in an epistolary fragment associated with Bugenhagen: Luther to Bugenhagen[?], July 1537[?], WA Br 8:176.

[86] Rörer's surviving minutes of the Wittenberg discussions of the Bible translation in 1539–41 are edited in WA DB 3:167–577; 4:1–278.

[87] The discussions over the revisions often provided the basis for marginal annotations in the German Bible: see the entries marked "[Gl.]" in WA DB 3–4. Cf. below, p. 479.

The doctor gave three rules, which should be carefully observed.[88] Since the Bible is a book from God, which He caused to be written down through the inspiration of His Spirit by prophets and apostles who had visibly seen and heard the Son of God Himself before and after His incarnation, no one, therefore, should undertake this work without fervent prayer.[89] For God's Word must be clarified by God's Spirit, as he also writes in his letter on translation: "This work requires a truly devout, faithful, diligent, reverent, Christian, learned, tried, and experienced heart,"[90] as well as good and apt[91] words, if you want to render the Bible correctly and understandably.

"Now, the Bible speaks primarily about God's being and will, and above all about the eternal Son of God, His incarnation and sacrifice, about His Church, about secular government, and about domestic life. If a text is not speaking about Christ and His Church, then it must be about secular authorities or the holy estate of marriage and domestic affairs. Those are the three holy hierarchies and estates of which the Bible speaks.[92] If the Jews and others dream up a new interpretation that speaks about neither God's Church nor about government nor about domestic affairs, then it should simply be thrown away and rejected. Then one must diligently take note of the characteristic of the Jewish words and the style and manner of speech of this language. For the holy language has its own style and figures of speech, which not all languages are able to express adequately."

Following this admonition, everyone indicated what he was able to show [about the text] based on the grammar, or on the basis of sound inference and coherence with what came before or after, or the testimony of scholars, until finally in the ǀyear 1542 this work was completed, by the grace of God.[93] Nevertheless, when the doctor was later engaged in writing against the Jews,[94] his understanding kept growing from day to day, and many fine passages

---

[88] The "three rules" are listed in *Table Talk* no. 5533 (1542–43), LW 54:446, though the version there differs somewhat from Mathesius' enumeration: first, that the Bible speaks about the three hierarchies; second, that in case of ambiguity the interpretation should be chosen that is in harmony with the New Testament; third, that when an interpretation of a particular passage conflicts with the whole of Scripture, it is to be rejected.

[89] Cf. *Preface to the German Writings* (1539), LW 34:285–86.

[90] *On Translating* (1530), LW 35:194.

[91] *Kirnige*

[92] On the "three estates" or "three hierarchies" established by God, see Luther, *Confession concerning Christ's Supper* (1528), LW 37:364; *On the Councils and the Church* (1539), LW 41:176–78.

[93] A new edition of the German Bible incorporating the committee's revisions was printed in 1541 but did not become available until 1542 because of delays in binding: WA DB 2:564, no. 69; see Brecht 3:107.

[94] See below, Mathesius, *History*, pp. 507–9, 514.

were rendered more plainly and clearly; after the doctor's death, these were inserted into the last [edition of the] Bible by Master Georg Rörer with the approval and consideration of the scholars in Wittenberg.[95] For example, the confession of Eve in Genesis 4 [:1] concerning her son Cain, whom she regarded as the promised Messiah: "I have received the Man, the Lord or God."[96] Again, in *The Last Words of David* the doctor later expressed this text [2 Sam. 7:19]: "*Ist das menschen recht*" ["Is that the law of man?"] this way: "*Das ist die weyse eines menschen, der Gott der Herr ist*" ["That is the way of a Man who is God the Lord"].[97] Herr Philip, too, later gave very fine renderings of some texts, such as Job chapter 19: "For I believe that my Redeemer lives, and in the last [days of the] world He will arise" [Job 19:25], whereas the old Bible speaks of our resurrection.[98] Dr. Ziegler also offered quite lovely explanations of some texts from the Hebrew, especially Isaiah 53 [:9]: "The Messiah has died poor in order to make us rich, and He has buried or sealed our godlessness in His grave."[99]

Again, in Habakkuk 2 [:2–4]: "Write down the prophecy on a tablet, so that those who are in course of their office—or, who preach—will have a certain form for how to speak properly about the certain coming of the promised Seed of the woman. For whoever believes will be righteous,

---

[95] I.e., the Wittenberg German Bible of 1546, printed after Luther's death but incorporating the last round of revisions which he had discussed with his Wittenberg colleagues. Unfortunately, though the Weimar edition uses the 1546 text in its edition of the New Testament translation (WA DB 6–7), it reverts to the 1545 text (the last completed in print while Luther was alive) in its edition of the Old Testament (WA DB 8–12). See the discussion by Otto Albrecht, WA DB 6:l–lxiii, and by Hans Volz, WA DB 8:xxxvii–xxxviii.

[96] See *On the Last Words of David* (1543), LW 15:319–23. The translation "I have the Man, the Lord" was included in the margin of the 1545 Wittenberg printing of the German Bible as well as in Rörer's afterword to that edition; it was taken into the text of the 1546 edition: see WA DB 8:46–47. Previous editions had translated the verse "I have obtained" [later: "have"] "the man of the Lord."

[97] *On the Last Words of David* (1543), LW 15:291, 298–99. Rörer mentions this new translation in his afterword to the 1543 Wittenberg Bible; it was incorporated into the text in the 1545 printing: see the introduction by Hans Volz, WA DB 8:lxxix; WA DB 9/1:320–21.

[98] This discussion does not appear in the protocols on Job 19 (WA DB 3:488), and Melanchthon's proposal does not seem to have been incorporated into the text of German Bibles during the sixteenth century. The Vulgate translation of Job 19:25b had read "and at the last I shall rise from the earth"; the DB reads: "and hereafter, He will awaken me from the earth." See WA DB 10/1:44–45; Stefan Michel, *Die Kanonisierung der Werke Martin Luthers im 16. Jahrhundert* (Tübingen: Mohr Siebeck, 2016), p. 78.

[99] This suggestion does not appear in the protocols on Isaiah 53 (WA DB 4:75), or in the text or marginal notes of Luther's Bible (WA DB 11/1:156–57), or in Luther's 1544 *Exposition of Isaiah 53*, WA 30/3:727–30 (LW 63).

pleasing, and saved, but whoever is stiff-necked and does not believe will be damned."[100]

Dr. Forster provided many texts with salutary and comforting explanations in his lexicon.[101] For example, he gave us a thoroughly Christian interpretation of Jacob's last words concerning Dan as referring to the promised Seed of the woman [Gen. 3:15]: "O Lord, I wait for Your salvation" [Gen. 49:18], [as if to say,] "Samson [Judg. 13:24–16:30] and Gideon [Judg. 6:11–8:32] will be unable to deliver me and my household from sin and death. You alone are the one true Helper, who will take away sin and death forever and restore righteousness and life to all who hope in You." The passage in Genesis 8 [:21] in which ˡGod speaks from heaven also became clearer later: where God promises that He will never again curse the world for the sake of the Man, that is, Jesus Christ; rather, He will bless all nations in Isaac's Seed, which is Christ, as St. Paul testifies [Rom. 9:7].[102]

During his lifetime, Doctor Luther was always glad to hear it[103] when someone could show him our Lord Christ in a passage,[104] even if it contradicted the glosses and interpretations of all the rabbis. He also admonished his people rather frequently to tear the corrupted texts of the wicked rabbis out of their hands.[105] God's book is so full of divine mysteries that we will never learn everything there is to know about it in this world. Instead, we should seek, think, search, examine, and ask, as Christ says in John 5 [:39], and the Bible is supposed to be called "Torah" because of the pondering and examining [cf. Ps. 1:2]. But we shall remain students as long as we live in this tarnished flesh and natural light, even though we have the firstfruits of the Spirit [Rom. 8:23]. May God preserve all theologians, so that they do not become masters in or over Scripture. "An elephant drowns in this sea," said

---

[100] No source for this interpretation beyond Mathesius' report could be identified.

[101] See Johannes Forster [Forstemius], *Dictionarium hebraicum novum* (Basel: Froben, 1557) [VD16 F1901], p. 359, s.v. יְשׁוּעָה.

[102] This interpretation of Gen. 8:21 does not appear in Forster's *Dictionarium* or in the materials surrounding the DB, where "for the sake of human beings" [*umb der Menschen willen*] is rendered in the plural.

[103] Literally: "could always tolerate it well."

[104] Cf. *Seven Penitential Psalms* (1517, 1525), LW 14:204 (cf. WA 1:119); sermon of August 5, 1545, LW 58:246–58; and *Table Talk* no. 5533 (1542–43), LW 54:446.

[105] See, e.g., *On the Last Words of David* (1543), LW 15:267–70, 343–44; *On the Jews and Their Lies* (1543), LW 47:228; *On the Shem Hamphorash and on the Lineage of Christ* (1543), WA 53:588.25ff., 644.30ff. (LW 61); *Table Talk* no. 5324 (1540), LW 54:408; *Table Talk* no. 5533 (1542–43), LW 54:445–46. Cf. Burnett, "Reassessing the 'Basel-Wittenberg Conflict.'" pp. 189–93.

Luther, based on St. Gregory. "A little lamb that seeks Christ and perseveres in doing so has a solid footing and passes through."[106]

It is well said, as Santes Pagnino[107] writes: "The diligence that Jerome and other great people applied to the Bible does not excuse our laziness and indolence. Instead, we should keep on studying as if we were to live forever, and live as if we were to die tomorrow." Once I was talking in Leipzig with Dr. Ziegler, the excellent Hebraist, and insisted on the doctor's version. He set before me the Hebrew text.[108] If we could rely on a translation alone, we would never need to study any more, not even the Hebrew Bible. Scripture, if read attentively, yields something new every day, as Dr. Bugenhagen says.[109]

I mention this here in the account of this work of translation in order to speak a word on behalf of all those who read, study, and examine Scripture today in humble Christian simplicity. I surely do not intend ever to make myself the patron of those who criticize and reject everything and yet do not create anything better, but only keep making things worse,[110] the kind of people to whom our doctor gave a very thorough answer in his letter on translation,[111] which Dr. Wenceslaus Linck published.[112] Many want to judge, but few can compose.[113] The doctor had many critics and correctors during his lifetime. Afterward, too, there was a young doctor who whipped his German Bible with a switch in the pulpit while saying that it should learn its lesson better.

---

[106] Gregory the Great, *Moralia in Job*, letter to Leander 4 (PL 75:515; FC 18:9). See Luther, *Labors on the Psalms* (1518–21/1519–21), WA 5:598 (LW 65); preface to *Lectures on Genesis* (1543), WA 42:2 (LW 62); *Table Talk* no. 5468 (1542), WA TR 5:168–69; sermon of April 6, 1534, WA 37:366; *Church Postil* (1540–44), sermon for Easter 3 on John 16:16–23, LW 77:205, paragraph 4. Cf. below, Mathesius, *History*, p. 561.

[107] Santes [Sancte, Xantes] Pagnino [Pagninus] (1470–1541) was an Italian Dominican who prepared a literal Latin translation of the Old Testament from the Hebrew under the patronage of Pope Leo X, published in 1528. See Bernard Roussel, "Pagnini, Sante," *OER* 3:194–95; Christoph Schmitt, "Pagninus, Santes," *BBKL* 6:1433–34. For the sentiment, see Pagnino, *Hebraicarum Institutionum libri IIII* (Paris: Robert Estienne, 1549) [USTC 150280], fol. a4r. For Luther's evaluation of Pagnino, see *Table Talk* no. 5535 (1542), WA TR 5:220; *Lectures on Genesis* (1535–45/1544–54), LW 1:297.

[108] Cf. Loesche, *Johannes Mathesius*, 1:134.

[109] Apparently Mathesius' recollection.

[110] See Thiele no. 478, p. 409.

[111] *On Translating* (1530), LW 35:175–202. See above, p. 478.

[112] On Linck, see above, Mathesius, *History*, p. 148 n. 48.

[113] *Vil wöllen richten/ aber wenig können dichten*; see Wander 1:582, "Dichten" no. 4. On criticisms of Luther's translation, see *Table Talk* no. 5469 (1542), WA TR 5:169–70; no. 5047 (1540), LW 54:382–84; Brecht 3:107–10.

Also in our day and age many such people have tried to translate the Old and New Testaments, some just the Psalter, into Latin[114] and German.[115] Likewise, the Jews also published a German translation of the five books of Moses, a literal rendering of the Hebrew,[116] in their Yiddish dialect.[117] Although such labors are not to be utterly condemned, and it is beneficial for diligent readers to compare these versions, what usually happens is what our doctor wrote in his preface to the old Latin Psalter.[118] He had hoped that the young Hebraists would produce something extraordinary and precious, but it turned out for him as it did for King Solomon, who had hoped for something wonderful from India and was brought apes and peacocks [1 Kings 10:22]. The majority make monkeys of themselves[119] and imitate either the rabbis or previous versions,[120] or they dress their work with peacock feathers, sprinkle in some Hebrew, embellish their work with Cicero's words and expressions, and lace it with Greek words.

---

[114] E.g., the Latin translations of Münster and Pagnino (see above, p. 477 n. 83 and p. 481 n. 107), as well as Erasmus' Latin translation of the New Testament, which was accompanied by his edition of the Greek text (see above, pp. 473–74 n. 64). Translations of the Psalter alone were made by Martin Bucer and Ulrich Zwingli, among others: see Bucer, S[acrorum] Psalmorum Libri Quinque ad Ebraicam Veritatem Versi (Strasbourg: Georg Ulricher, 1529) [VD16 B3145]; Zwingli, Enchiridion Psalmorum (Zurich: Christoph Froschauer, 1532) [VD16 B3151].

[115] E.g., the German translation by Jerome Emser, tacitly based on Luther's own (see above, Mathesius, History, p. 244) and the translations of the prophetic books by the Anabaptists Ludwig Hätzer and Hans Denck in Worms (see above, p. 474 n. 67) and in Zurich by Leo Jud (1482–1542). See R. Gerald Hobbs, "Bible: Translations of," OER 1:165–66. For Luther's complaint about the profusion of new translations, see Table Talk no. 5469 (1542), WA TR 5:169.

[116] schlecht wie die wort im Hebreischen stehn

[117] Current Deutsch. Yiddish translations of the Bible or portions thereof were published in 1544 in Augsburg by the Jewish convert Paulus Aemilius Romanus [Paolo Emili] (ca. 1510–75) [VD16 B2985] and in Constance by the Christian Hebraist Paul Fagius (1504–49) [VD16 ZV17559]. See Morris M. Faierstein, "Paulus Aemilius, Convert to Catholicism and Printer of Yiddish Books in Sixteenth-Century Augsburg," Judaica 71, no. 4 (2015): 349–65; Faierstein, "Paulus Fagius and the First Published Yiddish Translation of the Humash—Constance, 1544," Judaica 73, no. 1 (2017): 1–35. These two editions were therefore made by Christians, but a reprinting of Aemilius' text was made by Rabbi Jehuda Ben-Moses Naphtali in Cremona in 1560: see Edward Fram, "Some Preliminary Observations on the First Published Translation of Rashi's Commentary on the Pentateuch in Yiddish (Cremona, 1560)," Hebrew Union College Annual 86 (2015): 305–42.

[118] Luther, preface to the second edition of the corrected Wittenberg Latin Psalter (1537), WA DB 10/2:185–86 (LW 66).

[119] brauche Affenberg. Cf. Wander 1:39 and 5:723, "Affenberg" nos. 1–2; Thiele no. 131, p. 425.

[120] Cf. Luther's critiques of the Worms translation of the prophets in On Translating (1530), LW 35:194; and of Santes Pagnino and Sebastian Münster in Table Talk no. 5535 (1542), WA TR 5:220; Luther to Bugenhagen[?], July 1537[?], WA Br 8:176.

Dear friends, in honor of your German Bible, read ˈthe doctor's fine letter about his translation,[121] and you will discern the care, labor, and deliberation he put into it. "I have sat over a line or word for fourteen whole days with Master Philip and Aurogallus,"[122] he said, "before it came out speaking German."[123] As your pastor I exhort you, my parishioners and laity, both old and young, to recognize this treasure; thank God and His chosen instrument for the German Bible, and let it be your dearest, best, and most salutary book, the one which shows us the true way to eternal life. May you also listen with fervent prayer and true zeal to the interpreters whom God has sent you through a proper appointment and vocation.[124] Quality is the best bargain.[125]

It is useful for young people in schools to learn the languages and to read the Bible in Latin and Greek from their youth on. Regarding this, our dear Herr Philip advised taking one Bible (he recommended the old Latin Bible) and accustoming one's self to it from youth and learning it backward and forward.[126] The Bible produces and makes a theologian, especially if he knows the languages and searches for Christ in it with humility and fervent prayer. Eventually, if one wants to become a preacher, he should learn Hebrew, hold fast to this book as foundation, and inspect good people's translation or interpretation of the words of Scripture, noting which hits closer to the target, that is, to the grammatical sense. Finally, he should also endeavor to express this in good Latin in schools and in good German in churches.

It is, indeed, a great challenge for a German pastor to speak good German with the common man, even once he possesses a good acquaintance with the languages. Therefore, it is not bad advice that, as soon as someone has decided to dedicate himself to ministry in the Church, ˈhe should let the German Bible be his book of hours and daily reading.[127] If anyone is supposed to dispute in colloquies and councils and to offer a powerful refutation and persuasive appeal to the opponents—as in the case of a bishop, superintendent, doctor, or professor—he must be skilled both in rhetoric and in the languages. A German pastor should learn to speak of

---

[121] *On Translating* (1530), LW 35:175–202.

[122] Melanchthon and Matthaeus Aurogallus [Goldhahn] (see above, p. 475).

[123] *On Translating* (1530), LW 35:188.

[124] *richtige wahl und beruff*

[125] See Thiele no. 453, p. 396; Wander 2:1216, "Kauf" no. 2.

[126] *Localis und Literalis drinn werden*; i.e., acquainted with the topics [*loci*] of theological content as well as the letters [*litterae*] of the text.

[127] *sein Zornal und teglich handbuch*; i.e., the Bible should replace the traditional medieval prayer books (books of hours) modeled on monastic practice.

God and our religion in German churches using good German. A military chaplain studied in Wolff[128] near Vienna to put together a Greek sermon because he intended to preach among the Greeks in Constantinople, but plans fall far short, like new fabric that has shrunk.[129]

Once Doctor Johann Bugenhagen was listening to a preacher in Saxony who was reading the Gospel in German from a Greek Testament. "My [dear] doctor," he said, "give it a try and read the Gospel from the doctor's German [New] Testament. Surely that will turn out better."[130]

I knew a teacher who intended to become a preacher some day; he read his German Bible very diligently every morning. Another renowned teacher came to him and saw lying on his table this German book, in which he had made many notes and related as many passages and stories as he could to the catechism. "What?" he said. "You are reading German when you are supposed to be teaching languages?" The other replied, "I am a teacher now, but I intend to preach to German people one day. Therefore, I am equipping myself with words with which I will be able to express the Latin and Greek languages for the common man in a way that he can understand." When the [other] learned man also had to become a pastor in his old age and preached his first sermon, his parishioners all ran out of the church as if it were on fire.

I say this to exhort all who intend to devote themselves to the preaching office among Germans that they treasure the German Bible and constantly use its words, and not speak any line or stanza[131] that fails to incorporate at least one good biblical word. As that old preacher said, "German is what should be preached from the pulpit among Germans. Latin may be sung depending on the circumstances and what is best for the church."[132] Whoever is able to read Hebrew at universities and among his colleagues must be able to read and speak other languages as well. Our doctor, when he was in Smalcald, was more than a little annoyed by certain preachers who started off with Hebrew words and prattled on with *Adonai*, *Kyrie*, and *Domine*. "They do not make good preachers for the laity or peasants. They sprinkle in too much Latin, Greek, and Hebrew," he said at table. "Let us pray an Our Father in the name of Christ and commend everything to God. May

---

[128] Perhaps Wolfsthal, on the Danube, some 50 km east of Vienna, which was devastated in the Turkish invasion of 1529 (see above, Mathesius, *History*, pp. 256, 288). Loesche (*LH²*, p. 571) suggests Wolfersdorf by Neulengbach, some 45 km west of Vienna.

[129] For the expression, see above, p. 468.

[130] See *Table Talk* no. 5143 (1540), WA TR 4:682–83, where the preacher is identified as Urbanus Rhegius. On Rhegius, see above, p. 357 n. 203.

[131] *stöllichen oder gesetzlein*; terms describing the structure of the verse of the *Meistersinger*.

[132] Cf. *Table Talk* no. 6404 (n.d.), WA TR 5:644, where Mathesius himself is criticized for excessively ornate preaching; and no. 5143 (1540), WA TR 4:682–83.

He preserve our posterity in such simplicity! Amen."[133] Let that be enough for the present concerning the translation of the Bible into German.

Now when the [day's] work was done, our doctor sometimes kept his friends and assistants over for supper; that was an occasion for some very good talks. I heard that he disputed and asked questions at table about Ahab's breastplate in 1 Kings [22:34] because the German translation in the previous [edition of the] Bible had read: "Ahab was shot between the stomach and lungs."[134] Now it is rendered "between the armor and breastplate,"[135] where the sword hangs from the shoulder, as the gloss in the margin says.[136] Again, he circulated the question of how the word *Chail*[137] [Prov. 12:4] could be rendered in good German: whether it should be translated as "domestic"; or "honorable," "virtuous," "circumspect"; [or] "prudent." When some mentioned the new expression "very virtue-rich and valiant,"[138] [he said,] "We want to stay clear of the words of the ladies' salon and of 'stalwart and valiant ladies' in our homes and Bible."[139]

|When our doctor had labored until he was tired and weary, he was in good spirits at table; sometimes he organized a chorus. Once, in the company of good people, we sang the last words of Dido from Virgil: *Dulces exuviae.*[140]

---

[133] Luther complained about Andreas Osiander's criticism of his Bible translation, his preaching at Smalcald against Luther's doctrine of justification, and about his ostentatious display of erudition: see *Table Talk* no. 5047 (1540), WA TR 4:634–35; cf. *Table Talk* no. 5465 (1542), WA TR 5:167; no. 5004 (1540), WA TR 4:609; no. 5469 (1542), WA TR 5:169–70. On Osiander's sermon at Smalcald, which is not preserved in full, see Gottfried Seebass, *Das reformatorische Werk des Andreas Osiander* (Nürnberg: Verein für Bayerische Kirchengeschichte, 1967), pp. 154–55, and Melanchthon's description of reactions to the sermon in his letter to Hieronymus Baumgartner, October 24, 1550, MBW 6:103, no. 5927. Luther made similar criticisms of Karlstadt and of Zwingli for their displays of linguistic erudition: see *Table Talk* no. 5143 (1540), WA TR 4:683; no. 5006 (1540), WA TR 4:610; no. 4719 (1539), WA TR 4:446–48; no. 5469 (1542), WA TR 5:169–70. Volz, *Die Lutherpredigten des Johannes Mathesius*, p. 271, speculates that Mathesius has confused or conflated Luther's complaints about Zwingli at Marburg with the complaints about Osiander, but the *Table Talk* refers to Osiander's ostentatious use of the biblical languages as well.

[134] *zwischen dem Magen unnd Lungen*

[135] *zwischen Bantzer und Hengel*

[136] See WA DB 9/1:492–93 and the notes on revisions to 1 Kings 22 in WA DB 3:431.

[137] I.e., חַיִל.

[138] *vil tugentreich und gestrenge*; a courtly form of address for a woman of the minor nobility: see *DWB*, s.vv. "Gestreng" and "Tugendreich."

[139] See the protocol and notes on Prov. 12:4 in WA DB 4:11; cf. *Table Talk* no. 5330 (1540), WA TR 5:61.

[140] Virgil, *Aeneid* 4.651–54 (Loeb 63 [1916], pp. 466–67). For the musical setting, which appeared in Georg Rhau's 1538 *Sinfoniae Iucundae*, see WA 35:538–42. Although it was later ascribed to Luther, there is no basis for the musical attribution.

Herr Philip also chimed in, and when the song was done, he said, "Virgil wanted to compose a requiem for Anthony,[141] containing his last will and testament."[142] "Dear God," said Luther, "what wretched and miserable people the blind heathen are, together with their men of learning; how pitiably they die *sine crux Christi et lux verbi* ['without the cross of Christ and the light of the Word'].[143] Thus the great poet also concludes his book by depicting the demise of Prince Turnus: *Vitaque cum fremitu fugit indignata sub umbras*, 'I die in anger and depart from here with bitterness.'[144] That is why many of them took their own lives,[145] like the wretched and impetuous Dido. We thank God for the last words of David, Simeon, and Stephen [2 Sam. 23:1–7; Luke 2:29–32; Acts 7:59–60], who fell asleep calmly and joyfully in the true confession and invocation of the eternal Mediator, trusting the Lord Christ to raise and preserve their soul."

"Let us mark well the epitaphs and examples of Holy Scripture. Heathen wisdom is a much greater foolishness than the heathen think our Gospel to be, although their idolatry has abominably infiltrated all of the papacy, where people were also ignorant about how to die a blessed death."[146]

---

[141] Mark Anthony (83–30 BC) was a member of the Second Triumvirate with Octavian Caesar (Augustus), but allied himself with the Egyptian queen Cleopatra (r. 51–12 BC). After being defeated by Octavian's forces at the Battle of Actium in 31 BC, Anthony committed suicide the following year. See *OCD*, 3rd ed., s.v. "Anthony, Mark." Loesche (*LH²*, p. 571) suggests that the reference is to Robert Barnes, known as "Anthony Anglus" (see above, p. 422 n. 180), but this seems unlikely in the context.

[142] *Table Talk* no. 4976 (1540), WA TR 4:596.

[143] A proverbial expression in ungrammatical medieval Latin: see Wander 4:838, "Sterben" no. 185. It suggests death in despair, perhaps with concrete allusion to some of the physical apparatus involved in the last rites for the dying—a crucifix and a lamp or candle. For Luther's use of the expression, see, e.g., *Table Talk* no. 1365 (1532), WA TR 2:73; no. 2428 (1532), WA TR 2:461; no. 2517a (1532), WA TR 2:501; no. 2795b (1532), WA TR 2:665; no. 4379 (1539), WA TR 4:271; no. 5670 (1544), WA TR 5:310 and WA 48:479; no. 6572 (n.d.), WA TR 6:49; *Auslegung der ersten 25 Psalmen auf der Coburg* (1530), WA 31/1:264; *Lectures on Genesis* (1535–45/1544–54), LW 1:306.

[144] Literally: "With a roar, [his] life flees in indignation beneath the shades." Cf. Virgil, *Aeneid* 12.952 (Loeb 64 [1916], pp. 366–67), though the Virgilian text has *gemitu* ["with a sigh"] rather than *fremitu* ["with a roar"]. Cf. Loesche, *Johannes Mathesius*, 1:134.

[145] *rent jm mancher selbst sein hertz abe*; literally, "many tore out their own hearts." For Dido's suicide, see Virgil, *Aeneid* 4.663–65 (Loeb 63 [1916], pp. 466–67).

[146] It is unclear whether this paragraph should be regarded as a continuation of the report of Luther's *Table Talk* or as Mathesius' own commentary. For the thoughts, cf. *Preface to the Burial Hymns* (1542), LW 53:328; *Church Postil* (1540–44), sermon for Trinity 18 on 1 Cor. 1:4–9, LW 79:168.

Dr. Winsheim's[147] mother, with many others in these times, came to the right conclusion: Now, under the Gospel, many people have fallen asleep more peacefully and blessedly than in the papacy; therefore, the evangelical doctrine must be more certain and comforting than all the doctrines of monks, which have no power to comfort, assure, or give peace to any conscience. Many of [the monks] also came to a dreadful end, as is said, for example, about Fabri, Eck, and the monk in Ulm.[148]

¹In those days there was a student, whom the doctor liked to have at table, who brought him a pail of good must from Güttersbach.[149] It was very pleasant and fine, tempered with the pungency of wine. When the doctor put this before his guests, he asked, "How do you like this Pfeddersheimer?[150] Our Lord God intends to pour the world a good drink as a parting toast"—because very good wines had grown this fortieth year.[151] "If that nobleman were to ride back to Güttersbach now, he would have to pay his drinking money all over again to plant vines again in every corner. In the past when the wine was rough and sour, he advised throwing out all the wine and sowing the hillsides with hops."[152]

Around this time there was a clamor during supper that the Elbe River had turned altogether blood red. The doctor smiled, got his little Bible, and read to us from 2 Kings 3 [:22]. When the sun rose and cast its slanted rays

---

[147] On the Wittenberg Greek professor Veit Oertel, from Winsheim, see above, p. 299 n. 83. He and his wife, Anna Rüpel (d. 1590), had a son of the same name, Veit Oertel (1521–1608), who matriculated in Wittenberg in 1540, though the reference here is presumably to the mother of the older Veit Oertel, who is mentioned in *Table Talk* no. 5428 (1542), WA TR 5:139, in a conversation taking place at Mathesius' own farewell dinner on April 11, 1542.

[148] See *Table Talk* no. 5379 (1542), LW 54:415, where Fabri and Eck are said to have died amid blasphemies. On Johann Fabri, bishop of Vienna, who died on May 21, 1541, see above, p. 4 n. 4. On Luther's longtime opponent Johann Eck, see above, p. 154 n. 89. He died on February 10, 1543, but rumors of his death circulated after his illness at the Diet of Regensburg. The "monk from Ulm" may be a confusion for the Ulm nun who is reported to have died in terror over guilt at having hidden consecrated hosts in her cell: *Table Talk* no. 221 (1532), WA TR 1:94. Other suggestions include the Franciscan provincial Johann Winzler (d. 1554), who preached in Ulm after the Peasants' War; the Dominican theologian Johann Mensing (ca. 1475–1547), who may have taught in Ulm in 1514; and the Zwinglian preacher Conrad Sam (ca. 1483–1533), though he never seems to have been a monk: see Volz, *Die Lutherpredigten des Johannes Mathesius*, p. 272 on *LH* 324.33.

[149] "Must" [Latin *mustum*] is the pressed juice of the grape at the beginning of the process of fermentation. Güttersbach, in the Odenwald, some 40 km northeast of Heidelberg, does not seem to have been particularly distinguished for its viticulture.

[150] I.e., wine from the well-known vineyards around the town of Pfeddersheim, on the Pfrimm River in the Palatinate, near Worms (some 50 km west of Güttersbach).

[151] Cf. *Table Talk* no. 5326 (1540), WA TR 5:60, for the remark about the good wine of 1540. The rest of the episode is narrated by Mathesius alone.

[152] Perhaps a reference to the counts of Erbach, who had authority over Güttersbach.

across the water, the Edomites thought that all the water for which Elisha had prayed had turned red from the blood of the fallen kings. "No no!" said the doctor. "When the sun rises or sets and shines upon the water, it gives it a different appearance.[153] We are directed to the Word; and God the Father Himself [directs us] to Christ's mouth. We should never look for miraculous signs. It is in the Word and through the Word that the most glorious miracles occur today. The world and men of reason are presumptuous and long [for miracles] like the Pharisees, always wanting to have a sign while they ignore the Word [Matt. 12:38; 16:1–4]."

I wrote to my good friend Master Caspar Heidenreich,[154] who came to the doctor's table after me, about the visions and signs that were supposed to have been seen in Wiesenthal.[155] When he brought this up at table, the doctor responded, "Oh, dear Master Caspar, if you would like to see animals, castles, cities, and strange things in the sky, then talk to me. When a storm has just ended and there are many clouds, I will show you remarkable wonders. The world is always gaping after signs and often looks at a white dog high in the sky and takes it for a baker's apprentice;[156] it likes to believe in visions. The faithful hold fast to the Word and preserve it. Very often I have implored my God that He would not let me see any vision or sign nor speak to me in dreams, for I have enough to do in studying the Word;[157] it is

---

[153] For this episode, see *Table Talk* no. 4977 (1540), WA TR 4:597; cf. Mathesius to Spalatin, June 19, 1540, in Loesche, *Johannes Mathesius*, 2:232. Luther's remarks that follow are found only in Mathesius' report here.

[154] On Heidenreich (here spelled "Heidrich"), see above, p. 425 n. 7. He must have been Mathesius' direct source for this piece of *Table Talk*, which does not appear in other sources. See Volz, *Die Lutherpredigten des Johannes Mathesius*, p. 124.

[155] On June 4, 1543, a remarkable succession of images was seen in the clouds over Bohemian Wiesenthal [Loučná pod Klínovcem], near Joachimsthal: a man with a long black beard; a rock on which stood a tall man with a long nose wearing a long plume; two cities, one large and one small, over which something like a spiked pear appeared; a man on horseback carrying a banner in one hand and a child in the other; a man standing on a mountain who cut off another man's head; a man kneeling between two rocks, like Jesus on the Mount of Olives; a man in a long robe carrying sheep while being chased by a goat; two girls, one holding up her arm and the other playing a lute; a camel with a man wearing a plume standing on its back who is attacked by a lion; the lion, the girls, and the man with the sheep then approach the cities; finally, many lions with cannons surround the cities. This spectacle was described in a contemporary pamphlet: *Gar Wunderbarliche Newe zeytung vnd gschicht/ so im Wisenthal erschinen sind am himel/ nahent bey S. Joachimsthall/ den Vierdten Junij des XLIII. Jars* (Regensburg: Hans Kohl, 1543) [VD16 G398; see also VD16 ZV30188].

[156] For the proverb, about someone who is drunk or has poor eyesight (here with the addition of "high in the sky" to refer to clouds), see Wander 2:879, 890, "Hund" nos. 1372, 1605.

[157] See *Table Talk* no. 610 (1533), WA TR 1:287; no. 801 (1530), WA TR 1:382; *Vorlesung über Jesaia* (1527–30/1532–34), WA 25:120; *Table Talk* no. 508 (1533), LW 54:89–90; no. 2138

certain, true, solid; it provides wisdom, comfort, peace, and joy, and, to all who keep it, eternal life. May God protect us from false interpretations!"[158]

At this time in the autumn, the colloquy in Worms commenced, with many scholars from both parties assembled together.[159] The [representatives] from Wittenberg also went there, with the doctor's blessing. "I am stepping back,"[160] said the doctor, "because our God has provided many good people who understand His Word and have become superior to the opponents. They have gained and preserved nothing so far with their snorting and violence, because their religion and blasphemy has no foundation. Therefore, they act as the children of this world, who are wiser by nature in evil affairs than are the children of the Light and the clear Truth [Luke 16:8]. And since they are unable to make progress by means of the law, their books, threats, and violence, now they want to pull the wool over our eyes and negotiate in a deceptively conciliatory way, trying to see whether this stalling might do something for their rotten cause, because worldly wisdom and reason and

---

(1531), WA TR 2:334; no. 3049 (n.d.), WA TR 3:157; no. 4444a–b (1539), WA TR 4:315–16. Cf. below, Mathesius, *History*, pp. 543–44.

[158] *Glosen*; literally: "glosses." Cf. Mathesius, *History*, above, pp. 116, 217, 240, 261, 265, 314, 354, 480; and below, pp. 516, 549, 568.

[159] The Colloquy of Worms began on November 25, 1540, after preliminary internal discussions on each side, and continued through January 1541, when the imperial councillor Nicolas Perrenot de Granvelle (see above, p. 307 n. 145) adjourned the colloquy and announced its move to Regensburg. Each side sent thirty-three delegates, including eleven theologians as voting representatives (see WA Br 9:258–60). The electoral Saxon delegation consisted of Melanchthon, the Eisenach superintendent Justus Menius (see above, p. 385 n. 86), and the chancellor Franz Burchart (see above, p. 297 n. 72); Caspar Cruciger, the jurist Kilian Goldstein (see above, p. 299 n. 84) and the knight Hans von Dolzig (ca. 1485–1551) were also in attendance. Also among the Evangelicals were John Calvin (1509–64), who attended along with the Strassburg delegation of Martin Bucer and Wolfgang Capito (see above, pp. 171–72 n. 32 and p. 395 n. 5); Andreas Osiander and Wenceslaus Linck from Nürnberg (see above, p. 311 n. 170 and p. 148 n. 48); Martin Frecht from Ulm (see above, p. 354 n. 185 and p. 355 n. 188); Justus Jonas from Halle (see the introduction above, p. xxx); and Nicolaus von Amsdorf from Magdeburg (see above, p. 30 n. 15). The Scots Lutheran theologian Alexander Alesius (1500–1565; Günther Wartenberg, "Alesius, Alexander," *OER* 1:18–19), attending on behalf of Brandenburg, was officially counted as a Roman Catholic representative. The Roman Catholic delegation included Johann Eck from Bavaria (see above, p. 154 n. 89); Johann Gropper from Cologne (1503–59; John Patrick Donnelly, "Gropper, Johannes," *OER* 2:197); and Michael Helding from Mainz (1506–61; Friedrich Wilhelm Bautz, "Helding Michael," *BBKL* 2:696–98). For the documents surrounding the colloquy, see Klaus Ganzer and Karl-Heinz zur Mühlen, eds., *Das Wormser Religionsgespräch (1540/41)*, ADRRG 2/1–2; and the material published by Melanchthon: CR 3:2033–113; 4:5–91. See Vinzenz Pfnür, "Colloquies," *OER* 1:375–82; Sleidanus, *De statu religionis* (1558), book 13, pp. 371–74; Brecht 3:217–19.

[160] *Ich mach mich schwach.* Luther's words to the departing Wittenberg delegation are apparently Mathesius' own eyewitness report.

anti-Christian wickedness are unable to accomplish anything—or perhaps some people would drift off to sleep in the meantime.

"Go forth in the name of God as ambassadors of Jesus Christ, hold firmly to the simple Word, and concede nothing for our Lord Christ, for you have no authority to do so. In other matters, let yourselves be found lacking in nothing that fosters comity and unity. Christ, along with His Spirit and angelic guardians, shall be with you [cf. Matt. 28:20; John 14:16–17; Ps. 91:11], and I shall keep you in my prayers as long as I live. The adversaries have been put to flight and have a bad conscience; they are trafficking in rotten fish and in their crafty and clever tricks, but He who alone is wise and prudent [cf. Rom. 16:27; Jude 1:25] will catch them in their prudence [Job 5:13; 1 Cor. 3:19] and reveal their foolishness to everyone and put them to shame before long. He neither slumbers nor sleeps [Ps. 121:4], and He gives His Spirit to those who cry to Him [Luke 11:13]. He will also give you a mouth and wisdom, against which they will be unable to muster anything that will stand [cf. Luke 12:11–12; 21:15; Matt. 10:19–20]."

Then the representatives from Wittenberg went on their way and arrived in Worms, where the hares and bats, who shunned the light, were lying in wait:[161] they refused to engage in any negotiation and made impossibly far-reaching and unreasonable proposals, which were utterly unacceptable to our people.[162] Meanwhile, Christ's servants and ambassadors were equipping themselves: They divided up the doctors of the ancient church among themselves and read through them, so that they would be able to counter the Papists at every turn. After extensive negotiation, it was decided that each party should set apart one scholar who would publicly address the contested articles of the Augsburg Confession. Our party chose Herr Philip and assigned Dr. Cruciger and Musculus as his assistants to write down all that was said.[163] The opposing party proposed Dr. Eck.

---

[161] Cf. above, Mathesius, *History*, p. 412.

[162] The political position of the Roman Catholic delegation was complicated by the fact that several of the nominally Catholic estates—Brandenburg, Jülich-Cleve, and the Palatinate—were, in fact, evangelically inclined, making individual voting by the twenty-two representatives problematic. The Evangelical estates agreed on the Augsburg Confession as their joint position, but in the *Variata* form (see above, p. 332 n. 70), which gave the Catholic estates cause for objection.

[163] On Cruciger, see above, p. xx n. 19. Wolfgang Musculus (1497–1563), a member of the Augsburg delegation, was a former Benedictine monk who had come to Strasburg in 1528, where he was associated with Bucer and Matthias Zell (1477–1548). Musculus was called to Augsburg as a pastor in 1531 and served there until the Interim of 1548, after which he relocated to Switzerland. See J. Wayne Baker, "Musculus, Wolfgang," *OER* 3:103–4. On these arrangements at the colloquy, see Sleidanus, *De statu religionis* (1558), book 13, p. 372, where the "Musculus" who served as one of the secretaries is identified as Wolfgang rather than Andreas Musculus (1514–81; Robert Kolb, "Musculus, Andreas," *OER* 3:103), who was

The colloquy began early in 1541.[164] Herr Philip spoke like a precious and divinely instructed man [cf. John 6:45] and founded his discourse so firmly upon God's Word and sound reasons that Eck was unable to raise or maintain any solid objection against it. When the opponents realized that they with their Goliath were unable to gain anything against the little David and his sling [1 Samuel 17], ¹Granvelle[165] presented the imperial letter stating that the colloquy should be postponed until the next imperial diet.[166] The diet had already been scheduled, and Emperor Charles intended to attend it personally. This was the resolution and conclusion of the colloquy in Worms, at which our party received much praise from great people from other lands. Lord Granvelle is supposed to have said, "The protesting estates have a secretary"—he was referring to Doctor Cruciger—"more learned than all the Papists, for he manages to write down all the words that Herr Philip speaks while also reminding him what part of Eck's objection still has to be refuted."[167] I have seen the acts [of the colloquy] which were recorded on paper quite legibly as Melanchthon spoke.[168]

Our doctor mentioned a fine story. Eck came out with an argument well sharpened on every corner.[169] As Herr Philip considered this, he said, "I will respond tomorrow." Eck said, "It is dishonorable if one is unable to respond quickly and *ex tempore*." "Doctor," said the thoughtful man, "I am not seeking honor in this matter, but the truth. Tomorrow, God willing, you shall hear me."

Not long afterward, Emperor Charles went to the imperial diet in Regensburg, which was dutifully attended by many princes, bishops, and

---

a doctoral student in Wittenberg at the time. The information that the Evangelicals divided up the church fathers for review is Mathesius' contribution: see Volz, *Die Lutherpredigten des Johannes Mathesius*, p. 272; cf. Musculus' protocol of the preliminary discussions, ADRRG 2/1:470–72.

[164] I.e., actual discussions of doctrine began in the new year, lasting January 14–18, the end of 1540 having been spent negotiating the parameters for the discussion.

[165] On Nicholas Perrenot de Granvelle, see above, p. 489 n. 159.

[166] See Sleidanus, *De statu religionis* (1558), book 13, p. 373; ADRRG 2/1:208–10.

[167] For the anecdote, see *Table Talk* no. 5452 (1542), WA TR 5:162, and above, Mathesius, *History*, p. 307. Cf. the report of the Strassburg reformer Mathis Pfarrer (1489–1568), ADRRG 2/2:987.

[168] See ADRRG 2/1:213–61; CR 4:33–78. Mathesius may have seen either the edition published by Melanchthon or Cruciger's own manuscript; on Mathesius' friendship with Cruciger, see above, p. 298 n. 81.

[169] *sehr spitzigen und eckichten argument*; a wordplay on Eck's name, which means "an angle" or "a corner." Mathesius appears to be the source for this anecdote.

lords, as well as the papal legate Contarini,[170] in addition to the scholars of the protesting estates.[171] The colloquy begun in Worms was to be concluded here,[172] but because many prudent statesmen were averse to the colloquy, and other know-it-alls were striving to unite the two religions by application of their great powers of reason, a book was hammered out at this time which was intended to please both religions.[173] Out of it the Interim was patched together after Dr. Martin's death.[174] Many people were strongly urging unification, and good Emperor Charles ⏐wished to see peace and quiet, because the Turk was advancing on Germany with an army in force.[175]

Our people appealed to the Augsburg Confession and explained why they could not accept this new, inconsistent, and double-tongued book of patched-together religion. Legates were also dispatched to Wittenberg to ask Dr. Martin to promote and help defend the religious agreement.[176]

---

[170] Gasparo Contarini (1483–1542) was a Venetian cardinal who combined sympathy with the doctrine of justification by faith with a commitment to the papacy and the sacramental system of the church. He became a leader of reform-minded Catholics, chairing the papal commission whose Counsel (1538) was leaked and published with scorn by Luther: LW 34:231–67. See Elizabeth G. Gleason, "Contarini, Gasparo," OER 1:419–20.

[171] For the following account of the Regensburg Diet, see Sleidanus, De statu religionis (1558), book 13, pp. 374f., 378–79. Cf. Brecht 3:222–28; Brandi, Emperor Charles V, pp. 444–50; Pfnür, "Colloquies," OER 1:377–80. For the theologians participating, see below, p. 493 n. 178.

[172] The colloquy in Regensburg took place from April 27 to May 22, 1541. The proceedings of the colloquy at Regensburg were published separately by Melanchthon and by Martin Bucer in 1541: Melanchthon, Acta in conventu Ratisbonensi (Wittenberg: Joseph Klug, 1541) [VD16 M2385–87]; Bucer, Acta Colloquii in Comitiis Imperii Ratisbonae habiti (Strasbourg: Wendelin Rihel Sr., 1541) [VD16 B8831]. For a modern edition of documents surrounding the Regensburg colloquy, see Klaus Ganzer and Karl-Heinz zur Mühlen, eds., Das Regensburger Religionsgespräch (1541), ADRRG 3/1–2.

[173] The first draft of what became the Regensburg Book [Liber Ratisbonensis] was drafted secretly at Worms by Johann Gropper (see above, p. 489 n. 159) and Martin Bucer at the instigation of Granvelle: see ADRRG 2/1:574–701; CR 4:92–96. The final draft after the discussions at the colloquy can be found in ADRRG 3/1:268–391; CR 4:190–238. Luther received a copy of the draft from Elector Joachim II of Brandenburg in February 1541: see Luther to Joachim of Brandenburg, ca. February 21, 1541, WA Br 9:332–34.

[174] The Augsburg Interim of 1548 (see above, p. xxi n. 22) was initially drafted by Julius Pflug (1499–1564; Bernard Vogler, "Pflug, Julius," OER 3:252–53; see also below, p. 493 n. 178 and p. 500 n. 231),who had participated in the colloquy at Regensburg, as well as Michael Helding and Johann Gropper, who had participated at Worms (see above, p. 489 n. 159). See Kolb and Nestingen, Sources and Contexts, pp. 144–45.

[175] This Ottoman campaign would culminate in the capture of Buda in the fall of 1541. See Brandi, Emperor Charles V, pp. 444, 451–52; Fisher-Galati, Ottoman Imperialism and German Protestantism, p. 84.

[176] Mathesius is narrating events somewhat out of sequence. After the conclusion of the colloquy at Regensburg, a delegation consisting of the princes John and George of Anhalt (see above, p. 30 n. 16) and the theologians Alesius (see above, p. 489 n. 159) and Mathias von der

The doctor perceived what Satan had in mind: he wanted to make a breach in our religion. Therefore, he advised unity in whatever concerned ceremonies and external church usages. In articles of faith, which he had not set up but which belong to the eternal Son of God, there was nothing that he could change or yield. Therefore, he could not regard it as being advisable either to let uncertain, slippery, and ambiguous words and talk slip in in order to explain or to harmonize the chief articles. Scripture was like a ring that would no longer be whole if it were to break at any one place.[177]

Finally, when, at the most gracious request of Emperor Charles, three persons from each side[178] had agreed to a new colloquy and had been diligently admonished by the emperor himself to pursue these matters with the greatest resolve and diligence, the colloquy resumed. When some negotiators expressed themselves somewhat more mildly and moderately about the other party, Dr. Eck came into conflict with his own side; and after many negotiations, on the advice of the Papists, the discussion of all matters was referred to the Roman legate,[179] who intended to make a report to Rome, to the head of his church, the vicar of God,[180] who was supposed to decide all of these matters in a council.

Emperor Charles gave the protesting estates a fair resolution and assured them that he would as soon as possible seek to advance the council with the pope.[181] Thereupon this colloquy again came to a close.

Although no definite resolution was reached in religious matters, the foolishness of the opponents became even better known, and the Augsburg Confession was praised and accepted by many people. For the time was at hand when God with His Spirit and the steadfast declaration and confession of good people was going to reveal and slay the Antichrist. Therefore,

---

Schulenburg, representing Elector Joachim and Margrave George of Brandenburg, came to Luther in Wittenberg for discussions on June 10, 1541: see Brecht 3:225–26.

[177] For Luther's appraisal of the negotiations at Regensburg, see Luther and Bugenhagen to Elector John Frederick, May 10/11, 1541, WA Br 9:406–9; Luther to George of Anhalt, May 25, 1541, WA Br 9:419–20; Luther and Bugenhagen to John Frederick, June 24, 1541, WA Br 9:457, and June 29, 1541, WA Br 9:460–63. For the description of doctrine (or Scripture) as an unbreakable ring, cf. Luther, *Brief Confession* (1544), LW 38:307–8.

[178] Emperor Charles appointed the theologians Bucer, Melanchthon, and Johann Pistorius the Elder, from Hesse (ca. 1502–83; Eckhard Reichert, "Pistorius, Johannes," *BBKL* 7:648–49) on the Evangelical side, and Eck, Pflug, and Gropper on the Catholic side: ADRRG 3/1:78–79; Melanchthon to Luther, April 30, 1541, WA Br 9:384–85.

[179] I.e., Contarini: see above, p. 492 n. 170.

[180] On the pope as the vicar of God or of Christ, see above, p. 84 n. 5.

[181] Both the Catholic and the Evangelical estates at the diet rejected the Regensburg Book in early July 1541. The imperial recess of July 29 (to be edited in *DRA* 11) confirmed and extended the 1532 Peace of Nürnberg (see above, p. 347 n. 145), pending a general council: see Pfnür, "Colloquies," *OER* 1:379.

neither St. Peter's keys [Matt. 16:19][182] nor St. Paul's sword [Rom. 13:4][183] nor Antiochus' deceit [1 Macc. 1:31][184] nor the world's scheming would be of any more help. Day by day the truth of the pure doctrine ascended like the rising sun and drove away the darkness, mist, and gloomy clouds of the black Satan.

This year our doctor was very weak, and because of his blood pressure, he was hard of hearing for a time;[185] when he was even a little recovered, however, he worked without resting. Therefore, when his detractors charged him with having called his elector an insulting name[186] and with having instigated this whole matter of religion or of indulgences in order to please Elector Frederick, in addition to other charges, he wrote a book entitled *Against Hanswurst*,[187] in which he defends himself, as an honorable man. And because his opponents were always insisting so hard on the authority of the Church and of councils, and calling themselves "Catholics"—because there is no mention of the "Roman" Church in our children's Creed,[188] in which we are baptized—the doctor includes in his book defending himself the fine, instructive, and comforting articles about baptized and catechized children in the papacy.[189]

For because the Antichrist reclines in God's own temple, as St. Paul says [2 Thess. 2:4], and since through God's miraculous grace and promise the Church of God under the red whore[190] of Babylon still retained Baptism, the Ten Commandments, the Apostles' Symbol or Creed, and the Lord Christ's Our Father, along with the Sunday Gospels, the Passion of the Lord Christ, and many beautiful hymns and paintings, one must confess that God also had His portion in the Roman Church at all times, and especially among the children who received a proper and salutary Baptism in the name of

---

[182] I.e., papal authority. See above, Mathesius, *History*, pp. 165, 420–21.

[183] I.e., secular power. See above, Mathesius, *History*, pp. 420–21.

[184] Antiochus IV Epiphanes (r. 175–164 BC), the Seleucid king of Syria, attacked Jerusalem and sought to assimilate the Jews to Hellenistic culture and religion in a reversal of his father's policy. See *ODCC*, 3rd ed., s.v. "Antiochus Epiphanes."

[185] Luther suffered from a perforated eardrum and then from tinnitus: see Brecht 3:231.

[186] Duke Henry of Braunschweig-Wolfenbüttel accused Luther of having called the Saxon elector John Frederick "Hans Wurst" (see *Against Hanswurst* [1541], LW 41:187), a stock name for a carnival fool, identified by carrying a long leather sausage. See the introduction by Eric W. Gritsch, LW 41:182.

[187] *Against Hanswurst* (1541), LW 41:179–256. See Brecht 3:219–22.

[188] I.e., the Apostles' Creed: see above, p. 241 n. 58.

[189] *Against Hanswurst* (1541), LW 41:207–10. Cf. *Lectures on Galatians* (1531/1535), LW 26:24–25.

[190] *Braut*; see above, p. 236 n. 25.

the Father, Son, and Holy Spirit, albeit in a foreign language.[191] Captive Christendom, especially the married fathers and mothers, instructed their baptized children in the catechism and children's doctrine and taught them the holy Our Father and the Christian Creed or sent them to schools, where these things always remained.

Now, because these baptized and instructed children in the captivity of the Roman Church received a Christian Baptism and the Holy Spirit, Christ preserved His portion even in the papacy, and as the eternal Archbishop of our souls, He gladly received the children, who are dear to Him and whom He commands to have brought to Him [Matt. 19:14; Mark 10:14; Luke 18:16]; He also preserved these children in their Baptism, and through this He saved many in their years of childhood and adolescence.

The situation is different, however, with those who later abandoned this covenant of a good conscience [1 Pet. 3:21], knowingly fell away from their Baptism, and accepted the red whore's[192] character, oil or chrism, and mark[193]—who broke the oath their sponsors pledged to their God, Lord, and Savior in Baptism and made a new pledge and oath to the pope, letting themselves be anointed with his oil and promising him to help promote and advocate his lies and idolatry.

ᴵBaptized children, who have been sprinkled with the blood of Jesus Christ and sealed and pledged with the true anointing of the Holy Spirit [2 Cor. 1:22], are the dear *Hephzibah* [Isa. 62:4] and true Bride of Christ [Rev. 21:9] even under the papacy. The others, who forgot their first faith [1 Tim. 5:12] and broke faith with their Bridegroom and true lover, as Scripture says [Hosea 1:2; 2:13; Jer. 3:20; Heb. 6:4–12],[194] stray from the right path and turn into utterly desperate, shameful sacks and hides[195]— such are the good German words the doctor used to name the pope's church, names taken and derived from Scripture. For in Ezekiel 16 [:15–63] and many other places [e.g., Isa. 1:21; Jer. 2:20; Hosea 2:5; 9:1], when the Son of God speaks of the old harlot who had abandoned Him and His marriage covenant [e.g., Jer. 3:14; 31:32] (which He established with them in circumcision on the basis of the promised Seed of the woman), He calls this runaway hussy an archprostitute,[196] even as Scripture also calls this wicked

---

[191] I.e., in Latin.

[192] *Braut*

[193] I.e., in ordination: see above, Mathesius, *History*, pp. 146, 204, 206, 215.

[194] See *Against Hanswurst* (1541), LW 41:207–9.

[195] See *Against Hanswurst* (1541), LW 41:188, 199, 201, 208.

[196] See *Against Hanswurst* (1541), LW 41:188, 208.

and adulterous type a tart or trollop and an unholy, shameful, wanton whore [Revelation 17].

Those who have not read the books of the prophets and do not know the language of the Holy Spirit, which He has heard from the Son of God and caused to be written down by His prophets and preserved for us, will be offended by the words of this good book. The wanton world permits abominable licentiousness to slip and creep in among their clergy and laity and wants to gloss over its own harlotry when anyone talks about wicked deeds according to Scripture.

I mention this in defense of this salutary book, for which many good laity, who were not at all devoted to the Roman Church, gave sincere thanks to our God. In the papacy there were also many old laity who, because their whole life long they had never heard anything about their Baptism, took salutary comfort in Christ's suffering at their end and said their little prayer, which the old beguines or soul-women[197] who cared for the ill were accustomed to read for them to repeat. At age 7, I learned this little old prayer from such a dear old lady: "O great agony, O bloody wounds, O bitter death of the Son of God, come to my aid in my last need; when my heart breaks, O Lord Jesus Christ, do not abandon me!"[198]

When a poor layman and baptized Christian is held captive under the pope or Turk, if he can become free, he should do so.[199] If not, let him take comfort in his holy Baptism and send his children for this salutary washing [Titus 3:5] and bring them up in the fear of the Lord and in the children's catechism [cf. Eph. 6:4]; let him warn the child against the mark of disgrace and ungodly oaths that the consecrated clergy, patrons, and doctors must take for the Roman abomination if they want to be fit for and become partakers of his spiritual goods. If a good father of a household is unable to secure Baptism under the Turk, let him present the [matter] to the Lord Christ as he devoutly prays the Our Father, in the same way that children in the womb are brought to Him.[200]

---

[197] Beguines were Christian laywomen who gathered into organized associations which flourished especially in the thirteenth and fourteenth centuries, often under the guidance of Dominican or Franciscan friars, for purposes of devotion and of charitable work, including some spiritual care, from which they were called "soul-women" in Germany and the Low Countries. See *ODCC*, 3rd ed., s.v. "Beguines, Beghards."

[198] Cf. the versification of this prayer by Conrad Hoier [Höjer] (d. 1624) in Wackernagel 5:86, no. 124. See Loesche, *Johannes Mathesius*, 1:12.

[199] Luther wrote a preface for a book written by a man who had escaped the captivity of Turkish Muslims: preface to [George of Hungary,] *On the Ceremonies and Customs of the Turks* (1530), LW 59:255–62.

[200] Cf. *Comfort for Women Who Have Had a Miscarriage* (1542), LW 43:243–50.

The eternal Son of God, who also became the Virgin's Child for our sake and our children's, surely fills His paradise with baptized and sanctified children, to whom belongs the kingdom of heaven [Matt. 19:14; 11:25]. We were all born of father and mother under the fearsome wrath of God [cf. Eph. 2:3]; through Baptism, the Word, and faithful prayer we are begotten and chosen by God as new creatures and God's children and heirs. It is a perilous oath that people take in ordination and in monastic vows and when swearing to use one's sword, doctorate, or legal training to defend the pope's religion, reputation, and primacy along with his see and the heirs of St. Peter. But God's grace and mercy are greater than all the world's sin. He even saved many priests who loudly accused and helped to crucify the Lord of glory (Acts 6 [:7]), and He calls some from among the rich and great, who in the time of their ignorance [Acts 17:30] worshiped the Antichrist, 'drank from his chalice [Rev. 18:6], and protected his crown and religion—if they, like Aaron and Manasseh [Num. 12:10–11; 2 Chron. 33:12–13], repent and wholeheartedly turn back to their God, who had them circumcised or baptized. Let that be enough for the present concerning the good book that was published during the imperial diet in Regensburg!

After the imperial diet had ended, a new "diet" of devouring began.[201] Formerly, the clergy had devoured all sorts of property; now that the seat in Rome had begun to crack and the pope's bull had a bite taken out of it, anyone who abstained felt he was being cheated.[202] Once our doctor said at table:[203] "St. John's prophecy in Revelation 17 [:16] will come true. Even the pope's protectors are helping themselves and are unwilling to defend the holy sepulcher[204] for free. *Defensores Papae devoratores eius* ['The pope's defenders are his devourers'].[205] The great leaders remind me," he said, "of that clever dog who was carrying home his master's meat from the butcher. When dogs set at him on the way, he put down his basket and boldly defended himself. When he realized that he was outmatched, he was the

---

[201] *ein newer reißtag*; i.e., in the wake of the 1542 Diet of Speyer: see Sleidanus, *De statu religionis* (1558), book 14, p. 396; Brecht 3:358. Mathesius is playing on the word *Reichstag*. *Reiß* means a "rip," with the wordplay continued with images of tearing in the following sentences. The present translation shifts the metaphor to eating (to which the German text eventually turns) in order to maintain an English pun on "diet."

[202] Wander 4:1579, "Versäumen" no. 5.

[203] See *Table Talk* no. 4978 (1540), WA TR 4:597–98 (also Aurifaber); cf. *Table Talk* no. 5663 (1544), LW 54:472–74.

[204] See above, Mathesius, *History*, p. 401.

[205] This epithet appeared in the marginal note on Rev. 17:16 in Luther's German Bible beginning in 1530: see WA DB 7:463. Cf. *Table Talk* no. 3893 (1538), WA TR 3:690.

first to fall upon the basket.[206] Wise people surely see that priests' property (scraped together under a wicked pretext) is plunder.[207] Whoever abstains [from taking some], shame on him![208] This is how the little ox learns to plow from the old bull, over time.[209] But no one will get rich from this property or pass it down to the third generation of heirs;[210] they will wear their teeth down to painful stumps on this fat monastery food.[211]

"We urge and defend the true spiritual property when we have God's Word and the right use of the Sacraments in their purity[212] and the name of God is kept holy among us.[213] If we sincerely seek God's glory, kingdom, and will, surely we will not lack daily bread, even if it means the ravens bring us food [1 Kings 17:6]. We have to watch and let things happen as they will, *Quia vult vadere sicut vadit* ['because things will happen as they do']."[214]

[In view of the various events that transpired this year, some people, on the advice of lawyers and military counselors, began forging dogs' chains[215] and making alliances with other countries,[216] making reprisals and invoking the law of retribution,[217] attacking each other with pointed and sharpened

---

[206] *Table Talk* no. 4978 (1540), WA TR 4:597–98, where the fable is ascribed to Wolf Severus (see above, p. 339 n. 104).

[207] See above, Mathesius, *History*, p. 401.

[208] Cf. above, p. 497.

[209] Wander 3:1103, "Ochs" no. 239.

[210] See above, p. 402 n. 42.

[211] Cf. Wander 5:490, "Zahn" no. 140.

[212] Cf. AC VII 1 (Kolb-Wengert, pp. 42–43; *Concordia*, p. 34).

[213] See *Small Catechism* (1529) III 4 (Kolb-Wengert, p. 356; *Concordia*, p. 332).

[214] Cf. *Table Talk* no. 2143 (1531), WA TR 2:336. For the expression, see Wander 1:1424, "Gehen" no. 82; Luther uses it frequently, especially as a summary of the message of Ecclesiastes: see, e.g., *Notes on Ecclesiastes* (1526/1532), LW 15:27, 119; *Table Talk* no. 2018 (1531), WA TR 2:296. Luther refers to it as "a common saying of the monks": *Commentary on the Psalms of Degrees* (1532–33/1540), WA 40/3:212 (LW 66).

[215] A metaphor both for forging temporary alliances and for making preparations for war: see Wander 2:901, "Hundekette" nos. 1–2.

[216] In 1541, Duke William of Jülich-Cleves-Berg (1516–92) made an alliance with France against the emperor while the Smalcaldic League reopened negotiations over the treatment of French Protestants: see Sleidanus, *De statu religionis* (1558), book 13, p. 381.

[217] *repressalien und scheidenrecht zu gebrauchen*. On *Scheidenrecht*, see Herbert Wolf, *Die Sprache des Johannes Mathesius* (Cologne: Böhlau, 1969), p. 187; the word is not to be found in *DWB*. Perhaps, however, the meaning is "sequestration"? Duke Henry of Braunschweig-Wolfenbüttel had harassed the Evangelical cities of Goslar and Braunschweig by legal and military means, continuing military action even after legal sanctions had lapsed in 1540. In response, the Smalcaldic League, of which the cities were members, began to make its own legal and military preparations for their defense, culminating in the occupation and sequestration of the duchy of Braunschweig-Wolfenbüttel in July 1542. See Elector John Frederick to

quills,[218] heaping up many siegeworks, stockpiling artillery, and becoming entangled in convoluted negotiations. Sometimes our doctor would break out in impassioned words: "The pitcher carries water until it finally develops a crack, or else breaks entirely.[219] *Et quae non obsunt singula iuncta nocent* ['And things which individually are harmless cause injury when they are joined together'].[220] God and great lords can forgive a person's faults.[221] I will pray and help give counsel for peace and unity," he said, "for as long as I live. And I am certain that, even though some would like to stir up a tumult, no major war shall begin during my time."[222]

Our doctor was wary of the formation of alliances as well.[223] When there is too much snow clinging to a tree, if the tree or its crown does not break, it will still lose at least a few branches.[224] Enough of speaking from the pulpit about the business of chanceries and councils at court, business which we see only from the back side![225] It is not for everyone to know what such bells were made from and why they were cast, even as we cannot see into people's consciences.[226]

When the wagon gets stuck in the mud or the linchpin falls out and leaves the carriage all lying in a heap, one begins to reconsider the plan.[227] Josiah, the good king, also faltered when he started an unnecessary war [2 Chron. 35:20–24]. Jehoshaphat, too, made a mistake when he helped Ahab fight a war [1 Kings 22]. David likewise gave the command to undertake an unnecessary review of the army [2 Samuel 24]. Blessed is he who returns to the path, acknowledges his sin, takes comfort in the Lord Christ,

---

Luther, Bugenhagen, and Melanchthon, June 29, 1542, WA Br 10:88–91; Sleidanus, *De statu religionis* (1558), book 14, p. 410.

[218] On the polemical battle between Duke Henry of Braunschweig-Wolfenbüttel, and Elector John Frederick of Saxony, Landgrave Philip of Hesse, and many others, which saw the publication of scores of pamphlets in 1541–42—of which Luther's *Against Hanswurst* (above, pp. 494–95) was only a small piece—see Edwards, *Luther's Last Battles*, pp. 143–58.

[219] Wander 2:1642–43, "Krug" no. 20.

[220] A play on the legal maxim *Quae non prosunt* [or *valent*] *singula, iuncta* [or *multa*] *iuvant*. See Ovid, *Remedies for Love* 420 (Loeb 232 [1929], pp. 206–7); Detlef Liebs, *Lateinische Rechtsregeln und Rechtssprichwörter*, 6th ed. (Munich: C. H. Beck, 1998), p. 187, no. Q9.

[221] Cf. Wander 1:749, "Ehrte" no. 1.

[222] See Mathesius, *History*, above, p. 418; and below, p. 564.

[223] See above, Mathesius, *History*, pp. 359–60.

[224] Cf. Wander 1:90, "Anhang."

[225] Cf. Erasmus, *Adages* 3.1.53 (CWE 34:201–2), where "front and back" is a figure for complete knowledge.

[226] Cf. Wander 1:1730, "Glockengiesser." For a similar allusion to the dubious mixture used in casting bells, see above, Mathesius, *History*, p. 415 and n. 123 there.

[227] Cf. Wander 4:1731, "Wagen (Subst.)" no. 113.

and admonishes his people to rely for their protection on Jacob's God, who steadfastly keeps His Word and always stands by His people in their need, rescuing them in the end [Psalm 146].

ᴵAt the beginning of the year 1542, Dr. Luther consecrated a bishop in Zeitz,[228] following St. Paul's order [Titus 1:7; 1 Tim. 3:2] and the custom of the first churches.[229] He defended the Christian consecration he had performed with a public writing;[230] he let the legal experts and worldly-wise worry about the *ius patronatus* and *defensionis* ["right of patronage" and "of defense"].[231] One should promote God's honor and serve the people. Let everyone see to it that he does not put his sickle into another man's harvest [Deut. 23:25].[232] An imperial city violated the sovereign rights of the territorial lord and drove out its bishop. The doctor was supposed to help justify this after the fact, which did not please him.[233] [As it is said:] Whoever wants to marry should ask for advice before getting engaged.[234] Good advice comes far too late after a brash and impetuous deed.[235]

Many a good ruler is burdened in conscience because his peasants have no pastor at all or have a godless man to care for their souls. But what can he do differently? He appointed one man with good intent, and then those

---

[228] On January 20, 1542, Luther consecrated Nicolaus von Amsdorf (see above, p. 30 n. 15) as bishop of Naumburg-Zeitz, where he served until he was driven out in 1547 in the wake of the Smalcaldic War. See *Report on Luther's Sermon at the Consecration of Nicolaus von Amsdorf as Bishop of Naumburg* (1542), WA 49:xxvii–xxix; WA Br 9:599–601 (LW 61); Brecht 3:300–308; Robert Kolb, *Nikolaus von Amsdorf (1483–1565): Popular Polemics in the Preservation of Luther's Legacy* (Nieuwkoop: de Graaf, 1978), pp. 57–58; and Peter Brunner, *Nikolaus von Amsdorf als Bischof von Naumburg* (Gütersloh: Mohn, 1961), pp. 51–77.

[229] Cf. Melanchthon, Tr 13–15, 60–70 (Kolb-Wengert, pp. 332, 340–41; *Concordia*, pp. 296, 303–4); Luther, advice to the Naumburg Estates, January 19, 1542, WA Br 9:597–99.

[230] *Model for the Consecration of a True Christian Bishop* (1542), WA 53:219–60 (LW 61).

[231] The Saxon elector possessed these rights over the diocese of Naumburg. Although his authority to override the election of the cathedral chapter, which had elected Julius Pflug (see above, p. 492 n. 174), and to install Amsdorf as his own candidate instead was questionable under canon law, Luther left such legal questions to the elector's lawyers and offered a theological defense instead.

[232] Cf. Wander 5:549, "Sichel" no. 4.

[233] Apparently, the free imperial city of Augsburg, which in 1537 drove out Bishop Christoph von Stadion (see above, p. 175 n. 52) and the canons of the cathedral. The cup which Hans Honold bequeathed to Luther (see above, Mathesius, *History*, p. 443) may have been part of the plea of the Augsburg council to Luther to defend its action. See *Table Talk* no. 4874 (1540), WA TR 4:565; no. 4872 (1540), WA TR 4:564; and Luther, Jonas, Bugenhagen, Cruciger, and Melanchthon to Elector John Frederick, January 18, 1540, WA Br 9:29. On the expulsion of the Augsburg clergy, see Herbert Immenkötter, "Augsburg," *OER* 1:88–90; Tyler, *Lord of the Sacred City*, pp. 184–85.

[234] Wander 1:1152, "Freien" no. 86.

[235] Wander 3:1473, "Rath" no. 167.

to whom pastoral care was committed drove him out and chased him away, whereas the bishop of Samosata is left in peace.[236] So, too, the city and the lower nobility must commit the matter to God. If a [lord] who is in vassalage to another knows the truth, he admonishes his people and urges them to undertake a Christian pilgrimage and go to the holy Word and Sacraments, where God has publicly established this. The Israelites had only one temple, which those who were scattered visited every year from all over the world [cf. Deut. 12:5–7; 16:16], in addition to many proselytes and uncircumcised, God-fearing Gentiles [cf. Acts 2:5–11].

A good sermon is not too far away for those who take religion and their salvation seriously. Terrified people used to run to the ends of the earth,[237] and many noblemen journeyed over sand and sea to the empty grave of Christ.[238] This is the right way to do things: a territorial lord purchases only the peasants, their rent and services; the right to oversee the Church is not included in sale to anyone. ¦Therefore, every man for himself, and God for us all![239]

On Good Friday of this year the wafer war also began.[240] I heard many heartfelt sighs go forth and saw many eyes stream with tears among good people in Wittenberg at this time.[241] How this business sat with our peaceable doctor is expressed in the earnest letter which he addressed and sent

---

[236] An allusion to Paul of Samosata, bishop of Antioch, who was condemned as a heretic and proclaimed deposed at the Council of Antioch in 269. However, because of his personal wealth and support from the separatist empress Zenobia (ca. 240–ca. 274), he remained in control of his office for some years. On Paul and his heresy, see above, p. 388 n. 101.

[237] *zum finstern Stern*. According to *DWB*, s.v. "Stern(5)" 2, the German expression is a phonetic translation of the Latin *finis terrae*, "the end of the earth," with specific reference to Cape Finisterre in Gallicia, which was the terminus of the pilgrimage to St. James [Santiago] of Compostela. Luther frequently criticized such pilgrimages to faraway places in comparison with the ready presence of God's Word: see, e.g., *Lectures on Genesis* (1535–45/1544–54), LW 1:249–50; *Table Talk* no. 3588 (1537), LW 54:238.

[238] Frederick the Wise had made such a pilgrimage in 1493: see Mathesius, *History*, above, p. 136; and below, p. 577.

[239] Wander 2:1009, "Jeder" no. 17.

[240] The diocese of Meissen was under the joint protection of Elector John Frederick and Duke Maurice of Saxony. John Frederick decided to take direct control of the tax for support of war against the Turks, against the wishes of the Catholic bishop of Meissen and the Wurzen cathedral chapter, and sent in his own troops, which provoked Maurice to oppose his cousin's military occupation of ducal Saxon territory. The war began on Good Friday, April 7, 1542, and received the name "Wafer War" [*Fladenkrieg*] because when Philip of Hesse succeeded in negotiating a peace between the Saxon princes, and the opposing armies were disbanded on Holy Saturday, they were greeted with gifts of Easter cakes or wafers from the relieved populace. See Brecht 3:292–94; *Table Talk* no. 5428 (1542), WA TR 5:133–42.

[241] Mathesius was in Wittenberg for his ordination on March 29, 1542, and departed after April 11: see Loesche, *Johannes Mathesius*, 1:102–6.

to both commanders.[242] This man would not give counsel in favor of war or hostilities, as Herr Melanchthon and many good people testified of him.[243]

One other time when commanders were mobilizing, their territorial estates besought Dr. Luther to help advise against this.[244] He fell to his knees and advised, according to his motto, that they should keep silence [Isa. 30:15][245] and pursue peace [1 Pet. 3:11]. When they were unable to follow good counsel, however, and asked for his prayer on behalf of the military campaign, the doctor said, "I send my Our Father with you, but the Ten Commandments I cannot send with you. Old debts do not rust away,[246] and in time everything must be paid back. But one who manages to escape in the end and also confesses his error, as St. Bernard did,[247] lays hold of God's grace in the wounds of Christ. It is not ill for him to be here [cf. Matt. 17:4]. In the meantime, if someone's leg gets run over by a wheel, or his musket [recoils and] strikes him, or he gets stuck in the mud, let him sing 'patience,'[248] wait for the Lord, and say, 'I have sinned, Father'" [Luke 15:18, 21].

I mention this peace-loving man's counsels, advice, and faithful admonition to peace and unity with discreet words so that young preachers[249] may not interfere in secular affairs, help sound the call to arms, or wield the Bible

---

[242] Luther to Elector John Frederick and Duke Maurice, April 7, 1542, WA Br 10:32–36. This letter was published by Bugenhagen in 1547 in *Vermahnung zum Friede* (Wittenberg: Hans Lufft, 1547) [VD16 ZV10053], fols. A4r–C2r.

[243] See above, Mathesius, *History*, p. 317; cf. Brecht 3:199–203.

[244] In 1534, Philip of Hesse (see above, p. 70 n. 96) went to war to restore Duke Ulrich (1487–1550), who had been placed under imperial ban, to his rule over Württemberg. Philip was supported militarily by Strassburg (and financially by France) but received only diplomatic support from Elector John Frederick of Saxony. Luther and Melanchthon sought to dissuade Philip from the venture, though, in retrospect, Luther saw Philip's victory as providential. See Conrad Öttinger to Luther, early 1534, WA Br 7:4–5; *Table Talk* no. 5038 (1540), LW 54:379–82 (WA TR 4:625–30); Luther to Justus Menius, July 14, 1534, WA Br 7:89. See Brady, *Protestant Politics*, pp. 83–84; Brecht 3:28–29; James M. Estes, "Württemberg," *OER* 4:302–4.

[245] This verse in Latin—*In silentio et spe erit fortitudo vestra*—appeared around Luther's bust on the sandstone portal which Katharina gave him as a gift in 1540: see WA 48:99 n. 1.

[246] Wander 4:365, "Schuld" no. 4.

[247] On Bernard of Clairvaux, see above, p. lvi n. 191. For his deathbed repentance, see *LA* 1:102, no. 120; and Bernard, *Sermons on the Canticles* 20.1.1 (PL 183:867; CF 4:147), frequently quoted by Luther: see LW 60:264 n. 1.

[248] Cf. Rev. 14:12. Mathesius' reference to "singing" may allude to Ludwig Senfl's secular tenor song *Patientiam muß ich han*, though it ends with a rejection of "patience." See Senfl, *Sämtliche Werke*, 4:98–99, no. 104. There was also a religious *contrafactum* of the text: see Wackernagel 5:14, no. 17.

[249] See also Mathesius' criticism of Zwingli, above, *History*, p. 361.

in one hand and St. Peter's sword [John 18:10]²⁵⁰ in the other, but instead remember the doctor's prudence in such matters. His enemies who defended the pope's idolatry and opposed God's Word he boldly attacked with his pen, as a fearless hero, ¹and struck out on every side with the Our Father. Secular affairs for which he could provide no counsel with God's Word he had to let take their course. Therefore, dear friends, devote yourselves to the Word and prayer [cf. Acts 6:4; 1 Tim. 4:5], provide for your own people, and do not forget about Savonarola's dealings outside his own [office] [cf. 1 Pet. 4:15], which he also lamented when he met his end in the fire.²⁵¹ A military commander²⁵² once said to me: "Lords come into conflict and then are reconciled; poor fellows must remain poor fellows.²⁵³ Therefore, let none of them interfere in the quarrels of lords!" A friendship at court is quickly made, even as enmity at court does not last for long.

Do not forget about St. Peter, either, who asked his Lord if he should strike at the godless with his sword [Luke 22:49]. Before the answer came, he had drawn it [John 18:10], just as the heirs to his see failed to wait for the Lord Christ's answer. Meanwhile, let us follow St. Peter's doctrine and pursue peace, admonish to obedience as subjects, and sincerely pray for our lawful authorities [1 Pet. 2:13–20]. That is in accordance with God's Word and well-pleasing to Him; it helps promote the Gospel, preserves a good conscience, does not hinder our prayer, and will receive its reward and thanks in the end. Even if it means that on that account you must be denounced as a schismatic or sycophant, "just don't play games with the truth," as the miller said in the Passion play, "and see that you don't commit the crime [of which you are accused]; there will be a remedy against such lies and calumnies before long."²⁵⁴ *Experto credite Ruperto* ["Believe Rupert,

---

²⁵⁰ The medieval papacy claimed, on the basis of Luke 22:38; John 18:11; and Matt. 26:52, to control the "two swords" of spiritual and temporal power in Peter's name—the former directly and the latter by proxy. See Bernard of Clairvaux, *On Consideration* 4.3.7 (PL 182:776; CF 37:117–18); Boniface VIII, *Unam sanctam* (1302): Tierney, *Crisis of Church and State*, pp. 188–89.

²⁵¹ See above, Mathesius, *History*, p. 317; on Savonarola, see above, pp. 114–15 n. 4.

²⁵² Loesche (*LH²*, p. 338) suggests that Mathesius' source (*ein Feldöberster*) should be identified as the Joachimsthal mining administrator [*Berghauptmann*] Heinrich von Könneritz (ca. 1483–1551; see Hans Jürgen Rieckenberg, "Könneritz, Heinrich von," *NDB* 12:363). Volz (*Die Lutherpredigten des Johannes Mathesius*, p. 124 n. 1) suggests instead von Könneritz's son-in-law Wilhelm von Thumbshirn (d. 1551; see Theodor Distel, "Thumbshirn, Wilhelm von," *ADB* 38:166–67), the Saxon colonel [*Oberst*] who occupied Joachimsthal in March 1547. Cf. Loesche, *Johannes Mathesius*, 1:60, 167.

²⁵³ See Wander 2:556, "Herr" no. 503; 1:1604, "Gesell" no. 4.

²⁵⁴ Passion plays were dramas about Christ's Passion performed at the end of Passiontide by laymen from various guilds in late medieval towns. "Miller" here may identify either a character in the play (members of various estates of society were often depicted in hell) or the

who knows from experience"].²⁵⁵ That concludes the history of the doctor through the year 1542.

We thank the Lord Jesus for this man, His chosen instrument [cf. Acts 9:15], through whom He has scoured the tarnish from the pure doctrine and abolished the Babylonian captivity, and in whom He has also given us an example of beautiful and blessed virtues. Help, O Lord Jesus, that we may not forget the testimony and life of this man of great merit, and may use Your Word and Our Father ¹to protect ourselves against our enemies, wage the good warfare, preserve faith and a good conscience [1 Tim. 1:18–19], and let our gentleness shine brightly among all [cf. Phil. 4:5]. For You delight in peacemakers, and call and regard them as Your dear children [Matt. 5:9], and You scatter all who delight in war and contentiousness [Ps. 68:30; Isa. 41:12]. May You be highly exalted forever!

---

guildsman playing another role. The same scene is described in Mathesius, *Postilla Symbolica* (1588) [VD16 M1543], fol. 247r–v. The specific Passion play could not be identified (see Volz, *Die Lutherpredigten des Johannes Mathesius*, p. 324 on *LH* 338.23f.); cf. perhaps *Table Talk* no. 6187 (n.d.), WA TR 5:528, where Luther refers to a miller playing the role of Christ in a Passion play (cited by Wolf, *Die Sprache des Johannes Mathesius*, p. 43 n. 47). The saying ascribed to the "miller" was proverbial: see Wander 4:1139, "That" nos. 42 and 47; Luther, *Lectures on 1 Timothy* (1528/1909), LW 28:293; marginal note on Prov. 27:11, WA DB 10/2:90.

²⁵⁵ A Latin rhyming proverb (the name "Rupert" seems to be significant only for its rhyme with *experto*); cf. Wander 1:838, "Erfahrene" no. 1; and Virgil, *Aeneid* 11.283 (Loeb 64 [1916], pp. 256–57), where the expression appears without "Rupert." See also Luther, preface to Spangenberg, *German Postil* (1543), LW 60:285; Luther to Andreas Ebert, August 5, 1536, On Mathesius' own experience of going astray through involvement in political affairs at the time of the Smalcaldic War, see the introduction above, p. lxxxiv.

THE FOURTEENTH SERMON,[1]
ON THE HISTORY OF THE DOCTOR
FROM 1543 TO 1546

[Early 1564][2]

BELOVED friends in the Lord! It is said among the wise that anyone writing a book should often look back at the title, and anyone preaching should pay careful attention to the appointed text, so that he does not go astray and mix in extraneous matters.[3] Since I have undertaken to speak to you about the doctrine and life of the doctor, we shall carry on with our plan this time as well. As for the secular events[4] that took place in his last years, those we will deal with as miners do and consign them to the deep shaft.[5] Rarely does one accomplish anything beneficial by building upon the quarreling and division of princes. The negotiated agreement of princes[6] has paid many dividends. Here it behooves preachers to pay their assessment faithfully[7] with their Our Father; this pleases God and is a service to Christendom and the holy Gospel. If you wish to know something about the secular affairs of this period, you

---

[1] In the 1566 first edition, fol. 173r, this sermon is numbered again as the thirteenth. Cf. above, Mathesius, *History*, p. 424.

[2] On the dating of this sermon, see the introduction above, pp. lxxxvi–lxxxvii.

[3] Later attestations of such a proverbial saying (in the Latin form *Respice titulum, ne dum scribis, aberres a proposito*) include, e.g., Jean Hardouin and Claude Rigaud, eds., *Acta conciliorum et epistolae decretales, ac constitutiones summorum pontificum* (Paris: Imprimèrie Royale, 1715), p. v; the saying evidently must have been in circulation earlier.

[4] Among the significant secular events of these years not mentioned by Mathesius were the 1543 defeat of Duke William of Jülich-Cleve by the emperor after he had been abandoned by the French king and by the Smalcaldic League (see Walter Stempel, "Jülich-Cleve," *OER* 2:358) and the second defeat of Duke Henry of Braunschweig by the Smalcaldic League in the fall of 1545 (see Brecht 3:321–23 and Luther, *To the Saxon Princes* [1545], LW 43:251–88).

[5] *zum tieffen stollen verschreyben*. See *DWB*, s.v. "Stolle, Stollen" 3.g.

[6] *Fürsten vertrag*; in addition to its literal meaning, this was also the name of mines on the Schneeberg in Saxony (see above, Mathesius, *History*, p. 458) and in Joachimsthal: see Mathesius, *Sarepta*, fol. Oo4v.

[7] Cf. above, Mathesius, *History*, p. 459.

can satisfy your desire with Jovius,[8] Sleidanus,[9] Funck,[10] and others[11] who have diligently compiled the history of this period.

In the name of Jesus Christ we shall briefly and simply keep to the things which our doctor undertook from the year 1543 until his end, and how he completed his course and fell asleep, blessedly, in the Lord at Eisleben and was buried in Wittenberg. May God grant us grace, understanding, and strength to this end! Amen.

[Now, as all kinds of things were happening among friends and foes, some people moved from sharp quills[12] to take up sharp spears;[13] and some irenic princes and lords who had faithfully given their counsel and aid toward reconciliation and unity departed from this world.[14] Meanwhile, our doctor continued with his prayers and his [lectures on] Genesis[15] and counseled for peace as much as he could. He also spoke on behalf of his Lord and Savior Christ with the greatest vigor, defending His honor and name against the brood and spawn of the ancient serpent [Rev. 12:9; 20:2; John 8:44] and exhorting everyone to persevere steadfast in the true faith, with a good conscience and patience.

---

[8] Paulo Giovio [Jovius] from Como (1483–1552), bishop of Nocera, was author of numerous historical and biographical works, including the *Historiarum sui temporis libri XLV* (Paris: Michel de Vascosan, 1554) [USTC 204231] and the *Dialogus de bello Germanico* (Ingolstadt: Alexander Weißenhorn, 1547) [VD16 G2069]. See T. C. Price Zimmermann, *Paolo Giovio: The Historian and the Crisis of Sixteenth-Century Italy* (Princeton: Princeton University Press, 1995).

[9] On Sleidanus, see the introduction above, pp. lxx–lxxi.

[10] On Johann Funck, see the introduction above, p. xlvi and n. 149 there. His major historical work was the *Chronologia: hoc est omnium temporum et annorum ab initio mundi, usque ad hunc praesentem a nato Christo annum M. D. LII. computatio. Item commentariorum libri decem* (Königsberg: Hans Lufft, 1552) [VD16 F3382].

[11] On sixteenth-century histories of the Reformation, see the introduction above, pp. lxii–lxxi; cf. John Tonkin, "Reformation Studies," *OER* 3:398–401. Among the other historians whom Mathesius declines to name, one should probably think of the spiritualist Sebastian Franck (see above, p. 440 n. 100), whose *Chronica/ Zeÿtbůch und geschychtbibel* (Strassburg: Balthasar Beck, 1531) [VD16 F2064–2065] was widely read. On the popularity of historical literature in Joachimsthal, see Brown, *Singing the Gospel*, p. 121.

[12] See above, Mathesius, *History*, pp. 498–99.

[13] See above, Mathesius, *History*, pp. 499.

[14] Duke Henry IV of Saxony (see above, p. 313 n. 185; Mathesius, *History*, p. 421) died on August 18, 1541; George the Pious of Brandenburg-Ansbach (see above, p. 327 n. 42; Mathesius, *History*, pp. 329, 345, 492–93 n. 176) died on December 17, 1543.

[15] See above, Mathesius, *History*, p. 408.

Just as in 1539, at the request and insistence of a count in this land[16] who had sent him some Jewish books, he had published a letter *Against the Sabbatarians*,[17] who were drawing Christians to themselves and circumcising them, so now in 1543 the doctor was moved to write his precious book *On the Jews and Their Lies*.[18] He was not attempting to write a book about the Jews or against the Jews or in order to convert them;[19] rather, he was pleading on behalf of his Lord Christ against the shameful slanderers and thorny thistles, as David, their own king, calls them in his last words [2 Sam. 23:6].[20] He also cleaned away the poison and filth of the Jews and their rabbis from many fine passages in the Old Testament[21] and sought to warn Christians against their gross and shameful lies.

Earlier, in the year 1523, our doctor had also published a precious and thorough book: *That Jesus Christ Was Born a Jew*,[22] which he powerfully demonstrated on the basis of the passages in Genesis 3 [:15] and 22 [:18] and 2 Samuel 7 [:12–14] and Isaiah 7 [:14]. Additionally, in the second part, he instructed Christians about how the Jews are to be converted: namely, by persuading them from the prophecies of Jacob (Genesis 49 [:10]) and of Daniel [Dan. 9:24] that the promised Messiah had been supplied and had come in the flesh long ago. ᴵHe again treated this article very powerfully in his letter *Against the Sabbatarians*, using clear Scripture to refute the delusion and presumption of the Jews who claimed that their civil and ecclesiastical law should and must remain eternally because this had been promised to them for eternity, or *le-olam*,[23] as they interpret the word from Moses [e.g., Exod. 31:17].

So, then, in the year 1543, this book *On the Jews and Their Lies* was published, in which he dissolves and brings to naught the boasting of those

---

[16] I.e., Count Wolfgang Schlick of Falkenau: see above, Mathesius, *History*, p. 209 and n. 51 there.

[17] *Against the Sabbatarians* (1538), LW 47:57–98. The German original of the treatise appeared in March 1538; a Latin translation by Justus Jonas, which Mathesius may have in mind in his dating, appeared the following year, in 1539. See the introduction by Franklin Sherman, LW 47:62–63; Brecht 3:338–39.

[18] *On the Jews and Their Lies* (1543), LW 47:121–306; on the date of the printing, which may have begun in late 1542, see the introduction by Ferdinand Cohrs and Oskar Brenner, WA 53:415.

[19] *On the Jews and Their Lies* (1543), LW 47:137–38. Cf. Brecht 3:341.

[20] Cf. above, Mathesius, *History*, p. 273; *On the Last Words of David* (1543), LW 15:351–52.

[21] See above, Mathesius, *History*, pp. 478–80.

[22] *That Jesus Christ Was Born a Jew* (1523), LW 45:195–229. See Brecht 2:112–15; 3:334, 337.

[23] לְעוֹלָם. See *Against the Sabbatarians* (1538), LW 47:81–83; cf. *On the Jews and Their Lies* (1543), LW 47:206–7.

who proudly claimed that they were Abraham's seed and had received circumcision and the Law from God, who had also delivered the promised land of Canaan to them with great miracles, had given them the kingdom and temple, and had entrusted them with the Scriptures.

These are the articles that the doctor treats in the first part.[24] In the second, he gives solid proofs from Scripture that the Messiah has truly come in the flesh by again interpreting Jacob's prophecy in Genesis 49 [:10], the last words of David in 2 Samuel 23 [:2–7], the passage in Jeremiah 23 [:5], and the text in Haggai 2 [:7]. Finally, he comes to Daniel's seventy weeks in Daniel 9 [:24].[25]

Similarly, in the third part of this book[26] he opposes the abominable blasphemy of the Jews with which they abominably slander the eternal Son of God, our Lord Jesus Christ, and His noble mother, Mary. In the course of this, he provides good counsel and instruction both for the authorities and for Christian preachers about how they should deal with these abominable people who falsify the whole Bible with their lies and moreover know nothing about the true kingdom and people of the eternal Messiah.[27]

Also published this year[28] was the book against the invented *Shem Hamphorash*[29] of the Jews, in which the genealogy of our Lord Jesus Christ [Matt. 1:1–17; Luke 3:23–48] is explained very convincingly. The books by

---

[24] *On the Jews and Their Lies* (1543), LW 47:137–76.

[25] *On the Jews and Their Lies* (1543), LW 47:176–264.

[26] *On the Jews and Their Lies* (1543), LW 47:264–306.

[27] Mathesius does not detail Luther's shocking recommendations for confiscation and destruction of Jewish property and exile of Jews found in the third part of *On the Jews and Their Lies* (LW 47:268–74). He thus participates in a general reluctance on the part of the second generation of Lutherans to repeat Luther's advice or put it into practice: see Johannes Wallmann, "The Reception of Luther's Writings on the Jews from the Reformation to the End of the 19th Century," *LQ* (n.s.) 1, no. 1 (1987): 75–77; Reinhold Lewin, *Luthers Stellung zu den Juden: Ein Beitrag zur Geschichte der Juden in Deutschland während des Reformationszeitalters*, Neue Studien zur Geschichte der Theologie und der Kirche 10 (Berlin: Trowitzsch, 1911; repr., Aalen: Scientia, 1973), pp. 97–99.

[28] I.e., 1543.

[29] *On the Shem Hamphorash and on the Lineage of Christ* (1543), WA 53:579–648 (LW 61). The "Shem Hamphorash" (more accurately transliterated as *Shem ha-mephorash*) was a kabbalistic expansion of the name of God which was supposed to possess miraculous powers, to which the miracles of Jesus were attributed in Jewish polemic, as reported in the treatise of the fourteenth-century Carthusian Salvagus Porchetus (d. ca. 1315), *Victoria Porcheti adversus impios Hebreos* (Paris: Guillaume Desplains, 1520) [USTC 344420]. See *On the Jews and Their Lies* (1543), LW 47:256. On Porchetus' treatise and its context, see Edwards, *Luther's Last Battles*, pp. 132–42.

old Lyra,[30] Burgos,[31] and Margaritha[32]—ᶥand the one by Samuel[33] the good Jew, which Doctor Wenceslaus Linck[34] translated into German—are also good books and should be read diligently. But God granted this man such grace that since the time of the ancient prophets no books of greater power have been written and set forth against the Jews and their rabbis than in our own times.

For his own person, he would gladly have been of service to the Jews,[35] just as in the beginning he allowed some to be baptized and wrote

---

[30] On Nicholas of Lyra, see above, p. 456 n. 203. In addition to his *Postilla*, which drew on rabbinic exegesis of the Hebrew text, Lyra was also author of a polemical treatise, the *Libellus de perfidia Iudaeorum*, which was appended to the *Postilla*.

[31] Salomon Levi of Burgos, known as Paul of Burgos after his conversion from Judaism to Christianity, became a bishop and noted exegete (cf. above, p. 427 n. 18). In addition to his annotations [*Additiones*] to Lyra's *Postilla*, which were printed along with Lyra's text in early modern editions, Paul also wrote the *Scrutinium Scripturarum contra perfidiam Judaeorum*, also known as the *Dialogus Pauli et Sauli* (Strasbourg: Johann Mentelin, 1470) [GW 29971]. For Luther's opinion of Burgos' work, see, e.g., Luther to Johann von Staupitz, May 30, 1518, LW 48:67.

[32] Antonius Margaritha converted from Judaism to Christianity in 1522 and became a teacher of Hebrew, eventually becoming a professor in Vienna. He wrote *Der ganz jüdisch Glaub* (Augsburg: Heinrich Steiner, 1530) [VD16 M972–973], an exposition of the Jewish prayer book and ceremonies as hostile to Christianity. See Maria Diemling, "Anthonius Margaritha on the 'Whole Jewish Faith': A Sixteenth-Century Convert from Judaism and His Depiction of the Jewish Religion," in *Jews, Judaism, and the Reformation in Sixteenth-century Germany*, ed. Dean Phillip Bell and Stephen G. Burnett, Studies in Central European Histories 37 (Leiden: Brill, 2006), pp. 303–33; Peter von der Osten-Sacken, *Martin Luther und die Juden: Neu untersucht anhand von Anton Margarithas "Der gantz Jüdisch glaub" (1530/31)* (Stuttgart: Kohlhammer, 2002), pp. 162–208; and Walton, *Margaritha and the Jewish Faith*. On the use of Lyra, Burgos, and Margaritha by Luther, see *On the Jews and Their Lies* (1543), LW 47:130, 134, 257.

[33] *Das Jhesus Nazarenus der ware Messias dey, derhalben die Juden auff kaynen andern warten dürffen. Rabbi Samuelis*, trans. Wenceslaus Linck (Zwickau: Johann Schönsperger Jr., 1524) [VD16 S1568–1570]. This treatise was printed alongside Luther's works in Witt Ger 5 (1552), fols. 566v–583v. "Rabbi Samuelis" is Samuel de Fez [Marochitanus], an eleventh-century Jewish convert to Christianity under the Almoravid dynasty. On his identity and authorship of this text, which appeared in Latin translation at the beginning of the fourteenth century under the title *Epistola Rabbi Samuelis de Fes quam scripsit ad Rabbi Isaac magistrum Synagogue*, see Claire Soussen, "The Epistle of Rabbi Samuel de Fez: What Kind of a New Strategy against Judaism," in *Jews and Christians in Medieval Europe: The Historiographical Legacy of Bernhard Blumenkranz*, ed. Philippe Buc et al. (Turnhout: Brepols, 2016), pp. 131–46.

[34] On Linck, see above, p. 148 n. 48.

[35] See the beginning of Luther's letter to Josel [Rabbi Joseph Ben Gerson Lorchans] of Rosheim, June 11, 1537, WA Br 8:89–91 (translated in Brooks Schramm and Kirsi Stjerna, eds., *Martin Luther, the Bible, and the Jewish People: A Reader* [Minneapolis: Fortress, 2012], pp. 126–28).

commendations to good friends for some of them.[36] But they did not remain faithful, and some hired themselves out to kill him with poison.

With his knowledge, in 1540 I brought to his table a Jew who had been coming to church in Joachimsthal for some time and was requesting Baptism. "Jew," said Luther, "if you are serious, we will gladly serve you with the ministry of our church. I am favorably disposed toward all the Jews for the sake of one good Jew, who is of your race, yet born of a chaste virgin and *almah*[37] according to the prophecy of Isaiah [Isa. 7:14]. But you rarely keep your color."[38]

Since the Jew spoke very earnestly, he asked for his name and where he was from. The Jew answered, "Michael from Posen."[39] "My Jew," said the doctor, "someone warned me about a Jew of that name, but you look much too honest to be the one." Then the doctor began to tell at table an astonishing story about that Jew,[40] which I will also recount here. Certain bishops from outside the [Holy] Roman Empire secretly took counsel with the Jew Michael from Posen to have him slip our doctor some poison; they promised him a thousand gulden.[41] Although this secret, knavish council consisted of only four people, one of them gave our doctor warning by way of a renowned city,[42] which reported to him the name, appearance, and plan of the Jew. He intended to come to the doctor, to pose as an extraordinary man, skilled in many languages and having much experience, and to eat with him. At table, he would play with a poisoned pomander, let it fall into

---

[36] See, e.g., Luther to the baptized Jew Bernard [Jacob Gipher of Göppingen], June[?] 1523, WA Br 3:101–2 (in Schramm and Stjerna, *Luther, the Bible, and the Jewish People*, pp. 84–86); *Table Talk* no. 299 (1532), WA TR 1:124.

[37] עַלְמָה

[38] I.e., they rarely remain faithful. Cf. Wander 5:1248, "Farbe" no. 38.

[39] Posen [Poznań] is a town in western Poland. On Luther's 1540 interview with Michael, see *Table Talk* no. 5354 (1540), WA TR 5:83, though this source does not mention his connection with Joachimsthal or his disappearance (see below, p. 512). Cf. Brecht 3:339–40.

[40] The 1525 assasination plot against Luther and the letter of warning he received are described in Luther to Nicolaus von Amsdorf, January 23, 1525, WA Br 3:428; to Spalatin, February 11, 1525, WA Br 3:439; *Table Talk* no. 2501a–b (1532), WA TR 2:494–95; no. 2499b and 2501c (n.d.), WA 48:495. There is also a divergent account by the electoral physican Matthäus Ratzeberger (see above, p. 352 n. 170): see Christian Gotthold Neudecker, ed., *Die handschriftliche Geschichte Ratzebergers über Luther und seine Zeit* (Jena: Friedrich Mauke, 1850), pp. 70–72.

[41] According to the *Table Talk*, the promised bounty was 4,000 gulden; according to the 1525 letter to Amsdorf, it was 2,000 gulden. The origins of the plot among bishops is mentioned in *Table Talk* no. 2501c (n.d.), WA 48:495. According to Ratzeberger (*Geschichte*, p. 70), the plot was organized in Cracow.

[42] Breslau [Wrocław], in Silesia: see *Table Talk* no. 2501a–b (1532), WA TR 2:493, 494; and nos. 2499b and 2501c (n.d.), WA 48:495.

his cup, and drink half to the doctor;[43] himself, however, he would protect from the poison by taking good medicine in advance. The doctor was on his guard on account of this warning, and a watchman was also kept in the cloister[44] for some time.

In the meantime, another Jew came, claiming that he wanted to have the Bible published in Wittenberg in several languages. Many parts of the doctor's letter of warning matched this Jew, but the black hair was different; he was supposed to have blond hair. Therefore, this Jew was taken to the barber, and his hair was washed with very strong and caustic lye to see whether he had colored it black with gypsy dye. The master [barber] was so persistent that the Jew became indignant at this. But the color did not wash out, so they left the Jew alone.[45]

After seven or eight years, when they had completely forgotten about this matter and the doctor had lost his letter of warning, the real criminal Jew presented himself with his clever astrology to Master Philip,[46] who invited the doctor to come to his house and listen to this extraordinary man from afar.[47]

At table, the Jew spoke as an erudite adventurer of wide experience; he gave a good report on the Turkish, Indian, Armenian, and many other religions, and then added that, since he had seen so many faiths, he wanted to visit Wittenberg as well. He also presented himself to the doctor and wanted to play chess with him at his house,[48] having diligently learned about everything beforehand in the manner of Herod [cf. Matt. 2:7]. Everyone went home; when the doctor stepped upon the first stair in his house, it occurred to him: "What if this is the Jew about whom I have been warned?" "And

---

[43] Luther would then be expected to drink the other half of the cup, according to custom. See Tlusty, *Bacchus and Civic Order*, p. 126.

[44] I.e., Luther's residence.

[45] The 1525 appearance in Wittenberg of a Jewish traveler (or perhaps more than one), who was arrested on suspicion of attempting to poison Luther but then released, is described in Luther's letters to Amsdorf and Spalatin (see above, p. 510 n. 40). The account of the barber is Mathesius' own.

[46] On Melanchthon's interest in astrology, see *Table Talk* no. 3520 (1537), LW 54:219–20; no. 2834b (1532), LW 54:173. On Melanchthon's appreciation of astrology, see Claudia Brosseder, *Im Bann der Sterne: Caspar Peucer, Philipp Melanchthon und andere Wittenberger Astrologen* (Berlin: Akademie, 2004); Kusukawa, *Transformation of Natural Philosophy*.

[47] On the appearance of a remarkable Jewish traveler in Wittenberg in 1532, see Luther to Amsdorf, before February 9, 1533, WA Br 6:427; *Table Talk* no. 2501c (n.d.), WA 48:495. The visit is described without a clear indication of date in *Table Talk* no. 2499b (n.d.), WA 48:495; and no. 2501a–b (1532), WA TR 2:494–95.

[48] *Table Talk* no. 2501a–b (1532), WA TR 2:494, 495; no. 2499b (n.d.), WA 48:295. For Luther's interest in chess, see below, Mathesius, *History*, pp. 601–2.

I believe," said the doctor, "that my angel[49] reminded me of this. I looked for the letter and never found it, but I recalled many distinguishing marks which matched this Jew."

When the doctor left for Torgau early the next day,[50] he gave orders that no one was to be allowed into his room in his absence. The Jew came the next day but was not let in. Meanwhile, the matter became known, and people started rumoring that the hired Jew and assassin had arrived; the Jew got wind of this and disappeared within a few days.

"This Jew whom I brought to my table," the doctor said to his guest, "had the same name as you and was your fellow countryman, but I hope that you are not of his ilk. You do not look like him either." In sum, the doctor said, he would refer the Jew's case to the [other] scholars. Herr Philip, Doctor Cruciger,[51] and others took up the the the Jew's case, and when they examined him, they asked for a witness. The Jew called upon me. I advised them to bid the Jew to have acquaintances brought from Joachimsthal, where he had resided for quite some time, because I knew nothing more about him; I had seen him while preaching, and a count from elsewhere had given him refuge for a time in the guest room under the staircase.[52]

The Jew was loath to make the trip because of his poverty. I offered to provide him with food for the road, and my students[53] sent him off with letters [of commendation] and fine little books to read on the way, but the rascal did not arrive in Joachimsthal. Master Steude[54] had been going to baptize him, since he was not seeking any money from the sponsors.[55] Later,

---

[49] For Luther's idea of an angel assigned as protector to each Christian, see, e.g., *Small Catechism* (1529) Morning Prayer and Evening Prayer (Kolb-Wengert, pp. 363–64; *Concordia*, p. 344); *Sermon on the Angels* (September 29, 1530), WA 32:116–17 (LW 56).

[50] Assuming that the assassin came to Wittenberg in 1532, seven or eight years after the 1525 letter revealing the plot (see above, p. 510), the trip to Torgau mentioned here may have taken place on August 16, 1532, when Luther and Melanchthon were summoned to Elector John's deathbed at 5 o'clock in the morning: see Buchwald, *Luther-Kalendarium*, p. 89; *LH²*, p. 579.

[51] On Cruciger and Melanchthon, see above, p. xx n. 19 and pp. xxxix–xl.

[52] *ein frembder Graff hatt jhn auff ein zeyt im gasthof die treppen hinein geworffen.* Cf. *DWB*, s.v. "Treppe" B.1.a.

[53] I.e., the candidates for the first degree whom Mathesius served as pedagogue: cf. above, *History*, pp. 298–300 and n. 81 there; Loesche, *Johannes Mathesius*, 1:94.

[54] Sebastian Steude (1486–1566) was a graduate of the university at Leipzig who had first come to Joachimsthal in 1526 but left upon his marriage in 1528 and took up a new pastorate in Magdeburg. He returned to Joachimsthal as senior pastor in 1540, decisively institutionalizing Lutheranism in the town. Mathesius was called back to serve as preacher under him in 1542 and became senior pastor upon Steude's departure for Naumburg in 1545. See Brown, *Singing the Gospel*, pp. 35, 39–40; WA Br 9:500–501.

[55] *Patengelt*; see above, p. 459 n. 225; cf. *Ten Sermons on the Catechism* (1528), LW 51:186.

there was a rumor that he had been tortured to death on the wheel. "Where is your Jew?" the doctor said to me one day. "He really pulled the wool over your eyes."[56] |"The loss of money is less important," I said, "than if he had received Baptism from you by deceit."

"These are wretched and obdurate people," said the doctor. "They act deceitfully before and after Baptism. That is why the last will and testament of the baptized Jew who was provost in Cologne remains in effect.[57] For many years he held Mass, and when asked about his faith and confession he said, 'You will find my testament and confession together in my locked strongbox.' He had placed inside a cat and mouse cast from metal so that they were facing each other with this inscription: 'When this cat the mouse does chew, a baptized Jew shall be a Christian true.'[58]

"Psalm 109[59] bears down on them; and because they slander the blessed blood of Christ, the outcome is their eternal obduracy and damnation. They are ardent and bitter enemies of Christ, and to this day they still speak against the crucified Son of God with insolence, pride, and contempt, as their fathers and forefathers did, and allow themselves to be employed for all kinds of wickedness.

"Once some Jews came to me," the doctor continued. "When I held Holy Scripture up to them they said, 'We will deviate from our rabbis just as little as you do from your popes.' On the contrary," said the doctor, "we let go of everything else and adhere in our religion to the prophets and apostles alone. Then they asked for a letter of dismissal and a letter granting free and safe transit from the border guards and customs officers; I asked these [officials] to allow these wretched people to pass through for the sake of the Lord Jesus Christ. As the Jews went on their way, they found Christ's name in my letter and tore it up, because they refuse to have any part in our Christ."[60]

"Doctor," I responded, "there was a Jew lying deathly ill in an inn near us. When the others told him to greet Abraham, Isaac, and Jacob for them

---

[56] *er hat euch redlich angesetzt*

[57] See *Table Talk* no. 5354 (1540), WA TR 5:83; cf. *Table Talk* no. 7038 (n.d.), WA TR 6:352; Luther to the baptized Jew Bernard [Jacob Gipher of Göppingen], June[?] 1523, WA Br 3:102 (in Schramm and Stjerna, *Luther, the Bible, and the Jewish People*, p. 86).

[58] *Wenn dise katz die mauß frist, so wird ein getauffter Jud ein rechter Christ.* This story was sometimes associated with the papal nuncio Jerome Aleander: see above, p. 162 n. 128.

[59] Cf. *Summaries of the Psalms* (1531/1531–33), WA 38:54 (LW 65).

[60] On this encounter and Luther's letter, see *Table Talk* no. 5026 (1540), WA TR 4:619–20; cf. *Table Talk* no. 4795 (1541), WA TR 4:517–18; no. 3512 (1536), WA TR 3:369–70; *On the Jews and Their Lies* (1543), LW 47:191–92. Luther seems to mention it already in his sermon of November 5, 1526, WA 20:569–70.

but [added:] 'But Christ is no friend of yours,' the dying Jew replied, 'Nor I of Him.'"[61] And so he entered the garden of his Abraham.[62]

Our doctor also very frequently warned us that we should not engage in disputations with them: nothing would be accomplished with them, and it would be tiresome to hear nothing from them but diabolical blasphemy against Christ, as if from people possessed by devils.[63] In his last sermon,[64] which he delivered in Eisleben on the Sunday before he died, he concluded with an earnest admonition: if Jews are not converting to our Messiah, the authorities should not tolerate them in their lands, as public enemies and blasphemers of our Lord and as a general affliction and curse to the land, on account of which towns and villages would finally have to perish and fall to ruin, along with all the Jews.[65]

Now, once the doctor had cleaned away the Jews' lies from these fine texts in the Bible and had exposed their diabolical blasphemy and wickedness, he gave very powerful testimony this year[66] to the three persons of the Holy Trinity and the two natures in the single undivided person of the Lord Christ in the excellent book about the *Last Words of David* (or his "testament"),[67] which [Doctor Luther] wrote with a lofty spirit and in the greatest earnest. He also conducted public disputations on these articles a few times.[68]

When aged people who have been caught in severe and deep trials[69] and have fought hard with the devil write books, these books are powerful[70] and penetrate the heart. This book about our highest article [of faith], which the royal poet David wrote in his old age and which our doctor expounded a

---

[61] *Christus ist aber dir gram: Wider gram, sagt der sterbende Jude.* See *DWB*, s.v. "gram" B.4.b; cf. *Lectures on Titus* (1527/1902), LW 29:78 (WA 25:61.17).

[62] A Jewish expression for heaven: see, e.g., *Testament of Abraham* 20.14 (ANF 9:201).

[63] See, e.g., *On the Jews and Their Lies* (1543), LW 47:148–49.

[64] Although the *Admonition* was printed at the end of the group of Luther's final four sermons in Eisleben, it was likely delivered in connection with the next-to-last sermon, on February 7, rather than after the last sermon, on February 15, 1546. See the introduction by Christopher Boyd Brown, LW 58:402–4.

[65] *Admonition against the Jews* (1546), LW 58:458–59. Cf. below, p. 533.

[66] I.e., 1543.

[67] *On the Last Words of David* (1543), LW 15:265–352.

[68] See *Disputation concerning John 1:14* (1539), LW 38:235–77; *Disputation on the Divinity and Humanity of Christ* (1540), WA 39/2:93–121 (LW 73); *Doctoral Disputation of Erasmus Alberus, On the Unity of the Divine Essence* (1543), WA 39/2:253–56 (LW 73); *Doctoral Disputation of Peter Hegemon: On Original Sin and the Distinction of Persons in the Trinity* (1545), WA 39/2:339–401 (LW 73).

[69] *anfechtungen*

[70] *haben hend und füsse*; literally, "have hands and feet": see Wander 2:316, "Hand" no. 548.

short time before his own end, which Doctor Cruciger translated into Latin on his sickbed,[71] I recommend to young and old people alike, to be read attentively. In this way, each one may be confirmed in his true Christian faith, |be strengthened as King David was, and be warned against the claims of the heathen, rabbis, Turks, Servetans,[72] and all heretics.

Throughout this year, our doctor also continued his [lectures on the] first Book of Moses.[73] After the dreadful demise of Zwingli and Oecolampadius,[74] the Sacramentarians[75] began dressing up the views of their teachers, like the man who bought up the privy in which Arius died a putrid death, expelling his own lungs and liver, and had a beautiful building erected there.[76] They were, moreover, publishing pernicious books of every sort, which not only denegrated Christ's Supper but even weakened and undermined the whole of Christianity by beatifying honorable heathen.[77] Accordingly, in 1544 the

---

[71] Cruciger died on November 16, 1548, after a three-month illness, having completed his translation of *On the Last Words of David* the day before. See Melanchthon's preface, CR 7:581–85. Cruciger's translation appeared as *De Novissimis Verbis Davidis Commentatio* (Leipzig: Valentin Bapst, 1550) [VD16 L7166] and in Witt Lat 3 (1549), fols. 91v–131r.

[72] I.e., deniers of the Trinity, named after Michael Servetus: see above, p. 388 n. 102.

[73] On the *Lectures on Genesis*, see above, Mathesius, *History*, p. 408. In 1543, Luther would have progressed roughly from chapter 35 to chapter 37 (see the introduction by Jaroslav Pelikan, LW 6:ix–xi).

[74] See above, Mathesius, *History*, p. 314 and nn. 193–94 there.

[75] In the wake of the Wittenberg Concord of 1536 (see above, Mathesius, *History*, pp. 354–55), there had been some hope of reaching a common consensus on the Lord's Supper with the Swiss, even with Zwingli's successor in the Zurich church, Heinrich Bullinger (1504–75; J. Wayne Baker, "Bullinger, Heinrich," *OER* 2:227–30). Yet the ongoing publications of each side widened the gap, and Luther became alarmed at the spread of Sacramentarian ideas in Hungary and Italy. See Luther to Bullinger, May 14, 1538, WA Br 8:223–24; Zürich clergy to Luther, August 30, 1539, WA Br 8:546–47; Luther to Christoph Froschauer, August 31, 1543, WA Br 10:384–87; to the clergy of Eperjes [Prešov], April 21, 1544, WA Br 10:555–56; to Balthasar Alteri, November 12, 1544, WA Br 10:680–82. For discussion of the circumstances surrounding Luther's *Brief Confession* (1544), see the introduction by Martin E. Lehmann, LW 38:281–85; Edwards, *Luther and the False Brethren*, pp. 183–96.

[76] See Sozomen, *Historia Ecclesiastica* 2.30 (PG 67:1023–24; NPNF² 2:279–80); cf. Rufinus, *Historia Ecclesiastica* 10.13 (PL 21:486); Cassiodorus, *Historia Tripartita* 3.10 (PL 69:954–55); cf. Luther, *Church Postil* (1540–44), another sermon for Trinity Sunday, LW 78:29, paragraph 28.

[77] Zwingli's *Exposition of the Christian Faith* [*Christianae Fidei Expositio*] (CR 93.5:50–163; LCC 24:239–81), written in 1531 before Zwingli's death, was edited for posthumous publication in 1536 by his successor Heinrich Bullinger. The passage in which "Hercules . . . Theseus, Socrates, Aristides, Antigonus, Numa, Camillus, the Catos and Scipios" are listed among the blessed is LCC 24:275. For Luther's response, see *Brief Confession* (1544), LW 38:290–91. Mathesius likely also has in mind the whole project to produce a Zurich edition of Zwingli's collected works in 1544–45, which Martin Bucer and others feared would be a cause of offense

doctor wrote his *Brief Confession* concerning the Supper,[78] in which he once again openly confessed his faith and ardently attacked seven-cleft and discordant Sacramentarianism,[79] as he expressed himself in a letter soon afterward in these words:[80]

"Even if I were to live another hundred years and were able to refute all the sects that are to come, I can see that this would provide our posterity with but little rest, so long as the devil lives and rules. Therefore, I pray for a blessed end and have no desire for this life any longer."[81] After Arius died, too, people wanted to gloss over, reinterpret, and come to terms with his cause; but wicked causes, particularly in religion, only become worse. *Causa patrocinio non bona peior erit* ["A bad cause will be made worse by its patronage"][82]—as Hosius[83] and others who have yielded and recanted in religious matters powerfully help us to demonstrate. The people are pregnant with Nestorianism and Eutychianism.[84] I have done my part and leave my testimony and confession behind. May God preserve the simple with the straightforward Word, which alone strengthens the guileless, assures them, and gives them hope and life, ¹and may He protect our posterity from the vacuous glosses and theology of these Swiss babblers![85]

---

to Luther: see Reinhard Bodenmann, ed., in *Heinrich Bullinger Werke: Briefwechsel* (Zurich: Theologischer Verlag, 2011), 14:23–24.

[78] *Brief Confession* (1544), LW 38:279–319.

[79] See above, Mathesius, *History*, p. 261.

[80] The "letter" is presumably the preface to Witt Ger 2 (1548): "Dr. Martin Luther's Preface, Composed before His Passing" (WA 54:468–77), which was actually the work of Georg Rörer (see above, p. xxvi n. 45). The portion quoted here is found on LW 47:117 and WA 54:469.

[81] The direct quotation from Luther ends here (though the original German printing uses no quotation marks). The remainder of the paragraph must be regarded as Mathesius' own confession, his memory of an oral statement by Luther, or his loose paraphrase of sentiments to be found elsewhere in Luther's writings, placed in Luther's mouth.

[82] Cf. Ovid. *Tristia* 1.1.26 (Loeb 151 [1924], pp. 4–5).

[83] Hosius, bishop of Cordova (ca. 257–ca. 357), was one of Constantine's theological advisers and a staunch defender of the Nicene Creed through most of his life. In extreme old age, however, he succumbed to pressure to subscribe the creed of the semi-Arian Third Council of Sirmium (AD 357). See *ODCC*, 3rd ed., s.v. "Hosius, or Ossius."

[84] Nestorius (ca. 381–451) separated the divine and human natures of Christ (*ODCC*, 3rd ed., s.v. "Nestorianism"); Eutyches (ca. 378–after 454) confused the divine and human into a single nature (*ODCC*, 3rd ed., s.v. "Eutyches"). Luther connected the Sacramentarians with Nestorius and Caspar von Schwenkfeld with Eutyches. Cf. *Brief Confession* (1544), LW 38:307.

[85] *kauderwelschen oder Churwallen*. "Kauderwelsch" denoted foreign-sounding nonsense language in general, but with a specific allusion to the Romance [*Welsch*] languages of Italian and French—perhaps in this context a veiled allusion to John Calvin's French version of Reformed theology. In Chur, the distinctive Alemannic dialect of Swiss German [*Walserdeutsch* or *Walliserdeutsch*] prevailed—perhaps an allusion to Zwingli's own Swiss

Having thus taken his leave of the Turks, Jews, and Enthusiasts in his old age; having steadfastly confessed his faith in the Lord Jesus Christ; having boldly defended, lauded, and magnified his Lord, in whose name he was baptized and to whom he swore a solemn oath in this blessed covenant and afterward in his doctorate[86]—now, in the year 1545, he wanted to take leave of his and his Lord Jesus' chief adversaries as well and to make a book and an assortment of images as a valediction for the Roman pope. He is supposed to have said, "Trusting in the name and Word of Jesus Christ, I began contending with the pope and battled against his abominations and idolatrous lies; with him I want to bring things to a conclusion as well."[87] Accordingly, in 1545 he published the powerful and serious book *Against the Papacy, an Institution of the Devil, Promoted and Confirmed with Deceitful Signs*;[88] in the same year he also had many scathing images drawn in which he depicted the nature and abominations of the Antichrist for illiterate laity,[89] just as the Holy Spirit portrayed the red whore[90] of Babylon in the Revelation of John and as Master John Hus conveyed his case in images in which he set forth the Lord Christ and the Antichrist to all people.[91]

This is a harsh, scathing book, full of fiery words, in which he speaks about the abominations of the Antichrist, who has not only trampled on the majestic crown and neck of good emperors[92] but has even subjugated the Church of God to himself and robbed Christ of His honor, scepter, and priesthood, sprinkled himself with God's holy, precious blood, and beguiled and deceived the whole world [cf. 2 Thess. 2:10–11].

---

dialect, which Luther sometimes mocked: see, e.g., sermon for January 18, 1545, LW 58:218 and n. 10 there.

[86] See above, Mathesius, *History*, p. 129.

[87] Cf. above, Mathesius, *History*, p. 134. Mathesius seems to be the source for this declaration by Luther.

[88] *Against the Roman Papacy* (1545), LW 41:257–376; see Brecht 3:359.

[89] *Abbildung des Papsttums* (1545), WA 54:348–73. This work consisted of eight satirical (and often scatalogical) woodcuts on the papacy, designed by Luther and produced by Lucas Cranach. On these two works, see Edwards, *Luther's Last Battles*, pp. 185–200.

[90] *braut*; see above, p. 236 n. 25.

[91] The early Hussite Nicholas of Dresden (ca. 1380–ca. 1417) assembled a set of images contrasting the purity of the early church with the corruption of the present-day church under the papacy, the *Tabulae veteris et novi coloris*, also known as the *Cortina de Antichristo* or *Conversacio Christi opposita conversacioni Antichristi*; the work was sometimes ascribed to Hus himself. See Haberkern, *Patron Saint and Prophet*, pp. 56–58.

[92] See *Against the Roman Papacy* (1545), LW 41:297; preface to Barnes, *How Popes Adrian IV and Alexander III Showed Good Faith to Emperor Barbarossa* (1545), LW 60:349.

If you believe in accordance with Scripture that our God willed to use the mouth of His Spirit [cf. 2 Thess. 2:8][93] to bring this Antichrist and child of sin [cf. 2 Thess. 2:3] and incarnate devil into opprobrium and to slay him with His Word, then you will form an opinion that differs from that of the godless world. The Holy Spirit, too, can mock and be scathing. Adam brought himself into derision in Paradise after his reconciliation with the Spirit whom he had received: "This is is the tender man who became equal and truly like to God and His Son by biting into the apple!"—as the serpent's words are repeated here [Gen. 3:22; cf. Gen. 3:5].[94] Nor were all the words of mockery written down that Elijah used to chide and rebuke the idol of the worshipers of Baal and to command them to be slaughtered at the brook Kishon, out of his godly zeal [1 Kings 18:27, 40].

Elijah's mockery is prominent in the doctor's book as well, [written in these days] before the Antichrist is slaughtered and cast into the eternal and infernal lake of fire [Rev. 19:20]. God willing, the Lord will not be long in coming, and the whole world, which defends and protects its idol, shall experience it. But because this is a spiritual matter and belongs in front of a spiritual and impartial consistory or council, and we on earth are biased—some standing with the Antichrist and some with the Lord Jesus Christ—and no one can be his own judge,[95] we will look forward to the great Day of Judgment of the just Judge of all flesh and of all religions and will postpone the case until His coming. Then we shall learn whether injustice has been done to the Antichrist or to Doctor Luther, whether too much or too little was done to him, and whether cloistered monastic holiness and worldly favor have accomplished more than Luther's sharp quill.[96]

The world is wicked and corrupt; therefore, it only speaks favorably, according to its own notion, about wicked doings. God is jealous [Exod. 34:14] and a burning fire, and those who are kindled by His Spirit and driven to do spiritual battle against the enemies of God speak as enemies against the adversaries of their Lord and Savior. King David also sings this way in his Psalm 119: *Iniquos odio habui*, "I am hostile to the flighty spirits

---

[93] See above, p. 147 n. 44.

[94] See *Lectures on Genesis* (1535–45/1544–54), LW 1:222.

[95] A legal maxim found in the *Codex Iustinianus* 3.5.1: see Bruce W. Frier, gen. ed., *The Codex of Justinian: A New Annotated Translation, with Parallel Latin and Greek Text*, trans. Fred H. Blume (Cambridge: Cambridge University Press, 2016), 1:630–31; cf. Wander 3:1675, "Richter" nos. 80–83.

[96] Cf. above, Mathesius, *History*, p. 317.

and godless,[97] and I hate them vehemently," etc., *perfecto odio* ["with perfect hatred"] [Ps. 139:22], and wholeheartedly.

In and of itself the book is true and good, as a great ruler is supposed to have said when it was brought to him under his tablecloth on one occasion.[98] For nothing good and nothing untrue can be said of this supreme wickedness. If prudent secular people take offense at these harsh words, spoken in the spirit of Elijah, we must let that happen. We see that Christ's kingdom, name, and honor, His priesthood and sacrifice, His Church and Bride are praised in this book; this Lord will know how to excuse His servant at the proper time, for it is He who roused such fiery and burning zeal in His chosen instrument [cf. Acts 9:15] and used it for the benefit of His Church.

I hope the world will once again realize and confess this—if not sooner, then at least when it must take its place before the Lord Christ: whether God has been better served with papal hypocrisy or with the ardent zeal of Christ's servants. Let that suffice concerning this last book and testament of Doctor Luther against the papacy and its founder.[99]

This year[100] I visited Doctor Luther for the last time and brought along for him the song[101] in which our children drive out the Antichrist on *Laetare* Sunday,[102] as people used to drive out death[103] and as the ancient Romans

---

[97] Luther's translation of Ps. 119:113 refers to the "*Fladdergeister*" or "flighty spirits"; his marginal note reads: "'Flighty spirits' here refers to the inconstant spirits who are always finding and undertaking something new, as heretics customarily do": WA DB 10/1:515.

[98] For the positive reactions of Landgrave Philip of Hesse, Elector John Frederick of Saxony, and even King Ferdinand (who is most likely in view here) to Luther's *Against the Roman Papacy*, see Edwards, *Luther's Last Battles*, pp. 199–200.

[99] I.e., the devil, as the title of Luther's book suggests.

[100] I.e., 1545.

[101] On the song *Nun treiben wir den Papst hinaus*, apparently written by Mathesius with music (in four parts) composed or arranged by the Joachimsthal cantor Nicolaus Herman (see the introduction above, p. lxxxii), see Brown, *Singing the Gospel*, pp. 73–75 (with English translation) and pp. 239–40; Oettinger, *Music as Propaganda*, pp. 192–201. For the German text, see Wackernagel 3:30, no. 52; WA 35:569–70. The song was sometimes later ascribed to Luther, but Mathesius' account makes clear that it originated in Joachimsthal.

[102] *zu Mitterfasten*

[103] The medieval custom of driving out death on *Laetare* Sunday, in the form of a figure made by the children from straw and rags which was carried out of the town and thrown into the water, is described in Johannes Boemus (ca. 1485–1535), *Omnium gentium mores, leges et ritus* (Augsburg: Sigisimund Grimm, 1520) [VD16 B6316], fol. 59r; and in Paul Christian Hilscher, *De ritu dominica Laetare, quem vulgo apellant, den Tod austreiben* (Leipzig: Christoph Gunther, 1690) [VD17 12:138208A]. Cf. Steven E. Ozment, *Ancestors: The Loving Family in Old Europe* (Cambridge, MA: Harvard University Press, 2001), p. 72.

did with the images and Argei,[104] which they, too, threw into the water. He had this song printed and himself composed the caption: *Ex montibus & vallibus, ex sylvis & campestribus* ["From mountains and valleys, from forests and fields"].[105]

At that time, many stories were told at table about the Roman bishop and his clergy. [Luther] said, "Some good people have recognized the pope for what he is for a long time, even great lords," he said. "But as long as he was ascendant, no one could bring him down. The king of France would have liked to be rid of him, on account of Naples;[106] he sought counsel from all the universities in Christendom to see whether it was possible for a ruler to make war against the pope in genuinely secular affairs without any burden of conscience. But then the whole world abandoned him. This king could have used a Luther, or I could have used such a king," he said. "But the pope is to fall and die by the mouth of God's Spirit [cf. 2 Thess. 2:8], without any stroke of the sword, and Christ shall obtain His knighthood by eliminating the abominable and false prophets. Therefore, secular might had to keep still here."[107]

And—not to speak of St. Bernard,[108] Hus,[109] Gerson,[110] Savonarola,[111] Wesel,[112] Proles,[113] Dr. Summenhart,[114] and other good people who had little

---

[104] The Argei ["puppets"] were images in human form made of reeds which were placed in shrines around Rome in mid-March and then in May were thrown into the Tiber: see Ovid, *Fasti* 3.791f.; 5.621–62 (Loeb 253 [1931], pp. 178–79, 307–9, and the discussion, pp. 425–29) and *OCD*, 3rd ed., s.v. "Argei."

[105] *Ein lied fur die Kinder damit sie zu Mitterfasten den Babst außtreiben* (Wittenberg: n.n., 1545) [USTC 553911]. The broadsheet printing of the song is reproduced in R. W. Brednich, *Die Liedpublizistik im Flugblatt des 15. bis 17. Jahrhunderts*, 2 vols. (Baden-Baden: Koerner, 1974–75), vol. 2, plate 30.

[106] The kingdom of Naples had, since the end of the thirteenth century, been contested between France and Spain (Aragon), with the popes usually supporting the Spanish claim in order to avoid being encircled by French power. The French kings Charles VIII (r. 1483–98) and Louis XII (r. 1498–1515) had made war against papal armies and alliances; Luther is here referring to the campaigns of Louis XII against Pope Julius II from 1498 to 1504: see Michael Edward Mallet and Christine Shaw, *The Italian Wars 1494–1559: War, State and Society in Early Modern Europe* (New York: Pearson, 2012).

[107] Mathesius' account closely follows *Table Talk* no. 2733a (1532), WA TR 2:621; see also *Table Talk* no. 5079 (1540), WA TR 4:646; cf. above, Mathesius, *History*, p. 153.

[108] Bernard of Clairvaux, see above, p. lvi n. 191; Melanchthon, *Preface*, p. 61.

[109] John Hus: see the introduction above, pp. xxxvii–xxxviii and no. 103 there; Mathesius, *History*, p. 121.

[110] Jean Gerson: see above, p. 63 n. 49.

[111] Girolamo Savonarola: see above, pp. 114–15 n. 4.

[112] Johann Ruch[e]rath of Wesel, see above, p. 457 n. 211.

[113] Andreas Proles: see above, p. 457 n. 209.

[114] Konrad Summenhart [here: Summerhard]: see above, pp. 446–47 n. 143.

regard for the pope—I must recount a story I once heard in the [Black] Cloister[115] about how even the devil himself, the creator of this three-tiered crown,[116] mocked and ridiculed the pope's clergy.

One time, when many consecrated clerics were making their way to a possessed person in a grand procession with banners, candles, chanting, censers, their litany, and their *ora pro nobis*[117] to drive out the evil spirit, the devil loudly sang from the maniac: "*O popule meus, quid feci tibi?*" ["O my people, what have I done to you?"] [Mic. 6:3].[118] That is: "Are not all of you my comrades and my obedient people, whom I nourish and provide for? What do you have against me that you want to drive me out and harass me with your noise?" In sum of all, Luther's book and woodcuts[119] remain true, and (as the old miner said to the indulgence peddler on the Schneeberg)[120] the pope must be an evil and merciless man, who allows a poor soul to be tortured and tormented in purgatory so long for the sake of a penny.

This was the last time I saw and heard Doctor Martin; therefore, I gladly call to mind his last words to me.[121] On April 24, when he gave me a letter of consolation to Master Caspar Heidenreich,[122] whose little son died in Freiberg while he was away, I gave him my farewell blessing[123] and said, "Doctor, just one more word! Christ says 'which is given for you' [Luke 22:19]. Does this refer to the sacrifice on the cross or to the distribution of the true body of Christ in the Supper?" "*Utrumque!* ['Both!']" he said.[124] Then I saw him for the last time on this earth. God willing, I shall see him again with joy at the side of our Lord Christ and will be his table companion forever.

---

[115] Since Mathesius was never a monk himself, "cloister" here presumably refers to Luther's home (as above, Mathesius, *History*, p. 475).

[116] On the papal tiara, see above, p. 133 n. 107.

[117] On the litany, see Luther, *German Litany and Latin Litany Corrected* (1529), LW 53:153–70. In its late medieval form, which Luther adapted, it consisted chiefly of a long series of invocations of saints, to each of which the response was *ora pro nobis* ["pray for us"].

[118] This verse was also part of a liturgical chant, the so-called *Improperia* or "Reproaches" used in the Good Friday liturgy: see *ODCC*, 3rd ed., s.v. "Reproaches"; *Lutheran Service Book: Altar Book* (St. Louis: Concordia, 2006), p. 518.

[119] *gemelde*; literally, "painting[s]."

[120] See below, Mathesius, *History*, pp. 608–9.

[121] For the correct text as translated here, see *LH²*, p. 617 and the corrigenda on p. 619.

[122] Luther to Caspar Heidenreich [Heidrich], April 24, 1545, WA Br 11:76. On Heidenreich, see above, p. 425 n. 7; Mathesius, *History*, p. 488.

[123] *ich jhn gesegent*

[124] Mathesius is, of course, the source for this anecdote.

Now as the doctor faded and became weaker day by day, as the aged Abraham did [Gen. 25:8], having grown weary from his Moses,[125] the devil kept stirring up one offense after another in his parish. For (among other things) foul and filthy whores came in and infected many young students,[126] which pained our elder[127] [cf. 2 John 1] greatly, because his soul, like that of Lot in Sodom [2 Pet. 2:7] and that of the aged Polycarp,[128] was suffering torment every day. He preached and wrote against it[129] and was even so greatly troubled at it that he sought to abandon Wittenberg this year[130] and stayed for a time with the prince of Anhalt[131] in Merseburg.[132] But the university urged him to come back through honorable messengers, so he allowed himself to be persuaded,[133] just as in 1529 when he vowed that he would never enter the pulpit again.[134]

Dear old age is attended with weakness and fragility—young people should learn to take that in good part and learn to fear the sighs and tears of their elders. After returning home, he completed his [lectures on] Genesis on November 17, having labored with utmost diligence on them for ten years.[135] He publicly concluded his lectures of his with very affecting words. "Here now you have the dear[136] Genesis," he said in the lecture hall. "May our Lord God grant that others will do better after me. I can do no more. I am weak. *Orate Deum pro me* ['Pray to God for me'], that He would grant me a good and blessed final hour."[137] It is as he said when he began this

---

[125] I.e., from his *Lectures on Genesis* (1535–45/1544–54): see LW 8:333 and in the following paragraph.

[126] See Brecht 3:255–56.

[127] *senior*

[128] On Polycarp of Smyrna, see above, p. 41 n. 12; Mathesius, *History*, p. 418.

[129] See *Warning against Prostitutes* (May 13, 1543), WA 49:278–79 (*LSC*, pp. 292–94); sermon for June 7, 1545, LW 58:233–41. Cf. above, Mathesius, *History*, p. 418.

[130] See Brecht 3:262–63; the introduction by Christopher Boyd Brown, LW 58:233; Luther to Katharina Luther, July 28, 1545, LW 50:273–81, and Gottfried Krodel's introduction there. Luther left Wittenberg on July 25 and did not return until August 17.

[131] I.e., Prince George of Anhalt: see above, p. 30 n. 16. Luther consecrated him as bishop of Merseburg on August 2, 1545: see Brecht 3:307–8.

[132] Luther also preached in Merseburg on June 6, 1545, at the wedding of Sigismund of Lindenau (LW 51:355–67), and again, after a day in Halle (see *Sermon on John 5:39–43*, LW 58:242–58), on August 6 (*On Christ's Kingdom*, WA 51:11–22 [LW 66]).

[133] See Brecht 3:262–64.

[134] See above, Mathesius, *History*, p. 315.

[135] Cf. above, Mathesius, *History*, p. 408. See Brecht 3:136–40.

[136] Or, perhaps, "the book of" (*liber* for *lieber*): see WA 44:825 and n. 1; LW 8:333 n. 9.

[137] *Lectures on Genesis* (1535–45/1544–54), LW 8:333.

book: "This will be my final work; with this, God willing, my life will end."[138] The final thoughts are no doubt the best,[139] particularly if are they directed toward and spring from God's Word, and so the preaching and books of the aged are certainly to be noted and preserved.

In this book, our doctor manifested himself and spoke as a prophet of God, a servant of Jesus Christ, and a teacher and expositor of Holy Scripture, from which he brought forth for us much salutary instruction for patience, consolation, and steadfast hope, as a wise and experienced *pater lector*.[140] Many [lecturers] have surely written an *Iliad* after Homer[141] and slipped their fables from other places into this land, but not all have been welcome. Among you, my parishioners and students, I bear witness, in truth: In all my days, in which I have studied to understand the Scriptures of the prophets and apostles and to receive blessed and living consolation and strong hope amid grief and hardship, I have read through a considerable number of books, and no exposition more beautiful and comforting has ever come before my eyes in this world. The good books of other people also explain texts, outline the articles of our faith correctly and clearly, and refute the objections and arguments of the opponents with astuteness and skill. Our doctor bears witness to this with respect to Herr Philip and Brenz in particular.[142]

Yet whoever is desirous of seeing Christ in Genesis and of receiving instruction about the power of the living Word of God, about what sin is and what is the righteousness that alone avails and stands before God; whoever would learn how to hope confidently and to abide with our God, as well as how to be refreshed amid fear and extremity ˡand to discern how to make salutary use of the faults and faith of the great saints, or what things a teacher above all ought to focus on and pay heed to in Scripture, and how he can present and properly apply things old and things new [cf. Matt. 13:52] to his listeners as occasion arises, and would teach [them] to make proper and salutary use of them—then let him read this book, especially if he is caught under a holy cross and supposes that God is not home[143] and has utterly forgotten us! He will discover in fact and in experience what

---

[138] Preface to *Lectures on Genesis* (1543), WA 42:1 (LW 62). Cf. *Commentary on Psalm 90* (1534–35/1541), LW 13:75

[139] Wander 1:1400, "Gedanken" no. 26.

[140] Literally: "father reader," i.e., an ordained lecturer. Cf. below, Mathesius, *History*, pp. 542, 582.

[141] *Iliada post Homerum*; see Wander 2:1476, "kommen" no. 258; Theodor and Barbara Mahlmann, "*Iliada post Homerum scribere*: Prüfstein frühneuzeitlicher Autorschaft," in *Realität als Herausforderung*, ed. Ralf Bogner et al. (Berlin: de Gruyter, 2011), pp. 47–91.

[142] See above, Mathesius, *History*, p. 315.

[143] Wander 5:1109, "Daheim" no. 42.

our aged doctor has brought together in this book in his last days while he endured manifold trials.

I am herewith leaving behind my testimony about this blessed commentary so that my children and parishioners will not forget it and will learn to hold it in high regard throughout their lives—as should all those who desire to provide other people with salutary instruction about useful and necessary matters pertaining to the Church. My own [copy of the *Lectures on*] *Genesis*[144] will bear witness and attest this for me, especially the last parts, which I frequently perused and where I underlined and made notes for the sake of learning, teaching, and consoling.

Give heed to this exposition: it explained to me Christ's Word and will, and from it God breathed comfort, rest, and life into my wounded and troubled heart. For when our own cases coincide with the crosses of the patriarchs, and when the exposition penetrates to the heart, as if the doctor were personally speaking with us, the commentary lives and breathes,[145] and it refreshes and revives a person's heart.

I will mention just one little sentence, to the honor of God's Word and of this exposition and as an exhortation for you to treasure this book all the more. When our doctor describes the troubled heart and severe tribulation[146] of Jacob and Joseph in chapter 37, he concludes with these salutary and comforting words:[147] "Although Jacob intends to exhaust his heart in grief when robbed of his dearest son, and Joseph is betrayed and sold by his own brothers, and both think that God has forgotten them, nevertheless this is what God's disposition toward them was:

"'My Jacob, My Joseph'" ("My Mathesius," I add to these!), "I surely see what is oppressing and grieving you; I am not sleeping, but at the present time I do not will to remove from you what is burdening and distressing you or to console your heart. The time when I will rescue you is not yet at hand. You must first experience and learn who the devil, the world, your children, your brothers and friends, and death are, so that My grace may become all the sweeter to you and so that you may realize that I have compassionately provided for you amid your fear and pangs of death. For not a single little hair shall fall from your head without My knowledge and consent [cf. Matt. 10:30; Luke 12:7]. Take heart and be bold and endure and learn to accept and bear your cross with patience. I am faithful and will certainly keep [My promise]. I have promised to bless you and to deliver you; it will happen at the proper time. I will not and cannot be a liar to you

---

[144] Mathesius' own annotated copy of the *Lectures on Genesis* is apparently lost.

[145] *liebt* [= *leibt*] *und lebt*

[146] *anfechtung*

[147] *Lectures on Genesis* (1535–45/1544–54), LW 6:405–7, freely paraphrased.

[cf. Rom. 3:4]. Flesh and blood are impatient and grumble; but strive and fight against this, and rule over it in faith and the firm hope that your help is certain and determined and will be brought to pass at the proper time.'"

There are many other similar words of comfort in these last parts. For this, eternal praise and thanks to our God, who had this book put into writing for us by Moses as light, life, and consolation and had it translated and interpreted by Doctor Luther;[148] written down by Doctor Cruciger, Master Rörer, and Master Veit [Dietrich];[149] and prepared for publication by other good people.[150] Likewise, for the sake of my parishioners, I say thank you to those who had it translated into German and printed.[151] May God reward them all for their blessed effort and diligence and grant that their heirs may also draw comfort and patience from this book amid hardships.

|Ah, what a treasure it is, which cannot be paid for with all the world's possessions and rewards, to make a good book from which simple preachers can learn how they ought to teach correctly and comfortingly. There are indeed many authors of books, about which the wise King Solomon complained already in his days, but not all are spears and nails [Eccl. 12:11–12] that penetrate into the heart and leave comfort. The majority of authors either abandon the text or obscure it with unnecessary and excessive words, extraneous matters and questions, and refutations. Many do no more than to glorify themselves, slander, disparage, and judge other books, or heap together what other people's thoughts have been; they slip in and mix their own dreams and heresies into their commentaries; they do not address the

---

[148] Cf. above, Mathesius, *History*, p. 408.

[149] The notes on the lectures on Genesis by Georg Rörer and Caspar Cruciger (mentioned by Luther in his preface, WA 42:1 [LW 62]) do not survive; those of Veit Dietrich survive in part: see the introduction by Gustav Koffmane, WA 42:ix.

[150] *Lectures on Genesis* appeared in four volumes between 1544 and 1554, from presses in Wittenberg and Nürnberg. The first two volumes (Genesis 1–24) were edited by Veit Dietrich, using his own notes as well as the material from Rörer and Cruciger; after Dietrich's death in 1549, the Nürnberg Latin schoolteacher Michael Roting (1494–1588) and Luther's former student Jerome Besold (see above, p. 425 n. 8) completed the remaining work (Genesis 25–50), using in addition to Dietrich's notebooks notes by Besold and by Johann Stolz (ca. 1514–56) as well (see the introduction by Christopher Boyd Brown, LW 58:xxiv–xxv). See the introduction by Gustav Koffmane, WA 42:ix–x; the introduction by Otto Reichert, WA 44:xi–xiii; Brecht 3:136. On the controversy over the editorial work on the Genesis lectures, see Mickey Leland Mattox, *"Defender of the Most Holy Matriarchs": Martin Luther's Interpretation of the Women of Genesis in the Enarrationes in Genesis, 1535–1545* (Leiden: Brill, 2003), pp. 264–73.

[151] German translations of the exposition of chapter 25 and chapter 15 from the *Lectures on Genesis* appeared in 1551 and 1552, translated by the preachers Stephan Agricola of Mansfeld (ca. 1526–62) and Anton Otto (1505–65) of Nordhausen respectively; in 1558, a complete German translation of the lectures by the Nordhausen school rector Basilius Faber (ca. 1520–76) and Johannes Gudenus (d. 1566) appeared in Witt Ger 10–11. See the introduction by Gustav Koffmane, WA 42:xviii.

text to their present listeners, neither do they teach how to use it when in the pangs of death. Therefore, it is and remains true that, as many doctors have killed an emperor,[152] so also wretched or arrogant books do nothing but to darken and obscure the blessed and certain text and hinder people from arriving at the proper understanding.

The devil is very busy working to wrest the Bible and useful, good books from people's hands, for his domain[153] and desire are to tear the Word of God out of our hearts or to obscure and corrupt it with strange thoughts, dangerous interpretations, and useless matters. Therefore, it is pointless to give good advice to someone who will not listen to it.[154]

Now, once our exhausted and ill doctor had completed his Moses,[155] he never again lectured publicly;[156] sometimes he did preach. Moreover, his thoughts were occupied with death and the future life.[157] He liked to speak and hear about the hour of death and about those who fell asleep gently and blessedly in the true confession and invocation of the eternal Mediator. To be sure, from the time that he received his doctorate, his thoughts had likewise been continuously occupied with death,[158] and he had prayed for a blessed end and had sung his *In pace in id ipsum dormiam et requiescam* ["In peace, at the same time I shall sleep and rest"] [Ps. 4:8][159] long before.

Good people have recorded many fine sayings from which you can see how he sincerely longed for a blessed end and how he spoke many comforting words against the pains of death and hell.[160] I will recall a few of them

---

[152] Cf. Wander 1:154, "Arzt" no. 63.

[153] *eckerlein*; literally: "little field." Cf. Matt. 13:25.

[154] Cf. Wander 3:1486-87, "Rathen" no. 61.

[155] I.e., the *Lectures on Genesis*.

[156] See Jerome Besold, preface to the fourth volume of the *Lectures on Genesis*, WA 44:xxxv; Brecht 3:136.

[157] Cf. above, Bugenhagen, *Christian Sermon*, pp. 29–33; as well as Jonas, *Leichenpredigt auf Luther* (Schubart, *Die Berichte über Luthers Tod und Begräbnis*, no. 15, pp. 17–18), and Coelius, *Leichenpredigt* (Schubart, *Die Berichte über Luthers Tod und Begräbnis*, no. 28, pp. 29–32), both in *Zwo Tröstliche Predigt*, fols. B1v–B2r, fol. G1v.

[158] Cf. above, Mathesius, *History*, pp. 128–29.

[159] Cf. above, Mathesius, *History*, p. 353; below, p. 529. Psalm 4 was appointed for daily use in Compline: see *Rule of St. Benedict* 18.19 (Timothy Fry, ed., *RB 1980: The Rule of Saint Benedict in Latin and English with Notes* [Collegeville, MN: Liturgical Press, 1981], pp. 214–15).

[160] Jonas, *Leichenpredigt* (Schubart, *Die Berichte über Luthers Tod und Begräbnis*, no. 15, pp. 17–18), in *Zwo Tröstliche Predigt*, fols. B2r–C1r, mentions "more than twenty" sayings of comfort from the Bible and church fathers which Luther had written and explained in his Psalter (see above, Mathesius, *History*, pp. 429, 448) and in his prayer book and gives a selection, from which Mathesius seems to draw here, albeit not word for word. On the contents of the notes in Luther's lost Psalter, see WA 48:266–68.

now: "Whoever wants to enter the kingdom of heaven keeps God's commandments [Matt. 19:17]. Now, our God imposes on Adam, once he has been reconciled, that he shall return to ashes and that his wife shall bear much pain [Gen. 3:16, 19]. Faith cannot grow and increase without tribulation and the holy cross.[161] Sin does not cease before the hour of death; neither can we enter rest, peace, and joy until we are lying in the grave and rise again from it.[162]

"Alas, whoever flees the cross that God has laid upon Adam and his children for their benefit, whoever seeks to avoid physical death and cannot bear to have anyone speak of dying, he does not yet know what sin and the wages of sin are [cf. Rom. 6:23]. Nor does he know the Lord and His Word of life, which delivers us from death through His death, for He uses our death to put an end to all human misery. Therefore, all the saints have prayed from their hearts for a blessed end. The aged Simeon sings: 'Lord, let me now go sleep in peace and blessedly depart from here' [cf. Luke 2:29]. 'Oh, who will deliver me, wretched Paul, from my sinful and dead body?' [cf. Rom. 7:24]. 'Oh, let me depart!' [cf. Phil. 1:23]." Or, as pious Herr Philip interprets the text at the end of his life: "Dear Father, unyoke me. I have made myself weary pulling [the plow] in this wicked world."[163]

"Anyone who does not desire to die is not a Christian or living saint," the doctor said concerning Augsburg's Laminit (whom many people did regard as a living saint), because he could detect no trace of any desire or longing for death in her words.[164]

---

[161] I.e., affliction.

[162] Cf. Jonas, *Leichenpredigt* (Schubart, *Die Berichte über Luthers Tod und Begräbnis*, no. 15, pp. 17–18), in *Zwo Tröstliche Predigt*, fol. B4v.

[163] This elucidation of Rom. 7:17 (or possibly Phil. 1:23) is not to be found in Melanchthon's 1540 *Commentary on Romans* (CR 15:654), his 1556 *Enarratio* (CR 15:944), or his 1554 summary of Philippians dictated for Georg Major (CR 15:1287). For the sentiment, though without the image of the "yoke," see Melanchthon to Mathesius, November 14, 1559, CR 9:973 (MBW no. 9132). For the image of death as a release from the "yoke," see Lucas Lorbeer, *Die Sterbe- und Ewigkeitslieder in deutschen evangelischen Gesangbüchern des 17. Jahrhunderts* (Göttingen: Vandenhoeck & Ruprecht, 2012), p. 217.

[164] Anna Laminit, called Ursula (ca. 1480–1518), was a beguine of Augsburg who claimed to survive miraculously without any natural food. Coming to public attention about 1498, she attracted pilgrims from across Europe, including Emperor Maximilian and the artist Hans Holbein. After her public exposure as a fraud in 1514, she was a fugitive until she was arrested in Fribourg, in Switzerland, and executed by drowning in 1518. See Lyndal Roper, *The Holy Household: Women and Morals in Reformation Augsburg* (Oxford: Clarendon, 1989), pp. 262–63; B. Ann Tlusty, ed. and trans., *Augsburg during the Reformation Era* (Indianapolis: Hackett, 2012), pp. 239–41. Luther sought out Ursula in Augsburg during his return trip from Rome in 1512 (or 1511: see above, Mathesius, *History*, pp. 127–28; and Melanchthon, *Preface*, p. 64): *Table Talk* no. 4925 (1540), WA TR 4:582–83.

Again, it is a sure sign that the Word of life has taken hold of someone with a believing heart when this person desires to die and views death as nothing but gain [Phil. 1:21]. For whoever takes hold of the Lord and Giver[165] of life through the Word of life and keeps this Word shall not see or taste death eternally [cf. John 8:51].[166] A believer must for a time endure being bitten and gnawed by temporal death and must feel the pangs of death and fear of hell so that the Lord of life becomes all the more dear to him and he can groan all the more strongly against death [Rom. 8:23]. But this stinging and biting will not last forever.

When our doctor utterly despaired of his life in Smalcald,[167] he said that all fears of death and tribulation[168] had finally left him; he was very content in Christ, sincerely rejoiced to depart, and would gladly and joyfully have fallen asleep.[169] At table he said, "Therefore, I believe from God's Word and personal experience that whoever holds fast to God's Word shall not see death eternally [cf. John 8:51], but shall pass through it into eternal rest."[170]

One time he said, "Ah, how can a person be terrified and frightened of death if he believes God's Word: that Jesus Christ, the true Life, has died for us on the cross in His flesh and become the poison of death [Hosea 13:14 DB], which He has eliminated forever in His victory; He has turned our grave into a peaceful bed and sleeping chamber for us. Therefore, if you wish to die well, learn to know Christ, dead and risen, and look upon your own death in this one who died and lives. Then our death will be for us as a living sleep and eternal rest, until we rise again from the grave and our secret, hidden life is revealed to all the saints."[171]

Herr Menius[172] once wrote to our doctor about how a prior in Reinhardsbrunn had fallen asleep in full confidence and consolation. For after he had lain ill for a time in the monastery with some young brothers keeping vigil by him, one night he began speaking to one of them: "My son." The brother replied, "What do you wish, dear father?" "Ah, how the whole world oppresses and torments me, and all creatures are against me." That is what it means to feel the pangs of death. "Oh, father," the young brother said,

---

[165] Außtheyler

[166] Cf. above, Jonas and Coelius, *Report*, pp. 15–16.

[167] See above, Mathesius, *History*, pp. 402–3.

[168] anfechtung

[169] *Table Talk* no. 4991 (1540), LW 54:373–75.

[170] Cf. *Table Talk* no. 4835 (1543), WA TR 4:539; and a 1541 inscription: WA 48:157.

[171] Mathesius seems to be the source for this saying.

[172] On Justus Menius, see above, p. 385 n. 86. Menius' letter does not survive, and the anecdote does not seem to be transmitted elsewhere. Presumably the letter and the account of Luther's oral response to it date from Mathesius' 1540–42 stay in Wittenberg.

"but you have been far better than any of the rest of us." "None of this will stand before God's judgment," the ill man said. "*Etiam perdite vixi* ['I, too, have lived a damnable life'], as the good St. Bernard confesses.[173] But Christ the crucified is my testament and righteousness." Upon this, the good father flickered out like a little candle.

When the doctor read this story, he said, "This man, too, is among those who was saved in the papacy. Yes, surely it is and will ever be a peaceful and joyful death, if you know Christ who was crucified and died and take comfort in His victory and resurrection."

During his last years, the doctor made inscriptions in many people's books.[174] Most frequently, he interpreted passages that were aimed at providing comfort in the throes of death, even as he had collected many fine words of consolation for himself in his Psalter.[175] Believers die every day when they experience thoughts of death; they refresh themselves with living passages of the Gospel. Thus our doctor's discourse was chiefly about death and against it; he preached, wrote, sang, prayed, and spoke fervently against it. For example, in the last letters he wrote, he repeatedly asked that the recipient would help him sigh for a blessed last hour.[176]

From Coburg in 1530 he wrote to Ludwig Senfl,[177] asking him to compose a good requiem for him. Among other things, he mentioned that he had loved the verse in Psalm 4 [:8] since his youth; now these words were becoming ever dearer to him with every passing day, now that he understood them and was arming himself for death each hour because the world hated him and wanted to be rid of him, and he for his own part had also had quite enough of the world and this life. God, the faithful deliverer, would take His soul to Himself. Therefore, he was now desirous of singing and hearing this song: "I lie down and sleep in complete peace" [Ps. 4:8].[178]

In his sermon for Doctor Luther's funeral, Doctor Johann Bugenhagen, pastor in Wittenberg, recalled many fine stories, particularly of what the doctor had spoken with Master Ambrose Berndt and about his grave.[179] "The man fell asleep quite peacefully," he said. "He did not know that he died; neither does he know yet that he is dead, for he fell asleep in the Word

---

[173] See above, Mathesius, *History*, p. 502.

[174] See above, Jonas and Coelius, *Report*, pp. 15–16; and Mathesius, *History*, pp. 408, 426 and nn. 11–12 there.

[175] See above, p. 526 n. 160.

[176] See, e.g., Luther to Jacob Probst, January 17, 1546, WA Br 11:263–64.

[177] See above, Mathesius, *History*, pp. 352–53; Luther to Ludwig Senfl, October 4(?), 1530, LW 49:426–29.

[178] Cf. above, p. 526.

[179] See above, Bugenhagen, *Christian Sermon*, pp. 31–33.

and knowledge of Christ. Dear Lord Christ, grant me, too, such a peaceful and blessed hour of death before long, and take me, too, from this exile and valley of sorrow to Yourself." The pastor likewise testifies that [Luther] often asked them to help him pray to God for a blessed hour of death, because he was no longer of any use on earth.[180]

Now when the year 1546 arrived, as the Council of Trent went forward[181] while, in addition, an imperial diet and new colloquy were scheduled for Regensburg,[182] our doctor was summoned by his hereditary lords, the counts of Mansfeld, to resolve and arbitrate some quarrels and disputes that had risen among them.[183] This man was usually content to leave alone the affairs of the world and of rulers, as the accounts of many good people attest.[184] But he would not and could not refuse to serve his native land and hereditary lords with his Our Father and good counsel. Therefore, he set out with his three sons[185] on January 23. On the next day, he came to Doctor Jonas in Halle, where he preached on the Day of the Conversion of St. Paul.[186] At table, the doctor gave his host a toast and composed two lines of verse for it about the fragility of the glass: |"The weak and fragile Luther gives the vitreous Doctor Jonas a good toast from a fragile glass, that each may bear in mind his weakness."[187] Out of the abundance of the heart the mouth speaks [Matt. 12:34; Luke 6:45]; the man's thoughts were occupied with death; he began to die every day more and more and to desire rest; accordingly, not only God's Word but all creatures as well had to preach to him and console him.

---

[180] See above, Bugenhagen, *Christian Sermon*, p. 33.

[181] The Council of Trent opened on December 13, 1545. See Giuseppe Alberigo, "Trent, Council of," *OER* 4:173.

[182] The Diet of Regensburg had been announced for Epiphany 1546, but its opening was delayed until June. See *DRA* 17. The 1546 Colloquy of Regensburg began on January 27, 1546, and continued until March 10. See Vinzenz Pfnür, "Colloquies," *OER* 1:377–80.

[183] Mathesius' account of Luther's last journey and death is largely a summary of Jonas and Coelius, *Report*, above, pp. 7–22. See the extensive notes there.

[184] See above, Melanchthon, *Oration*, p. 47; Melanchthon, *Preface*, pp. 72–73.

[185] Johannes [Hans], Martin, and Paul Luther. See above, Jonas and Coelius, *Report*, p. 8.

[186] *On the Conversion of St. Paul, against the Monks* (January 26, 1546), LW 58:370–84. Luther in fact delivered this sermon on the day after the festival.

[187] *Der schwache und gebrechliche Luther bringt dem glesnern Doctor Jonas auß eim gebrechlichen glaß ein guten trunck, darauß sich ein jeder seiner schwachheyt zu erinnern habe.* Cf. *Table Talk* no. 6969 (n.d.), WA TR 6:299. Elsewhere, in *Sarepta*, fol. 285v (Loesche, *Mathesius: Ausgewählte Werke*, 4:299), Mathesius gives the original Latin form alongside a different German translation: *Dat vitrum vitreo Ionae vitrum ipse Lutherus, / Ut vitro fragili similem se noscat uterque.* The glass described here is identified with one preserved in the Germanisches Nationalmuseum, Nürnberg, inventory no. Gl206_a. Jonas and Coelius, *Report*, do not mention the episode with Jonas and the glass.

On the twenty-eighth of the month he sat himself in a little boat with his three sons and Dr. Jonas, because the Saale River had overflowed its banks. This was done not without peril and risk, for a stormy wind easily could have capsized the little boat. As he himself said then: "Would not it give the devil a fine game and great pleasure if I, with my three sons and yourself, were to drown in the water with you?"[188]

Afterward he came to Eisleben feeling extremely weak, which caused him to say on the way: "The devil always does this to me. Whenever I have some great task before me to accomplish, he first tries me in this way and attacks me."[189]

At his lodgings, he let himself be rubbed with warm towels, after which he felt better and sat at table with the others in the evening. Afterward he went to deal with the business at hand and gave his best advice along with the sincere prayer that God would speak His blessing as well, so that all things might be decided and arbitrated properly.

In addition to this, he did not forget his office: he faithfully attended to his prayers in the evening and morning; before going to bed at night, he stood for almost half an hour beneath his window, looked up to heaven, and consigned and cast all his cares and concerns upon the Lord, [praying] that God, who is faithful and true, would wrap up his poor little soul like a small bundle and faithfully protect it, and that He would remove him from this wicked world, the sooner the better, for he had had enough of life and had grown weary and tired of it.[190]

ᴵThe funeral sermons preached in Eisleben immediately after his death[191] also bear witness that he wholeheartedly desired that, if it were pleasing to God, he would not have to suffer long on his sickbed. And since he could feel that he walked and grew feeble like an exhausted old man, he often said, "I will not live long. Even if the pope and my adversaries were to get their hands on me and put me in their power, wanting to inflict much pain on me, which I have often sincerely desired for the glory of God and His Gospel, I would certainly perish quickly while in their hands."[192]

---

[188] See above, Jonas and Coelius, *Report*, p. 8.

[189] See above, Jonas and Coelius, *Report*, pp. 8–9.

[190] See above, Jonas and Coelius, *Report*, pp. 9–10, 14; cf. Jonas, *Leichenpredigt* (Schubart, *Die Berichte über Luthers Tod und Begräbnis*, no. 15, pp. 17–18), in *Zwo Leichen Predigt*, fol. B2v.

[191] Funeral sermons for Luther were preached in Eisleben by Jonas and Coelius: see the introduction above, p. xxxiii.

[192] Coelius, *Leichenpredigt* (Schubart, *Die Berichte über Luthers Tod und Begräbnis*, no. 28, pp. 29–32), in *Zwo Tröstliche Predigt*, fols. G1v–G2r.

Yet even though he was now weak and weary, he did not neglect his office. During these twenty-one days in Eisleben, he preached the Sunday Gospel four times,[193] and, as he had done before in his lectures on Genesis,[194] he faithfully exhorted people to the Sacrament, through which we are sealed and assured in our hearts that all of our sins are forgiven in and through the blood of Jesus Christ and that we are children, heirs, and members of Christ.[195] Twice in these days he received absolution: once publicly from the officiating minister, then also in private; and following this, he publicly received the true body and blood of the Lord Jesus Christ in the Supper.[196] In these days he said many comforting things at table and afterward, some of which are recalled in his funeral sermon.[197]

On February 7, he made his last inscription, written for the chief tax official of Hohnstein[198] in his *House Postil*: "John 8 [:51]: If anyone keeps My word, he will never see death." This he expounded as follows: "How unbelievable this saying is and contrary to manifest daily experience! Yet it is true: if anyone seriously contemplates God's Word in his heart, believes it, and falls asleep and dies in it, he slips away and ¦departs [into the Word] before he glimpses death or becomes aware of it, and has surely made a blessed departure in that Word which he has thus believed and contemplated."[199] This was to be the last thing he wrote,[200] even as the last thing he published was his propositions against the [theologians] of Louvain.[201]

---

[193] For Luther's sermons of January 31, February 2, and February 7, 1546, see LW 58:397–459; for his sermon of February 15, 1546, see LW 51:381–92. These were published together by Johann Aurifaber in June 1546.

[194] See, e.g., *Lectures on Genesis* (1535–45/1544–54), LW 1:248; 3:108, 146, 275; 4:179; 7:226; 8:33, 312–13; cf. above, Mathesius, *History*, p. 408.

[195] See, e.g., sermon of February 7, 1546, LW 58:447–48; sermon of February 15, 1546, LW 51:384–85, 391.

[196] See above, Jonas and Coelius, *Report*, p. 9. The *Report* does not mention the private absolution and says that Luther received the Lord's Supper twice while in Eisleben.

[197] See Jonas, *Leichenpredigt* (Schubart, *Die Berichte über Luthers Tod und Begräbnis*, no. 15, pp. 17–18), in *Zwo Leichen Predigt*, fol. C1r; also above, Jonas and Coelius, *Report*, pp. 9–11.

[198] Hans Gasmann: see above, Jonas and Coelius, *Report*, pp. 15–16.

[199] See above, Jonas and Coelius, *Report*, p. 16.

[200] In fact, the last thing written by Luther's hand seems to have been a note on a scrap of paper preserved as *Table Talk* no. 5677 (1546), LW 54:476; no. 5468 (1546), WA TR 5:168; see also WA 48:241 and RN; and the epilogue by Gottfried Krodel, LW 50:318. Luther also had with him in Eisleben a manuscript for a final treatise: *Against the Asses of Paris and Louvain* (1545–46), WA 54:444–68 (LW 61).

[201] *Against the Thirty-Five Articles of the Louvain Theologians* (1545), LW 34:339–60, published in the fall of 1545.

On February 15,[202] only two or three days before his end, he preached his last sermon from Matthew's Gospel, chapter 11, and taught well about the wisdom of the world and the wisdom of the saints, which God reveals to the simple [Matt. 11:25].[203] In conclusion, he gave a Christian admonition not to harbor and protect the stiff-necked Jews or to dispute much with them.[204] He also mentioned his weakness from the pulpit.[205]

On Wednesday, February 17, his fatigue was clearly noticeable, so that the counts asked him to set aside the business and to try to get some rest. But he did sit at the table for dinner, where he said many fine things. For example, he spoke about how God creates a new world every twenty years and fills His kingdom of heaven with children. "We old people must live long enough," he said, "to see the devil's backside and experience so much of the world's wickedness, treachery, and misery so that we may be witnesses that the devil is such a wicked spirit. The human race is like a fold of sheep with nothing but little lambs for slaughter standing in it."[206]

Among the things he said on this evening, the venerable father also called to mind the question to which I referred above:[207] that the saints will recognize each other in eternal life, even as Adam, before the fall, when he awoke from his sleep, clearly recognized that Eve, whom he had never seen before, was flesh and bone of his flesh and bone, wonderfully made to be his companion [Gen. 2:21–23].[208]

Afterward he stood up from his chair and said that his chest hurt him again and that he was concerned about it. Still, he went under the window and prayed according to his custom; then he was very weak. Those around him called the countess[209] and doctors, who rubbed him with warm towels. Count Albert[210] came and asked, "How are you doing, my dear doctor?" "There is no cause for concern, gracious lord, things are beginning to mend." Then he was twice given shavings of unicorn horn to swallow.[211] At nine

---

[202] There is debate over whether Luther's last sermon took place on Sunday, February 14, when Luther ordained two ministers, or on Monday, February 15. Mathesius' dating is the more likely. See Brecht 3:372.

[203] Sermon of February 15, 1546, LW 51:381–92.

[204] On the *Admonition against the Jews* (LW 58:458–59), which is probably to be dated to February 7 instead, see above, p. 514.

[205] Sermon of February 15, 1546, LW 51:392.

[206] See above, Jonas and Coelius, *Report*, p. 10. Cf. Brecht 3:375–77.

[207] See above, Mathesius, *History*, pp. 433–34; cf. Jonas and Coelius, *Report*, p. 11.

[208] See above, Jonas and Coelius, *Report*, p. 11.

[209] Anna Honstein-Klettenberg, the wife of Count Albert IV; see above, p. 13 n. 40.

[210] See above, p. xxviii n. 54.

[211] See above, p. 11 n. 27.

o'clock he lay down again on the couch. "If I might slumber for half an hour, I would hope that all would be remedied." Then he slept until about ten, got up again, and went into his room. When he crossed the threshold, he said, "In God's name I go to bed. Into Your hands I commend my spirit. You have redeemed me, O faithful God [Ps. 31:5]."[212] Then he lay down in his already warmed bed, shook hands with Dr. Jonas, Master Coelius, and the others, and bade them good night, saying, "Pray for our Lord God and His Gospel, that they may prosper, for the Council of Trent[213] and the wretched pope are raging harshly against Him." Remaining with him in the chamber that night were his two sons Martin and Paul, Dr. Jonas, his servant Ambrose,[214] and other servants.[215]

Here he rested peacefully until about one o'clock in the morning. When Dr. Jonas asked whether he was feeling weak again, he said, "Ah, Lord God, what pain I feel! Ah, dear Dr. Jonas! I think that I will remain here in Eisleben where I was born and baptized." To this Dr. Jonas replied, "Ah, Reverend Father, God our heavenly Father will help through Christ, whom you have preached." Then without assistance or escort he went into the room and repeated his previous words along the way: "*In manus tuas Domine commendo spiritum meum*" ["Into Your hands, O Lord, I commend my spirit" (Ps. 31:5)], and when he walked back and forth in the room once or twice, he lay on the couch and complained that there was intense pressure about his chest. Nonetheless, his heart was still spared.[216]

Then he was rubbed, and his host and the doctors were woken. Count Albert and his wife were also called and brought with them many restoratives and tonics. But our doctor said, "Dear God, I am departing. I will remain in Eisleben." Dr. Jonas comforted him and [said that] because he had called upon Jesus Christ, our High Priest and Mediator, it would get better, for he had let out a good sweat. The doctor answered, "No, it is a cold sweat of death. I shall yield up my spirit, for the illness is getting worse." And then he began, saying:

> O my heavenly Father, God and Father of our Lord Jesus Christ, God of all comfort: I thank You that You have revealed to me Your beloved Son, Jesus Christ, in whom I believe, whom I have preached and confessed, whom I have loved and worshiped, whom the wretched pope and all the ungodly

---

[212] In addition to its biblical source, this verse was also part of the brief responsory in the liturgy of Compline, which would have been part of Luther's daily prayer as a monk. Cf. *LSB* 255.

[213] See above, p. 530.

[214] On Ambrosius Rutfeldt [Rudfeldt], see above, p. 10 n. 18, p. 460 n. 230.

[215] See above, Jonas and Coelius, *Report*, pp. 11–13.

[216] See above, Jonas and Coelius, *Report*, p. 13.

dishonor, persecute, and blaspheme. I beseech You, my Lord Jesus, accept my little soul into Your keeping. O heavenly Father, though I am leaving this body and am torn away from this life, yet I know for certain that I will remain with You forever, and no one can snatch me out of Your hands [John 10:29].[217]

Then he continued speaking, in Latin: "For God so loved the world that He gave His only Son, that whoever believes in Him should not perish but have eternal life" [John 3:16]; and the words from Psalm 68 [:20; Ps. 67:21 Vg]: "We have a God who saves, and a Lord God who is able to deliver from death." But when all kinds of medicine were tried on him, he said again: "I am departing." And three times in very quick succession he said, "Father, into Your hands I commend my spirit. You have redeemed me, O faithful God." Then he fell silent. People shook, rubbed, ᴵcooled, and called to him, but he shut his eyes. Dr. Jonas and Master Coelius called loudly to him: "Reverend Father, is it your intention to die steadfast in Christ and His doctrines, as you have preached them?" He said, so that he could be heard plainly and understood, "Yes." Then he fell asleep in the name of Jesus Christ, without physical anguish, peacefully and in great patience, at three o'clock in the morning on February 18, which was the Day of Concord,[218] and he grew cold.[219]

This happened in the presence of many counts, lords, doctors, his own children, and other good people. May the eternal Son of God grant this faithful servant and witness of His a joyful resurrection, preserve all of us steadfastly in His holy Gospel until our end, and also grant us such a peaceful departure and hour of death in true invocation and confession of the Lord Jesus Christ! Amen, Lord Jesus Christ, Amen.

That is the blessed departure of the great and excellent prophet of God, Dr. Martin, through whom our God attacked the papacy and rescued many Christians from Babylonian captivity.[220]

On February 18, the remains were left where [Luther] had been staying, in Dr. Drachstedt's house.[221] After noon on the nineteenth, he was carried with great reverence into the main parish church, St. Andreas, in a beautiful procession that was honorably accompanied by many counts and lords in addition to the whole city, who deeply grieved [his death]. At that time Doctor Jonas preached a Christian funeral sermon, which has been printed.[222]

---

[217] See above, Jonas and Coelius, *Report*, p. 14.

[218] See above, Mathesius, *History*, p. 317 and n. 212 there.

[219] See above, Jonas and Coelius, *Report*, pp. 14–15.

[220] Cf. above, Mathesius, *History*, pp. 104, 107, 115, 157, 159, 229, 262, 264, 330, 504.

[221] See above, Jonas and Coelius, *Report*, p. 17.

[222] On Jonas' sermon, see above, p. 526 n. 157; Jonas and Coelius, *Report*, p. 17.

On the following day and night, the remains were kept in the church and were guarded by ten citizens. On the afternoon of the twentieth, once two painters[223] had made portraits of the deceased doctor, Master Michael Coelius preached another fine funeral sermon.[224] |Afterward the corpse, which was closed in a coffin made of pewter, was escorted out of the city with great reverence and wailing. In the evening, it was brought to Halle, where they received it with laudable Christian processions and guarded it again overnight in the Church of Our Dear Lady.[225]

On the twenty-first, the remains were brought to Bitterfeld at about noon. At the Saxon border, the elector of Saxony had it received by his commissaries and accompanied to Kemberg in the evening with customary and reverent ceremonies.[226]

On February 22, the remains arrived in Wittenberg at the Elster Gate. The entire university, honorable council, and whole citizenry accompanied it with beautiful ceremonies and singing through the whole length of the city and into the Castle Church. The elector's commissaries rode ahead, along with the counts of Mansfeld with approximately forty-five horse,[227] followed by the corpse and the late Doctor Luther's wedded wife[228] on a wagon. Next there followed his three sons; his brother Jacob Luther[229] and Ciliax Kaufmann,[230] his sister's son, both citizens of Mansfeld; and other relations. Then came the *magnificus dominus rector*[231] with some young princes, counts, and barons, who were residing in Wittenberg on account of their studies. Again, there was Doctor Gregor Brück;[232] Herr Philip;[233] Dr. Justus Jonas;[234] Dr. Pomeranus, the pastor;[235] Dr. Cruciger;[236] Dr. Hieronymus [Schurff][237]

---

[223] See above, Jonas and Coelius, *Report*, p. 18.

[224] See above, p. 526 n. 157.

[225] See above, Jonas and Coelius, *Report*, pp. 18–19.

[226] See above, Jonas and Coelius, *Report*, p. 19.

[227] See above, Jonas and Coelius, *Report*, pp. 19–20, which mentions forty-five horse from Mansfeld and sixty-five horse in total.

[228] *Doctor Luthers seligen eheliche Haußfraw.* On Katharina Luther, see above, p. xxxii n. 74.

[229] On Jacob Luther, see above, p. 57 n. 10.

[230] On Ciliax [Cyriacus] Kaufmann, see above, p. 20 n. 77.

[231] The university rector Augustine Schurff: see above, p. 20 n. 78.

[232] On Gregor Brück, see above, p. 21 n. 79.

[233] On Melanchthon, see the introduction above, pp. xxxix–xl.

[234] On Justus Jonas, see the introduction above, p. xxx.

[235] I.e., Johann Bugenhagen of Pomerania; see the introduction above, pp. xxxvi–xxxvii.

[236] On Caspar Cruciger, see above, p. xx n. 19, p. 298 n. 81.

[237] On Hieronymous [Jerome] Schurff, see above, p. 21 n. 83.

and all the other doctors and masters; the city council of Wittenberg; and the whole assembly of students and citizens. Christian funeral hymns were sung as the remains were placed in the Castle Church. Then Dr. Bugenhagen preached a comforting Christian funeral sermon[238] and, moved by extraordinary and ᴵdeep compassion, Herr Philip delivered a beautiful funeral oration in Latin, both of which have been printed.[239]

Afterward, Doctor Martin's body was laid in the grave and sown in the earth as a blessed grain of wheat [John 12:24; 1 Cor. 15:37], which shall be honorably and joyfully reawakened and raised for eternal glory at Christ's appearing.[240]

Come quickly, Lord Jesus [Rev. 22:20], and let us behold Your countenance with all the saints and abide with You in all eternity. Amen, Lord Jesus, Amen.

---

[238] For Bugenhagen's *Christian Sermon*, see above, pp. 25–35.

[239] For Melanchthon's *Oration*, see above, pp. 39–51. The preceding paragraph is based on Jonas and Coelius, *Report*, above, pp. 20–22.

[240] See above, Jonas and Coelius, *Report*, p. 22.

The Fifteenth Sermon,[1]
a Funeral Sermon
on the Anniversary of the Death
of Doctor Martin,
Who Blessedly Fell Asleep in Christ
in Eisleben on February 18, 1546

[February 18, 1564]

BELOVED friends in the Lord! It was today, on this eighteenth day of February, eighteen years ago, that our dear father, the venerable Herr Doctor Martin, blessedly fell asleep in Eisleben in the true confession and invocation of the eternal Mediator.

Now, because this day recalls his Christian departure to our minds, we would like to commemorate his death, funeral, and doctrine for ourselves as Christians, and to give sincere thanks to God for having raised up this excellent teacher and having through him rescued us from the Antichrist's doctrine, burnished the pure and blessed doctrine and restored it to our churches. At the same time, we want to ask the eternal Father in the name of Jesus Christ that He would not let us forget this Christian man and his doctrine, and that He would preserve us and our posterity steadfast in it, and that He would graciously protect us against all heresy and falsification of the Gospel.

For this is the way for us to celebrate a blessed Christian funeral: in order to glorify God and to affirm the truth of His Word. The heathen also commemorated their dead and praised their fine virtues; or they celebrated the anniversaries of their death by honoring and visiting the graves of their family and offering great gifts in sacrifice to their devils for the sins of the deceased, often even slaying live human beings for their sake. This abominable and diabolical idolatry, which detracts from the sacrifice and blood of Jesus Christ, also poured in a great flood into the Roman Church, where Mass was celebrated for the dead to deliver them from purgatory or to

---

[1] In the 1566 first edition, fol. 188v, this sermon is numbered as the fourteenth. Cf above, Mathesius, *History*, p. 463. The sermon was delivered in Joachimsthal on February 18, 1564.

alleviate their suffering and torment, or they commemorated their supposedly exalted saints in order to direct us to the merits and intercession of the
deceased. These celebrations were not right, even though the good people
among the heathen commemorated their parents in their *Parentalia*[2] and
wanted to reconcile them with the infernal idols.

The early Christian Church held its vigils and night watches at the
graves of the holy martyrs[3] in order to comfort the living in the face of death,
and so that they could comfort and encourage them from God's Word unto
a blessed end, a steadfast confession and witness in the face of the enemies
of Christendom. Each year they also honorably commemorated the apostles
and their faithful bishops and pastors of souls[4] in order to give their parishioners an annual reminder and admonition that they should not forget the
apostles' teaching or the witness of their pastors. Pure doctrine and the
sainted lights and pillars of the Church [cf. Gal. 2:9; Rev. 3:12] are easily
forgotten in this wicked and ungrateful world, because people are always
wanting to have something new.

Therefore, because the eternal and substantial Light, the Lord Jesus
Christ, has kindled a blessed light for us in our times and has provided a
great, extraordinary man and prophet, we will commemorate and celebrate
the sainted doctor in this funeral sermon and demonstrate and prove with
sound evidence that he was a true Christian doctor and expositor of Holy
Scripture, a steadfast witness of the Lord Jesus Christ, and a true prophet of
the Most High. May we thus all the more treasure his doctrine, exposition
[of Scripture], ¹and witness and abide steadfast in it until our end.

O eternal Son of God, You have raised up this man through Your Spirit,
entrusted Your Word to him, and performed many wonders through him in
the power of Your Word. Help us, that, to the glory of Your high priesthood
and eternal bishop's office and for the faithful exhortation of Your Church,
we may remember Your faithful servant in blessed honor, as obedient and
grateful students and children, and we may glorify You in him and in his
teaching forever and ever. Amen.

It is true, dear friends, that prophets, apostles, and holy lights of
Christendom are properly concerned with testifying and preaching about
God and His Son above all else. For such knowledge gives—and, indeed,
alone is—eternal life (John 17 [:3]). But since God and His Son give light to

---

[2] The *Parentalia* were a weeklong festival in honor of the family dead observed by the
Romans in mid-February. See Ovid, *Fasti* 2.533 (Loeb 253 [1931], pp. 94–95). See *OCD*,
3rd ed., s.v. "Parentalia."

[3] On vigils held by Christians at the graves of the martyrs on the anniversaries of their
death [*dies natales*], see *ODCC*, 3rd ed., s.v. "vigil."

[4] *Seelsorger*

this dark world through the mouths of sucklings and infants [Matt. 21:16]—and through their Spirit speak with us through prophets, apostles, and called servants of the Church—the Old and New Testaments testify in a great many places about what is characteristic of a true and faithful ambassador and servant of God, so that we may learn to recognize true teachers and distinguish them from the false prophets.

Now, the Bible instructs us that the true prophets and apostles are called and sent by the Son of God Himself, without intermediary, and that they teach what they themselves have heard from the Head of the Church, the eternal Son of God. Therefore, prophets and apostles devote themselves constantly and always to their calling and teach nothing but what they have been instructed by Christ Himself or by His Spirit in visions.

Bishops, pastors, and other servants of the Church should and must have their certain call and commission as well. That is why they have clear attestation and witness from the dear Christian Church ¹or from the people who have the legitimate command and authority to provide for the Church by appointing people to the teaching office.[5]

Therefore, it is necessary that a true ambassador of the Lord Christ not teach or bear witness to anything but what he has heard from the mouth of God's Son or has been instructed in miraculous visions and divine dreams. Or, if he has been sent out to be a doctor or to occupy the teaching office by legitimate means and a human call, it is necessary that he not teach or interpret anything but what has been recorded in the writings of the prophets and apostles through the Holy Spirit for our instruction, comfort, and admonition [cf. 2 Tim. 3:16] and has been confirmed and established by the miracles following, as Christ [says] [Mark 16:20].[6]

For just as prophets and apostles insist and rely upon only what they have heard from the mouth of God's Son, so, too, all legitimate ministers of the Church are to preach, write, and interpret nothing but the writings of the prophets and apostles, which alone are the rule and plumb line[7] and the one foundation and pillar of all truth to be taught and believed within Christendom [cf. 1 Tim. 3:14–15]; to these the ministers should devote themselves, and to these they should appeal.

Now, if the call is proper and legitimate; if the doctrine and interpretation are in accord and agreement with the faith in Christ [cf. Rom. 12:6], according to the measure and plumb line of the prophets and apostles; if such witness and exposition is freely and openly confessed before the people; and if a preacher boldly and steadfastly abides and perseveres in

---

[5] Cf. Luther, *Infiltrating and Clandestine Preachers* (1532), LW 40:379–94.

[6] *mit Christi folgenden wunderwercken*; or: "the subsequent miracles which Christ worked."

[7] Cf. FC SD Summary 9 (Kolb-Wengert, pp. 528–29; *Concordia*, p. 509).

his teaching, having drawn it from the well of the prophets and apostles, and confirms it, if God so wills, with his blood—then those who hear such a teacher or interpreter of Scripture may regard him as a genuine doctor, pillar, ᶦor blessed light of the true Church and may receive his teaching with assurance and confidence.

God is accustomed to clothe and adorn His chosen prophets and apostles with His Spirit from above and to confirm them with miracles, special grace, a prophetic spirit, and the witness of other people—all to the honor of His Word and to make it sure. Yet even when He raises up and commissions people through a human yet legitimate appointment, in order to serve His Church and combat its adversaries, He adorns such people also with special gifts and an excellent spirit and causes holy people to prophesy of their coming and supplies them with the testimony of great people. He endows them, too, with the gift of prophecy; He often has them shed their blood with long-suffering as a witness to their teaching; and He performs miracles through them so that all may perceive that their call and teaching are not simply human but have heavenly testimony as well. When God raises up extraordinary men,[8] He begins with them in a wondrous way and powerfully brings His cause to completion through them [cf. Isa. 28:29 DB], so that people can see and perceive that God is with those whom He has commissioned to be Christ's messengers and servants.

I mention this at the outset so that you may recognize the distinctions among God's ambassadors and messengers and what characteristics are required and necessary for a prophet, apostle, bishop, or true doctor. God, who dwells in the light which no one can approach [1 Tim. 6:16], sends His only-begotten Son forth from His heart to speak to us about the divine being and will and to explain the counsel of God, as the one who is in the bosom of the Father [John 1:18] and forever sees into the Father's heart and hears the Father speak [John 8:38, 40]. It is from the Son that the Holy Spirit, the other witness and ambassador of God, takes and receives this [message], as Christ says in John 16 [:13–15]. ᶦHe then speaks it through the appointed prophets and apostles, who are also witnesses and ambassadors of God, who have heard it from the Son of God Himself [1 John 1:1–5] and have been taught by the Spirit of God [John 14:26] with whom they have been wondrously clothed from above [Luke 24:49] and by whom they have been so powerfully moved. This oral and written witness is also firm and certain. Accordingly, God raised up legitimate Levites and priests in the tabernacle [cf. Numbers 3–4], who were born into the office, educated for it, and publicly confirmed in it. Likewise, through the prophets and apostles He also

---

[8] *Wunderleut*; see the introduction above, pp. lxxxix–xc; cf. Mathesius, *History*, above, pp. 104, 115, 197; and below, pp. 562, 567, 578, 593, 595.

causes witnesses and ambassadors to be chosen, ordained, and confirmed with prayer and the laying on of hands [Acts 14:23; 1 Tim. 4:14], and He adorns and confirms them, too, with the Spirit and gifts of the office, so that they understand the writings of the prophets and apostles, explain and interpret them in a proper and salutary way, and help to save the people [cf. 1 Tim. 4:16] through the Word of the prophets and apostles—which is actually the voice of the Son of God—when they call the people to repentance, remind them of their sins, direct them to Christ's blood and sacrifice, and exhort them to good works and new obedience.

Now, it is in this last group that our dear father Herr Doctor Martin belongs. He neither saw nor heard God and His Son in person, as the ancient prophets and apostles did. Often he even prayed in great earnest that God would not allow any angel to speak with him nor give him any visions or dreams.[9] He had enough and was content with the Word of the prophets and apostles and with having a called minister of the Church and Christian brother hold before him God's Word in accordance with Scripture.[10] And in every other way, he possessed all the elements and characteristics required of a true and Christian doctor of Holy Scripture, a witness of Christendom, a blessed minister of the Church, and an ambassador of the Lord Christ.

You have already been told at length about his call and commission in the accounts about him these past years. He received a blessed Baptism, learned the catechism from his parents, and then was sent to school.[11] However, when he entered the monastery against the will of his parents, became a member of the clergy, and submitted himself to the authority of his vicar and whole order (even as God wondrously leads His saints [Ps. 4:3 DB] and caused Moses to be placed in Egypt [Exod. 2:2–10] and Daniel in the Babylonian school [Dan. 1:1–6]), then, upon the decision and at the command of his whole order, his legitimate superior charged him with becoming first a *pater lector*,[12] and then a doctor of theology. And so

---

[9] See above, Mathesius, *History*, p. 489.

[10] Cf. *Smalcald Articles* (1537/1538) III IV and VIII 3–13 (Kolb-Wengert, pp. 319, 322–23; *Concordia*, pp. 278, 280–81).

[11] On Luther's Baptism, see above, Melanchthon, *Preface*, p. 56; Mathesius, *History*, pp. 114, 117. On Luther's schooling, see above, Melanchthon, *Preface*, pp. 57–59; Mathesius, *History*, pp. 117–22.

[12] I.e., a lecturer (cf. Mathesius, *History*, above, p. 523; and below, p. 582).

this took place with the knowledge, permission, command, and financial support of his territorial prince.[13]

There he received attestation from those who tested and examined him by virtue of their office and commission that he was suited for such an office [cf. 2 Tim. 2:2], and they solemnly called and promoted him to be a doctor of Holy Scripture in the name of the Holy Trinity, acting publicly in the name and at the behest of the Roman Imperial Majesty, the defender of Christendom, and by the human authority of the Roman pope, *iure humano* ["by human right"], and [with the consent of] their suffragan bishop at the time,[14] that he might serve the Christian Church with Holy Scripture, battle against false doctrine, and fight for and defend the pure doctrine.[15]

Now everything that pertains to a Christian call or commission which takes place through other persons as agents in legitimate fashion, as it should and can, is to be found in our "solemnly promoted doctor."[16] He himself frequently took comfort in his legitimate and Christian call and doctorate, using it to defend and protect himself against the devil.[17] The call and command are right.

Keep listening now to how the man carried out his office as doctor. ꞮHe was legitimately[18] called, set apart, and chosen to be a doctor, and was appointed and confirmed as a professor[19] and teacher of theology and a preacher and interpreter of God's Word, as his diploma[20] and public attestation and the matriculation register[21] in Wittenberg still affirm today.

Now we have no other writing or doctrine from God more certain than what has been recorded in the writings of the prophets and apostles from

---

[13] For Luther's entrance into the monastery, appointment as a teacher, promotion to doctor, and support from Johann von Staupitz and Elector Frederick, see above, Melanchthon, *Preface*, pp. 59–64; Mathesius, *History*, pp. 122–30.

[14] The suffragan bishop [*Weihbischof*] of Erfurt who ordained Luther a priest in the Cathedral of St. Mary on April 3, 1507, was Johann Bonemilch von Laasphe (ca. 1434–1510). See Rüdiger Weyer, "Bonemilch von Laasphe, Dr. Johannes," *BBKL* 29:199–204.

[15] See above, Mathesius, *History*, pp. 129–30.

[16] *solenniter promoto doctore*

[17] See above, Mathesius, *History*, pp. 129–30.

[18] *legitime*

[19] *Doctor*

[20] *format*; either Luther's university diploma (see Matthias Lexer, *Mittelhochdeutsches Handwörterbuch* [Leipzig: S. Hirtzel, 1872–78], 3:474, s.v. "formât") or in the sense of *litterae formatae*, i.e., a letter from the bishop certifying a member of the clergy to exercise clerical functions in another diocese (DuCange 3:565, s.v. "formatae"). In this case, Luther would have been moving from the diocese of Erfurt to the diocese of Brandenburg, which had jurisdiction over Wittenberg.

[21] Luther's 1508 matriculation at Wittenberg is recorded in Förstemann et al., *Album*, 1:28.

the mouth of Jesus Christ through the Spirit of God. Therefore, his call and commission entail that he must teach and bear witness to God's Word. Throughout his life, this Word went before him and followed him; that is why he renounced the wranglings of the sophists and scholastics as well as the doctrines of the heathen, Jews, Papists, Turks, and all heretics and fanatics.[22] He relied solely upon the *theologia* [cf. 1 Pet. 4:11], God's Word,[23] as he often said, "I began with the spoken Word of God, which prophets and apostles wrote down through the Spirit of God and which has the witness of the whole Christian Church. Upon this I stay and stand.[24] I began and have come thus far relying upon this Word; with God's help I shall also carry on to the end relying upon it.[25] Concerning this I swore a solemn oath and publicly pledged my poor soul to our God."

Note this well: The call is right. The doctrine is also certain, for our doctor bases and founds his cause on Scripture alone. With it he attacked the papacy, cleansed many churches, planted the true religion, comforted many hearts and made them joyful and blessed, so that they received his doctrine and have risked life and limb on its account.

He also taught his divine theology not merely in his monastic cell and cloister or from his ordinary professor's chair or from his pulpit, to which he was also ¹specially appointed and called by the honorable town council in Wittenberg,[26] but, as a doctor with a universal call and higher vocation,[27] he also had his teaching published and circulated among scholars and declared his readiness to defend the same and to give reason for his confession and hope. He also sent his teaching to the elected Roman emperor Charles[28] and to His Majesty's brother, Ferdinand, at that time archduke,[29] and to many princes and bishops.[30] And, finally, he wrote to

---

[22] Cf. above, Mathesius, *History*, pp. 131–36.

[23] *die Theologia und Gottes wort.* Cf. below, p. 547 n. 50.

[24] *drauff stehe und fusse ich*

[25] See above, Mathesius, *History*, pp. 435–36.

[26] See Brecht 1:150–51. Luther refers to his call from the Wittenberg council in *Eight Sermons at Wittenberg* (1522), LW 51:73.

[27] The doctorate conveyed (by papal authority) the *ius ubique docendi* (the right to teach everywhere).

[28] Luther to Emperor Charles, August 30, 1520, LW 48:175–79; to Charles, April 28, 1521, LW 48:203–9. See above, Mathesius, *History*, pp. 161, 178.

[29] No letter from Luther to King Ferdinand survives, though a forged letter from Ferdinand to Luther was in circulation, dated February 1, 1537: see WA Br 8:24–33.

[30] See Luther, *To the Christian Nobility* (1520), LW 44:115–217, where the emperor is also addressed (LW 44:124). For letters to bishops, see Luther to Bishop Jerome Scultetus of Brandenburg, February 13, 1518, WA Br 1:138–40; to Albert of Brandenburg, cardinal

the pope himself,[31] expressing himself unabashedly, without skulking in the dark as do those who boast of having the Spirit.[32] And then, when he was summoned to give an answer, he appeared and made a public confession before the papal legate in Augsburg.[33] He did so again in Leipzig, before those who at that time were regarded as (and claimed themselves to be) the most learned people,[34] and again in Worms, before Emperor Charles and the whole Roman Empire.[35] At the castle in Wittenberg, in the presence of the papal legate Vergerio,[36] he also declared his readiness to appear before the council in Mantua and speak.[37]

If a true doctor has been called and bases his doctrine solely on the writings of the prophets and apostles, then it also behooves him to confess it before the people and to stake his life upon it. Having now declared and vindicated his teaching openly and steadfastly before the highest [authorities] on earth, he stood firm upon it until his end. In the beginning, he proceeded with caution and trod lightly and carefully,[38] for with every passing day he kept gaining clarity[39] [cf. 2 Cor. 3:18 DB], as he wrote concerning

---

archbishop of Mainz and archbishop of Magdeburg, February 4, 1520, WA Br 2:27–29; to Bishop Adolph of Merseburg, February 4, 1520, WA Br 2:25–27.

[31] Luther, *Open Letter to Pope Leo X*, dated September 6, 1520, LW 31:334–43. See above, Mathesius, *History*, p. 158.

[32] Cf. above, Mathesius, *History*, p. 216.

[33] On Luther's hearing at the 1518 Diet of Augsburg, see above, Mathesius, *History*, pp. 147–52.

[34] On Luther's disputation in Leipzig in 1519, see above, Mathesius, *History*, pp. 154–56.

[35] For the Diet of Worms, see above, Mathesius, *History*, pp. 168–78.

[36] Pier Paolo Vergerio (1498–1565), from Capo d'Istria in the Venetian Republic, was a trained jurist who accompanied Cardinal Campeggio to Augsburg in 1530 (see above, p. 326 n. 40) and was sent back to Germany as nuncio to the court of King Ferdinand in 1533. In 1535, Vergerio was commissioned by Pope Paul III to win support in Germany for the envisioned general council. On this mission, he met Luther in Wittenberg in November 1535. See Brecht 3:174–76; *Table Talk* no. 6384 (n.d.), WA TR 5:633–35; no. 6388 (n.d.), WA TR 5:636–38. Vergerio was subsequently made bishop of Capo d'Istria in 1536 and attended the colloquies of Worms and Regensburg in 1540–41 (see above, Mathesius, History, pp. 489–93). By the mid-1540s, however, Vergerio had begun to develop Evangelical sympathies, and in 1549 he left Italy and was excommunicated by the Roman Church. He worked first as an Evangelical pastor in Graubünden in Switzerland, and from 1552 until the end of his life, he served as an adviser to the Lutheran Duke Christoph of Württemberg (r. 1550–68). Vergerio published extensively against the papal church and in support of Evangelical religion. See Anne Jacobson Schutte, "Vergerio, Pier Paolo," *OER* 4:228–29.

[37] On the proposed council at Manuta, see above, Mathesius, *History*, pp. 396–97, 400–401.

[38] See above, Mathesius, *History*, p. 143.

[39] *er kam von tag zu tage von einer klarheyt inn die ander*

himself.[40] Finally, he made his public confession in the book on the Supper;[41] he appealed to his later books, as the summary of his doctrine in the Augsburg Confession[42] and in the articles he prepared and summarized quite rightly and clearly for the council in Mantua[43] demonstrates.

ᴵHe remained steadfast in this doctrine until he was in his grave, as you heard in the previous sermon concerning his death.[44] He said many fine things in the last night before he died, in the end answering with a clear "Yes" when Doctor Jonas asked whether he wanted to remain steadfast in his doctrine and to fall asleep in it.[45] With this last "Yes," he affirmed and declared his firm and certain doctrine, on the basis of which he will appear with boldness before God's judgment and countenance.

Truly, dear friends, in these days there were many self-made[46] and uncalled, ungrounded, and inconstant teachers and preachers who ran of their own accord [Jer. 23:21] and infiltrated other churches without a call, who intruded their contentious books into other places without a command, often anonymously, and in the end fell away from their own books and sermons, or were suddenly and horribly slain in battle, outside of their calling, or met with terrors secretly, in the still of the night, or from evil spirits, and perished.[47] A bad beginning is rarely followed by a good middle and end.[48] Thus the obscure writings, deceitful testimonies and pernicious books of such people are not to be given any credence whatsoever, for one does not know who the people are, where they come from, or who gave them command to teach and write.

---

[40] Cf. *Preface to the Latin Writings* (1545), LW 34:327-38.

[41] Probably a reference to Luther's *Confession concerning Christ's Supper* (1528), LW 37:151-372, which includes a systematic confesson of faith (see above, Mathesius, *History*, pp. 261-62), rather than to Luther's more focused 1544 *Brief Confession*, LW 38:279-319; see above, Mathesius, *History*, pp. 515-16.

[42] See above, Mathesius, *History*, pp. 330-35; for the Augsburg Confession, see Kolb-Wengert, pp. 30-105; *Concordia*, pp. 27-63.

[43] The *Smalcald Articles* (1537) (Kolb-Wengert, pp. 297-328; *Concordia*, pp. 259-85): see above, Mathesius, *History*, pp. 356, 396-99.

[44] See above, Mathesius, *History*, pp. 533-35.

[45] See above, Jonas and Coelius, *Report*, p. 15.

[46] Cf. above, Mathesius, *History*, p. 240, describing Zwingli.

[47] I.e., Karlstadt, Oecolampadius, and Zwingli: see above, Mathesius, *History*, pp. 261, 314, 394-95.

[48] Cf. Wander 1:81; 5:761, "Anfang" nos. 75, 125; Luther, *Sermon Preached in the Castle at Leipzig*, June 29, 1519, LW 51:58.

It is reasonable and responsible for a rightly called[49] pastor to have his sermons printed in order to bear witness to the truth and to [the state of] his church, or as consolation and admonition for his parishioners and neighbors. But every teacher and author who professes a new doctrine of his own, seeks to cast suspicion and uncertainty on the writings and confession of other good people, stirs up division and dissension, splits the Church, disturbs and troubles hearts, and finds fault with the writings of all other preachers—¹as well as the governing authorities of such teachers who witness the spectacle and take delight in it—they shall have a difficult and perilous defense to make for themselves on that day when everyone will have to give a strict account for all his words and deeds before the judgment seat of God [Matt. 12:36].

I say this to honor and affirm the preaching and books of Doctor Martin Luther. He was called to be a doctor against his will and intentions and had to swear a solemn oath upon the oracles of God.[50] And since he wanted to act in accordance with this [oath] for the sake of his call and of conscience, in the beginning he engaged in disputations simply and sincerely for the honor of the papal supremacy, saying that the hawkers and peddlers of indulgences were to be stopped so that no ill fame for the Roman Church would result. He also requested protection from his diocesan bishop and from the primate[51] in Germany, as well as from the Holy Father.[52] Then he was challenged to defend himself like a knight and warrior of God and a *solemnis* ["duly appointed"] doctor of theology. And he defended himself bravely and honorably with the sword of God [Eph. 6:17], as a Christian hero, until his final hour, when he slung a powerful Our Father and mighty sighs against the great Goliath and his weaponry in Trent.[53] These [prayers] have gained considerably in strength since that time as shall, God willing, soon become all the more powerfully visible and manifest.

At the beginning,[54] however, we mentioned that great lights and pillars of the Christian Church also confirm and affirm their doctrine (which is actually God's) with their own blood, which is a beautiful rubric or red

---

[49] *ordenlicher*

[50] *die Theologia*. On Luther's doctoral oath, see above, Mathesius, *History*, pp. 129–30, 134.

[51] I.e., from Jerome Scultetus, bishop of Brandenburg (see above, p. 146 n. 41), and from Albert of Brandenburg (see above, Mathesius, *History*, p. 146), who as archbishop of Mainz was primate of Germany (see above, Mathesius, *History*, pp. 350–51). For Luther's letters to them, see above, Mathesius, *History*, p. 146 and nn. 40–41 there.

[52] See Luther, *Open Letter to Pope Leo X*, dated September 6, 1520, LW 31:334–43.

[53] See above, Jonas and Coelius, *Report*, p. 12; and Mathesius, *History*, p. 534; cf. above, Mathesius, *History*, p. 349. On the Council of Trent, see above, p. 401 n. 34.

[54] See above, pp. 539–40.

ink with which God's Word is illuminated, underlined, and emphasized. It is true that our doctor fell asleep very peacefully and honorably, and the whole world was neither able nor allowed to touch even a hair of his head [cf. Luke 21:18]. For it was God's will to preserve the man amid the lions, like Daniel [6:22], and like Jonah [2:10] in the whale, to the glory of His Word. Through this it is manifestly apparent that if God wishes you well, the whole world cannot do you any harm. If someone has God's protection and is watched over by the heavenly hosts, as Elisha was at Dothan [2 Kings 6:12–17], then not only all human power and might but even all the gates of hell must leave him in peace and undisturbed.

Doctor Martin had long felt deep regret that our God was demonstrating His power with this one person by allowing him to end his days in peace. Oh, how gladly would he have shed his blood to the glory of the crucified Lord Jesus Christ and of His Gospel concerning the blood of propitiation [Rom. 3:25]! Several times he even struggled with himself on this account and had to be comforted and encouraged through examples of God's dealings with holy people. As he said long before his death, amid his severe tribulations,[55] when he was surrounded by thoughts of death and the fear of hell: "Ah, how gladly would I, too, have shed my baptized blood for the honor of Christ and of His Word! But St. John, the beloved disciple of Jesus Christ, who himself wrote a mighty book against the Antichrist and the adversaries of the Son of God, also had to die upon his sickbed, as did many other great saints whom God snatched out of the jaws and hands of the tyrannical world and bloodthirsty clergy and infernal murderers."[56]

Moses [Deut. 34:7], Enoch [Gen. 5:24], and Elijah [2 Kings 2:11] did not shed their blood. Daniel, too, had to leave his lions without being torn to shreds [Dan. 6:22]. Neither did David have to sprinkle and underline his dear psalms with his blood [1 Kings 2:10; 1 Chron. 29:28]. Not all of God's saints were martyrs in the body. Yet about inward suffering, the world and untried Christians do not understand anything, even though excellent people have had [accounts of] their tribulation and spiritual battles written down in their psalms for our consolation and encouragment in patience. All who believe in Christ must be martyrs and have their crosses, but it is not given to all to shed their blood, and it is sufficient for their salvation if they, like the holy confessors, acknowledge and bear witness to Christ and His agony and blood.

---

[55] anfechtung

[56] This saying is found in Bugenhagen's report on Luther's Anfechtungen of July 6, 1527 (see above, Mathesius, History, pp. 258–59): Table Talk no. 2922b (1533), WA TR 3:83. Cf. Luther to Lambert Thorn, January 19, 1524, WA Br 3:238; to Hans Oldenburg, May 19(?), 1522, WA Br 2:535.

A strong and Christian confession of the Lord Christ and His blood of propitiation is far greater than all martyrs and particularly the silent blood of saints, not to mention the devil's martyrs, whom the evil spirit enchants and blinds so that they shed their blood in a deluded manner to adorn their heresy and dreams. Concerning the devil's martyrs of his time, St. Augustine said, "*Non poena sed causa facit martyrem*" ["Not the suffering but the cause makes the martyr"].[57] We stand far more firmly upon the confession and witness of the Christian confessors and doctors than upon the shedding of human blood. The blood of One has been shed; by it God's counsel and fatherly will are confirmed and attested and the whole world's sin and guilt is atoned and paid for. The blood of other people, who deny the divine blood of propitiation or trample on and mock the blood distributed to us in the Supper for the strengthening of our faith, is wicked blood, which cannot be used to confirm any uncertain and baseless doctrine or divisive and vacuous gloss.[58]

Now, though the devil and the world were unable to touch or to kill this man whom God anointed for us, he did not walk upon roses[59] all the time on earth. He was willing to have details about his fear of hell, mortal agony, and intense tribulation written down for the consolation of others, but the world was not worthy of it [cf. Heb. 11:38].[60] In the next life, when the goats are separated from the sheep [Matt. 25:33], the saints of God will hear about the inner suffering of the ancient patriarchs and many excellent people with great joy and heavenly gladness and will thank God for this for eternity.

Without acknowledging and trusting in the cross and suffering of Jesus Christ, no one can be acceptable to our God and become a child and heir of God. Apart from the holy cross which God lays upon His people out of love and for their benefit, no one can persevere and abide in the true faith and resist and subdue his own flesh and let it be cleansed. Likewise, no one can understand Scripture or taste and sense the sweet power and help of God apart from temptation.[61]

---

[57] Augustine frequently applies this maxim against the Donatists: see Letter 89 (PL 33:310; NPNF[1] 1:374); Letter 107 (PL 33:413); Letter 204 (PL 33:940); *Explanations of the Psalms* 34.2.13 (PL 36:340; NPNF[1] 8:85); Sermon 285.2 (PL 38:1293); Sermon 327.1 (PL 38:1451); and *Contra Cresconium* 3.47 (PL 43:525; CSEL 52:459). Cf. Luther, *Table Talk* no. 5231 (1540), WA TR 5:19; no. 6 (1531), WA TR 1:4.

[58] Cf. above, Mathesius, *History*, pp. 240–45, where Zwingli and the Sacramentarians are in view.

[59] See Thiele no. 49, pp. 74–76; Wander 3:1729, "Rose" no. 115.

[60] On the records of Luther's *Anfechtungen*, see the introduction above, p. xciv; Jonas and Coelius, *Report*, pp. 8–11; Mathesius, *History*, pp. 258–59, 375–76.

[61] *versuchung*. See above, Mathesius, *History*, p. 378.

These past years you have learned quite a bit about how the evil world assailed this man. For those who were important and great on earth and regarded themselves as holy, learned, and wise united with great zeal and determination and would have liked to suppress the man altogether, as shown by the papal bulls and several proscriptions and greater proscriptions, as well as severe resolutions and all kinds of machinations.[62]

The man was assailed[63] by Jews and Gentiles, some of whom went to Wittenberg and entered his cloister and chambers, seeking to take his life with poison and guns, as we recently recalled concerning the Jew Michael from Posen.[64] Thus a foreigner was arrested in his kitchen;[65] reportedly, a traveler carrying a small matchlock pistol[66] in his sleeve greeted him in front of the cloister and asked why he was going out alone. "I am in God's hands," the doctor said. "He is my defense and shield. What can a man do to me [cf. Ps. 119:114; 118:6]?" At that, the hired assassin turned pale and went out the gate trembling.[67]

One time I asked him whether he had ever been poisoned.[68] "Without a doubt," he said. "A great personage was heard to say that none would work on me. Once I was invited to be the guest of foreigners here [in Wittenberg]. When I came home, my whole body was in pain and anguish. When I went to sleep, an unpleasant sweat poured out of me, and I got a runny nose. My eyes were also dripping, and a filthy secretion ran out of my ears. Moreover, I had great pain while vomiting, and there was not a single passageway in my body that did not open at that time. This served as a good strong purgation, and the next morning I became quite cheerful and healthy. That time I surely must have received a strong poison. But the One who says, "If they drink any deadly thing, it will not hurt them"

---

[62] *mancherley acht und aber acht neben geschwinden abschieden unnd allerley praktiken*; see above, Mathesius, *History*, pp. 180–81 and nn. 68–69 there; cf. above, Mathesius, *History*, pp. 170–72.

[63] *an den Mann geschifftet*

[64] See above, Mathesius, *History*, pp. 510–11.

[65] *Table Talk* no. 5369 (1540), WA TR 5:98.

[66] *Zündbuchsen*. Such pistols existed in the early sixteenth century but were an expensive rarity. See Richard Holmes et al., eds., *The Oxford Companion to Military History* (Oxford: Oxford University Press, 2001), s.v. "pistols and revolvers."

[67] Cf. *Table Talk* no. 5369 (1540), WA TR 5:97–98; no. 2501a–b (1532), WA TR 2:494–95. An edited version of the report appeared in the first Eisleben volume of Luther's collected works and was reproduced in E 64:365–66. See also Ratzberger, *Geschichte*, pp. 69–70. Melanchthon alludes to assasination attempts against Luther in his *Postil*, CR 25:472; 20:526, no. 22, where the date is fixed as 1519.

[68] *Table Talk* no. 5253 (1540), WA TR 5:28–29. Cf. Ratzeberger, *Geschichte*, pp. 71–72.

[Mark 16:18], had spoken His blessing over it, and He saved me this time and other times from all misfortune."

Aside from this, he often recalled how the devil had tormented him inwardly and caused him burning pain, which sucked the marrow out of his bones and the strength out of his whole body. "Although my God," he said, "occasionally left me for a moment and let me sink into thoughts of death, He then very graciously picked me up again and abundantly comforted me, for which I will thank Him now and forever. The evil spirit also clearly wanted to frighten me with apparitions. For example, many nights while in my Patmos I could hear him clamoring;[69] and at Coburg, I could see him in the form of a star,[70] and in my garden I saw him as a wild black boar.[71] But my Christ strengthened me with His Spirit and Word, so that I paid no heed to the devil's poltergeist." I mention this, dear friends, so that you may see that God led His servant into the wilderness also [cf. Matt. 4:1], and allowed him to be tempted in many ways, and we will hear more about this battle from him himself on the Last Day.

As to the worldly-wise who claim that our doctor performed no miracles—one mocker wrote that the Evangelicals could not even help a lame or limping horse with their doctrine[72]—let me provide you with an answer:

Doctor Luther preached the doctrine which the Son of God had brought forth from the Father's bosom,[73] which He had proclaimed and recorded in the writings of the prophets and apostles through His Spirit, and which He confirmed from the beginning with great miracles in accordance with the prophecy of Moses [Deut. 13:1–5; 18:18–22]. Now, since the doctor brought forth no new doctrine, but only the attested doctrine of the patriarchs, prophets, and apostles, this well-founded and confirmed word had no need of any new miracles.

The Roman Church's new devilry of requiem Masses,[74] purgatory, and monastic life had need of miracles. Therefore, the Antichrist and adversary

---

[69] I.e., the Wartburg Castle, where Luther was kept in hiding in 1521–22. On apparitions there, see above, Mathesius, *History*, p. 185.

[70] Luther stayed in the Coburg Castle during the Diet of Augsburg in 1530. See above, Mathesius, *History*, pp. 267–68, 324. On apparitions there, see *Table Talk* no. 362 (1532), WA TR 1:153–54; protocol for revision of the Psalter, 1531, WA DB 3:6. See Volz, *Die Lutherpredigten des Johannes Mathesius*, p. 281.

[71] See *Table Talk* no. 5358b (1540), WA TR 5:87–88 (cf. the introduction by Georg Buchwald, WA 49:viii). See Volz, *Die Lutherpredigten des Johannes Mathesius*, p. 281.

[72] A charge made by Erasmus, *Freedom of the Will*, LCC 17:45, and repeated frequently by Catholic controversialists thereafter. Cf. Luther, *Bondage of the Will* (1525), LW 33:72, 75; *Vorlesung über Jesaja* (1527–30/1532–34), WA 25:223.

[73] Cf. above, Mathesius, *History*, p. 108.

[74] I.e., Masses said for the benefit of the souls of the dead.

of God, inspired by the devil, confirmed and attested his idolatry and lies with all kinds of deceitful powers, signs, and wonders among those who were lost, as St. Paul writes (2 Thessalonians [2:9–10]).

O Lord Jesus, thanks be to You for the confirmed Word of the prophets and apostles. Protect us against miracles, visions, and dreams. For the day of signs and wonders that was to follow the preaching of the Gospel has passed, and God's Word has resounded throughout the whole world and has been made manifest. We are directed by the heavenly Father to the mouth of Christ, and by Christ to the testimony of the apostles, upon which the house and Church of God was dedicated. But if anyone would still like to see Christ's power, victory, and miracles from our own people nonetheless, I can present some examples in honor of Doctor Luther's doctrine.

Take this as a mighty wonder and divine, unheard-of work: One man opposed the supposed head of Christendom, under whose feet all rulers, bishops, universities, and scholars lay prostrate, and ¹whose thunderbolt they all feared; they also took fright and trembled before a single monk who came running with a little missive from Rome.[75] Indeed, it is true, as the doctor wrote, that up to that time all kings and princes had to bow, stoop, and cower at the sight of a little letter from the pope.[76] But when God raised up our doctor, he single-handedly attacked the great Goliath with his quill and slingshot, making [the pope] so afraid that he roused the whole world, or at least those parts where Christ's name is spoken, against this one doctor. He also did whatever was humanly and diabolically possible on his own part: he banned, condemned, and burned his books and likeness; he delivered to his god for punishment all those who accepted this man's teaching and books or provided him with lodging or refuge.[77] But [Luther] let those who did not want to accept it rage, ban, and condemn, and he wrote a bold letter directly to the pope. *Qui moritur minis, illi pulsabitur bombis* ["One who dies in the face of threats will be rung to his grave with flatulence"].[78]

And still [Luther] had not been brought down; the great dragon [Rev. 20:2] or proud whore of Babylon had been unable to accomplish anything against him with her infernal cup [Rev. 17:4–5], though otherwise,

---

[75] I.e., a papal bull of excommunication or interdict.

[76] See Luther, *Commentary on Psalm 82* (1530), LW 13:42; *Preface to the Collected Wittenberg Theses* (1538), WA 39/1:6 (LW 72); *Table Talk* no. 5253 (1540), WA TR 5:28–29.

[77] In the bulls *Exsurge Domine* and *Decet Romanum pontificem*: see above, Mathesius, *History*, pp. 160–62, 168 and n. 8 there.

[78] See Wander 1:698–99, "Drohen" no. 27. Cf. Luther, *Bulla coenae domini* (1522), WA 8:704; *Table Talk* no. 3657 (1537), WA TR 3:492; Luther to Melanchthon, July 9, 1530, WA Br 5:456–57.

as the real Circe,⁷⁹ she had charmed the whole world. One of them after another fell in terror, along with her helpers, the helpers of her helpers, and all who had committed fornication with her, lain with her, and kissed her feet [cf. Rev. 18:3]. Take this, dear friends, as a great and unheard-of miracle: that a little David attacks such a great Goliath and giant [1 Samuel 17] and comes away from him unharmed. That is a miracle adorning and confirming Doctor Martin's teaching.

Now, Doctor Martin not only attacked the pope, which all the prudent world and the most learned men on earth regarded at the time as something impossible and absurd, but he also drove the Antichrist with his invented religion, lies, and false forms of worship out of his own parish, out of the hearts of many people who had been held captive, ˡand out of some kingdoms and principalities, and out of many chapters⁸⁰ and monasteries. For the Antichrist's folly had become known and evident to everyone, not merely among those who served at the pope's altar against their conscience and allowed themselves to be fed and fattened by his tithes. In truth, you could scarcely find among a thousand Papists even one who believed his idol's religion was right and true.

Moreover, our doctor reformed many lands and restored the pure doctrine and proper use of the Sacraments. He also taught and wrote against the Scholastics, all universities and monasteries, the pope, Turks, Jews, heretics, fanatics,⁸¹ and all who opposed the Son of God—no matter what the whole world would say or do about it.

This miracle—that one man should attack the triple tiara⁸² and expel his devilish lies, reestablish the true worship, visit and set in order churches and schools with God's Word, and should do so without having anyone able to touch a hair of his head—dear friends, this is a miracle through which Doctor Luther's course of life and teaching have been confirmed from above.⁸³ Of all the accounts in the Bible and the chronicles of the Church, I know of no one who faced more or greater opposition, bringing the whole world down upon himself in an instant, and yet came away unharmed, except for this German prophet.

---

⁷⁹ Circe was the enchantress who sought to trap Odysseus and who turned his men into swine: see Homer, *Odyssey* 10.203–574 (Loeb 104 [1919], pp. 372–99).

⁸⁰ On cathedral chapters or foundations [*Stiften*], see above, p. 159 n. 114.

⁸¹ *Schwermer*; see above, p. 195 n. 61.

⁸² I.e., the pope, identified by his crown: see above, p. 133 n. 107; Mathesius, *History*, pp. 133, 155–56, 521.

⁸³ For the defense of Luther against the charge of lacking miracles, cf. Johann Draconites (1494–1566), *Oratio de pia morte Doctoris Martini Lutheri* (Marburg: Andreas Kolbe, 1546) [VD16 D2507], fol. A8r–v.

Moreover, do not regard it as any ordinary sign or miracle that when the greatest leaders of this world summoned Doctor Luther before them, and listened to his and his followers' confession, as well as when they ultimately came to Wittenberg themselves, they left the city and university in peace with their doctrine.[84] Thus God willed to honor and attest this man's teaching.

Compared to that, what is it if the ¹devil helped a diseased horse under the name of St. Martin,[85] Leonard,[86] or Eligius,[87] to the eternal dishonor, denegration, and diminution of the omnipotence and glory of Jesus Christ? On the Last Day, we will hear and see what miracles the eternal Son of God has worked through His servant and instrument, as well as how many souls he has rescued and led out from Babylonian captivity,[88] how many consciences he has comforted, and how many bewitched souls he has liberated, awakened, and saved through Christ's powerful Word. Christ's kingdom is a spiritual kingdom, even as He is the Archbishop of our souls [1 Pet. 2:25]. Now, if anyone faithfully serves Christ and His kingdom through preaching and prayer, he is ministering to souls, though we will not perceive it until the Last Day.

And, that I may speak further on behalf of God's doctrine as proclaimed and explained to this world by Dr. Martin and his faithful assistants in recent times, hear now how it has been honored and confirmed by the prophecy and testimony of great and holy people.[89]

---

[84] I.e., at the Diet of Augsburg in 1530 and then when Charles V occupied Wittenberg in 1547. To say that the emperor left the university and its doctrine in peace under the Augsburg Interim is a Philippist interpretation of events (see the introduction above, pp. lxxiii–lxxiv, lxxxv). Mathesius himself is critical of the effects of the Interim elsewhere (see *History*, above, pp. 344–45, 414, 492; and below, pp. 561, 566), though he generally depicts Charles as sympathetic to the Lutherans: see *History*, above, pp. 168, 178–80, 322–23, 336–37, 346–47, 362; and below, pp. 558–59. On Emperor Frederick's position regarding the Lutherans, see the introduction above, p. xcii; and Mathesius, *History*, pp. 356–57.

[85] By the late Middle Ages, all three of these saints were regarded as patrons of horses. On St. Martin of Tours, see above, p. 34 n. 23, 117 n. 13. For his healing of horses, see *LA* 2:296.

[86] St. Leonard [Leonhard] of Noblac, a sixth-century Frankish hermit, was honored as a patron of horses in late medieval Bavaria and Swabia. See *LA* 2:243–46, no. 155; *ODCC*, 3rd ed., s.v. "Leonard."

[87] St. Eligius [Loy, Eloi], bishop of Noyon, was a seventh-century Frankish saint: see *LA* (Graesse) no. 239 (210), pp. 952–53; *ODCC*, 3rd ed., s.v. "Eligius." Later versions of his legend included a story in which Eligius shoed a resistant horse by cutting off and then miraculously restoring its leg: see David Hugh Farmer, *The Oxford Dictionary of Saints*, 5th ed. (Oxford: Oxford University Press, 2011), s.v. "Eloi."

[88] Cf. above, Mathesius, *History*, p. 157.

[89] Cf. above, Mathesius, *History*, pp. 120–22.

At present we will say only a little about the ancient prophets. Obadiah [1:20–21] clearly prophesies that the Zarephathites[90] and miners will come to the kingdom of Christ and that mining towns will produce many saviors and great, salutary preachers. Likewise, Jeremiah also prophesies in chapter 51 [:27] that the [kingdoms] of Ararat (or Armenia), Ashkenaz, and Minni[91] will aid in toppling and razing Babylon. Now the scholars attest that the Germans are Ashkenazi,[92] and that the Armenians and Minni, as miners, receive their name from mercury, or quicksilver, like the German Main [River],[93] which has its source in the metalliferous Fichtelberg,[94] and Mansfeld or "Menifeld" is also thought to have taken its name from mining long ago.[95]

The Revelation of St. John also mentions the fall and demise of the great and spiritual Babylon [Rev. 14:8], which, like ancient Jericho, was made to collapse into ruin by the blowing of trumpets and ᴵthe spiritual shout of war [Josh. 6:20]. Prophecies come from the Holy Spirit [cf. 2 Pet. 1:21] and are not perceived until they are fulfilled and come to pass. Now Dr. Martin was by birth a miner in Eisleben.[96] Therefore, what we have experienced makes clear and attests that God has accomplished great miracles through miners in the last days, and has caused the Roman Babylon, as Peter calls it [1 Pet. 5:13], to be brought down.

Elijah was a prophet and preacher to miners in the smelting works at Zarephath. Now Herr Melanchthon, that precious man, called our doctor *postremae aetatis Heliam*,[97] "the last Elijah," concerning whom a prophecy has always been preserved in Christendom: namely, that before the end of this world, Enoch and Elijah would return and, as the two blessed olive trees

---

[90] See Mathesius, *History*, above, pp. 117, 119; and below, pp. 574, 583, 589, 599.

[91] See below, Mathesius, *History*, pp. 585–86, 599. Mathesius gives the orthography of the name as "Meni."

[92] See *Lectures on Genesis* (1535–45/1544–54), LW 2:190.

[93] I.e., the White Main River. Cf below, Mathesius, *History*, pp. 585–86.

[94] The Fichtelberg is the highest mountain in the Saxon Erzgebirge, on the border with Bohemia.

[95] See below, Mathesius, *History*, p. 603. This etymology of Mansfeld is mentioned by the Mansfeld preacher Cyriakus Spangenberg (see the introduction above, p. lxxviii) as well, in his fourteenth sermon on Luther, delivered in November 1569, though he may well be dependent on Mathesius for the point: Spangenberg, *Theander Lutherus*, fol. 277r.

[96] See above, Mathesius, *History*, p. 117.

[97] Cf. Melanchthon to Spalatin, March 2, 1522, MBW T1:456–57 no. 218 (CR 1:565); cf. below, pp. 560–61; and above, Walter, *New Spiritual Song*, p. 98, stanza 59. On the identification of Luther with Elijah, see Rodney Peterson, *Preaching in the Last Days: The Use of the Theme of "Two Witnesses," as Found in Revelation 11:3–13, with Particular Attention to the Sixteenth and Seventeenth Centuries* (PhD diss., Princeton University, 1985), pp. 103–5.

[Rev. 11:3–4], would preach with great boldness about the peace of Jesus Christ and about His coming.[98]

The work and deed are here before our eyes: God raised up a miner's son, and the blessed black earth[99] rushed to join him; these two brought down the spiritual Babylon and proclaimed the beautiful peace that the Son of God gained for us through His blood and offers us in the Gospel. They also proclaimed that He would soon lead us home into His eternal rest. Our God knows all things that are to happen in the future and sees them before His eyes; He lets nothing great and wondrous transpire until He has first let it be seen and proclaimed by His prophets and seers, as He testifies in the prophet Amos [3:7]. That is why the patriarch Jacob sees and recognizes not only Samson [Gen. 49:16–18],[100] Gideon [Gen. 49:22],[101] David [Gen. 49:8],[102] and other great heroes but also the Son of God in the Virgin's womb and afterbirth [Gen. 49:10],[103] as well His faithful servants St. Paul, the little Benjamin [Gen. 49:27; Rom. 11:1; Phil. 3:5],[104] and the other disciples of Christ who were to be born from the tribe of Judah (Psalm 68 [:27]). Likewise, in his last words, Moses ˈspiritually sees the first Elijah and miners' preacher [Deut. 33:20–21];[105] Isaiah and Malachi spiritually see John, the Baptist and forerunner of Christ [Isa. 40:3; Mal. 3:1; 4:5]; and Obadiah spiritually sees the future Zarephathites and miners' pastors [Obad. 1:20–21].[106]

In addition to this ancient prophecy about the Reformation to take place before the Last Day, we now have more recent and very clear prophecies concerning our doctor and his teaching.

Master John Hus, the excellent martyr and true prophet of God, clearly stated in Constance: "Now you are roasting a goose"—for *hus* means "goose" in Bohemian,[107] which had cried out against the Italian bishop like the

---

[98] See below, Mathesius, *History*, p. 592. On the interpretation of the "two olive trees" in the Reformation era, see Petersen, *Preaching in the Last Days*.

[99] *schwartz erde*; i.e., Melanchthon, whose humanist name is a Greek translation of his German name Schwartzerd.

[100] *Simeon*; but probably Samson is meant: see *Lectures on Genesis* (1535–45/1544–54), LW 8:281–85.

[101] See *Lectures on Genesis* (1535–45/1544–54), LW 8:296.

[102] See *Lectures on Genesis* (1535–45/1544–54), LW 8:235.

[103] See *Lectures on Genesis* (1535–45/1544–54), LW 8:241–43.

[104] Cf. *Lectures on Genesis* (1535–45/1544–54), LW 8:306.

[105] Cf. Luther's marginal note on this verse, WA DB 8:673, translated in LW 8:290 n. 91.

[106] Cf. above, p. 555.

[107] See above, Bugenhagen, *Christian Sermon*, p. 28; and Mathesius, *History*, p. 121.

ancient Capitoline geese[108]—"but in a hundred years a *labod*[109] or swan will come, whose song you will have to hear, and [you will have to] leave him unroasted." Now Hus was burned at the stake in Constance in the year 1415. In 1516,[110] Doctor Luther began singing; he shouted out his song in the book about the papacy,[111] and no matter how many fires were stoked, he was not even singed because of it.

There was also an influential rumor in the Roman Curia that an eremite would attack the three-tiered crown. Therefore, Doctor Staupitz said to Luther: "I thought an anchorite or hermit[112] would do it, but now I see that it shall be an Augustinian monk."[113]

Again, Johann Hilten,[114] a Franciscan,[115] whom his brothers let die[116] in prison because he refused to receive the Lord's Supper in one kind outside of the Mass,[117] named 1516 as the year in which someone would come forth and attack the monasteries with their idolatry and bring them down. This time corresponds exactly. Surely this is, as I think, a true prophecy and preceding witness about Doctor Luther's blessed and powerful course of life and the Gospel.

Now when Doctor Luther had only begun to stir with his first propositions[118] and theses,[119] he shook the whole world. Good people, who still had the smoke from the burning of St. John Hus in their noses and were pained by the murder and lies of the Babylonian Church, lifted up their heads. As he read the first proposition concerning indulgences in his refectory, Doctor Fleck cried out: "Aha! He is the one who will do it!"[120]

---

[108] In the fourth century BC, the sacred geese in Juno's temple raised an alarm when the Gauls attacked at night. See Livy, *History of Rome* 5.47 (Loeb 172 [1924], pp. 158–59).

[109] The modern Czech word for swan is *labut'*.

[110] See above, Mathesius, *History*, p. 131.

[111] *On the Papacy in Rome* (1520). LW 39:49–104.

[112] *ein Kleusner oder Einsiedler*

[113] See *Table Talk* no. 147 (1532), WA TR 1:69; no. 3593 (1537), WA TR 3:438–40; no. 6435 (n.d.), WA TR 5:660. Staupitz and Luther belonged to the Order of Augustinian Hermits.

[114] On Hilten and his prophecy, see above, Mathesius, *History*, pp. 121–22.

[115] *Barfüsser Münch*: see above, Mathesius, *History*, pp. 145–46.

[116] *sterbeten*

[117] I.e., he either refused to receive Communion from the reserved Sacrament or refused to participate except when he was himself celebrating Mass (when the celebrant would receive the Sacrament in both kinds but all others in one kind only).

[118] See above, Mathesius, *History*, pp. 143–44.

[119] *Schlußreden*

[120] *Table Talk* no. 5480 (1542), WA TR 5:177. On Fleck, see above, Mathesius, *History*, pp. 145–46 and n. 35 there.

Again, Johann Reinecke comforted and encouraged our doctor when he set out for Worms to appear at the imperial diet.[121]

I have heard from an honorable nobleman who was in Worms at the time when the doctor arrived[122] that a court jester[123] (who became my own prophet later, when I first entered the court of his lord)[124] came up to our doctor with a processional cross used in funerals[125] and sang with a loud voice: "*Advenisti desiderabilis, quem expectabamus in tenebris*," "Welcome, dear guest, whom we in the darkness have long awaited."[126]

Later, in 1525, when a provost who was serving as princely counselor at the time tried to taunt him, I heard the following words with my own ears from the mouth of this wonderful man: "Priests in the council, pigs in the bath, dogs in the church—none of these have ever been any good."[127] Fools and children also speak the truth,[128] even as the Gergesene devils spoke the truth concerning the Son of God [Matt. 8:29], and the witch in Acts [Acts 16:17] spoke the truth about St. Paul.

But it would take too long to recount [all] the judgments which exalted and illustrious people have rendered concerning our doctor's teaching, so I will mention only a few examples.

When Emperor Charles V heard Doctor Luther's teaching confessed in Augsburg[129] with steadfast boldness, it is reported that he said, "This doctrine must have a better foundation and more permanence[130] than anyone

---

[121] On Reinecke, see above, Melanchthon, *Preface*, p. 57; and Mathesius, *History*, p. 118. Reinecke's contact with Luther before his 1521 travel to Worms is not otherwise documented. Volz suggests that Mathesius may have confused Reinecke's visit with Luther in the Coburg in June 1530 with the preparation for the 1521 trip: see Volz, *Die Lutherpredigten des Johannes Mathesius*, p. 127; above, Mathesius, *History*, p. 347.

[122] On Luther's entrance into Worms (without this anecdote), see above, Mathesius, *History*, p. 172. The "honorable nobleman" cannot be definitely identified: see Volz, *Die Lutherpredigten des Johannes Mathesius*, p. 123.

[123] This was Löffler, the court jester of Duke William of Bavaria: see Loesche, *Johannes Mathesius*, 1:27.

[124] On Mathesius' service in Munich, see above, *History*, pp. 257–58.

[125] *todten Creutz*. Cf. above, Mathesius, *History*, p. 486.

[126] This verse comes from an antiphon for Holy Saturday in which the Old Testament saints held until the advent of the Redeemer hail Christ's coming to break down the gates of hell: see PL 138:1081; Volz, *Die Lutherpredigten des Johannes Mathesius*, p. 123 n. 4.

[127] Wander 3:1231, "Pfaffe" no. 170; cf. Wander 2:847, "Hund" no. 689. Cf. above, Mathesius, *History*, p. 179.

[128] Wander 2:1296, "Kind" no. 570.

[129] See above, Mathesius, *History*, p. 335.

[130] *mehr grunds unnd bestands*; or: ". . . and more validity."

has imagined."[131] And when the clergy accused Doctor Luther before the emperor even more severely than did the old high priests with the innocent Lord Jesus Christ in the presence of the imperial governor and judge [Matt. 27:11–12], this man of noble blood immediately and impatiently responded: "If you priests were good, you would have no need of any Luther."[132]

In Venice, Dr. Martin's [exposition of the] Our Father was translated into Italian without his name.[133] Upon seeing it, the [censor] whose permission was required for printing said, "Blessed are the hands that have written this; blessed are the eyes that see it; blessed shall be the hearts that believe this book and cry out to God in this way."

Erasmus of Rotterdam, whom the greatest people on earth regarded as the wisest of men, publicly confessed that when our doctor interpreted Scripture there was more understanding and depth in one page than in all the volumes and books of the Scotists, Thomists, Albertists, Modernists, and Sophists.[134] And even though his words were sometimes rather sharp and severe, a severe physician was needed for the acute and severe illness of this world in these last days.[135]

A Turkish pasha in Hungary was listening to the preaching of an Evangelical man who articulated clear distinctions about government and urged people on the basis of clear doctrine to call upon the one God in the knowledge of His mercy. The Turk is reported to have said, "If all the clergy taught like this, Mohammed's kingdom and religion would not have stood so long or advanced so far."[136]

Here we should also mention the excellent martyrs and witnesses of Jesus Christ who shed their blood in the days of Doctor Luther as they boldly and steadfastly confessed and called upon the Lord Christ, surrendering life and limb as Christians for the teaching they learned in Wittenberg or from its books, such as Herr Leonhard Kaiser in Schärding[137] and many people in Brussels and in the Netherlands.[138] Again, there is the pious Franciscan

---

[131] See above, Mathesius, *History*, p. 347.

[132] See above, Mathesius, *History*, p. 342.

[133] See above Mathesius, *History*, p. 305.

[134] See above, Mathesius, *History*, p. 163; Melanchthon, *Oration*, p. 44.

[135] See above, Melanchthon, *Oration*, p. 45; cf. above, Mathesius, *History*, p. 133.

[136] Mathesius' source for this anecdote could not be determined.

[137] On Kaiser, see above, Mathesius, *History*, pp. 248–49.

[138] Under Hapsburg rule in the Low Countries, the Edict of Worms was enforced with great severity. See James D. Tracy, "Netherlands," *OER* 3:136–42. The Augustinians Heinrich Vos and Johann Esch, of Antwerp, were martyred in Brussels on July 1, 1523 (see Luther, *Letter to the Christians in the Netherlands* [1523], WA Br 12:73–80 [*LSC*, pp. 192–97]; *Ein neues Lied wir heben an* ["A New Song Here Shall Be Begun"], LW 53:211–16. Their fellow

whom the pope in Rome had hanged on account of Doctor Luther's doctrine.[139] Again, there is Doctor "Anthony" [Robert] Barnes, who was killed in England on account of the Gospel.[140] All these and many others confessed Doctor Martin's doctrine with their mouths, and with their blood they underscored and attested it.[141]

Now, when our doctor had run his course [cf. 2 Tim. 4:7] and was buried in Wittenberg, fine testimonies were offered concerning this man. Herr Philip, the pious Elisha,[142] publicly announced the man's death in the auditorium in Wittenberg and said, amid many tears: "*Occidit auriga et currus Israëlis*" ["Fallen is the horseman and chariot of Israel"] [2 Kings 2:12].[143] God had taken away the one who had led the Christian Church through word and prayer in the name and power of Christ and who, as the charioteer and horseman of the spiritual Israel, taught the proper way to blessed repentance. He [Melanchthon] also delivered a beautiful and powerful funeral oration[144] alongside other [preachers][145] at the funeral.

How often Master Philip repeated the beautiful old verse about our doctor: "*Nulla ferent talem saecla futura virum*,"[146] "No other man like this

---

Augustinian Lambert von Thorn was imprisoned and died in captivity in 1528: see Luther to Thorn, January 19, 1524, WA Br 3:237–39 (*LSC*, pp. 197–99). Meanwhile, Heinrich von Zütphen escaped, but was killed for his preaching in Dithmarschen in 1524: see Luther, *The Burning of Brother Henry* (1525), LW 32:261–86; and above, p. 163 n. 133.

[139] Giovanni Mollio (ca. 1500–1553), a Franciscan professor of theology and associate of the converts Bernardo Occhino (1487–1564) and Peter Martyr Vermigli (1500–1562), was hanged in Rome on September 5, 1553, for his defense of the doctrine of justification by faith. His story was published in Rabus, *Historien* 3 (1555) [VD16 R38], fols. 192v–202v. On Rabus, see the introduction above, pp. lxiii–lxiv.

[140] On Robert Barnes, see above, Mathesius, *History*, pp. 422–23.

[141] For the metaphor of blood as ink, cf. above, Mathesius, *History*, pp. 177, 317, 548, 549.

[142] For Melanchthon as Elisha, see the introduction above, p. xci; cf. below, Mathesius, *History*, pp. 592, 594.

[143] See the introduction above, p. xxxv. Cf. above, Mathesius, *History*, p. 316 and n. 204 there, pp. 555–56.

[144] See the introduction above, pp. xli–xliv; Melanchthon, *Oration*, pp. 39–51; cf. above, Mathesius, *History*, p. 537.

[145] I.e., Johann Bugenhagen: see the introduction above, pp. xxxvi–xxxvii; Bugenhagen, *Christian Sermon*, pp. 23–35; cf. Mathesius, *History*, p. 537.

[146] Melanchthon cites this verse as Plato's epitaph, composed by Aristotle, in his oration *On Aristotle* (1544), CR 11:651, trans. Asaph Ben-Tov in *Biography, Historiography, and Modes of Philosophizing*, ed. Patrick Baker (Leiden: Brill, 2017), pp. 274–75, apparently derived from Marsilio Ficino's (1433–99) *Platonis Vita* [*Life of Plato*], prefaced to his translation of Plato's works (Florence: St. Jacobus di Ripoli & Lorenzo d'Alopa, 1484) [GW M33912], fol. [6]v. For the Greek original, see M. L. West, *Iambi et Elegi Graeci ante Alexandrum Cantati*, 2nd ed. (Oxford: Oxford University Press, 1992), 2:44–45 (Aristotle 673). For its application to Luther, see Volz, *Die Lutherpredigten des Johannes Mathesius*, pp. 73f. n. 3.

will come again upon this earth." Doctor Wolf Severus, who had been the preceptor of the current Roman emperor, also wrote these two little lines about our doctor:[147]

Iapeti de gente prior maiorque Luthero,
Nemo fuit, sed nec, credo, futurus erit.

From Japheth's[148] blood and Gentile race
No greater light has e'er found place
Than Luther, whom our God did send
With him to bring things to an end.[149]

And surely the years that followed also confirmed what kind of man it was whom the Church had lost. He was indeed a true hero and lion, as one learned man proudly said when he received news of the doctor's death. "The lion is dead," he jeered. "Of the hares I am not afraid in the slightest."[150] But in the end, the hares roasted this hunter when he changed his teaching and sought to distort and muddle Doctor Luther's doctrine of justification. A hare or lamb armed with God's Word is greater than all elephants and panthers who boast in their supposed wisdom and despise other people.[151]

In the year following Doctor Luther's death, a great sovereign lord took counsel because of the war that had arisen. His counselor set before him our doctor's advice from 1531, when he counseled against taking up the sword against imperial authority.[152] Upon having the writing read to him, the

---

[147] On Wolfgang Schiefer [Severus], tutor to the future emperor Maximilian II from 1536 to 1538, see above, p. 339 n. 104. The dissemination of this hexameter couplet seems to depend on Mathesius: see Volz, *Die Lutherpredigten des Johannes Mathesius*, p. 28. Cf. Mathesius, *Sirach* (1586) [VD16 B4115], vol. 3, fol. 68r.

[148] On Japheth, see above, p. 105 n. 11.

[149] *Auß Japhets blut und Heyden stamm*
Kein Grösser Liecht auff erden kam.
Denn Doctor Luther, der grosse Mann,
Damit wil Gott beschlossen han.

[150] This remark on Luther's death is ascribed to the Nürnberg reformer Andreas Osiander (see above, p. 311 n. 170), on the claimed authority of direct witnesses in Königsberg, in Conrad Schlüsselburg, *Catalogus Haereticorum*, book 6 (Frankfurt a.M.: Peter Kopf, 1598) [VD16 S3038], pp. 43, 243. See Volz, *Die Lutherpredigten des Johannes Mathesius*, p. 150 n. 3. On Osiander's conflict with nearly all other Lutherans over the doctrine of justification, see above, Mathesius, *History*, p. 391 and n. 112 there, and Timothy J. Wengert, *Defending Faith: Lutheran Responses to Andreas Osiander's Doctrine of Justification, 1551–1559*, Studies in the Late Middle Ages, Humanism and the Reformation 65 (Tübingen: Mohr Siebeck, 2012).

[151] Cf. above, Mathesius, *History*, pp. 480–81.

[152] See above, Mathesius, *History*, pp. 359–60, on advice dating from 1530 but partly published (by Luther's opponents) in 1531. Luther's 1531 *Warning to His Dear German People* (LW 47:3–55) in fact makes provision for defensive armed resistance to the emperor.

leader remarked: "This book proves that Doctor Luther was not an unwise man. Blessed are those who have followed his faithful counsel."[153]

Finally, we ought not to forget this as well: that those who had been led astray and incited by the clergy ultimately not only left Doctor Luther's teaching uncondemned but also approved and accepted it at the end of their life, as has been credibly written.[154] For example, both lord emperors tolerated the Augsburg Confession[155] and admonished certain princes to abide in it and to beware of Calvinism.[156]

And because extraordinary men[157] also commonly confirm their office and doctrine with the gift of prophecy, as you heard at the beginning, let us conclude by recalling some of our doctor's prophecies, which have for the most part already been fulfilled by the present day and are becoming more visibly fulfilled every day. The doctor wrote to Prince George of Anhalt[158] that he was certain that no major war would arise in Germany during his lifetime, for his prayer was heard very attentively; but after his death they ought to be vigilant. Has this not come true? As soon as this prophet was gathered to his rest before the calamity [cf. Isa. 57:1–2], tumult[159] began in the German Empire, though God mercifully permitted this to take place so that many people might be led to repentance. Help, O God, so that our body may not be beaten by a more severe rod. Nebuchadnezzar came even into the Promised Land and carried some people away [2 Kings 24:11–16]. But when

---

[153] The source of this anecdote and the persons involved could not be determined. Perhaps Elector Joachim of Brandenburg is in view; he maintained neutrality in the Smalcaldic War (see the introduction above, pp. lxxiii, lxxxiv. See Bodo Nischan, "Brandenburg," *OER* 1:207–8.

[154] Probably a reference to Emperor Charles, as Mathesius depicts him. See above, *History*, p. 342. Loesche (*LH²*, p. 589) suggests that it may refer to rumors of the deathbed recantation of several of Luther's theological opponents, but they had not previously left Luther's teaching "uncondemned."

[155] On the toleration of the Augsburg Confession by the emperors, see above, Mathesius, *History*, pp. 341–42, 362, 554, 558.

[156] Probably a reference to the disquiet of Ferdinand and Maximilian at the efforts of the Elector Palatine Frederick III to introduce Reformed Protestantism in the Palatinate with the Heidelberg Catechism of 1563 (see above, p. 317 n. 213). See, e.g., Maximilian to Elector Frederick, April 25, 1563, in August Kluckhohn, ed., *Briefe Friedrich des Frommen, kurfürsten von der Pfalz* (Braunschweig: Schwetschke, 1868), 1:398–99; Bard Thompson, "Historical Background of the Catechism," in *Essays on the Heidelberg Catechism*, ed. Bard Thompson et al. (Eugene, OR: Wipf & Stock, 2016), chapter 1. On the attitudes of Charles and Ferdinand to the teaching of the Augsburg Confession, particularly on the doctrine of the Lord's Supper, see above, Mathesius, *History*, pp. 356–57.

[157] *wunderleut*; see the introduction above, pp. lxxxix–xc.

[158] On George of Anhalt, see above, p. 30 n. 16; cf. Mathesius, *History*, p. 418.

[159] I.e., the Smalcaldic War. See above, p. 233 n. 13; cf. Mathesius, *History*, p. 499.

few discerned the punishment and mended their ways, finally the whole kingdom and temple were utterly destroyed for a time [2 Kings 25:1–30].

At the colloquy in Marburg in 1529, Dr. Luther clearly prophesied that Oecolampadius and Zwingli would clasp their heads in their hands before three years had passed, and this is indeed what happened.[160] In 1532 the prophecy was fulfilled, as Zwingli's heart foretold him it would be, for the errant man was reported to say this there with burning tears: "With God as my witness, there is no one with whom I would rather be united than with those from Wittenberg."[161]

That same year our doctor was beset by severe tribulations, causing many of the others to despair of his life. "No," he said, "the devil is sorely afflicting me, but I will not die this time, so that the adversaries will not be able to gloat over my death too, as [they have] over [the death of] other people, claiming they had prayed me to death."[162]

Several times I and many others heard from his mouth what he said about a certain learned man,[163] whose name I refrain from mentioning to honor his students: "This man will yet become a heretic, because he does nothing but vaunt and swagger, and he thinks he can do everything on his own." This came to pass, as it did with many others.

He often repeated these words, which he spoke to me, also at table:[164] "Mathesius, you will see it. All who oppose this university and church in Wittenberg (as long as the pure doctrine remains here) will suffer a ship-wreck of their faith [1 Tim. 1:19] and become heretics." In my opinion,

---

[160] See above, Mathesius, *History*, pp. 309–13 (on the Marburg Colloquy); for Luther's prophecy, see above, Mathesius, *History*, p. 314.

[161] See Luther to Jacob Probst, June 1, 1530, WA Br 5:338–41; *Table Talk* no. 129 (1531), WA TR 1:53 (WA 48:393). The letter to Probst was printed in Johannes Timann, *Farrago sententiarum consentientium in vera et Catholica doctrina de Coena Domini* (Frankfurt a/M: Peter Braubach, 1555) [VD16 T1313], pp. 165–68, here p. 166. See Volz, *Die Lutherpredigten des Johannes Mathesius*, p. 282 on *LH* 395.12–15.

[162] See *Table Talk* no. 157 (1532), LW 54:23–24. Cf. above, Mathesius, *History*, pp. 258–59.

[163] Perhaps the "learned man" in view is Johann Rivius (1500–1553; Georg Müller, "Rivius, Johann," *ADB* 28:709), who had been rector of schools in Annaberg, Schneeberg, and Freiberg, and who, after their introduction of the Reformation, served the Albertine Saxon dukes as tutor to the future elector August (1526–86) and as organizer of the princely schools in Meissen; many of his former students had connections to Joachimsthal (Volz, *Die Lutherpredigten des Johannes Mathesius*, pp. 149–50 n. 6). See *Table Talk* no. 5148 (1540), WA TR 4:684. However, though Luther criticizes Rivius for arrogance (*Table Talk* no. 4492 [1539], LW 54:348), his lapse into heresy is difficult to document. A more likely target may be the Nürnberg reformer Andreas Osiander (see above, p. 311 n. 170), though Mathesius criticizes him by name elsewhere. Cf. *Table Talk* no. 3900 (1538), LW 54:290–91; no. 4763 (1530), WA TR 4:476–77; no. 5047 (1540), LW 54:382–84; no. 5048 (1540), WA TR 4:635–36; no. 5122 (1540), WA TR 4:672 n. 4 (cf. *LH*², p. 590 ad loc.).

[164] See above, Mathesius, *History*, p. 419.

time has shown this prophecy to be true. That is why ungrateful students who had been educated and nurtured in this university rebelled against this Mount Lebanon[165] and the doctrine they heard here, turning away from it and weaving in their own dreams. Some of them even wanted to grab our dead lion by his mane.[166] But the Lion of Judah [Rev. 5:5] has defended the teaching of His young lions and little rams and publicly preserved it to this day. May He continue to help and protect against those who secretly stab through the fence[167] and fish in front of the net.[168]

The doctor also said, "I do not expect that there will be any danger as long as people who have listened to us and accompanied us are alive. Once they have been carried off and have gone to sleep, then beware! The world loves to hear something new; clever Reason, too, loves to give voice to its new, unknown, and mysterious teaching. *Vilescit quotidianum* ["Everyday things become despised"].[169] But blessed are those who persist in simplicity in the simple Word and who know, invoke, and preach none but Christ the crucified."

In his preface to the prophet Daniel, our doctor thought that before the Lord Christ's appearance there would cease to be any pulpit in which God's Word was preached. Fathers would still preserve the catechism in their homes for a time, as in the days of Elijah [1 Kings 19:18].[170] But in the end, when Christ comes for judgment, He will find very little pure doctrine and faith on earth [Luke 18:8]. Help, eternal Son of God! Seal Your Word in our hearts and in the hearts of our children and posterity; do not let the devil tear it from their hearts; and graciously take us and them home, in the blessed confession and invocation of Your name. Amen.

The prophecies he made concerning kingdoms and principalities, which have, in part, already been fulfilled rather dramatically,[171] are like a festering sore that we cannot bear to touch. For many, this sore still has not completely dried up and healed. As he also frequently said, "I do not like

---

[165] See above, Mathesius, *History*, p. 237.

[166] *in bart greiffen*. Cf. above, Mathesius, *History*, pp. 319, 561. Cf. Wander 2:347, "Bart" no. 25.

[167] For the expression, see Mathesius, *History*, above, pp. 260, 413; and below, p. 595.

[168] See Wander 2:290, "Hamen" no. 6; Thiele, pp. 118–19, no. 101: i.e., seeking to poach fish that are being driven in front of another's net.

[169] See *Table Talk* no. 5015 (1540), LW 54:377–76. Cf. Wander 3:1007, "Neue (das)" no. 1. See also *Table Talk* no. 5469 (1542), WA TR 5:169–70.

[170] Luther, *Preface to Daniel [12]* (1545), WA DB 11/2:121–23 (LW 63). Cf. above, Mathesius, *History*, pp. 419, 435.

[171] *eben starck*

being a prophet,[172] for in my case the things generally come to pass. Pride and arrogance will never endure in the world."

In 1529, when the Turk was besieging Vienna, [Doctor Luther] was lecturing on Isaiah.[173] Among other things he said, "I hope that Daniel's prophecy [Dan. 7:20–27] will continue to come true. The Turk, the blasphemer of the Most High, has struck and broken off three horns or kingdoms from the Roman Empire. By doing so, he shall bring on his death. He may try his ambition against Germany; our sins could help him waltz in here and carry people away. He will not take possession of [the land] without a fight, I hope. For God also put a ring in the nose of Sennacherib [Isa. 37:29; 2 Kings 19:28] and set a boundary for him that he was unable to pass.

"The Roman Empire is to be the greatest and last of the empires, and in it, the greatest miracles of God are to be performed. This is where Christ was born, Jerusalem was destroyed, the Gospel was sent into the whole world; and, though the Antichrist has elevated himself above God and His Word [2 Thess. 2:4], God has allowed His Word to rise again in the Roman Empire and to be preached and confessed publicly before the Roman emperor. That is why I hope that the Last Day shall also come *stante et durante Romano imperio* ['while the Roman Empire stands and endures'].[174] For Daniel does not specify any kingdom after the Roman scepter."

This prophecy concerning the Turk is still applicable at the present time. May God continue to help the Roman Empire, so that the Turk and pope may be weakened and the holy Gospel brought into all the world through the head of this empire by means of public mandates, as happened during

---

[172] *Table Talk* no. 5064 (1540), LW 54:384; no. 5469 (1542), WA TR 5:169–70; no. 4379 (1539), WA TR 4:271; preface to Sutel, *Gospel on the Destruction of Jerusalem* (1539), LW 60:226; *Admonition to All Pastors* (1539), WA 50:486 (LW 61). Cf. *Appeal for Prayer against the Turks* (1541), LW 43:223; *Church Postil* (1540–44), sermon for Trinity 26 on Matt. 24:31–46, LW 79:350, paragraph 34).

[173] Cf. *Lectures on Isaiah* (1527–30/1532–34), LW 17:306, where Sennacherib's fate is discussed in parallel with deliverance from the Turk in Luther's own day. Daniel's prophecy is not mentioned in the surviving notes on Luther's Isaiah lectures but appears in other contemporary writings of his: see *Muster-Sermon against the Turks* (1529), WA 30/2:160, 161–79 (LW 63); letter to Nicholas Hausmann, October 26, 1529, WA Br 5:167.17, and November 10, 1529, WA Br 5:176.5f.; to Friedrich Myconius, October 17, 1529, WA Br 5:162, and December 2, 1529, WA Br 5:191–92; *Preface to Daniel* (1530), LW 35:294–313. See Volz, *Die Lutherpredigten des Johannes Mathesius*, pp. 170–71. Mathesius would have been a witness to these lectures on Isaiah: see above, Mathesius, *History*, p. 295. Mathesius presents here a kind of précis of the material in the *Muster-Sermon against the Turks*.

[174] An allusion to the words of Jordan of Osnabrück (ca. 1220–84; Heinrich Koch, "Jordanus von Osnabrück," *BBKL* 3:645–49) in his *De praerogativa Romani imperii*, incorporated in the *Memoriale* of Alexander de Roes (1225–88) (ed. Herbert Grundmann, Monumenta Germaniae Historica, Staatsschrifte des späteren Mittelalters 1/1 [Stuttgart: Anton Hiersemann, 1958], p. 98). The Latin phrase does not appear in Luther's corpus.

the reigns of Nebuchadnezzar [Dan. 3:29], Cyrus [2 Chron. 36:22–23; Isa. 44:28], Ahasuerus [Esth. 8:10], Theodosius, and Arcadius,[175] as testimony for the world in these last days, and so that the Son of God, before His return, may publicly vindicate and exculpate Himself and remain righteous throughout all eternity when the godless and those who despise His Gospel accuse Him falsely, out of diabolical envy.

In conclusion, hear also what our doctor prophesied about the papacy when he went to the house of Herr Spalatin[176] from the Coburg in 1530, along with the emissaries, and composed this verse:

Pestis eram vivens, moriens ero mors tua Papa.[177]

Alive, I was a plague to you;
   In death, O pope, I'll run you through.
A stroke you never shall endure:
   It is God's Word, the doctrine pure.[178]

Time has provided us with sufficient evidence of this from experience. For after the great imperial diet in Augsburg,[179] the papacy was weakened day by day. Once Doctor Luther was dead and the Interim[180] had been buried afterward, the pillars of the papacy were torn down as they were in Dagon's house in the days of Samson [Judg. 16:23–30], so that it is diminished daily. The prophecies of Daniel [Dan. 11:36], St. Paul [2 Thess. 2:3], and Luther are in agreement. No one else—however great, mighty, strong, learned, or ingenious he may be—shall ever help the last Antiochus to stand again.[181] Babylon the great must fall and be destroyed, for its time has come

---

[175] Under Emperor Theodosius the Great (see above, p. 322 n. 15), Nicene Christianity was declared to be the sole legal religion in the Roman Empire: see *ODCC*, 3rd ed., "Theodosius I." His son Arcadius (see above, p. 322 n. 16) reinforced the status of Nicene Christianity with numerous edicts: see Friedrich Wilhelm Bautz, "Arkadius," *BBKL* 1:217.

[176] On Spalatin, see above, p. 136 n. 121.

[177] See above, Bugenhagen, *Christian Sermon*, p. 35.

[178] *Weyl ich lebt, war ich dein gifft;*
Nach meinem todt laß ich dir ein stifft.
Der wird dich, Bapst, erwürgen gar,
Das thut Gotts wort, die reine lahr.

[179] The Diet of Augsburg in 1530, where the Augsburg Confession was presented: see above, Mathesius, *History*, pp. 320–67.

[180] On the so-called Augsburg and Leipzig Interims, see the introduction above, pp. xx–xxi and n. 22 there, p. lxxiii and n. 280 there, and p. lxxxv. The Interims were in effect in some form from 1547 to 1552; they were "buried" by the Passau Treaty of 1552 and Peace of Augsburg in 1555: see Günther Wartenberg, "Interims," *OER* 2:319–21; Herbert Immenkoetter, "Augsburg, Peace of," *OER* 1:91–93.

[181] On Antiochus Epiphanes (see above, p. 494 n. 184) as a type of antichrist, cf. Luther, *Preface to 1 Maccabees* (1533), LW 35:350–52.

[cf. Rev. 18:2, 10]. It will be brought down without the stroke of a sword and will finally be cast into the lake of fire [cf. Rev. 19:20–21], and in sulfur and pitch it will have eternal trouble and torment, like Sodom and Gomorrah [Gen. 19:24].

Now, so that we may draw to a close for the present: We have seen that our doctor was rightly and legitimately called to his professorship, and his teaching was at all times grounded solely upon the patriarchs, prophets, and apostles, on the Christian Creeds and confession of the true Christian Church, on the firm pillars of truth. These he also confessed before both high and low as a steadfast martyr and witness of God, and he stood firm upon them until his final breath. ¹His calling and course of life are attested and witnessed by strong and firm testimonies, before and during his lifetime and after his death, and many people have shed their blood for the sake of this doctrine. He was publicly excommunicated, proscribed, slandered, and defamed because of this, and, though most of the world opposed him, no devil, tyrant, heretic, or poison was able to kill him or to touch even a hair of his head, and he confirmed his doctrine with many certain prophecies as well as with other great gifts and graces. Thus it is certain that this doctor's course of life and his witness to Jesus Christ, like the preaching of other extraordinary men,[182] have been gloriously confirmed and attested, so that we need have no doubt that Doctor Luther's confession is the right doctrine, which is in agreement with Moses and with all blessed kings, prophets, apostles, pillars of the Church and lights, and the pure councils, and is the divine truth and blessed knowledge through which we receive eternal life through pure grace.

Oh, what meager witness the papacy as it stands today has from Scripture, even though the pope falsely calls himself St. Peter's heir and the rock upon which the Son of God, the one and eternal Rock [Matt. 16:18; 1 Cor. 10:4], has built His Church and congregation in the Word and preserved it until now.

Nor can Mohammed muster anything to justify or to prove his abominable blasphemy. Jews who fall away from Moses and the prophetic text and who call only upon their rabbinic fables and invented dreams likewise have no foundation or certainty for their interpretation. The heathen, too, who walked in their own darkness, without God and His Word, possess in all of their philosophers, poets, scholars, and histories nothing certain regarding the true religion, what God's essence and will are, what sin is, how to be delivered from sin and death ᴵor how to enter into eternal life, even though by virtue of their natural light and knowledge they do sometimes write not ineptly in their cleverly devised fables (as St. Peter calls them [cf. 2 Pet. 1:16])

---

[182] *wunderleut*; see the introduction above, pp. lxxxix–xc.

and wise maxims, and fine civil and domestic examples about discipline according to reason, and about honor, peace, and unity, and [the value of] a good name.

Heretics, fanatics, and false brethren do sometimes make use of Scripture, which they interpret to their liking and twist into their own false notions even as they boast of their spirit and their heavenly inspiration and motivation. But their dreams and deceptions are not in accord with the faith, as all true interpretation, books, and sermons are to be in accordance with St. Paul's doctrine [Rom. 12:6]. For they deny the Lord Jesus Christ and rob Him of either His divine or His human nature, or else they dishonor His eternal kingdom or priesthood and reject and trample the precious blood of reconciliation of Jesus Christ, God's Son, which alone cleanses us from all sins [1 John 1:7], reconciles us with God, and makes us to be children and heirs of God. Indeed, these idol-makers who boast of the name of God help the ancient serpent bite Christ's heel[183] and peaceful feet [Gen. 3:15; Rom. 10:15] and with all their erudition, spirit, zeal, and holiness attack the venerable preaching office amid great boasting. They also oppose the spoken and written Word of God, which the eternal and substantial Word brought forth from the heart and bosom of His Father and spoke from the beginning [John 1:1, 18]. The Holy Spirit has heard and received it from Him and caused it to be proclaimed and written down by the chosen and appointed witnesses of God, the patriarchs, prophets, and apostles, who also saw and heard Christ themselves; and it has been affirmed with great miracles.

Likewise, the flighty spirits [Ps. 119:113 DB],[184] who flutter away from the Word, employ a crafty and fraudulent guise and rationalistic, concocted glosses and interpretations that are discordant, vacuous, and ambiguous to assail the holy foundation and institution of the Lord Christ, our eternal High Priest and Archbishop, whom the Father Himself commanded us from heaven to hear [Heb. 2:17; 1 Pet. 2:25; Matt. 17:5]. For the ultimate intention of all heretics and fanatics is to assist their devil in furthering his lies and murder [cf. John 8:44] to confound and tear apart Christ's person and office as well as His Word and Sacraments and His estates: namely, the holy [estate of] governing authority and the estate of marriage.[185] In the end they all betray and clearly reveal themselves because they draw the sword, cause tumult, seek the life and property of the members and true witnesses of Christ, and soil and besmirch themselves with wicked lust and illicit sexual desire and intercourse at the prompting of their unclean spirit.

---

[183] See above, p. 104 n. 10.

[184] See above, Mathesius, *History*, p. 519 and n. 97 there.

[185] On the three estates, see above, p. 478 n. 92.

In short, Jews, Turks, heathens, monks, sophists, bishops, new councils, fanatics, heretics, flighty spirits, false brethren proclaim and profess nothing that is certain, solid, well-grounded, credible, coherent, and true with their mouths or in their books (Psalm 5 [:9]), but only sheer lies, murder, rebellion, unchastity, hypocrisy, and deceitfulness. And in the doctrine and conduct of those who claim to be the best, there is nothing but boasting, licentiousness, covetousness, and riotous living to be found.

So, then, this doctor, along with his faithful assistants and colleagues, bases his doctrine on the Word of the prophets and shines this light into the dark world and beclouded hearts, continually directing us to the only-begotten Son of God and His Word, which the Spirit of God wrote down through the prophets and apostles. His interpretation and exposition, or prophecy and prediction, are in accord, consistent, and congruent with the faith in Jesus Christ [Rom. 12:6]. ¦He gives the honor and glory to God and His Word alone and steadfastly teaches that we are saved by grace alone, through faith and trust in the unique blood of Jesus Christ, and not of ourselves or our works and righteousness or our new obedience, so that we cannot boast in ourselves, as St. Paul also writes in Ephesians 2 ([vv. 8–9]). Therefore, dear friends, today I exhort you to abide steadfast in this man's doctrine, witness, and true prophecy and exposition of Scripture and to persevere to the end of your lives together with your families. Meanwhile, thank God, who sent this chosen instrument to us in these lands in these last days and preserved him against all the gates of hell for twenty-nine years[186] in his legitimate calling. Do not be turned away from his confession or misled by swindlers and agitators,[187] who would like to suppress and destroy this man's reputation, office, and confession at the present day.

Through this man and his assistants God has liquated, cupellated, refined, and purified the blessed doctrine in Wittenberg, making it pass through the fire [cf. 1 Cor. 3:13; Ps. 12:6].[188] Beware of those who want to adulterate the silver again and stamp it with false images. For there are many clever, cunning, and shrewd people, and the world craves curiosities. That is why, as a member of the university and church in Wittenberg, as a grateful student of this doctor and of his most beloved friend, Herr Philip,[189] and as your rightly called, agèd pastor, I am warning you, my parishioners, lest you be tossed to and fro and carried about by every wind [of doctrine] [Eph. 4:14], led away from the Word of the Lord Christ, or made suspicious of His faithful servants among you in this church and university.

---

[186] I.e., from 1517 to 1546.

[187] *deumelern*

[188] *seigern, treyben, rein unnd superfein brennen unnd durchfeuren lassen*

[189] On Melanchthon and Luther's friendship, see above, Mathesius, *History*, pp. 403–4.

In the evil world of these last days there are many babblers, many book writers, and many dissemblers who ¹masquerade in angelic glory [cf. 2 Cor. 11:14] while speaking blandishments and gibberish.¹⁹⁰ Persist in what you have learned, and do not let the Word of the apostles and prophets, as God had it interpreted in Wittenberg, be wrenched out of your hands or torn out of your hearts and made detestable; rarely does a better judge and doctor come afterward.¹⁹¹ So shall you persevere in peace in the pure doctrine and blessedly depart from here in the truth with a good conscience, alongside your prophet and your pastor, and appear before the face of Jesus Christ with honor and joy, and abide eternally with God and all His true saints, whom the eternal Light and substantial Life has illuminated and sent out to us with His Word to testify and preach about Him. The world, which also boasts of its religion, turns the ambassadors and lights of God into saviors, mediators, and patrons, and in the best of their teaching they present us with their examples and holy lives in order to rob the Son of God of His priesthood.

We have only one Mediator, the Lord Jesus Christ [1 Tim. 2:5]; we confidently trust in His merit and intercession, not that of the deceased saints, as the true and speaking saints proclaim witness to us in their sermons, testimonies, and writings.

Let that suffice concerning Doctor Luther's doctrine, witness, and interpretation [of the Scriptures]. May God preserve us and those in our care in the same, as we ask with all our hearts. And may He protect this church and university from false doctrine, wicked examples, and diabolical and Babylonian forms of worship.

Amen, dear Lord Jesus, Amen!

---

¹⁹⁰ *schmeichel und kauderwelschen reden*; see above, Mathesius, *History*, p. 516 and n. 85 there.

¹⁹¹ Cf. Wander 4:538, "Selten" no. 2.

THE SIXTEENTH SERMON,[1]
ON THE FAR-RENOWNED CHRISTIAN UNIVERSITY
IN WITTENBERG,
AND HOW IT DEVELOPED,
ON THE OCCASION OF THE SCHOOL FESTIVAL
IN ST. JOACHIMSTHAL

[St. Gregory's Day, March 12, 1564][2]

D EAR friends in the Lord! Today our school is holding its festival,[3] and, according to the ancient and laudable custom, it is summoning the little children to school with heartfelt prayer and a solemn procession.[4] To the glory of God and in honor of this Christian school and congregation, therefore, we intend to hold a school sermon[5] about the Christian and widely renowned university in Wittenberg and how it came into being.

For then we will also have the opportunity to continue in our history of Doctor Luther and express our due and fitting gratitude to this university, our *alma [mater]*, because it is from this university that our God has attacked the Antichrist's abominations and idolatry and cleansed many hearts and churches, as well as planted and established His holy Gospel in the schools of nearly the entire Roman Empire and many other kingdoms.

---

[1] In the 1566 first edition, fol. 206v, this sermon is numbered as the fifteenth. Cf. above, p. 463 n. 1.

[2] On the dating of this sermon, see the introduction above, p. lxxxvii; Volz, *Die Lutherpredigten des Johannes Mathesius*, pp. 9–11. For a detailed evaluation of Mathesius' sources for the history of the University of Wittenberg, see Volz, *Die Lutherpredigten des Johannes Mathesius*, pp. 129–33.

[3] I.e., on March 12, the feast of St. Gregory the Great: see *LA* 1:171–84, no. 46. The day had been observed as a festival for schoolchildren since the time of Pope Gregory IV (r. 827–844). See *DWB*, s.v. "Gregorius." A reformed version of the festival had been celebrated in Joachimsthal since 1557: see Brown, *Singing the Gospel*, pp. 71–73; Mathesius, "Schulfestpredigt," in Loesche, *Mathesius: Ausgewählte Werke*, 4:29–54.

[4] *ehrlichem gepreng*

[5] Cf. Mathesius to Paul Eber, May 1, 1563, in Loesche, *Mathesius: Ausgewählte Werke*, 4:588: "I am continuing in the history of Herr Dr. Luther, and, God willing, I shall at our next school festival speak about the University of Wittenberg, out of gratitude."

To the glory of God, we in this valley can also boast in all truthfulness that we have received the pure doctrine of the Gospel from Wittenberg, along with the holy catechism and blessed administration of the venerable Sacraments. In addition, this church and school have been supplied from there for many years now; all of our ministers of the church and teachers in the school, as well as some ⌐children of our citizens, are [former] Wittenberg students,[6] who now honorably serve churches and schools both here and elsewhere, as well as many cities and courts.

For my part, I, too, should and can affirm truthfully that I am grateful to my Lord Christ and to the excellent people, my dear preceptors and friends in Wittenberg, and their good books for what I learned [there] and have taught here by God's grace and blessing about the true religion along with the liberal arts. Accordingly, I profess myself to be a member of this university and of the Wittenberg church for the rest of my life. I am obliged, moreover, by many a favor and by my promise and vows to laud and praise this church and university now and in all eternity and to defend them, to the extent my simplicity permits, against all those who accuse them and slanderously speak ill of them.

Therefore, beloved in the Lord, hear now about when and by whom this university was founded; what kind of illustrious people God appointed to serve there; the condition in which I found this university when our God first brought me there in 1529; what was being taught there in lectures and sermons at that time; and what fine people were being educated there, who still at the present day are rendering their Christian and laudable service to the Lord Christ's Gospel and to the honorable and liberal arts.

As many people know, having seen this esteemed city, Wittenberg is in the land of Saxony, on the Elbe River, between Torgau and Magdeburg, Leipzig and Jüterbog; and it is said to take its name from "White Mountain" or *Mons Libani* ["Mount Lebanon"][7] by God's providence, because, as Doctor Fleck preached when he helped dedicate this university,[8] God was going to send the true wisdom out into the whole [Holy] Roman Empire from this white mountain or mountain of life,[9] when ⌐He would cause His Gospel to be publicly preached at the end of the world as a bright flash [of lightning]

---

[6] On Joachimsthal students at Wittenberg, see Förstemann et al., *Album*, vols. 1–2; Lorenz, *Bilder aus Alt-Joachimsthal*, pp. 117–18; and Georg Buchwald, *Wittenberger Ordiniertenbuch*, 2 vols. (Leipzig: Weigand, 1894–95), s.v. "Joachimsthal." Cf. above, Mathesius, *History*, pp. 111–12, 292.

[7] See above, Mathesius, *History*, pp. 145, 237.

[8] On Johann Fleck and his sermon (and the question of the historicity of Mathesius' account), see above, Mathesius, *History*, pp. 145–46, 287.

[9] See above, Mathesius, *History*, pp. 307–8; cf. WA 48:680.

throughout the world [cf. Matt. 24:27] and vindicate Himself in the sight of many before revealing His Son at the final judgment.

Our reasons for calling this city *Mons Libani* ["Mount Lebanon"] and the Mountain of Wisdom,[10] which the wise child, the young Widukind,[11] is said to have built, are not trivial. After Jerusalem had been destroyed[12] and the Jews were scattered throughout the whole world, some of them resided in neighboring towns there and recognized that a new Jerusalem and Mount Zion would rise in that place and another promised land would be planted there, where the Son of God would finally make Himself heard again and have His Gospel preached as a witness before His coming.[13]

Therefore, the ancient inhabitants of this place called the next little village across the Elbe *Prata*,[14] or Ephrathah [Gen. 35:19; Mic. 5:2],[15] as Doctor Luther himself thought, because that is where the true breadbasket and granary would be, to which Christ would give His true bread of heaven and again teach the hearts of many people through the Word and Spirit—or, as St. Paul says [Gal. 4:19], form and clearly present [Himself in them]—and those afflicted by the papacy would eat again from the preached Christ and be satisfied and joyful [cf. Ps. 22:26]. Likewise, it is believed that the ancient inhabitants called the Elbe River—which has its origin in Bohemia on the Silesian border, under the Riesengebirge,[16] and is called the *Eilffe* because of its eleven tributaries[17]—*Phrat*, or the fertile Euphrates [cf. Gen. 2:14], because that is where faithful Abraham's children would be turned back

---

[10] See above, p. 145 n. 36.

[11] Widukind [Wittekind] (730–807)—whose name can be read as "wise child," though it probably originally meant "child of the woods"—was duke of the Saxons in their conflict against Charlemagne in 777–785; he finally converted to Christianity and accepted Frankish rule. See *Oxford Encyclopedia of the Middle Ages*, s.v. "Widukind." His association with Wittenberg is fictional; the town was founded in the twelfth century under the Ascanian dukes.

[12] I.e., after the Roman siege under Titus in AD 70. Cf. Luther, *Table Talk* no. 3990 (1538), LW 54:306.

[13] For the following linguistic speculation on the Hebrew origins of the towns around Wittenberg (which Luther calls a "jest"), cf. *Misuse of the Mass* (1521), LW 36:229; *De abroganda missa privata* (1521), WA 8:476; *On the Shem Hamphorash and on the Lineage of Christ* (1543), WA 53:600–601 (LW 61). See Volz, *Die Lutherpredigten des Johannes Mathesius*, p. 93.

[14] I.e., Pratau [Brate], some 3 km south of Wittenberg on the other side of the Elbe: see *Sermons on John 6–8* (1530–32/1565), LW 23:245.

[15] Bethlehem, the other name of Ephrathah, means "house of bread." Cf. Luther, *Church Postil* (1540–44), sermon for Christmas Day on Luke 2:1–14, LW 75:219–20, paragraphs 40–41.

[16] The Krkonoše Mountains, on the border of modern Poland and the Czech Republic.

[17] *Eilffe . . . eylff.* Cf. *Table Talk* no. 4125 (1538), WA TR 4:152.

to the God, religion, and the faith of their forefathers by the third and last Elijah [Mal. 4:5–6].[18]

And because good Israelites saw David's prophecy fulfilled [2 Sam. 23:6] when the Jewish thistleheads[19] were cut off and scattered throughout the whole world, they wanted to recall the root of *Isai* or Jesse [Isa. 11:10; Rom. 15:12] in their exile or, as it were, to prophesy that the root of Jesse would sprout and bloom anew in this place, and that the teaching of Jesus Christ in the Word would again be cleansed and purified in this region. That is why they named a little town not far from Wittenberg after Jesse.[20]

During their pilgrimage, they retained the old name "Sidon"[21] to honor and commemorate the ancient Zarephath, which was subject to the Sidonians [1 Kings 17:9; Luke 4:26], and the first Elijah and his parish in that glassworks and mining town,[22] much as Hector's wife established a little Troy for herself in Greece.[23] Therefore, they foresaw in their exile and conversion that God would appoint His Zarephathites and spiritual miners, smelters, and glassworkers in this region, who, in accordance with the prophecy of Obadiah [vv. 20–21],[24] would place the Romanists' broken silver back into the oven and smelt it, cupellate or liquate it, so that the Christian Church would bring forth refined and purified silver, as Psalm 12 [:6] says, and would separate and purge all dross and impurities from God's fine silver. We shall speak more of this later, when we call to mind the third Elijah, the son of the miner from Mansfeld.[25]

What if Dessau also took its name from "fatness,"[26] because God was going to place great princes and lords there who would suckle, nourish, and abundantly sustain God's Church and its servants from their fatness and breasts [Isa. 60:16], in addition to their public confession, which the princes of Anhalt have made with great discretion in our days in Christian writings in order to provide people with blessed teaching and strong encouragement?[27]

---

[18] On Luther as the third Elijah, see above, Walter, *New Spiritual Song*, p. 98, stanza 59; Mathesius, *History*, p. 555.

[19] See above, Mathesius, *History*, pp. 273, 507.

[20] I.e., Jessen, located on the Black Elster some 30 km east of Wittenberg.

[21] I.e., Seyda, some 20 km east of Wittenberg, between Zahna and Jessen.

[22] See above, Mathesius, *History*, p. 555.

[23] Andromache was married the third time to Hector's brother, Helenus, king of Epirus, who built a "little Troy" in Epirus: see Virgil, *Aeneid* 3:349 (Loeb 63 [1916], pp. 394–95).

[24] See above, Mathesius, *History*, p. 556.

[25] See below, pp. 582–83.

[26] I.e., דֶּשֶׁן [*deshen*]. Cf. Judg. 9:9; above, Mathesius, *History*, p. 266. Dessau, some 30 km west of Wittenberg, was the residence of the princes of Anhalt.

[27] On the princes of Anhalt, see above, p. 374 n. 36.

Zahna, which is only six miles[28] away from Wittenberg, also retains its Hebrew name and means a tavern or inn, even as Rahab [Josh. 2:1–21], the Christian innkeeper |or tavern keeper in Jericho, is called a *Zanah* [Josh. 2:1][29] because she gave lodging to Joshua's messengers in Jericho and because the future bloodline[30] of Jesus Christ is recognized through her [Matt. 1:5], and [His blood] is blessedly manifested and prefigured in her scarlet cord, which she hung from her house over the wall as a sign for protection [Josh. 2:18–19].[31]

For the true inn was to be located in Wittenberg and its surrounding villages, into which the eternal Samaritan and Protector of Christendom will bring those who have been robbed and wounded by the monastic murderers of souls, when the Roman bishops and chaplains have walked past them [cf. Luke 10:30–32]. Then He will commission the innkeeper to care faithfully for His [people who are] sick and afflicted and will give him two coins [Luke 10:35], the Old and New Testaments, with which he is to comfort and heal the poor and downcast consciences.[32]

I hope that this is what we have experienced, for indeed many troubled and contrite hearts, from which the spiritual robbers had taken all consolation and had stripped away everything, have stopped at this blessed inn and Christian haven, where they have found consolation, peace, life, teaching, salvation, and strength.

At this point I must mention a story I heard from Doctor Melchior Vend[33] when I traveled through Zahna with him. It was said that a nobleman once lived there who had endowed a single votive Mass. His deed of foundation included words to this effect: Since the Mass would eventually fall into disuse or be abolished, the interest from this foundation should be applied to the poorhouse for the needs of the poor. He confirmed this not only with

---

[28] *ein meil.* Zahna is 11 km east of Wittenberg. On the German mile, see above, p. 141 n. 9.

[29] Josh. 2:1 describes Rahab as a זוֹנָה. For the rabbinic argument that the word could mean "innkeeper" as well as "harlot" (an argument which Luther himself rejects), see *Lectures on Genesis* (1535–45/1544–54), LW 7:39; Josephus, *Jewish Antiquities* 5.2 (Loeb 490 [1930], pp. 164–65).

[30] *Blut*; or "blood."

[31] Cf. Luther, *First Lectures on the Psalms* (1513–15/1743–1876), LW 11:46, based on long patristic tradition: see, e.g., Ambrose, *On the Christian Faith* 5.10.127 (128) (PL 16:674; NPNF² 10:300). Cf. ACCS 4:14.

[32] For this allegorical interpretation of the parable of the Good Samaritan, cf. Luther, *Church Postil* (Roth's edition of the *Summer Postil* [1526]), sermon for Trinity 13 on Luke 10:23–37, Lenker 5:56–59; cf. sermon of August 30, 1523, WA 11:171–73. Cf. the patristic precedents in ACCS 3:179–81.

[33] On Melchior Vend [Fendt], see above, Mathesius, *History*, p. 304 n. 119. The anecdote and the Zahna nobleman in question could not be further identified.

his deed, signature, and seal but also by pushing his five fingers into the wax of the seal, so that his will and testament would always be inviolably upheld.

This praiseworthy nobleman had also foreseen that 'the idolatrous sacrificial Mass, which at that time was the sole and supreme form of worship and the mightiest pillar of the Roman Church, would eventually be torn down and abolished, along with celibacy, by a strong Samson [Judg. 16:28–30]. This is what has happened in our days in Wittenberg, the holy city and true holy Mount Zion and Moriah [1 Kings 8:1], for which we sincerely thank our Lord Jesus Christ, who celebrated for us an eternal Mass once for all on the tree of the holy cross and obediently offered up a perfect sacrifice to His Father for the eternal forgiveness of all our sins [cf. Heb. 10:12–18]. That is enough concerning the location and name of the city Wittenberg and the surrounding villages.

God, the eternal Father, who alone overthrows kingdoms and governments as He pleases [cf. Dan. 2:21], granted this region along the Elbe River together with the Electorate of Saxony to the estimable margraves of Meissen.[34] And when, in living memory, He gave to this land a highly estimable elector and wise master of the house, Duke Frederick of Saxony, who had great zeal and desire for true worship, this lord began establishing a collegiate foundation in his castle and beautiful church in Wittenberg.[35] He searched for the best people to be found in the papacy at that time and provided for the most pious ceremonies and liturgies to be had in any chapters in Germany. He also sought most diligently and at great expense after Roman relics—old knuckles and bones and discarded tatters[36]—in order to adorn his patron, St. Ursula, along with her eleven thousand virgins,[37] and to build himself a stairway or ladder to heaven. For since there was no mention

---

[34] When the Ascanian dynasty of Saxon electors, centered in Wittenberg, died out with the death of Albert III in 1422, Emperor Sigismund transferred the electorate and its territory to the Wettin margraves of Meissen, beginning with Frederick the Belligerent (r. 1423–28), who kept his seat of rule in Dresden. After the death of Elector Frederick II in 1464, his sons Ernest (r. 1464–86) and Albert III (r. 1464–1500) divided the territory in the 1485 Treaty of Leipzig. Albert inherited Dresden and the Meissen lands whereas Ernest inherited the electoral dignity and the old capital of Wittenberg, which his son Frederick (III) the Wise developed into the electoral residence. See Günther Wartenberg, "Saxony," OER 3:489–90.

[35] On Frederick the Wise, see above, p. 68 n. 82. On his construction of the Castle Church in Wittenberg and endowment of the All Saints' Foundation—i.e., a "chapter" consisting of clergy who were supported to celebrate Masses—see above, Mathesius, History, p. 136.

[36] On Frederick's collection of relics, see above, Mathesius, History, pp. 136–37.

[37] St. Ursula was remembered as the leader of 11,000 Christian virgins who were killed by the Huns near Cologne while traveling as pilgrims to Rome in the late fourth century. See LA 2:256–60, no. 158; ODCC, 3rd ed., s.v. "Ursula." Frederick the Wise was devoted to St. Ursula's Confraternity of the Eleven Thousand Virgins. See Ludolphy, Friedrich der Weise, p. 358. Cf. Luther to Georg Spalatin, December 14, 1516, LW 48:33.

of the blood, merit, and intercession of our eternal and sole Mediator in all the monasteries and foundations at that time, the aforementioned prince wanted to choose a special patron and mediator for himself and his land, ᶦone on whose merit and intercession he could confidently rely at the end of his life.

But since the pious lord felt that none of this would hold firm or stand fast[38] amid the pangs of death and fear of hell, and that it was able to give no sure and certain consolation and confidence, he undertook a lord's pilgrimage[39] over land and sea to the Holy Land, to visit the places where Christ had walked on the earth, shed His blood, and been laid in the noble grave.

Having honorably completed this pilgrimage, he followed the traveling court of Emperor Maximilian for some years and visited many excellent and erudite people in the Netherlands along the way.[40] He also received a report from his personal physician, Doctor Martin Mellerstadt,[41] who had diligently researched and visited the schools there, that the universities in these lands, which had originally been founded by those who had been driven out of Bohemia in the times of Hus,[42] were not properly and productively staffed at this time. Therefore, he began to form a plan, at the encouragement, gracious support, and prompting of his brother, the lord bishop of Magdeburg,[43] as well as the aforementioned Doctor Mellerstadt, to found a well-ordered university of his own and have it built in his electorate in accordance with the imperial Golden Bull,[44] seeing that he was an estimable elector of the [Holy] Roman Empire and that there was at that time no university in his

---

[38] *weder strich noch stich halten.* Cf. Wander 4:846, "Stich" no. 39.

[39] On Frederick's pilgrimage to Jerusalem, see above, Mathesius, *History*, p. 136.

[40] On Frederick's travel in the Netherlands, see Ludolphy, *Friedrich der Weise*, p. 146.

[41] On Martin Pollich von Mellerstadt, see above, p. 63 n. 53; Mathesius, *History*, p. 127.

[42] The University of Leipzig, in Meissen, had been founded after the withdrawal of the German nation from the University of Prague in 1409. The University of Erfurt, in Thuringia, had been founded in 1379.

[43] On Frederick's brother Ernest and his role in the university's founding, see above, Mathesius, *History*, p. 125.

[44] On the Golden Bull of 1356, see above, p. 323 n. 21. It makes no specific mention of a right of each elector to maintain a university (although the thirteenth article mentions the rights of electors over *universitates*, which refers to local corporations in general and not to schools). Such a right may have been taken as implied, however, by these articles and by the precedent of the founding of the University of Prague in 1348 by King Charles IV of Bohemia before his coronation as Holy Roman emperor in 1355. See Wolfgang D. Fritz, ed., *Die Goldene Bulle Kaiser Karls IV vom Jahre 1356* (Weimar: Böhlau, 1972), p. 69. Mathesius explicitly names such a right, based on the Golden Bull, in his *Ehespiegel*, fol. 254v. See Volz, *Die Lutherpredigten des Johannes Mathesius*, p. 129.

division of the principality.[45] He would establish it in Wittenberg, the capital city of the electorate, alongside his castle and foundation of canons.

When the crafty Satan realized what would become of this, the evil spirit sought to prevent it by means of friend and foe, both neighboring and at home, by means of scholars and the unlearned alike, who forcefully called attention to the expenses and difficulties that this would entail. But this great, extraordinary man[46] |followed the clock and compass[47] in his own heart, and in addition to his lord brother,[48] God had provided him with a number of good people who were tenacious and resolute. Doctor Mellerstadt, who was the *Lux mundi* ["light of the world"][49] and had received a doctorate in all three faculties,[50] offered his services to teach and lecture, having published some good Latin treatises at other universities after coming from the Netherlands.[51] These treatises were very pleasing to many good people who had started getting sick of the foolish *Moralogii*,[52] as well as the exercises in

---

[45] In the 1484 division of Saxony, the universities of Leipzig (in Meissen) and of Erfurt (in Thuringia) had gone to the Albertine line, leaving Ernestine Saxony with no higher school.

[46] *Wunderman*; see the introduction above, pp. lxxxix–xc.

[47] *seygersteller unnd antreyber*; see above, Mathesius, *History*, p. 316.

[48] See above, p. 577.

[49] An epithet given Mellerstadt by friends: see above, Mathesius, *History*, p. 127.

[50] On Mellerstadt, see above, p. 127 n. 73.

[51] Mellerstadt's publications before 1502 (mostly from Leipzig) included numerous medical works: editions of Mondino de Luzzi (1270–1326), *Anatomia* (Leipzig: Martin Landsberg, ca. 1493) [GW M25669-25671], and Arnoldus de Villa Nova (1235–1311), *Speculum medicinae* (Leipzig: Martin Landsberg, ca. 1495) [GW 02534]; his own *De complexione* (Leipzig: Jakob Thanner, n.d.) [GW M34675]; and an extended literary debate with the Leipzig professor of medicine Simon Pistoris (d. 1523) over syphilis: *Defensio Leonicena* (Magdeburg: Moritz Brandis, 1499) [GW M34676], *Disputationsankündigung* (Leipzig: Jakob Thanner, ca. 1500) [GW M3467610], *Castigationes in alabandicas declarationes Simonis Pistoris* (Leipzig: Thanner, 1500) [GW M34672], *Annotatio auctoritatum medicinae* (Nürnberg: Georg Stuchs, ca. 1501) [GW M34671], and *Responsio . . . in superadditos errores Simonis Pistoris in medicina* (Nürnberg: Georg Stuchs, 1501) [VD16 P3975]. He also published an edition of the jurist Pandulphus Collenucius' (1444–1504) *Agenoria* (Leipzig: Jakob Thanner, ca. 1500) [GW 07162]; books on astrology: *Compendium XV propositionum astrologicae* (Magdeburg: Bartholomäus Ghotan, 1482 or later) [GW M34673], as well as annual predictions which appeared from 1483 to 1490 under the title *Prognostikon* in Leipzig, Magdeburg, Nürnberg, Lübeck, and Cologne [GW M34683-34702]; and a number of poetic works: *Carmina et prognosticationes* (Leipzig: Markus Brandis/Konrad Kachelofen, 1485–86) [GW M34690-91], *Laconismos tumultuarius* (Leipzig: Jacob Thanner, 1502) [VD16 ZV12642], and a couplet celebrating Conrad Celtis' (1459–1508) edition of the works of the tenth-century Saxon canoness Hrotsvita of Gandersheim (*Opera Hrosvite* [Nürnberg, 1501] [VD16 H5278], fol. a4r).

[52] Mathesius writes *Morologii*, playing on the similarity of "ethics" in Latin [*mores*] and "fool" in Greek [*môros*], likely referring to Virgilius Wellendorffer's (fl. 1495) scholastic commentary on Aristotle's *Ethics*, published with a preface by Jerome Emser (see above,

cases and tenses,[53] and the *Parva Logicalia,*[54] and *pons asinorum,*[55] and whatever else there was of the old pagan trivialities.[56]

Now, this Mellerstadt was soon joined by the excellent man Doctor Staupitz,[57] the superior over several Augustinian monasteries, in addition to Doctor Wimpina[58] and many clerics from the Augustinian monastery who later became the first students, as I have seen in the university's matriculation register.[59] On the basis of such considerations and solicitations, the decision was made to found a university in Wittenberg for which the good elector would supply salaries and support from his own treasury.

In the year of Christ 1502, a day was set for installing the faculty and dedicating the university. Doctor Mellerstadt was appointed to be the first rector. In addition, many foreign and neighboring scholars were invited, including Doctor Fleck, who publicly preached at the dedication of the university and prophesied many good things about this university: for example, that the true wisdom would be disseminated from this White Mountain into the whole world.[60]

---

p. 156 n. 98): *Moralogium ex Aristotelis Ethicorum libris* (Leipzig: Wolfgant Stöckel, 1509) [VD16 W906].

[53] Cf. Luther's critique of these rote grammatical drills in *To the Councilmen of All Cities in Germany* (1524), LW 45:369.

[54] The *Parva Logicalia* was a name given to medieval supplements to Aristotle's work on dialectics. See, e.g., the work by Johann Eck (see above, p. 154 n. 89): *Bursa pavonis: Logices exercitamenta Appellata parva logicalia* (Strassburg: Matthias Hupfuff, 1507) [VD16 E281]. Cf. Melanchthon's critique in the *Erotemata dialectices,* CR 13:750; Luther, *Against the Roman Papacy* (1545), LW 41:304.

[55] The *pons asinorum,* or "bridge of asses," in logic was a diagram developed by Petrus Tartaretus (see above, p. 127 n. 75) for finding the middle term of a syllogism. See *Oxford Encyclopedia of Philosophy,* s.v. "*inventio medii.*"

[56] *paganterey und flasiarey* (cf. *DWB,* s.v. "Flause"). "Paganterey," however, may be derived instead from "Bachanten," or beginning students (see above, p. 133 n. 104) and would then mean something like "elementary."

[57] On Staupitz and his involvement in the establishment of the university, see above, Melanchthon, *Preface,* pp. 63–64; Mathesius, *History,* pp. 125–26.

[58] On Wimpina, see above, Melanchthon, *Preface,* p. 67 and n. 76 there; and p. 125 n. 62 and p. 151 n. 69. In fact, Mellerstadt had already come into conflict with Wimpina at Leipzig. Wimpina took part in the founding of the University of Frankfurt an der Oder in 1506 but had no role in the founding of Wittenberg. See Volz, *Die Lutherpredigten des Johannes Mathesius,* p. 130.

[59] In addition to Staupitz and the Tübingen Augustinian master Sigismund Epp, seven Augustinian hermits appear among the 416 students enrolled at Wittenberg in 1502–3: see Volz, *Die Lutherpredigten des Johannes Mathesius,* p. 131.

[60] On Fleck and Wittenberg as "White Mountain," see above, p. 572.

On the night before the morning on which these installations were to take place, some wicked provocateurs sought to convince the elector that he should give command in the morning to have the consecration or dedication of the new ˡuniversity postponed until a different time.[61] But because everything was prepared and things were already under way, the scholars proceeded and began this blessed work in the name of God. They escorted their rector and his scholars to the church, prayed to God and thanked Him for His favor. And since many people had gathered for this new university, the old doctors and the professors began holding lectures in the name of Christ and of the old St. Catharine, who at that time was regarded as the university's *Pallas* and goddess of wisdom, according to heathen custom, which is why the image in the university's seal included her.[62]

It would take too long to talk now about the doctors and professors who were there from the beginning. Doctor Mellerstadt and Staupitz received the commission to seek out good people and procure some Germans and Italians[63] from among the best that could found at that time in arts of every kind. Doctor Sibutus,[64] the poet, Master Vach,[65] and Master Staffelstein[66] lectured in the liberal arts; Ravennas,[67] the Italian, was also recruited to

---

[61] Volz, *Die Lutherpredigten des Johannes Mathesius*, p. 130, dismisses the historicity of this account as implausable for Frederick on psychological grounds. But the language [*wird der Churfürst . . . verwendet*] does not seem to demand that Frederick actually ordered a delay at the last minute, as Volz assumes, only that he was urged (unsuccessfully) to impose one.

[62] St. Catharine of Alexandria (d. ca. 310) was a virgin martyr who engaged in debate with pagan philosophers and orators; she was regarded as patron of scholars and schools. See *LA* 2:334–410, no. 172. Mathesius here compares her with the pagan goddess Athena. In Wittenberg, St. Catharine was the patroness of the arts (or philosophical) faculty and appeared on its original seal: see Friedensburg, *Geschichte der Universität Wittenberg*, p. 36 and Erich Gritzner, *Die Siegel der deutschen Universitäten in Deutschland*, Oesterreich und der Schweiz, J[ohann] Siebmachers grosses und allgemeines Wappenbuch 1/8/A (Nürnberg: Bauer & Raspe, 1906), table 33, no. 4.

[63] *wallen*; a German term that can apply to speakers of Romance languages generally, though especially those from Italy.

[64] Georg Sibutus (d. after 1528), who arrived in Wittenberg in 1505, was a humanist poet from the Vienna circle of Conrad Celtis. See Karl Hartfelder, "Sibutus, Georg," *ADB* 34:140–41.

[65] On Balthasar Fabricius from Vacha, see above, p. 297 n. 75.

[66] On Georg Elner from Staffelstein, see above, p. 302 n. 100.

[67] Petrus Ravennas (1448–1510) had studied law at Padua. In 1503, Frederick the Wise invited him to Wittenberg, where he gave his first public lecture on papal supremacy. He left Wittenberg in 1506 upon an outbreak of the plague. See Heinz Schmitt, "Ravennas, Petrus Franciscus," *BBKL* 33:1090–1123.

come there. Then the renowned Doctor Henning Göde[68] from Erfurt came to Wittenberg; he educated the illustrious jurists Dr. Gregor Brück,[69] Dr. Hieronymus Schurff,[70] Dr. Benedikt Pauli.[71] Lecturing on medicine were Dr. Peter Burkhard[72] and Dr. Stackmann,[73] whom I saw still in Wittenberg [in 1529]. By these men, Dr. Augustine Schurff,[74] Dr. Jacob Milich,[75] and Dr. Melchior Vend[76] were educated.

Dr. Hieronymus [Schurff] educated Dr. Ulrich Mordeisen,[77] Dr. Melchior Kling,[78] and Dr. Kilian Goldstein.[79]

And since it was now God's will to raise a voice out of this university to speak against the Antichrist in Rome, to burnish the doctrine of the obscured Gospel, and to have all the chaff and dregs of the monks, scholastics, sophists,

---

[68] Henning Göde (ca. 1450–1521) was a jurist educated at Erfurt who began teaching at Wittenberg in 1510. See *ADB* 2:495 (erroneously s.v. "Bode, Henning"). For Luther on Göde, see *Table Talk* no. 5254 (1540), WA TR 5:29–30.

[69] On Brück, see above, p. 21 n. 79; Mathesius, *History*, p. 335.

[70] On Hieronymus Schurff, see above, p. 21 n. 83; Mathesius, *History*, p. 173.

[71] On Pauli, see above, p. 304 n. 117. For Luther on Pauli, see *Table Talk* no. 4903 (1540), WA TR 4:575.

[72] Peter Burkhard [Mathesius: de Burcknedis; Burchard] (d. 1526) was professor of medicine in Wittenberg between 1518 and 1521, leaving amid the Wittenberg unrest to return to Ingolstadt, where he joined in condemning Luther's teaching in the seventeen articles of 1523. See Friedensburg, *Geschichte der Universität Wittenberg*, pp. 136–38.

[73] Heinrich Stackmann [Mathesius: Stackmair] (d. 1532) lectured in the arts faculty from 1513 until 1521, when he began teaching medicine after Burkhard's departure. See Friedensburg, *Geschichte der Universität Wittenberg*, pp. 132–33, 139. Melanchthon and Luther valued Stackmann as a colleague: see Kusukawa, *Transformation of Natural Philosophy*, pp. 49–51.

[74] On Augustine Schurff, see above, p. 20 n. 78.

[75] On Milich, see above, p. 298 n. 79.

[76] On Vend [Fendt], see above, p. 304 n. 119. Cf. above, p. 575.

[77] Ulrich von Mordeisen (1519–72) studied law at Wittenberg in 1534–35 and received his doctorate there in 1543. He served as rector of the university in 1545 and as a counselor and finally chancellor for Duke Maurice of Saxony. See Johannes Herrmann, "Mordeisen, Ulrich von," *NDB* 18:90–91. For Luther on Mordeisen, see *Table Talk* no. 5593 (1543), WA TR 5:269–70.

[78] Melchior Kling (1504–71) studied law in Wittenberg beginning in 1527 and received his doctorate in 1535, joining the faculty the following year and serving as rector in 1539. He was politically successful, working as counselor for Duke John Frederick, Archbishop Albert, and the counts of Mansfeld simultaneously. Luther regarded him with suspicion because of his efforts to defend and reform canon law. See *Table Talk* no. 3496 (1536), LW 54:214; LW 58:13 n. 34; Hiram Kümper, "Kling, Melchior," *BBKL* 24:940–42.

[79] On Goldstein, see above, p. 299 n. 84.

and penitentiaries[80] swept and strained out of it, Father Martin, who at that time ˈwas an Augustinian monk in Erfurt, came to Wittenberg at the urging and by the order of Dr. Staupitz. He lived as a sincere monk whose obedience in his monastery was beyond reproach, and he studied very diligently. And because Dr. Staupitz saw that this brother had great gifts and intelligence, he besought the elector of Saxony to have Friar Martin appointed to the university as a doctor and *pater lector.*[81]

It is here that he began to read his Bible and to engage in frequent disputations against the sophists and scholastics, until the crass and appalling words of Johann Tetzel, the Roman peddler of indulgences, induced Dr. Luther to draw up and post his propositions or theses[82] about the Roman flea market. From this arose the religious dispute which still has not been laid to rest, and which, if God so wills, shall remain unresolved until the Last Day, when the Lord Christ will visibly appear on a rainbow [cf. Rev. 4:3]. He shall issue His judgment against all of the writings, proceedings, resolutions, edicts, diatribes, and slanders that were disseminated at this time against the pure truth of God by the enemies of Christ's cross and many false brethren.

This is Doctor Martin Luther, a miner's son, who battled against the Roman Antichrist and monastic idolatry and deception, cleansed the Church, put the doctrine through the blast furnace, purified it in the cupellation furnace, and purged from it the Roman and monastic dross and contaminants in the liquation furnace.[83] Through this man, God exalted the university in Wittenberg and made it renowned all over the world. We owe thanks to our dear God and His only-begotten Son for this doctor, because we have been rescued from the Babylonian captivity and by grace have returned to the green meadows and pastures of God's Word and the fresh fountain of Israel [cf. Ps. 23:2]. ˈFor this swan[84] and miner's son had been prophesied not only by the excellent martyr and Christian from Bohemia Master John Hus—and afterward by Brother Johann Hilten in Eisenach and Dr. Proles in Leipzig, as you heard in the accounts concerning the doctor at another time[85] (and in addition, the creed of [St.] Ambrose also contains a

---

[80] Penitentiaries were officials delegated to administer and adjudicate the sacrament of penance, including indulgences. See *ODCC*, 3rd ed., s.v. "penitentiary."

[81] I.e., a lecturer: see above, Mathesius, *History*, pp. 523, 542. On the title "friar" [*Frater*], see above, Mathesius, *History*, pp. 126, 128–29; cf. p. 123 n. 47.

[82] *Positiones oder schlußreden*; see above, Mathesius, *History*, pp. 143–44.

[83] For these stages in the refining process (and the nomenclature), see the editorial note by Herbert Clark Hoover in Agricola, *De re metallica*, p. 492n.

[84] See above, Mathesius, *History*, pp. 121, 556–57.

[85] On Hus and Hilten and their prophecies, see above, Mathesius, *History*, pp. 121–22. On Proles, see above, p. 457 n. 209. According to Flacius, *Catalogus*, p. 582, though Proles was from

kabbalah and mystical prophecy of the year 1517 in the verse *Tibi Cherubin et Seraphin incessabili voce proclamant*,[86] in which the number of the year when the Gospel rose again in Germany is clearly to be found)—but also when the Holy Spirit prophesied through the patriarch Jacob in his last words concerning St. Paul, the Benjamite, that in the last days after Christ's ascension he would divide the spoil of the Son of God among the Gentiles [cf. Gen. 49:27];[87] and when Moses prophesied concerning the first Elijah [Deut. 33:20–21],[88] and Malachi concerning the second Elijah [Mal. 4:5], John the Baptist, that he would cast off the Law of the Jews, point to Christ, and turn the Gentiles to the faith of Abraham.[89] Similarly, the Holy Spirit also prophesied concerning this third Elijah [Matt. 17:11; Rev. 11:3], Dr. Martin Luther: that in the last days God would raise up teachers from among the miners and their children who would smelt, refine, liquate, and purify the teaching of the Antichrist and present the pure and uncontaminated silver to the Church of God.

Dear friends, let us miners' preachers speak on a firm footing about a miner's son among you miners, in accordance with Scripture and in the language of miners, concerning ancient prophecies that (praise God) are now being fulfilled. For an old kabbalah[90] or tradition has been preserved in Christendom that the third Elijah and Enoch, the blessed two olive trees [Rev. 11:4],[91] would reappear in the last days. There is also a clear prophecy in Obadiah[92] that the Zarephathites would come to Mount Zion [vv. 20–21],

---

Leipzig, his "prophecy" took place in the monastery of Himmelpforten near Wernigerode. See Volz, *Die Lutherpredigten des Johannes Mathesius*, p. 284 ad loc. Although Mathesius has not in fact narrated Proles' "prophecy" in the sermons on Luther as they were printed, Flacius relates that Proles said, "You have heard, brethren, the testimony of Holy Scripture, that by grace we are whatever we are, and by grace we have whatever we have. Whence, then, come this great darkness and these horrible superstitions? O brethren, Christianity stands in need of a strong and great reformation, which I see is now about to begin. . . . You see, brothers, that I am advanced in years and weak in body and powers, and I know that I am not endowed with such doctrine, diligence, and eloquence as this business requires. But the Lord will stir up a hero of the required age, powers, diligence, doctrine, intelligence, and eloquence, and he shall begin this reformation and set himself against the errors. God will give him the courage to dare to speak against the great men, and you will be witnesses of his salutary ministry, by God's grace."

[86] See above, Mathesius, *History*, p. 145.

[87] See above, Mathesius, *History*, p. 556.

[88] See above, Mathesius, *History*, p. 556.

[89] See above, Mathesius, *History*, p. 556.

[90] On Kabbalah, see above, p. 145 n. 30.

[91] See above, Mathesius, *History*, pp. 555–56.

[92] See above, Mathesius, *History*, p. 556.

through whom many of the Gentiles would be rescued in the last days ¹and the spiritual Edomites be defeated by the mouth of God.

It is also certain that the Zarephathites were miners, whom the first Elijah addressed in God's name⁹³ and to whom he preached the pure doctrine, turning many people to the God of their fathers, as John the Baptist did [Matt. 3:5–6]. This agrees with the prophecies of Isaiah and Malachi [Isa. 40:3; Mal. 4:5–6],⁹⁴ who speak of the second Elijah and of spiritual refiners. For when the voice calling in the wilderness appears [Matt. 3:3], it will purge the lead and litharge of the Pharisees and Sadducees from God's cakes of ore and refine out all the false doctrine; or, as Malachi says, the Son of God will establish a spiritual refinery through His Elijah and forerunner and will put the priests and their adulterated doctrine through the furnace and purify it [Mal. 3:3].

These texts speak in so many words about metallurgy and spiritual smelting, even as Jeremiah 51 [:27] expressly mentions miners when he calls to mind Ararat, Minni, and Ashkenaz,⁹⁵ who will thresh the daughters of Babylon and convert them [Jer. 51:33]. Dear friends, today, among miners, on the occasion of our school festival and *Quinquatria*,⁹⁶ [in honor] of the university in Wittenberg and of Dr. Luther, the miner's son, let me tell you something from the prophets about the calling and doctrine of our German prophet, the final one, as a testimony and for the sake of our blessed consolation and assurance.

There is no doubt that Jeremiah is speaking here about miners—even as God appointed him to be the overseer of a foundry and a refiner of his Israelite ore, in chapter 6 [:29]—for he mentions Minni by name [Jer. 51:27].⁹⁷ Now, Meni was a heathen or idolatrous mountain and the idol of merchants, as is made clear at the end of Isaiah [Isa. 65:11].⁹⁸ That is why the Arabs called

---

⁹³ *auff Göttliche weyse angelassen*

⁹⁴ See above, Mathesius, *History*, p. 556.

⁹⁵ See above, Mathesius, *History*, p. 555.

⁹⁶ The *Quinquatria* were an ancient Roman festival in honor of the goddess Minerva celebrated March 19–23. Among the other elements of the festival, children sought the goddess' favor for their studies. See Ovid, *Fasti* 3.809–48 (Loeb 253 [1931], pp. 180–83), esp. lines 815–16. A Christian version had been celebrated in Joachimsthal since 1561: see Loesche, *Johannes Mathesius*, 1:319.

⁹⁷ See Mathesius, *History*, above, p. 555; and below, p. 585.

⁹⁸ In Luther's German Bible, the ethnonym "Minni" [מִנִּי] and the name of the Babylonian god "Meni" [מְנִי] have the same spelling. Luther's marginal note on Isa. 65:11 identifies Meni as the "god of merchants" and compares him with the Roman god Mercury: see WA DB 11/1:182–83.

their mining towns *Minresi*, as Diodorus Siculus mentions too;[99] the Arabs also call metals *Minererz*,[100] |for they are made and generated from mercury and earth, as the name nicely conveys and all who are knowledgeable about nature affirm. This is the source of the Latin and German words *minium* and *Mennige*, and the word has remained in use among the Germans down to the present day as a name for quicksilver and cinnabar.[101]

Such Minni or miners will help tear down Babylon, Jeremiah says [Jer. 51:27]. Here he also mentions Ararat,[102] upon which Noah's ark settled in Armenia after the floodwaters dried up. For Ararat and Armenia are one and the same name. According to the Hebraists, Armenia means the "Mountain of Quicksilver and Metals,"[103] even as Arbela[104] is called the "Mountain of the Lord" or "Holy Mountain" in Hebrew.

Now, though the Armenians did help the Persian king tear down the physical Babylon, there is in fact another nation mentioned here: that of Ashkenaz,[105] whose people are descended from Japheth's son. Now, in the schools there is no doubt that the people of Ashkenaz are the honorable Germans, born from the great-grandson of Noah, Gomer's son [Gen. 10:2–3].[106] Tacitus[107] gives the name of the son of this German (that is, of Tusco) as Mannus. He is said to be the source of the name of the Main[108] (which springs from the Fichtel Mountains and flows past

---

[99] The Arabic words for "mine" and "town" are *maʿdin* [معدن] and *madina* [مدينة] respectively. Mathesius' source in Diodorus Siculus could not be clearly identified. Loesche (*LH²*, p. 596 ad loc.) suggests that Mathesius' statement derives from *Library of History* 3.42–43 (Loeb 303 [1933], pp. 212–13), which mentions similar names (especially in textual variants) but has nothing to do with mines.

[100] Perhaps *min al-ardz* [من الأرض], "from earth." Cf. Mathesius, *Sarepta*, fols. 41v–42r.

[101] These words and their etymological connection can be found in modern Latin and German dictionaries; both words were used to refer to lead tetraoxide (red lead) as well as to cinnabar (mercury sulfide).

[102] See above, Mathesius, *History*, p. 555. On Ararat, see *Lectures on Genesis* (1535–44/1544–54), LW 2:107–8; Matthaeus Aurogallus, *De hebraeis urbium, locorum, populorumque nominibus* (Wittenberg: Joseph Klug, 1526) [VD16 G2556], fol. C 4 4–v, s.v. אררט.

[103] Cf. Mathesius, *Sarepta*, fol. 18r. This etymology, which apparently takes "Armenia" as derived from "*har-minni*," is contradicted by Aurogallus, *De hebraeis urbium, locorum, populorumque nominibus*, fol. C3v, who derives it from the name "Aram."

[104] See 1 Macc. 9:1.

[105] See above, Mathesius, *History*, p. 555; cf. above, p. 119 n. 28.

[106] See above, p. 119 n. 28.

[107] Tacitus, *Germania* 2 (Loeb 35 [1915], pp. 130–31), where the name of the father is given as "Tuisto."

[108] I.e., White Main River; see above, Mathesius, *History*, p. 555.

the old Goldkronach[109] mining works in Franconia) and that of the old Mansfeld mines.[110] Likewise, the ancient German Minni and miners, who are descended from Ashkenaz, [are so called] because they work with fire alone[111] at the face of the mine[112] and in the refinery, and use fire to collect the metals from the stone. From this it follows very neatly that the prophet is speaking of German miners at the end of his book. If anyone wishes to see here the Roman Ascanius[113] or the lords of Ascania[114] or the Ascanian fortress on the Eine River,[115] he is free to do so—using a miner's liberty.[116]

At the end of his prophecy, Isaiah also mentions Tubal and Javan, the uncles of our Ashkenaz [Isa. 66:19].[117] [The descendants of] Javan ˈwe take to be Greeks,[118] but [the descendants of] Jubal[119] are actually miners, who take their name from what is produced by the earth;[120] and because of their traveling and wandering [wallen], we talk about such "wanderers" in Germany, Italy, and Spain, as well as the Celtic or Chur-wanderers;[121] that is the origin

---

[109] Goldkronach, near Bayreuth, had been a center of gold mining since the thirteenth century.

[110] See above, Mathesius, *History*, p. 555.

[111] Taking "Ashkenaz" as derived from the word "fire" [אֵשׁ (*esh*)]. Cf. Jerome, *De nominibus Hebraicis* (PL 23:773).

[112] Miners would break the rock face by heating it for days with a fire and then pouring cold water on it. See Agricola, *De re metallica* (trans. Hoover, pp. 118–20).

[113] Ascanius was the son of the Trojan hero Aeneas and the founder of the Italian city Alba Longa. See, e.g., Virgil, *Aeneid* 1.261–71 (Loeb 63 [1916], pp. 280–81). For the connection between Ashkenaz and Ascanius, see Aurogallus, *De hebraeis urbium, locorum, populorumque nominibus*, fol. C5r; for the connection between Ascanius and the Ascanienburg (or Schloss Askanien), see Ekkehard of Aura (1050–1126), *Chronicon Universale* (PL 154:1049).

[114] The Ascanians were an old German noble family, dating back to the eleventh century, who had ruled Brandenburg, Saxony (see above, p. 576 n. 34), and Anhalt, though by the sixteenth century Anhalt was the only remaining Ascanian principality.

[115] *Ascanienburg am Rein*; the Ascanienburg was the ancient fortress on the Wolfsberg mountain near Aschersleben, over the Eine River, which gave the Ascanian dynasty its name. "Rein" must therefore be a typographic error.

[116] *frey wie eim Bergman*; a humourous allusion to the special legal privileges accorded to miners [*Bergfreiheit*].

[117] See below, p. 587.

[118] I.e., "Ionians." Cf. Joel 3:6.

[119] Mathesius appears to conflate Tubal (Gen. 10:2) and Jubal (Gen. 4:21). Cf. Mathesius, *History*, above, p. 119; and below, p. 587.

[120] "Jubal" comes from the root יבל, which can mean "to produce." Cf. Deut. 33:22.

[121] Mathesius is connecting the verb *wallen* ("to wander" or "to go on pilgrimage") and the noun *Wahle*, which generally denotes people speaking Romance languages but was sometimes taken (as Mathesius apparently does here) to mean wandering peoples. The element was included in multiple place-names across Europe, though it is unclear whether Mathesius

of the word "*wallen*," [to wander] or to travel. In sum, we find German miners in the writings of the prophets, as is generally acknowledged. Isaiah prophesies that German men (or the ancient people of Lud [Gen. 10:22] and the wanderers [of Jubal]) will also come to the Gospel in the last days and help topple and overthrow Babylon [Isa. 66:19]. Now listen and learn something more concerning this.

It is true that Babylon was the chief city in the Chaldean Empire, where God's people were held in captivity. Nebuchadnezzar was a ruler over Babylon who erected a great statue[122] for the most abominable idolatry [Dan. 3:1]. Antiochus,[123] the Syrian king, was also a shameless and impious tyrant and antichrist who placed his abominations in God's temple in Jerusalem and led God's people astray and persecuted them [1 Macc. 1:54–61]. It is also certain that in Antiochus the prophet Daniel portrays for us the last antichrist in Rome and Constantinople,[124] as is explained for us by the Lord Christ in Matthew 24 [:15], by St. Paul in 2 Thessalonians 2 [:3–4], and by many ancient teachers of the Church.[125] In the same way, Isaiah, Obadiah, and Malachi, and especially Jeremiah,[126] in his last words, prophesied concerning the end times before the Last Day, when Gog and Magog [Ezekiel 38–39; Rev. 20:8][127] (the abominable Mohammedans), as well as the great spiritual Babylon or red whore at Rome, will be attacked with God's Word at the end of the world and will be struck down and destroyed in the hearts of many people.

St. Peter, who also calls the city of Rome "Babylon" [1 Pet. 5:13],[128] clearly agrees with this, as does the Revelation of St. John [cf. Rev. 14:8], which talks about the new temple and new Jerusalem from Ezekiel [Ezekiel 40–44; Rev. 21:2] and speaks quite plainly about the spiritual Babylon [Revelation 18], explaining for us the obscure prophecy that in the

---

is referring here to places or to people: see *DWB*, s.v. "Wahle." On the Swiss town of Chur in Graubünden, see above, Mathesius, *History*, p. 516 and n. 85 there.

[122] *ein grossen Rohland*; Mathesius compares the statue of Nebuchadnezzar with the statues of "Roland"—a man with crown and sword—that were erected in medieval German cities to symbolize their right to administer justice. See Dietlinde Munzel-Everling, *Rolande: Die europäischen Rolanddarstellungen und Rolandfiguren* (Dößel: Janos Stekovics, 2005).

[123] See above, Mathesius, *History*, p. 494.

[124] I.e., the papacy and the Turks.

[125] See, e.g., Jerome, *Commentary on Daniel*, prologue and commentary on Dan. 8:14; 9:21–45 (PL 537, 565–74; trans. Gleason Archer, *Jerome's Commentary on Daniel* [Grand Rapids: Baker, 1958], pp. 87, 129–35). For other patristic commentary, see ACCS 13:253, 291–92, 295–95, 299–301.

[126] See above, Mathesius, *History*, pp. 555–56.

[127] See above, Mathesius, *History*, p. 435.

[128] See above, Mathesius, *History*, p. 555.

last days ⸍the man of sin [cf. 2 Thess. 2:3], which is the Antichrist, will fall at Rome and throughout the world and be slain by God's Word. For even as Adam and Enoch at the very beginning prophesy about the Last Day and the ultimate fire (Genesis 4 [:17] and Jude [14]), so, too, also almost all the prophets speak about the end of the world, though in a veiled manner, using the destruction of physical cities. For example, a hidden prophecy about the final destruction of the Turk and the papacy is made by Joshua using the ban of destruction on the city of Jericho [Josh. 6:20; cf. Heb. 11:30]; by Daniel, using Antiochus [Dan. 11:36–39]; and by Jeremiah, using Babylon [Jeremiah 50–51].[129] In short, in the Babylon located in Chaldea, the Roman Babylonian captivity and its destruction were prefigured. This [destruction] was to be accomplished by German men and miners, or the descendants of Tubal and the wanderers.[130]

Dear friends, if you read chapter 51 in Jeremiah, you will see that the prophet prophesies not simply against the fortified city of Babylon, but primarily against its Baal[131] and blasphemous idolatry. That is what God intends to attack, destroy, and tear down through the words of the German miners, so that the Mass, celibacy, monasteries, and all their *Maosim* [Dan. 11:39][132] fall down in a heap, like the town hall of the Philistines when Samson tore down the two pillars in his old age [Judg. 16:25–30].[133] The fulfillment is now plain to see, praise God! The great Babylon has begun to fall, even though some, who have partaken of the Antichrist's treasures, are still helping to support it and shore it up. The pope's religion has become a laughingstock among the elderly and children, and so at mid-Lent here [the children] drive out the pope[134] as our forefathers drove out death, and as was done long ago in Rome with heretical images.[135] If only we would harmoniously carry the throne of grace [cf. Josh. 6:4; Rom. 3:25] around this Jericho and celebrate our Feast of Trumpets [Lev. 23:24][136] with crying out, preaching, praying, and deeply sighing, then we or our children would soon come to witness the high walls around Jericho and Babylon ⸍collapsing of themselves and lying

---

[129] See above, p. 585.

[130] See above, pp. 586–87.

[131] See above, Mathesius, *History*, p. 204.

[132] For the identification of *Maosim* with the Mass, see Luther, *Letter concerning His Book on the Private Mass* (1534), LW 38:232; *Preface to Daniel [12]* (1545), WA DB 11/2:73–75 (LW 63).

[133] See above, Mathesius, *History*, p. 566.

[134] See above, Mathesius, *History*, p. 519.

[135] See above, Mathesius, *History*, pp. 519–20.

[136] Cf. above, Mathesius, *History*, p. 329.

utterly destroyed forever [cf. Josh. 6:20, 26], without the stroke of a sword or a [single] canon [shot].

The fulfillment, I say, is plain to see; the whole papacy is in lamentation over it. But through whom has God accomplished this, if not through the German final prophet, Dr. Martin Luther? This blessed man is the true Zarephathite or, as God calls the overseer of His spiritual foundry in Jeremiah chapter 6 [:27], the true *Bachon*,[137] foreman of the silver works, and smelter, through whom God has pulverized the ore and initiated the refining in our days. He has valiantly set things in motion, and the Spirit of God has inspired him with boldness and caused him to preach and write with confidence, so that the Roman scrap silver and crude cakes of ore have been liquefied, and the monks' dross, like offscourings, has flowed off and been cast away. And now (praise God!) purified and refined silver has come forth and been committed as a tithe to God.[138]

And so that we would not doubt this, what was foretold by the prophets has become manifest. Dr. Luther was born in the Mansfeld district to a man who was a quarrier of slate, an honorable miner, and a smeltery owner. His father provided for him through mining,[139] and his furnace sustained him at the university in Erfurt, until God ordained that he be driven into the monastery, so that he would come to know the papacy as Daniel and Moses before him also had to become thoroughly acquainted with the folly of the Chaldeans and Egyptians [Exodus 2; Dan. 1:3–4, 20].

This is where God used our doctor as quicksilver,[140] as I heard from his own mouth: "As soon as I had been cast into the pond of monks, I broke open the dam, so that frogs and edible fish have totally disappeared, except that there are still some pike with sharp teeth who are devouring the monasteries' peasants and income in many places."[141]

Here I must mention some laudable mining towns in explanation of Jeremiah's prophecy.[142] Mansfeld[143] provided the true |miner or mining clerk, who laid to against the Antichrist, together with other good people who

---

[137] בָּחוֹן; i.e., an assayer of metals.

[138] Cf. below, pp. 591, 599.

[139] See Mathesius, *History*, above, pp. 117, 119; cf. Luther, *Sermon on Keeping Children in School* (1530), LW 46:250–51.

[140] Quicksilver was used in separating precious metals by amalgamation: see Agricola, *De re metallica* (trans. Hoover, pp. 297–300). However, the image here seems instead to be based on the idea that a small quantity of mercury would forever poison a water source: see *That These Words of Christ* (1527), LW 37:16; *Annotations on Matthew 1–18* (1534–35/1538), LW 67:207.

[141] *Table Talk* no. 351 (1532), WA TR 1:145.

[142] See above, Mathesius, *History*, p. 555.

[143] See above, Mathesius, *History*, p. 555.

performed their work industriously in accordance with their shift and con-
tract for some time, and continued to operate the mine for the duration of
the so-called "Interim."[144] Later the Hungarian mining towns likewise persevered in God's Word steadfastly and faithfully.[145]

Although God's Word was hindered among its neighbors, the Wild
Man[146] remained steadfast upon the new and blessed ore of the holy Gospel,
as free miners. Likewise, by God's grace and the most gracious permission of
their good authorities, to this day the mines in Bohemia have peacefully preserved the two kinds[147] as well as the blessed doctrine concerning the Lord
Christ, gracious forgiveness of sins, and true conversion or Christian repentance, which consists in the knowledge of sins and faith in Christ's Word
and a good conscience,[148] enjoying and availing themselves of the privilege
conceded to Joachimsthal.[149]

Was it not wondrous that, at the very time when God wanted to reforge
the Gospel[150] and to search the Roman tailings for ore, pulverize it, send it
through the oven, and smelt it, these laudable mining works were begun,
in God's gracious providence? Through Count Stephan Schlick and his
brothers,[151] our gracious counts and lords, God provided for us first both

---

[144] *biß man die zech auffm hinterim beleget.* "Hinterim" was a mocking title for the Interims
(see the introduction above, p. lxxxv), as in the saying *Das Interim hat den Schalk hinter ihm*
["The Interim has the fiend behind it"]. Cf. Wander 2:964, "Interim." Mathesius is depicting
as a heroic act the decision of Melanchthon, Bugenhagen, and others to continue teaching at
Wittenberg despite the imposition of the Interim.

[145] Lutheranism in the free mining towns of Hungary found itself challenged in the late
1550s under Hapsburg efforts to consolidate religious unity outside the empire (where the
Hapsburgs claimed that the religious provisions of the 1555 Peace of Augsburg did not apply).
The mining towns refused to submit to the authority of the archbishop of Esztergom and submitted their own Lutheran confession, the *Confessio Montana* or *Heptapolitana* of 1559. See
David P. Daniel, "Lutheranism in the Kingdom of Hungary," in *Lutheran Ecclesiastical Culture:
1550–1675*, ed. Robert Kolb (Leiden: Brill, 2008), pp. 477–78.

[146] I.e., the city of Braunschweig, whose coins bore the image of a wild man holding an
uprooted tree. Brandenburg, along with other Lutheran cities such as Magdeburg, sought to
resist the imposition of the Interim.

[147] I.e., both kinds for the laity in the Lord's Supper: see above, p. 159 n. 112.

[148] See AC XII (Kolb-Wengert, pp. 44–47; *Concordia*, p. 38).

[149] On the religious toleration conceded to Joachimsthal, see the introduction above,
p. lxxxiii.

[150] *auffm Euangelio anlassen*; the metaphor is that of reheating a metal object in the forge
so that it can be reshaped.

[151] On the Schlicks, see the introduction above, p. lxxxiii; on the individual counts, see
above, p. 138 n. 136 (Hieronymus, Lorenz, and Stephan), p. 208 n. 41 (Sebastian), p. 209 n. 51
(Wolfgang).

kinds, by virtue of the Bohemian *compactata*,[152] and then the cleansed doctrine and purified silver from God's spiritual smeltery in Wittenberg.

But though some bunglers worked some damage here in the beginning, making furnace bears[153] and causing loss through their lack of diligence, so that their brasque got kicked up[154] several times, our God replaced them with other smelters, who labored honorably for the benefit of both the lords and the shareholders. Consequently, (praise God!) in these thirty-one years[155] many beautiful and genuine cakes of silver have been set aside as tithes to God,[156] and a decent obedience, peace, discipline, and unity have been preserved down to the present along with the mechanical arts[157] |and the holy Gospel. May the Lord Jesus Christ, the supreme Lord of the mines, to whom we in this valley and Erzgebirge also give and measure out [our silver], give His help so that His Word and good ore may continue to be unearthed, and so that with God and a good conscience we and all pious miners may become rich here and then be saved eternally!

Enough has been said concerning Doctor Martin and his calling and course of life to explain the passage from Jeremiah, to honor the Christian university in Wittenberg, and to instruct and exhort our school and church, so that we may not on any account forget this most illustrious university and its people of great merit, and so that we do not staff our own [spiritual] mines and furnaces with master miners and smelters who know nothing of the Wittenberg lodestone,[158] workmanship, and metallurgy.

Now at the time when Doctor Martin openly confessed his teaching before the cardinal in Augsburg in 1518[159] and persisted steadfast in it, Dr. Johann Reuchlin[160] from Pforzheim sent his nephew Philip Melanchthon to Wittenberg at the gracious request of Duke Frederick, elector of Saxony, with a fine and comforting prophecy [that he would] get rid of the old

---

[152] See above, p. 343 n. 126.

[153] *jre sew machete*; a "sow" (in English terms, a "furnace bear" or "salamander") is an unwanted glob of molten iron stuck to the inside wall or to the floor of the hearth of a smelting furnace. See *DWB*, s.v. "Sau" C.1.

[154] *jre gestüb etlich mal auffstunden*; when glowing metal comes into contact with moisture, it sprays, thereby stirring up the brasque, a mixture of clay and coal dust that lines the hearth of a smelting furnace. Cf. *DWB*, s.v. "Gestübe" 2.a.

[155] Apparently, since the 1533 departure of the last non-Lutheran pastor, Johann Sylvius Egranus (see above, Mathesius, *History*, p. 291): see Brown, *Singing the Gospel*, p. 35.

[156] See above, p. 589.

[157] *gemeinen künsten*

[158] On the use of magnets in assaying, see Agricola, *De re metallica* (trans. Hoover, p. 247).

[159] See above, Mathesius, *History*, pp. 148–50.

[160] On Reuchlin, see above, p. 132 n. 100.

paganism[161] in the schools, praise the liberal arts and the languages, and establish a new university with the help of God. Many good people came to this young man, wanting to hear him. This is because he had quite correctly grasped pure theology from the doctor, and he helped to undermine the papacy and to cast it away with great mildness and helpful discretion for as long as he taught God's Word at his university. He summarized concisely and skillfully, with accuracy and sound discretion, what the doctor had set forth somewhat more richly and extensively in his writings and sermons.

This man was the second olive tree or the true Elisha [Rev. 11:4], who until his life's end, like us, openly acknowledged the great Elijah as his father and preceptor and as Israel's horseman and chariot.[162] He was also the earthen or graphite crucible,[163] in which the silver that Doctor Luther had purified was refined and tried by fire. This is the blessed black earth[164] that God provided for spiritual mining and smelting, who was the child of a *Choresh*[165] and gun-founder,[166] and was dried and roasted for smelting by the excellent and learned Reuchlin.[167] This earthen crucible stood in the fire for a long time, and in his public lectures and writings he faithfully endured in God's Word to the end, even though many an ungrateful student and neighbor gave him many hard hits and heavy blows.[168] The earth in which Dr. Luther carefully formed and shaped the Lord Christ was good; therefore, he did not allow himself to be thrown down or torn away from his calling.

These are the two miners who adorned Wittenberg and the Electorate of Saxony, gave the papacy burning pain, and gave countless benefits to the Christian Church. Moreover, they explained Scripture, translated the Bible into German, purified the liberal arts and returned them to their proper use, and educated many good people, working alongside the excellent and industrious Dr. Johann Bugenhagen from Pomerania, to whom the church and superintendency in Wittenberg were entrusted,[169] and Doctor Justus Jonas,

---

[161] *paganterey*; see above, p. 579.

[162] See above, Mathesius, *History*, p. 560; cf. above, Mathesius, *History*, p. 462.

[163] *der jrdener oder ipser tigel*; a graphite crucible, named in German after the Austrian town of Ybbs.

[164] See above, Mathesius, *History*, p. 556.

[165] חרשׁ; i.e., a craftsman. Cf. Gen. 4:22.

[166] Melanchthon's father, Georg Schwarzerdt (1459–1508), was armorer to the count Palatine Philip the Upright (r. 1476–1508).

[167] On Reuchlin, see above, p. 591.

[168] An allusion to the criticism of Melanchthon by other Lutherans—both Andreas Osiander and the Gnesio-Lutheran party—after Luther's death: see the introduction above, pp. xxi, lxxxiii–lxxxiv; cf. above, p. 199 n. 88, p. 280 n. 85.

[169] On Bugenhagen, see the introduction above, pp. xxxvi–xxxvii.

provost of the foundation,[170] who also served many people and churches with lecturing, preaching, and visitations. These great people knew and bore witness to the Lord Jesus with one spirit and concordantly opposed the fabricated dreams and glosses of the Antichrist, the fanatics, and the false brethren, and the turmoil they caused in the Church, with which they confused and troubled the hearts of many people. And yet each one of these scholars had his own gift, as Herr Philip ¹used to say so well: "Doctor Pomeranus is a *Grammaticus* ['grammarian'], who relies on the words of the text. I am a *Dialecticus* ['logician']; I look at how the text hangs together and what can be derived and deduced from it in a Christian manner and on good grounds. Dr. Jonas is an orator; he can brilliantly and clearly express, explain, and present the words of the text. Dr. Martin is *omnia in omnibus* ['all in all']; the speech and writing of this extraordinary man[171] and chosen instrument are powerful,[172] penetrate to the very heart, and leave behind their sharpness and consolation in the hearts of many people."[173]

In addition to these excellent people, Matthaeus Aurogallus from Chomutov taught Hebrew,[174] and many other students of Herr Melanchthon taught Greek and the liberal arts.

When God graciously sent me to this university in 1529, I still found Master Georg Elner from Staffelstein;[175] Master Volmar,[176] the excellent mathematician; Master Vach;[177] and Tulich[178] among the old professors there. Afterward the following began to lecture: Master Caspar Cruciger [the Elder],[179] Master Veit Winsheim the Elder,[180] Erasmus Reinhold,[181] Master Burchart from Weimar,[182] Master Amerbach,[183] and Master Jacob Milich,[184] all of whom had followed Herr Philip here and studied under

[170] On Jonas, see the introduction above, p. xxx.

[171] *wundermans*: see the introduction above, pp. lxxxix–xc.

[172] *hat hend und füß*; cf. above, Mathesius, *History*, p. 514.

[173] Mathesius appears to be the source for this much-quoted dictum by Melanchthon.

[174] On Aurogallus [Goldhahn], see above, p. 297 n. 71.

[175] On Elner, see above, p. 302 n. 100.

[176] On Johannes Volmar, see above, p. 298 n. 77.

[177] On Balthasar Fabricius of Vacha, see above p. 297 n. 75.

[178] On Tulich, see above, p. 297 n. 73.

[179] On Cruciger, see the introduction above, p. xx n. 19 and p. 298 n. 81.

[180] On Veit Oertel from Winsheim, see above, p. 299 n. 83.

[181] On Reinhold, see above, p. 299 n. 86.

[182] On Franz Burchart, see above, p. 297 n. 72.

[183] On Veit Amerbach [Trolmann], see above, p. 299 n. 85.

[184] On Milich, see above, p. 298 n. 79.

him. I knew Herr Georg Major[185] from Nürnberg, Hieronymus Weller[186] from Freiberg, Master Veit[187] from Nürnberg, Herr Viktorin Strigel,[188] David Chytraeus,[189] and Paul Eber[190] from Kitzingen as obedient and grateful students of the old Elijah and Elisha.[191] Indeed, (praise God!) the best churches and schools in the empire are staffed with Wittenberg scholars and masters. For Wittenberg produced outstandingly fine people, even as it still has fine and discreet teachers, who serve the Church of God and well-ordered schools with blessed fruits, |in love and friendship, while faithfully keeping the purified doctrine as they have heard and learned it from the Herr Doctor and Herr Melanchthon.

But as for the fact that some who were educated there somehow turned out to be ungrateful and quarrelsome disciples of Cassian and Damascene,[192] like Judas, Nicolaus [Acts 6:5; Rev. 2:6], and others who went out from Christ and His apostles [cf. 1 John 2:19]—that we must commend to our dear God. The raven had also been nourished in Noah's ark and was sent out but did not return [Gen. 8:7].[193] So it is nothing new in our times that many of them have suffered a shipwreck of faith [cf. 1 Tim. 1:19] and repaid their preceptors, who deserve respect, with no thanks but the devil's,[194] and that they preach Christ and His Gospel out of malice, hate, discord, vainglory, or desire for personal gain, like Balaam [Numbers 23–24], or fall away entirely. St. Paul deeply laments such false brethren and quarrelsome people who, with great and fervent zeal (as they claimed), helped afflict and trouble

---

[185] On Major, see above, p. 300 n. 88.

[186] On Weller, see above, p. 416 n. 127.

[187] On Veit Dietrich, see above, p. 278 n. 76.

[188] Victorin Strigel (1524–69) matriculated in Wittenberg in 1542 and became an avid student of Melanchthon and a leader of the "Philippist" party. He went on to teach in Jena, where he ran afoul of Matthias Flacius (see above, p. 112 n. 42) and other Gnesio-Lutherans for his emphasis on human capability and cooperation with God and for his limitation of the effects of original sin. Several of his positions were rejected in the Formula of Concord. See Arand et al., *Lutheran Confessions*, pp. 204–8; William R. Russell, "Strigel, Viktorin," *OER* 4:119–20.

[189] David Chytraeus (1530–1600) came to Wittenberg as a student in 1544. In 1550, he moved to Rostock, where he became a member of the theological faculty in 1563 and participated in the drafting of the Formula of Concord of 1577. See Friedrich Wilhelm Bautz, "Chytraeus, David," *BBKL* 1:1021–1122; Arand et al., *Lutheran Confessions*, pp. 271–73.

[190] On Eber, see above, p. 300 n. 89.

[191] See above, p. 592. On Mathesius' circle of acquaintances from Wittenberg, see Loesche, *Johannes Mathesius*, 1:191–94.

[192] See above, Mathesius, *History*, p. 291.

[193] Cf. *Lectures on Genesis* (1535–45/1544–54), LW 2:157–59.

[194] Cf. Wander 4:1130, "Teufelsdank" no. 2.

the Church of God, and he prays fervently against them, that God would abandon them to their sins and shame [Gal. 2:4; 5:12; Phil. 1:15–28; 3:17–19]. Likewise, in our times, Dr. Martin's prayer and prophecy against troublesome and deceitful people unfortunately had to become just as fervent, not only because they had become pernicious heretics but also because some of them had perished in a terrible and dreadful manner. I once heard this prophecy from his mouth: "Mathesius, you will see it. Those who impudently oppose this church and university in Wittenberg will surely become heretics and perish in terrors."[195]

God chose this university for Himself as His second Mount Zion and watchtower and provided it[196] with people who wisely and correctly preached repentance and forgiveness of sins, and He has watched over the university and these people for these forty years. If people will abide in the burnished and refined ¹doctrine in simplicity and in love and unity (as I have hope in God and good people), and will remain steadfast in the true and clear Word of God with simplicity and sincerity instead of looking to new and strange teachings or insidiously stabbing through the fence[197] and using human and rational wisdom to attack the acknowledged, publicly confessed, and well-founded truth, then this university and church will remain, even if all the gates of hell should oppose them together with the whole anti-Christian sect and the new zealots.[198]

Let us draw to a close now, for you will hear what remains to be said about the doctor in the history about him.[199] Today, at this school festival, we thank the Lord Jesus, who has established and preserved the Christian university in Wittenberg through excellent people; and who has appointed to this church and university outstanding and extraordinary people,[200] the likes of whom have not lived on the earth for many centuries; and who has caused many fine and useful people to be educated there who can be put to good use in churches, governments, and schools, and many good books to be explained and printed there, in addition to the German translation of the Bible.

---

[195] See above, Mathesius, *History*, pp. 419, 563–64.

[196] Reading *geben* with the 1556 edition for *gehen* in Loesche's text.

[197] See above, Mathesius, *History*, p. 260 and n. 167 there.

[198] I.e., the Roman Church on the one hand and the extreme Gnesio-Lutherans on the other.

[199] I.e., in the seventeenth sermon. Loesche (*LH²*, p. xvi) takes this as an indication that the sixteenth sermon as printed was delivered earlier, in the middle of the series. See the introduction above, p. lxxxvii.

[200] *treffliche wunderleut*; see the introduction above, pp. lxxxix–xc.

Today we also thank our faithful God, who has built up this imperial mining town with the Gospel;[201] has felicitously planted His Word here, together with the proper use of the holy Sacraments, and brought forth abundant fruit; has staffed this church and school with Wittenberg students and alumni; and has caused us to remain steadfast in love, friendship, reverence, and due gratitude toward our dear preceptors and friends. We also ask our faithful Father in the name of Jesus Christ[202] that He would repay His grace and rich blessing a thousandfold to the whole [ruling] house in Saxony, as well as to the church and university and the heirs and friends of Dr. Martin, Philip, Bugenhagen, and Cruciger, together with the whole city of Wittenberg and those who still provide our children and the children of our friends with counsel and aid, and that He would graciously preserve the land in gracious peace and prosperity. Today [we also ask that He would] preserve those from the church and university with His Spirit in pure doctrine, true faith, a good conscience, brotherly love, and unity in humility and obedience as subjects until the end. In addition, [we ask that He would] embrace our most gracious [imperial] and gracious [royal] authorities, the Roman emperor and Roman king and the whole house of Austria,[203] in addition to our old, gracious counts and lords, Lord Schlick and his heirs,[204] and both governments[205] here in Joachimsthal, as well as our church, school, and mines, and all who faithfully and simply teach and learn God's Word and the liberal arts in the church and school, along with all who support Joachimsthal in all honor and kindness, speaking a good word on its behalf where it is fitting, and especially those who receive the young students [cf. Matt. 18:5], who by Christ's command are led to His catechism and the discipline of the school, and [would] cause them them to be and to remain blessed vessels of mercy [Rom. 9:22–23].

May God also be with everyone with His Spirit and grant them to live, teach, and learn as Christians, that they may abide steadfast in the true doctrine with a good conscience, fall into a blessed sleep, rest in peace, joyfully

---

[201] Probably with a double reference to edification with the Gospel and to the synchronicity of Joachimsthal's founding with the beginning of Luther's public protest: see the introduction above, p. lxxxii.

[202] Emending the 1566 edition, which reads *im namen Jesu Christi, unsers getrewen Vattern* ["in the name of Jesus Christ, our faithful Father"] to *unsern getrewen Vattern*, with A. J. D. Rust, ed., *M. Johann Mathesius Leben Dr. Martin Luthers, in siebzehn Predigten* (Berlin: Crantz, 1841), p. 379.

[203] I.e., the Hapsburgs. In March 1564, Ferdinand I (d. July 1564) would still have been Holy Roman emperor and archduke of Austria and his son Maximilian II would have been the king of Bohemia (see the introduction above, p. lxxxiii).

[204] On the Schlicks, see above, p. 590 and n. 151 there.

[205] I.e., the government of the town and that of the mines.

rise from the dead, come with honor before God's judgment seat and countenance, and possess new joy and eternal life in the presence of God and
all His saints and angels. May the Holy Trinity help us to that end, and all
whom we have served here: God the eternal Father, through Jesus Christ,
His only-begotten Son, the fountain of all wisdom, and the Holy Spirit of
them both—highly exalted throughout all eternity! Amen.

The Seventeenth Sermon,[1]
on Doctor Luther's Blessed Stories and Sayings about Mining, in Honor of the Praiseworthy Mines in St. Joachimsthal

[Shrove Tuesday, March 6, 1565][2]

BELOVED friends in the Lord! The wise say that we must pay the occasion its due,[3] even as St. Paul tells us to make the most of the time [Rom. 12:11 DB; Eph. 5:16; Col. 4:5]. But since you miners hold your mining festival on this day[4] and faithfully come to church, and since our God has appointed me to be a miners' preacher and has transferred me from the mines to my studies,[5] I intend to speak again about the dear mines, to honor God, mining, and this, my beloved parish church. And because I have concluded the *Miners' Postil*[6] and the accounts about Doctor Luther's teaching and life,[7] in the present hour I will tell you as much as I know of what this miner's son said and thought about mining, and about his customary behavior toward honorable miners and toward my parishioners [in particular]. For Doctor Luther was born of a miner in Eisleben in the Harz Mountains, and there also he was baptized and made a member of Christ's Body by a miners' preacher.[8] His dear father, Hans Luther, also enabled him to study in Erfurt

---

[1] In the 1566 first edition, fol. 218v, this sermon is numbered as the sixteenth. Cf. above, p. 463 n. 1.

[2] On the dating of this sermon, see Volz, *Die Lutherpredigten des Johannes Mathesius*, p. 11; and the introduction above, p. lxxxvii.

[3] For the expression, see above, p. 266 n. 3.

[4] On the custom of observing Shrove Tuesday as a miners' festival in Joachimsthal, see Mathesius, *Sarepta*, fol. [5]r, fol. 1v; cf. above, Mathesius, *History*, p. 266.

[5] Mathesius was the son of a miner (see the introduction above, p. lxxx; cf. *Sarepta*, fol. [6]v), and in gratitude for his work as a teacher, he also had been made a shareholder of one of the Joachimsthal mines in 1538: see Loesche, *Johannes Mathesius*, 1:89.

[6] Mathesius' *Sarepta oder Bergpostil*: see the introduction above, p. lxxxvi.

[7] I.e., Sermons 1–15 of Mathesius, *History*.

[8] See above, Mathesius, *History*, p. 117.

by means of his honorable mining property and his two furnaces.[9] In the end, as you recently heard,[10] the doctor also faithfully commended his soul to the Lord Jesus Christ among miners in his hometown, where he made a Christian and blessed departure. ¹Of course, he is also one of the honorable Zarephathite miners and saviors, who will come to the holy Mount Zion and precious Christian Church in accordance with the prophecy of the prophet Obadiah [vv. 20–21][11] and will judge the bloodthirsty Edomites, tyrants, and murderers of souls. And he will destroy the great Babylon in accordance with Jeremiah's prophecy [Jer. 51:27][12] and help to raise up and bring to fulfillment the spiritual kingdom of the eternal King, our Lord Jesus Christ. This miner's son (praise God!) has intrepidly acted as a true Zarephathite with prayer, preaching, and writing for twenty-nine years on Mount Lebanon,[13] has driven off the spent slag from God's Church, and has tithed and devoted much beautiful, fine silver to God [cf. Ps. 119:140]. But you have already heard at length about his [calling] as doctor and his preaching these past years.

Today, learn and hear how this Minni or Ashkenaz[14] and German always bore love and goodwill toward mining and miners, and how he gladly spoke and listened to and about these with honor as occasion arose. It is natural for a man to be favorably inclined to his fatherland and the livelihood of his parents, and neither faith in Jesus Christ nor the Holy Spirit extinguishes such inborn love and goodwill, even though we have been born again from above [John 3:3] by God through the water and the Word [Eph. 5:26] as new creatures and God's children. So on this Shrove Tuesday, dear friends, listen to some fine stories from which you will also be able to take away some profitable teaching.

When our doctor began teaching the doctrine of true Christian repentance and exhorting everyone to contrition, sorrow, and blessed knowledge of the Lord Jesus Christ and to genuine new obedience, he also attacked the impure doctrine and false worship. With firm proofs drawn from the writings of the prophets and apostles, he overturned everything that had crept into the Church to the dishonor of Christ and of His blood, as well as ¹a great many scandalous practices. At this time, the old, hypocritical fasting fell away, along with the Shrovetide Carnival, which had become a truly

---

[9] See above, Mathesius, *History*, p. 119.

[10] See above, Mathesius, *History*, pp. 534–35.

[11] See above, Mathesius, *History*, p. 555.

[12] See above, Mathesius, *History*, p. 555.

[13] I.e., Wittenberg; see above, Mathesius, *History*, pp. 237, 307–8, 564, 572, 573.

[14] See above, Mathesius, *History*, pp. 555.

heathen festival,[15] when people not only weighed down their hearts with drunkenness and dissolute, wild gourmandizing [cf. Luke 21:34] but even engaged in all kinds of unchastity and insulted the old maids,[16] just as they had the custom of annually celebrating similar days of gluttony and gorging for the days of St. Martin[17] and Burchard[18] and others.[19]

Now once the people had been instructed to put away what is wicked and to hold on to what is good [1 Thess 5:21–22], and because indeed it would not be wrong to come together honorably and decently and to be joyful and of good cheer in cordial friendship in honorable public places, [such as] city halls, taverns, and at weddings, the honorable council in Wittenberg thought about ways to establish and preserve friendship, unity, and goodwill among [the citizens]. For this reason, [the council] resolved that they might gather in their city hall for several days in good *amity*,[20] and since there were two governments [in Wittenberg],[21] they issued invitations to people from the university.[22]

At this time, our doctor was also asked and invited to attend this honorable, esteemed gathering. But because he had cast aside the German days of fasting and gluttony by means of God's Word, it would not be right for him to give his teaching a bad name through his example, which his adversaries could have interpreted the wrong way. Therefore, he declined the invitation for himself, but bade them to be joyful and of good cheer in God's name and Christian discipline and to establish and preserve peace and unity. But he, as

---

[15] Luther does not, in fact, seem to have been particularly concerned with Carnival as an occasion for immorality. In the early Reformation, Carnival was often made an occasion for protest against the papacy: see Robert Scribner, "Reformation, Carnival and the World Turned Upside-Down," *Social History* 3, no. 3 (1978): 303–29.

[16] *die alten Megde in pflug spannete*; literally, "yoked the old maids to the plow." For the meaning, see Wander 3:1334, "Pflug" no. 63.

[17] On St. Martin, see above, pp. 34 n. 23, 114 n. 3, 117 n. 13 (cf. above, p. 554 n. 85). His festival on November 11 was traditionally observed with feasting on roast goose.

[18] St. Burchard [Burckhart] (d. ca. 755) was the first bishop of Würzburg. His feast day on October 14 was an occasion for extravagant revelry and drinking of new wine. See Friedrich Wilhelm Bautz, "Burchard," *BBKL* 1:816–17; Wander 5:1083, "Burchardstag"; WA 30/2:252 n. 36.

[19] In his collection of wedding sermons, the *Hochzeitspredigten*, Mathesius mentions "Christmas and Martin and Burchard's days" as special occasions for feasting and drinking: see Loesche, *Mathesius: Ausgewählte Werke*, 2:331. Cf. Luther, *Exhortation to All Clergy* (1530), LW 34:57.

[20] *inn guter charitate*

[21] I.e., the government of the town and of the university.

[22] The date of this occasion could not be determined.

a doctor and preacher, remained in his house and was also of good cheer in the Lord with his people.

On these days young people would run around in a disguise, according to the old heathen custom, provoking scandal.[23] |For a bad habit is not easy to get rid of.[24] Some came to the doctor's house (the cloister),[25] but to avoid [giving cause for] offense or evil rumor, none of them was let in.[26] Among others, there was an educated young man[27] who later served great electors with honor; he made his mark with his company.[28] They got themselves fitted in mining clothes and armed themselves like slate quarrymen with their picking hammers, without any childish pranks, for respectable fun.

If there is virtue within, as in the case of those who have studied well, it also makes itself manifest. Now, though this honorable company dressed up in costumes and had themselves announced to the doctor as miners born and raised at the mines, they acted like real miners and did not come before this great man with painted kings, popes, cardinals, devils, and sows,[29] or with carved knucklebone dice.[30] Instead, they came equipped with a finely

---

[23] Cf. the university decrees from 1540, 1541, and 1542, which criticize and seek to regulate the Carnival activities of the students: Friedensburg, *Urkundenbuch der Universität Wittenberg*, 1:223, no. 227 (February–March 1540); CR 4:99 (February 13, 1541); CR 4:779–81 (February 18, 1542).

[24] Cf. Wander 1:1679, "Gewohnheit" no. 22.

[25] Cf. above, Mathesius, *History*, pp. 475, 511, 521.

[26] This story about Luther and the students dressed as miners is also narrated by Spangenberg, *Theander Lutherus*, sermon 14 (November 11, 1569), fols. 278r–279r, where the printed marginalia in the 1589 edition purport to offer the names of the students who were involved (fol. 278v). Their documented dates of attendance in Wittenberg, however, do not all overlap. The most plausible date (with two of the three students verifiably present) would be 1523 or 1524.

[27] According to Spangenberg, this was Eberhard von der Tannen [Thann, Tann], who would have been a student at Wittenberg from 1512 to 1517 and who later served as counselor and ambassador for the Saxon electors (see above, p. 238 n. 37). It is possible that Tannen could have returned to Wittenberg in 1523 or 1524 after his further study in Erfurt, Bologna, Padua, and Freiburg.

[28] According to Spangenberg, the other participants included Wilhelm Nesen [Nesenus] (1493–1524; see Otto Kämmel, "Nesen, Wilhelm," *ADB* 23:438–41), a young humanist of great promise who drowned tragically in a boating accident in 1524, having attended Wittenberg since 1523 (cf. Luther's dedication to Nesen of his 1523 treatise *Against the Armed Man Cochlaeus*, WA 11:295–308 [LW 71]); and Philip Glüenspieß from Mansfeld (d. 1565), who studied in Wittenberg from 1519–24 (see WA Br 3:127, 413; 18:111).

[29] I.e., a deck of (painted) playing cards, which in German decks depicted or were named after the political and religious figures indicated. A "sow" appeared on the ace. See Timothy B. Husband, *The World in Play: Luxury Cards 1430–1540* (New York: Metropolitan Museum of Art, 2015), pp. 8–10.

[30] *abgeckten schelmebeine*

crafted chess game,[31] which the doctor, like many great and excellent people, liked to play.[32] When the doctor heard that a masquerade of honorable slate quarrymen was present, he said, "Those you can let in. They are my fellow countrymen and my dear father's fellow miners. Because these people spend the whole week underground in toxic air and vapors, they have to be allowed to enjoy some honorable fun and amusement on occasion."[33]

Upon this the company went to the doctor's table and set up their chess game. The doctor, as a practiced chess player, took up their challenge. "You miners," he said, "if you want to play deep into this game or go deep in the mines[34] without suffering loss and digging yourself into a hole you can't escape,[35] you should, as the saying goes, not stick your eyes in your pockets,[36] for in both situations you must be vigilant."

Then the doctor proceeded to checkmate his chess partner, who conceded the match to him, and they remained with him, joyfully singing and dancing in an honorable and decent manner. By nature our doctor was glad to enjoy himself where appropriate and was not against seeing the young people around him enjoying themselves and having good, clean fun. I am mentioning this story to give you a sense of how the character of an honorable miner also manifested itself in this miner's son, for he liked to have miners around him and was playful with and among them.

I also heard the doctor mention a mineral specimen or fine slate that had been unearthed in Mansfeld that was given to him as a token of esteem.[37]

---

[31] *staffieren sich mit eim künstlichen schachtspil. DWB*, s.v. "Karnöffel" 2, interprets this to mean that the students were wearing masks representing the chess figures, but Spangenberg, *Theander Lutherus*, fol. 278v, rewords it as *setzen ein künstliches Schachtspiel auff* ["set up a finely crafted chess set"].

[32] Luther was fond of chess, complimenting others on their chess skills and using chess analogies in his writing. See, e.g., Luther to Prince Joachim of Anhalt, June 12, 1534, WA Br 7:74; and above, Mathesius, *History*, p. 511.

[33] Cf. *Table Talk* no. 5173 (1540), WA TR 4:693.

[34] *wer inn diesem und andern tieffen schachten ziehen . . . will*; a play on words between *Schach[t]* ["chess"] and *Schacht* ["mine shaft"]. See *DWB*, s.v. "Schact" no. 1.

[35] *das seine mit unrat verbawen*

[36] Cf. Wander 1:178, 180, "Auge" nos. 257 and 322. See Luther, *Notes on Ecclesiastes* (1526/1532), LW 15:40.

[37] *Table Talk* no. 4961 (1540), WA TR 4:593. Aurifaber's version of this *Table Talk* indicates that the episode took place in 1538. It is also recounted in Spangenberg, *Theander Lutherus*, fol. 279r–v, and in sermon 8 (February 18, 1566), fol. 157r–v, based on an account by Hieronymus Weller, in which other witnesses of the fossil are identified as Luther's brother Jacob (see above, p. 57 n. 10), [Philip Glüenspieß], Melanchthon, Jonas, Cruciger, the jurist Basilius Monner (1500–1566; Teichmann, "Monner, Basilius," ADB 22:171), and Elector John Frederick. Glüenspieß is mentioned in the 1566 separate printing of Spangenberg's eighth sermon (VD16 S7677, fol. F6r) but not in the 1589 collected edition. See Volz, *Die*

In Eisleben, as you know, they are digging black slate that contains copper and silver. And seeing that God and nature have their delightful fun underground, too, all kinds of fish shapes were formed in the slate.[38] Such beautiful fish and animals have also been found in white rock in Bavaria by Kelheim, for example.[39] The scholars are in dispute about what causes such impressions in the rock, but the doctor said, "God, who makes His power manifest in the visible creatures, wants to be noticed underground in the mines as well, and to bear witness that this is His good gift."[40]

Now, on this slate there was an image of the pope with a three-tiered crown.[41] When [Luther] saw this, he said, "The pope shall be exposed, and this shall be done by a miner from Mansfeld. Perhaps that is why it derives its name from Minni and quicksilver, like the ancient German miners.[42] Therefore, since even the slate bears witness of this to us, we will not relent but utterly expose his foolishness to all the world, so that everyone will recognize that he has not come down from heaven above but has come up out of the deepest of depths below."

In about the year 1542, two citizens from Joachimsthal went to Wittenberg and visited the doctor; they also brought him a beautiful specimen of reddish-gold ore.[43] He displayed all manner of goodwill toward these two and invited them to be his guests. At table, one of them said, "Doctor, my colleague once severely attacked your reverence. When your reverence was burned [in effigy] at Altenberg during the Shrovetide Carnival,[44] he let

---

Lutherpredigten des Johannes Mathesius, p. 285 ad loc. Jacob Luther and Glüenspieß would presumbably have seen the stone in Mansfeld.

[38] See also Mathesius, *Sarepta*, preface, fol. c1r, and sermon 3, fol 48r (Loesche, *Mathesius: Ausgewählte Werke*, 4:73, 195).

[39] I.e., limestone fossils, found in the quarries around Kelheim, some 25 km southwest of Regensburg. The region is still recognized as a rich source of fossils. See Martin Röper, "East Bavarian Plattenkalk," *Zitteliana* B/26 (2005):57–70.

[40] Such fossils were described by Pliny, *Natural History* 36.29 (Loeb 419 [1938], pp. 108–9), and, in Luther's day, by Georg Agricola, in his *De natura fossilium* (Basel: Froben, 1546) [VD16 A922], pp. 181–82 (trans. Mark Chance Bandy and Jean A. Bandy [New York: Geological Society of America, 1955], p. 14). Luther himself offers a different explanation of such fossils— as the remains of the flood—in *Lectures on Genesis* (1535–45/1544–54), LW 1:98.

[41] Perhaps a fossil of a snail or nautiloid with a conical shell. On the papal tiara, see above, p. 133 n. 107.

[42] See above, Mathesius, *History*, p. 555.

[43] I.e., gold alloyed with copper or cinnabar. See Mathesius, *Sarepta*, sermon 3, fol. 48 (Loesche, *Mathesius: Ausgewählte Werke*, 4:195).

[44] Other sources recount that this ceremonial burning of Luther's image took place on the Geisingberg, near the town of Altenberg, at mid-Lent (Laetare Sunday) in 1522. See *LH²*, p. 602 ad loc.; Johann Georg Theodor Graesse, *Der Sagenschatz des Königreichs Sachsen*, 2nd ed. (Dresden: Schönfeld, 1874), 1:206–8; and Christoph Meissner, *Umständliche Nachricht von*

himself be used to play the judge, and he condemned your reverence to the fire like John Hus.[45] But now that he has been called to the Gospel and has recognized the truth through your doctrine, he is heartily sorry for this and comes asking for mercy and forgiveness of his foolish ignorance. He wishes from now on to become better through God's Word and your writings."

These words pleased the doctor, and he said, "Very well. Since he did that out of ignorance, and his papal fire did no harm to me or my doctrine, it is forgiven and forgotten in the name of the Lord." Seeing that this exchange produced a good and honorable laugh, the one who was absolved said, "O doctor, I thank your reverence. But I carry yet another large debt and ask that you would absolve me of it too. For I, a poor miner, have made a careless blunder in my mine and now owe about 500 gulden."

"Very well," said the doctor. "When you miners are poorest, your fortune blossoms, for then you are tenacious and take care of your mines in person, and need teaches you to pray, go to church, and be sober and temperate. Therefore, you are unaware yourselves of how rich you are. Go home, work faithfully, deal honestly, and believe and hope in God the Father Almighty, the true Ore-maker, in the name of His Son, who spoke silver and gold into the mouth of the fish [Matt. 17:27], keeps making ore grow, and gives it at the right time to those who persevere in their mines ʹand patiently abide with Him in heartfelt prayer. The rich God will be with you; upon His rich blessing and generous hand I absolve you also of all[46] of your debt." Before this miner had returned home, he received a message on the way that good ore had been found in his mine on the blessed Asar.[47] This he liquidated and paid dividends, repaying everything with a surplus left over.

Just as our doctor spoke to this man from Joachimsthal in a friendly and cheerful way, I can testify in truth, as one who has personally seen and heard, that he was always gracious and benevolent toward this valley, our gracious lords and other citizens and their children, and this church and its ministers. I have seen some of the letters that he wrote to our old gracious lords with his own hand. He dedicated one of his books to Count Sebastian [Schlick] of Elbogen, the one in which he gives a good report about the teaching of Hus.[48]

---

der Churfl. Sächß. Schrifftsäßigen freyen Zien-Berg-Stadt Altenberg (Dresden: Lesch & Hübner, 1747), pp. 18–22 (Volz, Die Lutherpredigten des Johannes Mathesius, p. 285 ad loc.).

[45] On Hus and his martyrdom, see the introduction above, pp. xxxvii–xxxviii and n. 103; Mathesius, History, p. 121.

[46] Reading von all ewer with the 1566 edition (fol. 221v) for von ewer of Loesche's text.

[47] For this Joachimsthal mine, begun in 1541, see Mathesius, Sarepta, fol. Oo3r.

[48] Against King Henry of England (1522), WA 10/2:180–222 (LW 61), with a letter of dedication to Sebastian Schlick (WA 10/2:180–82), dated July 15, 1522. On Count Sebastian Schlick, see above, p. 208 n. 41.

Likewise, [the book] against the Sabbatarians[49] [was dedicated to] Count Wolf [Schlick] of Falkenau, but without explicitly mentioning him.[50] This Christian count also let me read three of the doctor's letters.[51] In addition, the letter that the doctor wrote in 1532 to Count Hieronymus and Count Lorenz [Schlick] is still extant; at the request of Master Christoph Ering, he exhorted them in this letter not to tolerate the Anabaptists and Sacramentarians in their mines.[52] Upon this, these two aforementioned counts issued a public mandate that I found still [posted] in the old church[53] in 1532. He also wrote to your pastor, Master Steude, because of the Pickards.[54] Likewise, I have seen copies of other letters written to my parishioners, in which he exhorted one to be patient[55] and warned another against the teaching of Egranus.[56] I will pass over my letter,[57] |as well as how he wrote inscriptions in books for some citizens and me.[58]

---

[49] *Against the Sabbatarians* (1538), LW 47:57–98.

[50] The recipient of the treatise is identified in the printed edition only as "a good friend." See above, Mathesius, *History*, p. 209. On Count Wolfgang Schlick, see above, p. 209 n. 51.

[51] See above, Mathesius, *History*, p. 209.

[52] Luther to Hieronymus and Lorenz Schlick, October 9, 1532, WA Br 6:372–73. Christoph Ering (1491–1554) was pastor in Joachimsthal from 1529 to 1532: see Brown, *Singing the Gospel*, p. 35.

[53] I.e., in the chapel [*Spitalkirche*] next to the Joachimsthal cemetery, which had been built in 1516 and served as chapel for the poorhouse after the completion of the new town church in 1537 (see Brown, *Singing the Gospel*, pp. 100, 104). On the mandate, see above, Mathesius, *History*, p. 209.

[54] The surviving letter from Luther to Sebastian Steude (see above, p. 512 n. 54), April 25, 1541, WA Br 9:500–502, does not deal with relations with the Bohemian Brethren (known as the "Pickards": see Luther, preface to *Account of the Faith of the Brethren* [1533], LW 60:17–23). However, Luther's letter to Georg Major of the same date instructs him to write to the pastor in Joachimsthal about the "Waldensians" (WA 9:382–83), and Major's letter was presumably kept alongside Luther's. See also *Table Talk* no. 5165 (1540), WA TR 4:690, where the possibility of a "Pickard" preacher being called to Joachimsthal is raised.

[55] Luther to Nicolaus Herman, November 6, 1524, WA Br 3:369.

[56] Luther to Wolfgang Wiebel, October 9, 1532(?), WA 6:376. Wiebel was mayor of Joachimsthal in 1542, 1544, 1547, 1549, and 1553 (see Mathesius, *Chronica*). On Johannes Wildenauer of Eger [Egranus], see above, p. 222 n. 122.

[57] Luther to Mathesius, August 19, 1543, WA Br 10:372; cf. Luther's ordination letter for Mathesius, April 13, 1542, WA Br 12:470–71.

[58] Examples of Luther's book inscriptions for Joachimsthalers have not been identifed: see WA 48:xiii n. 1.

For a time he also had at his table our mayor's son[59] and those who have ministered to you in your church with the Word;[60] often he would tell them about great and necessary matters and would help provide [ministers] for your church. I should also mention how some of you from the council and other honorable miners have sat at his table, listened to him, and eaten and drunk with him.[61]

In 1541, when I received the call to Joachimsthal,[62] I brought seven of your emissaries along to the doctor's table, and he was very cheerful and in good spirits with them. And since there were some singers among them, he wanted to hear what kind of music there was in Joachimsthal. He also took a crystal glass reputed to have belonged to St. Elizabeth,[63] put it on the table, filled it himself, and passed around the drink.

Some children from Joachimsthal were undergoing their deposition at this time,[64] so he lent a hand himself and absolved them *a beanio* with very fine words.[65]

Now, when some mine owners appeared at the table with beautiful specimens, carved stones, and medallions, and expressed their thanks as honorable miners on behalf of their children, he began to speak about mining.[66] "I like to see how our rich God lets His treasures grow underground, by which He proves that He constantly provides for us and lets us see His mighty and creative hand. Besides this, I think about the ancient miners and mine

---

[59] Stephan Hacker, mayor of Joachimsthal in 1538 and 1540 (Mathesius, *Chronica*), sent his son of the same name to study in Wittenberg, where he boarded with Luther in 1540. See *Table Talk* no. 5261 (1540), WA TR 5:34–35.

[60] I.e., Mathesius himself.

[61] On Joachimsthal students in Wittenberg, see above, p. 112 n. 41; Volz, *Die Lutherpredigten des Johannes Mathesius*, p. 286 ad loc.; cf. above, p. 572 n. 6

[62] See the introduction above, pp. lxxxii, lxxxiv.

[63] St. Elizabeth of Hungary (1207–31) married Louis IV of Thuringia (r. 1217–27) and was a resident of the Wartburg castle centuries before Luther. Elizabeth was famous for her generosity to the poor and for her ascetic discipline after her husband's death on crusade in 1227. See *LA* 2:302–18, no. 168; *ODCC*, 3rd ed., s.v. "Elizabeth, of Hungary." Mathesius mentions (*Sarepta*, sermon 15, fol. 264r [Loesche, *Mathesius: Ausgewählte Werke*, 4:233]) that the glass had been displayed in the Wittenberg Castle Church before being given to Luther. (It is listed as the first relic in Lucas Cranach's 1509 catalog: *Dye Zaigung des hochlobwirdigen Hailigthumbs der Stifft-Kirche aller Hailigen zu Wittenburg* [VD16 Z250], fol. a3v.) The glass is preserved in the collections of the Veste Coburg.

[64] On the ceremony of advancing the youngest students to full membership in the university as scholars, see above, Mathesius, *History*, p. 455. Cf. DuCange, s.v. "Beanus."

[65] See *Table Talk* no. 4714 (1539), LW 54:362–63. The *beanus* was the cap worn by younger students.

[66] Mathesius is the source for this report.

owners whom Scripture lauds [cf. Deut. 8:7–9; Job 28:1–12], who traversed land and sea, entered India, and found vast riches.

"But we also ought not forget the fine saying of King David, to whom God's Word is more precious than all gold, even pure gold [Ps. 19:10; 119:127]. And whenever he sees a piece of ore or a smeltery, ⸢he always recalls the spiritual Mine Owner, our Lord Jesus Christ, and His mines. That is why the prophets and psalms contain many fine allegories in which the Holy Spirit presents the spiritual mines of God's Son to the miners. God's Word," he said, "has been put through the fire and purified, like refined silver that has gone through the fire seven times and in which there is no more blemish or impurity [Ps. 12:6]."

Again: "God casts away the godless like spent slag [Ps. 119:119]. If I had been in the mines more often and were charged with preaching among the miners, Scripture would guide me to present them with many fine and apposite allegories and images.

"This pleases me very much, and I have used this [approach] in interpreting the psalm.[67] The precious Christian Church is like a rich, solid, and noble vein that runs through the large mountains and cliffs, often being almost completely squeezed off. But the one who is mightier than all mountains often makes room for His vein, which has been allotted to His Son, so that it expands and yields what it should. Blessed are those who hold shares in this solid, rich vein running through a very solid rock and seek their salvation in it. Likewise, [blessed are] those who patiently and honorably pay their assessment[68] with true faith, sincere prayer, and Christian love. The dividend is certain, but there is much barren rock that must be cleared away from it.

"This allegory gives us a fine image, for even as it is hard work for you to excavate a shaft or cut through a mountain, so, too, will it require toil, work, and great expense to move ahead on this rich vein. For the kingdom of God also suffers violence [Matt. 11:12], and those who are violent—that is, who are zealous and persevere,[69] who are not frightened away by any water or misfortune or deterred by any solid rock—⸢they take it by force and gain a profit: the forgiveness of sins and eternal life.

---

[67] It is unclear which psalm (Psalm 12 or Psalm 119) or which interpretation is in view here. Loesche (*LH²*, p. 603) suggests Luther's interpretation of Ps. 12:6 in *Auslegung der ersten 25 Psalmen auf der Coburg* (1530), WA 31/1:305. See also Luther's hymn version of Psalm 12: "Ah God, from Heaven Look Down" (1523), LW 53:228 (WA Ar 4:178; Wackernagel 3:6, no. 3).

[68] Cf. above, Mathesius, *History*, p. 459.

[69] For this interpretation of Matt. 11:12, cf. *Annotations on Matthew 1–18* (1534–35/1538), LW 67:129–30.

"Now, just as Scripture often talks about miners and mines, so, too, it mentions the samples of gold that were shared with Christ and His Church. The samples of gold from the mines of the East [Matt. 2:11] will not be forgotten; this Indian or Arabian gold with which the Wise Men from the East honored Mary, the mother of God, and her dear little Son will be remembered not merely for as long as the world stands but for all of eternity as well.

"Oh, what blessed specimens of ore these are which are distributed to Christ and for the honor of His Church! An owner of one of the mines in Meissen, who wishes to remain anonymous, sent me two hundred silver gulden,[70] which I have distributed to poor students. This, too, shall have its honor on the Last Day.

"Who knows why exactly God let your Joachimsthal spring up along with the Gospel?[71] [Perhaps] so that His Church and many poor people whom God's Word had driven out of the monasteries would be sustained by it. Whatever I can to do serve your children and those in your care I do willingly and gladly. May God help you to raise many people who put their hand to Christ's vein and faithfully seek to promote His honor and the good of the Church." These and similar words were spoken this time and at other times at the doctor's table when some of our citizens were sitting there.

In closing, I want to mention one story that took place in 1545, when I saw and heard the doctor for the last time. I had some questions concerning religion, so I made a trip to Wittenberg.[72] Honorable and good people, who are still living, accompanied me and were invited along with me to sit at the doctor's table.

At that time the doctor was occupied with his last book, against the papacy.[73] He showed us some pictures in which he had the papacy depicted "for the laity," as he expressed it. At that time, a story[74] was told at table about how a miner asked an indulgence peddler on the Schneeberg whether what he had preached several times about the power of indulgences and the authority of the holy father was true: namely, that a person could release and ransom a soul from purgatory with one penny, as soon as it rang in the

---

[70] *gülden groschen*; a silver coin (*groschen*) of equivalent value to a gold gulden. The silver Joachimsthalers minted in Joachimsthal were themselves the most widely circulated example of this coinage.

[71] I.e., in 1516. See above, Mathesius, *History*, p. 137.

[72] On Mathesius' trip to Wittenberg in the spring of 1545, see above, Mathesius, *History*, pp. 519–21.

[73] *Against the Roman Papacy* (1545), LW 41:257–376, accompanied by the *Abbildung des Papsttums* (1545), WA 54:361–73. See above, Mathesius, *History*, p. 517.

[74] Cf. above, Mathesius, *History*, p. 521; Mathesius, *Sarepta*, sermon 2, fol. 24r–v (Loesche, *Mathesius: Ausgewählte Werke*, 4:123–24). Mathesius appears to be the source for this account.

bowl.[75] When the indulgence peddler affirmed this, the miner said, "Oh, what a merciless swindler the pope must be! He lets a poor soul wail in anguish in purgatory for so long for the sake of a penny when, in fact, he would be able, even if he had no other cash on hand, to muster up a few hundred thousand gulden and to free the poor souls all at once.[76] We poor people would gladly endow the amount of capital and whatever interest and fees would have accrued, if only we had an accurate accounting."

"Thank you, my old miner," said the doctor. "God willing, I would still like to send this excavator to the holy father in Rome at New Year's." Along with this, many other good things were said about income from mining:[77] that such money would be just as good as any other property gained by honest means. However, miners were a little too spendthrift. And because the money arrives in heaps and is met with joy, it usually departs again in heaps and amid wailing. And because many a miner will not be satisfied with a modest living, the goods he has gained will slip through his hands like water, or he will lose what is his like the dog in Aesop, who snapped at the shadow and lost the piece of meat he was holding in his mouth.[78]

At this time, a good wagon driver was taking me to Wittenberg. Along the way, he asked whether, since he was going with us to Rome, we would help arrange it so that he could see the real pope there too. When we had gone to be the doctor's guests, we arranged to be notified at table when our wagon driver had arrived to take us home. At table, a servant said, "*Auriga adest* ['The driver is here']." "Who is there?" said the doctor. "Doctor, it is our wagon driver, a good man, who drives us very diligently, has sung with us every morning, has not done any swearing, has never been drunk the whole trip, and never misses a sermon at home. He would like to see your reverence." "Let him in," said the doctor. The driver respectfully stood next to the door in keeping with the custom. The doctor asked him to come over to the table, offered him his hand, shook hands with him, and said, "When you see your comrades, tell them, 'I have had Doctor Luther, the greatest arch-heretic, by his hand.'" Then he offered him a toast from his glass. Our

---

[75] *im becken klüng.* Cf. above, Mathesius, *History*, p. 142.

[76] Cf. Luther, *Ninety-Five Theses* (1517), no. 82, LW 31:32; Mathesius, *History*, p. 144.

[77] Cf. *Table Talk* no. 5541 (1542), LW 54:450–51; no. 5173 (1540), WA TR 4:693; no. 5323 (1540), WA TR 5:58.

[78] For the fable, see Phaedrus, *Fables* 1.4 (Loeb 436 [1965], pp. 196–97; Perry no. 133); see also Oesterly, *Steinhöwels Äsop*, no. 5, pp. 85–86; Gibbs, *Aesop's Fables*, no. 263, p. 128. This was one of Luther's favorite fables: see Springer, *Luther's Aesop*, pp. 37–38 and *passim*. On Luther and Aesop, see above, Mathesius, *History*, pp. 267–70.

driver had never expected so great an honor, as he also joyfully recounted later many times among his fellows.[79]

Great people, deep humility, and an honorable mind do not despise the poor and lowly. For Christian faith and noble virtue come forth and make themselves manifest. If nothing is inside, nothing will come out.[80] How fine a thing it is, however, and how good to hear when men of great gifts let their light, affability, and friendliness shine upon lowly and simple people, following the good example of the Son of God, who also dealt with poor fishers like a good neighbor, tucking them in at night [cf. Matt. 14:25–27] and serving them food at table [cf. John 13:5; 21:3]. Or [there is] the example of great lords and princes who gladly allow their poor people to come before them, listen courteously, and quickly issue a decree, as is recounted in praise of many laudable Austrian lords and others.[81]

A pope who is a peasant remains a pope and a ¹peasant, even if he once again puts on a three-tiered crown and allows himself to be carried around and have his feet kissed;[82] and even if one were to dress a peasant in gold and set him upon the high altar, his boots will always be sticking out, as the Germans say.[83]

Here we will conclude our accounts about Doctor Martin for Shrove Tuesday. May it be no little honor to you miners, your mines, and the church in Joachimsthal that the man through whom God has expelled the abominable teaching of the monks from many hearts and churches was the son of a miner; that his teaching and books have come into this valley; that he had some of the ministers of your church ordained for you[84] and helped provide people for the church; that many honorable citizens and their children saw and heard him, ate and drank with him;[85] and that the doctrine which he inculcated has remained pure and uncontaminated among us in this church down to the present day; and that many people from these mountains have come through grace to the blessed knowledge of the eternal Mediator, have entered into their blessed rest in the true confession and invocation of this eternal Priest, and have become heirs and shareholders

---

[79] Mathesius is the source for this anecdote.

[80] Wander 2:961, "Innen" no. 1.

[81] Cf. Mathesius' description of King Ferdinand's morning audiences with common petitioners in his "Leichenrede": Loesche, *Mathesius: Ausgewählte Werke*, 4:368.

[82] Cf. above, p. 84 n. 4.

[83] Cf. Wander 1:269, "Bauer (der)," no. 340; Thiele no. 191, p. 691.

[84] Of the Joachimsthal clergy, only Mathesius was ordained by Luther himself. See Loesche, *Johannes Mathesius*, 1:103, 178–85; WA Br 12:470–71.

[85] See above, Mathesius, *History*, p. 606.

in the true and eternal heavenly host[86] solely on account of the precious blood and intercession of our one Patron. It is also to your credit that the greatest people and lights of the Church in Wittenberg visited the church and school in this valley and bore witness to our teaching.[87] Doctor Justus Jonas,[88] Dr. Cruciger,[89] Herr Philip,[90] Dr. Georg Major,[91] Dr. Paul Eber,[92] Dr. Pfeffinger,[93] Dr. Weller,[94] Dr. Medler,[95] Herr Joachim Camerarius,[96] Herr Fabricius,[97] and many excellent jurists[98] and physicians[99] have been glad to see this valley and have maintained good friendship with the ministers of your church and teachers of your school.

O Lord Jesus Christ, You have allowed Your mining works ǀto operate honorably in this place down to this present hour. Help us in patience to preserve and to abide in Your precious Gospel, which Dr. Luther burnished for us again, and which his students and table companions still supply for our use. [Help us do this] in true faith and a good conscience, along with due obedience as subjects and reverence toward our most gracious [imperial]

---

[86] The "heavenly host" was also the name of a Joachimsthal mine: "S. Jörgen im himlischen heersstoln" (see Mathesius, *Sarepta*, fol. Oo6r).

[87] See Loesche, *Johannes Mathesius*, 1:191–98.

[88] On Jonas, see the introduction above, p. xxx.

[89] On Caspar Cruciger, see the introduction above, p. xx n. 19 and p. 298 n. 81.

[90] On Melanchthon, see the introduction above, pp. xxxix–xl.

[91] On Major, see above, p. 300 n. 88.

[92] On Eber, see above, p. 300 n. 89.

[93] On Johann Pfeffinger, see the introduction above, pp. xxxii, lxxv.

[94] On Hieronymus Weller, see above, p. 416 n. 127.

[95] On Nicholas Medler, see above, p. 436 n. 71.

[96] On Camerarius, see the introduction above, p. xlv and n. 144 there.

[97] Georg Fabricius (1516–71), a student of Johann Rivius (see above, p. 563 n. 163) and an eminent classicist, helped to organize and reform the schools in Albertine Saxony. See Herbert, Schönebaum, "Fabricius, Georg," *NDB* 4:734–35; Loesche, *Johannes Mathesius*, 1:198.

[98] E.g., Caspar von Niedbruck (ca. 1525–57), counselor to King Ferdinand in Vienna. See Loesche, *Johannes Mathesius*, 1:198–99; Robert Holtzmann, "Niedbruck, Kaspar von," *ADB* 52:621–29.

[99] E.g., Georg Agricola, the author of *De re metallica* and *De natura fossilium*, who was town physician in Joachimsthal from 1527 to ca. 1530 (see above, p. 108 n. 24; p. 603 n. 40); the pharmacist and botanist Valerius Cordus (1515–44; Theodor Husemann, "Cordus, Valerius," *ADB* 4:479–80); and the Albertine ducal physician Johann Neff [Naevius], who was town physician in Joachimsthal from 1533 to 1544. See Loesche, *Johannes Mathesius*, 1:187–89; Volz, *Die Lutherpredigten des Johannes Mathesius*, pp. 124–25.

and gracious [royal] authorities.[100] Defend us also against all refiners and profiteering deceivers who slip false doctrine back in and seek to falsify pure silver. Dear Lord, also speak Your blessing over our praiseworthy mines, and let new veins be discovered and a rich new excavation begin, so that this laudable community, church, school, court, and justice may henceforth be preserved, and so that pious fathers of the house and poor widows may be able to raise their baptized children to glorify and serve You and to be heirs of heaven. May You, who are a rich God and give great blessing in the heavenly and earthly mines, be highly praised with Your Father and the Holy Spirit, along with all the sainted foremen, miners, and miners' preachers, here and in all eternity! Amen, O Lord Christ, Amen. And let faith grow in our hearts and mines, for You are the rich and almighty Son of God, Amen. And let everyone say with me a strong and sincere "Amen," in Christ's name! Amen.

---

[100] In 1565, Maximilian II would have been both Holy Roman emperor (since 1564) and king of Bohemia (since 1562). See the introduction above, p. lxxxiii and nn. 324–25 there; Mathesius, *History*, p. 423.

INDEX OF PERSONS

of, 342, 562n; Diet of Worms and, xc, 148, 151, 168–78, 545; Luther's appearance before, lxxvi, xc, 172–74, 464, 565; Luther's attitude toward, 161, 327, 359–60, 362, 363, 468, 544, 561n; Luther's proscription by (Edict of Worms), xl, 88, 180, 196, 324n, 453, 550; Peace of Nürnberg and, 347n, 362n, 365n, 369, 397–98, 422n; religious colloquies and, 467–68, 490–93; Smalcaldic War and, xxvn, lxx, lxxiii, 51n, 233n; support for council of the church by, 364, 396, 400, 407; sympathy for Luther by, xcii, 152, 178–79, 323, 339–40, 342, 347, 356–57, 362, 420, 493, 554, 558–59, 562; the Interims and, xxi, lxviii, lxxiii, lxxv, 554n; war against France and, 211n, 398, 422

Charles VIII (king of France, r. 1483–98), 520n
Chieregati, Francesco (1479–1539), 211n, 212n
Christopher (ca. 251), 294
Christopher (Christoffel, count of Mansfeld, 1520–91), 17–18
Cicero, Marcus Tullius (106–43 BC), 58, 296, 297, 482
Cimon (d. ca. 450 BC), 46
Clam, Johann, 302
Cleen, Dietrich von (1455–1531), 175n
Clement VI (pope, r. 1342–52), *Unigentus* of, 149n
Clement VII (pope, r. 1523–34), 323, 326
Cochlaeus, Johann (Dobnect/Dobneck von Wendelstein, 1479–1552), xxxiii, lxvii–lxx, xcv, 3, 4n, 12n, 177, 360n; *Commentary on the Deeds and Writings of Martin Luther from the Year of the Lord 1517 to the Year 1546 Related Chronologically to All Posterity*, lxviii–lxx, 122n; *Dialogus de Bello contra Turcas, in Antilogias Lutheri*, 4n; *Ein Auszug des Kaiserlichen Abschieds*, 360n; *Septiceps Lutherus*, lxviii, 4n
Cochlöffel. *See* Cochlaeus, Johann
Coelius, Michael (Caelius, 1492–1559), xxviii, xxxi, lxxx, 10–13, 15, 22, 534, 535; Luther's funeral sermon by, xxxiii, 17–18, 531n, 536; *Report on the Christian Departure of the Reverend Dr. Martin Luther from This Mortal Life*, xxxiii–xxxiv, xxxvi, xlvii, lxii, lxiii, lxvii, lxxiii, lxxxviii, xciii
Constantine I (ca. 272–337; emperor, r. 306–337), 247n, 318, 322, 399, 439; *Donation of* (spurious), 409, 473n
Contarini, Gasparo (1483–1542), 306n, 492, 493n
Cordatus, Conrad (1480–1546), xl, 407n, 416n

Corvinus, Antonius (Rabe, 1501–53), 384n
Cotta, Kunz, 119n
Cotta, Ursula, 119n
Cranach, Lucas ("The Elder," 1472–1553), xxxii–xxxiiin, 191n, 192n, 227n, 264n, 517n
Cratander, Andreas (d. 1540), xxii
Crautwald, Valentin (Krautwald, 1465?–1545), 260
Cronberg, Hartmut von (1488–1549), lxv
Cruciger, Caspar Jr. (1525–97), xxn
Cruciger, Caspar Sr. (1504–48), 416n, 419, 431, 512, 596, 602n, 611; as editor, stenographer, and translator of Luther, xx, xxiv–xxv, 188, 249, 270, 292, 298n, 372–73, 374n, 375n, 408, 426n, 515, 525; as Luther's "Elisha," xxn; as Mathesius' friend, lxxxi, 188n, 270n, 298n, 375; as professor of University of Wittenberg, 469–70, 593; as teacher in Wittenberg, 298; as translator of Melanchthon's *Oration at the Funeral of Dr. Martin Luther*, xliv, xlvi–xlix, li, 39n, 40n, 45n, 47n, 50n; at Luther's funeral procession, 21, 536; death of, 515n; Melanchthon's oration for, xlin; Melanchthon's Psalms commentary and, 370n; religious colloquies and, 306–7, 310–11n, 467, 489n, 490–91; translation of the Bible and, 475–77; Wittenberg Concord and, 354, 395–96
Cyrus ("The Great", r. 559–530 BC), 278, 322, 566

d'Ailly, Pierre (ca. 1350–1420), lvi, 62, 63n
Denck, Hans (ca. 1500–1527), 246, 380, 474n, 482n
Desprez, Josquin (ca. 1450–1521), 454
d'Étaples, Jacques Lefèvre (1455–1536), 440n
Dido, 485, 486
Dietleben, Kaspar (Caspar, Teutleben), 303–4
Dietrich, Veit (1506–49), xliv, xlix, 278, 309, 348, 358n; as editor and stenographer of Luther, 15n, 94n, 278n, 363n, 424, 428, 525; as Mathesius' friend, lxxxi, lxxxii, 267n, 354, 450n, 594; Smalcald conference and, 397n
Diodorus Siculus (ca. 80–20 BC), 585
Dolzig, Johann [Hans] von (ca. 1485–1551), 489n
Donatus, Aelius (fl. ca. 354), 117n
Döring, Christian (Düring, Aurifaber, ca. 1490–1533), 192n
Döring, Matthias (r. 1427–61), 146n
Dorothea of Denmark (duchess of Prussia, 1504–47), xli
Drachstädt, Carl, 303

SPECIAL INDEX
FOR MARTIN LUTHER
(TOPICS AND DOCUMENTS)